CONTEMPORARY AMERICAN DRAMATISTS

CONTEMPORARY LITERATURE SERIES

CONTEMPORARY AMERICAN DRAMATISTS

INTRODUCTION BY
HOLLY HILL

EDITOR
K.A. BERNEY

ASSOCIATE EDITOR
N.G. TEMPLETON

St J

St James Press

LONDON   DETROIT   WASHINGTON DC

Gale Research International Ltd.
PO Box 699
Cheriton House
North Way
Andover
Hants SP10 5YE
United Kingdom

or

Gale Research Inc.
835 Penobscot Bldg.
Detroit, MI 48226–4094
U.S.A.

ST. JAMES PRESS is an imprint of Gale Research International Ltd.
An Affiliated Company of Gale Research Inc.

A CIP catalogue record for this book is available from the British Library

ISBN 1–55862–214–4

Typeset by Florencetype Ltd, Kewstoke, Avon
Printed in the United Kingdom by Unwin Brothers Ltd, Woking

Published simultaneously in the United Kingdom and the United States of America

I(T)P   The trade mark ITP is used under license

IN MEMORY OF AND TRIBUTE TO M. ELIZABETH OSBORN,
AUTHOR, CRITIC, DRAMATURG, AND EDITOR

CONTENTS

EDITOR'S NOTE

The main part of *Contemporary American Dramatists* contains entries on English-language writers for the stage.

The selection of writers included in this book is based on the recommendations of the advisers listed on page xxi and is intended to reflect the best and most prominent of contemporary American playwrights (those who are currently active, as well as some who have died since 1950, but whose reputations remain essentially contemporary).

The entry for each writer consists of a biography, a complete list of published and/or produced plays and all other separately published books, a selected list of bibliographies and critical studies on the writer, and a signed essay. In addition, entrants were invited to comment on their work.

We have listed plays that were produced but not published; librettos and musical plays are listed along with other plays. The dates given are those of first publication/performance.

Some of the entries in the Dramatists section are supplemented in the Works section, which provides essays on a selection of the best-known plays written by the entrants.

The book concludes with a play, radio play, television play and screenplay title index.

ACKNOWLEDGEMENTS

We would like to thank the following for their help with this project: all the advisers and contributors; Barbara Archer; Deirdre Clark; Jackie Griffin; Lesley Henderson; Jane Kellock; Daniel Kirkpatrick; Roda Morrison, Humanities Publisher, Thomas Nelson; the staff of the London Theatre Museum; the staff of the British Library and Westminster Reference Library; and our friends and colleagues at St. James.

INTRODUCTION

American theatre at the end of the 1980s was beleaguered by dire forces. A national economic recession included government and private arts funding cutbacks that precipitated the closing of several institutional theatres and imperilled others. Even more ominous were battles to make censorship a policy of the National Endowment for the Arts or to abolish the agency altogether, led by religious/political conservatives whose objections ranged from using public monies for art they judged obscene, to arts funding in principle. Theatre institutions were also shaken by the aging of their founders, causing anxieties and some upheavals over their successors.

Both institutional and commercial theatre were challenged by new competition from cable television and home videos. On Broadway, mammoth production costs and rising ticket prices made serious new plays and musicals endangered species, and the success of spectacular British musicals hurt Americans' pride in their most vaunted indigenous form of theatre.

Minority voices were strident. Women and people of color had made advances, but white men of European heritage still dominated in all areas of theatre except in gender or ethnic-specific companies, most of which were never seen on Broadway, still the pinnacle of theatrical success. America's changing demographics, through which the combined population of people of color will outnumber whites before the end of the century, was reflected in increasing demands for access to or parity with white "mainstream" theatre. Gay men, long a closeted power on Broadway and theatre throughout the country, were also becoming more visible, impelled by the gay rights movement and the premature loss in the AIDS epidemic of major artists like Michael Bennett and rising talents like Scott McPherson. At the end of the 1980s, one wondered how American theatre would withstand, much less grow, amid all these pressures.

Just four years into the 1990s, there are signs of revitalization in theatre artists and institutions. In the fall of 1993, hope was renewed in the integrity of the National Endowment for the Arts with the appointment, by the first art-friendly President in over a decade, of the first artist to be the Endowment's Chair. Jane Alexander's reputation as an actress of exceptional talent and intelligence won her easy Congressional confirmation, even though she is also known as a liberal activist.

Financial problems continue to plague nonprofit and commerical theatre throughout America, but November of 1993 brought an event that most people considered impossible after *The Grapes of Wrath* closed shortly after winning the Best Play Tony award (usually a guarantee of a season's run) in 1990. Two two-part epic dramas, produced by the consortia of institutional theatres, commercial organizations and individuals that have developed to get serious work on Broadway, opened less that two weeks apart.

Both Tony Kushner's *Angels in America* (the first half of which had opened in the spring of 1993, winning the Pulitzer prize and Tony award) and Robert Schenkknan's *The Kentucky Cycle* (the first play ever to win a Pulitzer, in 1991, before it played in New York) were Broadway debuts for their authors. *Angels* is not only subtitled *A Gay Fantasia on National Themes*, but is by an openly gay author and staged by a gay African-American director, George C. Wolfe. Wolfe's spring 1993 designation as artistic director of the New York Shakespeare Festival founded by the late Joseph Papp is the first appointment of an African American to head a mainstream institutional theatre in New York. Progress, albeit modest, and decades in the making, as we shall see.

At the end of World War II, American theatre largely meant Broadway and touring productions of its hit plays and musicals. The dominant style in playwriting and production was realism, often in skeletal settings capable of suggesting real locales but accommodating quick shifts in place and time. Actors and directors were deeply influenced by the Method, the American interpretation of Stanislavsky's techniques fostered by the Actors Studio. Dedicated to finding the inner truth of a character and to naturalistic, as opposed to classical larger-than-life behavior, the Method included among its star practitioners Marlon Brando, Julie Harris, Geraldine Page, and Paul Newman (and, in the next generation Dustin Hoffman, Al Pacino, and Robert De Niro).

These styles blended felicitously in such landmark productions as Tennessee Williams' *A Streetcar Named Desire* (1947) and Arthur Miller's *Death of A Salesman* (1949). The most acclaimed dramatists in the postwar period, Williams and Miller exposed rends in the American social fabric and examined individual and social morality. Williams wrote in a poetic and impressionistic style, the intellectual Miller in a heightened vernacular and rhetoric.

Beyond Broadway, a Texas woman who had and continued to enjoy some success as a Broadway director, dreamed of an American national theatre consisting of a network of permanent companies established in cities throughout the country. In 1947, Margo Jones founded in Dallas the first fully professional (operating under an Actors Equity Association contract) nonprofit resident theatre in America. Her venture inspired Zelda Fichandler's 1952 Arena Stage in Washington, D.C. and Nina Vance's 1957 Alley Theatre in Houston. Though Margo Jones' theatre did not long survive her accidental death in 1955, the Arena and Alley thrive today, flagships in a network of some 300 resident theatres fostered by the movement's "Founding Mothers".

The 1950s was the last decade in which there appeared to be a consensus about how life in America was supposed to be: white males were supreme; women, children, and people of color were subservient; God and country were revered. Sexual morality was based upon the millenia-old double standard, as expressed on Broadway in comedies centered upon whether or not the heroine would lose her virginity before marriage. Even Neil Simon, the most successful comedy writer in American theatre history, applied the double standard to his first Broadway hit, *Come Blow Your Horn* (1962), with its "bad" girl who sleeps with the playboy hero and gets passed on to his younger brother, and its "good" girl who wins the playboy's heart and hand.

The Cold War, the Korean War, the hydrogen bomb, the McCarthy hearings and blacklists, and the first riots over school desegregation tore open America's moral and social fabric and began exposing its contradictions and hypocrisies in the 1950s, as Williams dramatized in such major works as *Cat on a Hot Tin Roof* (1955) and *The Night of the Iguana* (1961), and Miller in *The Crucible* (1953). No significant young American dramatist emerged during the decade, but the posthumus production of three Eugene O'Neill works—*Long Day's Journey into Night*, *A Moon for the Misbegotten* and *A Touch of the Poet*—embellished his reputation as a great (some say the greatest) American dramatist.

What American theatre in the 1950s is most noted for is the Off Broadway movement, whose first big success was a 1952 revival of Williams' *Summer and Smoke* (which had been given its first production at Margo Jones' Theatre '47 and flopped on Broadway the next year). The Circle in the Square production made a star of Geraldine Page, as did the theatre's 1956 revival of an O'Neill Broadway failure, *The Iceman Cometh*, starring Jason Robards, Jr. The Off Broadway movement used small theatre spaces to showcase talents in revivals of classics and worthy plays that had been Broadway failures, and to produce new and foreign writers like Brecht, Beckett, Genet, and Ionesco, whose form and content were too avant-garde for commercial theatres. Perhaps the best-known Off Broadway institution still surviving is the New York Shakespeare Festival, founded by Joseph Papp in 1954.

The 1960s began with a milestone, the first Broadway production of a full-length play by an African-American author. Lorraine Hansberry's *A Raisin in the Sun*, a finely crafted drama about three generations of an African-American family struggling to succeed and achieve personal dignity, also launched the careers of its director, Lloyd Richards, who would eventually discover and act as mentor to August Wilson, and actor-author-director Douglas Turner Ward, who became a founder of the Negro Ensemble Company in 1968.

Hansberry's career was cut short by her death from cancer in 1965. Tennessee Williams' star dimmed in the 1960s with a series of failures, while between *A View from the Bridge* in 1955 and *After the Fall* in 1964, Arthur Miller did not write for the stage. *After the Fall* was received by some as an ungallant gloss on his brief marriage to the tragic Marilyn Monroe, and while he has continued to write new plays and his early work has been revived on Broadway, Miller has never recaptured in America the esteem he was given in the first decade of his career. His body of work has been more honored in Britain.

The star dramatist of the 1960s was Edward Albee, whose first work, *The Zoo Story*, was presented off Broadway (on a double bill with Beckett's *Krapp's Last Tape*) in 1960, followed by three more Off Broadway one-acts and, in 1962, by *Who's Afraid of Virginia Woolf?* on Broadway. Particularly in his attacks on upper-middle class complacency in a style blending absurd humor, rhetorical flamboyance and existential musings in a usually naturalistic context, Albee helped to reflect American society as it pulled apart in the wake of political assassinations, the Civil Rights and Women's Movements, and the Vietnam War.

The 1950s had brought new foreign playwrights such as Osborne, Anouilh, and Giraudoux successfully to Broadway; the 1960s introduced Pinter and

Stoppard, and Peter Brook's seminal production of *Marat/Sade*. With the ascent of Absurdism to the aesthetic, if not usually the commerical firmament, social disintegration was mirrored in the breakup of conventional dramatic forms and spaces. Off Broadway became a victim of its own success as unions demanded better working conditions and productions grew too expensive; in even smaller spaces all over Manhattan Off Off Broadway was born.

At such pioneer theatres as Caffe Cino, LaMama, the Open Theatre and on other stages, fledgling playwrights like John Guare, Sam Shepard, Megan Terry, Jean-Claude van Itallie, and Lanford Wilson had their early works produced. As Stuart Little observed in *Off-Broadway: the Prophetic Theater* [Delta, 1972, p.188], "To the Off-Off Broadway playwright, the Absurdist writers Beckett, Genet and Ionesco were traditional theater." The venue was devoted to new writers and opposed to all taboos of form and content: homosexuality was among the diverse topics frankly explored, nudity and obscene language was common (by the end of the decade both had even reached Broadway in the musical *Hair*, developed at the New York Shakespeare Festival's Public Theater). Eventually the lines between Off and Off Off Broadway blurred, defined formally by the type of Equity contract the actors worked under. Beyond Broadway, there are throughout Manhattan strictly commercial ventures, institutional theatres that may operate under an Equity resident theatre contract, union-sanctioned and unsanctioned limited runs and workshops, and sometimes combinations of these running in different spaces under the same roof.

New playwrights also became a focus for nonprofit theatres, which burgeoned with the advent of private funding (starting with Ford Foundation grants in 1959) and government support (the NEA was established in 1965, followed by state and city arts councils). The National Playwrights Conference, which gives staged readings of new plays each July, was established at Connecticut's O'Neill Theater Center in 1966 and became an international model for playwright development programs. Most resident theatres created some venue for new work and several hold new play festivals attracting international attention.

Accompanying the Civil Rights Movement was a demand for more opportunities for artists of color. A series of plays dealing with the African-American experience in America, by such authors as Amiri Baraka, Ed Bullins, Adrienne Kennedy, and Douglas Turner Ward were produced Off Broadway. Ethnic-specific theatres like the Negro Ensemble Company, East West Players, El Teatro Compesino, INTAR Hispanic American Arts Center and Repertorio Espagnol were founded in the 1960s (more followed in the next decade, as did women's companies) to give African and Asian-American and Hispanic actors, designers, directors, playwrights, backstage and management personnel artistic homes. Some of the work began trickling into the mainstream; in 1969 the Negro Ensemble Company was awarded a special Tony award, and James Earl Jones, who had developed his talent playing Shakespearean as well as black characters Off Broadway and in resident theatres, won his first Best Actor Tony for *The Great White Hope*, which also introduced Jane Alexander to Broadway and her first Tony.

Homosexuality, alluded to as a subject for shame in such popular Broadway plays as Lillian Hellman's *The Children's Hour* (1934), *Tea and Sympathy*

(1953), and several Tennessee Williams dramas, was able to come out of the closet Off Broadway with the 1968 premiere of Mart Crowley's *The Boys in the Band*, about nine gay men (one of them black) at a birthday party. Off Off Broadway, openly gay playwrights like Doric Wilson had been writing about gay life for several years. *The Boys in the Band* brought the subject into the mainstream. Professional theatre companies (such as Wilson's TOSOS and The Glines) dedicated to presenting works about the gay experience began forming in the 1970s.

The 1960s also brought an abundance of experimental groups, many inspired by the writings of Antonin Artaud to rebel against written texts, others, inspired by such current events as student rebellions and Vietnam War protests to rebel against all authority and seek societal change. In 1961 the Bread and Puppet Theatre began to use both giant puppets and actors to enact parables denouncing war and materialism; the San Francisco Mime Theatre started in 1966 to promote such causes as civil and women's rights; the Performance Group formed in 1968 to create communal works with such diverse inspirations as Marilyn Monroe and the massacre of Vietnamese civilians by American troops, and to perform versions of classical plays in ambiances where the audience was not separated from the actors but arranged to be a part of the event—a practice for which the Group's founder Richard Schechner coined the term "environmental theatre."

Such groups flourished in the 1970s (some abide still), their experiments with text tending to make directors and/or actors rather than playwrights the primary creative artists in the theatre. Experimental work carried on that of the Absurdists in reimagining the theatrical experience not as linear (a play with a beginning, middle, and end) but as circular and open-ended, asking rather than answering questions or just inviting audiences to share an experience. Some groups, inspired by Polish director Jerzy Grotowski's 1968 book *Towards a Poor Theatre*, by performances of his Polish Laboratory Theatre, and by workshops he gave on visits to America, chose to work with limited technical resources, while other artists such as Robert Wilson incorporated new technology into their work and created multimedia events.

Experimental work existed beside that of resident theatres, which might produce both classics and new plays, and the play-development programs. The National Playwrights Conference alone, from its inception through the 1970s, introduced or fostered the work of many dramatists essayed in this book: Thomas Babe, Phillip Hayes Dean, Christopher Durang, Charles Fuller, Jack Gelber, John Guare, Oliver Hailey, Errol Hill, Israel Horovitz, David Henry Hwang, Albert Innaurato, Arthur Kopit, Leonard Melfi, Susan Miller, OyamO, John Pielmeier, Martin Sherman, Ted Talley, Ronald Tavel, Wendy Wasserstein, Richard Wesley and Lanford Wilson.

Apart from Neil Simon's ongoing Broadway successes, no playwright dominated in the 1970s (not surprising in a period of social and artistic unrest). There was considerable promise acknowledged in Christopher Durang's satiric comedies, David Rabe's Vietnam War trilogy, Lanford Wilson's plays of lyric realism, David Mamet's minimalist style and poetry forged from street language, and Sam Shepard's mixing of such elements as American drug culture, pop art, myth, gritty naturalism, and fantasy.

While American naturalistic acting style was vitalized by such young actors as Dustin Hoffman and Al Pacino, more demands were being made upon performers. Rigorous training was needed for the classics that were a staple of institutional theatres and for experimental work which required the physical virtuosity and the psychological openness taught by Grotowski. Many American universities began in the late 1960s to develop conservatory acting training programs, and when the first alumni of these debuted in New York in the 1970s—Kevin Kline, Mandy Patinkin, Patti LuPone, Meryl Streep—it seemed possible that America was headed for a Golden Age of acting. The tension between naturalistic and classical training, between inner-directed psychological probing of self and character and outer-directed vocal and physical skills responsive to all styles of theatre, remains constant in America. The essentailly naturalistic talent of Chicago's Steppenwolf Theatre Company, from which John Malkovitch emerged in the 1980s, and the classically-trained Kevin Kline, at home in Shakespeare, musical comedy, and film, testify to the range of American actors.

By 1980, the dream of a national theatre of resident companies had been altered by economics and geography. Many theatres could not afford to support a permanent company, and most actors would not commit themselves to long seasons away from New York or Hollywood, the only places where they could hope to make a national reputation and have a chance in films and television as well as theatre. Even the prestigious Repertory Theater of the Lincoln Center that opened in 1964 with the ideal of a resident company producing classical and new plays for Broadway had exhausted several managements.

A Broadway producing pattern that began when Margo Jones premiered *Summer and Smoke* at Theatre '47, solidified in the 1980s: plays, and sometimes whole productions, developed in nonprofit theatres Off Broadway, outside New York, or in the U.K., moved to Broadway for commerical runs. Even Neil Simon began to open his plays in resident theatres, and the blockbuster British musical *Les Miserables* moved to London's West End and on to Broadway after opening at the Royal Shakespeare Company. There are still some independent producers, but the consortium pattern prevails on Broadway. Probably the best thing about this is that it keeps most resident theatres across the country keenly interested in developing new work, and the worst is that some theatres focus on what they think will have a chance of success in New York at the expense of more original and daring work.

Christopher Durang, David Rabe, Lanford Wilson, and Sam Shepard wrote less for the theatre as the 1980s wore on, and while Edward Albee continued to write, most critics and audiences had ceased to acclaim his work in the 1970s. With *Glengary Glen Ross* (1984), David Mamet emerged as the foremost American dramatist of the period, though 1984 was also the year that August Wilson's first play was produced on Broadway. Both Mamet and Wilson are poets, but Wilson's style is as expansive as Mamet's is minimal. Wilson brought storytelling and plot back to the theatre after decades in which "plot" had been a bad word. Wilson's characters both spin and act out good yarns in the five plays that have so far appeared in his cycle exploring African-American life in each decade of the 20th century.

The first African-American playwright to win the accolades of three Pulitzer prizes as well as a Tony and numerous other awards, August Wilson made it into the mainstream via the National Playwrights Conference and the Yale Repertory Theater, both of which Lloyd Richards headed as artistic director. Richards has had a conscious and considerable influence in fostering the careers of artists of color and of women. The Best Play Tony-winner in 1987 was August Wilson, in 1988 David Henry Hwang, and in 1989 Wendy Wasserstein—all Conference alumni.

Wasserstein has become a highly successful commercial playwright with only four plays, the last two moving from institutional theatres to long runs on Broadway. Woman dramatists, seldom heard from in force on Broadway since the first women's movement inspired Susan Glaspell, Rachel Crothers, Sophie Treadwell and Zona Gale to write a number of plays on feminist themes (Gale won a Pulitzer in 1921, Glaspell in 1930), again found voices and listeners with the second women's movement in the 1960s. The first to move from fringe to mainstream theatre was African-American poet Ntozake Shange, whose *For Colored Girls* was a 1976 Broadway success; in the 1980s Beth Henley, Marsha Norman, and Wendy Wasserstein won Pulitzers with Broadway plays. Norman won a Tony in 1991 for her book of *The Secret Garden* musical.

Tonys and Pulitzers notwithstanding, women are still largely outsiders in mainstream theatre. A singular event in the spring of 1991 was the musical version of *The Secret Garden*, the first Broadway show for which the principal producer and the director, composer, librettist, set, costume and lighting designers were all women. The musical won a few Tonys and ran for over a season on Broadway and on a national tour. Still, while several women have been appointed artistic directors of major resident theatres in the last decade, few are hired to direct on Broadway.

How little women are regarded was demonstrated in March of 1992, when Joseph Papp's designated successor as artistic director of the New York Shakespeare Festival, JoAnne Akalaitis, was abruptly replaced with George C. Wolfe by the Festival Board. Akalaitis had powerful forces against her—she had made her international reputation as a director and writer in avant-garde theatre but had never directed on Broadway, she was in her fifties (not a fashionable age for women in America) and was described as abrasive (so was Papp, but abrasiveness in a man was evidently tolerable), she did not work a miracle during her twenty-month tenure and bring the Festival out of the recessionary slump it had sunk into before Papp's death, and the *New York Times* printed negative articles about her from the moment of her appointment. In summary, Akalaitis was not a member of Broadway's old boy network, whereas George C. Wolfe, just having written the book for and directed *Jelly's Last Jam* on Broadway, and engaged in staging *Angels in America*, was a new boy—and African American at that.

No one familiar with Wolfe's work could but rejoice in his appointment at the Festival, but in the theatre politics of the time few believed that the Board would have dared to replace a woman with a white man, or that any man being fired would have been treated to the humiliations Akalaitis suffered— being locked out of her office and scourged in the *New York Times*. Many women in theatre got the message that they didn't matter as much as they thought they were beginning to. Adding salt to the wound, the message came in the same season as David Mamet's *Oleanna*, seen by some as a savage attack on feminism. No wonder at the popularity of Wendy Wasserstein's characters, who may be feminists but who don't behave abrasively.

What white women lack, women and most men of color lack even more. The gains made by African Americans, with recognition of major talents in playwriting, directing, and acting, have reflected their role in the Civil Rights movement, but these gains are modest compared to the position of whites, and have yet to be equaled by Hispanic, Asian, and Native American artists. The Non-Traditional Casting Project, a nonprofit service organization founded in 1986, developed in response to the desire of artists and other theatre personnel to work across lines of gender, race, and also of physical disability. The Project is not only an advocate of minorities in theatre, film, and television, but towards the end of 1993 it had in operation a computer system that makes accessible via modem over 4,000 resumés (and photos of actors) to producers, casting directors, and others. The struggle truly to reflect American society on its stages and screens is sometimes branded with such slurs as "politically correct," but the fair-minded need only read the names and biographies of producers, directors, writers, designers, and actors in most theatre programs to understand how greatly women and people of color are still "minorities" even as they form the majority of America's population.

Another pressing problem in New York theatre is the power of the *New York Times* to influence the fate of individuals and shows. Up until the 1960s New York was much like London still is, with an abundance of newspapers and magazines. No single publication or critic dominated, but since the death of all but three Manhattan-based papers, New York theatre is in thrall to the *New York Times*. The relationship of the paper to the theatre community contains conflicts of interest—most pernicious is that the *New York Times* claims an unbiased position on the part of its critics (including not allowing them to vote on Tony or other awards) and in the assignment of its feature articles, while at the same time accepting enormous revenue for theatre advertising. But neither the paper nor any organization of theatre producers or artists has seriously addressed, much less been able to redress, such issues.

In the fall of 1993 the *New York Times* reshuffled its theatre critics, choosing, as usual, three white males. There are a few women mainstream theatre critics in New York and more across the country. In 1991 the *Denver Post* became the first mainstream newspaper to hire a person of color—and an African-American woman, to boot—as its chief theatre critic. Theatre journalists more representative of America's population may help eventually not only to bring fresh points of view into print but to draw more diverse audiences to both mainstream and ethnic theatres. More people of color are being added to the Boards and solicited as volunteers in institutional theatres; marketing strategies involve everything from ethnic groups to grade and high school programs to Broadway's Roundabout Theatre Company's cocktail-party and performance singles nights program, so successful that it was expanded to include gay singles nights.

American theatre is exploring solutions to the artistic, economic, and social problems confronting it as the 21st century approaches. Today there are a few signs more positive than that playwrights are confronting the misinformation in American history, often in epic form. August Wilson's cycle of plays about African Americans shows them as victims of white oppression but also depicts the oppressive forces within and between blacks. Robert Schenkkan's *The Kentucky Cycle* portrays human greed (and occasional nobility) from settlers cheating Native Americans, to industrialists robbing naive farmers of their land, to union members betraying their brethren.

In the fall of 1993, the Denver Center Theatre Company gave a world premiere to a dramatization of a book about a Sioux holy man, *Black Elk Speaks*. The play tells the story of America's settling from its natives' point of view, and began rehearsals with a Sioux blessing ceremony attended by Black Elk's descendants (two of whom were advisers for the production). It was not only the first mainstream play to have an entire cast of Native Americans and Hispanics, but in the Denver Theater Center's history it was the first to sell out early in its run, to receive standing ovations from the first preview to closing night, to attract native as well as white audiences, and to become the cover story for the national magazine *American Theatre*.

The most uplifting single development in American theatre today is the phenomenon of *Angels in America*. In this epic, Tony Kushner superbly weaves several stories, resolving them with both dramatic logic and unpredictably. His skill in plotting is of a theatrical tradition hallowed by Aristotle, while his mixing of forms (tragedy, comedy, melodrama, fantasy), styles (naturalism, camp, hallucinatory, classical) and periods (Middle Ages, Restoration, 1950s, the last decade) is Postmodern. His scheme for the work includes cross-gender casting; three actresses playing women and several men. His subject and themes not only embrace homosexuals suffering in the AIDS epidemic but all of humanity, struggling in a universe he depicts as abandoned by God. In the face of despair, Kushner finds courage, portraying human beings as able to progress without God, and compassion. Even the arch-villain of the work is granted a formal ceremony of forgiveness. Kushner's final words are to the audience, and they could acquire no greater power than in the theatre, which is not likely to die whatever anyone predicts, because only in live performance can such an exchange take place between playwright, actor, and audience: "The world only spins forward. . . . You are fabulous creatures, and I bless you. More life. The great work begins."

—Holly Hill

ADVISERS

Judith E. Barlow
C.W.E. Bigsby
Michael Billington
Katharine Brisbane
Ned Chaillet
Ruby Cohn

Tish Dace
Lizbeth Goodman
Anthony Graham-White
Nick Hern
Holly Hill
Joel Schechter

CONTRIBUTORS

Elizabeth Adams
Addell Austin Anderson
Frances Rademacher Anderson
Gary Anderson
Thomas Apple
Erica Aronson
Arthur H. Ballet
Judith E. Barlow
David W. Beams
Joss Bennathan
Susan Bennett
Linda Ben-Zvi
Gerald M. Berkowitz
Michael Bertin
C.W.E. Bigsby
Walter Bode
Gaynor F. Bradish
Jarka M. Burian
Bernard Carragher
Ned Chaillet
Bill Coco
Ruby Cohn
Tish Dace
Elin Diamond
Mark W. Estrin
John V. Falconieri
Michael Feingold
Leonard Fleischer
Kathy Fletcher
Leah D. Frank
Melvin J. Friedman
Steven H. Gale
Lois Gordon
Martin Gottfried
Anthony Graham-White
Prabhu S. Guptara
Dick Higgins
Errol Hill
Morgan Y. Himelstein
Foster Hirsch
William M. Hoffman

Jorge A. Huerta
Christopher Innes
John Istel
C. Lee Jenner
Burton S. Kendle
Liliane Kerjan
Helene Keyssar
Kimball King
Richard Kosterlanetz
John G. Kuhn
Michael T. Leech
Felicia Hardison Londré
Glenn Loney
James MacDonald
James Magruder
Thomas B. Markus
Thomas J. McCormack
Howard McNaughton
Walter J. Meserve
Louis D. Mitchell
Christian H. Moe
Paul Nadler
Osita Okagbue
Judy Lee Oliva
M. Elizabeth Osborn
Eric Overmyer
Sylvia Paskin
Roxana Petzold
Margaret Loftus Ranald
John M. Reilly
Sandra L. Richards
Arthur Sainer
Ellen Schiff
Elaine Shragge
Michael T. Smith
A. Richard Sogliuzzo
Carol Simpson Stern
Alan Strachan
Darwin T. Turner
Gerald Weales
Dennis Welland

LIST OF DRAMATISTS

George Abbott
JoAnne Akalaitis
Edward Albee
William Alfred
Robert Anderson
Robert Ardrey
George Axelrod

Thomas Babe
Jon Robin Baitz
James Baldwin
Amiri Baraka
Djuna Barnes
S.N. Behrman
Eric Bentley
Kenneth Bernard
George Birimisa
Lee Blessing
Eric Bogosian
Julie Bovasso
Lee Breuer
Kenneth H. Brown
Ed Bullins
Charles Busch

Lewis John Carlino
Lonnie Carter
Mary Chase
Paddy Chayefsky
Alice Childress
Frank Chin
Darrah Cloud
Rick Cluchey
Constance S. Congdon
Marc Connelly
Ron Cowen
Michael Cristofer
Rachel Crothers
Mart Crowley

Ossie Davis
Phillip Hayes Dean
Steven Dietz
Charles Dizenzo
Rosalyn Drexler
Martin Duberman
Christopher Durang

Lonne Elder III

Jules Feiffer
Lawrence Ferlinghetti
Harvey Fierstein
Horton Foote
Richard Foreman
María Irene Fornés
Paul Foster
Mario Fratti
Bruce Jay Friedman
Charles Fuller
George Furth

Frank Gagliano
Herb Gardner
Larry Gelbart
Jack Gelber
William Gibson
Frank D. Gilroy
James Goldman
Paul Goodman
Charles Gordone
Philip Kan Gotanda
Spalding Gray
Paul Green
Richard Greenberg
David Greenspan
John Guare
A.R. Gurney Jr.

Oliver Hailey
William Hanley
Lorraine Hansberry
William Hauptman
Allan Havis
Lillian Hellman
Beth Henley
James Leo Herlihy
Errol Hill
Robert Hivnor
William M. Hoffman
Joan Holden
Israel Horovitz
Tina Howe
David Henry Hwang

William Inge
Albert Innaurato

Len Jenkin

Lee Kalcheim
Garson Kanin
Adrienne Kennedy
Wendy Kesselman
Sidney Kingsley
Kenneth Koch
Harry Kondoleon
Arthur Kopit
H.M. Koutoukas
Ruth Krauss
Tony Kushner

Arthur Laurents
Jerome Lawrence
John Howard Lawson
Robert E. Lee
Romulus Linney
Robert Lowell
Craig Lucas
Charles Ludlam
Ken Ludwig

Eduardo Machado
Archibald MacLeish
Jackson Mac Low
David Mamet
Emily Mann
William Mastrosimone
Elaine May
Michael McClure
James McLure
Terrence McNally
Murray Mednick
Mark Medoff
Leonard Melfi
Arthur Miller
Jason Miller
Susan Miller
Ron Milner
Loften Mitchell
Tad Mosel

Richard Nelson
John Ford Noonan

Marsha Norman

Clifford Odets
Eugene O'Neill
Eric Overmyer
Rochelle Owens
OyamO

Suzan-Lori Parks
John Patrick
Robert Patrick
John Pielmeier
Miguel Pinero
Bernard Pomerance

David Rabe
Dennis J. Reardon
Keith Reddin
Ronald Ribman
Jack Richardson

Howard Sackler
Arthur Sainer
Milcha Sánchez-Scott
William Saroyan
Joan M. Schenkar
James Schevill
Murray Schisgal
Ntozake Shange
John Patrick Shanley
Wallace Shawn
Sam Shepard
Martin Sherman
Stuart Sherman
Neil Simon
Michael T. Smith
David Starkweather
Barrie Stavis
John Steppling
Karen Sunde

Ted Tally
Ronald Tavel
Megan Terry
Steve Tesich

Alfred Uhry

Luis Valdez

Jean-Claude van Itallie
Gore Vidal
Paula Vogel

Joseph A. Walker
Douglas Turner Ward
Wendy Wasserstein
Jerome Weidman
Arnold Weinstein
Michael Weller
Mac Wellman
Richard Wesley
Edgar Nkosi White

John White
Thornton Wilder
Tennessee Williams
August Wilson
Doric Wilson
Lanford Wilson
Robert M. Wilson
George C. Wolfe
Olwen Wymark

Susan Yankowitz

Paul Zindel

LIST OF WORKS

CONTEMPORARY AMERICAN DRAMATISTS

A

ABBOTT, George (Francis).

Born in Forestville, New York, 25 June 1889. Educated at Hamburg High School, New York; Rochester University, Rochester, New York, B.A. 1911; Harvard University, Cambridge, Massachusetts, 1912–13. Married 1) Ednah Levis in 1914 (died 1930), one daughter; 2) Mary Sinclair in 1946 (marriage dissolved 1951); 3) Joy Moana Valderrama in 1983. Founder, with Philip Dunning, Abbott–Dunning Inc., 1931–34. Recipient: Boston *Globe* award, 1912; Donaldson award, for directing, 1946, 1948, 1953, 1955; Tony award, 1955, 1956, 1960, and for directing, 1960, 1963, Special Tony, 1987; Pulitzer prize, 1960; New York Drama Critics Circle award, 1960; Lawrence Langner award, 1976; City of New York Handel medallion, 1976; Kennedy Center award, 1983. D.H.: Rochester University, 1961; H.H.D.: University of Miami, 1974. Address: 1270 Avenue of the Americas, New York, New York 10020, U.S.A.

Publications

PLAYS

The Head of the Family (produced 1912).
Man in the Manhole (produced 1912).
The Fall Guy, with James Gleason (produced 1924). 1928.
A Holy Terror: A None-Too-Serious Drama, with Winchell Smith (produced 1925). 1926.
Love 'em and Leave 'em, with John V.A. Weaver (also director: produced 1926). 1926.
Cowboy Crazy, with Pearl Franklin (produced 1926).
Broadway, with Philip Dunning (also director: produced 1926). 1927.
Four Walls, with Dana Burnet (also director: produced 1927). 1928.
Coquette, with Ann Preston Bridgers (also director: produced 1927). 1928.
Ringside, with Edward A. Paramore, Jr., and Hyatt Daab (also director: produced 1928).
Those We Love, with S.K. Lauren (also director: produced 1930).
Lilly Turner, with Philip Dunning (also director: produced 1932).
Heat Lightning, with Leon Abrams (also director: produced 1933).
Ladies' Money (also director: produced 1934).
Page Miss Glory (also director: produced 1934).
Three Men on a Horse, with John Cecil Holm (also director: produced 1935). 1935.

1

On Your Toes, music and lyrics by Richard Rodgers and Lorenz Hart (also director: produced 1936; revised version produced 1983).

Sweet River, adaptation of the novel *Uncle Tom's Cabin* by Harriet Beecher Stowe (also director: produced 1936).

The Boys from Syracuse, music and lyrics by Richard Rodgers and Lorenz Hart, adaptation of *A Comedy of Errors* by Shakespeare (also director: produced 1938).

Best Foot Forward, with John Cecil Holm (also director: produced 1941).

Beat the Band, with George Marion, Jr. (also director: produced 1942).

Where's Charley?, music and lyrics by Frank Loesser, adaptation of the play *Charley's Aunt* by Brandon Thomas (also director: produced 1948). 1965.

A Tree Grows in Brooklyn, with Betty Smith, adaptation of the novel by Smith (also director: produced 1951).

The Pajama Game, with Richard Bissell, music by Richard Adler and Jerry Ross, adaptation of the novel *7 Cents* by Bissell (also co-director: produced 1954). 1954.

Damn Yankees, with Douglass Wallop, music by Richard Adler and Jerry Ross, adaptation of the novel *The Year the Yankees Lost the Pennant* by Wallop (also director: produced 1955). 1956.

New Girl in Town, music and lyrics by Bob Merrill, adaptation of the play *Anna Christie* by Eugene O'Neill (also director: produced 1957). 1958.

Fiorello!, with Jerome Weidman, lyrics by Sheldon Harnick, music by Jerry Bock (also director: produced 1959). 1960.

Tenderloin, with Jerome Weidman, lyrics by Sheldon Harnick, music by Jerry Bock, adaptation of the work by Samuel Hopkins Adams (also director: produced 1960). 1961.

Flora, The Red Menace, with Robert Russell, music by John Kander, lyrics by Fred Ebb (also director: produced 1965).

Anya, with Guy Bolton, music and lyrics by Robert Wright and George Forrest, adaptation of the play *Anastasia* by Marcelle Maurette and Bolton (also director: produced 1965).

Music Is, music by George Adler, lyrics by Will Holt, adaptation of *Twelfth Night* by Shakespeare (also director: produced 1976).

Tropicana, music by Robert Nassif, lyrics by Nassif and Peter Napolitano (also director: produced 1985).

Frankie, music by Joseph Turin, lyrics by Gloria Nissenson, adaptation of *Frankenstein* by Mary Shelley (also co-director, with Donald Saddler: produced 1989).

SCREENPLAYS: *The Saturday Night Kid*, with others, 1929; *Why Bring That Up?*, with others, 1929; *Half-Way to Heaven*, with Gerald Geraghty, 1929; *All Quiet on the Western Front*, with Dell Andrews and Maxwell Anderson, 1930; *The Sea God*, 1930; *Manslaughter*, 1930; *Stolen Heaven*, 1931; *Secrets of a Secretary*, with Dwight Taylor, 1931; *The Pajama Game*, with Richard Bissell, 1957; *Damn Yankees* (*What Lola Wants*), 1958.

NOVELS

Broadway (novelization of stage play), with Philip Dunning. 1927.
Tryout. 1979.

OTHER

Mister Abbott (autobiography). 1963.

THEATRICAL ACTIVITIES

DIRECTOR: **Plays**—most of his own plays, and *Lightnin'* by Winchell Smith and Frank Bacon, 1918; *Chicago* by Maurice Watkins, 1927; *Spread Eagle* by George S. Brooks and Walter S. Lister, 1927; *Bless You, Sister* by John Meehan and Robert Riskin, 1927; *Gentlemen of the Press* by Ward Morehouse, 1928; *Jarnegan* by Charles Beahen and Garrett Fort, 1928; *Poppa* by Bella and Sam Spewack, 1928; *Louder, Please* by Norman Krasna, 1931; *The Great Magoo* by Ben Hecht and Gene Fowler, 1932; *Twentieth Century* by Ben Hecht and Charles MacArthur, 1932, 1971; *The Drums Begin* by Howard Irving Young, 1933; *John Brown* by Ronald Gow, 1934; *Kill That Story* by Harry Madden and Philip Dunning, 1934; *Small Miracle* by Norman Krasna, 1934; *Jumbo* by Richard Rodgers and Lorenz Hart, 1935; *Boy Meets Girl* by Bella and Sam Spewack, 1935; *Brother Rat* by John Monks, Jr., and Fred F. Finklehoffe, 1936; *Room Service* by John Murray and Allen Boretz, 1937; *Angel Island* by Bernie Angus, 1937; *Brown Sugar* by Bernie Angus, 1937; *All That Glitters* by John Baragwanath and Kenneth Simpson, 1938; *What a Life* by Clifford Goldsmith, 1938; *You Never Know* by Cole Porter, 1938; *The Primrose Path* by Robert Buckner and Walter Hart, 1939; *Mrs. O'Brien Entertains* by Harry Madden, 1939; *Too Many Girls* by George Marion, Jr., 1939; *Ring Two* by Gladys Harlbut, 1939; *The White-Haired Boy* by Charles Martin and Beatrice Kaufman, 1939; *The Unconquered* by Ayn Rand, 1940; *Goodbye in the Night* by Jerome Mayer, 1940; *Pal Joey* by John O'Hara, music by Richard Rodgers, lyrics by Lorenz Hart, 1940; *Sweet Charity*, by Irving Brecher and Manuel Seff, 1942; *Kiss and Tell* by F. Hugh Herbert, 1943; *Get Away Old Man* by William Saroyan, 1943; *A Highland Fling* by J.L. Galloway, 1944; *Snafu* by Louis Solomon and Harold Buchman, 1944; *On the Town* by Betty Comden and Adolph Green, 1944; *Mr. Cooper's Left Hand* by Clifford Goldsmith, 1945; *Billion Dollar Baby* by Betty Comden and Adolph Green, 1945; *One Shoe Off* by Mark Reed, 1946; *Beggar's Holiday* by John La Touche (restaged), 1946; *It Takes Two* by Virginia Faulkner and Sana Suesse, 1947; *Barefoot Boy with Cheek* by Max Shulman, 1947; *High Button Shoes* by Stephen Longstreet, music and lyrics by Jule Styne and Sammy Kahn, 1947; *Look Ma, I'm Dancin'* by Jerome Lawrence and Robert E. Lee, music by Hugh Martin, 1948; *Mrs. Gibbons' Boys* by Will Glickman and Joseph Stein, 1949; *Tickets Please* (revue; restaged and rewritten), 1950; *Call Me Madam* by Howard Lindsay and Russel Crouse, music and lyrics by Irving Berlin, 1950; *Out of This World* by Dwight Taylor and Reginald Lawrence (restaged), 1950; *The Number* by Arthur Carter, 1951; *In Any Language* by Edmund Beloin and Harry Garson, 1952; *Wonderful Town* by Joseph Fields and Jerome Chodorov, music by Leonard Bernstein, lyrics by Betty Comden and Adolph Green, 1953; *Me and Juliet* by Richard Rodgers and Oscar Hammerstein II, 1953; *Drink to Me Only* by Abram S. Ginnes and Ira Wallach, 1958; *Once upon a Mattress* by Jay Thompson and others, 1959; *Take Her, She's Mine* by Phoebe and Henry Ephron, 1961; *A Call on Kuprin* by Jerome Lawrence and Robert E. Lee, 1961; *A Funny Thing Happened on* *the Way to the Forum* by Burt Shevelove and Larry Gelbart, music and lyrics by Stephen Sondheim, 1962; *Never Too Late* by Sumner Arthur Long, 1962; *Fade Out—Fade In* by Betty Comden and Adolph Green, music by Jule Styne, 1964; *Help Stamp Out Marriage* by Keith Waterhouse and Willis Hall, 1966; *Agatha Sue, I Love You* by Abe Einhorn, 1966; *How Now, Dow Jones* by Max Shulman, 1967; *The Education of Hyman Kaplan* by Benjamin Zavin, 1969; *The Fig Leaves Are Falling* by Allan Sherman, 1969; *Norman Is That You* by Ron Clark and Sam Bobrick, 1970; *Winning Isn't Everything* by Lee Kalcheim, 1978. Films—*The Carnival Man,* 1929; *The Bishop's Candlesticks,* 1929; *Why Bring That Up?,* 1929; *Half-Way to Heaven,* 1929; *The Sea God,* 1930; *Manslaughter,* 1930; *Stolen Heaven,* 1931; *Secrets of a Secretary,* 1931; *My Sin,* 1931; *The Cheat,* 1931; *Too Many Girls,* 1940; *Kiss and Tell,* 1945; *The Pajama Game* (co-director, with Stanley Donen), 1957; *Damn Yankees* (co-director, with Stanley Donen), 1958. Television—*U.S. Royal Showcase,* 1952.

ACTOR: Plays—"Babe" Merrill in *The Misleading Lady* by Charles Goddard and Paul Dickey, 1913; in *The Queen's Enemies* by Lord Dunsany, 1916; Henry Allen in *Daddies* by John L. Hobble, 1918; Sylvester Cross in *The Broken Wing* by Charles Goddard and Paul Dickey, 1920; in *Dulcy* by Marc Connelly and George S. Kaufman, 1921; Texas in *Zander the Great* by Salisbury Field, 1923; Sverre Peterson in *White Desert* by Maxwell Anderson, 1923; Sid Hunt in *Hell-Bent fer Heaven* by Hatcher Hughes, 1924; Steve Tuttle in *Lazybones* by Owen Davis, 1924; Dynamite Jim in *Processional* by John Howard Lawson, 1925; Dirk Yancey in *A Holy Terror,* 1925; in *Cowboy Crazy,* 1926; Frederick Williston in *Those We Love,* 1930; title role in *John Brown* by Ronald Gow, 1934; Mr. Antrobus in *The Skin of Our Teeth* by Thornton Wilder, 1955.

George Abbott called his autobiography *Mister Abbott,* but *Mister Broadway* would have been more apt. Abbott notes: "From 1935 to this time [1963] I have, with the exception of a week or two, always had at least one play running on Broadway." Accepting without question the hit/flop mentality of the Broadway marketplace, Abbott is a professional showman whose canon is altogether undisturbed by the least suggestion of intellect. The Abbott production is a good show, a farce, a melodrama, a musical comedy; briskly paced, it is geared for the big laugh, the big climax, and its light-fingered, high-stepping rhythm naturally does not translate well to the library.

The Abbott play comes wrapped in two basic packages: the racy, slangy comedies and melodramas of the 1920s and 1930s, and the musical comedies of the 1940s and 1950s. In both kinds of plays, the colorful details of a milieu or particular way of life offer the appeal. Abbott's plots (Abbott almost always works with a collaborator) are neither especially compelling nor well constructed. The "gimmick" is the milieu: the politics in *Fiorello!,* baseball in *Damn Yankees,* factory routine in *The Pajama Game,* the red-light district in *Tenderloin.* Sports, politics, the working class: the Abbott musical takes for its field of action a significant aspect of American life, only to reinforce popular myths of Americana. Relentlessly unexploratory, an Abbott show is indebted almost exclusively to the conventions of Broadway folklore. Entertainments like *The Pajama Game* and *Fiorello!* introduce a spurious kind of rebellious hero—a gal who wants the workers to get a raise, a mayor who tries to buck the compromises and corruptions of the political machine. But reinforcing rather than countering cliché, the shows ultimately leave the status quo unruffled. On the stage, aided by the music, and by the charm and élan of Abbott direction, the weaknesses of the books are camouflaged; on the page, unadorned, the plays are dreary, devoid not only of "ideas" but of spirit as well.

Abbott's earlier collaborations are much more flavorful. *Broadway*, a melodrama that combines prohibition, gang warfare, and the clichés of the backstage musical, is a lively and engaging portrait of an era. The earthy dialogue captures the lingo of the gangster and the entertainer; the slang has its own peculiar kind of melody, and the story—murder and retribution—is comfortably situated against the prohibition nightclub setting. *Three Men on a Horse* does for bookies what *Broadway* does for hoods: gives them the status of popular myth. This time the genre is farce rather than melodrama, but the same perky, accurate yet subtly stylized dialogue prevails. In less successful, but equally "contemporary" plays like *The Fall Guy* and *Love 'em and Leave 'em*, Abbott and his collaborators regard from the same sly angle other scenes of the 1920s. The fall guy goes wrong with some hoods, is caught and reprimanded, and returns chastened to his long-suffering wife. *Love 'em and Leave 'em* is a harsh portrait of a dame on the make; she'll go out with the highest bidder, the one who can give her the most diamonds and furs. Her schemes of self-advancement are set against the problems of the tenants of a working-class rooming house. The plays seem quaint today, but these glimpses into an America of the past retain their undignified comic and melodramatic energy. Artifacts of popular culture, the plays record the values and the aspirations and the setbacks and the sins of various character types of a turbulent and appealing era.

A shrewd practical man of the theatre, Abbott has given Broadway audiences what they have wanted to see, and he has entertained them more often, and over a longer period of time, than any other professional in the history of the American theatre. That is revealing if not an especially happy statistic.

—Foster Hirsch

AKALAITIS, JoAnne.

Born in Chicago, Illinois, 29 June 1937. Educated at the University of Chicago, B.A. in philosophy 1960. Married Philip Glass (divorced); one daughter. Presented work and taught playwriting throughout North America, Europe, Australia, Nicaragua, Israel, and Japan. Co-founder of Mabou Mines, New York, 1970, and performer, designer, and director, 1970–90; playwright-in-residence, Mark Taper Forum, Los Angeles, 1984–85; artistic associate, Joseph Papp Public Theater, New York, 1990–91; artistic director, New York Shakespeare Festival, 1991–93. Recipient: Obie award, 1976, 1977, 1979, 1984; Guggenheim fellowship, 1981; Rosemund Gilder award, 1981; Drama Desk award, 1983; Rockefeller grant, 1984. Agent: Flora Roberts, 157 West 57th Street, New York, New York 10019, U.S.A.

Publications

PLAYS

Southern Exposure (produced 1979).
Dead End Kids: A History of Nuclear Power, music by David Byrne (produced 1980).
Green Card (produced 1986). 1991.
The Voyage of the Beagle, (opera), music by Jon Gibson (produced 1986).

SCREENPLAY: *Dead End Kids: A History of Nuclear Power*, 1986.

THEATRICAL ACTIVITIES

DIRECTOR: **Plays**—all her own plays; *Cascando* by Samuel Beckett, 1976; *Dressed Like an Egg*, based on the writings of Colette, 1977; *Request Concert* by Franz Xaver Kroetz, 1981; *Red and Blue* by Michael Hurson, 1982; *Through the Leaves* by Franz Xaver Kroetz, 1984; *The Photographer* by Philip Glass, 1984; *Endgame* by Samuel Beckett, 1985; *Help Wanted* by Franz Xaver Kroetz, 1986; *The Balcony* by Jean Genet;*American Notes* by Len Jenkin, 1988; *Leon & Lena (and Lenz)* by George Büchner, 1989; *The Screens* by Jean Genet, 1989; *Cymbeline* by Shakespeare, 1989; *'Tis Pity She's a Whore* by John Ford, 1990; *Henry IV, Parts One and Two* by Shakespeare, 1991; *Prisoner of Love* by Jean Genet, 1992; *Woyzeck* by Georg Büchner, 1992. **Film**—*Dead End Kids*, 1986.
ACTOR: **Plays**—Role in *Dressed Like an Egg*, 1977; *The Shaggy Dog Animation* by Lee Breuer, 1977; *Dark Ride* by Len Jenkin, 1981.

The title "avant-gardist" has stuck with JoAnne Akalaitis since she co-founded Mabou Mines. More anathema than blessing, it has prompted prejudice and a fundamental misunderstanding of her work. But Akalaitis is interested in the vicissitudes of human nature, a complex pursuit that requires her to delve deeply. Consequently, the theater of JoAnne Akalaitis has frequently been called "impenetrable," or "intimidating." Less interested in effect, she probes for cause: how does a noble quest become corrupt? (*Dead End Kids*; *The Voyage of the Beagle*); wherefore man's inhumanity to man? (*Green Card*). To do this, Akalaitis writes (and directs) with the focus on key links within the chain of events. Identified, the links are then viewed through a microscope. In much the same way that her physicists in *Dead End Kids* probe for the quintessence of an inanimate element, Akalaitis contemplates the cognizant animal.

One could take such a comparison further and say that, in a sense, to experience Akalaitis's theater is to sit in at the atomic level. At first sight, it appears chaotic: it is consuming, frenetic, kinetic, volatile, and often unforgiving. She eschews plot and narrative, alternately flashing, and contrasting, theory and practice. Dubious of rhetoric, she renders dialogue almost secondary in the process. The preservation of temporal and spatial continuity does not always accurately reflect cause and effect, and when it does not, Akalaitis arranges her own chronology. Not satisfied with actors simply reading dialogue and making the occasional gesture, she synthesizes a variety of media. Thus choreographer, composer, and photographer are as integral to the play as the text. Her atomic stage is rich in both image and language, and explicitly

reflects the intensity of everyday life. The result is an almost successful trans-
mogrification of theater, forming what critics have referred to as a "gestalt"—
the creation of an environment where it is impossible to distill any element
from the play without radically altering the work.

Akalaitis's concern with the shortcomings of language is perhaps best
reflected in *Green Card*, a rapid-fire montage of music, slides, songs, dance,
words, and film. It is a caustic satire concerning superficial values, bringing
face-to-face the Haves (citizens of the United States) and Have Nots (refugees
seeking asylum in the States). The play demonstrates how language is a trap
and how its subscribers are too easily held captive. Immigrants struggle to
understand the subtleties of the English language. "Learn English! Learn
English!" native speakers of Vietnamese, Yiddish, Spanish, Russian, Chinese
are warned or be faced with ignorance and confusion—even death. Yet when
they resolve to do so, what they learn is that they have not been adequately
prepared to comprehend it. For example, when a student asks for an explanation of the "REAL difference between 'I was writing' and 'I have written',"
the response is an impatient: "'I was writing' is the imperfect tense while 'I
have written' is the present perfect tense." Not quite sure what to make of this
answer, the student denigrates herself (acknowledging the inferiority of her
race) until the evening school teacher responds grandly: "The imperfect tense
refers to what WAS, while the present perfect tense refers to what HAS
BEEN."

To obtain a green card, that precious document promising a life with dignity
and reward to thousands of refugees, characters must compete on The Green
Card Show, the "game you have to play if you want to stay." Mocking the
consumer culture, Akalaitis transforms Ellis Island into a TV game show set
complete with canned applause and neon lights. If they win, the prize, of
course, is permission to stay in the country; to lose however, is to "get sent
back to where they belong." Akalaitis pummels characters and audience with
idioms, building to a frenzy: what is the difference between "burn up," "burn
down," "burnt out"; how does one get "carried away" without movement;
how do Zan and Rich "pull off" a joke—what is being removed and from
where? Her questions are ambiguous and mischievous enough to confuse a
native American-English speaker:

Q: What is the most contemporary use of the expression to TURN
     ONE ON or to TURN ONE OFF?
   a: Pretty women certainly TURN Charlie ON?
   b: Some of the Great Renaissance painters TURN me ON but some
       of the modern ones TURN me OFF.
   c. Minimalist post-modern performance art of the 1980's is a real
       TURN OFF for me.

Finally, language becomes more than just a trap—a prison and a kind of
torture as an immigrant is grilled by officials to reveal his history and recent
whereabouts. With search lights flashing across her stage and whistles at ear-
piercing decibels, Akalaitis's immigration officials weed out the sick and
undesirable and begin the examinations at break-neck speed. Struggling to
keep up and misunderstanding the occasional trick question, the applicant
begins blurting out responses half in English, half in Spanish.

This adroit manipulation of the traditional dramatic form is perhaps best experienced in *Dead End Kids*. Akalaitis has referred to this as an "impassioned repudiation of nuclear ineptitude." In context, it is a history of science (specifically, physics) beginning with 15th-century alchemists and ending in the present with the careless and devastating misuse of nuclear power. *Dead End Kids* is concerned with how, in spite of the best intentions, the human journey for knowledge is doomed. Released from its narrative, the play shifts into a whirling multimedia extravaganza. Switching to variety show format (circa 1962) our host and hostess primp and pose and gloss over any potentially distressing news items. Scenes change, and time shifts. Our hostess daydreams and the magic potions of an alchemist bubble forth. Another shift: suddenly, we are at a science fair where a young pupil and his perky teacher announce "This is the H bomb." Producing ingredients and parts from a bag, we are informed: "It's a question of design, not ingredients." "Be careful," our older guide counsels, "it would be such a pity to have even the tiniest explosion." Slides of Hiroshima and Nagasaki remind us just what sort of pity. "Spllllaaaaat! Nagasaki" reiterates Akalaitis. We witness explosion after explosion. Flash: a scene has changed; fragments fall and form new vignettes. She is as much an alchemist as the mysterious cloaked characters who mix potions and recite spells. The alchemist strives in vain to turn base metals into gold, while Akalaitis separates the elements of drama and recombines them to produce a strikingly original theater.

—Roxana Petzold

ALBEE, Edward (Franklin, III).

Born in Virginia, 12 March 1928; adopted as an infant. Educated at Rye County Day School, Lawrenceville, New Jersey, 1940–43; Valley Forge Military Academy, Pennsylvania, 1943–44; Choate School, Connecticut, 1944–46; Trinity College, Hartford, Connecticut, 1946–47; Columbia University, New York, 1949. Served in the U.S. Army. Radio writer, WNYC, office boy, Warwick and Legler, record salesman, Bloomingdale's, book salesman, G. Schirmer, counterman, Manhattan Towers Hotel, messenger, Western Union, 1955–58, all in New York; producer, with Richard Barr and Clinton Wilder, Barr/Wilder/Albee Playwrights Unit, later Albarwild Theatre Arts, and Albar Productions, New York. Founder, William Flanagan Centre for Creative Persons, Montauk, Long Island, New York, 1971, and Edward Albee Foundation, 1978. U.S. cultural exchange visitor to the U.S.S.R., 1963. Co-director, Vivian Beaumont Theater, New York, 1981; resident playwright, Atlantic Center for the Arts, New Smyrna Beach, Florida, 1982; Regents' professor of drama, University of California at Irvine, 1983–85. Recipient: Berlin Festival award, 1959, 1961; Vernon Rice award, 1960; Obie award, 1960; Argentine Critics award, 1961; Lola D'Annunzio award, 1961; New York Drama Critics Circle award, 1964; Outer Circle award, 1964; London *Evening Standard* award, 1964; Tony award, 1964; Margo Jones award, 1965; Pulitzer prize, 1967, 1975; American Academy gold medal, 1980; Brandeis University Creative Arts award, 1983, 1984; 10th Annual William

Inge award, 1990–91. D. Litt.: Emerson College, Boston, 1967; Litt.D.: Trinity College, 1974. Member, American Academy, 1966; member, Theater Hall of Fame, 1985. Agent: William Morris Agency, 1350 Avenue of the Americas, New York, New York 10019. Address: 14 Harrison Street, New York, New York 10013, U.S.A.

Publications

PLAYS

The Zoo Story (produced 1959). In *The Zoo Story, The Death of Bessie Smith, The Sandbox*, 1960.

The Death of Bessie Smith (produced 1960). In *The Zoo Story, The Death of Bessie Smith, The Sandbox*, 1960.

The Sandbox (produced 1960). In *The Zoo Story, The Death of Bessie Smith, The Sandbox*, 1960.

The Zoo Story, The Death of Bessie Smith, The Sandbox: Three Plays. 1960; as *The Zoo Story and Other Plays* (includes *The American Dream*), 1962.

Fam and Yam (produced 1960). 1961.

The American Dream (produced 1961). 1961.

Bartleby, with James Hinton, Jr., music by William Flanagan, adaptation of the story by Melville (produced 1961).

Who's Afraid of Virginia Woolf? (produced 1962). 1962.

The Ballad of the Sad Café, adaptation of the story by Carson McCullers (produced 1963). 1963.

Tiny Alice (produced 1964). 1965.

Malcolm, adaptation of the novel by James Purdy (produced 1966). 1966.

A Delicate Balance (produced 1966). 1966.

Breakfast at Tiffany's, music by Bob Merrill, adaptation of the story by Truman Capote (produced 1966).

Everything in the Garden, adaptation of the play by Giles Cooper (produced 1967). 1968.

Box and Quotations from Chairman Mao Tse-tung (as *Box-Mao-Box*, produced, 1968; as *Box and Quotations from Chairman Mao Tse-tung*, produced 1968). 1969.

All Over (produced 1971). 1971.

Seascape (also director: produced 1975). 1975.

Counting the Ways (produced 1976). In *Two Plays*, 1977.

Listening (broadcast 1976; also director: produced 1977). In *Two Plays*, 1977.

Two Plays. 1977.

The Lady from Dubuque (produced 1980). 1980.

Lolita, adaptation of the novel by Vladimir Nabokov (produced 1981). 1984.

Plays:
1. *The Zoo Story, The Death of Bessie Smith, The Sandbox, The American Dream*. 1981.
2. *Tiny Alice, A Delicate Balance, Box and Quotations from Chairman Mao Tse-tung*. 1982.
3. *Seascape, Counting the Ways, Listening, All Over*. 1982.

4.   *Everything in the Garden, Malcolm, The Ballad of the Sad Café.* 1982.
The Man Who Had Three Arms (also director: produced 1982).
Envy, in *Faustus in Hell* (produced 1985).
Marriage Play (produced 1987).

SCREENPLAY: *A Delicate Balance,* 1976.

RADIO PLAY: *Listening,* 1976.

NOVEL
Straight Through the Night. 1989.

OTHER
Conversations with Edward Albee, edited by Philip C. Kolin. 1988.

BIBLIOGRAPHY: *Edward Albee at Home and Abroad: A Bibliography 1958–June 1968* by Richard E. Amacher and Margaret Rule, 1970; *Edward Albee: An Annotated Bibliography 1968–1977* by Charles Lee Green, 1980; *Edward Albee: A Bibliography* by Richard Tyce, 1986.

CRITICAL STUDIES: *Edward Albee* by Richard E. Amacher, 1969, revised edition, 1982; *Edward Albee* by Ruby Cohn, 1969; *Edward Albee: Playwright in Protest* by Michael E. Rutenberg, 1969; *Albee* by C.W.E Bigsby, 1969, and *Edward Albee: A Collection of Critical Essays* edited by Bigsby, 1975; *Edward Albee* by Ronald Hayman, 1971; *From Tension to Tonic: The Plays of Edward Albee* by Anne Paolucci, 1972; *Edward Albee: The Poet of Loss* by Anita M. Stenz, 1978; *Who's Afraid of Edward Albee?* by Foster Hirsch, 1978; *Edward Albee: An Interview and Essays* edited by Julian N. Wasserman, 1983; *Edward Albee* by Gerald McCarthy, 1987; "Pure and Simple: the Recent Plays of Edward Albee" by Liliane Kerjan, in *New Essays on American Drama* edited by G. Debusscher, 1989.

THEATRICAL ACTIVITIES
DIRECTOR: several of his own plays.
ACTOR: **Radio Play**—Voice in *Listening,* 1988.

At the dawn of the 1960s Edward Albee introduced a humorous self-definition on stage with FAM, the "Famous American playwright," and YAM, the "Young American playwright," thus forecasting his exemplary career. Regarded as avant-garde when his first play, *The Zoo Story,* was produced in West Berlin on a double bill with Beckett's *Krapp's Last Tape,* he rocketed to fame when his director Alan Schneider decided to present *Who's Afraid of Virginia Woolf?* on Broadway.

Albee's beginnings established him as a master of language and absurd humour, with a fine ear for idiom and rhythm, a compassionate voice appealing for communication between ethnic communities as in *The Death of Bessie Smith,* between generations as in *The American Dream* or *The Sandbox,* or again between the dominant segments of society and the hipsters, the dropouts and the solitary dreamers as in *The Zoo Story.* For three decades, *The*

Zoo Story has remained a favourite and a classic in university festivals and café-theatres of the western world because of its intensity, its spiritual dénouement, and above all its ultimate confrontation with the Other. Will Jerry change the world having changed one man, Peter, his neighbour on a bench in Central Park? In *Who's Afraid of Virginia Woolf?* will George and Martha— named after the Washingtons—be able to face the future without inventing new lies in order to survive? The question mark in the title sets Albee's tone: an incessant double-game of truth and illusion, of success and failure, of transgression and regression. The evaluation of ideological choices, the recognition of sterility sound all the more acute as it takes place on a New England campus, thus emphasizing the responsibility of academics in the intellectual and social debate of the nation.

As always, Albee tosses questions to the audience, refusing to give easy answers, demanding stringency and honesty. He places his characters—the middle-aged bourgeoisie, as a rule—in a *huis-clos* ("closed doors," in other words, no exit) where they are confronted with loss (*The American Dream*), with death (*All Over, The Lady from Dubuque*), with moral dilemmas (*A Delicate Balance*), with their conceptions of God (*Tiny Alice*). As always he denounces betrayals, vices born of leisure among the idle rich, comfortable clichés.

Albee has been presented as the saviour of the American theater, coming forth in a period of void, evolving from Off-Broadway to Broadway, experimenting in every direction, blending the surreal, the poetic, the hermetic into a naturalistic tradition, committing himself to serious articulation of the existential questions of our time. He also flirts with vaudeville (*Counting the Ways*), science fiction (*Seascape*), adaptations, film scripts, libretti: every dramatic form has spurred his curiosity. An admirer of Tennessee Williams, he captures the pulse and the tensions inherent in our conflicting desires and transposes them into flamboyant symphonies or subtle interrelated chamber-music pieces (*Box and Quotations from Chairman Mao Tse-Tung, The Sandbox, The American Dream*).

The years have brought a sense of the essentials: Albee has described *The Lady from Dubuque* as "perfectly straightforward and clear." Indeed, since it is terminal cancer. But the two-act drama about three interwoven suburban couples suddenly visited by the elegant and motherly lady and her black companion is also a ritual of compassion with games of comfort, not of pain. *Listening*, commissioned as radio-play, explores "the sound of an idea" and once more the failure to communicate within a strange triangle: a cook, a nurse, and a patient mix blurred memories and fatal refusals.

Press critics have too often considered *Who's Afraid of Virginia Woolf?* as Albee's main contribution to American drama and misjudged his later ventures. The play, which has been performed around the world and popularized through its film version, belongs undoubtedly to the classic repertory of the century, thanks to its organic integration of allegory, brilliant wit, and grotesque parody: no one will forget the psychic violence, the internal turmoil, the shared fantasies, and final compassion. But Albee's overwhelming presence covers more ground and nurtures a broader ambition: to keep characters and audiences off-balance, impelling a slow internal transformation of the dramatic medium.

For Edward Albee, writing is an act of optimism. Born inside the trade, like Eugene O'Neill, he remains a radical. Wealthy by birth and after the colossal success of *Woolf*, which gave him the economic leeway not to have "to go around writing *The Son of Virginia Woolf*," his aim is to continue to take chances in the theatre and create his own style.

—Liliane Kerjan

See the essay on *Who's Afraid of Virginia Woolf?*

ALFRED, William.

Born in New York City, 16 August 1922. Educated at Brooklyn College, B.A. 1948; Harvard University, Cambridge, Massachusetts, M.A. 1949, Ph.D. 1954. Served in the U.S. Army, 1943–46. Associate editor, *American Poet*, Brooklyn, 1942–44. Instructor, 1954–57, assistant professor, 1957–59, associate professor, 1959–63, and since 1963 professor of English, Harvard University. Recipient: Brooklyn College Literary Association award, 1953; Amy Lowell traveling poetry scholarship, 1956; Brandeis University Creative Arts award, 1960; American Academy grant, 1965. Address: 31 Athens Street, Cambridge, Massachusetts 02138, U.S.A.

Publications

PLAYS

The Annunciation Rosary. 1948.
Agamemnon (produced 1953). 1954.
Hogan's Goat (produced 1965). 1966; revised version, as *Cry for Us All*, with Albert Marre, music by Mitch Leigh (produced 1970).
The Curse of an Aching Heart, music by Claibe Richardson (produced 1979). 1983.
Holy Saturday (produced 1980). In *Canto*, vol. 3 no. 1, 1979–80.

OTHER

Editor, with others, *Complete Prose Works of John Milton 1.* 1953.

Translator, *Beowulf*, in *Medieval Epics.* 1963.

MANUSCRIPT COLLECTIONS:
Houghton Library, Harvard University, Cambridge, Massachusetts; Brooklyn College Library.

William Alfred comments:

I write plays because I love people the way dog-lovers love dogs, indiscriminately, and want to capture as many as I can in all their baffled splendor.

"It is a fearful thing to love what death can touch." These words are uttered by Cassandra in poet-playwright William Alfred's blank verse version of the tragedy of Agamemnon. Yet they come not from Homer nor Aeschylus; they

were found on an ancient Vermont gravestone. The desperate sense of irremediable loss, both restrained and simple in this phrasing, is typical of Alfred's
best dialogue in his *Agamemnon*. It is at once economic, poetic, and dramatically effective. In reading or in playing, one does not have the vaguely
disquieting feeling that Alfred's characters are speaking English translations of
Sophocles or Anouilh. They are all too human, which at times diminishes the
magnitude of the tragic experience, especially when the dramatic diction tries
to evoke a kind of realism. Cassandra says to Agamemnon on the voyage back
from Troy: "A penny for your thoughts." Had she said "drachma" instead, it
would still be jarring.

Central to Alfred's idea of the events is Agamemnon's guilty concealment of
the true manner of his daughter Iphigenia's death at Aulis. On ship-board, he
has the tongue cut from a man who dares to utter the truth. He keeps it from
Cassandra, who divines it. Clytemnestra has been told her daughter died of
fever, but her oldest adviser actually saw the ritual slaying. Her co-regents have
said nothing of this, anxious to preserve order in the kingdom. Aegisthus, in an
awkward situation he'd like to escape from, feels used. The action moves back
and forth from the palace to Agamemnon's ship, as the moment of reunion
approaches. When Clytemnestra finally discovers the truth, she goes down to
the courtyard to receive—and to murder—her husband and Cassandra. This
action is heard from offstage by her advisers—and the audience.

It's curious that Alfred observes this nicety of the Attic Greek theatre—
scenes of horror offstage—when he is much more Shakespearean in his alternation of locales and intercutting of developing plotlines. He certainly makes
thoughtful use of the soliloquy, but there are moments in the play when poetic
ruminations detract from the potential power of the approaching confrontation by further foreshadowing it or by delaying it needlessly. Part of the
problem is that Alfred is a poet first and a playwright second. That he is also a
distinguished academic lends strength to his resources in rhetoric and cultural
allusion, but this may have made him less spontaneous as a dramatist.

Periodically, there comes a fervent cry for the "return of poetry to the
theatre," as though the victory of prose on stage were some kind of debasing of
the drama. T.S. Eliot—who later said he'd learned playwriting at the public's
expense—and Christopher Fry were hailed in the 1940s as new champions of
the verse drama. The danger to the theatre in such cyclic surgings of desire for
poetry on stage is that poetry-lovers and their favorite poets—encouraged to
write for the theatre—will be more interested in images and devices than in
characterisation and dramatic structure. When Alfred's tragic tale of ambition
and deceit in *fin de siècle* Brooklyn, *Hogan's Goat*, was initially produced by
the American Place Theatre which then specialized in staging works by poets
and novelists, it was praised for its poetic virtues.

What made *Hogan's Goat* interesting to audiences, beyond its lilting
Brooklyn Irish diction and homely but arresting images, was, however, its
strong plot and vivid characters. As in *Agamemnon*, Alfred's tragic hero,
Matthew Stanton, has concealed a terrible truth from his young wife. His
vaunting political ambitions are brought low with the threat of blackmail, and
he kills his wife in a frenzy when she tries to leave him, having learned their
marriage isn't legal, that he was the kept man of a powerful woman whom he
abandoned cruelly. There is power in the conflicts; complexity in the charac-

ters. Alfred's dialogue captures the idioms and rhythms of the Brooklyn Irish in the 1890s. *Hogan's Goat* recreates a bygone era in New York City's ethnic and political history in a vividly dramatic way. Best of all for ordinary audiences, the flow of Irish speech—heightened though it often is—is seldom perceived as poetry, but rather as passionate diction.

The critical and popular acceptance of *Hogan's Goat* led to a Broadway musical version, *Cry for Us All*, which failed. The essential failure was not in Alfred's drama, but in Albert Marre's notion that, with music by Mitch Leigh, this might be another Broadway hit like *Man of La Mancha*, also produced by Marre. As with the disappointing musical *Zorba!*, *Hogan's Goat* should have been an opera.

This disappointment didn't deter Alfred from offering Broadway in 1982 a charming suite of explorations among the Brooklyn Irish and their friends, *The Curse of an Aching Heart*. Subtitled "An Evening's Comedy," it is also a verse play, with some appealing songs by Alfred and music by Claibe Richardson. But the work failed to win a critical majority or a long run. Nonetheless, it remains a wryly and comically honest evocation of growing up in the big city in the 1920s and after. Its link with *Hogan's Goat* is its revelation of the hopes and defeats of descendants of figures noted in the earlier drama. It is not a sequential narrative; with a Prologue (1942) which looks backward, five one-act plays are offered, showing various stages in the lives of Frances Anna Duffy Walsh, her uncle Jo Jo, and their neighbors, friends, and lovers. The five minidramas are: *Friday Night Dreams Come True—1923*; *Clothes Make the Woman—1925*; *The Curse of an Aching Heart—1927*; *All Saints, All Souls—1935*; and *Holy Saturday—1942*. (The last play has been published and produced separately as well as *en suite*.) When Jo Jo inadvertently lets Fran know he is strongly attracted to her—even as he rages against her boyfriends, it shocks her. Until the end of the plays, when he's old and helpless and a healing occurs between them, she refuses to speak to him. These plays are not only an effective exercise in nostalgia, recreating games, folklore, values, prejudices, and style of the 1920s, 1930s, and 1940s, but they are also moving accounts of human strivings for contact and affection.

—Glenn Loney

ANDERSON, Robert (Woodruff).

Born in New York City, 28 April 1917. Educated at Phillips Exeter Academy, Exeter, New Hampshire, 1931–35; Harvard University, Cambridge, Massachusetts, 1935–42, A.B. (magna cum laude) 1939, M.A. 1940. Served in the U.S. Naval Reserve, 1942–46: lieutenant; Bronze Star. Married 1) Phyllis Stohl in 1940 (died 1956); 2) the actress Teresa Wright in 1959 (divorced 1978). Actor, South Shore Players, Cohasset, Massachusetts, summers 1937 and 1938. Assistant in English, Harvard University, 1939–42; teacher, Erskine School, Boston, 1941; teacher of playwriting, American Theatre Wing, New York, 1946–51, and Actors Studio, New York, 1955–56; member of the faculty, Salzburg Seminar in American Studies, 1968; writer-in-residence, University of North Carolina, Chapel Hill, 1969, and University of Iowa Writers Workshop, Iowa City, 1976, Member of the Playwrights Producing

Company, 1953–60; president, New Dramatists Committee, 1955–56, and Dramatists Guild, 1971–73; member of the Board of Governors, American Playwrights Theatre, 1963–79. Since 1965 member of the Council, and since 1980 vice-president, Authors League of America. Recipient: National Theatre Conference prize, 1945; Rockefeller fellowship, 1946; Writers Guild of America award, for screenplay, 1970; ACE award, for television, 1991. Member, Theater Hall of Fame, 1980. Agent: Mitch Douglas, International Creative Management, 40 West 57th Street, New York, New York 10019. Address: Roxbury, Connecticut 06783, U.S.A.

Publications

PLAYS

Hour Town, music and lyrics by Anderson (produced 1938).
Come Marching Home (produced 1945).
The Eden Rose (produced 1949).
Sketches in *Dance Me a Song* (produced 1950).
Love Revisited (produced 1951).
All Summer Long, adaptation of the novel *A Wreath and a Curse* by Donald Wetzel (produced 1952). 1955.
Tea and Sympathy (produced 1953). 1953.
Silent Night, Lonely Night (produced 1959). 1960.
The Days Between (produced 1965). 1965.
You Know I Can't Hear You When the Water's Running (produced 1967). 1967.
I Never Sang for My Father (produced 1967). 1968; screenplay published, 1970.
Solitaire/Double Solitaire (produced 1971). 1972.
Free and Clear (produced 1983).
The Last Act Is a Solo (televised 1991). 1991.

SCREENPLAYS: *Tea and Sympathy*, 1956; *Until They Sail*, 1957; *The Nun's Story*, 1959; *The Sand Pebbles*, 1966; *I Never Sang for My Father*, 1970.

RADIO AND TELEVISION PLAYS: *David Copperfield*, *Oliver Twist*, *Vanity Fair*, *The Glass Menagerie*, *Trilby*, *The Old Lady Shows Her Medals*, *The Petrified Forest*, *The Scarlet Pimpernel*, *A Farewell to Arms*, *Summer and Smoke*, *Arrowsmith*, and other adaptations, 1946–52; *The Patricia Neal Story*, 1980; *The Last Act Is a Solo*, 1991; *Absolute Strangers*, 1991.

NOVELS

After. 1973.
Getting Up and Going Home. 1978.

OTHER

Co-editor, *Elements of Literature* (anthology). 6 vols., 1988.

MANUSCRIPT COLLECTION: Harvard University Theatre Collection, Cambridge, Massachusetts.

CRITICAL STUDIES: *Life among the Playwrights* by John F. Wharton, 1974; *Playwrights Talk about Playwriting* edited by Lewis Funke, 1975; *Robert Anderson* by Thomas Adler, 1978; "A Dramatist's Inner Space," in *Dramatists Guild Quarterly*, Spring 1979; *The Strands Entwined* by Samuel Bernstein, 1980; *Represented by Audrey Wood* by Audrey Wood and Max Wilk, 1981.

Robert Anderson comments:

(1973) It is difficult and dangerous for a writer to talk about his own work. He should move on to whatever he is impelled to write about next without looking back and trying to analyze his work. Recently I read a doctoral thesis written about me and my plays. In many ways I wish I hadn't read it. I don't think it is wise for a writer to think about his "continuing themes" and recurring attitudes.

When I was near the end of writing *Tea and Sympathy*, my first wife begged me to tell her something of the subject of my new play. (I never discuss my work with anyone while I am writing.) I gave in and simply told her it took place in a boys' school. She said, "Oh, my God, not another play about a boys' school!" This almost stopped me. At that moment I hadn't been consciously aware that I had written other (unproduced) work with a boys' school background. I simply knew that I wanted to write that play. My wife's making me aware that I had worked that vein before almost stopped me from finishing the play.

People sometimes say, "Why don't you write about something besides marriage?" Strangely, it is only after I have finished a play that I am aware that I have written again about marriage. Each time I start a play, I certainly don't have the feeling that I am going over old ground. I feel I have something new and different nagging at me to be written. I do not consciously say, "This is my theme. I have done it reasonably well before. Let's try it again."

And these "plays about marriage" are seldom just that. *Solitaire/Double Solitaire* was not about marriage in the present and in the future, as some critics described it. It was about the loneliness of being alone and the loneliness of marriage. *The Days Between* was not about an academic marriage on the rocks but about a man who was ruining his life and his marriage by being unable to live the ordinary, unexciting days of life, "the days between." Marriage is often the arena of the plays, but not always the real subject matter.

As a matter of fact, the plays are rarely "about" what critics say they are about. *Tea and Sympathy* has always been described as "a play about homosexuality." In effect, it has nothing to do with homosexuality. It has to do with an unjust charge of homosexuality and what follows such a charge. It has to do with responsibility, which must extend beyond giving tea and sympathy; it has to do again with loneliness; it has to do with questioning some popular definitions of manliness; and, most important, it has to do with judgment by prejudice . . . and a great deal more, I hope.

You Know I Can't Hear You When the Water's Running was said to be "about" sex. The plays were told in terms of sex, but they were not about sex. As Elia Kazan said when he first read the manuscript, "They're about the same things as your other plays except this time it came out funny and sad." They are very sad plays. As Walter Kerr said of them, "Laugh only when it hurts."

I seem to have written largely about the family, or rather to have used the family as the arena. By and large English critics feel that American playwrights rather overwork this area of concern. Still, our three finest plays are, probably, *The Glass Menagerie*, *Death of a Salesman*, and *Long Day's Journey into Night*. I am glad that Williams, Miller, and O'Neill didn't scare when and if someone said to them, "not another play about the family!"

I have been amused that I have sometimes been considered a "commercial" playwright. I am amused because each of my plays has had an enormous struggle to get on. Nobody has thought of them as "commercial" till after they were successful. *Tea and Sympathy* was turned down by almost every producer and was on its way back into my files when the Playwrights Company optioned it and started me on my career. *You Know I Can't Hear You When the Water's Running* was turned down by everyone until two new producers "who didn't know any better" took a chance on it. I waited something like seven years before someone "took a chance" on *I Never Sang for My Father*. I think I can't be blamed for being amused when I hear myself described as "commercial," especially inasmuch as three of my plays have premiered in very non-commercial regional theatres, one opened Off-Broadway, and one launched The American Playwrights Theatre, a project which seeks to get the plays of "established" playwrights into the regional and college theatres rather than into Broadway theatres.

At various times in my youth I wanted to be an actor and a poet. I acted in college and summer theatres, and I was elected Harvard Class Poet on graduation. I think it is only natural that with these two "bents" I should end up a playwright, because in playwriting one finds the same kind of compression and essentialization one finds in poetry. Poems and plays are both the tips of icebergs.

Finally, I admire form. I took a course at Harvard with Robert Frost. One evening he was asked why he didn't write free verse. He replied, "I don't like playing tennis with the net down." I think that a great deal of the excitement in the theatre comes from using the limitations of the theatre creatively. Most plays, when they are adapted as movies, "opened up," lose their effectiveness, because part of their attraction was the way the playwright had found intensity and a creative impulse in dealing with the limitations of the theatre. Compare the play and the film of *Our Town*. I believe that form can be challenged, changed, stretched. But some kind of form seems to me of the essence of theatre.

I would wish that a person coming on my plays for the first time would not have any preconceived idea as to what they are "about." Each reader or spectator is a new collaborator, and he will, in a sense, write his own play and arrive at his own meanings, based on his own experience of life.

(1988) It has never been easier to get a play done some- place. It has never been more difficult to get a play done where a playwright can earn enough money to write the next play. Many years ago I wrote something which has been endlessly quoted and is still true: "You can make a killing in the theatre but not a living." If I had not been able to write movies and television from time to time, I could not have continued as a playwright. Most playwrights I know are moonlighters. When *Tea and Sympathy* was done in 1953, it cost forty thousand dollars to produce, with Elia Kazan, Jo Mielziner, and Deborah Kerr, all superb and expensive talents. I am told that my six character new play, *The Kissing Was Always the Best*, will probably cost close to a million dollars to produce on Broadway. I try not to think about this.

Robert Anderson first received limited recognition as a playwright in 1945 when his play *Come Marching Home* was awarded first prize in a National Theatre Conference contest. This was followed five years later by *Love Revisited* which was performed at the Westport County Playhouse. But it was Alan Schneider's Washington Arena production of *All Summer Long* that really marked his emergence as a writer of genuine power and considerable subtlety. Though it was not particularly well received when it eventually reached Broadway two years later, the success of *Tea and Sympathy* had by then established Anderson's reputation as a skilful and impressive playwright.

All Summer Long is a sensitive if somewhat portentously symbolic play about the loss of illusions and the inevitable dissolution of beauty, love, and innocence. The family, which is the focus for this elegy on human weakness, live beside a river which is slowly eroding the bank under their home—a none-too-subtle image of the collapse of genuine feeling within the family itself. Willie, the youngest boy, is on the verge of adolescence and his brother Don, a college sports star crippled in a motor accident, tries to protect him from his own emerging sexuality and from the cynicism and bitterness of the rest of the family, though ironically Don is unable to come to terms with the change in his own life. Anderson piles on the agony, with parents who no longer care for each other or their children, and a girl who tries to produce an abortion by throwing herself on an electrified fence. Though Willie and Don spend the summer trying to build a wall to hold out the threatening floodwaters, the forces of nature can no more be controlled on this level than they can in the lives of individuals growing more self-centered and lonely as they grow older. The play ends as the house collapses—an obvious image of the family itself which has long since disintegrated in human terms.

Though he has never since relied on such a melodramatic climax Anderson's work is never entirely free of a certain dramatic overstatement. In *All Summer Long* Don is not only a crippled sports star, itself something of a cliché, but the accident which caused his injury had been a result of his father's inadequacy. Similarly, in a later play, *Silent Night, Lonely Night*, a child dies because her mother is at that very moment preoccupied with reading a letter which reveals her husband's adultery. Her subsequent plunge into insanity is, perhaps, understandable, but serves to create a melodramatic setting for what is otherwise a subtle examination of human need. Nowhere, however, does Anderson control this tendency better than in what remains his best play, *Tea and Sympathy*, though even here there is a certain lack of subtlety in his portrait of a callous father and a weak and therefore vindictive schoolmaster who may well share the very sexual deviancy which he denounces in others.

Tea and Sympathy was Anderson's Broadway debut and earned him a deserved reputation for confronting delicate and even contentious issues with courage and effect—a reputation which he himself was to parody in his later

You Know I Can't Hear You When the Water's Running. The play is concerned with the plight of a 17-year-old boy in a New England boarding school
who is accused of being homosexual. Unsure of himself and tormented by his
fellow pupils, he turns to his housemaster's wife, whom he loves with adolescent passion and anguish. Horrified by her husband's inhumanity and genuinely concerned for the fate of the young boy, she finally allows him to make
love to her—the only way she can see him regaining his sexual self-confidence
and his faith in other people. The boy's father, long since divorced, has never
offered his son the slightest affection while his housemaster punishes the boy
for his own suppressed fears. As a perceptive indictment of the witch-hunt the
play was produced at a particularly appropriate moment, the height of the
McCarthy era. But it is a great deal more than this and despite the rather casual
psychological assumptions which underlie the portraits of both father and
housemaster the play was a perceptive comment on the failure of compassion
in a society which demanded conformity as the price of acceptance.

Anderson's next play, *Silent Night, Lonely Night*, again dealt with the
anguish of those who are deprived of the affection and understanding of those
who should be closest to them. Katherine, temporarily separated from a
husband whom she has just discovered to be unfaithful, finds herself alone in a
New England inn on Christmas Eve. Upset and lonely she dines with another
guest whose wife is in a nearby mental hospital—driven there by his own
infidelity. For this one night they manage to overcome their sense of guilt and
self-concern in order to offer one another the momentary consolation of true
compassion. The simple symmetry of the structure underlines the justice of
those who see Anderson primarily as a constructor of well-made plays, but
despite this and despite the melodramatic nature of the man's personal history
the play remains a delicate study which compares well with Anderson's earlier
work.

His next production, four one-act comedies presented under the title *You
Know I Can't Hear You When the Water's Running*, was not staged until eight
years later. Lightweight sketches which partly depend on and partly satirize the
new vogue for sexual explictness, they show little of his earlier sensitivity or
skill. The same nostalgic regret for the decay of love and the passing of youth is
manifested in two of the plays, "The Footsteps of Doves" and "I'll Be Home
for Christmas," but now it becomes the subject of rather tasteless jokes. The
spectacle of Anderson mocking his earlier convictions is not an altogether
attractive one, for the humour of the plays derives from precisely that cynical
worldly-wise detachment which he had previously seen as the enemy of the
human spirit. When he briefly comes close to a moment of true pathos, in "I'll
Be Home for Christmas," the integrity of the scene is lost in the sophisticated
banter of the rest of the play.

I Never Sang for My Father does little to redeem the weakness of this
composite play. Centering on the almost neurotic need of a son to win the love
of a bitter and virtually senile father, it reveals not only the terrifying gaps
which can open up between those who should be drawn to one another by all
the ties of natural affection and concern, but also the desperate absence of love
in a world full of people who choose to shelter and exile themselves in the
fragile shell of their own personalities. Yet, despite the emotive nature of his
subject, Anderson fails, in the last resort, to establish the tension which he

creates as anything more than a pathological study—a compassionate and detailed examination of individuals who, despite the familiarity of their situations, remain case studies rather than evocative projections of a universal state.

In some respects Anderson suggests comparison with dramatists like William Inge, Carson McCullers, and Tennessee Williams. Like them he has chosen to describe the plight of those whose romantic dreams founder on the harsh realities of modern life. Emotionally scarred and sexually vulnerable, his protagonists try to find their way in a world which frightens and dismays them. In *All Summer Long* and *Tea and Sympathy* the central figure, appropriately enough, is an adolescent—for the boy confronting sexuality and cruelty for the first time serves to emphasise simultaneously the ideals of youth and the cynicism and disillusionment of middle age. For Anderson this contrast constitutes the key to individual anguish and the mainspring of a pathos which he seems to regard as the truest expression of human experience. Clearly this is the stuff of which nostalgia and sentimentality are made and his work is open to both charges. Where Tennessee Williams balances his regret for the destruction of the innocent and the romantic with a grudging regard for the "Promethians" who dominate their surroundings, Anderson offers only a romantic regret that things cannot be other than they are. Where Inge and McCullers see the growth away from innocence into experience as a painful but necessary human process, Anderson tends to see it as the first stage in the extinction of genuine feeling and human compassion. If some people can sustain their innocence into maturity they do so, in his world it seems, only at the cost of their ability to act. It is a paradox which he is content to identify rather than examine with the kind of subtlety which Williams had brought to *The Glass Menagerie* and *Orpheus Descending*.

—C.W.E. Bigsby

ARDREY, Robert.

Born in Chicago, Illinois, 16 October 1908. Educated at the University of Chicago, 1927–30, Ph.B. 1930 (Phi Beta Kappa). Married Helene Johnson in 1938 (divorced, 1960); Berdine Grunewald, 1960; has three children. Theatre and film writer until 1958. Lecturer and consultant on the evolutionary origins of human behaviour, 1958–80. Recipient: Sergel Drama prize, 1935; Guggenheim fellowship, 1937; Sidney Howard Memorial prize, 1940; Theresa Helburn memorial award, 1961; Willkie Brothers grant, for anthropology, 1963. Fellow, Royal Society of Literature. *Died 14 January 1980.*

Publications

PLAYS

Star-Spangled (produced 1936). 1936.
Casey Jones (produced 1938).
How to Get Tough About It, (produced 1938).
Thunder Rock (produced 1939). 1940.
God and Texas. n.d.
Jeb (produced 1946). In *Plays of Three Decades,* 1968.

Sing Me No Lullaby (produced 1954). 1955.
Shadow of Heroes (produced 1958; as *Stone and Star*, produced 1961). 1958; in *Plays of Three Decades*, 1968.
Plays of Three Decades: Thunder Rock, 1939; *Jeb*, 1946; *Shadow of Heroes*, 1958. 1968.

SCREENPLAYS: *They Knew What They Wanted*, 1940; *A Lady Takes a Chance*, 1943; *The Green Years*, 1946; *The Three Musketeers*, 1948; *Madame Bovary*, 1949; *The Secret Garden*, 1949; *Quentin Durward*, 1955; *The Power and the Prize*, 1956; *The Wonderful Country*, 1959; *The Four Horsemen of the Apocalypse*, with John Gay, 1962; *Khartoum*, 1966; *The Animal Within* (documentary), 1975.

NOVELS
World's Beginning. 1944.
The Brotherhood of Fear. 1952.

OTHER
African Genesis: A Personal Investigation into the Animal Origins and Nature of Man. 1961.
The Territorial Imperative: A Personal Inquiry into the Animal Origins of Property and Nations. 1966.
The Social Contract: A Personal Inquiry into the Evolutionary Source of Order and Disorder. 1970.
Aggression and Violence in Man: A Dialogue Between Dr Louis Leakey and Mr Robert Ardrey. 1971.
The Hunting Hypothesis: A Personal Conclusion Concerning the Evolutionary Nature of Man. 1976.

MANUSCRIPT COLLECTION: Boston University.

Robert Ardrey wrote:

Like any other dramatist, in my earliest writings I was fascinated by the central question, Why do we act as we do? From the time of Aeschylus through Shakespeare to the present, any dramatist worthy of the term has been preoccupied by the problem of motivation. Fashions have changed with the centuries. We have looked to the intervention of the gods, as in the time of the Greeks. We have looked to society as in Ibsen, to rationality as in Shaw. In my own time we looked to Freud and to Marx for the determinisms of sex and economics. Always we have had the question, Why do we *act* as we do? And that is why in theatre we have such terms as acts, actors, actresses. The dramatist, throughout all ages, has been the poet of principal responsibility in such human investigations. And perhaps that is why, dissatisfied with all contemporary fashions of sex and economics, I left the theatre to pursue my investigations of the evolutionary sources of human behaviour. That we are four-dimensional beings, in whom the past lives as a portion of the present, is a thesis brought alive by such dramatists of genius as Harold Pinter. But for definitive investigation one must turn to stages larger than those of the theatre, always with the hope that any new understanding of our nature will be useful to the arts as to the sciences.

Any history of the American theatre would be deficient if it did not consider the plays of Robert Ardrey. His themes include many slices of American history and of the vast amalgam of cultures that America represents. But no playwright finds a place in history just for his themes and Ardrey's claim to acknowledgement must be attributed to his mastery over the components of dramatic literature. Settings are his particular forte, especially his native Midwest, but he set plays and scenarios all over the world, and, in particular, Africa, which he visited so often as an anthropologist and ethologist. He was a playwright who visualized staging problems long before the stage or movie director saw them, and guided these generally distraught persons to easy functioning. No wonder he was the golden boy of movie producers.

His characterizations—ordinary people in everyday situations—are made most convincingly real through his skill at re-creating ethnic speech patterns such as the Polish-American jargon (*Star-Spangled*), Southern American Black (*Jeb*), sub-standard speech of working class elements (*How to Get Tough About It, Casey Jones*), and so on. They are convincing and theatrically effective characters because Ardrey did not mimic them but represented them with a certain respect. This is because Ardrey respected all humanity and did not take up the clarion on behalf of the "down-trodden" or the underdog, but nurtured respect also for the anguished emotions of the powerful or the "overdog." Ardrey was not a political or even social writer, but a writer about the human soul, in settings that are charged generally with social problems which, though interesting, are mere scaffolding. His writing is infinitely closer to Ibsen than to Shaw. If his themes of anguish are dealt with on a philosophical plane with dialogue alone furnishing the dramatic tension, he fails. He is no Pirandello or Unamuno; but Brechtian he is and he demonstrated it in most of his plays. The exception—fundamental—is that Brecht takes historical themes from the past and far removed from the personal lives of his public. Ardrey always takes contemporary events, *current* events, thus risking the sympathy or antipathy of the public and its mood. If *Jeb, Shadow of Heroes, Star-Spangled*, and even *How to Get Tough About It* don't have the public following they deserve, it is the fault of the timing rather than of the plays. Let us examine several.

Thunder Rock is a fantastic-ontological play not too typical of Ardrey's repertoire. A man attempts to live in a fantastic world of his own ideation— and in isolation. He revives a group of immigrants who had lost their lives in a shipwreck ninety years earlier. The protagonist believes that he can create a better world through his fantasy only to come to realize through his resuscitated characters that the line beteen real and fantasy is indeed thin if existent at all. It is a quixotic world and Ardrey succeeds in winning sympathy for his protagonist: this gives the play a certain charm. In its interplay of real and fanciful it will remind one of *Six Characters in Search of an Author* (in fact, Ardrey brings back from the dead exactly six people) in that the six do impart a sense of doom inherent in man, and an instinctual distrust of "progressi-vism." If there is a weakness in this subtly developed play it is the character of the protagonist who does not quite convince us that his anguish is endemic and that his idealistic world is more than an experiment.

In *Thunder Rock* Ardrey demonstrated his skill in maintaining dramatic interest without a change of scenery, while in *Jeb* he ranges over half the United States, tying his shifting scenes together like a varied necklace.

Shadow of Heroes is the story of the Hungarian uprising and of the events leading to it. The characters are the historical figures that were actually involved, plus a light sprinkling of fictitious personages. Ardrey intended the play to be topical, to protest the tragic events of 1956. It is not surprising that this play would not be a box office success except during the moments of international concern concomitant with the events themselves.

By focusing beyond current events, another theme in *Shadow of Heroes* emerges: the tragedy of revolution —a transcendental tragedy which shows how revolution eats its children; and, as Giuseppe Mazzini pointed out, all governments imposed by force cannot, by this very fact, be tolerant, democra-tic or free. Ardrey shows, unwittingly perhaps, what revolution does to human relationships.

How to Get Tough About It is another piece of Americana, set in a Midwest steel town. Its action deals with strikes and strike breaking in the "good ole days" when labour unions and management first sat down at the bargaining table for their game of Chinese wrestling, while under the table they kicked each other in the shins or any other vulnerable spot; but the real internal action deals with human values and sensibilities dear to Ardrey's heart; love, friend-ship, loyalty. Towards the end of the play, in order to rescue his characters from falling into trite types, Ardrey leans to farce. It is too little and too late to save the play; but it indicates that the play would have to be lifted entirely from the realistic mode and turned into complete farce or into a musical comedy or into ballet —something that would give backbone to the now flaccid (*o tempora, o mores*) human values.

Casey Jones is a *tour de force* for a scenographer, but Ardrey was up to it —he had the ability to convince any stage designer that *anything* can be represented on stage. *Casey Jones*, as the title indicates, is about the life of a man devoted to the god of progress symbolized in locomotives and train schedules. Having sold his soul to that particular god it stands to reason that trains travelling at eighty miles an hour are superior to those travelling at seventy miles an hour, thus Casey Jones becomes a devotee of the faster train, *no matter what*. "You're a good citizen," says one of the characters to Casey Jones; but as Casey wears out his body and those dear to him, Ardrey implies that behind each good citizen there must be a good man, and Casey slowly realizes that a man travelling eighty miles an hour is not necessarily superior to the one travelling fifty miles an hour. His god of progress is indeed a demon, a female witch that has raped his soul. All that remains to him now is his life; and in an effort to retrieve his soul, he gives that "bitch" of a locomotive his life. In addition to its very valid tragic base, *Casey Jones* is good drama because, just as *The Odyssey* and *Moby Dick* make good sea yarns, its superstructure makes a good ironhorse yarn.

—John V. Falconieri

AXELROD, George.

Born in New York City, 9 June 1922. Served in the United States Army Signal Corps during World War II. Married 1) Gloria Washburn in 1942 (divorced 1954), two sons; 2) Joan Stanton in 1954, one daughter. Film director and producer. Recipient: Writers Guild of America West award, for screenplay, 1962. Agent: Irving Paul Lazar Agency, 211 South Beverly Drive, Beverly Hills, California 90212, U.S.A.

Publications

PLAYS

Sketches, with Max Wilk, in *Small Wonder* (produced 1948).
The Seven Year Itch: A Romantic Comedy (produced 1952). 1953.
Will Success Spoil Rock Hunter? (also director: produced 1955). 1956.
Goodbye Charlie (also director: produced 1959). 1959.
Souvenir, with Peter Viertel (produced 1975).

SCREENPLAYS: *Phffft!*, 1954; *The Seven Year Itch*, with Billy Wilder, 1955; *Bus Stop*, 1956; *Rally 'round the Flag, Boys* (uncredited), 1958; *Breakfast at Tiffany's*, 1961; *The Manchurian Candidate*, 1962; *Paris When It Sizzles*, 1963; *How to Murder Your Wife*, 1964; *Lord Love a Duck*, with Larry H. Johnson, 1966; *The Secret Life of an American Wife*, 1968; *The Lady Vanishes*, 1979; *The Holcroft Covenant*, with Edward Anhalt and John Hopkins, 1982.

RADIO WRITER: *Midnight in Manhattan* program, 1940; material for *Grand Old Opry*, 1950–52.

TELEVISION: For *Celebrity Time*, 1950.

NIGHT CLUB WRITER: *All about Love*, 1951.

NOVELS

Beggar's Choice. 1947; as *Hobson's Choice*, 1951.
Blackmailer. 1952.
Where Am I Now—When I Need Me? 1971.

THEATRICAL ACTIVITIES

DIRECTOR: **Plays**—*Will Success Spoil Rock Hunter?*, 1955; *Once More, With Feeling* by Harry Kurnitz, 1958; *Goodbye Charlie*, 1959; *The Star-Spangled Girl* by Neil Simon, 1966. **Films**—*Lord Love a Duck*, 1966; *The Secret Life of an American Wife*, 1968.

The playwriting career of George Axelrod well illustrates that dramatist of particular wit and imagination who manages to create marketable products for Broadway tastes and, for a brief period, enjoys the fame and fortune that successful commercial comedy brings. His brief period was the decade of the 1950s. *The Seven Year Itch* ran nearly three years in New York, with 1,141 performances and *Will Success Spoil Rock Hunter?* lasted a year and had 444 performances. Prior to his first success he had learned his trade writing for radio and television. Since this decade of playwriting he has had some success as a director, effectively directing such plays as Neil Simon's *The Star-Spangled Girl* for an audience acceptance that he was no longer able to reach as a dramatist.

In the history of American comic drama Axelrod might be mentioned as the author of two plays which say something about American tastes and attitudes during that post-World War II decade when audiences enjoyed a semi-sophisticated joke along with a semi-realistic view of themselves. Although the period for this enjoyment continued under the aegis of Neil Simon, Axelrod's imagination for such playwriting dried up. A later novel, *Where Am I Now— When I Need Me?*, is an artless attempt to capitalize on current free expression in writing as well as a kind of pathetic admission. In the span of theatre history in America the decade of the 1950s will be considered undistinguished and Axelrod's contribution will be measured, if at all, as an instance of conscious yet effective technique on the Broadway scale of carefully analysed entertainment.

Axelrod's success as a dramatist came with his ability to write clever, simply structured comedy that seemed a bit outrageous or naughty at first but was generally acceptable and comforting. Liberal circles have labelled him a writer of right-wing comedy in which right-wing morality always triumphs and have considered his success a disturbing feature of American comedy. Such observations have their place in history, but it is nonetheless true that such conservative comedy has a rich reputation in American comedy and for a decade Axelrod's polished and carefully tailored plays were the most imaginative of these slim pieces of professionally manufactured theatre. His plays satisfied an audience's needs. *The Seven Year Itch* tells of a New York businessman, Richard Shermans, who combines a humorous reluctance and eagerness as he spends a night with a girl after his wife has left the hot city for the summer months. *Will Success Spoil Rock Hunter?* toys with the Faustus theme as George MacCawley sells his soul ten percent at a time for fame, fortune and certain pleasures. But Axelrod always emphasized a definite, if sometimes late, morality. Richard is funny because his reluctance, his ineptness, and his remorse contrast hilariously with his view of himself as a seducer. At the final curtain a likeable hero emerges from an educational experience; even the girl, who slept with him because he could not be serious with her, begins to think that marriage should be worth a try. George also eats his cake and has it to enjoy. His fantasies are dramatically fulfilled, and he does not lose his soul. In this manner Axelrod presented safe, conservative entertainment that would run for at least a year. A few years later it is out of date, and with another generation it has lost most of its appeal.

Technically, Axelrod used the accepted devices of unpretentious comic entertainment. Verbal and visual jokes were a major part of a play's success with an audience. Perhaps that is why Axelrod has since substituted directing for playwriting. Topicality in the jokes was as much a part of a play's success as it was an appeal to snobbishness in the audiences. There are numerous local references to New York, and names were dropped in almost every scene. Obviously, Axelrod studied his audiences, considering them knowledgeable but not overly bright. Certain gags in *Will Success Spoil Rock Hunter?*—the positioning of the "Scarlet Letter" on a scantily clad model and the impossibility of making love in the sand—are repeated, and the staircase in *The Seven Year Itch*, described as giving "the joint a kind of Jean-Paul Sartre quality," is further explained as having "no exit." In *The Seven Year Itch* Axelrod enlivened his presentation with dramatic devices such as fantasy sequences, flashbacks, and soliloquies. Throughout all of his plays, ridiculing, making witty comments, and satirizing man and his society are standard ploys for humor. But Axelrod is neither innovator nor reformer, merely a professional entertainer. He satirized the usual things—the movies, psychiatrists, rental-novel sex, certain kinds of decadence, and so on. He had nothing to say to any thoughtful person, and he scarcely took himself seriously, suggesting as he did a thorough and comfortable acceptance of all that he ridiculed in his plays. John Gassner referred to his work as "imaginative fluff," and as such it has appeal for certain theatre audiences at certain times.

—Walter J. Meserve

B

BABE, Thomas.

Born in Buffalo, New York, 13 March 1941. Educated at high school in Rochester, New York; Harvard University, Cambridge, Massachusetts, B.A. 1963 (Phi Beta Kappa), graduate work, 1965–68; St. Catharine's College, Cambridge (Marshall scholar, 1963–65), B.A. 1965; Yale University School of Law, New Haven, Connecticut, J. D. 1972. Married Susan Bramhall in 1967 (divorced 1976), one daughter. Operated the Summer Players, Agassiz Theatre, Cambridge, Massachusetts, with Timothy S. Mayer, 1966–68; speechwriter for John Lindsay, Mayor of New York City, 1968–69. Recipient: CBS-Yale fellowship; Guggenheim fellowship, 1977; Rockefeller grant, 1978; National Endowment for the Arts fellowship, 1983. Agent: Agency for the Performing Arts, 888 Seventh Avenue, New York, New York 10016. Address: 103 Hoyt Street, Darien, Connecticut 06820, U.S.A.

Publications

PLAYS

Kid Champion, music by Jim Steinman (produced 1974). 1980.
Mojo Candy (produced 1975).
Rebel Women (produced 1976). 1977.
Billy Irish (produced 1977). 1982.
Great Solo Town (produced 1977). 1981.
A Prayer for My Daughter (produced 1977). 1977.
Fathers and Sons (produced 1978). 1980.
Taken in Marriage (produced 1979). 1979.
Daniel Boone (for children; produced 1979).
Salt Lake City Skyline (produced 1980). 1980.
Kathleen (produced 1980; revised version, as *Home Again, Kathleen*, produced 1981).
The Wild Duck, adaption of a play by Ibsen, translated by Erik J. Friis (produced 1981).
Buried Inside Extra (produced 1983). 1983.
Planet Fires (produced 1985). 1987.
Carrying School Children (produced 1987).
A Hero of Our Time (produced 1988).
Demon Wine (produced 1989). 1989.
Down in the Dumps (produced 1989).

Casino Paradise, with Arnold Weinstein, music by William Bolcom (produced 1990).
Junk Bonds (produced 1991). 1991.
Great Day in the Morning (produced 1992).

SCREENPLAYS: *The Sun Gods*, with Mike Wadleigh, 1978; *The Vacancy*, 1979; *Kid Champion*, 1979; *Lincoln and the War Within*, 1991; *Junk Bonds*, 1991.

RADIO PLAYS: *Hot Dogs and Soda Pop*, 1980; *The Volunteer Fireman*, 1981; *One for the Record*, 1986.

BALLET SCENARIOS: *When We Were Very Young*, music by John Simon, New York, 1980; *Twyla Tharp and Dancers*, 1980.

MANUSCRIPT COLLECTION: Harvard University Theatre Collection, Cambridge, Massachusetts.

THEATRICAL ACTIVITIES
DIRECTOR: **Plays**—*Two Small Bodies* by Neal Bell, 1977; *Justice* by Terry Curtis Fox, 1979; *Marmalade Skies* by M. Z. Ribalow, 1983; *The Pornographer's Daughter* by Terry Curtis Fox, 1984; *Life and Limb* by Keith Reddin, 1985; *Voices in the Head* by Neal Bell, 1986; *Finnegan's Funeral Parlor and Ice Cream Shoppe* by Robert Kerr, 1989; *A Night with Doris* by Stephanie Brown, 1989; *Sleeping Dogs* by Neal Bell, 1989; *Limbo Tales* by Len Jenkin, 1990.

Thomas Babe comments:

(1982) My position as an American playwright has been realized in the tension between a longing for eternal verities and my perverse desire, like any writer who thinks he's worth his salt, to complicate things. I've gotten in a lot of critical trouble on my native turf, most of which I've tried to weather, because when you push at the edges of things that people really care about, you find the breaking point. This is not to say what I've written is best; only to mention that the theater, in bad money times, has become more conservative in its choices as the funding has dried up while ticket prices go on rising. I've never gotten a prize, and I don't expect one, but I would love to continue to work. And that is all the impetus behind what I've done—that, and a few bucks for the bills. There is a myth that has been promulgated about the suffering of American playwrights; it is neither true nor fair to their ability to survive. I most suspect that the ability to survive is what's behind the best work done by my contemporaries in the last decade, and nearly every one of them has upped the ante every time out.

A Prayer for My Daughter insists that social and political corruption depend upon *co*-existing individual corruption and that personal corruption depends upon *pre*-existing social and political corruption. With this play Thomas Babe presents a pervasive, depressing, and compelling drama of post-

Watergate, post-fall-of-Saigon America. We witness one complex crime "committed" by the four principals, hear of a murder, and hear finally of a suicide. We cannot imagine an end to the extreme behavior of Kelly and Jack (the cops) and Sean and Jimmy (the crooks) because the law-keepers and the law-breakers seem to have exchanged equally meaningless roles and to have annihilated the rules of law and morality and the law of nature. Such men exist in symbiosis; the terrors of blind selfishness permeate their common membrane and generate a composite "cop-crook" which becomes the dominant creature in the environment. When the play closes, the sentiment of the old stand-by song "You are my sunshine"—sung intermittently by Jack throughout— becomes the lyric voiceover for Kelly's silent prayer "for [his] daughter" and it carries a terrible weight of meaning. Kelly and Jack function as the legal equivalent of Sean and Jimmy, whose end-product is two deaths, four killers, six victims.

The condition "daughter" renders all male-male and male-female relations radically and dangerously ill-defined, especially to the "daughters" themselves. Babe introduces the notion that man is partly composed of woman and therefore the struggle between men and women cannot be separated from the struggle within men. So long as human nature is misunderstood by the powerful, power will be destructive. Kelly's daughter kills herself with considerably less effect on Kelly than the elderly woman's murder which Sean and Jimmy are arrested for. And, although Sean and Jimmy seem at first to care for each other and to be more capable of caring than Kelly and Jack, neither has any loyalty, being perfectly ready to sell each other out when the moment comes. The love for *his* daughter which Jimmy expresses in Act II makes his being Sean's "daughter" strangely plausible, a plausibility reinforced when he becomes briefly Kelly's "daughter," whose vulnerability to Jimmy's "daughter-liness" seems equally homosexual and paternal. The tenderness each realizes in the other, however, does nothing to mitigate the nasty course of their encounter; just as Kelly's initial "fatherly" concern for Margie does nothing to mitigate her despair—or ours. Law and love seem less compatible than love and crime but love seems overwhelmed by both partners. Love is negated by partnerships of lawful and unlawful crime and by a partnership ordinarily thought above the law, the "natural" partnership of father and daughter. All power in this play, from the enforcement of the statutes to the beginnings of self-discovery, acts to make things worse.

Buried Inside Extra is a comic reverie on faith and duty with the absurd threat (taken seriously) of an A-bomb blast from within the *Times-Record* building on the morning of the paper's last edition; the sketchy love of the editor for the hard-nosed women's page editor; the "pill and placebo" love Jake gives his wife over the telephone; the epidemic of compromising, lying, and unfaithfulness in the name of "twenty-five cents of the best writing that can be written in the full knowledge that the writing will be thrown out the next day." These reporters are driven to provide the public with a substitute for experience; those who "have weak hearts . . . and don't drink . . . [and] only fuck about twice a year" are promised an "everything" defined as "true facts, clear impressions, informed guesses. . . . We will make our readers wear *our* shoes during the long night." Babe's "newsies" possess little wisdom, little sympathy, little contentment, and little self-esteem. Their already moribund paper will be defunct after this "extra" edition to cover the atom bomb scare. This newsroom can only generate stories from within itself; Liz's hiding (and hidden) father, Culhane (also a reporter), himself manufactures the bomb and phones the threat in because he knows that such news will cause Jake to print an extra edition. It's a way of prolonging life which Babe would have us consider to be the *modus operandi* of the press. Their own lives confused and conflicted, media people seek to clarify the lives of others by purveying the news, even if the clarity is fleeting and untrustworthy, even if the news moves society into yet more obscurity tomorrow, even if the headline proclaims and the columns elaborate a non-event. When all stories are taken at face-value and textualized as news, the distinction between true and false knowledge cannot function.

The edge to *Buried Inside* lies along the blade joining realism to parody. The *real* atom bombs exploded decades ago over Nagasaki and Hiroshima and reporters like these covered the story and made us *a* story, not *the* story. Babe uses Culhane's bomb as a device to explode any remaining fragments of trust in newspapers as truth-bearing instruments. Indeed, any trust in communication or in truth per se doesn't carry as far as Jake and Liz's choral, terminal "Write, you bastards." They know that everything beyond the headline article won't be read and won't be considered significant; that news will be "buried inside extra." This last edition will reconstruct events which might have led to *their* being "buried inside extra." Their willingness to make news out of themselves, to make reality conform to autobiography, at once represents the news business and business as usual in the 1970s.

With *Junk Bonds* Babe offers a comparatively unfocused and largely unaccountable play, especially since the stronger *Demon Wine* was produced not long before. Pressing questions of personal morality are paramount in each but substantial characters and a dynamic plot work only in *Demon Wine* in which the parallel but opposing *educations sentimentales* of an auto parts salesman and a mobster's son are experienced. It turns out that the child of organized crime embodies honor, the child of the people, dishonor; power breeds authenticity, powerlessness, a dangerous inauthenticity. The laying-out of full dilemmas seems to elicit Babe's strongest writing.

—Thomas Apple

BAITZ, Jon Robin.

Born in 1964 in California. Lived in Brazil, South Africa, and the United States. Playwright-in-residence, New York Stage and Film Company, 1989; currently co-artistic director, Naked Angels, New York. Recipient: Playwrights Horizons Revson fellowship, 1987; Rockefeller fellowship; New York *Newsday* Oppenheimer award, 1987; Playwrights U.S.A. award, 1988; Humanitas award, 1990. Agent: George Lane, William Morris Agency, 1350 Avenue of the Americas, New York, New York 10019, U.S.A.

Publications

PLAYS

Mizlansky/Zilinsky (produced 1985).
The Film Society (produced 1987). 1987.

Dutch Landscape (produced 1989).
The End of the Day (produced 1990).
The Substance of Fire (produced 1992). 1992.
Three Hotels (televised 1990; produced 1993).

TELEVISION PLAY: *Three Hotels*, 1990.

Before his writing career was 10 years old, Jon Robin Baitz was already perceived as many things. First, he was that rarity, a Hollywood playwright concentrating on the stage when every waiter in town had pretensions to being a screenwriter. When his second play appeared, a sophisticated and knowledgeable piece about apartheid, he was seen as South African. He was still well under 25. When that was followed by a disastrous new play at Los Angeles's Mark Taper Forum, he abandoned California for New York where his reputation became a cosmopolitan one.

Not all his audience was aware of it, but he was cosmopolitan from the first. His California credentials seemed impeccable, from his birth in Beverly Hills to studies at Beverly Hills High School. It was the time in between that gave him his international perspective.

As the son of an executive for Carnation Milk, Baitz spent most of his boyhood travelling, from Brazil to South Africa with spells in Israel, Holland, and England, before returning to California. His earliest plays were reports from the vastly different front lines of Hollywood and South Africa.

His first substantial play, *Mizlansky/Zilinsky*, was propelled by dialogue that possessed the same earthy vigour as David Mamet's *Glengarry Glen Ross*, a point noted by several critics. There are similarities, most surprisingly in the authorial distance from characters who are allowed to present themselves sympathetically despite a catalogue of obvious flaws. Then, too, like the real estate salesmen in Mamet's play, Baitz's characters Mizlansky and Zilinsky are deal-makers: cynical, independent producers in the backwaters of Hollywood who have moved on from financing movies to creating tax shelters. If they make a record of children's Bible stories, they can guarantee it will fail.

But Baitz's individuality is also apparent and the play, produced when he was just 21, revealed his gifts of observation and empathy. In sharp, disjointed scenes—described by the Los Angeles *Times* as a "little like listening to the Nixon tapes"—he allowed his people to reveal their character as they themselves judged it. Mizlansky, in particular, signing checks while facing bankruptcy and prison, must be taken on his own terms while his morally quibbling partner Zilinsky finds that confession to the Internal Revenue does not cleanse his soul.

For a dramatist beginning his career in Hollywood, such a clear-sighted view of the movie business could only be an advantage.

His second play, *The Film Society*, appeared to secure his reputation. He used his experience as a pupil in South Africa to create an all-white prep-school, like his own, that served as an apparently benign model of the country's white society sealed off from the black majority culture. Through the character of a teacher, Jonathan Balton, who founds a film society in the school, Baitz dynamically illustrates the feebleness of neutrality. The effort to ignore the explosive realities of apartheid by projecting flickering images of western civilization on the wall is doomed by the actuality of South Africa's real society, where the pent-up force of the subjugated black majority constantly threatens to explode.

The play was seen in New York and at London's Hampstead Theatre, and attracted the interest of Hollywood filmmakers. For a time, Baitz was the hottest dramatic talent produced by Los Angeles. With unusual and commendable loyalty, Baitz continued to write for the stage, but his next play, *Dutch Landscape*, was a famously unhappy experience for the playwright and his distinguished director, Gordon Davidson.

Perhaps prematurely, it attempted to confront his family life, compacting three continents' worth of experience into a muddled portrait of his relationship with his parents. Autobiographical conflict was partly buried by an uncomfortable return to the theme of apartheid and the undigested nature of the piece drew vitriolic reviews.

His subsequent departure for New York proved a canny move. The confidence in his work that had been damaged by *Dutch Landscape* was restored, and the strength that all his plays showed in portraying older men was reaffirmed when he created the character of a New York publisher resisting pressures to sell out.

The Substance of Fire was the play which finally gave Baitz his all-important New York credibility, earning him comparisons with Shakespeare, Chekhov, and Edward Albee. In the way of New York theatrical success nowadays, even Off-Broadway, it also brought him Hollywood deals ranging from commissions for adaptations to original screenplays which he would also direct. By the age of 29, Baitz was ready to put into practice the lessons of *Mizlansky/Zilinsky*.

—Ned Chaillet

BALDWIN, James (Arthur).

Born in New York City, 2 August 1924. Educated at Public School 139, Harlem, New York, and De Witt Clinton High School, Bronx, New York, graduated 1942. Worked as handyman, dishwasher, waiter, and office boy in New York, and in defense work, Belle Meade, New Jersey, in early 1940s; full-time writer from 1943; lived in Europe, mainly in Paris, 1948–56. Member, Actors Studio, New York, National Advisory Board of CORE (Congress on Racial Equality) and National Committee for a Sane Nuclear Policy. Recipient: Saxton fellowship, 1945; Rosenwald fellowship, 1948; Guggenheim fellowship, 1954; American Academy award, 1956; Ford fellowship, 1958; National Conference of Christians and Jews Brotherhood award, 1962; George Polk award, 1963; Foreign Drama Critics award, 1964; Martin Luther King, Jr., award (City University of New York), 1978. D.Litt.: University of British Columbia, Vancouver, 1963. Member, American Academy, 1964. *Died 30 November 1987.*

Publications

PLAYS

The Amen Corner (produced 1955). 1968.
Blues for Mister Charlie (produced 1964). 1964.

*One Day, When I Was Lost: A Scenario Based on "The Autobiography of
   Malcolm X"*. 1972.
A Deed from the King of Spain (produced 1974).
Screenplay: *The Inheritance*, 1973.

NOVELS
Go Tell It on the Mountain. 1953.
Giovanni's Room. 1956.
Another Country. 1962.
Tell Me How Long the Train's Been Gone. 1968.
If Beale Street Could Talk. 1974.
Just Above My Head. 1979.

SHORT STORIES
Going to Meet the Man. 1965.

VERSE
Jimmy's Blues: Selected Poems. 1983.
Gypsey and Other Poems. 1989.

OTHER
Notes of a Native Son. 1955.
Nobody Knows My Name: More Notes of a Native Son. 1961.
The Fire Next Time. 1963.
Nothing Personal, photographs by Richard Avedon. 1964.
A Rap on Race, with Margaret Mead. 1971.
No Name in the Street. 1972.
A Dialogue: James Baldwin and Nikki Giovanni. 1973.
Little Man, Little Man (for children). 1976.
The Devil Finds Work: An Essay. 1976.
The Price of a Ticket: Collected Nonfiction 1948–85. 1985.
The Evidence of Things Not Seen. 1985; as *Evidence of Things Not Seen,*
   1986.

BIBLIOGRAPHY: *James Baldwin: A Reference Guide* by Fred L. and Nancy
Standley, 1980.

CRITICAL STUDIES: *The Furious Passage of James Baldwin* by Fern Eckman,
1966; *James Baldwin: A Critical Study* by Stanley Macebuh, 1973; *James
Baldwin: A Collection of Critical Essays* edited by Kenneth Kinnamon, 1974;
James Baldwin: A Critical Evaluation edited by Therman B. O'Daniel, 1977;
James Baldwin by Louis H. Pratt, 1978; *James Baldwin* by Carolyn W.
Sylvander, 1980; *Talking at the Gates: A Life of James Baldwin* by James
Campbell, 1991.

THEATRICAL ACTIVITIES
DIRECTOR: **Film**—*The Inheritance*, 1973.

One of the best known modern authors in the United States, James Baldwin is least known as a dramatist. He was admired in the 1950s for the style and thought of his novels, the semi-autobiographical *Go Tell It on the Mountain* and *Giovanni's Room*, and for his personal and literary essays, first published in small avant-garde magazines, then collected as *Notes of a Native Son*. During the early 1960s, as increased attention was directed to the civil rights movement, Baldwin became recognized as a leading spokesman for black Americans. In a novel (*Another Country* and two collections of essays, (*Nobody Knows My Name* and *The Fire Next Time*), Baldwin seemed to articulate eloquently and persuasively the bitterness, the alienation, and the despair of black Americans. Some critics felt that Baldwin's statements reached a pinnacle in his first widely known drama, *Blues for Mister Charlie*. With an eye towards John Osborne and other British dramatists, some critics argued that Baldwin was "America's angriest young man." Just as few critics have recognized Baldwin's interest in drama, so most have missed the continuous message of the one-time preacher. In drama, as in his other writing, Baldwin repeatedly preached that people must love and understand other people if they wish to save the world from destruction.

Born and raised in New York City, Baldwin, the eldest of nine children, suffered in childhood from the oppression of Depression poverty and the religious enthusiasm of a fanatically devout father. During his youth he wavered between the church and literature. Undoubtedly influenced by his stepfather, at least seeking to please him, Baldwin became a teenaged minister in a faith which viewed romance (in literature or in life) as a snare for the godly. In junior high school, however, Baldwin had been a member of the literary society advised by Countee Cullen, the famous black poet and novelist. The opposing forces, Baldwin has written, met in a climactic confrontation when an excessively long sermon from the minister of Baldwin's church threatened to prevent Baldwin's attendance at a play for which he had tickets. When the minister chose to make an example of the quietly departing Baldwin, Baldwin became convinced that he could not endure the rigors of the faith. From this point Baldwin embraced literature as a faith with an emphasis upon the creed of love for fellow man.

After graduation from De Witt Clinton High School, Baldwin worked as a waiter while he tried to write a novel. With assistance from Richard Wright, the most famous black American novelist of the time, he secured a Saxton award, which temporarily relieved his financial needs. Despite occasional publication in little magazines, however, Baldwin increasingly despaired of his position as a black man and writer in the white-oriented United States. In 1948, he left for France, where, during the next ten years, he established a limited reputation as a creative writer and literary critic (the latter based partly on his rejection of Richard Wright, his former benefactor, as a novelist who sacrificed art to a message of social protest) and persuaded himself that he had discovered his identity.

As early as 1957 Baldwin had made a dramatic adaptation of his novel

Giovanni's Room, the story of a white American who discovers and surrenders to his latent homosexuality. Baldwin's recognition as a dramatist did not come until the season of 1963–64 when *Blues for Mister Charlie* became the controversial sensation of the New York stage while the quieter *The Amen Corner*, first produced at a black college in Washington, D.C., was receiving a professional production on the west coast. In both plays he tried to infuse the vitality of life which he felt to be missing from American drama.

Written after Baldwin had taken his first trip to Mississippi, to participate in civil rights demonstrations, *Blues for Mister Charlie* is based in part on two actual incidents. In one, a 14-year-old black youth from Chicago was tortured and killed while visiting his grandparents in Mississippi. The reason given by one killer was that the youth allegedly had flirted with a white woman. Although one murderer freely admitted the crime and a second did not deny it, both were acquitted by an all-white jury. In a second incident, a black man was killed by a white man. The reason was rumoured to be the fact that the black man protested against the white man's using the black man's wife as a concubine.

In *Blues for Mister Charlie* Baldwin focused on Richard Henry, a young black entertainer, who, after succumbing to dope, has returned bitter and frustrated to his Mississippi home. Within a short period of time, Henry becomes involved in an altercation with Lyle Britton, a white man known to have killed another black who objected to surrendering his wife to Britton's sexual exploitation. Britton kills Henry, is tried, and is acquitted.

Although some critics denounced the play as melodramatic and excessively bitter, Baldwin's major theme—his recurrent theme—is found in the tragedy of two secondary figures, who see the destruction of their hope for love between the races. One is a white journalist who, unlike his neighbours, has no prejudices against blacks. Once, in fact, he loved a black woman and wanted to marry her. At the critical moment in the play, however, this white "liberal" betrays himself and his black friends because, although he knows that Britton is guilty, he cannot force himself to testify that Britton's wife—a southern white woman—is lying. The second tragic figure is the Reverend Meridian Henry. All of his adult life, Reverend Henry has worked to improve the condition of his people by peaceful means. Even after his son's murder, he continues to urge black youths to limit themselves to non-violent protests in the manner of Mahatma Gandhi and Martin Luther King, Jr. After the acquittal of his son's murderer, however, the Christian minister decides that, in future, he and other blacks need to carry their guns even to church to protect themselves from the savages in their community.

The Amen Corner is the story of a woman minister who is forced to realize that love and compassion for human beings are more important than a fanatically rigid enunciation of God's law. After deserting her husband because he was inadequate to her needs after the death of their second child, Sister Margaret has become a minister who insists that members of her congregation and her son dedicate themselves to continuous sanctity. The return of her husband, who is dying, precipitates conflict by inspiring rebellion in her son and her congregation. By the end of the play, Margaret has been compelled to remember how human and loving she had been before the ministry. Now that she has regained compassion for human frailty, she is truly prepared for the first time to lead a congregation. But it is too late. Her son leaves her, her husband dies, and she can find no words to maintain her control over the faction of the congregation which has decided to replace her.

—Darwin T. Turner

BARAKA, Amiri.

Born Everett LeRoi Jones in Newark, New Jersey, 7 October 1934; took name Amiri Baraka in 1968. Educated at Central Avenue School, and Barringer High School, Newark; Rutgers University, Newark, New Jersey, 1951–52; Howard University, Washington, D.C., 1953–54, B.A. in English 1954. Served in the United States Air Force, 1954–57. Married 1) Hettie Roberta Cohen in 1958 (divorced 1965), two daughters; 2) Sylvia Robinson (now Amina Baraka) in 1967, five children; also two stepdaughters and two other daughters. Teacher, New School for Social Research, New York, 1961–64, and summers, 1977–79, State University of New York, Buffalo, Summer 1964, and Columbia University, New York, 1964 and Spring 1980; visiting professor, San Francisco State College, 1966–67, Yale University, New Haven, Connecticut, 1977–78, and George Washington University, Washington, D.C., 1978–79. Assistant professor, 1980–82, associate professor, 1983–84, and since 1985 professor of Africana studies, State University of New York, Stony Brook. Founder, *Yugen* magazine and Totem Press, New York, 1958–62; editor, with Diane di Prima, *Floating Bear* magazine, New York, 1961–63; founding director, Black Arts Repertory Theatre, Harlem, New York, 1964–66. Since 1966 founding director, Spirit House, Newark; involved in Newark politics: member of the United Brothers, 1967, and Committee for Unified Newark, 1969–75; chair, Congress of Afrikan People, 1972–75. Recipient: Whitney fellowship, 1961; Obie award, 1964; Guggenheim fellowship, 1965; Yoruba Academy fellowship, 1965; National Endowment for the Arts grant, 1966, award, 1981; Dakar Festival prize, 1966; Rockefeller grant, 1981; Before Columbus Foundation award, 1984; American Book award, 1984. D.H.L.: Malcolm X College, Chicago, 1972. Member, Black Academy of Arts and Letters. Address: Department of Africana studies, State University of New York, Stony Brook, New York 11794–4340, U.S.A.

Publications (earlier works as LeRoi Jones)

PLAYS

A Good Girl Is Hard to Find (produced 1958).
Dante (produced 1961; as *The 8th Ditch*, produced 1964). In *The System of Dante's Hell*, 1965.
The Toilet (produced 1964). With *The Baptism*, 1967.
Dutchman (produced 1964). With *The Slave*, 1964.
The Slave (produced 1964). With *Dutchman*, 1964.
The Baptism (produced 1964). With *The Toilet*, 1967.
Jello (produced 1965). 1970.
Experimental Death Unit #1 (also director: produced 1965). In *Four Black Revolutionary Plays*, 1969.

A Black Mass (also director: produced 1966). In *Four Black Revolutionary Plays*, 1969.
Arm Yrself or Harm Yrself (produced 1967). 1967.
Slave Ship: A Historical Pageant (produced 1967). 1967.
Madheart (also director: produced 1967). In *Four Black Revolutionary Plays*, 1969.
Great Goodness of Life (A Coon Show) (also director: produced 1967). In *Four Black Revolutionary Plays*, 1969.
Home on the Range (produced 1968). 1968.
Police. 1968.
The Death of Malcolm X, in *New Plays from the Black Theatre*, edited by Ed Bullins. 1969.
Rockgroup. 1969.
Four Black Revolutionary Plays. 1969.
Insurrection (produced 1969).
Junkies are Full of (SHHH . . .), and *Bloodrites* (produced 1970). In *Black Drama Anthology*, edited by Woodie King and Ron Milner, 1971.
BA-RA-KA, in *Spontaneous Combustion: Eight New American Plays*, edited by Rochelle Owens. 1972.
Black Power Chant. 1972.
Columbia the Gem of the Ocean (produced 1973).
A Recent Killing (produced 1973).
The New Ark's a Moverin (produced 1974).
The Sidnee Poet Heroical (also director: produced 1975). 1979.
S-1 (also director: produced 1976). In *The Motion of History and Other Plays*, 1978.
America More or Less, with Frank Chin and Leslie Marmon Silko, music by Tony Greco, lyrics by Arnold Weinstein (produced 1976).
The Motion of History (also director: produced 1977). In *The Motion of History and Other Plays*, 1978.
The Motion of History and Other Plays (includes *S-1* and *Slave Ship*). 1978.
What was the Relationship of the Lone Ranger to the Means of Production? (produced 1979).
At the Dim'crackr Convention (produced 1980).
Boy and Tarzan Appear in a Clearing (produced 1981).
Weimar 2 (produced 1981).
Money: A Jazz Opera, with George Gruntz, music by Gruntz (produced 1982).
Primitive World, music by David Murray (produced 1984).
General Hag's Skeezag (produced 1991).

SCREENPLAYS: *Dutchman*, 1967; *Black Spring*, 1967; *A Fable*, 1971; *Supercoon*, 1971.

NOVEL
The System of Dante's Hell. 1965.

SHORT STORIES
Tales. 1967.

VERSE

April 13. 1959.
Spring and Soforth. 1960.
Preface to a Twenty Volume Suicide Note. 1961.
The Disguise. 1961.
The Dead Lecturer. 1964.
Black Art. 1966.
A Poem for Black Hearts. 1967.
Black Magic: Collected Poetry 1961–1967. 1969.
It's Nation Time. 1970.
In Our Terribleness: Some Elements and Meaning in Black Style, with Fundi
    (Billy Abernathy). 1970.
Spirit Reach. 1972.
Afrikan Revolution. 1973.
Hard Facts. 1976.
Selected Poetry. 1979.
AM/TRAK. 1979.
Spring Song. 1979.
Reggae or Not! 1981.
Thoughts for You! 1984.

OTHER

Cuba Libre. 1961.
Blues People: Negro Music in White America. 1963.
Home: Social Essays. 1966.
Black Music. 1968.
Trippin': A Need for Change, with Larry Neal and A.B. Spellman. 1969(?).
A Black Value System. 1970.
Gary and Miami: Before and After. n.d.
Raise Race Rays Raze: Essays since 1965. 1971.
Strategy and Tactics of a Pan African Nationalist Party. 1971.
Beginning of National Movement. 1972.
Kawaida Studies: The New Nationalism. 1972.
National Liberation and Politics. 1974.
Crisis in Boston!!!! 1974.
Afrikan Free School. 1974.
Toward Ideological Clarity. 1974.
The Creation of the New Ark. 1975.
Selected Plays and Prose. 1979.
The Autobiography of LeRoi Jones/Amiri Baraka. 1983.
Daggers and Javelins: Essays 1974–1979. 1984.
The Artist and Social Responsibility. 1986.
The Music: Reflections on Jazz and Blues, with Amina Baraka. 1987.
An Amiri Baraka/ LeRoi Jones Poetry Sampler. 1991.

Editor, *Four Young Lady Poets.* 1962.
Editor, *The Moderns: New Fiction in America.* 1963.
Editor, with Larry Neal, *Black Fire: An Anthology of Afro-American Writing.*
    1968.

Editor, *African Congress: A Documentary of the First Modern Pan-African Congress.* 1972.

Editor, with Diane di Prima, *The Floating Bear: A Newsletter, Numbers 1–37.* 1974.

Editor, with Amina Baraka, *Confirmation: An Anthology of African American Women.* 1983.

BIBLIOGRAPHY: *LeRoi Jones (Imamu Amiri Baraka): A Checklist of Works by and about Him* by Letitia Dace, 1971; *Ten Modern American Playwrights* by Kimball King, 1982.

MANUSCRIPT COLLECTIONS: Howard University, Washington, D.C.; Beinecke Library, Yale University, New Haven, Connecticut; Lilly Library, Indiana University, Bloomington; University of Connecticut, Storrs; George Arents Research Library, Syracuse University, New York.

CRITICAL STUDIES: *From LeRoi Jones to Amiri Baraka: The Literary Works* by Theodore Hudson, 1973; *Baraka: The Renegade and the Mask* by Kimberly W. Benston, 1976, and *Imamu Amiri Baraka (LeRoi Jones): A Collection of Critical Essays* edited by Benston, 1978; *Amiri Baraka/LeRoi Jones: The Quest for a Populist Modernism* by Werner Sollors, 1978; *Amiri Baraka* by Lloyd W. Brown, 1980; *To Raise, Destroy, and Create: The Poetry, Drama, and Fiction of Imamu Amiri Baraka (LeRoi Jones)* by Henry C. Lacey, 1981; *Theatre and Nationalism: Wole Soyinka and LeRoi Jones* by Alain Ricard, 1983; *Amiri Baraka: The Kaleidoscopic Torch* edited by James B. Gwynne, 1985; *The Poetry and Poetics of Amiri Baraka: The Jazz Aesthetic* by William J. Harris, 1985.

THEATRICAL ACTIVITIES
DIRECTOR: several of his own plays.

Amiri Baraka comments:

My work changes as I change in a changing world.

In March 1964 when three one-act plays at different Off-Broadway locales introduced Amiri Baraka (LeRoi Jones) to city audiences, black theatre in America knew it had found a compelling voice summoning black playwrights to a new and urgent mission.

The first of these plays, *The 8th Ditch*, closed by action of civic authorities after a few days. Its fate foretold the playwright's continuing quarrel with officialdom. His second play, *The Baptism*, with its deliberate satire of subjects held sacred and taboo, served notice of Baraka's determination ruthlessly to strip the hypocritical masks that society wears to protect its vested interests. But it was in his third play and first professional production, *Dutchman*, that Baraka found his authentic voice to delineate a clearly perceived mission. That mission is nothing less than the cultural liberation of the black man in white America.

Dutchman, hailed by critic Clayton Riley as "the finest short play ever written in this country," spoke lucidly to black Americans of the savage destruction of their cultural identity should they continue to imitate or to flirt with an alien, though dominant, white lifestyle. White establishment critics praised Baraka's "fierce and blazing talent"; the *Village Voice* awarded *Dutchman* an Obie as the best American play of the season.

Baraka's next professional production consisted of two plays. *The Slave*, a two-act drama, and *The Toilet*, another one-acter, staged at the St. Mark's Playhouse in December 1964. *The Slave*, although it purports to speak of a coming race war between black and white and is called by Baraka "a fable," is frankly autobiographical in intent. Walker Vessels, a tall, thin Negro leader of a black army, enters the home where his former white wife, their two children, and her second husband are living together, apparently quite happily. The husband is a white liberal-minded professor who had taught Vessels in college. After a long, excoriating harangue in which he renounces his former life, Vessels shoots the white man, watches with indifference as his ex-wife is hit by a falling beam, and departs as shells from his black revolutionary forces demolish the house while the cries of children in an upstairs room mingle with the boom of guns and the shriek of falling debris. *The Toilet*, a curious work of teenage brutality and homosexual love set in a school lavatory, hints at the possibility of black and white coming together at some future time after the black man has earned his manhood and self-respect by defeating the white.

These two revolutionary plays were followed by an even more lurid and propagandistic work when *Experimental Death Unit #1* was staged at the St. Mark's Playhouse in New York in March 1965. In this short play Baraka concentrates on a night-time encounter between two white homosexuals and a black whore in a seamy section of the city. The climax occurs when a death unit of marching black militants enters and executes the three degenerates. The men are beheaded and their heads stuck on pikes at the head of the procession. The black liberation army, Baraka seems to say, has a duty to rid society not only of the oppressor but also of the collaborator. Black skin does not save one from the due penalty for betraying the revolution.

Writing of this second group of plays, white critics who a few months ago had hailed the rising star of playwright Baraka were now confounded. He had rejected the blandishments of popular (white) success held out to him and had become, to them, a bitter dramatist and violent propagandist preaching race hatred in virulent terms. Their attitude in the main confirmed Baraka's suspicions that the white culture would allow nothing but what it approved of to have credence and value.

A month after the production of *Experimental Death Unit #1*, Baraka imitated the actions of his fictitious character, Walker Vessels, by breaking with his past life. He left his white wife and two children, moved to Harlem, and founded the Black Arts Repertory Theatre School. The aim of the school was to train and showcase black theatrical talent, as well as teach classes in remedial reading and mathematics. It lasted for only a short time.

In a forum on Black Theatre held at the Gate Theatre, New York, in 1969, Baraka articulated the philosophic premise of the black arts movement, giving credit to Ron Karenga of San Francisco for having helped in its formulation. Black art, he affirmed, is collective, functional, and committed since it derives from the collective experience of black people, it serves a necessary function in the lives of black people (as opposed to the useless artifacts of most white art that adorn museums), and is committed to revolutionary change.

The short-lived Harlem-based theatre produced only one new play by Baraka: *Jello*, a hard-hitting satire on the once popular Jack Benny radio program advertising this product. The play, rejected by at least one established publisher because of its attack on a well-known stage personality, was performed on the streets of Harlem by the Black Arts Group. The straightforward plot casts Rochester, Benny's chauffeur and stereotype black handyman, as a militant who demands and gets full redress for years of subservience and oppression. In this play Baraka is less interested in attacking the white man than in erasing the myth of black inferiority which decades of white-controlled entertainment have helped to perpetuate. From this point Baraka was more conscious of addressing a black audience in his plays. His main characters were black, and whitey became either the symbolic beast whose ritualistic death is necessary for the emergence of black consciousness and nationhood, or else whitey will be pilloried mercilessly as completely irrelevant to the black struggle. Baraka declared:

> The artist must represent the will, the soul of the black community. [His art] must represent the national spirit and the national will. . . . We don't talk about theatre down here, or theatre up there as an idle jest but because it is necessary to pump live blood back into our community.

When the Black Arts Repertory Theatre closed in 1966, Baraka returned to his native Newark in New Jersey and formed the Spirit House Movers, a group of non-professional actors who performed his plays as well as the plays of other black writers.

In January 1969 Baraka formed the Committee for Unified Newark dedicated to the creation of a new value system for the Afro-American community. Aspects of this new system of values are evidenced in the wearing of traditional African dress, the speaking of Swahili language as much as English, the rejection of Christianity as a Western religion that has helped to enslave the minds of black people and the adoption of the Kawaida faith in its stead, and finally the assumption of Arabic names in place of existing Christian names. Jones became a minister of Kawaida faith and adopted his new name of Amiri Baraka prefixed by the title Imamu (Swahili for Spiritual Leader).

Baraka's work continues to dwell on themes of black liberation and the need to create a new black sensibility by alerting audiences to the reality of their lives in a country dominated by a culture that Baraka passionately believes to be alien and hostile to blacks. The urgent need to root out white ways from the hearts and minds of black people is constantly reiterated. White error is seen in *A Black Mass* as the substitution of thought for feeling, as a curiosity for anti-life. In *Home on the Range* the white family speaks a gibberish of unintelligible sounds and gazes glasseyed at the television box like robots of the computer society they have created. The devils in *Bloodrites* eat of the host and chant a litany of love immediately after attempting to shoot blacks in a glaring indictment of the hypocrisy of Christianity.

Baraka graphically dramatizes the problem by personifying the evil white lifestyle in the form of a devil or beast that must be slain if blacks are to gain their freedom. In *A Black Mass*, a play based on an Islamic fable, one of a trio of magicians persists in creating a wild white beast that he believes he can tame through love. The beast goes on a rampage and destroys everything in sight, including the magicians. *Madheart* has a Devil Lady who keeps a mother and sister of the Black Man in thrall, worshipping whiteness. In *Bloodrites*, whites are gun-toting devils that masquerade as artists, musicians, and hipsters to seduce blacks struggling towards spiritual reconstruction.

Baraka has been accused of preaching race hatred and violence as a way of life. In 1967 he was given the maximum sentence of three years in prison by a county judge for possession of revolvers during the Newark riots, a conviction that was condemned as victimization by the American Council of Civil Liberties and was later overturned by a higher court. It is true that violence permeates his plays, that Baraka seems to revel in bloodletting, but the intensity of his feeling and the power of his language have the effect of lifting violence to the level of a holy war against evil forces of supernatural potency. When the Devil Lady in *Madheart* boasts that she can never die, the Black Man responds "you will die only when I kill you" whereupon he stabs her several times, impales her with a stake and arrows, abuses her, stomps on her dead face, and finally drops her body into a deep pit from which smoke and light shoot up. Such needless overkill can only be understood in terms of magic and ritual.

Ritual, in fact, is the crucible that helps to transform the melodramatic incident in Baraka's plays into significant drama. Clay, the young black hounded by the vampire Lula in a subway train in *Dutchman*, realizes that the murder of a white is the only cure for the black man's neuroses, but he is too ingrained in white middle-class values to perform the rite that will liberate him. He dies as a result. Not so Walker Vessels in *The Slave*. When he shoots Easley, the white liberal professor, the latter's last words are "Ritual drama, like I said, ritual drama." Similarly, when Court Royal, the weak-kneed assimilationist in *Great Goodness of Life* is forced to shoot his militant son, this too is a rite that must be performed, "a rite to show that you would be guilty, but for the cleansing rite." In keeping with his philosophy that black theatre must be functional, Baraka has sought to make his plays identify with his audiences in form as well as content. Thus, *Bloodrites* calls for the sacrifice of a chicken whose blood is sprinkled into the audience. In *Police* the white cops are required to eat chunks of flesh from the body of the black policeman who has killed a member of his race and is forced by the black community to commit suicide. Such ritualistic acts reinforce the magical dimension of the struggle in which black people are engaged.

A second medium of identification is language. Baraka, the poet and littérateur, deliberately reaches for the vernacular and idiom of the urban black to pound home his message. *The Slave* is a fine example of the way in which college-educated Walker Vessels rejects the elegant but alienating discourse of which he is capable for the unifying language of the ghetto. The language in *Police* is pruned and compressed to a single drumbeat, with the syncopation and lyricism associated with that pervasive black musical instrument. The process of creating a new and appropriate language for black drama is pushed further in *Slave Ship* where the narrative element relies heavily on action and music rather than language, and where Yoruba instead of English is used in the first part of the production.

Finally, in his capacity as Spiritual Leader, Baraka uses the stage as a pulpit from which he exhorts his audiences to carry his message for revolutionary thinking and action into their daily lives. The Black Man in *Madheart* urges the audience to "think about themselves and about their lives when they leave this happening." A concluding narration in *A Black Mass* reminds the audience that the beasts are still loose in the world and must be found and slain. *Junkies* begins with an address by an Italian dope dealer who informs the audience that he succeeds by getting "niggers to peddle dope." The audience at *Police* are expected to leap on stage at one point of the play and join the characters in demanding vengeance on the black cop who shot and killed a black brother.

Baraka's theatre is blatantly agit-prop drama exalted to an elemental plane. Apart from *Slave Ship* the structure of his plays remains conventional but the dynamic of message, the boldness of conception, and the lyricism of language give his dramas a fierceness on the stage that defies complacency. Critics may praise or damn him, but Baraka is no longer writing for critical acclaim.

—Errol Hill

See the essay on *Dutchman*.

BARNES, Djuna (Chappell).

Born near Cornwall-on-Hudson, New York, 12 June 1892. Privately educated; studied art at the Pratt Institute, Brooklyn, New York, and the Art Students' League, New York, 1915. Married Courtenay Lemon c. 1917 (divorced, c. 1919). Journalist and illustrator, 1913–31: with Brooklyn *Daily Eagle*, 1913, and *Press*, *World*, and *Morning Telegraph*, all New York, 1914; actor in New York, 1920–22; columnist, *Theatre Guild Magazine*, New York, 1929–31; lived in Paris, 1922–37 (with periods in New York, 1922–23; 1926–27, 1929–31), London, 1937–39, and New York, 1940–82. Also an artist: exhibited at Art of This Century Gallery, New York, 1946. From 1961, trustee, New York Committee, Dag Hammarskjöld Foundation. Recipient: Merrill and Rothko grants. Member, American Academy. *Died 18 June 1982.*

Publications

PLAYS

Three from the Earth (produced 1919). In *A Book*, 1923.
Kurzy of the Sea (produced 1919).
An Irish Triangle (produced 1919). In *Playboy*, 1921.
To the Dogs, in *A Book*, 1923.
The Dove (produced 1926). In *A Book*, 1923.
She Tells Her Daughter. In *Smart Set*, November 1923.
The Antiphon (produced 1961). 1958; revised version, in *Selected Works*, 1962.

NOVELS

Ryder. 1928.
Nightwood. 1936.

SHORT STORIES

A Book (includes verse and plays). 1923; augmented edition, as *A Night among the Horses*, 1929; shortened version, stories only, as *Spillway*, 1962.
Vagaries Malicieux: Two Stories. 1974.
Smoke and Other Early Stories, edited by Douglas Messerli. 1982.

VERSE

The Book of Repulsive Women: Eight Rhythms and Five Drawings. 1915.
Creatures in an Alphabet. 1982.

OTHER

Ladies Almanack: Showing Their Signs and Their Tides; Their Moon and Their Changes; The Seasons as It Is with Them; Their Eclipses and Equinoxes; As Well as a Full Record of Diurnal and Nocturnal Distempers Written and Illustrated by a Lady of Fashion. 1928.
Selected Works. 1962.
Greenwich Village as It Is. 1978.
Interviews, edited by Alyce Barry. 1985.
I Could Never Be Lonely Without a Husband (interviews). 1987.
Selected Works. 1962.
Greenwich Village as It Is. 1978.
Bibliography: *Djuna Barnes: A Bibliography* by Douglas Messerli, 1976.

MANUSCRIPT COLLECTION: University of Maryland, College Park.

CRITICAL STUDIES: *Djuna Barnes* by James B. Scott, 1976; *The Art of Djuna Barnes: Duality and Damnation* by Louis F. Kannenstine, 1977; *Djuna: The Life and Times of Barnes* by Andrew Field, 1983, as *The Formidable Miss Barnes*, 1983; *Silence and Power: A Re-evaluation of Barnes*, edited by Mary Lynn Broe, 1986.

THEATRICAL ACTIVITIES

ACTOR: **Plays**—in *Power of Darkness* by Tolstoy, 1920; in *The Tidings Brought to Mary* by Paul Claudel, 1922.

Best known as the author of the novel *Nightwood*, Djuna Barnes turned to drama early and late in her career. Three one-act plays were performed by the Provincetown Players and three published in *A Book*. In 1958 she published *The Antiphon*, a play that is Jacobean in feeling and language.

Two of her three one-act plays used that stock character, a Woman with a Past. In *Three from the Earth* such a woman is confronted by three brothers who ask for the return of their father's letters to her. The curtain falls on the revelation that the youngest brother is the woman's son. In *To the Dogs* such a woman denies love to the neighbour who vaults through her window. Cowed, the neighbour retreats, but the play is ambiguous as to which of the two is going "to the dogs". *The Dove* focuses on a young girl living with two old maid sisters who relish their collection of knives, guns, and romantic fantasies. The young girl taunts each of the old maids to use a weapon, but she alone shoots a gun—at a painting of prostitutes. None of these plays can be taken seriously, but *The Antiphon* is an astonishing if anachronistic achievement.

The title *The Antiphon* indicates its style; one verse speech seems to call forth its verse reply, in poetic rather than dramatic structure. The language is stiff and archaic on the lips of its 20th-century characters. Set in 1939, on the eve of World War II, the play reveals sexual sin and a hint of expiation, as in Jacobean drama. To 17th-century Burley Hall in England come Miranda and her coachman companion from Paris. Her mother Augusta and her two merchant brothers have been summoned from America by a third and absent brother, Jeremy.

Act I reveals that Augusta has betrayed her aristocratic Burley lineage, marrying an American Mormon, Titus Higby Hobbs of Salem, by whom she has four children. Titus has tortured his wife, brutalized his sons, offered his daughter Miranda for rape by a middle-aged Cockney. Though he has been dead some years, his memory is stronger in Burley Hall than that of the nobles who owned it. And his immortality is the heritage of his two merchant sons, who plan to murder their mother. Daughter Miranda has a checkered past as actress, writer, and woman of the world, and there are hints that she is having an affair with her coachman, Jack Blow. Only Augusta's brother Jonathan, who never left Burley Hall, is untainted by the life of Titus Higby Hobbs.

Though diction and verse of *The Antiphon* are Jacobean, the three-act structure has the tidiness of a well-made play. After the Act I explosion, Act II develops accusations and defence, climaxed when the merchant sons don masks of pig and ass in order to taunt Augusta and Miranda, mother and daughter. A grotesque masque is interrupted by the entrance of coachman Jack Blow with a doll's house, a miniature of Hobb's Ark, the family home in America, with its memories of Titus's seven mistresses, and the rape of the 17-year-old Miranda. Obliquely, the shared family past leads to the Act III confrontation between mother and daughter. Each woman recognizes herself in the other as they slowly mount the side staircase in an antiphon of accusation. At the top Augusta realizes that her sons have abandoned her in her ancestral home, but she refuses to accept the limitation of that home, and she drives her daughter down the stairs, accusing her of conspiracy. At the bottom of the staircase Augusta Burley Hobbs rings down a giant curfew bell, killing both women. Augusta's brother Jonathan and Miranda's erstwhile coachman, actually her brother Jeremy, gaze at the two dead women, and Jeremy muses: "But could I know/Which would be brought to child-bed of the other?" Through the rhythmed, imaged dialogue, the death of the women comes to symbolize the death of an aristocratic lineage, too easily seduced by the violence of a commoner.

—Ruby Cohn

BEHRMAN, S(amuel) N(athaniel).

Born in Worcester, Massachusetts, 9 June 1893. Educated at Providence Street School, and Classical High School, both Worcester; Clark College (now Clark University), Worcester, 1912–14; Harvard University, Cambridge, Massachusetts (in George Pierce Baker's 47 Workshop), A.B. 1916 (Phi Beta Kappa); Columbia University, New York, M.A. 1918. Married Elza Heifetz in 1936; one son and two step-children. Advertising writer and book reviewer,

New York Times, 1917–18; reviewer, *New Republic*, New York, and free-lance publicist until early 1920s; columnist, *New Yorker*, from 1927. Founder, with Robert E. Sherwood, Elmer Rice, Maxwell Anderson, Sidney Howard, and John F. Wharton, Playwrights Company, 1938. Trustee, Clark University. Recipient: American Academy grant, 1943; New York Drama Critics Circle award, 1944; Writers Guild of America West award, for screenplay, 1959; Brandeis University Creative Arts Award, 1962. LL.D.: Clark University, 1949. Member, American Academy, 1943, and American Academy of Arts and Sciences. *Died 9 September 1973.*

Publications

PLAYS

Bedside Manners: A Comedy of Convalescence, with J. Kenyon Nicholson (produced 1923). 1924.
A Night's Work, with J. Kenyon Nicholson (produced 1924). 1926.
The Man Who Forgot, with Owen Davis (produced 1926).
The Second Man (produced 1927). 1927.
Love Is Like That, with J. Kenyon Nicholson (produced 1927).
Serena Blandish, from the novel by Enid Bagnold (produced 1929). In *Three Plays*, 1934.
Meteor (produced 1929). 1930.
Brief Moment (produced 1931). 1931.
Biography (produced 1932). 1933.
Love Story (produced 1933).
Three Plays: Serena Blandish; Meteor; The Second Man. 1934.
Rain from Heaven (produced 1934). 1935.
End of Summer (produced 1936). 1936.
Amphitryon 38, with Roger Gellert, from a play by Jean Giraudoux (produced 1937). 1938.
Wine of Choice (produced 1938). 1938.
No Time for Comedy (produced 1939). 1939.
The Talley Method (produced 1941). 1941.
The Pirate, from a play by Ludwig Fulda (produced 1942). 1943.
Jacobowsky and the Colonel, from a play by Franz Werfel (produced 1944). 1944.
Dunnigan's Daughter (produced 1945). 1946.
Jane, from a story by W. Somerset Maugham (produced 1946; as *The Foreign Language*, produced 1951). 1952.
I Know My Love, from a play by Marcel Achard (produced 1949). 1952.
Let Me Hear the Melody (produced 1951).
Fanny, with Joshua Logan, music by Harold Rome, from a trilogy by Marcel Pagnol (produced 1954). 1955.
Four Plays: The Second Man; Biography; Rain from Heaven; End of Summer. 1955.
The Cold Wind and the Warm (produced 1958). 1959.
The Beauty Part (produced 1962).
Lord Pengo: A Period Comedy, based on his book *Duveen* (produced 1962). 1963.
But for Whom Charlie (produced 1964). 1964.

SCREENPLAYS: *Liliom*, with Sonya Levien, 1930; *Lightnin'*, with Sonya Levien, 1930; *The Sea Wolf*, with Ralph Block, 1930; *The Brat*, with others, 1931; *Surrender*, with Sonya Levien, 1931; *Daddy Long Legs*, with Sonya Levien, 1931; *Delicious*, 1931; *Rebecca of Sunnybrook Farm*, with Sonya Levien, 1932; *Tess of the Storm Country*, with others, 1932; *Brief Moment*, 1933; *Queen Christina*, with Salka Viertel and H.M. Harwood, 1933; *Cavalcade*, 1933; *Hallelujah, I'm a Bum* (*Hallelujah, I'm a Tramp, Lazy Bones*), with Ben Hecht, 1933; *My Lips Betray*, 1933; *As Husbands Go*, with Sonya Levien, 1934; *The Scarlet Pimpernel*, with others, 1934; *Anna Karenina*, with others, 1935; *A Tale of Two Cities*, with W.P. Lipscomb, 1935; *Conquest* (*Marie Walewska*), with others, 1937; *Parnell*, with John van Druten, 1937; *The Cowboy and the Lady*, with Sonya Levien, 1938; *Waterloo Bridge*, with others, 1940; *Two-Faced Woman*, with others, 1941; *Quo Vadis*, with others, 1951; *Me and the Colonel*, with George Froeschel, 1958; *Stowaway in the Sky* (English narration), 1962.

OTHER

Duveen. 1952.
The Worcester Account (*New Yorker* sketches).1954.
Portrait of Max: An Intimate Memoir of Sir Max Beerbohm. 1960; as
   Conversation with Max, 1960.
The Suspended Drawing Room. 1965.
The Burning-Glass. 1968.
People in a Diary: A Memoir. 1972; as *Tribulations and Laughter: A Memoir,*
   1972.

BIBLIOGRAPHY: *Maxwell Anderson and S.N. Behrman: A Reference Guide* by William Klink, 1977.

CRITICAL STUDIES: *Life Among the Playwrights* by John F. Wharton, 1974; *S.N. Behrman* by Kenneth T. Read, 1975; *S.N. Behrman: The Major Plays* by William Klink, 1978.

S.N. Behrman's work encompasses more than 35 plays, most of which can be considered high comedy. Through his sophisticated social comedies walk an array of urbane, often intellectually articulate characters meeting in elegant surroundings on America's eastern seaboard, or abroad. The dramas convey Behrman's thematic concerns with the dangers of intolerance and the problems of success with its attendant moral questions and tensions arising when related to matrimony, money, politics, and love. The author's protagonists tend to be dispassionate observers of life rather than fighters for a cause. Frequently they confront fanatic or passionate points of view with an unheroic attitude of compromise. A tolerant, liberal humanistic view is the crux of Behrman's comic vision. Often at the center of his plays is a mature and radiant woman acting as a lodestone toward whom all the other characters are drawn. Forgiving and liberal in spirit, she clashes with more intense opponents to emerge triumphant, strengthened by her grace and magnanimity. Because Behrman's protagonists compromise rather than cope with issues, his plays are apt to seem inconclusive and are often faulted for structural looseness and insufficient plot progression. However, such shortcomings are redeemed in his best plays by lively, witty characters and incisive dialogue within which Behrman's humanistic vision is clearly implied.

In addition to finely-drawn female characters (providing vehicles for actresses the like of Ina Claire, Ruth Gordon, Katherine Cornell, and Lynn Fontanne), Behrman peopled his world with character-types bearing symbolic significance. These figures recur in his plays in different guises, such as the politically conservative man of power (commonly a financier or businessman); the failed, if modestly talented, artist; the emancipated woman; the success-motivated financial or professional genius; and the idealistic Marxist.

In *The Second Man*, the author's first major play, the limitedly talented writer Clark Storey is matrimonially desired by two women: an understanding rich woman offering financial security, and an emancipated young flapper who is beloved by an unexciting but talented and prosperous scientist. The plot's two love triangles are resolved when all characters prove true to themselves. Storey pragmatically chooses the wealthy lady, accepting his opportunistic nature, and the flapper agrees to marry her reliable scientist-suitor. The play is well realized with interesting characters surrounding a witty, unheroic protagonist.

Biography introduces Behrman's most masterfully created protagonist in Marion Froude, a charming and worldly portrait painter who views life and the many men she has loved with kindly detachment. Offered a lucrative commission to write her autobiography for a popular magazine by an intense and socially embittered young journalist named Richard Kurt, Marion accepts the offer and, soon, Kurt's developing love for her. When she learns, however, of Kurt's expectation that her memoirs scandalously expose her many celebrated acquaintances, Marion destroys her manuscript and, consequently, her relationship with Kurt who thinks her compromising attitude indulgent toward society's evils. Encountering this fanatic outlook, Marion refuses to abandon her own. Particular objects of Kurt's enmity are a pompous Senatorial candidate (a re-emerged former lover from Marion's youth) and his wealthy and powerful political mentor who has exerted pressure to have the memoirs quashed. No other play of Behrman's so skillfully develops and interweaves character, story, and theme, emphasizing a protagonist embodying his humanistic beliefs.

Variations of Marion Froude appear in several subsequent Behrman comedies. *End of Summer* revolves around a wealthy and charming, but impressionable, divorcee who is infatuated with a fortune-hunting doctor. When she learns that the physician loves her daughter rather than she, she sadly, but firmly, dismisses him, as does her daughter. Dealing with the often conflicting quests of love and money, the author draws a compelling portrait of his central woman in a social environment of interesting characters. In *Rain from Heaven* a liberal and wise English woman mediates a stormy debate of socio-political ideals among weekend guests at her country home. Among them are a German-Jewish music critic, an anti-semitic American aviator, and a dictatorial American millionaire bent on uniting youth in favor of Fascism. Accenting the world-wide turmoil of the 1930's, the author sharply raises and opposes the issues of political intolerance and racism.

In *No Time for Comedy*, an understanding actress wife temporarily accepts her playwright husband's affair with another woman while he attempts to turn from composing light comedies to serious drama in keeping with darkening times. Seeing his attempts are unsuccessful, she persuades him to write a comedy about his own love triangle which leads him to recover his true stylistic abilities and to return to his wife. That the secondary character of the wife emerges as a more forceful depiction than that of the writer-protagonist is a shortcoming in a play successfully dramatizing Behrman's self-admitted concern about a comic writer's proper path in a turbulent age.

Other noteworthy dramatic works in the latter portion of Behrman's career touch on problems of marriage, romance, and racism, and encompass several adaptations. *Amphitryon 38*, adapted from Giraudoux's play, is an entertaining bedroom farce employing the Amphitryon legend. *Jacobowsky and the Colonel*, an ironically amusing, if structurally diffuse, version of Franz Werfel's play, brings together a Jew and an anti-Semite fleeing from the Nazis in World War II. Based on Marcel Pagnol's trilogy and written in collaboration with Joshua Logan, *Fanny*—Behrman's only musical—charmingly treats the burdens of long-parted lovers. *The Cold Wind and the Warm* stands strongly as an affecting, semi-autobiographical memoir about a youthful friendship. Behrman did not continue to write for the theater after his last play, *But for Whom Charlie*, in 1964.

S.N. Behrman left a substantial legacy of social comedies, the best being notable for richly-drawn characters, dialogue filled with wit and the intelligent discussion of ideas, and a humanistic *Weltanschauung* advocating tolerance. As a dramatist, his comic view of the world greatly enriched the theater and its literature.

—Christian H. Moe

BENTLEY, Eric (Russell).

Born in Bolton, Lancashire, England, 14 September 1916; moved to the United States, 1939; became citizen, 1948. Educated at Bolton School; Oxford University, B.A. 1938, B.Lit. 1939; Yale University, New Haven, Connecticut, Ph.D. 1941. Married 1) Maja Tschernjakow (marriage dissolved); 2) Joanne Davis in 1953; twin sons. Teacher, Black Mountain College, North Carolina, 1942–44, and University of Minnesota, Minneapolis, 1944–48; Brander Matthews professor of dramatic literature, Columbia University, New York, 1952–69; freelance writer, 1970–73; Katharine Cornell professor of theatre, State University of New York, Buffalo, 1974–82. Professor of comparative literature, University of Maryland, College Park, 1982–89. Charles Eliot Norton professor of poetry, Harvard University, Cambridge, Massachusetts, 1960–61; Fulbright professor, Belgrade, 1980. Drama critic, *New Republic*, New York, 1952–56. Recipient: Guggenheim fellowship, 1948; Rockefeller grant, 1949; American Academy grant, 1953; Longview award, for criticism, 1961; Ford grant, 1964; George Jean Nathan award, for criticism, 1967; CBS fellowship, 1976; Obie award, 1978; Theater Festival gold medal, 1985. D.F.A.: University of Wisconsin, Madison, 1975; Litt.D.: University of East Anglia, Norwich, 1979. Member, American Academy of Arts and Sciences, 1969. Agent: Jack Tantleff, 375 Greenwich Street, Suite 700, New York, New

York 10013; or, Joy Westendarp, International Copyright Bureau, 22A
Aubrey House, Maida Avenue, London W2 1TQ, England. Address: 194
Riverside Drive, Apartment 4–E, New York, New York 10025, U.S.A.

Publications

PLAYS

A Time to Die, and A Time to Live: Two Short Plays, adaptations of plays by
   Euripides and Sophocles (as *Commitments,* produced 1967). 1967.
Sketches in *DMZ Revue* (produced 1968).
The Red White and Black, music by Brad Burg (produced 1970). 1971.
*Are You Now or Have You Ever Been: The Investigation of Show-Business by
   the Un-American Activities Committee 1947–1958* (produced 1972). 1972.
The Recantation of Galileo Galilei: Scenes from History Perhaps (produced
   1973). 1972.
Expletive Deleted (produced 1974). 1974.
From the Memoirs of Pontius Pilate (produced 1976). In *Rallying Cries,* 1977.
Rallying Cries: Three Plays (includes *Are You Now or Have You Ever Been,
   The Recantation of Galileo Galilei, From the Memoirs of Pontius Pilate*).
   1977; as *Are You Now or Have You Ever Been and Other Plays,* 1981.
The Kleist Variations: Three Plays. 1982.
   1. *Wannsee* (produced 1978).
   2. *The Fall of the Amazons* (produced 1979).
   3. *Concord* (produced 1982).
Larry Parks' Day in Court (produced 1979).
Lord Alfred's Lover (produced 1979). 1981; in *Monstrous Martyrdoms,* 1985.
Monstrous Martyrdoms: Three Plays (includes *Lord Alfred's Lover, H for
   Hamlet, German Requiem*). 1985.
Round Two. In *Gay Plays: Four,* edited by Michael Wilcox, 1990.
The First Lulu, adaptation of a play by Frank Wedekind (produced 1993).
   1993.

OTHER

*A Century of Hero-Worship: A Study of the Idea of Heroism in Carlyle and
   Nietzsche, with Notes on Other Hero-Worshipers of Modern Times.* 1944;
   as *The Cult of the Superman,* 1947.
The Playwright as Thinker: A Study of Drama in Modern Times. 1946; as *The
   Modern Theatre: A Study of Dramatists and the Drama,* 1948.
Bernard Shaw: A Reconsideration. 1947; revised edition as *Bernard Shaw
   1856–1950,* 1957; as *Bernard Shaw,* 1967.
In Search of Theater. 1953.
The Dramatic Event: An American Chronicle. 1954.
What Is Theatre? A Query in Chronicle Form. 1956.
The Life of the Drama. 1964.
The Theatre of Commitment and Other Essays on Drama in Our Society.
   1967.
*What Is Theatre? Incorporating "The Dramatic Event" and Other Reviews
   1944–1967.* 1968.
Theatre of War: Comments on 32 Occasions. 1972.

The Brecht Commentaries 1943–1980. 1981.
The Pirandello Commentaries. 1985.
The Brecht Memoir. 1986.
Thinking about the Playwright: Comments from Four Decades. 1987.
The Life of the Drama. 1991.

Editor, *The Importance of "Scrutiny": Selections from "Scrutiny," A Quarterly Review, 1932–1948.* 1948.
Editor and part translator, *From the Modern Repertory.* Series 1 and 2, 1949–52; series 3, 1956.
Editor, *The Play: A Critical Anthology.* 1951.
Editor, *Shaw on Music.* 1955.
Editor and part translator, *The Modern Theatre.* 6 vols., 1955–60.
Editor and part translator, *The Classic Theatre.* 4 vols., 1958–61.
Editor and translator, *Let's Get a Divorce! and Other Plays.* 1958.
Editor and part translator, *Works of Bertolt Brecht.* 1961–.
Editor and part translator, *The Genius of the Italian Theatre.* 1964.
Editor, *The Storm over "The Deputy."* 1964.
Editor, *Songs of Bertolt Brecht and Hanns Eisler.* 1966.
Editor, *The Theory of the Modern Stage: An Introduction to Modern Theatre and Drama.* 1968.
Editor and part translator, *The Great Playwrights: Twenty-Five Plays with Comments by Critics and Scholars.* 2 vols., 1970.
Editor, *Thirty Years of Treason: Excerpts from Hearings before the House Committee on Un-American Activities 1938–1968.* 1971.
Editor and translator, *Dramatic Repertoire.* 1985–.

Translator, *The Private Life of the Master Race,* by Brecht. 1944.
Translator, *Parables for the Theatre: The Good Woman of Setzuan, and The Caucasian Chalk Circle,* by Brecht. 1948; revised edition, 1965.
Translator, with others, *Naked Masks: Five Plays,* by Pirandello. 1952.
Translator, *Orpheus in the Underworld* (libretto), by Hector Crémieux and Ludovic Halévy. 1956.
Translator, *The Wire Harp,* by Wolf Biermann. 1968.

RECORDINGS: *Bentley on Brecht,* 1963; *Brecht Before the Un-American Activities Committee,* 1963; *A Man's a Man,* Spoken Arts, 1963; *Songs of Hanns Eisler,* 1965; *The Elephant Calf/Dear Old Democracy,* 1967; *Bentley on Biermann,* 1968; *Eric Bentley Sings The Queen of 42nd Street,* 1974.

MANUSCRIPT COLLECTION: Boston University Library.

CRITICAL STUDY: *The Play and Its Critic: Essays for Eric Bentley* edited by Michael Bertin, 1986.

THEATRICAL ACTIVITIES

DIRECTOR: **Plays**—*Sweeney Agonistes* by T.S. Eliot, 1949; *Him* by e.e. cummings, 1950; *The House of Bernarda Alba* by García Lorca, 1950; *The Iceman Cometh* (co-director) by Eugene O'Neill, 1950; *Purgatory* by W.B. Yeats, and *Riders to the Sea* and *The Shadow of the Glen* by J.M. Synge, 1951; *The Good Woman of Setzuan* by Brecht, 1956.

Eric Bentley quotes

from an interview with Jerome Clegg (1988):

Clegg: Why on earth did you have to write a play? For you are nothing if not critical.

Bentley: Maybe the impulse was to write a counter-play.

Clegg: Counter to what?

Bentley: A (good) performance of the Anouilh Antigone—in its integrity, not in the Galantiere adaptation-distortion—had riled me. So I had to write a "correct" Antigone; set Anouilh straight. The same with Brecht.

Clegg: Meaning?

Bentley: He made such absurd demands upon his people. What else could Mother Courage have done?

Clegg: Galileo?

Bentley: Brecht wilfully chose to misunderstand him. The recantation could not possibly be taken as a betrayal of Marxism.

Clegg: So it was historical correctness you were after? Oh, you and your scholarly background!

Bentley: Rubbish. There would be no possible "historical correctness" for Antigone. It is a human correctness that interests me. Telling a story more honestly—truer to *our* time, if you will, not necessarily truer to some other time.

Clegg: Someone had called your dramatic works "no nonsense plays."

Bentley: Can one tell the Jesus story without nonsense? There would be no precedents.

Clegg: The New Testament nonsense?

Bentley: A very over-rated book.

Clegg: "Better than the New Testament"—is that a good description of your Jesus-Pilate play?

Bentley: I hope so. Shaw spoke of himself as "better than Shakespeare" with something like that in mind.

Clegg: He also put a question mark after the phrase.

Bentley: As I do.

Clegg: What was your first play? I want to know how all this got started.

Bentley: Which is the wickedest of all your wicked questions.

Clegg: Answer it.

Bentley: My first play wasn't a play of mine at all, it was other people's plays.

Clegg: Especially Bertolt Brecht's.

Bentley: Actually, my first-play-that-was-really-someone-else's-play was not a Brecht, it was a Meilhac and Halévy.

Clegg: Who dey?

Bentley: Jacques Offenbach. The first time I launched out on my own was when I re-did the libretto to Offenbach's *Orpheus* for the New York City Opera Company.

Clegg: Everyone loved it.

Bentley: The press hated it. Except the communist paper.

Clegg: So you took up the Commie cause in *Are You Now or Have You Ever Been?*

Bentley: Well, that was some centuries later, and it wasn't the commie cause.

Clegg: But you do champion causes. What came next?

Bentley: *Lord Alfred's Lover?*

Clegg: Exactly. Your gay liberation play.

Bentley: Touché.

Clegg: After which I lose you. No causes but lots of Heinrich von Kleist.

Bentley: My three Kleist Variations. In which lots of Kleist got thrown overboard—and not all causes were forgotten . . .

Clegg: No?

Bentley: No! Didn't you interview me on this point, and isn't your interview the preface to *The Kleist Variations*, published sometime, somewhere?

Clegg: Is it? Oh, yes. What's your latest?

Bentley: Another gay item.

Clegg: But prompted by a non-gay item, Schnitzler's *Reigen? La Ronde?*

Bentley: Transposed to the 1970's and New York. *Round Two.*

The majority of Eric Bentley's plays are history plays, dealing with historical figures who have either attained the status of myth, or who are on the verge of entering the popular imagination. Bentley consequently is free to work upon our assumptions about his characters, and he usually works towards a radical point: the shoring-up of individual identity against the inroads of institutional power, be it of the church or the state.

He is a Shavian dramatist in that, not only does language matter, but his talent makes it central to his plays. He may rely upon a stage-grouping, he may use every available stage nuance; in the end, it is the pure dialectic of impassioned speech that gives his plays their force.

He is Shavian as well in the less obvious sense of writing plays against the stage, the stage being but the reflection of our melodramatic lives. Against the commonly held belief that our enemies are evil personified and that ours is a kill-or-be-killed world, he will grant the antagonist an argument and create a scene in which both sides are right from their own perspective. His plays are thus historical tragedies, not mere spectacles of put-upon humanity.

We can see all of these ingredients at work in his early play *The Recantation of Galileo Galilei*, his response to the *Galileo* of Bertolt Brecht. A close comparison of the two makes for fascinating reading. If Brecht writes inspired science fiction, with a cast of inquisitors who are mostly clowns, Bentley carries the conviction of political reality, his play building to the climax of the trial which Brecht necessarily avoids. Brecht's *Galileo* may be the greater play, its epic scope, easy manner, and fine touch of folk wisdom bearing the marks of genius. Nevertheless, Bentley's mastery of the issues, his sense of the argument, and his scene of contention create a trial that is the best set-piece since Shaw's *Saint Joan*.

As for the protagonists: if Brecht's appetitive man ends in cynicism and despair, of this false confession before the threat of torture becoming his true confession of self-hatred for having caved in, Bentley reverses the human dilemma, making his Galileo lie for the greater good. This refined man is a naïve intellectual headed for a rude awakening, but an awakening nevertheless. The cynicism of Brecht's protagonist is shifted in Bentley's play to the shoulders of a real antagonist, the Jesuit scientist and priest, Scheiner.

If Bentley's Galileo is an ideological man who fights for the ideal, his Oscar Wilde, by contrast, fights for the right to be himself. The description nicely fits the title of the play, *Lord Alfred's Lover*, which implies, of course, that Wilde is not yet established as himself. The playwright's masterstroke is to "tell" the story of the trials through the expedient of the aging Bosie's confession to a priest; he thereby not only wins sympathy for Bosie, but also subverts the intentions of those who would praise Wilde at Bosie's expense (the adulation of Wilde when carried to an extreme sounding suspiciously like gay-bashing, the Bosies of the world be damned!). By joining the two fates, Bentley encompasses the scope of the homosexual journey, which begins with Bosie, the man who never made peace with himself, and ends with Wilde, the man who did but at a cost.

Since the conventional audience reads the title for their definition of Wilde, Bentley establishes Wilde against their reading. The notorious homosexual is their creation, his notoriety being their contribution to the case. They would prefer the portrait of a self-destructive man, which absolves them of guilt. They get instead, the portrait of their victim, which does not.

Of course it is rash of Bentley to suggest that the gay Prime Minister Rosebery actively conspired against Wilde, but this is a mere quibble given the fine scene he creates for them at Reading Gaol. Threatened by association with Wilde, influential homosexuals may have helped to bring him down; in any case, while we can argue that their "imaginary conversation" never took place, we can also imagine it as taking place every day in the minds of people who are forced into acting against themselves.

In a totally different key is a series of plays collectively known as *The Kleist Variations*. Contemporary readings of the plays of Heinrich von Kleist, they reveal the earlier playwright in a more metaphysical vein. To Kleist's astounding vision, Bentley offers the challenge of a whole new world of sexual politics, political hatreds, and apocalyptic fears.

Concord, the variation of Kleist's *Broken Jug*, is typical of the three plays. Set in Puritan New England during the early days of the Republic, it turns the tables on a sexual bounder and makes him the victim of Puritan hatred (read: "family values") instead. A "monstrous martyrdom" comically turned, it exposes the same hypocrisy that hit Wilde and Galileo, while it inspires the same hope.

—Michael Bertin

BERNARD, Kenneth.

Born in Brooklyn, New York, 7 May 1930. Educated at City College of New York, B.A. 1953; Columbia University, New York, M.A. 1956, Ph.D. 1962. Served in the United States Army, 1953–55: private. Married Elaine Reiss in 1952; two sons and one daughter. Instructor, 1959–62, assistant professor, 1962–66, associate professor, 1967–70, and since 1971 professor of English, Long Island University, Brooklyn. Advisory editor, 1973–75, assistant editor, 1976–78, and since 1979 fiction editor, *Confrontation*, Brooklyn. Vice-president, New York Theatre Strategy, 1972–79. Recipient: Rockefeller grant, 1971, 1975; Guggenheim fellowship, 1972; Creative Artists Public Service grant, 1973, 1976; National Endowment for the Arts grant, for fiction, 1977; Arvon poetry prize, 1980. Address: 800 Riverside Drive, New York, New York 10032, U.S.A.

Publications

PLAYS

The Moke-Eater (produced 1968). In *Night Club and Other Plays*, 1971.
The Lovers. In *Trace*, 1969; in *Night Club and Other Plays*, 1971.
Marko's: A Vegetarian Fantasy. In *Massachusetts Review*, 1969.
Night Club (produced 1970). In *Night Club and Other Plays*, 1971.
The Monkeys of the Organ Grinder (produced 1970). In *Night Club and Other Plays*, 1971.
The Unknown Chinaman (produced 1971). In *Playwrights for Tomorrow 10*, edited by Arthur H. Ballet, 1973.
Night Club and Other Plays (includes *The Moke-Eater, The Lovers, Mary Jane, The Monkeys of the Organ Grinder, The Giants in the Earth*). 1971.
Mary Jane (also director: produced 1973). In *Night Club and Other Plays*, 1971.
Goodbye, Dan Bailey. In *Drama and Theatre*, 1971.
The Magic Show of Dr. Ma-Gico (produced 1973). In *Theatre of the Ridiculous*, edited by Bonnie Marranca and Gautam Dasgupta, 1979.
How We Danced While We Burned (produced 1974). With *La Justice; or, The Cock That Crew*, 1990.
King Humpy (produced 1975). In *2Plus2*, 1985.
The Sensuous Ape. In *Penthouse*, 1975.
The Sixty Minute Queer Show, music by John Braden (produced 1977).
La Justice; or, The Cock That Crew, music by John Braden (produced 1979). With *How We Danced While We Burned*, 1990.
La Fin du Cirque (produced 1984). In *Grand Street*, 1982.
The Panel (produced 1984).
Play with an Ending; or, Columbus Discovers the World (produced 1984).
We Should . . . (A Lie) (produced 1992). In *Curse of a Fool*, 1992.
Curse of a Fool (includes *One Thing Is Not Another, Nevertheless, We Should . . . (A Lie)*). 1992.

SHORT STORIES
Two Stories. 1973.
The Maldive Chronicles. 1987.
From the District File. 1992.

MANUSCRIPT COLLECTIONS: Lincoln Center Library of the Performing Arts, New York; University of Minnesota, Minneapolis.

CRITICAL STUDIES: introduction by Michael Feingold to *Night Club and Other Plays*, 1971; *The Original Theatre of New York* by Stefan Brecht, 1978; *Contemporary American Dramatists 1960–1980* by Ruby Cohn, 1982; *The Darkness We Carry: The Drama of the Holocaust* by Robert Skloot, 1988; article by Rosette LaMont in *Stages*, 1992.

THEATRICAL ACTIVITIES
DIRECTOR: **Play**—*Mary Jane*, 1973.

Kenneth Bernard comments:

I like to think of my plays as metaphors, closer to poetic technique (the coherence of dream) than to rational discourse. I am not interested in traditional plot or character development. My plays build a metaphor; when the metaphor is complete, the play is complete. Within that context things and people do happen. I would hope the appeal of my plays is initially to the emotions only, not the head, and that they are received as spectacle and a kind of gorgeous (albeit frightening) entertainment. The characters in my plays can often be played by either men or women (e.g., *The Moke-Eater*, *Night Club*): only a living presence is necessary, one who reflects the character component in the play rather than any aspect of non-stage individuality: they are instruments to be played upon, not ego-minded careerists: they must "disappear" on stage. More important than technique, etc., are passion and flexibility. The defects of this preference are offset by strong directorial control: each play in effect becomes a training program. My plays use music, dance, poetry, rhetoric, film, sounds and voices of all kinds, costume, color, make-up, noise, irrationality, and existing rituals to give shape (e.g., the auction, the magic show). The audience must be authentically pulled into the play in spite of itself. It must not *care* what it all means because it is enjoying itself and feels itself involved in a dramatic flow. What remains with the audience is a totality, the metaphor, from which ideas may spring—not ideas from which it has (with difficulty) to recreate the dramatic experience.

Kenneth Bernard's major plays have been produced mainly by the Play-House of the Ridiculous, under John Vaccaro's direction. This collaboration provides the best avenue of approach to an understanding of Bernard's plays. The "Ridiculous" style, with its shrilly pitched, frenzied extravagance, its compulsively and explicitly sexual interpretation of every action, the elaborate make-up and costumes that lend confusion to the antics of transvestites of both sexes, the general aura of bleakness and violence that adds despair to even the company's most optimistic productions—that style is a reasonable physicalization of the world Kenneth Bernard evokes.

The two interlocking themes of Bernard's drama are cruelty and entertainment. His characters are perpetually threatening each other with tortures, mutilations, particularly painful modes of execution, and these vicissitudes are constantly placed in a theatrical "frame" of some sort, as intended for the amusement of a group, or of the torture-master, or of the audience itself, implicated by its silent consent to the proceedings. In Bernard's first full-length work, *The Moke-Eater*, the setting is a prototypical American small town, the hero the stock figure of a traveling salesman, desperately ingenuous and jaunty, who suddenly finds himself, when his car breaks down, confronting the sinister, inarticulate townspeople and their malevolent boss, Alec. Alec alternately cajoles and bullies the salesman into submitting to a humiliating series of charades, nightmarish parodies of small-town hospitality, climaxing in his realization that he is trapped when he drives off in the repaired auto, only to have it break down outside the next town . . . which turns out to be exactly the same town he has just left. (In the Ridiculous production, an additional frisson was added to the salesman's re-entrance by having the townspeople, at this point, attack and eviscerate him—a fate which Alec describes earlier in the play as having been inflicted on a previous visitor.)

Later plays by Bernard present the spectacle of cruelty with the torturer, rather than the victim, as protagonist. *Night Club* displays Western civilization as a hideous, inept cabaret show, controlled by an androgynous master of ceremonies named Bubi, who, like Alec in *The Moke-Eater*, cajoles and bullies both audience and performers into humiliating themselves. In fact, the theatre audience first sees the company performing the show as a parody of itself: the grotesque nightclub acts all emerge out of the "audience," which meanwhile cheers, catcalls, attacks the club's one waitress, and generally behaves boorishly. The acts themselves include a ventriloquist (male) trapped in a virulent love-hate relationship with his dummy (female), who spouts obscenities; a juggler (recalling the "Destructive Desmond" of Auden and Isherwood's *The Dog Beneath the Skin*) who throws valuable antiques into the air and declines to catch them; an impersonator, obsessed with his own virility, whose imitations veer from a sex-starved southern belle to a sadistic Nazi; and "The Grand Kabuki Theatre of America," which lends the patina of Japanese ceremoniousness to a vulgar soap-opera-like story about a pregnant college girl. Eventually, the nightclub show culminates, at Bubi's behest, in mass copulation by the "audience," accompanied by the William Tell Overture; for a climax, the one member of the audience who declines to perform is summarily dragged onstage and decapitated, while he repeatedly screams, "The menu says there's no cover charge!" In a similar vein, Bernard's *The Magic Show of Dr. Ma-Gico* is a series of violent encounters, more courtly in tone but just as unpleasant, based on fairy-tale and romance themes. (A maiden, to test her lover's fidelity, transforms herself into a diseased old crone and forces him to make love to her; a king is challenged to pick up a book without dropping his robe, orb, and scepter; in both cases the man fails.) *Auction* (unproduced) is a surreal, aleatory version of a rural livestock auction, whose items include a pig-woman and an invalid who sells off his vital organs one by one. The world-picture contained in these plays is essentially that of a continuous nightmare, and while the surface action and language change (Bernard's language is exceptionally varied in texture, going from the loftiest politeness to the most degraded abuse), the emotional thrust of the material is constantly the same: towards revealing the sheer ludicrous horror of existence. In his collaboration with the Play-House of the Ridiculous, Bernard has carried the Artaudian project of raising and exorcizing the audience's demons about as far as it is likely to get through the theatrical metaphor.

—Michael Feingold

BIRIMISA, George.

Born in Santa Cruz, California, 21 February 1924. Attended school to the ninth grade; studied with Uta Hagen at the Herbert Berghof Studios, New York. Served in the United States Naval Reserve during World War II. Married Nancy Linden in 1952 (divorced 1961). Worked in a factory, as a disc jockey, health studio manager, clerk, salesman, bartender, page for National Broadcasting Company, bellhop; counterman, Howard Johnson's, New York, 1952–56; typist, Laurie Girls, New York, 1969–70. Artistic director, Theatre of All Nations, New York, 1974–76. Recipient: Rockefeller grant, 1969. Address: 627 Page Street, Apartment 6, San Francisco, California 94117, U.S.A.

Publications

PLAYS

Degrees (produced 1966).
17 Loves and 17 Kisses (produced 1966).
Daddy Violet (produced 1967). In *Prism International*, 1968.
How Come You Don't Dig Chicks? (produced 1967). In *The Alternate*, 1981.
Mister Jello (produced 1968; revised version produced 1974).
Georgie Porgie (produced 1968). In *More Plays from Off-Off-Broadway*, edited by Michael T. Smith, 1972.
Adrian (produced 1974).
Will the Real Yogonanda Please Stand Up? (produced 1974).
A Dress Made of Diamonds (produced 1976).
Pogey Bait! (produced 1976). In *Drummer*, 1977.
A Rainbow in the Night (produced 1978).
A Rose and a Baby Ruth (produced 1981).

MANUSCRIPT COLLECTION: Joe Cino Memorial Library, Lincoln Center Library of the Performing Arts, New York.

THEATRICAL ACTIVITIES

DIRECTOR: **Plays**—*The Bed* by Robert Heide, 1966; *The Painter* by Burt Snider, 1967; *Georgie Porgie*, 1971; *A Buffalo for Brooklyn* by Anne Grant, 1975.

George Birimisa comments:

(1973) I write about the people I know. At this point in my life many of my friends are homosexual. I try to write honestly about them. In writing honestly about them I believe that my plays (in particular *Georgie Porgie*) mirror the terror of a schizophrenic society that is lost in a world of fantasy. In *Daddy Violet* I believe I showed how the individual's fantasy can lead to the burning of women and children in Vietnam. The problem with my plays is that many critics label them as homosexual plays. In the United States we live at the edge of a civilization that is near the end of the line. I feel that it is important for me to throw away every fantasy and get down into the total terror of this insane society. Only then can I truly write a play that is God-affirming, that is full of light. In my new play, tentatively titled *It's Your Movie*, I'm trying to write about the only alternative left in a demonic society—the nitty-gritty love of brother for brother and sister for sister. I know I must go through the passions of the flesh before I can break through to love my brother and sister. Anything else is an illusion. I also believe that the American male is terrified of his homosexuality and this is one of the chief reasons why he is unable to love his brother. His repression creates fires of the soul and this is translated into wars and violence. If all the "closet queens" would step out into the sunshine it would be a different country. I believe the above is what I write about in my plays.

(1977) At last I have discovered that four letter word LOVE. My early plays were screams of anger and rage. I was really screaming at myself because I was a microcosm of the good and evil of the western world, and I finally realize that it is possible to walk through death and destruction, and care . . . really care.

(1992) I just re-read my comments of 1973 and 1977. *Pompous*. I gave up the theatre for the last 10 years but I'm back in it. This time it's for my personal enjoyment. Period.

George Birimisa's early play *Daddy Violet* is built on a series of cathartic acting exercises which, through a process of association and hallucinatory transformation, evoke a battle in the Vietnam war. The cruelty and destruction of the war are connected, using a technique based on improvisation, with the actor's self-loathing and sexual immaturity.

Birimisa is a fiercely moral writer; his plays are filled with compassionate rage against needless suffering, furious impatience with the human condition, desperately frustrated idealism. He links the pain of human isolation to economic and social roots.

Mister Jello starts out with a mixed bag of characters: a waspish aging transvestite, a bitchy social worker, a dreamy boy flower child, a business-like prostitute, and fat, foolish Mister Jello, who likes to pretend to be a little boy and have the prostitute as his mommy discipline him. Birimisa sets their antagonisms in perspective by reference to the social philosopher Henry George.

Georgie Porgie is a series of vignettes about homosexual relationships, almost all bitter and ugly in tone, interspersed with choral episodes quoted from Friedrich Engels. The contrast between Engels's idealistic vision of human liberty and Birimisa's variously stupid, contemptible, pitiful, self-despising characters, all imprisoned in their own compulsions, is powerful and painful.

Birimisa's writing is often crude, the language vulgar, the humor cruel, the events shocking; the author has been preoccupied with psychic pain and the consequences of neurotic patterns, and his work makes up in self-examining integrity and emotional intensity what it eschews of seductiveness and beauty. In 1976 he made what is for Americans a mythic move from East to West, from New York first to Los Angeles, then to San Francisco. In the more affirmative pre-AIDS climate of gay liberation there, he attempted to go beyond the rage and desperation of the earlier plays to a more positive view: *Pogey Bait!* was well received in Los Angeles and ran for several months.

—Michael T. Smith

BLESSING, Lee (Knowlton).

Born in Minneapolis, Minnesota, 4 October 1949. Educated at schools in Minnetonka, Minnesota; University of Minnesota, Minneapolis, 1967–69; Reed College, Portland, Oregon, 1969–71, B.A. in English 1971; University of Iowa, Iowa City, 1974–79, M.F.A. in English 1976, M.F.A. in speech/theater 1979. Married Jeanne Blake in 1986; two stepchildren. Teacher of playwriting, University of Iowa, 1977–79, and Playwrights' Center, Minneapolis, 1986–88. Recipient: American College Theater Festival award, 1979; Jerome Foundation grant, 1981, 1982; McKnight Foundation grant, 1983, 1989; Great American Play award, 1984; National Endowment for the Arts grant, 1985, 1988; Bush Foundation fellowship, 1987; American Theater Critics Association award, 1987; Marton award, 1988; Dramalogue award, 1988; Guggenheim fellowship, 1989. Agent: Lois Berman, Little Theatre Building, 240 West 44th Street, New York, New York 10036; or, Jeffrey Melnick, Harry Gold Agency, 3500 West Olive, Suite 1400, Burbank, California 91505. Address: 2817 West 40th Street, Minneapolis, Minnesota 55410, U.S.A.

Publications

PLAYS

The Authentic Life of Billy the Kid (produced 1979). 1980.
Oldtimers Game (produced 1982). 1988.
Nice People Dancing to Good Country Music (produced 1982; revised version produced 1984). 1983; revised version included in *Four Plays*, 1990.
Independence (produced 1984). 1985; included in *Four Plays*, 1990.
Riches (as *War of the Roses*, produced 1985). 1986; included in *Four Plays*, 1990.
Eleemosynary (produced 1985). 1987; included in *Four Plays*, 1990.
A Walk in the Woods (produced 1987). 1988.
Two Rooms (produced 1988). 1990.

Cobb (produced 1989). 1991.
Down the Road (produced 1989).
Four Plays (includes *Eleemosynary*, *Riches*, *Independence*, *Nice People Dancing to Good Country Music*). 1990.
Lake Street Extension (produced 1992).
Fortinbras. 1992.

TELEVISION PLAY: *Cooperstown*, 1993.

A cast of characters including a foul-mouthed nun who recites the back of cereal boxes instead of prayers, an eccentric grandmother who believes she can fly using homemade wings, an American photographer who is taken hostage in Beirut, and a Russian diplomat who prefers talking about Willie Nelson instead of nuclear arms control, reflects Lee Blessing's penchant for writing about the illogical state of the human condition. Themes embrace both public and private politics, centering around the battle to establish, nurture, and maintain human relationships. Style and subject-matter are eclectic, though Blessing's plays have certain features in common. His plays are usually short with small casts and sketchy plots.

The most interesting of his early works is *Nice People Dancing to Good Country Music*. A comedy set on a deck above a Houston Bar, it pairs together two unlikely women in order to explore the notions of discovery and acceptance. A would-be nun, Catherine, who is asked to leave the convent due to inappropriate behavior, comes to stay with her raucous aunt, who manages the bar. Catherine gets a secular education from her aunt, and from a customer of the bar, who advises her not "to remarry the world, just to date it a little." Understatement and double entendre help establish the environment necessary for the odd but realistic characters. There are a few instances in which the language is too clever and not in line with the character's personal voice. However, it is Blessing's creative use of language that distinguishes much of his work.

Eleemosynary is also a one-act play with eccentric female characters, but here Blessing uses language both as a dramatic device and as an ongoing theme. Three generations of the Westbrook women tell their stories through recollections of their shared histories, each trying to find independence but each wanting the security that dependence provides. The grandmother warns her daughter about having a child: "You'll just be something a child needs" while the daughter reveals her thoughts about her mother: "I spent my free time being delighted not to be around my mother, and wondering how she was." The granddaughter, who uses a spelling bee to bring them all together, wins the bee with the word "eleemosynary" only to realize that words neither guarantee communication nor establish relationships. In fact, the characters use words to avoid communication. Most effective is Blessing's ability to use words both to engage and to disengage the characters' emotions and their relationships with each other.

Plot is subordinate to theme in *Eleemosynary*, but structure is less traditional than Blessing's other work, with the exception of *Two Rooms*, a poignant dramatization of the imprisonment of an American hostage in Beirut and the effect it has on his wife. Blessing uses symbolism to advantage, using light and darkness to represent certain issues and maintaining a comparison of the wife's situation with that of an African hornbill bird. Hers is a desperate attempt to maintain hope while her husband's situation is exploited by the media and ignored by the government: "After they mate, the male walls the female up, in the hollow of a tree. He literally imprisons her. . . . After the eggs are hatched, he breaks down the wall again, and the whole family is united. . . . It hasn't been a prison at all. It's been . . . a fortress."

Blessing's concern about relationships is played out differently in *Independence* and *Riches*. Like *Eleemosynary*, *Independence* explores female relationships in a family void of men. The burden of maintaining familial relationships is borne by three daughters and their mentally unstable mother. However, the mother is often remarkably lucid though blatantly sardonic: "That's what family means—each generation destroying itself willingly, for what comes after." The linguistic rhythm is not as strong as it is in *Eleemosynary* and *Two Rooms*, but the plot is more cohesive. Blessing often writes about the rituals that define and reflect individuality. In *Independence* the oldest daughter forces the family to partake in a "tea time" ritual hoping that the experience will change their behavior. A funny scene, the exercise fails to effect change.

In *Riches* the husband's ritual of blowing his nose, "a big blow, then three little ones," prompts the wife's realization that she no longer wishes to be married. The play attempts to explore the notion that love is not enough to sustain a relationship. Unfortunately the first act moves slowly, in contrast with a physically violent second act. There are some interesting observations regarding human behavior: how people come to logical conclusions in rather illogical ways and some creative contrasting images. Still, the play lacks substantive dramatic action. *Riches* is similar in treatment to *Down the Road*, about a husband and wife writing team who conduct a series of interviews with a serial killer. And, like the husband and wife of *Riches*, in the end they suffer a failed marriage, theirs due to the unsuccessful results of their dealings with the murderer. The play seems truncated, but the issue of journalistic ethics serves as a unifying factor and makes the play dramatically more viable than *Riches*.

A Walk in the Woods is Blessing's most commercially successful play and has appeared on Broadway. It is based on an actual walk in the woods by Russian and American diplomats Yuli A. Kvitsinsky and Paul H. Nitze. However, the play is about personal politics and deals more with the process of how two superpowers negotiate, rather than the outcome. The plot is negligible, subordinate to the theme of American idealism versus Russian pragmatism underlying mundane conversations on topics ranging from Italian shoes to the lyrics of country music. The play's structure is cyclical, which is problematic and results in an unsatisfying ending because in the end nothing has changed; no agreement has been reached; no revelations are made. It is similar in style to an earlier and lesser play, *Oldtimers Game* in that both are vehicles for social and political issues but neither play explores these issues in any depth.

Blessing's work reflects an interest in characters whose past interferes with their future. Cyclical structures coupled with non-traditional plots create a unique style in which character and language are pivotal dramatic elements, and unique observations about relationships create impassioned moments on stage.

—Judy Lee Oliva

BOGOSIAN, Eric.

Born in Boston, Massachusetts, 24 April 1953. Educated at Woburn High School and Woburn Drama Guild, Massachusetts, 1971–73; University of Chicago, 1973–74; Oberlin College, Ohio, 1975–76, B.A. in theater 1976. Director, The Kitchen, New York, 1977–81. Recipient: National Endowment for the Arts and New York State Arts Council grants; Drama Desk award, 1986; Obie award, 1986, 1990; Berlin Film Festival Silver Bear, 1988. Agent: George Lane, William Morris Agency, 1350 Avenue of the Americas, New York, New York 10019, U.S.A.

Publications

PLAYS

Men Inside (produced 1981).
Voices of America (produced 1982).
Funhouse (produced 1983).
Talk Radio (produced 1985; revised version produced 1987). 1988.
Drinking in America (produced 1986). 1987.
Sex, Drugs, Rock & Roll (produced 1988). 1991.
An American Chorus (produced 1989).
Dog Show (produced 1992).
Notes from Underground (produced 1992). 1993.

SCREENPLAY: *Talk Radio*, 1988.

THEATRICAL ACTIVITIES
ACTOR: **Plays**—all his own plays.

Eric Bogosian's brand of performance is strongly influenced by rock concerts, Pop art, video-art, happenings, mixed media, and the blending of "high" and "low" art. Influenced by performance artists such as Cindy Sherman, Spalding Gray, Laurie Anderson, and Robert Longo, Bogosian grew impatient with traditional theater and experimented in the 1970s with alternative forms. He developed his one-man show, dazzling and offending his audience with his rogue's gallery of American males. The black stud, the spaced-out hippy, the virulently anti-semitic caller on a radio talk show, the rock star, the gang-bangers, the punks, and the homeless, all were played by this gifted theater artist in his black trousers, white oxford button-down collar shirt or T-shirt, and black ref shoes. At first his act was built around his imaginary entertainer-/comedian, Ricky Paul, who ranted and gloated about the deplorable condition of the modern world. The set was generally sparse—a chair, a table, a microphone, and stand. Later, he eliminated Ricky Paul and simply played his

medley of unlikely, zany, often nasty, but unforgettable characters. The monologists usually offer a warped, often angry, quasi-autobiographical account of
their dispossessed selves.

Bogosian creates characters who challenge his vocal range, permitting him
to play with the different accents and idioms of urban black English, a Texas
drawl, burly ethnic American, or Hispanic speech. At its best, the dialogue
reflects the finely observed language of the hustler, druggy weirdo, Archie
Bunker racist, or rock groupie. Lacing together a stream of monologues and
appropriated media images, he created his satiric or parodic assemblages,
*Funhouse, Men Inside, Drinking in America, Talk Radio, Sex, Drugs, Rock &
Roll,* and *An American Chorus.* A successful stand-up comic in Lower
Manhattan's late-night clubs and also trained in dance, Bogosian energizes his
monologues, propelling them with the power of the rock star—a characteristic
of such consummate stage actors as Anthony Sher—and feeding off his
audience's desire to be offended while entertained.

Bogosian began offering his monologues in New York performance art
spaces such as Performance Space 122, The Kitchen, the Snafu Club, and
Franklin Furnace. RoseLee Goldberg describes him as one of the founders of
"artists' cabaret," a new genre spawned in New York discos. Beginning as a
solo performer, Bogosian drew on Lenny Bruce, the New York deejay Alan
Freed, the underground performer Brother Theodore, Bob Dylan, Jimi
Hendrix, and Laurie Anderson for his inspiration. By 1982, his work crossed
over from the vanguard into the mass cultural status, twice winning awards for
best play, becoming the subject of films and cable specials, and appearing in
book form. It is currently rumored that he is finished with monologues
featuring himself and plans to write plays for others to act in.

Influenced by our media age and what is known as the hyperreal, Bogosian's
works are best understood against the backdrop of the writings of Roland
Barthes and Jean Baudrillard. Barthes's dissection of mass culture and its
mythologies influence Bogosian's exploration of a cross-section of American
cultural stereotypes. Baudrillard's analysis of the codes, structures, and practices of our consumer society are also helpful in situating Bogosian's themes.
Bogosian's perspective on his material and his cultural critique address many
of the same phenomena that are searchingly analyzed by Barthes and
Baudrillard.

Bogosian's works are full of advertising slogans—for Kronenbrau beer,
Nyquil, and Remington cigarettes—and numerous references to McDonalds,
BMWs, Volvos, Peruvian cocaine, 'ludes, Jimi Hendrix, Janis Joplin, Cassius
Clay, and other idols of American pop culture. His preoccupation with the
media's ability to level all images and numb the mind informs his choice of the
clichés and banalities uttered by his monologists.

Baudrillard defined the hyperreal as a condition in which simulations come
to constitute reality itself. Drawing upon Marshall McLuhan's concept of
implosion and his famous slogan that "the medium is the message,"
Baudrillard argues that the boundary between image or simulation and reality
implodes in the postmodern world: people cannot differentiate between the
real and its simulations. He finds ammunition to support this contention—one
he has later modified—by citing the simulations of politics created by Reagan
where the public elects the image not the man, the simulations of religions

foisted on us by television evangelists, and the simulations of rape or homelessness or trials produced by television shows.

Bogosian's monologists can be read as simulations. Some of his callers on his talk show sentimentally echo the banal lyrics of Diana Ross to "reach out and touch" or Bruce Springsteen's "Arms Across America" AIDS concerts as though they form the basis of their moral beliefs. In *Sex, Drugs, Rock & Roll*, he ridicules the rock lyrics that revolutionized an era: "Freedom's just another word for nothing left to lose," or "Wanna die before I get old." Bogosian finds America's love affair with the confessional mode deeply disturbing, particularly as it is served by television, radio, and rock. With a humor that is often corrosive and with caustic wit, he offers his critique of American postmodern culture.

Barry Champlain, the radio host in *Talk Radio*, exploits the simulation. When a drugged caller pleads for help, saying that he cannot get his strung-out girlfriend to wake up, Champlain knows the call is a hoax. When he invites the caller onto the talk show, he is willing to take the risk that perhaps the caller might just really do what the killer of real-life Alan Berg did, namely kill him. Alan Berg was an ex-Chicago talk show host famous for his insulting and abusive manner. In 1984 he was machine-gunned to death in the driveway of his home in Denver, Colorado by members of a Neo-Nazi hate group angered by his radio persona. Bogosian intensifies the play's taut atmosphere by staging a moment when the caller in the studio reaches into his pocket, drawing out a flash camera, not a gun, which he shoots. The moment is exactly of the kind that disturbs. Its hyperreality almost washes out the ground of reality. At one level, it is possible that the crazy caller will kill the talk show host. Such events happen in life. But are they merely imitations of what has been staged on television or marketed on talk shows? Bogosian's play raises this troubling thought at the same time as it saturates the audience in the hyperreal. The portrait of the hyper-active, egocentric, abusive talk-show host, mercurial in his mood and full of self-loathing, shows us a man just at the edge of a breakdown as every bit as disturbing as some of the pathetic or chilling life stories confessed to him by his callers. Still more frightening is the way the play mirrors its audience, making it question its own insatiable appetite for sex, violence, trouble, and confession.

In the film version of *Talk Radio* Oliver Stone changed the ending of Bogosian's stage version. The film's penultimate scene involves the shooting and death of Barry Champlain while the final images show us a postmodern mediascape in which the boundaries between information and entertainment, politics and image, implode. Callers are talking about Barry's death; they incorporate it into media patter. It has the same unreal feel about it that developed surrounding the television coverage of the Gulf War when the images that played nightly on CNN threatened to replace the reality. Bogosian's stage play is even more effective. There is no dead talk-show host; rather there is a world of sound, of talk, of narratives, most contrived, seemingly filled with beliefs for which there is no real referent. In this respect his stage play achieves some of the more nihilistic effects of Baudrillard's deeply pessimistic thinking of the 1970s.

In *Drinking in America* and *Sex, Drugs, Rock & Roll* Bogosian refines his skill at portraiture, using largely the same male types and media images and clichés, but focusing the image more sharply. Describing a schizoid America that wants to "live in piggish splendor and be ecologically responsible . . . wants to have the highest principles but win the popularity contest," Bogosian confesses to wanting both to be a big baby and a responsible citizen. In *Sex, Drugs, Rock & Roll* he says he has created 12 monologues that "take the nasty side of myself and put them out there for everyone to see." The play opens with a there-but-for-the-Grace-of-God-go-I beggar panhandling the audience. The down-and-out ex-convict shamelessly pleads with the audience to do something, give their money to him, not to the blacks in South Africa ten thousand miles away. His repeated "thank you" and "bless you" segue into the next piece, a hypocritical autobiographical promotional spiel of a British rock 'n' roll star and ex-druggie telling his imaginary talk show host how the youth of the day should avoid his mistakes and "just say No." The other monologues include a grubby derelict cursing at the gutter; a stud bragging about the size of his penis; the host of a stag party revelling in the evening of women, porn, and drugs; Candy, talking dirty to her phone-sex caller; a wheeler-dealer; a paranoic, self-hating misogynist; and other equally obnoxious yet wholly believable types.

Bogosian is skilled both as an actor and writer. His dramatic monologues are raucous, often abrasive, rich in their specificity of character, and often capable of making their audience thoroughly uncomfortable. His characters are too recognizable. Their faults, pushed to excess and rendered without judgment, remind the audience of its own complicity in this culture of commodification and the hyperreal.

—Carol Simpson Stern

BOVASSO, Julie (Julia Anne Bovasso).

Born in Brooklyn, New York, 1 August 1930. Educated at City College of New York, 1948–51. Married 1) George Ortman in 1951 (divorced 1959); 2) Leonard Wayland in 1959, (divorced 1964). Founder (director, producer, actress), Tempo Playhouse, New York, 1953–56. Teacher, New School for Social Research, New York, 1965–71, Brooklyn College, New York, 1968–69, and Sarah Lawrence College, Bronxville, New York, 1969–74; playwright-in-residence, Kentucky Wesleyan University, Owensboro, 1977. President, New York Theatre Strategy. Recipient: Obie award, Best Actress, and Best Experimental Theatre, 1956; Triple Obie award, Best Playwright-Director-Actress, 1969; Rockefeller grant, 1969, 1976; New York Council on the Arts grant, 1970; Guggenheim fellowship, 1971; Public Broadcasting Corporation award, 1972; Vernon Rice award, for acting, 1972; Outer Circle award, for acting, 1972. *Died 1991.*

Publications

PLAYS

The Moon Dreamers (also director: produced 1967; revised version produced 1969). 1972.

Gloria and Esperanza (also director: produced 1968; revised version produced 1970). 1973.

Schubert's Last Serenade (produced 1971). In *Spontaneous Combustion: Eight New American Plays*, edited by Rochelle Owens, 1972.
Monday on the Way to Mercury Island (produced 1971).
Down by the River Where Waterlilies Are Disfigured Every Day (produced 1972).
The Nothing Kid, and Standard Safety (also director: produced 1974). *Standard Safety* published 1976.
Super Lover, Schubert's Last Serenade, and The Final Analysis (also director: produced 1975).

THEATRICAL ACTIVITIES

DIRECTOR: **Plays**—many of her own plays; and *The Maids* by Jean Genet, 1953; *The Lesson* by Eugène Ionesco, 1955; and *The Typewriter* by Jean Cocteau; *Three Sisters Who Were Not Sisters* by Gertrude Stein; *Escurial* by Michel de Ghelderode; and *Amédée* by Eugène Ionesco, 1956; *Boom Boom Room* by David Rabe, 1973.

ACTOR: **Plays**—*A Maid in The Bells* by Leopold Lewis, 1943; Gwendolyn in *The Importance of Being Earnest* by Wilde, 1947; title role in *Salome* by Wilde, 1949; Belissa in *Don Perlimplin* by Garcia Lorca, 1949; Lona Hessel in *Pillars of Society* by Ibsen, 1949; title role in *Hedda Gabler* by Ibsen, 1950; Emma in *Naked* by Pirandello, 1950; Countess Geschwitz in *Earth Spirit* by Wedekind, 1950; Zanida in *He Who Gets Slapped* by Andreyev, 1950; title role in *Faustina* by Paul Goodman, 1952; Anna Petrovna in *Ivanov* by Chekhov, 1952; Margot in *The Typewriter* by Jean Cocteau, 1953; Madeleine in *Amédée* by Eugène Ionesco, 1955; Claire, 1955, and Solange, 1956, in *The Maids* by Jean Genet, and The Student in *The Lesson* by Eugène Ionesco, 1956; Henriette in *Monique* by Dorothy and Michael Blankfort, 1957; Luella in *Dinny and the Witches* by William Gibson, 1959; The Wife in *Victims of Duty* by Eugéne Ionesco, 1960; Lucy and Martha in *Gallows Humor* by Jack Richardson, 1961; Mistress Quickly in *Henry IV*, 1963; Madame Rosepettle in *Oh Dad, Poor Dad . . .* by Arthur Kopit, 1964; Mrs Prosser in *A Minor Miracle* by Al Morgan, 1965; Fortune Teller in *The Skin of Our Teeth* by Thornton Wilder, 1966; Madame Irma in *The Balcony* by Jean Genet, 1967; Agata in *Island of Goats* by Ugo Betti, and Constance in *The Madwoman of Chaillot* by Giraudoux, 1968; Gloria in *Gloria and Esperanza*, 1970; The Mother in *The Screens* by Jean Genet, 1971. **Films**—*Willie and Phil*, 1980; *The Verdict*, 1982; *Daniel*, 1983; *Betsy's Wedding*, 1990. **Television**—Rose in *From These Roots* series, 1958–60; Pearl in *The Iceman Cometh* by O'Neill, 1960; *Just Me and You*, 1978; *The Last Tenant*, 1978; *King Crab*, 1980; *The Gentleman Bandit*, 1981; *Doubletake*, 1985; and other performances in *US Steel Hour, The Defenders*, and other series, 1958–63.

The Bovasso world is highly orchestrated; the work appears to be driven, indeed hounded, by an ideological aesthetic. Julie Bovasso, one of America's more interesting actresses, became as a playwright a kind of mad mathematician, marshalling people and events into lunatic propositions and hallucinatory equations. The work sometimes marches to a drumbeat, sometimes sidles up to you, sometimes stridently calls out to the heavens, sometimes chuckles to itself. Throughout, there is the strong sense of the child infiltrating the grown-up theatre breathlessly, stealthily while the adults are asleep, relocating the furniture, putting bells on the cat, all to see how it will come out, to see whether the cunning proposition will prove itself.

The Moon Dreamers, one of Brovasso's earlier pieces, uses as the core of its narrative a simple situation in which wife, husband, and mistress can't agree as to who is to vacate the apartment. But into the situation, Bovasso, with a sense of increasing lunacy, introduces the wife's mother (Jewish), a lawyer (specified as dark-haired) who turns out to be the wife's second cousin, a doctor who turns out to be a childhood admirer of the wife's, an Indian chief who turns out to be a Japanese Buddhist, and a chief of police who turns out to be a French midget. Doctor, Lawyer, Indian chief, as well as Jewish momma and Gallic Fuzz. All these argue and split hairs in an increasingly complicated situation that on its surface is humorous but nevertheless suggests it is going somewhere other than farce. Around this core, Bovasso adds another layer, what she designates as an "Epic" world as opposed to the "Personal" world. The characters of the Epic world are in shadows, there is barely dialogue for them and they seem to exist principally as witnesses. But there are dozens of them, soldiers, black stockbrokers, gangsters, belly dancers, snake dancers, Spanish royalty. The domestic squabble is thus both knotted with what we might call the presence of banal archetypes and overseen by graver archetypes until it simply ceases to be what it has been. That is, it seems to become nothing that we can intellectually comprehend—until the end when the appearance of the astronaut, a kind of *deus ex machina*, makes a comprehensive statement about humanity—but rather something that we must allow to wash over us if we want to continue sensing it at all. Any information seems to be taken out of our hands and we must become like children or Martians witnessing an unknown world.

Monday on the Way to Mercury Island is filled with both dialogue and silent actions that recur numerous times, sometimes repeated identically, sometimes with variations. As in The Moon Dreamers, these are sometimes banal and sometimes extraordinary. But even the banal elements usually suggest something beyond themselves. The repetition tends to ritualize these sounds and movements without providing a philosophical base. A formal, austere aesthetic seems to be at work. The ritual tends here to make the theatre more into play, a relentlessly earnest if also whimsical play. But there appears to be a political thesis at work. Servants and peasants rise at last against socialite masters. The latter are painted as corrupt and soft, the former as steadfast and hard. But even here the intellectual content seems subordinate to the flowering theatrics, to the rhythms and colours of spectacle.

Down by the River Where Waterlilies Are Disfigured Every Day is another vast landscape, another epic with vivid theatrics. The Bovasso trait of mixed, merged, or transferred identities is strong here. Phoebe and Clement, lovers for many years, exchange clothes and then sexes. Count Josef, leader of the established order, is at work on a statue of Pango, head of the revolutionary forces, breathing life and the qualities dear to him into the figure that is attempting to end his own life. Revolt is strong here. Overturned lives, overturned order. In Monday the peasants end by burying the aristocrat. In Waterlilies the children toss the old world onto the garbage heap in the town square. But again one has the sense that the playing out of the act takes precedence over the intellectual meaning of the act, that the logic of aesthetics and of forming is ultimately the prime mover.

—Arthur Sainer

BREUER, Lee.

Born in Philadelphia, Pennsylvania, 6 February 1937. Educated at the University of California, Los Angeles, B.A. 1958; San Francisco State University. Married Ruth Maleczech in 1978; two children. Director, San Francisco Actors' Workshop, 1963–65; free-lance director in Europe, 1965–70. Since 1970 co-artistic director, Mabou Mines, New York; since 1982 staff director, New York Shakespeare Festival; co-artistic director, Re Cher Chez studio. Teacher, Yale University School of Drama, New Haven, Connecticut, 1978–80, Harvard University Extension, Cambridge, Massachusetts, 1981–82, and New York University, 1981–82. Board member, Theatre Communications Group, New York. Recipient: Obie award, 1978, 1980, 1984; Creative Artists Public Service grant, 1980; National Endowment for the Arts fellowship, 1980, 1982; Rockefeller grant, 1981; Los Angeles Drama Critics Circle award, 1986; Tony award, 1988. Lives in New York City. Agent: Lynn Davis, Davis-Cohen Associates, 513–A Avenue of the Americas, New York, New York 10011. Address: Mabou Mines, c/o Performing Arts Journal, 325 Spring Street, Suite 318, New York, New York 10013, U.S.A.

Publications

PLAYS

The Red Horse Animation, music by Philip Glass (produced 1970; revised version, produced 1972). In *The Theatre of Images*, edited by Bonnie Marranca, 1977.

The B-Beaver Animation, music by Philip Glass, adaptation of a work by Samuel Beckett (produced 1974).

The Saint and the Football Players (produced 1976).

The Lost Ones, adaptation of the fiction by Samuel Beckett (produced 1977).

The Shaggy Dog Animation (produced 1977).

Animations: A Trilogy for Mabou Mines. 1979.

A Prelude to Death in Venice (produced 1980). In *New Plays USA 1*, edited by James Leverett, 1982.

Sister Suzie Cinema, music by Bob Telson (produced 1980). 1987.

The Gospel at Colonus, music by Bob Telson, adaptation of *Oedipus at Colonus* by Sophocles (produced 1982). 1989.

Hajj (produced 1983). In *Wordplays 3*, 1984.

The Warrior Ant, music by Bob Telson (produced 1988).

Lear, adaptation of *King Lear* by Shakespeare (produced 1990).

THEATRICAL ACTIVITIES

DIRECTOR: Plays—all his own plays; *The House of Bernarda Alba* by García Lorca, 1963; *Mother Courage* by Brecht, 1967; *The Messingkauf Dialogues*

by Brecht, 1968; *Play* by Samuel Beckett, 1969, 1970; *Come and Go* by Samuel Beckett, 1975; *Mr. Frivolous* by Wallace Shawn, 1976; *Earth Spirit* by Wedekind, 1976(?); *Sunday Childhood Journeys to Nobody at Home* by Arthur Sainer, 1980; *Lulu* by Wedekind, 1980; *The Tempest*, 1981; *From the Point of View of the Salt* by Liza Lorwin, 1986.
ACTOR: **Play**—in *Wrong Guys* by Ruth Maleczech, 1981.
CHOREOGRAPHER: **Play**—*Measure for Measure*, 1976.

Lee Breuer is a dramatist as well as auteur-director, and was a founding member of the Mabou Mines experimental theatre collective in New York, a company in which he remains vitally active. His "performance poems," as he calls his playtexts, merge the American tradition of the self-conscious, extended lyric poem (Whitman, Ginsberg) with the main tendencies of European modern drama. After beginning his directorial work with the San Francisco Actors' Workshop, Breuer studied with the Berliner Ensemble and with actors who worked with Grotowski, so he knows both "presence" and the complexities of self-conscious presentational form.

The greater part of Breuer's dramatic writing is structured in the form of a labyrinthine monologue that he then "animates" in a richly physicalized stage setting and performance. The monologues telescope many identities into a single voice that in turn splices together fragments of many linguistic worlds: street language, colloquialisms, phrases from sports, science, Latin, spiritualism, etc., and above all pop imagery from the movies and the media. Through juxtaposition he develops a complex mode of irony, dominated by a sophisticated use of punning. This artistic strategy allows the poem and its speakers to subvert the efficacy of the expressive language of emotion without denying the reality of the emotion itself. Breuer's approach to dramatic language plays with the illusions of performance, emphasized by the *bunraku* puppets he so admires and often uses in his stagings of the poems.

His early poems are brief modernist beast fables in which the animal figure tells a human story. A single voice is taken up by several performers to project a fragmented self. *The Red Horse Animation* is an interior monologue about a lone voice seeking a shape for its life, as performers gyrate in evocation of a message-carrying horse. In its struggle the horse's life is stifled by the father's ethos of drudge-work and money. Just as the voice starts to feel mind and imagination coming together, the image of the horse—and potential poet—tears itself apart and dissolves into silence. *The B-Beaver Animation* tells of a stutterer—the artist who can't get his words out. He seeks to build a dam to protect his Missus and The Brood, who function as a chorus for his thoughts, which are dammed up with the detritus of his everyday experience, his learning, and his fantasies.

While working on these Animations, Breuer experimented with performance art, and both lines of work converged during the late 1970s, culminating in the hours-long *The Shaggy Dog Animation*. Here two distinct voices speak for a pair of *bunraku*-style puppets in American contemporary dress, supported by live performers who animate the puppets' bodies and their words. The story is that of the exploitative John Greed who falls in love with a faithful dog-woman who calls herself Your Dog Rose. She submits to him as one of the "bitches of the city" who are "prisoners of love." Her shaggy-dog life includes a trip to Venice, California, for moviemaking, and a return to New York where she enters the art world. At her opening she shows a painted fireplug, and the art establishment comes down on her for seeing only the surface of things. She goes on to have puppies, and in a last bitter street fight with John, she ends it with him. Still, their voices merge to become one voice, as powerful in memory as they were in life.

With *A Prelude to Death in Venice* Breuer's stagings shift to solo performance, here with a triple persona: of a puppeteer (Bill); the puppet John Greed; and the movie agent Bill Morris. Expanded from a brief section of *Shaggy Dog*, life is presented as a succession of late-night calls into a pair of city street payphones which frame the figure like the two thieves framed Christ on Golgotha. He suffers the indignities of family and the movie world, with tirades to Mother, his Agent (who's "into producing reality" and is in fact himself), and finally his father. Throughout, Thomas Mann's *Death in Venice* provides an overlay of imagery and ironic contrast. Exasperated by his failed plan to shoot a movie in Venice, California, Bill the puppeteer kills John his puppet-self and thus is able to call down his father and deliver himself to momentary freedom.

A monologue of even greater complexity emerges with *Hajj*, in which an American actress seated at her make-up table summons the memory of her East European father who committed suicide. They sleep together, suffer together, and he shoots himself before she can repay the money she borrowed from him, which stands for an emotional debt, too. In this fateful recollection that is her version of the traditional Moslem's trip to ancient Mecca, her father's image is superimposed upon her own, and even upon that of her son—all through a sophisticated interaction of live performer, mask, film, and video imagery. No unmasking will separate their identities, for they vibrate within one another.

Beginning in 1980, Breuer initiated a series of experiments in music-theatre with the composer Bob Telson, aiming for a synthesis of popular and high art on the order of the Brecht-Weill collaborations. Their first piece was *Sister Suzie Cinema*, a brief "Doo-Wop Opera" in which young black singers dream of a union with images on a movie-house screen. Imagination becomes reality as the ground gives way and they ride to their paradise on a huge airplane wing.

In a major experiment with Telson, *The Gospel at Colonus*, Breuer rips the Oedipus story from its Greek context and thrusts it into the world of exultation that is American black gospel singing. While this radical adaptation maintains the central events and figures of Sophocles's final masterpiece, it augments the Greek conventions with the black preacher's dramaturgy of chanting and shouting together with an onstage congregation. By the end, the audience too joins this great chorus, standing, clapping, and joyously singing along.

The transposition of the Sophoclean drama spins forward yet another strand of Breuer's auteur-directorial vision, which is, in his words, "to recreate [classic] texts through American lenses." Most recently, in his *Lear*, as a company statement tells us: "Shakespeare's *King Lear* takes on a whole new aspect in a radical, matriarchal version transported to America's Deep South, circa 1957, updating with its interracial casting and gender-switching, to question the family unit, old age, and the traditional structure of power."

Breuer's most ambitious effort to date is another collaboration with Telson, *The Warrior Ant*. It remains a work-in-progress, some parts already performed, which is projected as a 12-part mock epic poem to be played in four evening-long performances. In this mythological biography modeled upon those of the Japanese *samurai*, the hero Ant is mis-conceived in rape and chooses the path of individuality over that of the society of the Hill. There is a Virgilian dream-journey to hell where he discovers his true father who is termite and not ant. Renouncing the world in order to transcend this essential war within, of newly discovered parental rape-identity, he moves toward the sky by climbing a Redwood tree. Years later, reaching the top, he copulates with the Death Moth and discovers that he loves death best. Drawing upon multiple and seemingly contradictory theatrical resources and cultures—Japanese, Latino, African and more—Breuer is orchestrating in fabulous abandonment, a polyphonic cultural symphony in dramatic form.

Most jubilantly in his collaborations with Telson, music and song have led Breuer to worlds of dramatic reconciliation. But even here, as in all his work, Breuer's poetry of the theatre is predicated upon a radical synthesis of performance genres—illusory play that also is a feat of illumination.

—Bill Coco

BROWN, Kenneth H.

Born in Brooklyn, New York, 9 March 1936. Educated at a preparatory school in Brooklyn. Served in the United States Marine Corps, 1954–57. Mail clerk, 1951–54; bartender and waiter, New York and Miami, 1958–63; bank clerk, New York, 1960; cigarette sales-man, New York, 1961; resident playwright, Living Theatre, New York, 1963–67; private tutor, 1966–69, and resident playwright, 1968–69, Yale University School of Drama, New Haven, Connecticut; visiting lecturer (improvisational acting), Hollins College, Virginia, 1969; visiting lecturer (history of theatre), Hunter College, New York, 1969–70; associate professor in performance (theatrical production), University of Iowa, Iowa City, 1971. Recipient: Venice Film Festival gold medal, 1964; Rockefeller fellowship, 1965, and grant, 1967; ABC-Yale University fellowship, 1966, 1967; Guggenheim fellowship, 1966; Creative Artists Public Service grant, 1974. Agent: Mary Yost, 59 East 54th Street, New York, New York 10022. Address: 150 74th Street, Brooklyn, New York 11209, U.S.A.

Publications

PLAYS

The Brig (produced 1963). 1965.
Devices (produced 1965).
The Happy Bar (produced 1967).

Blake's Design (produced 1968). In *The Best Short Plays 1969*, edited by
Stanley Richards, 1969.
The Green Room (produced 1971).
The Cretan Bull (produced 1972).
Nightlight (produced 1973). 1973.

SCREENPLAYS: *The Brig*, 1965; *Devices*, 1967.

NOVEL
The Narrows. 1970.

OTHER
You'd Never Know It from the Way I Talk (lectures and readings). 1990.

MANUSCRIPT COLLECTION: New York Public Library.

Kenneth H. Brown comments:

I began as a playwright quite by accident. It was the best means to convey my
experiences as a confined prisoner in a Marine Brig. All my plays since have
been either direct or symbolic representations of my life experiences. As such, I
have been classified by one theatre historian as an accidental playwright, a title
I gladly accept since I adhere to the belief that all things of personal import in
my life have come about as a result of pure chance. I do not take to writing as a
daily chore that must be done. It is, for me, a labor of love and, as such, I
engage in it only when moved to do so. As I get older, I am constantly amazed
by the body of works accumulated through this philosophy.

Although Kenneth H. Brown has published poetry, a novel, *The Narrows*, and
a collection of lectures and readings, *You'd Never Know It from the Way I
Talk*, his most significant achievements to date have been in drama. *The Brig*, a
stark and appalling indictment of militarism, stamped Brown as one of the
more gifted and experimental of American dramatists of the 1960s. It placed
him in a tradition with Artaud and proved him able to create what neither
Artaud nor Ionesco accomplished, "theatre of cruelty" complete with a metaphysics of language. His next published play, *Blake's Design*, gave further
support to the belief that Brown was a dramatist who defied labels. Moving
away from the stark, purposefully flat prose of *The Brig*, Brown played with
the catchy rhythms of vaudeville, embellished his prose giving it a lyrical
quality, and turned away from naturalism to expressionism. Of *The Cretan
Bull*, Brown says he produced a "very funny play about complete strangers
who meet in Central Park at dawn and confront a very odd set of circumstances." Again Brown went in new directions, experimenting with another
style, and exploring different themes. In *Nightlight*, a play produced at the
Hartford Stage Company to strong critical acclaim, Brown says he wrote
about "the elements of violence that are now threatening the safety of decent
citizens in our big cities."

Though *The Brig* and *Blake's Design* are very different, they share many
common elements. In both, an egalitarianism makes Brown select characters
for his drama who reflect the ethnic and racial mix that makes up American

society. In both Brown draws on music and popular songs: in *Blake's Design* the songs and dances are handled in a manner reminiscent of a vaudeville skit; in *The Brig* music is subverted and becomes an instrument of torture. The sarcastic, strident, sneering tone of a guard's voice is played contrapuntally against a clear, impersonal, unaffected voice. The breaking of a command is answered by its own often inaudible flat echo. The hideous dissonant martial music that is the tool of the fascist or authoritarian state, the kind of music that breaks a man's mind and makes him crawl like a maggot at any command, is produced by clashing garbage can lids together as if they were cymbals. Yet more hellish music derives from the sound of a voice resonating against a toilet bowl as one of the prisoners, using the cubicle as his confessional, cries out his litany of wrongs in obedience to the guard's orders. Dance, too, figures in the plays. In *Blake's Design* Muvva and Zack sing of Zack's necrophilia with his dead, black wife while they do a soft shoe dance. In *The Brig* dance is a ritual in which the prisoners suffer repeatedly at the hands of the guards. The dance is one where men shrink, recoil, and double-over in response to the quick, sharp blows delivered by the truncheons of the Warden or the guards. This violent dance pattern is varied with a pattern of running across the stage and halting at every white line in conformity with the procedure outlined in the *Marine Corps Manual*. Finally, both plays employ a point of view that is reminiscent of naturalism. A dispassionate exact observer records precisely the world in all its minutiae as if the reality being depicted were a hard surface that can only be penetrated once it has been fully sounded. But for all these seeming similarities, the plays are, in fact, very different, both in style and in theme.

The Brig is a blatantly political play, or rather, "concept of theater," as Brown would have it called. A penal institute in Camp Fuji, the brig is the place where Marines are sent to be punished for any infraction of military orders. The set of the play duplicates as nearly as possible the specifications of the brig and its actions reenact the rules that govern its workings as set down in the *Marine Corps Manual*. The play opens with the waking of the prisoners at dawn and it closes with the putting out of the light at night. Between dawn and night, we see the prisoners repeat again and again the same gestures and motions as they are forced to dress and undress, eat and march, clean and stand at attention, for no other reason than to fulfill an order and submit to power. Nameless (they are called by number—only the guards have names), the prisoners grovel, crawl, abuse themselves, whimper silently, and try desperately to carry out any order to the letter while the military guards sadistically delight in finding new indignities for them to suffer and new punishments for their supposed failures. The discipline is without restraint or reason. Senselessly the prisoners are humiliated, beaten, and abused. The only logic that governs events is the relentless logic of power and physical force. In the course of the day, one prisoner is released, a new one enters, and a third is released to an even worse form of institutional imprisonment, the asylum. Number 26, after two weeks in the brig which follows upon 16 years of honorable military service, finds himself, against all orders and common sense, crying out his name, James Turner, and in so doing demonstrating that in the brig seemingly sane behavior is in fact insane. For two hours, the senses of the audience are assaulted as the prisoners are hollered at and harassed by the guards. Plot and character development in the ordinary sense are absent from the play. Language, stripped of all warmth, finally negates itself. The members of the audience are left responding to sounds, intonations, incantations, and not denotative meanings. They experience an agony of feeling which derives from the immediacy of the violence unleashed both on the stage and in themselves and which has little reference to the world of reason that has systematically been destroyed by the extremes to which it has been pushed on the stage.

Blake's Design depicts Zack's struggle to free himself from both his past—the black woman whose dead body he has slept with for ten years—and his illusions—Blake, or call him God, is one of them—in order to tell his son the truth, live in the present, and move out of his dark basement apartment upstairs and into the light. Zack's mulatto son, Sweek, and his two women, Muvva, with whom he has shared his bed, dead wife, and son for ten years, and Modrigal, his half-oriental mistress, all talk rather self-consciously throughout the play about man's weakness, his lies, and that part of himself which he does not know or understand and so calls God, or Blake, in an effort at understanding. The play ends when Zack unburdens himself, tells the truth, closes the door on his past, and mounts the stairs. The symbolism is rather obvious and the long talks about Blake tend to be tiresome, but the characters themselves are well imagined and the quick staccato exchanges between Sweek and Zack and the shuffling dances and songs save the play.

Brown's talents are considerable; he was one of the few genuinely original American dramatists to emerge in the early 1960s. It is the public's loss that Brown now finds the social and political environment in the United States inhospitable to writers of genuine creative talent. In his collection of lectures, he laments the breakdown in the relationship between theatre and community in the United States and starkly outlines the difficulties of trying to pursue the vocation of a writer in our era. He no longer finds his own art relevant to this crass, materialistic society. He finds this admission deeply sobering, not only because it speaks of his own failure, but because it speaks of a larger societal loss, A society that does not nurture its own art also fails itself.

—Carol Simpson Stern

BULLINS, Ed.

Born in Philadelphia, Pennsylvania, 2 July 1935. Educated in Philadelphia public schools; at William Penn Business Institute, Philadelphia; Los Angeles City College, 1958–61; San Francisco State College, 1964–65, and M.F.A. candidate since 1990; Antioch University, San Francisco, B.A. 1989. Served in the United States Navy, 1952–55. Married Trixie Warner (marriage ended). Playwright-in-residence and associate director, New Lafayette Theatre, New York, 1967–73; editor, *Black Theatre* magazine, New York, 1969–74; producing director, Surviving Theatre, New York, from 1974; writers unit coordinator, New York Shakespeare Festival, 1975–82; Mellon lecturer, Amherst College, Massachusetts, from 1977; public relations director, Berkeley Black Repertory, Berkeley, 1982; promotions director, Magic Theater, 1982–83; group sales coordinator, Julian Theater, 1983; playwriting teacher, Bay Area Playwrights Festival, and People's School of Dramatic Arts,

1983; instructor, City College of San Francisco, 1984–88; lecturer, Sonoma State University, California, 1987–89, and University of California, Berkeley, 1989. Recipient: Rockefeller grant, 1968, 1970, 1973; Vernon Rice award, 1968; American Place grant, 1968; Obie award, 1971, 1975; Guggenheim grant, 1971, and fellowship, 1976; Creative Artists Public Service grant, 1973; National Endowment for the Arts grant, 1974, 1989; New York Drama Critics Circle award, 1975, 1977. D.L.: Columbia College, Chicago, 1976. Address: 3617 San Pablo Avenue, #118, Emeryville, California 94608, U.S.A.

Publications

PLAYS

Clara's Ole Man (produced 1965). In *Five Plays*, 1969.

How Do You Do? (produced 1965). 1965.

Dialect Determinism, or, The Rally (produced 1965). In *The Theme Is Blackness*, 1973.

The Theme Is Blackness (produced 1966). In *The Theme Is Blackness*, 1973.

It Has No Choice (produced 1966). In *The Theme Is Blackness*, 1973.

A Minor Scene (produced 1966). In *The Theme Is Blackness*, 1973.

The Game of Adam and Eve, with Shirley Tarbell (produced 1966).

In New England Winter (produced 1967). In *New Plays from the Black Theatre*, edited by Bullins, 1969.

In the Wine Time (produced 1968). In *Five Plays*, 1969.

A Son, Come Home (produced 1968). In *Five Plays*, 1969.

The Electronic Nigger (produced 1968). In *Five Plays*, 1969.

Goin' a Buffalo: A Tragifantasy (produced 1968). In *Five Plays*, 1969.

The Corner (produced 1968). In *The Theme Is Blackness*, 1973.

The Gentleman Caller (produced 1969). In *A Black Quartet*, edited by Clayton Riley, 1970.

Five Plays. 1969; as *The Electronic Nigger and Other Plays*, 1970. *We Righteous Bombers* (as Kingsley B. Bass, Jr.), adaptation of a work by Camus (produced 1969).

The Man Who Dug Fish (produced 1969). In *The Theme Is Blackness*, 1973.

Street Sounds (produced 1970). In *The Theme Is Blackness*, 1973.

The Helper (produced 1970). In *The Theme Is Blackness*, 1973.

A Ritual to Raise the Dead and Foretell the Future (produced 1970). In *The Theme Is Blackness*, 1973.

The Fabulous Miss Marie (produced 1970). In *The New Lafayette Theatre Presents*, edited by Bullins, 1974.

Four Dynamite Plays: It Bees Dat Way, Death List, The Pig Pen, Night of the Beast (produced 1970). 1971.

The Duplex: A Black Love Fable in Four Movements (produced 1970). 1971.

The Devil Catchers (produced 1970).

The Psychic Pretenders (produced 1972).

You Gonna Let Me Take You Out Tonight, Baby (produced 1972).

Next Time, in *City Stops* (produced 1972).

House Party, music by Pat Patrick, lyrics by Bullins (produced 1973).

The Theme Is Blackness: The Corner and Other Plays (includes *Dialect Determinism, or, The Rally*; *It Has No Choice*; *The Helper*; *A Minor Scene*;

The Theme Is Blackness; The Man Who Dug Fish; Street Sounds; and the scenarios and short plays *Black Commercial No. 2, The American Flag Ritual, State Office Bldg. Curse, One-Minute Commercial, A Street Play, A Short Play for a Small Theatre,* and *The Play of the Play*). 1973.

The Taking of Miss Janie (produced 1975). In *Famous Plays of the '70's,* 1980.

The Mystery of Phyllis Wheatley (produced 1976).

I Am Lucy Terry (for children; produced 1976).

Jo Anne!!! (produced 1976).

Home Boy, music by Aaron Bell, lyrics by Bullins (produced 1976). *Daddy* (produced 1977).

Sepia Star, or Chocolate Comes to the Cotton Club, music and lyrics by Mildred Kayden (produced 1977).

Storyville, music and lyrics by Mildred Kayden (produced 1977; revised version produced 1979).

Michael (also director: produced 1978).

C'mon Back to Heavenly House (produced 1978).

Leavings (produced 1980).

Steve and Velma (produced 1980).

Bullins Does Bullins (also director: produced 1988).

I Think It's Gonna Work Out Fine, with Idris Ackamoor and Rhodessa Jones (produced 1990).

American Griot (produced 1990).

Salaam, Huey Newton, Salaam (produced 1991). In *Best Short Plays of 1990,* edited by Howard Stein and Glenn Young, 1991.

Raining Down Stars: Sepia Stories of the Dark Diaspora, with Idris Ackamoor and Rhodessa Jones (produced 1992).

SCREENPLAYS: *Night of the Beast,* 1971; *The Ritual Masters,* 1972.

NOVEL

The Reluctant Rapist. 1973.

SHORT STORIES

The Hungered One: Early Writings. 1971.

VERSE

To Raise the Dead and Foretell the Future. 1971.

OTHER

Editor, *New Plays from the Black Theatre.* 1969.

Editor, *The New Lafayette Theatre Presents: Plays with Aesthetic Comments by 6 Black Playwrights.* 1974.

BIBLIOGRAPHY: *Ten Modern American Playwrights* by Kimball King, 1982.

CRITICAL STUDIES: *Drumbeats, Masks, and Metaphor: Contemporary Afro-American Theatre* by Geneviève Fabre, translated by Melvin Dixon, 1983; *Toward Creation of a Collective Form: The Plays of Ed Bullins* by Nicholas Canaday, in *Studies in American Drama*, 1986.

THEATRICAL ACTIVITIES

DIRECTOR: Play—*Michael*, 1978; *Bullins Does Bullins*, 1988; *Savage Wilds*, 1988; *Tripnology* by J. Woodward, 1992.

ACTOR: Play—Role in *The Hotel Play* by Wallace Shawn, 1981; role in *The Real Deal* by J. Woodward, 1988; role in *The Burial of Prejudice* by J. Woodward, 1991.

Ed Bullins comments:

I write plays for a number of reasons but the most simple and direct truth of the matter is that it is my work.

Though he is the most prolific, and one of the most active, figures in black American theater, Ed Bullins resists close identification with the prominent contemporary styles. With Black House and Black Arts/West in San Francisco he participated in projects to create a revolutionary theater; yet, at the same time he was capable of satirizing revolutionary ideologues in *Dialect Determinism*. He can adapt the mode of realism for his Twentieth-Century Cycle, but deflect a critic's attempt to discern its autobiographical theme with the remark that specific reference is not apt for symbolic writing like his own. Bullins's statements are often, in fact, less a commentary than an enactment of the theatrical devices of black language. There is the pretended innocence of "shuckin" that allows him to deny association with militants, the inflated language of the put-on self-description ("Ed Bullins, at this moment in time, is almost without peer in America—black, white or imported"), and the ironic humor producing elaborate games about racial stereotypes in and around his plays. Like the originators of those linguistic techniques Bullins stays loose so that he can survive the pressures of the moment and continue to evolve through performance after performance.

The best known of his works are set in the 1950s, a period that matches historically the personal deracination of the characters. They are urban people completely divorced from the southern past, the soil, and traditional culture. Shown without the coloration of myth in either their own or their creator's consciousness, they are neither idealized folk primitives so dearly beloved in the past to friendly white writers on the Negro, nor the agents of imminent revolution ardently desired by some black spokespersons. Their ghetto is both physical and moral. Excluded from accomplishments beyond those of subsisting they cannot transcend private passion or see any possibility of redemption in community. In *Clara's Ole Man*, for instance, a young student hoping to make out with a woman stumbles into a cast of grotesques who fulfill a projected sense of menace by calling in a street gang to beat him senseless.

The Twentieth-Century Cycle—about which Bullins says, in his put-on voice "there is already talk of this collective project surpassing greatness in its scope, though the work is not that astonishing, relative to Bullins' abilities" — develops its first installment, *In the Wine Time*, from a prologue in which a male narrator lyrically describes the beautiful woman who represents the goals he innocently hopes to achieve. As counterpoint the body of the play reveals through its slowly moving dialogue of a summer evening the disappointments of the youth's exhausted aunt, the frustrated hopes of her husband, and the diversion of their ambitions into a contest over the boy. Structured as an initiation play, *In the Wine Time* carries the protagonist to a point where he destroys his own future with an act of casual violence. *In New England Winter* picks up the leading character, now free from the prison sentence he receives for the pointless assault in the previous play, and juxtaposes him to yet another young man and group of small-time hustlers. Scenes of a planned robbery intermix with memories of a love idyll that is at first attractive, like the prologue of *In the Wine Time*, and is then revealed to have been a period of desperate escape. The human needs people have for each other issue in sadomasochistic relationships, gratuitous brutality, and a deadly lack of sustained feeling.

With *The Duplex*, subtitled *A Black Love Fable in Four Movements*, the theme of the cycle is fully established: the impossibility of love, and by implication broader community, and the reflexive self-destruction of character. Again the movement is of a young man gaining experience in the social world. Steve Benson hesitates between submission to the anodynes of alcohol and sex and the resolution to direct his own life. The forces for submission are so powerful that hesitation seems the only plausible action for him in the brief time of the play; self-sufficiency would be too unlikely. Application of the playwright's naturalism is so overwhelming that race hardly seems the point of the plays in the cycle, though it certainly provides the circumstances that prod characters along their desperate ways. Cast out and angry they invert their creativity: social insignificance releases energy in violence and sexual dominance; the contempt of an external society is mirrored in a lumpen style and contempt for life itself.

Still, Bullins stops short of dehumanizing his characters. In *The Fabulous Miss Marie* the vital and vulgar heroine demonstrates the vigor that sustains humanity, and in the other cycle plays Bullins rejects either a portrayal of characters as victims or the easy sentiment of pity, equally dehumanizing. His identification with the plight of his people in the industrial slums of the northeastern cities and sunshine ghettoes of southern California instead advances the idea that the public world we know in terms of social and economic problems is lived in the experience of personal troubles and private feelings. If the inhabitants of the 1950s ghetto appear to be trapped, it is because Bullins sees in politics and the philosophy of art no release for their humanity. We have got to see the problem, he says, in the depths of personality before we can honestly propose any solution.

The dramaturgy of Bullins's cycle, as well as such a pre-cycle play as *Goin' a Buffalo*, exploits the entire theatrical ambience for effect. The decor of *Goin' a Buffalo* consists of all-white walls and a crimson carpet. The set of *The Duplex* is a non-realistic gradation of planes that contest with the realism of the dramatic action and dialogue to give credence to the view that the plays are, indeed, intended to be seen symbolically. Nearly all the plays call for musical accompaniment attuned to situation and shifting lighting effects to spot significant relationships, while the directions for movements on stage suggest choreography.

In the late 1970s Bullins carried his interest in the associated stage arts into collaboration on the musicals *Storyville* and *Sepia Star*. At other times in his career he wrote sketches, one-act plays, children's dramas, scenarios, even radio commercials. In this variety of production one sees the historical problem of the black playwright searching for a sympathetic audience. The expectations of white playgoers subtly educe, even against a writer's will, some accommodation, or else they create a strong need for defiance. Meanwhile blacks who share the writer's cultural experience and language find their theater in the events of the church and other institutions, rather than on Broadway which for more reasons than one has been called the great white way. In an approach to the latter part of the problem Bullins became involved in the Black Arts Alliance on the west coast and, then, invested ten years' time in New York attempting to establish in the contemporary city the New Lafayette Theatre as a successor to the original Lafayette Stock Company that laid the foundations of black legitimate theater from 1917 to 1932.

The creation of such political plays as those collected in *Four Dynamite Plays* can also be understood as part of Bullins's effort to engender in audiences the conviction that drama can be the arena for serious examination of black values. *Death List* from this collection portrays a rifleman intoning indictments of popular leaders while the play's other character, Blackwoman, explains the extenuating circumstances of each alleged betrayal of black interests. Getting no response to her pleas for mercy Blackwoman asks if the potential assassin himself is not the actual enemy of the people. There is no resolution of the opposition. The action simply ends with the offstage sound of shots; presumably it is time for the audience to debate the issue.

Bullins's confrontation of the white members of his dual audience generally takes the form of instructive, but not necessarily didactic, writing. The cycle plays are works meant to inform whites as much as to produce recognition for blacks. Then, too, a play such as *Daddy* can be taken, as it was by New York reviewers, to be an exploration of the feelings animating the man who abandons his family to better himself and the substitute father who replaces him. The abstracts of social science quantify the behavior that produces broken homes; Bullins tries to humanize it.

The theater has taken a breather from militancy, and Bullins has assumed a retrospective attitude toward the revolutionary period. *House Party* satirizes political figures, and *The Taking of Miss Janie* converts the politics of the 1960s into a drama of inter-racial rape. All-black theater, too, seems to be a thing of the past for Bullins. Though there are several active companies in America, and New York's Negro Ensemble Company looks to be the genuine successor to the famous American Negro Theater of the 1940s, as well as the old Lafayette Players, Bullins sees community theater in a drift. For the present at least the outlet for his remarkable productivity will be the mainstream American theater. He has been supervising the playwrights workshop of the New York Shakespeare Festival, recovering the roots of black show business for musical theater, and trying to shape his instructional plays into the style of domestic drama. Bullins will stay loose, avoid getting backed into a corner, and survive to give the American stage in one or another of its forms his intensely dramatic vision.

—John M. Reilly

BUSCH, Charles (Louis).

Born in New York City, 23 August 1954. Educated at High School of Music and Art, New York, 1968–72; Northwestern University, Evanston, Illinois, 1972–76, B.S. Worked as office temporary receptionist, quick sketch pastel portrait artist, ice-cream scooper, encyclopedia salesman, sports handicapper, 1976–84, New York and Chicago, Illinois. Co-founder, 1984, and since 1984 playwright-in-residence, Theatre-in-Limbo, New York. Agent: Jeffrey Melnick, Harry Gold Agency, 3500 West Olive, Suite 1400, Burbank, California 91505; or, Marc Glick, Glick and Weintraub, 1501 Broadway, Suite 2401, New York, New York 10036–5503, U.S.A.

Publications

PLAYS

Charles Busch, Alone with a Cast of Thousands (includes *Hollywood Confidential*, 1978, *A Theatrical Party*, 1980, *After You've Gone*, 1982, *Phantom Lovers*, 1983, produced on U.S. tours).
Before Our Mother's Eyes (produced 1981).
Vampire Lesbians of Sodom (produced 1984). In *Four Plays*, 1990.
Sleeping Beauty or Coma (produced 1984). In *Four Plays*, 1990.
Theodora, She-Bitch of Byzantium (produced 1984). In *Three Plays*, 1992.
Times Square Angel: A Hard-Boiled Christmas Fantasy (produced 1984; revised version produced 1985). In *Three Plays*, 1992.
Gidget Goes Psychotic (produced 1986). 1986.
Pardon My Inquisition; or, Kiss The Blood Off My Castanets (produced 1986). In *Three Plays*, 1992.
Psycho Beach Party (produced 1987). In *Four Plays*, 1990.
Ankles Aweigh, music and lyrics by Sammy Fain and Dan Shapiro (also co-director: produced 1987). 1987.
The Lady in Question (produced 1989). In *Four Plays*, 1990.
Four Plays. 1990.
House of Flowers, adaptation of the libretto by Truman Capote (produced 1991). 1991.
Red Scare on Sunset (produced 1991). 1991.
Three Plays. 1992.

MANUSCRIPT COLLECTION: Lincoln Center Library of Performing Arts, New York.

CRITICAL STUDY: *Downtown* by Michael Musto, 1986.

Theatrical activities

Director (with Dan Siretta): Plays—*Ankles Aweigh*, 1987.

Actor: Plays—all his own plays including: Virgin Sacrifice and Madeleine Astarte in *Vampire Lesbians of Sodom*; Irish O'Flanagan in *Times Square Angel*; Chicklet in *Psycho Beach Party*; title role in *Theodora, She-Bitch of Byzantium*; Maria Garbonza and the Marquesa Del Drago in *Pardon My Inquisition*; Gertrude Garnet in *The Lady in Question*; Fauna Alexander in *Sleeping Beauty*; Mary Dale in *Red Scare on Sunset*.

Charles Busch comments:

I identify strongly with the actor-managers of the 19th century. All of my plays have been written to give my company, Theatre-in-Limbo, and myself opportunities to act. Like the theatrical monsters I emulate, I believe passionately in the eternal power of melodrama, old-fashioned comedy rhythms, and the glamorous star vehicle. I've tried to celebrate these forms and conventions as well as parody them. An audience can be thrilled by the chase but also laugh at their own easy manipulation. However, I've also tried to employ old movie and theatrical genres as starting-off points to then reflect issues of importance to me, both personal and political. Ultimately, I remain hopelessly stagestruck and I write in order to act. It's not enough for an audience to read my stories, I am compelled to get up there and tell it to them myself.

Actor-playwright Charles Busch and his cohorts at Theatre-in-Limbo are proving themselves worthy successors to Charles Ludlam, whose death in 1987 was an irretrievable loss to the comic vein of American theatre. In eight years, Busch's work has moved from burlesque sketch comedies performed for late-night coterie audiences to two-act, Off-Broadway productions with open runs. Less aesthetically dangerous and more intellectually accessible than Ludlam's sublime scavenges of Western art, Busch's deft fruit salads of B-movie conventions, femme attitudes, and subversive politics, are enormously popular with audiences and critics of all persuasions.

Although Busch insists in preface after preface that his heroines needn't be performed by men in drag, much of the power in his work is derived from a cross-dressing, decidedly gay perspective. Without Busch himself expertly glossing—indeed, outdoing—Norma Shearer or Betty Hutton or Greer Garson on the stage, making us question the construction of gender and genre, his plays might seem of little more consequence than television spoofs of best-forgotten moments in American cinema. Yet no matter how outsized the role in Busch's menagerie, from a silent screen vamp to a 12-year-old Nazi, they are meant to be performed with a sincerity and a realism that forestalls any unwelcome complicity from the audience.

The double bill of *Sleeping Beauty or Coma* and *Vampire Lesbians of Sodom* started as a weekend party for friends and became one of the longest-running plays in Off-Broadway history. In *Sleeping Beauty*, a send-up of Carnaby Street in the swinging sixties, a fashion designer, a supermodel, and a photographer hit the heights of mod London and crash semi-permanently on shoddy tabs of acid. *Vampire Lesbians* time-travels from ancient Sodom to Hollywood in the 1920s to contemporary Las Vegas to tell the tale of rival succubi who wind up as competing entertainment divas. At the conclusion, each discovers she needs the other (if only to revile her)—the rewards of feminine friendship, treated embryonically in this fairytale, is a theme that runs through all of Busch's work.

Times Square Angel is Busch's first attempt at a cinematic saga, and he continues to tailor roles for his troupe of regulars much as Molière or Preston Sturges did. Irish O'Flanagan goes from the slums of Hell's Kitchen to the top of the post-war entertainment industry, trading in her heart along the way. One Christmas Eve, with the help of a wayward angel, Irish learns the true meaning of life. Although this fantasia on *It's a Wonderful Life* overreaches itself narratively, *Times Square Angel* is full of Busch's deliriously hard-boiled dialogue.

Funnier still is *Psycho Beach Party*, an amalgam of 1960s beach movies, *Sybil*, and *Mommie Dearest*. In addition to all the surfboards, dance numbers, and petting sessions compulsory to the sandflick genre, Busch's characters are unconscious heralds of non-conformism. Chicklet must free herself by integrating her multiple personalities, and, rather than suppress their attraction for each other, beach rats Yo Yo and Provoloney openly declare their forbidden homosexual love. Liberation is again the theme when Busch returns to the 1940s with *The Lady in Question*, an anti-Nazi war melodrama. Like Irish O'Flanagan, internationally acclaimed concert pianist Gertrude Garnet is an impossibly selfish woman who only discovers her humanity through sacrifice. After her sidekick Kitty is strangled by the evil Lotte Von Elsner, Gertrude rescues a political prisoner and escapes into Switzerland on skis with the man she loves. Busch's growth as a writer is impressive; familiarity with the intertexts, among them, in this case, Hitchcock's *Notorious* and the dreadful 1950s *Bad Seed*, enhances one's appreciation of *The Lady in Question* but isn't necessary if one is to laugh at its comedy or be held in real suspense by its plot.

No less artful than his other screen "adaptations," *Red Scare on Sunset*, Busch's latest offering, was greeted with less enthusiasm. When Mary Dale, played by Busch, names names on the air in order to free Hollywood of Communist menace, audiences were confused by the author's intentions. In a culture that in a very short while has become increasingly hostile to homosexuals and to art, one can no longer afford to satirize the left with impunity. Busch is not a political writer *per se*, but his choice of material and his production style are an inherent critique of the American myths of family, assimilation, career, love, showbiz, power, and luxury. They celebrate personal freedom against the forces of evil implicity gathering just beyond the footlights. In addition to his gay audience, Busch is popular with the aging Baby Boomers given over to refabricating the hoary artifacts and attitudes of their past; yet, beneath the cartoon contours of his Hollywood tropes, Busch challenges an easy, ravenous predilection for camp by creating moments of genuine feeling. His insistence that his work be performed "straight," lends to his best plays an undeniable charm and a salutary tension.

—James Magruder

C

CARLINO, Lewis John.

Born in New York City, 1 January 1932. Educated at El Camino College, California; University of Southern California, Los Angeles, 1956–60, B.A. (magna cum laude) in film 1959 (Phi Beta Kappa), M.A. in drama 1960. Served in the United States Air Force, 1951–55. Married Denise Jill Chadwick; three children from previous marriage. Recipient: British Drama League prize, 1960; Huntington Hartford fellowship; Yaddo fellowship; Rockefeller grant. Lives in California. Agent: Gilbert Parker, William Morris Agency, 1350 Avenue of the Americas, New York, New York 10019, U.S.A.

Publications

PLAYS

The Brick and the Rose: A Collage for Voices (produced 1957). 1959.
Junk Yard. 1959.
Used Car for Sale. 1959.
Objective Case (produced 1962). With *Mr. Flannery's Ocean*, 1961.
Mr. Flannery's Ocean (includes *Piece and Precise*) (produced 1962). With *Objective Case*, 1961.
Two Short Plays: Sarah and the Sax, and High Sign. 1962.
The Beach People (produced 1962).
Postlude, and Snowangel (produced 1962).
Cages: Snowangel and Epiphany (produced 1963; *Epiphany* produced 1974). 1963.
Telemachus Clay: A Collage for Voices (produced 1963). 1964.
Doubletalk: Sarah and the Sax, and The Dirty Old Man (produced 1964; *Sarah and the Sax* produced 1971). 1964.
The Exercise (produced 1967). 1968.

SCREENPLAYS: *Seconds*, 1966; *The Fox*, with Howard Koch, 1967; *The Brotherhood*, 1968; *Reflection of Fear*, with Edward Hume, 1971; *The Mechanic*, 1972; *Crazy Joe*, 1973; *The Sailor Who Fell from Grace with the Sea*, 1976; *I Never Promised You a Rose Garden*, with Gavin Lambert, 1977; *The Great Santini*, 1980; *Resurrection*, 1981.

TELEVISION PLAYS: *And Make Thunder His Tribute* (*Route 66* series), 1963; *In Search of America*, 1971; *Doc Elliot* (pilot), 1972; *Honor Thy Father*, from the novel by Gay Talese, 1973; *Where Have All the People Gone?*, with Sandor Stern, 1974.

Novels
The Brotherhood. 1968.
The Mechanic. 1972.

Theatrical activities
Director: Films—*The Sailor Who Fell from Grace with the Sea*, 1976; *The Great Santini*, 1980; *Class*, 1983.

Between June, 1963 and May, 1964—less than a year's time—four one-act plays and one full-length work by Lewis John Carlino were produced Off-Broadway in New York. They ranged from the vast talent and imagination of *Telemachus Clay* to the burgeoning maturity of *Cages* to the unfulfilled *Doubletalk*. With these plays, Carlino established himself as an American playwright of exceptional quality and promise. The theatre did not hear from him again for four years, as he turned to screenwriting (*Seconds*, *The Brotherhood*). In 1968 he made his Broadway debut with the sloppy and self-indulgent *The Exercise*, and the catastrophe seems to have driven him permanently from the theatre.

If critics, financial uncertainty, and the unpredictable duration of a play's run are the theatre's risks, however, film writing has its own dangers. Like too many artistic writers caught up in the American commercial maelstrom, Lewis John Carlino was lost in the hurly-burly of a marketplace too busy to notice or care. Nevertheless, the originality and craftsmanship of his stage work endure. He is a playwright who should not forget or be forgotten.

His first notable New York production was a bill of one-act plays—*Cages*. The curtain raiser, *Snowangel*, is a minor look at a constricted intellectual and an earthy prostitute, spelling out the predictable point. The main work of the program, however, is devastating.

Called *Epiphany*, it is about an ornithologist who is discovered by his wife in a homosexual act. In reaction he turns into a rooster. The Kafkaesque metaphor is theatrically powerful, visually striking, and provocative in context. But as he becomes that rooster, clucking and strutting, it turns out that he is laying eggs. Having really wanted to be a hen, he has suffered a breakdown only to find his wife all too willing to strip the coxcomb from the mask he has donned. He need no longer pretend to virility. She turns him into a female and stays to keep him that way.

Although the play came at a time when every other drama seemed to condemn women as man's arch-enemy, Carlino's imaginative story and powerful structure transcended the cliché. The dramatic scheme is faultless and the writing is for actors—something too few playwrights seem capable of doing.

As is often the case, a well received play generates production of a writer's earlier work and, within six months, Carlino's *Telemachus Clay* was presented Off-Broadway. One could only again ponder the judgment of producers for here was a drama of tremendous poetry, artistry and stage life—a drama that would never have been presented had it not been for the notices *Cages* received.

Like so many first plays, *Telemachus Clay* is a story of the artist as a young man, in this case drawn parallel to Odysseus's son. It is subtitled *A Collage for Voices*, as indeed it is, the actors perched on stools, facing the audience. The 11 of them play a host of characters, changing time and location with the magic of poetry weaving the fabric of story, thought, event, and emotion in overlapping dialogue and sound.

This is a device that risks pretension and artiness, but in *Telemachus Clay* it succeeds on the sheer beauty of language and the structural control. There are thoughts and dreams, flashbacks, memories, overheard conversation—a score of effects beyond conventional structure and justifying the form. Like *Cages* the play suffers from immature message making, but like it, too, there is a marvellous sense of theatre, of dialogue, of fantasy, and of humor.

Doubletalk underlined the flaws rather than the strengths of these earlier plays—instead of picking up on his technical finesse, strong dialogue, and sense of stage excitement, Carlino stumbled on his inclination toward point-making and his trouble with plots. These two one-act plays used coy notions instead of stories—an old Jewish lady having a chance meeting with a black musician; a virgin having a chance meeting with an aged poet. This coyness came to a head with *The Exercise*—a play about actors, improvisations, reality, and theatricality that threatened to bring Pirandello from his grave if only to blow up New York's Actors Studio, to which this play was virtually a bouquet.

The work output is slim, certainly inconsistent, and no peak of development was ever achieved. Yet, Carlino's playwriting is unmistakably artistic. Its uncertain flowering is tragically representative of too many American writers for the stage.

—Martin Gottfried

CARTER, Lonnie.

Born in Chicago, Illinois, 25 October 1942. Educated at Loyola University, Chicago, 1960–61; Marquette University, Milwaukee, B.A. 1964, M.A. 1966; Yale University School of Drama, New Haven, Connecticut (Molly Kazan award, 1967; Shubert Fellow, 1968–69), M.F.A. 1969. Married Marilyn Smutko in 1966 (divorced 1972). Taught writing at Marquette University, 1964–65, Yale University School of Drama, 1974–75, Rockland Community College, Suffern, New York, University of Connecticut, Storrs, and New York University, 1979–86; Jenny McKean Moore Fellow, George Washington University, Washington, D.C., 1986–87. Recipient: Peg Santvoord Foundation fellowship, 1969, 1970; Guggenheim fellowship, 1971; National Endowment for the Arts grant, 1974, 1983; CBS Foundation grant, 1974; Connecticut Commission on the Arts grant, 1976, 1988; Open Circle award, 1978; PEN grant, 1978. Address: Cream Hill Road, West Cornwall, Connecticut 06796, U.S.A.

Publications

PLAYS

Adam (produced 1966).
Another Quiet Evening at Home (produced 1967).

If Beauty's in the Eye of the Beholder, Truth Is in the Pupil Somewhere Too (produced 1969).
Workday (produced 1970).
Iz She Izzy or Iz He Ain'tzy or Iz They Both, music by Robert Montgomery (produced 1970). In *The Sovereign State of Boogedy Boogedy and Other Plays*, 1986.
More War in Store, and Time Space (produced 1970).
Plumb Loco (produced 1970).
The Big House (produced 1971).
Smoky Links (produced 1972).
Watergate Classics, with others (produced 1973). In *Yale/Theatre*, 1974.
Cream Cheese (produced 1974).
Trade-Offs (produced 1976).
Bleach (produced 1977).
Bicicletta (produced 1978). In *The Sovereign State of Boogedy Boogedy and Other Plays*, 1986.
Victoria Fellows (produced 1978).
Sirens (produced 1979).
The Sovereign State of Boogedy Boogedy (produced 1985). In *The Sovereign State of Boogedy Boogedy and Other Plays*, 1986.
The Sovereign State of Boogedy Boogedy and Other Plays (includes *Iz She Izzy or Iz He Ain'tzy or Iz They Both, Waiting for G, Bicicletta, Necktie Party*). 1986.
Mothers and Sons (produced 1987).
Necktie Party (produced 1987). In *The Sovereign State of Boogedy Boogedy and Other Plays*, 1986.
Gulliver (produced 1990).
Waiting for Lefty Rose (produced 1991).
I.B. Randy Jr. (produced 1992).

RADIO PLAYS: *Certain Things about the Trombone*, 1982; *Lulu*, 1983.

TELEVISION PLAY: *From the Top*, 1976.

While Lonnie Carter was studying playwriting at Yale University School of Drama he spent most of his time not writing plays, but rather attending movie retrospectives of Buster Keaton, Charlie Chaplin, the Marx Brothers, and W.C. Fields. Spending hours watching these classic comedies, he saw something in the basic physiognomy of the characters that he was trying to do verbally in his own plays. He then decided to write his own slapstick farce, *The Big House*, using a Marx Brothers film as a springboard.

Employing the original plot of the film, in which three con-men take over a prison and lock up the warden, he used the film's basic characters of Groucho, a cockney Chico, Harpo, and a minister made up to look like Chaplin. Carter's only additions were a few songs and dances. Basically what Carter ended up with was a hodge-podge of 1920s and 1930s movie comedies. The play is filled with low comedy hijinks, pratfalls galore, and very broad burlesque humor. The action proceeds at such a furious pace that by the middle of the second act the audience is out of breath and the playwright out of plot. The main trouble with Carter's *The Big House* lies in the plot and structure. It would have been fine as a one-act play or mini-musical, but it didn't work as a full-length play.

The most popular play Carter has written is called *Iz She Izzy or Iz He Ain'tzy or Iz They Both*. It had its premiere at Yale in 1970, and has since been performed regularly by university and high school drama groups. *Izzy* is set in a chaotic contemporary courtroom where a schizoid judge (Justice "Choo-Choo" Justice; half-male and half-female) is on trial for having committed the premeditated murder of his female self. In *Izzy* Carter once again uses many familiar movie gags, and supplements the action by songs with lovely lyrics that show off his audacious wit. A good example is the song sung by the frustrated Justice (Choo-Choo) Justice near the end of the play: "I'd like to have a baby/A lass or little laddie/But when it saw its mommy/Would it say 'Daddy'?"

Smoky Links is about a revolution on a mythical Scottish golf course. The main revolutionary is a symbolic Oriental golf pro who threatens the whole club while turning the Scottish accent around with his Oriental pronunciation.

In *Smoky Links*, as in most of his plays, Carter wrestles with the subject of justice. All of his main characters, Wolfgang Amadeus Gutbucket in *The Big House*, Justice (Choo-Choo) Justice in *Izzy*, and the Oriental Golf Pro in *Smoky Links*, are in some way frustrated by the law. But the characters' attitude towards justice and the law remains mostly ambiguous, except in the case of the Marx Brothers in *The Big House*. The Marx Brothers are dyed in the wool anarchists and never offer any alternative except total disruption.

Except for the highly derivative *The Big House*, Carter's sharp humor and verbal somersaults remind one more of Restoration comedy or the satires of Rabelais than the oldtime Hollywood comedies. The influence of films is strong, but Carter has also a special, quite obvious talent that has yet to be developed to its fullest extent.

—Bernard Carragher

CHASE, Mary (née Coyle).

Born in Denver, Colorado, 25 February 1907. Educated in Denver public schools; Denver University, 1922–24: University of Colorado, Boulder, 1924–25. Married Robert Lamont Chase in 1928; has three sons. Reporter, *Rocky Mountain News*, Denver, 1928–31; freelance correspondent, International News Service and the United Press, 1932–36; publicity director, NYA, Denver, 1941–42, and for Teamsters Union, 1942–44. Recipient: Pulitzer prize, 1945. Litt.D.: University of Denver, 1947. *Died 20 October 1981.*

Publications

PLAYS

Me, Third (produced 1936; as *Now You've Done It*, produced 1937).
Sorority House (produced 1939). 1939.
Too Much Business. 1940.
A Slip of a Girl (produced 1941).
Harvey (produced 1944). 1944.

The Next Half Hour (produced 1945).
Mrs McThing (produced 1952). 1952.
Bernardine (produced 1952). 1953.
Lolita (produced 1954).
The Prize Play. 1961.
Midgie Purvis (produced 1961). 1963.
The Dog Sitters. 1963.
Mickey, based on *Loretta Mason Potts.* 1969.
Cocktails with Mimi (produced 1973). 1974.

OTHER

Loretta Mason Potts (juvenile). 1958; as *Colin's Naughty Sister*, 1959.
The Wicked Pigeon Ladies in the Garden (juvenile). 1968.

A comedy about a gentle alcoholic and his friend—who happens to be a six-foot-tall, invisible rabbit—made Mary Chase a significant name in the American theatre. *Harvey* won the Pulitzer prize for the 1944–45 season and had one of the longest runs ever achieved on Broadway. It was made into a successful film and it has been successfully revived on American television.

Harvey was Chase's second play to be performed in New York. Her first, *Now You've Done It*, lasted only a few weeks back in 1937, giving little indication that her next comedy would be so popular. But in retrospect we can see the same setting in a western city, the same whimsy, and the same inverted morality that found fuller expression in *Harvey*. *Now You've Done It* is a comedy about a young man who seeks nomination to Congress. When he is opposed by the established party leaders, he is rescued by his mother's maid, whose former job in a brothel gives her a powerful hold on most of the male politicians in town. Mary Chase got a few good laughs out of her mischievous mixture of politics and prostitution.

In *Harvey* (originally titled *The Pooka*), Chase recounted the efforts of a widow, Veta Louise Simmons, to cure her alcoholic brother, Elwood P. Dowd, whose invisible rabbit friend has become an embarrassment to the family. She takes Elwood to Dr Chumley's Rest, a private psychiatric hospital, for shock treatment, but rescues him from the doctor because she fears that the cure will turn her harmless brother into an ogre.

The original production was a smash hit. Produced by Brock Pemberton—against the advice of his knowing Broadway friends—and staged with great fun and charm by Antoinette Perry, *Harvey* had an inspired cast. As Elwood P. Dowd, Frank Fay was making a Broadway comeback, having lost a fortune in Hollywood and having overcome—as rumour had it—his own problem with alcohol. New York audiences empathized nightly with his personal triumph as an actor almost as much as they cheered Elwood's quiet triumph over Dr Chumley. Underplaying the role, Fay projected decency and gentleness along with a warm alcoholic glow, without ever descending to vulgarity or cuteness. Josephine Hull created Veta Louise with all her scatterbrained mannerisms but with the inner compassion that made her Elwood's sister beyond any doubt. These were two of the great American performances of the 1940s.

But even after Fay was succeeded by actors such as James Stewart, who did descend to cuteness, *Harvey* remained popular. The play had substance even without the great acting.

Harvey's strength derived from its highly theatrical use of illusion and reality. Chase followed the tradition of plays like Thornton Wilder's *Our Town* that violated the laws of time and space, but she treated these dislocations of reality with a deadpan playfulness. Her comic motif of supernatural whimsy was like that of Noël Coward's *Blithe Spirit*, but she replaced his brittle sophistication with homespun compassion.

Though Harvey can hardly be regarded as a Christ symbol, Mary Chase dramatized a conflict between faith and disbelief. She suggested that the person who has faith in something invisible is mistakenly regarded as insane by "'normal" society. Amid her comedy, she suggested further that faith and illusion should triumph over reality, that the psychiatrists were crazy, and that the abnormal were really sane. The punch line of the play is delivered by the cabby who warns Veta Louise about the shock treatment that Elwood is about to receive: "Lady, after this he'll be a perfectly normal human being, and you know what bastards they are!" Veta Louise pounds on the door of the treatment room and rescues her brother. Better a gentler alcoholic with faith in his invisible rabbit than a normal human bastard with no illusions and no ideals.

Audiences cheered Veta Louise on to her rescue of Elwood. Just as they applauded for Tinker Bell in *Peter Pan*, they gave Harvey an enthusiastic curtain call, one invisible paw held by Frank Fay and the other by Josephine Hull. The spectators may have been applauding the escape from reality to alcoholic illusion. But, on the other hand, they may have been cheering for the ideals of individualism, decency, and friendship.

Whatever audiences responded to in *Harvey's* invisibility gave the play much of its humour as well as its meaning. During the Boston tryout an actor in a rabbit costume played the role for one performance. So great was the loss of laughs that Harvey was rendered invisible for ever more.

A year after *Harvey*, Mary Chase tried a serious drama with a supernatural motif. In *The Next Half Hour* she wrote about an Irish immigrant woman who believed in little people and banshees. But the play failed quickly. Comedy was really her forte, she apparently decided, because her next three plays were comic treatments of illusion and reality.

In *Mrs McThing* Mary Chase told the story of the wealthy Mrs Howard V. Larue III, whose son is stolen away by a witch (Mrs McThing) and replaced by a model boy. Aided by the witch's daughter, Mrs Larue rescues her real son, who has become involved with a gang of comically incompetent gangsters. Like Harvey, the witch remained invisible, except for a moment in the last scene. Just as *Harvey* mixed real alcohol and whimsy, *Mrs McThing* mixed whimsy with fake gangsters and fairy-tale witchcraft. This play was written for children, but it had a moderate success with adults who went to see Helen Hayes and Brandon de Wilde as mother and son. The Jean Arthur-Boris Karloff *Peter Pan*, a mixture of pirates and whimsy, had also been fairly popular with adults a few years earlier.

Later in 1952, Mary Chase brought her whimsy back to earth with *Bernardine*, a comedy about a group of teen-age boys who search without much success for sexual experience with "fast" women. They daydream of the accessible, but imaginary, Bernardine, who "lives" in Sneaky Falls. But since the sexual revolution, their fantasies seem quaintly dated.

No matter how sexual mores change, nothing remains so timely as a six-foot-tall invisible rabbit. In 1961 Chase again tried the mixture of insanity and whimsy in *Midgie Purvis*, but, even with Tallulah Bankhead in the title role, the play failed. Mary Chase never succeeded in matching the comic perfection of *Harvey*. It is her classic.

—Morgan Y. Himelstein

CHAYEFSKY, Paddy.

Born Sidney Chayefsky in the Bronx, New York, 29 January 1923. Educated at DeWitt Clinton High School, Bronx, graduated 1939; City College, New York, B.S. in social science 1943. Served in the U.S. Army, 1943–45: private; Purple Heart. Married Susan Sackler in 1949; one son. Worked for a printer, New York, 1946; writer in Hollywood, late 1940s; gag writer for Robert Q. Lewis, New York, 1950. President, Sudan Productions, 1956, Carnegie Productions, 1957, S.P.D. Productions after 1959, Sidney Productions after 1967, and Simcha Productions after 1971, all New York. Council member, Dramatists Guild, from 1962. Recipient: Screen Writers Guild award, 1954, 1971; Oscar, for screenplay, 1955, 1971, 1976; New York Film Critics award, 1956, 1971, 1976; British Academy award, 1976. *Died 1 August 1981.*

Publications

PLAYS

No T.O. for Love, music by Jimmy Livingston (produced 1945).
Printer's Measure (televised 1953). In *Television Plays*, 1955.
Middle of the Night (televised 1954; revised version, produced 1956). 1957.
Television Plays (includes *The Bachelor Party*; *The Big Deal*; *Holiday Song*; *Marty*; *The Mother*; and *Printer's Measure*). 1955.
The Bachelor Party (screenplay). 1957.
The Goddess (screenplay; stage version produced 1971). 1958.
The Tenth Man (produced 1959). 1960.
Gideon (produced 1961). 1962.
The Passion of Josef D. (also director: produced 1964). 1964.
The Latent Heterosexual (produced 1968). 1967.

SCREENPLAYS: *The True Glory* (uncredited), with Garson Kanin, 1945; *As Young as You Feel*, with Lamar Trotti, 1951; *Marty*, 1955; *The Bachelor Party*, 1957; *The Goddess*, 1958; *Middle of the Night*, 1959; *The Americanization of Emily*, 1964; *Paint Your Wagon*, with Alan Jay Lerner, 1969; *The Hospital*, 1971; *Network*, 1975; *Altered States*, 1979.

RADIO PLAYS: *The Meanest Man in the World, Tommy,* and *Over 21* (all in *Theater Guild of the Air* series), 1951–52; scripts for *Cavalcade of America*.

TELEVISION PLAYS: Scripts for *Danger* and *Manhunt* series; *Holiday Song*, 1952; *The Reluctant Citizen*, 1952; *Printer's Measure*, 1953, *Marty*, 1953, *The Big Deal*, 1953, and *The Bachelor Party*, 1953; *The Sixth Year*, 1953; *Catch My Boy on Sunday*, 1953; *The Mother*, 1954; *Middle of the Night*, 1954; *The Catered Affair*, 1955; *The Great American Hoax*, 1957.

NOVEL
Altered States. 1978.

CRITICAL STUDY: *Paddy Chayefsky* by John M. Clum, 1976.

The Broadway drama of the 1950s was dominated by Arthur Miller and Tennessee Williams, the one focussing on ordinary people and using their stories to make political and social comment, and the other writing about the very human psychological and spiritual pains of society's outcasts and freaks. Almost every other playwright of the period can be placed somewhere on a continuum between the two giants; and one way of defining the early work of Paddy Chayefsky is as giving the Williams treatment to Miller characters. That is, in his most successful early plays, for television and film as well as for theatre, Chayefsky dissects the ordinary lives of ordinary people and finds tiny but moving drama within.

Among his theatrical plays, only *Middle of the Night* is as successful as his television play, *Marty*, in blending an accurate and intermittently satiric depiction of a milieu with the serious treatment given to the central story. The play is about a 53-year-old widower who falls in love with an unhappily married woman who is 30 years younger. She appreciates and returns his devotion, but friends and family on both sides are shocked by the mismatch, which seems to violate basic cultural taboos, and the lovers themselves are led to doubt their right to happiness. As in *Marty*, the very small question of whether these unremarkable people will stay together and have an ordinary chance of happiness is made a meaningful one through an unpatronizing respect for the reality of their emotions.

The careful balance of social reportage, satire, and sentimentality begins to break down in Chayefsky's next play, *The Tenth Man*, as he moves from what had been his area of strength—the characterization of ordinary people—toward a more abstractly philosophical focus. The play is about a congrega-tion of elderly Jews who decide that the schizophrenic grand-daughter of one of them is really possessed by a demon and decide to exorcise it. They actually affect the dead-spirited young man they dragged off the street to participate in the ceremony; with renewed faith and love, he proposes to the girl. But the human story of the damaged young people reaching toward each other is buried in vague discussions about the nature of sanity and faith, and theatri-cally overpowered by the string of easy and patronizing jokes at the expense of the bored and confused old men.

That this movement away from small melodrama and toward philosophy mixed with social satire was deliberate is made obvious in the biblical play *Gideon*, which has almost no real human interaction, but rather builds to an interesting and challenging debate between Gideon and God about how man finds belief in an omnipotent deity too difficult and frightening because it leaves no place and dignity for humans. The ideas are not fully integrated into the play, coming almost as afterthoughts, and one must wade through too much easy humor built on the demythologized characterizations—God as a petulant old man, Gideon as a dim country hick—to get to them. Still, they are there, and give what would otherwise be a trivial play some weight.

After two commercial failures—*The Passion of Josef D.*, a misguided attempt to tell the story of Stalin through Brechtian devices which Chayefsky had not mastered, and *The Latent Heterosexual*, a satire on the dehumanizing power of success—Chayefsky left the theatre to concentrate on his parallel career as a screenwriter, where his best work resembled *Gideon* in placing thought-provoking ideas in otherwise unremarkable contexts.

Except for those who know him only from such late filmscripts as *The Hospital* and *Network*, Paddy Chayefsky will probably be remembered primarily as the author of *Marty*, a 1953 television play later expanded into a film. The title character is a New York butcher in his 30's, overweight and socially awkward, who is stuck in an extended adolescence of living with his mother and idly hanging out with his buddies. He meets an equally plain schoolteacher at a dance, and they clumsily begin a small courtship—and that is just about it. The material is obviously very fragile, and Chayefsky's skill lies in making the small story seem meaningful while still acknowledging its comic aspects, and without lapsing into preciousness.

Such films as *The Bachelor Party*, *The Americanization of Emily* and *Network* have in common the fact that they are all very conventional formula pieces into which Chayefsky was able to squeeze one or two scenes, discussions, or characterizing touches of unexpected depth. And that, indeed, might be the summation of Chayefsky's accomplishment on stage and screen: while less ambitious and talented writers settled for convention, and more ambitious writers stretched or challenged it, Paddy Chayefsky wrote little plays and films that were just a little deeper and better than one expected them to be.

—Gerald M. Berkowitz

CHILDRESS, Alice.

Born in Charleston, South Carolina, 12 October 1920. Educated at schools in Harlem, New York; Radcliffe Institute for Independent Study (scholar), Cambridge, Massachusetts, 1966–68, graduated 1968. Married to the musician Nathan Woodard; one daughter. Actor and director, American Negro Theatre, New York, 1941–52; columnist ("Here's Mildred"), Baltimore *Afro-American*, 1956–58. Artist-in-residence, University of Massachusetts, Amherst, 1984. Recipient: Obie award, 1956; Woodward School Book award, 1975; Paul Robeson award, for screenplay, 1977; Virgin Islands Film Festival award, 1977; Radcliffe Graduate Society medal, 1984; African Poets Theatre award, 1985; Audelco award, 1986; Harlem School of the Arts Humanitarian award, 1987. Agent: Flora Roberts Inc., 157 West 57th Street, New York, New York 10019, U.S.A.

Publications

PLAYS

Florence (also director: produced 1949). In *Masses and Mainstream*, October, 1950.

Just a Little Simple, adaptation of stories by Langston Hughes (produced 1950).

Gold Through the Trees (produced 1952).

Trouble in Mind (produced 1955). In *Black Theatre: A Twentieth-Century Collection of the Work of Its Best Playwrights*, edited by Lindsay Patterson, 1971.

Wedding Band (produced 1966). 1974.

The World on a Hill, in *Plays to Remember*. 1968.

Young Martin Luther King (produced 1969).

String, adaptation of a story by Maupassant (produced 1969). With *Mojo*, 1971.

Wine in the Wilderness (televised 1969; produced 1976). 1970.

Mojo (produced 1970). With *String*, 1971.

When the Rattlesnake Sounds (for children). 1975.

Let's Hear It for the Queen (for children). 1976.

Sea Island Song (produced 1977).

Gullah (produced 1984).

Moms: A Praise Play for a Black Comedienne, music and lyrics by Childress and Nathan Woodard (produced 1987).

SCREENPLAY: *A Hero Ain't Nothin' But a Sandwich*, 1977.

TELEVISION PLAYS: *Wine in the Wilderness*, 1969; *Wedding Band*, 1973; *String*, 1979.

NOVEL

A Short Walk. 1979.

OTHER

Like One of the Family: Conversations from a Domestic's Life. 1956.

A Hero Ain't Nothin' But a Sandwich (for children). 1973.

Rainbow Jordan (for children). 1981.

Those Other People (for children). 1989.

Editor, *Black Scenes: Collections of Scenes from Plays Written by Black People about Black Experience*. 1971.

CRITICAL STUDIES: articles by Gayle Austin and Polly Holliday, in *Southern Quarterly*, Spring 1987; *Their Place on Stage: Black Women Playwrights in America* by Elizabeth Brown-Guillory, 1988.

THEATRICAL ACTIVITIES

DIRECTOR: Play—*Florence*, 1949.

ACTOR: Plays—*Dolly* in *On Strivers Row* by Abram Hill, 1940; Polly Ann in *Natural Man* by Theodore Browne, 1941; Blanche in *Anna Lucasta* by Philip Yordan, 1944.

Alice Childress's contribution to 20th-century American theatre is remarkable. She came to playwriting after 11 years as an actor with the American Negro Theatre and, in her writing career, has many achievements which mark her importance as a playwright.

Her 1952 play, *Gold Through the Trees*, was the first by a black woman to be produced professionally. The Obie award she won for *Trouble in Mind* was the first for a woman playwright. *Wedding Band* was the first play to show an inter-racial relationship on the stage. Indeed, Childress's commitment to develop her playwriting in the context of a theatre for, and of, black people has been often demonstrated. Alongside the many plays, she has edited a book of scenes for black actors and has written for young audiences too.

Childress's plays invariably deal with emotional relationships and the tensions within them. Sometimes the cause of such tension is overt as in the inter-racial relationship of Julia and Herman (in *Wedding Band*). Other times it is caused by fears which are provoked by the inevitable insecurity of being black in a white person's world. In her history-drama *When The Rattlesnake Sounds* (based on the life of escaped slave and underground railway-worker Harriet Tubman), Celia reveals a very real fear of being found working with Harriet for whom there is a $40,000 reward outstanding. In *Mojo* Irene faces an imminent hospital treatment where she sees herself lying on a white sheet in a white room where a white man with a white mask will put her to sleep so that another white man in a white suit can cut her open.

Childress shows again and again in her drama how marginalized position breeds fear and tension within a community. This is perhaps best portrayed in the action of *String*, a play set at an annual block association picnic. Here, Joe is suspected of stealing a wallet for two simple reasons: first, because he was seen picking something up (in fact a piece of string that one of the women had dropped), and second, because of his unconventional appearance and behaviour. L.V. Craig, the owner of the lost wallet, has all the power and credibility because of his appearance—he is wearing a suit—and his ownership of a bar. The action shows Joe to be the most honest and also the most misunderstood person in the community. Everyone recognizes the deceit of Craig—he cheats his customers and has apparently shot a man some time previously—but nevertheless respects him because of his economic position. Like much of her writing, *String* demonstrates that justice is determined both in terms of race and class.

Childress's work contributed significantly to a developing black women's theatre and her texts foreground her own personal experience. Childress was born in South Carolina, where her great-grandmother had been a slave, and raised in Harlem. The importance of her roots was acknowledged when the South Carolina Commission for the Arts asked her to prepare a play to tour in the state's schools and in response Childress wrote *Gullah*, a musical play for which her husband, Nathan Woodard, wrote the score. "Gullah" is a language spoken only on some of the islands off the South Carolina coast and Childress wanted to capture the poetry of these people (which included her stepfather). The South Carolina Commission for the Arts, however, objected to the title, because of its sometime use to disparage country people, and substituted *Sea Island Song*. This act was itself a testament to Childress's sense that her work is inevitably read out of context (in other words, in the context of the dominant white culture and its prejudices and sensitivities). *Gullah*, as does much of Childress's writing, recoups and celebrates black American history for black Americans.

Perhaps the most significant contribution of Childress's playwriting, however, is her creation of many major female characters. Cynthia in *Wine in the Wilderness* leads Tommy (Tommorrow Marie) away from idealized (male) notions of the women's role towards a sense of her own self. As Tommy projects her new-found confidence, she not only attracts the artist, Bill, but becomes the model to represent the future in the triptych of past, present, and future that he is painting. In the two-hander *Mojo*, it is Irene who shows her ex-husband, Teddy, how his success has been conceived in "white" terms. It is not coincidental that Teddy's girlfriend (never seen on stage) is a white woman. Here, as in other Childress plays, the events which touch the characters' lives are those which affect the working-class black community in America—drugs, family violence, teenage pregnancy, exploitation by white consumerism. Against such a background, however, Childress creates characters who behave with dignity and humanity. There are no easy solutions in Childress's plays, but realistic, honest, and brave ways of coping.

The plays achieve Childress's aim to present the experience of black Americans. She intends to present ordinary people in their everyday world; she looks not to the extraordinary few winners, but to the many and commonplace losers. Her plays show a keen awareness, too, of class and of gender. Childress has acknowledged that in many ways she has been doubly disadvantaged because she writes both as a black and as a woman. She has commented that it is not that critics have always and necessarily dealt with her work unfairly, but that their criteria are always theirs (thus primarily white and male). Hers, then, is a theatre of resistance. The plays have been successful in the mainstream (perhaps particularly marked by the translation of some into television productions), but Childress has apparently never compromised her aims in order to gain that success. For this reason, she has been a remarkable role model for other black and women writers.

—Susan Bennett

See the essay on *Wedding Band*.

CHIN, Frank (Chew, Jr.).

Born in Berkeley, California, 25 February 1940. Educated at the University of California, Berkeley, 1958–61; University of Iowa, Iowa City, 1961–63; University of California, Santa Barbara, A.B. in English 1966. Clerk, Western Pacific Railroad Company, Oakland, California, 1962–65; brakeman, Southern Pacific Railroad, Oakland, 1966; production writer and story editor, King-T.V. and King Screen Productions, Seattle, Washington, 1966–69; lecturer in Asian American Studies, University of California, Davis, San Francisco State College, 1969–70, and University of California, Santa Barbara, 1980; lecturer in creative writing, University of California, Berkeley, 1972, and lecturer in English, University of Oklahoma, Norman, 1988; film consultant, Western Washington State College, Bellingham, 1969–70; founder and artistic director, Asian American Theater Workshop, San Francisco, 1973–77.

Recipient: Joseph Henry Jackson award, 1965; James T. Phelan award, 1966; East-West Players award, 1971; Jack J. Flaks Memorial grant, 1972; San Francisco Foundation fellowship, 1974; Rockefeller grant, 1975; National Endowment for the Arts grant, 1975, 1980; Before Columbus-American Book award, 1981, 1989; Rockefeller American Generations grant, 1991. Address: 2106 Lemoyne Street, #5, Los Angeles, California 90026, U.S.A.

Publications

PLAYS

The Chickencoop Chinaman (produced 1972). With *The Year of the Dragon*, 1981.
The Year of the Dragon (produced 1974). With *The Chickencoop Chinaman*, 1981.
Gee, Pop! (produced 1974).
America More or Less, with Amiri Baraka and Leslie Marmon Silko, music by Tony Greco, lyrics by Arnold Weinstein (produced 1976).
Lullaby, with Leslie Marmon Silko, from a story by Silko (produced 1976).
American Peek-a-Boo Kabuki, World War II and Me (produced 1985).
Flood of Blood: A Fairy Tale (for children). In the *Seattle Review*, vol. 11 no. 1, 1988.

TELEVISION PLAYS: *Seattle Repertory Theatre: Act Two* (documentary), 1966; *The Bel Canto Carols* (documentary), 1966; *A Man and His Music* (documentary), 1967; *Ed Sierer's New Zealand* (documentary), 1967; *Seafair Preview* (documentary), 1967; *The Year of the Ram* (documentary), 1967; *And Still Champion . . .! The Story of Archie Moore* (documentary), 1967; *Mary*, 1969; *Rainlight Rainvision* (for *Sesame Street* series), 1969; *Chinaman's Chance* (documentary), 1971.

NOVEL

Donald Duk. 1991.

SHORT STORIES

The Chinaman Pacific and Frisco R.R. Co. 1988.

OTHER

Rescue at Wild Boar Forest (comic book). 1988.
The Water Margin, or Shui Hu (comic book). 1989.
Lin Chong's Revenge (comic book). 1989.

Editor, with others, *Aiiieeeee! An Anthology of Asian American Writers*. 1974.
Editor, with Shawn Wong, *Yardbird Reader, volume 3*. 1974.
Editor, with others, *The Big Aiiieeeee!*. 1991.

Frank Chin comments:

Asian American theatre is dead without ever having been born, and American theatre, like American writing has found and nurtured willing Gunga Dins, happy white racist tokens, with which to pay their lip service to yellows and call it dues. No thanks.

My theatrical sense combined with my ruthless scholarly nature and need to make things right to produce ceremonial events that restored history and civility inside Japanese America, and between the Japanese Americans and Seattle and Portland. The events, called "Day of Remembrance," dramatically publicized the campaign to redress the constitutional grievances suffered by all persons of Japanese ancestry during World War II. I put together groups of Japanese-American leaders and activists to lead a return to the county fairgrounds outside of Seattle and Portland that had been converted into concentration camps for the Nikkei in 1942. The Day of Remembrance included participation by the National Guard, local politicians, a display of art and artifacts from the concentration camps, a huge pot luck dinner, and a couple thousand Japanese Americans in both cities.

Otherwise, I am out of theatre. I will not work with any theatre, producer, writer, director, or actor who has played and lives the stereotype. So, I write fiction, essays, and articles.

I have written extensively on Chinese- and Japanese-American history, culture, literature, and presence in popular local newsmagazines, television documentaries, and scholarly journals.

I have taught Asian-American history and ideas using storytelling, theatre, and writing games, in four- to five-week-long workshops for the Asian-American Studies Program at Washington State University, in Pullman, Washington; the American Thought and Literature Department at Michigan State University, in East Lansing, Michigan; in five Portland high schools for the Bilingual/ESL program of Portland Public Schools.

In response to American west-coast public schools teaching the white racist characterisation of Chinese fairytales and childhood literature as teaching misogynistic ethics and despicable morals as fact, I have, like the Cantonese and Chinese before me, wherever Chinese literature and language are banned, taken to the comic book as a tactic for making the real accessible in a hostile literary and learning atmosphere.

I am the principal editor and author of the introductory essays of *Aiiieeeee!: An Anthology of Asian American Writers*, the most influential critical work in Asian-American literature, and *The Big Aiiieeeee! The Big Aiiieeeee!* explores Chinese- and Japanese-American history and stereotyping through the history of western Christian thought and writing, Chinese- and Japanese-American writing, and the Asian fairytales and childhood literature that informed the immigrants and the structures of their political and artistic institutions from *tongs* and *tanemoshi* to railroad building and music.

Frank Chin's two full-length plays, *The Chickencoop Chinaman* and *The Year of the Dragon*, were presented at the American Place Theatre, New York, in 1972 and 1974, and the latter was presented to a national television audience by the Public Broadcasting Service. The historical priority of his achievement might tempt one to call Chin the doyen of Asian-American playwrights, but that would be misleading because he attacks his fellow writers—as he and his fellow-editors put it in *The Big Aiiieeeee!*—for "ventriloquising the same old white Christian fantasy of little Chinese victims," victims of their own sadoma-sochistic culture and of their denial of their own identity in a quest for honorary whiteness. He also claims Maxine Hong Kingston, Amy Tan, and David Henry Hwang "fake all of Asian American history and literature." He attributes the success of Hwang's M. *Butterfly* to the portrayal of the central Chinese character as "the fulfillment of white male homosexual fantasy, literally kissing ass." He remains, then, something of the Angry Young Man who is the central character in both his full-length plays.

Indeed, *The Chickencoop Chinaman* can be compared to *Look Back in Anger*. In both, we are meant to recognize the truth of the central character's highly rhetorical attacks upon society, while in the course of the play he himself is presented in such a way as to lose our sympathy. As Tam's friend Kenji says almost at the end of the play:

> I used to think it was funny, brave, man, the way you ripped everybody up with your tongue, showing 'em up for clowns and bullshit. Your tongue was fast and flashy with the sounds, man, savin your ass from this and that trouble, making people laugh, man, shooin in the girls, I used to know why you were mean and talkin all the time. I don't anymore, and you're still talkin the same crazy talk.

Tam acknowledges that he is a loner and a loser. Chin seems to try to save Tam from total alienation by having him end the play preparing Chinese food—perhaps because "food's our only common language" (*The Year of the Dragon*) —while he reminisces about his grandparents. *Look Back in Anger* ends with a similarly sentimental turn-around.

The image of "The Chickencoop Chinaman making whooppee in a bird-cage" recurs in both plays. The subject of Chin's plays is the difficulty Asian-American men have in establishing an independent and personal identity when doubly isolated: from a culture whose experiences the American-born Chinese has not directly known and of whose language he knows only a smattering, and from a dominant white society whose members see only stereotypes and seek to push one back—psychologically, if not physically—into the cage of Chinatown. Thus, Tam's speech "jumps between black and white rhythms and accents" for he has "no real language of my own to make sense with, so out comes everybody else's language that don't conceive." This metaphor links the sterility of the protagonist's language, however hyper-active, with a lack of manhood that all three Asian-American men in *The Chickencoop Chinaman* feel. Similarly, the corresponding slick-speaking central character in *The Year of the Dragon*, Fred, swings between a phony Chinatown accent that he employs as a tourist guide and casual American English. Tam visits his friend Blackjap Kenji, who has adopted a black lifestyle, and who is sheltering Lee, who has had husbands of "all colors and decorator combinations." She passes for white but is in fact part-Chinese. Her Chinese ex-husband Tom turns up to claim her. Tam has told us that his name has been miscorrected to Tom, and Tom is an obvious alter ego. (They are even given the same line about their visits: "I didn't mean to come/walk into no situ-ation.") Tom represents the choice Tam has not made, to become a buttoned-down, assimilated, published writer. Symbolically, he has married white, but both Tom and Tam are separated from their wives—as though neither staying in the culture nor leaving it is a satisfactory solution.

That dilemma is the subject of *The Year of the Dragon*. Again, there is a character—Fred's sister—who has "married out" and become a published author, of a successful cookbook incorporating some of Fred's tourist patter. The ironic cultural contrasts pile up. Fred's "China-crazy" white brother-in-law speaks Mandarin and admires traditional Chinese culture, while Fred speaks a little Cantonese and is contemptuous of the Chinatown culture around him. Fred's father, feeling the approach of death, has brought his first wife and Fred's real mother from China (to the dismay of his Chinese-American wife); since she speaks no English, she is a mostly silent reminder of the ties to the old country. In the younger generation, Fred's younger brother is a juvenile delinquent, responsive to his peers rather than to the authority of the family.

Fred has always spoken of wanting to get out of Chinatown and write. He helped his sister get out, and now her success and his father's death at the end of the play give him that opportunity. But Chinatown is his subject and he fears that his inspiration will dry up away from it. Deeper than that, his decision is determined by his relationship to his father, the *paterfamilias* whom Chin names simply Pa. Pa disparages the one little-magazine publication Fred has achieved, and does not introduce Fred to his fellow seniors in Chinatown (this is based on an anecdote from Chin's own life). Pa is about to give a speech at the New Year's parade in which he will acknowledge Fred's achievement in the community, but he collapses and dies in a confrontation with Fred:

> *Fred.* You gotta do somethin for me. Not for your son, but for me.
> *Pa.* Who you? You my son. Da's all. What else you ting you are.

The final irony is that he will continue as his father's son rather than pursue his individual dreams.

If *Chickencoop Chinaman* is akin to Osborne, *The Year of the Dragon* is more like Odets in its tightly plotted family conflicts and in tone. The ideal seems to be, as Fred expresses it, that "[we] get together and we're talkin a universe, and sing." But in the hierarchical Chinese family, that does not happen.

Flood of Blood: A Fairy Tale is a lively children's play performed by a travelling Chinese troupe in which Chin mixes the Ark story, the princess to be rescued from a dragon, and shades of Turandot.

—Anthony Graham-White

CLOUD, Darrah.

Born in Illinois, 11 February 1955. Educated at Goddard College, Plainfield, Vermont, B.A. 1978; University of Iowa, Iowa City, M.F.A. in creative writing 1980, M.F.A. in theater 1981. Married David Emery Owens in 1992. Recipient: University of Iowa fellowship, 1978; National Endowment for the Arts grant, 1984; Drama League award, 1991. Lives in Catskill, New York. Agent: Peregrine Whittlesey Agency, 345 East 80th Street, New York, New York 10021, U.S.A.

Publications

PLAYS

The House Across the Street (produced 1982).
The Stick Wife (produced 1987). 1987.
O, Pioneers! adaptation of the novel by Willa Cather, music by Kim D.
   Sherman (produced 1989).
Obscene Bird of Night (produced 1989).
The Mud Angel (produced 1990).
Braille Garden (produced 1991).
Genesis (produced 1992).
The Sirens (produced 1992).

SCREENPLAY: *The Haunted*, 1991.

MANUSCRIPT COLLECTION: New Dramatists, New York.

Darrah Cloud comments:

I am haughty enough to think that I might be able to speak for people who can't speak for themselves, so I write plays. Since I began meeting tremendous and brilliant actresses with no good parts to play, I have been obsessed with writing parts for women. And as a woman, I have found a language within my gender that is secret and which I want to reveal, so that it becomes a part of the norm. For in language is perspective, and in perspective is a whole new way of looking at things. I want women's ways of looking at things to be more prevalent in the world.

I think that I always write for my mother. I imagine her in the audience and I know what makes her laugh, what affects her, what she'll believe and what she won't. In that sense, I am always writing my mother as well. I guess I am constantly showing my mother to my mother, in order to let her see herself as not alone, as understood and appreciated, if only by me. My male characters are my mother. And so, obviously, are my female characters. If there is a dog in the play, it's always the dog my mother picked out for us when we were little. I am currently writing a musical about the life of Crazy Horse. Crazy Horse, in his struggle against an encroaching white world, and toward his own fulfillment as a human being, Crazy Horse is my mother.

Sometimes I put my grandmother in because she's short and funny. I have yet to write my sister. This is a goal.

I grew up in the Midwest, and there too, is a unique language based not on what is said, but on what is not said. To be midwestern is to have to intuit the subtext of conversations. If one is talking about the weather, one might actually mean something quite different; something like, "I love you," or "my wife just died and I'm lost." The weather is a very important conversational tool in the Midwest. What is not said, but felt, implied in the moment, is what I love best to write. The congress of emotions that prevent the manifestation of explanations. That creates gestures that say more than words. Open mouths with nothing coming forth from them. This strikes me as always more honest than words. I am always trying to get at the truth of a moment. And so my characters rarely say what they feel, unless they're lying, which is more honest, to me.

I believe in ghosts. I believe that animals are so much more highly evolved than people that they have gotten over language and ambition and live to live. Sometimes I think they contain the spirits of dead people.

Darrah Cloud's best work uses notable historical events as the context for her dark, satiric commentary on American domestic bliss. The result is an antic cartoonish realism that occasioned one critic to describe an early "macabre comedy" as "'Father Knows Best' as written by Joe Orton." However, Cloud's later plays, while sharing some of this loony-tune tone, tend more toward Gothic tragicomedy than farce. Fundamentally, Cloud's plays explore the means by which the violence at the heart of American society reflects itself in the dysfunction of family life—and vice versa. The plays, set in prototypical U.S. towns and cities—Birmingham, Alabama, rural Wisconsin, the suburbs of Chicago—invariably drop their sense of humor by the final fade-to-black, ending enigmatically, but ultimately questioning the poverty of American lower- and middle-class life.

Cloud's dialogue alternates passages of great lyrical beauty reminiscent of the arias Sam Shepard often wrote for his characters with scenes marked by the absurdity of a clipped, repetitious vernacular that, as David Mamet and Samuel Beckett before him discovered, creates its own powerful poeticism. All the plays contain central characters, most often female, whose struggle against their victimization tests their will, morality, and sanity. Cloud's focus on females caught in the grip of mid-American morality and restrictive social norms made her a natural choice to adapt Willa Cather's frontier fable, *O, Pioneers!*, for the stage. Although filmed for television, the production's success was limited. Perhaps Cloud felt her eccentric sense of humor thwarted when harnessed to the slow-burn emotionalism of Cather's novel.

The Mud Angel explores Cloud's feminist themes allegorically. In this bizarre play a rural Wisconsin farm family, symbolically named Malvetz, owns a horse named Shadow whose part is written as a speaking role to be portrayed by a female actor. The action centers around the tensions derived from the mother's threat to sell the valued yet victimized family pet. (*Braille Garden* seems a departure, focusing on a recently married couple and the consequences of the bridegroom's mysterious incapacitation that leaves him in bed, weak and frightened.)

Cloud offers her most fully developed investigation of society's subjugation of women in *The Stick Wife*. The title refers to Jessie, a woman struggling against her domesticated, dominated (identity-less) status as spouse of the Ku Klux Klan member responsible for the bombing of a Birmingham church in 1963 that resulted in the murder of four young black girls. Cloud's parallel between sexism and racism is a conscious one; she once noted in an interview how women in a patriarchical society must deny their true feelings much like slaves once did, forced to hide "their vibrant, inner life behind the 'Yes, Master' pose." The play begins with Ed leaving home to commit his despicable deed. Jessie prefers to ignore her husband's actions; when her neighbor tries to tell her that someone has bombed "a colored church," Jessie responds by pulling her dress up over her head. Jessie pays a high price for her existence: she has lost all contact with her two grown children. When alone, she experiences delusions of self-importance, playing a movie star relating her life story to an imaginary Hollywood interviewer; and she hallucinates "white ghosts" (perhaps fleeting images of her husband's evil alternate identity). The action takes place exclusively in Jessie's backyard, dominated by the clothes-line on which she hangs the white sheets that double as Ed's KKK costume and as symbols of her complicity in his crimes by virtue of their marriage bed. In this play based on a true incident, Jessie tries to free herself neither by divorcing her husband nor running away, but by secretly informing on him.

Cloud sets the action of the second act on the day of President Kennedy's assassination, two months after Ed has been indicted and imprisoned for murder. However, the independence Jessie has gained from her surreptitious action dissipates—Ed is acquitted and returns home. The ending mirrors the beginning: Ed says, "Here we go again," and although he senses something about Jessie has changed, he stalks out of the house as the lights fade on her repeatedly asking him, "Where are you going?" Jessie's helpless question mirrors the uncertainty felt by many Americans during a period marked by the violent murder of its moral and political leaders.

Cloud's earlier exploration of the violence of American life, *The House Across the Street*, contains the seeds of many of these themes. The title refers to the home in which a mass-murderer, very loosely based on John Wayne Gacy, lived. The farcical black comedy focuses on the ironically named Fortune family who never noticed anything amiss in their sedate suburban community, even though their front window looked out on the murderer's house. Donald, a thirteen-year-old budding amateur scientist (he performs experiments on his comatose Grandma), and his kid sister Donna resemble characters from a Charles Addams cartoon. Impertinent, hip, and wizened choristers, they watch the police unearth more and more bodies across the street from their front window. For Donald, this ghoulish activity is "like watchin' a movie." Donald's gleeful shouts accompanying each discovery of a body punctuate the play, much to his mother's frustration. For like Jessie in *The Stick Wife*, Lillian, the matriarch of the family, tries to shut out ugliness by insisting on shutting the front window's blinds, as if such willed ignorance offers protection from the terrors of contemporary reality.

Cloud humorously shows such efforts to be futile. The coroner Norman Bird (a nod here to Hitchcock's Norman Bates), enters late in the first act and to Lillian's horror tracks mud from the murder site all over the carpets. Unfortunately, Cloud's dramatic energy soon spins out of control: as body-bags sprout in the living room and the catatonic grandmother returns to consciousness, a heavy-handed Freudian family feud ensues that reads like a second-rate Albee one-act. Yet within this morass Cloud still manages to summon powerful imagery to state her themes—at the point Grandma crawls into a body-bag, a succinct metaphor for American's willingness to view its elders as disposable. Although occurring in an early and uneven play, such hilarious and heartbreaking moments help mark Cloud as a playwright of original and incisive vision.

—John Istel

CLUCHEY, (Douglas) Rick(land).

Born in Chicago, Illinois, 5 December 1933. Served in the U.S. Army, 1949–51. Married Teri Cluchey in 1951; one son and one daughter. Convicted of armed robbery in 1955; sentenced to life imprisonment at San Quentin State Prison, California; paroled, 1966. Founder and executive director, San Quentin Prison Theatre Group, 1957–66.

Publications

PLAYS

The Cage (produced 1965). 1970.
The Wall Is Mama (produced 1974).
The Bug, with R.S. Bailey (produced 1974).

THEATRICAL ACTIVITIES

DIRECTOR: **Plays**—*In the Zone* by Eugene O'Neill, *Hughie* by Eugene O'Neill, *The Caretaker* by Harold Pinter, *Deathwatch* by Jean Genet, *Krapp's Last Tape* by Samuel Beckett, *The Cage, The Wall Is Mama, The Iceman Cometh* by Eugene O'Neill, *The Execution of Eddie Slovik, Escurial* by Michel de Ghelderode, and *Don Juan in Hell* by Shaw, 1957–75; *Endgame* by Samuel Beckett, London, 1978.

ACTOR: **Plays**—in his own directed plays, and in *Stalag 17* by Donald Bevan and Edmund Trzcinski, *Time Limit* by Henry Denker and Ralph Berkey, *Room Service* by John Murray and Allen Boretz, *Of Mice and Men* by John Steinbeck, *Inherit the Wind* by Jerome Lawrence and Robert E. Lee, *Brother Orchid, Waiting for Godot* by Samuel Beckett, *The Dock Brief* by John Mortimer, *Endgame* by Samuel Beckett, *The Advocate* by Robert Noah, *The Brig* by Kenneth H. Brown, *The Dumb Waiter* by Harold Pinter, *People Need People* by H.F. Greenberg, *Krapp's Last Tape* by Samuel Beckett, and *The Bug*, 1957–77; 5 roles in *Edmond* by David Mamet, 1982.

Rick Cluchey comments:

(1977) I became involved with theatre while serving time at San Quentin. Prior to November 1957, no live drama had been seen within the walls of the prison since the turn of the century when Sarah Bernhardt's troupe entertained the convicts. Thus, when the San Francisco Actors Workshop production of Samuel Beckett's *Waiting for Godot* was staged in our north dining hall, the several hundred inmates who saw the play fairly howled their satisfaction, and the Warden gave his approval to the formation of our own drama group. Our theatrical program took time developing. Drama activity was in the main looked upon as something for sissies and homosexuals, child molesters and rapists. This attitude took time to overcome, but the program gradually gained acceptance and approval. Since no female was allowed to participate, and no inmates were allowed to impersonate females, we were limited to plays with all-male casts.

I began as an actor, and for several years (with the help of Al Mandell and, later, Ken Kitch of the San Francisco Actors Workshop) studied acting and directing. Since plays were difficult to find, I began to investigate possibilities of adapting plays for our use. I discovered that the plays of Beckett appeared void of any expository elements and seemed to take on wholly their own reality. There followed a period of several years when we experimented with the works of Beckett, producing *Waiting for Godot*, *Endgame*, and *Krapp's Last Tape*. We staged productions twice a year for the general public, and weekly for inmates. Martin Esslin visited the workshop in 1963 and was impressed that we were preparing John Mortimer's *The Dock Brief*, and sent us Mrozek's early play *Out at Sea*, which we also produced. Other productions were Solzhenitsyn's *One Day in the Life of Ivan Denisovich* and Kenneth H. Brown's *The Brig*.

Throughout the decade of theatre activity at San Quentin, the inmates themselves were directly responsible for all aspects of production. Outside professional assistance was welcome and warmly received, but only on an advisory level. As a theatre the workshop was committed to social and political themes; oddly the focus of much of this activity, although censored by the prison staff, seemed to point to conditions outside the walls of our own prison. But certainly prison as such was an ongoing theme, although nothing could directly be said of our own four-walled hell.

Sadly the San Quentin workshop was closed down in 1967, though almost all of the convicts who'd worked to bring the program to fruition had already been paroled. In May 1967 the first outside production of the Quentin group was staged in Walnut Creek, California, the beginning of a ten-year journey.

Though Rick Cluchey has lived in relative freedom since December 1966, when he was paroled from his life sentence, he remains metaphorically in prison. Not only is the underworld the subject of his three plays, but he responds as director to confined spaces in which passions rise to explosion. Innocent of orthography and syntax, he writes of the world he knows in the idiom he knows.

While Cluchey was still in San Quentin prison, he composed *The Cage* for performance by the prison theatre group. "We asked the Warden for permission to perform the play," recalls Cluchey, "and he said fine—as long as it isn't about my prison." So Cluchey set his play in France, and the Warden exclaimed after the performance: "I had no idea French prisons were so bad." Though Cluchey had read Genet, the prison was his very own.

Cluchey has reworked the play, but the kernel remains invariant: Jive, a college graduate charged with murdering his girlfriend, is imprisoned in the same "cage" as three lifers—ex-prize fighter Doc, crippled homosexual Al, and mad Hatchet. Both Doc and Al make advances to the newcomer, but Hatchet, whose insanity takes a virulently religious form, places Jive on trial. Hatchet's two cell-mates are accustomed to lending themselves to his fixations and they play Jive's defense counsel and prosecuting attorney. Hatchet is both judge and executioner, finally sentencing Jive to death and strangling him on stage. As Hatchet washes his murderous hands in the toilet-bowl, he addresses the gods: "I have done your will," but then points into the audience to conclude the play: "Your will."

The Wall Is Mama is nominally set outside prison, in the shady darkness of Mother's Bar on the Bowery in New York City. However, the characters have been in prison and are still caged by their criminal past. Duke, a black heroin user and dealer, claims to have kicked dope and is encouraged by his ex-mistress, bar owner Bea. However, two white members of the dope ring believe he has siphoned off heroin for his own use, and they torture him to reveal its whereabouts. Nearly unconscious with pain, Duke nevertheless defies them until Bea seizes their gun and drives them from her bar. In Act 2, several hours later, a homosexual addict seduces a Marine in the presence of Duke, Bea, and a pseudo-preacher. The Marine addresses Duke much as did the gang killers. In a dope trance, Duke then reverts to childhood, seeing Bea as his mother. As she cuddles him, the white killers shoot both. For these rejects of society, the wall *is* mama.

The Bug, written with R.S. Bailey, a San Quentin colleague, is a work in progress. A woman is harassed by obscene phone calls. Two policemen hide in an adjoining apartment, with electronic equipment that will ostensibly identify the source of the calls. But the play merges invasion of privacy into alleged obscenity.

Circumstances have walled Cluchey's life, but he has exchanged the enclosed space of prison for the enclosed space of theatre—an exchange that has liberated him and deepened public perception of prison-fostered brutalities.

—Ruby Cohn

CONGDON, Constance S.

Born in Rock Rapids, Iowa, 26 November 1944. Educated at Garden City High School, Kansas, 1963; University of Colorado, Colorado Springs, B.A. 1969; University of Massachusetts, Amherst, M.A., M.F.A. 1981. Married Glenn H. Johnson, Jr. in 1971; one son. Car hop, Bob's A & W Root Beer, 1960–63, columnist, Garden City Telegram, 1962–3, and grocery checker, Wall's IGA, 1963–65, all in Garden City; library clerk, Pikes Peak Regional District Library, 1965–66; library clerk, University of Colorado, 1966–69, and leather worker, What Rough Beast, 1969–70, all Colorado Springs; instructor in remedial writing, St. Mary's College of Maryland, St. Mary's City, 1974–76; instructor in rhetorical writing, University of Massachusetts, Amherst, 1977–81; instructor in English composition and theatre, Western New England College, Springfield, Massachusetts, 1981–83; literary manager, 1981–88, and playwright-in-residence, 1984–88, Hartford Stage Company, Connecticut, 1984–88. Recipient: American College Theatre Festival National Playwriting award, 1981; Great American Play Contest prize, 1985; National Endowment for the Arts fellowship, 1986–87; Rockefeller award, 1988; Arnold Weissberger award, 1988; Dramalogue award, 1990; Oppenheimer award, 1990; Guggenheim fellowship, 1991. Agent: Peter Franklin, William Morris Agency, 1350 Avenue of the Americas, New York, New York 10019, U.S.A.

Publications

PLAYS

Gilgamesh (produced 1977).
Fourteen Brilliant Colors (produced 1977).

The Bride (produced 1980).
Native American (produced 1984).
No Mercy (produced 1986). 1985; in *Seven Different Plays*; edited by Mac Wellman, 1988.
The Gilded Age, adaptation of the novel by Mark Twain (produced 1986).
Raggedy Ann and Andy (for children), adaptation of the books by Johnny Gruelle, music by Hiram Titus (produced 1987).
A Conversation with Georgia O'Keeffe (produced 1987).
Tales of the Lost Formicans (produced 1988). 1990.
Rembrandt Takes a Walk (for children), adaptation of the book by Mark Strand and Red Grooms (produced 1989). In *Plays in Process 4: Plays for Young Audiences*, vol.10 no.12, 1989.
Casanova (produced 1989).
Time Out of Time (produced 1990).
Mother Goose (for children), music by Hiram Titus (produced 1990).
The Miser, adaptation of the play by Molière (produced 1990).
Madeline's Rescue (for children), adaptation of the book by Ludwig Bemelmans, music by Mel Marvin (produced 1990).
Beauty and the Beast (for children; produced 1992).

CRITICAL STUDIES: "An Interview with Constance Congdon" by Nancy Klementowski and Sonja Kuftinec, in *Studies in American Drama*, vol.4, 1989; "Constance Congdon: A Playwright Whose Time Has Come" by Susan Hussey, in *Organica*, Winter 1990; "Trying to Find a Culture: An Interview with Connie Congdon" by Lisa Wilde, in *Yale/Theatre*, vol.22 no.1, Winter 1990; article by Craig Gholson, in *Bomb*, Fall 1991; "Connie's *Casanova*" by M. Elizabeth Osborn, in *Theatre Week*, June 3–9, 1991.

Constance Congdon comments:

I have an eclectic taste in theatre, although I usually hate everything I see on Broadway. My main influences are Thornton Wilder, The Wooster Group, Caryl Churchill, also rhythm and blues and country western music, Richard Wilbur, Joni Mitchell. The American critical scene is still culturally embarrassed and defensive and trying to be something it's not—cold, cynical, politically strident, trying to out-European the changing Europeans. The American art scene is still dominated by too many people from "good" schools who have intellectual agendas that have nothing to do with what I go to theatre for. I go to have an experience that taps the mystery of living, one that comes from great passion on the part of the artist, one that has something to do with awakening or calling up the spirit that is in every theatre.

I come from about as far away from the Ivy League as is possible and am proud of it. I see myself more as an "outside artist"—one of those people who makes sculpture out of car parts in their backyard. I don't live in New York although I enjoy going in to see the work of my friends which is very good and usually found in small theatres painted flat black with bad seats and great risk or big fun (or both) going on onstage.

When I start to write a play, I imagine an empty theatre space and see who or what turns up—this is my opening image and, if I mess with it, I always pay for it and lose my way in the play. I feel that the first things I create in a new play are like coded messages for the rest of the play, and I just return to them for clues about the rest of the play. The code is in metaphor, image, and given circumstances and I just need to see it. In *Native American*—the only naturalistic play I ever wrote—I saw, very clearly, the image of a cowboy lying face down on a couch with a sheet covering him. I also saw that the couch was outside on a porch. Then I saw an old Hudson automobile up on blocks. Some of these images were memories, I realize now, but at the time, they seemed all new and rich. Why the cowboy was on the couch, face down, gave me, bit by bit, the story and then the theme. I also knew that the play had to take place in consecutive real time. I trust these early strong impulses.

I need to entertain myself and surprise myself, so my plays are usually different from each other in style—I don't like to repeat myself. I make my living doing adaptations, and I don't recommend it to young playwrights, but it's better, for me, than teaching or trying to get media work.

Constance Congdon was a published poet before she was a playwright. Her plays come to her as a series of images; they are made up of many small scenes, sometimes comic, often emotionally direct, with dialogue that goes straight to the heart of the matter. When these scenes are linked together, the result reflects the world's true complexity.

Though the lives of ordinary decent people, the pleasure and pain of sexuality, the damaging effects of gender stereotypes are primary Congdon concerns, her central subject is loss. Her very first play was a dramatization of *The Epic of Gilgamesh*, at its heart the inconsolable grief of the hero at the death of his beloved friend Enkidu. The award-winning drama *No Mercy* deals with the testing of the first atomic bomb and its after-effects, but it is fundamentally about faith, and the loss of faith—in science, in religion, in life itself. Watching the scientist J. Robert Oppenheimer cross and recross the stage—the play takes place in 1945 and 1985 simultaneously, and he is lost in time—we wonder if he is dreaming this world, whose other inhabitants are the kind of undistinguished Americans this writer lovingly brings to life. Our uncertainty about who rules the play's universe is part of the point: we are watching characters lose *their* certainty, then pick themselves up and go on.

By far the most successful of Congdon's plays to date is *Tales of the Lost Formicans*, which looks at the life of contemporary suburbia through the eyes of aliens, a perspective which shows this taken-for-granted world to be complicated, mysterious, and absurd. Behind this tragicomedy lies the death of Congdon's father, many years ago, from what we now call Alzheimer's disease, but the play is really about *America's* Alzheimer's. The father in *Formicans* is far from the only character who's confused. His recently divorced daughter has moved back home with her teenaged son, who expresses in pure form the anger and distress everyone in the play feels. By donning sunglasses the play's actors become the aliens who are trying to make sense of this disoriented civilization; *Formicans* suggests that we ourselves are the aliens, attempting to distance ourselves from our own feeling. Finally we're not sure whether "real" aliens are "really" telling the story; as in *No Mercy*, this not knowing reflects our actual position in the actual world.

The opening words of Congdon's *Casanova* are the scream of a young woman in labor: "What—is—LOVE!" The playwright's answer to this most fundamental of questions is characteristically complex. An epic play not quite under control at its first showing, *Casanova* is Congdon's richest text, and may one day be seen as a revelation of the way of our own world.

Casanova's focus on sexuality and gender was presaged by an early play, *The Bride*, which brings to mind both *Our Town* and *Spring Awakening* in its depiction of the sexual awakening of four teenagers during the 1950s. In *Casanova* Congdon uses more than 60 years of her central character's life to present the full range of sexuality in men, women, and children. The famous lover is played by two actors: during the first act the old man who is writing his memoirs watches the irresistible boy he once was; after intermission Young Casanova is horrified to witness what he has become.

Congdon's *Casanova* is a feminist corrective to those one-sided memoirs; the author's deepest sympathy goes to the very young girls this man loves and leaves. Yet Young Casanova is almost wholly appealing; Congdon sees that his society gives him permission to behave as he does, that he is not so different from other men. She shows us the complicity of women: having no other power, mothers pimp their daughters, using their beauty and virginity for their own ends. The older Casanova commits monstrous acts, including rape and child seduction, but at the same time we see that he is aging, frightened, as trapped in his sexual role as any female.

In *Casanova* bedrock biological difference makes women inevitably vulnerable. Yet there is hope in the play, and it lies in those characters who transcend the usual limits of gender. The two women who come through their encounters with Casanova unscathed are bisexual, and the play's exemplar of lasting devotion is Bobo, an aging transvestite. Once tutor to Casanova's daughter, Bobo is still taking care of her 30 years later. He is Casanova's equal and opposite force, and the most memorable incarnation yet of Congdon's special feeling for gay men.

Congdon's talent flows in many directions. Her poetic gift lends itself to opera librettos; her comic sense has enlivened a series of delightful plays for the Children's Theatre of Minneapolis. Her one-woman piece about painter Georgia O'Keeffe lets her speak of her own love of the West and her complicated feeling about the position of women artists. What knowledgeable theatre people across the country have said for years is becoming more widely known: Constance Congdon is one of the most original and revelatory writers in the American theatre today.

—M. Elizabeth Osborn

CONNELLY, Marc(us Cook).

Born in McKeesport, Pennsylvania, 13 December 1890. Educated at Trinity Hall, Washington, Pennsylvania, 1902–07. Married Madeline Hurlock in 1930 (divorced, 1935). Reporter and drama critic, Pittsburgh *Press* and *Gazette-Times*, 1908–15; moved to New York, 1915: freelance writer and actor, 1915–33; reporter, New York *Morning Telegraph*, 1918–21; helped found the *New Yorker*, 1925; wrote screenplays and directed in Hollywood,

1933–44; professor of playwriting, Yale University Drama School, New Haven, Connecticut, 1947–52; U.S. commissioner to Unesco, 1951; adviser, Equity Theatre Library, 1960. Council member, Dramatists Guild, from 1920; member of the executive committee, U.S. National Committee for Unesco. Recipient: Pulitzer prize, 1930; O. Henry award, for short story, 1930. President, Authors League of America and National Institute of Arts and Letters, 1953–56. *Died 21 December 1980.*

Publications

PLAYS

$2.50 (produced 1913).

The Lady of Luzon (lyrics only), book by Alfred Ward Birdsall, music by Zoel Parenteau (produced 1914).

Follow the Girl (lyrics only, uncredited; produced 1915).

The Amber Empress, music by Zoel Parenteau (produced 1916; as *The Amber Princess*, produced 1917).

Dulcy, with George S. Kaufman (produced 1921). 1921.

Erminie, revised version of the play by Henry Paulton (produced 1921).

To the Ladies!, with George S. Kaufman (produced 1922). 1923.

No, Sirree!, with George S. Kaufman (produced 1922).

The 49ers, with George S. Kaufman (produced 1922).

West of Pittsburgh, with George S. Kaufman (produced 1922; revised version, as *The Deep Tangled Wildwood*, produced 1923).

Merton of the Movies, with George S. Kaufman, from the story by Harry Leon Wilson (produced 1922). 1925.

A Christmas Carol, with George S. Kaufman, from the story by Dickens. In *Bookman*, December 1922.

Helen of Troy, New York, with George S. Kaufman, music and lyrics by Harry Ruby and Bert Kalmar (produced 1923).

Beggar on Horseback, with George S. Kaufman, music by Deems Taylor, from a play by Paul Apel (produced 1924). 1925.

Be Yourself, with George S. Kaufman, music and lyrics by Lewis Genzler and Milton Schwarzwald, additional lyrics by Ira Gershwin (produced 1924).

The Wisdom Tooth: A Fantastic Comedy (produced 1926). 1927.

The Wild Man of Borneo, with Herman J. Mankiewicz (produced 1927).

How's the King? (produced 1927).

The Green Pastures: A Fable Suggested by Roark Bradford's Southern Sketches "Ol' Man Adam an' His Chillun" (produced 1930). 1929.

The Survey (skit). In *New Yorker*, 1934.

The Farmer Takes a Wife, with Frank B. Elser, from the novel *Rome Haul* by Walter D. Edmonds (produced 1934). Abridgement in *Best Plays of 1934–1935*, 1935.

Little David: An Unproduced Scene from "The Green Pastures." 1937.

The Good Earth, with others, (screenplay). In *Twenty Best Film Plays*, edited by John Gassner and Dudley Nichols, 1943.

Everywhere I Roam, with Arnold Sundgaard (produced 1938).

The Traveler. 1939.

The Mole on Lincoln's Cheek (broadcast 1941). In *The Free Company Presents*, edited by James Boyd, 1941.

The Flowers of Virtue (produced 1942).
A Story for Strangers (produced 1948).
Hunter's Moon (produced 1958).
The Portable Yenberry (produced 1962).
The Green Pastures (screenplay), edited by Thomas Cripps, 1979.
The Stitch in Time (produced 1981).

SCREENPLAYS: *Whispers*, 1920; *Exit Smiling*, with others, 1926; *The Bridegroom, The Burglar, The Suitor*, and *The Uncle* (film shorts), 1929; *The Unemployed Ghost* (film short), 1931; *The Cradle Song*, 1933; *The Little Duchess* (film short), 1934; *The Green Pastures*, 1936; *The Farmer Takes a Wife*, 1937; *Captains Courageous*, with John Lee Mahin and Dale Van Emery, 1937; *The Good Earth*, with others, 1937; *I Married a Witch*, with Robert Pirosh, 1942; *Reunion (Reunion in France)*, with others, 1942; *The Imposter* (additional dialogue), 1944; *Fabiola* (English dialogue), 1951; *Crowded Paradise* (additional scenes), 1956.

RADIO PLAYS: *The Mole on Lincoln's Cheek*, 1941.

NOVEL
A Souvenir from Qam. 1965.

OTHER
Voices Off-Stage: A Book of Memoirs. 1968.

CRITICAL STUDY: *Marc Connelly* by Paul T. Nolan, 1969.

Marc Connelly attracted attention between 1920 and 1924 as co-author with George S. Kaufman of several popular social comedies about contemporary America, beginning with *Dulcy*. *To the Ladies!* seems more original in apparently celebrating the business acumen of women, but, for all its mockery of male superiority, it is unregenerately chauvinistic. The woman's role, except for one improbably successful impromptu after-dinner speech, is as the supportive wife, winning advancement for her husband by what is presented as persuasive advocacy, but in fact is an opportunist piece of near-blackmail, reinforced by sentimentality. That the husband seems congenitally unlikely to succeed in the post she secures for him is ignored entirely, as is the unlikelihood of the employer's gullible blindness to the man's manifestly inept mediocrity. Described once as "a hilarious American counterpart to Barrie's *What Every Woman Knows*" (written 14 years earlier), the play's greatest merit is having brought Helen Hayes into starring prominence. It was followed by *Merton of the Movies* and the unpublished musical *Helen of Troy*, both equally popular.

   In *Beggar on Horseback* a less ambivalent satiric aim comes at least nearer to realisation. The authors' established association with the smart set of New York humorists known as the Algonquin Wits gave the dialogue a sharper edge and guaranteed a receptive audience, but the preface to the published text, by one of the best-known of the group, Alexander Woollcott, is over-generous. The most inventive of their joint plays, though based on a German original, it contrasts the impecunious insecurity of the artist's integrity with the monied attractions of a capitalist business world. It contains a dream-sequence with elements of surrealism and expressionism which gave it, in 1924, an avant-garde interest, but which could have been more tightly controlled and better exploited. Like two Sinclair Lewis novels, *Main Street* and *Babbitt*, the play promises a vigorous satire on the "booster" American business ethic of the 1920s and has the necessary witty acuteness of observation. Had Connelly accepted Lewis's invitations to partner him in play-writing, however, their joint products would have been as limited as their individual works: both writers are among what Lewis revealingly called "those of us who hesitated about being drafted into the army of complacency". Satire cannot be satisfactorily based on mere hesitation. Neither, for all its imaginative vitality, can *Beggar on Horseback* be claimed, as it sometimes is, to be an important progenitor of the "theatre of the absurd": here again, it tries to ride on the backs of two different horses at once.

The Kaufman-Connelly partnership ended amicably in 1924, after they had followed *Beggar on Horseback* with *Be Yourself*, their second musical. Connelly wrote on his own, between 1925 and 1930, two more comedies, a musical comedy, a series of ten one-act plays, and numerous short stories, including some for the *New Yorker*, which he helped to found. He also acted in and directed the plays of others. The only readily-accessible piece of his writing of this period is an undistinguished one-acter, *The Traveler*. Its hero is seen leaving Grand Central Station on the Twentieth Century Limited, the Chicago express. After brief but enthusiastic conversations with two of the train's staff he alights with his luggage at its first stop, 125th Street, still in New York City. We are to see his short trip home as invested with a glamour that will sustain him until he can afford to repeat it in a year's time, but the suburban little man's pathetic zest for new experience is neither comic nor moving.

For the small-town Pennsylvanian grandson of an Irish Catholic immigrant to be remembered primarily for an all-black play based on the unsophisticated religion of the ethnic minority in the American South seems wildly improbable, yet it was as the author of *The Green Pastures* that Connelly became known internationally. That it is hard to imagine a successful revival of the play now is less a sign of progress than a matter of regret. Its artless translation of Old Testament stories into the idiom and ethic of a race but lately itself delivered from slavery is neither as patronising, as *faux-naif*, nor as reactionary as it would be judged today. To Connelly it was "an attempt to present certain aspects of a living religion in the terms of its believers". He acknowledged the "terrific spiritual hunger and the greatest humility" with which "these untutored black Christians . . . have adapted the contents of the Bible to the consistencies of their everyday lives", and 1930s audiences accepted it in that spirit. Comparisons have been drawn with the medieval English mystery plays when, for example, a heavenly celebration resembling a Louisiana Sunday School treat is initiated by "de Lawd God Jehovah", incarnate as a black minister, solemnly pronouncing, "Let de fish fry proceed". Major critics compared it favourably with its acknowledged source, Roark Bradford's original fiction *Ol' Man Adam an' His Chillun*, and responded warmly to the integrity of its concept and its sympathetic image of the blacks. The humour, the inventiveness, the interweaving of text with serio-comic spectacle and the music of the spirituals, and the directness of the piece, however sentimental and over-long, sufficiently explain its original popularity but would probably embarrass today's audiences.

It is inevitable, if less than wholly fair, to remember Connelly only as the author of *The Green Pastures*. His most carefully researched work, it is undeniably his greatest artistic achievement. Easy-going and enthusiastic, he continued to spread his energy over an area too wide for the good of his reputation, and there is less social philosophy than nostalgic complacency in his work. The small-town attitude to life that underlay the Algonquin wit was symbolised in his acting success in the 1940s in the role of the Stage Manager in the New York and London productions of Thornton Wilder's *Our Town*.

—Dennis Welland

COWEN, Ron(ald).

Born in Cincinnati, Ohio, 15 September 1944. Educated at the University of California, Los Angeles, B.A. in English 1966; Annenberg School of Communications, University of Pennsylvania, Philadelphia, 1967–68. Taught classes in theatre at New York University, Fall 1969. Associate trustee, University of Pennsylvania. Recipient: Wesleyan University fellowship, 1968; Vernon Rice award, 1968; Emmy award, 1986, and Peabody award, 1986, for television play. Lives in Pacific Palisades, California. Agent: William Morris Agency, 151 El Camino, Beverly Hills, California 90212, U.S.A.

Publications

PLAYS

Summertree (produced 1967). 1968.

Valentine's Day (produced 1968; revised version, music by Saul Naishtat, produced 1975).

Saturday Adoption (televised 1968; produced 1978). 1969.

Porcelain Time (produced 1972).

The Book of Murder (televised 1974).1974.

Lulu, adaptation of plays by Wedekind (produced 1974; as *Inside Lulu*, produced 1975).

TELEVISION PLAYS: *Saturday Adoption*, 1968; *The Book of Murder*, 1974; *Paul's Case*, from the story by Willa Cather, 1977; *I'm a Fool*, from the story by Sherwood Anderson, 1979; *An Early Frost*, with Daniel Lipman, 1985.

The ethical crisis arising from America's involvement in the Vietnam war was a major concern for American writers in the 1960s. *Summertree*, the most successful American play of the decade to deal with this subject, was written by Ron Cowen at the age of twenty. (David Rabe's *The Basic Training of Pavlo Hummel* and *Sticks and Bones* may prove to be more significant works, but they appeared after the initial national tension over the war had peaked.) *Summertree*, which was widely produced and made into a Hollywood film, was perhaps successful more because of its timeliness than its intrinsic worth.

The play is an excessively sentimental telling of an inconsequential young man's death and life in Vietnam. As the protagonist (Young Man) lies fatally wounded under a jungle tree, he hallucinates flashback episodes from his civilian and military experience: sometimes he is twenty, sometimes he is ten. The jungle tree becomes the backyard tree in which he once built a treehouse. His recollections are of his Mother and Father, his Girl and his Buddy (Soldier). These characters are drawn by Cowen in broad strokes that critics of the production were prone to see as American archetypes: the essential constellation of personae. A critic of a less emotionally charged era is prone to see them as uninspired caricatures.

The play's most successful attribute is its three-act, cinematic structure which provides a degree of dramatic irony and gives the play substance. Its least successful is its banal dialogue. When the Young Man says to his father, late in the final act, "I want to tell the back yard goodbye," there is a cloying sentimentality which renders the moment bathetic. Yet for an audience tired of both the brutality of the war and the hysteria of the anti-war protests which shook the land in 1967, the play (and even its dialogue) struck sympathetic chords.

The play is a product of its cultural climate in yet another sense. It was written by Cowen while he was a student at the University of Pennsylvania. When the play was first presented, in the summer of 1967 at the Eugene O'Neill Memorial Theatre Foundation in Waterford, Connecticut, it underwent major re-writings at the request of its director. As it was prepared for New York production by the Repertory Theater of Lincoln Center, additional changes were introduced. The play—far more than the average commercial project—became the reflection of many concerned person's attitudes towards the war. Small wonder it found a receptive ear and was awarded the Vernon Rice award for that turbulent year. (When the movie script was being prepared this procedure got out of control. Cowen wrote a first screenplay, Rod McKuen was hired to do a second, and the shooting script was finally the work of Hollywood pros Edward Hume and Stephen Yafa. The final script owes shockingly little to Cowen's initial intentions, images, or characters.)

Cowen's subsequent career has been somewhat erratic. In 1968 *Saturday Adoption* was telecast on CBS Playhouse and in 1974 ABC aired *The Book of Murder*. Both were critical failures. The first dealt with a socially conscious young man's failures to change the world through his father's money or his pupil's achievements; the second is a coy murder mystery. Cowen's trademarks are easily seen in both: the cinematic structure, the sentimental and nostalgic tone, the domestic circumstance, the conflict over money. His weaknesses are in evidence as well: the badly motivated actions, the clichéd characters, and the clumsy dialogue which the critic for *Variety* called "goody two-shoes language." *I'm a Fool*, a television adaptation of Sherwood Anderson's story, was more successful, and *An Early Frost* won an Emmy award.

Cowen has completed subsequent stage scripts, but none has been given major production. He assisted on the book for *Billy* which flopped on Broadway in 1968. His musical *Valentine's Day* was show-cased at the Manhattan Theatre Club in 1975 but reviewed as an "unsatisfying experience." It included the Cowensque line, "I want to tell the apartment goodbye." *Inside Lulu* was a banal work, loosely based on the Wedekind plays, and created by Section Ten, the off-off-Broadway improvisational group. Cowen was their literary collaborator.

In retrospect, *Summertree* appears very much to be in the tradition of television soap opera and it is appropriate that Cowen should continue to write for the television medium. As long as his language, characters and situations remain banal, autobiographical, and domestic it is unlikely he will produce a major work. *Summertree* appears to have been less the work of a *wunderkind* than a timely reflection of a culture's anxieties.

—Thomas B. Markus

CRISTOFER, Michael.

Pseudonym for Michael Procaccino. Born in White Horse, New Jersey, 22 January 1945. Educated at Catholic University, Washington, D.C., 1962–65; American University, Beirut, 1968–69. Recipient: Los Angeles Drama Critics Circle award, for acting, 1973, for playwriting, 1975; Pulitzer prize, 1977; Tony award, 1977; Obie award, for acting, 1980. Agent: Joyce Ketay Agency, 334 West 39th Street, New York, New York 10024, U.S.A.

Publications

PLAYS

The Mandala (produced 1968).
Plot Counter Plot (produced 1971).
Americomedia (produced 1973).
The Shadow Box (produced 1975). 1977.
Ice (produced 1976).
Black Angel (produced 1978). 1984.
C.C. Pyle and the Bunyon Derby (produced 1978).
The Lady and the Clarinet (produced 1980). 1985.
Love Me Or Leave Me, adaptation of the screenplay by Isobel Lennart and Daniel Fuchs (produced 1989).

SCREENPLAYS: *Falling in Love*, 1985; *The Witches of Eastwick*, 1987.

THEATRICAL ACTIVITIES

DIRECTOR: **Plays**—*Candida* by Shaw, 1981; *Forty-Deuce* by Alan Bowne, 1981.
ACTOR: **Plays**—roles at the Arena Stage, Washington, D.C., 1967–68, Theatre of Living Arts, Philadelphia, 1968, and Beirut Repertory Company, Lebanon, 1968–69; in *Yegor Bulichov* by Gorky, 1970–71; Jules in *The Justice Box* by Michael Robert Davis, 1971; *The Tooth of Crime* by Sam Shepard, 1973; *Ajax* by Sophocles, 1974; Colin in *Ashes* by David Rudkin, 1976; *The Three Sisters* by Chekhov, 1976; *Savages* by Christopher Hampton, Trofimov in *The Cherry Orchard* by Chekhov, 1976; Charlie in *Conjuring an Event* by Richard Nelson, 1978; title role in *Chinchilla* by Robert David MacDonald, 1979. **Films**—*An Enemy of the People*, 1976; *The Little Drummer Girl*, 1984. **Television**—*Sandburg's Lincoln*, 1975; *Crime Club*, 1975; *The Last of Mrs. Lincoln*, 1975; *The Entertainer*, 1976; *Knuckle*, 1976.

Michael Cristofer's development as a playwright, a development that includes *Plot Counter Plot*, *The Mandala*, and *Americomedia* and climaxed with *The Shadow Box* (Pulitzer prize and Tony award), is as instructive a lesson in how to become a playwright as *The Shadow Box* is an exciting addition to recent American drama. Like Harold Pinter and certain other contemporary dramatists, Cristofer is a gifted actor—and, with the Circle in the Square production of Shaw's *Candida*, director—and his own practical experience with theater is everywhere apparent in the play's skillful theatricality. In addition his association with the Mark Taper Forum and its director Gordon Davidson has provided a unifying center. The coalescence of three one-act plays through a series of workshops into a single contrapuntal drama, *The Shadow Box* is a process seldom possible without a secure producing environment.

The play, apparently based upon the terminal illness of two friends and Kubler-Ross's research into the state of mind of dying patients, demonstrates how the shadow of death intensifies life, merges individuality into community, and reduces times and places into a single here and now. Perhaps reflecting its origin as three draft one-act plays, *The Shadow Box* is built upon threes. Cristofer presents a trinity of characters, each surrounded by two other characters important in his personal life: Joe, a blue-collar worker, his wife, and adolescent son; Brian, an extravagant writer-intellectual, his lover, and his former wife; and Felicity, a lady of uncertain age, and both her spinster daughter and her dead daughter whose imaginary letters keep her alive. The play's set seems also to be in triplicate: three vacation cottages in the woods in a medically and psychologically controlled estate for the dying, each cottage with "*A front porch, a living room area, and a large kitchen area.*" But it is through the set's omnipresent visual image, and the constant cross-cutting this makes possible, that death's power to reduce diversity to communality and a common ground is constantly reiterated: the three cottages are in effect presented as one, and the trio of characters, who never actually meet, alternately inhabit, as the lights go down and come up, the various playing areas. The pastoral setting and the domesticity made possible by the cottage also unobtrusively place death in the context of external nature and the echoes of everyday life.

If Cristofer has a sure theatrical sense and a feeling for essential dimensions of the human experience, he also has a sense for the other indispensable ingredient of drama: language. Like a number of recent dramatists he has deliberately attempted to reverse the trend toward non-verbal theater—really the concern of dance—that characterized so much drama in the 1960s and early 1970s. The movement made important contributions but forgot the necessity to be memorably articulate. Cristofer's concern for verbal complexity is apparent immediately in the title *The Shadow Box*. In modern drama especially, titles index a play's concerns, and this one works on several complementary levels of reference. It refers to a late 19th-century device in which figures were superimposed against a chosen landscape or setting. The stationary quality of such scenes and their arbitrary arrangement express the predetermined situation of the terminally ill who are placed in a deliberately arranged environment. The term, which refers as well to a method of covering a motion picture screen so that film can be shown in daylight, expresses the play's analysis of the usually unseen, and the verb "to shadow box" connotes a fight, like the fight with death, which is ultimately an illusion. If the play begins with an emphasis upon words, it ends with an extraordinary "coda" in which life is celebrated in the face of death. The characters speak in choral fashion exchanging brief words and phrases and conclude with repetitions of the affirmative "Yes" and the final "This moment."

   Ice is set in a cabin in Alaska and shows a trio of characters caught in a situation that symbolizes death in life. The subsequent *Black Angel* and *The Lady and the Clarinet* have now been seen in New York, but these somewhat counterpart plays do not sustain the promise of *The Shadow Box*. The former studies a man, Martin Engel, an apparent Nazi war criminal, and analyzes "hate," and the latter is a portrait of a woman, Luba, and her experiences with "love." Both plays interestingly suppress facts and narrative clarity and make use of simultaneous time, but in neither case are the central characters themselves created in enough depth or uniqueness to occasion or to support the playwright's relentless analyses of them. But these plays do continue Cristofer's important interest in the collaborative arts of theater.

—Gaynor F. Bradish

CROTHERS, Rachel.

Born in Bloomington, Illinois, 12 December 1878. Educated at Illinois State University Normal High School, Bloomington, graduated 1891; New England School of Dramatic Instruction, certificate 1892; Stanhope-Wheatcroft School of Acting, New York, 1897. Elocution teacher, Bloomington, 1892–96; teacher, Stanhope-Wheatcroft School, 1897–1901; founder, Stage Women's War Relief Fund, 1917; president, Stage Relief Fund, 1932–51; founder and first president, American Theatre Wing, and organized American Theatre Wing for War Relief, 1940. Recipient: Megrue prize, 1933; Chi Omega award, 1939. *Died 5 July 1958.*

Publications

PLAYS

Elizabeth (produced 1899).
Criss-Cross (produced 1899). 1904.
Mrs. John Hobbs (produced 1899).
The Rector (produced 1902). 1905.
Nora (produced 1903).
The Point of View (produced 1904).
The Three of Us (produced 1906). 1916.
The Coming of Mrs. Patrick (produced 1907).
Myself, Bettina (produced 1908).
Kiddie. 1909.
A Man's World (produced 1910). 1915.
He and She (produced 1911; as *The Herfords*, produced 1912). In *Representative American Plays*, 1917; revised edition, 1925.
Young Wisdom (produced 1914). 1913.
Ourselves (produced 1913).
The Heart of Paddy Whack (produced 1914). 1925.

Old Lady 31, from the novel by Louise Forsslund (produced 1916). In *Mary the Third*, 1923.
Mother Carey's Chickens, with Kate Douglas Wiggin, from the novel by Wiggin (produced 1917). 1925.
Once upon a Time (produced 1917). 1925.
A Little Journey (produced 1918). In *Mary the Third*, 1923.
39 East (produced 1919). In *Expressing Willie*, 1924.
Everyday (produced 1921). 1930.
Nice People (produced 1921). In *Expressing Willie*, 1924.
Mary the Third (produced 1923). In *Mary the Third*, 1923.
Mary the Third; Old Lady 31; A Little Journey: Three Plays. 1923.
Expressing Willie (produced 1924). In *Expressing Willie*, 1924.
Expressing Willie; Nice People; 39 East: Three Plays. 1924.
Six One-Act Plays (includes *The Importance of Being Clothed; The Importance of Being Nice; The Importance of Being Married; The Importance of Being a Woman; What They Think; Peggy*). 1925.
A Lady's Virtue (produced 1925). 1925.
Venus (produced 1927). 1927.
Let Us Be Gay (produced 1929). 1929.
As Husbands Go (produced 1931). 1931.
Caught Wet (produced 1931). 1932.
When Ladies Meet (produced 1932). 1932.
The Valiant One. 1937.
Susan and God (produced 1937). 1938.

SCREENPLAY: *Splendor*, 1935.

CRITICAL STUDY: *Rachel Crothers* by Lois C. Gottlieb, 1979.

THEATRICAL ACTIVITIES
Directed and staged her own plays.

Rachel Crothers was America's most successful woman playwright during the early decades of the 20th century. From the turn of the century until the late 1930s her plays were a staple of the New York stage, with productions of two dozen full-length works. Her career was made still more astonishing by the fact that she usually directed her own plays and sometimes produced, designed, and (in the case of the 1920 revival of *He and She*) starred in them. In an era when women directors were even rarer on Broadway than women playwrights, Brooks Atkinson of the *New York Times* called Crothers "one of the best directors we have".

Crothers was among the first American dramatists to attempt the problem play, already popular in Europe. These dramas comprise her most important early works and, in fact, may be her most enduring legacy to American drama. *A Man's World* is a perceptive look at the double standard of morality—an issue Crothers would continue to explore throughout her career. The heroine of the play is Frank Ware, an independent "New Woman", who is a writer, social activist, and single mother of an adopted son. When Frank eventually renounces her suitor, she does so not because he had impregnated a young single woman but because he fails to acknowledge that he, a man, shares equal responsibility for the consequences of their affair. Critics compared her rejection of him to Nora's slamming the door of her "doll's house" in Ibsen's play.

Also powerful, in different ways, is *He and She*, which presents the dilemma of a talented woman artist caught between her desires for a career and the needs of her teenage daughter. Although Crothers resolves the play along conventional lines—family taking priority over career—she is sensitive enough to present the difficulty of the choice involved, a choice being faced by more and more women of the period.

After a spate of cloyingly sentimental comedies like *Old Lady 31* (based on Louise Forsslund's novel) and *39 East*, Crothers turned to the form that would dominate the last two decades of her career and earn her great commercial success: social comedies about women of the upper and upper-middle classes. The action is typically set in an opulent house, and the dialogue—particularly toward the end of Crothers' career—is the witty repartee of high comedy. Although the works of the early 1920s tend to focus on flappers at odds with their parents, while the later ones center on more experienced women, they share a concern with the choices and challenges facing women in a world of shifting moral values.

Among the most effective of the plays of the 1920s is a dark comedy entitled *Mary the Third*. While Crothers' comedies usually end with that most conventional of conclusions, the uniting of hero and heroine, her picture of marriage is often so bleak that the traditional ending scarcely qualifies as a happy one. Young Mary has seen the flaws in her grandmother's marriage, a union based on wheedling and deception, as well as her parents' marriage, an angry clash of disparate personalities that her mother says went sour after only five years. Mary is an articulate spokeswoman for what Crothers believed was wrong with the American marriage: young people wed before they had a chance to know their prospective mates, and women's economic dependence kept them hostages to their husbands. When Mary finally accepts the proposal of her conservative suitor, responding to much the same urges that her mother and grandmother did, her decision can only be viewed with deep irony.

Numerous characters in Crothers' later plays comment on the prevalence of sexual affairs and divorce, reflecting the changing social climate in post-World-War-I America, but none of Crothers' heroines seems to find a satisfying alternative to the flawed institution of marriage. Kitty Brown, in *Let Us Be Gay*, divorces her unfaithful husband and then tries a life of sexual adventure herself, only to discover that neither free love nor a budding business career can replace the husband she still misses.

Crothers' last produced play was also her most successful: *Susan and God*, a satirical portrait of a woman infected by a European religious enthusiasm much like the Oxford Movement. A better effort—both more substantial and wittier—is *When Ladies Meet*. Ringing still one more change on the love triangle that is a virtual constant throughout her canon, the playwright presents talented, self-sufficient Mary Howard, a novelist in love with her married publisher, Rogers Woodruff. When Mary meets his wife, the two discover empathy for each other and a realization of how badly he has treated all women. Instead of forgiving him one more time, as conventional comedy would demand, Claire Woodruff abandons her husband because of his cruelty to Mary.

Rachel Crothers was very much a Broadway playwright: she considered the art theaters of the 1910s and 1920s a "very grave menace" to the New York stage, and her plays of the 1930s largely ignored the economic disaster that had struck the nation and the theatrical world. The author of well-crafted plays that are rarely structurally innovative, she proclaimed that "realism at its best . . . is the highest form of dramatic writing". Crothers' critique of a society that treats women unfairly comes from an often traditional point of view likely to alienate many late 20th-century audiences. Her "answer" to the question of the double standard is to hold both sexes to a rigid code of morality and, along with most of her generation, Crothers seems unable to imagine women successfully synthesizing career and family.

But if Crothers is scarcely the daring artist and feminist some defenders would claim her to be, neither is she simply a prolific crafter of conventional comedies. Like her character Mary Howard, who hoped in her writing to "say something *new* and *honest*—from a woman's standpoint", Crothers saw her work as a '*Comédie Humaine de la Femme*' that traces women's "evolution" in modern society. The best of her problem plays and comedies combine a genuine sense of what works on stage with a thoughtful investigation of such serious issues as the double standard, the conflict between career and domestic responsibility, the challenges of the new sexual freedom, the loneliness of the career woman, and the hollowness of many marriages—problems that time and the slow currents of social change have still not resolved.

—Judith E. Barlow

CROWLEY, Mart.

Born in Vicksburg, Mississippi, 21 August 1935. Educated at St. Aloysius High School, Vicksburg; Catholic University, Washington, D.C., graduated 1957. Worked for Martin Manulis Productions, 1963, and Four Star Television, 1964; Secretary to the actor Natalie Wood, 1964–66; from 1979 producer, *Hart to Hart*, television series. *Died 1991.*

Publications

PLAYS

The Boys in the Band (produced 1968). 1968.
Remote Asylum (produced 1970).
A Breeze from the Gulf (produced 1973). 1974.

SCREENPLAY: *The Boys in the Band*, 1970.

TELEVISION PLAY: *There Must Be a Pony*, from the novel by James Kirkwood, 1986.

Michael, the host of the homosexual birthday party in Mart Crowley's highly successful *The Boys in the Band*, through whose agency it becomes a shattering summation of all ironic birthdays, is also a character in Crowley's other two plays, *Remote Asylum* and *A Breeze from the Gulf*.

In *The Boys in the Band*, in the aftermath of his drunken manipulation and mockery of his friends, Michael's hysterical guilt quiets into the memory of his father dying in his arms with the words, "I don't understand any of it. I never did." In *Remote Asylum* this scene is re-enacted at an exotic clifftop mansion in Acapulco, where Michael is a guest. The wealthy American owner, Ray, mute from cancer and abjectly mothered by his wife Irene, with furtive liquor and a shrine to the Madonna his sole remaining prerogatives, expires in Michael's arms as Michael speaks the confession-absolution for him. Finally, in *A Breeze from the Gulf* the original scene is enacted as Michael's father, Teddy, the insecure, conventionally Catholic owner of a pool hall who jocularly took a drink "just to be somebody", dies of alcoholism cradled in his son's arms. Since Michael's father is diminutive whether as "Daddy" or Teddy, his wife Loraine has taken to Demerol and to the protective and flirtatious smothering of her son, expressed in the adolescent Michael's asthma. Though Michael depends on Teddy and Teddy's God to keep his mother well, both let him down. At the climax of the first act, when Teddy threatens to have Loraine committed, Michael cracks a gin bottle over his head and curses God for betraying the bargain in which Michael stopped masturbating for his mother's sake. Thus Crowley's recurring image is of the death or bafflement of the masculine principle, not least in Michael himself.

The Boys in the Band was a sensational success in New York and was soon filmed. Although conventional in form, depending on a naturalistic verve in the styles with which the homosexual subculture disports itself, it marks a breakthrough in dramatizing that milieu from within. Its perspective of the comforting if not always comfortable camaraderie of a gay circle allows Crowley to project the internal conflict of the homosexual in the sphere and relationships in which it arises, besides exploiting the native mix of defiant role-playing and wry self-consciousness. Crowley may be said to invert the older pattern in that the outsider in this ensemble play is the one heterosexual character. Historically the importance of the play is that, in the idiom of its characters, it brings out of the closet the species of male "bitch" (in Eric Bentley's word) or that generic ambivalence notoriously felt but dissembled in the plays of Williams and Albee. Significantly these dramatists are integrated into Crowley's dialogue as the upper end of the camp culture with which his characters identify.

The homosexuals assembled in a smart New York duplex are demonstrative in several senses, ranging from giddy effeminacy through a pair of more masculine and stable lovers, a black, and a dumb hustler hired for $20 as a birthday present, to the host Michael, preoccupied with his thinning hair and feckless lifestyle, remembering his possessive mother and weak father, and drinking heavily until his self-hatred is turned on the others in the second act "game". The unexpected presence of Michael's heterosexual college friend Alan focuses the fantasy of the straight man who can be had, and he is the intended victim of the game in which Michael compels the others to telephone the one individual they have truly loved. With surprising candour the game is evidence for a view of homosexuality as the dissimulated impulse to emasculate the other men. The tables are turned on Michael when Alan calls his wife and when the lovers Hank and Larry repair the breach of jealousy by sentimentally phoning each other, but what lingers from this epiphany of love is the disembodiment of the telephone as an acute symbol of the severance of love and carnal expression which is the homosexual's plight, of the promiscuous Larry no less than the dehumanized hustler, Cowboy. Possibly the limitation of the play is that, beyond the desperate fraternity of the group, it finds no better image of love with which to transcend the self-centredness and compulsion of sex. Michael says at the end, "You show me a happy homosexual and I'll show you a gay corpse". The dialogue preserves a witty flash and bite and refuses to solemnize the gambits of gay life, except for a persistent referent of self-pity, but intellectually, for all its epigrammatic edge and tartness, the camp ambience is a kind of glamorizing soft-focus suggestive of Hollywood models like Mankiewicz's *All About Eve* (which one of the boys can recite verbatim). In the end the dialogue is all about "Evelyn", the archetypal guilty mother who loved her son for his failures.

In *Remote Asylum* Michael depends on liquor and pills and a familial relationship with the lovers Diana and Tom, whom he accompanies to the Acapulco retreat of the older Americans Irene and Ray. Both Diana and Tom are flying from broken marriages, and Tom, a golden boy of tennis, is nearly as infantile as Michael. But the terrible example of the emasculating Irene, in whose barrenness and barren luxury the maternal haven is exposed for good and all, inspires Tom to a knowledge that responsibility as well as love is necessary for survival. And even Michael, after identifying with the dying Ray both as father and father confessor, flees the mad asylum of Irene. This play recalls Tennessee Williams in its vivid coastal scene and bizarre symbolism: the towers rising above the terrace set; the recurrent cry of a baby for which there appears to be no explanation (though Michael claims to be a ventriloquist); the magnified shadow of a rat, and the grotesquely cackling and jangling homosexual Mexican servants, "La Damita" and "El Dorado", who cavort in obscene travesty of the Americans, of sex itself, and who savagely beat Michael in the drained swimming pool. The pool, scene also of lovemaking between Diana and Tom, in which Irene voyeuristically shares from atop her tower, is the ironic womb of Michael's yearnings. Simultaneously the audience hears Diana climaxing, the sleeping moans of the drunken Ray, and the cry of the baby. Set against masculine debility and the neuter freaks of Irene's household is the primitive virility of the native chauffeur Carlos who, besides befriending the helpless Ray, secretes and protects his peasant girl-wife and baby, and in the end coolly sells his body to Irene, meeting her on equal if ambiguous terms.

A *Breeze from the Gulf*, a three-character play spanning ten years of family life in a Mississippi town, also recalls Williams in the neurotic, drug-dependent Loraine, particularly in the final scene when she is being readied for the sanatorium and in her last speech about moments of happiness as "a breeze from the gulf". For that matter, in the miasma of alcohol and drugs, comparisons arise with O'Neill. And the familiarity of the basic situation lends itself to Michael's compact summary in the other two plays. The ineffectual Teddy censures his son's spelling and stands by while Loraine bathes, babies, and woos Michael. Loraine's own weakness—social insecurity, hypochondria, and dependence on drugs—becomes the classic feminine mode of domination.

But for all this, and the increasing extremities of conflict, the play has a remarkable integrity of felt experience owing to the naturalness, thrift, and energy of Crowley's dialogue. The first act is a lyric evocation of the family bond regardless of warps, of the intimate rites and instinctive if groping affirmations that, however universal, are *sui generis* in the matrix Michael "remembers". The irony of the second act is that Michael, out of his crucible of dependency and with now the addition of rankling resentments, must return from college to take bitter responsibility for both his parents. In the brutal duel of the final scene he compels Loraine to make her perennial trip to the sanatorium. Sex remains the fatality in Crowley's world, but here it is indivisible from love, and by that token the moral centre passes from the self-pity of *The Boys in the Band* to the compassion of which Teddy speaks. This also he does not "understand", but where his last words have been objectified with harrowing and poignant force, it is the authentic form and distillate of Crowley's play.

There Must be a Pony is a television play based on the novel by James Kirkwood. This drama of a flamboyant aging actress, her relationship to her sensitive son and to a new lover with whom the teenager also identifies, seems continuous with the Crowley ambience: Hollywood and Tennessee Williams. Though the lover's masculine strength and appeal and his much-needed *reliable* quality, appear to derive from his being outside the tinsel show-business world of mother and son, in the end he lets them down. His so positive role in their lives proves to be a "role" in the wrong sense —a false identity which undermines the good he has done and finally destroys him. So there is the familiar ambiguity of the masculine model, the familiar letdown, and possibly the irony that for all her instability and excesses the actress is more "real" than the rational people on whom she depends.

—David W. Beams

D

DAVIS, Ossie.

Born in Cogdell, Georgia, 18 December 1917. Educated at Waycross High School, Georgia; Howard University, Washington, D.C., 1935–39; Columbia University, New York, 1948; studied acting with Paul Mann and Lloyd Richards. Served in the United States Army, 1942–45: surgical technician. Married Ruby Ann Wallace (i.e., the actress Ruby Dee) in 1948; two daughters and one son. Janitor and clerk, New York, 1938–41; member of the Rose McClendon Players, Harlem, New York, 1940–42; then writer, actor, and director; off-Broadway stage manager, 1954–55; co-host, *Ossie Davis and Ruby Dee Story Hour* and *With Ossie and Ruby* television programs. Recipient: Frederick Douglass award, 1970; Emmy award, for acting, 1970; American Library Association Coretta Scott King award, for children's book, 1979. Agent: The Artists Agency, 10000 Santa Monica Boulevard, Suite 305, Los Angeles, California 90067. Address: P.O. Box 1318, New Rochelle, New York 10802, U.S.A.

Publications

PLAYS

Goldbrickers of 1944 (produced 1944).
Alice in Wonder (produced 1952; revised version, as *The Big Deal*, produced 1953).
Purlie Victorious (produced 1961). 1961; revised version, with Philip Rose and Peter Udell, music by Gary Geld, as *Purlie* (produced 1970), 1970.
Curtain Call, Mr. Aldridge, Sir (produced 1963). In *The Black Teacher and the Dramatic Arts*, edited by William R. Reardon and Thomas D. Pawley, 1970.
Escape to Freedom: A Play about Young Frederick Douglass (for children; produced 1976). 1978.
Langston (for children). 1982.
Bingo!, with Hy Gilbert, music by George Fischoff, lyrics by Gilbert, adaptation of a play by William Brashler (also director: produced 1985).

SCREENPLAYS: *Gone Are the Days!*, 1963; *Cotton Comes to Harlem*, with others, 1970; *Black Girl*, with J.E. Franklin, 1973; *Countdown at Kusini*, with others, 1976.

TELEVISION WRITING: *Schoolteacher*, 1963; *Just Say the Word*, 1969; *Today Is Ours*, 1974; *For Us the Living*, 1983; scripts for *Bonanza*; *NYPD*; *East Side, West Side*; and *The Eleventh Hour* series.

THEATRICAL ACTIVITIES

DIRECTOR: **Plays**—*Take It from the Top* by Ruby Dee, 1979; *Bingo!*, 1985. **Films**—*Cotton Comes to Harlem*, 1970; *Kongi's Harvest*, 1970; *Black Girl*, 1973; *Gordon's War*, 1973; *Countdown at Kusini*, 1976. **Television**—*The Perpetual People Puzzle* (co-director), 1972; *Today Is Ours*, 1974.

ACTOR: **Plays**—in *Joy Exceeding Glory*, 1941; title role in *Jeb* by Robert Ardrey, 1946; Rudolf in *Anna Lucasta* by Philip Yordan, 1947; Trem in *The Leading Lady* by Ruth Gordon, 1948; Lonnie Thompson in *Stevedore* by George Sklar and Paul Peters, 1948; Stewart in *The Smile of the World* by Garson Kanin, 1949; Jacques in *The Wisteria Trees* by Joshua Logan, 1950, 1955; Jo in *The Royal Family* by George S. Kaufman and Edna Ferber, 1951; Gabriel in *The Green Pastures* by Marc Connelly, 1951; Al in *Remains to be Seen* by Howard Lindsay and Russel Crouse, 1951; Dr. Joseph Clay in *Touchstone* by William Stucky, 1953; The Lieutenant in *No Time for Sergeants* by Ira Levin, 1955; Cicero in *Jamaica* by E.Y. Harburg and Fred Saidy, 1957; Walter Lee Younger in *A Raisin in the Sun* by Lorraine Hansberry, 1959; Purlie in *Purlie Victorious*, 1961; Sir Radio in *Ballad for Bimshire* by Loften Mitchell, 1963; in *A Treasury of Negro World Literature*, 1964; Johannes in *The Zulu and the Zayda* by Howard DaSilva and Felix Leon, 1965; *Take It from the Top* by Ruby Dee, 1979; Midge in *I'm Not Rappaport* by Herb Gardner, 1987. **Films**—*No Way Out*, 1950; *Fourteen Hours*, 1951; *The Joe Louis Story*, 1953; *The Cardinal*, 1963; *Gone Are the Days!*, 1963; *Shock Treatment*, 1964; *The Hill*, 1965; *A Man Called Adam*, 1966; *The Scalphunters*, 1968; *Slaves*, 1969; *Sam Whiskey*, 1969; *Let's Do It Again*, 1975; *Countdown at Kusini*, 1976; *Hot Stuff*, 1980; *Harry and Son*, 1984; *Avenging Angel*, 1985; *I'm Not Rappaport* by Herb Gardner, 1986; *School Daze*, 1988; *Do the Right Thing*, 1989; *Jungle Fever*, 1991. **Television**—*The Green Pastures* (*Showtime* series), 1951; *The Emperor Jones* (*Kraft Theater* series), 1955; *The Defenders* series, 1961–65; *Death Is the Door Price* (*The Fugitive* series), 1966; *The Outsider*, 1967; *The Third Choice* (*The Name of the Game* series), 1969; *Night Gallery* series, 1969; *Teacher, Teacher*, 1969; *The Sheriff*, 1971; *Billy: Portrait of a Street Kid*, 1980; *Roots: The Next Generation*, 1981; *King*, 1981; *The Tenth Level*, 1984; and *Seven Times Monday*, *The Doctors*, *The Nurses*, *Twelve O'Clock High*, *Bonanza*, *Hawaii Five-O*, and *All God's Children* series.

Ossie Davis is extraordinary on two counts. Loften Mitchell says in *Black Drama*, "For this tall, intelligent, graying, proud man came into the theater, interested in writing. Fortunately and unfortunately, it was learned that he is a good actor—a phenomenon rare for a writer, and detrimental as well. Mr. Davis went on to job after job working regularly as a Negro actor, never quite getting as much writing done as he wanted to do." But, despite his greater acclaim as director and actor, two of his plays are lasting contributions to dramatic literature.

The early 1950s were difficult years for black playwrights to try to get their works produced. One of the plays that did happen to make the boards—directed and produced in September 1952, in Harlem by the playwright and his friends, Maxwell Glanville, Julian Mayfield, and Loften Mitchell among others—was Davis's *Alice in Wonder*. The production, impoverished as it was, also included two of Mayfield's one-acters, *A World Full of Men* and *The Other Foot*. At the Elks Community Theater the talented group of spirited black artists "ushered in a hit show with few people in the audience" (Loften Mitchell in the *Crisis*, March 1972). Eventually Davis's charming play was optioned off to Stanley Greene and was produced successfully in downtown New York. Davis later expanded it into a full piece, *The Big Deal*.

Alice in Wonder—a reputable beginning for a gifted man—is a delightful piece. It is set in upper Harlem ("cadillac country," as Davis calls it). Alice (Ruby Dee in the original production) sees her husband Jay (Maxwell Glanville) given a sizeable contract by one of the leading television networks. In the meantime, Alice's brother (Ed Cambridge) has involved himself in a number of political affairs—one of which is an effort to restore the passport of a militant black singer. The network director asks Jay to go to Washington to testify before a government committee and to denounce the singer. Complications arise and Alice—who refuses to compromise her principles— sees that Jay is about to "sell out." She packs up and leaves. The ethos of this play is racial tension and all that it means, and it showed what Davis could do as a writer.

Purlie Victorious—warmly received by the alert New York critics at the Cort Theater, 29 September 1961—moved beyond an embryonic idea of laughter as a cure to racial bigotry, and became a dramatic experiment, and an artistic dream. The play is farcical, mocking, sparkling, resounding in ethnic wit, rapid, and unyielding as satire. Purlie Judson, a man of impatience, with a flowery evangelical style, moved by messianic mission for his race ("Who else is they got?") goes South determined to turn Big Bethel (an old barn) back into a church as an integrated symbol of freedom. Every racial cliché of southern life—and northern life for that matter—the white pro-Confederate Colonel, the Jim Crow system, the "colored" mammy and all that that image brings to mind, the Uncle Tom figures, the plantation store, the parochial cops, the stalking country sheriff, the NAACP, the Supreme Court, the church—and all that it symbolizes in both the white man's and the black man's psychology— integration, constitutional rights—are given a Swiftian examination. *Purlie Victorious* is a series of irresistible mirrors in which men are forced to see the folly of hatred, the insanity of bigotry, and the fruitlessness of racial supremacy theories. As Davis himself says (in *Contemporary Drama*, edited by Clinton T. Oliver and Stephanie Sills, 1971), "What else can I do but laugh? . . . The play is an attempt, a final attempt to hold that which is ridiculous up to ridicule—to round up all the indignities I have experienced in my own country and to laugh them out of existence."

The dialogue is scintillating, poetic, and realistic. There are many puns, ironic uses of idiomatic expressions, and an acute awareness of the black American's sense of melody and rhythm. The satire is sharply focused with the clever use of malapropisms and misnomers: "This is outrageous—This is a catastrophe! You're a disgrace to the Negro profession! . . . That's just what she said all right—her exactly words . . . When I think of his grandpaw, God rest his Confederate soul, hero of the Battle of Chickamauga—. . . My ol' Confederate father told me on his deathbed: Feed the Negroes first—after the horses and cattle—and I've done it evah time! . . . You know something, I've been after these Negroes down here for years: Go to school, I'd say, first chance you get—take a coupla courses in advanced cotton picking. But you'd think they'd listen to me: No sireebob. By swickety!" Like many other comic works *Purlie Victorious* is an angry play. Davis allows his anger to smolder through a gem-lit comedy, and he permits his work to romp and bound through southern settings and bromidic racial situations of the most impoverished and demeaning variety. But Davis is ever in control. Like Molière he knows that people laugh at beatings, mistaken identities, disguises, clever repartee, buffoonery, indecency, and themselves when taken off guard. Thus the satire—ever corrective in the hands of an artist—is both crude and polished in aiming its fire at personal and general prejudices.

The struggle to keep the mask in place in comedy becomes a conflict between intelligence and character, craft and habit, art and nature. In Davis's principles of writing and performing there is a beautiful balance between poetry and realism.

—Louis D. Mitchell

DEAN, Phillip Hayes.

Born in Chicago, Illinois. Educated at schools in Pontiac, Michigan. Taught acting at the University of Michigan, Ann Arbor. Recipient: Dramatists Guild Hull-Warriner award, 1972; Drama Desk award, 1972. Address: c/o Dramatists Play Service, 440 Park Avenue South, New York, New York 10016, U.S.A.

Publications

PLAYS

This Bird of Dawning Singeth All Night Long (produced 1968). 1971.
The Sty of the Blind Pig (produced 1971). 1972.
American Night Cry (includes *Thunder in the Index, This Bird of Dawning Singeth All Night Long, The Minstrel Boy*) (produced 1974). *Thunder in the Index* and *The Minstrel Boy*. 1972.
Freeman (produced 1973). 1973.
The Owl Killer. 1973.
Every Night When the Sun Goes Down (produced 1974). 1976.
If You Can't Sing, They'll Make You Dance (also director: produced 1978).
Paul Robeson (produced 1978). 1978.

THEATRICAL ACTIVITIES

DIRECTOR: **Play**—*If You Can't Sing, They'll Make You Dance*, 1978.

Phillip Hayes Dean, who had been working intermittently as a playwright since the 1950s, emerged as a dramatist to watch when the Negro Ensemble Company produced *The Sty of the Blind Pig* late in 1971. The title is the name of the red-light house in which Blind Jordan, one of the last of the blind street singers, was born and which he describes in a graphic passage as a place of blood and violence and the "smell of butchered pig." (Pork would figure more directly as an image of black self-corruption in *Every Night When the Sun Goes Down*.) Blind Jordan's presence emphasizes the condition of the other three characters, whose worlds are collapsing: Weedy, the acid-tongued churchwoman, sure of her own righteousness despite a years-long affair with her minister, who goes on the annual convocation to Montgomery just in time for the 1955 bus boycott and finds the new church unrecognizable; her brother Doc, who imagines that if he can get a little money together he can become Sportin' Jimmy Sweet again in a Memphis that has disappeared; and Alberta, Weedy's daughter. She is the central figure in the play, a woman caught between a past she never really had and a future she cannot embrace; at the end, she assumes the voice and manner of her mother. The off-stage event, the burgeoning civil rights movement, is putting an end to whatever community Weedy and Doc know although the characters never see anything other than a bunch of "young folks" with "nappy hair" heading South for some reason. The most effective scene in *The Sty of the Blind Pig* is the one in which Alberta re-enacts a funeral service in which her fervor is clearly sexual, a mark of the personal and social repression in which she lives, but the strength of the piece lies in the characters as a group, the querulous sense of family even in a state of disintegration, and in the mysterious and disquieting presence of Blind Jordan.

The three plays that make up *American Night Cry*, some of which predate *The Sty of the Blind Pig*, are fables of white fear and black oppression, images of mutuality which end in madness, murder, and suicide. *Thunder in the Index*, *This Bird of Dawning Singeth All Night Long*, and *The Minstrel Boy* are all long on accusation, but the confrontations, despite Dean's talent for grotesque gamesplaying, are too obviously in the service of the ideational thrust of the plays. The programmatic quality of the work and the assumption of inevitable violence prepare the way for the Moloch plays. Both *Freeman* and *Every Night When the Sun Goes Down* are set in Moloch, a small industrial city in Michigan obviously suggested by Pontiac, where Dean lived for a time, but appropriately named Moloch because that god was worshipped through the sacrificial burning of children; both plays end in fire. *Freeman* is a family play in which the titular protagonist is an ambitious and bright man constantly defeated by his inability to work in the practical world of compromise, thwarted by his working-class family, his frightened wife, and his foster brother, who has become a successful doctor. In the end, he torches the community center that he sees as a symbol of accommodation to white power and is saved from arrest at the cost of incarceration in a mental hospital. A more fully developed version of the main character in *Thunder in the Index*, Freeman is interesting dramatically as a man whose best impulses are self-destructive and harmful to those around him. Such a description may be an act of white liberal co-option, softening Dean for the mainstream of American theater, for the play is more ambiguous about Freeman. It suggests, primarily through the belated understanding of his father, that Freeman is not an instance of black hubris but of a man driven mad by an uncongenial society whose final act of violence is the inevitable end of his frustrated quest. Certainly, such a reading is suggested by *Every Night When the Sun Goes Down*. Set in a decrepit bar-hotel, peopled by whores, pimps, drunks, and crazies, it brings Blood back from prison, inspirited by a new sense of self, as a prophet who enlists this motley crew in a firebomb attack on their own environment. "And God gave Noah the Rainbow sign. No more water, the fire next time."

Paul Robeson is an unusual play in the Dean canon unless one sees the destruction of the political activist in the second act as the inevitable end of the black hero who outwitted the forces of oppression in Act 1 to become a football star, a lawyer, a famous singer and actor. Yet the celebratory frame of the play belies so Dean-like a movement. Neither convincingly Paul Robeson nor effectively Phillip Hayes Dean, it remains an anomaly in the playwright's work perhaps because Dean had his dramatic image forced on him by Robeson's biography. One of Dean's theatrical virtues is that he has a knack for non-realistic fables in which his best characters have room to develop realistically. At his weakest, the expected development never takes place; such is the case with *If You Can't Sing, They'll Make You Dance*, in which an unlikely triangle allows the protagonist's ineffectuality to expose his macho self-image. At the other extreme is *The Sty of the Blind Pig*, in which the fable, implicit in Alberta's wondering if Blind Jordan was "ever really here," gains power from those who act it out. It is not that "every character comes from some man or woman," as Dean has said, but that every character becomes a man or woman. The other plays lie between these two, at their strongest when invention and idea are less visible than the people who embody them.

—Gerald Weales

DIETZ, Steven.

Born in Denver, Colorado, 23 June 1958. Educated at the University of Northern Colorado, Greeley, 1976–80, B.A. 1980. Member, Playwrights' Center, 1980–91, co-founder, Quicksilver Stage, 1983–86, and artistic director, Midwest PlayLabs, 1987–89, all Minneapolis; resident director, Sundance Institute, Utah, 1990; associate artist, A Contemporary Theatre, Seattle, 1990–91. Recipient: Jerome Foundation fellowship, 1982, 1984; McKnight fellowship in directing, 1985, in playwriting 1989; Theatre Communications Group fellowship in directing, 1987; Society of Midland Authors award, 1988; National Endowment for the Arts fellowship, 1989. Agent: Wiley Hausam, International Creative Management, 40 West 57th Street, New York, New York 10019. Address: 4416 Thackeray North East, Seattle, Washington 98105, U.S.A.

Publications

PLAYS

Brothers and Sisters, music by Roberta Carlson (produced 1982).
Railroad Tales (produced 1983).
Random Acts (produced 1983).
Carry On (produced 1984).
Wanderlust (also director: produced 1984).
Catch Me a Z, music by Greg Theisen (produced 1985).
More Fun Than Bowling (produced 1986). 1990.
Painting It Red, music by Gary Rue, lyrics by Leslie Ball (produced 1986). 1990.

Burning Desire (produced 1987).
Foolin' Around with Infinity (produced 1987). 1990.
Ten November, music and lyrics by Eric Bain Peltoniemi (produced 1987). In
   Plays in Process, vol. 9 no. 4, 1987; 1990.
God's Country (produced 1988). 1990.
Happenstance, music by Eric Bain Peltoniemi (produced 1989).
After You (produced 1990). In *More Ten-Minute Plays from Actor's Theatre
   of Louisville*, edited by Michael Dixon, 1992.
To the Nines (produced 1991). In *The Twentieth Century*, edited by Dan
   Fields, 1991.
Halcyon Days (produced 1991). 1991.
Trust (produced 1992). 1992.
Lonely Planet (produced 1992).

SCREENPLAY: *The Blueprint*, 1992.

THEATRICAL ACTIVITIES

DIRECTOR: **Plays**—many of his own plays; *Standing on My Knees* by John
Olive, 1982; *21–A* by Kevin Kling, 1984; *The Voice of the Prairie* by John
Olive, 1985; *Harry and Claire* by Jaime Meyer, 1985; *A Country Doctor* by
Len Jenkin, 1986; *Auguste Moderne* by Kevin Kling, 1986; *T Bone N Weasel*
by Jon Klein, 1986; *Lloyd's Prayer* by Kevin Kling, 1987; *The Einstein Project*
by Paul D'Andrea and Jon Klein, 1987; *The Wild Goose Circus* by Russell
Davis, 1990; *Tears of Rage* by Doris Baizley, 1991; *New Business* by Tom
William, 1991; *Home and Away* by Kevin Kling, 1992; and many readings
and workshops at the Playwrights' Center, Minneapolis, 1980–91. **Opera**—
Saint Erik's Crown by Eskil Hemberg, 1989.

Steven Dietz comments:

At the core of my interest in the theatre is a quote from Bertolt Brecht: "The
modern theatre musn't be judged by whether it manages to interest the
spectator in the theatre itself—but whether it manages to interest him in the
world."

To that end, I have devoted many of my plays to investigations of factual
events. I believe the theatre is a rehearsal of the concerns of the present
moment. I believe that, as workers in this marvelous grand accident of an art
form, we have a mandate to be the explorers, not the curators, of our society.
Our daunting challenge, one we seldom rise to meet, is to run through the
minefields before our culture does. To make the mistakes, confront the idiocy
and revel in the excesses (social, sexual, religious, political) of our culture in
the metaphorical safety of the theatre (where we can watch, learn, and
judge)—before these same things hit us head-on in the bloody maelstrom of the
world.

I believe that, at its best, the theatre can serve as a social forum, a place
where members of a community can gather to confront those things which
affect them. A place for reasoning and rage, laughter and loss, recognition and
discussion.

I believe that, at its best, the theatre is a combustible mix of fun, fury, and eloquence.

Of the generation of young dramatists coming of age in the 1990s, Steven Dietz is unique in a number of ways. Although he works largely out of Seattle, his plays are frequently seen in theatres around the country, including in New York City. He is prolific, diverse, and has a "voice" which is always changing and yet recognizable as his own. Dietz pays careful attention to an issue that most playwrights of his generation and background tend to ignore or glide over: politics.

A few years ago, with *More Fun Than Bowling*, Dietz's dramaturgy came to public attention in a theatre in St. Paul, Minnesota. The theatre company is now defunct but the "voice" of Steven Dietz was unmistakable: macabre, funny, lunatic, hard-hitting, and finally disturbing in a way that many other plays of his contemporaries failed to be. Dietz showed, almost proudly, that he cared, that he had compassion, that he was not just another cool observer. The promise of *More Fun Than Bowling* has been realized recently in even more compelling work.

God's Country captured a good deal of attention because it dared to take on the headlines. The murder of radio talk show host, Alan Berg by Neo-Nazis is the mainspring of this play, where Dietz tackles thorny questions and comes up with lucid explanations. A fairly small cast is called on to play a wide range of characters in this docu-drama which dramatizes Voltaire's statement that "Anyone who has the power to make you believe absurdities has the power to make you commit injustices," which Dietz quotes in the published text of the drama. Alan Berg, "a bleeding heart with an acid tongue," had outraged the far right with his Denver talk show, his challenges to make-believe "facts." He was murdered for attempting to be reasonable and sane. As with much modern docu-drama, Dietz unfortunately resorts too often to having his characters tell us the play rather than show it to us. There is a plethora of speeches directly to the audience in this court-room drama. But montages of voices and images work well to create the atmosphere and the sense of irrationality which the madmen-murderers palm off as "salvation." The Jew-haters are themselves pathetic and dangerous, believing the "absurdities" which their leaders manufacture out of whole cloth.

In later plays, Dietz resorts to direct audience-address even more frequently, and while the speeches themselves are interesting and even fascinating, they replace dramatic conflict between characters on the stage which might have been more effectively achieved through dialogue and action.

In *Halcyon Days*, Dietz turns his attention to the American invasion of Grenada. Here again he relies on long speeches which are essentially narrative rather than theatrical. And again, we have a montage of short, snappy scenes and representative characters ranging from senators to goofy, laid-back medical students, from gift shop clerks to presidential speech writers. While the central issue of the invasion of this tiny island became moot almost instantly, what saves the play as theatre and should guarantee it a future life is its wit. As Senator Eddie notes, "There are no comics in D.C. Comics would be redundant." Sadly, the senator's own life is engulfed by the tragedy, and comedy itself becomes redundant. Dietz proves over and over again that he can write very funny material, as when he has a character attack the murder of language: he calls it "linguicide". Euphemisms hide reality: "The old are chronologically gifted. The hungry are nourishment-free. And the homeless are architecturally-inconvenienced. . . . Murdered civilians become collateral damage, and the starving thousands . . . become disenfranchised indigenous people of color." Strong stuff emerges from hilarious spoofery, but Dietz, like many Americans, is outraged at the way his country's leaders behave and speak and lie. Such political stands are rare in American drama, but Dietz makes them work, by and large.

Trust once again uses the open stage to represent a variety of essentially cinematic settings. When Dietz lets his dialogue rip along, he is absolutely first rate, but he frequently slips back into monologue, relating the action to the audience. The fault, if it is a fault at all, is common enough in his generation of playwrights, but in *Trust* it seems intrusive. And yet Dietz has the 1990s generational jargon, attitude, value system, casual yet twitchy behavior, down pat.

Dietz's most recent play is *Lonely Planet*. It seems very different from the preceding works, except that the language is absolutely on the mark and the point that is being made is sadly only too recognizable. Two men, Jody and Carl, play games of truth and lies with each other in a map store, with the world as seen by the astronauts hanging behind them. Dietz pays direct homage to Ionesco's *The Chairs*, and in time his stage is filled with chairs, with memories which may or may not be "true." Carl complains that he is bored, but eventually we learn that his boredom is with death, which the chairs symbolize. The two characters duel with maps, play with the world, but their inner struggle emerges as we see their fear and share their anxiety. AIDS is out there, waiting, and the chairs are the chairs of their dead friends. This play is heavy in symbolism, but despite its grim center there is wit and irony which is ". . . the penicillin of modern thought." Dietz is at his best when he has Jody ponder, "We remember the wrong things. We remember the combination to our high school gym locker, we forget the name of the woman who taught us to swim. We remember the capitals of states and forget our parents' birth-days." In the end, on our lonely planet, we have only memory, however faulty, and each other.

In *Lonely Planet*, Dietz treats the audience as a character to be addressed, to have things directed at. But here the device is relevant and important because it integrates the audience as a part of the action; we should not remain passive.

—Arthur H. Ballet

DIZENZO, Charles (John).

Born in Hackensack, New Jersey, 21 May 1938. Educated at New York University, B.A. 1962. Married Patricia Hines in 1964. Instructor in playwriting, New York University 1970–71, and Yale University, New Haven, Connecticut, 1975–76. Recipient: Yale University-ABC fellowship, 1966, and CBS fellowship, 1975; Guggenheim fellowship, 1967; National Endowment for the Arts grant, 1972. Agent: Helen Harvey Associates, 410 West 24th

Street, New York, New York 10011. Address: 106 Perry Street, New York, New York 10014, U.S.A.

Publications

PLAYS

The Drapes Come (televised 1965; produced 1965). 1966; in *Off-Broadway Plays 1*, 1970.
An Evening for Merlin Finch (produced 1968). 1968; in *Off-Broadway Plays 1*, 1970.
A Great Career (produced 1968). 1968.
Why I Went Crazy (produced 1969; as *Disaster Strikes the Home*, produced 1970).
The Last Straw, and Sociability (produced 1970). 1970.
Big Mother and Other Plays (includes *An Evening for Merlin Finch* and *The Last Straw*). 1970.
Big Mother, music by John Braden (produced 1974). In *Big Mother and Other Plays*, 1970.
Metamorphosis, adaptation of works by Kafka (produced 1972).
The Shaft of Love (produced 1975).

TELEVISION PLAY: *The Drapes Come*, 1965.

OTHER

Phoebe (for children), with Patricia Dizenzo. 1970.

Charles Dizenzo's plays were first produced in the off-off-Broadway workshop movement of the 1960s. Since then they have been presented by the Repertory Company of Lincoln Center, the David Merrick Arts Foundation, and the American Place Theater in New York, and in theatres in Europe.

A good example of Dizenzo's work is a pair of one-act comedies first presented at Lincoln Center's experimental Forum Theater. The first play, *A Great Career*, is an office play built on the assumption that office life is impossible, but that for all the meaningless work and the petty quarrels among employees, the office is as much "womb as tomb," or, as the heroine snarlingly calls it as the play opens, "a home away from home." It is about a harried clerical worker named Linda who has a report to prepare. During the course of the action she explodes, gets herself fired, and then realizing that there is no place else to go that is not the same she literally begs to be taken back. This description makes the play sound more painful than funny, and Dizenzo obviously wants his audience to hang on to that side of the story. The ending certainly encourages them to. We see Linda crawling around the stage picking up the papers that she scattered during her defiant scene, as a fellow employee tells her about the new bookkeeper who tried to commit suicide unsuccessfully in the men's room. In *A Great Career* Dizenzo shows the emasculating nature of office life by having men play women and women turning out to be men.

In *An Evening for Merlin Finch* the sterility of the office gives way to the silent violence of the home. Darlene Finch, an insensitive middle-class middle-American housewife, is plagued by a vengeful mother who materializes in the shape of her son Merlin. This becomes her vision of hatred and guilt. As he demonstrates in all of his plays Dizenzo is fascinated with the normality within a sick society. His plays point up the compromises which sink the soul of modern man into a dismal acceptance of everyday predicaments. Merlin, the focus of concern, is forced to play his bassoon for company. Each observation his parents make is a body blow and each gesture of contact a refusal. Merlin's life turns out to be an eternal adolescence and as he blows away on his bassoon his slim identity evaporates before our eyes. His mother's ignorance and hostility continuously undercut the comic image of Merlin's silly instrument. Here Dizenzo's dry black humor together with a carefully constructed situation exposes and explodes the Finches' severely distorted family life.

Another Dizenzo play which in its own bizarre and comic way explodes the quiet violence of family life is *Disaster Strikes the Home* (also presented under the title *Why I Went Crazy*). In this play Dizenzo submerges his audience into a complete and outrageous comic world. Once again the sexes are changed: wives are played by men, husbands by women. The reversal is not a gimmick, but a surrealistic view of the sexual strangulation that exists in the American household. Dizenzo counterpoints these outlandish images with careful, and empty, colloquial speech. The violent role reversals that take place in weak marriages epitomize Dizenzo's nightmare view of American family life.

Dizenzo's playwriting is always startlingly inventive and for the most part consistently amusing. By distorting the real world he illuminates the dark emotional silences between people which is something many contemporary playwrights attempt but seldom achieve. Although his writing has none of the manicured edge of Albee's or Ionesco's, and in places is in serious need of tightening, Dizenzo has a keen ear for the truthful phrase and a fine farceur's instint for pace. His theatrical vision is controlled and iconoclastic; he imitates no one, relying totally on his own creative talents, thereby fostering a theatrical voice which is both unique and thoroughly American.

—Bernard Carragher

DREXLER, Rosalyn.

Born in New York City, 25 November 1926. Self-educated. Married Sherman Drexler in 1946; one daughter and one son. Painter, sculptor, singer, and wrestler; taught at the University of Iowa, Iowa City, 1976–77. Recipient: Obie award, 1965, 1979, 1985; Rockefeller grant, 1965 (2 grants), 1968, 1974; *Paris Review* fiction prize, 1966; Guggenheim fellowship, 1970; Emmy award, 1974. Agent: (drama) Helen Harvey Associates, 410 West 24th Street, New York, New York 10011; (literary) Georges Borchardt Inc., 136 East 57th Street, New York, New York 10022, U.S.A.

Publications

PLAYS

Home Movies; and Softly, and Consider the Nearness, music by Al Carmines (produced 1964). In *The Line of Least Existence and Other Plays*, 1967.
Hot Buttered Roll (produced 1966). In *The Line of Least Existence and Other Plays*, 1967; with *The Investigation*, 1969.

The Investigation (produced 1966). In *The Line of Least Existence and Other Plays*, 1967; with *Hot Buttered Roll*, 1969.
The Line of Least Existence (produced 1967). In *The Line of Least Existence and Other Plays*, 1967.
The Line of Least Existence and Other Plays. 1967.
The Bed Was Full (produced 1972). In *The Line of Least Existence and Other Plays*, 1967.
Skywriting, in *Collision Course* (produced 1968). 1968.
Was I Good? (produced 1972).
She Who Was He (produced 1973).
The Ice Queen (produced 1973).
Travesty Parade (produced 1974).
Vulgar Lives (produced 1979).
The Writers' Opera, music by John Braden (produced 1979).
Graven Image (produced 1980).
Starburn, music by Michael Meadows (produced 1983).
Room 17–C (produced 1983).
Delicate Feelings (produced 1984).
Transients Welcome (includes *Room 17–C*, *Lobby*, *Utopia Parkway*) (produced 1984). 1984.
A Matter of Life and Death (produced 1986).
What Do You Call It? (produced 1986).
The Heart That Eats Itself (produced 1987).
The Flood (produced 1992).
Occupational Hazard. In *Women on the Verge: 7 Avant-Garde American Plays*, edited by Rosette C. Lamont, 1993.

NOVELS

I Am the Beautiful Stranger. 1965.
One or Another. 1970.
To Smithereens. 1972; as *Submissions of a Lady Wrestler*, 1976.
The Cosmopolitan Girl. 1975.
Dawn: Portrait of a Teenage Runaway (as Julia Sorel). 1976.
Alex: Portrait of a Teenage Prostitute (as Julia Sorel). 1977.
Rocky (novelization of screenplay; as Julia Sorel). 1977.
See How She Runs (novelization of screenplay; as Julia Sorel). 1978.
Starburn: The Story of Jenni Love. 1979.
Forever Is Sometimes Temporary When Tomorrow Rolls Around. 1979.
Bad Guy.1982.

OTHER

Rosalyn Drexler: Intimate Emotions. 1986.

Rosalyn Drexler comments:

I try to write with vitality, joy, and honesty. My plays may be called absurd. I write to amuse myself. I often amuse others.

Almost all my reviews have been excellent, but I am not produced much. It seems that every theatre wants to premiere a play. (That's how they get grants.)

Therefore, if a play is done once, good or bad, that's it for the playwright—unless she is Ibsen, Shaw . . . etc.

Playwriting is my first love, I'm considered established, but I have just begun.

Rosalyn Drexler came to prominence as a novelist and playwright at a time when the absurdist symbolism of Albee was very much in vogue. Her own work of the 1960s has sometimes been called "pop art," and it has also been billed as "An Evening of Bad Taste"; whichever, it seems very much a reaction against the intellectualism and pretentiousness which surrounded the theatre of the absurd. She has remained true to her early style in the 1980s, and has found sympathetic—and still emphatically "alternative"—production milieus with groups like the Omaha Magic Theater.

Bad taste is often both the subject and the style of Drexler's plays, manipulating the audience into compromising corners. *The Investigation* presents itself as a simple if not naïve parable about a police interrogation of an adolescent murder suspect, a timid, puritanical boy who is eventually bullied by the police into suicide. Some critics found it a fashionable tract against police brutality, and hence a very slight work. The characters are, as usual in Drexler, two-dimensional, but the boy is so colourless that he is unengaging as an object of sympathy. The detective, on the other hand, is so resourceful that his techniques of sadistic attrition become the main theatrical dynamic. Much of the detective's imaginative energy is invested in verbal reconstruction of the grotesque rape and murder, putting the boy in the central role. As the audience receives no evidence from any external source, there remains the possibility that the facts which the detective narrates may be correct, and that what appears to be his sadism is in fact nausea at an outrageous crime. In the second scene there is a surprising technical twist when the murder victim's twin sister introduces herself to the audience and volunteers to re-enact the crime, using a boyfriend of hers as the accused boy. That this is parodic is obvious—they congratulate each other on their performances and show no sadness that a girl has been killed—but the mechanics of the parody are obscure. Does the scene represent the detective's hypothesis? or the boy's nightmare? or public assumptions about what happens when repression meets precociousness? The only possibility to be eliminated is that the scene shows what really happened. When questions like these are left open at the end of a play, the author can hardly be accused of triteness.

If questions are generated prodigally, Drexler also seems to have many techniques for ensuring that her plays do not become too meaningful; the title-piece for her collection, *The Line of Least Existence*, may consist of profundity or malapropism. Verbal vandalism certainly does exist in that play, but so also does an utterly unpretentious playfulness, in which words are discovered and traded just for their phatic values. Because Drexler's dramatic world is never remotely naturalistic, the reference of words is often totally unclear; one wonders whether "least existence" actually defines the dramatic cosmos as a sort of limbo, especially when at the end the central character, with a heroic irresponsibility, commits his wife and himself to a mental asylum. In *Hot Buttered Roll*, Mr Corrupt Savage, a senile bedridden billionaire, exercises his waning appetites with the assistance of a call girl and an amazonian bodyguard who from time to time throws him back into bed. The cast also includes two pimps, a "purveyor of girly girls" and a "purveyor of burly girls," but the essential action seems to be in a bunker, where all connections and relationships have been severed and the use of appetite is tentative and vicarious. As with the detective in *The Investigation*, the more scabrous parts of the dialogue sometimes have a vatic quality, so that the impact is often in its vagueness or suggestiveness. Thus the play's central image is never clearly stated, but seems to be that of (gendered) man as a sort of transplant patient, his facilities being monitored externally, his needs being canvassed through a huge mail-order system, and his responses being tested by the bizarre performances by the call girl at the foot of the bed. Very similar in rationale is *Softly, and Consider the Nearness*, in which a woman uses a television set as a surrogate world of experience.

In a later play, *Skywriting*, there are only two characters, and their referential functions are trimmed back even further: the unnamed Man and Woman seem to be archetypes, and as such make this an important work, a transition from the pop plays of the 1960s towards the mythical work of the 1970s. Beyond the fact that the diction seems closer to Drexler's Bronx than to Eden, the play is not located in any time or place. The two characters, segregated on either side of the stage, argue about the possession of a huge (projected) picture postcard of clouds. As in Shepard, the sky is perceived as a fantasy arena, and the characters instinctively take a territorial attitude to it, invading each other's minds as they defend their sexuality. This is a very clever and economical play, in which the primordial merges with the futuristic before dissolving in a throwaway ending. *She Who Was He* investigates the world of myth and ritual in an exotic, distant past; the style is lavish and operatic, but the attempt at transcendence has been problematic for audiences. In her Obie-winning *The Writers' Opera*, Drexler returns to her more familiar mode, the perversely illogical associative collage of stereotypical items. The pretentiousness and fickleness of the art world is the satirical target in this play, and this world is reflected in the domestic behaviour of the central characters, where a transsexual finds himself in an Oedipal relationship with his son. Such events differ only in degree from the ingredients of her first stage success, *Home Movies*, where outrageous farcical grotesquerie revolves round the prodigal and inventive sexuality of the characters. There, as throughout Drexler's large output of plays, novels, and novelizations, her most characteristic trait, the ridiculous pun, typifies an author who defies critical assessment while at the same time—in her own inimitable phrasing—she "shoots the vapids."

—Howard McNaughton

DUBERMAN, Martin (Bauml).

Born in New York City, 6 August 1930. Educated at Yale University, New Haven, Connecticut, 1948–52, B.A. 1952 (Phi Beta Kappa); Harvard University, Cambridge, Massachusetts, 1952–57, M.A. 1953, Ph.D. 1957. Tutor, Harvard University, 1955–57; instructor and assistant professor (Morse Fellow, 1961–62), Yale University, 1957–62; assistant professor, 1962–65, associate professor, 1965–67, and professor of history, 1967–71,

Princeton University, New Jersey. Since 1971 distinguished professor, Lehman College Graduate Center, and founder, 1986, Center for Lesbian and Gay Studies, City University of New York. Recipient: Bancroft prize, for history, 1962; Vernon Rice award, 1964; American Academy award, 1971; Manhattan Borough Presidents gold medal, 1988; George Freedley prize, 1990; Lambda Book award, 1990 (twice); Myer award, 1990. Address: 475 West 22nd Street, New York, New York 10011, U.S.A.

Publications

PLAYS

In White America (produced 1963). 1964.
Metaphors, in *Collision Course* (produced 1968). 1968.
Groups (produced 1968).
The Colonial Dudes (produced 1969). In *Male Armor*, 1975.
The Memory Bank: The Recorder, and The Electric Map (produced 1970; *The Recorder* produced 1974). 1970.
Payments (produced 1971). In *Male Armor*, 1975.
Soon, music by Joseph Martinez Kookoolis and Scott Fagan, adaptation of a story by Kookoolis, Fagan, and Robert Greenwald (produced 1971).
Dudes (produced 1972).
Elagabalus (produced 1973). In *Male Armor*, 1975.
Male Armor: Selected Plays 1968–1974 (includes *Metaphors*, *The Colonial Dudes*, *The Recorder*, *The Guttman Ordinary Scale*, *Payments*, *The Electric Map*, *Elagabalus*). 1975.
Visions of Kerouac (produced 1976). 1977.
Mother Earth: An Epic Drama of Emma Goldman's Life. 1991.

SCREENPLAYS: *The Deed*, 1969; *Mother Earth*, 1971.

OTHER

Charles Francis Adams 1807–1886. 1961.
James Russell Lowell. 1966.
The Uncompleted Past (essays). 1969.
Black Mountain: An Exploration in Community. 1972; revised edition, 1992.
About Time: Exploring the Gay Past. 1986; revised edition, 1992.
Paul Robeson. 1989.
Cures: A Gay Man's Odyssey. 1991.

Editor, *The Antislavery Vanguard: New Essays on the Abolitionists*. 1965.
Editor with Martha Vicinus and George Chauncey, Jr., *Hidden from History: Reclaiming the Gay and Lesbian Past*. 1989.

In White America was first produced in October 1963, at a time of great optimism in American social consciousness. It was the era of the New Frontier. The play was an immediate, sustained, and internationally acclaimed success. Its author, however, was a playwright by avocation only, and his subsequent theatrical productivity has proven to reflect his true profession in subject matter, theory of communication, and evolution. Martin Duberman is a professor of history at Lehman College, a professional historian of recognized accomplishment, and author of several works in that field: *James Russell Lowell, Charles Francis Adams, The Uncompleted Past, Black Mountain: An Exploration in Community,* and *About Time.*

In White America is less a "play" in any traditional literary sense than an "evening of theatre"—it is an assemblage of documents from the history of the black American's experience of 200 years' suffering. As an historical event reflecting the social fabric of its time, the piece is significant, and at the time of its presentation it was a moving experience for all audiences. It weaves together dialogues, documents, songs, and narration with impressive sensitivity for theatrical construction and it suggests a possible form for playwrights to explore. In a 1963 essay, "Presenting the Past," Duberman argued that "the past has something to say to us . . . a knowledge of past experience can provide valuable guidelines, though not blueprints, for acting in the present." Clearly his professional concern for history provided him with his subject matter (he did not create material; he selected, edited, and shaped it). His teaching duties, moreover, led him to a belief in the theatrical and dramatic potential of oral communication: a lecturer can be more than informative. "The benefits of a union between history and drama," Duberman wrote, "would not by any means be all on one side. If theater, with its ample skill in communication, could increase the immediacy of past experience, history, with its ample material on human behavior, could broaden the range of theatrical testimony." In his preface to the printed play he added, "I chose to tell this story on the stage, and through historical documents, because I wanted to combine the evocative power of the spoken word with the confirming power of historical fact." It was the assessment of critics of the time that Duberman had succeeded in all respects. The play stimulated an awakening social consciousness, was vital in the enactment, and communicated its thesis most effectively.

In the late 1960s Duberman's attitudes towards the uses of the past and the efficacy of wedding history to theatre began to change. Perhaps the disenchantment of the New Left that followed the Kennedy and King assassinations influenced his thinking. His work for the theatre abandoned the path suggested by *In White America,* and he began to write fiction-invented drama.

Male Armor collects seven plays written between 1968 and 1974. Two are full-length. Four of the one-acts had been published previously. None had received successful production in the commercial theatre. In his introduction to the collection, Duberman professes that the plays explore a common theme, "What does it mean to be a 'man'?" The collection's title, he explains, is meant to recall Wilhelm Reich's concept of "character armor"—the devices we employ to protect ourselves from our own energy, particularly our sexual energy. Each of the plays investigates the way we build protective roles which then dominate us. For Duberman, the way to destroy these confining roles is, apparently, androgyny, either practiced or metaphorical.

Metaphors, The Electric Map, and *The Recorder* are all highly literate sparrings between consenting adults which explore the themes of power struggle and homosexuality. In *Metaphors* a young applicant to Yale University nearly seduces his admissions interviewer. *The Electric Map* and *The Recorder,* which had an unsuccessful off-Broadway production under the title *The Memory Bank,* are also duologues. The former is set before an elaborate, electrified map of the Battle of Gettysburg, and self-consciously uses this visual analogue to puff up a foolish domestic quarrel between two brothers into what the author hopes will be something akin to universality. There is a predictable undertone of latent homosexuality to the trite and poorly motivated action. *The Recorder* is an interview of the friend of a great man by an academician-historian. In it, Duberman is intrigued by the ineffectiveness and inaccuracy of historical inquiry, and the play unquestionably reflects his growing disenchantment with the study of history, as well as his growing use of sexuality as a dramatic subject. By the time of these plays, Duberman was referring to himself as "more a writer than a historian."

The newest play in *Male Armor* is *Elagabalus*, a six-scene realistic play about Adrian, a self-indulgent and affluent androgynist. Duberman writes, "Adrian is playful and daring. His gaiety may be contaminated by petulance and willfulness, but he *is* moving toward an *un*-armored territory, moving out so far that finally he's left with no protection against the traditional weaponry brought to bear against him . . . other than the ultimate defense of self-destruction." In his quest for self, Adrian stabs himself fatally in the groin, and the final image the writer offers is a gratuitous freeze-frame from the porno film "Big Stick" in which a teenage girl sucks sensuously on a popsicle. This reader was reminded of the adage that many people (Adrian? Duberman?) who are looking for themselves may not like what they find. Adrian is a boring character whose self-destruction does not seem significant.

The Uncompleted Past is a collection of Duberman's critical and historical essays which concludes with an expression of his disenchantment with the study of history and reveals why his theatrical development had moved towards fiction (in which area he appears undistinguished) and away from the documentary (in which his initial acclaim was achieved). He writes,

> For those among the young, historians and otherwise, who are chiefly interested in changing the present, I can only say . . . they doom themselves to bitter disappointment if they seek their guides to action in a study of the past. Though I have tried to make it otherwise, I have found that a "life in history" has given me very limited information or perspective with which to understand the central concerns of my own life and my own times.

It seems probable that *In White America* will stand as Duberman's major writing for the theatre, and that it will prove more significant as an event of cultural history than as either an innovation in theatrical form or the first work in the career of a significant playwright—thus belying the very attitudes towards history and theatre which Duberman has recently held.

—Thomas B. Markus

DURANG, Christopher (Ferdinand).

Born in Montclair, New Jersey, 2 January 1949. Educated at Harvard University, Cambridge, Massachusetts, 1967–71, A.B. in English 1971; Yale University School of Drama, New Haven, Connecticut, 1971–74, M.F.A. in playwriting 1974. Drama teacher, Southern Connecticut College, New Haven, 1975, and Yale University, 1975–76. Recipient: CBS fellowship, 1975; Rockefeller grant, 1976; Guggenheim grant, 1979; Obie award, 1980, 1985;

Lecomte de Nouy Foundation grant, 1981; Dramatists Guild Hull-Warriner award, 1985. Agent: Helen Merrill Ltd., 435 West 23rd Street, Suite 1A, New York, New York 10011, U.S.A.

Publications

PLAYS

The Nature and Purpose of the Universe (produced 1971). In *The Nature and Purpose of the Universe; Death Comes to Us All, Mary Agnes; 'dentity Crisis*, 1979.

'dentity Crisis (as *Robert*, produced 1971; as *'dentity Crisis*, also director: produced 1975). In *The Nature and Purpose of the Universe; Death Comes to Us All, Mary Agnes; 'dentity Crisis*, 1979.

Better Dead Than Sorry, music by Jack Feldman, lyrics by Durang (produced 1972).

I Don't Generally Like Poetry But Have You Read "Trees"?, with Albert Innaurato (produced 1972).

The Life Story of Mitzi Gaynor; or, Gyp, with Albert Innaurato (produced 1973).

The Marriage of Bette and Boo (produced 1973; revised version produced 1979). *Yale/Theatre* 1973; revised version (produced 1985), 1985.

The Idiots Karamazov, with Albert Innaurato, music by Jack Feldman, lyrics by Durang (produced 1974).*Yale/Theatre*, 1974; augmented edition, 1981.

Titanic (produced 1974). 1983.

Death Comes to Us All, Mary Agnes (produced 1975). In *The Nature and Purpose of the Universe; Death Comes to Us All, Mary Agnes; 'dentity Crisis*, 1979.

When Dinah Shore Ruled the Earth, with Wendy Wasserstein (produced 1975).

Das Lusitania Songspiel, with Sigourney Weaver, music by Mel Marvin and Jack Gaughan (produced 1976; revised version produced 1976; revised version produced 1980).

A History of the American Film, music by Mel Marvin (produced 1976). 1978.

The Vietnamization of New Jersey (produced 1977). 1978.

Sister Mary Ignatius Explains It All for You (produced 1979). 1980.

The Nature and Purpose of the Universe; Death Comes to Us All, Mary Agnes; 'dentity Crisis: Three Short Plays. 1979.

Beyond Therapy (produced 1981). 1983.

The Actor's Nightmare (produced 1981). With *Sister Mary Ignatius Explains It All for You*, 1982.

Christopher Durang Explains It All for You (includes *The Nature and Purpose of the Universe, 'dentity Crisis, Titanic, The Actor's Nightmare, Sister Mary Ignatius Explains It All for You, Beyond Therapy*). 1982.

Baby with the Bathwater (produced 1983). 1984; with *Laughing Wild*, 1989.

Sloth, in *Faustus in Hell* (produced 1985).

Laughing Wild (produced 1987). With *Baby with the Bathwater*, 1989.

Cardinal O'Connor and *Woman Stand-up*, in *Urban Blight* (musical revue), based on an idea by John Tillinger, music by David Shire, lyrics by Richard Maltby Jr. (produced 1988).

Christopher Durang at Dawn (cabaret) (produced 1990).
Naomi in the Living Room (produced 1991).
Seeking Wild (produced 1992).

SCREENPLAY: *Beyond Therapy*, with Robert Altman, 1987.

TELEVISION WRITING: *Comedy Zone* series; *Carol Burnett Special.*

THEATRICAL ACTIVITIES

DIRECTOR: **Play**—*'dentity Crisis*, 1975; *And the Air Didn't Answer* by Robert
Kerr, 1989.

ACTOR: **Plays**—Gustaf in *Urlicht* by Albert Innaurato, 1971; Darryl in *Better
Dead Than Sorry*, 1972; Performer in *The Life Story of Mitzi Gaynor; or,
Gyp*, 1973; Performer in *I Don't Generally Like Poetry But Have You Read
"Trees"?*, 1973; Bruce in *Happy Birthday, Montpelier Pizz-zazz* by Wendy
Wasserstein, 1974; Chorus in *The Frogs* by Burt Shevelove and Stephen
Sondheim, 1974; Student in *The Possessed* by Camus, 1974; Alyosha in *The
Idiots Karamazov*, 1974; Emcee in *When Dinah Shore Ruled the Earth*, 1975;
Performer in *Das Lusitania Songspiel*, 1976, 1980; Young Cashier in *The
Hotel Play* by Wallace Shawn, 1981; Matt in *The Marriage of Bette and Boo*,
1985; role in *Laughing Wild*, 1987; Ubu's Conscience in *Ubu Roi*, adaptation
of Alfred Jarry's play by Larry Sloan and Doug Wright, 1989; *Christopher
Durang at Dawn*, 1990. **Film**—*The Secret of My Success*, 1987; *Housesitter*,
1992.

Handsomely surviving a Catholic boyhood in New Jersey and Ivy League
education at Harvard and Yale (M.F.A. in playwriting), Christopher Durang
has been critically ranked in the top echelon of American playwrights. Most of
his plays have been popular with regional and off-the-mainline theatres, and
reflect their author's penchant for parody with favorite targets being drama
and film, literature, American social history and popular culture, parochial
religion, and the middle-class family. National recognition arrived with the
1978 Broadway production on *A History of the American Film*. Most critics
applauded Durang's satiric skills that coalesced in this inventive multi-leveled
profile of the films and social history of the last 50 years.

Using a revue-type format and song lyrics by Durang, *American Film* trots
out the clichés, stereotypes, and superficial attitudes toward events that bom-
barded American culture from *Orphans of the Storm* to *Earthquake*. The
characters interchange as screen spectators and actors, as we follow the thorny
path of the naively innocent heroine from poverty with a callous Cagney-like
lover through speakeasies, prison, high society, wartime, to heavenly ascen-
sion. The play spoofs specific films of the 1930s and 1940s, film genres, and
screen stars representing our personified ideals of toughness or innocence. And
the audience watches itself identifying with the black and white morality of the
western, the jingoism of World War II, and the neurotic narcissism of the
postwar period. More than a revue with some skits wearing thin by the second
act, this satiric farce is impudently effective.

Literature and drama, respectively, fall under attack in *The Idiots
Karamazov*, written with Albert Innaurato, and *The Vietnamization of New*

Jersey. The first is an irreverent send-up of Dostoevsky's novel and western literature's great books; its action combines chaotic slapstick with a profusion of literary allusions comprehensible largely to the cognoscenti. Displaying sharper comedic ability, the second play is an absurdist parody of David Rabe's anti-Vietnam play *Sticks and Bones* and of American anti-war dramas thrusting collective guilt upon docile audiences. Comic recognition, however, rests too heavily on knowledge of Rabe's drama.

The theatre and drama as satirical subjects again surface in *The Actor's Nightmare*, a hilarious curtain-raiser in which a befuddled accountant clad as Hamlet, without benefit of lines or rehearsal, finds himself on stage in a phantasmagoric play whose actors veer from Coward's *Private Lives* and Beckett plays to *Hamlet* and Robert Bolt's *A Man for All Seasons*. Ultimately thrust into a scene from the last play, the baffled hero becomes Sir Thomas More facing a suddenly realistic execution, and despite his last minute, out-of-character recanting, is not seen on stage for the curtain call—an end resembling that of Tom Stoppard's Rosencrantz and Guildenstern.

Setting his sights on personal relationships and the deficiencies of psychiatrists, Durang in *Beyond Therapy* chronicles the tale of two Manhattan singles in their thirties, a bisexual male lawyer and a female journalist concerned about getting herself married, who meet through a personals ad. The curious couple are ineptly coached through a courtship of insults, rejections, and threats by their respective psychiatrists: the woman's shrink, a male chauvinist who seduces his female patients, and the man's, a daffy lady who constantly carries a Snoopy doll and confuses words. In a more optimistic ending than Durang normally gives, the couple jointly reject their therapists and consider having a continued relationship perhaps even leading to marriage. There is a dazzling display of funny lines and jokes on contemporary mores, gender identity, and psychiatry. Credibility is stretched with two such divergent lovers even considering a relationship, a problem not mitigated by the lack of a final resolution scene or a well-developed farcical plot to connect the many short two-character scenes. Yet these shortcomings have not prevented the play from becoming a favorite with community and regional theatres.

Dogmatic parochial education receives barbs in Durang's Obie-winning *Sister Mary Ignatius Explains It All for You*. The title character is a sin-smelling teaching nun who tyrannizes her students. During a lecture she is interrupted by the return of four former students who loathe her. The group ranges from a happy homosexual and unwed mother to a rape victim and a suicidal alcoholic; their recriminations rouse the nun to shoot them, and class servility is restored. The satire is sharp and wildly funny in this gem of black humor.

Absurdist portraits of the American family particularly abound in five Durang plays. *The Nature and Purpose of the Universe, Death Comes to Us All, Mary Agnes*, and *'dentity Crisis* are three short black comedies treating victimized females losing life, sanity, or identity at the hands of callous families and the traditional Catholic view of women. Although losing their bite in farcical chaos, the plays project subjects more maturely developed in two later works. The first is *Baby with the Bathwater*, a satirical farce on parenting in which two self-absorbed parents idiotically raise a male child (confusing his true gender for 15 years) who survives to young adulthood desperate to avoid his own upbringing's mistakes when becoming a father himself. The play's string of cartoon-like scenes progressively pall, despite the satirical feast they offer, and would profit from sharper variety and a greater buttressing of reality. More effective is the revised (1985) Obie-winning *The Marriage of Bette and Boo*, a trenchantly amusing dissection of the contemporary Catholic family. In 33 inventive scenes related by the family's only son and treated with farcical brilliance, a marriage moves through three decades of alcoholism, divorce, surrounding relatives representing failures of the married and single state, and a priest who dodges counsel-session questions by imitating frying bacon. At the center stand the dipsomaniac Boo and the dimwit Bette, who persists after a first surviving child producing stillborn babies against medical advice. Admitting an autobiographical connection, the playwright gives us the outrageously satiric view of society that characterizes his best work.

Durang's satiric concern with the perils of modern urban life continues in two works written since 1987. *Laughing Wild* consists of two monologues individually delivered by a man and a woman who expose their dreams and frustrations resulting from separate daily lives in which they encounter and expound upon rude taxi drivers, waiting in line, inane talk shows, attitudes of the Catholic Church towards sexual matters, and each other as they clash over a purchase of canned tuna fish in a supermarket aisle. In the play's final section the two strangers meet to re-enact the supermarket incident with varying interpretations, talk more of their overlapping dreams, and reach a hesitant truce. This funny and inventive comedy has proved popular with regional and fringe theatres. Less successful, *Naomi in the Living Room* is a dark absurdist comedy treating a self-absorbed, psychotic middle-class mother (Naomi) who rudely receives her son and his wife for a brief visit during which her son cross-dresses and behaves like his wife. The couple departs at the wife's insistence, leaving the mother in her loveless, sterile urban home.

Durang's work rises above collegiate-like preciosity to reveal a gifted satirist and farceur whose American absurdist view of the world is most delightfully successful when he furnishes a floor of reality under the dance of his characters. As a satirist writing for the stage, he is a member of an endangered species who deserves the theatre's nurturing if he is to continue to flourish. He is a needed talent in the American theatre.

—Christian H. Moe

E

ELDER, Lonne, III.

Born in Americus, Georgia, 26 December 1931. Educated at New Jersey State Teachers College (now Trenton State College); Yale University School of Drama, New Haven, Connecticut (John Hay Whitney fellow and American Broadcasting Company Television writing fellow, 1965–66; John Golden fellow and Joseph E. Levine fellow in film-making, 1967). Served in the U.S. Army, 1952. Married Judith Ann Johnson in 1969; two sons. Worked as a docker, waiter, and professional gambler; coordinator of the Playwrights-Directors Unit, Negro Ensemble Company, New York, 1967–69; writer, Talent Associates, New York, 1968; writer/producer, Cinema Center Films, Hollywood, 1969–70; writer, Universal Pictures, Hollywood, 1970–71, and Radnitz/Mattel Productions, Hollywood, 1971; writer/producer, Talent Associates, Hollywood, 1971; writer, MGM Pictures and Columbia Pictures, Hollywood, 1972. Recipient: Stanley Drama award, 1965; American National Theatre Academy award, 1967; Outer Circle award, 1970; Vernon Rice award, 1970; Stella Holt Memorial Playwrights award, 1970. Address: c/o Farrar Straus and Giroux, 19 Union Square West, New York, New York 10003, U.S.A.

Publications

PLAYS

Ceremonies in Dark Old Men (produced 1965; revised version produced 1969). 1969.
Charades on East 4th Street (produced 1967). In Black Drama Anthology, edited by Woodie King and Ron Milner, 1971.
Seven Comes Up—Seven Comes Down (produced 1977–78).
Splendid Mummer (produced 1988).
King, music by Richard Blackford, lyrics by Maya Angelou and Alistair Beaton (produced 1990).

SCREENPLAYS: Sounder, 1972; Melinda, 1972; Sounder Part 2, 1976; Bustin' Loose, with Roger L. Simon and Richard Pryor, 1981.

TELEVISION PLAYS: Camera 3 series, 1963; The Terrible Veil, 1964; NYPD series, 1967–68; McCloud series, 1970–71; A Woman Called Moses, from a book by Marcy Heidish, 1978.

MANUSCRIPT COLLECTION: Boston University.

THEATRICAL ACTIVITIES

ACTOR: **Plays**—Bobo in *A Raisin in the Sun* by Lorraine Hansberry, 1959; Clem in *Days of Absence* by Douglas Turner Ward, 1965.

A screenwriter, television scriptwriter, and dramatist, Lonne Elder III is best known in the theatre for his acclaimed work, *Ceremonies in Dark Old Men*. In the tradition of Lorraine Hansberry's *A Raisin in the Sun*, *Ceremonies* examines the struggles of an African-American family in Harlem trying to find a way to break out of the cycle of poverty and despair. In the play, the Parker family recognize few options to improve their bleak condition. An ex-vaudevillian and family patriarch, Russell Parker, depended on his now deceased wife to be the primary breadwinner for much of their 30 years of marriage. Though he earns little money as a barber, Russell finds it difficult to submit himself to the humiliation of working in the subservient jobs to which his lack of education and experience restrict him. His adult sons, Theo and Bobby, also would rather be unemployed than accept menial work. In contrast, Russell's daughter —Adele—personifies the work ethic and takes over the role of her mother by supporting and caring for the men of the family. Theo sees only one way to break this cycle through an illegal, quick money scheme.

Theo teams with Blue Haven, who ostensibly poses as a community leader, to make and sell whisky and run a numbers racket. Theo wins the support of his brother and convinces his father to join the scheme by using his barbershop as a front for the operation. Theo believes the plan will end their money problems and their dependence on his sister. In effect, he thinks it will help to heal familial wounds and bring them all closer together. Ironically, despite Theo's intent, the scheme creates more strife within the already troubled family. Bobby shuns the whisky business to join Blue Haven's thievery ring instead. Russell steals money from the till and spends more than his share of the profits on women and other pursuits. Adele becomes involved with dubious elements of the community which leads to her abuse by a male acquaintance. Theo feels used by other family members as he works day and night for the business, yet enjoys few of its rewards. At the play's end, Theo decides to give up the business and join Adele in seeking other ways to overcome their predicament. However, a price must be paid for the games the family chose to play. Bobby loses his life in a robbery attempt; and Russell is revealed as a self-centered man who places his own well-being above that of his family. With this work, Elder joins the few playwrights able to dramatize the realities of the impoverished of Black America and, specifically, the desperate, seemingly futile search of African-American males to attain a sense of dignity and financial independence.

Elder's other dramatic works lack the craft and intense emotional impact of *Ceremonies*. Commissioned by Mobilization for Youth, Inc. of New York City, *Charades on East 4th Street* was written as a vehicle to encourage young people to use legal means to protest against police brutality, however, the play seems little more than a vicarious means whereby an audience can experience the terrorization of a policeman. On the city's Lower East Side in the basement of a movie theatre, six youths hold a police officer hostage, threatening to execute him with a guillotine. Accused of raping the sister of one of the youths and brutally beating the brother of another, the officer is given little opportunity to defend himself against the charges. Adam, the group leader, initially appears to be the officer's only protector as he seems to find ways to stop the others from carrying out their death sentence. However, by the play's end, Adam is revealed as the only one willing to injure the accused. With the officer's neck on the guillotine, Adam admits it was actually his own sister who was the rape victim and forces his prisoner to admit to the crimes. He frees the man from the guillotine, but breaks both of his arms in vengeance even as the officer pleads his innocence once again. Incredibly—given their seemingly enthusiastic participation in the officer's terrorization—the other youths ultimately disapprove of Adam's actions and vow that they will now work in nonviolent ways to combat police brutality.

A better written and more recent work is *Splendid Mummer*, based on the life of the famous 19th-century tragedian Ira Aldridge. Although born in the United States, Aldridge found fame on European stages, since discriminatory practices barred him from acting in the dramatic theatre of his native land. This demanding one-man show depicts various aspects of Aldridge's life from his teenage years as a valet and protégé of actor Henry Wallack to his triumphant, mature performances as Othello and Lear. While the play is laudatory towards its subject, it does not shy away from revealing less attractive aspects of Aldridge: his imperious manner or his demeanor toward his marriages and romantic conquests. By the play's end, this challenging monodrama arouses one's interest in learning more about this complex, talented man known as the "celebrated African Roscius."

—Addell Austin Anderson

F

FEIFFER, Jules (Ralph).

Born in the Bronx, New York, 26 January 1929. Educated at James Monroe High School, New York; Art Students' League, New York, 1946; Pratt Institute, Brooklyn, 1947–48, 1949–51. Served as a cartoon animator and graphic artist in the U.S. Army Signal Corps, 1951–53: private. Married 1) Judith Sheftel in 1961 (separated 1971, divorced 1983), one daughter; 2) Jennifer Allen in 1983, one daughter. Assistant to the cartoonist Will Eisner, 1946–51 (ghostwriter, *The Spirit* comic, 1949–51); drew cartoon *Clifford*, 1949–51; freelance cartoonist and artist, 1951–56. Since 1956 cartoonist (*Feiffer*), *Village Voice*, New York, and since 1959 syndicated in other newspapers and magazines. Faculty member, Yale University School of Drama, New Haven, Connecticut, 1973–74. President, Dramatists Guild Foundation, 1982–83. Since 1976 director, Corporation of Yaddo, Saratoga Springs, New York. Recipient: Oscar, for cartoon, 1961; George Polk Memorial award, 1962; London Theatre Critics award, 1968; Obie award, 1968; Outer Circle award, 1968, 1969; Pulitzer prize, for cartoon, 1986; Los Angeles Critics Circle award, 1988; Venice Film Festival award, for screenplay, 1989; George and Elisabeth Marton award, 1990–91. Address: 325 West End Avenue, New York, New York 10023, U.S.A.

Publications

PLAYS

The Explainers (produced 1961).
Crawling Arnold (produced 1961). In *Best Short Plays of the World 1958–1967*, edited by Stanley Richards, 1968.
The World of Jules Feiffer (produced 1962).
Interview, in *Harper's*, June 1962.
You Should Have Caught Me at the White House, in *Holiday*, June 1963.
Little Murders (produced 1966). 1968.
The Unexpurgated Memoirs of Bernard Mergendeiler (produced 1967). In *Collision Course*, 1968.
God Bless (produced 1968). In *Plays and Players*, January 1969.
Feiffer's People (produced 1968).
Dick and Jane, in *Oh! Calcutta!* (produced 1969). 1970.
The White House Murder Case (produced 1970). 1970.
Munro (produced 1971).
Carnal Knowledge: A Screenplay (revised version produced 1988). 1971.

Silverlips, in *VD Blues* (televised 1972). 1973.
Watergate Classics, with others (produced 1973).
Cohn of Arc, published in *Partisan Review*, vol. 40, no. 2, 1973.
Knock, Knock (produced 1976). 1976.
Hold Me! (produced 1977). 1977.
Grown Ups (produced 1981). 1982.
A Think Piece (produced 1982).
Rope-a-Dope, in *Urban Blight* (musical revue), based on an idea by John
    Tillinger, music by David Shire, lyrics by Richard Maltby, Jr. (produced
    1988).
Elliot Loves (produced 1989). 1989.
Anthony Rose (produced 1989).

SCREENPLAYS: *Munro* (animated cartoon), 1960; *Carnal Knowledge*, 1971;
Little Murders, 1971; *Popeye*, 1980; *I Want to Go Home*, 1989.

TELEVISION PLAYS: *Silverlips* in *VD Blues*, with others, 1972; *Kidnapped*
(*Happy Endings* series), 1975.

NOVELS
Harry, The Rat with Women. 1963.
Ackroyd. 1977.
Tantrum: A Novel-in-Cartoons. 1979.

OTHER
Sick, Sick, Sick. 1958.
Passionella and Other Stories. 1959.
The Explainers. 1960.
Boy, Girl. Boy, Girl. 1961.
Hold Me! 1963.
Feiffer's Album. 1963.
The Unexpurgated Memoirs of Bernard Mergendeiler. 1965.
The Penguin Feiffer. 1966.
Feiffer on Civil Rights. 1966.
Feiffer's Marriage Manual. 1967.
*Pictures at a Prosecution: Drawings and Text from the Chicago Conspiracy
    Trial*. 1971.
Feiffer on Nixon: The Cartoon Presidency. 1974.
Jules Feiffer's America from Eisenhower to Reagan, edited by Steven Heller.
    1982.
Outer Space Spirit 1952, with Will Eisner and Wallace Wood, edited by Denis
    Kitchen. 1983.
Marriage Is an Invasion of Privacy and Other Dangerous Views. 1984.
Feiffer's Children. 1986.
Ronald Reagan in Movie America: A Jules Feiffer Production. 1988.

Editor, *The Great Comic Book Heroes*. 1965.

Jules Feiffer is, first of all, a cartoonist. Long before he began to write plays, he had made a reputation as a satirist with an uncanny knack for catching the psychological, social, and political clichés which are the refuge and the cross of the college-educated middle class that provides him with an audience as well as a subject matter. His talent has always been as much verbal as visual; his ear as good as his hand. His cartoons are ordinarily strips in which two characters pursue a conversation, panel by panel, until the congenial platitudes dissolve into open aggression, naked greed, impotence, ineffectuality, pain; a variation is the strip in which a single figure—I almost said performer—speaks directly to the reader. The line between this kind of cartoon and the revue sketch is a narrow one, and a great many of Feiffer's early cartoons have crossed that line. Most of the material in *Feiffer's People* and *Hold Me!* presumably began as cartoon dialogue. Even those short works written for the theatre—*Dick and Jane*, the Feiffer sketch from *Oh! Calcutta!*, or the early one-acter *Crawling Arnold*—seem little more than extended cartoons with the stage directions standing in for the drawing.

Inevitably, Feiffer's full-length plays have been viewed—and condemned in some cases—as the work of a cartoonist. There is justice in the viewing, if not in the condemnation, for—as so often with satirists—Feiffer works in terms of stereotypes, of those figures identified by a single idiosyncrasy or a pattern of related compulsions. Even the two young men in *Carnal Knowledge* are societal types rather than psychological studies, although the labels by which we identify them may be written in the kind of psychological language that one expects to find in the balloons of Feiffer's cartoons. Feiffer tends to see his figures as more realistic than my description suggests. Just before the off-Broadway revival of *Little Murders*, Feiffer told an interviewer (*New York Times*, 26 January 1969) that his characters "are very, very real to me. I care about them as people." Yet, elsewhere in the same interview, he identified the family in the play as "a nice, Andy Hardy type family," and the Hardy family films were straight stereotype. If we read *real* in the Feiffer quotation as *true*—that is, identifiable—then the characters are real, as Andy Hardy is, as the figures in his cartoons are; we look at them and say, *oh yes, I know him*, meaning, *oh, yes, I know the type.*

The important thing about Feiffer as a playwright is that he produces unified dramatic structures—related, in some of their elements, to his cartoons and to revue sketches—in which apparently disparate material is held together by a controlling idea. In *Little Murders* the random violence that is the ostensible subject is simply the most obviously theatrical evidence of a general collapse that is reflected in technological malfunction (the failed electricity) and the impotence of traditional power-and-virtue figures (the comic turns of the judge, the detective, the priest). When Feiffer's nice American family begins to shoot people on the street, the event is not so much a culmination of the action as an open statement of what has been implicit all through the play. That last scene; the disintegration, physical and political, in *The White House Murder Case*; the sexual ignorance, and failure, that calls itself "Carnal Knowledge"—all these suggest that Feiffer has about as black a view of American society and of human possibility as one can find in the contemporary theatre.

After *Knock, Knock*, an uncharacteristic fantasy of commitment, *Grown Ups* comes home to familiar Feiffer territory with a self-pitying protagonist, faced with personal and professional collapse and a parental support system which is the presumed cause of his misery; on stage, his daughter, used as a weapon by all the adults, is something of a trial for the audience, but the television version of the play, ending with the camera on the little girl, successfully emphasizes the child as victim and the continuity of loving destructiveness within the family. A *Think Piece* concentrates on the trivia of daily existence to show, as the author says, "the nothingness that constitutes so much of our lives."

Elliot Loves and *Anthony Rose* explore familiar Feiffer themes, once again in darkly comic contexts. The titular hero of *Elliot Loves*, a nonrealistic gathering of four sketch-like scenes, is a man so unable to stop questioning, teasing, and testing his love that he ends with only a telephone cord holding him, tentatively, to his beloved. Anthony Rose is a successful playwright who turns up at a rehearsal of *The Parent Lesson*, a 25-year-old hit of his, and proceeds to rewrite it to conform to his new view of the world; the villainous father and the wronged sons exchange guilt and innocence. In the process, he takes over the production, undermining the company even as he calls them his family—a scary label since he has destroyed his own family and every theater group with which he has worked. *Elliot Loves* is the more polished script, but *Anthony Rose* is more interesting—particularly in its assumption that an author, at whatever age, uses his art to get back at the real world.

—Gerald Weales

FERLINGHETTI, Lawrence (Mendes-Monsanto).

Born in Yonkers, New York, 24 March 1919; lived in France, 1920–24. Educated at Riverdale Country School, 1927–28, and Bronxville Public School, 1929–33, both New York; Mount Hermon School, Greenfield, Massachusetts, 1933–37; University of North Carolina, Chapel Hill, B.A. in journalism 1941; Columbia University, New York, 1947–48, M.A. 1948; Sorbonne, Paris, 1948–50, Doctorat de l'Université 1950. Served in the U.S. Naval Reserve, 1941–45: lieutenant commander. Married Selden Kirby-Smith in 1951 (divorced 1976); one daughter and one son. Worked for *Time* magazine, New York, 1945–46; French teacher, San Francisco, 1951–53. Co-founder, 1952, with Peter D. Martin, and since 1955 owner, City Lights Bookstore, and editor-in-chief, City Lights Books, San Francisco, delegate, Pan American Cultural Conference, Concepción, Chile, 1960. Also a painter: individual show—Ethel Guttmann Gallery, San Francisco, 1985. Recipient: Etna-Taormina prize (Italy), 1968. Address: City Lights Books, 261 Columbus Avenue, San Francisco, California 94133, U.S.A.

Publications

PLAYS

The Alligation (produced 1962). In *Unfair Arguments with Existence*, 1963.
Unfair Arguments with Existence: Seven Plays for a New Theatre (includes
  The Soldiers of No Country, Three Thousand Red Ants, The Alligation, The

Victims of Amnesia, Motherlode, The Customs Collector in Baggy Pants, The Nose of Sisyphus). 1963.
The Victims of Amnesia (produced 1989). In *Unfair Arguments with Existence,* 1963.
The Customs Collector in Baggy Pants (produced 1964). In *Unfair Arguments with Existence,* 1963.
The Soldiers of No Country (produced 1969). In *Unfair Arguments with Existence,* 1963.
3 by Ferlinghetti: Three Thousand Red Ants, The Alligation, The Victims of Amnesia (produced 1970). In *Unfair Arguments with Existence,* 1963.
Routines (includes 13 short pieces). 1964.

NOVELS

Her. 1960.
Love in the Days of Rage. 1988.
When I Look at Pictures. 1990.

VERSE

Pictures of the Gone World. 1955.
A Coney Island of the Mind. 1958.
Tentative Description of a Dinner Given to Promote the Impeachment of President Eisenhower. 1958.
One Thousand Fearful Words for Fidel Castro. 1961.
Berlin. 1961.
Starting from San Francisco. 1961; revised edition, 1967.
Penguin Modern Poets 5, with Allen Ginsberg and Gregory Corso. 1963.
Where Is Vietnam? 1965.
To Fuck Is to Love Again; Kyrie Eleison Kerista; or, The Situation in the West; Followed by a Holy Proposal. 1965.
Christ Climbed Down. 1965.
An Eye on the World: Selected Poems. 1967.
After the Cries of the Birds. 1967.
Moscow in the Wilderness, Segovia in the Snow. 1967.
Repeat After Me. 1967(?).
Reverie Smoking Grass. 1968.
The Secret Meaning of Things. 1968.
Fuclock. 1968.
Tyrannus Nix? 1969; revised edition, 1973.
Back Roads to Far Towns after Basho. 1970.
Sometime During Eternity. 1970(?).
The World Is a Beautiful Place. 1970(?).
The Illustrated Wilfred Funk. 1971.
A World Awash with Fascism and Fear. 1971.
Back Roads to Far Places. 1971.
Love Is No Stone on the Moon: Automatic Poem. 1971.
Open Eye, with *Open Head,* by Allen Ginsberg. 1972.
Constantly Risking Absurdity. 1973.

Open Eye, Open Heart. 1973.
Populist Manifesto. 1975.
Soon It Will Be Night. 1975(?).
The Jack of Hearts. 1975(?).
Director of Alienation. 1975(?).
The Old Italians Dying. 1976.
Who Are We Now? 1976.
White on White. 1977.
Adieu à Charlot. 1978.
Northwest Ecolog. 1978.
The Sea and Ourselves at Cape Ann. 1979.
Landscapes of Living and Dying. 1979.
The Love Nut. 1979.
Mule Mountain Dreams. 1980.
A Trip to Italy and France. 1981.
The Populist Manifestos, Plus an Interview with Jean-Jacques Lebel. 1981.
Endless Life: The Selected Poems. 1981.
Over All the Obscene Boundaries: European Poems and Transitions. 1984.
Roman Poems. 1986.
Since Man Began to Eat Himself. 1986.
Wild Dreams of a New Beginning. 1988.

RECORDINGS: *Poetry Readings in "The Cellar,"* with Kenneth Rexroth, 1958; *Tentative Description of a Dinner to Impeach President Eisenhower and Other Poems,* 1959; *Tyrannus Nix? and Assassination Raga,* 1971; *The World's Greatest Poets 1,* with Allen Ginsberg and Gregory Corso, 1971; *Lawrence Ferlinghetti,* 1972; *Into the Deeper Pools . . .,* 1984.

OTHER
Dear Ferlinghetti/Dear Jack: The Spicer-Ferlinghetti Correspondence. 1962(?).
The Mexican Night: Travel Journal. 1970.
A Political Pamphlet. 1975.
Literary San Francisco: A Pictorial History from Its Beginnings to the Present Day, with Nancy J. Peters. 1980.
An Artist's Diatribe. 1983.
Leaves of Life: Fifty Drawings from the Model. 1983.
Seven Days in Nicaragua Libre, photographs by Chris Felver. 1984.

Editor, *Beatitude Anthology.* 1960.
Editor, with Michael McClure and David Meltzer, *Journal for the Protection of All Beings 1* and *3.* 2 vols., 1961–69.
Editor, *City Lights Journal.* 4 vols., 1963–78.
Editor, *Panic Grass,* by Charles Upton. 1969.
Editor, *The First Third,* by Neal Cassady. 1971.
Editor, *City Lights Anthology.* 1974.
Editor, with Nancy J. Peters, *City Lights Review 1 [3].* 2 vols., 1987–89.

Translator, *Selections from Paroles by Jacques Prévert.* 1958.

Translator, with Anthony Kahn, *Flowers and Bullets, and Freedom to Kill*, by
  Yevgeny Yevtushenko. 1970.
Translator, with Richard Lettau, *Love Poems*, by Karl Marx. 1977.
Translator, with Francesca Valente, *Roman Poems*, by Pier Paolo Pasolini.
  1986.

BIBLIOGRAPHY: *Lawrence Ferlinghetti: A Comprehensive Bibliography to 1980*
by Bill Morgan, 1982.

MANUSCRIPT COLLECTION: Bancroft Library, University of California, Berkeley.

CRITICAL STUDIES: *Ferlinghetti: A Biography* by Neeli Cherkovsky, 1979;
Lawrence Ferlinghetti: Poet-at-Large by Larry Smith, 1983; *Constantly
Risking Absurdity: The Writings of Lawrence Ferlinghetti* by Michael Skau,
1989; *Ferlinghetti: The Artist in His Time* by Barry Silesky, 1990.

Poet of the Beat Generation, Lawrence Ferlinghetti has published two volumes
of short plays in prose. Ferlinghetti's plays, like his poems, are influenced by
French Existentialist attitudes to love and death, but, like his fellow Beats, he
replaces French Existentialist commitment by disaffiliation. Even before
he turned to plays, Ferlinghetti "performed" his poems, sometimes with jazz
accompaniment. His first volume of plays, *Unfair Arguments with Existence*,
uses a casual American idiom for depicting existence as we know it in modern
industrial society. The progression of the seven plays in this volume is from the
roughly realistic to the distinctly symbolic. The next to last play is a monologue, and the last play spurns all dialogue, striving for a more improvisational
effect.
  In the longest Argument with Existence, *The Soldiers of No Country*, a 60-
year-old priest and a 20-year-old deserter compete for the love of 35-year-old
Erma. Watching this grotesque triangle in a womblike cave are many silent
people who fall, one by one, to the ground. After the priest's victory, Erma
stumbles out of the cave, and the deserter threatens the priest. Though the play
seems to end in ubiquitous death, a baby cries within the cave, implying the
possibility of rebirth.
  Hope is fainter in the next two Arguments. *Three Thousand Red Ants* is an
associational conversation between Fat and Moth, a married couple in bed. At
the end Fat turns binoculars on the audience and exclaims that he sees a
breakthrough, to which his wife replies under the bedclothes: "Your own!
Humpty Dumpty!" In *The Alligation* Ladybird is fixated on her pet alligator,
Shooky, though a Blind Indian warns her that this is dangerous. When
Ladybird stretches full length on Shooky, he rolls over on top of her, and the
Blind Indian calls to the audience for help. Both plays pose audience help as an
implicit question.
  Influenced by the Theatre of the Absurd, the next three Arguments are
extended metaphors for the human condition. In *The Victims of Amnesia* a
Night Clerk converses with a woman shown at four stages of diminishing
age—Marie, Young Woman, Girl, Baby—all embraced in the name Mazda. At
the play's end the Night Clerk *cum* Fate inveighs against all life, as the play
explodes into smashing light bulbs of many sizes. But finally a single small bulb

flickers in the dark before the theatre lights come up. Similarly, *Motherlode* theatricalizes the undimmed faith of a dying miner, even after the crass commercial Schmucks have despoiled the land. After the miner's death, with Schmuck triumphant, the birds still call "Love! Love!". *The Customs Collector in Baggy Pants* is set on a life-boat "full of flush-toilets which we call civilization." Assailed by a storm outside and the storm of flushing toilets on the boat, the Customs Collector shouts his determination not to die or capitulate. Ferlinghetti punctuates the Absurd with hope.

In *The Nose of Sisyphus*, however, hope is all but extinguished. In a playground that is a metaphor for the world, Sisyphus uses his false nose to try to push a globe up a slide, while assorted human beings try to scale a jungle gym. Though Sisyphus cannot persuade the people to help him, he does succeed in leading their chants. But a whistle-blowing Big Baboon slides down the slide, toppling Sisyphus, frightening the people, and robbing Sisyphus of globe and nose. Alone on stage, the Big Baboon tosses the false nose into the audience. At best, one can hope for another Sisyphus to arise from the audience.

The Nose of Sisyphus is the last play in *Unfair Arguments with Existence*, and Ferlinghetti incorporates it as the last of the 13 pieces in his second volume of plays, *Routines*. He defines a routine as

> a song and dance, a little rout, a routing-out, a run-around, a "round of business or amusement": myriads of people, herds, flowerbeds, ships and cities, all going through their routines, life itself a blackout routine, an experimental madness somewhere between dotage and megalomania, lost in the vibration of a wreckage (of some other cosmos we fell out of).

All 13 *Routines* focus on visual metaphors, but they read rhythmically, with the free flexible rhythms of Ferlinghetti's poems. Their subjects are love, death, and the totalitarian establishment. Just before *The Nose of Sisyphus* appears *Bore*, a call to action: "Routines never end; they have to be broken. This little routine to end all routines requires the formation of a worldwide society dedicated to the non-violent disruption of institutionalized events." Play tries to infiltrate life in Ferlinghetti's final play.

—Ruby Cohn

FIERSTEIN, Harvey (Forbes).

Born in Brooklyn, New York, 6 June 1954. Educated at Pratt Institute, Brooklyn, B.F.A. 1973. Drag performer and actor from 1970: professional debut at Club 82 and La Mama Experimental Theatre Club, New York, 1971; roles in more than 60 plays and in several films. Recipient: Rockefeller grant; Ford grant; Creative Artists Public Services grant; Obie award, 1982; Tony award, 1983 (for writing and acting), 1984; Oppenheimer award, 1983; Drama Desk award, 1983 (for writing and acting); Dramatists Guild Hull-Warriner award, 1983; Los Angeles Drama Critics Circle award, 1984; Ace award, 1988. Agent: George Lane, William Morris Agency, 1350 Avenue of the Americas, New York, New York 10019, U.S.A.

Publications

PLAYS

In Search of the Cobra Jewels (produced 1972). 1972.
Freaky Pussy (produced 1973).
Flatbush Tosca (produced 1975). 1975.
Torch Song Trilogy (produced 1981). 1981.
  The International Stud (produced 1978).
  Fugue in a Nursery (produced 1979).
  Widows and Children First! (produced 1979).
Spookhouse (produced 1982). In *Plays International*, July 1987.
La Cage aux Folles, music and lyrics by Jerry Herman, adaptation of the play
  by Jean Poiret (produced 1983).
Manny and Jake (produced 1987).
Safe Sex (includes *Manny and Jake, Safe Sex, On Tidy Endings*) (produced
  1987). 1987.
Forget Him (produced 1988).
Legs Diamond, with Charles Suppon, music and lyrics by Peter Allen (pro-
  duced 1988).

SCREENPLAY: *Torch Song Trilogy*, 1989.

Actor/drag queen Harvey Fierstein began writing plays at age 20 so as to create
roles for himself. His first attempt concerned his efforts to clean Harry
Koutoukas's apartment, a horrifying task which he undertook so that playwright would write a script for him. Instead, Fierstein wrote about the house-
cleaning experience in a musical—*In Search of the Cobra Jewels*, complete
with a chorus of cockroaches—in which both writers appeared as themselves.
Because Fierstein wanted to play a whore, he wrote *Freaky Pussy*, whose seven
cross-dressing hookers live in a subway men's room. Then, longing to sing
Tosca, he wrote *Flatbush Tosca*. His next, though still unproduced, play,
Cannibals, anticipates a plot element in *La Cage aux Folles*, as two kids run off
and bring shame on their tribe because they want to be straight.

The next year Fierstein began writing his Tony award-winning role, Arnold
Beckoff (i.e. "beckon" versus "back off"), in the first of the *Torch Song
Trilogy* plays, *The International Stud*, and the plump pixie, wit, political
activist, and outspoken critic of a heterosexist society finally began attracting
the attention of audiences beyond the confines of the experimental off-off-
Broadway La Mama. In dialogue at once droll, direct, and distressing ("A
thing of beauty is a joy till sunrise"), Arnold compulsively carries the torch for
bisexual Ed; his winning that stud degrades him nearly as much as does the
initial pursuit and the eventual loss. Yet he accompanies each act of dependence, each self-destructive kvetch with which he pushes Ed away from him,
with a laconic quip which lets us know that Arnold understands what he's
doing. Like the torch singer who capitalizes on her pain with "music to be
miserable by," Arnold often allows his vulnerability to careen crazily into
masochistic self-pity.

Fierstein suits his form to his content by employing presentational styles in
the first two plays. Thus Arnold's egocentricity finds expression when he gazes

into a mirror during the opening of *The International Stud*, which also isolates
Arnold and Ed in a series of self-absorbed monologues; although this is a two-
character play (plus torch singer), they appear together only in the last scene,
after Fierstein creates the effect of a backroom orgy by employing Arnold
alone. *Fugue in a Nursery* picks up Arnold and ex-lover Ed a year after the end
of their affair, as Arnold and his new flame Alan visit Ed and the "other
woman" Laurel at Ed's summer home. Only slightly matured out of pure
narcissism, the four, in contrapuntal scenes played upon a giant bed, engage in
frequently rearranged pairings with occasionally intersecting dialogue. They're
sophisticated enough to suit the fugal accompaniment (by string quartet) and
plot construction, but sufficiently infantile for Arnold's bedroom to be termed
"the nursery."

If *Fugue*'s duologues seem an experimental version of Noël Coward or
William Wycherley, the representational domestic drama *Widows and
Children First!* begins with more conventional sit-com plotting and balances
deflation of sentiment with effective sentimentality. Five years after *Fugue*, we
find Arnold in a period of widowhood following Alan's death—bludgeoned
with baseball bats by homophobes. Ed has left Laurel, Arnold mothers his
"hopelessly homo" foster son, 15-year-old David, while visiting Mrs. Beckoff
rebukes her own homosexual son Arnold, giving us therefore two mothers,
two widows, two sons, two referees for fights—yet only four characters.
Although Arnold and Ed have matured to some degree, Ed still doesn't know
what he wants and Arnold still displays a penchant for acting in ways not in his
own best interest. In a moving microcosm of human paradox, Mrs. Beckoff
disapproves of David when she, hilariously, mistakes him for Arnold's lover,
but grows still more shocked when she learns the tie is filial. Arnold demands
respect of his mother without necessarily giving it in return. David waxes wise
about how to help Arnold, yet doesn't apply much insight to himself. Arnold
objects to his mother's distress at homosexuality, yet loves an equally fearful
man.

Fierstein's rich thematic panoply—including loneliness, loss, self-esteem,
homophobia, and honesty ("What's the matter? Catch your tongue in the
closet door?")—numbers among its concerns frequent allegiance to the sort of
family values to which right-wing zealots love to claim sole proprietorship.
Arnold can't be impersonal about sex, longing instead for romance, commitment, monogamy, and children to mother. Such conventional values imbue
most of Fierstein's work ever since his groundbreaking trilogy and contribute
to his popularity among heterosexual as well as gay audiences.

Spookhouse embodies contradictory attitudes towards the possibility of
raising decent kids. The conscientious but destructively naïve gay social
worker believes in the social system and the future. As in Tennessee Williams's
The Glass Menagerie, the obnoxious mother's grit provides the only glue
holding together her neurotic—and in this case lower-class—family, but she
knows the system has failed her kids and wants her sociopathic son imprisoned. Set in a disintegrating Coney Island amusement park ride and the home
above it, *Spookhouse* serves as metaphor for the horrors in our lives we can't
control. ("Life's scary enough without paying for added attractions.") These
haunt us even in our safe places, such as our homes, and pop out at us when
we're unable to cope with them. This black-comic melodrama, replete with

rape, incest, murder, and arson, taps into our anxieties, particularly our pessimism pertaining to parenting and the urban bureaucracy, which victimizes both its clients and its employees.

The dysfunctional but straight Janiks in *Spookhouse* contrast with the stable gay family in *La Cage aux Folles*, a musical which provides a refreshing perspective refuting homophobic stereotypes. Married in all but law, Albin and Georges exceed their devotion to each other only in their love for son Jean-Michele, who poorly repays Albin's mothering by banishing him from the family flat when the boy's fiancée and her right-wing parents visit to inspect their future in-laws. Unlike the French farce original by Jean Poiret, Fierstein poignantly focuses on Jean-Michele's insensitivity and ingratitude and celebrates the commitment between the two middle-aged men, a night club owner and his androgynous drag-queen star. In addition to dramatizing loving domestic relationships, Fierstein again stresses the importance of being oneself ("I Am What I Am") and respecting oneself and others, particularly (c.f. the biblical injunction to honor them) parents.

Although this tender comedy ran on Broadway for four and a half years, Fierstein's second foray onto the musical stage proved less successful, probably because he merely attempted to salvage the work of an inexperienced librettist. When Fierstein inherited clothing designer Charles Suppon's book for the 1940s gangster musical *Legs Diamond*, scored by Australian Peter Allen, he revised characters and dialogue but retained the structure. The less said about this disastrous vanity production for the composer/star the better. The one-act, pre-AIDS comedy *Forget Him*, on the other hand, deserves an audience. The Fierstein stand-in, Michael, has paid a finder's fee for the perfect lover—handsome, rich, smart, athletic, and attentive. Yet he demands his money back because Eugene's blindness and deafness—or Michael's own insecurities—leave him troubled that someone even better, the title's "him," will come along.

With the *Safe Sex* trilogy Fierstein finally turns to the effect of AIDS on gay men's lives, representing this impact in part by means of presentational set metaphors (like *Fugue*'s bed and the spooks in *Spookhouse*). For *Manny and Jake*, he dramatizes disease-carrier Manny's ex-lovers—many now corpses—with dummies. In the title play, he visualizes for us how the men's relationship has been thrown off-balance by placing them on a seesaw, although a more recent New York revival puts them in bed, which makes the seductiveness and terrors more real.

Fear, indeed, informs all three plays. Manny, who used to live for sex, paralyzes himself with worry over infecting more men, even while praying for the renewal of romantic possibilities he regards as now blighted by his HIV status; implicitly he rejects the option of safer sex and simply laments his loss. His parallel in the title play, Ghee (played by Fierstein), also permits fears to inhibit him. HIV-negative, Ghee's terrified avoidance of sex by means of verbal attacks, retreats, and reprises really masks a greater problem: fear of intimacy. The teeter-totter metaphor expresses a relationship imbalanced by scares from AIDS, letting a lover get close, and potential loss of both lover and life. Despite the pain at their core, *Manny and Jake* offers a lyrical elegy to sexual joy, while *Safe Sex* satirically mocks both Ghee's anxieties and his macho lover's unwashed ardor.

In the final treatment of fear, loss, and—dare we?—trust, *On Tidy Endings*, Fierstein employs a fully representational style and setting (repeating in this trilogy the same progression from presentational to realistic which he first used in *Torch Song*). The Fierstein character, Arthur, mourns his lover's death from AIDS, while he confronts Colin's ex-wife, there with legal papers pertaining to their shares of the inheritance. Part of that legacy turns out to be the disease, which ironically has spared Arthur but stricken the woman, probably working hard to win Arthur's trust not only for her sake but for that of her son, who needs to overcome his own grief, rage, and homophobia so as to continue to benefit from Arthur's maternal care. Like *Torch Song Trilogy*, *On Tidy Endings* prompts our laughter and tears at a son and alternately bickering and affectionate widows.

—Tish Dace

See the essay on *Torch Song Trilogy*.

FOOTE, (Albert) Horton (Jr.).

Born in Wharton, Texas, 14 March 1916. Educated at the Pasadena Playhouse Theatre, California, 1933–35; Tamara Daykarhanova Theatre School, New York, 1937–39. Married Lillian Vallish in 1945; two daughters and two sons. Actor with American Actors Theatre, New York, 1939–42; theatre workshop director and producer, King-Smith School of Creative Arts, 1944–45, and manager, Productions Inc., 1945–48, both Washington, D.C. Recipient: Oscar, for screenplay, 1963, 1983; William Inge award, for lifetime achievement in theater, 1989. D.Litt.: Austin College, Sherman, Texas, 1987; Drew University, Madison, New Jersey, 1987; American Film Institute, Los Angeles, California. Lives in New York City and Wharton, Texas. Agent: Lucy Kroll Agency, 390 West End Avenue, New York, New York 10024, U.S.A.

Publications

PLAYS

Wharton Dance (produced 1940).
Texas Town (produced 1941).
Out of My House (also co-director: produced 1942).
Only the Heart (produced 1942). 1944.
Two Southern Idylls: Miss Lou, and The Girls (produced 1943).
The Lonely (produced 1943).
Goodbye to Richmond (produced 1943).
Daisy Lee, music by Bernardo Segall (produced 1944).
Homecoming, In My Beginning, People in the Show, The Return (produced 1944).
Themes and Variations (produced 1945?).
Celebration (produced 1948).
The Chase (produced 1952). 1952.
The Trip to Bountiful (televised 1953; produced 1953). 1954.
The Oil Well (televised 1953; produced 1991).
The Midnight Caller (televised 1953; produced 1958). 1959.

John Turner Davis (televised 1953; produced 1958). In *A Young Lady of Property*, 1955.

The Dancers (televised 1954; produced 1963). In *A Young Lady of Property*, 1955.

The Travelling Lady (produced 1954). 1955.

A Young Lady of Property: Six Short Plays (includes *A Young Lady of Property, The Dancers, The Old Beginning, John Turner Davis, The Death of the Old Man, The Oil Well*). 1955.

Harrison, Texas: Eight Television Plays (includes *The Dancers, The Death of the Old Man, Expectant Relations, John Turner Davis, The Midnight Caller, The Tears of My Sister, The Trip to Bountiful, A Young Lady of Property*). 1956.

Flight (televised 1957). In *Television Plays for Writers*, edited by A.S. Burack. 1957.

Old Man, adaptation of a story by Faulkner (televised 1958). In *Three Plays*, 1962.

Roots in a Parched Ground (as *The Night of the Storm*, televised 1960). In *Three Plays*, 1962.

Tomorrow, adaptation of the story by Faulkner (televised 1960). In *Three Plays*, 1962.

Three Plays. 1962.

The Screenplay of To Kill a Mockingbird. 1964.

Gone with the Wind, music and lyrics by Harold Rome, adaptation of the novel by Margaret Mitchell (produced 1972).

The Roads to Home (includes *The Dearest of Friends, A Nightingale, Spring Dance*) (also director: produced 1982). 1982.

Courtship (produced 1984). In *Courtship, On Valentine's Day, 1918*, 1987.

1918 (televised 1984). In *Courtship, On Valentine's Day, 1918*, 1987.

On Valentine's Day (televised 1985). In *Courtship, On Valentine's Day, 1918*, 1987.

Tomorrow (television play) and *Tomorrow* (screenplay), in *Tomorrow and Tomorrow and Tomorrow* (also includes Faulkner's story "Tomorrow"), edited by David G. Yellin and Marie Conners. 1985.

The Road to the Graveyard (produced 1985). 1988.

Blind Date (produced 1986). 1986.

Lily Dale (produced 1986). In *Roots in a Parched Ground, Convicts, Lily Dale, The Widow Claire*, 1988.

The Widow Claire (produced 1986). In *Roots in a Parched Ground, Convicts, Lily Dale, The Widow Claire*, 1988.

Courtship, On Valentine's Day, 1918. 1987.

Roots in a Parched Ground, Convicts, Lily Dale, The Widow Claire. 1988.

The Man Who Climbed the Pecan Trees (produced 1988). 1989.

Selected One-Act Plays, edited by Gerald C. Wood. 1988.

Habitation of Dragons (also director: produced 1988).

Cousins, and The Death of Papa. 1989.

To Kill a Mockingbird, Tender Mercies, The Trip to Bountiful: Three Screenplays. 1989.

Dividing the Estate (produced 1989).

Talking Pictures (produced 1990).

SCREENPLAYS: *Storm Fear*, 1955; *To Kill a Mockingbird*, 1962; *Baby, The Rain Must Fall*, 1964; *Hurry Sundown*, with Thomas Ryan, 1966; *Tomorrow*, 1972; *Tender Mercies*, 1983; *1918*, 1984; *The Trip to Bountiful*, 1985; *On Valentine's Day*, 1985; *Courtship*, 1986; *Convicts*, 1989; *Of Mice and Men*, 1991.

TELEVISION PLAYS: *Ludie Brooks*, 1951; *The Travelers*, 1952; *The Old Beginning*, 1952; *The Trip to Bountiful*, 1953; *A Young Lady of Property*, 1953; *The Oil Well*, 1953; *Rocking Chair*, 1953; *Expectant Relations*, 1953; *The Death of the Old Man*, 1953; *The Tears of My Sister*, 1953; *John Turner Davis*, 1953; *The Midnight Caller*, 1953; *The Dancers*, 1954; *The Shadow of Willie Greer*, 1954; *The Roads to Home*, 1955; *Drugstore: Sunday Noon*, 1956; *Flight*, 1957 (UK title: *Summer's Pride*, 1961); *Member of the Family*, 1957; *Old Man*, 1958; *Tomorrow*, 1960; *The Shape of the River*, 1960; *The Night of the Storm*, 1960; *The Gambling Heart*, 1964; *The Displaced Person*, from a story by Flannery O'Connor, 1977; *Barn Burning*, from the story by Faulkner, 1980; scripts for *Gabby Hayes Show*, 1950–51; *Habitation of Dragons*, 1991.

NOVEL
The Chase. 1956.

CRITICAL STUDIES: "On Valentine's Day" by Samuel G. Freedman, in the New York *Times* Magazine, February 9, 1986; "Roots in a Parched Ground: An Interview with Horton Foote" by Ronald L. Davis, in *Southwest Review*, Summer 1988.

THEATRICAL ACTIVITIES
DIRECTOR: **Plays**—*Out of My House* (co-director, with Mary Hunter and Jane Rose), 1942; *Goodbye to Richmond*, 1946.
ACTOR: **Plays**—role in *The Eternal Road* by Franz Werfel, 1937; with One-Act Repertory Company: Robert Emmet in *The Coggerers*, Lorenzo in *The Red Velvet Goat*, and Chief Outourou's Brother in *Mr. Banks of Birmingham*, 1939; *Railroads on Parade*, 1939; *Yankee Doodle Comes to Town*, 1940; *The Fifth Column* by Ernest Hemingway, 1940; Pharmacist in *Texas Town*, 1941.

In *1918*, Horace Robedaux, the principal character of Horton Foote's Orphans' Home cycle, asks Foote's rich and perennial question: "How can human beings stand all that comes to them?". A little later, his mother-in-law indirectly answers him: "You just stand it. You keep going." Between the question and the answer lies Foote's deeply realized Texan world, where the fundamentals and the universals of many kinds of relationships are played out. We see and hear in the accents of everyday talk how sons and daughters, mothers and fathers, lovers, drunks, and crazies "stand it" and "keep going." We are not preached at, nor are the scenes or characters calculated to point morals. Instead, the plays—each of which can stand on its own dramatically— present simply and inexorably, the stuff of life. And since the cycle is set in the

earlier parts of this century, our sense acts unconsciously to join that past to
our own. And so the past becomes actual, both in its differences and in its
similarities. There are few large-scale events; World War I, for instance, seems
very far from, yet very much part of, *1918*. The central characters engage in
getting and losing jobs, missing trains, flunking out of school, as well as
fathering and losing children and marrying the one they love. Although life can
be very bleak, Foote somehow justifies the bleakness; despite ourselves, we do
not feel desperate or depressed. Through the cycle Texas becomes our world,
and Horton Foote's people become our people.

The rhetoric of Foote's work suggests that the language we regularly use be
taken as fully adequate to our condition, and that our condition consists
precisely of the people we know, the work we do, the era in which we live.
Things like a new dress (*Roots in a Parched Ground*) are significantly related
to 'flu epidemics (*1918*) and Foote's methodical vision delineates the relationship and discovers the particulars of its reality. Nothing and no one is
unrelated, even by choice. The Texas of 1912 and the New York City of 1992
work in the same categories of truth and falsehood, love and death, happiness
and unhappiness, rejection and acceptance. The cycle lives through the
coming-of-age of Horace Robedaux. From the days just before his father's
early death we become part of his family because we know him at the
beginning of self-definition and experience with him the sorrows and the joys.
He never assumes the role of representative, however, because Foote has made
his character a living one which now and again makes surprising decisions.
The familiarity we have established does not breed contempt but rather
respect. Horace endures partly on our behalf and our response to that endurance is to understand ourselves better—a classical purpose of theatre.

Much of Foote's drama treats the common man and woman realistically in
disturbing but strangely comforting stories. The pathos which ordinary people
undergo, the nobility of the neglected and the forgotten, the profound humor
in unsuspected houses and families, the suffering around every corner, the
substantiality of the taken-for-granted, the high stakes wagered in backstairs
games—these constitute his subject. Foote's realism pertains to times and
places he has both lived in and imagined; his ear for speech is true, his
characters recognizable and individualized. The Orphans' Home cycle offers
us aspects of life itself and it deserves to be staged as a cycle so that its full
subtlety and strength can be realized.

Foote is a writer schooled in the television screenplay; a regional writer; a
folk writer; a miniaturist. But, thanks to all that, he is a writer of considerable
power. His one-act *The Man Who Climbed the Pecan Trees* treats only part of
the subject of the cycle, namely, the spiritual barrenness of the arid southeast-
Texas landscape. Much like Horace, Stanley has grown up in a family devoid
of judgment and passion. But, unlike him, his family still "functions" because
his mother keeps it alive despite its break-up. (By contrast, Horace's mother
moves to Houston and leaves him to fend for himself.) The husband and father
is dead before the play begins but the mother (Mrs. Campbell) keeps him alive
too, in a series of inane sentimentalities which function to deaden him further
and to stultify memory itself; so much so in Stanley's case that finally he can't
say where in the world he is or where he's been—a fate that might well have
been Horace's.

As it turns out, the same source of energy by which Mr. Campbell has gone on living since his death will now sustain his son, Mr. Stanley Campbell—Mrs. Campbell's platitudes which deny even the truth of sentiment in Stanley's obsessive lyric: "In the gloamin', Oh, my darlin'." Her manner of speaking will pen him (is penning him) in a dead-end. At play's end, he sits beside his mother, firmly on the ground but no longer of this earth. Ironically, until he "falls" back into infantile dependency, Stanley, among the evaders and euphemists, has been the truth-teller, one who sees things for what they are, even if the facts are partial. Foote's "facts" may be partial, too, but the impartiality of the theatre allows him to give us an almost complete version of American society.

—Thomas Apple

FOREMAN, Richard.

Born in New York City, 10 June 1937. Educated at Scarsdale High School, Scarsdale, New York; Brown University, Providence, Rhode Island, 1955–59, B.A. 1959; Yale University School of Drama, New Haven, Connecticut, 1959–62, M.F.A. 1962. Married 1) Amy Taubin in 1962 (divorced 1971); 2) Kate Manheim in 1992. Writer with New Dramatists and Actors Studio, both New York, 1962–65; associate director, Film-Maker's Cinematheque, New York, 1967–68. Since 1968 founding director, Ontological-Hysteric Theatre, New York. Recipient: Obie award, 1970, 1973, 1983, 1986 (for directing), 1987, sustained achievement award, 1988; National Opera Institute grant, 1971; National Endowment for the Arts grant, 1972, 1974, and distinguished artists fellowship, 1989; Creative Artists Public Service award, 1972, 1974; Rockefeller grant, 1975; Guggenheim fellowship, 1975; Ford Foundation grant, 1980; American Academy and Institute of Arts and Letters award, 1992. Agent: Gregor F. Hall, Bookport International, 429 Third Street, Suite 2B, Brooklyn, New York 11215. Address: 152 Wooster Street, New York, New York 10012, U.S.A.

Publications

PLAYS

Angelface (also director: produced 1968).

Elephant-Steps, music by Stanley Silverman (also director: produced 1968).

Ida-Eyed (also director: produced 1969).

Real Magic in New York, music by Stephen Dickman (produced 1969).

Total Recall: Sophia = (Wisdom) Part 2 (also director: produced 1970).

Dream Tantras for Western Massachusetts, music by Stanley Silverman (also director: produced 1971).

HcOhTiEnLa; or, Hotel China (also director: produced 1971). Excerpts in *Performance 2*, April 1972.

Evidence (also director: produced 1972; selection, as *15 Minutes of Evidence*, produced 1975).

Dr. Selavy's Magic Theatre, music by Stanley Silverman, lyrics by Tom Hendry (also director: produced 1972).

Sophia = (Wisdom) Part 3: The Cliffs (also director: produced 1972). In *Performance* 6 (New York), May–June 1973.

Particle Theory (also director: produced 1973).

Honor (also director: produced 1973).

Classical Therapy; or, A Week under the Influence . . . (also director: produced 1973).

Pain(t) (also director: produced 1974).

Vertical Mobility: Sophia = (Wisdom) Part 4 (also director: produced 1974). In *Drama Review 63*, June 1974.

RA-D-IO (Wisdom); or, Sophia = (Wisdom) Part 1, music by David Tice (produced 1974).

Pandering to the Masses: A Misrepresentation (also director: produced 1975). In *The Theatre of Images*, edited by Bonnie Marranca, 1977.

Hotel for Criminals, music by Stanley Silverman (also director: produced 1975).

Rhoda in Potatoland (Her Fall-starts) (also director: produced 1975).

Thinking (One Kind) (produced 1975).

Le Théâtre de Richard Foreman, edited by Simone Benmussa and Erika Kralik. 1975.

Plays and Manifestos, edited by Kate Davy. 1976.

Livre de Splendeurs (Part I) (produced 1976).

Lines of Vision, music by George Quincy, lyrics by María Irene Fornés (produced 1976).

Slight (produced 1977).

Book of Splendors (Part II): Book of Levers: Action at a Distance (also director: produced 1977). In *Theater*, Spring 1978.

Blvd. de Paris (I've Got the Shakes) (produced 1978).

The American Imagination, music by Stanley Silverman (produced 1978).

Luogo + Bersaglio (Place + Target) (produced 1979).

Madame Adare, music by Stanley Silverman (produced 1980).

Penguin Touquet (also director: produced 1981).

Café Amérique (produced 1982).

Egyptology: My Head Was a Sledgehammer (produced 1983).

George Bataille's Bathrobe (produced 1984).

Miss Universal Happiness (also director: produced 1985).

Reverberation Machines: The Later Plays and Essays. 1985.

Africanis Instructus, music by Stanley Silverman (also director: produced 1986).

The Cure, music by Foreman (produced 1986). In *Unbalancing Acts*, 1992.

Film Is Evil, Radio Is Good (also director: produced 1987). In *Unbalancing Acts*, 1992.

Love and Science (also director: produced 1987). 1991.

Symphony of Rats (also director: produced 1988). In *Unbalancing Acts*, 1992.

What Did He See? (also director: produced 1988). In *Unbalancing Acts*, 1992.

Lava (also director: produced 1989). In *Unbalancing Acts*, 1992.

Eddie Goes to Poetry City: Part 1 (also director: produced 1990).

Eddie Goes to Poetry City: Part 2 (also director: produced 1991).

The Mind King (also director: produced 1992).
Unbalancing Acts: Foundations for a Theater. 1992.
The Richard Foreman Trilogy (includes *In the Mind*, *My Father Was Already Lost*, *The Field of White Light*) (produced 1992).

SCREENPLAYS: *Out of the Body Travel*, 1975; *City Archives*, 1977; *Strong Medicine*, 1978.

MANUSCRIPT COLLECTIONS: Lincoln Center Library of the Performing Arts, New York; Anthology Film Archives, New York.

CRITICAL STUDIES: "Richard Foreman's Ontological-Hysteric Theatre" by Michael Kirby, in *Drama Review*, June 1973; *Richard Foreman and the Ontological-Hysteric Theatre* by Kate Davy, 1981.

THEATRICAL ACTIVITIES

DIRECTOR: **Plays**—most of his own plays (also designer); *The Threepenny Opera* by Brecht, 1976; *Stages* by Stuart Ostrow, 1978; *Don Juan* by Molière, 1981; *Three Acts of Recognition* by Botho Strauss, 1982; *Die Fledermaus* by Johann Strauss, 1984; *Dr. Faustus Lights the Lights* by Gertrude Stein, 1984; *Golem* by H. Levick, 1984; *My Life My Death* by Kathy Acker, 1985; *The Birth of the Poet* by Kathy Acker, 1985; *Largo Desolato* by Václav Havel, 1986; *End of the World* by Arthur Kopit, 1987; *The Fall of the House of Usher* by Arthur Yorinks and Philip Glass, 1988, revised version, 1992; *Where's Dick?* by Michael Korie and Stewart Wallace, 1989; *Woyzeck* by Georg Büchner, 1990; *Don Giovanni* by Mozart, 1991.

Richard Foreman comments:

In 1968 I began to write for the theatre which I wanted to see, which was radically different from any style of theatre that I had seen. In brief, I imagined a theatre which broke down all elements into a kind of atomic structure—and showed those elements of story, action, sound, light, composition, gesture, in terms of the smallest building-block units, the basic cells of the perceived experience of both living and art-making.

The scripts themselves read like notations of my own process of imagining a theatre piece. They are the evidence of a kind of effort in which the mind's leaps and inventions may be rendered as part of a process not unique to the artist in question (myself) but typical of the building-up which goes on through all modes of coming-into-being (human and non-human). I want to refocus the attention of the spectator on the intervals, gaps, relations and rhythms which saturate the objects (acts and physical props) which are the "givens" of any particular play. In doing this, I believe the spectator is made available (as I am, hopefully, when writing) to those most desirable energies which secretly connect him (through a kind of resonance) with the foundations of his being.

Richard Foreman's statement "I have developed a style that shows how it is with us, in consciousness. I don't speak in generalities. I show the mind at work, moment-by-moment" is perhaps the best starting point from which to approach his theatre. His plays eschew plot, characters, development, and even emotions in the attempt to dramatize the process of thinking itself. Each moment in the theatre corresponds to a moment in consciousness, and the relationships between them, or between the moments in the theatre, may not be immediately obvious. In *Rhoda in Potatoland* actors discuss writing, but digress to a dinner of potatoes. As in any train of thought ("Do you think using the associative method," says Foreman's Voice in *Pandering to the Masses.* "Everybody does you know."), potatoes become part of the freight, and the play begins to compare everything to a potato. After a digression for an all-girl band and a shoe store, a sign announces "THE RETURN OF THE POTATOES" and with the entrance of four human-sized potatoes, the Voice says

> Now this is where the interesting part of the
> evening begins. Everything up to now was
> Recognizable.
> Now, however
> The real potatoes are amongst us
> And a different kind of undertanding is possible
> for anybody who wants a different kind of
> understanding.

Thereafter "potato" becomes a kind of counter, a word that can replace another word or form comparisons and links with other objects. Even when the word is replaced by other words, Foreman follows the linguistic philosophy of Ludwig Wittgenstein, as he interprets it: "Use anything, to mean anything, but the system must have a rigor."

To perform consciousness rigorously, Foreman developed techniques which allow tight control over the presentation. He directs his plays using a core of performers, who have little or no classical theater training. Foreman's actors speak their lines flatly, without inflection. In some of the performances, the actors only murmur key words of their pre-recorded dialogue. Their words are frequently repeated, their sentences broken into fragments, and their phrases echoed by another actor. Foreman further ends the identity of actor and character through movement. Actors' gestures are also repeated in a hieratic style until they lose their original significance and acquire a new one from the course of the play.

The visual side of Foreman's theatre is crucial. Backdrops are used to present a fleeting image, to introduce a stray thought. Small stages reproduce the larger scene, and the actors themselves freeze into tableaux. Strings, ropes, and pieces of wood or paper stretch across the stage, link props or actors, or divide the stage into smaller frames. Buzzers, lights, and noises create other aural and visual "frames," to isolate words and actions.

No description of this odd theatre can suggest the power that these slow, measured plays can build. As the performances progress, the incomprehensible actions and incidents take their place in an overall design, not with a logical inevitability, but with a psychological appropriateness. As in Gertrude Stein's landscape plays, dialogue and incident are meant to be seen all together and simultaneously, not as a sequential development. A part of the power of the plays arises from the effort of the spectator in deciphering each individual moment like the facet in a Cubist painting, and then assembling them into a whole.

Foreman has described his plays as being what happens in his mind as he is writing a play. Recently, however, he has been increasingly directing other playwright's works, and it is possible that this expansion of his artistic universe is infecting his playwriting. *Egyptology* hints at a real setting (Egypt), and includes Louis XIV, who may have come from Foreman's having directed Molière's *Don Juan. Miss Universal Happiness* topically includes Central American guerrillas even as it asserts that "the self you seek is inside you." *The Cure* not only provides a moment of emotional contact, but even a hesitant attempt at synthesis and statement: "The pain is the cure," says one of the characters. All of this is undoubtedly happening in Foreman's mind, and while we may debate whether such a detailed presentation of one man's mind is appropriate to the theatre, that is precisely the kind of debate Foreman would enjoy: "The play's over. You're left with your own thoughts. Can you really get interested in them or are they just occurring."

—Walter Bode

FORNÉS, María Irene.

Born in Havana, Cuba, 14 May 1930; emigrated to the United States, 1945; became citizen, 1951. Educated in Havana public schools. Lived in Europe, 1954–57; painter and textile designer; costume designer, Judson Poets Theatre and New Dramatists Committee productions, 1965–70; teacher at the Teachers and Writers Collaborative, New York, privately, and at numerous drama festivals and workshops, from 1965. President, New York Theatre Strategy, 1973–80. Recipient: Whitney fellowship, 1961; Centro Mexicano de Escritores fellowship, 1962; Office for Advanced Drama Research grant, 1965; Obie award, 1965, 1977, 1979, 1982, 1984, 1985, 1988; Cintas Foundation fellowship, 1967; Yale University fellowship, 1967, 1968; Rockefeller fellowship, 1971, 1985; Guggenheim fellowship, 1972; Creative Artists Public Service grant, 1972, 1975; National Endowment for the Arts grant, 1974; American Academy award, 1985; Home Box Office award, 1986. Agent: Helen Merrill Ltd., 435 West 23rd Street, 1A, New York, New York 10011. Address: 1 Sheridan Square, New York, New York 10014, U.S.A.

Publications

PLAYS

The Widow (produced 1961). As *La Viuda*, in *Teatro Cubano*, 1961.

Tango Palace (as *There! You Died*, produced 1963; as *Tango Palace*, produced 1964; revised version produced 1965). In *Promenade and Other Plays*, 1971.

The Successful Life of Three: A Skit for Vaudeville (produced 1965). In *Promenade and Other Plays*, 1971.

Promenade, music by Al Carmines (produced 1965; revised version produced 1969). In *Promenade and Other Plays*, 1971.

The Office (produced 1966).

A Vietnamese Wedding (produced 1967). In *Promenade and Other Plays*, 1971.

The Annunciation (also director: produced 1967).

Dr. Kheal (produced 1968). In *Promenade and Other Plays*, 1971.

The Red Burning Light; or, Mission XQ3 (produced 1968). In *Promenade and Other Plays*, 1971.

Molly's Dream, music by Cosmos Savage (also director: produced 1968). In *Promenade and Other Plays*, 1971.

Promenade and Other Plays. 1971; revised edition, 1987.

The Curse of the Langston House, in *Baboon!!!* (produced 1972).

Dance, with Remy Charlip (also co-director: produced 1972).

Aurora, music by John FitzGibbon (also director: produced 1974).

Cap-a-Pie, music by José Raúl Bernardo (also director: produced 1975).

Lines of Vision (lyrics only), book by Richard Foreman, music by George Quincy (produced 1976).

Washing (produced 1976).

Fefu and Her Friends (also director: produced 1977). In *Wordplays 1*, 1980.

Lolita in the Garden, music by Richard Weinstock (also director: produced 1977).

In Service (also director: produced 1978).

Eyes on the Harem (also director: produced 1979). ·

Blood Wedding, adaptation of a play by García Lorca (produced 1980).

Evelyn Brown: A Diary (also director: produced 1980).

Life Is Dream, adaptation of a play by Calderón, music by George Quincy (also director: produced 1981).

A Visit, music by George Quincy (also director: produced 1981).

The Danube (also director: produced 1982). In *Plays*, 1986.

Mud (also director: produced 1983; revised version, also director: produced 1985). In *Plays*, 1986.

Sarita, music by Leon Odenz (also director: produced 1984). In *Plays*, 1986.

Abingdon Square (produced 1984). In *Womenswork*, edited by Julia Miles, 1993.

The Conduct of Life (also director: produced 1985). In *Plays*, 1986.

Cold Air, adaptation of a play by Virgilio Piñera (also director: produced 1985). 1985.

Drowning, adaptation of a story by Chekhov, in *Orchards* (produced 1985). 1986.

The Trial of Joan of Arc on a Matter of Faith (also director: produced 1986).

Lovers and Keepers, music by Tito Puente and Ferrando Rivas, lyrics by Fornés (also director: produced 1986). 1987.

Art, in *Box Plays* (produced 1986).

The Mothers (also director: produced 1986).

Plays. 1986.

A Matter of Faith (produced 1986).

Uncle Vanya, adaptation of the play by Anton Chekhov (also director: produced 1987).

Hunger (also director: produced 1988).
And What of the Night? (includes *Hunger*; *Springtime*; *Lust*; *Charlie*)(also
   director: produced 1989). In *Women on the Verge: 7 Avant-Garde
   American Plays*, edited by Rosette C. Lamont, 1993.
Oscar and Bertha (produced 1991).

MANUSCRIPT COLLECTION: Lincoln Center Library of the Performing Arts, New
York.

CRITICAL STUDIES: "The Real Life of María Irene Fornés," in *Theatre Writings*
by Bonnie Marranca, 1984; "Creative Danger" by Fornés, in *American
Theatre*, September 1985; preface by Susan Sontag to *Plays*, 1986; "The
Madwoman in the Spotlight: The Plays of María Irene Fornés", in *Making a
Spectacle: Feminist Essays on Contemporary Women's Theatre*. 1989.

THEATRICAL ACTIVITIES

DIRECTOR: **Plays**—several of her own plays; *Exiles* by Ana Maria Simo, 1982;
Uncle Vanya by Anton Chekhov, 1987; *Going to New England* by Ana Maria
Simo, 1990.

María Irene Fornés's scripts and dialog can seem cryptic because they pivot
on an objectifying abstraction, a realistic detail, free-floating pronouns, or
unstated constructs. Always current in forms and themes, her plays refuse
(Susan Sontag says) to settle for "reductively psychological" or "sociological"
explanations as the underlying truth. By 1982 her plays, designs, lyrics, and
directing had earned Fornés a special Obie for "Sustained Achievement." She
has long walked the stylistic edges of the avant-garde and experimental theater
off-Broadway—especially since *Tango Palace*, *The Successful Life of Three*,
and *Promenade*. If recently a few have blamed her directing for handicapping
her own plays, M.E. Osborn finds her influence as a master teacher of
playwriting increasingly acclaimed. This Cuban-American, by her plays, translations, projects, and workshops, has developed powerful, new Hispanic-
American playwrights and repertory.
   Fornés's playful attention to verbal and visual imagery from the first challenged audiences with freakishly or theatrically exalted characters, both innocent and experienced. In later, seriously passionate plays, comic provocations
of a laugh or grimace reveal her fresh point of view. Even the fairly consistent,
selective realism of many of her more recent and substantial works moves with
the odd undulations of an idiosyncratic heart and mind. These and her
considered theatricality give rise to a startling magic. Fornés is a sometimes
poignant, often humorous, and always intense playwright.
   An antic symbiosis of sadism and masochism in life and art locks the naïve
Leopold and the strenuous Isidore into *Tango Palace*. The arrogant harangue
of *Dr. Kheal*, the raucous road-show of *The Red Burning Light*, and the
Jarry-Beckett scatology of *Oscar and Bertha* now seem too familiar as comic-
didactic theater pieces. Their modes and themes work better in the songs and
the Crosby-Hope *Road*-show format of *Promenade*. In their journey from cell
to cell, Prisoners 105 and 106 must constantly trick or elude the pursuing
Jailer—a dumb, sexually overactive beast. Tunnelling out of prison into a

snooty banquet, 105 and 106 meet Miss Cake, ally themselves with the Servant (she seeks the meaning of life) and escape after robbing the rich Guests who nod off from stupid self-indulgence. Seeking her lost babes, Mother too joins the lengthening line of their pursuers. She and the fugitives play a tender double Pietà with two soldiers on the battlefield, before the tyrannical Mayor sends them back to jail, to escape again. The cruelty and criminality are casual. After Mother's tucking-in and the Servant's fond farewell, the prisoners remain alone, like everyone else, neither informed nor changed by their adventures.

Molly's Dream uses the Dietrich poses and bar setting of Hollywood westerns to ridicule the machismo and romance of male myths like *Bus Stop* and *The Misfits*. Movie timing and allusion activate a young couple and an older man through 10 semi-burlesque scenes in *The Successful Life of Three*. Their looks at each other (he "disdainful", she "stupid") become part of the dialog, as such a "look" becomes a whole scene in the later *Abingdon Square*. The figures and patterns of these plays of the 1960s recur with permutations throughout Fornés's works: a lover and/or beloved as jailer, spunky companions and victims, a wiser servant, a tyrannical teacher, an older man, a casual stranger, a self-loathing woman, or a mysteriously ill person. Bright "outrageousness" steps toward liberation, but *Abingdon Square* ends with a tableau of the angelically illuminated Michael appearing behind the Pietà of Marion cradling dead old Juster.

The Danube creates a bloated horror of America's naïve international meddling and policies from a European perspective. In Budapest, 1938 to whenever, nice American Paul meets sweet Eve over "Basic Sentences," chronicled in units (scenes) of Hungarian-English lessons: they marry, fall ill with a mysterious sickness, and blame each other. The last two, most difficult lessons are repeated as puppet shows and human scenes until Paul and Eve, contorted and red-spotted, both exit in a white flash explosion of pistol shot or nuclear blast. Such violence seems the inevitable doom of human agonies in Fornés's vision.

An understanding of the Hispanic family and religious heritage informs her musical chronicle *Sarita* (set in the South Bronx, 1939–47) and her viciously spare *The Conduct of Life* (set in a Latin American country). Trapped in poverty between Cuban and Yankee values and Catholic-pagan gods, Sarita from age 13 tries to follow her mind away from her incinerating passion for Julio but can't, despite his ruthless betrayals and the understanding of her "nice" new American husband Mark. Momentary vignettes and songs lead her through deepening self-hatred to stab her lover-destroyer to death. Is Mark's holding her hand in the hospital a hope of healing? *The Conduct of Life* distributes the male-dominated woman's role among three characters in relation to Orlando, who is rising on the mutilated minds and bodies of his victims to become state torturer. He ridicules the intellectual, spiritual aspirations of his wife Leticia who tolerates his humiliations and betrayals. While he ignores the older servant Olimpia who seethes with anger but will survive, he rapes, enslaves, and installs in his cellar (as servant) 12-year-old Nena. Nena "receives" those who hurt her "since maybe they are in worse pain than me." Adaptive and resisting her knowledge of his evil, Leticia grovels toward her husband and remains petulantly childish with Olimpia—until she must finally accept her responsibility and her identity with both Orlando and his victims. She shoots him and gives the child Nena the gun to shoot her. The play is a fascinating exploration of the consequences of moral distancing in human actions.

In *Fefu and Her Friends*, seven accomplished women arrive to plan a panel on education. Fefu, who considers herself alternately bright and "loathsome," proves herself "outrageous" by fixing toilets and shooting (only blanks?) her offstage husband through the window with a rifle. After falling, he dusts himself off; men are lucky. Only ballerinas lack the heavy female insides, observes friend Julia, crippled, dying of a malady, and suffering hallucinations. After the first living-room scene, Fornés divides the audience into four groups and leads them backstage to stand in the kitchen, backyard, study, and Julia's bedroom respectively, in intimate proximity to actors performing their brief scene four times; then all return to auditorium and stage. Even the ferocious Fefu who must save Julia, to maintain her own self-respect and survival, cannot do so. Fefu shoots again outside and Julia dies behind her with a red cross of blood on her forehead.

"Springtime," the most tender and the only published act of four in Fornés's powerful drama of human reachings, incest, and degradation, *And What of the Night?*, consists of 14 short scenes. The overextension of this short-scene construction device tends to fragment *Abingdon Square* (in two acts, 32 scenes), a frequently moving chronicle of the love and marriage between poor 15-year-old Marion and wealthy Juster (aged 50) from 1908 to 1917.

In *Mud*, another of her best, Fornés compassionately represents the intricacies of relationships among three characters: Mae and Lloyd (both 25) and the older Henry. Behind their ignorant and repetitiously brutal language, both Mae and Lloyd yearn to receive and provide nourishment in the form of food, health, sex, and learning. The actors reflect their attempts to recreate themselves out of the red mud into a next phase by exiting one scene to pivot visibly in the doorway and re-enter for the next. Mae brings semi-literate Henry in to read a pamphlet on Lloyd's sickness and to teach her to read. Not wanting to live like an animal, Mae mistakes the meaner-spirited Henry for "heaven." Lloyd weeps but learns to read, cure himself, and nurse Henry who becomes more greedy, mocking and crippled. "Lloyd is good, Henry. And this is his home," Mae says before fleeing it and the men's destructive combat. Lloyd chases her, shoots and brings her back—to die like a starfish.

Perhaps, Fornés's plays imply that depriving others is a necessary way of life, as in the eternal game of euchre which occupies the four characters at the end of the grotesque little *Oscar and Bertha*, or the bleak heap that may finally absorb all in *And What of the Night?*

—John G. Kuhn

See the essay on *The Conduct of Life*.

FOSTER, Paul.

Born in Penns Grove, New Jersey, 15 October 1931. Educated at schools in Salem, New Jersey; Rutgers University, New Brunswick, New Jersey, 1950–54, B.A. 1954; St. John's University Law School, New York, 1954, 1957, LL.B. 1958. Served in the U.S. Naval Reserve, 1955–57. Since 1962 co-founder and president, La Mama Experimental Theater Club, New York; U.S. Department of State lecturer, 1975, 1976, 1977; Fulbright lecturer, Brazil, 1980; taught at University of California, San Diego, 1981, and New York University, 1983. Recipient: Rockefeller fellowship, 1967; Irish Universities award, 1967, 1971; New York Drama Critics Circle award, 1968; Creative Artists Public Service grant, 1972, 1974; National Endowment for the Arts grant, 1973; Arts Council of Great Britain award, 1973; Guggenheim fellowship, 1974; Theatre Heute award, 1977; Bulandra Foreign Play award, 1983. Address: 242 East 5th Street, New York, New York 10003, U.S.A.

Publications

PLAYS

Hurrah for the Bridge (produced 1962). 1965; in *Balls and Other Plays*, 1967.
The Recluse (produced 1964). In *Balls and Other Plays*, 1967.
Balls (produced 1964). In *Balls and Other Plays*, 1967.
The Madonna in the Orchard (produced 1965). As *Die Madonna im Apfelhag*, 1968; as *The Madonna in the Orchard*, 1971; in *Elizabeth I and Other Plays*, 1973.
The Hessian Corporal (produced 1966). In *Balls and Other Plays*, 1967.
Balls and Other Plays. 1967.
Tom Paine (produced 1967; expanded version produced 1967). 1967.
Heimskringla; or, The Stoned Angels (televised 1969; produced 1970). 1970.
Satyricon (produced 1972). In *The Off-Off-Broadway Book*, edited by Bruce Mailman and Albert Poland, 1972; in *Elizabeth I and Other Plays*, 1973.
Elizabeth I (produced 1972). 1972; in *Elizabeth I and Other Plays*, 1973.
Elizabeth I and Other Plays. 1973.
Silver Queen Saloon (as *Silver Queen*, music by John Braden, lyrics by Foster and Braden, produced 1973; revised version, as *Silver Queen Saloon*, produced 1978). 1976; with *Marcus Brutus*, 1977.
Rags to Riches to Rags (produced 1974).
Marcus Brutus (produced 1975). 1976; with *Silver Queen Saloon*, 1977.
A Kiss Is Just a Kiss (televised 1980; produced 1983).
The Dark and Mr. Stone 1–3 (produced 1985–86).

SCREENPLAY: *Cinderella Story*, 1985.

TELEVISION PLAYS: *Heimskringla, or, The Stoned Angels*, 1969; *A Kiss Is Just a Kiss*, 1980; *Mellon*, 1980; *Smile*, 1981; *The Cop and the Anthem*, from the story by O. Henry, 1984.

SHORT STORIES

Minnie the Whore, The Birthday Party, and Other Stories. 1962.

OTHER

Translator, with others, *Kasimir and Karoline*; *Faith, Hope, and Charity*; *Figaro Gets a Divorce*; *Judgement Day*, by Ödön Von Horváth. 1986.

MANUSCRIPT COLLECTION: Lincoln Center Library of the Performing Arts, New York.

CRITICAL STUDIES: *The New Bohemia* by John Gruen, 1966; "The Theatre of Involvement" by Richard Atcheson, in *Holiday*, October 1968; "The World's a Stage," in *MD Publications*, October 1968; *Up Against the Fourth Wall* by John Lahr, 1970; *Le Nouveau Théâtre Américain* by Franck Jotterand, 1970; *Selvsyn-Aktuel Litteratur og Kulturdebat* by Elsa Gress, 1970; *Now: Theater der Erfahrung* by Jens Heilmeyer and Pia Frolich, 1971; *The Off-Off-Broadway Book* edited by Bruce Mailman and Albert Poland, 1972.

The theatrical reputation of Paul Foster essentially belongs to the 1960s, when, as a highly innovative contributor to the off-off-Broadway movement, he showed greater audacity than Albee and at one stage appeared to be the mentor to the emergent Sam Shepard. The diversity of Foster's early work is much greater than his often-argued debt to Beckett would suggest. As well as abstraction, symbolism, and existentialism—for which European models may be suggested—his plays up to *Tom Paine* all have a highly idiosyncratic lyrical vein which was peculiarly suited to the ensemble techniques of the La Mama Experimental Theater Club, where all his best work was premiered. In *Hurrah for the Bridge* an old waif, pulling a cart piled high with junk, appears to be victimised by an expressionistic group of leather-jacketed urban predators, though their autonomy is demonstrated by his eventual death at their hands, at which point he is visited by the down-and-out angel he idolises. *The Recluse* is more distinctively American in style, in its presentation of an old basement grotesque accompanied by her semi-animate mannequins and her pet cat, stuffed, which she hides in a drawer and keeps the best milk for. Foster's sympathies with the Happening and kinetic art, hinted at in these earliest plays, become rather more explicit in *Balls*, strictly a puppet play in which two pendant table tennis balls swing in and out of light; human representation comes only through recorded voices over, a nostalgic dialogue between the only two cadavers remaining in a coastal cemetery which is being eroded by the sea.

Foster's first approach to an ostensibly non-fictional subject was in *The Hessian Corporal*, subtitled "a one-act documentary play," but more like a parable for the theatre on the theme of the immorality of war, historicised to the Hessian recruitment of 1776. Though this was an important new development for Foster, it differs from his later "historical" works in that its focus is not a famous individual; his concern here is with the exploited nonentity, and the play has a social resonance which approaches the sentimental, although its relevance to Vietnam disguised this in the premiere. However, even Foster's most famous play, *Tom Paine*, is only superficially a historical portrait in any sense; in the face of surging ensemble playing and an insistent line of lyrical narrative, individuality crystallises only briefly before dissolving back into a faceless, collective context. The play poses questions about individuality; it presents conflicting elements in the traditional portrait of Paine, the visionary and the alcoholic, but by theatricality (such as fragmenting Paine and sharing him among several actors) there arises the implicit question whether such elements can coexist in the world of history or whether such a Paine is just a monster from myth. Several prominent critics felt that the play was not about a person but about a way of looking at a society, about collective impulses towards revolution. Paine himself is, theatrically and metatheatrically, a trigger device for common-sense reappraisal of the world that matters, a world which comes into focus haphazardly through the blurring devices of Paine's alcoholism and the ensemble performance.

Nor is *Elizabeth I* any more a history play or documentary. Again, two actors play the title role, but not this time to achieve schizoid characterisation; one actress does Queen Elizabeth, while the other does Elizabeth the Player Queen, a member of an itinerant company presenting a fairy-tale, cartoon-style play about the queen in the late 16th century. A few episodes, such as those concerning the death of Mary of Scotland, have some urgency, but the sterner tone and historical momentum of *Tom Paine* are all but absent; the play is generally much more frolicsome, and there is no sense of continuity between the events depicted and the world of the modern audience. A similar tone of historical vandalism permeates an earlier television play, *Heimskringla*, in which Leif Eriksson's discovery of Newfoundland is presented initially with the aura of a dramatised saga, with a massed choric incantation generating the action; however, an anachronistic flippancy soon permeates the action, with a diagram showing how to fill the stage with bubbles, and by the second-act "love-in" all intellectual pretensions have been abandoned. From this perspective, *Satyricon* would seem an almost logical development for Foster: a stage embellishment of Petronius's work in which the decadence of the *Cena* is supplemented by appearances from various Bacchantes, Petronius himself, and Nero and Agrippina (who together enact the Foundation of Rome, the emperor playing Romulus while she plays the she-wolf). The comic grotesquerie of this play moves beyond cartoon caricature into theatrical pop art, an appropriate contribution to the Theatre of the Ridiculous. A later play with a Roman setting, *Marcus Brutus*, attempts to return to an individual focus, but again fails to target the play on contemporary issues.

Foster's subsequent plays have been diverse, and have included film scripts, but the stylistic assurance that marked his work up to *Tom Paine* has not been seen again. His sole work to attract substantial critical interest has been *A Kiss Is Just a Kiss* in which Humphrey Bogart sits centre stage and splices together personal memory and public film clips. Bogey seems intended—like Tom Paine—to offer a lens to our world, but in performance the play has lacked cohesion. Foster has never been a playwright in any conventional sense; he has been a literary collaborator in group-developed work, and his idiosyncratic habit of writing stage directions as imperatives defies any acceptance of his scripts as literature.

—Howard McNaughton

FRATTI, Mario.

Born in L'Aquila, Italy, 5 July 1927; emigrated to the United States, 1963;
became citizen, 1974. Educated at Ca'Foscari University, Venice, 1947–51,
Ph.D. in language and literature 1951. Served in the Italian Army, 1951–52:
lieutenant. Married 1) Lina Fedrigo in 1953 (marriage dissolved); 2) Laura
Dubman in 1964; three children. Translator, Rubelli publishers, Venice,
1953–63; drama critic, *Sipario*, Milan, 1963–66, *Paese Sera*, Rome, 1963–73,
L'Ora, Palermo, 1963–73, and since 1963 *Ridotto*, Venice. Taught at Adelphi
University, Garden City, New York, and New School for Social Research,
New York, 1964–65, Columbia University, New York, 1965–66, and Hofstra
University, Hempstead, New York, 1973–74. Since 1968 member of the
Department of Romance Languages, Hunter College, New York. Recipient:
RAI-Television prize, 1959; Ruggeri prize, 1960, 1967, 1969; Lentini prize,
1964; Vallecorsi prize, 1965; Unasp-Enars prize, 1968; Arta-Terme award,
1973; Eugene O'Neill award, 1979; Richard Rodgers award, 1980. Agent:
Samuel French Inc., 45 West 25th Street, New York, New York 10010.
Address: 145 West 55th Street, Apartment 15–D, New York, New York
10019, U.S.A.

Publications

PLAYS

Il Campanello (produced 1958). In *Ridotto*, 1958; as *The Doorbell* (produced
   1970), in *Ohio University Review*, 1971.
La Menzonga (The Lie) (produced 1959). In *Cynthia*, 1963.
A (produced 1965). In *Ora Zero*, 1959; translation in *Fusta*, 1976.
La Partita (The Game) (produced 1960). In *Ridotto*, 1960.
Il Rifiuto (produced 1960). In *Il Dramma*, October 1965; as *The Refusal*
   (produced 1972), in *Races*, 1972.
In Attesa (produced 1960). 1964; as *Waiting* (produced 1970), in *Poet Lore*,
   Autumn 1968.
Il Ritorno (produced 1961). In *Ridotto*, 1961; as *The Return* (produced
   1963); in *Four by Fratti*, 1986.
La Domanda (The Questionnaire) (produced 1961). In *La Prora*, 1962.
Flowers from Lidice, in *L'Impegno*, 1961; in *Dramatics*, October 1972.
L'Assegno. 1961; translated by Adrienne S. Mandel as *The Third Daughter*
   (produced 1978).
Confidenze (produced 1962). 1964; as *The Coffin* (produced 1967), in *Four
   Plays*, 1972.
Gatta Bianca al Greenwich (produced 1962). In *Il Dramma*, March 1962, as
   White Cat, in *Races*, 1972.
Il Suicidio (produced 1962). In *Cynthia*, 1962; as *The Suicide* (produced
   1965), in *Four by Fratti*, 1986.
La Gabbia (produced 1963). In *Cynthia*, 1962; as *The Cage* (produced 1966),
   in *The Cage, The Academy, The Refrigerators*, 1977.
The Academy (produced 1963). As *L'Accademia*, 1964; as *The Academy*, in
   The Cage, The Academy, The Refrigerators, 1977.
La Vedova Bianca (produced 1963). In *Ridotto*, 1972; as *Mafia* (produced
   1966), 1971.

La Telefonata (produced 1965). 1964; as *The Gift* (produced 1966), in *Four Plays*, 1972.

I Seduttori (produced 1972). In *Il Dramma*, 1964; as *The Seducers*, music and lyrics by Ed Scott (produced 1974), with *The Roman Guest*, 1972.

I Frigoriferi (produced 1965). In *Ora Zero*, 1964; as *The Refrigerators* (produced 1971), in *The Cage, The Academy, The Refrigerators*, 1977.

Le Spie (produced 1967). In *The Spies*, in *Fusta*, 1978.

Eleonora Duse (produced 1967). 1972.

Il Ponte (produced 1967). In *Ridotto*, 1967; as *The Bridge* (produced 1972), 1970.

The Victim (produced 1968). As *La Vittima*, 1972; as *The Victim*, in *Eleonora Duse, The Victim, Originality*, 1980.

Che Guevara (produced 1968). In *Enact*, April 1970; 1980.

Unique (produced 1968). In *Ann Arbor Review*, 1971.

L'Amico Cinese (produced 1969). In *Ridotto*, 1969; as *The Chinese Friend* (produced 1972), in *Enact*, October 1972.

L'Ospite Romano (produced 1971). 1969; as *The Roman Guest*, with *The Seducers*, 1972.

La Panchina del Venerdi (produced 1970); as *The Friday Bench* (produced 1971), in *Four Plays*, 1972.

Betrayals. 1970; in *Drama and Theatre*, 1970.

The Wish (produced 1971). In *Four Plays*, 1972.

The Other One (produced 1971). In *Races*, 1972.

The Girl with a Ring on Her Nose (produced 1971). In *Janus*, 1972.

Too Much (produced 1971). In *Janus*, 1972.

Cybele (produced 1971).

The Brothel (produced 1972). In *Mediterranean Review*, 1971.

The 75th (produced 1974). In *Arcoscenico*, January 1972; in *Dramatika*, 1976.

Notti d'amore. In *Tempo Sensibile*, July 1972.

The Letter (produced 1978). In *Tempo Sensibile*, September 1972; in *Wind*, 1974.

The Family (produced 1972). In *Enact*, October 1972.

Four Plays. 1972.

Three Minidramas. In *Janus*, 1972.

Rapes (produced 1972). In *Races*, 1972.

Races: Six Short Plays (includes *Rapes, Fire, Dialogue with a Negro, White Cat, The Refusal, The Other One*). 1972.

Dialogue with a Negro (produced 1975). In *Races*, 1972.

Teatro Americano (includes *Fuoco, Sorelle, Violenze, Fami- glia*). 1972.

L'Ungherese (produced 1974). In *Tempo Sensibile*, 1972.

Dolls No More (produced 1975). In *Drama and Theatre*, Winter 1972–73.

Chile 1973 (produced 1974). In *Enact*, October, November, and December 1973; in *Parola del Popolo*, 1974.

New York: A Triptych (produced 1974).

Patty Hearst. In *Enact*, 1975; in *Parola del Popolo*, 1975.

Madam Senator, music and lyrics by Ed Scott (produced 1975).

Originality (produced 1975). In *Eleonora Duse, The Victim, Originality*, 1980.

The Only Good Indian . . ., with Henry Salerno (produced 1975). In *Drama and Theatre*, 1975.

Tania, music by Paul Dick (produced 1975).

Two Centuries, with Penelope Bradford (produced 1976).

Kissinger (produced 1976). In *Enact*, 1976.

Messages, in *Dramatika*, 1976.

The Cage, The Academy, The Refrigerators. 1977.

Lunch with Fratti: The Letter, Her Voice, The Piggy Bank (produced 1978). *The Piggy Bank* in *Scholia Satyrica*, 1977.

La Croce di Padre Marcello. 1977.

The Biggest Thief in Town (produced 1978).

Birthday. n.d.

David, Son of Sam. In *Ars-Uomo*, 1978.

Six Passionate Women. In *Enact*, 1978.

Two Women (produced 1981). In *Zone Press*, 1978.

Sette Commedie. 1979.

The Fourth One (produced 1980).

Caccia al Morto, Mafia. 1980.

The Pill (produced 1980). In *Scholia Satyrica*, 1980.

Eleonora Duse, The Victim, Originality. 1980.

Nine, book by Arthur Kopit, music and lyrics by Maury Yeston, adaptation of the screenplay *8 1/2* by Federico Fellini (produced 1981). 1983.

Half. In *Other Stages*, 1981.

Elbow to Elbow, adaptation of a play by Glauco Disalle (produced 1982).

Il Pugnale Marocchino (produced 1982). 1982.

Viols, Feu (two plays) (produced 1983).

Four by Fratti (includes *The Suicide, The Return, The Victim, Eleonora Duse*). 1986.

Our Family, Toys (two plays). 1986.

A.I.D.S. (produced 1987).

V.C.R. (produced 1988).

Encounter (musical) (produced 1989).

Two Centuries, with Penelope Bradford (produced 1990).

Lovers (produced 1992).

Sex Commedie di Fratti. 1992.

Translations for Italian television: plays by David Shaw, Reginald Rose, Thomas W. Phipps, R.O. Hirson, J.P. Miller.

VERSE

Volti: Cento Poesie (Faces: 100 Poems). 1960.

BIBLIOGRAPHY: in *Ora Zero*, 1972; in *Four Plays*, 1972.

MANUSCRIPT COLLECTION: Lincoln Center Library of the Performing Arts, New York.

CRITICAL STUDIES: articles by Robert W. Corrigan, in *New Theatre of Europe II*, 1964, and in *Masterpieces of the Modern Italian Theatre*, 1967; by Paul T. Nolan, in *Ora Zero*, 1972, and in *La Vittima*, 1972; *Mario Fratti* by Jane

Bonin, 1982; "Italian-American Playwrights on the Rise" by G.C. Di Scipio, in *Journal of Popular Culture*, Winter 1985.

Mario Fratti comments:

I keep writing plays, at least one a year, because I have something to say. It is my way of being involved with the world that surrounds me. It is my way to comment on the jungle we are living in. Greed and hatred prevail today. I am trying to create characters who are the victims of greed and hatred. I indicate ways to unmask them.

Mario Fratti arrived in New York in 1963 as foreign correspondent for the Italian press. He had already achieved some distinction in Italy as a playwright, and made his American debut that same year with a production of *The Academy* and *The Return* at the Theatre De Lys, starring Ron Liebman. Although a critical success, this first production failed to establish Fratti as an important New York playwright. Undaunted, Fratti continued writing prolifically. Translations of his plays appeared in prominent American literary journals and anthologies; his words were produced throughout the United States and abroad, and were evaluated in several academic studies. Fratti was a phenomenon: a European playwright based in New York achieving national and international recognition without being produced in New York. While most playwrights struggled to "crack" the New York theatrical scene, Fratti imposed himself upon the city by the weight of his international success (more than 300 productions).

Fratti is fascinated with the idea of life as theatre. Existing in an unknowable universe, caught in social systems beyond his control, man becomes an actor wearing an endless array of public and private masks as a means of survival. In such a world, deceit, treachery, and violence are commonplace. While this theme is explored by other modern writers, Fratti is unique for embracing clarity rather than obscurity in the theatre, convinced that the playwright must be the "quintessence of clarity" both for the actor and the audience. Otherwise, he is only "an hysterical poet talking to himself in front of a mirror." Fratti's rich theatrical imagination and impeccable craftsmanship assure clarity.

Comparable to the plots of the commedia dell'arte, many of his plays hinge on a deception, but the results are frequently pathetic or tragic rather than comic. While the characters are passionate, and the situation tense, the structure is coldly logical and tight, progressing like a mystery thriller: the audience's sympathies shift from one character to another; each seems to be on the side of right and the truth is elusive. However, the conclusion is not the revelation of a murderer but a provocative idea regarding the human condition. "I want to open a door in the minds of the audience," states Fratti.

In *The Cage*, Cristiano's pessimism is convincing and his isolation seems justified. Ultimately, however, his moralizing proves destructive; his murder of Pietro, the presumably cruel husband, is the megalomaniacal act of a man who would play God with other peoples' lives. Sanguemarcio, the invalid degenerate of *The Coffin*, pays to hear lurid tales of violence and perversion, aided by his trusted friend, Paoletto, who provides him with storytellers. But the tales are lies; Paoletto is a thief and parasite using the old degenerate for profit. Sanguemarcio dies when he discovers that his one trusted friend was just another of life's frauds. Fratti, however, never moralizes: deceived and deceiver are caught in a hopeless struggle for survival.

The dominant metaphor in Fratti's plays is the trap: characters trapped in situations which they attempt to escape from by violence or deception. Most of the plays are set indoors: oppressive rooms, a cage: concretized images of entrapment. Even the short, percussive titles of his plays suggest traps that have been sprung. But Fratti is not another modern pessimist. While dramatizing life's *Inferno*, he believes in man's basic goodness: "I believe in man, man notwithstanding." In *The Bridge*, a courageous policeman risks his life to save potential suicide victims, recalling a biblical parable that it is better to save one lost sheep than keep a flock. The Priest of *The Roman Guest* learns a new liberalism in America, confronts a prejudiced mob, and returns to Italy with a more profound sense of Christianity. *Che Guevara* is a heroic yet realistic depiction of the Argentinean revolutionary, a man who views his actions as expedient rather than superhuman, necessary steps toward the positive evolution of society.

Fratti also has a subtle sense of comedy. Works such as *The Academy* and *Waiting* are humorous explorations of deceit and self deception. In *The Academy*, set in postwar Italy, a fascist attempts to revenge himself upon America by maintaining an academy for gigolos in pursuit of wealthy American women. The heroine of *Waiting* feigns docility in order to lure her seducer into marriage and then punish him by making his future life a hell. *The Refrigerators*, a dark comedy, is a bizarre parable of contemporary American life and technology, a unique departure from the essential realism of Fratti's drama. Transvestism and perversion are rampant, and the madcap events have a Marx Brothers quality.

America has had a significant influence on Fratti: "This society with all its problems and conflicts is fascinating. It's the ideal society for a modern dramatist." He now writes in English as well as Italian, and evidences a remarkable ear for American dialogue: a terseness and directness that suit the compactness of his dramatic structure. Living in the heart of Manhattan's theatre district, Fratti is continually stimulated by the city, inspired by the most seemingly insignificant event or occurrence around him. "I am a great observer. Faces are incredibly revealing. Just an expression can give me an idea for a play." He describes the scene that provided him with the idea for *The Chinese Friend*, a one-act masterpiece of racial prejudice, filled with nuances regarding America's foreign policy in the Far East: "A very handsome, and elegantly attired American family passed me on the street. They seemed to be overly solicitous to a Chinese gentleman, who was, apparently, their guest."

Thematically, cynicism has tended to override Fratti's humanism in recent years. The world is too much with him of late, embittered by the cruelty, violence, and obsessive war mentality in the post-Vietnam period. But he remains deeply concerned about the poor, the underdog, the perennially helpless victims of life's more skilful and deceptive players. A recurring metaphor is exposure: men and women enmeshed in a futile battle of the sexes, exposing their penchant for foolishness, deceit, and treachery. In his darker plays, the exposure concerns buried guilts, jealousies, hatreds that end in senseless tragedy.

In the comedy *Six Passionate Women* voyeurism and self exposure dominate the lives of the film industry characters of the play. A man hater, appropriately named Mrs. Gunmore, sets out to avenge herself upon the film director, Nino, for what she regards as the male chauvinism and contempt for women evident in his work. *Nine* also centers on the travails of a film director, Guido Contini, but he is treated more sympathetically than Nino. "Sometimes I neglect you," Guido tells his suffering wife; but asks her to forgive him for his waywardness and exposure of their private life on film; it is his way of "creating and recreating." Adapted from Fellini's $8^{1}/_{2}$, *Nine* dramatizes the central character's attempts toward self-understanding by exploring his guilts, desires, fantasies through his characters. The work also satirizes the film industry's incongruous marriage of crass materialism and art through the character of the German financier, Weissnicht, who backs Guido's latest film.

The Third Daughter and *Birthday* are two dark plays concerned with the theme of a father's incestuous desire for his daughter. In *The Third Daughter* Ilario decides to avenge himself upon his adulterous wife by having the offspring of her infidelity, their third daughter Alda, have an affair with a young man, thus destroying her purity, and so torment his wife. The sordid tale is complex in its implications regarding family ties, hatreds, jealousies, desires. Ilario's actual daughters are acting out their own love-hate relationship with their father: hating him for his cruel treatment of their mother, and for his preferring his stepsister to them. He has not only denied them paternal love, but aroused their jealousy, based upon their own repressed incestuous desires. *Birthday* is a fascinating dramatization of incest that becomes madness. A father annually enacts the imagined return of his runaway daughter on her birthday. Women are brought in to assume the role coached by the servant, who encourages them to please the man, and satisfy his incestuous desires.

In *The Piggy Bank* deception and exposure again prevail. A clever prostitute frightens off clients, who have paid in advance, by pretending to have venereal disease; she uses her victims, and is in turn used by her husband; a vicious game of survival with no real winners. *The Letter* is one of Fratti's short chamber plays; excellent acting vehicles—brief, intense, ambivalent.

Fratti is one of off-off Broadway's most frequently performed playwrights, a tribute to his originality and willingness to explore uncomfortable truths about contemporary life. He finds fertile ground for his drama in the most apparently insignificant moments in the passing scene of everyday life, and has a notebook filled with ideas for plays. "Look, I'll never be able to use them all in my lifetime." Let's hope he's wrong.

—A. Richard Sogliuzzo

FRIEDMAN, Bruce Jay.

Born in New York City, 26 April 1930. Educated at De Witt Clinton High School, Bronx, New York; University of Missouri, Columbia, 1947–51, Bachelor of Journalism 1951. Served in the United States Air Force, 1951–53: lieutenant. Married 1) Ginger Howard in 1954 (divorced 1977), three children; 2) Patricia J. O'Donohue in 1983, one daughter. Editorial director, Magazine Management Company, publishers, New York, 1953–56. Visiting professor of literature, York College, City University, New York, 1974–76. Address: P.O. Box 746, Water Mill, New York 11976, U.S.A.

Publications

PLAYS

23 Pat O'Brien Movies, adaptation of his own short story (produced 1966).
Scuba Duba: A Tense Comedy (produced 1967). 1968.
A Mother's Kisses, music by Richard Adler, adaptation of the novel by Friedman (produced 1968).
Steambath (produced 1970). 1971.
First Offenders, with Jacques Levy (also co-director: produced 1973).
A Foot in the Door (produced 1979).

SCREENPLAYS: *The Owl and the Pussycat*, 1971; *Stir Crazy*, 1980; *Doctor Detroit*, with others, 1983; *Splash*, with others, 1984.

NOVELS

Stern. 1962.
A Mother's Kisses. 1964.
The Dick. 1970.
About Harry Towns. 1974.
Tokyo Woes. 1985.
Violencia. 1988.
The Current Climate. 1989.

SHORT STORIES

Far from the City of Class and Other Stories. 1963.
Black Angels. 1966.
Let's Hear It for a Beautiful Guy and Other Works of Short Fiction. 1984.

OTHER

The Lonely Guy's Book of Life. 1978.
Editor, *Black Humor.* 1965.

CRITICAL STUDY: *Bruce Jay Friedman* by Max F. Schulz, 1974.

THEATRICAL ACTIVITIES

DIRECTOR: **Play**—*First Offenders* (co-director, with Jacques Levy), 1973.

It has always been the temptation of fiction writers to turn to the theatre. From Balzac through Henry James 19th-century novelists tried their hand at playwriting, with quite mixed results. Most of us are now interested in only one of Balzac's plays, *Mercadet*, and that probably because of its influence on *Waiting for Godot.* James's plays are readily available in Leon Edel's fine edition but only specialists seem to bother to read them. The same is true for most of the plays of the other 19th-century novelists-turned-dramatist. This rule-of-thumb applies also to certain of our contemporaries: Saul Bellow and John Hawkes, for example, have turned from first-rate fiction to the theatre; the results have been somewhat frustrating and disappointing.

The case of Hawkes is instructive because his plays seem largely extensions of his novels and elaborate on certain of their themes. Hawkes had already published four superb novels by the time he brought out his collection of plays, *The Innocent Party*, in 1966. It would seem that he turned to the theatre only after he felt his position as a novelist was fairly assured. Bruce Jay Friedman appeared to follow the same pattern although he turned to playwriting earlier in his career than Hawkes. The change from fiction to drama was also managed, from all indications, with fewer problems. *Scuba Duba* and *Steambath* are clearly more stageable, if less literary, than Hawkes's plays.

But like the plays in *The Innocent Party* Friedman's work for the theatre is thematically very much tied to his fiction. *Scuba Duba* and *Steambath* use the ambience, character types, and other literary props familiar to readers of Friedman's novels and collections of stories. Guilt, failure, and frustration are words which come to mind when we look at any part of his *oeuvre*.

Scuba Duba bears the subtitle "a tense comedy"; so might almost anything else Friedman has written because laughs come always at the expense of overbearing psychic pain in all of his work. Harold Wonder, the 35-year-old worrier who uses a scythe as a more aggressive kind of security blanket, has rented a chateau in the south of France. As the play opens he laments the fact that his wife has just run off with a black man. Harold's urban Jewish intonation is evident even in his first speech: "I really needed this. This is exactly what I came here for." He feels the need to communicate his *tsuris* to anyone who will listen. An attractive young lady, Miss Janus, is all too willing to help out, but Harold—like most of Friedman's other heroes—seems especially drawn to his psychiatrist and his Jewish mother. The former, aptly named Dr. Schoenfeld, who appears in the first act as a "cut-out" and returns in the flesh in Act 2, warns him in accustomed psychiatric fashion: ". . . you've never once looked at life sideways . . ." Harold's mother seems cut from the same cloth as the mothers in Friedman's novels *Stern, A Mother's Kisses*, and *The Dick*. Harold speaks to her long-distance and the telephone conversation which follows should be familiar to readers of the fiction of Philip Roth, Wallace Markfield, Herbert Gold, and other American Jewish writers. Harold's mother's voice is perfectly tuned: "That's all right, Harold. I'll just consider that my payment after thirty-six years of being your mother."

As the play develops the stage gets more and more crowded. A namedropping French landlady, an American tourist who demands proximity to a Chinese restaurant, a thief with an aphoristic turn ("All men are thieves"), an anti-American gendarme, a "wild-looking blonde" named Cheyenne who prefers "Bernie" Malamud and "those urban Jews" to C.P. Snow—all appear at one time or other. The main confrontation occurs in the second act when Harold's wife appears, followed shortly by two black men, one of whom is her lover. Harold's reaction involves much of the ambivalence experienced by Friedman Jews when in the company of blacks. The hero of Friedman's first novel, for example, went out of his way to express an affection he was never certain was compelling enough: ". . . Stern, who had a special feeling for all Negroes, hugged him [Crib] in a show of brotherhood."

Harold, *schlemiel* that he is, ends up by losing his wife and vows to "get started in my new life." Stern and Kenneth LePeters (the hero of *The Dick*) make similar resolutions and LePeters even goes to the point of leaving his wife and planning an extended trip with his daughter.

Friedman has been grouped with the so-called black humorists on several occasions. In a foreword he wrote for a collection of stories, *Black Humor* (which included his own story "Blank Angels"), he remarked: "There *is* a fading line between fantasy and reality . . ." This is evident in *Scuba Duba* but perhaps even more in *Steambath*. Almost half way through the first act, the protagonist Tandy makes the shocked discovery: ". . . We're dead? Is that what you were going to say? That's what I was going to say. That's what we are. The second I said it, I knew it. Bam! Dead! Just like that! Christ!" Until this point in the play all indications are of a *real* steambath; then everything suddenly dilates into symbol and "fantasy," with no noticeable change in the dramatic movement. (John Hawkes used the steambath in the fifth chapter of his novel *The Lime Twig* with somewhat the same symbolical intent.)

Tandy is clearly not quite ready for death and protests the Attendant's (read God) decision through the remainder of the play. He seems very like Kenneth LePeters at the end of *The Dick*. He is on the verge of doing things he likes—writing a novel about Charlemagne, working for a charity to help brain-damaged welders, courting a Bryn Mawr girl who makes shish kebab—after divorcing his wife and giving up his job "teaching art appreciation over at the Police Academy." Tandy shares his frustration with a blonde girl named Meredith in somewhat the way Harold Wonder shared his plight, conversationally, with Miss Janus in *Scuba Duba*.

Max Schulz, in a very good book on the American Jewish novel, *Radical Sophistication*, speaks of Friedman's manner as having something "of the stand-up comic." This is especially noticeable in *Steambath*. Its humor favors the incongruous and unlikely. One can almost hear Woody Allen pronouncing some of the lines with considerable relish, like Tandy's incredulous response when he realizes that God is a Puerto Rican steambath attendant or when he discovers what he stands to lose by being dead: "No more airline stewardesses . . . *Newsweek* . . . Jesus, no more *Newsweek*."

Much of the humor has to do with popular culture. Bieberman, who makes intermittent appearances, is very much taken with the actors and baseball players of the 1940's. Other characters refer to the impact made by such essentials of television as the David Frost Show and pro football (American style). Names of every variety, including those of defeated political candidates (Mario Procaccino) and editors of magazines (Norman Podhoretz), are introduced incongruously and irreverently in the conversations. Theodore Solotaroff believes that

> nostalgia has a particular attraction for many Jewish writers: some of them, like Gold or Bruce Jay Friedman or Wallace Markfield or Irwin Faust, seem to possess virtually total recall of their adolescent years, as though there were still some secret meaning that resides in the image of

Buster Brown shoes, or Edward G. Robinson's snarl, or Ralston's checkerboard package.
How much to the point of this remark is *Steambath*!

There is a good deal of the spirit of the second-generation American Jew in Friedman's plays as well as in his novels. He has caught this verbal rhythm and pulse beat in much the way that Philip Roth and Woody Allen have.

—Melvin J. Friedman

FULLER, Charles (H., Jr.).

Born in Philadelphia, Pennsylvania, 5 March 1939. Educated at Villanova University, 1956–58, and La Salle College, 1965–67, both Philadelphia. Served as a petroleum lab technician in the U.S. Army in Japan and Korea, 1959–62. Married Miriam A. Nesbitt in 1962; two sons. Bank loan collector, counselor at Temple University, and city housing inspector, all Philadelphia, 1960s; co-founder and co-director, Afro-American Arts Theatre, Philadelphia, 1967–71; writer and director, *The Black Experience* program, WIP Radio, Philadelphia, 1970–71. Recipient: Creative Artists Public Service grant, 1975; Rockefeller grant, 1976; National Endowment for the Arts grant, 1976; Guggenheim fellowship, 1977; Obie award, 1981; Audelco award, 1981, 1982; Pulitzer prize, 1982; New York Drama Critics Circle award, 1982; Outer Circle award, 1982; Hazelitt award, 1983; Mystery Writers of America Edgar Allan Poe award, for screenplay, 1985. D.F.A.: La Salle College, 1982; Villanova University, 1983. Lives in Philadelphia. Agent: Esther Sherman, William Morris Agency, 1350 Avenue of the Americas, New York, New York 10019, U.S.A.

Publications

PLAYS

The Village: A Party (produced 1968; as *The Perfect Party*, produced 1969).
The Rise, in *New Plays from the Black Theatre*, edited by Ed Bullins. 1969.
In My Many Names and Days (produced 1972).
Candidate (produced 1974).
In the Deepest Part of Sleep (produced 1974).
First Love (produced 1974).
The Lay Out Letter (produced 1975).
The Brownsville Raid (produced 1975).
Sparrow in Flight, music by Larry Garner, based on a concept by Rosetta LeNoire (produced 1978).
Zooman and the Sign (produced 1980). 1982.
A Soldier's Play (produced 1981). 1982.
We (includes *Sally*, *Prince*) (produced 1988).
Eliot's Coming, in *Urban Blight* (musical revue), based on an idea by John Tillinger, music by David Shire, lyrics by Richard Maltby, Jr. (produced 1988).
Jonquil (produced 1990).

SCREENPLAY: *A Soldier's Story*, 1984.

TELEVISION PLAYS: *Roots, Resistance, and Renaissance* series, 1967; *Mitchell*, 1968; *Black America* series, 1970–71; *The Sky Is Gray*, from the story by Ernest J. Gaines (*American Short Story* series), 1980; *A Gathering of Old Men*, 1987.

An angry, consuming energy which propels the protagonist towards violence, an irony which humanizes him while depriving the viewer of easy categorizations: these elements characterize Charles Fuller's style. Within an American theatre tradition Fuller's work both acknowledges the seminal position of Amiri Baraka and extends the vision of the tumultuous 1960s beyond a rigid, racial schematization which in conferring upon blacks the status of victims of oppression, seemingly robbed them of any responsibility for or power over the circumstances in which they found themselves.

A former bank loan collector, college counsellor, and city housing inspector, Fuller initially gained a measure of national recognition in 1976 with *The Brownsville Raid*. Though presently out of circulation, the play is of interest because it prefigures the approach adopted in the later *A Soldier's Play*. *The Brownsville Raid* is a dramatization of the investigation into a 1906 shooting spree which culminated in President Teddy Roosevelt's unwarranted, dishonorable discharge of an entire black infantry brigade. With historical accounts as his starting point, Fuller skilfully interweaves a "whodunnit" plot with a compelling portrait of a black corporal who has his faith in the Army shattered when he refuses to comply with his officers' demand for a scapegoat. Both black and white men are presented with strengths and faults; what emerges is a composite picture of men and a society whose vision is distorted by racism.

In both *Zooman and the Sign* and *A Soldier's Play* racism appears not as a specific, external event to which the black protagonists must react; rather, its negative values have been so internalized that, propelled by their own frantic despair, the characters move relentlessly towards self-destruction. In the first play, about a father's search for his daughter's killer, a knife-toting, drug-running, 15-year-old casually admits to the audience at the outset that he is the killer. Although Zooman attempts to mask a mounting sense of entrapment with calculated bravado, his direct conversations with the audience about familial disintegration, unwanted homosexual encounters, and detention for uncommitted crimes characterize him as an alienated youth whose experiences have taught him that "niggahs can't be heroes," that blacks seemingly have no control over the atrophy engulfing their families and communities. These monologues, delivered in a street-wise, frenetic style which is nonetheless reminiscent of black toast traditions and Muhammad Ali's alliterative poetry, have the effect of humanizing Zooman, of placing him in a context where his asocial behavior becomes more understandable, and his affinity to the larger society more apparent.

Just as Zooman believes that blacks are helpless, so too do the neighbors of the slain girl, for no one will come forth as witnesses to the crime. The father's erecting a sign accusing them of moral complicity triggers only hostile recriminations from the neighbors and argument within the family itself. Symbolic of a community's failure to foster a more active, ennobling sense of its own possibilities, the sign occasions the final violence wherein Zooman is accidentally killed in his attempt to tear it down. Another black child lies dead in the street, another family grieves, and another sign goes up as momentary monument to incredible waste.

An ultimately pervasive irony, which empties the landscape of possible victors and reveals instead a society maimed by racism, is equally evident in *A Soldier's Play*. Unlike Zooman, Sergeant Waters espouses the black middle-class values of hard work, education, and racial pride as the means of self-advancement. Like Zooman, Waters, in seeking a sphere in which to exercise a masculine sense of control and dignity, has had only limited success, for he operates within the segregated Army of World War II. The search for his killer triggers a series of flashbacks which reveal him as a vicious, petty tyrant bent upon literally ridding the race of all those blues-singing, hoodoo-oriented men who he says prevent advancement; yet, they also create a measure of sympathy for this ambitious man, consumed by misplaced faith, self-hatred, and guilt.

The eventual identification of two black recruits as Waters's murderers defies the expectation, carefully nurtured by the playwright, that overt white hostility is the motivating factor. Additionally, it raises questions concerning the definition of justice, for the infantrymen have just received their long-awaited orders to ship out, in effect being granted license to kill in Europe a tyranny similar to what Waters represents at home. Compounding the irony further, Fuller provides a postscript which subverts the dramatic experience: the investigating officer reveals that the entire incident is recorded in military documents as meaningless black-on-black crime; Waters is inadvertently listed as an heroic war casualty; and the entire company is destroyed in combat. Thus, the Army learns nothing from this sorry episode.

To date, Fuller's dramatic world is dominated by driven, destructive men trying to carve out a viable place within a hostile environment. Though his characters inhabit a bleak landscape, his audiences need not: through the dramatic experience they can appreciate how racism distorts an entire society and choose to stop the human destruction.

—Sandra L. Richards

FURTH, George.

Born George Schweinfurth in Chicago, Illinois, 14 December 1932. Educated at Northwestern University, Evanston, Illinois, B.S. in speech 1954; Columbia University, New York, 1955–56, M.F.A. 1956. Served in the U.S. Navy, 1958–62. Stage, film, and television actor from 1956; member of the Drama Department, University of Southern California, Los Angeles, 1979. Recipient: New York Drama Critics Circle award, 1970; Outer Circle award, 1970; Drama Desk award, 1970; Tony award, 1971. Agent: The Lantz Office, 888 Seventh Avenue, New York, New York 10106. Address: 3030 Durand Drive, Hollywood, California 90068, U.S.A.

Publications

PLAYS

Company, music and lyrics by Stephen Sondheim (produced 1970). 1970.
Twigs (includes *Emily, Celia, Dorothy, Ma*) (produced 1971). 1972.
The Act, music by John Kander, lyrics by Fred Ebb (produced 1977). 1987.

Merrily We Roll Along, music and lyrics by Stephen Sondheim, adaptation of
the play by George S. Kaufman and Moss Hart (produced 1981).
The Supporting Cast (produced 1981). 1982.
Precious Sons (produced 1986). 1988.
Music Minus One (produced 1992).

MANUSCRIPT COLLECTION: Northwestern University School of Speech,
Evanston, Illinois.

THEATRICAL ACTIVITIES

DIRECTOR: Plays—*The Supporting Cast*, 1986; *Precious Sons*, 1988.
ACTOR: Plays—Jordan in *A Cook for Mr. General* by Steve Gethers, 1961;
Junior Tubbs in *Hot Spot*, 1963; Skip in *Tadpole* by Jules Tasca, 1973; Butler
in *Tiny Alice* by Edward Albee; Arnold in *The Supporting Cast*, 1982. Films—
The Best Man, 1964; *The New Interns*, 1964; *A Rage to Live*, 1965; *A Very
Special Favor*, 1965; *The Cool Ones*, 1967; *Games*, 1967; *Tammy and the
Millionaire*, 1967; *The Boston Strangler*, 1968; *How to Save a Marriage—And
Ruin Your Life*, 1968; *Nobody's Perfect*, 1968; *P.J.*, 1968; *What's So Bad
about Feeling Good?*, 1968; *Butch Cassidy and the Sundance Kid*, 1969; *Myra
Breckinridge*, 1970; *Blazing Saddles*, 1974; *Shampoo*, 1975; *Airport '77*,
1977; *Cannonball Run*, 1981; *MegaForce*, 1982; *The Man with Two Brains*,
1983; *Doctor Detroit*, 1983. Television—*Tammy*, *Broadside*, *Mary Hartman*,
Mary Hartman and *The Dumplings* series.

George Furth's career to date, his book for Stephen Sondheim's *Company*
excepted, has been a tantalising series of near misses. Adroit as his work is,
especially when he has risked innovations with the actual form of mainstream
playwriting, he has rarely strayed from the narrow range of concerns that can
occupy the successful Broadway play.

Twigs is essentially four one-act plays with a linking thread, providing a
versatile actress with the chance to play three different sisters and their mother
in the course of the evening. Taking its title from Alexander Pope ("Just as the
twig is bent, the tree's inclined"), the plays are set in four different kitchens all
on the same prior-to-Thanksgiving Day. All the sisters have their problems,
seen mainly through a comedic lens, although the slick lines and sight-gags of
the first playlet in which the garrulous recently-widowed Emily finds a possible
new romance are in sharp contrast to the second, in which Celia, married to a
crudely unfeeling slob whose ex-army buddy joins them for Thanksgiving,
trembles on the verge of another nervous breakdown. This play begins in a
vein of rumbustious comedy but gradually reveals an undertow of bleak pain.
Furth does not always have time to paint in the sublest of brush strokes, one of
the hazards of the one-act format; perhaps unsurprisingly, the most successful
episode is the final one in which the sisters' terminally ill Mother, a formidable
old lady, decides that before she dies the "Pa" with whom she has lived for so
long will do right by her and marry her. The ensuing wedding scene with an
understandably flustered priest may be fairly broad comedy but it has a gleeful
relish, skirting the boundaries of taste, which fuels it with zest.

Furth, with an actor's background, gives all his cast good opportunities, as
well as providing a virtuoso showcase for the central performer. The play had

a moderate Broadway success, which was more than he achieved with *The Supporting Cast*. Set in a luxurious Malibu beachhouse, with a bushfire and a minor earthquake among the traumas of the day, the play is happiest in the realms of a wisecracking or visual comedy; it milks a recurring sight-gag of characters walking into glass patio doors, and the dialogue is crammed with sardonic one-liners, the most pungent coming from the sharp-tongued Mae. Like all the characters, all friends of first-time novelist Ellen whose novel's publication requires waivers from the real-life prototypes of her characters, Mae represents East Coast unease with Californian living ("Someone must have tipped this country on its end and everything that wasn't screwed down fell into California," as Florrie from Brooklyn puts it). The play's slight plot rests on the mixed reactions to the book before outrage turns to ego-preening; aiming for a high-octane zany comedy the play becomes progressively more desperate in its contrivances simply to keep events moving.

All of which made Furth's most recent play perhaps somewhat surprising. *Precious Sons* managed only a short run, even in a Broadway season starved of good new plays. It has many of the hallmarks of an autobiographical play: set in Furth's native Chicago in the summer of 1949, it is a solidly naturalistic play centered on the lower-middle-class household of Fred Small, hard-working and tough father in poor health, Bea his slapdash, indomitably optimistic wife, and their two very different sons (the younger with dreams of becoming an actor, the elder sneaking off to wed his Prom sweetheart), for both of whom Fred is desperate for better lives. It is a long, and sometimes flawed play (somewhat confused over Bea's motives at crucial points, especially her attitude to a projected promotion of Fred's) but offering magnificent acting opportunities, particularly in the loving, brawling volatile relationship between Fred and Bea. The play, set as it is in 1949, inevitably recalls the playwrights of that period—Inge, Miller, Williams (indeed Williams figures strongly in the story, with Freddy the younger son auditioning for the touring company of *A Streetcar Named Desire*, producing a wonderful scene in which Bea has to read Blanche to Freddy's Newspaper Boy)—but deserved a more considered critical reaction than the faint praise it received on Broadway.

Furth has had considerable success with his streamlined books for various musicals including *Company* (although *The Act* required little more than linking dialogue between Liza Minnelli's numbers) but there are signs in his work to date that there is possibly a major play yet to come from him.

—Alan Strachan

G

GAGLIANO, Frank (Joseph).

Born in Brooklyn, New York, 18 November 1931. Educated at Queens College, New York, 1949–53; University of Iowa, Iowa City, B.A. 1954; Columbia University, New York, M.F.A. 1957. Served in the U.S. Army, 1954–56. Married Sandra Gordon in 1958; one son. Freelance copywriter, New York, 1958–61; promotion copywriter, McGraw-Hill Text-Film Division, New York, 1962–65. Associate professor of drama, Florida State University, Tallahassee, 1969–72; lecturer in playwriting and director of the E.P. Conkle Workshop, University of Texas, Austin, 1972–75. Since 1975 Benedum professor of playwriting, University of West Virginia, Morgantown. Visiting professor, University of Rhode Island, Providence, 1975. Recipient: Rockefeller grant, 1965, 1966; Wesleyan University-O'Neill Foundation fellowship, 1967; National Endowment for the Arts grant, 1973; Guggenheim fellowship, 1974. Lives in Pittsburgh. Agent: Gilbert Parker, William Morris Agency, 1350 Avenue of the Americas, New York, New York 10019. Address: Theatre Arts Center, University of West Virginia, Morgantown, West Virginia 26506, U.S.A.

Publications

PLAYS

Night of the Dunce (as *The Library Raid*, produced 1961; revised version, as *Night of the Dunce*, produced 1966). 1967.

Conerico Was Here to Stay (produced 1965). In *The City Scene*, 1966.

The City Scene (includes *Paradise Gardens East* and *Conerico Was Here to Stay*) (produced 1969). 1966.

Father Uxbridge Wants to Marry (produced 1967). 1968.

The Hide-and-Seek Odyssey of Madeleine Gimple (produced 1967). 1970.

The Prince of Peasantmania (Inny), music by James Reichert (produced 1968; revised version produced 1970). 1968.

Big Sur (televised 1969; revised version produced 1970). 1971.

In the Voodoo Parlour of Marie Laveau: Gris-Gris, and The Comedia World of Byron B (produced 1973; as *Gris-Gris, and The Comedia World of Lafcadio Beau*, produced 1974; revised version, as *Voodoo Trilogy*, produced 1977; revised version, as *In the Voodoo Parlour of Marie Laveau*, produced 1983).

Congo Square, music by Claibe Richardson (produced 1975).

189

The Resurrection of Jackie Cramer, music by Raymond Benson (produced 1976).
The Private Eye of Hiram Bodoni (produced 1978).
The Total Immersion of Madeleine Favorini (produced 1981).
San Ysidro (cantata), music by James Reichert (produced 1985).
From the Bodoni County Songbook Anthology, Book 1 (produced 1986).
Hanna (produced 1992).

TELEVISION PLAY: *Big Sur*, 1969.

MANUSCRIPT COLLECTIONS: Lincoln Center Library of the Performing Arts, New York; O'Neill Theatre Center Library, Waterford, Connecticut.

CRITICAL STUDIES: *Stages: The Fifty-Year Childhood of the American Theatre* by Emory Lewis, 1969; *The Nature of Theatre* by Vera M. Roberts, 1971.

Frank Gagliano comments:

My whole effort in dramatic writing has been to keep a center while allowing myself the freedom of following any *seemingly* absurd path that seems to make sense. Form and impulse; the artist's great tightrope act. My favorite playwrights are Shakespeare, Georg Büchner, Chekhov, Verdi, and Bach.

Frank Gagliano is an experimental artist, uncompromising in his quest for a dramatic form that synthesizes his passion for music, language, and metaphysical themes of Christian idealism in an age of terror, disorder, perversion, and violence. "Mindlessness scares me and I'm in a mindless age," cries the heroine of *The Total Immersion of Madeleine Favorini*. Her words express the playwright's own torment. But Gagliano resembles a medieval dramatist, theatricalizing the terrors of hell to effect salvation, yet fascinated by the evils he deplores. In his plays, images of decay, violence, and death prevail over those of transcendence and salvation.

Gagliano is at war with himself. His drama is often an unresolved battleground of contradictory themes, language, and structure; winged allegories soar toward some unperceived light, burdened by the very demons they hope to evade. It is a brilliant, painful quest for truth, a journey for playwright and spectator in which the ridiculous and sublime combine in uneasy balance. Gagliano never plays it safe, and that is his great virtue as an artist.

His two-act opera, *Inny*, exemplifies the allegories of his earlier work. The dominant metaphor is that of the odyssey toward some form of self-realization, though the play's structure is far more logical and compact than that of his later plays. Innocent, "Inny," rightful heir to the throne of Peasantmania, is prevented from ruling by forces of political, social, and religious corruption that dominate the country. In his struggle to obtain power, Inny journeys from innocence to wisdom. Despite the evils endured, Inny remains spiritually pure, a Christ on the throne ready to suffer for man's transgressions and leading him to salvation: "I must stay . . . I'll never understand this—the ones who chased me, beat me, betrayed me . . . I love them all."

Inny is a grand operatic spectacle of pageants, processions, dances, choruses, battles; an entourage of jaded, cruel aristocrats, hags, heroines, fools, and a wise jester, symbol of art, who ultimately dies a horrid death with Inny's beloved, Glorabella. The dominant image of the play is a huge, foreboding eye that hangs overhead: "God's surrealistic yo-yo?" cries the jester, "but where's the string?" Is the horror heaven sent, the cruel plaything of a less than benign God, or the devil's toy? The ultimate answers are beyond us; all we know for certain is that man pursues senseless evil. The innocent and wicked suffer alike. All we can hope for is that wise, beneficent, courageous leaders like Inny may ultimately triumph.

The Private Eye of Hiram Bodoni is a flawed, sprawling work intended for television, part comedy, part surrealistic nightmare. Bodoni, a private eye, is hired to discover the cause of the unexplained death of the star of a television soap opera. However, the plot is merely a device to explore the lives of the characters through their personal recollections, flashbacks, and fantasies. Although it offers some imaginative visual images and poetic dialogue, the play is confused and unresolved.

In the Voodoo Parlour of Marie Laveau, "an unsung chamber opera," is a three-character play in which a man and woman seek help and revenge from a voodoo sorceress. Under Marie Laveau's spell, the two characters give vent to nightmare and sexual fantasy:

> I wish that was me
> being humped by a donkey
> while the chic of New Orleans
> marveled at me.

The woman's gross allusion revolts the man, who dreams of pure, idealized love. Verbal images of lurid sexuality dominate the play's language, but never gratuitously, only as essential to theme and action. Marie Laveau's parlor is a microcosm of New Orleans at the turn of the century, a city of Mardi Gras, witchcraft, perversion, racial hatred, and violence. The play gains its intensity by the very limitations of its theme. Rather than Gagliano's usual depiction of the characters' torments as symptomatic of a vaster social malaise, *Marie Laveau* is concentrated on the characters as ends in themselves. The parallel to 19th-century melodramatic plots of love and revenge is deliberate—a self-contained world of passion, violence, and death. The settings and costumes are simple yet theatrically effective: a bare space, masks, skulls, bizarre headgear, the horrid implements of the voodoo ritual. The hypnotic spell of the ritual is perfectly suited to Gagliano's odyssey metaphor, the evocation of nightmare and fantasy. Through an imaginative use of scenery, costumes, and operatic dialogue, Gagliano creates a Genet-like transcendence through evil. *Marie Laveau* is powerful drama that lends itself naturally to music.

In *The Total Immersion of Madeleine Favorini* Gagliano again uses the metaphor of the journey into self through a protagonist's total immersion in fantasy, nightmare, and dreams. Madeleine, a timid librarian locked in a gynecologist's stirrups for two weeks, wanders back in fantasy to Sicily, land of her ancestors. On her journey she encounters various forms and characters:

a Stalactite, the Wax Prometheus, the Goddess Materna. The actress playing Madeleine transforms herself into each of them (the other actor and actress also assume a variety of identities). Madeleine becomes imbued with the Dionysian and Christian spirit of this ancient land, an earth mother absorbing all humanity into her giant womb. In a brilliant sequence of dialogue, Madeleine and her deceased grandfather, Pazzotesto (Crazy Head), rhapsodize over the wonders of basil that covers the landscape of Sicily, creeping "up from the bottom of the green Mediterranean . . . on the beach . . . the roads, rooftops. The toilets have basil seats. The bells of the great cathedrals are covered with basil and cushion their clang." At the conclusion of the play, Madeleine is freed from the restrictions of the harsh, decadent society that nurtured her. She ascends to freedom on a crescendo of pure language. "Yes! Yes! I know what I want. I know what I mean! I want to become—language! Language!"

These final moments of the play seem to represent Gagliano's desire to free himself from the limits of drama. This work is a form of theatricalized literature or poetry rather than drama. Action becomes the exploration of character and theme instead of the resolution of some essential dramatic conflict. Gagliano's emphasis upon language as the dominant structural element of his drama can become excessive and unfocused. He has a tendency to use dialogue for the sheer richness of sound and imagery. Yet, his dialogue can also be stirring or even frightening, revealing a character's desperate need for freedom and salvation. Gagliano's drama is in transition, and its direction is unclear, but he remains one of the most daring, imaginative, and poetic playwrights of the American theatre.

—A. Richard Sogliuzzo

GARDNER, Herb(ert).

Born in Brooklyn, New York, 28 December 1934. Educated at the High School of Performing Arts, New York, graduated 1952; Carnegie Institute of Technology, Pittsburgh; Antioch College, Yellow Springs, Ohio. Married the actress Rita Gardner in 1957. Cartoonist: created *The Nebbishes* syndicated cartoon strip. Recipient: Screenwriters Guild award, 1966; Tony award, 1986; Outer Circle award, 1986; John Gassner award, 1986. Lives in New York City. Address: c/o Samuel French Inc., 45 West 25th Street, New York, New York 10010, U.S.A.

Publications

PLAYS

The Elevator (produced 1952). 1952.

A Thousand Clowns (produced 1962). 1962.

The Goodbye People (produced 1968). 1974; revised version (produced 1979), included in *A Thousand Clowns, Thieves, The Goodbye People*, 1979.

Who Is Harry Kellerman and Why Is He Saying Those Terrible Things about Me? (screenplay). 1971.

Thieves (produced 1974). In *A Thousand Clowns, Thieves, The Goodbye People,* 1979.
Love and/or Death (produced 1979).
A Thousand Clowns, Thieves, The Goodbye People. 1979.
I'm Not Rappaport (produced 1985). 1986.
Conversations with My Father (produced 1992).

SCREENPLAYS: *A Thousand Clowns,* 1965; *Who Is Harry Kellerman and Why Is He Saying Those Terrible Things about Me?,* 1971; *Thieves,* 1976.

TELEVISION PLAY: *Happy Endings,* with others, 1975.

NOVEL
A Piece of the Action. 1958.

Critics keep trying to point out serious ideas in Herb Gardner's plays, but the playwright consistently wards off their attempts with a comic flourish. Clearly a thoughtful man, obviously stimulated by certain prevailing attitudes of mankind, he insists that he is a writer of comedy and that his objective is to entertain audiences. Surely this is a noble and inspiring trait in a modern dramatist, particularly during a period in history when social issues are forcibly intruded into theatres at every opportunity. Unlike Robert Sherwood who, though concerned with the human condition, hid his serious thoughts behind a facade of light comedy, the like-minded Gardner looks carefully around and, like Chekhov, is genuinely amused by what he sees—the fancied and the futile attempts of man to escape the real world, the indefatigable quality of old age. Gardner, then, proceeds to use the comic techniques that bring his plays to Broadway—*A Thousand Clowns, The Goodbye People, Thieves,* and *I'm Not Rappaport.*

The world that seems funny to Gardner, however, sometimes arrests the attention of others as extremely sad. There is Max Silverman in *The Goodbye People.* This exuberant but completely unrealistic old gentleman wants to erase 20 years from passing time, rebuild his hot-dog stand on Coney Island, and bring his "Hawaiian Ecstasies" to an eager public. Moreover, he wants to do this in February, so convinced is he that his dreams can awaken "ecstasy" in a dull world. There is old Nat in *I'm Not Rappaport,* a defiant, irascible Jewish radical who refuses to be intimidated by either the establishment or the underworld and rejects any movement that intrudes upon his independence. There are all the pathetic people around the apartment building in *Thieves,* each with a problem to which no one listens, each a thief and each being robbed by passing time. And from *A Thousand Clowns* there are Murray who is tortured by the world he sees, Leo who wants to believe in himself but cannot, and Arthur who purposefully surrenders to the establishment but survives. He catches the wind and goes with it. Mainly, Gardner's characters appear to catch the cold wind straight in their faces, defiantly, stubbornly, and disastrously—and die, in one sense or another, romantically and in the glow of stage sentiment.

The comic appeal of Gardner's plays comes from his mastery of comic technique and his philosophy as a writer. Although not a storyteller and, as his plays show, somewhat contemptuous of traditional plotting in a play, he likes to hear people talk. He is also a dreamer who, like Nat, can make up little scenes which may appear as a line, a speech, or an incident—a joke, a monologue, or an episode. Like Max Silverman, Gardner does not believe in standing around and watching. One must act, wage battle even while knowing that victory is impossible. Like Murray he is afraid of "dying alive." Although called a "laureate of losers," Gardner has a sense of comic balance that contradicts this description. He sees humor, not sadness. Losers stand around; fighters keep the soul alive, and Gardner's characters, synthetic and romanticized or caricatured as they may be, are ever hopeful, even in their fantastic, ridiculous, or childishly recalcitrant attempts to escape whatever worlds surround them. Gardner sees his people as survivors, and in juxtaposing their acts with those of others in the world he experiences he creates dramatic tension in silly-serious, comic-tragic, and pathetic-horrible situations while revealing a real comic irony.

Structurally, Gardner's plays include a lavishly encumbered stage and a love story. As visual metaphors there are the incredibly messy room in *A Thousand Clowns*, the beach that sprouts fireworks in *The Goodbye People*, the terrace in *Thieves*, and the bench in *I'm Not Rappaport*. Gardner truly loves the long monologue, the quick repartee of stand-up comedians, and the one-line gag. Jewish humor, local New York humor, visual jokes, absurd comparisons, and the unexpected retort vie for attention in a selected accumulation of odd people. In *Thieves* a character complains that "all I ever got from this neighborhood was four knife scars, two broken noses and a fruitcake wife! And they all hurt when it rains." Gardner's comedies are assuredly enhanced by good actors: his monologues are a comedian's food and wine; his dialogue can be as sprightly and as touching as the actor can create. Music also is significant in his plays to please or assault the ear as the clutter on stage may accost the eye. Within this grand expression of comic theatre where dreams cannot be answered but believing in dreams is deemed necessary, Gardner presents his characters, mainly in episodes involving the rituals of lovemaking in the modern world. Then, he stops; conclusions are not his métier.

The comic possibilities that have brought Gardner success, however, may also serve to limit his acceptance with future audiences. During the 1960s, for example, audiences applauded the rebellious youth's single-minded escape into fantasy from a real world where they found people living as "fakes." Today's audiences are more interested in contending with this real world. Carlton, the young thief in *Thieves*, is not funny to them, nor is Sally, who contends seriously and unsuccessfully with a stubbornly inhuman father. It is scarcely funny to a generation concerned with people starving in the streets that the doorman is not sleeping but dead. Gardner presents father-daughter relationships in *The Goodbye People*, *Thieves*, and *I'm Not Rappaport*, each one funny to him, each one geared to the comic sense of a different audience. In *I'm Not Rappaport* he catches the pathos as well as the comedy and with this development in his dramaturgy may advance beyond the comic banter of temporal pleasure.

—Walter J. Meserve

GELBART, Larry.

Born in Chicago, Illinois, 25 February 1928. Educated at John Marshall High School, Chicago; Fairfax High School, Los Angeles. Served in the U.S. Army, 1945–46. Married Pat Marshall in 1956; two daughters and three sons. Radio and television writer from 1947; producer or co-producer of television series including *The Marty Feldman Comedy Machine*, 1971, *M*A*S*H*, 1972–76, *Karen*, 1975, *United States*, 1980, and the *Academy Awards Show*, 1985. Artist-in-residence, Northwestern University, Evanston, Illinois, 1984–85. Recipient: Sylvania award, 1958; Emmy award, 1958, 1973; Tony award, 1963, 1990 (twice); Peabody award, 1964, 1975; Montreux Television Festival Golden Rose award, 1971; Humanitas award, 1976; Edgar Allan Poe award, 1977, 1990; Writers Guild of America award, 1977, 1978, 1982; Christopher award, 1978; Laurel award, 1981; Los Angeles Film Critics award, 1982; New York Film Critics award, 1982; National Society of Film Critics award, 1982; Pacific Broadcasting Pioneers award, 1987; Lee Strasberg award, 1990; Outer Critics Circle award, 1990 (twice); Drama Desk award, 1990; New York Drama Critics Circle award, 1990; Beverly Hills Theater Guild Spotlight award, 1991. Member, Motion Picture Academy of Arts and Sciences. D. Litt: Union College, Schenectady, New York, 1986. Address: 807 North Alpine Drive, Beverly Hills, California 90210, U.S.A.

Publications

PLAYS

My L.A. (revue; produced 1948).

The Conquering Hero, with Burt Shevelove, adaptation of the work by Preston Sturges, music by Moose Charlap, lyrics by Norman Gimbel (produced 1960).

A Funny Thing Happened on the Way to the Forum, with Burt Shevelove, music and lyrics by Stephen Sondheim, adaptation of plays by Plautus (produced 1962; revised version produced 1971). 1963.

Jump (produced 1971).

Sly Fox, adaptation of *Volpone* by Ben Jonson (produced 1976). 1978.

Mastergate (produced 1989). 1990; with *Power Failure*, 1993.

City of Angels, music by Cy Coleman, lyrics by David Zippel (produced 1989). 1990.

Power Failure (produced 1991). With *Mastergate*, 1993.

Peter and the Wolf (narration for ballet) (produced 1991).

SCREENPLAYS: *The Notorious Landlady*, 1962; *The Thrill of It All*, with Carl Reiner, 1963; *The Wrong Box*, with Burt Shevelove, 1966; *Not with My Wife, You Don't*, with Norman Panama and Peter Barnes, 1966; *Oh, God*, 1977; *Movie Movie*, 1978; *Neighbors*, 1981; *Tootsie*, 1982; *Blame It on Rio*, 1984; *Barbarians at the Gate*, 1992.

RADIO WRITING: *Danny Thomas* ("Maxwell House Coffee Time"), 1945; *The Jack Paar Show*, 1945; *Duffy's Tavern*, 1945–47; *The Eddie Cantor Show*, 1947; *Command Performance* (Armed Forces Radio Service), 1947; *The Jack Carson Show*, 1948; *The Joan Davis Show*, 1948; *The Bob Hope Show*, 1948.

TELEVISION WRITING: *The Bob Hope Show*, 1948–52; *The Red Buttons Show*, 1952; *"Honestly, Celeste!"* (*The Celeste Holm Show*), 1953; *The Patrice Munsel Show*, 1954–62; *The Pat Boone Show*, 1954; *Caesar's Hour*, 1955–57; *The Art Carney Specials*, 1958–59; *The Danny Kaye Show* (consultant), 1963; *The Marty Feldman Comedy Machine*, 1971; *M*A*S*H* series, 1972–76; *Karen*, 1975; *United States*, 1980; *Academy Award Show*, 1985, 1986; *Mastergate*, 1992.

RECORDINGS: *Peter and the Wolf*, 1971; *Gulliver*, adaptation of the novel by Swift, 1989.

THEATRICAL ACTIVITIES

DIRECTOR: **Plays**—*A Funny Thing Happened on the Way to the Forum*, 1986. **Television**—several episodes of *M*A*S*H* series.

Larry Gelbart comments:

If anything I've ever written in any way reflects this dream-like existence that passes for life, I can only hope that the mirror I've held up to it is sufficiently cracked.

In an age of often homogenised comedy, Larry Gelbart has helped to keep the tradition of American satirical writing alive. He has more than a trace of George S. Kaufman's lean, sharp style and, like Kaufman, he has also written for the musical theatre, undoubtedly helping the economic style and satiric thrust of his plays.

He is, in fact, one of the few book-writers of musicals whose scripts could survive without the music. *A Funny Thing Happened on the Way to the Forum*, co-authored with Burt Shevelove, was a glorious reminder back in 1962, at a time when the musical tended towards refinement, that the American musical stage had one foot in its indigenous past of vaudeville and burlesque as well as one in European operetta. *Funny Thing* exploited with gleeful zest the happy marriage between the staples of Plautine farce and those of the Orpheum Circuit's world of top bananas and bump-and-grind. Its fusion of low comedy and high-precision plotting makes it one of the endearingly funny musical comedies.

Gelbart, working solo, also later restored faith in the comedy element of musical comedy in his book for *City of Angels*, opening in 1989 at the close of a decade dominated by the sung-through spectacles of the Lloyd–Webber dominated British ascendancy.

The show came out of Gelbart's collaboration on a flop revue, *My L.A.*, which showed him "just how theatrically marvellous that marvellously theatrical city was," and his wry evocation of L.A.'s contrasted mean streets and Bel Air poolsides, filtered through pastiche of classic detective fiction and *films noirs*, helped give his script its acrid wit. It is an extremely layered script, building up complex levels of irony, but always moving the story forward, essential for a musical. It tells the story of a novelist (Stine), gradually selling out to Hollywood crassness, while simultaneously presenting scenes from his work which mirror those in his life. His work is an adaptation of one of his movies into a screenplay built around a fictional ex-cop turned private eye (Stone), the Stone scenes creating an on-stage classic private-eye movie. The Hollywood of the 1940s is created in technicolour while the movie is staged in monochrome, the two worlds coalescing as the levels of reality and fantasy combine into a hall of mirrors. Again, Gelbart's script was genuinely funny— not least in its portrait of a wonderfully monstrous movie mogul, Buddy Fidler—as it joyfully skewered Tinseltown pretensions.

Gelbart's other big theatrical success was also a study of human duplicity, greed, and gullibility—his nimble 1976 re-working of *Volpone* set in the rumbustious Barbary coast world of San Francisco at the turn of the century. *Sly Fox* has a satirical energy that gives Jonson's original some key twists. Purists might carp that he diminishes a masterpiece, but Gelbart really uses Jonson's play as a trampoline for some fast and furious fun. His language—a sinewy, muscular prose—finds a bold American equivalent for Jonson's verse, not least in his re-working of Volpone's great speeches to his gold as Foxwell S. Sly hymns his treasure-chest. And his trial scene, with his no-nonsense Judge (played by the same actor as plays Sly) presiding over a courtroom filled with cheats and chisellers, is side-splitting, especially in the evidence of the venal good-time girl Merrilee Fancy, giving her occupation to the court as "a pleasure engineer."

Gelbart's other theatrical efforts have been less successful. *Jump*, a frenetic farce centered round a zany New York family, sank under a dismal London production and *Mastergate* flopped on a Broadway no more hospitable than usual to political satire. Both were uneven pieces, but hopefully these failures will not keep Gelbart away from the theatre for long.

—Alan Strachan

GELBER, Jack.

Born in Chicago, Illinois, 12 April 1932. Educated at the University of Illinois, Urbana, B.S. in journalism 1953. Married Carol Westenberg in 1957; one son and one daughter. Writer-in-residence, City College, New York, 1965–66; adjunct professor of drama, Columbia University, New York, 1967–72. Since 1972 professor of drama, Brooklyn College, City University of New York. Recipient: Obie award, 1960, for directing, 1972; Vernon Rice award, 1960; Guggenheim fellowship, 1963, 1966; Rockefeller grant, 1972; National Endowment for the Arts grant, 1974; CBS-Yale fellowship, 1974. Address: Department of English, Brooklyn College, Bedford Avenue and Avenue H, Brooklyn, New York 11210, U.S.A.

Publications

PLAYS

The Connection (produced 1959). 1960.
The Apple (produced 1961). 1961.
Square in the Eye (produced 1965). 1966.
The Cuban Thing (also director: produced 1968). 1969.
Sleep (produced 1972). 1972.

Barbary Shore, adaptation of the novel by Norman Mailer (also director:
produced 1973).
Farmyard, adaptation of a play by Franz Xaver Kroetz (also director: pro-
duced 1975). In *Farmyard and Four Other Plays*, by Kroetz, 1976.
Rehearsal (also director: produced 1976).
Starters (produced 1980).
Big Shot (also director: produced 1988).
Magic Valley (produced 1990).

SCREENPLAY: *The Connection*, 1962.

NOVEL
On Ice. 1964.

BIBLIOGRAPHY: *Ten Modern American Playwrights* by Kimball King, 1982.

CRITICAL STUDIES: *Seasons of Discontent* by Robert Brustein, 1965; *Les U.S.A.:
A la Recherche de Leur Identité* by Pierre Dommergues, 1967; *Tynan: Right
and Left* by Kenneth Tynan, 1967; *Now: Theater der Erfahrung* edited by Jens
Heilmeyer and Pia Frolich, 1971; *The Living Theatre* by Pierre Biner, 1972;
Theatricality by Elizabeth Burns, 1972; *Off Broadway* by Stuart Little, 1972;
People's Theatre in Amerika by Karen Taylor, 1973; introduction by Richard
Gilman to *The Apple, and Square in the Eye*, 1974.

THEATRICAL ACTIVITIES
DIRECTOR: **Plays**—several of his own plays, and works at Lincoln Center, New
Theatre Workshop, and the American Place Theatre, including *The Kitchen* by
Arnold Wesker, 1966, *Kool Aid* by Merle Molofsky, 1971, *The Kid* by Robert
Coover, 1972, *The Chickencoop Chinaman* by Frank Chin, 1972, *Eulogy for a
Small-Time Thief* by Miguel Piñero, 1977, and *Seduced* by Sam Shepard,
1979; *Indians* by Arthur Kopit, 1968; *The Man and the Fly* by José Ruibal,
1982; *The House of Ramon Iglesia* by José Rivera, 1983; *The Dolphin
Position* by Percy Granger, 1983; *Mink on a Gold Hook* by James Ryan,
1986; *The Independence of Eddie Rose* by William Yellow Robe Jr., 1989;
George Washington Dances by David Margulies, 1992.
ACTOR: **Film**—*Another Woman*, 1988.

Jack Gelber, playwright, award-winning director, and teacher, has had one of
the most important and innovative careers in contemporary American drama,
and in discussing this career there are two aspects of it that must be taken into
account: the kind of influence his plays had upon the improvisational and
group drama of the 1960s and early 1970s, and the particular vision the plays
themselves present.

The most influential of his plays is *The Connection*, produced by the Living
Theatre in 1959, and its theatrical characteristics introduce the Gelber technique: the play and production represent, or seem to represent, an attack upon
the "written" play. The usual authority figures of playwright and producer are

parodied, plot is suppressed, and improvisation takes their place as the actors, supposedly junkies and musicians drawn from everyday life, improvise a play from their personal lives to the complementary accompaniment of Charlie Parker-type jazz. Dramatic time is ambiguous and also improvised, with the specifically allocated length of the musical passages its clearest measure. Gelber deliberately avoids detailed psychological characterization and concentrates upon communal, representative figures although three of the characters, with specific functional roles, are especially vivid: Cowboy, the "connection" who incites the events: Sister Salvation, the unexpected guest who places the play in perspective; and Leach, the everyman of the play's world who overdoses on heroin. This "spontaneous" making of a play, the seemingly improvised action with its jazz accompaniment, the use of photographers to validate another version of the happenings, the interaction with the spectators, all combine to break down the usual relationship between actors and audience, reality and illusion, play and life. The subsequent group theater movement with its distrust of authority, its emphasis upon spontaneity and community, and its attack upon the text was clearly foreshadowed, even partly suggested, by the success of Gelber's play. But it is important to note that *The Connection* is itself a carefully written text.

Gelber's subsequent plays explore and expand these characteristics of *The Connection*. *The Apple* is communal and without central characters; its action is deliberately ambiguous and chaotic; and the actors shift in and out of character and participation. *Square in the Eye* is a family play about Ed Stone, a teacher, his wife, the children, and grandparents. Here various theatrical styles, including stand-up comedy and movies, undermine realism, and the chronology of events is purposefully disrupted. In *Sleep* two sleep scientists replace the playwright; the world of the play is a sleep laboratory; time is measured in sleep cycles; and the hero Gil, whose dreams coalesce into a kind of psychological action, proves on examination to be an average everyman. His sleeping and dreams, which correspond to the waking sleep of the addicts in *The Connection*, question the nature of reality, and in the play's most important speech one of the scientists expands the ambiguity into social statement: "The fact is that we have wired up a scientifically selected sample of the entire population and we have found, I know you won't believe this, we have found that they are technically asleep." In *Rehearsal*, publicly admired by several of his fellow dramatists, a play is in rehearsal; the nervous director cannot control the performance; and the producer is an incompetent alcoholic. The theater itself becomes the setting as the play emerges from the "interpolated" digressions initiated by the actors.

These formal characteristics suggest, of course, a view of life, and it is his second play, *The Apple*, that most clearly provides its symbol. The play invites the audience to make what it will of the apple and its connotations are many, but the biblical reference to what Milton calls "the fruit of that forbidden tree" is inescapable. The Gelber dramatic world describes a society that seems to have begun with a mythic expulsion, a communal and pragmatic place without heroes where man has become his ordinary self and disappointment and death are inevitable. It is a world where a secure reality is generally illusory and a world where drugs and call it sleep become the refuge of the human imagination which cannot recall it to order.

Gelber's writing, like the title of his best known play, has many connections, connections with the contemporary theater and the world it reflects, and he is paradoxically both the American playwrights' playwright and the chronicler of the American everyman.

—Gaynor F. Bradish

GIBSON, William.

Born in New York City, 13 November 1914. Educated at the City College of New York, 1930–32. Married Margaret Brenman in 1940; two sons. Since 1966 co-founding president, Berkshire Theatre Festival, Stockbridge, Massachusetts. Recipient: Harriet Monroe Memorial prize (*Poetry*, Chicago), 1945; Sylvania award, for television play, 1957. Agent: Flora Roberts Inc., 157 West 57th Street, New York, New York 10019. Address: Stockbridge, Massachusetts 01262, U.S.A.

Publications

PLAYS

I Lay in Zion (produced 1943). 1947.

Dinny and the Witches: A Frolic on Grave Matters (produced 1945; revised version produced 1959). With *The Miracle Worker*, 1960.

A Cry of Players (produced 1948). 1969.

The Ruby (as William Mass), libretto based on the play *A Night at an Inn* by Lord Dunsany, music by Norman Dello Joio. 1955.

The Miracle Worker: A Play for Television (televised 1957). 1957; stage version (produced 1959), with *Dinny and the Witches*, 1960; published separately 1960.

Two for the Seesaw (produced 1958). In *The Seesaw Log: A Chronicle of the Stage Production*, 1959.

Golden Boy, with Clifford Odets, adaptation of the play by Odets, music by Charles Strouse, lyrics by Lee Adams (produced 1964). 1965.

American Primitive (as *John and Abigail*, produced 1969; as *American Primitive*, produced 1971). 1972.

The Body and the Wheel: A Play Made from the Gospels (produced 1974). 1975.

The Butterfingers Angel, Mary and Joseph, Herod the Nut, and the Slaughter of 12 Hit Carols in a Pear Tree: A Christmas Entertainment (produced,1974). 1975.

Golda (produced 1977). As *How to Turn a Phoenix into Ashes: The Story of the Stage Production, with the Text, of Golda*, 1978; *Golda* published 1978.

Goodly Creatures (produced 1980). 1986.

Monday after the Miracle (produced 1982). 1983.

Handy Dandy (produced 1984). 1986.

Raggedy Ann and Andy, music and lyrics by Joe Raposo (produced 1984; as *Rag Dolly*, produced 1985; as *Raggedy Ann*, produced 1986).

SCREENPLAYS: *The Cobweb*, 1954; *The Miracle Worker*, 1962.

TELEVISION PLAY: *The Miracle Worker*, 1957.

NOVELS
The Cobweb. 1954.
Necromancer. 1984.

VERSE
Winter Crook. 1948.

OTHER
A Mass for the Dead. 1968.
*A Season in Heaven, Being a Log of an Expedition after That Legendary Beast,
   Cosmic Consciousness*. 1974.
Shakespeare's Game. 1978.

William Gibson began as a novelist and poet, earning a reputation with a
bestselling novel (*The Cobweb*) and a collection of verse (*Winter Crook*). An
early playwriting interest resulted in a short verse drama about the Apostle
Peter (*I Lay in Zion*), well-tailored for church groups, which predicted larger
dramas to come.

Gibson's first success on the Broadway stage came in 1958 with *Two for the
Seesaw*, a two-character drama about an embittered and lonely Nebraska
lawyer in New York, separated from his wife, and his affair with a generous-
hearted Bronx gamine down on her luck as a dancer. Although mutual love
and dependency develop between these two disparate people, the lawyer's
home ties are strong enough ultimately to draw him back to his wife. The
drama's chief appeal lies in its engaging portrait of the dancer, whose colorful
individuality and guileless love in the face of what she realizes is a doomed
relationship grasps one's attention and sympathy. The role marked the
author's uncommon ability to create strong parts for women and brought
recognition to the actress Ann Bancroft who continued to portray other
Gibson heroines. The play won praise from the critics and a substantial
Broadway run resulting in a film contract for Gibson. Later it was adapted by
others as the basis of the successful musical *Seesaw*. In *The Seesaw Log* Gibson
chronicles with liveliness the page-to-stage odyssey of *Two for the Seesaw* in
which he reveals his disenchantment with the professional production process
without minimizing the significant contribution of his collaborators.

In 1959 Gibson's short-lived off-Broadway production of *Dinny and the
Witches*, a satirical fantasy with song whose good intentions exceeded its
effectiveness, was followed by his greatest success: *The Miracle Worker*.
Originally written as a teleplay, the biography-drama portrays the teacher
Anne Sullivan's turbulent but triumphant struggle to free her savagely recalcitrant pupil, Helen Keller, from the prison of a sightless and soundless body.
Encompassing the time it takes the young teacher to gain mastery over the
seemingly ungovernable child in order to teach her language, the play is
brought to a poignant resolution when Helen, having had her hand repeatedly
doused under the water pump, excitedly discovers the connection between
words and things as she writes the word "water" in her teacher's palm.

Somewhat uneven and clumsy structure results from an insufficient transformation of the drama from its television form. Although critics faulted the play for its sentimentality and deficiencies in craft, they and the public agreed on its theatrical impact in presenting a compassionate portrait of the heroic teacher who made possible the greatness of Helen Keller. The play's success led to a 1962 film scripted by Gibson. Less critically successful was the 1982 sequel *Monday after the Miracle*, which focuses on the lively courtship and marriage of Anne Sullivan, still Helen Keller's companion and protector 17 years later, to the journalist John Macy, who comes to live in the Boston-area household of the two women and unavoidably disturbs their dependent relationship. Macy, unable to subordinate his private and professional needs to the now famous and articulate Helen, who is first in his wife's priorities and also sexually awakened by his presence, must leave. Critically indicted for being less emotionally powerful in material and effect than its predecessor, this thoughtful play about the difficult choices between duty and happiness offers compelling characterizations of its three leading figures and deserved better than its brief Broadway run.

Extending his experience in 1965 by collaborating on the book for a musical version of Clifford Odets's *Golden Boy*, Gibson transforms the white violinist-turned-boxer hero into a non-musical black pugilist. Aided by Sammy Davis, Jr. in the title role and a well-adapted book, the musical's New York production won moderate success.

A return to biography in the late 1960s was marked both by *American Primitive*, a lively documentary portraying John and Abigail Adams through their letters over three stormy years, and *A Cry of Players*, Gibson's dramatization of young Will Shakespeare's scantily recorded Stratford years and those of his wife Anne, who emerges as a full-bodied character enlisting our compassion. Young Will is characterized as a restless, free-living profligate, frustrated by the limitations of his village and the constricting ties of his family, who survives public punishment for poaching to join Will Kempe's troupe of players for the destiny that awaits him in London. That critics validly observed that the writer's penchant for poetic speech was marred by his lapses into either pretentious or prosaic dialogue and did not offer sufficient approval to let the play endure on Broadway, did not diminish the drama's popularity with community and college theatres.

Less successful than his other ventures into biography, Gibson's *Golda* offers the decisive days of the Arab-Israeli Yom Kippur War of 1973 as a dramatic frame to surround an episodic portrait of Israel's Golda Meir. As the Prime Minister deals with strategy crises and conflicting generals, she recalls in a series of flashbacks key public and private moments in her life stretching from her childhood to her ultimately troubled marriage and strong commitment to Zionism. Despite several strong scenes and a periodically enlivening profile of the protagonist's humor and humanity, the play failed to compress sufficiently the abundant scope of the material and to disclose the private person behind the public one. Yet Gibson merits credit for attempting to dramatize so worthy and so difficult a subject who was then still living.

In the 1980s Gibson wrote two works considerably slighter than *Monday after the Miracle*: *Handy Dandy*, a thematically pointed comedy about a conservative judge and a radical anti-armaments nun constantly brought into his court; and the book for the musical *Raggedy Ann*, concerning a doll springing to life to solve a sick young girl's parental problems, whose 1986 New York production lasted only briefly.

Gibson's work in several media demonstrates both his literary and dramatic gifts, which have resulted in some important plays of sensitivity and substance. Largely successful in dramatizing actual figures, Gibson has secured his place in American letters as an effectual writer of biography-drama.

—Christian H. Moe

GILROY, Frank D(aniel).

Born in New York City, 13 October 1925. Educated at De Witt Clinton High School, Bronx, New York; Dartmouth College, Hanover, New Hampshire, B.A. (magna cum laude) 1950; Yale University School of Drama, New Haven, Connecticut, 1950–51. Served in the U.S. Army, 1943–46. Married Ruth Dorothy Gaydos in 1954; three sons. Since 1964 member of the Council, and president, 1969–71, Dramatists Guild, New York. Recipient: Obie award, 1962; Outer Circle award, 1964; Pulitzer prize, 1965; New York Drama Critics Circle award, 1965; Berlin Film Festival Silver Bear, 1971. D. Litt.: Dartmouth College, 1966. Lives in Monroe, New York. Address: c/o Dramatists Guild, 234 West 44th Street, New York, New York 10036, U.S.A.

Publications

PLAYS

The Middle World (produced 1949).

A Matter of Pride, adaptation of the story "The Blue Serge Suit" by John Langdon (televised 1957). 1970.

Who'll Save the Plowboy? (produced 1962). 1962.

The Subject Was Roses (produced 1964). 1962; in *About Those Roses; or, How Not to Do a Play and Succeed, and the Text of "The Subject Was Roses"*, 1965.

Far Rockaway (televised 1965). With *That Summer—That Fall*, 1967.

That Summer—That Fall (produced 1967). With *Far Rockaway*, 1967.

The Only Game in Town (produced 1968). 1968.

Present Tense (includes *Come Next Tuesday, Twas Brillig, So Please Be Kind, Present Tense*) (produced 1972). 1973.

The Next Contestant (produced 1978). 1979.

Dreams of Glory (produced 1979). 1980.

Last Licks (produced 1979; as *The Housekeeper*, produced 1982).

Real to Reel (produced 1987).

Match Point (produced 1990).

A Way with Words (produced 1991).

Grang (produced 1991).

Give the Bishop My Faint Regards (produced 1992).

Any Given Day (produced 1993).

SCREENPLAYS: *The Fastest Gun Alive*, with Russel Rouse, 1956; *Texas John Slaughter*, 1958; *Gunfight at Sandoval*, 1959; *The Gallant Hours*, with Beirne Lay, Jr., 1960; *The Subject Was Roses*, 1968; *The Only Game in Town*, 1969; *Desperate Characters*, 1971; *From Noon till Three*, 1976; *Once in Paris*, 1978; *The Gig*, 1985.

TELEVISION PLAYS: *A Matter of Pride*, 1957; *Who Killed Julie Greer?* and *Up Jumped the Devil (Dick Powell Show)*, 1960–61; *Far Rockaway*, 1965; *The Turning Point of Jim Malloy*, 1975; *Gibbsville* series, from stories by John O'Hara, 1976; *Nero Wolfe*, from the novel *The Doorbell Rang* by Rex Stout, 1979; *Burke's Law* series; and since 1952 plays for *U.S. Steel Hour, Omnibus, Kraft Theater, Studio One, Lux Video Theatre*, and *Playhouse 90*.

NOVELS

Private. 1970.
From Noon till Three: The Possibly True and Certainly Tragic Story of an Outlaw and a Lady Whose Love Knew No Bounds. 1973; as *For Want of a Horse*, 1975.

OTHER

Little Ego (for children), with Ruth G. Gilroy. 1970.
I Wake Up Screening. 1993.

THEATRICAL ACTIVITIES

DIRECTOR: **Films**—*Desperate Characters*, 1971; *From Noon till Three*, 1976; *Once in Paris*, 1978; *The Gig*, 1985. **Television**—*The Turning Point of Jim Malloy* (pilot film), 1975; *Gibbsville* series, 1976; *Nero Wolfe*, 1979.

Frank D. Gilroy's bittersweet comedies consider men and male rituals: their alienation and loneliness, their difficulty communicating with and understanding women, and their insecurities in dealing with one another.

In Gilroy's first commercial success, *Who'll Save the Plowboy?*, the characters set the pattern of relationships found in his later work. Gilroy introduces us to three lives characterized by frustration, failure, and an inability to communicate honestly. Albert, the Plowboy of the title, and Helen, his wife, confront Larry, the now-dying man who saved the Plowboy's life during the war. Albert builds a castle of lies to impress his war buddy with non-existent postwar success and accomplishment, with fantasies of a happy marriage, and an imaginary strong and healthy son. Albert struts through the script like a rooster who doesn't notice that the hen house is empty. In *Plowboy* Gilroy begins to delineate the little humiliations, the deceits, and the burdensome pretenses of being a man. He also introduces us to the sexually unresponsive, adulterous woman who talks incessantly about insignificant and inappropriate things. These are the characters who populate all of Gilroy's work. In spite of *Plowboy*'s exposition and plot development, the shorthand that will become a trademark of a Gilroy script is apparent: the short, snappy repartee; the one-liner insights; the quick expressions of anger and bitterness.

The Subject Was Roses won the Pulitzer prize and is still the epitome of his style and thematic concerns. Elegant in its spareness, this play all but eliminates plot and concentrates on a moment of precisely outlined dramatic time. The World War II experiences of Timmy, another veteran, are a backdrop for the parental battlefield in his home, where his warring parents alternately use him as the cannon with which to shoot one another down. Gilroy hones his ability to communicate a complex set of emotions by focusing in exquisite detail on ordinary objects. When Nettie's waffles stick in the waffle iron, spoiling the first breakfast she's made her son in three years, her tears have less to do with a hungry son than they do with her fear of ruining an already tenuous mother-son relationship, her sense of inadequacy as a woman, and her inability to cope with losing her baby to an adult world.

Because of their terror of exposing their inner selves, Gilroy's characters are divided rather than united by emotions. They smash into one another and spin away without pausing to examine the damage. Toward the end of *The Subject Was Roses*, Timmy says: "I suspect that no one's to blame. . . . Not even me." This disavowal of any responsibility for the mess they've made of their lives is a common factor among all of Gilroy's characters.

Impressed with his Pulitzer prize and subsequent personal publicity, Gilroy admits to having felt a pressure to write something worthy of all his new-found fame. The result was the disastrous *That Summer—That Fall*, in which he tried to wed the Phaedra and Hippolytus legend to modern characters living in Manhattan's Little Italy. The play had 12 performances, and as Gilroy now says: "It proved that a boy from the Bronx shouldn't mess with the Greeks." That experience released him from what he perceived as the burden of being a Pulitzer prize-winning playwright, and enabled him to return to his own ideas and terse dramaturgy.

It is in his one-act plays that Gilroy is best able to concentrate the power of his simple descriptive style. He takes an incident and rapidly sets time, mood, and place by zeroing in on the minutest detail. In *The Next Contestant*, for example, a man who is about to be married becomes a guest on a television game show, and is challenged to call up an ex-girlfriend, who knows he's engaged, and get a date with her. If he achieves his goal, he will win a washer and dryer, a bedroom suite, a radio, television, stereo, wall-to-wall carpeting, luggage, an all-expenses-paid vacation in Miami Beach, and more. The heart of this very short play is the quick and emotionally painful telephone conversation between the contestant and the jilted ex-girlfriend. Gilroy shows the manipulation, the deceit, and the subsequent devastating disillusionment.

Gilroy is an idea man more than a plot man, and this can and does hinder him in his full-length work. *Last Licks* presents a variation on his stock characters who are involved with a one-act's worth of idea. A father, a son, and, in this case, the father's mistress, present a typical Gilroy triangular relationship filled with deception, emotional and physical sadism, drinking bouts, and tales of extramarital affairs.

Gilroy builds entire lives around rebuke and repentance. *Last Licks* is resplendent with repressed emotions and bitter speeches. Like so many of his plays, it is an often comic, but more often quite painful skirmish between the sexes, in which the primary sympathy is with the men's involvement with the world and with each other.

—Leah D. Frank

GOLDMAN, James.

Born in Chicago, Illinois, 30 June 1927; brother of the writer William Goldman. Educated at the University of Chicago, Ph.B. 1947, M.A. 1950; Columbia University, New York, 1950–52. Served in the U.S. Army, 1952–54. Married 1) Marie McKeon in 1962 (divorced 1972), one daughter and one son; 2) Barbara Deren in 1975. Since 1966 member of the Council, Dramatists Guild, and since 1967 member of the Council, Authors League of America. Recipient: Oscar, 1969; Writers Guild of America West award, 1969; Writers Guild of Great Britain award, 1969; New York Film Critics award, 1969; New York Drama Critics Circle award, 1972; Olivier award, 1987; *Evening Standard* award, 1987; Society of West End Theatres award, 1987. Agent: Owen Laster, William Morris Agency, 1350 Agency of the Americas, New York, New York 10019, U.S.A.

Publications

PLAYS

They Might Be Giants (produced 1961). 1970.
Blood, Sweat and Stanley Poole, with William Goldman (produced 1961). 1962.
A Family Affair, with William Goldman, music by John Kander (produced 1962).
The Lion in Winter (produced 1966). 1966.
Follies, music and lyrics by Stephen Sondheim (produced 1971; revised version produced 1985). 1971.
Robin and Marian (screenplay). 1976.

SCREENPLAYS: *The Lion in Winter*, 1968; *They Might Be Giants*, 1970; *Nicholas and Alexandra*, with Edward Bond, 1971; *Robin and Marian*, 1976; *White Nights*, with Eric Hughes, 1985.

TELEVISION PLAYS: *Evening Primrose*, music and lyrics by Stephen Sondheim, 1966; *Oliver Twist*, 1983; *Anna Karenina*, with Simon Langton, from the novel by Tolstoy, 1985; *Anastasia: The Mystery of Anna Anderson* series, 1986.

NOVELS

Waldorf. 1965.
The Man from Greek and Roman. 1974.
Myself as Witness. 1979.
Fulton County. 1989.

James Goldman at his best is a second-rate Neil Simon: both are dramatists who entertain rather than engage their audiences. Whether he is writing situation comedies (in collaboration with his brother), *A Family Affair* and *Blood, Sweat and Stanley Poole*, historical dramas, *The Lion in Winter* and *Nicholas and Alexandra*, or a musical, *Follies*, his work is always predictable, never ranging outside of the already-tested limits of the form. Only his skillful handling of dialogue occasionally redeems his plays, but even this cannot compensate for his deficiency in imagination, nor can it conceal that his characters are stock, plots mechanical, and themes imperfectly realized.

A Family Affair and Blood, Sweat and Stanley Poole play like the pseudo-comedies that could be seen between 6 and 10 p.m. any weeknight on American television throughout the late 1950s and early-to-middle 1960s. One concerns itself with the bustle and bickering that typically occurs when two families attempt to plan a wedding and the guardian of the bride wants a simple, elegant "family affair" while the mother of the groom longs for something a bit fancier. The other involves an army officer, 1st Lieutenant Stanley Poole, who has been bribing the education officer, Malcolm, with goods from the supply room to pass him on the army proficiency tests. The hero-of-the-day is Private Robert Oglethorpe who runs a "cram" course for the army officers, making it possible for Poole to replace the pilfered supplies, free himself from his bondage to Malcolm, and retain his military rank by passing the proficiency exams. The plot is mechanical, the jokes are stale, the characters too familiar, and the situation—Oglethorpe's classroom for the army's dunderheads—plays like a classroom scene from Our Miss Brooks or Sergeant Bilko, replete with all the cute gimmicks and mnemonics that teach the adult student to learn the names of the five Great Lakes or to recognize "the Symphony that Schubert wrote and never finished." Even the two Goldmans' sense of theatricality falters in this play. The slapstick accident where the good guys mangle and mutilate the villainous Captain Malcolm's coveted Jag takes place off-stage and can only be recounted, supposedly hilariously, by the conspirators on the stage. The climax of the play comes when the clumsy Private Oglethorpe, who previously got headaches whenever even the word "bayonet" was mentioned, catches the rifle Malcolm throws at him and brilliantly executes the manual of arms. The first action better fits a movie or television program than a play; the second simply lacks enough intrinsic importance to carry even the climax of a silly piece of canned comedy.

Goldman finds better success in another genre, the history or chronicle play, which had its revival in the 1960s with Luther, Lawrence of Arabia, and most successfully, A Man for All Seasons. Well done, the chronicle play examines and revitalizes characters from the past whose significance is unchallenged. It brings the past to life and, more importantly, it shows how the present has worked upon the past making it relevant. Goldman, however, seems to have overlooked this most important aspect of historical drama. It is not surprising that the dramatist of They Might Be Giants left the contemporary world and looked to the past to supply him with the heroes he sought, but it is regrettable that he only went to the past to acquire material and not to relate it to modern concerns. In The Lion in Winter Henry II of England and Eleanor of Aquitaine engage in a battle of wits as each attempts to outdo the other and settle the questions of succession, which son will marry the king's mistress, and which son will inherit the Vexin and Aquitaine. Henry, the aging monarch, still the roaring, regal lion, seeks to possess both his mistress and his wife and both their lands in order to pass England and that portion of France which is England's to John, his youngest and weakest son. Eleanor fights fiercely to hold Henry, and, failing that, to guarantee that England and her precious Aquitaine are willed to Richard Coeur de Lion. Geoffrey, the middle and cleverest son, plays brother against brother and son against father as he, too, struggles to protect what he believes should be his own. Alais, the lovely mistress, is pawn to Henry and his aged and imprisoned wife throughout the play. The dialogue in the play is witty, intelligent, pithy, and often mercurial. Henry and Eleanor alternately rage at each other and ask each other for pity in a manner reminiscent of George and Martha's quarrels in *Who's Afraid of Virginia Woolf?* But finally, the play is too contrived, the games of oneupmanship grow stale, and the audience begins to doubt that anything so real as the fate of the kingdom is at stake. The Christmas Court ends in a stalemate; the question of succession is postponed to another year; Eleanor and Henry conclude acknowledging to each other that their real enemy is time and that it will win. Goldman, meanwhile, seems to have forgotten that there was ever a real historical question raised in the play. History, and not the play, is left to tell us how the question of succession was resolved. The natures of the regal pair and not succession seem to have been the stuff of the play, but Goldman never demonstrates why these natures matter or who this King and Queen are.

More recently Goldman tried his hand at musical comedy; but he seems no more likely to be successful with this form than with the others. The book for *Follies* suffers from the same flaws that plagued his earlier works. The occasion is a reunion called by an impresario of the Weismann Follies' girls. Back to the crumbling music hall that had its heyday thirty years earlier come the show-girls who had danced for the era between the two wars. Among the guests are two girls, Sally and Phyllis, and their husbands, Buddy and Ben. As the evening progresses, we watch these pairs when they were young and in love, thirty years ago, and now, when they are old and discontented and flirting with the possibility that they can undo time and their marriages and return to the men who had jilted them before they married so long ago. The soap opera tale can be guessed. After an evening in which the couples dance and sing down memory lane and exorcize their regrets in a Follies Loveland, the couples leave their fancied past and return to drab realities and each other. The lyrics and music do much to redeem the play, and the gauzy interplay of past and present, shadows and substance, is visually well-handled and extremely well-suited to a musical that has taken sentimentality and nostalgia for its theme. A revised version of *Follies*, which Goldman and Stephen Sondheim worked on together, was a 1987 hit in London.

Goldman's difficulty in creating fully realized characters of his own fresh imagining and his lack of a significant theme continue to plague his work.

—Carol Simpson Stern

GOODMAN, Paul.

Born in New York City, 9 September 1911. Educated at the City College of New York, B.A. 1931; University of Chicago, Ph.D. 1940 (received, 1954). Married twice: two daughters. Reader for Metro-Goldwyn-Mayer, 1931; instructor, University of Chicago, 1939–40; teacher of Latin, physics, history, and mathematics, Manumit School of Progressive Education, Pawling, New York, 1942; also taught at New York University, 1948; Black Mountain College, North Carolina, 1950; Sarah Lawrence College, Bronxville, New York, 1961; University of Wisconsin (Knapp professor), Madison, 1964;

Experimental College of San Francisco State College, 1966; University of Hawaii, Honolulu, 1969, 1971. Former editor, *Complex* magazine, New York; film editor, *Partisan Review*, New Brunswick, New Jersey; television critic, *New Republic*, Washington, D.C.; editor, *Liberation* magazine, New York, 1962–70. Recipient: American Council of Learned Societies fellowship, 1940; Harriet Monroe prize, *Poetry*, Chicago, 1949; National Institute of Arts and Letters grant, 1953. Fellow, New York Institute of Gestalt Therapy, 1953; Institute for Policy Studies, Washington, D.C., 1965. *Died 3 August 1972.*

Publications

PLAYS

Childish Jokes: Crying Backstage. 1938.
The Tower of Babel, in *New Directions in Prose and Poetry 5.* 1940.
2 Noh Plays (produced 1950). In *Stop-Light,* 1941.
Stop-Light: 5 Dance Poems (Noh plays: *Dusk: A Noh Play, The Birthday, The Three Disciples, The Cyclist, The Stop Light*). 1941.
The Witch of En-Dor, in *New Directions,* 1944.
Faustina (produced 1949). In *Three Plays,* 1965.
Theory of Tragedy, in *Quarterly Review of Literature,* vol.4, 1950.
Jonah (produced 1950; revised version produced 1966). In *Three Plays,* 1965.
Abraham (cycle of *Abraham* plays; produced 1953). *Abraham and Isaac* in *Cambridge Review,* November 1955.
The Young Disciple (produced 1955). In *Three Plays,* 1965.
Little Hero (produced 1957). In *Tragedy and Comedy: Four Cubist Plays,* 1970.
The Cave at Machpelah, music by Ned Rorem (produced 1959). In *Commentary,* June 1958.
Three Plays. 1965.
Tragedy and Comedy: Four Cubist Plays (includes *Structure of Tragedy, After Aeschylus; Structure of Tragedy, After Sophocles; Structure of Pathos, After Euripides; Little Hero, After Molière*). 1970.

NOVELS

The Grand Piano; or, The Almanac of Alienation. 1942.
The State of Nature. 1946.
The Dead of Spring. 1950.
Parents Day. 1951
The Empire City. 1959.
Making Do. 1963.

SHORT STORIES

The Facts of Life. 1945.
The Break-up of Our Camp and Other Stories. 1949.
Our Visit to Niagara. 1960.
Adam and His Works: Collected Stories. 1968.

VERSE

Ten Lyric Poems. 1934.
12 Ethical Sonnets. 1935.

15 Poems with Time Expressions. 1936.
Homecoming and Departure. 1937.
Childish Jokes: Crying Backstage. 1938.
A Warning at My Leisure. 1939.
Pieces of Three, with Meyer Liben and Edouard Roditi. 1942.
Five Young American Poets, with others. 1942.
The Copernican Revolution. 1946; revised edition, 1947.
Day and Other Poems. 1954.
Red Jacket. 1955.
Berg Goodman Mezey, with Stephen Berg and Robert Mezey. 1957.
The Well of Bethlehem. 1957.
The Lordly Hudson: Collected Poems. 1962.
Hawkweed. 1967.
North Percy. 1968.
Homespun of Oatmeal Gray. 1970.
Two Sentences. 1970.

OTHER

Art and Social Nature (essays). 1946.
Kafka's Prayer. 1947.
Communitas: Means of Livelihood and Ways of Life, with Percival Goodman.
   1947; revised edition, 1960.
Gestalt Therapy: Excitement and Growth in the Human Personality, with
   Frederick Perls and Ralph Hefferline. 1951.
The Structure of Literature. 1954.
*Censorship and Pornography on the Stage, and Are Writers Shirking Their
   Political Duty?* 1959.
Growing Up Absurd: Problems of Youth in the Organized Society. 1960.
The Community of Scholars. 1962.
Utopian Essays and Practical Proposals. 1962.
Drawing the Line. 1962.
The Society I Live in Is Mine. 1963.
Compulsory Mis-Education. 1964.
People or Personnel: Decentralizing and the Mixed System. 1965.
Mass Education in Science. 1966.
Five Years: Thoughts During a Useless Time. 1966.
Like a Conquered Province: The Moral Ambiguity of America. 1967.
The Open Look. 1969.
New Reformation: Notes of a Neolithic Conservative. 1970.
Speaking and Language. 1972.
Little Prayers and Finite Experience. 1972.
Don Juan; or, The Continuum of the Libido, edited by Taylor Stoehr, 1979.

Editor, *Seeds of Liberation.* 1965.

Paul Goodman wrote:

Writing for the theatre has always given me the most satisfaction—it is
sociable.

I write *for* the actors and the available space.

I think my plays are my best works. They have uniformly failed. I have never received a favourable review.

I could write for the stage only if connected with a company. Since The Living Theatre left the USA I have had no such company—and we were already at variance. My spirit is Calderon, Racine, Goethe, Seami, whereas they went in the direction they went.

Most of my ideas about theatre and direction are expressed in the Preface to *Three Plays*.

Teacher, essayist, novelist, city-planner, psychoanalyst, Paul Goodman has made sporadic forays into drama, in several styles. Like Pound and Yeats, Goodman was fascinated by the Japanese Noh play, which he described as "imita[ting] a State, of the soul or of nature." In 1941 he published *Stop-Light*, five dance plays patterned on the Noh. In these brief pieces a Traveler comes to a place, witnesses the dance of the spirit of the place, and thereby gains a new perception. In the first two plays, the Traveler, like the author, is named Paul; in the next three plays, the Traveler is Poet, Cyclist, and Driver. Cumulatively, then, Goodman's Traveler becomes a kind of Everyman.

More conventionally Western in form, *Jonah* renders the Old Testament story in modern colloquial idiom. As in the Bible, Goodman's Jonah takes ship for Tarshish; he is thrown overboard in a storm and is swallowed by a whale in whose stomach an angel appears. The angel leads Jonah to a Nineveh that resembles New York. The city ignores his jeremiads, and Jonah feels like a fool when the Lord spares Nineveh, but the angel gradually teaches Jonah humility and acceptance of the Lord's mercy.

In Goodman's *Faustina*, however, the protagonist is not so receptive to education. Faustina, the wife of Emperor Marcus Aurelius, is consumed with lust for the Gladiator, Galba. In spite of his Stoicism, the Emperor is envious, so he allows his wife to persuade him to have Galba killed. The Emperor nevertheless tries to present death mercifully, denigrating life. Though Galba screams at his death, he does learn the Emperor's lesson, and it is the Emperor who finally has to call for help.

The Bible rather than Stoicism was Goodman's main dramatic source. The Living Theatre performed his five-part play, *Abraham*, but only excerpts have been published. In 1955 Goodman wrote *The Young Disciple,* which he described as inspired by his "psychological analysis of the Gospel of Mark." Goodman's Young Disciple is a rationalist who loves Our Master for his humanity. And yet the Disciple scorns the mob who make up humanity. Only after the mob stones Our Master, then repents, does the Young Disciple begin to feel part of them: "I am almost at home here with these superstitious people. I do not love them yet, but that will come in time. And found our church." More startling than this conversation is the play's vocabulary of love. Our Master expresses his love for the world as "fucking", and his last appearance is in a dance, reminiscent of the Noh play's search for Yugen.

In 1970 Goodman published four short plays that he designates as "Cubist." Goodman believed that Cubism plays with the medium in which it works, and in his Cubist plays he claimed to emphasize dramatic plot and thought by playing with them. *Structure of Tragedy, After Aeschylus* carries reminiscences of the *Oresteia*, as *Structure of Tragedy, After Sophocles* does of *Oedipus Tyrannos*. Yet such reminiscences play with the (five-part) choral *form*, rather than the *plot* of Greek tragedy. *Structure of Pathos, After Euripides* resembles *The Bacchae* in which the passions of Pentheus and Dionysius are abstracted from the plot. The final play, *Little Hero, After Molière*, recalls the antics of Scapin, and yet the comic chorus reaches back to Aristophanes.

Zen, Stoicism, Old Testament, New Testament, Greek Tragedy, and slapstick comedy—all were grist to Goodman's theatre mill. From the several sources emerges the signature of their author—searching, eclectic, reasonable, and humanitarian.

—Ruby Cohn

GORDONE, Charles (Edward).

Born in Cleveland, Ohio, 12 October 1925. Educated at Elkhart High School, Indiana; University of California, Los Angeles; Los Angeles State College (now University), B.A. in drama 1952; New York University Television Workshop. Served in the U.S. Air Force. Married Jeanne Warner in 1959; two sons and three daughters. Instructor, Cell Block Theatre, Yardville and Bordontown prisons, New Jersey, 1977–78; taught playmaking, New School for Social Research, New York, 1978–79. Founder, with Godfrey Cambridge, Committee for the Employment of Negro Performers, 1962. Recipient: Obie award, for acting, 1964; Pulitzer prize, 1970; New York Drama Critics Circle award, 1970; Vernon Rice award, 1970; American Academy award, 1971. Address: 17 West 100th Street, New York, New York 10025, U.S.A.

Publications

PLAYS

A Little More Light Around the Place, adaptation of the novel by Sidney Easton (produced 1964).

No Place to Be Somebody: A Black-Black Comedy (also director: produced 1967). 1969.

Gordone Is a Muthah (miscellany; produced 1970). In *The Best Short Plays 1973*, edited by Stanley Richards, 1973.

Baba-Chops (produced 1974).

The Last Chord (produced 1976).

A Qualification for Anabiosis (produced 1978; revised version, as *Anabiosis*, produced 1979).

MANUSCRIPT COLLECTION: Schomburg Collection, New York.

CRITICAL STUDY: "Yes, I Am a Black Playwright, But . . ." by Gordone, in *New York Times*, 25 January 1970.

THEATRICAL ACTIVITIES

DIRECTOR: Plays—about 25 plays, including *Rebels and Bugs*, 1958, *Faust* by Goethe and *Peer Gynt* by Ibsen, 1959, and *Tobacco Road* by Erskine Caldwell, *Three Men on a Horse* by George Abbott and John Cecil Holm,

Detective Story by Sidney Kingsley, *Hell Bent fer Heaven* by Hatcher Hughes, and Eugene O'Neill's "Sea Plays," 1960; *No Place to Be Somebody*, 1967 (and later productions); *Leaving Home* by Marcia Haufrecht, 1978; *After Hours* by Virgil Richardson (co-director, with Lucien Fiiyer), 1981.

ACTOR: **Plays**—in *Fortunato*; Logan in *The Climate of Eden* by Moss Hart, 1952; in *Mrs. Patterson* by Greer Johnson and Charles Sebree, 1957; The Valet in *The Blacks* by Jean Genet, 1961; George of *Of Mice and Men* by Steinbeck, 1964; Jero in *The Trials of Brother Jero* by Wole Soyinka, 1967; in *Gordone Is a Muthah*, 1970. **Television**—*The Climate of Eden*, 1961.

Charles Gordone comments:

Always the search for IDENTITY.

Charles Gordone first came to public attention as an actor in the tumultuous 1961 New York production of Genet's *The Blacks*. In addition to Gordone, the cast for that production included James Earl Jones, Cicely Tyson, Godfrey Cambridge, and Cynthia Belgrave. Like the first production of *A Raisin in the Sun*, *The Blacks* inspired most of its cast members to continue and extend the 1960s renaissance of black theater. As a member of the cast of *The Blacks*, Gordone was deeply involved in discussions of the politics of the play and of the relationship of theater to the black movement.

Although Gordone continued to work in and around theater throughout the 1960s, it was not until 1969, with the first production of his major play, *No Place to Be Somebody*, that his voice was clearly heard. Gordone had difficulty finding a producer for the play until Joseph Papp agreed to do it. The production quickly won public and critical applause. Gordone received a Drama Desk award as one of the three most promising playwrights of the year, and the play received the Pulitzer prize.

No Place to Be Somebody aptly fits a category or genre of drama defined by W. E. B. Du Bois early in this century: it is a "play of the contact of black and white." More than most plays by black American dramatists, and certainly more than most plays of the late 1960s, *No Place to Be Somebody* quickly establishes a world in which black characters and white characters not only inhabit the same space but come into direct conflict with each other. Johnny Williams, the owner of Johnny's bar where the play is set, is a young, angry black man who is obsessed with "Charlie fever," the play's organizing metaphor for black rage against white power. Johnny's rage does not take a strictly separatist form; some of his most important and ambiguous relationships are with vulnerable whites. He serves as the abusive pimp for two prostitutes—one black, the other white. He has an affair with the white, liberal college daughter of a lawyer who holds information useful to Johnny. He employs as bartender a white man whose dreams of being a "black" musician are undermined both by his ethnicity and his drug addiction. Since all of these white characters are weak and dependent on Johnny, we can read his contact with whites as a mode of reverse cultural exploitation; that is true of the structure of the relationships, but, within each one, there is at least a moment when Johnny reveals enough human concern to suggest that something in addition to power is at stake. The complexities of Johnny's motivations are only hinted, however, and could be taken in a number of directions in performance.

Johnny's foil and eventually his foe is Gabe, a "fair-skinned" black man who plays a role and a half as unemployable actor and the author of the play-in-progress. Gabe haunts Johnny's bar from its internal and external fringes. As a Brechtian narrator, Gabe initiates each scene with a commentary on the play's intentions and limitations; he informs us, for example, that No Place to Be Somebody is not a social protest play. Gabe is not satisfied in his external role; he enters the world of the play, in disguise one might say, as an actor-poet who distracts and provokes the company at the bar but can not get cast in any other show in town because he is neither white nor black enough in appearance. Gabe's voice opposes Johnny's "Charlie fever" throughout the play, but his voice does not suffice. In the end, Gabe kills Johnny, and in so doing destroys both his black brother and the character created by the playwright-at-work.

No Place to Be Somebody is an unabashedly derivative play whose sources make odd and only sometimes harmonious bedfellows. The constrained bar-room setting of the play is reminiscent of The Lower Depths, The Iceman Cometh, and The Time of Your Life; expressionistic conventions such as Gabe's lyrics and rhapsodies and Machine Dog, a materialized hallucination, interrupt the interactions on stage much as they do in the plays of Tennessee Williams and Ed Bullins; Gabe's final speeches and his appearance costumed as a black woman in mourning recall Baraka's Dutchman and Hawthorne's sin-laden Puritans. As many reviewers commented, the play also manages to accelerate its activity so that we find ourselves suddenly confronted with melodrama replete with an over-abundance of on-stage corpses.

In No Place to Be Somebody Gordone took on the difficult task of writing a drama that would at once illuminate the complex and discordant responses of black Americans to white American culture and would embrace what he himself called the "broader human context." In the 1970s he moved to the midwest and continued his struggle to "tell the story of the human comedy" through directing for the theater. His later writing includes an attempt to extend the form of the American musical with a musical version of No Place to Be Somebody. Anabiosis explores his tendency to "get sidetracked," and has been revised several times.

—Helene Keyssar

GOTANDA, Philip Kan.

Born in Stockton, California, 17 December 1949. Educated at the University of California, Santa Barbara, B.A. in Asian studies; Hastings College, Nebraska, J.D. Co-founder, Asian American Musicians Organization; artist-in-residence, Okada House, Stanford University, California. Recipient: Rockefeller grant, 1980–81. Address: 7, 229 Willard North, San Francisco, California 94118, U.S.A.

Publications

PLAYS

Bullet Headed Birds (produced 1981).
A Song for a Nisei Fisherman (produced 1982).

The Dream of Kitamura (produced 1985). In *West Coast Plays*, 15/16, 1983.
The Wash (produced 1985). In *Between Worlds: Contemporary Asian-American Plays*, edited by Misha Berson, 1990.
Yankee Dawg, You Die (produced 1987). 1989.
Fish Head Soup (produced 1987).
Day Standing On Its Head (produced 1994).

One sees in the work of a number of Asian-American playwrights the attraction of Asian theatre styles. Thus, Philip Kan Gotanda's earliest published play, *The Dream of Kitamura*, includes the use of masks and the crucial act from the past which haunts the characters is re-enacted with puppets. By contrast, his next two plays are realistic in their action, though *The Wash* has three locations simultaneously present throughout and *Yankee Dawg, You Die*—like *The Dream of Kitamura*—uses an abstract set of *shoji* screens.

The nonrealism of *The Dream of Kitamura* is to be seen not only in the mode of presentation but in the plotting. At the beginning of the play we hear a voice, over the chanting of a Buddhist sutra, that tells us "A crime has been committed. A robbery. A double murder. There was a witness." What we find is Rosanjin enthroned like Beckett's Hamm and so fearful of the vengeance of the demon mask Kitamura that he has hired two guards to protect him. In different pools of light we see the various interchanges between the characters, especially between Rosanjin's daughter and the young guard. At the play's end we learn that the murderer was not Rosanjin but his wife Zuma, the young guard is the victims' baby they could not find, and the older guard was witness to the crime and rescuer of the baby. Gotanda's refracted and often ritualized presentation suggests Rosanjin's state of mind even though the action does not take place within his consciousness.

The Wash takes us deep into the psyches of a married but now separated couple, perceived with deep sympathy and totally involving us in their parallel situations. After decades of marriage, in which she played a traditional supportive role, Masi has walked out on her husband Nobu. Every week she comes by to collect his dirty washing and return his clean clothes. He hardly acknowledges her visits, but his hurt is expressed by his retreating into building an elaborate kite such as he flew in his childhood. The play follows her into an affair and a new marriage with a widower, he into a very tentative relationship with a widow who runs a neighborhood restaurant at which he has come to eat regularly. He, however, cannot adjust to his wife's leaving and when she announces her remarriage isolates himself in his apartment, refusing to answer the door or the telephone. Yet Gotanda provides a subplot which allows him to suggest some hope for change in Nobu. One of two daughters has married a black man and Nobu has refused to consider this as anything but a disgrace, but when in this crisis she visits with her young son he slowly accepts the child and gives him the kite.

On the one hand, this is the story of anybody, although it is unusual in presenting such struggles for self-fulfilment among retired people in their sixties. On the other, it has particular significance for Asian-Americans. First, the central problem has been and is Nobu's internalized prohibition on the expression of emotion, perhaps even stronger in the Nisei (second-generation Japanese-Americans) because of the difficult lives they faced, notably the wartime internment to which Nobu's mind keeps returning. Even in the one scene where he asks Masi to stay the night he does so by asking her to make him breakfast (it is evening when he says this). It is this too that makes him embarrassed by the restaurant owner's small advances. Second, the length of time that it has taken Masi to face up to recognizing her own needs reflects a sense of obligation and of the importance of the family; it is perhaps only when her daughters are in their thirties that she feels free to consider herself. Third, as Michael Toshiyuki Uno, the director of the 1988 film of *The Wash*, has suggested, "if you're talking about Asian-American images in the past, there is no sexuality," and *The Wash* deals openly with sexual as well as psychological needs.

Yankee Dawg, You Die is a smaller play, in cast and in subject. It is a series of encounters between two Japanese-American film actors, the elder of whom took a Chinese name in the 1940s to improve his acceptability. This is one of the series of professional compromises that the play addresses. The young actor is at the point of moving from an Asian-American theatre company to "the industry," film and television. He expresses a mixture of admiration for the older actor's success and contempt for the compromises he has made to achieve it. At the play's end, the two friends, as they have become, try out for the same movie; the young actor takes the part of Yang, the Evil One—exactly the kind of stereotyped role he has attacked the older man for accepting— while the older actor turns down a role to appear in an independent no-budget Asian-American film.

The message is clearly put in the play's opening speech, which is repeated midway and again at the end. We see the older actor delivering a speech that he had in some long-ago war movie in which he played a Japanese soldier guarding American prisoners:

> You stupid American G.I. I know you try and escape. You think you can pull my leg. I speakee your language. I graduate UCLA, Class of '34. I drive big American car with big-chested American blond sitting next to . . . Heh? No, no, no, not "dirty floor." Floor clean. Class of '34. No, no, not "dirtyfloor." [. . .] What is wrong with you? You sickee in the head? What the hell is wrong with you? Why can't you hear what I'm saying? Why can't you see me as I really am?

Most of the rest of the play depicts the stereotyped media images of Asian-Americans and the frustrations the performers feel.

Gotanda's plays are diverse. His future work may be unpredictable, but also eagerly awaited.

—Anthony Graham-White

See the essay on *The Wash*.

GRAY, Spalding.

Born in Providence, Rhode Island, 5 June 1941. Educated at Fryeburg Academy, Maine; Emerson College, Boston, B.A. 1965. Actor in summer stock, Cape Cod, Massachusetts, and in Saratoga, New York, 1965–67; with Performance Group, New York, 1969–75; founder, with Elizabeth LeCompte, the Wooster Group, New York, 1975. Recipient: National Endowment for the Arts fellowship, 1977; Rockefeller grant, 1980; Guggenheim fellowship, 1985; Obie award, 1985. Agent: Suzanne Gluck, International Creative Management, 40 West 57th Street, New York, New York 10019. Address: c/o The Wooster Group, Box 654, Canal Street Station, New York, New York 10013, U.S.A.

Publications

PLAYS AND MONOLOGUES

Scales (also director: produced 1966).

Sakonnet Point, with Elizabeth LeCompte (produced 1975).

Rumstick Road, with Elizabeth LeCompte (also co-director: produced 1977).

Nayatt School, with Elizabeth LeCompte (produced 1978).

Three Places in Rhode Island (includes *Sakonnet Point*, *Rumstick Road*, *Nayatt School*), with Elizabeth LeCompte (produced 1978).

Point Judith: An Epilog, with Elizabeth LeCompte (produced 1979).

Sex and Death to the Age 14 (produced 1979). In *Sex and Death to the Age 14* (collection), 1986.

Booze, Cars, and College Girls (produced 1979). In *Sex and Death to the Age 14*, 1986.

India and After (America) (produced 1979).

Nobody Wanted to Sit Behind a Desk (produced 1980). In *Sex and Death to the Age 14*, 1986.

A Personal History of the American Theater (produced 1980).

Interviewing the Audience (produced 1981).

47 Beds (produced 1981). In *Sex and Death to the Age 14*, 1986.

In Search of the Monkey Girl, with Randal Levenson (produced 1982). 1982.

8 × Gray (produced 1982).

Swimming to Cambodia, parts 1 and 2 (produced 1984). 1985; in *Swimming to Cambodia: The Collected Works*, 1987.

Travels Through New England (produced 1984).

Rivkala's Ring, adaptation of a story by Chekhov, in *Orchards* (produced 1985). 1986.

Terrors of Pleasure: The House (produced 1985; as *Terrors of Pleasure: The Uncut Version*, produced 1989). In *Sex and Death to the Age 14*, 1986.

Sex and Death to the Age 14. 1986; augmented edition, including *Swimming to Cambodia*, parts 1 and 2, as *Swimming to Cambodia: The Collected Works*, 1987.

Monster in a Box (produced 1990). 1991.

Impossible Vacation. 1992.

Gray's Anatomy (produced 1993).

SCREENPLAY: *Swimming to Cambodia*, 1987.

TELEVISION PLAY: *Bedtime Story*, with Renée Shafransky, 1987.

THEATRICAL ACTIVITIES

DIRECTOR: **Plays**—*Scales*, 1966; *Rumstick Road* (co-director, with Elizabeth LeCompte), 1977.

ACTOR: **Plays**—roles in all of his own plays and in numerous other plays; Hoss in *The Tooth of Crime* by Sam Shepard, 1973; role in *North Atlantic* by Jim Strahs, 1984; Stage Manager in *Our Town* by Thornton Wilder, 1988. **Films** —*The Killing Fields*, 1984; *True Stories*, 1986; *Swimming to Cambodia*, 1987; *Clara's Heart*, 1989. **Television**—*Bedtime Story*, 1987.

Like Eugene O'Neill—also a New England playwright—Spalding Gray creates histrionic exorcisms of private demons. Such an autobiographical dramatist that he cheerfully admits to narcissism, Gray—again like O'Neill—in his early work is obsessed with his family and with doctors. Although Gray's subjects have evolved into his more recent experiences, his work always, unabashedly, concerns himself. An actor before he began writing roles, Gray appears in his pieces as well.

Gray initially created personal plays in collaboration with the director Elizabeth LeCompte, with whom he constructed four works named after places from his boyhood. *Sakonnet Point* recalls discontinuous images of his preschool summer beach vacations; it's as non-verbal as the infant Gray. This quiet piece built around objects and simple activities contrasts to the often frenetic and noisy *Rumstick Road*, which includes tape recordings of actual family members and of the psychiatrist who treated his mother prior to her suicide. So important are the recordings that the operator of the tape machine sits above the set in full view. Below is a doctor's examination table, on either side of which there is a room. One, containing a window through which we see a tent, is associated primarily with Gray's re-enacted past, while the other, containing a screen and slide projector, is associated more often with Gray's probing the past by stimulating his memories with mementos and tapes. The most interesting is a recording of the insensitive doctor, who tells Gray his mother's insanity is hereditary, "but don't be frightened."

Although still more fragmented and surreal, the third of Gray's *Three Places in Rhode Island*, called, after a childhood school, *Nayatt School*, begins with a seemingly straightforward lecture on T. S. Eliot's *The Cocktail Party*, from which Gray and LeCompte's script derives at least half its dialogue. While it deconstructs the Eliot play, *Nayatt School*'s imagery remains that of *Rumstick Road*: a red tent, insanity, death, Christian Science's suspicion of doctors, and preservation of past experience on tapes, film, and records—though the latter eventually are destroyed. Gray's earnest academician, a pedant intoning without passion his passion for the Eliot play, sits at a long table midway between the audience above and playing space below, where one of the rooms in *Rumstick Road* has been turned around, so we peer into it through the window. From quiet beginnings, *Nayatt School* increases its speed, ferocity, iconoclasm, and discontinuity. Farce chases punctuate scenes with a mad doctor and a parody of a horror film in which a scientist lets a giant blob of protoplasm run amok ("Get me a rewrite man quick—it's still growing"). Mindless antisocial amenities of alcohol, cigarettes, and disco music are partaken by children dressed as sophisticated adults, until characters strip and—literally—climb the walls.

Even more apocalyptic is the Gray and LeCompte part of the Rhode Island trilogy's epilogue, *Point Judith* (which also incorporates a send-up of machismo by Jim Strahs called *Rig*). Once more recur the red tent and the room frame, preservation of the past on records and film, windows which invite us in yet cut us off, and madness—this time in part by deconstruction of O'Neill's *Long Day's Journey into Night*, drowned out by a buzzer, wind, and Berlioz and accompanied by frantic farce in which objects (particularly a reversed vacuum cleaner billowing exhaust), writhing ribbons of light, and whirling bodies create cataclysmic discord. As a quieter coda, a film of men dressed as nuns and the trademark room frames concludes the piece.

After *Point Judith* Gray tired of fragmentation and deconstruction. In search of a controlled narrative form, he returned to the monologue format he'd employed in the opening of *Nayatt School* and constructed three intensely personal solo pieces. In these and his subsequent experiments in unilateral repartee, Gray reflects upon such intimate, often embarrassing details of his private life as what sort of things he did with his penis at the age of twelve. (A variation is *Interviewing the Audience*, in which, after speaking candidly of his own life, he grills spectators upon *their* experiences.) Although he condenses time and occasionally embellishes details, Gray does not fabricate. "A poetic journalist," as he terms himself, he may rearrange events to increase the humor or drama, but candor compels him to confess in *Swimming to Cambodia* (about corruption, both national and personal) that he vomited on the beach, made half as much money as others in *The Killing Fields*, was obsessed about losing his money, and patronized prostitutes. *Terrors of Pleasure* examines memories of being outfoxed by a con artist and of humiliation in Hollywood.

Whereas in those monologues Gray is largely victimized, in others he reveals his ineptitude at getting laid. Among his Woody Allen-style anxiety tales about bumbling towards the sack and fumbling in it is his ineffectual attempt to escape his confirmed heterosexuality in sex with another man. "I figured no one will know about it," Gray muses—and 200 spectators laugh.

This self-deprecatory raconteur who carries a dozen "public memories" around in his head—a nearly Homeric achievement—writes of shame—"pretty hard to maintain in New York City"—and pain, of fear, freaks, and failure, of embarrassment, banality, discomfort, and death, of greed and exploitation. With minimalist means, he confronts his paranoia and, employing a Buddhist idea, he recycles negative energy, a healing process for us as well as for him.

—Tish Dace

GREEN, Paul (Eliot).

Born near Lillington, North Carolina, 17 March 1894. Educated at Buies Creek Academy (now Campbell College), North Carolina, graduated 1914; University of North Carolina, Chapel Hill, 1916–17 and 1919–21, AB 1921 (Phi Beta Kappa), graduate study, 1921–22; Cornell University, Ithaca, New York, 1922–23. Served in the U.S. Army Engineers, 1917–19, partly in France and Belgium: lieutenant. Married Elizabeth Atkinson Lay in 1922; one son and three daughters. School principal, Olive Branch, North Carolina, 1914–17; lecturer, then associate professor of philosophy, 1923–39, professor of dramatic art, 1939–44, and professor of radio, television, and motion pictures, 1962–63, University of North Carolina; editor, *Reviewer* magazine, Chapel Hill, 1925; president, National Folk Festival, 1934–45, National Theatre Conference, 1940–42, and North Carolina State Literary and Historical Association, 1942–43; created large-scale "symphonic dramas" on historical themes, from late 1940s; member, U.S. Executive Committee, and National Commission, Unesco, 1950–52; Rockfeller Foundation lecturer in Asia, 1951; director, American National Theatre Company, 1959–61; delegate, International Conference on the Performing Arts, Athens, 1962. Recipient of several prizes, including: Pulitzer prize, 1927; Yale School of Drama award, 1964; Susanne M. Davis award, 1966; National Theatre Conference citation, 1974; American Theatre Association award, 1978. Litt.D.: Western Reserve University, Cleveland, 1941; Davidson College, North Carolina, 1948; University of North Carolina, 1956; Berea College, Kentucky, 1957; University of Louisville, Kentucky, 1957; Campbell College, Buies Creek, North Carolina, 1969; Duke University, Durham, North Carolina, 1980; DFA: North Carolina School of the Arts, Winston-Salem, 1976. Member, American Academy, 1941. *Died 4 May 1981.*

Publications

PLAYS

Surrender to the Enemy (produced 1917).

Souvenir (produced 1919).

The Last of the Lowries (produced 1920). In *The Lord's Will and Other Carolina Plays*, 1925.

The Long Night. In *Carolina Magazine*, 1920.

Granny Boling. In *Drama*, August–September 1921.

Old Wash Lucas (The Miser) (produced 1921). In *The Lord's Will and Other Carolina Plays*, 1925.

The Old Man of Edenton (produced 1921). In *The Lord's Will and Other Carolina Plays*, 1925.

The Lord's Will (produced 1922). In *The Lord's Will and Other Carolina Plays*, 1925.

Blackbeard, with Elizabeth Lay Green (produced 1922). In *The Lord's Will and Other Carolina Plays*, 1925.

White Dresses (produced 1923). In *Lonesome Road*, 1926.

Wrack P'int (produced 1923).

Sam Tucker. In *Poet Lore*, Summer 1923; revised version, as *Your Fiery Furnace*, in *Lonesome Road*, 1926.

Fixin's, with Erma Green (produced 1924). 1934.

The No 'Count Boy (produced 1925). In *The Lord's Will and Other Carolina Plays*, 1925; revised (white) version, 1953.

In Aunt Mahaly's Cabin: A Negro Melodrama (produced 1925). 1925.

Quare Medicine (produced 1925). In *In the Valley and Other Carolina Plays*, 1928.

The Man Who Died at Twelve O'Clock (produced 1925). 1927.

The Lord's Will and Other Carolina Plays (includes *Black-beard; Old Wash*

Lucas (The Miser); The No 'Count Boy; The Old Man of Edenton; The Last of the Lowries). 1925.

The Prayer Meeting. In Lonesome Road, 1926.

The End of the Row. In Lonesome Road, 1926.

In Abraham's Bosom (produced 1926). With The Field God, 1927.

The Hot Iron. In Lonesome Road, 1926; revised version as Lay This Body Down (produced 1972), in Wings for to Fly, 1959.

Lonesome Road: Six Plays for the Negro Theatre (includes In Abraham's Bosom, one-act version; White Dresses; The Hot Iron; The Prayer Meeting; The End of the Row; Your Fiery Furnace). 1926.

The Field God (produced 1927). With In Abraham's Bosom, 1927.

Bread and Butter Come to Supper. 1928; as Chair Endowed (produced in Salvation on a String, 1954).

Saturday Night. In In the Valley and Other Plays, 1928.

The Man on the House. In In the Valley and Other Plays, 1928.

The Picnic. In In the Valley and Other Plays, 1928.

Supper for the Dead (produced in Salvation on a String, 1954). In In the Valley and Other Carolina Plays, 1928.

Unto Such Glory (produced 1936). In In the Valley and Other Carolina Plays, 1928.

The Goodbye (produced 1954). In In the Valley and Other Carolina Plays, 1928.

Blue Thunder; or, The Man Who Married a Snake. In One Act Plays for Stage and Study, 1928.

Old Christmas. In Wide Fields, 1928.

In the Valley and Other Carolina Plays (includes Quare Medicine; Supper for the Dead; Saturday Night; The Man Who Died at Twelve O'Clock; In Aunt Mahaly's Cabin; The No 'Count Boy; The Man on the House; The Picnic; Unto Such Glory; The Goodbye). 1928.

The House of Connelly (produced 1931). In The House of Connelly and Other Plays, 1931; revised version (produced 1959), in Five Plays of the South, 1963.

Potter's Field (produced 1934). In The House of Connelly and Other Plays, 1931; revised version, as Roll Sweet Chariot: A Symphonic Play of the Negro People, music by Dolphe Martin (produced 1934), 1935.

Tread the Green Grass, music by Lamar Stringfield (produced 1932). In The House of Connelly and Other Plays, 1931.

Shroud My Body Down (produced 1934). 1935; revised version, as The Honeycomb, 1972.

The Enchanted Maze: The Story of a Modern Student in Dramatic Form (produced 1935). 1939.

Hymn to the Rising Sun (produced 1936). 1939.

Johnny Johnson: The Biography of a Common Man, music by Kurt Weill (produced 1936). 1937; revised version, 1972.

The Southern Cross (produced 1936). 1938.

The Lost Colony (produced 1937). 1937; revised versions, 1939, 1946, 1954, 1980.

Alma Mater. In The Best One-Act Plays of 1938, edited by Margaret Mayorga, 1938.

Out of the South: The Life of a People in Dramatic Form (includes *The House of Connelly; The Field God; In Abraham's Bosom; Potter's Field; Johnny Johnson; The Lost Colony; The No 'Count Boy; Saturday Night; Quare Medicine; The Hot Iron; Unto Such Glory; Supper for the Dead; The Man Who Died at Twelve O'Clock; White Dresses; Hymn to the Rising Sun*). 1939.

The Critical Year: A One-Act Sketch of American History and the Beginning of the Constitution. 1939.

Franklin and the King. 1939.

A Start in Life (broadcast 1941). In The Free Company Presents, edited by James Boyd, 1941; as *Fine Wagon*, in *Wings for to Fly*, 1959.

The Highland Call: A Symphonic Play of American History (produced 1939). 1941; revised version, 1975.

Native Son (The Biography of a Young American), with Richard Wright, from the novel by Wright (produced 1941). 1941; revised version, 1980.

The Common Glory: A Symphonic Drama of American History (produced 1947). 1948; revised version, 1975.

Faith of Our Fathers (produced 1950).

Peer Gynt, from the play by Ibsen (produced 1951). 1951.

The Seventeenth Star (produced 1953).

Serenata, with Josefina Niggli (produced 1953).

Carmen, from the libretto by H. Meilhac and L. Halévy, music by Bizet (produced 1954).

This Declaration. 1954.

Salvation on a String (includes *Chair Endowed; The No 'Count Boy; Supper for the Dead*; produced 1954).

Wilderness Road: A Symphonic Outdoor Drama (produced 1955; revised version produced 1972). 1956.

The Founders: A Symphonic Outdoor Drama (produced 1957). 1957.

The Confederacy: A Symphonic Outdoor Drama Based on the Life of General Robert E. Lee (produced 1958). 1959.

Wings for to Fly: Three Plays of Negro Life, Mostly for the Ear But Also for the Eye (includes *The Thirsting Heart; Lay This Body Down; Fine Wagon*). 1959.

The Stephen Foster Story: A Symphonic Drama Based on the Life and Music of the Composer (produced 1959). 1960.

Fine Wagon, from the radio play *A Start in Life*. In *Wings for to Fly*, 1959.

The Thirsting Heart (produced 1971). In *Wings for to Fly*, 1959.

Five Plays of the South (includes revised versions of *The House of Connelly; In Abraham's Bosom; Johnny Johnson; Hymn to the Rising Sun; White Dresses*). 1963.

Cross and Sword: A Symphonic Drama of the Spanish Settlement of Florida (produced 1965). 1966.

The Sheltering Plaid. 1965.

Texas: A Symphonic Outdoor Drama of American Life (produced 1966). 1967.

Sing All a Green Willow (produced 1969).

Trumpet in the Land (produced 1970). 1972.

Drumbeats in Georgia: A Symphonic Drama of the Founding of Georgia by James Edward Oglethorpe (produced 1973).
Louisiana Cavalier: A Symphonic Drama of the 18th Century French and Spanish Struggle for the Settling of Louisiana (produced 1976).
We the People: A Symphonic Drama of George Washington and the Establishment of the United States Government (produced 1976).
The Lone Star: A Symphonic Drama of Sam Houston and the Winning of Texas Independence from Mexico (produced 1977).
Palo Duro: A Sound and Light Drama (produced 1979).

SCREENPLAYS: *Cabin in the Cotton*, 1932; *State Fair*, with Sonya Levien, 1933; *Dr. Bull*, 1933; *Voltaire*, with Maude T. Howell, 1933; *The Rosary*, 1933; *Carolina*, 1934; *David Harum*, 1934; *Time Out of Mind*, 1947; *Roseanna McCoy*, 1949; *Red Shoes Run Faster*, 1949.

RADIO PLAY: *A Start in Life*, 1941.

NOVELS
The Laughing Pioneer: A Sketch of Country Life. 1932.
This Body the Earth. 1935.

SHORT STORIES
Wide Fields. 1928.
Salvation on a String and Other Tales of the South. 1946.
Dog on the Sun: A Volume of Stories. 1949.
Words and Ways: Stories and Incidents from My Cape Fear Valley Folklore Collection. 1968.
Home to My Valley. 1970.
Land of Nod and Other Stories: A Volume of Black Stories. 1976.

VERSE
Trifles of Thought. 1917.
The Lost Colony Song-Book. 1938.
The Highland Call Song-Book. 1941.
Song in the Wilderness, music by Charles Vardell. 1947.
The Common Glory Song-Book. 1951.
Texas Song-Book. 1967.
Texas Forever. 1967.

OTHER
Contemporary American Literature: A Study of Fourteen Outstanding American Writers, with Elizabeth Lay Green. 1925; revised edition, 1927.
The Hawthorn Tree: Some Papers and Letters on Life and the Theatre. 1943.
Forever Growing: Some Notes on a Credo for Teachers. 1945.
Dramatic Heritage (essays). 1953.
Challenge to Citizenship (address). 1956.

Drama and the Weather: Some Notes and Papers on Life and the Theatre.
  1958.
The University in a Nuclear Age (address). 1963.
Plough and Furrow: Some Essays and Papers on Life and the Theatre. 1963.

BIBLIOGRAPHY: *Fifty Southern Writers after 1900: A Bio-Bibliographical Sourcebook* by Joseph M. Flora and Robert Bain, 1987.

CRITICAL STUDIES: *Paul Green* by Walter S. Lazenby, 1970;
Paul Green by Vincent Kenny, 1971.

North Carolinian Paul Green became noted nationally as a dramatist in the 1920s for plays depicting the harsh existence of the whites and blacks of the rural South. He won particular attention as a white writer with an uncommon understanding of the black experience. Many of his full-length plays were produced on Broadway from 1926 to 1941. Later in his career, Green translated a love of country into national themes in regionally-produced historical dramas. Often criticized for flaws in dramaturgical craftsmanship, Green nevertheless was a distinctive American playwright with a keen understanding of man's delicate, often despairing relationship to the earth, and to his fellow man.

The playwright's early one-act plays, designed for small regional theatres and published in anthologies, deal with Southern poor folk wrestling with the often insurmountable hostility of nature and neighbor, deceived by religion as panacea, with few characters surviving the frustration or suffering. Several representative works can be cited. *The Lord's Will* introduces a self-appointed preacher who ignores his family's crushing ills to "preach the Word". *Unto Such Glory* looks farcically at a religious zealot justifiably tricked by a shrewd layman. Notably focusing on the black culture is *The No 'Count Boy*, whose title-character is a shiftless, persuasive young dreamer who nearly succeeds in enticing a girl with similar dreams to abandon her hard-working suitor and take to the open road.

In *White Dresses* a pretty Mulatto interprets a Christmas gift to mean her beloved white employer-lover will marry her, until she realizes that his father has arranged her marriage to a black admirer. These plays are compactly structured, employ details of folklore and local color well known by the author, and sensitively display compassion for society's downtrodden and humor toward its fools.

An outstanding one-act play, *Hymn to the Rising Sun*, was first produced in New York in 1936. Set in a Southern prison camp on 4th July, the play relates a chain gang's brutal treatment. The sadistic warden whips a young white prisoner who is tormented by a black fellow prisoner's punishment, suffering, and death in a "sweat box". Telling characterizations, graphic stage images, and irony effectively expose the brutality inherent in incarceration.

Three full-length plays about the black experience, presented in New York, reflect a similar mood of anger and indictment. *In Abraham's Bosom*, Green's first full-length work, was produced in 1926 by the Provincetown Players. Despite critical surprise and controversy it won the Pulitzer Prize. It is the story of a self-educated black man who wishes to raise the lot of the Negro through education, and with the aid of his white father opens a school in rural North Carolina against white planters' opposition and blacks' apathy. Frustrated in continuing his school after his father's death, he kills his deceiving white half-brother and consequently is killed by a Klan posse. While flawed in construction and in stereotypical characterizations of secondary figures, the folk tragedy holds power in its despairing compassion for the plight of blacks and in its portrait of a relentlessly driven protagonist.

Roll Sweet Chariot delivers a trenchant indictment in depicting a marginally-existing black community that is facing callous severance by road construction. Green termed the play a "symphonic drama" because it synthesizes such elements as sound, music, dance, and pantomime—an influence of expressionistic and Brechtian techniques studied during a European stay. Neither commercially nor artistically successful, this ambitious work's form came to be better realized in his subsequent history-dramas.

Continuing his concern with the fate of blacks in America, Green collaborated with Richard Wright in dramatizing Wright's novel *Native Son*, in which a black chauffeur's unintentional killing of a white woman leads to his trial and conviction. The 1941 Mercury Theatre production, directed by Orson Welles, projected a sterner attitude toward repression of blacks than Green had intended. Flawed, but dramatically powerful, it achieved commercial success despite mixed critical reviews.

Green wrote sympathetically about white people too. *The Field God*, an early drama, concerns a rural Southern farmer driven to conform to his neighbors' puritanical Christianity, which he ultimately rejects to find God in his own creative existence. The play failed in New York in 1927, with critically observed deficiencies of plot and character, but it underlines Green's distrust of the inflexible, uncharitable ways of so-called "Christians."

In 1931 *The House of Connelly*, patterned after Chekhov's *The Cherry Orchard*, proved more significant than *The Field God*, chronicling the decay of a landed Southern aristocratic family. Originally a tragedy, the 1931 Group Theatre production interpolated a marriage of the weak surviving son to a poor white woman, thereby providing a hopeful note of redemption and continuation of the family estate. Commercially unsuccessful, the play nonetheless earned attention for its poignant treatment of a dying white aristocracy amidst the anguish of blacks.

In *Johnny Johnson*, a 1936 Group Theatre production, Green enlisted expressionism and Kurt Weill's music to create a powerful anti-war play centering on a pacifist soldier in World War I who is wounded and suffers consequent disillusionment. His attempts, with laughing gas, to force the military high command to decree war's end result in arrest and committal to an asylum for the insane, where he consolidates his pacifist beliefs before returning home to be ignored as a peace-promulgating toy peddler. Satirizing jingoism and the military, Green offers an international theme proving his ability to extend beyond regional themes and subjects.

In 1937, Green began the last decades of his career with *The Lost Colony*, a "symphonic drama" about the first British settlement in North America, which continues to thrive in summertime amphitheatre performances on North Carolina's Roanoke Island, near the subject's historical site. Green subsequently wrote other outdoor epic dramas of the American heritage, several of which also enjoy continuity in similar regional theatres from Virginia to Texas.

Paul Green's canon of history-dramas, contributing to an awareness of American history, represents a significant achievement. Furthermore, his plays treating the themes of the biracial South reflect a compassionate understanding rarely expressed by other dramatists of his time. His place as a distinctive voice in American theatre is secure.

—Christian H. Moe

GREENBERG, Richard.

Born in East Meadow, New York, 22 February 1958. Educated at local schools; Princeton University, Princeton, New Jersey, 1976–80, A.B. in English 1980; Harvard University, Cambridge, Massachusetts, 1980–81; Yale University School of Drama, New Haven, Connecticut, 1982–85, M.F.A. in drama 1985. Member, Ensemble Studio Theater, New York. Recipient: Oppenheimer award, 1985; Dramalogue award, 1991. Lives in New York City. Agent: George Lane, William Morris Agency, 1350 Avenue of the Americas, New York, New York 10019, U.S.A.

Publications

PLAYS

The Bloodletters (produced 1984).
Life Under Water (produced 1985). 1985.
Vanishing Act (produced 1986). 1987.
The Author's Voice (produced 1987). 1987.
The Maderati (produced 1987). 1987.
The Hunger Artist, with Martha Clarke and company, adaptation of a work by Franz Kafka (produced 1987).
Eastern Standard (produced 1988). 1989.
Neptune's Hips (produced 1988).
The American Plan (produced 1990). 1990.
The Extra Man (produced 1991).
Jenny Keeps Talking (produced 1992).
Pal Joey, adaptation of the musical by Rodgers and Hart (produced 1992).

SCREENPLAYS: *Ask Me Again*, 1989; *Life Under Water*, 1989.

TELEVISION PLAY: *The Sad Professor*, in the *Trying Times* series, 1989.

Richard Greenberg comments:

Self-indulgently, I consider all my work to date to constitute a public apprenticeship. My last several plays have had quite classically constructed stories. This is a deliberate process of self-teaching, an effort to master the fundamentals of story-telling as a kind of jumping-off place for whatever the future brings. I'm non-ideological but I prefer plays that *become* ideas to those that provide forums for ideas.

Richard Greenberg's comedies explore what it is to be young, semi-gifted, white, and wealthy in Reagan-era America, with all the attendant education, anxiety, and ennui that such status confers. Exclusively set in New York City or some fashionable nearby resort, Greenberg's plays are populated by females with names better suited to pets—Minna, Rena, Dewy, and Jinx—and WASPy, dithering men saddled with names that are the inheritance of their "hegemony"—Keene, Kip, Spence, and Sky. Greenberg treats his characters with a mixture of fascination, cynicism, and envy. Often an uneasy tension exists: are they adorable but misguided eccentrics or despicably vacuous victims of their wealth and breeding?

Greenberg's characters are articulate to a fault. Where exceptions occur, the inability to express oneself properly becomes a running joke—in *The Maderati* the "Method Actor" Danton mumbles inaudibly while mediocre poet Keene never finishes his similes. In *The Author's Voice*, a hilarious and brilliant little one-act play updating the Cyrano de Bergerac story by way of the "Twilight Zone," a handsome but untalented writer is punished for relying on a misshapen gnome-like creature to provide the book he must deliver to his publisher.

Greenberg's fixation with the power of language, syntax, and literacy is evident throughout his work. Responding to the formal elocution of Eva, a German emigrée nicknamed "Czarina" in *The American Plan*, Gil exclaims, "What a sentence—wonderful!—Americans never take grammar to that kind of extreme." In *Life Under Water*, Kip tries to seduce Amy-Beth by describing a fictitious green light at the end of her dock. She responds: "That's the goddamn 'Great Gatsby.' I can read! Oh, you sensitive boys with your quotations." This is an example not only of Greenberg's propensity for making literary references, but for having other characters—and therefore the audience —recognize them.

Greenberg's one-act comedies are in many ways his most original and intriguing work; his full-length plays lack their appealing fairytale tone and surreal quality. Written in five scenes, *Vanishing Act* is a Pirandellian experiment that unfolds in a dreamy landscape peopled by wealthy but largely useless characters searching for ways to prevent physical or emotional dissipation. In the play, Minna brushes her younger sister Anya's hair while telling her a bedtime story about a woman named Carla whose husband is murdered and dismembered. The last scene jumps ahead several years to find Carla, the character in Minna's story, onstage telling *her* daughter a bedtime tale about Minna's family. As one narrative "vanishes" into another, Greenberg's structural sleight-of-hand jostles the audience's sense of reality, making manifest the infuriatingly ephemeral nature of life and art. No other Greenberg play takes such structural risks.

Life Under Water uses 17 short scenes to evoke incisively the emotionally submerged existence of pampered young people at a fashionable Hamptons beach house. Kip, a hapless teenager, runs away from home and meets Amy-Joy and her friend Amy-Beth, recently released from a mental institution. Although a short romance flares up between Kip and Beth, Kip can't sustain any sense of commitment—emblematic of many Greenberg characters (Kip and Beth could be an early sketch for Nick and Lili in *The American Plan*).

The Maderati is a broad farce satirizing a crowd of self-involved New York artists and pseudo-intellectuals. Greenberg fully embraces the traditional farce form, concluding with a *faux* murder and the couples neatly arrayed in a final tableaux. The genre and the subject allow Greenberg to give full rein to his verbal games. After the depressed poet Charlotte has been committed to an insane asylum, Dewy erroneously believes she's died, while Keene thinks she's hospitalized for an abortion. Both believe Danton should not be out of town:

Keene: He should be by her bedside.
Dewy: You mean by her *bier*.
Keene: Buying her beer, buying her flowers, buying her anything she wants.

Both *The American Plan* and *The Extra Man* feature strong, slightly demonic figures—the Miss Haversham-like Eva and the blocked writer Keith, respectively—who destructively manipulate the love affairs of those they care for most, ostensibly out of some subliminal jealousy (although sheer boredom and lack of amusement is offered as a more frightening, though unconvincing, motivation). Both plays describe the difficulty of loving another person because of the need for honesty, strength, determination, commitment, and openness—qualities invariably lacking in these cynical times. Unfortunately, the characters are so spineless and emotionally inept that they fail to generate much sympathy.

Eastern Standard most successfully details its characters' struggles to make commitments. The first act's three scenes occur at the same lunch hour and at the same restaurant, but with three different couples center-stage. In this way the action that was peripheral in one scene becomes central in another. The main character Stephen, an architect specializing in monstrous postmodern office towers ("I *am* urban blight") meets his gay friend Drew, a painter of some renown, while the girl he's loved only from a distance, Phoebe, waits to meet her brother Peter, a TV writer recently diagnosed as having AIDS. When May, a mentally unstable homeless woman, hits Peter with her Perrier bottle, Stephen has his excuse to meet his love object as he and Drew come to Peter's rescue. Act Two takes place at Stephen's Hamptons beach house, to which he's invited everyone present at the restaurant that day—eventually including May, the baglady, and Ellen, the waitress. Here all the characters struggle, not always convincingly, with commitment—Ellen to her acting career, May to sanity, Peter to the solitude imposed by the discovery he has AIDS, Drew to his artwork and his cynicism, and Stephen and Phoebe to their love for each other. Unusually for a Greenberg play, they also struggle actively with their liberal guilt, trying to gauge their personal responsibility for homelessness, an assessment occasioned by May's presence. But once it is clear no one is willing to prevent her return to the streets, May steals their valuables and disappears. The play ends rather glibly, with Drew breaking through Peter's emotional defenses, and Stephen and Phoebe engaged to each other and committed to designing and financing buildings for the homeless. As they toast their happiness, it's clear May couldn't steal what is most valuable to them—their newfound love for each other and their heightened social consciousness—highly unusual qualities for characters in the rarified world of Richard Greenberg's plays.

—John Istel

GREENSPAN, David.

Born in Los Angeles, California, 17 March 1956. Educated at Beverly Hills High School, graduated 1974; University of California, Irvine, B.A. in drama 1978. Lives with William Kennon. Busboy and waiter, New York, 1978–88; playwright-in-residence, HOME for Contemporary Theatre and Art, New York, 1987–90; director and playwright-in-residence, New York Shakespeare Festival, 1990–92. Recipient: Brooklyn Arts and Cultural Association award, 1984; Art Matters grant, 1987, 1988, 1989; Revson fellowship, 1989; Rockefeller fellowship, 1989; Albee Foundation residency, 1989; Yaddo residency, 1991. Agent: Wiley Hausam, International Creative Management, 40 West 57th Street, New York, New York 10019, U.S.A.

Publications

PLAYS

Vertices, Man in a/the Chair, Pieces in the Dark, Recent Hemispheres (monologues and short pieces; produced 1981–86).
The Horizontal and the Vertical (produced 1986).
Dig a Hole and Bury Your Father (produced 1987).
Jack (produced 1987). In The Way We Live Now, edited by M. Elizabeth Osborn, 1990.
Principia (produced 1987).
The Home Show Pieces (includes Doing the Beast, Too Much in the Sun, Portrait of the Artist, The Big Tent) (produced 1988). In Plays in Process, 1993.
The Closet Piece (produced 1989).
2 Samuel 11, Etc. (also director: produced 1989). In Plays in Process, 1990.
Dead Mother, or Shirley Not All in Vain (produced 1991). In Grove New American Theatre Anthology, 1992.
Son of an Engineer (produced 1994).

THEATRICAL ACTIVITIES

DIRECTOR: Plays—Sexual Perversity in Chicago by David Mamet, 1984; Danny and the Deep Blue Sea by John Patrick Shanley, 1986; Kate's Diary by Kathleen Tolan, 1989; Wanking 'Tards by Nicky Silver, 1990; Gonza the Lancer by Chikamatsu Monzaemon, 1990; The Way of the World by William Congreve, 1991.

David Greenspan comments:

I think of my writing as an act of self-exploration and a form of entertainment. Sometimes I engage in research and spend long hours studying history or biography. I also work from observation and memory. Always the external instigators are filtered through the fabric of my inner life and associations.

For several years I wrote a series of autobiographical plays that dramatized private details of my personal life, attempting to capture the pedestrian obsessions and conflicts that occupy much of my experience. More recently, I have been attempting to move beyond the strictly autobiographical, and explore myself in terms of a wider social context.

David Greenspan is the most nakedly personal of playwrights. He became a writer for the theatre when he started performing excerpts from his journals, and he still often takes the central role in his pieces, which he also invariably directs. Greenspan's mother died of lupus when he was a boy; her specter shadows his entire body of work, and the tensions of a troubled family are dramatized again and again. Homoerotic fantasy is another key component of Greenspan's writing, but here, as elsewhere, his real focus is the mind, not the body. His true subject is not sex, but obsession and longing. He seeks to capture the process of thinking—especially, thinking about feeling.

Yet Greenspan's highly emotional art has always been formally experimental. Samuel Beckett, Gertrude Stein, and Robert Wilson are his acknowledged masters. Greenspan has described his early pieces as "very abstract—word-associated, fragmented, stream-of-consciousness, nonsensical in the strictest sense of the word." To include performers other than himself, he used numbers to indicate who was to speak which lines of these texts. There is little sense of character; what's dramatized is a single consciousness.

Greenspan's recent texts resemble plays more closely; they contain vivid characters who often have their own convincing voices. Yet the playwright still identifies them as Character 1 or Speaker 2, emphasizing the distance between actors and characters on the one hand, and between characters and the actual people who inspired them on the other. Any sort of actor might play any sort of character. Various actors can play the same character at different points in the play. Actors can stop playing their characters and start discussing them. Identity is fluid. Transformation, role-playing, and pretending are paramount.

The one-act *Jack* is a good introduction to Greenspan's work. It's an AIDS play, a lovely and elegiac piece for three women Speakers who stand upstage at music stands—"ideally, the image is one of floating busts," writes Greenspan —and a male Character 8 who sits surrounded by seven empty chairs. On the page the Speakers' words are printed in three columns; in the theatre they are overlapping waves of sound. In this verbal music, repetition and variation gradually build a portrait of the dead Jack. At other moments one voice breaks clear to deliver a monologue, long or short, as often about Jack's difficult mother as about Jack himself. At the center of the piece is a depiction of a primal Greenspan location: a dark park where men come for sex. It is a locus of longing, a fallen Eden, a trap. Late in the play Character 8—Jack—finally speaks, telling about getting lost as a small boy on a crowded beach, about finally seeing his father and embracing him, crying.

The Home Show Pieces and *Dead Mother, or Shirley Not All in Vain* are much bigger works, uneven, ungainly, and fascinating. *Home* contains some of this writer's wittiest scenes: in its opening section Character 1 is in bed, trying to read, then trying to hump the mattress between the interruptions of a series of phone calls which reveal his loneliness. Some years later, Character 1 sits on the toilet indulging in fantasies of fame, a playwright claiming not to read his reviews while revealing extensive knowledge of them.

The central character in *Dead Mother* is a young man, Harold, who impersonates his mother to help his brother win the woman he wants to marry. There is comedy in this *Charley's Aunt* situation, of course, but also intense drama. In one remarkable scene Harold looks into a mirror, at once accusing the mother whose identity he has put on and, as the mother, striking back. The unexpected appearance of Harold's father, who thinks he's seeing his dead wife's ghost, gives Harold the opportunity to attack his father, expressing his mother's grievances along with his own. The masquerade enables Harold not only to speak long-hidden truths to his family, but to know himself; in the end he leaves his marriage and the family business to disappear into a homosexual life.

Greenspan's most impressive and successful piece to date is *2 Samuel 11, Etc.*, which retells the David and Bathsheba story from the woman's point of view, setting it against a complex contemporary narrative that works its way to a story of a young man's encounter with a sexually predatory old man. Both narratives are evolving in the mind of Character 1, a writer, who spends the second half of the play standing in his shower recounting the second story, telling it through the dialogue of 11 characters.

Character 1 is also onstage during the first half, but all the speaking is done by Character 2: Bathsheba as she is re-imagined by the writer. As the expression of the male writer's mind, the female character speaks not only Bathsheba's story—which is wonderfully told, and filled with a complex mixture of revulsion and sympathy for the old king who seduces her, has her husband killed, and takes her into his harem—but also the homoerotic fantasies that overwhelm the writer, and the telephone conversations that represent the intrusion of everyday realities.

It's all you can do to keep up with the complicated post-intermission narrative, but the first half of *2 Samuel* is utterly clear, and so there's space for rich comedy. "I've got to find a way to get this down on paper," says Character 2, speaking for her author, who is masturbating with one hand and writing with the other. Bathsheba's jaundiced view of Old Testament patriarchy also brings wicked laughter, and there's shocking power in the juxtaposition of the Bible and what Greenspan himself calls the "pornographic ruminations" coming out of her mouth. This time the author has embodied his ideas and obsessions in a context so potent that the result is unforgettable theatre.

—M. Elizabeth Osborn

GUARE, John (Edward).

Born in New York City, 5 February 1938. Educated at Joan of Arc Elementary School, and St. John's Preparatory School, New York; Georgetown University, Washington, D.C., 1956–60, A.B. 1960; Yale University School of Drama, 1960–63, M.F.A. 1963. Served in the U.S. Air Force Reserve, 1963. Married Adele Chatfield-Taylor in 1981. Assistant to the manager, National Theatre, Washington, D.C., 1960; member, Barr/Wilder/Albee Playwrights Unit, New York, 1964; founding member, Eugene O'Neill Playwrights Conference, Waterford, Connecticut, 1965; playwright-in-residence, New York Shakespeare Festival, 1976–77; adjunct professor of playwriting, Yale

University, 1978. Council member, Dramatists Guild, 1971; vice-president, Theatre Communications Group, 1986. Recipient: ABC-Yale University fellowship, 1966; Obie award, 1968, 1971, 1991; *Variety* award, 1969; Cannes Film Festival award, for screenplay, 1971; New York Drama Critics Circle award, 1971, 1972, 1991; Tony award, 1972, 1986; Joseph Jefferson award, 1977; Venice Film Festival Golden Lion, National Society of Film Critics award, New York Film Critics Circle award, and Los Angeles Film Critics award, all for screenplay, 1980; American Academy Award of Merit Medal, 1981; New York Institute for the Humanities fellowship, 1987; Hull-Warriner award, 1990. Lives in New York City. Address: c/o R. Andrew Boose, Collyer and Boose, 1 Dag Hammarskjold Plaza, New York, New York 10017–2299, U.S.A.

Publications

PLAYS

Theatre Girl (produced 1959).
The Toadstool Boy (produced 1960).
The Golden Cherub (produced 1962?).
Did You Write My Name in the Snow? (produced 1963).
To Wally Pantoni, We Leave a Credenza (produced 1965).
The Loveliest Afternoon of the Year, and Something I'll Tell You Tuesday (produced 1966; *The Loveliest Afternoon of the Year* produced 1972). 1968.
Muzeeka (produced 1967). In *Off-Broadway Plays*, 1970; in *Cop-Out, Muzeeka, Home Fires*, 1971.
Cop-Out (produced 1968). In *Off-Broadway Plays*, 1970; in *Cop-Out, Muzeeka, Home Fires*, 1971.
Home Fires (produced 1969). In *Cop-Out, Muzeeka, Home Fires*, 1971.
Kissing Sweet (televised 1969). With *A Day for Surprises*, 1971.
A Day for Surprises (produced 1970). With *Kissing Sweet*, 1971.
The House of Blue Leaves (produced 1971). 1972; with *Bosoms and Neglect*, 1993.
Two Gentlemen of Verona, with Mel Shapiro, music by Galt MacDermot, lyrics by Guare, adaptation of the play by Shakespeare (produced 1971). 1973.
Cop-Out, Muzeeka, Home Fires. 1971.
Taking Off (screenplay), with others. 1971.
Optimism; or, The Misadventures of Candide, with Harold Stone, based on a novel by Voltaire (produced 1973).
Rich and Famous (produced 1974). 1977.
Marco Polo Sings a Solo (produced 1976; revised version produced 1977). 1977.
Landscape of the Body (produced 1977). 1978.
Take a Dream (produced 1978).
Bosoms and Neglect (produced 1979). 1980; with *The House of Blue Leaves*, 1993.
In Fireworks Lie Secret Codes (produced in *Holidays*, 1979; also director: produced separately, 1981). 1981.

Nantucket series:
   Lydie Breeze (produced 1982). 1982.
   Gardenia (produced 1982). 1982.
   Women and Water (produced 1984; revised version produced 1985). 1990.
Three Exposures (includes *The House of Blue Leaves, Landscape of the Body,
   Bosoms and Neglect*). 1982.
Hey, Stay a While, music by Galt MacDermot, lyrics by Guare (produced
   1984).
Gluttony, in *Faustus in Hell* (produced 1985).
The Talking Dog, adaptation of a story by Chekhov, in *Orchards* (produced
   1985). 1986.
The House of Blue Leaves and Two Other Plays (includes *Landscape of the
   Body* and *Bosoms and Neglect*). 1987.
Moon over Miami (produced 1989).
Six Degrees of Separation (produced 1990). 1990.
Four Baboons Adoring the Sun (produced 1992). In *Antaeus*, 1992.

SCREENPLAYS: *Taking Off*, with others, 1971; *Atlantic City*, 1980.

TELEVISION PLAY: *Kissing Sweet* (*Foul!* series), 1969.

MANUSCRIPT COLLECTION: Beinecke Library, Yale University, New Haven,
Connecticut.

CRITICAL STUDY: article and checklist by John Harrop, in *New Theatre
Quarterly 10*, May 1987.

THEATRICAL ACTIVITIES
DIRECTOR: **Play**—*In Fireworks Lie Secret Codes*, 1981.

In dramatizing philos/aphilos, the love/hate relationships in the American
family, John Guare locates sources of humor in suffering, penning stinging
satires, corrosive black comedies, and screwball farces about such subjects
as bereavement, humiliation, betrayal, and guilt. An ironist who frequently
eschews pathos, fantasist Guare speaks to our brutal realities; his comedies can
move us to tears. His freewheeling imagination unfettered by the constraints of
realism as he employs such presentational devices as narration, soliloquies and
asides to the audience, and poetic speech, Guare nevertheless grounds his plays
in contemporary American life, especially the sudden end of a family unit.
   This paradoxical playwright has described one of his plays as a union of
Feydeau and Strindberg. Not surprisingly, Guare depicts marriage as bondage
between self-absorbed people who can't care for others, since narcissism
precludes nurturing. When egocentric misfits nevertheless marry and breed,
they create nightmares frequently culminating in death. Women (often more
sympathetic than this dramatist's men) especially suffer from romantic or
domestic ties, but sons also are victimized by family life.
   His early one-acts provide the characters with bizarre backgrounds which

distance us. The wayward husband in *The Loveliest Afternoon of the Year*, "a seeing eye person for blind dogs," recounts his sister's dismemberment by a polar bear and his father's death by scalding from a calliope's steam. "You're from Ohio," he explains to his mistress. "You come from a nice family. You don't understand the weirdness, the grief that people can spring from." Perhaps she gains that understanding when she dies; the man's wife shoots and kills them both.

Guare's early neo-absurdist plays also include the dreadful marital squabbles of *Something I'll Tell You Tuesday*; the characters so removed from humanity in *A Day for Surprises* that Pringle is pregnant, not with a baby, but with *The Complete Works of Dr. Spock*; and the eradication of reproductive capacity in the S&M *Cop-Out*. In *Home Fires* Guare mocks the lengths to which the Schmidts go to avoid acknowledging their family name and ties. *Muzeeka*'s Brechtian short episodes and scene titles indict marriage, which causes Argue (an anagram for Guare) to sell out his creativity, flee to kinky sex, and then ultimately escape via suicide. Marriage proves one of the rotten institutions comprising the American dream.

The House of Blue Leaves keeps the pain at a distance with increasingly antic farce, as nuns in Artie Shaughnessy's Queens apartment pursue a soldier disguised as an altar boy, prompting him to toss a bomb into the arms of the deaf movie star. In order to dramatize familial resentments of the humiliations relatives inflict on one another, Guare creates Artie, a zookeeper/composer whose singing voice is as cracked as his wife's mind. Artie's son Ronnie hates Uncle Billy for having made a fool of him, and he loathes his father for never ceasing to remind him of it. Instead of murdering his real father, Ronnie resorts to symbolic patricide by trying to kill the Pope. Because Artie can't stand his wife Bananas witnessing his failures and her knowledge that he has plagiarized his songs, he kills her. Among a group of hopeless narcissists, only Bananas can love others; therefore she is "mad." Guare dramatizes this family as unreal, phony, illusory, impermanent—like the bare tree in which blue birds momentarily perch. The family home, not the mental institution, constitutes the real "house of blue leaves."

In the cartoon *Rich and Famous*, one of the plays replete with arctic imagery, Bing turns to his parents for comfort but encounters, not warmth, but ice. They shoot him—and he shoots back—because he has failed to fulfill their own dreams. They would prefer a mentally retarded son to one who wants his own life.

In the even more baroque *Marco Polo Sings a Solo*, set in the Arctic Circle, icy images dominate, though mixed with metaphors of fire. The characters, narcissists who live only for themselves, engage in solos or quests alone. Stony McBride even owes his birth to a transexual impregnated by her own sperm— the ultimate image of self-absorption. Guare describes the play as a "comedy coming out of each character's complete obsession with self." In a house carved out of ice, all three marriages disintegrate, but it's as though Ibsen's Nora (one wife has attended 41 productions of *A Doll's House*) has been walled in by a gigantic igloo without doors—or egress.

Landscape of the Body dramatizes relatives as helpless victims, or, as Guare puts it, "people drifting with their heads cut off." Here family members long for love, but their insecurities destroy them. After his father abandons them,

Bert and his mother Betty try to begin a new life in New York, but he fears his mother won't return from a search for a husband, grabs a friend in his terror, and dies because his pal, misinterpreting this as a homosexual pass, in his own turn panics, killing and decapitating Bert. Betty's own anxieties had sent her away on a trip with an (unsuitable) admirer; those fears cost her the only person with whom she could share love (a parallel to Artie murdering his loving wife, Bananas).

Bosoms and Neglect likewise concerns loss, anxiety, egomania, and aching loneliness. Despite the farce with which Guare maneuvers Scooper, his aging mother and new girl friend, *Bosoms* forces us to experience the excruciating pain of family life. Scooper worries more about neglected authors than about his neglect of his mother or her neglect of her breast and uterine cancer—the areas of her body where he was gestated and nurtured. After Scooper tries to murder his mother, she lays bare her own regrets, anguish, and humiliation in an effort to offer him salvation, but his selfishness already has prompted him to leave the room. Horrifyingly, as she provides him with the key to understanding his recurrent nightmare, his blind mother cannot know he's not there to hear her.

Such images of loneliness, frequent throughout his career, achieve especial poignancy in *Landscape of the Body, Bosoms and Neglect,* and most of Guare's subsequent work. Even as he hones his ability to dramatize people cut off from other's affections, however, Guare shifts direction in another respect. While he tends to focus in the first couple of decades on families with sons, thereafter, with one exception, he writes also about daughters and sisters in his full-length plays.

That exception, *Moon over Miami* resembles the playwright's work of 20 years earlier in its blistering, Ortonesque satire targeting corruption among FBI agents, politicians, and religious con artists (a salesman of bibles which "leave out the sad parts," such as Jesus dying). The characters comprise such grotesques as agent Otis Flimbsby (weird because honest), con-man Shelley Slutsky, his mother (who sings only lewd and scatological songs in her nightclub act), and a chorus of mermaids. Beginning in Alaska, then shifting to Miami, *Moon* features more images of ice and heat, as well as extravagant efforts to connect with others. Agent Wilcox even recognizes that disillusioning people or leaving them can kill them. Suggested by the ABSCAM federal sting operation, *Moon* indicts fraud and deception. Flimsby encounters only unscrupulous charlatans except for his girlfriend, who hopes "to find a better world where Bambi runs free and Dumbo flies high and Pinocchio tells the truth and Sleeping Beauty is wide awake."

Guare originally undertook *Moon over Miami* as a film for John Belushi, who died inopportunely, as though he were a character in one of the dramatist's black-comic farces. Guare encountered better luck with another violent but amusing film script, the award-winning *Atlantic City.* Initially it depicts a bleak view of families: Sally's husband has run away with and impregnated her sister Chrissy. Yet Lou becomes a surrogate father for Sally, and Chrissy finds a surrogate mom in Grace. Perhaps substitute or chosen families nurture more tenderly and effectively than biological relatives.

In two 1980s one-acts Guare examines alienation between lovers without offspring. *In Fireworks Lie Secret Codes* concerns belonging or not belonging on the part of a gay male couple and their friends, whereas *The Talking Dog* dramatizes the unsuitable mating of a woman and her boyfriend: she agrees to both physical and emotional risk taking, while he hang glides—but hangs back from commitment.

Sabotaging or betraying relationships likewise figures prominently in Guare's full-length plays of the 1980s and early 1990s. The ambitious Nantucket trilogy evokes comparison to Eugene O'Neill's New England plays. Beginning during the Civil War, then continuing through the subsequent three decades, these melodramas offer an American fable illuminating the country's origins, nature, and future direction—just as Guare's William Dean Howells urges aspiring writer Joshua to do. The presentational and episodic *Women and Water* moves fluidly back and forth across time and permits Lydie Breeze to confide her thoughts to us directly. Guare dramatizes murder, rape, arson, and suicide in a melodrama which veers off into both satire and Senecan tragedy of blood guilt and a ghost's vengeance. Moving between hope and disillusion, Guare touches upon both betrayal, patricide, greed, lies, and the punishment of sins, and the healing of wounds and the ideals of a golden age. He balances water as a life-sustaining force against the image of the watery grave. Out of the Battle of Cold Harbor (when 17,000 men died) and other misery grows Lydie's resolution to take three men—Joshua, Dan, and Amos—and found the commune of Aipotu—Utopia spelled backwards.

The more realistic and linear *Gardenia*, though it also features murder, takes as its central image blossoms: their birth and nurturance with water, their flowering, deflowering, and withering. Other emblematic details include Lydie's conviction that her patient's baby died in punishment of the parents (innocence and guilt, sin and redemption figure prominently) and Joshua's prison assurance to the Brighton Mauler that going home constitutes a happy ending (an ironic view considering what lies ahead of Joshua). As Guare further examines ideals and disillusionment, hope and its loss, healing of old wounds and inflicting new ones, and the loneliness which engulfs Lydie, he maintains suspense by withholding from us the killing's cause.

To learn that we need *Lydie Breeze*, replete with more murder, rape, and suicide, as well as madness and syphilis. Yet this summer on Nantucket provides a sunny ending, permitting peace with the past and hope for Lydie's daughter, even while clearly suggesting a future fraught with further narcissism and corruption. This coming-of-age play of Lydie Hickman ends on the significant word "alone."

Six Degrees of Separation depicts a man singularly alone, an outsider in several senses. Black, gay, self-educated, poor, and homeless, Paul's separation from the pampered and privileged residents of condos bordering Central Park seems massive, yet, in scenes both searing and amusing, he cons them into accepting him as one of them. In this touching and hilarious commentary on human interconnections—or, often, disconnections, which separate us from ourselves as well as each other—society matron Ouisa Kittredge figures "Everybody on this planet is separated by only six people." Ouisa fears failure to forge links but also appears anxious about letting people get close, past those distancing devices at which the Kittredges and their friends excel.

As he did with *Landscape of the Body*, Guare lifted found materials from newspaper headlines: an African-American, claiming he's both Sidney Poitier's son and a friend of the Kittredge's college-student offspring, arrives in their posh apartment claiming he's been mugged in the park. When the Kittredges and several friends learn they've all, after hearing the same tale, given overnight lodging and small sums to the young man, they figure they've been victimized by a con artist. Yet he's spent their money on them (plus a male hustler) and he's stolen nothing. His goal: becoming one of them, part of the family, and receiving parental love from Ouisa and her husband. With dramaturgy sporting monologues, dreams, jumps in time and place, and chats with the audience, Guare shows Paul's impressive bid for a foster family and the Kittredge's eventual failure to provide the affection and approval he craves.

As double-sided as the Kittredges' Kandinsky, *Six Degrees'* multiple ironies and dual tone have won it many admirers. Less popular but rich in its own right, *Four Baboons Adoring the Sun* flashes both forward (three years later, for narrative, though Guare clarifies the chronology only on the page, not the stage) and back to the courtship of Penny and Philip. The present portrays their married life in Sicily, where they dig up artifacts of the past, ostensibly archeological finds, but actually the damage to their lives which may render their union too fragile to endure.

Within 24 hours, in a classical Italian setting, events evolve which we know will end tragically, because a god, Eros, predicts disaster in the first lines: "The start of another perfect day./Something will go wrong." The newly-weds are joined by their total of nine children from their former marriages. Eros targets their first born, Wayne and Halcy, at 13 craving the romantic and sexual bliss secured by their parents, who try to thwart their youngsters' wishes. The title, which refers to a statue in which the eyes have been burned out from worshipping the sun, suggests both the ecstatic joy of love and the danger of worshipping Eros. Of each pair of lovers, the men depart, and the women remain to survive tragedy and respond affirmatively to Eros's injunction "From out of the part of your soul that's not broken, adore the Sun." If Guare in this and other plays offers hope of battered spirits reviving and flourishing, clearly those will spring from among his resilient women.

—Tish Dace

See the essay on *The House of Blue Leaves.*

GURNEY, A(lbert) R(amsdell), Jr.

Born in Buffalo, New York, 1 November 1930. Educated at St. Paul's School, Concord, New Hampshire, 1944–48; Williams College, Williamstown, Massachusetts, 1948–52, B.A. 1952; Yale University School of Drama, New Haven, Connecticut, 1955–58, M.F.A. 1958. Served in the U.S. Naval Reserve, 1952–55. Married Mary Goodyear in 1957; two sons and two daughters. Since 1960 member of the faculty, and since 1970 professor of literature, Massachusetts Institute of Technology, Cambridge. Recipient: Drama Desk award, 1971; Rockefeller grant, 1977; National Endowment for the Arts award, 1982; American Academy and Institute of Arts and Letters award of merit, 1987; San Diego Theater Critics Circle award, 1988. D.D.L.: Williams College, 1984. Agent: Gilbert Parker, William Morris Agency, 1350

Avenue of the Americas, New York, New York, 10019. Address: 74 Wellers Bridge Road, Roxbury, Connecticut 06783, U.S.A.

Publications

PLAYS

Three People, in *The Best Short Plays 1955–56*, edited by Margaret Mayorga. 1956.

Turn of the Century, in *The Best Short Plays 1957–58*, edited by Margaret Mayorga. 1958.

Love in Buffalo (produced 1958).

The Bridal Dinner (produced 1962).

The Comeback (produced 1965). 1967.

The Rape of Bunny Stuntz (produced 1966). 1976.

The David Show (produced 1966). 1968.

The Golden Fleece (produced 1968). In *The Best Short Plays 1969*, edited by Stanley Richards, 1970.

The Problem (produced 1969). 1968.

The Open Meeting (produced 1969). 1969.

The Love Course (produced 1970). In *The Best Short Plays 1970*, edited by Stanley Richards, 1971; published separately, 1976.

Scenes from American Life (produced 1970; revised version produced 1988). In *Four Plays*, 1985.

The Old One-Two (produced 1973). 1971.

Children, suggested by the story "Goodbye, My Brother" by John Cheever (produced 1974). 1975; in *Four Plays*, 1985.

Who Killed Richard Cory? (produced 1976). 1976; revised version, as *Richard Cory* (produced 1984), 1985.

The Middle Ages (produced 1977). In *Four Plays*, 1985.

The Wayside Motor Inn (produced 1977). 1978.

The Golden Age, suggested by the story "The Aspern Papers" by Henry James (produced 1981). 1985; in *Love Letters and Two Other Plays*, 1990.

What I Did Last Summer (produced 1981). 1983; in *Love Letters and Two Other Plays*, 1990.

The Dining Room (produced 1982). 1982; in *Four Plays*, 1985.

Four Plays. 1985.

The Perfect Party (produced 1986). 1986; in *The Cocktail Hour and Two Other Plays*, 1989.

Another Antigone (produced 1986). 1988; in *The Cocktail Hour and Two Other Plays*, 1989.

Sweet Sue (produced 1986). 1987.

Don't Fall for the Lights (dialogue only) with Terence McNally and Richard Maltby, Jr., and *White Walls*, in *Urban Blight* (musical revue), based on an idea by John Tillinger, music by David Shire, lyrics by Richard Maltby, Jr. (produced 1988).

The Cocktail Hour (produced 1988). In *The Cocktail Hour and Two Other Plays*, 1989.

Love Letters (produced 1988). In *Love Letters and Two Other Plays*, 1990.

The Cocktail Hour and Two Other Plays (includes *The Perfect Party*, *Another Antigone*). 1989.

Love Letters and Two Other Plays (includes *The Golden Age, What I Did Last Summer*). 1990.
The Snow Ball, adaptation of his own novel (produced 1991).
The Old Boy (produced 1991).
Public Affairs. 1992.
Later Life (produced 1993).

SCREENPLAYS: *The House of Mirth*, 1972; *The Hit List*, 1988.

TELEVISION PLAY: *O Youth and Beauty*, from a story by John Cheever, 1979.

NOVELS
The Gospel According to Joe. 1974.
Entertaining Strangers. 1977.
The Snow Ball. 1985.

MANUSCRIPT COLLECTION: Sterling Library, Yale University, New Haven, Connecticut.

A.R. Gurney, Jr., comments:

What attracts me about the theatre are its limitations as well as its possibilities. Indeed, its best possibilities may lie in its limitations. I am as much concerned about what to leave out as about what to put in. Offstage characters and events give a kind of pressure and resonance to what is shown onstage. In fact, offstage comprises the infinite possibilities and resources of film and television. Anyone who writes plays these days is forced to explore the very restrictions of this enduring old medium. I am particularly drawn to it because I like to write about people who themselves are beginning to stretch out and push against the walls.

In recent years A. R. Gurney, Jr.'s reputation in his native America has risen sharply and his work also continues to be performed in Britain. This has been partly due to changes in the organisation of the American theatre. After Gurney's first full-length play, *Scenes from American Life*, was produced at the Forum Theatre at Lincoln Center in 1971, he had virtually nowhere else to go with his work after the Center regime changed, especially at a time when his main concern—WASP manners and mores—was out of fashion. But with a changing society that produced the Yuppie generation, Gurney's plays (especially *The Dining Room* which marked his breakthrough in the U.S.) finally found their audiences. He also formed a continuing and productive link with the Playwrights' Horizon group in New York. His work continues to expand the technical skill and that fascination with theatrical flexibility that has marked it from the outset.

Scenes from American Life is, as the title implies, a kind of montage of Americana. With a small cast including an onstage-pianist linking scenes, it uses an almost cinematic technique of dissolving and overlapping scenes to build up a series of WASP life from the 1930s to the immediate future—a christening, a debutante dance, a modern Encounter Therapy session, and so on. Its ingenious structure at points recalls Thornton Wilder, but in its concern with archetypal American rituals and family ties, not to mention the device of an offstage character (the omnipresent Snoozer), the play indicated that Gurney had his own voice.

Offstage characters dominate his one-act plays to a great extent: *The Golden Fleece* is about a suburban couple, friends of Jason and Medea, whom the audience never sees, and in the very funny *The Open Meeting* a discussion group discovers startling new relationships while awaiting the arrival of a vanished founder member. Much of their edge derives from characters who never appear; as in Greek drama, the Gods remain offstage but people are influenced by them (or, as Gurney has said "people find their gods in other people"), and Gurney often uses or adapts classical motifs. *The Love Course* and *The Old One-Two* are both sharp satires on liberal-academic attitudes, but *The Old One-Two* develops a strain of Plautine farce as a hip young college Dean discovers an unexpected relationship with his adversary, an old-fashioned professor.

Children, first produced in London during the fallow years at home for Gurney, was "suggested by" John Cheever's 1940s story "Goodbye, My Brother"; the story, like the play, takes place in a New England summer home and has a violent confrontation between two brothers, a crucial offstage event in the play. In structure the play is much tighter than *Scenes from American Life*, covering one Saturday on a July 4th weekend in the lives of a well-to-do WASP family vacationing at their Massachusetts summer home. It is a deceptively simple study of the tensions in the family caused by the eldest son, Pokey, who rules his family as an offstage presence (only one of the offstage "Gods" in the piece—the dead father is a kind of God to all the characters). In a long final speech the Mother reverses her decision to re-marry and talks to Pokey (finally visible as a shadow on the terrace on which the play passes) casting him out to preserve the family. The scene is a fitting summation to the play which subtly exposes (not least in its aptly sparse dialogue, devoid of metaphor) a culture in erosion.

Who Killed Richard Cory?, an exploration around a WASP lawyer who in middle age finds "liberation," is a more confident handling of the techniques of *Scenes from American Life*, confirming Gurney's special ability to suggest the unease under the surface of average American life. Even more confident was *The Dining Room*, a long-running New York success later produced widely in regional theatres and abroad, a sign that Gurney's world was less recondite than it had seemed when he began his career. The dining room in which the play is set represents many such rooms in different places and times from the Depression to the present; the play is both a dissection of and an elegy to a civilisation in flux, a world centred round rituals and family occasions. Using a small cast to represent a large canvas of characters—children, patriarchs, servants, and adulterous adults alike—its stagecraft is breathtakingly assured. It can move from sharply observed social comedy as a Thanksgiving lunch collapses into disarray when the grandmother slides into happy senility to a poignant late scene in which an upright dying father instructs his son in the arrangements for his funeral.

Gurney continues to be encouragingly prolific. *What I Did Last Summer* is a touching and often very funny play centred round an adolescent boy spending a wartime summer with his mother and family on the Canadian borders, befriending a dynamic eccentric woman while the family's father—another of Gurney's potent offstage presences—is away in the Pacific. Less successful was *The Golden Age*, an updated version of "The Aspern Papers," faintly reminiscent of the kind of star-vehicle play of Gurney's childhood. Despite an intriguing central situation—Henry James's Juliana transformed into Isobel Hastings Hoyt, fabled New York legend, possibly the original of Daisy in *The Great Gatsby* and possessor of Fitzgerald manuscripts—the play never quite worked either in London or New York (despite Constance Cummings and Irene Worth, respectively), mainly because of Gurney's inability to create a satisfactory character for his variation on James's investigative scholar. But he was quickly back to form with both *Another Antigone*, a full-length return to the culture-clash world of his academic background one-act plays, and *The Perfect Party*, a successful example of that rarity, an American artificial comedy of manners. Set in the house of a college professor hosting what he plans as "the perfect party" reflecting late 20th-century American life, the event to be reviewed by a critic from "a leading New York newspaper," the play spirals into Wildean comedy as the professor, to keep the beautiful critic's interest, finds himself embroiled in a plot with distinct echoes of *The Importance of Being Earnest*.

Gurney also adapted his novel *The Snow Ball* for the stage, an ambitiously large-cast play incorporating several scenes involving ballroom dancing, centred round the final revival of the tradition of the Snow Ball, a winter dance in Buffalo, New York. Through the various characters the play traces across several decades—its central pair comprise the socially different Jack and the rich girl Kitty, champion dancers whose lives go separate ways—Gurney again subtly conveys the changes in a city and a culture.

His autobiographical *The Cocktail Hour* was a social comedy in the Philip Barry tradition based on a playwright's return to his Buffalo family to tell them about his new play, based—to some resulting consternation—on that family, a visit which opens up some old resentments and secrets. And Gurney had an extraordinary runaway success with *Love Letters*—a simple two-handed piece in which two actors seated at a desk read letters over a 40-year period between a WASP couple, a buttoned-up man with political leanings and a more Bohemian, mixed-up woman. Once again, in this understated play, Gurney managed to cover a lot of ground as he traced the pair's relationship, beginning with formal notes after childhood parties and following them through marriages, her divorce and love affairs and their own brief affair to her death. The play was also very successful overseas, except in England where misconceived casting made the piece seem sentimentally trite. Gurney charted new ground in *The Old Boy*, his latest play, an unsettling piece, handling its time-shifts with considerable skill, in which a WASP politician revisits his old private school and has to face the truth, which might compromise his career ambitions, that his old roommate died of AIDS. His handling of WASP traditions and mores was as subtle as ever, but there was a new astringency in this play which Gurney reworked extensively following its first production in New York at Playwrights Horizons, a continually welcoming home for Gurney's work.

—Alan Strachan

H

HAILEY, Oliver.

Born in Pampa, Texas, 7 July 1932. Educated at the University of Texas, Austin, B.F.A. 1954; Yale University School of Drama, New Haven, Connecticut (Phyllis S. Anderson fellow, 1960, 1961), M.F.A. 1962. Served in the U.S. Air Force, 1954–57; captain in the reserves. Married Elizabeth Ann Forsythe in 1960; two daughters. Feature writer, Dallas *Morning News*, 1957–59; story editor, *McMillan and Wife* television series, 1972–74; creative consultant, *Mary Hartman, Mary Hartman* television series, 1976–77; co-producer, *Another Day* television series. Recipient: Vernon Rice award, 1963; Writers Guild award, for television writing, 1982. Agent: Shirley Bernstein, Paramuse Artists Associates, 1414 Avenue of the Americas, New York, New York 10019. Address: 11747 Canton Place, Studio City, California 91604, U.S.A.

Publications

PLAYS

Hey You, Light Man! (produced 1962). In *The Yale School of Drama Presents*, edited by John Gassner, 1964.
Child's Play: A Comedy for Orphans (produced 1962).
Home by Hollywood (produced 1964).
Animal (produced 1965). In *Picture, Animal, Crisscross*, 1970.
Picture (produced 1965). In *Picture, Animal, Crisscross*, 1970.
First One Asleep, Whistle (produced 1966). 1967.
Who's Happy Now? (produced 1967). 1969.
Crisscross (produced 1969). In *Picture, Animal, Crisscross*, 1970.
Picture, Animal, Crisscross: Three Short Plays. 1970.
Orphan (produced 1970).
Continental Divide (produced 1970). 1973.
Father's Day (produced 1970). 1971; revised version (produced 1979), 1981.
For the Use of the Hall (produced 1974). 1975.
And Where She Stops Nobody Knows (produced 1976).
Red Rover, Red Rover (produced 1977). 1979.
And Furthermore (produced 1977).
Triptych (produced 1978).
I Can't Find It Anywhere, in *Holidays* (produced 1979).
I Won't Dance (produced 1980). 1982.
And Baby Makes Two (produced 1981).

About Time (produced 1982). In *A.M./P.M.*, 1983.
24 Hours. In *A.M./P.M.*, 1983.
Round Trip (produced 1984).
The Father, adaptation of a play by Strindberg (produced 1984). 1984.
Kith and Kin (produced 1986). 1988.

SCREENPLAY: *Just You and Me, Kid*, with Leonard Stern, 1979.

TELEVISION PLAYS: *McMillan and Wife* series (9 episodes), 1971–74; *Sidney Shorr: A Girl's Best Friend*, 1981; *Isabel's Choice*, 1981.

CRITICAL STUDY: *Showcase One* by John Lahr, 1969.

Oliver Hailey comments:

(1973) My plays are primarily the attempt to take a serious theme and deal with it comedically. Though the idea for a particular play often begins as something quite serious, I try not to start writing until I have found a comic point of view for the material.

In the case of my play that is most autobiographical, *Who's Happy Now?*, it took ten years to find that comic attitude. There had been nothing particularly funny about my childhood—and yet I felt that to tell the story without a comic perspective was to put upon the stage a story too similar to many that had been seen before. With the comic perspective came the opportunity for a much fresher approach to the material—and also, strangely, it allowed me to deal with the subject on a much more serious level than I would have risked otherwise.

Because, finally, my plays are an attempt to entertain—and when they cease to entertain—no matter how "important" what I am trying to say—they fail as plays.

Despite considerable early promise Oliver Hailey has yet to achieve either critical or commercial success in the theatre. While some of his plays have been well received in university and regional playhouses, the full-length works presented in New York City all had brief runs.

Hey You, Light Man!, written and first produced at Yale University, contrasts the reality-stained world of banal domesticity with the more glamorous role-playing offered by the stage. Hailey's hero, an unhappily married actor named Ashley Knight, flees from his dreadful family to live on a stage set. There he meets a lonely young widow who has fallen asleep during a performance and is locked in the theatre. Lula Roca's husband, a stagehand, was accidentally killed by some falling equipment and her three children were all lost at a national park. One fell into a waterfall at the same time that another fell off a mountain. A third was taken by a bear. Ashley and Lula, an unlikely pair, change the direction of each other's life. Lula's experience with the illusory world of the stage permits her to develop her imaginative powers so as to face the future with new hope. Ashley, on the other hand, for whom reality could only be dreary, sees in Lula new possibilities in life off the stage and is able to make a final escape from his domestic prison. Much of the play's

humor and charm stems from Lula's endearing innocence, but Hailey's somewhat redundant elaboration of his illusion vs. reality theme weakens the play.
A number of oddball characters appear, but the playwright's straining for an
eccentric originality is apparent. At times, however, his dialogue achieves the
intended poetic effect, and his tender concern for his odd couple results in
some touching moments.

First One Asleep, Whistle, which had only one performance on Broadway,
reflects some of the same concerns as *Hey You, Light Man!* but lacks its offbeat
charm. The milieu is again theatrical, the heroine an actress in television
commercials. She has a daughter by a man not her husband and during the
course of the play has an affair with a married man. This time her lover is an
emotionally immature actor who is separated from his wife. As in *Light Man*
the lovers eventually part, the actor returning to his wife, unaware that his
mistress is pregnant. Elaine, the actress, has somehow been strengthened by
this latest affair and remains confident that she will survive without a man. The
ill-fated romance is complicated by the presence of Elaine's seven-year-old
daughter whose innocent responses to her mother's unconventional life are the
principal sources of the play's occasional humor. While Hailey avoids a
sentimental "happy" ending, his characters are never very interesting and the
play remains at the level of semi-sophisticated soap opera.

Who's Happy Now? also deals with domestic difficulties, but the setting is
far removed from the urbane New York scene. The play takes place in Texas
during the years 1941–55 and focuses on the confused reactions of a young
man to the bizarre relationship between his parents. His father, a strong-willed
and crude butcher, has managed to keep both his wife and mistress happy,
despite the efforts of his son to alter the situation. The mistress, a waitress
named Faye Precious, has lost her husband as a result of a freak accident and
respects her butcher/lover (aptly named Horse) despite his continuing affection
for his wife. The hero is an aspiring songwriter, his ambition inspiring disgust
in Horse, and the play is a kind of comic variation of the Oedipal struggle.
Who's Happy Now? contains some diverting musical numbers, but the
mixture of irony and sentiment results in a confused tone. The frame of the
play involves the hero attempting to explain to his mother, through the
medium of drama, what he really felt about his parents. Such a device seems
intended to point out the disparity between actual experience and its painful,
often inaccurate, re-creation on stage, a theme Hailey deals with elsewhere.
There are other theatrical techniques that serve to distance the audience from
potentially mawkish material, but the effects, while at times inventive, ultimately manage to make a play too diffuse in impact. Despite Hailey's genuine
ironic gifts, his play suffers from the lack of a firm larger design.

Continental Divide is closer to pure farce as it contrasts a wealthy couple
from Long Island with the down-at-heel parents of their future son-in-law. The
latter couple are visitors from their native Arkansas and the juxtaposition of
rich and poor is mined of its limited potential for original insight and humor.
Mr. John, the father of the groom, had killed his first wife and during the
course of the play manages to wound his host twice. There are other farcical
events, and whatever satiric thrusts intended by the playwright are subordi-
nated to the broad comic effects.

Hailey's best play, *Father's Day*, despite some highly favorable reviews, ran for only one performance on Broadway. It marked a return to the urbane New York scene, and the dialogue has a pungency and bite. The characters are three divorced couples briefly reunited on Father's Day. The play focuses primarily on the complex feelings of the women, as it uncovers their ambivalent desires for both independence and security. The comic tone on the surface barely conceals the pathos of their situation, and the play has a toughminded quality normally absent in a conventional sex comedy. The characters, especially the women, are sharply drawn and while *Father's Day* at times suffers from an overly eager attempt to be topical, the playwright's verbal energy is sufficient to sustain the work. Hailey demonstrates his usual compassion and refusal to impose standard moral judgments. Here he has avoided his tendency to employ striking, if redundant or irrelevant, theatrical effects. At the close of the play, there is a reference to Chekhov's *The Three Sisters* suggesting that Hailey saw a parallel to his unhappy trio in the Russian classic. While *Father's Day* lacks the depth and resonance of Chekhov's work, its tenderness and its willingness to understand the bitterness and frustration of unfulfilled lives make the parallel not altogether inapt.

In addition to his full-length plays, Hailey has written several shorter works. *Picture*, a labored one-act play or "demonstration" is similar to *Who's Happy Now?* in its concern with the problems in recreating the past through the medium of drama. *Crisscross* is a strained sketch in which Santa Claus is crucified by his father, a carpenter resentful of his son's desire for independence. *Animal* is a brief, but effective, monologue by a mother desperately struggling to impose her will on her rebellious daughter.

It is perhaps too early to make any definitive judgment on Hailey's playwriting career. What does seem evident at this point is that he has failed in his efforts at employing conventional commercial formulas to sustain an often original point of view. Despite his refusal to provide emotionally satisfying conclusions to his plays, his dramas seem too designed to please, too eager to be charming and clever. His major themes appear rooted in the dislocations of family life and while he is often adept in revealing the sadness beneath the laugh, the shifting tone of his plays results in uncertain dramatic effects. The characters are ultimately "liberated," although their freedom contains no guarantee of happiness or security. Hailey's fondness for obvious comic devices prevents the emergence of the genuine artist he at times reveals himself to be.

—Leonard Fleischer

HANLEY, William.

Born in Lorain, Ohio, 22 October 1931. Educated at Cornell University, Ithaca, New York, 1950–51; American Academy of Dramatic Arts, New York, 1954–55. Served in the U.S. Army, 1952–54. Married 1) Shelley Post in 1956 (divorced 1961); 2) Patricia Stanley in 1962 (divorced 1978); two daughters. Recipient: Vernon Rice award, 1963; Outer Circle award, 1964. Agent: Georges Borchardt Inc., 136 East 57th Street, New York, New York 10022. Address: 179 Ivy Hill Road, Ridgefield, Connecticut 06877, U.S.A.

Publications

PLAYS

Whisper into My Good Ear (produced 1962). In *Mrs. Dally Has a Lover and Other Plays*, 1963.
Mrs. Dally Has a Lover (produced 1962; revised version, produced 1988). In *Mrs. Dally Has a Lover and Other Plays*, 1963.
Conversations in the Dark (produced 1963).
Mrs. Dally Has a Lover and Other Plays. 1963.
Today Is Independence Day (produced 1963). In *Mrs. Dally Has a Lover and Other Plays*, 1963.
Slow Dance on the Killing Ground (produced 1964). 1964.
Flesh and Blood (televised 1968). 1968.
No Answer, in *Collision Course* (produced 1968). 1968.

SCREENPLAY: *The Gypsy Moths*, 1969.

RADIO PLAY: *A Country Without Rain*, 1970.

TELEVISION PLAYS: *Flesh and Blood*, 1968; *Testimony of Two Men*, with James and Jennifer Miller, from the novel by Taylor Caldwell, 1977; *Who'll Save Our Children*, from a book by Rachel Maddox, 1978; *The Family Man*, 1979; *Too Far to Go*, from stories by John Updike, 1979; *Father Figure*, 1980; *Moviola: The Scarlett O'Hara War* and *The Silent Lovers*, from the novel by Garson Kanin, 1980; *Little Gloria . . . Happy at Last*, from the book by Barbara Goldsmith, 1982; *Something about Amelia*, 1984; *Celebrity*, 1984.

NOVELS

Blue Dreams; or, The End of Romance and the Continued Pursuit of Happiness. 1971.
Mixed Feelings. 1972.
Leaving Mt. Venus. 1977.

With a trio of one-act plays and one full-length drama William Hanley achieved a reputation in American drama which seems to have satisfied him. During a three-year period he made his appearance, created a play—*Slow Dance on the Killing Ground*—which not only reflected relevant contemporary issues but provided three acting vehicles, and disappeared from the New York theatre scene.

In spite of some serious dramaturgical weaknesses in his work Hanley was one of the few American playwrights who infused a certain amount of vitality into American drama of the early 1960s. His one-act plays are somewhat unstructured, talky, two-character plays. They are essentially conversations, but they involve perceptive thought, poetic tenderness, and the problems and feelings of generally believable people. Hanley's major concern is communication, that sometimes impossible connection between two people. Language, therefore, is important to him and his plays occasionally show a too luxuriant use of it, just as these same plays become overly concerned with discussion. Understandably, then, his sense of humanity, which is allied to his feelings for communication, frequently erupts in a distasteful sentimentality. He believes in the optimism which such sentiment suggests, however; and although his characters would seem to stumble around in an unhappy world, they do see something better. It is this vague idea of something better which he once explained as the major thought he wished his audiences for *Slow Dance on the Killing Ground* would take with them. It was a shrewd comment, however, for throughout man's history such points of view have not only been acceptable but ardently desired, especially in the theatre.

Whisper into My Good Ear presented the conversation of two old men who are contemplating suicide but change their minds. One can find a good ear for his problems: friends have value. Hanley's most popular one-act play, *Mrs. Dally Has a Lover*, is a conversation between a middle-aged Mrs. Dally and her 18-year-old lover. Before they part as the curtain falls and their affair ends the difficulty of conversation is dramatized as they are drawn in and out of their respective psychological shells. The sympathy created in this play for Mrs. Dally is further explored in *Today Is Independence Day* where she talks with her husband Sam who almost leaves her but decides to stay. Mrs. Dally also makes decisions about her own attitudes, and, although the ending of the play is sad and essentially unhappy, it is an affirmation of living.

The same comment can be made for *Slow Dance on the Killing Ground*, his only full-length Broadway success. (*Conversations in the Dark*, a discussion of the problems of husband-wife infidelity, closed in Philadelphia.) Act 1 of *Slow Dance* introduces us to three characters. None of the three—a young black genius, a middle-class white girl, a Jew who has denied his heritage and his family—can escape the violence of the world, that killing ground. In Act 2 each is unmasked, and in Act 3 a mock trial shows each one guilty. Although the play suggests that nothing can be done, there is a cohesiveness among the characters, a joint decision toward commitment and responsibility on this "killing ground," which tends to remove the play from sentimental and simply clever melodrama. Instead Hanley's insight into his characters and his obvious theme of contemporary significance have challenged critics to see *Slow Dance* as a quite substantial theatre piece.

—Walter J. Meserve

HANSBERRY, Lorraine (Vivian).

Born in Chicago, Illinois, 19 May 1930. Educated at the Art Institute, Chicago; University of Wisconsin, Madison, 1948–50. Married Robert Nemiroff in 1953 (divorced 1964). Journalist, 1950–51, and associate editor after 1952, *Freedom*, New York. Recipient: New York Drama Critics Circle award, 1959. *Died 12 January 1965.*

Publications

PLAYS

A Raisin in the Sun (produced 1959). 1959.
The Sign in Sidney Brustein's Window (produced 1964). 1965.
To Be Young, Gifted, and Black: A Portrait of Hansberry in Her Own Words,
    adapted by Robert Nemiroff (produced 1969). 1971.

Les Blancs, edited by Robert Nemiroff (produced 1970). In *Les Blancs: The Collected Last Plays,* 1972.
The Drinking Gourd. In *Les Blancs: The Collected Last Plays,* 1972.
What Use Are Flowers? In *Les Blancs: The Collected Last Plays,* 1972.
Les Blancs: The Collected Last Plays (includes *Les Blancs; The Drinking Gourd; What Use Are Flowers?*), edited by Robert Nemiroff. 1972.

SCREENPLAY: *A Raisin in the Sun,* 1961.

OTHER

The Movement: Documentary of a Struggle for Equality. 1964; as *A Matter of Colour,* 1965.
To Be Young, Gifted, and Black: A Portrait of Hansberry in Her Own Words, edited by Robert Nemiroff. 1969.

CRITICAL STUDIES: *Lorraine Hansberry* by Anne Cheney, 1984; "Diverse Angles of Vision: Two Black Women Playwrights"by Margaret B. Wilkerson in *Theatre Annual,* 40, 1985.

In her short life, Lorraine Hansberry completed two plays and left three others uncompleted; a sixth theatre piece was assembled by others out of excerpts from her dramatic and nondramatic writing. But her reputation must rest on her first produced play, *A Raisin in the Sun,* the first play by a black woman to be staged on Broadway, and one of the very few plays by black authors to be mainstream successes before the 1960s.

A Raisin in the Sun is the story of the Younger family: matriarch Lena, her adult son and daughter, Walter Lee and Beneatha, and Walter Lee's wife Ruth and son Travis, all living in a Chicago slum apartment. The father's death has left the family with $10,000 in insurance money, and much of the first act is devoted to a debate on what to do with the windfall, Walter Lee wanting to invest it in a liquor store and Lena holding out for buying a house in a better part of town. As the head of the family, Lena wins, and uses some of the money as a down payment on a house in a white neighborhood, only to be visited by a representative of the neighbors offering to buy back the house, to prevent the black family from moving in. He is sent away, but called back when Walter Lee impulsively loses the rest of the money in a swindle. In the play's climax, Walter Lee finds the strength to send the man away again, and the family prepares for the move.

There are two plot lines to *A Raisin in the Sun.* The more obvious one concerns the family's attempt to raise itself, and its encounter with one more example of racial prejudice. Curiously, while that plot is built on the fact that the Youngers are black, it does not really *depend* on it. It would take very little rewriting to make the play one about Jews, the Irish, Italians, or any working-class group unwelcome in a restricted neighborhood; and probably much of the play's power and success comes from white audiences' recognition of an experience not very foreign to their own.

The second, more subtle, story line of the play is built on the conflicts within the family, particularly between Lena and Walter Lee, which expose one of the tragic paradoxes of black family life in America: generations of prejudice have limited the potential and weakened the will of black men, forcing the women (who, for various reasons, have not been quite as broken in spirit) to be strong; yet the women know that every step they take to help their men is an addition to their emasculation. The argument between Walter Lee and his mother over how to spend the insurance money is not just monetary; it is a contest for the role as head of the family. By all objective considerations Lena's plan is far superior; but her insisting on it is also a slap in the face for her son, and she knows it. When Walter Lee loses his share, he is clearly in the wrong, and yet too much of his manhood is at stake to allow the women to condemn him too harshly.

The play dramatizes the delicate balance and subtle adjustments the women must constantly make in the very real and vital struggle to protect their men from further indignities. Having won the first-act battle, Lena makes a point of giving Walter Lee the rest of the money, to make use of (implicitly, to make foolish use of) as he sees fit, because the act of respect in giving him this authority is worth more than the money. When Walter Lee calls the white man back to sell him the house, the women see that this is not just a financial setback, but a final capitulation to failure, and unite to save his soul. And when Walter Lee finds in himself the strength to reject the racists a second time, and the white man turns to Lena for help, she can reply, "My son said we was going to move and there ain't nothing left for me to say", as a joyous abdication of power. It is in these, and similar, quiet insights into the dynamics of family life, more than in the conflict with racism, that *A Raisin in the Sun* offers its greatest insights into the American black experience.

The Sign in Sidney Brustein's Window, Hansberry's only other completed play, was a commercial and critical failure, though it did attract some passionate supporters. It is a sympathetic study of the plight of the white liberal. The title character, a right-thinking but apolitical man, is slowly drawn into action, working to support a reform candidate in a city election; the titular sign is a banner declaring his political commitment. But dedication, and even victory, does not change the world, and Sidney discovers that people who believe the right things can be personally corrupt or weak in ways that invalidate their theoretical commitment: the candidate sells out, a black friend proves to be prejudiced, a homosexual friend is sexually manipulative. Driven to the point of despair, Sidney regains his determination to fight for the good in spite of all the obstacles and defections along the way.

The play is excessively talky, and secondary characters are either underwritten (such as the politician) or overwritten (as with Sidney's conservative sister-in-law, too complexly developed for the minor role she plays). A character on whom the plot turns does not even appear until Act III, while the important subplot of Sidney's marital problems is never integrated with the other action or themes. Still, it is a failure of accomplishment rather than of conception, and one can see the core of a play that might have been stronger had Hansberry (who was terminally ill at the time of production) been able to work on it more.

—Gerald M. Berkowitz

See the essay on *A Raisin in the Sun.*

HAUPTMAN, William (Thornton).

Born in Wichita Falls, Texas, 26 November 1942. Educated at Wichita Falls
Senior High School, graduated 1961; University of Texas, Austin, B.F.A. in
drama 1966; Yale University School of Drama, New Haven, Connecticut,
M.F.A. in playwriting 1973. Married 1) Barbara Barbat in 1968 (divorced
1977), one daughter; 2) Marjorie Erdreich in 1985, one son. Instructor in
playwriting, Adelphi College, Garden City, New York, 1973–75, and Yale
University School of Drama, 1976; performer with Cadillac Cowboys rockabilly band, La Jolla, California, Summer 1985. Recipient: CBS grant, 1976;
National Endowment for the Arts grant, 1977; Obie award, 1977;
Guggenheim grant, 1978; Boston Theatre Critics Circle award, 1984; Tony
award, 1985; San Diego Drama Critics Circle award, 1985; Drama logue
award, 1986; Jesse Jones award, for fiction, 1986. Agent: Rick Leed, Agency
for the Performing Arts, 888 Seventh Avenue, New York, New York 10106.
Address: 240 Warren Street, Apartment E, Brooklyn, New York 11201,
U.S.A.

Publications

PLAYS

Heat (produced 1972; revised version produced 1974). 1977.
Shearwater (produced 1973). In *Performance*, vol. 1, no. 5, March–April
    1973.
Domino Courts (produced 1975). With *Comanche Cafe*, 1977.
Comanche Cafe (produced 1976). With *Domino Courts*, 1977.
The Durango Flash (produced 1977).
Big River, music and lyrics by Roger Miller, adaptation of the novel
    Adventures of Huckleberry Finn by Mark Twain (produced 1984). 1986.
Gillette (produced 1985; revised version produced 1986). 1985.

TELEVISION PLAY: *A House Divided* series (3 episodes), 1981.

NOVEL
The Storm Season. 1992.

SHORT STORIES
Good Rockin' Tonight. 1988.

William Hauptman comments:

I find as I get older I'm more interested in writing what I know about, and what
I really know about is working class, because that's where I'm from. . . . When
you get older you realize that there's a reason why the forms exist; they've been
created by a process that's hundreds of years long. Story and character are still
the most important things. The style comes and goes, but stories about people
remain.

There is a remarkable wholeness about William Hauptman's dramatic writing
that transcends the working-class milieu in which his plays are set. His

characteristic preoccupations surface even in *Big River*, his Tony award-winning book for the 1985 Broadway musical based upon Mark Twain's *Adventures of Huckleberry Finn*. An awareness of the outdoors, the land, and forces of nature permeates this writing and generates some striking scenic images. That visual sensibility is supplemented by his strongly imagistic use of sound: the distant dog bark that ends *Domino Courts*, the low rumble that seems to comment upon Carroll's line "Now we can have some peace and quiet, right, honey?" in *Heat*, a passing train, the howl of a coyote, droning cicadas, and specific musical selections that often mock a character's pipe dreams.

All of his plays are episodically constructed; like the early Tennessee Williams, William Hauptman might be better described as a "scenewright" than a playwright. That loose construction, however, is metaphorically appropriate for these studies of characters infected by wanderlust. The car on the road or the raft on the river offer them an aimless mobility that might bring "the answer" to drifters like Huck and Jim in *Big River*, Mickey and Bobby in *Gillette*, and Roy in *Domino Courts*, or to those who merely dream of travel, like Ronnie in *Comanche Cafe* and Joe Billy in *Heat*. Above all, Hauptman's characters seem to be in search of their own identities. Huck Finn declares in song his determination "to be nobody but himself." "Hell—let's be ourselves," Floyd pleads with Roy, whom he accuses of flaunting a "phony personality." In *Heat* Carroll says, "I've got a club. When you belong you can be anyone you want." Mickey, the fortyish drifter in *Gillette*, says "You look at that town and you see all the towns that ever were, and every person you've ever been. . . . There's somebody inside me who's bigger and better than I've ever been yet." But his young friend Bobby, a novice on the road, seeks to define himself in terms of an occupation.

Friendship between two men is the basis for all of Hauptman's full-length plays as well as for the one-act *Domino Courts*. Huck and Jim, Mickey and Bobby, Carroll and Harley, and Floyd and Roy all experience a pattern of alternating closeness and estrangement in their relationships. Each craves self-sufficiency but fears loneliness. The pattern is reiterated structurally by an alternation of scenes set in town with scenes set on the river or prairie or desert. When they are in town, the men feel trapped and have to get away from "civilization"; but out in the country, with the town's lights twinkling in the distance, they feel as if they are missing out on some action. Similarly, they are often torn between their need for freedom and their desire for the comfort of a woman's love. Mickey sums up the conflict most of them have faced: "Long time ago, I decided not to go for the house and kids. I was going for the other dream—freedom and a big score at the end of the road."

Women cause the greatest stress on the men's friendships. *Gillette* deals most directly with this problem, for both Mickey and Bobby must choose between binding themselves to the women who seem to be so right for them or remaining buddies as before. In *Domino Courts* Floyd and Roy get at each other through their women. In both of these plays and in *Heat*, the men often behave like little boys showing off for the women or for each other. They speak of "staying up all night" as if it were a special affirmation of manhood. Between women this sort of bonding is rare in Hauptman's plays; they are usually too afraid of losing their man. Occasionally that wariness will be dissolved in a spontaneous appreciation of "something in common," as in

Heat when Susan and Billie find that they have both shoplifted. They devote much effort to learning, as Ronnie says in *Domino Courts*, "how to deal with men," even as they tell each other: "Don't cry, honey, no man's worth it." It is a major breakthrough when a woman like Jody in *Gillette* learns that she need not be dependent upon a man.

Hauptman's best writing to date is probably *Gillette*, about a couple of oil rig roughnecks who dream of making "big coin" in a northeastern Wyoming boom town. Originally published in Theatre Communications Group's "Plays in Process" series in 1985, it was extensively revised by Hauptman for its 1986 production at La Jolla Playhouse. *Variety's* review sums up the appeal of this compelling portrait of blue-collar America: "It is earthy, rousing, contemporary and tough-minded—a very funny, well-written, well-staged, well-played serious comedy with a Saroyanesque strain in oddly touching moments. And like Saroyan, Hauptman's long suit is dialog and the creating of strong, highly individual, often eccentric characters."

—Felicia Hardison Londré

HAVIS, Allan.

Born in New York City, 26 September 1951. Educated at City College, New York, B.A. 1973; Hunter College, New York, M.A. 1976; Yale University, New Haven, Connecticut, M.F.A. 1980. Married Cheryl Riggins in 1982. Film instructor in children's program, Guggenheim Museum, New York, 1974–76; writer-in-residence, Case Western Reserve University, Cleveland, Ohio, 1976; theatre critic, *Our Town*, New York, 1977; playwriting instructor, Foundation of the Dramatists Guild, New York, 1985–87, Ulster County Community College, Stone Ridge, New York, 1986–88, Old Dominion University, Norfolk, Virginia, 1987, Sullivan County Community College, Loch Sheldrake, New York, 1987, and since 1988, University of California at San Diego, La Jolla. Recipient: John Golden award, 1974, 1975; Case Western Reserve University Klein award, 1976; Dramatists Guild/CBS award, 1985; Playwrights USA award, 1986; National Endowment for the Arts fellowship, 1986; Rockefeller fellowship, 1987; Guggenheim fellowship, 1987; New York State Foundation for the Arts fellowship, 1987; Albee Foundation for the Arts fellowship, 1987; Kennedy Center/American Express grant, 1987; MacDowell fellowship, 1988; McKnight fellowship, 1989; Hawthornden fellowship, 1989; University of California Faculty Summer fellowship, 1989; California Arts Council fellowship, 1991; Rockefeller residency, Bellagio Centre, Italy, 1991. Agent: Helen Merrill, 435 West 23rd Street, New York, New York 10011, U.S.A.; or Peters, Fraser, and Dunlop Group, 503/4 The Chambers, Chelsea Harbour, Lots Road, London SW10 0XF, England. Address: 531 Palomar Avenue, La Jolla, California 92037, U.S.A.

Publications
PLAYS

The Boarder and Mrs. Rifkin (produced 1974).
Oedipus Again (produced 1976).
Watchmaker (produced 1977).

Heinz (produced 1978).
Interludes (produced 1978).
Family Rites (produced 1979).
The Road from Jerusalem (produced 1984).
Holy Wars (produced 1984).
Morocco (produced 1984). In *Plays in Process*, 1985; in *Morocco, Mink Sonata, Hospitality*, 1989.
Mink Sonata (also director: produced 1986). In *Morocco, Mink Sonata, Hospitality*, 1989.
Duet for Three (produced 1986).
Mother's Aria (also director: produced 1986).
Einstein for Breakfast (produced 1986).
Haut Goût (produced 1987). In *Plays in Process*, vol.8 no.5, 1987.
Hospitality (produced 1988). In *Morocco, Mink Sonata, Hospitality*, 1989.
Morocco, Mink Sonata, Hospitality. 1989.
A Daring Bride (produced 1990).
Lilith (produced 1990). 1991.
Adoring the Madonna (produced 1992).

OTHER

Albert the Astronomer (for children). 1979.

THEATRICAL ACTIVITIES

DIRECTOR: **Plays**—some of his own plays.

"We had a passion for strange dark risks," says Claire, the modern-day demon lover in Allan Havis's *Lilith*, getting at the essence of the mysterious and disturbing work of this American playwright. Havis's plays tend toward the Kafka-esque. Their worlds are nightmares of unreason in which a well-off white American male, often Jewish, is lured by the siren song of the Other—a woman, or a man of dark skin: an Arab, a Haitian. Whether or not a formal investigation is taking place, dialogue is filled with the threat of attack, the tension of defense. The white man is victimized, betrayed. He may be goaded to murder; nonetheless his antagonist always wins.

Havis is a cryptic storyteller. Critic James Leverett wrote of one play that characters "encounter one another in circumstances that are fraught but far from clear." This is generally true, and the playwright's elegant and elliptical language resists reduction to straightforward meaning or moral. Still, the sexual and racial tensions at the heart of Havis's plays are uncomfortably familiar, and this dramatist's most important achievement may prove to be the revelation of what it feels like to be a white male, an American, in an age in which he senses his long ascendancy coming to an end.

Morocco, Havis's best and most successful play to date, was described by Mel Gussow in the New York *Times* as "an absorbing cat-and-mouse game in which one cannot always distinguish the cat from the mouse." The first act consists of 10 brief scenes representing 10 days during which Kempler, a Jewish-American architect, attempts to secure his wife's release from a Moroccan jail. Kempler's antagonist, the nameless Arab Colonel who runs the prison, is given to remarks like "Is this secrecy Jewish?" Havis knows his audience will think the worst of the Moroccan and the best of the architect and his banker wife, and therefore assume that a charge of prostitution and a diagnosis of syphilis have been trumped up—at least until they witness the tension-filled second-act conversation between husband and wife, which takes place at an expensive restaurant in Spain "some days later." Increasingly it seems possible that Mrs. Kempler, who is part Arab and part Spanish gypsy, is in fact promiscuous; it is also apparent that her husband is inclined to jealousy, paranoia, and masochism. The third act finds him back in the Colonel's office, confessing to the murder of his wife—who promptly appears to collect her husband. She takes him away only after her exchanges in Arabic with the Colonel show that Kempler is the odd man out. This play takes place—the phrase is Gussow's—in "a Morocco of the mind."

Haut Goût mines similar terrain. A rich Jewish doctor insists on taking leave from his New York suburban life to spend several months in Haiti testing a milk formula he has developed to combat infant mortality. This innocent abroad promptly finds himself entangled with the ruler of the island, who incarnates Americans' most prejudicial notions about such figures: Le Croix is an army general, a communist, a torturer, a heroin addict, a homosexual— and, as Dr. Gold discovers, a person with AIDS (though that term is not used). Gold resists Le Croix's persistent sexual advances, but is nonetheless under his spell; the doctor is less successful in standing up to Latch, the U.S. State Department official who pressures him to murder the general. (Latch, we are given to understand, arranged the deaths of seven babies in Gold's study— deaths the doctor naïvely blames himself for.) Gold gives Le Croix a lethal injection and returns home a broken man, but in the last scene the general turns up in Scarsdale with his perpetual attendant, a woman said to be able to raise the dead. They poison Dr. Gold, and Le Croix ends the play with talk of togetherness in death. Filled with the guilt of the privileged, the American has sought his own destruction.

A sinister view of United States government is central to the ironically titled *Hospitality*, in which two Immigration agents—one white, one black—work to break two detainees, one a female Colombian journalist, the other a rightwing Israeli politician. They induce diarrhea in the woman; she gives names; in the end she is released, though it is now impossibly dangerous for her to return home. The Jew is beaten, and his insulin is withheld; he dies of a stroke. Happy Logan, the agent who administered the beating, is in a neat reversal the designated victim of the subsequent investigation. His presumed buddy, the black agent Fuller, will not help him, and may have set him up. His personal as well as professional life a shambles, Logan kills himself. He is a particularly clear example of a white American destroyed through his dealings with the Other.

Mink Sonata, at least initially, attempts a lighter tone. The most absurdist of these plays, its focus is the relationship between an affluent father and his troubled daughter, Roberta. She has an alter ego, Blake, "stylish, self-confident and very attractive"; played by the same actress, Blake enables sexual fantasies to surface. Nearly every relationship in a Havis play is notable for talk about what would ordinarily be subliminal sexual tension.

There is considerable comedy, too, in the first act of *Lilith*, in which Adam and his pre-Eve wife wrangle before a Voice, that of an archangel conducting the hearing that will result in the couple's separation and the creation of

Adam's new mate. "Strindberg as directed by Mike Nichols" is Havis's description of his post-intermission depiction of present-day Claire's power to disrupt family life by seducing Arnold (the act's Adam), sexually initiating his 10-year-old son, and, at moments, casting her spell over Eppy, the wife and mother who is the act's Eve. Throughout the play Adam is inept and helpless in the face of Lilith's determination to have children; once again male power is shown to be illusory.

—M. Elizabeth Osborn

HELLMAN, Lillian (Florence).

Born in New Orleans, Louisiana, 20 June 1905 (some sources give 1906). Educated at New York University, 1924–25; Columbia University, New York, 1925. Married the writer Arthur Kober in 1925 (divorced 1932). Reader, Horace Liveright publishers, New York, 1924–25; reviewer, New York *Herald-Tribune*, 1925–28; theatrical play reader, 1927–30; reader, Metro-Goldwyn-Mayer, 1930–32; began long relationship with Dashiell Hammett in 1930; teacher at Yale University, New Haven, Connecticut, 1966, and at Harvard University, Cambridge, Massachusetts, Massachusetts Institute of Technology, Cambridge, and University of California, Berkeley. Recipient: New York Drama Critics Circle award, 1941, 1960; American Academy gold medal, 1964; Paul Robeson award, 1976; MacDowell medal, 1976. M.A.: Tufts College, Medford, Massachusetts, 1940; Litt.D: Wheaton College, Norton, Massachusetts, 1961; Rutgers University, New Brunswick, New Jersey, 1963; Brandeis University, Waltham, Massachusetts, 1965; Yale University, New Haven, Connecticut, 1974; Smith College, Northampton, Massachusetts, 1974; New York University, 1974; Franklin and Marshall College, Lancaster, Pennsylvania, 1975; Columbia University, 1976. Vice-president, National Institute of Arts and Letters, 1962; Member, American Academy of Arts and Sciences, 1960, and American Academy, 1963. *Died 30 June 1984.*

Publications

PLAYS

The Children's Hour (produced 1934). 1934.
Days to Come (produced 1936). 1936.
The Little Foxes (produced 1939). 1939.
Watch on the Rhine (produced 1941). 1941.
Four Plays (includes *The Children's Hour; Days to Come; The Little Foxes; Watch on the Rhine*). 1942.
The North Star: A Motion Picture about Some Russian People. 1943.
The Searching Wind (produced 1944). 1944.
Watch on the Rhine, with Dashiell Hammett. In *Best Film Plays of 1943–44,* edited by John Gassner and Dudley Nichols, 1945.
Another Part of the Forest (also director: produced 1946). 1947.
Montserrat, from a play by Emmanuel Roblès (also director: produced 1949). 1950.
Regina, music by Marc Blitzstein (produced 1949).

The Autumn Garden (produced 1951). 1951.

The Lark, from a play by Jean Anouilh (produced 1955). 1956.

Candide, music by Leonard Bernstein, lyrics by Richard Wilbur, John LaTouche, and Dorothy Parker, from the novel by Voltaire (produced 1956). 1957.

Toys in the Attic (produced 1960). 1960.

Six Plays. 1960.

My Mother, My Father and Me, from the novel *How Much?* by Burt Blechman (produced 1963). 1963.

The Collected Plays (includes *The Children's Hour; Days to Come; The Little Foxes; Watch on the Rhine; The Searching Wind; Another Part of the Forest; Montserrat; The Autumn Garden; The Lark; Candide; Toys in the Attic; My Mother, My Father and Me*). 1972.

SCREENPLAYS: *The Dark Angel,* with Mordaunt Shairp, 1935; *These Three,* 1936; *Dead End,* 1937; *The Little Foxes,* with others, 1941; *Watch on the Rhine,* with Dashiell Hammett, 1943; *The North Star,* 1943 ; *The Searching Wind,* 1946; *The Children's Hour (The Loudest Whisper),* with John Michael Hayes, 1961; *The Chase,* 1966.

OTHER

Three. 1979; contents separately published as:
  An Unfinished Woman: A Memoir. 1969.
  Pentimento: A Book of Portraits. 1973.
  Scoundrel Time. 1976.
Maybe: A Story. 1980.
Eating Together: Recollections and Recipes, with Peter Feibleman. 1984.
Conversations with Hellman (interviews), edited by Jackson R. Bryer. 1986.

Editor, *Selected Letters,* by Chekhov, translated by Sidonie K. Lederer. 1955.

Editor, *The Big Knockover: Selected Stories and Short Novels,* by Dashiell Hammett. 1966; as *The Hammett Story Omnibus,* 1966; as *The Big Knockover* and *The Continental Op* (2 vols.), 1967.

BIBLIOGRAPHY: *Lillian Hellman: An Annotated Bibliography* by Steven H. Bills, 1979; *Lillian Hellman: A Bibliography 1926–1978* by Mary M. Riordan, 1980.

CRITICAL STUDIES: *Lillian Hellman* by Jacob H. Adler, 1969; *Lillian Hellman: Playwright* by Richard Moody, 1972; *The Dramatic Works of Lillian Hellman* by Lorena Ross Holmin, 1973; *Lillian Hellman* by Doris V. Falk, 1978; *Lillian Hellman* by Katherine Lederer, 1979; *Lillian Hellman: Plays, Films, Memoirs: A Reference Guide* by Mark W. Estrin, 1980; *Stage Left: The Development of the American Social Drama in the Thirties* by R.C. Reynolds, 1986; *Lillian Hellman: The Image, the Woman* by William Wright, 1986; *Lilly: Reminiscences of Lillian Hellman* by Peter Feibleman, 1988; *Lillian Hellman: Her Legend and Her Legacy* by Carl Rollyson, 1988.

Theatrical activities
Director: Plays—*Another Part of the Forest*, 1946; *Montserrat*, 1949.
Narrator: *Marc Blitzstein Memorial Concert*, 1964.

Lillian Hellman is one of America's major dramatists. She entered a male-dominated field when she was nearly thirty and wrote some dozen plays in three decades. Her early model was Ibsen, and she shared his love of tightly knit plots and emphasis on sociological and psychological forces. Her best plays, like Ibsen's, are those in which a powerful character cuts loose and transcends the limitations of the play's rigid symmetry and plot contrivance. Along with Clifford Odets, the other significant writing talent of the 1930s, Hellman showed a keen interest in Marxist theory and explored the relationship between the nuclear family and capitalism. Hellman, more than Odets, held ambiguous views of man and society. Her antagonists are not wholly the products of environment but seem at times innately malicious. The quest for power fascinated the author and her characters became famous for their ruthlessness and cunning. Most of her plays verge on melodrama but are admired for their energetic protagonists and swift-moving plots.

In her first play, *The Children's Hour*, Hellman showed how the capricious wielding of power could ruin innocent people. Two young women at a girl's school are falsely accused of having a lesbian relationship by a disturbed child. They are brought to trial by outraged parents and eventually lose their case—and their school. One of the teachers commits suicide and, too late, the child's treachery is discovered. The homosexual motif, though discreetly handled, accounted for the play's notoriety in 1934; but the abuse of power by an arrogant elite is its enduring theme.

Usurping power is also the motivating force in Hellman's best-known play, *The Little Foxes*, at once a political statement and a complex study of family dynamics. The rapacious Hubbard family represents a new brand of Southern capitalist who subordinates all traditions and human values to the goal of acquiring wealth and property. The strength of the play lies in Hellman's implicit comparison of the Hubbard siblings' rivalries with the competitiveness of Americans in the free enterprise system. The role of Regina Hubbard, who withholds her dying husband's heart medicine and who outwits her equally greedy brothers in a major business coup, has become a favorite vehicle for American actresses.

At the beginning of World War II Hellman wrote *Watch on the Rhine* and *The Searching Wind*, both of which dealt with the fascist menace. The former play contains some witty repartee and suspenseful moments; but its solutions to the international crisis are simplistic, and it is better described as an adventure story than a thesis play.

When the War ended, Hellman returned to the easy-to-hate Hubbard family in *Another Part of the Forest*. Unfortunately the exaggerated spitefulness and hysteria of the characters and the unrelieved high-tension atmosphere of this play become nearly ludicrous. The concept of personal manipulation had become an obsession with the author, and a correlation seemed to have developed between her studies of social and societal exploitation and her own excessive control over plot characterization and stage effects. Perhaps the playwright realized this, because in her last plays she turned from Ibsen to Chekhov for inspiration. Both *The Autumn Garden* and *Toys in the Attic* recall the mood and ambiguous moral judgments of Chekhov. Neither of these plays has a truly pernicious villain, and most of the characters seem to be suffering from a Chekhovian paralysis of will. The atmosphere is deterministic and the plots are truer to life. What has changed is that all bids for personal power prove self-defeating—the predatory are caught in traps of their own making and hardly struggle before acknowledging defeat. Nevertheless these plays also include sharp, amusing verbal exchanges and the famous blackmail scenes associated with Hellman. Blackmail, present in all of her plays, is Hellman's favorite metaphor for personal manipulation; but in the later works she uses blackmail and other devices with greater subtlety, and presents a somewhat blurred but more convincing vision of stumbling modern man and his society.

Hellman's dramatic mode, based on her adherence to continental models, was bound to an earlier era. Most of her experiments with screenwriting proved frustrating. Her best later works were autobiographical sketches: in *An Unfinished Woman*, *Pentimento*, and *Scoundrel Time* she revealed her penetrating intelligence but tacitly acknowledged that her insights and talents were better suited to the historical memoir.

—Kimball King

See the essay on *The Children's Hour*.

HENLEY, Beth (Elizabeth Becker Henley).

Born in Jackson, Mississippi, 8 May 1952. Educated at Southern Methodist University, Dallas, B.F.A. 1974; University of Illinois, Urbana, 1975–76. Actress, Theatre Three, Dallas, 1972–73, with Southern Methodist University Directors Colloquium, 1973, and with the Great American People Show, New Salem, 1976; teacher, Dallas Minority Repertory Theatre, 1974–75. Recipient: Pulitzer prize, 1981; New York Drama Critics Circle award, 1981; Oppenheimer award, 1981. Lives in Los Angeles. Agent: Gilbert Parker, William Morris Agency, 1350 Avenue of the Americas, New York, New York 10019, U.S.A.

Publications

PLAYS

Am I Blue? (produced 1973; revised version produced 1981). 1982.
Crimes of the Heart (produced 1979). 1982.
The Miss Firecracker Contest (produced 1980). 1985.
The Wake of Jamey Foster (produced 1982). 1983.
The Debutante Ball (produced 1985). 1991.
The Lucky Spot (produced 1987). 1987.
Abundance (produced 1989). 1991.
Control Freaks (also director: produced 1992).

SCREENPLAYS: *The Moon Watcher*, 1983; *True Stories*, with Stephen Tobolowsky, 1986; *Crimes of the Heart*, 1987; *Nobody's Fool*, 1987; *Miss Firecracker*, 1990.

Herself a former actor, Beth Henley writes substantial roles for other women. Her eccentric southerners, sharply sketched and spouting dialogue penned in Mississippi dialect, comprise a huge collection of oddballs and misfits with whom we sympathize.

As Henley's exotics pursue their unfulfilled dreams, they inhabit a Southern, gothic, whimsical world likely to make us laugh and wince in about equal measure. When she appears primed to veer into pathos, Henley generally undercuts sentimentality with eccentric characters or grotesque action. Although generally optimistic in response to adversity, even as she makes us care about her independent outsiders and generates suspense about what will happen to them, the playwright employs human idiosyncrasy or the macabre to humorous effect.

Death claims more characters than we might expect in comedy: Aunt Ronelle and Turnip (*The Miss Firecracker Contest*), Jamey and the arson victims (*The Wake of Jamey Foster*), Violet's brother, dead by his own hand, and the murdered man (*The Debutante Ball*), Sue Jack's mother and Cassidy's parents (*The Lucky Spot*), and Bess's Indian chief (*Abundance*). Henley's most famous play, *Crimes of the Heart*, kills off Billy Boy, Old Granddaddy, and the sisters' mother, as well as her cat. Meg exhibits a death wish, and Babe attempts suicide hours after shooting her abusive husband Zachery. Several sets of offstage parents have died leaving orphans. Even when not lethal, violence—physical as well as psychological—occurs in nearly every Henley play.

The gentlest of these, her early *Am I Blue?*, dramatizes an encounter between 16-year-old hippie, Ashbe, and college freshman John Polk, her preppy, awkward, overweight new friend. When they meet in New Orleans in 1968, Ashbe encourages John to avoid going along mindlessly with his frat brothers' values. Yet hope for their future must be tempered by the pressures John will experience to conform and by Ashbe's parental neglect.

For *The Lucky Spot* Henley goes further back, to Christmas Eve 1934, and to the Depression in Pigeon, a Louisiana bayou village. Reed Hooker aims to cheer up the local rural folk and turn a profit by converting the ramshackle house he won in a poker game into a taxi-dance hall, despite its location far from anyone likely to have the price of a dance. He's joined in this enterprise by untidy, 15-year-old Cassidy Smith, whom he also won in that card game, and whom he has impregnated. Reed unleashes violence against men and women alike, but then so does his wife, released from prison for Christmas through Cassidy's contrivance, because she hopes Sue Jack and Reed will divorce; of course, that's not what happens. The happy ending (as close to sentimentality as Henley comes) proves simultaneously predictable and implausible. Yet the play does amuse intermittently, while it suggests that in this lucky spot dreams sometimes come true, indeed that happiness need not elude us. These are losers, but—without any of O'Neill's irony in *The Iceman Cometh*—hopeful losers, still, appropriately, looking at life through rose-colored glasses.

In *The Wake of Jamey Foster*, a more bitter play, the disillusioned dreamer has already died from a kick in the head by a cow, leaving to his survivors their own disappointed dreams, rage, humiliation, depression, and, ironically, hope. When we meet the newly widowed Marshael Foster in her dilapidated, rural home in Mississippi, she is gnawing on a chocolate Easter rabbit and reading a ladies' magazine. Her wild sister Collard (nicknamed Collard Greens) arrives wearing a muddy red evening gown and cowboy boots and without a change of clothes for the funeral. Collard's dreams of becoming a lawyer have been dashed by the I.Q. test she took, aged 12, so she has consoled herself (or tried to destroy herself) by caressing "death and danger with open legs". Marshael's backward brother, Leon, jerks out turkey innards for a living, while his 17-year-old girlfriend, Pixrose, aims to become a dog bather, and Marshael's friend Brocker unsuccessfully tried to raise hogs. Henley conveys such salient details about her hilarious human menagerie's dreams in exposition composed of stunning *non sequiturs*.

Like other Henley characters, these wage war with their relatives: Jamey's mean brother, Wayne, offends his priggish wife, Kathy, so badly that she locks herself in the bathroom. And Jamey had left Marshael for a young baker, who sends a pie to the wake, giving Marshael a chance to hurl it to the floor from the upstairs landing. Naturally, Pixrose and Marshael and her siblings are orphans, while Jamey's parents project off-stage malevolence. Marshael neglects her own bereaved children. Pixrose recounts the funniest, and yet most pathetic familial discord: her pyromaniac mother and father had committed suicide separately while nearly killing her and her brother as well.

The somewhat more lighthearted *The Miss Firecracker Contest* also mixes pain with our pleasure. Again, Mississippi relatives have failed to nurture each other. Mean Aunt Ronelle, who grew furry after a monkey's pituitary gland was substituted for hers, raised orphaned Carnelle along with her own children —beautiful but egocentric Elain and difficult Delmount—but she instilled little self-esteem in her niece. Siding with those who fail to achieve perfection, popularity, and success, Henley directs our compassion towards insecure Carnelle, while keeping us laughing at her hopeless hope of winning the beauty contest. While Cousin Elain, a former winner who dislikes her husband and children, prepares her speech on "My Life as a Beauty", Carnelle practises baton-twirling and tap-dancing, setting herself up for humiliation. Born into a culture with little tolerance of difference and which prefers women to boast beauty rather than brains, spunky Carnelle wins respect not only for her tenacity in pursuing her goal, but for her indomitable spirit after she has endured one indignity too many. "I'll always remember you", comments a friend, "as the one who could take it on the chin".

Pulitzer prize-winning *Crimes of the Heart*, another Mississippi comedy, dramatizes all the themes which Henley considers, a few at a time, in other plays: hope, loneliness, respect, control, domestic violence, and death. The three sisters (echoes of Chekhov probably intended) as well as their four men suffer from their own crimes of the heart: two pairs—Lenny and Charlie, Meg and Doc—have languished and anguished because the women lacked the courage to remain in the relationships, while Babe has shot husband Zachery and got young Willie Jay in trouble. Yet the women also have been damaged by others' crimes of the heart, for Zachery abused Babe, and the Magrath sisters were orphaned by their mother's suicide. Although initially having little self-esteem and courage, however, they take control of their lives by making affirmative choices. Even Lenny, in one of several expertly written farcical scenes, chases a tormenting cousin out of the house with a broom.

Two less well-known, but also bizarrely amusing plays, *The Debutante Ball* and *Abundance*, likewise portray gutsy women coping with a world in which men abuse their women. The former, set in the present in Hattiesburg, ostensibly concerns the preliminaries to a pregnant, guilt-ridden, suicidal teenager's ignominious debut, overseen by a mother intent upon re-establishing her reputation after she was found innocent of murdering her daughter's father. Both lighter and darker than such a synopsis suggests, the play unfolds the cause of their troubles in some of Henley's funniest scenes. By the play's end, the debutante appears bound for happiness, as does her neglected half-sister, who heads into the sunset with her step-father's deaf-mute niece.

The more pessimistic *Abundance* concerns two men and their two mismatched mail-order brides, living during the last quarter of the 19th-century in the Wyoming Territory, where they have less to fear from the Wild West than they do from each other. Romantic Bess and pragmatic Macon all but trade places. After Bess is abducted by Indians, they betray their own values and each other's trust, and Bess fulfills Macon's dream. Their power struggles and dashed hopes—Bess's for domestic bliss and Macon's for adventures she can turn into a novel—constitute familiar Henley themes. But the play especially resembles *The Debutante Ball*; both dramatize the love/hatred within families that erupts in violence. Their effective poignancy combined with humor in dramatizing abused women's shaky self-esteem contributes significantly to late 20th-century drama.

—Tish Dace

HERLIHY, James Leo.

Born in Detroit, Michigan, 27 February 1927. Educated at Black Mountain College, North Carolina, 1947–48; Pasadena Playhouse, California, 1948–50; Yale University School of Drama, New Haven, Connecticut (RCA Fellow), 1956–57. Served in the U.S. Naval Reserve, 1945–46; petty officer. Taught playwriting at City College, New York 1967–68; distinguished visiting professor, University of Arkansas, Fayetteville, 1983. *Died 20 October 1993.*

Publications

PLAYS

Streetlight Sonata (produced 1950).

Moon in Capricorn (produced 1953).

Blue Denim, with William Noble (produced 1958). 1958.

Crazy October, adaptation of his story "The Sleep of Baby Filbertson" (also director: produced 1958).

Terrible Jim Fitch (produced 1965).

Stop, You're Killing Me (includes *Terrible Jim Fitch*; *Bad Bad Jo-Jo*; *Laughs, Etc.*) (produced 1968; *Bad Bad Jo-Jo* produced 1970; *Laughs, Etc.* produced 1973). 1970.

NOVELS
All Fall Down. 1960.
Midnight Cowboy. 1965.
The Season of the Witch. 1971.

SHORT STORIES
The Sleep of Baby Filbertson and Other Stories. 1959.
A Story That Ends with a Scream and Eight Others. 1967.

OTHER
The Sleep of Reason, photographs by Lyle Bongé. 1974.

MANUSCRIPT COLLECTION: Boston University.

THEATRICAL ACTIVITIES
DIRECTOR: **Play**—*Crazy October*, 1958.
ACTOR: **Plays**—roles at the Pasadena Playhouse, California; in *The Zoo Story* by Edward Albee, 1961; title role in *Terrible Jim Fitch*, 1965. **Films**—*In the French Style*, 1963; *Four Friends (Georgia's Friends)*, 1981.

> So I'll get on a bus to Hell.
> Which will probably be
> another San Pedro—or Times Square or Tia Juana or
> Dallas—and I'll make out all right. I can make out in places
> like Hell. I've had practice.
> —*Terrible Jim Fitch*

Embattled innocence and vulnerable corruption, often shading into each other, define the limits of James Leo Herlihy's drama. The innocent, struggling in a hostile society they inadvertently threaten, sometimes perish, sometimes triumph, and occasionally become embodiments of the corruption they once challenged. In Herlihy's unpublished fantasy *Moon in Capricorn*, Jeanne Wilkes has an actual star in her heart, a condition producing untrammelled happiness, often objectified in her tendency toward impromptu dancing. Such behavior causes incomprehension, pain, and hostility in those around her (including a typical Herlihy psychotic cripple), and ultimately Jeanne's own death. Another unpublished play, *Crazy October*, derived from Herlihy's story "The Sleep of Baby Filbertson," focuses on a mother who tyrannizes her simple-minded son until he unearths a literal family skeleton that could destroy her, a reversal suggesting both the victory of innocence and its transmutation into corrupt power. Despite the presence of Tallulah Bankhead in a showy role, the play failed to reach New York, perhaps because the conventional plot line, which punishes the wicked Mrs. Filbertson, lacked an irony consistent with the black-comic atmosphere and characterizations.

Herlihy's least representative play, *Blue Denim*, written in collaboration with William Noble, was both a critical and financial success and became a popular film. In some ways the archetypal version of the misunderstood adolescent theme of the 1950s, *Blue Denim* partially transcends the genre through clever scenic symbolism and a sympathetic portrait of the adults. The setting, the Detroit home of Major Bartley, his wife, their 23-year-old daughter Lillian, and 15-year-old son Arthur, provides simultaneous views of both the main-floor existence of the family and the basement refuge of Arthur and his friends, Janet and Ernie, a combination hideaway and copy of the adult world upstairs (the boys' beer parodies the Major's serious brandy drinking). Though the play fails to explore the full possibilities of the semi-underground life of the adolescents, the setting suggests that their rebellion (the sexual union of Janet and Arthur, Janet's abortion, the boys' forgery to help pay for the abortion) will be short-lived. The young are already aping their elders.

The bluejeans of the title, a familiar image in Herlihy, stress Arthur's sexual vulnerability (in Herlihy's novels like *Midnight Cowboy* and *All Fall Down* the garment displays sexual aggressiveness or commercial availability). The innocence of Arthur and Janet causes her pregnancy and encounter with a shady abortionist. However, the painful experience does not destroy the youngsters, nor turn them into variants of the abortionist or Lillian's gangster suitor. Ultimately, Arthur and Janet will become part of the world of the Major, a muted version of Herlihy's familiar grotesque, whose "game leg" results not from 18 years army service but from a ludicrous fall on a department store escalator. Though Arthur seems the logical protagonist and achieves an insight into his relationship with his parents, Janet's plight generates more interest; unfortunately, most of her anguish occurs offstage, and Arthur's once-removed reactions seem too inarticulate to reveal either his own feelings or to echo Janet's. Thus, in a sense, Major Bartley, the faintly ridiculous, faintly grotesque personification of the American Legion outlook, emerges as the focal figure and the catalyst in Arthur's maturation. Though the Major's sudden prominence unbalances the play, his changing role seems designed less to please a predominantly middle-aged Broadway audience than to convey the decency latent in such a man: his belief that feeding Arthur huge quantities of food will effect the desired reconciliation may be simplistic, but works convincingly in the play and amusingly underscores Arthur's youthfulness.

Herlihy's next dramatic work, *Stop, You're Killing Me*, is a collection of three one-act plays that experiment in varying ways with the monologue and attempt to create a nightmare vision of a violent America. In *Laughs, Etc.*, a single-character play in the Ruth Draper tradition, Gloria, the middle-aged wife of a lawyer, reminisces to unseen friends and husband about her recent party at which she fed vicariously off the lives of some East Village neighbors and the young female addict they had befriended. Gloria's nastiness inadequately disguises a vulnerability stemming from her childlessness, the source of her quasi-sexual, quasi-maternal obsession with her "safe" homosexual neighbors. Gloria's stress on her essential purity, as she describes the effect of a popular song heard across the courtyard, is predictably ludicrous: "It was as if we were all seven again, and taking our first Holy Communion together. There was this feeling of the oneness of humanity, the sort of thing Dostoevski raved about." However, the irony becomes obtrusive when Gloria, having spent generously for the party, refuses to provide $35 in drug money for the girl, who dies the next day from the forced withdrawal. Not only is it difficult to understand why none of the men living in an expensive building could find the necessary money, but it is also difficult to accept the play's assessment of the girl as a violated innocent whom only Gloria sees as grotesque: "Then Michael said,

Gloria, I hope you'll try to bring her out, will ya? Try to get to know her a little? She's very worthwhile, she has all kinds of original thoughts, insights, ideas, she has her own little window on the world." This view seems as falsely sentimentalized as Gloria's reaction to the song. Despite Gloria's shallowness and bitchery, it is easy to share her indignation at the charge that ". . . this same dreadful Gloria is responsible for shelling out thirty-five smackeroos to save the life of every drug fiend in Manhattan." The play fails to make a $35 drug purchase an index either to the girl's purity or Gloria's compassion, and seems a rigged attempt to flay the would-be hip bourgeois. Since Gloria's auditors apparently respond to her lines, the monologue does not intensify her sense of isolation and remains merely a technical exercise.

   Bad Bad Jo-Jo begins with what is essentially a telephone monologue by Kayo Hathaway, creator of the pop novel and movie figures, Bad Bad Jo-Jo and Mama, allegorical right-wing dispensers of violent law and order in a mother-dominated society. A poster depicts them as "a little old lady with tiny eyeglasses and sensible shoes leading an enormous apelike young man by a chain. The young man wears an Uncle Sam hat that is too small for him." The play parodies the Frankenstein myth when two young men invade Kayo's home and don the garb of Jo-Jo and Mama in order to murder their creator ritualistically. Though Kayo protests, "Is it really and truly necessary to point out to you that I do not kill people? I am in show business," he is responsible for the violence he commercializes. The play, least effective of the three because of its predictable conclusion and use of camp humor to satirize a camp culture hero like Kayo, merely dwells on varieties of corruption and creates neither a sense of justice at Kayo's death, nor sufficient irony to define the climax as more than an exercise in sadism.

   Terrible Jim Fitch, Herlihy's best play, focuses on a man who robs churches, a character with rich folklore resonance and the allegorical dimensions of Spenser's Kirkrapine. In a variation of Strindberg's method in *The Stronger*, Jim addresses his monologue to the silent, but responsive Sally Wilkins, a former singer whose face he once scarred in a fit of rage. The motel room setting helps build a powerful sense of Jim's loneliness and frustration, as he half-threatens, half-begs a reaction from Sally:

> What am I talking about, Sal, something about sleeping in cars? Help me! Answer me, goddam you. . . . Some day, some day, lady, you are not gonna answer me, and God help—I got it! Sleeping in cars! One night in a saloon in Key West, I got in a fist fight and when it was daylight I went to sleep in a car and had this dream about philosophy. There! I remembered—without anybody helping me.

Jim eventually loses his battle for control in the face of loneliness heightened by Sally's unspoken hostility (her behavior underlines the effectiveness of the monologue); but Jim is sometimes capable of raw tenderness: "If I was God, I'd hear you." However, his final plea apparently goes unanswered and leads to Sally's death: "Come on Sally, let me quit now. I'm beggin you. What's my name? Just say what my name is. You don't have to call me darling with it, but just say that one thing. Say my name. Once." The play illuminates Jim's blend of "criminal mentality" and vulnerability, and implies their genesis without sociological jargon or condescension. The inevitability of the conclusion heightens the tension and helps create that fusion of corruption and innocence toward which all Herlihy's plays aspire.

—Burton S. Kendle

HILL, Errol (Gaston).

Born in Trinidad, 5 August 1921; naturalized U.S. citizen. Educated at the Royal Academy of Dramatic Art (British Council scholar), London, diploma 1951; University of London, diploma in dramatic art 1951; Yale University, New Haven, Connecticut, B.A., M.F.A. 1962, D.F.A. 1966. Married Grace L.E. Hope in 1956; four children. Drama tutor, University of the West Indies, Kingston, Jamaica, 1952–58; creative arts tutor, University of the West Indies, Trinidad, 1958–65; teaching fellow in drama, University of Ibadan, Nigeria, 1965–67; associate professor of drama, Richmond College, City University, New York, 1967–68. Associate professor of drama, 1968–69, professor of drama, 1969–76, Willard professor of drama and oratory, 1976–89, and since 1989 emeritus professor, drama department, Dartmouth College, Hanover, New Hampshire. Chancellor's distinguished professor, University of California, Berkeley, 1983. Founder, Whitehall Players, Trinidad; editor, Caribbean Plays series, University of the West Indies, 1954–65. Editor, *ATA Bulletin of Black Theatre*, Washington, D.C., 1971–76. Recipient: Rockefeller fellowship, 1958, 1959 and teaching fellowship, 1965–67; Theatre Guild of America fellowship, 1961; Bertram Joseph award for Shakespeare Studies, 1985; Barnard Hewitt award, for theatre history, 1985; Guggenheim fellowship, 1985; Fulbright fellowship, 1988. Address: 3 Haskins Road, Hanover, New Hampshire 03755, U.S.A.

Publications

PLAYS

Oily Portraits (as *Brittle and the City Fathers*, produced 1948). 1966.
Square Peg (produced 1949). 1966.
The Ping Pong: A Backyard Comedy-Drama (broadcast 1950; produced 1953). 1955.
Dilemma (produced 1953). 1966.
Broken Melody (produced 1954). 1966.
Wey-Wey (produced 1957). 1958.
Strictly Matrimony (produced 1959). 1966; in *Black Drama Anthology*, edited by Woodie King and Ron Milner, 1971.
Man Better Man (produced 1960). In *The Yale School of Drama Presents*, edited by John Gassner, 1964; in *Plays for Today*, edited by Hill, 1986.
Dimanche Gras Carnival Show (produced 1963).
Whistling Charlie and the Monster (carnival show; produced 1964).
Dance Bongo (produced 1965). 1966; in *Caribbean Literature: An Anthology*, edited by G.R. Coulthard, 1966.

RADIO PLAY: *The Ping Pong*, 1950.

OTHER

The Trinidad Carnival: Mandate for a National Theatre. 1972.

Why Pretend? A Conversation about the Performing Arts, with Peter Greer. 1973.

Shakespeare in Sable: A History of Black Shakespearean Actors. 1984.

The Jamaican Stage 1655–1900. 1992.

Editor and Contributor, *The Artist in West Indian Society: A Symposium.* 1964.

Editor, *A Time and a Season: 8 Caribbean Plays.* 1976.

Editor, *Three Caribbean Plays for Secondary Schools.* 1979.

Editor, *The Theater of Black Americans: A Collection of Critical Essays.* 2 vol., 1980.

Editor, *Plays for Today.* 1986.

Editor, *Black Heroes: Seven Plays.* 1989.

BIBLIOGRAPHY: *Black Theatre and Performances: A Pan-African Bibliography* by John Gray, 1990.

MANUSCRIPT COLLECTION: Baker Library, Dartmouth College, Hanover, New Hampshire.

THEATRICAL ACTIVITIES

DIRECTOR: **Plays**—more than 120 plays and pageants in the West Indies, England, the United States, and Nigeria.

ACTOR: **Plays**—more than 40 roles in amateur and professional productions in the West Indies, England, the United States, and Nigeria.

Errol Hill comments:

I was trained first as an actor and play director. I began writing plays when it became clear to me, as founder of a Trinidad theatre company (the Whitehall Players, later merged with the New Company to become the Company of Players), that an indigenous West Indian theatre could not exist without a repertoire of West Indian plays. The thrust of my work as playwright has been to treat aspects of Caribbean folk life, drawing on speech idioms and rhythms, music and dance, and to evolve a form of drama and theatre most nearly representative of Caribbean life and art. As drama tutor for the University of the West Indies I carried this message to every part of the Caribbean and have written plays by way of demonstrating what could be done to provide a drama repertoire for Caribbean theatre companies.

Errol Hill demonstrates a remarkable talent in two separate but closely associated artistic fields—namely, playwriting and literary criticism. Presently Chairman of the Department of Drama at Dartmouth College, he is the author of one-act plays and full-length dramas; he has edited the Caribbean Plays series and is the author of many articles and reports. *The Trinidad Carnival:*

Mandate for a National Theatre is a definitive contribution to the study of a rich folklore.

Man Better Man, Hill's most outstanding theatrical success, tells of a young suitor for the hand of Petite Belle Lily. The suitor's method is to challenge the village stick-fighting champion to a decisive duel. The young lover resorts to the supernatural means of his vibrant culture. He goes to the village obeah-man, Diable Papa, and is subsequently cheated by the quack magician. He receives a herb, "Man Better Man"—a known cure which guarantees invincibility. With characteristic humility, Hill once wrote to me the following explanation:

> It [*Man Better Man*] was for me little more than an experiment in integrating music, song, and dance into dramatic action, and using the calypso form with its rhymed couplets to carry the rhythm and make the transitions occur more smoothly. . . . I never had an orchestral score of the music for the play. Since most of it is traditional-based, with a few numbers "composed by me," . . . I simply provided a melodic line and left it to each production to create their own orchestration. Much of the music should appear to be improvised anyway with, ideally, the musicians carrying their instruments as part of the chorus on stage.

Hill's play celebrates, in a ritualized form, the triumphal pleasure of comedy. Richard F. Shepard said in the *New York Times* (3 July 1969): "Mr. Hill has encapsuled an authentic folk tale flavor, letting us know something about a people, his people, whose history antedates steel drum bands. It is quaint, yet not condescending; ingenuous, yet not silly." On the surface the musical play gleams with a tropical panache; beneath are the threatened subtleties and hidden meanings. Thus that magic, that mystery which the festive Greeks knew very well, is engaged—no, released—by Hill on a richly set Caribbean stage. The connection between the author's skill in portraying effects obtained by the juxtaposition of the real with the assumed—one of the several functions of comedy—and his symbolic comic vision is the dynamic element of this work.

C. L. R. James was deeply moved when Hill produced and directed a lengthy skit in Trinidad of dramatic, musical, festive, and political impact. He observed that the audience enjoyed it while "the authorities" did not approve. Hill's venture to me is completely West Indian, and completely Greek. Sir William Ridgeway in *The Origin of Tragedy* (1910) and *The Dramas and Dramatic Dances of Non-European Races* (1915) could have been speaking of West Indian drama as well as Greek tragedy when he states that the heavy emphasis on ghosts, burial rites, and ancestor worship could not be derived from such a deity as Dionysus alone. The art must be related to hero and ancestor worship and the cult of the dead. For example, in *Man Better Man* Hannibal, Calypsonian, enjoys a position roughly analogous to the Anglo-Saxon court *scop*. He immortalizes the island's heroes in song, and his repertoire constitutes a veritable oral chronicle. Pogo's homeric cataloguing of famous stick-fighters displays the continuity of the heroic tradition. Villagers manifest an awareness that they see tradition-in-the-making. "Excitement for so/More trouble and woe/A day to recall/When you grow old."

Medieval courtly conventions are carried off to the Caribbean setting in the most graceful and lyrical moods. Courtly love comes forward and all action stems from Tim Briscoe's desire to win a woman's affection through a demonstration of physical prowess. He expresses his longing in courtly love terms for Petite Belle Lily. Tim displays those familiar symptoms of "heroes"—the conventional lover's malady—when he says "I cannot eat by day, come the night/Cannot sleep, what a plight." Petite Belle Lily shows her indifference—perhaps medieval, perhaps Petrarchan—to her lover's sorry state which is so fitting and proper to her courtly heroine-like state. The stick-fight itself—traditionally accompanied by a calinda—between Tim and Tiny Sata is reminiscent of a medieval tournament whose proceedings are governed by ritualized and rigid customs. Aspects of trial-by-combat are ever-present, along with strong emphasis on personal honor and its defence. Indeed, stick-fighting is envisioned among these island dwellers as a folk institution. The fighter is a true folk hero, like Beowulf or Achilles, who embodies not only the primitive drive of the islanders, but also the qualities which they esteem most highly—physical courage, prowess in battle, personal honor. The reigning champion becomes a personification of the communal ideal.

The tension between Diable Papa—a fake and a counterfeit who, by means of voodoo, makes money from the primitive fears of the people—and Portagee Joe supplies the intellectual focus of the drama. The obeahman—the holder of all the local rituals, spells, and incantations—represents the power of illusion and mass deception. Portagee Joe, who successfully challenges Diable Papa's authority, is the typical "village atheist"—whose cynicism or rationalism keeps him outside the circle of communal belief. "The social significance of the play lies in the relationship between Portagee Joe and his customers: They were not 'niggers' to him and he is not 'white' to them," writes Mrs. Stanley Jackson, in a letter to the *New York Times*. "A man could be judged as a man seventy years ago in Trinidad. . . . The author of *Man Better Man* knew his material extremely well."

Lastly, Diable Papa, who is a fraud, nevertheless reflects some picaresque influences. He is reminiscent of the medieval and Tudor horrific-comic depiction of stock diabolic figures. But the obeahman is balanced against the broader irony of the play's resolution. Tim Briscoe qua anti-hero, although defeated, emerges as a hero in spite of himself. Diable Papa, confounded by supposedly "supernatural" happenings and spectral visitations, is actually victimized by the very beliefs he has fostered in the villagers.

The drama is a picture of thoughtful delight. The audience—even the reader—becomes an extension of the stage. One cannot help recalling throughout the work Michael Rutenberg's advice to directors: "Break through the proscenium!" The ceremonial interaction of chorus, dancers, actors, and calypsonian sequences—responsorial in nature (counter-melodies are used by Diable Papa and Minee)—and the lively verse—incantatorial in quality and reflecting the natural rhythmic delivery of the West Indian speech pattern—all go to picture and re-emphasize the profundity of life, dying, and existence when tragic and comic values meet in confrontation.

—Louis D. Mitchell

HIVNOR, Robert (Hanks).

Born in Zanesville, Ohio, in 1916. Educated at the University of Akron, Ohio, A.B. 1936; Yale University, New Haven, Connecticut, M.F.A. 1946; Columbia University, New York, 1952–54. Served in the U.S. Army, 1942–45. Married Mary Otis in 1947; two sons and one daughter. Political cartoonist and commercial artist, 1934–38; instructor, University of Minnesota, Minneapolis, 1946–48, and Reed College, Portland, Oregon, 1954–55; assistant professor, Bard College, Annandale-on-Hudson, New York, 1956–59. Recipient: University of Iowa fellowship, 1951; Rockefeller grant, 1968. Address: 420 East 84th Street, New York, New York 10028, U.S.A.

Publications

PLAYS

Martha Goodwin, adaptation of the story "A Goat for Azazel" by Katherine Anne Porter (produced 1942; revised version broadcast, 1959).
Too Many Thumbs (produced 1948). 1949.
The Ticklish Acrobat (produced 1954). In *Playbook: Five Plays for a New Theatre*, 1956.
The Assault upon Charles Sumner (produced 1964). In *Plays for a New Theatre: Playbook 2*, 1966.
Love Reconciled to War (produced 1968). In *Break Out! In Search of New Theatrical Environments*, edited by James Schevill, 1973.
"I" "Love" "You" (produced 1968). In *Anon*, 1971.
DMZ (includes the sketches *Uptight Arms, How Much?*, *"I" "Love" "You"*) (as Osbert Pismire and Jack Askew; produced 1969).
A Son Is Always Leaving Home. In *Anon*, 1971.
Apostle/Genius/God. In *Bostonia*, January/February, 1990.

CRITICAL STUDIES: "The Pleasure and Pains of Playgoing" by Saul Bellow, in *Partisan Review*, May 1954; *The Theatre of the Absurd* by Martin Esslin, 1961, revised edition, 1968; *American Drama since World War II* by Gerald Weales, 1962; *The New American Arts* edited by Richard Kostelanetz, 1965; by Albert Bermel, in *New Leader*, 1966; by A. W. Staub, in *Southern Review*, Summer 1970.

The economics of theatre are all too cruel to art: because a play costs so much more to produce than, say, a novel, many important texts are rarely, if ever, presented. Those particularly victimized by such economic discrimination include older playwrights who have neither the time nor energy necessary to launch non-commercial productions on their own. There is no doubt, in my judgment, that Robert Hivnor has written two of the best and most original American postwar dramas, but it is lamentable that our knowledge of them, as well as his reputation, must be based more upon print than performance and that lack of incentive keeps yet other plays half-finished. The first, called *Too Many Thumbs*, is more feasible, requiring only some inventive costuming and masks to overcome certain difficulties in artifice. It tells of an exceptionally bright chimpanzee, possessed of a large body and a small head, who in the course of the play moves up the evolutionary ladder to become, first, an intermediate stage between man and beast, and then a normal man and ultimately a god-like creature with an immense head and a shrivelled body. The university professors who keep him also attempt to cast him as the avatar of a new religion, but unending evolution defeats their designs. Just as Hivnor's writing is often very funny, so is the play's ironically linear structure also extremely original (preceding Ionesco's use of it in *The New Tenant*), for by pursuing the bias implicit in evolutionary development to its inevitable reversal, the play coherently questions mankind's claim to a higher state of existence. *The Ticklish Acrobat* is a lesser work, nonetheless exhibiting some true originality and typically Hivnorian intellectual comedy; but here the practical difficulty lies in constructing a set whose period recedes several hundred years in time with each act.

Hivnor is fundamentally a dark satirist who debunks myths and permits no heroes; but unlike other protagonist-less playwrights, he is less interested in absurdity than comprehensive ridicule. *The Assault upon Charles Sumner* is an immensely sophisticated history play, regrettably requiring more actors and scenes than an unsubsidized theatre can afford, and an audience more literate than Broadway offers. Its subject is the supreme example of liberal intellectuality in American politics—the 19th-century Senator from Massachusetts, Charles Sumner, who had been a distinguished proponent of abolition and the Civil War. Like Sumner's biographer David Donald, Hivnor finds that Sumner, for all his saintliness, was politically ineffectual and personally insufferable. The opening prologue, which contains some of Hivnor's most savage writing, establishes the play's tone and thrust, as it deals with the funeral and possible afterlife of the last living Negro slave. "Sir, no American has ever been let into heaven." "Not old Abe Lincoln?" the slave asks. "Mr. Lincoln," Sumner replies, "sits over there revising his speech at the Gettysburg. . . ."

Extending such negative satire, Hivnor feasts upon episodes and symbols of both personal and national failure, attempting to define a large historical experience in a single evening. While much of the imagery is particularly theatrical, such as repeating the scene where Preston Brooks assaults Sumner with a cane, perhaps the play's subject and scope are finally closer, both intrinsically and extrinsically, to extended prose fiction.

—Richard Kostelanetz

HOFFMAN, William M.

Born in New York City, 12 April 1939. Educated at the City University, New York, 1955–60, B.A. (cum laude) in Latin 1960 (Phi Beta Kappa). Editorial assistant, Barnes and Noble, publishers, New York, 1960–61; assistant editor, 1961–67, and associate editor and drama editor, 1967–68, Hill and Wang, publishers, New York; literary adviser, *Scripts* magazine, New York, 1971–72; visiting lecturer, University of Massachusetts, Boston, Spring, 1973; playwright-in-residence, American Conservatory Theatre, San Francisco, 1978, and La Mama, New York, 1978–79. Since 1980 Star professor, Hofstra University, Hempstead, New York. Recipient: MacDowell Colony fellowship, 1971; Colorado Council on the Arts and Humanities grant, 1972; Carnegie Fund grant, 1972; PEN grant, 1972; Guggenheim fellowship, 1974; National

Endowment for the Arts grant, 1975, 1976; Drama Desk award, 1985; Obie award, 1985; New York Foundation for the Arts grant, 1985. Lives in New York City. Agent: International Creative Management, 40 West 57th Street, New York, New York 10019, U.S.A.

Publications

PLAYS

Thank You, Miss Victoria (produced 1965). In *New American Plays 3*, edited by Hoffman, 1970.

Saturday Night at the Movies (produced 1966). In *The Off-Off-Broadway Book*, edited by Albert Poland and Bruce Mailman, 1972.

Good Night, I Love You (produced 1966).

Spring Play (produced 1967).

Three Masked Dances (produced 1967).

Incantation (produced 1967).

Uptight! (produced 1968).

XXX (produced 1969; as *Nativity Play*, produced 1970). In *More Plays from Off-Off-Broadway*, edited by Michael T. Smith, 1972.

Luna (also director: produced 1970). As *An Excerpt from Buddha*, in *Now: Theater der Erfahrung*, edited by Jens Heilmeyer and Pia Frolich, 1971.

A Quick Nut Bread to Make Your Mouth Water (also director: produced 1970). In *Spontaneous Combustion: Eight New American Plays*, edited by Rochelle Owens, 1972.

From Fool to Hanged Man (produced 1972). In *Scenarios*, 1982.

The Children's Crusade (produced 1972).

Gilles de Rais (also director: produced 1975).

Cornbury, with Anthony Holland (produced 1977). In *Gay Plays*, edited by Hoffman, 1979.

The Last Days of Stephen Foster (televised 1977). In *Dramatics*, 1978.

A Book of Etiquette, music by John Braden (produced 1978; as *Etiquette*, produced 1983).

Gulliver's Travels, music by John Braden, adaptation of the novel by Swift (produced 1978).

Shoe Palace Murray, with Anthony Holland (produced 1978). In *Gay Plays*, edited by Hoffman, 1979.

The Cherry Orchard, Part II, with Anthony Holland (produced 1983).

As Is (produced 1985). 1985.

TELEVISION WRITING: *Notes from the New World: Louis Moreau Gottschalk*, with Roger Englander, 1976; *The Last Days of Stephen Foster*, 1977; *Whistler: 5 Portraits*, 1978.

VERSE

The Cloisters: A Song Cycle, music by John Corigliano. 1968.

Wedding Song. 1984.

OTHER

Editor, *New American Plays 2, 3 and 4*. 3 vols., 1968–71.

Editor, *Gay Plays: The First Collection*. 1979.

MANUSCRIPT COLLECTIONS: University of Wisconsin, Madison; Lincoln Center Library of the Performing Arts, New York.

THEATRICAL ACTIVITIES

DIRECTOR: Plays—*Thank You, Miss Victoria*, 1970; *Luna*, 1970; *A Quick Nut Bread to Make Your Mouth Water*, 1970, 1972; *XXX*, 1970; *First Death* by Walter Leyden Brown, 1972; *Gilles de Rais*, 1975.
ACTOR: Plays—Frank in *The Haunted Host* by Robert Patrick, 1964; Cupid in *Joyce Dynel* by Robert Patrick, 1969; Twin in *Huckleberry Finn*, 1969. Film—*Guru the Mad Monk*, 1970.

William M. Hoffman comments:

(1982) In 1980 the Metropolitan Opera commissioned me to write a libretto for their 1983–84 season. The composer chosen was John Corigliano. We decided to complete the trilogy of operas on Figaro, using Beaumarchais's last play, *La Mère coupable* (*The Guilty Mother*), as our port of embarkation.

This libretto capped a decade of work with historical materials. My subjects included Gilles de Rais, the actual Bluebeard of 15th-century France; *Gulliver's Travels* and Emily Post's *Book of Etiquette* (1934 edition), in musical adaptation; James McNeill Whistler, Stephen Foster, and Louis Moreau Gottschalk, in plays for television; and Jesus.

My three collaborations with Anthony Holland were also historically founded. *Cornbury* is based on the life of the transvestite English governor of New York in the early 18th century. *Shoe Palace Murray* is located in New York in the 1920s. And *The Cherry Orchard, Part II* is set in Russia of the 1905–17 era.

But now after finishing the libretto, I have returned to the more personal material of my earliest plays, which all took place in contemporary times. I am currently working on a semiautobiographical play and a novel set in my neighborhood, SoHo.

William M. Hoffman's early work *Spring Play* is about a young man leaving home, girlfriend, and innocence and coming to New York City, where he meets a variety of exciting, corrupting people and experiences, and comes to some grief in his growing up. The style of the play is romantic and poetic, a kind of hallucinatory naturalism. Since then Hoffman has edited several anthologies of new American plays, and his awareness of contemporary styles and modes of consciousness is reflected in his own work. *Thank You, Miss Victoria* is a brilliant monologue in which a mother-fixated young business executive gets into a bizarre sado-masochistic relationship on the telephone. *Saturday Night at the Movies* is a bright, brash comedy, and *Uptight!* a musical revue. The eccentrically titled play *XXX* has as characters Jesus, Mary, Joseph, the Holy Ghost, and God. It retells the story of Jesus's life in a personal, free-form, associative, hip, provocatively beautiful fashion. The play is conceived as an ensemble performance for five actors. *Luna* is a light show. *A Quick Nut Bread to Make Your Mouth Water* is an ostensibly improvisatory play for three actors constructed in the form of a recipe, and the nut bread is served to the audience at the finish of the performance. In one production the author himself directed, he incorporated a group of gospel singers into the play.

Hoffman has explored forms other than drama, seeking a renewal of dramatic energies, attempting to expand theatrical possibilities and the audience's awareness. *From Fool to Hanged Man* is a scenario for pantomime, based on imagery from the Tarot. By contrast with much of Hoffman's earlier work, which made a point of the possibility of enlightenment, in which innocence was rewarded at least with edifying experience, here the innocent hero moves blindly, almost passively, through a bleak succession of destructive encounters and is finally hanged. The beauty of the work only emphasizes its despair. Characteristically, the forces at work are not worldly or political but seem to exist in the individual state of mind. *The Children's Crusade* is another dance-pantomime of naive and sentimental innocence brought down by the mockery and hostility of the corrupt, historically worn-out world. The theme parallels a widespread shift of attitude in the United States; to follow Hoffman's work is to observe a representative contemporary consciousness.

Although *Gilles de Rais* embraces depravity, most of Hoffman's subsequent work treats lighter subjects. In this vein are *The Cherry Orchard, Part II*, *Shoe Palace Murray*, and *Cornbury*, all collaborations with Anthony Holland. *The Cherry Orchard, Part II* is a political satire, incorporating lyrical and melodramatic elements, which opens and closes with the final moments of Chekhov's play and co-opts the character of Irina from *The Three Sisters*. It traces the evolution between 1903 and 1918 of a group of Moscow intellectuals from Tolstoyan pacifists to Bolsheviks. Comedies both, *Shoe Palace Murray* takes place in a New York footwear store in 1926, while *Cornbury* dramatizes the life of an early governor of New York, a transvestite who ruled in Queen Anne's leftover clothing. With the songwriter John Braden, Hoffman has also written two musicals, *Gulliver's Travels* and *A Book of Etiquette*. Another musical project—suggested by the third play in Beaumarchais's trilogy *The Guilty Mother*—is the libretto to *A Figaro for Antonia* for the composer John Corigliano, commissioned by the Metropolitan Opera.

As Is returns to serious matters: the mysterious and, so far, incurable illness AIDS, which in America has struck male homosexuals particularly hard. Blending humor with rage and sorrow, playing freely with time and place, *As Is* makes its larger social commentary within the context of an old-fashioned love story—only here the lovers are gay men, one of whom has a fatal, infectious disease. Hoffman's most popular play to date, *As Is* transferred from the Circle Repertory Company to Broadway.

—Michael T. Smith and C. Lee Jenner

HOLDEN, Joan.

Born in Berkeley, California, 18 January 1939. Educated at Reed College, Portland, Oregon, B.A. 1960; University of California, Berkeley, M.A. 1964. Married 1) Arthur Holden in 1958 (divorced); 2) Daniel Chumley in 1968, three daughters. Waitress, Claremont Hotel, Berkeley, 1960–62; copywriter, Librairie Larousse, Paris, 1964–66; research assistant, University of California, Berkeley, 1966–67. Since 1967 playwright, publicist, 1967–69, and business manager, 1978–79, San Francisco Mime Troupe. Editor, Pacific News Service, 1973–75; instructor in playwriting, University of California, Davis, 1975, 1977, 1979, 1983, 1985, 1987. Recipient: Obie award, 1973; Rockefeller grant, 1985. Address: San Francisco Mime Troupe, 855 Treat Street, San Francisco, California 94110, U.S.A.

Publications

PLAYS

L'Amant Militaire, adaptation of a play by Carlo Goldoni, translated by Betty Schwimmer (produced 1967). In *The San Francisco Mime Troupe: The First Ten Years*, by R. G. Davis, 1975.

Ruzzante; or, The Veteran, adaptation of a play by Angelo Beolco, translated by Suzanne Pollard (produced 1968).

The Independent Female; or, A Man Has His Pride (produced 1970). In *By Popular Demand*, 1980.

Seize the Time, with Steve Friedman (produced 1970).

The Dragon Lady's Revenge, with others (produced 1971). In *By Popular Demand*, 1980.

Frozen Wages, with Richard Benetar and Daniel Chumley (produced 1972). In *By Popular Demand*, 1980.

San Fran Scandals, with others (produced 1973). In *By Popular Demand*, 1980.

The Great Air Robbery (produced 1974).

Frijoles; or, Beans to You, with others (produced 1975). In *By Popular Demand*, 1980.

Power Play (produced 1975).

False Promises/Nos Engañaron (produced 1976). In *By Popular Demand*, 1980.

The Loon's Rage, with Steve Most and Jael Weisman (produced 1977). In *West Coast Plays 10*, Fall 1981.

The Hotel Universe, music by Bruce Barthol (produced 1977). In *West Coast Plays 10*, Fall 1981.

By Popular Demand: Plays and Other Works by The San Francisco Mime Troupe (includes *False Promises/Nos Engañaron*; *San Fran Scandals*; *The Dragon Lady's Revenge*; *The Independent Female*; *Frijoles*; *Frozen Wages* by Holden, and *Los Siete* and *Evo-Man*). 1980.

Factperson, with others (produced 1980). In *West Coast Plays 15–16*, Spring 1983.

Americans; or, Last Tango in Huahuatenango, with Daniel Chumley (produced 1981).

Factwino Meets the Moral Majority, with others (produced 1981). In *West Coast Plays 15–16*, Spring 1983.

Factwino vs. Armaggedonman (produced 1982). In *West Coast Plays 15–16*, Spring 1983.

Steeltown, music by Bruce Barthol (produced 1984).

1985, with others (produced 1985).

Spain/36, music by Bruce Barthol (produced 1986).

The Mozamgola Caper, with others (produced 1986). In *Theater*, Winter 1986.

Ripped van Winkle, with Ellen Callas (produced 1988).
Seeing Double, with others (produced 1989).
Back to Normal, with others (produced 1990).
The Marriage of Figaro, adaptation of a play by Beaumarchais (produced 1990).

MANUSCRIPT COLLECTION: University of California, Davis.

CRITICAL STUDIES: "*Hotel Universe*: Playwriting and the San Francisco Mime Troupe" by William Kleb, in *Theater*, Spring 1978; "Joan Holden and the San Francisco Mime Troupe," in *Drama Review*, Spring 1980, and *New American Dramatists 1960–1980*, 1982, both by Ruby Cohn.

Joan Holden comments:

I write political cartoons. For years, I was ashamed of this. I agreed meekly with those critics who said, "*mere* political cartoons." To please them, and led astray by well-wishers who'd say, "You can do more—you could write *serious* plays," I've tried my hand, from time to time, at realism. Each time I've been extremely impressed, at first, with the solemnity of what I've written. Rereading those passages, I always find I've written melodrama. The fact is, I'm only inspired when I'm being funny. Writing comedy is not really a choice: it's a quirk. On a certain level, making things funny is a coward's way of keeping pain at arm's length. But that same distance allows you to show certain things clearly: notably, characters' social roles, their functions in history. These generalities, not the specifics which soften them, interest caricaturists—who have serious reasons for being funny, and in whose ranks I now aspire to be counted.

For 20 years, I've written for a permanent company, for particular actors, directors, and composers, and in collaboration with them. This has put conditions on my writing; it has also supplied a nearly constant source of ideas, and a wonderful opportunity to learn from mistakes.

Joan Holden has been the principal playwright of the San Francisco Mime Troupe, which has always performed with words as well as gesture. Although chance led to this association, a 30-year career was launched.

The Holden/Goldoni *Military Lover/L'Amant Militaire* drew large audiences to nearly 50 park performances, and Holden wrote: "Comedy, which in its basic action always measures an unsatisfactory reality against its corresponding ideal, may be the revolutionary art form *par excellence*." It became Holden's art form *par excellence*, pitting satirized Establishment figures of unsatisfactory reality against the satisfactory dream of working-class harmony and celebration.

After the Mime Troupe went collective in 1970, *The Independent Female* expressed the new spirit. *Commedia* characters gave way to those of soap opera with satiric telltale names—Pennybank for a business tycoon, Heartright for a junior executive, Bullitt for a militant feminist. A pair of lovers is faced with an obstacle to their marriage, as in soap opera. But subverting the genre,

Holden identifies the obstacle as the young ingénue's growing independence. Instead of dissolving the obstacle for a happy curtain clinch, Holden sees a happy ending in sustained feminist revolt which the audience is asked to link to working class revolt.

The Dragon Lady's Revenge is grounded in another popular form, the comic strip, with assists from Grade B movies, and its intricate plot involves the corrupt American ambassador in Long Penh, his soldier son, a CIA agent Drooley, and the titular Dragon Lady, as well as the honest native revolutionary Blossom. Holden shifted from global to local politics with *San Fran Scandals* blending housing problems into vaudeville. Science fiction and detective story were then exploited for *The Great Air Robbery*.

In the mid-1970s the San Francisco Mime Troupe reached out beyond the white middle class, actively recruiting Third World members, and Holden's scripts reflect their new constituency. *Frijoles* (Spanish for beans) zigzags from a Latin American couple to a North American couple, joining them at a food conference in Europe, and joining them in identical class interests. As *Frijoles* travels through space, *Power Play* travels through time in order to indict the anti-ecological monopoly of the Pacific Gas and Electric Company.

By 1976, America's bicentennial year, Holden was in firm command of her style: a specific issue attacked through a popular art form; simple language and clean story line; swift scenes often culminating in a song. The group wished to present a play on the uncelebrated aspects of American history—the role of workers, minorities, women. Based on collective research, Holden scripted *False Promises*, which deviated from her usual satiric formula in presenting heightened realism of working-class characters. They continue to appear in such subsequent plays as *Steeltown* and the final play of the Factwino trilogy. In *Factperson* the person of the title is an old black baglady with the power to cite facts that contradict the lies of the media. In *Factwino vs. Armaggedonman* "the double-headed dealer of doom" or the military-industrial powers subjugate an old black wino with alcohol, but in the most recent Factwino play he emerges triumphant through his own research beneath lies: "Everybody has to find their own power." *Ripped van Winkle* is a hilarious reversion to satire, when a 1960s hippy awakens from a 20-year acid trip, adrift in Reaganomics. Local or global, probing character, or tickling caricature, Holden theatricalizes current events with theatrical verve.

—Ruby Cohn

HOROVITZ, Israel (Arthur).

Born in Wakefield, Massachusetts, 31 March 1939. Educated at the Royal Academy of Dramatic Art, London, 1961–63; City College, New York, M.A. in English 1972. Married 1) Elaine Abber in 1959 (marriage annulled 1960); 2) Doris Keefe in 1961 (divorced 1972), one daughter and two sons. 3) Gillian Adams in 1981, twin daughter and son. Stage manager, Boston and New York, 1961–65; playwright-in-residence, Royal Shakespeare Company, London, 1965; instructor in playwriting, New York University, 1967–69; professor of English, City College, 1968–73; Fanny Hurst professor of theatre, Brandeis University, Waltham, Massachusetts, 1973–75. Founder, New York

Playwrights Lab, 1977; founder, 1980, and producer and artistic director, Gloucester Stage Company, Massachusetts. Columnist, *Magazine Littéraire*, Paris, 1971–77. Recipient: Obie award, 1968, 1969; Rockefeller fellowship, 1969; Vernon Rice award, 1969; Drama Desk award, 1969; *Jersey Journal* award, 1969; Cannes Film Festival Jury prize, 1971; New York State Council of Arts fellowship, 1971, 1975; National Endowment for the Arts fellowship, 1974, 1977; American Academy award, 1975; Fulbright fellowship, 1975; Emmy award, 1975; Christopher award, 1976; Guggenheim fellowship, 1977; French Critics prize, 1977; Los Angeles Drama Critics Circle award, 1980; Goldie award, 1985; Eliot Norton Prize, 1986; Boston Best Play award, 1987. Agents: William Morris Agency, 1350 Avenue of the Americas, New York, New York 10019, U.S.A., and 31–32 Soho Square, London W1V 6AP, England.

Publications

PLAYS

The Comeback (produced 1958).
The Death of Bernard the Believer (produced 1960).
This Play Is about Me (produced 1961).
The Hanging of Emanuel (produced 1962).
Hop, Skip, and Jump (produced 1963).
The Killer Dove (produced 1963).
The Simon Street Harvest (produced 1964).
The Indian Wants the Bronx (produced 1966). In *First Season*, 1968; in *Off-Broadway Plays*, 1970.
Line (produced 1967; revised version produced 1971). In *First Season*, 1968.
It's Called the Sugar Plum (produced 1967). In *First Season*, 1968; in *Off-Broadway Plays*, 1970.
Acrobats (produced 1968). 1971.
Rats (produced 1968). In *First Season*, 1968.
Morning (in *Chiaroscuro* produced 1968; in *Morning, Noon, and Night* produced 1968). In *Morning, Noon, and Night*, 1969.
First Season: Line, The Indian Wants the Bronx, It's Called the Sugar Plum, Rats. 1968.
The Honest to God Schnozzola (produced 1968). 1971.
Leader (produced 1969). With *Play for Trees*, 1970.
Play for Trees (televised 1969). With *Leader*, 1970.
Shooting Gallery (produced 1971). With *Play for Germs*, 1973.
Dr. Hero (as *Hero*, produced 1971; revised version, as *Dr. Hero*, produced 1972). 1973.
The Wakefield Plays (produced 1978). In *The Wakefield Plays* (collection), 1979.
   1. *Alfred the Great* (also director: produced 1972). 1974.
   2. *Our Father's Failing* (produced 1973).
   3. *Alfred Dies* (produced 1976).
Play for Germs (in *VD Blues*, televised 1972). With *Shooting Gallery*, 1973.
The First, The Last, and The Middle: A Comedy Triptych (produced 1974).
The Quannapowitt Quartet (produced 1976). 3 plays in *The Wakefield Plays* (collection), 1979.

1. *Hopscotch* (also director: produced 1974). With *The 75th*, 1977.
2. *The 75th* (produced 1977). With *Hopscotch*, 1977.
3. *Stage Directions* (produced 1976). With *Spared*, 1977.
4. *Spared* (also director: produced 1974). With *Stage Directions*, 1977.

Turnstile (produced 1974).

The Primary English Class (produced 1975; also director: produced 1975). 1976.

Uncle Snake: An Independence Day Pageant (produced 1975). 1976.

The Reason We Eat (produced 1976).

The Lounge Player (produced 1977).

Man with Bags, adaptation of a play by Eugène Ionesco, translated by Marie-France Ionesco (produced 1977). 1977.

The Former One-on-One Basketball Champion (produced 1977). With *The Great Labor Day Classic*, 1982.

Cappella, with David Boorstin, adaptation of the novel by Horovitz (produced 1978).

The Widow's Blind Date (produced 1978). 1981.

Mackerel (produced 1978; revised version produced 1978). 1979.

A Christmas Carol: Scrooge and Marley, adaptation of the story by Dickens (produced 1978). 1979.

The Good Parts (produced 1979). 1983.

The Great Labor Day Classic (in *Holidays*, produced 1979). With *The Former One-on-One Basketball Champion*, 1982.

The Wakefield Plays (collection; also includes *The Quannapowitt Quartet* except for *The 75th*). 1979.

Sunday Runners in the Rain (produced 1980).

Park Your Car in Harvard Yard (produced 1980).

Henry Lumper (produced 1985). 1990.

Today, I Am a Fountain Pen, adaptation of stories by Morley Torgov (produced 1986). 1987.

A Rosen by Any Other Name, adaptation of a novel by Morley Torgov (produced 1986). 1987.

The Chopin Playoffs, adaptation of stories by Morley Torgov (produced 1986). In *An Israel Horovitz Trilogy*, 1987.

North Shore Fish (produced 1986). 1989.

Year of the Duck (produced 1986). 1988.

An Israel Horovitz Trilogy (includes *Today, I Am a Fountain Pen*; *A Rosen by Any Other Name*; *The Chopin Playoffs*). 1987.

Faith, Hope, and Charity (three one-acts) with Terrence McNally and Leonard Melfi (produced 1988). 1989.

Strong-Man's Weak Child (also director: produced 1990).

Fighting over Beverly (produced 1993).

SCREENPLAYS: *Machine Gun McCain* (English adaptation), 1970; *The Strawberry Statement*, 1970; *Believe in Me* (*Speed Is of the Essence*), 1970; *Alfredo*, 1970; *The Sad-Eyed Girls in the Park*, 1971; *Camerian Climbing*, 1971; *Acrobats*, 1972; *Fast Eddie*, 1980; *Fell*, 1982; *Berta*, 1982; *Author! Author!*, 1982–83; *Light Years*, 1985; *A Man in Love*, with Diane Kurys, 1988.

TELEVISION PLAYS: *Play for Trees*, 1969; *VD Blues*, with others, 1972; *Start to Finish*, 1975; *The Making and Breaking of Splinters Braun*, 1976; *Bartleby the Scrivener*, from the story by Melville, 1978; *A Day with Conrad Green*, from a story by Ring Lardner, 1978; *The Deer Park*, from the novel by Norman Mailer, 1979.

NOVELS
Cappella. 1973.
Nobody Loves Me. 1975.

MANUSCRIPT COLLECTIONS: Lincoln Center Library of the Performing Arts, New York; Sawyer Free Library, Gloucester, Massachusetts.

CRITICAL STUDIES: *Thirty Plays Hath November* by Walter Kerr, 1969; *Opening Nights* by Martin Gottfried, 1970; *The Playmakers* by Stuart W. Little and Arthur Cantor, 1970; in *Études Anglaises*, Summer 1975.

THEATRICAL ACTIVITIES
DIRECTOR: **Plays**—several of his own plays in English and French, and *Chiaroscuro: Morning, Noon and Night*, by Horovitz, Leonard Melfi, and Terrence McNally, 1968. **Film**—*Acrobats*, 1972. **Television**—*VD Blues*, 1972.
ACTOR: **Film**—*The Strawberry Statement*, 1970.

Israel Horovitz comments:

(1988) Much of life has changed for me.

I used to aspire to run 10 kilometers under 30 minutes. Breaking 40 minutes for the same distance is now quite satisfactory.

My family and my work remain as they were to me before: holy.

(1993) Not much has changed. Happy to break 45 minutes for 10 kilometers.

Israel Horovitz has produced a large volume of work since the 1970s, leaving audiences with the impression of a writer with broad concerns, varying aesthetic impulses, and an impish overview of the human condition. The Horovitz work wants to reach out to a community we call America; often it addresses that community in rudimentary terms, in buoyant cadences, in colloquial jargon (and the colloquialisms will change with the times) about the perverse innocence of the New World, and about the blatant, if also diluted, examples of good and evil within it. And all this is revealed in good-humoured fashion by an older brother who can speak to that afternoon headache known to us as the Land of the Free and the Home of the Brave. Morning in America is not to be recycled, but Afternoon in America is having its extended, slightly sickening nap. Israel is somewhat inducing it to sleep on and somewhat inducing it to get on its feet, and Horovitz is positioned as a kind of Puckish moralist-voyeur over an uneasy, fitfully napping, sometimes racist Gulliver.

First performed in 1968 at the Astor Place Theatre in New York City, *The*

Indian Wants the Bronx presents a luminous title, suggesting what in fact it isn't. This Indian isn't a Native American demanding the return of ancestral lands which have been renamed the Grand Concourse and Tremont Avenue; instead he is a Hindu momentarily trapped in Manhattan by two juvenile hoods while waiting for a bus to take him to his English-speaking son somewhere in the bombed-out vista still known as the Bronx. The Indian, named Gupta, has just landed in the U.S., has neither a working knowledge of what passes for English nor of the habits of white slum kids idling between self-induced bouts of trouble. Gupta, unfortunately dependent on the kindness of strangers to help him relocate the son he is visiting and from whom he has momentarily been separated, is caught in a luckless encounter. We gather from the moment Horovitz's two louts, Joey and Murph, come careening into view, disturbing the silence of a September night on upper Fifth Avenue with their aggressive rendition of a rock-and-roll number (the import of which is that "Baby, you don't care"), that Gupta is in for an ugly encounter, at least a touch of misery before he is ever reunited with his son. The louts, before they turn their attention to Gupta, have been trying to make the September night unbearable for a lady they call Pussyface, a social worker whose caseload has included Joey and Murph. Pussyface's apartment apparently faces the afore-mentioned bus stop and the lady is being serenaded with snippets and variations from the "Baby, you don't care" cycle. We deduce that "baby" is either out of town, fast asleep, indifferent to, or highly annoyed at the public attention presently being showered on her. The impromptu concert goes on intermittently, the boys curse, sulk, and play ugly physical games, but in due time they begin to terrorize the Indian. Why do they terrorize him? He's an innocent, an alien, and the play needs tension.

The work's major problem is that it is essentially an anecdote which Horovitz has to loosen into movement. An anecdote is a self-enclosed organism which is perfectly satisfied with itself; it moves nowhere on its own, one has to "make something" of it. The anecdote may have threads but having been unravelled, even threads need to be transformed. In *Indian* there is no plausible reason for the bus never arriving except that it's necessary for Horovitz's story; also necessary is that Gupta speak not a word of English and that he be on his own in a strange city, unable to make contact with his son except through a phone number that he can't read. Horovitz sets up the conditions whereby Gupta has to be terrorized. But the terrorizing is an arbitrary development, and one has to ask, what do we learn from it other than that human actions are sometimes arbitrary?

Albee's *Zoo Story* can be viewed as a similarly arbitrary work. That is, the writing of the narrative takes on an arbitrariness, and it pushes the story into another arbitrariness. In the Horovitz play, there is even less necessity than in the Albee. People in the world do sometimes terrorize one another but not always. One would think that something in Joey and Murph, which might only be understood viscerally, has to give way and take over in order to manifest the terror. In André Gide's *Lafcadio's Adventures* there is an arbitrary murder, but it is a willed arbitrariness; Gide's hero wants not to resist the impulse to arbitrariness. Perhaps Horovitz needed to employ arbitrariness for the sake of theatricality.

Henry Lumper, some two decades later, begins with necessity. Horovitz creates, sets, and produces the play in Gloucester. It deals with serious concerns of the Gloucester townspeople that are familiar to many: drugs, mass unemployment, deception, alcoholism, violence, community dislocation and, as in *Indian*, our relationship to those we see as aliens. In the 1970s, disciples of Reverend Moon, more popularly known as "Moonies," moved into the fishing village of Gloucester, creating much tension and bitterness among townspeople who envisioned the cult movement destabilizing the village. As Horovitz tells it, the area was also invaded by condo developers buying up precious waterfront property and drug runners moving in on the fishing industry. Overlaid on this contemporary drama is Shakespeare's *Henry IV*, with the Bolingbrokes and the Percys as principal players, and Prince Hal, or alcoholic loser Hal Boley, as the principal among principals. Hal Boley can't find himself, it's post-Vietnam, Hal can't commit, he's into drugs, booze, and erotic pleasures. He will eventually redeem himself, tackle the issues, become a responsible Boley, put the town back on its feet, and provide moral clarification for a community under siege.

Horovitz has given us a contemporary morality play, a work that has to do both with economics and with saving the soul of a people. In its best moments, and there are many of them, *Henry Lumper* is a moving, heartfelt work, with clarity and believable people. Horovitz uses an open stage and cinematic devices, quick dissolves between characters, so that a whole layer of subjectivity is beautifully present. One might argue that Shakespeare simply gets in the way of the story and one wastes time hunting for parallels. But the work has fine strengths and here Horovitz has moved far beyond the arbitrariness and unconvincing staginess of *Indian*. It's a play, perhaps too heavily coated with morality, that nevertheless moves as if under its own steam and that's a significant movement.

—Arthur Sainer

HOWE, Tina.

Born in New York City, 21 November 1937. Educated at Sarah Lawrence College, Bronxville, New York, B.A. 1959; Chicago Teachers College, 1963–64. Married Norman Levy in 1961; one son and one daughter. Since 1983 adjunct professor, New York University; since 1990 visiting professor, Hunter College, City University of New York. Recipient: Rosamond Gilder award, 1983; Rockefeller grant, 1983; Obie award, 1983; Outer Critics Circle award, 1983, 1984; John Gassner award, 1984; National Endowment for the Arts grant, 1984; Guggenheim fellowship, 1990. Honorary degree: Bowdoin College, Brunswick, Maine, 1988. Agent: Flora Roberts Inc., 157 West 57th Street, New York, New York 10019, U.S.A.

Publications

PLAYS

Closing Time (produced 1959).
The Nest (produced 1969).
Museum (produced 1976). 1979.

Birth and After Birth, in *The New Women's Theatre*, edited by Honor Moore. 1977.
The Art of Dining (produced 1979). 1980.
Appearances (produced 1982).
Painting Churches (produced 1983). 1984.
Three Plays (includes *Museum, The Art of Dining, Painting Churches*). 1984.
Coastal Disturbances (produced 1986). 1987.
Approaching Zanzibar (produced 1989). 1989.
Coastal Disturbances: Four Plays (includes *Painting Churches, The Art of Dining, Museum*). 1989.
Teeth. In *Antaeus*, no.66, Spring 1991.
Swimming (produced 1991).

CRITICAL STUDIES: *Creating Theater: The Professionals' Approach to New Plays* by Lee Alan Morrow and Frank Pike, 1986; *Interviews with Contemporary Women Playwrights* edited by Kathleen Betsko and Rachel Koenig, 1987; *A Search for Postmodern Theater: Interviews with Contemporary Playwrights* by John L. DiGaetani, 1991.

Tina Howe is a marvelously perceptive observer of contemporary mores, and much of the pleasure one receives from her plays comes from her comic skewering of pretentious amateur art critics, couples moaning orgasmically over the yuppie menu of their dreams, and thoroughly enlightened parents thoroughly unable to cope with their monstrous four-year-old. At their best, however, her comedies probe beneath the surface to reveal the inextricable mixture of the humorous and horrific to which modern culture—including art, ritual, and table manners—is a barely adequate response.

Although it already hints of better things to come, *The Nest* is the least satisfying of Howe's full-length plays. The influence of Ionesco and Beckett, whose work Howe admires, is evident here in the use of repeated scenes as well as in the heavy reliance on verbal and physical farce. Still, this play about a trio of female roommates lacks the satirical and emotional bite of her subsequent creations even as it offers glimpses of her prodigious imagination.

"Family life has been over-romanticized; the savagery has not been seen enough in the theatre and in movies," Howe once complained. She attempts to fill this gap with *Birth and After Birth*, a sometimes hilarious, often frightening portrait of the Apples. As their name implies, the Apples (including a four-year-old son played by an adult actor) are a parody of the TV-fare all-American family, continually declaring how happy they are and continually belying this claim. What keeps *Birth and After Birth* from being simply another satire on Ozzie and Harriet is not only Howe's accurate portrait of the physical and emotional brutality inherent in family life but her disturbingly negative exploration of why women choose to have—or not to have—children. Despite the often broad slapstick, *Birth and After Birth* is one of Howe's darkest comedies.

Museum is less a plotted play than a wonderful series of comic turns as visitors—singly and in groups—wander through an exhibit entitled "The Broken Silence." As Howe has acknowledged in interviews, all of her plays are about art, and *Museum* examines the complex interrelationships among creator, creation, and viewers. On one level, *Museum* reveals what fools art makes of us (witness the young woman painstakingly copying an all-white canvas); on another level, however, it shows that artworks cannot fully exist except in the presence of an audience, foolish or not. Finally, in one of the comically horrific monologues that seem an essential part of the Howe landscape, a museum-goer recounts a foraging expedition she took with Agnes Vaag, a young artist represented in the show but never seen on stage. The story reveals the frightening, non-rational roots of art. Vaag, at once a mysterious being who makes "menacing constructions" out of animal carcasses and a ludicrous figure who lugs suitcases through state parks, may well be Howe's archetypal artist.

Another loosely knit comedy, *The Art of Dining* combines Howe's obsession with food (first manifest in *The Nest*) and her concern with art and its consumption. Because the fragility of art is a repeated motif throughout Howe's canon, in a sense food is for her the ultimate artistic medium: it must be destroyed to be appreciated. Set in a restaurant, *The Art of Dining* contains one of Howe's most brilliant creations, Elizabeth Barrow Colt, a wonderfully comic and pathetic figure who embodies every cliché about writers; comfortable only in the world of the imagination, she's a genius with a pen but a total failure with a soup spoon. In *The Art of Dining*'s spectacular conclusion—all the restaurant guests gathered around a flaming platter of crepes tended by the female chef—Howe uses Elizabeth to point out the connection between art and ritual as well as the redemptive power of artistic creation, a theme that runs through several of Howe's works.

Howe's biggest critical success to date is *Painting Churches*, in some ways her most conventional play as well as one of her most lyrical. Returning to the favorite subject of the American playwright—the nuclear family—Howe gives us a comedy about the necessity of acceptance: a daughter accepting the inevitable decline of her aging parents, parents accepting their daughter as a capable adult (and artist). Howe's quirky sense of humor and her distinctive verbal and visual idiom mark the work as uniquely her own, however familiar her starting point. Although Howe denies that she is an autobiographical writer, there is obviously a kinship between the playwright and Mags Church, the young artist who learns that the portrait she is painting of her parents reveals her as well as them. In a moving final tour-de-force that erases the line between Mags' painting and Howe's play, the stripped-bare stage becomes the portrait, the aging characters rescued from decline for the space of a magical moment.

Howe favors unusual settings—a museum, a restaurant kitchen—and the beach locale of *Coastal Disturbances* is as much metaphor as place: like human beings and their relationships, the sand and ocean remain essentially the same over millennia yet change from moment to moment. The main character is a young woman photographer; appropriately, the play is divided into numerous short scenes that rely heavily on visual effects—resembling, in other words, a sequence of snapshots. Although the central situation, a love triangle, is not Howe's most original, her verbal and especially her visual wit are amply in evidence.

Swimming shares the beach location and largely affirmative vision of *Coastal Disturbances*, while *Teeth* is a serio-comic meditation on fear set, appropriately, in a dentist's office. These two add to the small but growing canon of Howe's one-act plays, which also includes *Appearances*, an encounter between a dressing room attendant and a painfully awkward customer. *Approaching Zanzibar*, Howe's latest major work, is a "road play" that follows a family of four on a cross-country trip to visit a dying relative (an elderly artist reminiscent of Georgia O'Keeffe). The Blossoms' journey is both physical and metaphysical as they engage in hilarious—and sometimes nasty— travel games while wrestling with anxieties about change, loss, and death. Not only is this the first of Howe's plays to exploit multiple settings, but its relatively large cast also represents a deliberate attempt on the playwright's part to include a wider range of characters in terms of ethnicity as well as age. Despite being one of Howe's most complex and ambitious works, however, *Zanzibar* received mixed reviews and enjoyed only a brief New York run.

Howe has acknowledged her debt to Absurdist writers, a debt more apparent in her earlier work than in her most recent plays. Like many other American playwrights, Howe doesn't quite share the nihilistic vision of her European counterparts; although salvation is transitory and more likely to be aesthetic than religious or social, there are moments of redemption in most of her plays. Her work has grown in emotional depth over the years and her focus on art and the artist has become stronger. Women artists are her favored protagonists: she writes from a clearly female perspective even if not from a consistently feminist one. Howe's comedies reveal a playwright with a fine sensitivity to the terrors of existence, a splendidly anarchic sense of humor, and a willingness to take risks on the stage.

—Judith E. Barlow

HWANG, David Henry.

Born in Los Angeles, California, 11 August 1957. Educated at Stanford University, California, 1975–79, A.B. in English 1979; Yale University School of Drama, New Haven, Connecticut 1980–81. Married Ophelia Y.M. Chong in 1985. Recipient: Dramalogue award, 1980, 1986; Obie award, 1981; Golden Eagle award, for television writing, 1983; Rockefeller fellowship, 1983; Guggenheim fellowship, 1984; National Endowment for the Arts fellowship, 1985; Tony award, 1988; Outer Critics Circle award, 1988; Drama Desk award, 1988; Asian/Pacific American Artists Media award, 1991; Los Angeles Drama Critics Circle award, 1991. Lives in Los Angeles. Agent: Paul Yamamoto and William Craver. Writers and Artists Agency, 70 West 36th Street, #501, New York, New York 10018, U.S.A.

Publications

PLAYS

FOB (produced 1978). In *Broken Promises: Four Plays*, 1983.

The Dance and the Railroad (produced 1981; in *Broken Promises*, produced 1987). In *Broken Promises: Four Plays*, 1983.

Family Devotions (produced 1981). In *Broken Promises: Four Plays*, 1983.

Sound and Beauty (includes *The House of Sleeping Beauties* and *The Sound of a Voice*) (produced 1983; *The House of Sleeping Beauties* in *Broken*

Promises, produced 1987). *The House of Sleeping Beauties* in *Broken Promises: Four Plays*, 1983; *The Sound of a Voice*, 1984.

Broken Promises: Four Plays. 1983.

Rich Relations (produced 1986).

As the Crow Flies (produced 1986).

Broken Promises (includes *The Dance and the Railroad* and *The House of Sleeping Beauties*) (produced 1987).

1000 Airplanes on the Roof, music by Philip Glass (produced 1988). 1989.

M. Butterfly (produced 1988). 1989.

FOB and Other Plays (includes *The Dance and the Railroad*, *The House of Sleeping Beauties*, *1000 Airplanes on the Roof*, *Family Devotions*, *The Sound of a Voice*). 1990.

The Voyage, music by Philip Glass (produced 1992).

Bondage (produced 1992). In *The Best American Short Plays 1992–1993*, edited by Howard Stein and Glenn Young, 1993.

TELEVISION PLAY: *Blind Alleys*, 1985.

THEATRICAL ACTIVITIES

DIRECTOR: **Plays**—*A Song for a Nisei Fisherman*, 1980, and *The Dream of Kitamura*, 1982, both by Philip Kan Gotanda; *FOB*, 1990.

David Henry Hwang comments:

I'm interested in the dust that settles when worlds collide. Sometimes these worlds are cultural, as in my explorations of a Chinese past meeting an American present. Sometimes they are spiritual, as in *Rich Relations*, where the gung-ho materialism of a California family struggles with its Christian mysticism. Most of the time I also try to walk the fine line between tragedy and comedy. I'm fascinated by America as a land of dreams—people pursue them and hope some day to own one.

"The element it shares with my previous work has to do with a concern for identity," says David Henry Hwang in the introduction to *1000 Airplanes on the Roof*. "To me, all the really interesting human dilemmas are basically internal searches." His comment is as misleading as it is true, for the internal searches in his plays are hedged by external pressures and prejudices. This fact is obvious in the title (*Broken Promises*) which Hwang gave to the collection of his first four plays. Historically, the promise that was broken for so many Chinese immigrants was the dream of the Gold Mountain, an America where fortunes could be picked up off the street. Hwang, the son of immigrants, conventionally educated at choice American universities, is not only interested in the broken promises of the past, but is also concerned about the loss implicit in an embracing of the emblems of American success and the confusions embodied in being a hyphenated person, a Chinese-American.

Essentially a non-realistic dramatist, Hwang does not develop his characters in the conventional way by the accumulation of psychological details. They emerge through formal presentational modes as varied as Chinese opera (*The Dance and the Railroad*) and the television sitcom (*Family Devotions*). Neither the opera nor the sitcom is allowed to retain its classic form, however, for artistically as well as ideationally Hwang is preoccupied in the early plays with the ground on which the hyphenated American struggles to define himself. The tension of inclusion/exclusion which marks these plays operates in a less narrowly ethnic context in the later work, and the early use of non-realistic techniques (the role-playing in *FOB*, for instance) prepares the way for the extreme theatricality of *M. Butterfly* and *1000 Airplanes*, in which Jerome Sirlin's projections come close to upstaging both Philip Glass's music and Hwang's text.

FOB is a three-way struggle between Dale, who is accepted—almost—as something other than "a Chinese, a yellow, a slant, a gook"; Grace, his first-generation cousin who has been in the States since she was a child; and Steve, the bumptious newcomer, the FOB (Fresh Off the Boat). The final pairing of Steve and Grace, who sometimes become the hero Gwan Gung and Fa Mu Lan, the Woman Warrior, suggests that the Chinese in America must hold onto some sense of being Chinese, but it is instructive that at the end they are heading for a fashionable disco in a rented limousine. There is a similar but more moving cross-over in *The Dance and the Railroad*, in which Lone tries to separate himself from his fellow immigrant workers by going to the mountain-top to practice the movements of Chinese opera. Ma, who wants both to dance with Lone and to be one of "the guys" down below, improvises—with Lone's blessing—an opera, at once comic and touching, which uses the vocabulary of traditional art in a new American context and which frees Lone of his need to stand apart. In *Family Devotions*, it is the visiting uncle from the mainland, more Chinese than Communist, who teaches his great nephew that, before he can escape the twin traps of materialism and Christianity which his family represents, he must recognize his face—reflected in the back of the violin that will open his path to the future—and carry his Chinese self into his American world.

Between *Family Devotions* and *M. Butterfly*, seven years later, there were several plays—including the elegantly suggestive, Japanese-based *Sound and Beauty*—but it was with *M. Butterfly* that Hwang scored his greatest success. Much of that success came from the surface slickness of the work, in part the contributions of the director and the designer, and the somewhat lurid content of the story around which the play is built. Yet, *M. Butterfly* is Hwang's most complex treatment of the crises of identity, one that allows for political, sexual, and social considerations more convoluted than those in the early work. The scandalous story, borrowed from a real event, is the account of a French diplomat and his mistress, a Chinese actress on whom he thought he had fathered a child, charged with spying; the trial reveals, to the apparent surprise of the diplomat, that the mistress is a man. In the end, the diplomat dons the robes discarded by his lover and, like Madame Butterfly, kills himself to prove that there is a love deep enough to die for. The suicide is simply an audience-pleasing charade unless playgoers recognize the act as an illustration of the arbitrariness and elusiveness of sexual and ethnic stereotypes. The assumptions underlying the affair—Western male assumptions—are that both women and Asians are submissive, accepting the invasion of the male, the

Westerner. It is an admonitory tale for a time in which such assumptions are under attack.

With *1000 Airplanes on the Roof*, Hwang's protagonist is stripped of ethnic identification. He or she (the role was designed to be played by either a man or a woman) is ill-at-ease in the ordinary world in which he presumably lives, constantly on the run from both the here-and-now, and a half-remembered encounter with extraterrestrials, a painful but transcendent event. An interview with a doctor allows him to disown all extraordinary elements in his life, frees him from the threat implied in recurrent lines ("It is better to forget. It is pointless to remember. No one will believe you. You will have spoken heresy. You will be outcast."), lets him see "only the glow of neon" in the sky but robs him of the sound like a thousand airplanes on the roof. Although the "science fiction music-drama" gives Hwang his most experimental vehicle to date, his text is largely a platitude about the contemporary sense of alienation. Neither his words nor Glass's music have the force or the imagination of Sirlin's design. Perhaps it is time for Hwang to jump (space)ship and get back to the land of broken promises and broken butterflies.

—Gerald Weales

See the essay on *M. Butterfly*.

I

INGE, William (Motter).

Born in Independence, Kansas, 3 May 1913. Educated at Montgomery County High School, Independence, graduated 1930; University of Kansas, Lawrence, 1930–35, A.B. 1935; Peabody Teachers College, Nashville, Tennessee, 1935–36, M.A. 1938; Yale University, New Haven, Connecticut, 1940. Announcer, KFH Radio, Wichita, Kansas, 1936–37; teacher at Columbus High School, Kansas, 1937–38, Stephens College, Columbia, Missouri, 1938–43, and Washington University, St. Louis, 1946–49; arts critic, St. Louis *Star-Times*, 1943–46; story consultant, *Bus Stop* television series, 1961–62; lecturer, University of North Carolina, Chapel Hill, 1969, and University of California, Irvine, 1970. Recipient: George Jean Nathan award, 1951; Pulitzer prize, 1953; New York Drama Critics Circle award, 1953; Donaldson award, 1953; Oscar, for screenplay, 1962. *Died 10 June 1973.*

Publications

PLAYS

The Dark at the Top of the Stairs (as *Farther Off from Heaven*, produced 1947; revised version, as *The Dark at the Top of the Stairs*, produced 1957). 1958.

Come Back, Little Sheba (produced 1950). 1950.

Picnic: A Summer Romance (produced 1953). 1953; revised version, as *Summer Brave* (produced 1962), in *Summer Brave and Eleven Short Plays*, 1962.

Bus Stop (produced 1955). 1955.

Glory in the Flower (produced 1959). In *24 Favorite One-Act Plays*, edited by Bennett Cerf and Van H. Cartmell, 1958.

Four Plays (includes *Come Back, Little Sheba; Picnic; Bus Stop; The Dark at the Top of the Stairs*). 1958.

The Tiny Closet (produced 1959). In *Summer Brave and Eleven Short Plays*, 1962.

A Loss of Roses (produced 1959). 1960.

Splendor in the Grass (screenplay). 1961.

Natural Affection (produced 1962). 1963.

Summer Brave (produced 1973). In *Summer Brave and Eleven Short Plays*, 1962.

Summer Brave and Eleven Short Plays (includes *To Bobolink, For Her Spirit; A Social Event; The Boy in the Basement; The Tiny Closet; Memory of*

Summer; The Rainy Afternoon; The Mall; An Incident at the Standish Arms; People in the Wind; Bus Riley's Back in Town; The Strains of Triumph). 1962.

Where's Daddy? (as Family Things, Etc., produced 1965; as Where's Daddy?, produced 1966). 1966.

The Disposal (as Don't Go Gentle, produced 1968; as The Last Pad, produced 1972). In Best Short Plays of the World Theatre 1958–1967, edited by Stanley Richards, 1968; revised version, as The Disposal, music by Anthony Caldarella, lyrics by Judith Gero (produced 1973).

The Call. In Two Short Plays, 1968.

A Murder. In Two Short Plays, 1968.

Midwestern Manic (produced as part of The Love Death Plays, 1975). In Best Short Plays 1969, edited by Stanley Richards, 1969.

Overnight (produced 1969).

Caesarian Operations (produced 1972).

Margaret's Bed. In Best Short Plays of the World Theatre 1968–1973, edited by Stanley Richards, 1973.

Love Death Plays: Dialogue for Two Men; Midwestern Manic; The Love Death; Venus and Adonis; The Wake; The Star (produced 1975).

Screenplays: Splendor in the Grass, 1961; All Fall Down, 1962; Bus Riley's Back in Town, 1965.

TELEVISION PLAYS: Out on the Outskirts of Town, 1964.

NOVELS

Good Luck, Miss Wyckoff. 1971.

My Son Is a Splendid Driver. 1972.

CRITICAL STUDIES: William Inge by R. Baird Shuman, 1966, revised edition, 1987; Memories of Splendor: The Midwestern World of William Inge by Arthur F. McClure, 1989; The Life of William Inge: The Strains of Triumph by Ralph F. Voss, 1989.

William Inge is the quintessential mid-20th century Midwestern American playwright. His reputation rests on four plays written during the 1950s: Come Back, Little Sheba; Picnic; Bus Stop; and The Dark at the Top of the Stairs. These dramas were among the most popular and critically acclaimed theatrical works in America during the playwright's lifetime, and they continue to be popular staples in repertory companies across the United States.

Inge's success lies primarily in his understanding of his audience. He consciously wrote plays for what is now called "Middle America", and his Midwest settings and characters express common perceptions held about that segment of the American population. He was not interested in dramatic experimentation or innovation in format or characterization. Inge's works focus on the narrow interests of an audience with little knowledge of, or concern for, world affairs: the world of Inge's audience is the world of a small town.

Inge chose characters and themes that his audience were familiar with, and to which they could relate easily. In *Come Back, Little Sheba*, a childless married couple, like George and Martha in Edward Albee's *Who's Afraid of Virginia Woolf?*, must face the reality of life. In *Picnic* Flo, Madge, Millie, Rosemary, and Helen are affected by the appearance of Hal, a sexually attractive man from outside the community. *Bus Stop* is a romantic comedy about a Montana cowboy and a Kansas City nightclub performer. In *The Dark at the Top of the Stairs*, a family confronts the small-town prejudices that lead to the suicide of the daughter's country-club dance partner, a young Jew. The one common element that runs through Inge's four major plays is his utilization of similar images to depict life in a small Midwestern town—images that reflect the setting itself, the character types, and the characters' thoughts.

Inge commented that *Come Back, Little Sheba*, which is set in "late spring", a time of hope and renewal, "was a fabric of life, in which the two characters (Doc and Lola) were a species of the environment". The inner strength of these two people under stress is demonstrated in actions reflecting their Midwestern American culture and its underlying beliefs and traditions.

Picnic contains many of the same common denominators that grow out of a small, Midwestern town setting. Hal Carter is perceived as a threat to the peaceful balance in the town because of the new ideas and experiences from the outside that he embodies. Ironically, one of Hal's motivations is the desire to establish a family, and the family is one of the most important elements in Midwestern society. It is significant that the action takes place on Labor Day, for holidays are important in the Midwest, and as a celebration of summer's end and the beginning of the harvest season the stereotypical picnic symbolically conveys the image of bourgeois values commonly associated with Midwesterners.

Another Midwestern locale, a restaurant/bus stop in a *"small Kansas town"*, is the setting of *Bus Stop*, and the characters are essentially Midwesterners in their attitudes and backgrounds. Again, the value placed on establishing a family is a major motivating force; Bo and Cherie can overcome Bo's uncivilized past and her unsavory career because of their desire to become a family. And, once more, the action takes place in the spring. As the storm that temporarily isolates those in the restaurant illustrates, this season can be very unsettled, yet ultimately it is a time of hope.

The family in a Midwestern context is the theme of *The Dark at the Top of the Stairs* too. By placing the Flood family's residence *"in a small Oklahoma town close to Oklahoma City"*, Inge juxtaposes two disparate cultures to demonstrate the strength of the traditional family. This strength is epitomized when Rubin and Cora reaffirm their love, and familial ties lead Cora's older sister to renew their relationship. Sammy Goldenbaum dies because he has neither family nor Midwestern traditions to sustain or support him.

Inge was the first American dramatist to gain prominence on the basis of his presentation of the people and philosophies of the Midwest. His solid but conventional plays are filled with images that reinforce his small-town themes in a positive, affectionate manner. He was successful in presenting to the world a limited but accurate picture of a specific people in a specific place at a specific time.

—Steven H. Gale

See the essay on *Picnic*.

INNAURATO, Albert.

Born in Philadelphia, Pennsylvania, 2 June 1947. Educated at Temple University, Philadelphia, B.A.; California Institute of the Arts, Valencia, B.F.A. 1972; Yale University School of Drama, New Haven, Connecticut, M.F.A. 1975. Playwright-in-residence, Playwrights Horizons, New York, 1983; adjunct professor, Columbia University, New York, and Princeton University, New Jersey, 1987. Recipient: Guggenheim grant, 1975; Rockefeller grant, 1977; Obie award, 1977; National Endowment for the Arts grant, 1986, 1989; Drama League award, 1987. Agent: George Lane, William Morris Agency, 1350 Avenue of the Americas, New York, New York 10019. Address: 325 West 22nd Street, New York, New York 10011, U.S.A.

Publications

PLAYS

Urlicht (produced 1971). In *Bizarre Behavior*, 1980.
I Don't Generally Like Poetry But Have You Read "Trees"?, with Christopher Durang (produced 1972).
The Life Story of Mitzi Gaynor; or, Gyp, with Christopher Durang (produced 1973).
The Transfiguration of Benno Blimpie (produced 1973). 1976.
The Idiots Karamazov, with Christopher Durang, music by Jack Feldman, lyrics by Durang (also director: produced 1974). 1974; augmented edition, 1981.
Earth Worms (produced 1974). In *Bizarre Behavior*, 1980.
Gemini (produced 1976). 1977.
Ulysses in Traction (produced 1977). 1978.
Passione (also director: produced 1980). 1981.
Bizarre Behavior: Six Plays (includes *Gemini, The Transfiguration of Benno Blimpie, Ulysses in Traction, Earth Worms, Urlicht, Wisdom Amok*). 1980.
Coming of Age in SoHo (also director: produced 1984; revised version produced 1985). 1985.
Best Plays (includes *Coming of Age in SoHo, The Transfiguration of Benno Blimpie, Gemini*). 1987.
Gus and Al (produced 1987). 1989.
Magda and Callas (produced 1988). 1989.

THEATRICAL ACTIVITIES

DIRECTOR: Plays—*The Idiots Karamazov*, 1974; *Passione*, 1980; *The Transfiguration of Benno Blimpie*, 1983; *Herself as Lust*, 1983; *Coming of Age in SoHo*, 1984.
ACTOR: Play—*I Don't Generally Like Poetry But Have You Read "Trees"?*, 1973.

In his Introduction to his collection of plays *Bizarre Behavior* the extraordinarily talented Albert Innaurato expresses understandable annoyance at the frequency with which critics misunderstand his plays or insist upon discussing connections between them. But to misread is always the critic's risk and to search out the connections, when they do indeed exist, one of his obligations.

When considered together, Innaurato's individual plays delineate, as the work of such an important and promising dramatist must, a unique, powerfully held vision of the human condition. This vision is characterized by the skillful manipulation of vividly contrasting dramatic elements that ignite the plays' tensions and yield to their reconciliations. Most prominent among these are satiric farce, comedy, and pathos; the beauty-and-the-beast combination of the grotesque and the beautiful; and the religious and the blasphemous. Among a rather extensive list of more specific dualities are his characters' outward appearances and contrasting inner realities; their often "bizarre behavior" and their rather different inner impulses; and a frequent doubling of times and places that parallel these dichotomies of character and action. Innaurato also explores the psychological terrain of sexual ambiguity, seems to exploit aspects of the disease of overeating, bulimia, with the necessary purgation, here Aristotelian rather than Roman-orgy in nature, and from music borrows the concepts of aria and counterpoint.

The multiple dualities of *Gemini*, his most commercially successful play, with a run of over four years at a small Broadway house, are indicated by the title from which the hero Francis Geminiani, "plump" and "a little clumsy," derives his name. At the time of his 21st birthday, his fellow Harvard students, the attractive and very WASP Judith Hastings and her freshman younger brother, arrive for an unexpected visit to his Italian and Catholic South Philadelphia home. At his symbolic coming of age, climaxed by a disastrous birthday feast, Francis is forced to investigate openly his inner life and to admit that he is attracted emotionally not only to the sister but to her brother as well. But despite the potential pathos of the central situation, as Harvard and South Philadelphia, his college friends and his overfed, rough-talking, but good-hearted neighbors collide, the results are a raucous comic festival, as lively as an Italian street *festa* and funnier than anything Neil Simon could devise. In *Passione* Innaurato returns to South Philadelphia to explore the emotional problems of a middle-aged couple and to contrast the parents with their happy son, a clown, who is incongruously married to the fat lady of the circus.

Innaurato's most recent, more interesting, and less successful play *Coming of Age in SoHo* is a kind of counterpart or sequel to *Gemini* and brings to the foreground some of its preoccupations. The hero Bartholomew Dante has left his wife to write in a loft in SoHo and like his predecessor also comes of age, this time at 36. There is again much wild humor, triggered here by his wife's South Philadelphia family headed by her father, the Mafia don Cumbar' Antonio, and the unexpected entrance of three boys, the brothers Odysseus ("WASP culture") and Trajan from St. Paul's and Harvard, and his own forgotten son Puer, the result of a long-ago affair with a German terrorist. But the play's intent is serious. The brothers with their classical names, poor Puer ("boy" and the *puer* complex) who seeks a brother and finds his father, and the Dante-Beatrice allusions index the play's assemblage of elements of what might be called the *gemini* concept: the linkage of narcissism, dual or ambivalent identity, and creativity. Aspects of this concept underlie Albee's much earlier *The American Dream* and are present in the plays of Peter Shaffer, particularly *Equus*.

But the brilliant, darkly beautiful *The Transfiguration of Benno Blimpie*, Innaurato's finest work thus far, belongs to a differently imagined South

Philadelphia than *Gemini* and is more characteristic of his other plays. The fat, unattractive Benno, with his delicate inner life, is eating himself to death. As he controls the play's dramatic time, he comments upon and verbally participates in scenes of his past emotional yearnings and rejections. The play ends with a startling cannibalistic image as Benno, before the quick black-out, "*lowers the meat cleaver as though to cut off some part of himself.*"

The same dark intensity is present in *Earth Worms*, one of the most widly imaginative plays by any recent dramatist. Arnold Longese, the sexually ambiguous hero, manages to beget a child with a country girl from the south. He brings her back to South Philadelphia, and there they are surrounded by his blind grandmother who lives on the floor, two transvestites, and a group of hustlers. At the end of the play the grandmother dies, the family home is becoming a whorehouse, and the hero is mutilated by three vindictive nuns. Ingredients for an unintended comedy? Perhaps. But here they combine into Magritte-like fragments of a vivid tragicomic nightmare. The short play *Urlicht* belongs to a similar dramatic world, features outrageously comic religious situations, and is peopled in part by incongruous nuns.

Innaurato's plays clearly make allusions to his awareness of the grandeur and comedy of the classical past. *Gemini* and *Ulysses in Traction*, with its implications of inhibited enterprise, make the suggestions in their titles; the mad nuns who become like giant cockroaches as they swarm over the hero of *Earth Worms* recall the Furies. But in their effects the plays bring to mind that modern gothic playwright Michel de Ghelderode, and they seem more properly gothic and medieval. Francis in *Gemini* and Arnold in *Earth Worms* wander like modern everymen through their distorted worlds, and Innaurato's most memorable characters resemble frightening or wildly comic gargoyles. But in familiar phrases from Shakespeare and Yeats, most of his characters have "that within which passeth show": they have Dionysus's "beating heart" rather than stone "in the midst of all."

—Gaynor F. Bradish

J

JENKIN, Len (Leonard Jenkin).

Born in New York City, 2 April 1941. Educated at Columbia University, New York, 1958–63, 1969–71, B.A. in English 1962, M.A. 1963, Ph.D. in English 1972. Has one daughter. Lecturer in English, Brooklyn College, New York, 1965–66; associate professor of English, Manhattan Community College, 1967–79. Since 1980 associate professor, Tisch School of the Arts, New York University. Since 1983 associate artistic director, River Arts Repertory Company, Woodstock, New York. Recipient: Yaddo fellowship, 1975; National Endowment for the Arts fellowship, 1979, 1982; Rockefeller fellowship, 1980; Christopher award, 1981; American Film Festival award, 1981; Creative Artists Public Service grant, 1981; Obie award, 1981 (for writing and directing), 1984; MacDowell fellowship, 1984; Guggenheim fellowship, 1987. Agent: Scott Hudson, Writers and Artists Agency, 19 West 44th Street, Suite 1000, New York, New York 10036, U.S.A.

Publications

PLAYS

Kitty Hawk (produced 1972).
Grand American Exhibition (produced 1973).
The Death and Life of Jesse James (produced 1974).
Mission (produced 1975).
Gogol: A Mystery Play (also director: produced 1976). In *Theatre of Wonders: Six Contemporary American Plays*, edited by Mac Wellman, 1986.
Kid Twist (produced 1977).
New Jerusalem (produced 1979).
Limbo Tales (includes *Highway, Hotel, Intermezzo*) (also director: produced 1980). 1982.
Five of Us (produced 1981). 1986.
Dark Ride (also director: produced 1981). 1982.
Candide; or, Optimism, adaptation of the novel by Voltaire (produced 1982). 1983.
A Country Doctor, adaptation of a story by Kafka (also director: produced 1983).
My Uncle Sam (also director: produced 1984). 1984.
Madrigal Opera, music by Philip Glass (produced 1985).
American Notes (also director: produced 1986). 1988.

A Soldier's Tale, adaptation of a libretto by Ramuz, music by Stravinsky (produced 1986).
Poor Folks Pleasure (also director: produced 1987).
Pilgrims of the Night (also director: produced 1991).

SCREENPLAYS: *Merlin and Melinda*, 1977; *Blame It on the Night*, 1985; *Welcome to Oblivion*, 1989; *Nickel Dreams*, 1992.

TELEVISION PLAYS: *More Things in Heaven and Earth*, 1976, and *See-Saw*, 1977 (*Family* series); *Road Show* (*Visions* series), 1976; *Eye of the Needle* (*Quincy* series), 1977; *Games of Chance* (*Incredible Hulk* series), 1979; *Family of Strangers*, 1980; *Days and Nights of Molly Dodd*, 1989.

NOVEL
New Jerusalem. 1986.

OTHER
Editor, with Leonard Allison and Robert Perrault, *Survival Printout*. 1973.

THEATRICAL ACTIVITIES
DIRECTOR: some of his own plays.

Len Jenkin comments:

I always like the opening: the houselights fade, the room goes black, the voices around me quiet, the first lights come up in the toybox, and the figures start to move.

Once that's over, for something to hold me, as author or audience, there needs to be a continuing sense of *wonder*, as powerful as that in fairy tales, moonlight, or dreams. This can be present in any sort of work for the stage—realistic to sublimely outrageous—and it's a quality that can't be fused into or onto something with clever staging or sideways performances. It's gotta be there, in the text and through and through.

The other thing that needs to be there for what I'd consider to be "Theatre" to exist is what I call *heart*. This doesn't mean I want to look at people struggling bravely through their emotional problems. It means that the author is not primarily an entertainer; that he/she is instead a preacher, and a singer, and a human being. And that the deep twined nature of what binds us and what makes us free is going to be out there on the stage.

I want to see theatre energetically stomping around the U.S.A. and the rest of the world. Put on plays by the highway side. I want to see tractor-trailers full of men in hats and beautiful women, pulling into town and setting up on the high school football field. I'll be glad to be in the cab of the first truck in line—the one that says "ALIVE" in a bullet on its side.

In *American Notes* one character might be speaking of almost any of Len Jenkin's characters when he says, "You have fallen through an American crack, and them is deep." Another says, "You know, there's a lot of people who think their life is what happens to them. Get a job, get married, eat an ice cream cone. It's a great life. There's another kind of people who don't connect what happens to them with their lives at all. Their life is something else . . . hopefully."   It is about the latter that Jenkin writes. Yearning for something outside their lives, his characters are interested in the sleazy dreams offered by supermarket tabloids and carnival pitchmen, and in extraterrestrial beings. *American Notes* is more than an *Our Town* of the current rural depression for, as in most of Jenkin's plays, the characters are isolated beings, who are as likely to address the audience in monologues as engage with other characters.

The central characters of *Gogol*, *Five of Us*, and *Dark Ride* are all artists of a kind: a playwright, a writer who is more successful at writing pornographic romances pseudonymously than the artistic novel in his desk drawer, the translator of a meaningless and maybe fake Chinese mystical work. Journalists, would-be writers, and an ex-director of slasher films haunt the margins of his plays. Other purveyors of dreams are the salesmen, offering encyclopedias, love potions, views of the crocodile Bonecrusher, or novelties to trick and surprise people. This last salesman, the eponymous Uncle Sam, might speak for Jenkin when he says "These gags break the rules in people's heads. If there weren't any rules, I'd be outta business." Jenkin plays with theatrical conventions and seems to disclaim any deeper intentions. As 10 characters repeat, one after another, at the end of *Dark Ride*, "I'm not interested in philosophy. Just tell me how it ends." But, as Jenkin's epigraph to *American Notes*, from Blake's "America: A Prophecy," suggests, "Tho' obscur'd, this is the form/Of the Angelic land," his plays are driven by deeper concerns, spelled out most clearly in *American Notes*:

> Last few weeks, I've seen a lot of dreams with my eyes open, just riding down the road. I drive through these towns, one after the other, and they all got a main street, and on it is a place to buy groceries, Food Town—a place to eat, Marv's Broiler—and a place to get fucked-up, Hi-Hat tavern. And when you go through these places in America, the question is always "Anybody home?" The answer is obvious. No. Basically, there is nobody home in America, Pauline. Except you.
>
> There are people out there, after all. They go way back, and they came outta the sky and the dirt, just like us. And they got secrets, just like us.

His plays commonly center upon quests, presented wryly—even mockingly—as what might be called *drames noirs*.

Gogol, *Dark Ride*, and *My Uncle Sam* all portray rather absurd quests in which gangsters or the police dog the footsteps of the central character as he stumbles toward an unclear goal. And most of the decidedly unreligious pilgrims of *Pilgrims of the Night* who wait through the night at a ferry terminal in the middle of nowhere, are hoping to contact extraterrestrials who are reported to have crashed in the forest across the river. All these plays have narrator figures and an episodic structure full of seedy eccentrics who typically offer the audience an introductory account of themselves. *My Uncle Sam*, one of the most fascinating of Jenkin's plays, has various levels of commentary upon the action: from the Author; from his Uncle Sam in old age; from Sam when young and on his quest; from an audio cassette from the Universal Detective Agency that instructs him step by step; and from a series of

Narrators dressed appropriately for the successive settings. His version of *Candide*, which might be described as an un-quest play, has an equally elaborate set of narrative devices and characters. In both *Candide* and *Gogol* a play within the play is presented; in *Pilgrims of the Night* the characters arrange to while away the night by telling stories, which we see enacted.

This overt, sometimes flamboyant, theatricality brings a joyousness or aesthetic pleasure that gives the audience something of that transfiguring experience whose want his characters unconsciously or consciously feel. For example, in "Hotel," one of his *Limbo Tales*, a "starved, stalled, and stranded" salesman talks to the audience in his hotel room. On either side of him are the other two rooms with only a large audio speaker in each: from one we hear a writer painfully composing "Kubla Khan," interrupted not by a person from Porlock but by a lightning-rod salesman, and from the other a teenage drug-addict who is visited by acquaintances who leave with her last 20 dollars. And yet the salesman gets a phone call from his dead father; before he leaves to avoid eviction he quotes the Bible, "For ye shall go out with joy, and be led forth with peace: the mountains and the hills shall break forth before you into singing, and all the trees of the field shall clap their hands"; and finally, with his room and the stage empty, we see the shadow of a dove briefly on the windowshade and hear the writer begin to type again. Like *Waiting for Godot*, Jenkin's plays are about the inability of man not to hope.

—Anthony Graham-White

K

KALCHEIM, Lee.

Born in Philadelphia, Pennsylvania, 27 June 1938. Educated at Trinity College, Hartford, Connecticut, B.A.; Yale University School of Drama, New Haven, Connecticut, one year. Recipient: Rockefeller grant, 1965; Emmy award, 1973. Agent: Susan Schulman, 454 West 44th Street, New York, New York 10036. Address: RD #2, West Center Road, West Stockbridge, Massachusetts 01266, U.S.A.

Publications

PLAYS

A Party for Divorce (produced 1963).
Match Play (produced 1964). In *New Theatre in America*, edited by Edward Parone, 1965.
. . . And the Boy Who Came to Leave (produced 1965). In *Playwrights for Tomorrow 2*, edited by Arthur H. Ballet, 1966.
An Audible Sigh (produced 1968).
The Surprise Party (produced 1970).
Who Wants to Be the Lone Ranger (produced 1971).
Hurry, Harry, with Jeremiah Morris and Susan Perkis, music by Bill Weeden, lyrics by David Finkle (produced 1972).
Prague Spring (produced 1975).
Win with Wheeler (produced 1975). 1984.
Winning Isn't Everything (produced 1978).
Breakfast with Les and Bess (produced 1983). 1984.
Friends (produced 1984; also director: revised version, produced 1989).
Moving (produced 1991). 1991.
The Tuesday Side of the Street (produced 1991).

TELEVISION PLAYS: *Reunion*, 1967; *Let's Get a Closeup of the Messiah*, 1969; *Trick or Treat*, 1970; *All in the Family* series, 1971–72; *Is (This) Marriage Really Necessary*, 1972; *The Class of '63*, 1973; *The Bridge of Adam Rush*, 1974; *The Comedy Company*, 1978; *Marriage Is Alive and Well*, 1980.

Lee Kalcheim comments:

I am a realist. So, my plays are realistic. Comic. Dramatic. Strongly based on characters. I grew up with the realistic writers of the 1950s. Found myself sitting in the middle of the avant garde movement with an inherited style. And then as the theatre began to be less faddish (in New York) it became apparent that I could indeed maintain my love of character—of reality—and survive as a playwright. My work in improvisational theatre and film began to broaden my work. My later work became more fragmented or film like. Less . . . livingroomish. But I realized that for all the excitement of theatrical effects (I have tried various experiments with mixed media), the thing that still moved me most, standing in rehearsal watching my plays, were those one to one scenes. Those scenes where two people faced each other, wanting something from each other. Those scenes where something happened between people. They washed out all the media effects, or unusual transitions, or whatever. They were theatre at its strongest. And I suppose I keep coming back to those in my plays. I do write film. But I keep coming back to the theatre for the excitement of those live, vibrant scenes—that put flesh and blood out there in front of you.

"It makes me very sad and very happy to be a playwright," was Lee Kalcheim's answer to a request for a statement which could introduce this piece about him. It serves well. Kalcheim is indeed a melancholy and a joyful chronicler. But what made him almost unique among the American dramatists of his generation was his ability to bustle, hustle, and earn his own way *as a writer*. While most "young playwrights" are weaving their tortured ways through the mazes of foundations and endowments and theatre boards seeking grants, honoraria, subsistences, and other encouraging hand-outs, Kalcheim energetically and quite successfully went into the *business* of writing.

He has a good mind and that intelligence which reflects both cool observations and warm insights into the characters he creates. More than storytelling, Kalcheim is people-telling. His plays, he says, are about "human ideas": as a playwright he is less concerned with the usual ideas *per se* than he is with the humanness of those ideas, with the humanity which generates those ideas.

Moreover, as even a quick reading or viewing of his work for the stage reveals, Kalcheim is fascinated by human loneliness. What for other, more abstract writers is a concern with the condition of loneliness, for Kalcheim becomes both a compassionate and an uninvolved concern for the human being as an alone creature: yes, both passionate and uninvolved, both sad and happy. People trying—desperately, lazily, sadly, hopefully, hilariously, pathetically, ridiculously—to make contact with other people is what his plays not only are but are about.

At the end of *An Audible Sigh*, one of the characters, Gale, says, "You see . . . I want to be loved, but I don't want to have strings attached." And there, indeed, is the rub. Kalcheim's people are lonely, loving but afraid of being loved and even of being un-lonely. They sometimes seem to enjoy their loneliness and find sanctuary in their states of not being loved. Driven in part by fear of being possessed and by desire to possess, the characters are intensely vulnerable. Their bulwarks seem all terribly sturdy and well-planned but facing in the wrong direction.

In play after play, Kalcheim examines these qualities. Even more personally, he exhibits a unique ability to watch and be part of the action, *and* to double the effect, to watch the watchers (himself included) and the actors. Again and again, Kalcheim seems to be writing much the same play—each time in a different guise but each time about the same qualities, sensibilities. If these feelings and events are indeed his own experiences (love, divorce, joining, separation, regret, hope, need, fear, tenacity, escape), he is quite excellent at turning that experience into theatrical action, because Kalcheim the writer is a very astute observer of Kalcheim the man.

Moreover, his technique works unusually well: he juxtaposes comedy and drama with almost metronomic regularity, but at the critical heart of the matter is a much more important and profound juxtaposition: The Fear of Death poised against An Immortality Assured, if one may capitalize such sentiments any more.

Kalcheim has been writing since he was eleven years old, and he says that when his first playlet was produced, he wept at the recognition of his own voice "up there." If he has turned now more and more to film and television to earn a living, his first and enduring love is perhaps not a person (ironically) but the theatre. As with many media writers, Kalcheim plays the game of running down his own television writing, but nonetheless he speaks with justified pride about the way his voice is now heard "up there."

—Arthur H. Ballet

KANIN, Garson.

Born in Rochester, New York, 24 November 1912. Educated at local schools to age 15; attended American Academy of Dramatic Arts, New York, 1932–33. Served in the U.S. Army Signal Corps, 1941–42; private; Air Force, 1942–43, and the Office of Strategic Services, 1943–45; captain, on Staff on SHAEF (European Theatre Operations). Married the actress and playwright Ruth Gordon in 1942 (died 1985). Jazz musician, Western Union messenger, stock boy and advertising proofreader at Macy's, New York, burlesque comedian, and summer camp social director, 1929–32; assistant to the playwright and director George Abbott, q.v., 1935–37; radio interviewer and actor; on production staff, Samuel Goldwyn Productions, Hollywood, 1937–38. Since 1938 freelance director and producer: formed Kanin Productions, 1967. Recipient: New York Film Critics Circle award, 1945; Oscar, for documentary, 1946; Sidney Howard Memorial award, 1946; Donaldson award, for play and direction, 1946; American Academy of Dramatic Arts award of achievement, 1958; New York Public Library Literary Lion award, 1985; elected to the Theater Hall of Fame, 1985. Agent: William Morris Agency, 1350 Avenue of the Americas, New York, New York 10019. Address: 200 West 57th Street, New York, New York 10019, U.S.A.

Publications

PLAYS

Born Yesterday (also director: produced 1946). 1946.
The Smile of the World (also director: produced 1949). 1949.
The Rat Race (also director: produced 1949). 1950.
The Live Wire (also director: produced 1950). 1951.

The Amazing Adèle, adaptation of a play by Pierre Barillet and Jean-Pierre Grédy (also director: produced 1950).

Fledermaus, adaptation of the libretto by Haffner and Genée, music by Johann Strauss, lyrics by Howard Dietz (also director: produced 1950). 1950.

The Good Soup, adaptation of a play by Félicien Marceau (also director: produced 1960).

Do Re Mi, music by Jule Styne, lyrics by Betty Comden and Adolph Green, adaptation of his own novel (also director: produced 1960).

A Gift of Time, adaptation of *Death of a Man* by Lael Tucker Wertenbaker (also director: produced 1962). 1962.

Come on Strong, based on his own stories (also director: produced 1962). 1964.

Remembering Mr. Maugham, adaptation of his own book (produced 1966).

Adam's Rib, with Ruth Gordon (screenplay). 1972.

Dreyfus in Rehearsal, adaptation of a play by Jean-Claude Grumberg (also director: produced 1974). 1983.

Peccadillo (also director: produced 1985).

Happy Ending (also director: produced 1989).

SCREENPLAYS: *Woman of the Year* (uncredited), 1942; *The More the Merrier* (uncredited), 1943; *From This Day Forward*, with Hugo Butler, 1946; *Born Yesterday* (uncredited), 1950; *It Should Happen to You*, 1953; *The Girl Can't Help It*, with Frank Tashlin and Herbert Baker, 1957; *The Rat Race*, 1960; *High Time*, 1960; *Where It's At*, 1969; *Some Kind of a Nut*, 1969; with Ruth Gordon—*A Double Life*, 1947; *Adam's Rib*, 1949; *The Marrying Kind*, 1952; *Pat and Mike*, 1952.

TELEVISION PLAYS: *An Eye on Emily, Something to Sing About*, and *The He-She Chemistry* (*Mr. Broadway* series), 1963–64; *Josie and Joe; Hardhat and Legs*, with Ruth Gordon, 1980; *Scandal*, 1980.

NOVELS

Do Re Mi. 1955.
Blow Up a Storm. 1959.
The Rat Race. 1960.
Where It's At. 1969.
A Thousand Summers. 1973.
One Hell of an Actor. 1976.
Moviola: A Hollywood Saga. 1979.
Smash. 1980.
Cordelia? 1982.

SHORT STORIES

Cast of Characters: Stories of Broadway and Hollywood. 1969.

OTHER

Remembering Mr. Maugham. 1966.
Tracy and Hepburn: An Intimate Memoir. 1971.
Hollywood: Stars and Starlets, Tycoons and Flesh-Peddlers, Movie-Makers

and Moneymakers, Frauds and Geniuses, Hopefuls and Has-Beens, Great Lovers and Sex Symbols. 1974.
It Takes a Long Time to Become Young. 1978.
Together Again! The Stories of the Great Hollywood Teams. 1981; as *Great Hollywood Teams*, 1982.

THEATRICAL ACTIVITIES

DIRECTOR: **Plays**—assistant director, to George Abbott, of *Three Men on a Horse* by Abbott and John Cecil Holm, 1935, *Boy Meets Girl* by Bella and Sam Spewack, 1935, *Brother Rat* by John Monks, Jr., and Fred F. Finklehoffe, 1936, and *Room Service* by John Murray and Allen Boretz, 1937; director of *Hitch Your Wagon* by Sidney Holloway, 1937; *Too Many Heroes* by Dore Schary, 1937; *The Ragged Path* by Robert E. Sherwood, 1945; *Years Ago* by Ruth Gordon, 1946; *Born Yesterday*, 1946; *How I Wonder* by Donald Ogden Stewart, 1947; *The Leading Lady* by Ruth Gordon, 1948; *The Smile of the World*, 1949; *The Rat Race*, 1949; *The Amazing Adèle*, 1950; *The Live Wire*, 1950; *Fledermaus*, 1950, 1966; *Into Thin Air* by Chester Erskine, 1955; *The Diary of Anne Frank* by Frances Goodrich and Albert Hackett, 1955; *Small War on Murray Hill* by Robert E. Sherwood, 1957; *A Hole in the Head* by Arnold Schulman, 1957; *The Good Soup*, 1960; *Do Re Mi*, 1960, 1961; *Sunday in New York* by Norman Krasna, 1961; *A Gift of Time*, 1962; *Come On Strong*, 1962; *Funny Girl* by Isobel Lennart, 1964; *I Was Dancing* by Edwin O'Connor, 1964; *A Very Rich Woman* by Ruth Gordon, 1964; *We Have Always Lived in the Castle* by Hugh Wheeler, 1966; *Remembering Mr. Maugham*, 1969; *Idiot's Delight* by Robert E. Sherwood, 1970; *Dreyfus in Rehearsal*, 1974; *Ho! Ho! Ho!* by Ruth Gordon, 1976; *Peccadillo*, 1985. **Films**—*A Man to Remember*, 1938; *Next Time I Marry*, 1938; *The Great Man Votes*, 1939; *Bachelor Mother*, 1939; *My Favorite Wife*, 1940; *They Knew What They Wanted*, 1940; *Tom, Dick and Harry*, 1941; *Night Shift*, *Fellow Americans*, and *Ring of Steel* (documentaries), 1942; *Woman of the Year*, 1942; *German Manpower* (documentary), 1943; *Night Stripes* (documentary), 1944; *Battle Stations* (documentary), 1944; *A Salute to France* (*Salut à France*) (documentary), with Jean Renoir, 1944; *The True Glory* (documentary), with Carol Reed, 1945; *Where It's At*, 1969; *Some Kind of Nut*, 1969. **Television**—*Born Yesterday*, 1956.
ACTOR: **Plays**—Tommy Deal in *Little Ol' Boy* by Albert Bein, 1933; Young Man in *Spring Song* by Bella and Sam Spewack, 1934; Red in *Ladies' Money* by George Abbott, 1934; Al in *Three Men on a Horse* by George Abbott and John Cecil Holm, 1935; Izzy Cohen in *The Body Beautiful* by Robert Rossen, 1935; Green in *Boy Meets Girl* by Bella and Sam Spewack, 1935; Vincent Chenevski in *Star Spangled* by Robert Ardrey, 1936; Garson Kanin in *Remembering Mr. Maugham*, 1969. **Film**—*Bachelor Mother*, 1939. **Radio**—*March of Times* news re-enactments, *The Goldbergs*, *Aunt Jenny's Real Life Stories*, *The Theatre Guild on the Air*, *Five-Star Final*, *The NBC Theatre*, *The Honeymooners*—*Grace and Eddie*, 1935–37.

Born Yesterday is conventionally cited as Garson Kanin's only commercial and critical success, his only twin birth. The other plays are either dismissed utterly or damned with faint praise. But such a division into the worthwhile and the worthless assumes both that the number of times a writer can earn money and praise matters definitively, and that an accomplishment must be repeatable to be substantial. That *Born Yesterday* is great drama cannot be argued conclusively. But to argue that its quality seems anomalous and, therefore, negligible begs the question rather than answering it. (In this respect, the anomalies are the Arthur Millers and the Neil Simons.) When Harry Brock, king junk dealer and influence-strongman, and his floozie, Billie Dawn, meet Paul Verrall, *New Republic* reporter, in the nation's capital, a dose of culture makes a "dumb blonde" wise and a powerful "low-life" weak. The combined force of the embattled ideals of the American Revolution and the reality of love defeat post-war domestic corruption in the same way that the force of democracy had just defeated Nazi Germany, Fascist Italy, and Imperial Japan. Kanin brings the higher, eminently practical yet optimistic lessons of the war home.

Played today, his play reveals, among other things, that 50 years of *The New Republic* and other "popular" voices have not managed to restrain plutocracy in Washington. *Born Yesterday* can be seen as the post-war theatrical analog of *Mr. Smith Goes to Washington*; we feel a similar vindication of the small people, especially since the United States and the Allies had won a famous victory. But when Ed Devery (a former Assistant U.S. Attorney General gone to seed) toasts the "dumb chumps and all the crazy broads, past, present, and future—who thirst for knowledge—and search for truth. . . . and civilize each other—and make it so tough for sons-of-bitches like you [the bribed Senator Hedges]—and you [Brock]—and me," we are embarrassed at the extreme ironies we hear in the word "broads," and in the phrases "civilize each other," and "make it so tough." That world isn't this world, and the difference obtains as much in the national life and character as in the dramatic literature. Paul and Billie did—and would continue to—"make it tough" for the Brocks and their cronies, and audiences and readers could be assured that the balance of power had shifted *representatively* in *Born Yesterday*. Hitler and Mussolini had been joined by Brock, Devery, and Hedges on the junkpile of history. We know different—and differently. Kanin catches the innocence of a people victorious and generous, a condition of mind almost wholly lacking and a state of the nation almost wholly nostalgic now. *Born Yesterday* is a period piece which reconstitutes American's original brash promise and it does so with real humor and point. After all, Judy Holliday became a *bona fide* star in *Born Yesterday* and her brief, brilliant career can be said to form a counterpart to the brief and brilliant career of the Billie Dawns and Paul Verralls; in retrospect, Kanin's *brilliant* career lasted about as long. The first flush of peace seems to have conferred a hard-won yet easy freedom which the 1950s and 1960s continually wore away. Kanin's highest achievement took place while peace was becoming the Cold War and once that time settled in, his special command of a time of innocence lost its relevance.

As a man of the working theatre, Kanin (actor, director, playwright) knew its special requirements; that he succeeded in Hollywood as well as in New York testifies to *working* knowledge. The popular theatre lives by such versatile, common, and regular talents. Yet acting, directing, and writing for the stage should not be so described, except relatively since almost no one manages to sustain over 40 years a career, let alone careers, in show business. To manage it argues something uncommon and extraordinary. And Kanin managed it. Practical lessons are best learned not from works of genius but from works of the accomplished; the commercial theatre needs productive perseverance of the kind Kanin lived by, not simply in terms of continuity but energy and creativity, too. *Born Yesterday* belongs to the grand tradition of Broadway comedy, just as Kanin belongs four-square to the grand tradition of Broadway.

His later plays such as *The Rat Race* and *A Gift of Time* fall short of *Born Yesterday*'s standard, offering little but schematic plots and clichéd dialogue. By this time, however, Kanin had basically left writing for a stage he had been apparently in process of leaving for some years. He spent much of his effort in directing plays by others and in writing essays and fiction. Judging a dramatist involves assessing the ongoing exigencies of the theatre to which the play is offered. Demands which emphasize commercial viability impose curious restrictions on playwrights. Producing texts of high aesthetic or social merit often seems irreconcilable with producing scripts of high earning potential.

—Thomas Apple

KENNEDY, Adrienne (Lita, née Hawkins).

Born in Pittsburgh, Pennsylvania, 13 September 1931; grew up in Cleveland, Ohio. Educated in Cleveland public schools; Ohio State University, Columbus, B.A. in education 1953; Columbia University, New York, 1954–56. Married Joseph C. Kennedy in 1953 (divorced 1966); two sons. Joined Edward Albee's workshop in 1962. Lecturer in play- writing, Yale University, New Haven, Connecticut, 1972–74, Princeton University, New Jersey, 1977, and Brown University, Providence, Rhode Island, 1979–80; chancellor's distinguished lecturer, University of California, Berkeley, 1986. Member of the Board of Directors, PEN, 1976–77. Recipient: Obie award, 1965; Guggenheim fellowship, 1967; Rockefeller grant, 1967, 1969, 1973; New England Theatre Conference grant; National Endowment for the Arts grant, 1972; CBS-Yale University fellowship, 1973; Creative Artists Public Service grant, 1974. Agent: Bridget Aschenberg, 40 West 57th Street, New York, New York 10019. Address: 325 West 89th Street, New York, New York 10024, U.S.A.

Publications

PLAYS

Funnyhouse of a Negro (produced 1964). 1969.
The Owl Answers (produced 1965). In *Cities in Bezique*, 1969.
A Beast's Story (produced 1965). In *Cities in Bezique*, 1969.
A Rat's Mass (produced 1966). In *New Black Playwrights*, edited by William Couch, Jr., 1968.
The Lennon Play: In His Own Write, with John Lennon and Victor Spinetti, adaptation of works by Lennon (produced 1967; revised version produced 1968). 1968.
A Lesson in Dead Language (produced 1968). In *Collision Course*, 1968.
Boats (produced 1969).

Sun: A Poem for Malcolm X Inspired by His Murder (produced 1969). In
   Scripts 1, November 1971.
Cities in Bezique: 2 One-Act Plays: The Owl Answers and A Beast's Story.
   1969.
An Evening with Dead Essex (produced 1973).
A Movie Star Has to Star in Black and White (produced 1976). In *Wordplays*
   3, 1984.
Orestes and *Electra* (produced 1980). In *In One Act*, 1988.
Black Children's Day (produced 1980).
A Lancashire Lad (for children; produced 1980).
Solo Voyages (includes excerpts from her previous plays; produced 1985).
In One Act (includes *Funnyhouse of a Negro, The Owl Answers, A Lesson in*
   Dead Language, A Rat's Mass, Sun, A Movie Star Has to Star in Black and
   White, Electra, Orestes). 1988.
The Ohio State Murders (produced 1990).
She Talks and Beethoven: 2 One-Act Plays. In *Antaeus*, no.66, Spring 1991.

OTHER
People Who Led to My Plays (memoirs). 1987.
Deadly Triplets: A Theatre Mystery and Journal. 1990.
The Alexander Plays. 1992.

Adrienne Kennedy comments:

My plays are meant to be states of mind.

As black power gathered strength in America in the 1960s, the dramatist
Adrienne Kennedy, who is black, was discovering more uses for the word
Negro. She marks the beginnings of celebratory blackness with *Funnyhouse of*
a Negro in which a woman's personal history of miscegenation, rape, and
madness inscribes the larger history of black experience in white America, a
history that Americans now sanitize and democratize under the rubric "race
relations." Kennedy makes no totalizing claims to represent anyone, but the
play's motifs resonate sharply in collective history.
   In her New York apartment, Kennedy's "Negro-Sarah" enshrines an enormous statue of Queen Victoria and, in the course of the play, splits into a
hunchbacked Jesus, the Duchess of Hapsburg, the African liberation leader
Patrice Lumumba, and even Queen Victoria—each denoted as "One of
Herselves." This is history and identity in a funnyhouse of distorted mirrors
whose reflections are as unthinkable in racist America emerging from the
1950s as Sarah herself, child of a light-skinned black woman supposedly raped
by her missionary black husband in Africa. Slowly Sarah's incarnations emerge
from darkness to narrate bits of the original trauma: the missionary zeal of the
father who "wanted the black man to rise from colonialism," the mother who
"didn't want him to save the black race and spent her days combing her hair
. . . and would not let him touch her in their wedding bed and called him
black," the daughter conceived in violence, who rejects the father but re-

sembles him and watches her mother lapse into madness, then death, the remembered sign for which is hair falling out.

Throughout the play, shining hairless skulls appear in dialogue and enacted fantasy until Sarah tries to stifle her father's (and her race's) claim on her by bludgeoning him with an ebony mask. Yet he returns: "He keeps returning forever, coming back ever and keeps coming back forever." Sarah's white friends whose (Victorian) culture "keep [her] from reflecting too much upon the fact that [she is] a Negro" cannot protect her from this returning and recurring repressed racial memory, signified by the repeated sound of knocking and the obsessively repeated images of fallen hair, kinky and straight, on a white pillow; of yellowness, the sickly white color of Sarah's skin; of swarming ravens and of death's-heads. The expressionistic funnyhouse of Sarah's memory defies linear logic. Her father hangs himself—or does not—in two versions of the story, but the last play image shows Sarah herself hanged, reclaimed by the jungle that engulfs the stage. Sarah's split subjectivity bears the scars of Afro-American history; her identification with her m ther and murderous repression of her father's culture engage the discourses of feminism and psychoanalysis, and reveal the desire and exclusion embodied in Kennedy's "Negro."

The Owl Answers brilliantly extends these issues through the laminated identities of Kennedy's protagonist, She who is Clara Passmore who is the Virgin Mary who is the Bastard who is the Owl, whose history generates another violently skewed family romance, this time with a poor black mother and the "Richest White Man in the Town." Gradually a story emerges of a bastard daughter of miscegenous union, adopted by the Reverend Passmore, renamed Clara, but who carries her black mother's color and a passion for her white father's culture, "the England of dear Chaucer, Dickens and dearest Shakespeare," whose works she reads as a child in the Passmore library, and later disseminates as a "plain, pallid" schoolteacher in Savannah, Georgia. The glorious fathers of literary history merge with those of Christian myth as God's white dove (associated with Reverend Passmore's preaching) replaces the jungle father's black ravens in *Funnyhouse*. Her black mother called a whore, the adopted Clara identifies with the Virgin Mary, but in a fantasy visit to England the white fathers who have colonized her desire refuse Clara access to St. Paul's where she imagines burying her own white father, and lock her in the Tower of London. Rejected by her father, but unable to bury or repress him, Clara is imprisoned in her own history. In the play's associative logic the Tower is also a New York subway car in which the adult Clara, lost in guilt and rage, picks up a Negro man, introduces herself as Mary, addresses him as God, and tries to stab him.

The surrealistic Tower (dominant white culture) and the High Altar (sacrificial Christianity) are the phallic edifices against which Clara Passmore measures her being. Ultimately she transforms into the screeching Owl, symbol of her black mother and her criminal origins: "The Owl was [my] beginning." Although her adopted status allows her to "pass more," Clara belongs to the owls as she cannot belong to the world of "Buckingham Palace, . . . the Thames at dusk, and Big Ben" or the "Holy Baptist Church . . . on the top of the Holy Hill." Near the end of the Play, Clara kneels to pray: "I call God and the Owl answers."

This summary conveys nothing of Kennedy's surrealistic spectacle: "There is the noise of the train, the sound of moving steel on the track." "The WHITE BIRD's wings should flutter loudly"—a cacophony that should evoke, says Kennedy, "a sense of exploding imprisonment."

Two shorter works, *A Lesson in Dead Language* and *A Rat's Mass*, add new elements of Kennedy's bestiary. In the first Western culture in the form of a Latin lesson and a schoolteacher, costumed from waist up as a White Dog, and Christian doctrine in the form of enormous statues of Jesus, Joseph, Mary, two Wise Men, and a shepherd, instruct and overwhelm seven little girls, whose initiation into menstruation marks them (and their white dresses) as guilty. In *A Rat's Mass* redemptive authority resides in a schoolmate, Rosemary, who refuses to expiate the incestuous crime of Brother and Sister Rat; and the sister goes mad. In this as in all of Kennedy's beautifully crafted plays, cultural exclusion translates into sexual terror and guilt, the signs of "Negro" womanhood.

Funnyhouse of a Negro won an Obie, but Kennedy's work is rarely discussed or performed in the United States.

—Elin Diamond

See the essay on *A Movie Star Has to Star in Black and White.*

KESSELMAN, Wendy (Ann).

Teaching fellow, Bryn Mawr College, Pennsylvania, 1987. Also a composer and songwriter. Recipient: Meet the Composer grant, 1978, 1982; National Endowment for the Arts fellowship, 1979; Sharfman award, 1980; Susan Smith Blackburn prize, 1980; Playbill award, 1980; Guggenheim fellowship, 1982; Ford Foundation grant, 1982; McKnight fellowship, 1985; ASCAP Popular award, for musical theatre, 1992. Agent: George Lane, William Morris Agency, 1350 Avenue of the Americas, New York, New York 10019; and, Jane Annakin, William Morris Agency Ltd., 31–32 Soho Square, London W1V 6AP, England. Address: P.O. Box 680, Wellfleet, Massachusetts 02667, U.S.A.

Publications

PLAYS

Becca (for children), music and lyrics by Kesselman (produced 1977). 1988.

Maggie Magalita (produced 1980). 1987.

My Sister in This House, music by Kesselman (produced 1981; revised version produced 1987). 1982.

Merry-Go-Round (produced 1981).

I Love You, I Love You Not (one-act version produced 1982; full-length version produced 1986). 1988.

The Juniper Tree: A Tragic Household Tale, music and lyrics by Kesselman (produced 1982). 1985.

Cinderella in a Mirror (produced 1987).

The Griffin and the Minor Cannon, music by Mary Rodgers, lyrics by Ellen Fitzhugh (produced 1988).

A Tale of Two Cities, adaptation of the novel by Dickens (produced 1992).

The Butcher's Daughter (produced 1993).

Fiction (for children)
Franz Tovey and the Rare Animals. 1968.
Angelita. 1970.
Slash: An Alligator's Story. 1971.
Joey. 1972.
Little Salt. 1975.
Time for Jody. 1975.
Maine Is a Million Miles Away. 1976.
Emma. 1980.
There's a Train Going by My Window. 1982.
Flick. 1983.
Sand in My Shoes. 1993.

Critical study: "Wendy Kesselman: Transcendence and Transformation" by Jay Dickson, in *Harvard Advocate*, 1986.

Theatrical activities
Actor: **Play**—role in *The Juniper Tree*, 1983.

Already an author of children's books, Wendy Kesselman began her playwriting career with *Becca*, a play ostensibly for a young audience, though older spectators responded to the implicit subtext of parental neglect and a brother's abuse of his sister. Kesselman charms tiny tots with her book, lyrics, and music, particularly the songs for caged animals (parrot, salamander, grasshopper, and bullfrog) and the creatures (rats, Ida the Spider, escaped snake, and witches) who terrify Becca when her bullying brother Jonathan, as a means of controlling her, locks her in the closet. Yet Kesselman teaches as well as entertains: relegated to his room by parents who never appear but by implication both ignore him and dictate his every move, Jonathan mirrors that behavior by neglecting to provide his pets with food and water and tyrannizing his sister, treating her like a toy doll, not a person. He eventually learns to respect others, relinquishes his pets (after Becca tells them they can free themselves), and stops hitting and threatening his sister. Jonathan changes because Becca changes first, finding the courage to put a stop to his dehumanizing treatment, to take control of her own life, and to toss onto the closet floor the long white dress which reduced her to a mere object. The most amazing moment in this startling feminist parable occurs when Becca rebels against her tormentor and it finally dawns on us that she is not a doll.

Becca prefigures Kesselman's later dramas in its use of her own music, its parallels (Becca and the pets) and contrasts (the pets versus the creatures, Becca versus Jonathan), and its themes of loneliness, maturation, violence to soul and body, fear, family relations, control, and courage. Kesselman continues to write about children and adolescents and about gender inequities, while expanding this exploration to include conflicts fueled by disparities of class, age, and culture. Further, she imbues her plays with a feminist sensibility to the ways patriarchal, social, and economic structures stunt women's minds and stifle their souls.

Kesselman's early masterpiece *My Sister in This House* exemplifies the way in which she keeps her viewpoint implicit, never preaching, always dramatizing. She constructs the play in a dazzling series of parallels and contrasts, satirizing life in the drawing room and dining room, while portraying with compassion life in the kitchen and garret. Conversations between the maids and between the mother and daughter for whom they slave frequently intersect, the concerns of each economic class reflecting those of the other. But so great is the social stratification separating them that not until the play's bloody climax do the two sets of women converse across class lines. Instead the Danzards beckon or point or nod or, when the white glove detects dust, scowl. Yet the sisters and the two women who employ them share a common obstacle to their humanity and self-actualization: female existence in a time and place (France in the early 1930s) which permit their sex only a domestic function. Conservative arbiters of conduct require women without men to repress their sexuality as well as their needs for personal and professional fulfillment. While the women in both social strata lead empty lives, at least the sisters provide each other with the tender love and sex missing from their vacuous employers' existence. Yet the young women's inability to control their own economic destinies dooms both them and their bourgeois nemeses, as the impulse towards aggression, though stifled, on both sides builds and builds.

When Jean Genet based *The Maids* on the same horrendous Le Mans double murder committed by incestuous sisters, he wasn't attempting to create sympathetic portraits of the killers, but Kesselman accepts that challenge. She succeeds by depicting impoverished innocents trapped in a claustrophobic world devoid of stimulation, affection, or purpose except for each other's solace. After the mutual enthusiasm of the Danzards and the sisters gives way to suspicion and fear, Madame explodes with a venomous denunciation which guarantees that the sisters will be thrown on the street without references, food, or shelter; this tragedy can end only in the destruction of all four bleak lives.

A prize-winning composer as well as a dramatist, Kesselman has supplied music for most of her texts. By the end of *My Sister*, we're already deeply affected by the play's action, but Kesselman enhances its impact by the recurrence of the musical refrain "Sleep my little sister, sleep." In *The Juniper Tree: A Tragic Household Tale* Kesselman renders the drama's macabre murder, dismemberment, cannibalism, revenge, and resurrection both funnier and more horrifying by describing and enacting events with lovely solos and eerie duets. As usual, Kesselman takes a child's perspective in dramatizing this Grimm's fairy-tale about parental abuse. Both narrating and acting out the plot in the style of story theatre, *The Juniper Tree* portrays the irrational but compulsive murder of a child by (as in her *Cinderella in a Mirror*) a wicked stepmother, who compounds the crime by blaming her own daughter for the boy's death, then cooking him and serving him as soup for supper. Among Kesselman's funny, folksy touches are the men's descriptions of their personal activities, the father's ravenous appetite—gruesomely comic—and the daughter's disgust at her father's gross table manners while he unknowingly devours his son.

Merry-Go-Round, using as music only a title song, considers childhood largely by depicting its outcome in young adults: we see a similar child within each quite different grown-up. The play's structure jumps from present to past, not with flashbacks, but with the adults re-enacting the earlier scenes. After they reconnect with their past selves, their roots, their early powerful bond broken by their parents, and their loneliness after Michael moved away, Daisy and Michael consummate sexually their earlier relationship, coming full circle —as the title suggests. Kesselman keeps all this understated, implicit, subtle, but authentically evokes the feelings engendered by a reunion of former soul mates.

In *Maggie Magalita* Kesselman depicts an immigrant adolescent struggling to win acceptance from her classmates in New York City while responding with embarrassment to her Spanish-speaking grandmother. Eventually their culture clash educates them both, after screaming arguments, sullen rejection, and cruelties to the aging Abuela which correspond to what her tormentors inflicted upon little Magalita before she became Americanized into Maggie. In addition to her characteristic theme of loneliness—Magalita's as well as Abuela's—Kesselman dramatizes such values as respect for those who are different, self-acceptance, and courage when confronting pressures to conform. Although set largely in the family apartment, the episodes shift freely from present to past and among such other locales as the zoo, the seashore, and Maggie's high-school. The playwright visually expresses her protagonist's transformation from Latin American to North American when the teenager dons flashy sunglasses and earrings and a baggy T-shirt bearing a photo of a rock group.

In *I Love You, I Love You Not* the dramatist narrows this confrontation of cultures and generations to its essentials: wilful adolescent Daisy (a favorite name?) and Nana, her grandmother from the Old World. Jewish rather than Hispanic, Daisy (the flower used in playing the ambivalent petal-plucking game of the play's title) actually wants to learn the language of her heritage (in this case German) so as to deprive her parents of the capacity to speak privately in her presence, whereas Nana, a Holocaust survivor, hates the tongue of her persecutors, who killed Nana's sisters and parents. As in *Becca*, Kesselman keeps Daisy's parents off-stage, but employs them as a formidable hostile presence. Like this playwright's other domestic dramas, this one also compels our attention to the love/hate relations within a family. While the high-strung teenager spends this weekend in her rites of passage to maturity skirmishing with her grandmother, her parents intrude by telephone as they attempt to remove her from her grandmother's nurturing care. "Care" proves the operative word. Never maudlin—indeed, Daisy proves spoiled, narcissistic, self-indulgent, childish—*I Love You, I Love You Not* dramatizes the volatile but nurturing relationship between an emotionally needy, insecure youngster and the woman who can develop her fragile "Daisy" into hardier stock with survival skills, capable of overcoming her intolerance, guilt, and especially fears.

In the late 1980s Kesselman began work on two more musical plays, each set in France during the Revolution. Both again in some part concern young people, contrast classes, and dramatize events in brief episodes, and each ends with execution by guillotine. In *A Tale of Two Cities* she adapts Dickens' novel, whereas *The Butcher's Daughter* breaks audacious new ground. *A Tale of Two Cities* employs the parallels of Charles and Sydney, young Thérèse and young Lucie, the burning of shoemaking tools and burning the Bastille, Lucie's imprisoned father and then little Lucie's imprisoned father. Kesselman also utilizes flashbacks, building suspense about events we can't fully comprehend when we first observe them, until we grasp how Thérèse Defarge's sister was raped on her wedding day by the Évremondes, who killed her husband, father, and brother. The latter's moving song "Quieting the Frogs" proves one of the best among Kesselman's extraordinary compositions for musical theatre.

The Butcher's Daughter's parallels constitute the play's whole structure, as we follow the destinies of two young women, one adopted by a butcher, the other the daughter of the executioner who decapitates the butcher's daughter at the end, when the executioner's daughter hangs herself. A grandmother lives in each household; images of blood permeate the play, which indicts such male-driven acts as capital punishment and incest. Once more, the world proves pernicious to women of any talent or spirit, so utterly denying them autonomy and equity they cannot survive. Kesselman selects as one of her central figures the pioneer playwright and feminist Olympe de Gouges, and both women's spirits soar. The women interact only twice, for a few wordless but indelible moments. Linking the two protagonists, the street singer Pierrot knows, loves, and celebrates them both—just as Kesselman sings of women young and old, timid and bold, some of the most memorable female characters in contemporary drama.

—Tish Dace

KINGSLEY, Sidney.

Born Sidney Kirshner in New York City, 22 October 1906. Educated at Townsend Harris Hall, New York, 1920–24; Cornell University, Ithaca, New York (state scholarship), 1924–28, B.A. 1928. Served in the U.S. Army, 1941–43: lieutenant. Married the actress Madge Evans in 1939 (died 1981). Actor in the Tremont Stock Company, Bronx, New York, 1928–29; thereafter play-reader and scenario writer for Columbia Pictures; full-time writer and stage director from 1934. President, Dramatists Guild, 1961–69; member, New Jersey Motion Picture and TV Authority, and chair, 1976–80. Recipient: Pulitzer prize, 1934; New York Theatre Club medal, 1934, 1936, 1943; New York Drama Critics Circle award, 1943, 1951; Donaldson award, 1951; American Academy Award of Merit Medal, 1951, Gold Medal, 1986. D.Litt: Monmouth College, West Long Branch, New Jersey, 1978; Ramapo College, Mahwah, New Jersey, 1978.

Publications

PLAYS

Men in White (produced 1933). 1933.
Dead End (produced 1935). 1936.
Ten Million Ghosts (produced 1936).
The World We Make, from a novel by Millen Brand (produced 1939). 1939.
The Patriots (produced 1943). 1943.
Detective Story (produced 1949). 1949.

Darkness at Noon, from the novel by Arthur Koestler (produced 1951). 1951.
Lunatics and Lovers (produced 1954). Condensed version in *Theater 1955*,
   1955.
Night Life (produced 1962). 1966.

SCREENPLAYS: *Homecoming*, with Paul Osborn and Jan Lustig, 1948.

CRITICAL STUDY: *American Drama Between the Wars* by Jordan Y. Miller and
Winifred L. Frazer, 1991.

THEATRICAL ACTIVITIES
DIRECTOR: **Plays**—all his own plays except *The Patriots*.

Certain of Sidney Kingsley's plays have probably outlived his reputation. *Dead
End*, for example, is likely to evoke recognition among those who are indifferent to the name of its author, largely through its renown on the cinema screen.
(Warner Brothers made a series of films after the original adaptation, all of
which featured the "Dead End Kids".) But Kingsley, in his time, was acknowledged as "a man of the theatre", one who could be relied on for a solid piece of
work with each new play.
   It is therefore surprising that his canon is relatively small, compared to the
prolific output of his best-known contemporaries. His era, the 1930s, saw only
four plays from him, one of which was an adaptation, and another a commercial failure. *Men in White* won for him a Pulitzer prize at the age of 27, and
Dead End is commonly cited in accounts of American Depression drama—it
ran for 687 performances. But despite his critical and commercial success, he
may even be remembered as a "one-play author" by the casual theatre-goer.
   The "one-play" tag, at least, is erroneous. Both *The Patriots* and *Darkness
at Noon*, written in successive decades, were awarded New York Circle of
Critics Awards. *Detective Story* was made into an all-celebrity film, which is
regularly revived on television. Kingsley always wrote well, if sparingly, and
every one of his plays has its distinct architecture. He created whole worlds in
his plays, bringing onto sumptuously-detailed sets entire cross-sections from
his chosen sphere, frequently in a specific socio-historical context. And if his
naturalism stood in the way of experimentation like Elmer Rice's *The Adding
Machine*, it was never the gimcrack of later television serials or quasi-pulp
fiction.
   Kingsley's writing addressed genuine social issues, sometimes much in
advance of other dramatists. Even the failure *Ten Million Ghosts* deals with
the devastating consequences of large-scale munitions production. American
drama had to wait 11 more years before another play, Arthur Miller's *All My
Sons*, came anywhere near the seriousness of this theme. Each world of a
Kingsley play, too, is as distinct from the others as any one author's could be.
Men in White features articulate, professional men; the street urchins in *Dead
End* use a demotic speech that is hard to decipher on the page; *The Patriots*
focuses on the tempestuous relationship between Jefferson and Hamilton; and
Darkness at Noon (taken from the Arthur Koestler novel) departs from the
American scene altogether.
   Kingsley was bold enough to address social issues that still feature in today's

headlines. *Men in White* and *Detective Story* present abortion almost as a commonplace solution for the disempowered. The random violence in *Dead End* remains a staple of documentaries about juvenile crime. Kingsley's extensive treatment of psycho-analysis in *The World We Make* reveals how superficial its appearance is in the Moss Hart and Kurt Weill musical play, *Lady in the Dark*.

Detractors regularly point out the irksome reliance on familiar plot devices in a Kingsley play. One or two, it is true, come dangerously close to the stock formula of "stranded passengers". One key-turning line ("Didn't you ever make a mistake?") even appears in two of the plays. But the resolutions, finally, cannot be said to be "comfortable", and characterisation is never wholly subservient to a melodramatic conclusion however vulnerable Kingsley may have been to the "problem play" formula. The protagonists of *Dead End* and *Detective Story* are sufficiently rounded never to polarise sympathy absolutely.

The physical defect of the character "Gimpty" in *Dead End* is presented in such a way that its relevance to the theme of urban decay supercedes any possible sentimental interpretation. Gimpty's semi-requited attachment to the mistress of a businessman is convincing precisely because such a defect would adequately define their relationship. It is in the transformation of the character into a clean-limbed but impoverished architect in the film version of *Dead End* that the relationship lacks credibility.

Rarely in Kingsley is the protagonist the play's spokesman. Gimpty betrays boyhood loyalty in his attempt to do right. Macleod's dilemma in *Detective Story* hardly makes him attractive, but it does put into focus the conflicts of an inner-city policeman who resolutely refuses to "look the other way". Jefferson's recourse to traditional political manoeuvring in *The Patriots* points up the limitations in the American political system rather than any venal traits in the personalities of Jefferson, Washington, or Hamilton.

The level of political debate in any Kingsley play is always less extensive than it is in Robert E. Sherwood's plays. Kingsley is far better at identifying a problem than at providing solutions, which restricts his work as "thesis drama". But it is hard to find fault with the careful articulation of issues, and this could occasionally result in positive action outside the theatre. Congressman Robert Wagner initiated a national campaign of slum clearance specifically based on viewing *Dead End*. Less sensationally, other of the plays prefigured reforms in medical care, criminal incarceration, and "head start" education.

An inability to anticipate future social trends may explain the failure of Kingsley's later work. In both *Lunatics and Lovers* and *Night Life* he remained contemporaneous, and the attention to detail is as scrupulous as ever. There is nothing bogus about the characterisation of the gangsters in *Night Life*; it is at least as convincing as Sidney Howard's is in *Lucky Sam McCarver*. Nonetheless, at a time when the Teamsters' boss James Hoffa was under indictment, and his exposure threatened the fabric of the Kennedy administration (Hoffa's eventual murder was never solved), Kingsley's depiction of racketeering offered nothing new, and was seen, very clearly, as parochial.

By this time his crusading realism had become the province of the more adventurous television detective serials. Kingsley is worthy of remembrance, though, for the enduring quality of his slender output. In percentage terms, he scored higher than any other major American dramatist, though his name was to feature less frequently in both the popular press and in the annals of American drama.

—James MacDonald

KOCH, Kenneth.

Born in Cincinnati, Ohio, 27 February 1925. Educated at Harvard University, Cambridge, Massachusetts, A.B. 1948; Columbia University, New York, M.A. 1953, Ph.D. 1959. Served in the U.S. Army, 1943–46. Married Mary Janice Elwood in 1955; one daughter. Lecturer in English, Rutgers University, New Brunswick, New Jersey, 1953–54, 1955–56, 1957–58, and Brooklyn College, 1957–59; director of the Poetry Workshop, New School for Social Research, New York, 1958–66. Lecturer, 1959–61, assistant professor, 1962–66, associate professor, 1966–71, and since 1971 professor of English, Columbia University. Associated with *Locus Solus* magazine, Lans-en-Vercors, France, 1960–62. Recipient: Fulbright fellowship, 1950, 1978; Guggenheim fellowship, 1961; National Endowment for the Arts grant, 1966; Ingram Merrill Foundation fellowship, 1969; Harbison award, for teaching, 1970; Frank O'Hara prize (*Poetry*, Chicago), 1973; American Academy award, 1976; American Academy of Arts and Letters award of merit, 1987. Address: Department of English, 414 Hamilton Hall, Columbia University, New York, New York 10027, U.S.A.

Publications

PLAYS

Bertha, music by Ned Rorem (produced 1959). In *Bertha and Other Plays*, 1966.

The Election (also director: produced 1960). In *A Change of Hearts*, 1973.

Pericles (produced 1960). In *Bertha and Other Plays*, 1966.

George Washington Crossing the Delaware (in *3 x 3*, produced 1962). In *Bertha and Other Plays*, 1966.

The Construction of Boston (produced 1962). In *Bertha and Other Plays*, 1966.

Guinevere; or, The Death of the Kangaroo (produced 1964). In *Bertha and Other Plays*, 1966.

The Tinguely Machine Mystery; or, The Love Suicides at Kaluka (also co-director: produced 1965). In *A Change of Hearts*, 1973.

Bertha and Other Plays (includes *Pericles, George Washington Crossing the Delaware, The Construction of Boston, Guinevere; or, The Death of the Kangaroo, The Gold Standard, The Return of Yellowmay, The Revolt of the Giant Animals, The Building of Florence, Angelica, The Merry Stones, The Academic Murders, Easter, The Lost Feed, Mexico, Coil Supreme*). 1966.

The Gold Standard (produced 1969). In *Bertha and Other Plays*, 1966.

The Moon Balloon (produced 1969). In *A Change of Hearts*, 1973.

The Artist, music by Paul Reif, adaptation of the poem "The Artist" by Koch (produced 1972). Poem in *Thank You and Other Poems*, 1962.

A Little Light (produced 1972).
A Change of Hearts: Plays, Films, and Other Dramatic Works 1951–1971
(includes the contents of *Bertha and Other Plays*, and *A Change of Hearts*;
E. Kology; *The Election*; *The Tinguely Machine Mystery*; *The Moon
Balloon*; *Without Kinship*; *Ten Films: Because, The Color Game,
Mountains and Electricity, Sheep Harbor, Oval Gold, Moby Dick, L'Ecole
Normale, The Cemetery, The Scotty Dog*, and *The Apple*; *Youth*; and *The
Enchantment*). 1973.
A Change of Hearts, music by David Hollister (produced 1985). In *A Change
of Hearts* (collection), 1973.
Rooster Redivivus (produced 1975).
The Art of Love, adaptation of a poem by Mike Nussbaum (produced 1976).
The Red Robins, adaptation of his own novel (produced 1978). 1979.
The New Diana (produced 1984).
Popeye among the Polar Bears (produced 1986).
One Thousand Avant-Garde Plays (produced 1987). 1988.
The Construction of Boston, music by Scott Wheeler (produced 1989).
Some Avant-Garde Plays (produced 1990).

SCREENPLAYS: *The Scotty Dog*, 1967; *The Apple*, 1968.

NOVEL
The Red Robins. 1975.

SHORT STORIES
Interlocking Lives, with Alex Katz. 1970.
Hotel Lambosa and Other Stories. 1993.

VERSE
Poems. 1953.
Ko; or, A Season on Earth. 1960.
Permanently. 1960.
Thank You and Other Poems. 1962.
Poems from 1952 and 1953. 1968.
When the Sun Tries to Go On. 1969.
Sleeping with Women. 1969.
The Pleasures of Peace and Other Poems. 1969.
Penguin Modern Poets 24, with Kenward Elmslie and James Schuyler. 1973.
The Art of Love. 1975.
The Duplications. 1977.
The Burning Mystery of Anna in 1951. 1979.
From the Air. 1979.
Days and Nights. 1982.
Selected Poems 1950–1982. 1985.
On the Edge. 1986.
Seasons on Earth. 1987.
Selected Poems. 1991.

OTHER

John Ashbery and Kenneth Koch (A Conversation). 1965(?).
Wishes, Lies, and Dreams: Teaching Children to Write Poetry. 1970.
Rose, Where Did You Get That Red? Teaching Great Poetry to Children. 1973.
I Never Told Anybody: Teaching Poetry Writing in a Nursing Home. 1977.

Editor, with Kate Farrell, *Sleeping on the Wing: An Anthology of Modern Poetry, with Essays on Reading and Writing.* 1981.
Editor, with Kate Farrell, *Talking to the Sun: An Illustrated Anthology of Poems for Young People.* 1985.

THEATRICAL ACTIVITIES

DIRECTOR: **Plays**—*The Election,* 1960; *The Tinguely Machine Mystery* (co-director, with Remy Charlip), 1965.

Kenneth Koch is a genuine man of letters, though that epithet seems inappropriate for a writer whose natural instincts are comic and parodic. In addition to writing much first-rate poetry and some striking fiction, he has been one of America's best teachers of writing—not only inspiring several promising younger poets, but also popularizing the idea of poetry writing in elementary education. His book *Wishes, Lies, and Dreams* details his own experience in the New York City public schools, and thus establishes a pedagogical example that is currently imitated all over the United States. Koch has also written short plays over the past three decades, most of which originated as responses to his personal experience as a graduate student of literature, a college professor, a serious poet, and a participant in the New York art scene. Perhaps because of their occasional inspiration, many of these shorter works remained too attached to their original circumstances to be presented again. His second collection, *A Change of Hearts*, includes several new pieces, all of which are typically Kochian, none particularly better than his past work.

On one hand, Koch is a bemused absurdist and a giggler, incapable of taking anything too seriously, whose plays exploit situations and/or subjects for their available humor. On the other, he is a "New York School" poet capable of extraordinary acoherent (as distinct from incoherent) writing, such as the marvelous nonsense of these concluding lines from his early play, *Pericles*:

And we stood there with pure roots
In silence in violence one two one two
Will you please go through that again
The organ's orgasm and the aspirin tablet's speechless spasm.

In structure, his plays tend to be collections of related sketches, strung together in sequences of varying duration, allowing imaginative leaps between the scenes. The best also reveal his debt, both as playwright and as poet, to the French surrealists and dadaists.

Bertha and Other Plays collects most of Koch's early works in chronological order. The very best, *George Washington Crossing the Delaware*, originated as a response to Larry Rivers's painting of the same title (and the play is appropriately dedicated to the artist). Koch's compressed historical play ridicules several kinds of clichés: the myths of American history, the language of politicians, war films, military strategies, patriotism, and much else. The theme of Koch's multiple burlesques, here and elsewhere, is that the accepted familiar versions are no more credible than his comic rewritings. The play also reveals Koch's love of Apollinaire's great poem *Zone* (1918) by scrambling space and time. The British general refers at one point to "the stately bison," which did not enter popular mythology until the 19th-century and certainly could not be seen on the East Coast; and the play takes place in "Alpine, New Jersey," which is nowhere near the Delaware River.

In the ten short-short scenes of his earlier mini-epic, *Bertha*, whose text runs less than ten pages, Queen Bertha of Norway uses power to assuage her evident madness, attacks Scotland only to halt at the frontier, shoots lovers for their sins, only to win the confidence, nonetheless, of both her armies and their captives. (The historical source of this burlesque is less obvious than for *George Washington*, but several possibilities come to mind.) Koch's book also includes *Guinevere*, an early work with some marvelous nonsense writing; and "Six Improvisational Plays," four of which are prose texts that suggest a performance (much like a script for a "happening"); and the book closes with scenes from *Angelica*, an opera about 19th-century French poetry that was written for the American composer Virgil Thomson but never performed.

Koch's more recent plays are likewise filled with marvelous moments. In *The New Diana*, essentially a satire of the myth of poets and their muses, he has live turkeys appear, speaking indigenous language: CAGED TURKEY: Mishiki wai nowuga gan! Ish tang. TURKEY ON TABLE: Nai shi mai ghee itan, korega. *Popeye among the Polar Bears*, likewise a series of vignettes, has the wit and representational freedom we've come to associate with Koch's verse plays. *The Red Robins* is, by contrast, an adaptation of Koch's sole novel, published a few years before; it differs from other Koch theater in having considerably longer speeches.

In the mid-1980s he developed a working relationship with Barbara Vann and her colleagues at the Medicine Show, a New York Off-Broadway theater, which produced an operatic version of *A Change of Hearts* (from his second collection).

Whereas Koch is clearly a major American poet, is he yet a major playwright? His dramatic texts are unique in the ways that all major work is unique. They are radical enough for Ruby Cohn to write (in *New American Dramatists 1960–1980*, 1982), "I find the plays of poet Kenneth Koch, which I have never seen performed, too childish to examine in a book intended for adults." Such dismissal would not occur unless Koch's texts took risks with theatrical language and yet, to my senses, they don't take enough risks within their premises and don't sustain their innovations to sufficient length. There is nothing in Koch's theater equal to his two book-length poems, *When the Sun Tries to Go On* (written in 1953, but not published until 1969) and *Ko; or, A Season on Earth*—but symptoms of such ambition abound in his work. It should also be noted that Koch, like his poetic colleagues John Ashbery and Frank O'Hara (both of whom also wrote plays), belongs to the counter-tradition of American playwriting—a theater of poets and novelists that emphasizes not naturalism but fantasy; not character but circumstance; not events but essence.

—Richard Kostelanetz

KONDOLEON, Harry.

Born in New York City, 26 February 1955. Educated at Hamilton College, Clinton, New York (Bradley Playwriting prize, 4 times), 1974–77, B.A. 1977; Yale University, New Haven, Connecticut (Kazan award, 1979, 1980), M.F.A. 1981. Member, playwrights and directors unit, Actors Studio, New York, 1978–80, and Manhattan Theatre Club, 1982–84. Instructor in playwriting, New School for Social Research, 1983–84, and Columbia University, 1985–87, both New York. Recipient: International Institute of Education fellowship, 1977; Oppenheimer award, 1983; Obie award, 1983; New York Foundation for the Arts grant, 1984; National Endowment for the Arts grant, 1985. Agent: George Lane, William Morris Agency, 1350 Avenue of the Americas, New York, New York 10019, U.S.A.

Publications

PLAYS

The Cote d'Azur Triangle (produced 1980). 1985.
The Brides, music by Gary S. Fagin (also director: produced 1980; as *Disrobing the Bride*, also director: produced 1981). In *Wordplays 2*, 1982.
Rococo (produced 1981).
Andrea Rescued (produced 1982). 1987.
Self Torture and Strenuous Exercise (produced 1982). In *The Best Short Plays 1984*, edited by Ramon Delgado, 1984; 1991.
Slacks and Tops (produced 1983). 1983.
Christmas on Mars (produced 1983). 1983.
The Vampires (produced 1984). 1984.
Linda Her, and The Fairy Garden (produced 1984). 1985.
Anteroom (produced 1985). 1985.
Play Yourself (produced 1988).
The Poet's Corner (produced 1988; with *The Little Book of Professor Enigma*, as *Harry Kondoleon's Nightmare Alley*, produced 1992).
Zero Positive (produced 1988). 1989.
Love Diatribe (produced 1990). 1991.
Harry Kondoleon's Nightmare Alley (includes *The Poet's Corner* and *The Little Book of Professor Enigma*) (produced 1992).

TELEVISION PLAY: *Clara Toil*, 1982.

NOVEL
The Whore of Tjampuan. 1987.

VERSE
The Death of Understanding. 1986.

THEATRICAL ACTIVITIES

DIRECTOR: **Plays**—*The Brides*, 1980; *Disrobing the Bride*, 1981; *The Vampires*, 1984; *Rich Relations* by David Henry Hwang, 1986.

With just a handful of plays, Harry Kondoleon has mapped out a territory where the brittle wit of high comedy of manners and the breakneck plot-twists of farce fuse with the primal fears, monstrous egotism, and logic of dreams. There, the bedrock of social existence—loving partnerships, family life, the company of friends—are depicted as barely preferable to purgatory. There is no suggestion that these are bourgeois constraints. The elemental world—as represented by children (dead and alive) and fairies—is viewed as damaged and damaging. No one is innocent in this world. Salvation is not a possibility. It is a measure of Kondoleon's unique—one is tempted to say warped—perspective that all this is presented as hilarious.

A voice out of bedlam wailing of love and loss, to the formal rhythm of the tango: this is Screamin' Jay Hawkins's rendition of "I Put a Spell on You." This song is integral to *The Vampires* (but could serve as anthem to any Kondoleon play). Zivia, a zombie 13-year-old, plays it as she wanders around her aunt and uncle's chic home, mainlining heroin and wondering what happened to her brother. Dispatching her to an ashram only creates new problems. Meanwhile, her elders are establishing aberrant and obnoxious behaviour as normative. Particularly notable is Uncle Ian, who has taken to sleeping during the day and biting his wife in the neck at night.

Linda Her is set in a sparse bedroom on a humid night in a summer cottage upstate somewhere. Carol walks out on her sleeping husband, his daughter, her best friend. She does this because Linda Her, the most popular girl in her husband's nursery class, died. Some years ago. ". . . I picture her so clearly. This very beautiful, bright girl, who everyone likes, with her whole life ahead of her and then one day many years later boom you find out she doesn't exist anymore—isn't that scary?" asks Carol. And goes.

Linda Her is the curtain raiser and complement to *The Fairy Garden*. The stark bedroom is replaced with a lush garden and the ornate lives of its inhabitants. Mimi and Roman are men and lovers and best friends with Dagny who is married to Boris, but he is old and ugly and she wants to live with her boyfriend The Mechanic. So Dagny cuts off Boris's head. Luckily a fairy appears who restores Boris's head to his shoulders and elopes with him. (The Fairy, it should be noted, is more fond of diamonds than Zsa Zsa Gabor and charges for wishes granted.) Mimi leaves Roman for Dagny which leaves The Mechanic to seduce Roman except that Roman prefers the agony of being alone to the pain of being dependent and vulnerable.

This is soap opera taken to demented and dislocating extremes. Everyone acts out of boredom, malice, and self-interest, communicating only to feed and confirm their obsessive urges. "I thought Boris was kind of cute in a boyish innocent kind of way, and he'd be fun to kiss and hold for a few minutes," the Fairy tells Roman while predicting that Mimi and Dagny—who have torn Roman's world apart—will be together, "A week, two weeks, maybe even a month." Kondoleon takes groups at crisis point, but though the group fragments and realigns, no change occurs. The pace merely accelerates.

When asked his wish, Roman (Kondoleon's most fully realized character) replies, "I want the world to disappear," and—in a remarkable visual coup— the Fairy (kind of) obliges. Like Carol's flight into the unknown or Ian's vampirism, Roman is yearning for a state of otherness, in a world where death—or at least oblivion—is preferable to life suffused with loss.

This does not sound like the stuff of comedy. Yet there has been no playwright this side of Joe Orton who relishes the awfulness of people in the way Kondoleon does. This mordant delight is contagious. There is also the vicarious thrill of observing characters totally unfettered by propriety. Best of all there is the dialogue, where the barbed wisecrack and the hysterical outburst attain new heights of elegance and wit. With all this to delight in, it is a shame that there is a tinge of misogyny. For no apparent reason, the female characters are even more horrendous than the male.

Kondoleon's outlandish vision is usually taken as satirical but could equally be his perception of reality. This ambiguity only serves to make the plays more complex and interesting. Like the creature in *Alien*, Kondoleon has burst forth, spewing the entrails of American domestic comedy in his wake. He is the most arresting playwright at work in America today.

—Joss Bennathan

KOPIT, Arthur (Lee).

Born in New York City, 10 May 1937. Educated at Lawrence High School, New York, graduated 1955; Harvard University, Cambridge, Massachusetts, A.B. (cum laude) 1959 (Phi Beta Kappa). Married to Leslie Ann Garis; two sons and one daughter. Playwright-in-residence, Wesleyan University, Middletown, Connecticut, 1975–76; CBS fellow, 1976–77, adjunct professor of playwriting, 1977–80, Yale University, New Haven, Connecticut. Since 1981 adjunct professor of playwriting, City College, New York. Since 1982 Council member, Dramatists Guild. Recipient: Shaw Travelling fellowship, 1959; Vernon Rice award, 1962; Outer Circle award, 1962; Guggenheim fellowship, 1967; Rockefeller grant, 1968, 1977; American Academy award, 1971; National Endowment for the Arts grant, 1974; Wesleyan University Center for the Humanities fellowship, 1974; Italia prize, for radio play, 1979; Tony award, 1982. Lives in Connecticut. Agent: Audrey Wood, International Creative Management, 40 West 57th Street, New York, New York 10019, U.S.A.

Publications

PLAYS

The Questioning of Nick (produced 1957). In *The Day the Whores Came Out to Play Tennis and Other Plays*, 1965.
Gemini (produced 1957).
Don Juan in Texas, with Wally Lawrence (produced 1957).
On the Runway of Life, You Never Know What's Coming Off Next (produced 1957).
Across the River and into the Jungle (produced 1958).

To Dwell in a Place of Strangers, Act 1 published in *Harvard Advocate*, May 1958.
Aubade (produced 1958).
Sing to Me Through Open Windows (produced 1959; revised version produced 1965). In *The Day the Whores Came Out to Play Tennis and Other Plays*, 1965.
Oh Dad, Poor Dad, Mamma's Hung You in the Closet and I'm Feelin' So Sad: A Pseudoclassical Tragifarce in a Bastard French Tradition (produced 1960). 1960.
Mhil'daim (produced 1963).
Asylum; or, What the Gentlemen Are Up To, And As for the Ladies (produced 1963; *And As for the Ladies* produced, as *Chamber Music*, 1971). *Chamber Music* in *The Day the Whores Came Out to Play Tennis and Other Plays*, 1965.
The Conquest of Everest (produced 1964). In *The Day the Whores Came Out to Play Tennis and Other Plays*, 1965.
The Hero (produced 1964). In *The Day the Whores Came Out to Play Tennis and Other Plays*, 1965.
The Day the Whores Came Out to Play Tennis (produced 1964). In *The Day the Whores Came Out to Play Tennis and Other Plays*, 1965.
The Day the Whores Came Out to Play Tennis and Other Plays. 1965; as *Chamber Music and Other Plays*, 1969.
Indians (produced 1968). 1969.
An Incident in the Park, in *Pardon Me, Sir, But Is My Eye Hurting Your Elbow?*, edited by Bob Booker and George Foster. 1968.
What's Happened to the Thorne's House (produced 1972).
Louisiana Territory; or, Lewis and Clark—Lost and Found (also director: produced 1975).
Secrets of the Rich (produced 1976). 1978.
Wings (broadcast 1977; produced 1978). 1978.
Nine (book), music and lyrics by Maury Yeston, from an adaptation by Mario Fratti of the screenplay *8½* by Federico Fellini (produced 1981). 1983.
Good Help Is Hard to Find (produced 1981). 1982.
Ghosts, adaptation of a play by Ibsen (produced 1982). 1984.
End of the World (produced 1984; as *The Assignment*, produced 1985). 1984.
Bone-the-Fish (produced 1989; revised version as *The Road to Nirvana*, produced 1991). 1991.
Phantom, music and lyrics by Maury Yeston (produced 1991). 1992.

RADIO PLAY: *Wings*, 1977.

TELEVISION PLAYS: *The Conquest of Television*, 1966; *Promontory Point Revisited*, 1969; *Starstruck*, 1979; *Hands*, 1987; *Hands of a Stranger* series; *Phantom of the Opera* series; *In a Child's Name*.

BIBLIOGRAPHY: *Ten Modern American Playwrights* by Kimball King, 1982.

CRITICAL STUDY: *Sam Shepard, Arthur Kopit, and the Off Broadway Theater* by Doris Auerbach, 1982.

THEATRICAL ACTIVITIES

DIRECTOR: Plays—*Oh Dad, Poor Dad, Mamma's Hung You in the Closet and I'm Feelin' So Sad*, 1963; *Louisiana Territory*, 1975. Television—*The Questioning of Nick*, 1959.

"Do I exaggerate?" asks Michael Trent in his first speech in *End of the World*. "Of course. That is my method. I am a playwright." The line is a comic one which becomes ironic in the face of a theme—the prospect of global annihilation—which turns even the grandest theatrical exaggeration into austere understatement. Out of context, the words provide a suitable description of the way Arthur Kopit works.

At 23, fresh out of Harvard, Kopit escaped—or appeared to escape—the cocoon of university production when *Oh Dad, Poor Dad, Mamma's Hung You in the Closet and I'm Feelin' So Sad* was published by a house that specializes in serious drama and went on to production in London and New York. A fashionable success, it established Kopit as a dramatist, but it also saddled him with the label "undergraduate playwright" which stayed with him long after the playfulness of *Oh Dad* had given way to the mixed-genre method that marks his best and most complex plays. One reason the epithet stuck is that the work that immediately followed *Oh Dad* lacked the flash of that play and offered little substance in consolation. *The Day the Whores Came Out to Play Tennis and Other Plays*, which contained some of his student work along with his post-*Oh Dad* efforts, seemed to confirm the critics who saw him simply as a clever young man noodling around.

Such a judgment is far too dismissive. Although some of *Oh Dad*'s games—the parody references to Tennessee Williams, for instance—seem too cute in retrospect, it is an early indication of the dramatic virtues that have become increasingly apparent in Kopit's work: a facility with language, an ear for the clichés of art and life, an eye for the effective stage image (the waltz scene in which Madame Rosepettle breaks Commodore Roseabove, for instance), a strategic use of caricature, the talent for being funny about a subject that is not at all comic. All of these are in evidence in *Oh Dad* and all of them are in the service of a serious theme (or one that seemed serious in 1960)—the emasculation of the American male by the too protective mother, the iron-maiden temptress and the little girl as seducer.

In an interview in *Mademoiselle* (August 1962), Kopit said, "Comedy is a very powerful tool . . . You take the most serious thing you can think of and treat it as comically as you can." Although he invoked Shaw, *Oh Dad* is the immediate reference. Since then, he has thought of more serious things—war, death, nuclear destruction—and has treated them seriously. And comically, as *Indians* and *End of the World* indicate. The Bantam edition of *Indians* (1971) prints a long interview with John Lahr in which Kopit identifies his play as a response to "the madness of our involvement in Vietnam," but he chose to approach the subject obliquely, going back to the eviction of the American Indian from his land. The play shows the distance between official words and deeds, the power of platitude and the way in which myths are made and used. The central figure is Buffalo Bill, who begins as a friend of the Indians and ends—a star of his own show—as an apologist for slaughter. The play moves back and forth between comic and serious scenes, from the broad farce of the play within the play and the cartoon Ol' Time President to the powerful accusatory ending in which the Wild West Show is invaded by the dead Indians. For some, the funny scenes fit uncomfortably with the solemn subject matter, but they are not simply entertaining decoration. The comedy is thematic. The disastrous production of the Ned Buntline melodrama at the White House is both an instance of the creation of myth and a critique of it.

End of the World is a similar fusion of genres. It concerns a playwright who is commissioned to write a play about the dangers of nuclear proliferation—as Kopit was, in fact—and finds that he can only do so by writing a play about a playwright who . . . The parody private-eye frame of the play (the playwright as detective), the agents' lunch at the Russian Tea Room and the three interviews in which the rationale of nuclear stockpiling and scenarios of destruction are presented as comic turns are all central to the play's assumption that there are personal, artistic, and official ways of not facing up to the impending horror. What Michael Trent learns in the play is that all the nuclear strategists know the situation is hopeless but do not believe what they know, and that he was chosen to write the play because, like the men he interviews, he has an attraction to evil and destruction. A painful and funny play, it provides no solution, only an insistence on the probability of catastrophe and, unlike the conventional post-bomb melodrama, no promise of rebirth.

If *Indians* and *End of the World* share dramatic method, *Wings* is an indication of Kopit's unpredictability. There are funny lines in the play, but it is primarily a lyric exploration of death. It is about a woman who suffers a stroke, struggles to make her fragmented speech fit her still coherent thoughts and, after a second stroke, becomes eloquent as she sees herself flying into the unknown. A wing-walker in her youth, her profession/art provides the main metaphor for her final sense of exhilarating discovery. The play evokes both the concerned narrowness of medicine's perception of the woman and the imagination that continues to carry her above her stammering exasperation with herself and those around her. It is an indication—along with *Indians* and *End of the World*—that Kopit is wing-walking far above the bravura flight of *Oh Dad*.

—Gerald Weales

See the essay on *Indians*.

KOUTOUKAS, H.M.

Born in Endicott, New York, 4 June 1947. Educated at Harpur College, Binghamton, New York; Maria Ley-Piscator Dramatic Work- shop, New School for Social Research, New York, 1962–65; Universalist Life Church, Modesto, California, Ph.D. Associated with the Electric Circus and other theatre groups in New York; founder Chamber Theatre Group, New York; member, the Ridiculous Theatrical Company, New York. Recipient: Obie award, 1966; National Arts Club award; Professional Theatre Wing award. Agent: Nino Karlweis, 250 East 65th Street, New York, New York 10021. Address: c/o Judson Church, Washington Square, New York, New York 10012, U.S.A.

Publications

PLAYS

The Last Triangle (produced 1965).

Tidy Passions; or, Kill, Kaleidoscope, Kill (produced 1965). In *More Plays from Off-Off-Broadway*, edited by Michael T. Smith, 1972.

All Day for a Dollar (produced 1966).

Medea (produced 1966).

Only a Countess (produced 1966).

A Letter from Colette (also director: produced 1966).

Pomegranada, music by Al Carmines (produced 1966).

With Creatures Make My Way (produced 1967).

When Clowns Play Hamlet (also director: produced 1967).

View from Sorrento (produced 1967).

Howard Kline Trilogy (produced 1968).

Christopher at Sheridan Squared (produced 1971).

French Dressing (revue), with others (produced 1974).

Grandmother Is in the Strawberry Patch (produced 1974).

The Pinotti Papers (produced 1975).

One Man's Religion (produced 1975).

Star Followers in an Ancient Land, music by Tom O'Horgan and Gale Garnett (also director: produced 1975).

The Legend of Sheridan Square (produced 1976).

Turtles Don't Dream (also director: produced 1977).

Too Late for Yogurt (also director: produced 1978).

The Butterfly Encounter, music by David Forman (produced 1978).

A Hand Job for Apollo (produced 1988).

When Lightning Strikes Twice (includes *Awful People Are Coming Over So We Must Be Pretending to Be Hard at Work and Hope They Will Go Away, Only a Countess May Dance When She's Crazy*) (produced 1991). 1991.

THEATRICAL ACTIVITIES

DIRECTOR: **Plays**—several of his own plays.

H. M. Koutoukas wrote a very large number of plays—several dozen—in the decade beginning about 1963. Most of them he produced himself in a wide variety of situations. He is the quintessential off-off-Broadway dramatist: in addition to showing his work in the usual coffee houses, churches, and lofts, he put on plays in art galleries, concert halls, movie theatres, and, on commission, at parties as private entertainment for the rich. He gained a considerable though largely underground following, but this did not bring him readier access to stages. The theatre scene has changed, there is less personal rapport between producers and artists, more commercial pressure, and since the mid-1970s Koutoukas's output has declined.

His plays have a special tone and flavor that are all his own and immediately recognizable. He often writes in verse, and the characters and situations are the product of a highly fanciful imagination and an elaborately refined sensibility. Most of his plays are designated "camps" rather than drama or comedies, and the style is flamboyantly romantic, idiosyncratic, sometimes self-satirizing, full of private references and inside jokes, precious, boldly aphoristic, and disdain-ful of restrictions of sense, taste, or fashion. Koutoukas is perhaps the last of the aesthetes. Underlying the decoration, his characteristic themes concern people or creatures who have become so strange that they have lost touch with ordinary life, yet their feelings are all the more tender and vulnerable—the deformed, the demented, the rejected, the perverse.

Medea is an adaptation of the Greek play in which the action is set in a laundromat, and in the author's production Medea was played by a man. On the surface a ridiculous notion, the play vividly articulates the situation of a woman from a more primitive, natural, expressive culture trapped among the over-civilized, calculating Greeks and conveys a sympathetic insight into her desperation. The characters in *Tidy Passions; or, Kill, Kaleidoscope, Kill* include a high priestess and several withces of a broken-down cobra cult, a dying dove, Narcissus, and Jean Harlow, who proclaims, "Glamour is dead." *With Creatures Make My Way* is set in a sewer where the single character, neither man nor woman, finally consummates an eternal love with a passing lobster. *A Letter from Colette*, in the naturalistic mode, sweetly tells of romance between an aging woman and a handsome young delivery boy. *Pomegranada* opens in the Garden of Eden and is about tarnish. *Christopher at Sheridan Squared* is an hallucinatory documentary about the Greenwich Village street where Koutoukas has lived for years.

In the mid-1980s Koutoukas re-emerged as an actor and theatrical persona-lity. He presented his students, the School for Gargoyles, in his play *A Hand Job for Apollo*, and appeared at La Mama in *The Birds*. Joining the Ridiculous Theatrical Company, he won acclaim for his performances in revivals of several plays by the late Charles Ludlam, appearing in London as well as New York. His plays *Awful People Are Coming Over So We Must Be Pretending to Be Hard at Work and Hope They Will Go Away* and *Only a Countess May Dance When She's Crazy*, under the collective title *When Lightning Strikes Twice*, were presented by the Ridiculous, starring Everett Quinton, in 1991.

—Michael T. Smith

KRAUSS, Ruth (Ida).

Born in Baltimore, Maryland, 25 July 1911. Educated in public elementary schools; at Peabody Institute of Music, Baltimore; New School for Social Research, New York; Maryland Institute of Art, Baltimore; Parsons School of Art, New York, graduate. Married David Johnson Leisk (i.e., the writer Crockett Johnson) in 1940 (died 1975). Address: c/o Scholastic Books, 730 Broadway, New York, New York 10003, U.S.A.

Publications

POEM-PLAYS

The Cantilever Rainbow. 1965.
There's a Little Ambiguity Over There among the Bluebells and Other Theatre Poems. 1968.
If Only. 1969.
Under Twenty. 1970.

Love and the Invention of Punctuation. 1973.
This Breast Gothic. 1973.
If I Were Freedom (produced 1976).
Re-examination of Freedom (produced 1976). 1981.
Under 13. 1976.
When I Walk I Change the Earth. 1978.
Small Black Lambs Wandering in the Red Poppies (produced 1982).
Ambiguity 2nd (produced 1985).

PRODUCTIONS INCLUDE: *A Beautiful Day, There's a Little Ambiguity Over There among the Bluebells, Re-Examination of Freedom, Newsletter, The Cantilever Rainbow, In a Bull's Eye, Pineapple Play, Quartet, A Show, A Play*—It's a Girl!, *Onward, Duet* (or *Yellow Umbrella*), *Drunk Boat, If Only, This Breast,* many with music by Al Carmines, Bill Dixon, and Don Heckman, produced since 1964.

FICTION (for children)
A Good Man and His Good Wife. 1944; revised edition, 1962.
The Carrot Seed. 1945.
The Great Duffy. 1946.
The Growing Story. 1947.
Bears. 1948.
The Happy Day. 1949.
The Big World and the Little House. 1949.
The Backward Day. 1950.
The Bundle Book. 1951.
A Hole Is to Dig: A First Book of First Definitions. 1952; 1963.
A Very Special House. 1953.
I'll Be You and You Be Me. 1954.
How to Make an Earthquake. 1954.
Charlotte and the White Horse. 1955.
Is This You? 1955.
I Want to Paint My Bathroom Blue. 1956.
The Birthday Party. 1957.
Monkey Day. 1957.
Somebody Else's Nut Tree and Other Tales from Children. 1958.
A Moon or a Button. 1959.
Open House for Butterflies. 1960.
"Mama, I Wish I Was Snow" "Child, You'd Be Very Cold." 1962.
Eye Nose Fingers Toes. 1964.
The Little King, The Little Queen, The Little Monster, and Other Stories You Can Make Up Yourself, illustrated by the author. 1966.
This Thumbprint: Words and Thumbprints, illustrated by the author. 1967.
Little Boat Lighter Than a Cork. 1976.
Minestrone: A Ruth Krauss Selection, illustrated by the author. 1981.
Big and Little. 1987.

VERSE (for children)
I Can Fly. 1950.
A Bouquet of Littles. 1963.

What a Fine Day for . . ., music by Al Carmines. 1967.
I Write It. 1970.
Everything under a Mushroom. 1974.
Somebody Spilled the Sky. 1979.

MANUSCRIPT COLLECTION: Dupont School, Wilmington, Delaware.

Ruth Krauss comments:

All the "works"—or "plays"—are essentially poems—with an approach from
the words themselves, rather than ideas, plot, etc. (This division cannot be
made in so cut-and-dried a fashion.) The interpretation is *mostly* left completely to the director—i.e., one line can be made to take dozens of forms in
actual presentation.

Part of the philosophy behind this is: say *anything*—and leave it to the
director to see what happens. This does not always work out for the best—
depending on the director.

The nature of Ruth Krauss's work is that it is bursting with health, bursting
with greenery, with fresh promise. This nutritional assault, this vitality asserts
itself beyond all the emotions of the day, all of which, sadness, wistfulness, and
hilarity, appear ephemeral beside the steady residue of glowing good health.

But health seems to issue from a steadying optimism and a kind of bravery,
an ability to look the universe in the eye. Nothing cannot be looked at, nothing
is so awful that it cannot be faced, perhaps mended, always accepted.

But the world that she sees appears to be without serious menace, without
horror; it appears to be essentially benign, so that in effect what Krauss faces is
what she perhaps nearsightedly envisions. The bursting sense to her work is
matched by a quieter sense, one of comic wistfulness. And one of whimsy. The
world viewed in comic tranquility.

I recall a series of Krauss whimsies. A number of years ago the Hardware
Poets, long since gone not only from Manhattan but from the planet, presented
an evening of her works which, if memory doesn't betray me, had the generic
term of seven-second plays. I may be inventing this name but they certainly *felt*
like seven-second plays. They were little, exploding, comic pellets which
appeared, exploded and disappeared in dazzling succession for many long
minutes. Or what appeared to be many long minutes. They were delightful
charmers, about nothing that I can now possibly recall, except the essential
sense of them—comic energy organisms, dramatic meteorites which lasted
long enough to be retained forever in the spirit.

My sense of Krauss's work is that it consists of fragmented interruptions in
the more sombre concourse of human events, healthy winks from over the
fence. The fragments give off the sense also of interrupting shards of sunlight in
a universe grown perceptibly greyer as the years go on. Here are excerpts from
a Krauss fragment, a monologue called *If Only* which Florence Tarlow,
a performer with an especially dry wit, delivered with comic gravity at the
Judson Poets Theatre in New York:

If only I was a nightingale singing
If only I was on my second don't-live-like-a-pig week
If only the sun wasn't always rising behind the next hill
If only I was the flavor of tarragon
If only I was phosphorescence and a night phenomena at sea
If only Old Drainpipe Rensaleer as we used to call him hadn't hit bottom
    in Detroit the time he made a fancy dive and got absentminded and
    forget to turn and all his shortribs got stove in he got sucked down the
    drain-pipe because the grate wasn't on
If only I didn't have to get up and let our dog out now
If only the glorious day in April because it has no beginning or end that
    all Flatbush had awaited impatiently between creation and construc-
    tion had come
If only I was Joyce and had written Finnegans Wake only then I'd be gone
If only somebody would kiss me on the back of the neck right now
If only those degraded bastards hadn't monkeyed around with the Oreo
    Sandwich pattern

Krauss is a playwright to turn to when both the flesh and spirit grow weak.
                                                                    —Arthur Sainer

KUSHNER, Tony.

Born in New York City, 16 July 1956. Grew up in Lake Charles, Louisiana.
Educated at Columbia University, New York, B.A. 1978; New York
University, M.F.A. in directing 1984. Since 1989 guest artist, New York
University Graduate Theatre Program, Yale University, New Haven,
Connecticut, and Princeton University, New Jersey. Director, Literary Services,
Theatre Communications Group, New York, 1990–91; playwright-in-
residence, Juilliard School of Drama, New York, 1990–92. Recipient:
National Endowment for the Arts directing fellowship, 1985; Princess Grace
award, 1986; New York State Council on the Arts playwriting fellowship,
1986; New York Foundation for the Arts playwriting fellowship, 1987; John
Whiting award, 1990; Kennedy Center/American Express Fund for New
American Plays award, 1990, 1992; Bay Area Theater Critics award, 1991;
National Arts Club Kesselring award, 1991; Will Glickman playwriting prize,
1992; *Evening Standard* award, 1992. Lives in Brooklyn. Agent: Joyce Ketay,
334 West 89th Street, New York, New York 10024, U.S.A.

Publications

PLAYS

Yes, Yes, No, No (for children; produced 1985). In *Plays in Process*, vol. 7, no.
    11, 1987.
Stella, adaptation of the play by Goethe (produced 1987).
A Bright Room Called Day (produced 1987). 1991.
Hydriotaphia (produced 1987).
The Illusion, adaptation of a play by Pierre Corneille (produced 1988; revised
    version produced 1990). 1991.

Widows, with Ariel Dorfman, adaptation of the novel by Dorfman (produced 1991).
Angels in America, Part One: Millennium Approaches (produced 1991). 1992. 1994.
Angels in America, Part Two: Perestroika (produced 1992). 1994.

Tony Kushner dreams on a grand scale. He creates manifestations of Satan, Death, and the soul as readily as other dramatists invent ordinary humans. A passionate political thinker and devoted student of Bertolt Brecht, Kushner writes plays suffused with historical consciousness and often filled with political argument. Behind the torrents of his language lie models of extravagant prose—his play *Hydriotaphia* was inspired by the 17th-century essayist Sir Thomas Browne—and the poetry of centuries. Though Kushner has an acute ear for the ways all sorts of people speak, his dialogue frequently breaks into poetry, which can rhyme or be very free. A Romantic with a capital R, he is also a gay activist; his work is death-haunted, yet full of hope.

Kushner has shot to prominence with his two-part, roughly seven-hour *Angels in America*. *Angels* is the first significant Kushner play to be rooted wholly in contemporary life; it depicts the catastrophe of AIDS in New York City. This emotionally powerful subject works to bring the recondite stuff of Kushner's earlier plays to a much larger audience.

The Illusion, freely adapted from Corneille's *L'illusion comique*, shows Kushner reveling in romance. The play is full of poetic hyperbole at once indulged in and mocked, but above all enjoyed. Kushner's braggart soldier Matamore is a Don Quixote, the embodiment of the play's absurd and melancholy beauty. The love of theatre, of its magic and its transformations, at this play's heart is a key element in *Angels* as well.

Kushner wrote his first important play, *A Bright Room Called Day*, in "deepest-midnight Reagan America"; since then it has been extensively revised. In the Weimar Germany of 1932–33 a circle of friends disintegrates under the pressures of Hitler's rise to power, one after another forced into hiding or exile until just one woman, Agnes, is left cowering in her apartment. This story is periodically interrupted by Zillah Katz, a contemporary American "with Anarcho-Punk tendencies," who in the version staged at New York's Public Theater in 1991 comes to Berlin and lands in the same apartment; finally she and Agnes inhabit each other's dreams. Kushner keeps rewriting Zillah's lines because she is there to draw parallels with the current political situation in the United States. "Overstatement is your friend: use it," advises Zillah, comparing Reagan and Bush to Hitler. For subsequent productions, Kushner writes, he "will cheerfully supply new material, drawing appropriate parallels between contemporary and historical monsters and their monstrous acts, regardless of how superficially outrageous such comparisons may seem. To refuse to compare is to rob history of its power to inform present action."

One of the bravest of *Bright Room*'s characters, a woman artist named Gotchling, says that "the dreams of the Left are always beautiful." Her words catch at the essence of Kushner's art: "As an artist I am struck to the heart by these dreams. These visions. We progress. But at great cost." Words very like these recur at the end of *Angels in America*.

Subtitled "A Gay Fantasia on National Themes," *Angels* is an epic play for eight actors, its theatricality heightened by casting them in a number of roles—often characters of the opposite sex—in addition to their primary one. Twin plots center on two troubled couples. Prior has AIDS and his lover Louis, unable to cope, leaves him. Joe and Harper are Mormons; their marriage is falling apart because Joe is losing his lifelong battle to repress his homosexuality and Harper's way of dealing is to retreat into Valium-assisted visions. As in a 19th-century novel, the two stories interweave: Louis and Joe become lovers; Harper and Prior meet in a mutual hallucination. Joe and Louis both work at a Federal Court building in Brooklyn, giving scope for plenty of political argument between the conservative Mormon and the liberal Jew.

Even more important to the play's political nexus is Roy M. Cohn, Joe's father-figure and the embodiment of the naked desire for power that underlies politics and corrupts it. Kushner has made of this historical figure a monster, a profane, bigoted, brazen criminal. He is also the life-force incarnate. Cohn fights the whole world, and revels in the struggle. A gay man dying of AIDS (however closeted, however much he insists he has liver cancer), he is furious and unafraid. He brings to *Angels in America* acid comedy and demonic energy; he summons complicated feeling; and after he dies he comes back to dominate yet more scenes.

Millennium Approaches is not only the first part's title; it is the feeling that underlies the entire work. Prior's illness seems to open him to a sense of apocalypse; at the end of Part One an angel crashes through his bedroom ceiling. In the second part, *Perestroika*, Prior journeys to heaven to reject the role of prophet, to reject the angel's message of stasis, to ask for more life. By the January 1990 epilogue, set at the Bethesda angel's fountain in Central Park, where no water flows in winter, he has been living with AIDS for five years. Prior and his friends tell us the story of the original fountain of Bethesda: when the Millennium comes—"not the year two thousand, but the capital M Millennium"—the waters that heal all pain will flow again.

Angels in America is a work of such size and scope, so filled with poetry and felt thought, that it brings to mind *Faust* and *Peer Gynt*. Whether its resolution will meet with the acclaim that greeted *Millennium Approaches* in San Francisco and London has yet to be seen. What's already clear is that *Angels* is one of the most ambitious, exciting, and talented plays ever written in America. In it one encounters an enormously gifted young writer coming into his full power.

—M. Elizabeth Osborn

See the essay on *Angels in America*.

L

LAURENTS, Arthur.

Born in Brooklyn, New York, 14 July 1917. Educated at Cornell University, Ithaca, New York, B.A. 1937. Served in the U.S. Army, 1940–45: sergeant; radio playwright, 1943–45 (Citation, Secretary of War, and *Variety* radio award, 1945). Stage director. Director, Dramatists Play Service, New York, 1961–66. Council member, Dramatists Guild, from 1955. Recipient: American Academy award, 1946; Sidney Howard Memorial award, 1946; Tony award, for play, 1967, for directing, 1984; Vernon Rice award, 1974; Golden Globe award, 1977; Screenwriters Guild award, 1978; elected to the Theatre Hall of Fame, 1983; Sydney Drama Critics award, for directing, 1985. Agent: Shirley Bernstein, Paramuse Artists, 1414 Avenue of the Americas, New York, New York 10019. Address: Dune Road, Quogue, New York 11959, U.S.A.

Publications

PLAYS

Now Playing Tomorrow (broadcast 1939). In *Short Plays for Stage and Radio*, edited by Carless Jones, 1939.

Western Electric Communicade (broadcast 1944). In *The Best One-Act Plays of 1944*, edited by Margaret Mayorga, 1944.

The Last Day of the War (broadcast 1945). In *Radio Drama in Action*, edited by Erik Barnouw, 1945.

The Face (broadcast 1945). In *The Best One-Act Plays of 1945*, edited by Margaret Mayorga, 1945.

Home of the Brave (produced 1945; as *The Way Back*, produced 1949). 1946.

Heartsong (produced 1947).

The Bird Cage (produced 1950). 1950.

The Time of the Cuckoo (produced 1952). 1953.

A Clearing in the Woods (produced 1957). 1957; revised version, 1960.

West Side Story, music by Leonard Bernstein, lyrics by Stephen Sondheim (produced 1957). 1958.

Gypsy, music by Jule Styne, lyrics by Stephen Sondheim, adaptation of a book by Gypsy Rose Lee (produced 1959; also director: produced 1973). 1960.

Invitation to a March (also director: produced 1960). 1961.

Anyone Can Whistle, music by Stephen Sondheim (also director: produced 1964). 1965.

Do I Hear a Waltz?, music by Richard Rodgers, lyrics by Stephen Sondheim (produced 1965). 1966.
Hallelujah, Baby!, music by Jule Styne, lyrics by Betty Comden and Adolph Green (produced 1967). 1967.
The Enclave (also director: produced 1973). 1974.
Scream (also director: produced 1978).
The Madwoman of Central Park West, with Phyllis Newman, music by Peter Allen and others, adaptation of the play *My Mother Was a Fortune Teller* by Newman (also director: produced 1979).
A Loss of Memory (produced 1981). In *The Best Short Plays* 1983, edited by Ramon Delgado, 1983.
Nick and Nora, music by Charles Strowse, lyrics by Richard Maltby, Jr. (also director: produced 1991).

SCREENPLAYS: *The Snake Pit*, with Frank Partos and Millen Brand, 1948; *Rope*, with Hume Cronyn, 1948; *Anna Lucasta*, with Philip Yordan, 1949; *Caught*, 1949; *Anastasia*, 1956; *Bonjour Tristesse*, 1958; *The Way We Were*, 1973; *The Turning Point*, 1977.

RADIO PLAYS: *Now Playing Tomorrow*, 1939; *Hollywood Playhouse, Dr. Christian, The Thin Man, Manhattan at Midnight*, and other series, 1939–40; *The Last Day of the War, The Face, Western Electric Communicade*, and other plays for *The Man Behind the Gun, Army Service Force Presents* and *Assignment: Home* series, 1943–45; *This Is Your FBI* series, 1945.

TELEVISION: *The Light Fantastic*, 1967.

NOVELS
The Way We Were. 1972.
The Turning Point. 1977.

MANUSCRIPT COLLECTION: Brandeis University, Waltham, Massachusetts.

THEATRICAL ACTIVITIES
DIRECTOR: **Plays**—*Invitation to a March*, 1960; *I Can Get It for You Wholesale* by Jerome Weidman, 1962; *Anyone Can Whistle*, 1964; *The Enclave*, 1973; *Gypsy*, 1973, 1974, 1989; *My Mother Was a Fortune Teller* by Phyllis Newman, 1978; *Scream*, 1978; *The Madwoman of Central Park West*, 1979; *So What Are We Gonna Do Now?* by Juliet Garson, 1982; *La Cage aux Folles* by Jean Poiret, adapted by Harvey Fierstein, 1983, 1985, 1986; *Birds of Paradise* by Winnie Haltzman and David Evans, 1987; *Nick and Nora*, 1991.

Arthur Laurents comments:

Too much of today's theatre brings "The Emperor's New Clothes" to my mind. Style is considered content; formlessness is considered new technique; character is reduced to symbol and/or type; and story has been banished—not necessarily a loss—in favor of incident which is usually too thin and too undramatic to fuse an entire play. Moreover, the dominant tone is modish pessimism or militancy, both of which can be as sentimentally romantic as effulgent optimism.

All a matter of taste, of course. My own is for a heightened theatricality and for new forms—but I still believe that form is determined by content and requires control. I want characters in a play, I want to be emotionally involved; I want social content; I want language and I want a *level* of accessibility. (I suspect obscurantism of being the refuge of the vague, the uncommitted, and the chic.) Although I do not demand it, I prefer optimism—even if only implied. For I think man, naturally evil or not, is optimistic. Even the bleakest has hope: why else does he bother to write?

For the United States, for New York, I want subsidized theatres with permanent companies playing repertory. I think that is the most important need of the American playwright and would be of the greatest aid in his development.

One of the most promising dramatists appearing immediately after World War II was Arthur Laurents. His first success in New York, *Home of the Brave*, showed both his skill as a dramatist and his insight into human nature as he dramatized the ethnic and individual problems of a Jewish soldier in a battle situation. During the following 15 years Laurents wrote four plays—*The Bird Cage, The Time of the Cuckoo, A Clearing in the Woods*, and *Invitation to a March*—which continued to demonstrate his theatrical powers and his inclination to write serious drama. Unfortunately, in neither area—theatricality or intellectual penetration—was he able to sustain or develop a first-rate drama for the American commercial theatre. Perhaps he recognized either the personal or public impasse. At any rate, toward the end of this period Laurents had begun to devote more of his talents to musical comedy with considerable success. His creation of the books for *West Side Story* and *Gypsy* gave these musicals the careful integration and character development which distinguish them among modern musicals. During the next decade he collaborated on musicals but without significant success, and seemed to abandon his career in legitimate drama—a disappointment for critics who had felt his earlier promise.

Laurent's seriousness as a dramatist was most evident in the themes that he chose to develop. The fearful uncertainties of the lonely person trying to find a meaningful identity in a world full of frustrations and strangers—this is a dominant theme in his works. Generally, his major character was trying to discover the essentials of love which Laurents seemed to believe would lead to a revelation of self. Although his psychological penetration into his major characters suggests a generally acute perception of humanity, his dramatized solutions tend more consistently toward theatricality than a probing concern for mankind. In other words, the problems that he considers—a person's fears, frustrations, feeling of alienation—place Laurents among these seriously concerned with modernity, but his insistence that sex is fundamental to all such problems limits both his psychology and his insight.

In three of his four plays since his initial success his major characters have been women whose psychological problems have driven them toward disaster. (The other play, *The Bird Cage*, tells the story of Wally, a vicious egomaniac and owner of a night club, whose abuse of everyone stems from his own sexual frustrations.) In *The Time of the Cuckoo* Leona Samish is that warm but lonely woman whose pathos rests in her inability to know and have faith in herself or accept the love of others. Sorry for herself and bitter towards life and thus unable to get what she most desires, she is that dangerous person who destroys. Virginia, the heroine of *A Clearing in the Woods*, sees herself as the destroyer although she wants desperately to be loved. Discovering that someone does truly care, she can work toward a position where she accepts both herself and the real world around her. *Invitation to a March* tells of a girl who, at first, wants to "march" along with the ordinary world and its seemingly inherent problems of love, sex, and divorce. But she changes, rejects the "march" and finds love with one who said "come dance with me." Uncharacteristically for a Laurents play, a strongly made decision becomes the climax of this one, and perhaps both the author and his characters abandon the ordinary world as idealism seems a possible alternative to drudgery. Unfortunately, no further step has been dramatized.

Although Laurents has not been an innovator in technical theatre, he has courageously employed distinctive techniques in his plays. While *The Bird Cage* employs a rather obvious use of theatrical symbol, the "clearing in the woods" with its "magic circle" is well integrated into the structure of the play where three characters—Ginna, Nora, Jigee—act out particular ages in the heroine's life and tease her for her inability to accept what "they" contribute to her present problems. The frequent "front" delivery to the audience in an attempt to indicate unspoken and personal feelings was unsuccessful even in a semi-fantasy such as *Invitation to a March*. Music becomes a dominant part of several of his plays, as might be expected of a dramatist interested in musical comedy. In all of Laurents's theatre works his care in the creation of his characters is a major asset. Whether in musical comedy or straight drama, through an integration of theme and theatrical technique Laurents has tried to express his views on psychological and social life in the modern world.

—Walter J. Meserve

LAWRENCE, Jerome.

Born in Cleveland, Ohio, 14 July 1915. Educated at Ohio State University, Columbus, B.A. 1937; University of California, Los Angeles, 1939–40. Director of summer stock, Connellsville, Pennsylvania, then Pittsfield, Massachusetts, summers 1934–37; reporter and telegraph editor, Wilmington *News-Journal*, Ohio, 1937; editor, New Lexington *Daily News*, Ohio, 1937–38; continuity editor, KMPC Radio, Beverly Hills, California, 1938, 1939; senior staff writer, Columbia Broadcasting System, Hollywood and New York, 1939–41; scenario writer, Paramount Pictures, Hollywood, 1941. Expert consultant to the Secretary of War during World War II: co-founder of Armed Forces Radio Service, and radio correspondent in North Africa and Italy (wrote and directed the official Army-Navy programs for D-Day, VE Day and VJ Day). Since 1942 partner, Lawrence and Lee, and since 1955 president, Lawrence and Lee Inc., New York and Los Angeles. Founder and national president, Radio Writers Guild; co-founder and president, American Playwrights Theatre, 1970–85; co-founder and judge, Margo Jones award; founder and board member, Writers Guild of America; council member, Dramatists Guild and Authors League of America; member of the advisory board, Eugene O'Neill Foundation, American Conservatory Theatre, 1970–80, Board of Standards of the Living Theatre, Plumstead Playhouse, Stella Adler Theater, and Ohio State University School of Journalism. Professor, Banff School of Fine Arts, Alberta, Canada, 1950–53; member, U.S. State Department Cultural Exchange Panel, 1962–70. Master playwright, New York University, 1967, 1968; visiting professor of playwriting, Ohio State University, 1969; lecturer, Salzburg Seminar in American Studies, 1972; visiting professor, Baylor University, Waco, Texas, 1976; William Inge lecturer, Independence Community College, Kansas, 1983, 1986–91; professor of playwriting, University of Southern California, Los Angeles, 1984–92. Contributing editor, *Dramatics* magazine, Cincinnati. Recipient: New York Press Club award, 1942; *Radio-TV Life* award, 1948, 1952; Peabody award, 1949, 1952; *Radio-TV Mirror* award, 1952, 1953; *Variety* award, 1954, 1955; Donaldson award, 1955; Outer Circle award, 1955; British Drama Critics award, 1960; Moss Hart Memorial award, 1967; Ohio State University Centennial award, 1970, and Alumni medal, 1985; American Theatre Association award, 1979; International Thespian Society Directors award, 1980; William Inge award, 1983; Valentine Davies award, 1984; Emmy award, 1988 (twice); Southeastern Theater Conference award, 1990; elected to Theater Hall of Fame and College of Fellows of the American Theatre, 1990. D.H.L.: Ohio State University, 1963; D.Litt.: Fairleigh Dickinson University, Rutherford, New Jersey, 1968; College of Wooster, Ohio, 1983; D.F.A.: Villanova University, Pennsylvania, 1969. Agent: Robert Freedman Dramatic Agency, 1501 Broadway, New York 10036; and, Mitch Douglas, International Creative Management, 40 West 57th Street, New York, New York 10019. Address: 21056 Las Flores Mesa Drive, Malibu, California 90265, U.S.A.

Publications

PLAYS

Laugh, God!, in *Six Anti-Nazi One-Act Plays*. 1939.

Tomorrow, with Budd Schulberg, in *Free World Theatre*, edited by Arch Oboler and Stephen Longstreet. 1944.

Inside a Kid's Head, with Robert E. Lee, in *Radio Drama in Action*, edited by Erik Barnouw. 1945.

Look, Ma, I'm Dancin', with Robert E. Lee, music by Hugh Martin, conceived by Jerome Robbins (produced 1948).

The Crocodile Smile, with Robert E. Lee (as *The Laugh Maker*, produced 1952; revised version, as *Turn on the Night*, produced 1961; revised version, as *The Crocodile Smile*, also director: produced 1970). 1972.

Inherit the Wind, with Robert E. Lee (produced 1955). 1955.

Shangri-La, with Robert E. Lee and James Hilton, music by Harry Warren, adaptation of the novel *Lost Horizon* by Hilton (produced 1956). 1956.

Auntie Mame, with Robert E. Lee, adaptation of the work by Patrick Dennis (produced 1956). 1957; revised version, music by Jerry Herman, as *Mame* (produced 1966), 1967.

The Gang's All Here, with Robert E. Lee (produced 1959). 1960.

Only in America, with Robert E. Lee, adaptation of the work by Harry Golden (produced 1959). 1960.

A Call on Kuprin, with Robert E. Lee, adaptation of the novel by Maurice Edelman (produced 1961). 1962.

Sparks Fly Upward, with Robert E. Lee (as *Diamond Orchid*, produced 1965; revised version, as *Sparks Fly Upward*, produced 1967). 1969.

Live Spelled Backwards (produced 1966). 1970.

Dear World, with Robert E. Lee, music by Jerry Herman, based on *The Madwoman of Chaillot* by Giraudoux (produced 1969).

The Incomparable Max, with Robert E. Lee (also director: produced 1969). 1972.

The Night Thoreau Spent in Jail, with Robert E. Lee (produced 1970). 1970.

Jabberwock: Improbabilities Lived and Imagined by James Thurber in the Fictional City of Columbus, Ohio, with Robert E. Lee (produced 1972). 1974.

First Monday in October, with Robert E. Lee (also director: produced 1975). 1979.

Whisper in the Mind, with Norman Cousins and Robert E. Lee (produced 1990).

The Plays of Lawrence and Lee, edited by Alan Woods (includes: *Inherit the Wind, Auntie Mame, The Gang's All Here, Only in America, A Call on Kuprin, Diamond Orchid, The Night Thoreau Spent in Jail, First Monday in October*). 1992.

The Angels Weep. In *Studies in American Drama: 1945 to the Present*. 1992.

SCREENPLAYS, with Robert E. Lee: *My Love Affair with the Human Race*, 1962; *The New Yorkers*, 1963; *Joyous Season*, 1964; *The Night Thoreau Spent in Jail*, 1972; *First Monday in October*, 1982.

RADIO PLAYS: *Junior Theatre of the Air* series, 1938; *Under Western Skies* series, 1939; *Nightcap Yarns* series, 1939, 1940; *Stories from Life* series, 1939, 1940; *Man about Hollywood* series, 1940; *Hollywood Showcase* series, 1940, 1941; *A Date with Judy* series, 1941, 1942; *They Live Forever* series, 1942; *Everything for the Boys* series, 1944; *I Was There* series; with Robert E. Lee—*Columbia Workshop* series, 1941–42; *Armed Forces Radio Service Programs*, 1942–45; *The World We're Fighting For* series, 1943; *Request Performance* series, 1945–46; *Screen Guild Theatre* series, 1946; *Favorite Story* series, 1946–49; *Frank Sinatra Show*, 1947; *Dinah Shore Program*, 1948; *The Railroad Hour*, 1948–54; *Young Love* series, 1949–50; *United Nations Broadcasts*, 1949–50; *Halls of Ivy* series, 1950–51; *Hallmark Playhouse* series, 1950–51; *Charles Boyer Show*, 1951; other freelance and special programs, 1941–50.

TELEVISION PLAYS: *Lincoln, The Unwilling Warrior*, 1975; with Robert E. Lee—*The Unexpected* series, 1951; *Favorite Story* series, 1952–53; *Song of Norway*, 1957; *West Point*, 1958; *Actor*, music by Billy Goldenburg, 1978.

OTHER

Oscar the Ostrich (for children; as Jerome Schwartz). 1940.
Actor: The Life and Times of Paul Muni. 1974.

Editor, *Off Mike: Radio Writing by the Nation's Top Radio Writers.* 1944.

BIBLIOGRAPHY: in *Studies in American Drama: 1945 to the Present.* 1992.

MANUSCRIPT COLLECTIONS: Lawrence and Lee Theatre Research Institute, Ohio State University, Columbus; Lincoln Center Library of the Performing Arts, New York; Kent State University, Ohio; Widener Library, Harvard University, Cambridge, Massachusetts; Ziv-United Artists film and transcription library.

CRITICAL STUDY: "The Greatest Sport in the World" (interview with Christopher Meeks), in *Writer's Digest*, March 1986.

THEATRICAL ACTIVITIES

DIRECTOR: **Plays**— *You Can't Take It with You* by George S. Kaufman and Moss Hart, *The Imaginary Invalid* by Molière, *Anything Goes* by Howard Lindsay and Russel Crouse, *The Green Pastures* by Marc Connelly, *Boy Meets Girl* by Bella and Sam Spewack, *H.M.S. Pinafore* and *The Pirates of Penzance* by Gilbert and Sullivan, and *Androcles and the Lion* by Shaw, in summer stock, 1934–37; *Mame*, 1969; *The Incomparable Max*, 1969; *The Crocodile Smile*, 1970; *The Night Thoreau Spent in Jail*, 1972; *Jabberwock*, 1974; *Inherit the Wind*, 1975; *First Monday in October*, 1975.

Jerome Lawrence comments:

Robert E. Lee and I have been called by various critics: "the thinking man's playwrights." In our plays and in our teaching we have attempted to be part of our times. We have done all we can to encourage truly national and international theatre, not confined to a few blocks of real estate in Manhattan or London's West End. Thus, we have sought to promote the growth of regional and university theatres through the formation of American Playwrights Theatre, to bring new and vital and pertinent works to all of America and all of the world.

It has been my privilege to travel to more than a hundred countries, often on cultural-exchange missions. At home, through the years, we have tried to encourage new and untried playwrights, stimulating their work through teaching and through the annual Margo Jones Award.

In our plays we have hoped to mirror and illuminate the problems of the moment—but we have attempted to grapple with universal themes, even in our comedies. We have tried for a blend between the dramatic and the entertaining: our most serious works are always leavened with laughter (*Inherit the Wind* is an example) and our seemingly frivolous comedies (*Auntie Mame*, *Mame*, *Jabberwock*) have sub-texts which we hope say something important for the contemporary world. We are pleased and gratified that our plays have been translated and produced in 34 languages.

We are lovers of the living theatre and intend to continue working and living in it.

"Eatable things to eat and drinkable things to drink," comments a shocked character in Dickens's short story "Mugby Junction," describing a visit to France. The British railway station buffet is the object of Dickens's scorn, and the news that French railways provide edible and easily assimilated food causes the staff of Mugby Junction's restaurant to come close to catatonic fits.

Many a critic, professional *or* amateur, might, in snobbish chorus, make similar comments about the works of collaborators Jerome Lawrence and Robert E. Lee. "Playable plays to play—or readable plays to read!" might be their disbelieving cry. The expressions of disapproval and disdain might be almost as extreme as those of the 19th-century railway grotesques, for both playability and readability are cardinal points of the works of Lawrence and Lee. Their plots are tight, their characters cleanly developed, their dialogue smooth. Actors like them for they present strong speeches and well developed scenes, and although this might be considered old-fashioned playwriting it is clear that audiences like it too. Their most successful work, *Inherit the Wind* (first presented at the National Theatre in New York, April 1955, after a run in Dallas under a great encourager of new talent, Margo Jones) was the third longest-running serious play in the history of Broadway. It is based on the famous Scopes Trial in Tennessee (the "Monkey Trial") when Darwinism and traditional religion had a head-on crash in a rural American setting. It featured Paul Muni and Ed Begley, who made the dialogue of this solid courtroom drama flow back and forth like a mounting tide. The script is very readable; although not deep it is most engaging in a theatrical, if not an intellectually involving way. The effect of putting two great contemporary orators, pitted one against the other, as the core of the play makes for compelling speeches, and the device of the trial itself provides a rounded dramatic vehicle, still open-ended enough to allow one of the protagonists to stand at the end weighing copies of the Bible and Darwin while planning the appeal. Today's audience (even though we would like to think ourselves beyond quaint beliefs) can still become emotionally involved over God versus gorilla. Good and forceful fare, it has been produced around the world.

Many of the works of Lawrence and Lee are lighter, mirroring their ability to zero in on the essentially sentimental underbelly of the average Broadway audience. Their evident enjoyment of the sentimental is one of their secrets. By far the largest part of the Broadway audience is out for fun, a pleasurable look at the land of never-never, which is why the musical when successful is always such a huge money-spinner. Lawrence and Lee pull off a clever trick with *Inherit the Wind* for it has many elements of the musical, yet gives patrons the self-importance of feeling they have seen something serious. They are also at home in creating an impossible character like *Auntie Mame*, first produced in New York in 1956. This giddy American dame was adored onstage, although she probably would not have been tolerated for more than a moment beyond Manhattan or Wilshire Boulevard. Many of the members of the audience would have come from suburban patios like the satirized Upsons (whose house in Connecticut is called "Upson Downs"—Lawrence has a weakness for rather ponderous puns in conversation and his own California house is called "Writers to the Sea") but the social comment is kept gentle and the medicine is never too strong. An amusing evening and intended to be nothing more no doubt, yet for this writer the play only sparked into life when Beatrice Lillie played the part in the London production.

Auntie Mame became the very successful musical *Mame* (May 1966) which Lawrence and Lee also wrote, featuring the then relatively unknown Angela Lansbury. Their collaboration on a monolithic musical called *Dear World* based on the Giraudoux play *The Madwoman of Chaillot* was less successful. However, it's hard to find fault with writers when faced with the complexities of producing musicals in New York City where music, lyrics, choreography, special songs, production numbers, direction, elaborate costumes, and stagger- ing scenery—along with equally staggering costs—seem often to overwhelm the basic book.

Nevertheless Lawrence and Lee seem happier when they are away from the big-time musical stage, as witness their commitment to a play entitled *The Night Thoreau Spent in Jail*. This play, first presented at Ohio State University in 1970, is an interesting experiment. Some years ago, intent on trying to circumvent the sterile Broadway scene where serious plays are concerned, the partners set up American Playwrights Theatre in Columbus, Ohio. It was a deliberate move away from New York in a laudable attempt to develop new audiences for serious drama, with the plays of dramatists, known and un- known, presented in a new "circuit"—the network of resident and university theatres across America. Each writer was guaranteed a number of *different* productions in various spots on this new circuit and many were produced before Lawrence and Lee launched one of their own—*Thoreau*, a subject of particular interest to young audiences, for it deals with one of the first cases of civil disobedience in America. Later collaborations include *Jabberwock* and *First Monday in October*.

Their hand with humour can, unfortunately, be a little heavy, and when tackling such a delicate exponent of the art as Max Beerbohm in *The Incomparable Max* they became caught in a morass that was anything but Maxian. There are times when the pair cleaves dangerously close to the jungle of clichés.

Lawrence and Lee collaborate easily—each has a veto, "but it's a positive one" says Lawrence. They both feel they can, and do, learn from criticism. Their contribution to American drama is perhaps most significant when one looks at the number of nations that know them from the many translations of their principle works. *Inherit the Wind* has been translated into 28 different languages while the citizens of Ireland, Israel, Holland, Germany, Bangladesh, and Russia, among others, have been given an eye-opening view of a Yankee philosopher's protest in *Thoreau*.

—Michael T. Leech

LAWSON, John Howard.

Born in New York City, 25 September 1894. Educated at the Halstead School, Yonkers, New York; Cutler School, New York, graduated 1910; Williams College, Williamstown, Massachusetts, 1910–14, BA 1914. Served in the American Ambulance Service in France and Italy during World War I. Married 1) Kathryn Drain in 1919 (divorced 1923), one son; 2) Susan Edmond in 1925, one son and one daughter. Cable editor, Reuters Press, New York, 1914–15; lived in Paris for two years after the War; director, New Playwrights Theatre, New York, 1927–28; screenwriter in Hollywood, 1928–47. Council member, Authors League of America, 1930–40; founding president, 1933–34, and member of the executive board, 1933–40, Screen Writers Guild. One of the "Hollywood Ten": served a one-year sentence for contempt of the House Un-American Activities Committee, 1950–51. *Died 11 August 1977.*

Publications

PLAYS

Servant-Master-Lover (produced 1916).
Standards (produced 1916).
Roger Bloomer (produced 1923). 1923.
Processional: A Jazz Symphony of American Life (produced 1925). 1925.
Nirvana (produced 1926).
Loudspeaker (produced 1927). 1927.
The International (produced 1928). 1928.
Success Story (produced 1932). 1932.
The Pure in Heart (produced 1934). In *With a Reckless Preface: Two Plays*, 1934.
Gentlewoman (produced 1934). In *With a Reckless Preface: Two Plays*, 1934.
Marching Song (produced 1937). 1937.
Algiers, with James M. Cain (screenplay). In *Foremost Films of 1938*, edited by Frank Vreeland, 1939.
Parlor Magic (produced 1963).

SCREENPLAYS: *Dream of Love*, with others, 1928; *The Pagan*, with Dorothy Farnum, 1929; *Dynamite*, with Jeanie Macpherson and Gladys Unger, 1929; *The Sea Bat*, with others, 1930; *Our Blushing Brides*, with Bess Meredyth and Helen Mainard, 1930; *The Ship from Shanghai*, 1930; *Bachelor Apartment*, with J. Walter Rubin, 1931; *Success at Any Price*, with others, 1934; *Blockade*, 1938; *Algiers*, with James M. Cain, 1938; *They Shall Have Music*, with Irmgard Von Cube, 1939; *Four Sons*, with Milton Sperling, 1940; *Earthbound*, with Samuel C. Engel, 1940; *Sahara*, with others, 1943; *Action in the North Atlantic*, with others, 1943; *Counter-Attack* (*One Against Seven*), 1945; *Smash-Up—The Story of a Woman*, with others, 1947.

OTHER

Theory and Technique of Playwriting. 1936; revised edition, as *Theory and Technique of Playwriting and Screenwriting*, 1949.

*The Hidden Heritage: A Rediscovery of the Ideas and Forces That Link the
  Thought of Our Time with the Culture of the Past.* 1950.
Film in the Battle of Ideas. 1953.
*Film: The Creative Process: The Search for an Audio-Visual Language and
  Structure.* 1964; revised edition, 1967.

CRITICAL STUDIES: *People's Theater in America* by Karen M. Taylor, 1973;
Stage Left: The Development of the American Social Drama in the Thirties by
R.C. Reynolds, 1986.

John Howard Lawson's eight major plays markedly reflect a commitment to
social protest and a zest for theatrical experimentation. Also they exemplify
the root concept of Lawson's dramatic theory expressed in his *Theory and
Technique of Playwriting and Screenwriting,* namely that dramatic conflict is
social conflict predicated on the exercise of the *conscious will,* whereby the
protagonist must strive to understand the world in order to be able consciously
to choose a course of action. Lawson's first two major plays, *Roger Bloomer*
and *Processional,* focus on an initially naive or socially unaware central figure
who follows a rugged path from ignorance or indifference to self-discovery and
social awareness.

The young protagonist of *Roger Bloomer* is the naïve son of a materialistic
midwestern businessman who rejects a Yale education to follow a dissatisfied,
home-town, working girl to New York, where she ultimately commits suicide.
Wrongly accused of responsibility for her death, the title character is thrown in
jail, where, at the drama's climax, he undergoes an expressionistic dream
sequence in which distorted apparitions from his past and his imagination
appear to free him from his inner turmoil of fears and guilt and prepare him for
maturity at the conclusion. Both the stylized nature of the dream sequence
projecting convoluted aspects of American life, and, in previous scenes, the
mechanical and exaggerated behavior of characters accenting the influence of
empty capitalistic values identify *Roger Bloomer* as an early example of
American expressionism pre-dating Elmer Rice's *The Adding Machine.*
Faulted by self-conscious poetic language, simplistic characters, and sentimentalized romance, the play has flaws, which, from our contemporary perspective, curtail its durability.

Processional eclectically combines elements of expressionism, jazz, and
vaudeville to make a sardonic statement about American social problems. Set
in a West Virginia coal-mining community divided by a strike, the play
presents caricatured figures of capitalistic authority, from businessman and
reporter to law officers and the Ku Klux Klan, while also offering a cartoon-
like one-dimensionality to working-class characters and such aspects of
American life as a strike, a July 4th celebration, the press, the military,
vigilantism, and romance.

The hero is the tough, brawling, politically-unaware miner Dynamite Jim
Flimmins, who defies, and is relentlessly pursued by, anti-labor authorities
until finally caught and blinded. During the pursuit Jim suffers confinement, in
a series of hiding places, which generates revelations through such expressionistic devices as "voices", causing his conversion from ignorant brawler to
inchoate political anarchist. Along the way he impregnates a town girl whom,

at the play's conclusion, the blinded protagonist marries as the strike is unexpectedly settled and a presidential telegram arrives ironically proclaiming that "all men are brothers". The author discloses his social criticism while sardonically presenting the flaws of both sides in the labor struggle. Although dated in its content and approach, *Processional* remains an interesting example of 1920's American protest drama and possesses a lively eclectic style.

Loudspeaker employs farce to examine critically American politics in its essential absurdity. Here the protagonist is the unethical Babbitt, with gubernatorial ambitions which he ultimately realizes, but at the cost of a falsely idealized family life being exposed as a sham. Cartoon-like characters and a cliché-ridden romance detract from the drama's credibility, yet Lawson's observations on politics and political aspirants can find parallels today.

The International extravagantly, if somewhat incoherently, mixes song, dance, choral movement, and vaudevillian and epic-theatre devices to attack an acquisitive society. Set in Tibet, the sprawling plot concerns the rebellion of a businessman's son converted to world revolution by his love for a female Soviet agent, with whom he dies a martyr's death for a noble, but ill-fated, cause. Romance is again treated sentimentally, and the language throughout is more rhetorical than realistic.

In later plays Lawson turned from theatrical experimentation to realism, while maintaining his social criticism. *The Pure in Heart* follows the fortunes of an innocent small-town heroine to the big city, where her determination to be an actress brings her into a backstage world of unprincipled sophisticates and to an ex-convict, with whom she falls in love. A romance develops which ends in death, in a callous world destructive of innocence and humanity.

Success Story chronicles the rise and fall of slum-born and success-driven New Yorker Sol Ginsberg, who betrays his left-wing beliefs and a loving girlfriend for a successful advertising career and his employer's materialistic mistress, whom he marries. His lust for wealth and power ultimately destroy him, demonstrating the author's overstated view that capitalistic values corrupt.

In *Gentlewoman*, its author dramatizes the ineffectual sterility of upper-class society. Into the milieu of the rich and well-educated comes unpolished Rudy Flannigan, a Lawson proletarian hero who finds his strong attraction to the urbane title character, Gwyn Ballentine, reciprocated. A relationship between them is short-lived, for she is too much imprisoned by her ingrained values to live without wealth and to accept Rudy as he is, and he realizes that remaining with Gwyn will compromise his proletarian ideals. The title character is one of Lawson's most successfully drawn.

Marching Song, Lawson's most didactic work, overstates the theme of group solidarity as a requisite for social action in the midst of capitalistic exploitation. The play eschews the stylistic devices of *Processional*, but chooses a similar locale: a company town beset by a labor dispute. Striking workers, portrayed as heroically noble and victimized, suffer cruel reprisals to win a costly victory after seizing a power station.

In overview, Lawson's plays lack contemporaneity and durability. His ideological themes have grown outdated—particularly in the light of recent world events. His theatrical experiments, which do not always mix styles and effects successfully, are now familiar and better-integrated elements of modern drama. Many of his characters lack humanly credible three-dimensionality and are not well-served by stilted or artificial language. Despite these shortcomings, however, Lawson is historically significant as an early innovator of American expressionism and as a major contributor to American social protest drama of the 1920s.

—Christian H. Moe

LEE, Robert E(dwin).

Born in Elyria, Ohio, 15 October 1918. Educated at Northwestern University, Evanston, Illinois; Drake University, Des Moines, Iowa; Ohio Wesleyan University, Delaware, 1935–37. Served in the U.S. Army, 1942–45: expert consultant to the Secretary of War, 1942; co-founder, Armed Forces Radio Service; writer-director, Armed Forces Radio Service, Los Angeles, 1942–45: Special Citation, Secretary of War, 1945. Married Janet Waldo in 1948; one son and one daughter. Astronomical observer, Perkins Observatory, Delaware, Ohio, 1936–37; director, WHK-WCLE Radio, Cleveland, 1937–38; director, Young and Rubicam, New York and Hollywood, 1938–42; professor of playwriting, College of Theatre Arts, Pasadena Playhouse, California, 1962–63. Since 1942 partner, Lawrence and Lee, and since 1955 vice-president, Lawrence and Lee Inc., New York and Los Angeles; since 1966, lecturer, University of California, Los Angeles. Co-founder and judge, Margo Jones award; co-founder, American Playwrights Theatre. Recipient: New York Press Club award, 1942; City College of New York award, 1948; *Radio-TV Life* award, 1948, 1952; Peabody award, 1949, 1952; *Radio-TV Mirror* award, 1952, 1953; *Variety* award, 1954, 1955; Donaldson award, 1955; Outer Circle award, 1955; British Drama Critics award, 1960; Moss Hart Memorial award, 1967; William Inge award, 1988; elected to Theater Hall of Fame and College of Fellows of the American Theatre, 1990. Lit.D.: Ohio Wesleyan University, 1962; M.A.: Pasadena Playhouse College of Theatre Arts, 1963; H.H.D.: Ohio State University, Columbus, 1979; Litt.D.: College of Wooster, Ohio, 1983. Agent (Attorney): Martin Gang, 6400 Sunset Boulevard, Hollywood, California 90028. Address: 15725 Royal Oak Road, Encino, California 91436, U.S.A.

Publications

PLAYS

Inside a Kid's Head, with Jerome Lawrence, in *Radio Drama in Action*, edited by Erik Barnouw. 1945.

Look, Ma, I'm Dancin', with Jerome Lawrence, music by Hugh Martin, conceived by Jerome Robbins (produced 1948).

The Crocodile Smile, with Jerome Lawrence (as *The Laugh Maker*, produced 1952; revised version, as *Turn on the Night*, produced 1961; revised version, as *The Crocodile Smile*, produced 1970). 1972.

Inherit the Wind, with Jerome Lawrence (produced 1955). 1955.

Shangri-La, with Jerome Lawrence and James Hilton, music by Harry Warren, adaptation of the novel *Lost Horizon* by Hilton (produced 1956). 1956.

Auntie Mame, with Jerome Lawrence, adaptation of the work by Patrick

Dennis (produced 1956). 1957; revised version, music by Jerry Herman, as *Mame* (produced 1966), 1967.

The Gang's All Here, with Jerome Lawrence (produced 1959). 1960.

Only in America, with Jerome Lawrence, adaptation of the work by Harry Golden (produced 1959). 1960.

A Call on Kuprin, with Jerome Lawrence, adaptation of the novel by Maurice Edelman (produced 1961). 1962.

Sparks Fly Upward, with Jerome Lawrence (as *Diamond Orchid,* produced 1965; revised version, as *Sparks Fly Upward,* produced 1967). 1969.

Dear World, with Jerome Lawrence, music by Jerry Herman, based on *The Madwoman of Chaillot* by Giraudoux (produced 1969).

The Incomparable Max, with Jerome Lawrence (produced 1969). 1972.

The Night Thoreau Spent in Jail, with Jerome Lawrence (produced 1970). 1970.

Jabberwock: Improbabilities Lived and Imagined by James Thurber in the Fictional City of Columbus, Ohio, with Jerome Lawrence (produced 1972). 1974.

Ten Days That Shook the World, based on reports from Russia by John Reed (also director: produced 1973).

First Monday in October, with Jerome Lawrence (produced 1975). 1979.

Sounding Brass (produced 1975). 1976.

Whisper in the Mind, with Norman Cousins and Jerome Lawrence (produced 1990).

The Plays of Lawrence and Lee, edited by Alan Woods (includes: *Inherit the Wind, Auntie Mame, The Gang's All Here, Only in America, A Call on Kuprin, Diamond Orchid, The Night Thoreau Spent in Jail, First Monday in October*). 1992.

SCREENPLAYS, with Jerome Lawrence— *My Love Affair with the Human Race,* 1962; *The New Yorkers,* 1963; *Joyous Season,* 1964; *The Night Thoreau Spent in Jail,* 1972; *First Monday in October,* 1982; with John Sinn— *Quintus,* 1971.

RADIO PLAYS: *Empire Builders* series, 1938; *Opened by Mistake,* 1940; *Flashbacks* series, 1940–41; *Three Sheets to the Wind,* 1942; *Task Force,* 1942; *Ceiling Unlimited,* 1942; *Meet Corliss Archer,* 1942; *Suspense,* 1943; *The Saint* 1945; with Jerome Lawrence— *Columbia Workshop* series, 1941–42; *Armed Forces Radio Service Programs,* 1942–45; *The World We're Fighting For* series, 1943; *Request Performance* series, 1945–46; *Screen Guild Theatre* series, 1946; *Favorite Story* series, 1946–49; *Frank Sinatra Show,* 1947; *Dinah Shore Program,* 1948; *The Railroad Hour,* 1948–54; *Young Love* series, 1949–50; *United Nations Broadcasts,* 1949–50; *Halls of Ivy* series, 1950–51; *Hallmark Playhouse* series, 1950–51; *Charles Boyer Show,* 1951; other freelance and special programs, 1941–50.

TELEVISION PLAYS: *A Colloquy with Paul,* 1961; with Jerome Lawrence— *The Unexpected* series, 1951; *Favorite Story* series, 1952–53; *Song of Norway,* 1957; *West Point,* 1958; *Actor,* music by Billy Goldenburg, 1978.

OTHER

Television: The Revolution. 1944.

BIBLIOGRAPHY: in *Studies in American Drama: 1945 to the Present.* 1992.

MANUSCRIPT COLLECTIONS: Lawrence and Lee Theatre Research Institute, Ohio State University, Columbus; Lincoln Center Library of the Performing Arts, New York; Kent State University, Ohio.

CRITICAL STUDY: "The Greatest Sport in the World" (interview with Christopher Meeks), in *Writer's Digest,* March 1986.

THEATRICAL ACTIVITIES

DIRECTOR: Plays—*Only in America,* 1960; *The Night Thoreau Spent in Jail,* 1970; *The Gang's All Here,* 1972; *Ten Days That Shook the World,* 1973.

Robert E. Lee comments:

The devil's name is Dullness. An eraser is sometimes more essential than a pencil. But merely to entertain is fatuous. Writing for today is really writing for yesterday; I try to write for tomorrow.

See the essay on Jerome Lawrence and Robert E. Lee.

LINNEY, Romulus.

Born in Philadelphia, Pennsylvania, in 1930. Educated at Oberlin College, Ohio, A.B. 1953; Yale University School of Drama, New Haven, Connecticut, M.F.A. 1958. Served in the U.S. Army, 1954–56. Actor and director in stock for 6 years; stage manager, Actors Studio, New York, 1960; has taught at the Manhattan School of Music, University of North Carolina, Chapel Hill, University of Pennsylvania, Philadelphia, Brooklyn College, Princeton University, New Jersey, Columbia University, New York, Hunter College, New York, and Connecticut College, New London. Recipient: National Endowment for the Arts grant, 1974; Obie award, 1980, for sustained achievement, 1992; Guggenheim fellowship, 1980; Mishima prize, for fiction, 1981; American Academy award, 1984; Rockefeller fellowship, 1986; American Theater Critics Association award, 1988, 1990; Helen Hayes award, 1990. Lives in New York City. Agent: Gilbert Parker, William Morris Agency, 1350 Avenue of the Americas, New York, New York 10019, U.S.A.

Publications

PLAYS

The Sorrows of Frederick (produced 1967). 1966.
The Love Suicide at Schofield Barracks (produced 1972). With *Democracy and Esther,* 1973; one-act version (produced 1984), in *The Best Short Plays 1986,* edited by Ramon Delgado, 1986.
Democracy and Esther, adaptation of the novels by Henry Adams (as *Democracy,* produced 1974; revised version produced 1975). With *The Love Suicide at Schofield Barracks,* 1973; as *Democracy,* 1976.

Holy Ghosts (produced 1974). With *The Sorrows of Frederick*, 1977.
The Seasons, Man's Estate (produced 1974).
Appalachia Sounding (produced 1975).
Old Man Joseph and His Family (produced 1977). 1978.
Childe Byron (produced 1977; revised version produced 1981). 1981.
Just Folks (produced 1978).
The Death of King Philip, music by Paul Earls (produced 1979). 1984.
Tennessee (produced 1979). 1980.
El Hermano (produced 1981). 1981.
The Captivity of Pixie Shedman (produced 1981). 1981.
Goodbye, Howard (produced 1982). In *Laughing Stock*, 1984.
Gardens of Eden (produced 1982).
F.M. (also director: produced 1982). In *Laughing Stock*, 1984.
April Snow (produced 1983). In *Three Plays*, 1989.
Laughing Stock (includes *Goodbye, Howard*; *F.M.*; *Tennessee*) (produced 1984). 1984.
Wrath, in *Faustus in Hell* (produced 1985).
Sand Mountain (includes *Sand Mountain Matchmaking* and *Why the Lord Come to Sand Mountain*) (produced 1986). 1985.
A Woman Without a Name (produced 1986). 1986.
Pops (includes *Can Can, Claire de Lune, Ave Maria, Gold and Silver Waltz, Battle Hymn of the Republic, Songs of Love*) (produced 1986). 1987; *Ave Maria* produced as *Hrosvitha* in *Three Poets*, 1989.
Heathen Valley, adaptation of his own novel (produced 1986). 1988.
Yancey (produced 1988). In *Three Plays*, 1989.
Juliet (produced 1988). In *Three Plays*, 1989.
Pageant, with others, music and lyrics by Michael Rice (produced 1988).
Precious Memories, adaptation of a story by Chekhov (also director: produced 1988); as *Unchanging Love* (produced 1991), 1991.
Three Plays (includes *Juliet, Yancey, April Snow*). 1989.
Three Poets (includes *Komachi, Hrosvitha, Akhmatova*; also director: produced 1989). 1990.
2 (produced 1990). In *Six Plays*, 1993.
Ambrosio (produced 1992). In *Seventeen Short Plays*, 1992.
Seventeen Short Plays (includes *Ambrosio, The Love Suicide at Schofield Barracks, Sand Mountain Matchmaking, Why the Lord Come to Sand Mountain, Komachi, Hrosvitha, Akhmatova, Can Can, Claire de Lune, Gold and Silver Waltz, Songs of Love, Juliet, Yancey, The Death of King Philip, El Hermano, The Captivity of Pixie Shedman, Goodbye, Howard*). 1992.
Six Plays (includes *F.M., Childe Byron, Tennessee, 2, April Snow, Heathen Valley*). 1993.

TELEVISION PLAYS: *The 34th Star*, 1976; episodes for *Feelin' Good* series, 1976–77.

NOVELS

Heathen Valley. 1962.
Slowly, By Thy Hand Unfurled. 1965.
Jesus Tales. 1980.

OTHER

Editor, with Norman A. Bailey and Domenick Cascio, *Ten Plays for Radio*. 1954.

Editor, with Norman A. Bailey and Domenick Cascio, *Radio Classics*. 1956.

MANUSCRIPT COLLECTION: Lincoln Center Library for the Performing Arts, New York.

THEATRICAL ACTIVITIES

DIRECTOR: **Plays**—*F.M.*, 1982; *Sand Mountain Matchmakers*, 1989.

Romulus Linney comments:

My plays and novels are drawn from either historical subjects or memories of my childhood in Tennessee and North Carolina, or direct personal experiences.

Romulus Linney has worked at the writer's trade as playwright, novelist, and television scriptwriter. His dramatic writing thus far has garnered awards and resulted in more than 15 plays produced on and off Broadway, in American regional theatres, and abroad. Widely ranging in subject and structure, Linney's plays show him to be a distinctive writer of uncommon literacy.

Linney often develops in his dramas a pattern of action in which his protagonists enter or mature in environments where they confront values repressive of their own worth as individuals. Usually tempted or victimized by such values, these characters experience them while testing or evaluating them against their own needs and beliefs and ultimately reaching a decision to accept or reject them. This pattern is evident in at least six plays: *The Love Suicide at Schofield Barracks*, *Democracy*, *Holy Ghosts*, *A Woman Without a Name*, *Tennessee*, and *The Sorrows of Frederick*.

Within the framework of a military inquiry, *The Love Suicide at Schofield Barracks* reveals the events behind the bizarre double suicide in 1970 of an army general and his wife in Hawaii at a Schofield Barracks Officers' Club party. As witnesses testify, a compassionate portrait emerges of a patriotic professional soldier whose beliefs become so shattered by Vietnam that with his wife he perpetrates—in the guise of a classic Japanese drama—a ritualistic suicide expressing disapproval of the war and America's conduct. The play generates considerable tension as the event is finally pieced together, and makes a strong statement about war and individual responsibility for national morality. The author also has written an equally powerful one-act version preserving the original's skillfully orchestrated characters.

Democracy, a combined dramatization of two Henry Adams 19th-century novels, introduces a wealthy widow and an agnostic photographer, two attractive and intelligent women who enter Washington's 1875 presidential society during the corruption-ridden Grant administration, to be individually charmed, courted, and proposed to by two attractive men of high station whose beliefs they abhor. They courageously reject the men and leave Washington. Major characters are richly drawn; the values of 19th-century American democracy are examined in a manner both provocative and dramatic.

In *Holy Ghosts* a runaway wife flees a boorish husband to find sanctuary with a Pentecostal sect whose members seek redemption from self-loathing by surviving the handling of poisonous snakes. When the husband angrily comes to reclaim his newly converted wife and lets his low self-esteem turn him into a convert during the cult's ritual, the wife abandons the sect, resolving to achieve independence and self-realization. This theatrically intriguing drama of redemption colorfully recreates the rural Southern milieu and its dispossessed. Also rising above domestic strife and despair by achieving self-recognition is the title character in *A Woman Without a Name*, a drama adapted from Linney's novel *Slowly, By Thy Hand Unfurled*. She is an uneducated, small-town Southern wife and mother tormented both by her turn-of-the-century family's afflictions and by its unfair calumny of her regarding its travails. With despairing self-doubt she records memories of family experiences in a journal as characters come forward re-enacting events and interacting with her as participant, and becomes progressively literate and liberated as she absolves herself of guilt and discovers her self-worth in a starkly yet imaginatively conceived portrait of feminine endurance and self-discovery. Similarly effective, the Obie-winning *Tennessee* portrays an elderly 1870 Appalachian woman, her family's sole survivor, who recalls her youth and realizes that her late husband cheated her of independence by tricking her into a frontier marriage's stern service. The richly rounded protagonist and vividly detailed exposition create a definitive world of the past with present parallels. (Appearing in a short-play trilogy collectively entitled *Laughing Stock*, *Tennessee* accompanies two efficacious comedies: *Goodbye, Howard*, about three sisters' confused death-watch over a brother; and *F.M.*, focusing on a talented rough-diamond student writer who shocks dilettante classmates in a creative writing course.)

The Sorrows of Frederick offers a psychological portrait of Prussia's philosopher-king Frederick the Great. In a series of sharply-etched scenes, Linney unravels the chronicle of a father-dominated prince who as a king forsakes great artistic and intellectual gifts to pursue power and finds himself a victim of his life at its end. Enriched by elevated dramatic language and fully rounded characterizations, the drama revivifies Frederick and, like the afore-mentioned five dramas, exemplifies Linney's concern with characters resolving their destinies by their choice of values. Treating a less regal tyrant, *2* thoughtfully examines the character of Hermann Goering during the 1945–46 Nuremberg trials as he reveals the self-deception and unrepentant Nazi prejudices existing within all nations and all would-be world conquerors.

Apparent in Linney's work is a penchant for comedy, romance, and the one-act form which is demonstrated by two collective works of short plays, *Sand Mountain* and *Pops*. Strong in homespun humor, *Sand Mountain* encompasses two Appalachian folklore yarns about, respectively, a discriminating young widow who rejects a bragging band of eligible men for a truth-telling widower, and the visit of Jesus and St. Peter, in human disguise, to a mountaineer family. *Pops*, consisting of six comically rich one-acts, treats forms of love, young and

old, from the romantic to the aesthetic. Among the collection's funniest works
are those of a progeny-opposed oldsters' romance (*Songs of Love*) and a 10th-
century abbess's defense of Hrosvitha's, and her own, right to create art (*Ave
Maria*). The latter, retitled *Hrosvitha*, accompanies *Komachi*, an adapted
Japanese Nō drama, and *Akhmatova*, demonstrating the Russian poetess's
calm ethical courage in confronting a Stalinist inquisition in an admirable
short-play collection entitled *Three Poets*.

In a darker mode, two more recent works trenchantly depict the tight rural
world of Appalachia: *Unchanging Love*—based on a Chekhov story and
formerly entitled *Precious Memories*—exposes the corruption and lack of
social compassion within a merchant family; and Linney's adaptation of his
novel *Heathen Valley*, whose narrator-protagonist disavows and opposes
church hierarchy and dogmatism to advocate his community's need for social
goodness.

A writer of substance and range, Romulus Linney creates plays that crackle
with challenging issues and theatricality, and evince by the spectrum of their
structural variety an imaginative craftsman. He is a major talent among
contemporary dramatists.

—Christian H. Moe

LOWELL, Robert (Traill Spence, Jr.).

Born in Boston, Massachusetts, 1 March 1917. Educated at schools in
Washington, D.C. and Philadelphia; Brimmer School, Boston; Rivers School;
St Mark's School, Southboro, Massachusetts, 1930–35; Harvard University,
Cambridge, Massachusetts, 1935–37; Kenyon College, Gambier, Ohio,
1938–40, A.B. (summa cum laude) 1940 (Phi Beta Kappa); Louisiana State
University, Baton Rouge, 1940–41. Conscientious objector during World War
II: served prison sentence, 1943–44. Married 1)the writer Jean Stafford, in
1940 (divorced, 1948); 2)the writer Elizabeth Hardwick in 1949 (divorced,
1972), one daughter; 3)the writer Caroline Blackwood in 1972, one son.
Editorial assistant, Sheed and Ward, publishers, New York, 1941–42; teacher
at the University of Iowa, Iowa City, 1950, 1953, and Kenyon School of
Letters, Gambier, Ohio, 1950, 1953; lived in Europe, 1950–52; teacher at
Salzburg Seminar on American Studies, 1952, University of Cincinnati, 1954,
Boston University, 1956, Harvard University, 1958, 1963–70, 1975, 1977,
and New School for Social Research, New York, 1961–62; professor of
literature, University of Essex, Wivenhoe, Colchester, 1970–72. Consultant in
Poetry, Library of Congress, Washington, D.C., 1947–48; visiting fellow, All
Souls College, Oxford, 1970. Recipient: Pulitzer prize, 1947; American
Academy grant, 1947; Guggenheim fellowship, 1947, 1974; Harriet Monroe
Poetry award, 1952; Guinness prize, 1959; National Book award, 1960; Ford
grant, for poetry, 1960, for drama, 1964; Bollingen Poetry Translation prize,
1962; New England Poetry club Golden Rose, 1964; Obie award, for drama,
1965; Sarah Josepha Hale award, 1966; Copernicus award, 1974; National
Medal for Literature, 1977. Member, American Academy. *Died 12 September
1977.*

Publications

PLAYS

Phaedra, from the play by Racine (produced 1961). In *Phaedra and Figaro*, 1961.

The Old Glory (*Benito Cereno* and *My Kinsman, Major Molineux*) (produced 1964). 1964; expanded version, including *Endecott and the Red Cross* (produced 1968). 1966.

Prometheus Bound, from a play by Aeschylus (produced 1967). 1969.

The Oresteia of Aeschylus. 1978.

VERSE

Land of Unlikeness. 1944.

Lord Weary's Castle. 1946.

Poems 1939–1949. 1950.

The Mills of the Kavanaughs. 1951.

Life Studies. 1959.

Imitations. 1961.

For the Union Dead. 1964.

Selected Poems. 1965.

The Achievement of Lowell: A Comprehensive Selection of His Poems, edited by William J. Martz. 1966.

Near the Ocean. 1967.

The Voyage and Other Versions of Poems by Baudelaire. 1968.

Notebook 1967–68. 1969; augmented edition, as *Notebook*, 1970.

The Dolphin. 1973.

History. 1973.

Poems: A Selection, edited by Jonathan Raban. 1974.

Selected Poems. 1976; revised edition, 1977.

Day by Day. 1977.

OTHER

The Collected Prose, edited by Robert Giroux. 1987.

Editor, with Peter Taylor and Robert Penn Warren, *Randall Jarrell 1914–1965*. 1967.

Translator, *Poesie*, by Eugenio Montale. 1960.

BIBLIOGRAPHY: *Lowell: A Reference Guide* by Steven Gould Axelrod and Helen Doese, 1982.

CRITICAL STUDIES: *Lowell* by John Crick, 1974; *Pity the Monsters: The Political Vision of Lowell* by Alan Williamson, 1974; *Lowell: Life and Art* by Steven Gould Axelrod, 1978; *American Aristocracy: The Lives and Times of James Russell, Amy, and Robert Lowell* by C. David Heymann, 1980; *Lowell* by Burton Raffel, 1981; *Lowell: A Biography* by Ian Hamilton, 1982.

Robert Lowell was the most considerable American poet of his generation to write for the stage. His first play was a verse translation of Racine's *Phèdre*, and though it is faithful to the French text, Lowell's imagery and energy seep into the English. Similarly, Lowell's translation of Aeschylus' *Prometheus Bound* shows his modern existential awareness of man's precarious fate. These translations have invigorated two classical tragedies into English, but Lowell's most important achievement in drama is the three plays of *The Old Glory*. Dramatizing stories of Hawthorne and Melville, Lowell has refracted America's past through the lens of the present. His plays are linked by the theme of revolution and the image of the American flag, the Old Glory. The three plays show that every declaration of independence is grounded in violence, however lofty the banner.

Based on Hawthorne stories, the first two plays of Lowell's trilogy are set in American colonial times, but for Lowell the seed of imperial America is already present in 17th-century Puritan Massachusetts and in 18th-century Boston. Lowell's third play, based on Melville's novella *Benito Cereno*, foreshadows the Civil War and contemporary racial conflict. In all three dramas a single act of rising tension explodes into violence. Far from patriotic celebration, these three plays underline the ambiguities and cruelties of revolutionary action.

Endecott and the Red Cross, the first play of the trilogy, takes its subject and title from a Hawthorne short story, but Lowell also uses another Hawthorne story about Endecott, "The Maypole of Merry Mount", as well as Thomas Morton's *New English Canaan*. Morton's account serves as background for the two Hawthorne stories. Unlike Hawthorne, Lowell provides his Puritan protagonist Endecott with an Anglican antagonist Morton, and the play implies that Endecott's Puritans and Morton's Anglicans shared a taste for commerce. Economic competition sharpens ideological conflict, and during the course of the play that conflict becomes irreconcilable, erupting into Endecott's rebellion against English rule.

Lowell's Endecott can remember his courtly youth, before the death of his wife turned him into a soldier needing a stern faith. Highly self-conscious, Lowell's Endecott understands his own Puritanism, and he is still prey to gentle memories, so that he countermands the punitive dicta of Elder Palfrey. And yet, he recounts to Elder Palfrey a dream in which he, Endecott, is Elder Palfrey, preacher and executioner. That dream, invented by Lowell, portrays men who commit cruelties in the name of rigid religions. Even as Endecott narrates the dream, he perceives its symbolic prophecy; a rigid English ruler will force upon the colony his governor and his religion, and an equally rigid opponent will have no recourse but rebellion.

By the end of the play, Endecott as Endecott acts out his dream; opposing the king's rule in Morton, he addresses his soldiers in words that are "half truth, half bombast". Originally as moderate as Morton, he has acquired the cruel rigidity of Elder Palfrey. "A Bible in his left hand and a loaded pistol in his right", he orders Merry Mount destroyed and captive Indians executed. In cutting the Red Cross flag of England from its staff, Endecott has taken the first violent step that will result in the supremacy of the Old Glory.

The second play of Lowell's trilogy, based on Hawthorne's *My Kinsman, Major Molineux*, takes place a century and a half later, on the eve of the American Revolution. The protagonist, eighteen-year-old Robin, comes to Boston to seek his fortune, hoping for favour from his kinsman, Major Molineux, British governor. Within the few hours that Robin spends in the city, his country innocence gradually gives way to complicity in the lynching of his kinsman.

Lowell emphasizes the impact of events upon Robin by giving him a younger brother, who is at once more innocent and more self-absorbed during their long day in the city, in which they are initiated into corruption and rebellion. In the play's last scene Robin and his brother finally see their kinsman, Major Molineux, tarred and feathered by the rebels. Even as Robin pities his kinsman, Robin "unconsciously" waves the rebel Rattlesnake flag in his face as his brother "unthinkingly" offers dirt to be flung at the Major. The latter remains courageously loyal to the English king, and is finally silenced by Lowell's infernal figures, the Ferryman knocking him senseless with an oar and a masked colonel stabbing him with his sword. When the Major is dead, the crowd cries: "Long live the Republic! Long live the Republic!" Slowly, the crowd disperses until Robin and his brother are alone. But they are immutably tainted. Robin's brother echoes the words he has heard: "Major Molineux is dead." Robin, leading his brother back to the city, affirms: "Yes, Major Molineux is dead." They are independent now, and neither of them mentions that the Major was their kindly kinsman.

As in *Endecott and the Red Cross* the flag emerges as the central image. In *My Kinsman,* Major Molineux the Union Jack is emblematic of British authority, and the Rattlesnake flag of the Boston rebellion. Endecott had to cut down the Red Cross to prepare the way for the Old Glory, and the Boston rebels have to raise their Rattlesnake in the same cause. The Old Glory will wave over gory ground.

In *Benito Cereno* Lowell follows the events of the Melville novella, to subvert its intention. Only in this third play does the Old Glory actually appear, as the standard of Yankee Captain Delano's ship. Lowell's play opens with a "machinelike" salute to the American flag, which will soon be opposed by the pirate flag on the slave-ship *San Domingo* —a black skull and crossbones on white ground. But slavery as piracy is a metaphor of implicit and gradual meaning in Lowell's play about white slavers and black slaves, which takes place, ironically, on American Independence Day.

When Lowell's Captain Delano boards the *San Domingo* captained by Don Benito Cereno, he disapproves of the dirt and lack of discipline. Once aboard, Delano is almost hypnotized by the heat and the buzzing insects, the rambling Captain Cereno and the unctuous slaves. Patronizing and friendly to Spanish Benito Cereno, Delano is patronizing and oppressive to the black Babu. While Don Benito is taking his siesta, Babu shows Captain Delano four brief plays within the play, symbolizing the cruel complexity of race relations. Later Delano is a spectator at scenes that stage like plays within the play: an African king festooned with chains, Babu shaving Cereno with the Spanish flag as towel, a formal dinner with "La Marseillaise" as background music.

When Delano's boatswain Perkins (invented by Lowell) warns Delano that the blacks are the masters of Cereno's slave ship, the Yankee captain is incredulous but courageous. With the blacks in open and vengeful command, Delano watches with disapproval as Don Benito is forced to walk across the Spanish flag to kiss a skull, as his boatswain takes the same path. When his own turn comes, Delano points his gun at Babu. American seamen arrive in the nick of time, and Babu rises a white handkerchief but cries out: "The future is with us." Delano retorts: "This is your future." and shoots him dead. Melville's Delano is a man of good will with limited perceptions. Lowell's Delano is a man whose good will is eroded by his limited perceptions. Behind his smoking gun, the Old Glory is not visible, but its presence is felt.

The Old Glory is an unglorious view of American history. Lowell's dramatizations rely on imagery and analogy rather than conventional characters. Endecott and the Red Cross incorporates an aborted Maypole ritual; My Kinsman, Major Molineux is a voyage through an Inferno; Benito Cereno is mesmerizing in its plays within plays within the play of black and white. Each member of the trilogy lives in its own theatrical atmosphere, but Robert Lowell's language provides dramatic dialogue that is highly imaged and rhythmed, relevant, and resonant.

—Ruby Cohn

LUCAS, Craig.

Born in Atlanta, Georgia, 30 April 1951. Educated at Boston University, Massachusetts, B.F.A. (cum laude) 1973. Since 1987 associate artist, South Coast Repertory, Costa Mesa, California, and since 1989 member, Circle Repertory, New York. Recipient: Dramalogue award 1986; Los Angeles Drama Critics award, 1986; George and Elizabeth Marton award, 1986; Guggenheim fellowship, 1987; Rockefeller grant, 1989; Tony award, 1989; Outer Critics Circle award, 1989; Obie award, 1990; Sundance Film Festival Audience award, 1990. Lives in New York City. Agent: Peter Franklin, William Morris Agency, 1350 Avenue of the Americas, New York, New York 10019, U.S.A.

Publications

PLAYS

Marry Me a Little, with Norman Rene, music and lyrics by Stephen Sondheim (produced 1980).
Blue Window, music by Craig Carnelia (produced 1984). With Reckless, 1989.
Three Complaints, music by Stewart Wallace (produced 1985).
Missing Persons (produced 1985).
Three Postcards, music and lyrics by Craig Carnelia (produced 1987).
Prelude to a Kiss (produced 1988). 1990.
Reckless, music by Craig Carnelia (produced 1988). With Blue Window, 1989.
Orpheus in Love (libretto), music by Gerald Busby (produced 1992).
Throwing Your Voice (produced 1992).
Credo, excerpts published in One on One: The Best Men's Monologues for the Nineties, edited by Jack Temchin, 1993.

SCREENPLAYS: Longtime Companion, with Norman Rene, 1990; Prelude to a Kiss, with Norman Rene, 1991.

TELEVISION PLAY: Blue Window, with Norman Rene, 1987.

MANUSCRIPT COLLECTION: Boston University, Special Collections, Boston, Massachusetts.

THEATRICAL ACTIVITIES

ACTOR: **Plays**—role as Confederate Sniper in *Shenandoah* by James Lee Barrett, 1975, and Nathan, 1976–77; Gentleman of the Court in *Rex*, book by Sherman Yellen, music by Richard Rodgers, lyrics by Sheldon Harnick, 1976; male singer and standby Max Jacobs in *On the Twentieth Century*, book and lyrics by Betty Comden and Adolph Green, music by Cy Coleman, 1978; member of the company, *Sweeney Todd, the Demon Barber of Fleet Street*, book by Hugh Wheeler, music and lyrics by Stephen Sondheim, 1979; *Marry Me A Little* by Lucas and Norman Rene, music and lyrics by Stephen Sondheim, 1980.

Several of Craig Lucas's plays are prefaced by epigraphs from other authors, which give pointers to the journeys taken in his work. W. H. Auden's aptly-titled "Leap Before you Look" provides the motto to *Reckless*, at the startling opening in which the heroine Rachel, a happy suburban housewife, anticipating a happy Christmas with her husband and kids, is suddenly told by her husband that he has taken out a contract on her life. As an intruder breaks in downstairs, Rachel climbs out of the bedroom window. Windows in Lucas's world have something of the mystery of the nursery window in *Peter Pan*, and in *Reckless* Rachel's defenestration begins one of the roller-coaster journeys on which Lucas takes his audiences.

　　Reckless is an unusual Christmas fable—fleeing into the snowy night, Rachel is given a lift by Lloyd, who takes her to the Springfield, Massachusetts home which he shares with the crippled Pooty, who is also deaf and dumb. But as Pooty reveals to Rachel later, she so adored Lloyd when she first saw him at the centre for the physically handicapped where he works that she has only pretended to be deaf and dumb because she felt that only if she were somehow needier than others would she get special attention from Lloyd. This is only one of several revelations in the play—that Lloyd walked out on a wife with multiple sclerosis is another ("The past is the nightmare you wake up to every day," he says)—as it traces Rachel's journey through a wacky parody of television game-shows ("Your Money or your Wife?") and her encounters with different doctors, all played by the same actor (Lucas has some sharp fun at psychiatry's expense in these sections), to eventual self-discovery and maturity. It ends with Rachel as a doctor herself, interviewing her now-adolescent son (who, of course, does not recognise her) who has had problems sleeping, troubled by his family's past, in a scene which climaxes in a curiously affecting sense of reconciliation at another Christmas time.

　　The audience goes on another journey in *Blue Window*, a play of dazzling technical achievement, which takes place in five separate New York apartments simultaneously. It's Sunday night and Libby is preparing to give a party (relying on her friend Griever for telephonic advice); other guests include a lesbian couple and a composer and his girl. Before, during, and after the party, Lucas weaves their conversations into a complex mesh of overlapping dialogue, scoring verbal music against an abstract blue setting and building up against this slightly sterile background the patterns of young(ish) professional mid-1980s Manhattan, anxious and self-defensively wry (especially in Griever's often outrageous cadenzas) with some splendid running sight-gags (Libby's encounter with a caviare jar breaks off a cap on a tooth, forcing her to mask her mouth for much of the evening). On the page, it might seem over-wistful and fatally arch, but in performance *Blue Window* combines social comedy with a melancholy substrain to potent effect.

Lucas's association with the Circle Repertory Company in New York continued with a recent play, *Prelude to a Kiss*, which then moved to Broadway for a long run. E. M. Forster's *aperçu* from *Howard's End* that "Death destroys a man, but the idea of death is what saves him" suggests the dark urban fairytale at the centre of the play.

Prelude to a Kiss represents the boldest of Lucas's journeys to date. In Manhattan, a young man (Peter) falls in love with a young girl (Rita) he meets at a party. There are just a few clues (Rita's insomnia, for example) that suggest perils lurking behind the idyll of their courtship. At their wedding at Rita's parents' New Jersey home, an unsettling incident occurs, with an uninvited old man kissing Rita and then going on his way. Rita seems oddly affected by the encounter, and her oddness increases on the couple's Jamaican honeymoon. By the disturbing close of Act One, we have begun to realise that a transmigration of souls has taken place, and the second act traces Peter's dilemma; with Rita's soul residing in the body of an old man dying of cancer, can he still love her? Love makes Peter resourceful enough to engineer a way by which to regain Rita's soul, and the play ends with their reunion after a typical Lucas tragi-comic journey. The play occasionally falls into the trap of becoming overslick, even fey, but obliquely—as he does in much of his work—Lucas reaffirms the power of love in an age of fears which compromise it. And the hairpin bends Lucas has to negotiate in the rides he creates give his best work a sense of exhilarating adventure.

—Alan Strachan

LUDLAM, Charles.

Born in Floral Park, New York, 12 April 1943. Educated at Hofstra University, Hampstead, New York, 1961–65, B.A. in Drama, 1965. Member, John Vaccaro's Play-House of the Ridiculous, New York, 1965–67; founding director, Ridiculous Theatrical Company [RTC], 1967, for which he wrote, acted, and directed until his death. Lecturer, University of Massachusetts, Amherst, 1972, University of New London, Connecticut, 1974 and 1975, American University, Washington, DC, 1976, New York University, 1977 and 1979–80; adjunct associate professor, Yale University, New Haven, Connecticut, 1982–83; directed for the Santa Fe Opera Company, 1985–86. Recipient: Obie award, 1969, 1973, 1975, 1977, 1985, 1987; Drama Desk award, 1982, 1985; Rosamund Gilder award, 1986. *Died 28 May 1987.*

Publications

PLAYS

Big Hotel (produced 1967).
Conquest of the Universe; or, When Queens Collide (produced 1967).

Turds in Hell, with Bill Vehr (produced 1969). In *Drama Review*, September 1970.

The Grand Tarot (produced 1969; revised version produced 1971).

Bluebeard (produced 1970). In *More Plays from Off-Broadway*, edited by Michael Smith, 1972; published separately, 1987.

Eunuchs of the Forbidden City (produced 1971). In *Scripts 6*, April 1972.

Corn, music by Virgil Young (produced 1972).

Camille: A Tear-Jerker, from a play by Dumas *fils* (produced 1973).

Hot Ice (produced 1973). In *Drama Review*, June 1974.

Stage Blood (produced 1975). 1979.

Professor Bedlam's Educational Punch and Judy Show (puppet play; produced 1975).

Caprice (produced 1976; revised version, as *Fashion Bound*).

Jack and the Beanstalk (for children; produced 1976).

The Adventures of Karagöz (produced 1976).

Der Ring Gott Farblonjet, music by Jack McElwaine (produced 1977).

Aphrodisiamania (dance scenario; produced 1977).

The Ventriloquist's Wife (produced 1978).

Anti-Galaxie Nebulae, with Bill Vehr and Everett Quinton (puppet play; produced 1978).

Utopia Incorporated (produced 1978).

The Enchanted Pig (produced 1979). 1989.

The Elephant Woman (produced 1979).

A Christmas Carol, from the story by Dickens (produced 1979).

Reverse Psychology (produced 1980). 1989.

The Production of Mysteries, music by Peter Golub (libretto; produced 1980).

Love's Tangled Web (produced 1981). 1989.

Secret Lives of the Sexists (produced 1982).

Exquisite Torture (produced 1982).

Galas (produced 1983).

Le Bourgeois Avant-Garde (produced 1983).

The Mystery of Irma Vep (produced 1984). 1987.

Salammbó, from the novel by Flaubert (produced 1985).

The Artificial Jungle (produced 1986). 1987.

Die Fledermaus (libretto; produced 1986).

Medea. 1988.

Isle of the Hermaphrodites; or, The Murderered Minion.

How Not to Write a Play.

Complete Plays (includes all original plays). 1989.

SCREENPLAYS: *The Sorrows of Dolores; The Museum of Wax.*

OTHER

Ridiculous Theatre: Essays and Opinions. 1993.

CRITICAL STUDIES: "A Brief Life" by Steven Samuels in Ludlam's *Complete Plays*, 1989; *New American Dramatists 1960–1990* by Ruby Cohn, 1991.

THEATRICAL ACTIVITIES

DIRECTOR: **Plays**—most of his own plays, and *Whores of Babylon* by Bill Vehr, 1968. **Film**—*The Sorrows of Dolores*, 1981.
ACTOR: **Plays**—many of his own plays, and *Whores of Babylon* by Bill Vehr, 1968. **Films**—*Lupe*, 1966; *Imposters*, 1979.

Actor, director, designer, and playwright Charles Ludlam, founder of New York's Ridiculous Theatrical Company, employed all his diverse theatrical skills for one overriding purpose—to make people laugh. In his 20-year career—cut short by his untimely death from AIDS—he proved himself a comic master.

Ludlam's playwriting achievements include almost 30 plays, plus a dance scenario, two films, a couple of puppet serials, a frame tale for a cabaret, and two opera librettos. In writing and mounting them, Ludlam adhered to principles that comedy should combine humor and pathos, should dramatize serious themes by means of farce, wit, parody, melodrama, and satire, should concern hypocrisy and moral paradox, and should take risks.

Like Joe Orton, Ludlam often shows himself a strict moralist, even though his standards may differ from the norm. Whereas several Ludlam plays explicitly personify good and bad angels, or devils versus angelic figures, or feature death as a character or force, Ludlam more often indicts the objects of his ridicule for violating his own humanistic standards (as when the lovers in *The Artificial Jungle* live by an amoral "law of the jungle"). Although conservatives might label his obscenity and scatology proof of moral iconoclasm, his work suggests nothing is sacred only in areas such as sex, which have always been the province of satirists and farceurs. But even as he frees our inhibitions, moving spectators quickly from incredulity at his daring to joining him in raucous belly laughs, Ludlam demonstrates outrage at hypocrisy, cruelty, greed, con-games, sycophancy, and other violations of his own moral imperatives.

Ludlam staged his indictments of human folly and Aristophanic celebrations of the free spirit with overtly theatrical, yet traditional methods—what Ludlam called "lost strains in theatre craft"—such as footlights, thunder sheets, wind machines, and outrageous but carefully crafted costumes designed by Ludlam's successor as Artistic Director of the RTC, Everett Quinton.

Ludlam tends to acknowledge, in presentational fashion, that spectators are watching a play rather than observing real life. In *Big Hotel* one character laments, "two deaths in one play", while another complains, "I've lost the thread of the narrative". In *Conquest of the Universe*, Tamberlaine plans to go to the theatre to see the play in which we're watching him; later Zabina protests: "That was the worst line I've ever had to say in *any* play". In addition, characters discuss the play and/or the playwright in *Hot Ice*, *Stage Blood*, *How Not to Write a Play*, and *The Ventriloquist's Wife*. Rarely does Ludlam's theatricality fail: in one play he invents a hunchback, pinhead, sex maniac who sneaks into a convent disguised as Santa Claus and is met by a nun on roller skates; in another, he creates for a gay actor (originally played by Ludlam himself) the role of a straight job-applicant, who impersonates a gay physical culture expert, who's pretending to be a heterosexual anti-feminist woman, who's mistaken by a female bedmate for a lesbian!

Of course, Ludlam lifts his plots and gags from all of Western culture, particularly its films, books, plays, and operas. Although partly parodying his originals, Ludlam also reveres them; he sticks so closely to his sources in his classic adaptations that his departures prove all the more hilarious. Ludlam rifles from Chaucer, Shakespeare, and numerous other dramatists, novelists (including the Brontës, Dickens, and Zola), fairy tales (*Cinderella, Rumpelstiltskin, Beauty and the Beast, Bluebeard,* and *Jack and the Beanstalk*), films (*Grand Hotel, Sunset Boulevard, White Heat,* and *Double Indemnity*), and even Wagner's *Ring* and the American Declaration of Independence.

Each script revels in wordplay — "gownless evening strap", "molten irony", "I'm too Jung to be Freudened", "the plot sickens", "the Enema of the People" — and puns proliferate. Careful attention rewards the listener with verbal gems harder to catch on first hearing. Even the mock-heroic plays, where opportunity presents itself less often, interrupt the bombast with delicious colloquialisms.

Ludlam employs all the other tried-and-true sources of humor, from pie-in-the-face slapstick in *Camille* and *Hot Ice*, to bedroom farce in *Bluebeard, Reverse Psychology,* and *Secret Lives of the Sexists,* and cross-dressing in numerous plays. One of his most successful farces, *How to Write a Play,* finds the character of Ludlam at his typewriter, trying to meet a script deadline while mobbed by a suicidal woman, gay seniors, a belly dancer, a balloon folder, and a gorilla; in the midst of all this he's forced to try to raise money for his theatre by impersonating his (fictional) twin sister. Yet Ludlam likewise succeeds with horror farce (*Salammbô*) and black comedy (*The Artificial Jungle*). Ludlam's topical targets of satire include diets high in sugar, fat, and chemical additives; cryogenic freezing of corpses; the fashion industry; psychiatrists and modern art; seeming excesses and pretensions in avant-garde music, dance, and theatre (and their critics); and feminists. And Ludlam builds entire scripts from the self-parody of melodrama. Thus we laugh at the material itself, exaggerated only mildly, in such plays as *Salammbô, A Christmas Carol, Medea, Isle of the Hermaphrodites; or, The Murdered Minion, Love's Tangled Web,* and *Exquisite Torture.*

Ludlam mixes ridicule with reverence in his best known works. Thus, when he played Camille, his sincerity moved spectators to tears, even while he carefully revealed the hairy chest beneath the *décolletage,* intentionally undercutting the perfect verisimilitude. Ludlam also travesties, yet pays tribute to, the Victorian penny-dreadful in his *tour de force, The Mystery of Irma Vep.* This side-splitting Gothic horror spoof concerns Lord Edgar's marriage to a new wife, Lady Enid, even though the loyalties of the servants, Jane and Nicodemus, still belong to their first mistress, Irma Vep (the name is an anagram of vampire). Joining in the mayhem at the manor are a monster, an Egyptian con-artist, a mummy, and an apparition of Irma Vep. Moreover, in the original production Nicodemus transformed into a werewolf — onstage — as Ludlam simultaneously acted both, plus the role of Lady Enid.

Although he directed his plays, Ludlam did not star in them all. His famous parts included Norma Desmond in *Big Hotel,* the title roles in *Camille* and *Galas,* and the 13-year-old virgin priestess of the moon in *Salammbô* (all in drag), as well as Hamlet in *Stage Blood,* Dr. Silver in *Reverse Psychology,* Dr.

Rufus Foufas in *Le Bourgeois Avant-Garde*, Dickens' Scrooge in *A Christmas Carol*, the Ventriloquist in *The Ventriloquist's Wife*, and the title role in *Bluebeard*. A balding gnome, he became gorgeous in women's roles. Ludlam likewise possessed a beautifully trained and versatile voice, physical exuberance and agility, expert timing, mobile features, and a gift for mimicry.

—Tish Dace

LUDWIG, Ken.

Born in York, Pennsylvania, 15 March 1950. Educated at York Suburban High School, 1968; Haverford College, Pennsylvania, B.A. (magna cum laude) 1972; Trinity College, University of Cambridge, England, LL.M. 1975; Harvard Law School, Cambridge, Massachusetts, J.D. 1976. Married Adrienne George in 1976; one daughter. Attorney (Of Counsel), Steptoe and Johnson, law firm, Washington, D.C., 1976–89. Recipient: Helen Hayes award, 1991–92; Tony award, 1992. Lives in Washington, D.C. Agent: Gilbert Parker and Peter Franklin, William Morris Agency, 1350 Avenue of the Americas, New York, New York 10019, U.S.A.

Publications

PLAYS

Class Night (sketches) (produced 1970).
Divine Fire (produced 1979).
Sullivan and Gilbert (produced 1983). 1989.
Postmortem (produced 1984). 1989.
Dramatic License (produced 1985).
Lend Me a Tenor (as *Opera Buffa*, produced 1985; as *Lend Me a Tenor*, produced 1986). 1986.
Crazy for You, adaptation of *Girl Crazy* by George and Ira Gershwin (produced 1991).

THEATRICAL ACTIVITIES

DIRECTOR: **Play**—*Who's Afraid of Virginia Woolf* by Edward Albee, 1972.

Ken Ludwig comments:

The tradition of stage comedy that I admire most is what scholars call "high comedy" and I like to call "muscular comedy." It's the kind of comedy which, while firmly rooted in reality and the emotions of the characters, bursts off the stage, has a story filled with unexpected twists and turns, contains a broad range of characters from different levels of society, and abounds in word play—all in all, a reflection of our real lives, but somehow "bigger." The most distinguishing hallmark of this kind of comedy is some form of confusion, deception, or mistake, either in the workings of the plot or at the core of the structure.

The tradition began about 2,000 years ago with that irreverent Roman, Plautus. It re-emerged in the comedies of Shakespeare where mistaken identities and deception abound (*viz.*, in my opinion, the greatest comedies ever written, *Twelfth Night*, *As You Like It*, *Much Ado About Nothing*, and *A Midsummer Night's Dream*). Then came Goldsmith and Sheridan (*She Stoops to Conquer* and *The Rivals*) in the 18th century. In the 19th century the tradition is best seen in the comic operas of Rossini and Donizetti. And in our own century the tradition re-emerges in the stage comedies of Kaufman and Hart, Hecht and MacArthur, the screen comedies of Lubitsch and Sturges, and in the uniquely American musical comedies that were written in the 1920s and 1930s.

This is the form of drama, which, when it has greatness about it, touches me most deeply. My goal as a writer is to reinvent this tradition for our own times.

It is hardly surprising that Ken Ludwig should have achieved his biggest success to date with *Crazy for You*, his 1990s reworking of the 1930s book to the old Gershwin musical *Girl Crazy*. Music runs like a seam through Ludwig's plays and it was surely that musical sense and his sharp ear for the rhythm and shaping of a scene that made him the ideal choice to reconstruct the show's libretto affectionately.

Sullivan and Gilbert, Ludwig's play about the volatile relationship between Gilbert and Sullivan, may not tread any noticeably new ground, but it integrates the accompanying Savoy Opera songs with adroit smoothness, and the play has some astute scenes revealing the pitfalls of artistic collaboration.

Lend Me a Tenor is that rarity, a completely successful modern farce. Leading comedy writers have either failed signally in this tricky field (Neil Simon with *Rumours*) or skirted with homage to the form (such as Alan Ayckbourn paying tribute to Ben Travers in *Taking Steps*), with—in Britain at least—only Ray Cooney left to fly the flag for farce. So *Lend Me a Tenor* was doubly welcome—a farce which had all the classic Swiss-watch precision of plotting as it handled the spiralling complexities of its initially simple central situation, while retaining wit and heart. In a hotel suite in 1930s Cleveland, an imperious Opera House manager faces disaster when the Italian tenor ("Il Stupendo") booked to sing Otello at an important charity gala falls into a drunken stupor and is presumed dead (the scene of this assumption, involving the misunderstanding of the goodbye note from the tenor's jealous wife, may be a familiar farce staple—Ayckbourn uses it too in *Taking Steps*—but here it's superbly funny, because so credibly plotted and planted). To save the day, the impresario's dogsbody, Max, besotted by his employer's daughter, gets the chance to realise his operatic ambitions when he puts on blackface to win acclaim as Otello. Of course Il Stupendo awakes and dresses in costume, leading to a post-performance second act of hair's-breadth near-misses as real and substitute Otellos enter and exit through the suite's multiple doors, while the aphrodisiacs of fame and seductive music figure more strongly as various swooning females crowd the suite.

The play works well (it achieved an especially buoyant success in Jerry Zaks's high-octane New York production) not just because of its meticulous timing and passages of climactic lunacy (reaching the heights of some vintage Marx Brothers sequences), but also because of the spine of the plot, the old standby of understudy blossoming into star, given extra mileage here by a genuinely appealing central character; the audience moves progressively towards Max throughout the play as he looks like winning both his girl and musical fame.

Theatrical ambitions are also at the heart of Ludwig's expert book for *Crazy for You*—his hero, Bobby Childs, dreams of a dancing career in the Zangler Follies in 1930s New York, but is forced to act for his affluent family law firm to reposses a bankrupt Western township. Out in Deadrock, Nevada, there just happens to be a disused theatre and Bobby falls for the owner's daughter. Ludwig then cheekily re-works his central *Tenor* device with Bobby impersonating the flamboyant Zangler, only for the real Zangler to turn up. The script has a blithe, spring-heeled invention that will no doubt have producers besieging Ludwig for more of the same, but it is to be hoped that he will also come up with another play as funny as *Lend Me a Tenor*.

—Alan Strachan

M

MACHADO, Eduardo.

Born in Havana, Cuba in 1953. Moved to the United States in 1956. Lives in New York. Agent: William Craver, The Writers and Artists Agency, 19 West 44th Street, Suite 1000, New York, New York 10036, U.S.A.

Publications

PLAYS

Rosario and the Gypsies, music by Rick Vartorella (produced 1982).
The Modern Ladies of Guanabacoa (produced 1983). In *The Floating Island Plays*, 1991.
Broken Eggs (produced 1984). In *On New Ground* (an anthology of Hispanic plays), edited by Betty Osborne, 1986.
Fabiola (produced 1985). In *The Floating Island Plays*, 1991.
When It's Over, with Geraldine Sher (produced 1986).
Wishing You Well (produced 1987).
Why to Refuse (produced 1987).
A Burning Beach (produced 1988).
Don Juan in New York City (produced 1988).
Garded (opera libretto) (produced 1988).
Once Removed (produced 1992). In *Plays in Process*, vol. 9, no. 3, 1988.
The Day You'll Love Me, adaptation of the play by José Ignacio Cabrujas (produced 1989).
Cabaret Bambu (produced 1989).
Related Retreats (also director: produced 1990).
Pericones (produced 1990).
Stevie Wants to Play the Blues, music by Fredric Myrow, lyrics by Machado and Myrow (produced 1990).
In the Eye of the Hurricane (produced 1991). In *The Floating Island Plays*, 1991.
The Floating Island Plays (includes *The Modern Ladies of Guanabacoa*, *Fabiola*, *Broken Eggs*, *In the Eye of the Hurricane*). 1991.
Across a Crowded Room (produced 1991).

TELEVISION PLAYS: *Death Squad*, 1989: *China Rios, HBO*, 1989; *In the Heat of Saturday Night*, 1990.

362

THEATRICAL ACTIVITIES
ACTOR: **Play**—role in *A Visit* by Maria Irene Fornés, 1981.

With his teacher and mentor Irene Fornés, Eduardo Machado stands at the
forefront of Hispanic-American drama, which is an increasingly important
component of theatre in the United States. His plays, unlike those of Fornés,
are not innovative in form. The best of them—Machado is prolific, and his
work uneven—bring Chekhov to mind: in the tempestuous and yet ordinary
life of a household may be seen the end of an era, the remaking of a society.
The highly individual characters are viewed with a critical yet compassionate
eye. The plays are tragicomic, filled with absurdity, pettiness, energy, and grief.

Sent from his homeland as a child, the Havana-born Machado knows at first
hand the loss of privilege, the experience of exile. In all his major work this
dramatist seeks the meaning of his people's history. *A Burning Beach* symbolically represents Cuban society in the late 19th century, at the time of the short-
lived uprising led by the poet José Martí; this decadent world of Yankee
imperialists, landowners of Spanish descent, and Afro-Cuban servants is
clearly doomed. The Bay of Pigs débâcle is the background event in *Once
Removed*, which chronicles the misadventures of an emigrant family in Florida
and then in Texas; Machado's most satiric play, it is also full of affectionate
admiration for the bumbling perseverance of its displaced persons. But the
richest of Machado's works is the quartet published as *The Floating Island
Plays*. Autobiographically based, they make up an epic 20th-century drama,
encompassing the stories of several Cuban families linked by marriage and
then by exile in the United States. This is poetic history, in which details of
characters' lives shift to meet the needs of an individual play, and it is high
comedy, laying bare personal and societal shortcomings at every turn.

Each of the *Floating Island* plays shows an extended family struggling with
fundamental change. Set in the Cuba of 1928–31, *The Modern Ladies of
Guanabacoa* depicts the domestic rituals of a society that is conservative,
Catholic, and patriarchal. As the title suggests, these values are under siege,
and in the end the head of the household, a proud Basque who excels at
womanizing rather than moneymaking, is shot dead, possibly by an enraged
husband, possibly by a government displeased by the expansion of the family's
bus routes, possibly at the instigation of his son-in-law, a taxi driver who is
using the family money and his own ability to make their fortune. Remarkably
fair to all his characters, the playwright nonetheless exhibits throughout his
work a special sympathy for those out of power: women, homosexual men, all
those from a lower class and with darker skin. Not that such Machado
creations are weak people. Women, here and in other plays, are the survivors;
they frequently get what they want. In these home-centered plays they are
often dominant figures.

Fabiola covers the period 1955–67, and introduces *Floating Island*'s central
catalytic (though offstage) event—the rise of Fidel Castro. Portraying a
wealthy family related by marriage to that of the previous play, this work is the
quartet's least comic and most daring. Its terrain is Gothic, at its heart the
desperate love of one brother for another. The less committed partner in this
incestuous relationship must flee the country; his needier brother finally slits

his wrists as yet more family members leave for the United States. Years of luxury end in anguish and guilt.

In the Eye of the Hurricane dramatizes the nationalization of the bus company established in the first play. It is 1960, and the taxi driver, in his climb to wealth, has apparently forgotten where he came from. He and his wife, attempting to keep their buses through public protest, are shocked when their efforts are made ludicrous by a lack of support: the populace cheers the takeover. Family members who lent romantic support to Castro's revolution come to see what it really means.

The resolution—if that is the right word—of this epic story takes place in 1979 at a country club in suburban Los Angeles, where three generations of displaced Cubans gather for a wedding. *Broken Eggs* is the blackest of comedies. Though these Cuban-Americans are once again reasonably well off, their tight family structure has come apart. The bride's parents have divorced and her father is remarried to an Argentinian. Nearly everyone is drug-dependent: the older generation downs valium and alcohol, the younger snorts cocaine. Though family lives throughout the *Floating Island Plays* are filled with squabbles, tensions, and power struggles, nastiness has reached a new level. Yet for all this we see that both the family and Cuba are inescapable. More than one character in more than one play quotes Christopher Columbus: "This is the most beautiful land that human eyes have seen." The loss of Eden is the quintessential American theme. Machado knows that you can't go home again.

—M. Elizabeth Osborn

MacLEISH, Archibald.

Born in Glencoe, Illinois, 7 May 1892. Educated at schools in Glencoe; Hotchkiss School, Lakeville, Connecticut, 1907–11; Yale University, New Haven, Connecticut (editor, *Yale Literary Magazine*), 1911–15, A.B. 1915 (Phi Beta Kappa); Harvard Law School, Cambridge, Massachusetts, 1915–17, 1919, LL.B. 1919. Served in the U.S. Army, 1917–19; captain. Married Ada Hitchcock in 1916; one daughter and three sons. Lecturer in Government, Harvard University, 1919–1921; attorney, Choate Hall and Stewart, Boston, 1920–23; lived in Paris, 1923–28; editor, *Fortune* magazine, New York, 1929–38; curator, Niemann Foundation, Harvard University, 1938; librarian of Congress, Washington, D.C., 1939–44; director, U.S. Office of Facts and Figures, 1941–42, assistant director, Office of War Information, 1942–43, and assistant Secretary of State, 1944–45, Washington, D.C,; chair of the U.S. Delegation to the Unesco drafting conference, London, 1945, and member of the executive board, Unesco, 1946. Rede lecturer, Cambridge University, 1942; Boylston professor of rhetoric and oratory, Harvard University, 1949–62; Simpson lecturer, Amherst College, Massachusetts, 1963–67. Recipient: Shelley Memorial award, 1932; Pulitzer prize, for verse, 1933, 1953, for drama, 1959; New England Poetry club Golden Rose, 1934; Bollingen prize, 1952; National Book award, 1953; Sarah Josepha Hale award, 1958; Tony award, 1959; National Association of Independent Schools award, 1959; Academy of American Poets fellowship, 1965; Oscar, for documentary, 1966; Presidential Medal of Freedom, 1977; National Medal for Literature, 1978; American Academy Gold Medal for Poetry, 1979; M.A.: Tufts University, Medford, Massachusetts, 1932; D. Litt.,: Wesleyan University, Middletown, Connecticut, 1938; Colby College, Waterville, Maine, 1938; Yale University, 1939; University of Pennsylvania, Philadelphia, 1941; University of Illinois, Urbana, 1947; Rockford College, Illinois, 1952; Columbia University, New York, 1954; Harvard University, 1955; Carleton College, Northfield, Minnesota, 1956; Princeton University, New Jersey, 1965; University of Massachusetts, Amherst, 1969; York University, Toronto, 1971; LL.D.,: Dartmouth College, Hanover, New Hampshire, 1940; Johns Hopkins University, Baltimore, 1941; University of California, Berkeley, 1943; Queen's University, Kingston, Ontario, 1948; University of Puerto Rico, Rio Piedras, 1953; Amherst College, Massachusetts, 1963; D.C.L.: Union College, Schenectady, New York, 1941; L.H.D.: Williams College, Williamstown, Massachusetts, 1942; University of Washington, Seattle, 1948. Commander, Legion of Honour (France); Commander, el Sol del Peru: President American Academy, 1953–56. *Died 20 April 1982.*

Publications

PLAYS

Nobodaddy. 1926.
Union Pacific (ballet scenario), music by Nicholas Nabokoff (produced 1934). In *The Book of Ballets*, 1939.
Panic: A Play in Verse (produced 1935). 1935.
The Fall of the City: A Verse Play for Radio (broadcast 1937). 1937.
Air Raid: A Verse Play for Radio (broadcast 1938). 1938.
The States Talking (broadcast 1941). In *The Free Company Presents*, edited by James Boyd, 1941.
The American Story: Ten Broadcasts (includes *The Admiral*; *The American Gods*; *The American Name*; *Nat Bacon's Bones*; *Between the Silence and the Surf*; *Discovered*; *The Many Dead*; *The Names for the Rivers*; *Ripe Strawberries and Gooseberries and Sweet Single Roses*; *Socorro, When Your Sons Forget*) (broadcast 1944). 1944.
The Trojan Horse (broadcast 1952). 1952.
This Music Crept by Me upon the Waters (broadcast 1953). 1953.
J.B.: A Play in Verse (produced 1958). 1958.
The Secret of Freedom (televised 1959). In *Three Short Plays*, 1961.
Three Short Plays: The Secret of Freedom, Air Raid, The Fall of the City, 1961.
Our Lives, Our Fortunes, and Our Sacred Honor (as *The American Bell*, music by David Amram, produced 1962). In *Think*, July-August 1961.
Herakles: A Play in Verse (produced 1965). 1967.
An Evening's Journey to Conway, Massachusetts: An Outdoor Play (produced 1967). 1967.
The Play of Herod (produced 1968).
Scratch, from *The Devil and Daniel Webster* by Stephen Vincent Benét (produced 1971). 1971.
The Great American Fourth of July (produced 1975). 1975.

Six Plays (includes *Nobodaddy, Panic, The Fall of the City, Air Raid, The Trojan Horse, This Music Crept by Me upon the Waters*). 1980.

SCREENPLAYS (documentaries): *Grandma Moses*, 1950; *The Eleanor Roosevelt Story*, 1965.

RADIO PLAYS: *The Fall of the City*, 1937; *King Lear*, from the play by Shakespeare, 1937; *Air Raid*, 1938; *The States Talking*, 1941; *The American Story* series, 1944; *The Son of Man*, 1947; *The Trojan Horse*, 1952; *This Music Crept by Me upon the Waters*, 1953.

TELEVISION PLAY: *The Secret of Freedom*, 1959.

VERSE

Songs for a Summer's Day (A Sonnet-Cycle). 1915.
Tower of Ivory. 1917.
The Happy Marriage and Other Poems. 1924.
The Pot of Earth. 1925.
Streets in the Moon. 1926.
The Hamlet of A. MacLeish. 1928.
Einstein. 1929.
New Found Land: Fourteen Poems. 1930.
Before March. 1932.
Conquistador. 1932.
Frescoes for Mr. Rockefeller's City. 1933.
Poems 1924–1933. 1933; abridged edition, as *Poems*, 1935.
Public Speech. 1936.
Land of the Free—U.S.A. 1938
Dedication: Motet for Six Voices, music by Douglas Stuart. 1938.
America Was Promises. 1939.
Freedom's Land, music by Roy Harris. 1942.
Actfive and Other Poems. 1948.
Collected Poems 1917–1952. 1952.
Songs for Eve. 1954.
New York. 1958.
Collected Poems. 1963.
The Wild Old Wicked Man and Other Poems. 1968.
The Human Season: Selected Poems 1926–1972. 1972.
New and Collected Poems 1917–1976. 1976.
On the Beaches of the Moon. 1978.

OTHER

Housing America, with others. 1932.
Jews in America, with others. 1936.
The Irresponsibles: A Declaration. 1940.
The Next Harvard, As Seen by MacLeish. 1941.
A Time to Speak: The Selected Prose. 1941.
The American Cause. 1941.
American Opinion and the War: The Rede Lecture. 1942.

A Time to Act: Selected Addresses. 1943.

Poetry and Opinion: The Pisan Cantos of Ezra Pound: A Dialog on the Role of Poetry. 1950.

Freedom Is the Right to Choose: An Inquiry into the Battle for the American Future. 1951.

Art Education and the Creative Process. 1954.

Poetry and Journalism. 1958.

Emily Dickinson: Three Views, with Louise Bogan and Richard Wilbur. 1960.

Poetry and Experience. 1961.

The Dialogues of MacLeish and Mark Van Doren, edited by Warren V. Bush. 1964.

The Eleanor Roosevelt Story. 1965.

A Continuing Journey. 1968.

The Great American Frustration. 1968.

Champion of a Cause: Essays and Addresses on Librarianship, edited by Eva M. Goldschmidt. 1971.

Riders on the Earth: Essays and Recollections. 1978.

Letters 1907–1982, edited by R.H. Winnick. 1983.

Reflections, edited by Bernard A. Drabeck and Helen E. Ellis. 1986.

Editor, with E.F. Prichard, Jr., *Law and Politics: Occasional Papers of Felix Frankfurter 1913–1938.* 1962.

Other journalism pieces, lectures, and pamphlets published.

BIBLIOGRAPHIES: *A Catalogue of the First Editions of MacLeish* by Arthur Mizener, 1938; *MacLeish: A Checklist* by Edward J. Mullaly, 1973.

CRITICAL STUDIES: *MacLeish* by Signi Lenea Falk, 1965; *MacLeish* by Grover Smith, 1971.

Were it not for the success of *J.B.: A Play in Verse,* Archibald MacLeish would be just another of the many modern poets who yearned to hear their verse in the theatre without accommodating that verse to the exigencies of the theatre. MacLeish was sporadically drawn to the theatre over five decades, since he published his first play, *Nobodaddy,* in 1926. Of his plays, two are drawn from classical myth, two from the Bible, one from a modern American story.

Nobodaddy is a biblical play, but the title is an invention of the poet William Blake, who designated the God of orthodox religion by this word composed of "nobody" and "daddy". In MacLeish's play God is absent from the three acts resting on Genesis—the fall of Adam in Acts I and II, Cain's murder of Abel in Act III. In the absence of God, Eve offers her human love first to Adam and then to Cain. Father and son are men who pit their questioning minds against an indifferent universe, and human love does not fulfil them.

In the socially conscious 1930s MacLeish shifted his attention from the universe to society. While the 1929 financial crash was fresh in people's minds, MacLeish wrote *Panic,* a verse play about the panic produced by the bank failures. The play is influenced by German Expressionist contrast between the caricature protagonist-banker McGafferty and the mass of men whom he wrongs. Though McGafferty refuses to panic at the bank failure, he finally shoots himself rather than face the accusations of those he has ruined.

MacLeish's next two plays (written for radio but also produced on the stage) contain the collective protagonist and social resonances of Expressionist drama. In *The Fall of the City* the city falls because it will not defend itself against invaders. In *Air Raid* the village inhabitants are destroyed because they will not take shelter from enemy planes in the early days of air raids. In each play the collective victim cannot believe in the dangerous reality of destructive war.

Though MacLeish's play *The Trojan Horse* was written over a decade after the radio plays, it too uses a collective protagonist that consents to its own destruction. Disregarding warnings, the people of Troy admit the deadly horse, and the play ends on Cassandra's prophecies of doom for the city. A year later, however, MacLeish wrote a verse play in a quite different key, *This Music Crept by Me upon the Waters*. The Shakespearean title already suggests a mood play, where the drama lies largely in the music of the lines. A moonrise on the Caribbean is of such exquisite beauty that two of the ten characters are inspired to base a new, shared life on its enchantment. Elizabeth and Peter plan to leave their respective husband and wife, but they do not wish to injure them. Faced with the sudden disappearance of Peter's wife, the romantic couple renounce their hope of a new union. At the play's end, Peter's wife is found prosaically cooking potatoes, but the poetic inspiration has "crept by", never to return.

By the time MacLeish dramatized the Job story in his *J.B.*, he had experimented with mood play, Expressionist play, and modern relevance of myth in a variety of meters. *J.B.* is a composite of earlier MacLeish techniques, and the new whole coheres through the playlong viability of a play within the play. MacLeish's inner play is the Job story, but his frame draws upon an area that has fascinated modern artists—the circus. "A travelling circus . . . has been on the roads of the world for a long time", and "the raking of the rings and the hang of the canvas give a sense that the audience too is inside the huge, battered, ancient tent."

In the acting version of *J.B.* (unfortunately less widely distributed than the reading version), the play opens as two nameless roustabouts finish putting up the circus tent, and two circus vendors enter with their wares. Frame and inner play are joined when the roustabouts take minor roles in the play within the play: soldiers who announce the war death of Job's son, reporters who bring the news of the automobile accident in which two more children die, policemen who describe the rape and murder of Job's youngest daughter, and finally Civil Defense officers during an atomic war.

More important is the consistent framing role of the circus vendors, Zuss and Nickles, who feel impelled to stage the Job story. A little uneasily, they don the masks of God and Satan, and they later register surprise at the biblical words they emit through their masks. But they frequently remove the masks, to comment on the story that they witness. Paradoxically, they become more involved in the story as their roles diminish, and their involvement is consistent in viewpoint—Zuss speaking for orthodox acceptance of God's will and Nickles for rebellious and sometimes cynical youth.

What Zuss and Nickles half create and half observe is the Job story in a modern American setting. J.B. is first seen as a successful businessman, surrounded by a loving family at Thanksgiving dinner. But soon, as in the Bible, disaster descends: J.B. loses his children, his fortune, his home, and his health. At the end of Act I he pleads: "Show me my guilt, O God!" But God remains mysterious, as in the Bible. Job's biblical comforters appear in contemporary guise—Freudian, Marxist, and clergyman—who yield no more comfort than their ancestors. Uncomforted, deserted by his wife, J.B. offers to repent. Finally, however, J.B. asserts his innocence and his dignity, rejecting the attitudes of both Zuss and Nickles, rejecting both, "Yes in ignorance" and "No in spite." Towards the end of MacLeish's *J.B.* Zuss and Nickles exit separately. The frame dissolves into the Job story, which becomes the portrait of Everyman. J.B. is beaten but not vanquished, and his wife returns to him in love. Frail human love is J.B.'s answer to the Voice out of the Whirlwind.

MacLeish's *J.B.*, a humanized Job play, was followed by his *Herakles*, a humanized Greek tragedy, based on *Mad Herakles* of Euripides. Like the Greek tragedy, the American play splits in two. Euripides shows the triumphant return of Herakles in time to rescue wife and sons from their enemy, but, mad, Herakles himself then slays wife and sons. MacLeish writes about a proud, monomaniacal American scientist who visits Athens after receiving the Nobel prize. In the second half of MacLeish's play the scientist's wife and child visit Delphi, where they witness Herakles' story as a play within the play. The relationship of Herakles and Megara reflects that of the scientist and his wife. Like J.B.'s wife, Megara pleads for human love, but the ancient hero is no humanist, and Herakles spurns Megara in order to vie with the gods, as did Adam and Cain in MacLeish's first play, *Nobodaddy*. The implication is that such heroic hubris is also the sin of modern American science.

Through various verse forms and settings, MacLeish espoused a simple dignified humanism in the face of disaster. And this persistent optimism, couched in a rhythmic and readily apprehended language, embellished with a setting at once colourful and meaningful, made for his unusual success on the commercial stage—in *J.B.*

—Ruby Cohn

MAC LOW, Jackson.

Born in Chicago, Illinois, 12 September 1922. Educated at the University of Chicago, 1939–43, A.A. 1941; Brooklyn College, New York, 1955–58, A.B. (cum laude) in Greek 1958. Formerly married to the painter Iris Lezak; two children. Freelance music teacher, English teacher, translator, and editor, 1950–66; reference book editor, Funk and Wagnalls, 1957–58, 1961–62, and Unicorn Books, 1958–59; copy editor, Alfred A. Knopf, 1965–66, all in New York. Member of the editorial staff, and poetry editor, 1950–54, *Now, Why?* (later *Resistance*), a pacifist-anarchist magazine; instructor, American Language Institute, New York University, 1966–73; poetry editor, *WIN* magazine, New York, 1966–75. Recipient: Creative Artists Public Service grant, 1973, 1976; PEN grant, 1974; National Endowment for the Arts fellowship, 1979. Address: 42 North Moore Street, New York, New York 10013, U.S.A.

Publications

PLAYS

The Marrying Maiden: A Play of Changes, music by John Cage (produced 1960).
Verdurous Sanguinaria (produced 1961). 1967.
Thanks: A Simultaneity for People (produced 1962).
Letters for Iris, Numbers for Silence (produced 1962).
A Piece for Sari Dienes (produced 1962).
Thanks II (produced 1962).
The Twin Plays: Port-au-Prince, and Adams County, Illinois (produced 1963). 1963.
Questions and Answers. . . . : A Topical Play (produced 1963). 1963.
Asymmetries No. 408, 410, 485 (produced 1965).
Asymmetries, Gathas and Sounds from Everywhere (produced 1966).
A Vocabulary for Carl Fernbach-Flarsheim (produced 1977). 1968.

PERFORMANCE SCORES AND BROADSIDES: *A Vocabulary for Sharon Belle Mattlin* [*Vera Regina Lachman, Peter Innisfree Moore*], 1974–75; *Guru-Guru Gatha,* 1975; *1st Milarepa Gatha,* 1976; *1st Sharon Belle Mattlin Vocabulary Crossword Gatha,* 1976; *Homage to Leona Bleiweiss,* 1976; *The WBAI Vocabulary Gatha,* 1977, revised edition, 1979; *A Vocabulary Gatha for Pete Rose,* 1978; *A Notated Vocabulary for Eve Rosenthal,* 1978; *Musicwords (for Phill Niblock),* 1978; *A Vocabulary Gatha for Anne Tardos,* 1980; *Dream Meditation,* 1980; *A Vocabulary Gatha for Malcolm Goldstein,* 1981; *1st [2nd] Happy Birthday, Anne, Vocabulary Gatha,* 1982; *Unstructured Meditative Improvisation for Vocalists and Instrumentalists on the Word "Nucleus,"* 1982; *Pauline Meditation,* 1982; *Milarepa Quartet for Four Like Instruments,* 1982; *The Summer Solstice Vocabulary Gatha,* 1983; *Two Heterophonics from Hereford Bosons 1 and 2,* 1984; *Phonemicon from Hereford Bosons 1,* 1984.

RADIO WRITING: *Dialog unter Dichtern/Dialog among Poets,* 1982; *Thanks/Danke,* 1983; *Reisen/Traveling,* 1984; *Locks,* 1984.

COMPOSER: Incidental music for *The Age of Anxiety* by W.H. Auden, produced 1954; for *The Heroes* by John Ashbery, produced 1955.

VERSE

The Pronouns: A Collection of 40 Dances—for the Dancers—6 February-22 March 1964. 1964.
August Light Poems. 1967.
22 Light Poems. 1968.
23rd Light Poem: For Larry Eigner. 1969.
Stanzas for Iris Lezak. 1972.
4 Trains, 4–5 December 1964. 1974.
36th Light Poem: In Memoriam Buster Keaton. 1975.
21 Matched Asymmetries. 1978.
54th Light Poem: For Ian Tyson. 1978.

A Dozen Douzains for Eve Rosenthal. 1978.
Phone. 1978.
Asymmetries 1–260: The First Section of a Series of 501 Performance Poems.
   1980.
Antic Quatrains. 1980.
From Pearl Harbor Day to FDR's Birthday. 1982.
"Is That Wool Hat My Hat?" 1983.
Bloomsday. 1984.
French Sonnets, Composed Between January 1955 and April 1983. 1984.
The Virginia Woolf Poems. 1985.
Representative Works 1938–1985. 1986.
Twenties, 100 Poems. 1991.

RECORDINGS: *A Reading of Primitive and Archaic Poems*, with others; *From a Shaman's Notebook*, with others.

CRITICAL STUDIES: "Jackson Mac Low Issue" of *Vort 8*, 1975, and *Paper Air*, vol. 2, no. 3, 1980.

THEATRICAL ACTIVITIES
ACTOR: **Plays**—in *Tonight We Improvise* by Pirandello, 1959, and other plays.

Jackson Mac Low is recognized as America's leading dramatist of the aleatoric school, which uses chance-structured materials and is best known by its principal musical exponent, John Cage. Mac Low's works for the theatre have been performed in the U.S.A., Canada, Germany, Brazil and England, although few have ever been commercially published in a complete form.

   Mac Low's original interest was musical composition, though after 1939 he became increasingly involved in poetry. During the 1940s Mac Low contributed to such anarchist publications as *Now, Why?* (later called *Resistance*) and was poetry editor for *WIN*, for the Workshop In Nonviolence. Most of his poems are, however, designed for live performance and Mac Low has described himself as a "Writer and Composer of Poetry, Music, Simultaneities, and Plays."

   The most active phase of his theatre activity begins with Prester John's Company in New York in 1949 (one of the most interesting early off-off-Broadway groups), as co-director and actor in various Paul Goodman plays, and continues in a long association with the Living Theatre beginning in 1952, originally as composer for productions of John Ashbery's *The Heroes*, W.H. Auden's *The Age of Anxiety*, etc., but also as an actor, and eventually as dramatist.

   The major phase of his dramatic corpus begins also with his association with the Living Theatre and, at about the same time, with John Cage. There are two sets of "Biblical Poems" and a "Biblical Play," performed in 1955, and a major play called *Lawrence*, based on writings by D.H. Lawrence. These pieces are extremely static and resemble Gagaku oratorios of words. The climax of this group of works is *The Marrying Maiden* performed in repertoire by the Living Theatre in 1960–61 with a sound score by John Cage. This play is totally lyrical and abstract, and it includes actions to be determined by the performers using a randomizing process. The Living Theatre's production was extremely conventional and inappropriate; it failed to bring out the uniqueness of the piece which was, as a result, unpublished except as an acting script and has not been performed since. About the works of this time, Mac Low has written:

> All during the 1940s and 1950s, many poems of mine in all modes express a pacifistic and libertarian political viewpoint strongly related to religious attitudes derived from Taoism, Buddhism, and mystical Judaism (Chassidism and Cabala). . . . These religious and political views, along with the more libertarian schools of psychotherapy [e.g. Paul Goodman], helped make me receptive to the use of chance operations and to the interpenetration of art works and the environment. . . .

Mac Low's performance works are structured as social models in which each participant participates as a co-equal and direction is self-guidance and by working-out, rather than being along doctrinaire, authoritarian, or imposed-visionary lines. The sound of the lines is as important as the sense (the sound often *is* the sense), resulting in a uniquely musical theatre experience.

After *The Marrying Maiden* the plays become more choric—there is action, usually in unison and repetitive—though the texts remain more musical than semantic. As with *Lawrence*, the pieces take their names from some aspect of their source material. For instance, one major work of this period is *Verdurous Sanguinaria*, which is derived from a botanical text on wild flowers. Another is *The Twin Plays*, mentioned before, two plays with identical action in all respects, but one of which uses combinations of the letters in the name "Port-au-Prince" and the other proverbs collected from "Adams County Illinois" which become the names for their respective plays. Another of these works is *Questions and Answers Incredible Statements the Litany of Lies Action in Freedom Statements and Questions All Round Truth and Freedom in Action; or, Why Is an Atom Bomb Like a Toothbrush? A Topical Play* which takes political texts reflecting Mac Low's views, treats it as a litany, then randomizes the actions.

Simultaneous with Mac Low's theatre work (and not necessarily completely separate from it) Mac Low's poems were developing in parallel blocks. There are early works such as *Peaks and Lamas* (1957, included in the magazine *Abyss*, Spring 1971). There is *Stanzas* for *Iris Lezak*, a massive cycle of over 400 pages, written more or less immediately after *The Marrying Maiden* and in some ways paralleling it. And at the end of *Stanzas*, the work develops into the *Asymmetries*, another large cycle (unpublished in any complete form but, like the Iris Lezak stanzas, often performed). These poems are overwhelmingly ear-oriented. They include long silences, difficult to approximate on a printed page apart from performance. They may be "poetry" but they partake of theatre, especially of the heard elements. Many are "simultaneities," by Mac Low's term, but theatre in fact.

Starting in the late 1950s the theatre of Happenings began to develop, with its emphasis on the simple image. The acme of Happenings was the Fluxus group, which performed in Europe, Japan, and the U.S.A. many works by George Brecht, Ben Vautier, Ay-o, Dick Higgins, Bob Watts, Wolf Vostell, Yoko Ono, Chieko Shiomi, and others. In 1962 and the years immediately following, the Fluxus group published and performed a number of Mac Low pieces. Mac Low's third major body of performance works relates to the

Fluxus kind of piece. Many of these pieces, such as *Thanks* or *Questioning*, have sets of directions and intentions as scripts, and these are filled in improvisatorially by the performer. Others, such as the *Gathas* (a series begun in 1961), are purely choric "simultaneities," in which the readers read the sounds in any direction. Still other performance pieces are "buried" in other cycles, such as the *8th Light Poem* which is a scenario, written in a fairly typical Happenings vein. There also exist film scenarios from this period and in this style, the best known of which is *Tree* in which the cameraman is asked to photograph a tree, unmoving and static, through a day.

Mac Low's cycle of odes, highly personal poems in classical form, do not use chance in any direct way and suggest a more direct and semantic phase in his work.

—Dick Higgins

MAMET, David (Alan).

Born in Flossmoor, Illinois, 30 November 1947. Educated at Rich Central High School; Francis W. Parker School; Neighborhood Playhouse School, New York, 1968–69; Goddard College, Plainfield, Vermont, B.A. in English 1969. Married 1) Lindsay Crouse in 1977 (divorced), one daughter; 2) Rebecca Pidgeon in 1991. Actor in summer stock, 1969; stage manager, *The Fantasticks*, New York, 1969–70; lecturer in drama, Marlboro College, Vermont, 1970; artist-in-residence, Goddard College, 1971–73; founder and artistic director, St. Nicholas Company, Plainfield, Vermont, 1972, and St. Nicholas Players, Chicago, 1974–76; faculty member, Illinois Arts Council, 1974; visiting lecturer, University of Chicago, 1975–76 and 1979, and New York University, 1981; teaching fellow, Yale University School of Drama, New Haven, Connecticut, 1976–77; associate artistic director, Goodman Theatre, Chicago, 1978–84; associate director, New Theater Company, Chicago, 1985. Since 1988 associate professor of film, Columbia University, New York. Contributing editor, *Oui* magazine, 1975–76. Recipient: Joseph Jefferson award, 1974; Obie award, 1976, 1983; New York State Council on the Arts grant, 1976; Rockefeller grant, 1976; CBS-Yale University fellowship, 1977; New York Drama Critics Circle award, 1977, 1984; Outer Circle award, 1978; Society of West End Theatre award, 1983; Pulitzer prize, 1984; Dramatists Guild Hull-Warriner award, 1984; American Academy award, 1986; Tony award, 1987. Agent: Howard Rosenstone, Rosenstone/Wender, 3 East 48th Street, 4th Floor, New York, New York 10017, U.S.A.

Publications

PLAYS

Lakeboat (produced 1970; revised version produced 1980). 1981.
Duck Variations (produced 1972). With *Sexual Perversity in Chicago*, 1978;
   in *American Buffalo, Sexual Perversity in Chicago, Duck Variations*, 1978.
Mackinac (for children; produced 1972?).

Marranos (produced 1972–73?).

The Poet and the Rent: A Play for Kids from Seven to 8:15 (produced 1974). In *Three Children's Plays*, 1986.

Squirrels (produced 1974).1982.

Sexual Perversity in Chicago (produced 1974).With *Duck Variations*, 1978; in *American Buffalo, Sexual Perversity in Chicago, Duck Variations*, 1978

American Buffalo (produced 1975). 1977; in *American Buffalo, Sexual Perversity in Chicago, Duck Variations*, 1978.

Reunion (produced 1976). With *Dark Pony*, 1979.

The Woods (also director: produced 1977). 1979.

All Men Are Whores (produced 1977). In *Short Plays and Monologues*, 1981.

A Life in the Theatre (produced 1977). 1978.

The Revenge of the Space Pandas; or, Binky Rudich and the Two-Speed Clock (produced 1977). In *Three Children's Plays*, 1986.

Dark Pony (produced 1977). With *Reunion*, 1979.

The Water Engine: An American Fable (produced 1977). With *Mr. Happiness*, 1978.

Prairie du Chien (broadcast 1978; produced 1985). In *Short Plays and Monologues*, 1981; with *The Shawl*, 1985.

American Buffalo, Sexual Perversity in Chicago, Duck Variations: Three Plays. 1978.

Mr. Happiness (produced 1978). With *The Water Engine*, 1978.

Lone Canoe; or, The Explorer, music and lyrics by Alaric Jans (produced 1979).

The Sanctity of Marriage (produced 1979). With *Reunion* and *Dark Pony*, 1982.

Shoeshine (produced 1979). In *Short Plays and Monologues*, 1981.

A Sermon (also director: produced 1981). In *Short Plays and Monologues*, 1981.

Short Plays and Monologues (includes *All Men Are Whores, The Blue Hour: City Sketches, In Old Vermont, Litko, Prairie du Chien, A Sermon, Shoeshine*). 1981.

Edmond (produced 1982). 1983.

The Disappearance of the Jews (produced 1983).

Glengarry Glen Ross (produced 1983). 1984.

Red River, adaptation of a play by Pierre Laville (produced 1983).

Five Unrelated Pieces (includes *Two Conversations; Two Scenes; Yes, But So What*) (produced 1983). In *Dramatic Sketches and Monologues*, 1985.

The Dog (produced 1983). In *Dramatic Sketches and Monologues*, 1985.

Film Crew (produced 1983). In *Dramatic Sketches and Monologues*, 1985.

4 A.M. (produced 1983). In *Dramatic Sketches and Monologues*, 1985.

Vermont Sketches (includes *Pint's a Pound the World Around, Deer Dogs, Conversations with the Spirit World, Dowsing*) (produced 1984). In *Dramatic Sketches and Monologues*, 1985.

The Frog Prince (produced 1984). In *Three Children's Plays*, 1986.

The Spanish Prisoner (produced 1985).

The Shawl (produced 1985). With *Prairie du Chien*, 1985.

The Cherry Orchard, adaptation of a play by Chekhov (produced 1985). 1987.

Cross Patch (broadcast 1985; produced 1990). In *Dramatic Sketches and Monologues*, 1985.
Goldberg Street (broadcast 1985; produced 1990). In *Dramatic Sketches and Monologues*, 1985.
Vint, adaptation of a story by Chekhov, in *Orchards* (produced 1985). 1986.
Dramatic Sketches and Monologues (includes *Five Unrelated Pieces*, *The Power Outrage*, *The Dog*, *Film Crew*, *4 A.M.*, *Food*, *Pint's a Pound the World Around*, *Deer Dogs*, *Columbus Avenue*, *Conversations with the Spirit World*, *Maple Sugaring*, *Morris and Joe*, *Steve McQueen*, *Yes*, *Dowsing*, *In the Mall*, *Cross Patch*, *Goldberg Street*). 1985.
Goldberg Street: Short Plays and Monologues. 1985.
Three Children's Plays. 1986.
Speed-the-Plow (produced 1987). 1988.
House of Games (screenplay). 1987.
Things Change, with Shel Silverstein (screenplay). 1988.
Where Were You When It Went Down? in *Urban Blight* (musical revue), based on an idea by John Tillinger, music by David Shire, lyrics by Richard Maltby, Jr. (produced 1988).
Bobby Gould in Hell (produced 1989). In *Oh Hell!*, 1991.
Uncle Vanya, adaptation of the play by Chekhov (produced 1990). 1989.
Five Television Plays (includes *A Waitress in Yellowstone*, *The Museum of Science and Industry Story*, *A Wasted Weekend*, *We Will Take You There*, *Bradford*). 1990.
We're No Angels (screenplay). 1990.
Three Sisters, adaptation of the play by Chekhov. 1991.
Homicide (screenplay). 1992.
Oleanna (produced 1992). 1993.
Jolly. In *The Best American Short Plays 1992–1993*, edited by Howard Stein and Glenn Young, 1993.

SCREENPLAYS: *The Postman Always Rings Twice*, 1981; *The Verdict*, 1982; *The Untouchables*, 1987; *House of Games*, 1987; *Things Change*, with Shel Silverstein, 1988; *We're No Angels*, 1990; *Homicide*, 1991; *Glengarry Glen Ross*, 1992; *Hoffa*, 1992.

RADIO PLAYS: *Prairie du Chien*, 1978; *Cross Patch*, 1985; *Goldberg Street*, 1985; *Dintenfass*, 1989.

VERSE
The Hero Pony. 1990.

OTHER
Writing in Restaurants (essays). 1986.
The Owl (for children), with Lindsay Crouse. 1987.
Warm and Cold (for children), with Donald Sultan. 1988.
Some Freaks (essays). 1989.
On Directing (essays). 1991.
The Cabin. 1992.

BIBLIOGRAPHY: *Ten Modern American Playwrights* by Kimball King, 1982.

CRITICAL STUDIES: *David Mamet* by C.W.E. Bigsby, 1985; *David Mamet* by Dennis Carroll, 1987.

THEATRICAL ACTIVITIES

DIRECTOR: **Plays**—*Beyond the Horizon* by O'Neill, 1974; *The Woods*, 1977; *Twelfth Night*, 1980; *A Sermon*, 1981. **Films**—*House of Games*, 1987; *Things Change*, 1988; *Homicide*, 1991.

David Mamet's rise to the forefront of American drama has been seen as the triumph of the minimalist, of the theatre poet indulging in language for its own sake, of the apologist for the big-mouthed home-baked philosopher. His plays have been attacked for their lack of clarity, for their plotlessness, for their obscenity, for their articulation of a poetics of loss without any compensatory dimensions. Critics have said his work is without subtext; others have implied that it consists of nothing but subtext. All of this is true in one sense or other, but the stridency of response is itself an indicator that the Mamet phenomenon has implicated the audience as a vital constituent of what happens in the play: clarity is a commodity which is as much in the audience's hands as in the characters'.

Most of Mamet's plays seem in some way fragmentary. Though he did not begin screen-writing until the 1980s, with *The Postman Always Rings Twice*, his plays almost from the start looked like something made on the editing table, with sometimes brutal cross-cutting. The 30 brief scenes which make up *Sexual Perversity in Chicago* do have a chronological linearity that is absent from the 14 episodes of *Duck Variations*, but it is left to the audience—placed by the title as voyeur of perversity—to read through the displacement activity that passes as dialogue and write its own construction of the homosocial sexuality behind the talk. Mamet's use of the fragment cogently illustrates the response theorists' view of the audience function as "creatively filling in gaps."

Like the presentation of behaviour, the philosophies that spill out of Mamet's early characters are fractured slogans chipped out of a broader cultural context. These contexts are always so well-known as to have their own mythology. The gangster, the real estate salesman, the Jewish patriarch, the sexual hijacker—each has an ethic that has been articulated and endorsed by decades of film and popular culture. That the characters are losers in the face of the myth does nothing to invalidate the myth, but it does open up the dimension of loss. The failure of the three would-be crooks in *American Buffalo* to achieve any part of their scheme does not undermine the notion of the big burglary as a faith to live by, any more than the males in *Sexual Perversity* will cease to live in hope of the big sexual coup. But the reading of this as loss, meaninglessness, or sterility is ambivalent because the texture of language brings a lyricism that is both bonding and possibly healing, if not regenerative. *American Buffalo* ends with compassion. *The Disappearance of the Jews* may be about the disappearance of something, but that does not mean that nothing is left. Whether they reach for fiction or for rhetoric, the characters seldom stop reaching.

Bonding may be loveless or even adversarial in Mamet. *Glengarry Glen Ross* has its four salesmen wedged within the real estate system, a system that says that two of them must be debased, to become waste products, the condition of so many Mamet characters. But the predatory cycle takes in not only the salesmen themselves, but also clients, who are trapped by the wonderful spirals of sales blather into buying junk land. Again, language is the bond: the first act ends with Roma's virtuoso cadenza on the general theme of the human condition, and the sudden—brilliantly comic—revelation that he is talking to a complete stranger. But the laughter is also reflexive, in that the audience has been absorbed in the bar-room philosophy almost as much as the client.

Mamet has not been averse to describing some of his plays as "classical tragedies," apparently because of their tone and themes of rejection and betrayal. But it is also noticeable that in these plays he moves beyond episodic structure to give a precisely defined diachronic placing which observes unities of both place and time. The whole claustrophobic action of *American Buffalo* occurs in a junkshop within a single day, while *The Woods* dramatises the recurrent Mamet question—why don't men and women get on?—by putting the two characters in a cabin in the woods for a single night. Though in both plays the characters are firmly positioned within a social fantasy system, their more sustained action has gratified critics who want to give Mamet characters an individual psychology.

That Mamet's plays look at gender delineations as well as sexuality is clear from the content of the male fantasies that pervade his work. But the gendering of characters through fantasy as well as through social constructions means that female characters in particular can be ambivalent in stature. This is especially clear when, as in *The Shawl* and *Speed-the-Plow*, two male characters confront a woman who intrudes on their relationship. In the latter play, some Hollywood tycoons run up against a temporary secretary who, given a script to read, comes up with a verdict that divides them. The secretary can be played dumb or shrewd, as a product of the male gaze or as a generator of it, like the non-appearing woman in *A Life in the Theatre*.

A similar complexity of female characterisation is in his first filmscript for his own direction, *House of Games*, and in the sequel to *Speed-the-Plow*, *Bobby Gould in Hell*. Structurally, both of these may be seen as modern morality plays, a genre Mamet had experimented with in *Edmond*, a descent into the hell of New York. Here, the American Everyman figure of the title is precipitated through the grotesqueries of the city's lower depths and brought to the brink of his own judgement, sketched with an extravagance that contrasts sharply with the economy of the earlier plays. But *Edmond* is also important for its reminder that Mamet is primarily a regional playwright, who writes plays not *for* New York but *at* it.

—Howard McNaughton

See the essay on *American Buffalo*.

MANN, Emily.

Born in Boston, Massachusetts, 12 April 1952. Educated at Radcliffe College, Cambridge, Massachusetts, B.A. in English 1974 (Phi Beta Kappa); University of Minnesota, Minneapolis (Bush Fellow), 1974–76, M.F.A. in theater arts 1976. Married Gerry Bamman in 1981 (divorced), one son. Associate director, Guthrie Theatre, Minneapolis, 1978–79; resident director, BAM Theater Company, Brooklyn, New York, 1981–82; member of the board, 1983–87, and vice-president of the board, 1984–86, Theatre Communications Group, and director, New Dramatists workshop for play development, 1984–91, both New York. Since 1989 artistic director, McCarter Theatre Center for the Performing Arts, Princeton, New Jersey; artistic associate, Crossroads Theatre, New Brunswick, New Jersey, 1990; lecturer, Council of the Humanities and Theatre and Dance program, Princeton University, New Jersey, 1990. Recipient: Obie award, 1981 (for writing and directing); Guggenheim fellowship, 1983; Rosamond Gilder award, 1983; National Endowment for the Arts grant, 1984, 1986; Creative Artists Public Service grant, 1985; Edinburgh Festival Fringe first award, 1985; McKnight fellowship, 1985; Dramatists Guild award, 1986; Playwrights USA award, 1986; Helen Hayes award, 1986; Home Box Office U.S.A. award, 1986. Lives in Princeton, New Jersey. Agent: George Lane, William Morris Agency, 1350 Avenue of the Americas, New York, New York 10019, U.S.A.

Publications

PLAYS

Annulla, An Autobiography (as *Annulla Allen: The Autobiography of a Survivor*, also director: produced 1977; revised version, as *Annulla, An Autobiography*, produced 1985). 1985.
Still Life (also director: produced 1980). 1982; in *Coming to Terms: American Plays and the Vietnam War*, edited by James Reston, Jr., 1985.
Execution of Justice (produced 1984; also director: produced 1986). In *New Playwrights 3*, edited by James Leverett and Elizabeth Osborn, 1986.
Nights and Days, adaptation of a play by Pierre Laville, in *Avant-Scène*, July 1984.
Betsey Brown, adaptation of the novel by Ntozake Shange, book by Shange and Mann, music by Baikida Carroll, lyrics by Shange, Mann, and Carroll (also director: produced 1989).

THEATRICAL ACTIVITIES

DIRECTOR: Plays—*Cold* by Michael Casale, 1976; *Ashes* by David Rudkin, 1977; *Annulla Allen*, 1977; *Surprise, Surprise* by Michel Tremblay, 1978; *On Mount Chimborazo* by Tankred Dorst, 1978; *Reunion* and *Dark Pony*, by David Mamet, 1978; *The Glass Menagerie* by Tennessee Williams, 1979, and 1990; *He and She* by Rachel Crothers, 1980; *Still Life*, 1980 and 1986; *Oedipus the King* by Sophocles, 1981; *A Tantalizing* by William Mastrosimone, 1982; *The Value of Names* by Jeffrey Sweet, 1982 and 1984; *A Weekend near Madison* by Kathleen Tolan, 1983; *Execution of Justice*, 1985 and 1986; *A Doll's House* by Ibsen, 1986; *Hedda Gabler* by Ibsen, 1987; *Betsey Brown*, 1989 and 1990; *The Three Sisters* by Chekhov, 1991.

Emily Mann has referred to her work as "theatre of testimony." Documentary drama is her métier, and recent history has provided her subjects ranging from the horrors of war, to peacetime violence, to the revolution in gender roles and sexual politics. Her first three stage plays are based wholly or in part on interviews with the people whose stories she tells.

Annulla, An Autobiography is the prototype. Mann visited the protagonist, a survivor of Nazism, in 1974, and the work hews so closely to what the playwright heard in Annulla Allen's London kitchen that she credits her as co-author. The short play turns Annulla's own words into an uninterrupted monologue. Annulla's privileged girlhood in Galicia is a distant memory, eclipsed by the Nazi terror. Her self-assurance and unsemitic good looks helped her escape the camps and rescue her Jewish husband from Dachau. Now widowed, she cares for a demanding invalid sister. However compelling her harrowing story, Annulla insists, "It is not me who is interesting, it is my play." An enormous manuscript covers her kitchen table, stage center. Annulla's play argues for global matriarchy as the solution to evil and barbarism. "If women would only start thinking, we could change the world," she observes, declaring women incapable of the monstrous acts of Hitler or Stalin.

Still, Annulla is unable to read out representative passages from her work in progress. The manuscript is so disorganized and the need to get dinner for her ailing sister so pressing that she loses patience sifting through the jumbled pages. Therein lies Mann's point. However reasoned Annulla's thesis or promising her creativity, she is chronically distracted by more traditional female roles and by the anxieties and guilt which stem from her terrible past. Annulla can no more impose order on her play than she can on her life. Mann does not try to do that for her. In setting down the unmediated monologue of this scarred but plucky woman, Mann makes a statement about her own role. *Annulla* testifies to the freedom for creativity exercised by the playwright who recognizes that, by sheer accident of time and place, she was spared the life of her co-author and subject.

In *Still Life* Mann again draws on interviews with real people who become the *dramatis personae*. She calls this work a documentary, specifying that it be produced with that genre's characteristic objectivity. That tone is the first of the ironies that mark this work about the virulent psychic and emotional conditioning suffered by a Vietnam veteran and about the troubled society to which he returns. As a Marine, Mark learned that he could kill civilians as easily as enemy soldiers. After the war, he cannot get rid of the memory of having wielded power over life and death. His obsession is alternately the source of rage, guilt, and physical pleasure. Incapable of talking either to those who were not in Vietnam, or to those who were, Mark turns to drugs, crime, and domestic violence. He is not too self-centered to appreciate that his wife, Cheryl, whom he abuses, is as much of a casualty of the war years as he. Cheryl wants to return to the securities of a traditionalism more alive in her memories than in post-1960s America. She longs to play the roles her mother did, noting that, except in wartime, it is women who protect men—a point of view strikingly antithetical to that of Annulla Allen. Mark's mistress Nadine has done battle with all manner of "naughtiness." "A woman with many jobs and many lives," in Mann's words, Nadine describes herself as being so busy that she sleeps with her shoes on. The observation is metaphoric. Nadine steps over troubled waters, never feeling the cold or agitation, and never plunging beneath the surface. Mark can tell Nadine his ugly truths, for absolutely nothing offends, disturbs, or even touches her.

Still Life is staged so as to make palpable the lack of genuine communication between Mark, who lives in the past, Cheryl, who yearns for an unrealizable future, and Nadine, who hovers above an unexamined present. The three characters sit side by side behind a table, like members of a panel discussion— or witnesses at a trial. They talk about, but rarely to, one another, their intersecting speeches often juxtaposed ironically. So, for example, Nadine's innocence about her near fatal pregnancies overlaps the ingenuous Cheryl's shock in coming upon Mark's pictures of war casualties. Projections on a screen behind the actors underscore the hopelessness of anyone's enjoying the full understanding of others. Gruesome pictures of horribly mutilated war injured, for instance, illustrate Mark's inability to talk to his parents who supported the war. Indeed, this seething play whose self-possessed characters never touch one another on stage ironically reflects a society where people, however uncommunicating, are continually in violent and destructive collision.

The notion of the audience as jury, implicit in *Still Life*, is central to *Execution of Justice*. Significantly, the work was commissioned by the Eureka Theatre of San Francisco. Its subject is the 1978 murder of George Moscone, Mayor of San Francisco, and Harvey Milk, a City Supervisor and the first avowed homosexual voted into high public office. The play brings to the stage the case of the People against Dan White, the assassin. It demonstrates the instability of White, who had been elected a City Supervisor, resigned, changed his mind and, when Moscone refused to reappoint him to his former post, vented his rage by shooting him and Milk. Mann bases her script on the transcript of the trial, reportage, extensive interviews with some of the principals, as well as what she calls in a prefatory note "the street." The play neatly synthesizes background pertinent to the case, such as the evolution in the social and political spheres caused by the migration to San Francisco of a large homosexual population. It recreates the climate of fear provoked by the mass deaths in Jonestown, Guyana, and the reputed connections between James Jones and liberal elements in San Francisco. The play captures effectively the unprecedented violence that stalked American political life in the 1970s.

As the testimony piles up, one appreciates the implausible defense arguments (e.g., the famous "Twinkies defense," which attributed criminal behavior to the accused's junk food diet) and its unlikely claim that the murders were purely politically and not homophobically motivated. *Execution of Justice* shows that what was really on trial was conservative values, outraged and threatened by the growing power of the gay community. The use of video projections and film clips from documentaries intensify the passions of the trial; the inclusion of reporters and photographers heightens its immediacy. Though Mann treats this explosive material with an even hand, there is no question that she wants the audience as jury to find that Dan White's conviction and light jail sentence for the lesser charges of voluntary manslaughter amount to the miscarriage of justice referred to in the play's title.

Mann's penchant for transforming life to the stage takes a new turn with *Betsey Brown*, a rhythm and blues musical. She came to the project at the invitation of Ntozake Shange who began it as a short story, turned it into a performance piece produced in 1979 at the Kennedy Center as *Boogie Woogie Landscapes*, and finally rewrote it as a novel. Shange and jazz trumpeter-composer Baikida Carroll approached Mann for help in reworking the piece for the stage. The result was a full-fledged collaboration, a musical whose 28 songs color and interweave the various strands of a distinctly contemporary story.

The eponymous Betsey Brown is a young African-American woman who comes of age in St. Louis of 1959. The first stirrings of the civil rights movement form the background for a number of issues the play explores. The most obvious is, of course, racism, both within the black community and from white society threatened by integration. At least as consequential is the question of a role model for teen-age Betsey. On one side is her mother, a "modern" woman who briefly abandons her family to pursue her own intellectual needs. Notwithstanding, she is genuinely concerned about educating her daughters to become cultivated members of a society which hardly encourages the self-actualization of black women. On the other side is the comforting figure of the Browns' housekeeper, a traditional woman who sings gospel songs with exquisite conviction. Her other accomplishments include commonsensical strategies for pleasing a man and consoling a crying child. Reviews of *Betsey Brown*'s premiere prove the success of the work in moving beyond its delineation of the tensions and beauties of black life to dramatize universal problems of parental responsibilities to children in a radically changing world.

In addition to her work for the stage, Mann has written three screenplays (none yet produced). *Naked* (1985), based on the book by Jo Giese Brown, is subtitled *One Couple's Intimate Journey Through Infertility. Fanny Kelly* (1985) dramatizes the true story of an intrepid pioneer woman captured by the Sioux. *You Strike a Woman, You Strike a Rock* (1990) is a script on the Greensboro Massacre, commissioned by NBC Theatre. These scripts are distinguished by tight, suspenseful plots as well as the credible characterizations that Mann has made her signature.

—Ellen Schiff

MASTROSIMONE, William.

Born in Trenton, New Jersey, 19 August 1947. Educated at Pennington Preparatory School, New Jersey, 1963–66; Tulane University, New Orleans, 1966–70; Rider College, Trenton, New Jersey, 1973–74, B.A. in English 1974; Rutgers University, New Brunswick, New Jersey, 1974–76, M.F.A. 1976. Recipient: Los Angeles Drama Critics Circle award, 1982; Outer Circle award, 1983; John Gassner award, 1983. Agent: George Lane, William Morris Agency, 1350 Avenue of the Americas, New York, New York 10019. Address: 715 First Avenue West, Apartment 202, Seattle, Washington 98119, U.S.A.

Publications

PLAYS

The Woolgatherer (produced 1979). 1981.
Extremities (produced 1980). 1984.
A Tantalizing (produced 1982). 1985.
Shivaree (produced 1983). 1984.
The Undoing (produced 1984).
Nanawatai (produced 1984). 1986.

Tamer of Horses (produced 1985; revised version produced 1986; revised version produced 1987).
Cat's-Paw (produced 1986). 1987.
The Understanding (produced 1987).
Sunshine (produced 1989).

SCREENPLAYS: *Extremities*, 1986; *The Beast*, 1988.

TELEVISION PLAY: *Sinatra* series, 1992.

MANUSCRIPT COLLECTION: Boston University.

When *Extremities* opened off-Broadway in 1982, it proved to be one of the most controversial plays of the season, on or off Broadway. Some critics suggested that William Mastrosimone's tense drama about a would-be rapist and his implacable woman captor attracted audiences because there wasn't more powerful fare available. Some dismissed the play as an exercise in old-fashioned melodrama, with onstage violence to whet the visual appetites of jaded television viewers. Actually, Mastrosimone, inspired by a 55-year-old woman rape victim—as he explained in "The Making of Extremities," had touched a raw nerve among theatre-goers in general and women in particular. The fear of and revulsion against, violent, vicious, and unprovoked sexual attacks were very real. That angry or unbalanced male members of some minority groups were perceived as the usual rapists found resonance in the play, whose very disturbed potential ravisher is named Raul. This, some suggested, was invoking racial stereotypes, and confronting a seemingly helpless young woman, Marjorie, with this cunning, shifty criminal seemed a deliberate attempt to exploit current fears.

This is unfair to Mastrosimone, although he clearly cares more for victims' rights and safety than he does for those of wrong-doers. In *Extremities* the naked threat of violence and violation is presented almost immediately, but fortunately Marjorie is able to turn the tables and take Raul captive. His deviousness and threats, as the play progresses, make her decide—driven by rage—to kill him and bury the body in her garden. Her roommates return and react variously, suggesting standard social reactions to such a situation when it is merely hypothetical. At the close, there is a catharsis—somewhat schematic —for both Raul and Marjorie, but it offers no magic solutions to the problem. In addition to the exercise of physical violence on stage, Mastrosimone offers audiences a tightly constructed cat-and-mouse plot, whose outcome is not easily guessed. What is especially appealing, however, as in other Mastrosimone plays, is his ability not only to capture the rhythms and idioms of conversation of various social groups, but also to make them the proper expression of his characters. David Mamet is often praised for his ear for common or raffish speech; Mastrosimone is also adept, but in a different way. Where Mamet's characters may seem involved in an aimless stream-of-consciousness, Mastrosimone's are generally trying to achieve some end, to move the plot forward at the very least.

In *The Woolgatherer*, there is almost no major plot action. Rose, a fragile, disturbed girl, who displaces her terrors and misadventures on a mythical friend, Brenda, brings home Cliff, a trucker looking for a sexual encounter. Their banter—his jocular, angry, or uncomprehending; hers tense, poetic, pained—are the substance of the play, as they come to know and trust each other. The title refers to her collection of men's sweaters, begged from previous visitors. *A Tantalizing*, a one act play, is also a two-character exercise, but this time it's the man, Ambrose, who is unbalanced. Dafne, a young woman who has watched this once well-dressed, confident lawyer spend his days in a parking lot, doing imaginary business on a disconnected telephone he carries with him, has brought him to her apartment, though it's not clear why. No matter what comforts or refreshments she offers him, he is peremptory, corrective, fussy, revealing reasons for his failure in life. At the close, she succeeds in getting him to lay aside his ragged clothing for some of her late father's fine garb.

Mastrosimone can manipulate three or more characters on stage at the same time, with effective exchanges of dialogue, but he seems to prefer confrontations between two people, with others brought on—if at all—only when required by the plot. *Shivaree* has echoes of *Butterflies Are Free*, with the difference that Chandler, its protagonist, is hemophiliac, not blind. His overprotective mother drives a cab to pay the bills, while he saves ice-cream money to pay for a session with a prostitute. He finds himself and romance, however, with a neighboring exotic dancer named Shivaree.

Nanawatai deals with the fates of a Soviet tank-team, trapped in a mountain cul-de-sac by Afghan rebels. The title is supposedly the tribal word for sanctuary: once uttered, enemies must protect the one who begs it. A Russian soldier claims it and is spared. Later, his former comrades do so as well, but implacable Afghan women, impatient with the seeming softness of their men, slaughter the helpless Soviets. Interestingly, this was premiered in Norway rather than the United States.

Cat's-Paw goes beyond *Extremities* in dealing with topical terrors and in subtly satirizing American manners and mores. Jessica Lyons, a weekend television anchor-woman, who wants a major news scoop to improve her position, is brought blindfolded to make a television interview with Victor, who has just blown up a car loaded with explosives outside the Environmental Protection Agency in Washington, D.C. He and his small group are using terror tactics to protest government failures to protect the public from toxic wastes. To that end, he's kidnapped a culpable minor EPA official, David Darling, whom he threatens to kill. Lyons's past television coups have shown her unblinking in the face of horrors; Victor hopes to use her talents to get his message to the world and, perhaps, blow up the White House as she reports the event on television. The willingness of the media to exploit—or to trivialize—horrors to win audiences, the very real threat of toxic wastes and official coverups, and the various aspects of terrorism are all effectively used dramatically. It's especially provocative that the maniacal killer seems to espouse all the pieties of the Sierra Club and be willing to destroy unknown innocents for the greater good of mankind. The verbal sparring between Victor and Lyons is notable; the situation, cinematic.

In *The Undoing* there are overtones of Tennessee Williams: Lorraine Tempesta, who runs a chicken-slaughtering and dressing shop, drinks too much, longs for a man, and harasses her dating daughter. A year before, her husband Leo had been killed in a terrible traffic accident; at the site, she laughed. Now she's overcome with guilt. Into the shop comes a one-eyed man who wants to help out. He proves to be the driver of the other wrecked car, come to make amends. There's also a kind of Greek-Italian chorus, two old women, Mrs. Corvo and Mrs. Mosca.

Tamer of Horses combines elements familiar in other Mastrosimone plays. Childless Ty and Georgiane have taken a youthful black offender, Hector, as a foster child. Ty, orphaned and separated from his brother Sam, who died young as a criminal, wants to give another youth in trouble a chance for a new life. Ty, who is a classics teacher, reaches Hector through a retelling of *The Iliad*, but he cannot break him of old thieving, lying ways. Especially chilling is Hector's recreation of a subway mugging. Touched by the two and their caring, Hector nonetheless departs. With his talent for authentic ethnic dialogue and his apparent belief that one cannot even teach a *young* dog new tricks, Mastrosimone has found a voice and themes for the audiences of his time.

As so many other talented younger playwrights, Mastrosimone has found cinema and television more lucrative markets than the theatre. Nonetheless he has told an interviewer he prefers the "instant gratification," which a writer can get in the theatre from both audience and critics. He can also discover rapidly what audiences and critics think, reactions which are delayed or muted with film and television. A novice in film-making, he was so disgusted with what was done to *Extremities* that he walked out in mid-production. *The Beast* is based on his drama of the Soviet-Afghan confrontation, *Nanawatai*.

The Understanding is autobiographical in tone, dealing with a sternly independent immigrant Italian father—a stone-carver—in Tenafly, New Jersey, and his alienated son. The father threatens to shoot officials who want to evict him from the stone house he built himself in order to build a freeway ramp. His son, Raff, arrives, ostensibly to introduce his fiancée, Janice, but actually to persuade the old man to leave his home peacefully. Old wounds are probed and new threats explored. Father and son arrive at an understanding on two levels.

Also with a small cast, *Sunshine*—which the writer is adapting for the screen—also probes emotional wounds. Sunshine is a "porn queen" stripper who performs for ogling males in a glass-booth under seductive pink lights. At home she has a pet lobster in a glass-tank, an obvious symbol. Repulsed by her life, she flees to take shelter from a murderous husband with Nelson, a burned-out paramedic. He protects himself from the world with indifference, but she manages to get under his skin. They are both in glass-booths, but finally they also have an understanding. The idea came from a nine-hour talk with an actual stripper who took shelter with Mastrosimone from her porn-king spouse. The play, he says is "about the effect pornography has on the people who perform it."

—Glenn Loney

MAY, Elaine.

Born Elaine Berlin in Philadelphia, Pennsylvania, 21 April 1932; moved to Los Angeles, California, 1942. Daughter of theatre director Jack Berlin and actress Jeannie Berlin. Studied acting under Maria Ouspenskaya, 1947; attended University of Chicago and Playwrights Theatre in Chicago, 1950. Married 1) Marvin May, 1949; daughter: Jeannie Berlin; 2) the lyricist Sheldon Harnick (divorced 1963). Member of the improvisational theatre group, The Compass Players, 1953–57; performed in New York clubs with Mike Nichols, 1957; made several television appearances, 1960; directed, and acted in the theatre, 1960s; also wrote and performed for radio; recorded comedy albums. Address: c/o Julian Schlossberg, Castle Hill Productions, 1414 Avenue of the Americas, New York 10019, USA.

Publications

PLAYS

An Evening with Mike Nichols and Elaine May (sketches; produced 1960).
A Matter of Position (produced 1962).
Not Enough Rope (produced 1962).
Adaptation (also director; produced 1969). 1971.
Mr Gogol and Mr Preen (produced 1991).

SCREENPLAYS: *A New Leaf*, 1970; *Such Good Friends* (uncredited), 1971; *Mickey and Nicky*, 1976; *Heaven Can Wait*, with Warren Beatty and Buck Henry, 1978; *Tootsie*, with Larry Gelbart (uncredited), 1982; *Ishtar*, 1987.

THEATRICAL ACTIVITIES

DIRECTOR: Plays—*The Third Ear* (revue), 1964; *Adaptation, and Next* by Terrence McNally, 1969. Films—*A New Leaf*, 1970; *The Heartbreak Kid*, 1972; *Mickey and Nicky*, 1976; *Ishtar*, 1987.
ACTOR: Plays—debut as child actor; also *An Evening with Mike Nichols and Elaine May*, 1960; Shirley in *The Office* by María Irene Fornés, 1966. Films—*Enter Laughing*, 1966; *Luv*, 1967; *A New Leaf*, 1970; *California Suite*, 1978; *In the Spirit*, 1990. Television—since 1959. Cabaret—at The Second City, Chicago, and The Compass, Chicago and New York, 1954–57; Village Vanguard and Blue Angel, New York, 1957; Town Hall, New York, 1959.

Although in the 1980s and 1990s there has been a proliferation of women directors in Hollywood, Elaine May, along with Dorothy Arzner and Ida Lupino, paved the way for these contemporary careers. May entered show business at the age of six as an actor, spending her childhood on the road with her father's travelling theatre company. From 1954 to 1961, she had a stage partnership with Mike Nichols. May then became more interested in play-writing and went on to film acting roles and screenwriting. She was valued in Hollywood as a "script-doctor" and used her considerable ability in this area when other more prestigious film-work was not available. Her films fall into the conventional Hollywood genres, mainly comedy, although her work usually has a subtext of darker psychological depth and resonance.

Some critics have seen her work as derogatory to women but her male characters are also weak and dependent. They exhibit mutual needs (see, for example, May and Matthau in *A New Leaf*). Her main protagonists are openly neurotic victims who, like the protagonists in Woody Allen's films, triumph by achieving what they want, namely, a love relationship earned through pain. The secondary characters in May's films are generally pragmatists who get on in life by using other people. She sees this social pragmatism as a neurotic weakness, and once again like Woody Allen, has more admiration for sensitive people who make no secret of their vulnerability.

The plots of her films explore the way in which men see women as objects who can be used to fulfil a fantasy or "save" them. Both Matthau in *A New Leaf* and Grodin in *The Heartbreak Kid* see their "love-objects" as a means of gaining money, sex, and security but have their defensive pragmatism stripped away from them until they are exposed as equally dependent and vulnerable as the women. In both of the films, the women appear to be the victims but end up triumphant.

However, Elaine May's work is not restricted to exploring male/female conflicts. In *Mickey and Nicky*, she enters the world of mobsters, *film noir* terrain, and provides a bitter and complex exploration of male friendship. *Ishtar* (made at Columbia in 1987 with the largest budget ever entrusted to a woman director) is a film about male-buddies-on-the-road rather in the Bob Hope and Bing Crosby vein—a genre which took her back to her show-business origins.

Elaine May believes above all in comedy—she says, "You can drink this wine straight or you can drink it funny. You can kill somebody straight or you can kill them funny. Funny is closer to life . . . Humour is just a way of looking at things. I mean you can look at it this way and it's a disaster. And you can look at it this way, and it's funny". But in all her films, the humour is subversive, revealing a remarkably dark and injured world where everyone betrays everyone else.

—Sylvia Paskin

McCLURE, Michael (Thomas).

Born in Marysville, Kansas, 20 October 1932. Educated at the University of Wichita, Kansas, 1951–53; University of Arizona, Tucson, 1953–54; San Francisco State University, B.A. 1955. Married Joanna Kinnison in 1954 (divorced), one daughter. Assistant professor, 1962–77, associate professor, 1977, and since 1978 professor, California College of Arts and Crafts, Oakland. Playwright-in-residence, American Conservatory Theatre, San Francisco, 1975; associate fellow, Pierson College, Yale University, New Haven, Connecticut, 1982. Editor, with James Harmon, *Ark II/Moby I*, San Francisco, 1957. Recipient: National Endowment for the Arts grant, 1967, 1974; Guggenheim fellowship, 1971; Magic Theatre Alfred Jarry award, 1974; Rockefeller fellowship, 1975; Obie award, 1978. Agent: Helen Merrill

Ltd., 435 West 23rd Street, New York, New York 10011. Address: 5862 Balboa Drive, Oakland, California 94611, U.S.A.

Publications

PLAYS

!The Feast! (produced 1960). In *The Mammals*, 1972.

Pillow (produced 1961). In *The Mammals*, 1972.

The Growl, in *Four in Hand* (produced 1970). In *Evergreen Review*, April–May 1964.

The Blossom; or, Billy the Kid (produced 1964). 1967.

The Beard (produced 1965). 1965; revised version, 1967.

The Shell (produced 1970). 1968; in *Gargoyle Cartoons*, 1971.

The Cherub (produced 1969). 1970.

The Charbroiled Chinchilla: The Pansy, The Meatball, Spider Rabbit (produced 1969). In *Gargoyle Cartoons*, 1971.

Little Odes, Poems, and a Play, The Raptors. 1969.

The Brutal Brontosaurus: Spider Rabbit, The Meatball, The Shell, Apple Glove, The Authentic Radio Life of Bruce Conner and Snoutburbler (produced 1970; *The Meatball* and *Spider Rabbit* produced 1971; *The Authentic Radio Life of Bruce Conner and Snoutburbler* produced 1975). In *Gargoyle Cartoons*, 1971.

Gargoyle Cartoons (includes *The Shell, The Pansy, The Meatball, The Bow, Spider Rabbit, Apple Glove, The Sail, The Dear, The Authentic Radio Life of Bruce Conner and Snoutburbler, The Feather, The Cherub*). 1971.

The Pansy (produced 1972). In *Gargoyle Cartoons*, 1971.

Polymorphous Pirates: The Pussy, The Button, The Feather (produced 1972). *The Feather* in *Gargoyle Cartoons*, 1971.

The Mammals (includes *The Blossom, !The Feast!, Pillow*). 1972.

The Grabbing of the Fairy (produced 1973). 1978.

The Pussy, The Button, and Chekhov's Grandmother; or, The Sugar Wolves (produced 1973).

McClure on Toast (produced 1973).

Gorf (produced 1974). 1976.

Music Peace (produced 1974).

The Derby (produced 1974; revised version produced 1981).

General Gorgeous (produced 1975). 1982.

Two Plays. 1975.

Sunny-Side Up (includes *The Pink Helmet* and *The Masked Choir*) (produced 1976). *The Pink Helmet* in *Two Plays*, 1975; *The Masked Choir* in *Performing Arts Journal*, August 1976.

Minnie Mouse and the Tap-Dancing Buddha (produced 1978). In *Two Plays*, 1975.

Two for the Tricentennial (includes *The Pink Helmet* and *The Grabbing of the Fairy*) (produced 1976).

Range War (produced 1976).

Goethe: Ein Fragment (produced 1977). In *West Coast Plays 2*, Spring 1978.

Josephine the Mouse Singer, adaptation of a story by Kafka (produced 1978). 1980.

The Red Snake (produced 1979).
The Mirror (produced 1979).
Coyote in Chains (produced 1980).
The Velvet Edge. 1982(?).
The Beard, and VKTMS: Two Plays, (*VKTMS* produced 1988). 1985.

TELEVISION PLAY: *The Maze* (documentary), 1967.

VIDEO: *Love Lion*, 1991.

NOVELS
The Mad Cub. 1970.
The Adept. 1971.

VERSE
Passage. 1956.
Peyote Poem. 1958.
For Artaud. 1959.
Hymns to St. Geryon and Other Poems. 1959.
The New Book: A Book of Torture. 1961.
Dark Brown. 1961.
Two for Bruce Conner. 1964.
Ghost Tantras. 1964.
Double Murder! Vahrooooooohr! 1964.
Love Lion, Lioness. 1964.
13 Mad Sonnets. 1964.
Poisoned Wheat. 1965.
Unto Caesar. 1965.
Mandalas. 1966.
Dream Table. 1966.
Love Lion Book. 1966.
Hail Thee Who Play. 1968; revised edition, 1974.
Muscled Apple Swift. 1968.
Plane Pomes. 1969.
Oh Christ God Love Cry of Love Stifled Furred Wall Smoking Burning.
   1969(?).
The Sermons of Jean Harlow and the Curses of Billy the Kid. 1969.
The Surge. 1969.
Hymns to St. Geryon, and Dark Brown. 1969.
Lion Fight. 1969.
Star. 1971.
99 Theses. 1972.
The Book of Joanna. 1973.
Transfiguration. 1973.
Rare Angel (writ with raven's blood). 1974.
September Blackberries. 1974.
Solstice Blossom. 1974.
Fleas 189–195. 1974.
A Fist Full (1956–1957). 1974.

On Organism. 1974.
Jaguar Skies. 1975.
Man of Moderation. 1975.
Flea 100. 1975.
Ah Yes. 1976.
Antechamber. 1977.
Antechamber and Other Poems. 1978.
Fragments of Perseus. 1978.
Letters. 1978.
Seasons, with Joanna McClure. 1981.
The Book of Benjamin, with Wesley B. Tanner. 1982.
Fragments of Perseus (collection). 1983.
Fleas 180–186. 1985.
Selected Poems. 1986.
Rebel Lions. 1991.

OTHER

Meat Science Essays. 1963; revised edition, 1967.
Freewheelin' Frank, Secretary of the Angels, as Told to Michael McClure by Frank Reynolds. 1967.
Scratching the Beat Surface. 1982.
Specks (essays). 1985.
Testa Coda. 1991.

Editor, with David Meltzer and Lawrence Ferlinghetti, *Journal for the Protection of All Beings 1 and 3.* 2 vols., 1961–69.

BIBLIOGRAPHY: A *Catalogue of Works by Michael McClure 1956–1965* by Marshall Clements, 1965.

MANUSCRIPT COLLECTIONS: Simon Fraser University, Burnaby, British Columbia; University of California, Berkeley.

CRITICAL STUDIES: "This Is Geryon," in *Times Literary Supplement,* 25 March 1965; interview in *San Francisco Poets* edited by David Meltzer, 1971, revised edition, as *Golden Gate,* 1976; "Michael McClure Symposium" in *Margins* 18, March 1975.

THEATRICAL ACTIVITIES
ACTOR: Films—*Beyond the Law,* 1968; *Maidstone,* 1971.

Michael McClure comments:

Theatre is an organism of poetry—weeping, and laughing, and crying, and smiling, and performing superhuman acts—on a shelf in space and lit with lights.

Michael McClure's curious and highly personal amalgams of Artaud, pop art playfulness, surrealism, and Eastern mysticism seek to bridge the Romantic gap, to join the mind and body in what he calls *spiritmeat*. His first attempt in this ambitious project was a succès de scandale, *The Beard*, in which two archetypes of American dreams, Jean Harlow and Billy the Kid, confront each other outside time and place. Harlow's challenge, "Before you can pry any secrets from me, you must first find the real me! Which one will you choose?" counterpoints Billy's "You're divine," and "You're a bag of meat," two McClurean identities. *The Beard* avoids the implied metaphysics of meaty divinity, since rational argument could only intensify the split between the senses and the spirit. Instead, Billy and Harlow's verbal duel becomes increasingly sexual and violent, pulsating to an ecstatic climax rather than a resolution.

McClure has tried to extend our concept of what humanity is, first by emphasizing man's animality. *!The Feast!* was written in grahr language, sound-poetry based on animal grunts growls, howls and groans, which gradually evolved into mystical imagery:

> There's no light in the closed rose but a tiny black cherub sleeps there and sings to the creatures that walk in the cliffs of the Lily's pollen, moving from shadow to light in the drips of rain. The seen is as black as the eye seeing it.

At its best, such language is difficult to sustain in the theatre and for *Gargoyle Cartoons* and subsequent plays up to *Minnie Mouse and the Tap-Dancing Buddha* McClure returned to the more direct statement of *The Beard*. These plays present his metaphysics in what is almost a parody of Beat slang: "from the moment of birth till the hour we're zapped and boogie to the grave, we're thoroughly enwrapped in the realms of being. How can we know nothing, and know especially that even nothing isn't something, if there's always *Being* there?" Although these bald statements have little dramatic value, the best of the plays are oddly unsettling glimpses of human nature, and humans and nature. The combination spider and rabbit of *Spider Rabbit* wanders absent-mindedly onstage, and decides to show and tell. Producing a head from his bag he saws it open: "BOY AM I HUNGRY! This is the brain of a soldier. BOY, do I hate war. (The head quivers as Spider Rabbit proceeds to eat it with the spoon.) I'M OUT OF CARROTS. BOY, DO I HATE WAR." Few of the plays blend social satire and sight gag so sharply, but they all have a reckless playfulness, a freedom to explore the theatre's sensuous possibilities and the audience's expectations about the theatre.

Despite their frequent childishness, McClure felt these plays illustrated the universe's basic nature, which embraces the silly and shallow as well as the profound. More recently, however he decided "I'd carried that stream of comedies where the universe created the plays to an extreme that completed my expectations and satisfactions in that mode. So at this time, I've nothing further to say in that vein." Since then (about 1978), his work has focused largely on the relation of art to society. In *Goethe: Ein Fragment*, Mephistopheles offers a callow, arrogant young Goethe a deal: if Goethe will write a play that immortalizes the devil, the playwright will receive a second life. This alternate life is the play called *Faust*, and with this arrangement,

McClure plays with the relative importance of the artist and his creation. Not only is the devil a more sympathetic character than Goethe, both of them frequently become subordinate to the play *Faust*. As Mephistopheles says, "Everything real or imagined exists everywhere at once," and McClure suggests that what is imagined is less mortal than ordinary reality, a state that is performed behind a scrim in *Goethe: Ein Fragment*.

Like *Goethe* and the clumsy *The Red Snake* (based on James Shirley's 1641 *The Cardinal*), McClure's *Josephine the Mouse Singer* is drawn from existing literature, Kafka's delicate and eloquent short story. The play won an Obie award for its script before it was produced in New York, and its best dialogue is the narration taken directly from Kafka. However, McClure effectively dramatizes the central problem: Is Josephine's art, brilliant as it is, more important than the dull grey mouse society? Josephine, proud and demanding, is willing to break all the rules of society in order to give it better art, but at the same time she threatens to destroy it. Neither, Kafka nor McClure is foolhardy enough to try to resolve this dilemma, but in dramatizing it, McClure produced some of the best writing of his career.

—Walter Bode

McLURE, James.

Born in Louisiana. Address: c/o Dramatists Play Service, 440 Park Avenue South, New York, New York, 10016, U.S.A.; and, Chappell Plays Ltd., 129 Park Street, London W1Y 3FA, England.

Publications

PLAYS

Lone Star (produced 1979). 1980.
Pvt. Wars (produced 1979). 1980.
1959 Pink Thunderbird (includes *Lone Star* and *Laundry and Bourbon*) (produced 1980).
Laundry and Bourbon (produced 1980). 1981.
The Day They Shot John Lennon (produced 1983). 1984.
Thanksgiving (produced 1983).
Wild Oats: A Romance of the Old West, adaptation of the play by John O'Keeffe (produced 1983). 1985.
Lahr and Mercedes (produced 1984).
The Very Last Lover of the River Cane (produced 1985).
Max and Maxie (produced 1989). 1989.

THEATRICAL ACTIVITIES

ACTOR: **Plays**—in *The Death and Life of Jesse James* by Len Jenkin, 1978; *Music Hall Sidelights* by Jack Heifner, 1978.

James McLure is a playwright and actor who became recognized for two one-acts, *Lone Star* and *Pvt. Wars*, that were produced on Broadway in 1979. It is *Lone Star* that best characterizes the nature and dilemma of McLure's favorite protagonist: a southwestern country bumpkin, good ole boy veteran who returns as an adult to a tamer and duller world which both baffles and bores him. This character or his counterpart, appearing in several McLure plays, is a displaced romantic unable to function well in an adult world that no longer operates by his values.

Set in the littered backyard of a small-town Texas bar, *Lone Star* focuses on the swaggering figure of Roy, a former high school hero now back in town after a hitch in Vietnam and not adjusting well. He drinks Lone Star beer and gasses with his hero-worshipping but slower younger brother about his military and amorous exploits and his three loves: his wife, his country, and his 1959 pink Thunderbird convertible. At the evening's end only one love is left intact, for Roy learns that his brother has slept with his young wife and that his cherished Thunderbird has been borrowed and demolished by a fatuous hardware store clerk ever jealous of Roy. Though the symbols of Roy's youth are destroyed or tarnished, he bounces back at the conclusion dimly realizing he can no longer merely muse on the past. Validly praised by critics for its earthy humor and the salty regional idiom of its roistering language, the short play represents McLure at his most effective.

Less successful than its companion piece, *Pvt. Wars* is a black comedy set in an Army hospital where three recuperating Vietnam veterans tease, torment, and even solace each other to disguise their anxiety about returning to the uncertainties of civilian life. Like *Lone Star*'s Roy, they will have to confront a different world. The trio includes a Georgia hillbilly (Gately) given to fiddling with a dead radio, a street-wise hipster (Silvio) addicted to "flashing" nurses even though he is now possibly impotent, and a prissy rich kid (Natwick) who misses his mother. The men's encounters, depicted in 12 sketch-like scenes, project an off-beat humor; but the play's episodic structure forces too fragmentary a quality on the action and characters.

Conceived as a companion piece to *Lone Star* and set in the latter's same mythical Texas town at the home of Roy and his wife Elizabeth, *Laundry and Bourbon* is a short comedy introducing three women on a hot summer afternoon. Elizabeth, the intelligent young lady of the house, folds laundry and sips bourbon while chatting with a gabby neighbor, Hattie. Their talk is interrupted by the self-righteous and unwelcome Amy Lee, the gossipy wife of the hardware clerk met in *Lone Star*. Amidst self-generated bits of gossip, Amy Lee purposefully blurts out that Roy has been seen with another woman. Displaying an inner strength and an understanding of her husband's turmoil since returning from Vietnam, Elizabeth realizes Roy's need for her and her love for him and resolves to be waiting for him when he returns home whatever the opinion of others. In this comedy McLure's humor, characters, and dialogue are richly successful. It stands alongside *Lone Star* as the playwright's strongest work.

Wild Oats is a loose adaptation of John O'Keeffe's 18th-century comedy of the same name keeping the plot structure of the original while transferring the action's locale and characters to the legendary American Old West. The plot and characters are a send-up of old-fashioned melodrama's clichés and stereotypes involving long-lost sons found and forgiven, long-estranged parents reunited, and mistaken identities ultimately revealed. While *Wild Oats* suffers from a surfeit of complications and characters, it yet emerges as an amusing theatrical romp disclosing its author's promising hand for theatricality and parody.

The Day They Shot John Lennon is comprised of a series of encounters between a group of strangers gathered at the New York City site of John Lennon's assassination. The disparate group, whose motives vary from curiosity and shock to theft, includes the veterans Silvio and Gately (of *Pvt. Wars*) now out of Army hospital and practicing pickpockets. Caught in a theft, Gately reveals his serious mental disturbance and Silvio his protective overseeing of his friend. The total group's interaction throughout point up the assassination's larger significance: that violence and ugliness continue to exist in the communal soul and are too soon forgotten even when witnessed. McLure credibly portrays contemporary urbanites with point and poignancy, demonstrating that his territory goes beyond the southwest.

That he is an actor as well as a writer contributes to McLure's strengths, which include a sharp eye for character, a gifted ear for regional idiomatic speech, and an uncommon comic flair extending to the examination of American myths and mores. If he can stretch effectively beyond the one-act form in which he is most comfortable, McLure should have a productive future.

—Christian H. Moe

McNALLY, Terrence.

Born in St. Petersburg, Florida, 3 November 1939. Educated at schools in Corpus Christi, Texas; Columbia University, New York (Evans Traveling Fellow, 1960), 1956–60, B.A. in English 1960 (Phi Beta Kappa). Stage manager, Actors Studio, New York, 1961; tutor to John Steinbeck's children, 1961–62; film critic, *Seventh Art*, New York, 1963–65; assistant editor, *Columbia College Today*, New York, 1965–66. Since 1981 vice-president, Dramatists Guild. Recipient: Stanley award, 1962; Guggenheim fellowship, 1966, 1969; Hull Warriner award, 1973, 1987, 1989; Obie award, 1974; American Academy award, 1975. Agent: Gilbert Parker, William Morris Agency, 1350 Avenue of the Americas, New York, New York 10019. Address: 218 West 10th Street, New York, New York 10014, U.S.A.

Publications

PLAYS

The Roller Coaster in *Columbia Review*, Spring 1960.

And Things That Go Bump in the Night (as *There Is Something Out There*, produced 1962; revised version, as *And Things That Go Bump in the Night*, produced 1964). In *The Ritz and Other Plays*, 1976.

The Lady of the Camellias, adaptation of a play by Giles Cooper based on the play by Dumas fils (produced 1963).

Next (produced 1967). In *Sweet Eros, Next, and Other Plays*, 1969.

Tour (produced 1967). In *Apple Pie*, 1969.

Botticelli (televised 1968; produced 1971). In *Sweet Eros, Next, and Other Plays*, 1969; in *Off-Broadway Plays 2*, 1972.

Sweet Eros (produced 1968). In *Sweet Eros, Next, and Other Plays*, 1969; in *Off-Broadway Plays 2*, 1972.

i Cuba Si! (produced 1968). In *Sweet Eros, Next, and Other Plays*, 1969.

Witness (produced 1968). In *Sweet Eros, Next, and Other Plays*, 1969.

Noon (in *Chiaroscuro* produced 1968; in *Morning, Noon, and Night*, produced 1968). In *Morning, Noon, and Night*, 1968.

Apple Pie (includes *Next, Tour, Botticelli*). 1969.

Last Gasps (televised 1969). In *Three Plays*, 1970.

Bringing It All Back Home (produced 1969). In *Three Plays*, 1970.

Sweet Eros, Next, and Other Plays. 1969.

Three Plays: i Cuba Si!, Bringing It All Back Home, Last Gasps. 1970.

Where Has Tommy Flowers Gone? (produced 1971). 1972.

Bad Habits: Ravenswood and Dunelawn (produced 1971). 1974.

Let It Bleed, in *City Stops* (produced 1972).

Whiskey (produced 1973). 1973.

The Ritz (as *The Tubs*, produced 1973; revised version, as *The Ritz*, produced 1975). In *The Ritz and Other Plays*, 1976.

The Ritz and Other Plays (includes *Bad Habits, Where Has Tommy Flowers Gone?, And Things That Go Bump in the Night, Whiskey, Bringing It All Back Home*). 1976.

Broadway, Broadway (produced 1978).

It's Only a Play (produced 1982). 1986.

The Rink, music by John Kander, lyrics by Fred Ebb (produced 1984). 1985.

The Lisbon Traviata (produced 1985). In *Three Plays*, 1990.

Frankie and Johnny in the Claire de Lune (produced 1987). In *Three Plays*, 1990.

Don't Fall for the Lights (dialogue only), with A.R. Gurney and Richard Maltby, Jr., *Street Talk*, and *Andre's Mother* in *Urban Blight*, (musical revue), based on an idea by John Tillinger, music by David Shire, lyrics by Richard Maltby, Jr. (produced 1988).

Faith, Hope, and Charity, with Israel Horovitz and Leonard Melfi (produced 1988). 1989.

Prelude and Liebstod (produced 1989).

Up in Saratoga (produced 1989).

Three Plays (includes *The Lisbon Traviata, Frankie and Johnny in the Claire de Lune, It's Only a Play*). 1990.

Kiss of the Spider Woman, adaptation of the novel by Manuel Puig, music by John Kander, lyrics by Fred Ebb (produced 1990).

Lips Together, Teeth Apart (produced 1991). 1992.

L'Age d'Or (produced 1993).

Love! Valour! Compassion (produced 1993).

SCREENPLAYS: The *Ritz*, 1976; *Frankie and Johnny*, 1991.

TELEVISION PLAYS: *Botticelli*, 1968; *Last Gasps*, 1969; *The Five Forty-Eight*, from the story by John Cheever, 1979, *Mama Malone series*, 1983.

It's a long way from Terrence McNally's one-act plays to the rather woozy *And Things That Go Bump in the Night* to the manic antics of *The Ritz* to the hilarious bitchiness of *The Lisbon Traviata* to the wistful sadness of *Lips Together, Teeth Apart* to the upbeat quirkiness of the characters in *Frankie and Johnny in the Claire de Lune* and back to the sharp and incredibly funny goings-on in *It's Only a Play*.

There are a number of unifying elements which are evident in all of McNally's plays: a love of music and theatre; a clever, often biting, wit; a sense of where middle-America thinks it is; and an aura of the confessional with the characters as penitents and the audience as priest. This latter characteristic in lazy writers simply takes the form of narrative monologue but in McNally's work it can be genuinely revealing and often hilarious.

One-act plays seem slightly out of fashion these days, but they are wonderful entrances to production for new writers, and well over 20 years ago McNally was pumping out some biting and successful playlets. One favorite is *Whiskey*, which is as funny at times as any one-act play since *Box and Cox*. It begins with the disastrous appearance of a drunken television cast at the Houston Astrodome and eventually exposes an endearing bunch of fakers. What is clear in this play, as in so many of McNally's pieces, is his infatuation with and amusement by theatre and show people.

Other one-act plays which should continue to find productions include *Tour*, which is a funny and very accurate portrait of an American couple abroad; they are an easy target, however, and McNally later finds more amusing Americans to tease. For those of us who saw James Coco as the reluctant and shy draftee in *Next*, this short play will always be a highlight of off-Broadway. *Botticelli* is different in almost every way as we see two soldiers in Vietnam playing the word-game Botticelli as they "kill a gook"; what is truly frightening (and provokes anger) in this one-act play is the fact that these Americans are intelligent, clever, and educated, yet they have become murderers.

McNally wrote *Hope*, the middle play in *Faith, Hope, and Charity*, which is located in Central Park. As with a good many of McNally's plays, many brand products are named; the device seems to locate the time and the characters but can at times be overdone. In *Hope* several characters wait on Easter Sunday for the sun to rise, which it almost fails to do. The sadness in the play is reflected in an exchange in which a nun says, "Sometimes I think that Christ died in vain. Isn't that terrible?" and another character replies, "Sometimes I think everyone dies in vain. Isn't that worse?" Heavy stuff, indeed, and a portent of heavier stuff to come with the age of AIDS.

With *Sweet Eros*, in which a young lady is tied to a chair and tormented, McNally achieved a good deal of notoriety, but the play flounders in a monologue, which seems to be the purpose of the work itself. Likewise, *Witness* is basically one very long funny speech by a window cleaner, given a memorable performance by the late James Coco again.

Given the nature of one-act plays, however, McNally's considerable reputation as one of America's leading playwrights will rest instead on his full-length plays. *And Things That Go Bump in the Night* received a lot of attention, in part because of its homosexual hero and its experimental format, but also because at heart the play is honest and fascinating. It takes itself very seriously indeed. A later work, *Where Has Tommy Flowers Gone?*, brings to the foreground some of McNally's favorite leitmotifs: the theatre, the outsider, the long monologue with the hero addressing the audience as a character in the play. Theatre and cinema references abound in Tommy's monologues, and the dramatic conventions which are routed in Tommy's various drag outfits are explored skillfully and with good humor. Again, products and product names are almost the "scenery" of this play, but beneath it all is a boy so alienated from the world that he is making a bomb to blow the whole thing up. Thus again, beneath the humor of *Where Has Tommy Flowers Gone?*, there is a deep and disturbing anger which lifts the play from mere frippery to something more profound.

Recently, McNally has written at least four major theatre pieces, all of which have had major success with audiences, just as did the earlier, commercial *The Ritz*, which takes place in a gay bathhouse.

Lips Together, Teeth Apart brings together two men and two women at a house on Fire Island. The brother of one of the women has died of AIDS, and she is deciding what to do with the place. McNally juggles his onstage and offstage characters with enormous skill, combining the running gags and an abiding sense of tragedy, death, fear, and loneliness. Chloe says, quite wisely, as she babbles incessantly, "I talk too much probably because it's too horrible to think about what's really going on." The contrast between this sense of horror and death is sharp as the gays next door noisily celebrate the Fourth of July—if we cannot laugh and at least pretend, we all wallow in sadness and self-pity. There is much in McNally's *Lips Together, Teeth Apart* which echoes the best of Chekhov. This is a play which is much more than merely topical and clever, giving us four distinct and touching characters; it is a play that confronts a deep ache in most of us.

Frankie and Johnny in the Claire de Lune, on the other hand, is a realistic bringing-together of two unheroic figures: a brassy, frightened waitress and her suitor, Johnny, who is hardly the hunk of the week. Together, in Frankie's walk-up, one-room apartment, they find and lose each other, and find themselves finally. Another of McNally's devices is used here very successfully: the integration of appropriate music which comes from "real" sources and is not merely background or mood-inducing pabulum. Frankie and Johnny talk and love and talk some more, but not for a moment are we, the audience, bored or alienated, because we find our own real or hoped-for love in these characters. The film version seemed less intimate but was equally moving, and once the film has had its run, it is likely that the play will continue to have a life of its own in theatres all over the world. It deserves a returning audience.

The Lisbon Traviata is both an achingly funny play and a sad commentary on a love affair that is not just breaking up, but is already broken to pieces. The "opera queens" who dote on, and live for, opera divas are hoist on their own petards. Mendy, the "queen" who has to, simply absolutely must, have a copy of Maria Callas (who else?) singing the "Lost One" in Lisbon, is one of the funniest (and most pathetic) characters of modern drama. A lonely man, he wants so much to be loved but his caustic wit and his obsessions would frighten off a saint. Stephen knows that his relationship with Mike is over, that Paul has come between them, but he cannot quite accept his loss. McNally has created a poignant and very funny play. It may (even now) shock some audiences, but it will survive and thrive in theatre wherever humor, self-exploration, and honesty are permitted.

The funniest play in recent years is *It's Only a Play*. Not since Michael Frayn's *Noises Off* has there been a farce about theatre and theatre people to equal the sheer joy and madness of this play. *It's Only a Play* is an almost perfect reflection of what it was to produce a play on Broadway. (Is it McNally's own *The Ritz* that he is remembering?) The maniacal characters "celebrating" the opening night at the producer's smart apartment are so brilliantly drawn that one need never have seen a theatre person to know that that these are the real thing, properly exaggerated for farce. In the fabled tradition of *The Torchbearers* (those inept amateurs) and *Light up the Sky* (those greedy professionals), McNally has skewered his beloved showbusiness, and I honestly cannot remember a play at which the audience screams with laughter in just this way. It is all outrageous, improbable, and absolutely on the mark.

It is safe to assume that Terrence McNally is not only a leading American playwright but a caring, skillful, and successful man who has only just begun to explore his theatrical territory with these diverse and wonderful plays. He's well beyond "promised"; he has delivered.

—Arthur H. Ballet

MEDNICK, Murray.

Born in Brooklyn, New York, 24 August 1939. Educated at Fallsburg Central School, New York; Brooklyn College, 1957–60. Artistic co-director, Theatre Genesis, New York, 1970–74. Founder with others and since 1978 artistic director, Padua Hills Playwrights Workshop and Festival, Los Angeles, California. Playwright- in-residence, Florida State University, Tallahassee, 1972, State University of New York, Buffalo, 1973, California State University, Long Beach, 1973, La Verne College, California, 1978–82, and Pomona College, Claremont, California, 1983, 1984. Recipient: National Endowment for the Arts grant, for poetry, 1967; Rockefeller grant, 1968, 1972; Obie award, 1970; Guggenheim grant, 1973; Creative Artists Public Service grant, 1973; Los Angeles Theatre League Ovation Lifetime Achievement award, 1992. Address: 10923 Ayres Avenue, Los Angeles, California 90064, U.S.A.

Publications

PLAYS

The *Box* (produced 1965).
The Mark of Zorro (produced 1966).
Guideline (produced 1966).
Sand (produced 1967). In *The New Underground Theatre*, 1968.
The Hawk: An Improvisational Play, with Tony Barsha (produced 1967). 1968.
Willie the Germ (produced 1968). In *More Plays from Off-Off-Broadway*, edited by Michael T. Smith, 1972.
The Hunter (produced 1968). 1969.
The Shadow Ripens (also director: produced 1969).
The Deer Kill (produced 1970). 1971.
Cartoon (produced 1971).
Are You Lookin'? (also director: produced 1973).

Black Hole in Space (produced 1975).

Taxes (also director: produced 1976). In *Wordplays 3*, 1984.

The Coyote Cycle (7 plays) (also director: produced 1978–80; complete cycle produced 1984). In *West Coast Plays*, 1981; *Coyote V: Listening to Old Nana*, in *Plays from Padua Hills*, edited by Mednick, 1983.

Solomon's Fish (produced 1979).

The Actors' Delicatessen, with Priscilla Cohen (produced 1984).

Scar (also director: produced 1985).

Zohar (also director: produced 1985).

The Pitch (produced 1985). In *Articles*, 1986.

Face (produced 1986).

Heads (produced 1987).

Shatter 'n Wade (produced 1990). In *Best of the West*, edited by Mednick, 1991.

TELEVISION PLAYS: *Iowa*, 1977; *Blessings*, 1978.

OTHER

Editor, *Plays from Padua Hills*. 1983.

Editor, *Best of the West*. 1991.

THEATRICAL ACTIVITIES

DIRECTOR: **Plays**—several of his own plays, and *Blue Bitch* by Sam Shepard, 1973.

ACTOR: **Plays**—*The Actors' Delicatessen*, 1984; *Zohar*, 1985.

Murray Mednick is one of the important American dramatists who came of age in the 1960s. In the decade beginning in 1965 he produced some dozen plays, developing increasing technical strength, clarity, and complexity and extending his vision with passionate conviction. His plays and the worlds they evoke are often dominated by ugly, crushing economic and personal pressures that lie behind the American pretense of equality and social justice. The humor is often bitter. Another recurring feature has been the attempt to place contemporary experience in the context of native American myth.

Mednick did most of his early work at Theatre Genesis, a church-sponsored theater on the lower East Side in New York. A poet before he turned to drama, he wrote several one-act plays in the mid-1960s, then moved onto larger forms. *Sand* shows an ageing, used-up American couple who are visited by a formal ambassador, their horrible regressive stupor unbroken by the news that their son is dead in the (Vietnam) war. The dead soldier's body is brought in at the end on a meat hook. *Willie the Germ* is about a down-and-out man working as a dishwasher for a grotesque family of Coney Island freaks who endlessly seduce him into incomprehensible machinations that always get him into trouble. He yearns to escape but is kept in his place by put-downs and an invisible electric force field operated by an anonymous Button-Pusher in the audience. At the end he is destroyed and castrated by the monstrous representatives of "society."

Mednick has also created plays with groups of actors, using improvisation to draw material from their lives and imaginations into a form devised by the dramatist. *The Hawk* is a play about a drug pusher and his victims. The victims' self-revealing monologues were developed by the actors and framed in a formal, ritualistic structure. The play employed a novel and experimental set of technical acting devices and was remarkably successful in shaping very loose, idiosyncratic material within an elegantly disciplined and cohesive form. *The Shadow Ripens* was based on an Eskimo legend and embodied the idea of descending to dangerous non-rational depths of being in quest of wisdom and authenticity.

Mednick continued to produce plays that emphasized language and carefully crafted writing. *Are You Lookin'?* is a fragmented, highly subjective study of the effect of heroin use on personal emotional life. *The Hunter* depicts a hip, tight friendship between two men. They are united by a common enemy, a middle-aged hunter obsessed with the Civil War, whom they nail to a tree; and they are driven to mutual mistrust by a woman. The play's pared-down, ambiguous style shows Mednick moving toward the visionary.

The young hero of *The Deer Kill* has moved to an old farm seeking a simple, virtuous life. His good nature and well-being are sorely tried—by crazed friends from the city, one of whom kills himself, by his unfaithful wife, and by the local authorities, because his dog has killed a deer. The play is more realistic than Mednick's early work, a clear, rich, and affecting study of the struggle to live morally in contemporary America.

In the middle 1970s Mednick, Brooklyn-born, moved from New York to Los Angeles, where he has continued to broaden and deepen his achievement. The cartoon-like *Taxes*, his take on the vaunted California lifestyle, ironically recapitulates the devices of the freshly historic New York avant-garde. The playwright's biting clarity of vision communicates a new compassion for his characters.

With Maria Irene Fornés, John Steppling, and Sam Shepard, Mednick founded the Padua Hills Playwrights Workshop and Festival in Los Angeles in 1978, and he continues as artistic director.

Padua Hills took the form of theater without a theater—natural settings were the only stage available. This led to Mednick's extraordinary *The Coyote Cycle*, seven plays developed between 1978 and 1984. Drawing on Native American imagery, including the Coyote/Trickster tradition and the Hopi creation myths, as well as contemporary culture and experimental theatre, *The Coyote Cycle* is an environmental warning and prayer for planetary salvation. All-night performances of the cycle have taken audiences into rugged landscapes for a unique theatrical and conceptual experience.

By the early 1990s Mednick had also written *Scar*, *Shatter 'n Wade*, and *Heads*. In *Scar*, set in the New Mexico mountains, a successful rock musician encounters a "loser" from his past who forces him to confront deep responsibilities to earth and being. The teeming, finely honed talk in *Shatter 'n Wade* implies sharp contemporary anxieties and aggressions, its mounting menace and fear mirroring society at the raw interface with individual consciousness. The direct, apocalyptic *Heads* is clean, mean, and powerful, unflinchingly mythic, and beautifully spare in its language.

Mednick uses theater as a free poetic medium, and the dark intensity of his vision, as well as the intelligence of his forms, fuses many levels of meaning. His latest works have won fervent admiration, and he continues to enlarge the meaning, artistry, and emotional effect of his plays.

—Michael T. Smith

MEDOFF, Mark (Howard).

Born in Mount Carmel, Illinois, 18 March 1940. Educated at the University of Miami, 1958–62, B.A. 1962; Stanford University, California, 1964–66, M.A. 1966. Married Stephanie Thorne in 1972 (second marriage); three daughters. Supervisor of publications, Capitol Radio Engineering Institute, Washington, D.C., 1962–64. Instructor, 1966–71, assistant professor, 1971–74, associate professor, 1974–79, since 1979 professor of drama (currently head of the department of theatre arts), since 1975 dramatist-in-residence, and artistic director, 1982–87, American Southwest Theatre Company, all at New Mexico State University, Las Cruces. Chair of the Awards Committee, American College Theatre Festival, 1985–86. Recipient: Drama Desk award, 1974, 1980; New Mexico State University Westhafer award, 1974; John Gassner award, 1974; Joseph Jefferson award, for acting, 1974; Guggenheim fellowship, 1974; Tony award, 1980; Outer Circle award, 1980; New Mexico Governor's award, 1980; Society of West End Theatre award, 1982; Obie award, 1984. D.H.L.: Gallaudet College, Washington, D.C., 1981. Agent: Gilbert Parker, William Morris Agency, 1350 Avenue of the Americas, New York, New York 10019. Address: Department of Theatre Arts, New Mexico State University, Las Cruces, New Mexico 88003, U.S.A.

Publications

PLAYS

The Wager (produced 1967). 1975.

Doing a Good One for the Red Man (produced 1969). In *Four Short Plays*, 1974.

The Froegle Dictum (produced 1971). In *Four Short Plays*, 1974.

The War on Tatem (produced 1972). In *Four Short Plays*, 1974.

The Kramer (produced 1972). 1976.

When You Comin Back, Red Ryder? (produced 1973). 1974; in *The Hero Trilogy*, 1989.

The Odyssey of Jeremy Jack (for children), with Carleene Johnson (produced 1975). 1974.

Four Short Plays (includes *The Froegle Dictum, Doing a Good One for the Red Man, The War on Tatem, The Ultimate Grammar of Life*). 1974.

The Wager: A Play, and Doing a Good One for the Red Man, and The War on Tatem: Two Short Plays. 1975.

The Halloween Bandit (produced 1976).

The Conversion of Aaron Weiss (produced 1977).

Firekeeper (produced 1978).

The Last Chance Saloon (also director: produced 1979).

Children of a Lesser God (produced 1979). 1980.

The Hands of Its Enemy (produced 1984). 1987.

The Majestic Kid, music by Jan Scarborough, lyrics by Medoff and Scarborough (produced 1985). In *The Hero Trilogy*, 1989.
Kringle's Window (produced 1985).
The Heart Outright (produced 1986). In *The Hero Trilogy*, 1989.
The Hero Trilogy (includes *When You Comin' Back, Red Ryder?*, *The Majestic Kid*, *The Heart Outright*). 1989.
Big Mary. 1989.

SCREENPLAYS: *Good Guys Wear Black*, with Bruce Cohn and Joseph Fraley, 1978; *When You Comin' Back, Red Ryder?*, 1979; *Off Beat*, 1986; *Apology*, 1986; *Children of a Lesser God*, with Hesper Anderson, 1987; *Clara's Heart*, 1988; *City of Joy*, 1992.

RADIO PLAYS: *The Disintegration of Aaron Weiss*, 1979.

NOVEL
Dreams of Long Lasting. 1992.

THEATRICAL ACTIVITIES
DIRECTOR: **Plays**—some of his own plays; *Waiting for Godot* by Samuel Beckett; *The Effect of Gamma Rays on Man-in-the-Moon Marigolds* by Paul Zindel; *Jacques Brel Is Alive and Well and Living in Paris*; *The Birthday Party* by Harold Pinter; *One Flew over the Cuckoo's Nest* by Dale Wasserman; *Equus* by Peter Shaffer; *The Hotel Baltimore* by Lanford Wilson; *Head Act* by Mark Frost; *The Hold Out* by Tony Stafford; *Xmor* by Jan Scarborough and Barbara Kerr; *Vanities* by Jack Heifner; *A Flea in Her Ear* by John Mortimer; *Deadline for Murder*.
ACTOR: **Plays**—Andrei Bolkonski in *War and Peace*; Marat in *Marat/Sade* by Peter Weiss; Pozzo in *Waiting for Godot* by Samuel Beckett; Teddy in *When You Comin Back, Red Ryder?*; Harold Gorringe in *Black Comedy* by Peter Shaffer; Bro Paradock in *A Resounding Tinkle* by N.F. Simpson; Lenny Bruce in *The Soul of Lenny Bruce*; Dysart in *Equus* by Peter Shaffer; Deeley in *Old Times* by Harold Pinter; Scrooge in *A Christmas Carol*; Bellman in *The Hands of Its Enemy*, 1984.

Mark Medoff comments:

My work is simply a reflection of my own spirit, my fears, sorrows, and fires.

Mark Medoff's characters are nostalgic, hoping for redemption in the face of a disappearing way of life. This life exists in various forms: in some of Medoff's plays we mourn the lost idealism of the 1960s, in some the disappearing myth of the west. In all of them characters are defending against a changing world, whether through violence, verbal wit, or the hope of love.

The Kramer is a dream play depicting a power-hungry young man's seemingly gratuitous attempt to take over a secretarial school and simultaneously transform the lives of everyone in it. In a touch of rather heavy-handed symbolism Kramer's profile is marred by a cancerous mole. The men in his way—the obligatory conservative supervisor, the unambitious secretary Artie Malin—are no match for Kramer's cynicism, his verbal game-playing, or his eventual transition from verbal to physical violence. Or the women either. Kramer's persuasiveness is based on his apparent ability to know, verbatim, the past lives of his antagonists. He easily persuades Judy Uichi to leave her Japanese amputee husband on the grounds that: "the idealism of your youth having dissipated, he's a lodestone around your neck." Equally as easily he persuades Artie Malin to leave his unattractive wife, Carol May. Ironically, it is Carol May, who seems to be Kramer's weakest opponent, who is actually his only true adversary. Carol May is the only character who seems capable of genuine feeling, and it is her voice that we remember: "You understand you're trying to drown me. . . . Why are you doing this? . . . Is it me—or is it that you just want to destroy things? . . . Haven't you ever loved another person very, very much?"

Teddy in *When You Comin Back, Red Ryder?* is, like Kramer, a figure of violence who far exceeds everyone around him in both intelligence and physical strength. But Teddy is a more complex character. Though initially his disruption of the New Mexico diner appears as gratuitous as Kramer's takeover, it becomes evident that Teddy's real threat is not only his violence but also his ability to destroy the illusions around which lives are constructed. Teddy shares Kramer's uncanny insight into others' pasts, and his readings of people are both cruel and accurate. If Teddy is evil he is also a catalyst for change, forcing decisions and realizations that have long been avoided. In addition, Medoff allows an insight that we don't get into Kramer: we see what Teddy is mourning. Calling himself one of the "disaffected" youth, he asks of the old western heroes, "What in the hell happened to those people?" and announces at the end of the play, "This is the last dance then, gang. Time's gone and I'm gonna ride off into the sunrise." Teddy's tragedy is both his misused brilliance and his ability to accept life's divergence from myth.

The Wager is in many ways a transition between Medoff's earlier works and *Children of a Lesser God*. Leeds shares with Kramer and Teddy the qualities of violence, verbal wit, and cruel if brilliant insight. But the violence here is transformed to suggest emotional vulnerability. As in *The Kramer* the protagonist's only real match is a woman. The verbal pyrotechnics between Leeds and Honor are clearly a defense against their attraction to one another. Leeds's ability to overcome this defensiveness, even if with great resistance, and Honor's recognition that words are often destructive to understanding suggest greater depth of character than that possessed by any of Medoff's earlier protagonists, and, in addition, for Medoff, a change of key.

The singular quality of *Children of a Lesser God* is its lyricism, relying on the same fluid and dream-like staging employed in *The Kramer*. The play begins and ends in James's memory. James, like his predecessors, is bright and somewhat disaffected, a former Peace Corps volunteer who tells us, "I saved Ecuador." Unlike his predecessors, he retains in the face of the cynicism of his somewhat stereotypical supervisor and students at a school for the non-hearing both some measure of idealism and an openness to feeling, although his tendency to what Robert Brustein has called "pop psychoanalysis" can become annoying. Also unlike his predecessors, James shares the stage. He has a co-protagonist.

Sarah Norman, one of James's non-hearing students, who signs because she will not speak, provides the play with much of its lyrical eloquence. The relationship between James and Sarah, initially a power struggle between teacher and student, becomes a love affair and then reverts to a power struggle. The issues Medoff explored in earlier works are now complicated by the conflict between power and feeling. James acknowledges the inherent ambiguity of his motives: do they stem from a desire to help or a desire to control? Sarah, for her part, is "determined to preserve her wholeness inside a deaf world . . . deafness . . . is a condition of being 'other,' and this otherness has its sufficient rewards." She signs to James: "I live in a place you can't enter. It's out of reach. . . . Deafness isn't the opposite of hearing, as you think. It's a silence full of sound. . . ." Their final confrontation is a recognition of simultaneous love and difference—a difference that is, despite love, irresolvable, James acknowledging: "Yes, I'm a terrific teacher: Grow, Sarah, but not too much. Understand yourself, but not more than I understand you. Be brave, but not so brave you don't need me anymore," and Sarah: "I'm afraid I would just go on trying to change you. We would have to meet in another place; not in silence or in sound but somewhere else. I don't know where that is now."

The play's eloquence is, paradoxically, inherent in its characters' inability to make themselves understood. The fact is that the two protagonists speak separate languages. Although this linguistic difference is muted by James's simultaneous translation of Sarah's signing, the play does give an indication, at least, of the imperative to understand those who are "inarticulate" in our language. Those who are non-vocal, Medoff suggests, do not necessarily have nothing to say. The struggle to be heard is a common theme, and Brustein, in his review, expresses his irritation, calling the play "a chic compendium of every extant cliché about women and minority groups. . . ." But the frequency with which a theme is explored does not necessarily relate to its importance; if anything the repetition of an idea may indicate the necessity of coming to terms with it. Gerald Weales has written of this play that: "Since no marriage—however close, however loving—can make two people one . . . the special cases of James, as teacher, and Sarah, as unwilling pupil, can become metaphors for any marriage." James's final nostalgia for a love that is real and yet not realizable is at the heart of the play's poignance, a poignance the later screenplay, by resorting to a happy ending, fails to retain.

Two later plays by Medoff are less successful in their reiteration of earlier themes. Aaron, in the musical *The Majestic Kid*, is like Leeds, concerned with issues of love and distance, with lost idealism. But the characters are unrealized. Aaron's love affair with Lisa is abrupt and therefore unimportant. It is difficult to know how to take the Laredo Kid, a movie character brought to life who knows all the old western plots by heart—movie as karma?—but cannot decipher the present script. And the ideological and political concerns of Aaron's long-time lover and co-worker, A.J., jar with her flip one-liners. *The Hands of Its Enemy* also concerns a woman who cannot hear. But *Enemy* is more conceptional than *Children*, a play within a play which juxtaposes a psychological exploration of the characters of a playwright and her director with the rehearsal process for their play. The central theme again centers around issues of distance and the need to trust, but here the struggle is at times cloying and overdone.

At his weakest Medoff may occasionally go too far in one direction or the other, becoming either gratuitous or overly sentimental. But in his best plays he is able to combine a frighteningly realistic depiction of the cruelties we wittingly or unwittingly commit with a simultaneous acknowledgement of our tremendous vulnerability.

—Elizabeth Adams

See the essay on *Children of a Lesser God.*

MELFI, Leonard (Anthony).

Born in Binghamton, New York, 21 February 1935. Educated at Binghamton Central High School; St. Bonaventure University, New York, 1956–57; American Academy of Dramatic Arts. Worked as a waiter and carpenter, lecturer, New York University, 1969–70. Columnist ("Notes of a New York Playwright"), *Dramatists Guild Quarterly*, New York. Recipient: Eugene O'Neill Memorial Theatre Foundation award, 1966; Rockefeller grant, 1966, 1967; Guggenheim fellowship, 1978. Lives in New York City. Agent: Helen Harvey Associates, 410 West 24th Street, New York, New York 10011, U.S.A.

Publications

PLAYS

Lazy Baby Susan (produced 1965).

Sunglasses (produced 1965).

Pussies and Rookies (produced 1965).

Ferryboat (produced 1965). In *Encounters*, 1967.

Birdbath (produced 1965). In *Encounters*, 1967; in *New Short Plays 1*, 1968.

Times Square (produced 1966). In *Encounters*, 1967.

Niagara Falls (produced 1966; revised version produced 1968). In *New Theatre for Now* (*New Theatre in America 2*), edited by Edward Parone, 1971.

Lunchtime (produced 1966). In *Encounters*, 1967.

Halloween (produced 1967). In *Encounters*, 1967.

The Shirt (produced 1967). In *Encounters*, 1967.

Encounters: 6 One-Act Plays. 1967.

Disfiguration (produced 1967).

Night (in *Chiaroscuro* produced 1968; in *Morning, Noon, and Night*, produced 1968). In *Morning, Noon, and Night*, 1969.

Stars and Stripes, in *Collision Course* (produced 1968). 1968.

Stimulation (produced 1968).

Jack and Jill (produced 1968; revised version, produced as part of *Oh! Calcutta!*, 1969). 1969.

The Breech Baby (produced 1968).

Having Fun in the Bathroom (produced 1969).

The Raven Rock (produced 1969).

Wet and Dry, and Alive (produced 1969).

The Jones Man (produced 1969).

Cinque (produced 1970). In *Spontaneous Combustion: Eight New American Plays*, edited by Rochelle Owens, 1972.

Ah! Wine! (produced 1974).
Beautiful! (produced 1974).
Horse Opera, music by John Braden (produced 1974).
Sweet Suite (produced 1975).
Porno Stars at Home (produced 1976). 1980.
Eddie and Susanna in Love (produced 1976).
Fantasies at the Frick; or, (The Guard and the Guardess) (produced 1976). 1980.
Butterfaces (produced 1977).
Taxi Tales (five plays; produced 1978). In *Later Encounters*, 1980.
Rusty and Rico, and Lena and Louie (produced 1978). In *Later Encounters*, 1980.
Later Encounters: Seven One-Act Plays (includes *Taxi Tales—Taffy's Taxi, Tripper's Taxi, Toddy's Taxi, The Teaser's Taxi, Mr. Tucker's Taxi—Rusty and Rico, Lena and Louie*). 1980.
Amorous Accidents (produced 1981).
The Dispossessed (produced 1982).
Eve Is Innocent (produced 1983).
Rosetti's Apologetics, music by Mark Hardwick (produced 1983).
The Little Venice Makes a Good Drink (produced 1985).
Lily Lake (produced 1986).
Faith, Hope, and Charity, with Terrence McNally and Israel Horovitz (produced 1988). 1989.

SCREENPLAY: *La mortadella (Lady Liberty)*, 1971.

TELEVISION PLAYS: *The Rainbow Rest*, 1967; *Puck! Puck! Puck!*, 1968; *What a Life!*, 1976.

CRITICAL STUDY: *American Playwrights: A Critical Survey* by Bonnie Marranca and Gautam Dasgupta, 1981.

THEATRICAL ACTIVITIES
ACTOR: **Plays**—Knute Gary in *Beautiful!*, 1974; Room Service in *Sweet Suite*, 1975; Richard DeRichard in *The Dispossessed*, 1982; Rosetti in *Rosetti's Apologetics*, 1983. **Films**—*La mortadella (Lady Liberty)*, 1971; *Rent Control*, 1983.

Leonard Melfi comments:

A personal statement introducing my plays?

Well . . . "I borrow from life and pay back my debt by giving my imagination."

Or, maybe . . . "Plays about my fellow human beings in and out of trouble, like all of us at various times. In other words: celebrating the human condition, the miracle and mystery of life, no matter what."

Or, maybe . . . "I take people who wake up in the morning and ask themselves: 'Are you happy?', and then they answer immediately to themselves: 'Yes, I am!' . . . and I throw them together with the other group, who, when they ask themselves the very same question, always answer immediately: 'No, I'm not!' (There's always a play in that situation!)."

Why I feel so great about writing plays (among other certain reasons)? Well, once in my father's roadhouse restaurant and bar in Upstate New York where I grew up, a bunch of hunters walked in to drink and eat and my father was behind the bar. One of the men asked: "By the way: what does your son down in New York City do anyway?" And my father smiled and proudly replied (he had gone as far as the sixth grade): "My son does the same thing that Shakespeare did!"

It's just like a sort of Utopia . . . all those windows with all those people behind all of those windows: living and breathing and trying to love too. Well, I just love it all, my dear Louie Pussycat! All of them trying like holy hell and holy heaven to be wholly holy happy as much as it's humanly possible in all of our rather only half-happy lives instead of our wholly happy lives . . . !

Lena of *Lena and Louie* shows the best and the worst of Leonard Melfi's playwriting. The exuberance and visionary optimism are as typical of his work as the shallow sentiment and flabby prose. Although Melfi has never fulfilled the promise of his early plays, and may have reneged on it, he has consolidated his dramatic territory and remained constant to it.

Melfi gained his first foothold in theatre when he began writing one-act plays for Ellen Stewart's Cafe La Mama, one of the birthplaces of off-off-Broadway. To fit the one-act form, Melfi stripped his characters of all but one or two qualities, usually the need for love or the need for sex, or both. Similarly, the plays of *Encounters* revolved around those brief moments when human contact becomes possible. Such moments are particularly rare in large cities, and Melfi's plays are as New York as pavement, filled with specific references to the city and its people. Presented at La Mama, they were always on intimate terms with their audiences.

The plays range in style from a necessarily narrowed realism to a highly stylized fantasy occasionally reminiscent of Michael McClure's cartoon plays. *Birdbath*, one of Melfi's best known plays, brings together a superficially composed young man and an excessively nervous young woman who can speak of little but her mother. Their encounter brings out the man's obsessive need to write and the woman's murder of her mother that morning, and the bond between them that results from these revelations brings them together, and the play ends with Frankie's valentine to Velma. In contrast, *Times Square* is a masquelike fantasy about the people who inhabit New York's most offensive block of sex-shows and other adult temptations. The characters, however, are childlike, hopeful dreamers whose innocence is only confirmed by the fluid, anything-can-happen life of Times Square. When the angelic Melissa Sobbing is hit by a car, she is revivified with a kiss, and for a moment Times Square really is a street of dreams.

Melfi's world has its nightmares too, which come with a sudden violence that counterpoints oddly its romance. In *Encounters* the violence exploded into the romance with a sharpness and suddenness that enriched the plays. In *Later Encounters* and Melfi's longer plays the dark side of New York has been increasingly absorbed and softened by the light. Although Lena and Louie freeze to death in Central Park, their deaths are an apotheosis. They die "in each other's arms, with the two most beautiful smiles on their faces: smiling like one has never seen smiling ever before in one's life; smiling smiles that told of things like, well, things like . . . forever!"

Melfi's longer plays are essentially enlarged one-acts, with small casts and limited aims. In *Porno Stars at Home* the characters begin an evening with their facades intact, smoothly congratulating themselves on their style and dash. Before the evening is out, they've reduced their styles to shreds, and are trying desperately to put them back together. Unfortunately, their psychological strip uncovers little of interest, little more than "Baby, all I do all of the time is to try and not be scared anymore, that's all," or "I just want something to hang on to before it's too late." Although an able craftsman of the theatre, Melfi has so far failed to pursue his well-worn themes and situations into new territory.

—Walter Bode

MILLER, Arthur.

Born in New York City, 17 October 1915. Educated at Abraham Lincoln High School, New York, graduated 1932; University of Michigan, Ann Arbor (Hopwood Award, 1936, 1937), 1934–38, A.B. 1938. Married 1) Mary Slattery in 1940 (divorced 1956), one son and one daughter; 2) the actress Marilyn Monroe in 1956 (divorced 1961); 3) the photographer Ingeborg Morath in 1962, one daughter. Worked in automobile supply warehouse, 1932–34; member of the Federal Theatre Project, 1938; writer for CBS and NBC Radio Workshops. Associate professor of drama, University of Michigan, 1973–74. International president, PEN, London and New York, 1965–69. Recipient: Theatre Guild award, 1938; New York Drama Critics Circle award, 1947, 1949; Tony award, 1947, 1949, 1953; Pulitzer prize, 1949; National Association of Independent Schools award, 1954; American Academy Gold medal, 1959; Brandeis University Creative Arts award, 1969; Peabody award, for television play, 1981; Bobst award, 1983; National Arts Club medal of honor, 1992; City University of New York Edwin Booth award, 1992; Commonwealth award, 1992. D.H.L.: University of Michigan, 1956; Honorary degree: Hebrew University, Jerusalem, 1959; Litt.D.: University of East Anglia, Norwich, 1984. Member, American Academy, 1981. Lives in Connecticut. Agent: Kay Brown, International Creative Management, 40 West 57th Street, New York, New York 10019, U.S.A.

Publications

PLAYS

Honors at Dawn (produced 1936).
No Villain (They Too Arise) (produced 1937).
The Pussycat and the Expert Plumber Who Was a Man, and *William Ireland's*

Confession. In *100 Non-Royalty Radio Plays,* edited by William Kozlenko. 1941.

The Man Who Had All the Luck (produced 1944). In *Cross-Section 1944,* edited by Edwin Seaver, 1944.

That They May Win (produced 1944). In *Best One-Act Plays of 1944,* edited by Margaret Mayorga, 1945.

Grandpa and the Statue. In *Radio Drama in Action,* edited by Erik Barnouw. 1945.

The Story of Gus. In *Radio's Best Plays,* edited by Joseph Liss. 1947.

The Guardsman, radio adaptation of a play by Ferenc Molnár, and *Three Men on a Horse,* radio adaptation of the play by George Abbott and John Cecil Holm, in *Theatre Guild on the Air,* edited by William Fitelson. 1947.

All My Sons (produced 1947). 1947; in *Collected Plays,* 1957.

Death of a Salesman: Certain Private Conversations in Two Acts and a Requiem (produced 1949). 1949.

An Enemy of the People, adaptation of a play by Ibsen (produced 1950). 1951.

The Crucible (produced 1953). 1953; augmented version (with additional scene, subsequently omitted), 1954.

A View from the Bridge (produced 1955). With *A Memory of Two Mondays,* 1955; revised version (produced 1956), 1956.

A Memory of Two Mondays (produced 1955). With *A View from the Bridge,* 1955; in *Collected Plays, 1957.*

Collected Plays (includes *All My Sons, Death of a Salesman, The Crucible, A Memory of Two Mondays, A View from the Bridge*). 1957.

After the Fall (produced 1964). 1964.

Incident at Vichy (produced 1964). 1965.

The Price (produced 1968). 1968.

Fame, and The Reason Why (produced 1970). *Fame* in *Yale Literary Magazine,* March 1971.

The Creation of the World and Other Business (produced 1972). 1973; in *Collected Plays 2,* 1981; revised version, as *Up from Paradise,* music by Stanley Silverman (also director: produced 1974), 1984.

The Archbishop's Ceiling (produced 1977; revised version produced 1984). 1984; with *The American Clock,* 1989.

The American Clock, adaptation of the work *Hard Times* by Studs Terkel (produced 1979). 1983; with *The Archbishop's Ceiling,* 1989.

Playing for Time, adaptation of a work by Fania Fenelon (televised 1980; produced 1986). 1981; in *Collected Plays 2,* 1981.

Collected Plays 2 (includes *The Misfits, After the Fall, Incident at Vichy, The Price, The Creation of the World and Other Business, Playing for Time*). 1981.

Eight Plays (includes *All My Sons, Death of a Salesman, The Crucible, A Memory of Two Mondays, A View from the Bridge, After the Fall, Incident at Vichy, The Price*). 1981.

Two-Way Mirror (includes *Elegy for a Lady* and *Some Kind of Love Story*) (also director: produced 1982). 1984.

Danger! Memory! (includes *I Can't Remember Anything* and *Clara*) (produced 1987). 1986.

Speech to the Neighborhood Watch Committee in *Urban Blight* (musical revue), based on an idea by John Tillinger, music by David Shire, lyrics by Richard Maltby, Jr. (produced 1988).
Plays 3 (includes *The American Clock, The Archbishop's Ceiling, Two-Way Mirror*). 1990.
Everybody Wins (screenplay). 1990.
The Last Yankee (produced 1991). 1991.
The Ride Down Mount Morgan (produced 1991). 1992.

SCREENPLAYS: *The Story of G.I. Joe* (uncredited), 1945; *The Witches of Salem*, 1958; *The Misfits*, 1961; *Everybody Wins*, 1990; *The Crucible*, 1992.

RADIO PLAYS: *The Pussycat and the Expert Plumber Who Was a Man, William Ireland's Confession, Grandpa and the Statue, The Story of Gus, The Guardsman, Three Men on a Horse*, early 1940s; *The Golden Years*, 1987.

TELEVISION PLAY: *Playing for Time*, 1980.

NOVELS
Focus. 1945.
The Misfits (novelization of screenplay). 1961.

SHORT STORIES
I Don't Need You Any More. 1967.

OTHER
Situation Normal. 1944.
Jane's Blanket (for children). 1963.
In Russia, photographs by Inge Morath. 1969.
The Portable Arthur Miller, edited by Harold Clurman. 1971.
In the Country, photographs by Inge Morath. 1977.
The Theater Essays of Arthur Miller, edited by Robert A. Martin. 1978.
Chinese Encounters, photographs by Inge Morath. 1979.
"Salesman" in Beijing. 1984.
Timebends (autobiography). 1987.

BIBLIOGRAPHY: "Arthur Miller: The Dimension of His Art: A Checklist of His Published Works," in *Serif*, June 1967, and *Arthur Miller Criticism (1930–1967)*, 1969, revised edition as *An Index to Arthur Miller Criticism*, 1976, both by Tetsumaro Hayashi; *Arthur Miller: A Reference Guide* by John H. Ferres, 1979.

MANUSCRIPT COLLECTIONS: University of Texas, Austin; University of Michigan, Ann Arbor; New York Public Library; Library of Congress, Washington, D.C.

CRITICAL STUDIES (a selection): *Arthur Miller*, 1961, and *Miller: A Study of His Plays*, 1979, revised edition as *Miller the Playwright*, 1983, both by Dennis Welland; *Arthur Miller* by Robert Hogan, 1964; *Arthur Miller: The Burning Glass* by Sheila Huftel, 1965; *Arthur Miller: Death of a Salesman: Text and Criticism* edited by Gerald Weales, 1967; *Arthur Miller* by Leonard Moss, 1967, revised edition, 1980; *Arthur Miller, Dramatist* by Edward Murray, 1967; *Arthur Miller: A Collection of Critical Essays* edited by Robert W. Corrigan, 1969; *Psychology and Arthur Miller* by Richard I. Evans, 1969; *The Merrill Guide to Arthur Miller* by Sidney H. White, 1970; *Arthur Miller: Portrait of a Playwright* by Benjamin Nelson, 1970; *Arthur Miller* by Ronald Hayman, 1970; *Twentieth-Century Interpretations of The Crucible* edited by John H. Ferres, 1972; *Studies in Death of a Salesman* edited by Walter J. Meserve, 1972; *Critical Essays on Arthur Miller* edited by James J. Martine, 1979; *Arthur Miller: New Perspectives* edited by Robert A. Martin, 1982; *Arthur Miller* by Neil Carson, 1982; *Twentieth-Century Interpretations of Death of a Salesman* edited by Helene Wickham Koon, 1983; *Conversations with Arthur Miller* edited by Matthew C. Roudané, Jackson, 1987; *File on Miller* edited by C.W.E. Bigsby, 1988.

THEATRICAL ACTIVITIES
DIRECTOR: **Plays**—*The Price*, 1969; *Up from Paradise*, 1974; *Two-Way Mirror*, 1982; *Death of a Salesman*, 1983, 1992.
ACTOR: **Play**—Narrator in *Up from Paradise*, 1974. **Television**—*The Civil War*.

Arthur Miller comments:

I have, I think, provided actors with some good things to do and say. Beyond that I cannot speak with any certainty. My plays seem to exist and that's enough for me. What people may find in them or fail to find is not in my control anymore; I can only hope that life has not been made less for what I've done, and possibly a bit more.

How may a man make of the outside world a home?

I am constantly awed by what an individual is, by the endless possibilities in him for good and evil, by his unpredictability, by the possibilities he has for any betrayal, any cruelty, as well as any altruism, any sacrifice.

Arthur Miller writes primarily about man's relationship to society and the issues of personal identity and human dignity. Throughout, he has used the realistic form. His statement of purpose—to write "a drama of the whole-man"—conveys his interest in psychology as well as morality. Miller frequently uses what T.S. Eliot called the "objective correlative" ("a set of objects, a situation, a chain of events which shall be the formula of that *particular* emotion") in order to combine an extraordinarily forceful theater with uncanny psychological insights and lyrical and poetic vision. His aim is a theater that "teaches, not by proposing solutions but by defining problems."

The *Collected Plays* of 1957 portray the individual struggling against the laws of society, family, and even selfhood—torn between either the dreams the dog-eat-dog world has imposed upon him and his essential goodness, or torn between his deepest wishes for the simple life and the needs he feels obliged to meet. Set against a ruthless capitalist system that ignores or uses the common man, his identity frequently consists of merely accommodating himself to an essentially alien universe (society) and the act of painstakingly supporting his family. Sometimes, however, he learns that he never was in fact connected with family or job, let alone society, or that the values of each were equally spurious.

Miller's first successful play, *All My Sons*, portrays the conflict between the idealistic son (Chris) and his materialistically corrupted father (Joe Keller). To retain his business, Keller has shipped out defective plane parts which have ultimately caused the deaths of many fliers. The seeds of the great *Death of a Salesman* are here—from the stage setting (with the Keller's house and the impinging presence of the more successful neighbors) to the use of poetic images (wind, the car), to even specific rhetorical cadences ("Nobody in this house dast take her faith away"). Here is the eternally forgiving, self-deluding wife-mother; her idealistic sons (one has committed suicide for his principles); the poignant and misguided bond between father and son; and the father's suicide to expiate a lifetime of wrong commitment. Here is Miller's vision of the terrible rat-race of ordinary, business reality, and one's better knowledge of the need to love other men. One bears a responsibility to the other, and "can be better! Once and for all you can know there's a universe of people outside and you're responsible to it." This, however, becomes increasingly difficult to enact, as one's love for his family may also tear him apart: "There's nothin' he could do that I wouldn't forgive. Because he's my son. Because I'm his father and he's my son."

Miller's masterpiece, *Death of a Salesman*, measures the enormous gap between America's promise of inevitable success and the devastating reality of one's concrete failure. Commitment to false social values blinds one to the true values of human experience—the comforts of personal relationships, of family and friendship, of love. Identity and commitment are again the subject. Willie Loman, who might well exemplify Miller's definition of the tragic hero (in his important essay "Tragedy and the Common Man"), has completely sold himself to what is at best an anachronistic dream—that anyone can get ahead. This is what he has been brought up to believe, the promise of his mythic (salesmen) heroes. While Willie has pursued this for 40 years and has sold it to his two sons, he is blind to its contemporary meaninglessness and to his own (and their) failure. But Willie *is* a great salesman—of the old American dream—and even his wife, the loyal Linda, lives in a world of self-generating lies and illusions. What Willie comes to realize on this single day of the play—his "recognition scene"—is that he has totally overlooked his true wealth, that he is a deeply loved father. Ironically, armed with this knowledge, he defies the system that has until now defeated him. He commits suicide to give his sons the only thing his society respects—cash. In defiance, irony, and profound bitterness, Miller sends Willie to his death with the same illusion he has lived by—though Willie is now fully aware of and in control of it. This is Miller's most bitter picture of the system that uses the little man—that eats the orange and throws away the peel. As tattered and self-pitying as Willie sometimes appears, he is one of the theater's most poignant and moving figures.

Miller has connected the origins of *The Crucible* with McCarthyism, with the "political, objective knowledgable campaign from the far Right [which] was capable of creating not only a terror, but a new subjective reality, a veritable mystique which was gradually assuming even a holy resonance." Specifically about the Salem witch trials of 1692, the play also treats the national paranoia, hysteria, and general immorality that characterized the McCarthy witch-hunts. Miller bitterly attacks the society that rewards the suppression of freedom in the name of "right" and conformity. Two lines summarize his focus: the rhetorical "Is the accusor always holy?" and "You must understand . . . that a person is either with this court or he must be counted against it, there be no road between." Although this has been called a modern morality play, Miller goes beyond black/white characterizations to portray his figures' petty rivalries and moral ambiguities. He probes the political, social, and psychological needs of both those who capitulate and those who resist. Mr. Proctor, after defying the court's demands, finally regains his name (also important to Willie and Keller) and dies in another act of defiance. Once again, Miller illustrates his conviction that one can assert his "personal dignity" and "act against the scheme of things that degrades." As he puts it in *All My Sons*, one can be "better."

A Memory of Two Mondays, which Miller has expressed an especial fondness for, brings back the depression years. It was produced initially with *A View from the Bridge*, which treats the hardworking and likeable Eddie Carbone who, out of blind love toward his niece-ward, informs on the illegal immigrants he is presumably safeguarding; one is his niece's boyfriend. Blind to what really drives him ("You can never have her"), and defiant of community, family, and natural law, he endures public humiliation for his act of treason. His grief is overwhelming as he cries the familiar: "I want my name"; he draws a knife and once again Miller's protagonist precipitates his own death. Although the play is, as Miller intended, simpler than *Salesman*, it recalls it in many ways: two men in conflict with a third, an authority figure; the (surrogate) father's blind worship of his charge ("She's the best"); the ever-supportive and loving wife; it also retains certain expressionistic elements (the narrator functions like a Greek chorus and frames each section in mythic terms).

For the next nine years, Miller wrote short stories, prose essays (the important "The Shadow of Gods"), and the screenplay *The Misfits*. With *After the Fall* he turns from the family and one's obligation to connect with the social world to a more existential statement: the recuperative and regenerative powers of love, the question of personal or universal guilt, and the necessity of man to justify himself to himself (rather than the system)—the need for human community and love, and the fact that one *is* his brother's keeper. Despite the many critical attempts to pigeonhole *After the Fall* autobiographically (with Maggie as Miller's wife, Marilyn Monroe), Miller has said that the play is no more autobiographical than his other work. It treats, he continues, the self-destructiveness of a character who views herself as "pure victim." In this stream-of-consciousness drama, Quentin, the protagonist, subjects all of his values to scrutiny. His statement—"the bench was empty. No judge in sight.

And all that remained was the endless argument with oneself, this pointless litigation of existence before any empty bench"—and the tone of the entire piece redefines Miller's conviction that one must come to terms with his own acts and values. As Quentin confronts his parents, wives, and the various situations of his recent and past life, Miller suggests that we all bear the mark of Cain; we are all born after the fall and are responsible for all our acts. After such knowledge *is* forgiveness: the play ends with the affirmative "Hello."

Themes of commitment, responsibility, and integrity continue in *Incident at Vichy*, where the aristocrat Von Berg (the mirror image of Quentin) transfers his own freedom to the Jewish Leduc and accepts his own death. Miller raises questions about sacrifice and guilt ("the soul's remorse for his own hostility"). The play investigates the need we all have for scapegoats and the suffering "other." "You must face your own complicity," he writes, "with . . . your own humanity." One must accept not only his own evil (and goodness) but also the sacrifices and kindness of others.

The Price returns to two brothers, the poles of love and money, the sacrifices and selfishness of each, and the terrible lack of relationship that always existed between the two—the terrible "price" that rivalry and lovelessness exact. Unlike Von Berg in *Incident*, the brothers have given nothing, and they therefore have nothing. Gregory Solomon, the antiques dealer, teaches that one must give without expecting repayment; he understands the gratuitousness of love. One must embrace community while realizing the utter isolation that is finally the human condition.

Although in 1972 Miller said that his plays were becoming more mythical, *The Creation of the World and Other Business* (about God's conflict with Lucifer over the behavior of Adam and Eve, and Cain and Abel) is an existential query into the nature of individual responsibility. Miller's most recent works have been less than successful. *The American Clock* is a series of vignettes in which the fate of a Depression family—the not particularly heroic Baums—is intertwined with that of a remarkably heroic nation during the 1930s. An overly ambitious effort, Miller describes it "as though the whole country were really the setting"; it was intended, he explains, to be "a mural for the theater inspired by Studs Terkel's *Hard Times*." The two minidramas of *Two-Way Mirror*, on the other hand, are extremely modest, although they are intended as "passionate voyages through the masks of [agonizing] illusion." *Elegy for a Lady* focuses on a middle-aged man who, while selecting a gift for his dying mistress, indulges in a conversation on the pain of love with the boutique proprietress. In *Some Kind of Love Story* a detective visits an old girlfriend, now a call girl, who may be the key figure in clearing a murder suspect. The 20—minute *The Last Yankee* treats two men—one, an affluent businessman with seven children; the other, a carpenter with no children—who meet in a mental hospital. They are waiting to visit their wives, both of whom suffer from severe depression. The men discuss the possible reasons for their wives' illness, in the course of which they realize that the women's symptoms, and obviously their causes—specifically, their marriages—are totally different. At the end of the play, as the social and economic rivalries between the men become dominant, Miller evokes a subtle perspective on the ubiquitousness of human need and self-absorption, both of which inevitably destroy personal relationships.

The Ride Down Mount Morgan is presumably a "comedy" about bigamy, although Miller himself describes his sombre subject as "what it takes out of a man to get everything he wants in marriage and life." While there are some comic moments, the play really focuses on marital deception and responsibility. Miller portrays a 50ish husband named Lyman Felt—a Willy Loman gone astray, a one-time poet, now salesman (insurance) magnate, who has gone the limits of marital infidelity. Lyman is a nine-year bigamist, who has negotiated "two sublimely happy marriages . . . without being humbled." Throughout the play, Lyman (and Miller) rationalizes his clearly immoral life. That is to say, as he "loves each wife equally," he prides himself on his efforts to understand true selfhood. "You can either be true to yourself or to other people," he says, and, "A loser lives someone else's life. I've lived my own life." The play is constructed as a series of flashbacks in Lyman's hospital room following his car accident on icy Mount Morgan. It is here that the two wives, Leah and Theodora (one a young Jewish businesswoman; the other, a WASPY older woman) first meet and learn the truth. Ultimately, each rejects him as a deceptive liar. Miller said of the play: "We have no solution to this problem. We have an instinctual life, and we have a social life," a variation of Lyman's remark to his lawyer: "Look, we're all the same." Perhaps more pertinent to Miller's audience, however, is Lyman's revelation: "I know what's wrong with me—I could never stand still for death! Which you've got to do, by a certain age, or be ridiculous—you've got to stand there nobly and serene and let death run his tape out your arms and around your belly and up your crotch until he's got you fitted for that last black suit. And I can't. I won't! So I'm left wrestling with this anachronistic energy which God has charged me with and I will use it till the dirt is shoveled into my mouth."

—Lois Gordon

See the essay on *Death of a Salesman*.

MILLER, Jason.

Born John Miller in Long Island City, New York, 22 April 1939. Educated at St. Patrick's High School, Scranton, Pennsylvania; Scranton University, B.A. 1961; Catholic University, Washington D.C., 1962–63. Married Linda Gleason in 1963 (divorced 1973); one daughter and two sons. Stage and film actor. Recipient: New York Drama Critics Circle award, 1972; Tony award, 1973; Pulitzer prize, 1973. Address: c/o Screen Actors Guild, 7750 Sunset Boulevard, Los Angeles, California 90046, U.S.A.

Publications

PLAYS

Three One-Act Plays: Lou Gehrig Did Not Die of Cancer, It's a Sin to Tell a Lie, The Circus Lady (produced 1970). 1972.
Nobody Hears a Broken Drum (produced 1970). 1971.
That Championship Season (produced 1972). 1972.
Screenplay: *That Championship Season*, 1982.

TELEVISION PLAY: *Reward*, 1980.

VERSE
Stone Step. 1968.

THEATRICAL ACTIVITIES

DIRECTOR: **Film**—*That Championship Season*, 1982.
ACTOR: **Plays**—Edmund in *Long Day's Journey into Night* by O'Neill; Tom in *The Glass Menagerie* by Tennessee Williams; Pip in *Pequod* by Roy S. Richardson, 1969; Poker Player in *The Odd Couple* by Neil Simon, 1970; Assistant in *The Happiness Cage* by Dennis J. Reardon, 1970; Rogoshin in *Subject to Fits* by Robert Montgomery, 1971; in *Juno and the Paycock* by O'Casey, 1971. **Films**—*The Exorcist*, 1972; *The Nickel Ride*, 1975; *The Devil's Advocate*, 1977; *Marilyn—The Untold Story*, 1980; *Twinkle, Twinkle Killer Kane (The Ninth Configuration)*, 1980; *Monsignor*, 1982; *Toy Soldiers*, 1984. **Television**—*A Home of Our Own*, 1975; *F. Scott Fitzgerald in Hollywood*, 1976; *The Dain Curse*, 1978; *Vampire*, 1979; *The Henderson Monster*, 1980; *The Best Little Girl in the World*, 1981; *A Touch of Scandal*, 1984.

Jason Miller's *That Championship Season* is a solid, vibrant play. The solidity comes in part from the familiar structure of the play—too familiar, at points—but Miller's freshness of detail saves the evening.

The event that occasions the drama has been used a lot: it is a reunion, in this case of four members of a champion high-school basketball team of twenty years ago. The fifth man on stage is the now-retired coach who has taught them that winning is all that counts—in basketball and in life. As Walter Kerr pointed out, the set itself is familiar—limp lace curtains and a steep staircase that recalls the conventional naturalism of William Inge's *The Dark at the Top of the Stairs*.

In fact, the experienced play-goer knows within two minutes what the arc of things will be: the men have come together to celebrate and live again their triumph, but before the night is out it will be revealed how everything has gone rotten somehow. And so it turns out. One of the players is now mayor of the small Pennsylvania town, and he is proud of it. But underneath he is a loser—and indeed it is obvious he will be thrown out of the forthcoming election.

Another team-mate has been his chief financial backer—a man made rich through the strip-mining that ecologists condemn. But now he sees the mayor will lose, so he wants to shift his backing to another candidate.

A third player is now a school principal who wants to be superintendent. When the mayor tells him that he can't back him because it will hurt his own candidacy, the superintendent angrily blurts out that the strip-miner is sleeping with the mayor's wife, and he says he'll tell the whole town if they don't support him. But he is a mediocrity; he knows it, his own young son knows it, and everyone on stage knows it. The coach calls his bluff, knowing he is even too much of a mediocrity to do something so substantial as tell the town about the mayor's wife.

The fourth player is now an alcoholic but he nevertheless sees things more clearly than the rest. It is he who brings up Martin. In basketball there are five players: Martin was the fifth, and at first he is mourned as if dead. Ultimately it is revealed that he has simply gone away, turning his back on the coach and his dogmas. It was Martin who, at the coach's direction, broke the ribs of the "nigger" who was the star of the other team, and it's clear that's the only reason our boys won.

The play uncovers the dark underside of that old triumph and the abject failure beneath any gloss of current success. The coach is shown to be a bigot, a right-wing supporter of Joe McCarthy, a champion of the ugly ethic that to win is to be good.

So the route of the play is familiar and so are the figures. But the figures are not cardboard—Miller fills in their dimension with the rich detail of an orthodox novelist. And the play is not without surprises. In particular it is verbally surprising. Lines are fresh and newly honed. And the humor is painfully superb. Cautioning the mayor not to exploit the fact of his handicapped child, the alcoholic says, "You lose the mongoloid vote right there." And he denies he has a liquor problem: "I can get all I want."

Miller's limitation, at least in this play, is his conventionality, his predictability. But many regard the theatrical experimentation on the American scene as unrewarding, and other traditionalists have lost the vitality that Miller found in this play. It's a somber comment on American theatre that one of the most promising plays of the early 1970s could have been written in the early 1950s.

—Thomas J. McCormack

MILLER, Susan.

Born in Philadelphia, Pennsylvania, 6 April 1944. Educated at Pennsylvania State University, University Park, B.A. 1965; Bucknell University, Lewisburg, Pennsylvania, M.A. 1970. Instructor in English, Pennsylvania State University, 1969–73; lecturer in playwriting, University of California, Los Angeles, 1975–76; playwright-in-residence, Mark Taper Forum Theatre, Los Angeles, 1975. Recipient: Rockefeller grant, 1975; National Endowment for the Arts grant, 1976; Obie award, 1979. Agent: Joyce Ketay Agency, 334 West 89th Street, New York, New York 10024, U.S.A.

Publications

PLAYS

No One Is Exactly 23. In Pyramid 1, 1968.
Daddy, and A Commotion of Zebras (produced 1970).
Silverstein & Co. (produced 1972).
Confessions of a Female Disorder (produced 1973). In Gay Plays, edited by William M. Hoffman, 1979.
Denim Lecture (produced 1974).
Flux (produced 1975; revised version produced 1977).
Cross Country (produced 1976). In West Coast Plays , 1978.
Nasty Rumors and Final Remarks (produced 1979).
Arts and Leisure (produced 1985).
For Dear Life (produced 1989).
It's Our Town, Too (produced 1992).

TELEVISION PLAYS: *Home Movie* (*Family* series); *One for the Money, Two for the Show*, with Nedra Deen; *A Whale for the Killing*; *Visions* series.

In Susan Miller's *Arts and Leisure*, the character J.D. Salinger inquires of the Professor—about a student's films—"Does her work astonish you?" Miller's startling explorations of women's minds and hearts do just that, especially creating the shock of recognition in spectators who, like her characters, write, teach, or experience turbulent relationships. Miller's plays most frequently explore issues of intimacy and of evolving sexual identity. In contrast to her self-protective Dina in *Flux*, who pleads "I'm not eager to expose private agonies," Miller persists in such probing, in plays characterized by their whimsy yet potential violence, passion yet playfulness.

Most of Miller's full-length plays include a tap dance, and nearly all her funny dramas or poignant comedies end on an upbeat note—with Jake's optimism, with Ronnie's self-discovery, with Jess regaining her confidence, with Salinger gladly relinquishing his manuscripts, with Perry beginning a new life; in fact, the last line of *Cross Country* finds Perry greeting new companions. Although the title of *Nasty Rumors and Final Remarks* suggests that Raleigh's demise concerns Miller, actually the dramatist focuses on the life of this quicksilver woman, who can't be confined by her hospital bed or defined by her friends, lovers, or offspring; hence, even Raleigh after her stroke seems affirmative. So does Miller's reply to the Republican's 1992 convention; although *It's Our Town, Too*, because it follows the structure of her model by Thornton Wilder, ends at the graveyard, it affirms respect for those who are different, for values other than those of fundamentalist Christians, and for families other than the old-fashioned model of homemaker mother, wage-earning father, two children, and a dog.

Miller's language provides part of her plays' fascination. She builds her rhythms into her lines so their catchy cadences prove actor-proof. In natural dialogue, fragmented but also filled with expressive turns of phrase, her characters fumble to express their panic or pleasure, occasionally achieving eloquent accuracy. *Cross Country*, for instance, says of Perry's wrenching herself out of her marriage to take off in search of professional and personal fulfilment: "There is a moment, like the black holes in space, of complete and irrevocable loss. To allow that moment is to let go of the sides of time, to fall into another place where it is not likely any of your old friends will recognize you again." Often Miller's lines provide witty insights into women's lives, as when a character remarks that, because we are so often interrupted while looking after others, "Women live longer just to finish their conversations."

Miller chooses as her characters writers and others in the arts, usually women in crisis or transition, experiencing problems living with others or in their own skin. One of several protagonists bearing names unusual for women, Ronnie in *Confessions of a Female Disorder* makes the transition from puberty to marriage and career while struggling to avoid confronting her attraction to women. The title expresses both Ronnie's love of women and a female penchant for abnegation. Perry leaves her marriage to find herself. *Flux*'s iconoclast Jess, on the edge and unable to contain her emotions or control those she inspires in others, turns on her students to her considerable charms instead of to English, making a mess in the classroom and in her personal life

as well. *Nasty Rumors and Final Remarks* takes dying Raleigh on an adventure
of self-discovery; nobody else could tame her enough to know her. Catherine
and Jake in *For Dear Life* differ too profoundly to sustain their relationship:
she always expects the worst, while her husband flees her pessimism, which
begins to infect him. Yet, ironically, she proves correct in her fears that their
marriage will crumble.

Such early Miller works as the Jewish-American rites-of-passage black
comedy *Silverstein & Co.* and her one-act *No One is Exactly 23* employ
absurdist styles. As her craft developed, however, Miller suited her form to her
objective, often combining presentational and representational conventions in
the same play and varying her structure to fit her purpose. Although frequently
employing surface verisimilitude, Miller sticks to that style throughout only
in *Arts and Leisure*, in which the Professor and Ginny break into the New
Hampshire farmhouse of J.D. Salinger—"the Greta Garbo of American
letters"—threatening to blow up his home unless the reclusive but compulsive
writer turns over all his unpublished manuscripts. Establishing immediate
suspense and then sustaining it throughout, Miller confines the action to less
than 24 hours on a single set.

At the other extreme, Miller's most surprising play structurally, *Cross
Country*, employs huge chunks of narration (distributed among the cast, rather
than assigned to a single narrator) as well as stage directions which the actors
speak aloud, as in chamber theatre. This highly episodic play dramatizes some
scenes in a single sentence, or gives one line to two characters who interact on
stage simultaneously, but in fact separately, with protagonist Perry. Miller
begins by describing what happens after the play's middle, and the narrative
occurs mostly in the past tense. After repeatedly jumping around in its chronology, however, *Cross Country* eventually moves forward to Perry's new life
on the West Coast.

Miller experiments with chronology in another fashion with *For Dear Life*,
which disrupts linear progression through time by moving from a "present" in
Act I, to 18 years later in Act II, to 16 years before that in Act III. In other
words, Act III occurs about two years after Act I, but the intervening act
flashes far forward. The style, meanwhile, moves from mostly representational
to often presentational. Miller unifies the unusual construction with a speech
which we watch Jake prepare during the first act and which his son quotes at
the end of the play, when he's supposed to be one year old—but we see him
then as the teenager he was in the previous act. The disrupted chronology of
the play's construction permits Miller to show us in Act III the problems which
cause the divorce which Act II has already shown us does occur. The couple in
the third act wait for their happiness to end—as we know it must. Not only Act
II but the title also tells us that they are hanging on for dear life, clinging to a
relationship as though to a lifeline, even though logic dictates letting go.

Confessions of a Female Disorder, perhaps the most fluid of all Miller's
unconventionally constructed plays, takes Ronnie from her first menstrual
period and the start of her search for a man through her gathering with other
women in her kitchen to begin exploring facets of themselves. So presentational and episodic is this play that Miller hops Ronnie out of a shower straight
into her shrink's office in mid-lather and pops husband David in "out of
sequence," a line which acknowledges to spectators that we all know this is a

play, not a slice of life. "Cheerleaders" and "Lettermen" jump in and out of the action both to comment and to take minor roles (such as the guys who offer her a sexual experience superior to her first time); when coercing her into marriage, Ronnie's shrink turns into a minister.

Although Miller has revised *Flux* several times, each version employs presentational, episodic scenes conveying the quality of dreams and nightmares which do for the collapse of female self-esteem what Arthur Miller (no relation) did for male disintegration in *Death of a Salesman*. Moving freely from the classroom, Saul's bedroom, Jess's house, Jess's office, and her mentor's office or classroom, Miller dramatizes Jess's disorienting mismatch of expectations with those of her students and partner. Such construction and style convey what Jess and her students experience emotionally rather than factually; thus, the mentor performs a con artist's shell game, the students don pyjamas and brush their teeth in the classroom, and a voice-over about student evaluations accompanies an orgy. Clearly Jess and her students populate each other's dreams.

Miller's most unusual temporal distortions occur in *Nasty Rumors and Final Remarks*; while Raleigh experiences a cerebral haemorrhage on one side of the stage, others elsewhere deal with its aftermath. Only one preliminary scene has established Raleigh's personality before the stroke. As time passes, Raleigh begins narrating and describing herself in the third person, past tense (somewhat like *Cross Country*); while she's supposed to be in a coma and dying, we see her talking to us and eavesdropping on her male lover, her female lover, her friend. Raleigh's ramblings round the hospital are intersected by flashbacks which dramatize her relationships to these people who have gathered to wait for her death. These presentational episodes connect so seamlessly in a montage of past events and present passions that we scarcely notice the technique, till everyone gathers to bid goodbye to the dead woman.

Raleigh has proven unreliable, unpredictable, unfaithful, and unnerving to all who care about her. Yet when the play ends, we miss her, as we do all Miller's protagonists—usually brilliant, beautiful, bisexual women who fascinate and bewilder their admirers, who cannot tame their whirlwind natures. In dramatizing them Miller explores such themes as how to couple successfully, how to balance professional and personal fulfillment, how to know and be oneself, and how to behave responsibly towards others without betraying oneself. Miller balances her evocation of anxiety and loneliness with a sense of elation at rising to the challenges of intimacy and career. Repeatedly she achieves the trademark Miller effect of locating our hidden lacerations, then tickling those wounds till we're convulsed.

—Tish Dace

MILNER, Ron(ald).

Born in Detroit, Michigan, 29 May 1938. Educated at Northeastern High School, Detroit; Highland Park Junior College, Detroit; Detroit Institute of Technology; Columbia University, New York. Writer-in-residence, Lincoln University, Pennsylvania, 1966–67; taught at Michigan State University, East Lansing, 1971–72. Founding director, Spirit of Shango theatre company, and Langston Hughes Theatre, Detroit. Recipient: John Hay Whitney fellowship,

1962; Rockefeller grant, 1965. Address: c/o Crossroads Theatre Company, 320 Memorial Parkway, New Brunswick, New Jersey 08901, U.S.A.

Publications

PLAYS

Who's Got His Own (produced 1966). In *Black Drama Anthology*, edited by Milner and Woodie King, 1971.
The Monster (produced 1969). In *Drama Review*, Summer 1968.
The Warning: A Theme for Linda (produced 1969). In *A Black Quartet: Four New Black Plays*, 1970.
(M)Ego and the Green Ball of Freedom (produced 1971). In *Black World*, April 1971.
What the Wine-Sellers Buy (produced 1973). 1974.
These Three (produced 1974).
Season's Reasons (produced 1976).
Jazz Set, music by Max Roach (produced 1979).
Crack Steppin' (produced 1981).
Roads of the Mountaintop (produced 1986).
Don't Get God Started, music and lyrics by Marvin Winans (also director: produced 1987).
Checkmates (produced 1987).

OTHER

Editor, with Woodie King, *Black Drama Anthology*. 1971.

Playwright Ron Milner is considered one of the more exciting writers who came to national prominence during the explosive Black Theatre movement of the 1960s. Much like his contemporaries, Ed Bullins and Amiri Baraka, he was influenced by both the social and political conditions of those times. A native Detroiter, Milner, who has often been called "the people's playwright," has had his works described as being rich in the authentic texture of life in the urban black setting. He has repeatedly been praised for his powerful use of language and observation of character. His characters often examine their self-perceptions and identity while questioning their place in a complex and oppressive world. This introspection enables them to come to a new under-standing of themselves, thereby changing how they relate to that world.

Reminiscent of Lorraine Hansberry's *A Raisin in the Sun*, Milner's first full-length play, *Who's Got His Own*, portrays the damaged relationships of a recently widowed mother with her alienated son and embittered daughter. The drama explores the impact that living in a racist society has on black manhood. Opening with the funeral of the domineering patriarch, the son—Tim, Jr.—is forced to address the conflicting feelings of disgust and love he has for his father. After Mrs. Bronson reveals several unspoken truths about her husband, Tim, Jr. and his sister, Clara are better able to understand their father in a new way, thereby coming to terms with those feelings.

Milner's next play, a one-act drama called *The Warning: A Theme for Linda*, again examines the theme of black manhood. However, unlike *Who's*

Got His Own, the issue is dealt with entirely through the unpleasant and whimsical experiences of women. Linda, a 17-year-old girl living in an impoverished section of Detroit, daydreams about men and what it means to be a woman. In contrast to her fantasies, Linda's alcoholic mother and resentful grandmother tell her of their disastrous encounters with men, warning her to stay clear of them. Finally, after deciding to discard both the imaginary men of her dreams and those of the stories told by her mother and grandmother, Linda instead decides to begin a serious, sexual relationship with her boyfriend, Donald. She confronts him with the challenge of sharing their futures together as equals in mind, body, and soul.

In 1973, Milner combined his concern for the temptations besetting urban black youth with an examination of the destructive black role models of pimps and drug-dealers created by Hollywood. Set in Detroit, *What the Wine-Sellers Buy* deals with a young high-school boy choosing between good and evil. The boy, Steve Carlton, is forced to decide whether to follow the advice of a pimp named Rico who suggests that he turns his girlfriend into a prostitute to raise money for Steve's sick mother. By following Rico's advice, Steve would simultaneously satisfy his mother's medical needs while condemning his girlfriend Mae to a life of depravity. Steve's struggle with his conscience allowed Milner again to address the theme of black male responsibility. Finally, Steve comes to the correct moral decision by understanding that the cost would be too high for himself and his girlfriend.

Set in Detroit in the late 1980s, *Checkmates* depicts the vast differences in the value systems of two generations of African-American couples: a young upwardly mobile professional pair, and their older, middle-class, traditionally-minded landlords. Milner shows the world in which we live as one devoid of the strong moral and social values it once had. Initially the younger couple — Sylvester and Laura — appear to have it all: successful careers, good looks, love, and financial security. As the play progresses, their commitment to one another is tested as they confront growing individual needs. For Laura, it is her desire for a career that justifies having an abortion without Sylvester's knowledge. Sylvester displays self-centeredness when he becomes physically abusive after increased feelings of paranoia regarding his job and the discovery of Laura's abortion. Eventually the distrust created between Laura and Sylvester pushes them both into the arms of other lovers. Their "anything goes" code of behavior actually helps to create a division in their relationship during times of strife. Rather than bringing them closer, Sylvester and Laura's troubles enlarge the division between them which eventually makes their love for one another seem futile, and finally leads to divorce.

In contrast, through reminiscent flashbacks we see that the older couple of Frank and Mattie have also dealt with infidelity, physical abuse, and the frustrations of racism on the job. However, in each of these experiences Frank and Mattie chose personal sacrifice over self-centered behavior; children were not seen as being in conflict with individual desires, and adultery and physical abuse was simply not tolerated. It is through their lives that we see how these sacrifices for the marriage have strengthened their relationship. Because of their more traditional value system, Frank and Mattie's world is more stable. Theirs is a code of behavior which helps them live through troubled times.

—Gary Anderson

MITCHELL, Loften.

Born in Columbus, North Carolina, 15 April 1919. Educated at De Witt
Clinton High School, Bronx, New York, graduated 1937; City College, New
York, 1937–38; Talladega College, Alabama, B.A. in sociology 1943;
Columbia University, New York, 1947–51, M.A. Served in the United States
Naval Reserve, 1944–45: seaman second class. Married Helen Marsh in 1948;
two sons. Actor, stage manager, and press agent, 115th Street People's Theatre
and Harlem Showcase, New York, 1946–52; social worker, with Gypsy
families, 1947–58, and in Day Center Program for Older Persons, 1959–66.
Department of Welfare, New York; professor of African-American Studies
and Theatre, State University of New York, Binghamton, 1971–85, now
professor emeritus. Editor, NAACP *Freedom Journal*, 1964. Recipient:
Guggenheim fellowship, 1958; Rockefeller grant, 1961; Harlem Cultural
Council award, 1969; State University of New York Research Foundation
award, 1974; Audelco award, 1979. Address: 88–45 163rd Street, Jamaica,
New York 11432, U.S.A.

Publications

PLAYS

Shattered Dreams (produced 1938).
Blood in the Night (produced 1946).
The Bancroft Dynasty (produced 1948).
The Cellar (produced 1952).
A Land Beyond the River (produced 1957). 1963.
The Phonograph (produced 1961).
Tell Pharaoh televised 1963; (produced 1967). In *The Black Teacher and the
    Dramatic Arts*, edited by William R. Reardon and Thomas D. Pawley, 1970.
Ballad for Bimshire, with Irving Burgie (produced 1963; revised version
    produced 1964).
Ballad of the Winter Soldiers, with John Oliver Killens (produced 1964).
Star of the Morning: Scenes in the Life of Bert Williams (produced 1965;
    revised version produced 1985). In *Black Drama Anthology*, edited by
    Woodie King and Ron Milner, 1971.
*The Final Solution to the Black Problem in the United States; or, The Fall of
    the American Empire* (produced 1970).
Sojourn to the South of the Wall (produced 1973; revised version produced
    1983).
The Walls Came Tumbling Down, music by Willard Roosevelt (produced
    1976).
Bubbling Brown Sugar, concept by Rosetta LeNoire, music by Danny Holgate,
    Emme Kemp, and Lilian Lopez (produced 1976). 1985.
Cartoons for a Lunch Hour, music by Rudy Stevenson (produced 1978).
A Gypsy Girl (produced 1982).
Miss Waters, To You, concept by Rosetta LeNoire (produced 1983).

SCREENPLAYS: *Young Man of Williamsburg*, 1954; *Integration: Report One*,
1960; *I'm Sorry*, 1965.

RADIO WRITING: *Tribute to C.C. Spaulding*, 1952; *Friendly Advisor* program, 1955; *The Later Years* program, 1959–62.

TELEVISION PLAYS: *Welfare Services*, 1960s; *Tell Pharaoh*, 1970.

NOVEL
The Stubborn Old Lady Who Resisted Change. 1973.

OTHER
Black Drama: The Story of the American Negro in the Theatre. 1967.
Editor, *Voices of the Black Theatre*. 1975.

MANUSCRIPT COLLECTIONS: State University of New York, Binghamton; Boston University; Talladega College, Alabama; Schomburg Collection, New York.

CRITICAL STUDIES: *Negro Playwrights in the American Theatre 1925–1959* by Doris E. Abramson, 1969; article by Ja A. Jahannes, in *Afro–American Writers after 1955* edited by Thadious M. Davis and Trudier Harris, 1985.

THEATRICAL ACTIVITIES
ACTOR: **Plays**—with the Progressive Dramatizers and the Rose McClendon Players, both New York; Victor in *Cocktails*, and Aaron in *Having Wonderful Time* by Arthur Kober, 1938; Angel in *The Black Messiah* by Dennis Donoghue and James H. Dunmore, 1939.

For his work as a black theatre historian, the American theatre owes a great debt to Loften Mitchell. His books—*Black Drama* and *Voices of the Black Theatre*—and numerous essays contain invaluable information and insights on Afro-American contributions to the theatre. Mitchell's plays reflect his passionate interest in the black theatre and black American history in general. With few exceptions, his plays and librettos inform the audience of the tribulations and achievements of well known black entertainers and historical figures.

Black pride, unity, and perseverance during times of adversity form recurrent themes in Mitchell's plays. These concepts are often voiced in rhetorical discourses by characters drawn along simplistic, ideological lines. His protagonists based on historical individuals speak and act as though already aware of the significance of their achievements to future generations. After the black characters have suffered in conflicts with external forces motivated by racial prejudice and self-interests, the plays end on a triumphant note as the blacks learn how to endure the hardships and, in some cases, prevail over their adversaries.

Tell Pharaoh surveys the history of black Americans; the characters speak of their illustrious African heritage, bitter experiences as slaves, and ongoing struggles for the same civil rights and opportunities enjoyed by white Americans. The drama identifies black American heroes and martyrs, and celebrates the contributions of blacks to various aspects of American life. As in most of his works, Mitchell includes a tribute to his beloved Harlem and uses music to set the mood and underscore the sentiments of the play. The concluding harangue against Pharaoh—a symbolic persecutor of blacks, Latins, Asians, Indians, and other groups—dates the work and typifies the rhetoric of the revolutionary activists of the 1960s.

Based on real events, *A Land Beyond the River* depicts the story of a rural, black South Carolina community which through the judicial system sought the right to send its children to any school receiving public funds. In Mitchell's dramatization, a sickly but courageous black woman—Martha Layne— proposes the law suit and her husband—Joseph—rallies the support of other black citizens and a sympathetic white physician. "Uncle Toms" and white bigots attempt to undermine their efforts. Intimidating threats and the burning of the Layne home aggravate Martha's precarious condition and result in her death. The events create dissension among the blacks and encourage most to accept a local court decision to provide a "separate, but equal" school for blacks. However, in a stirring speech punctuated with biblical references, Joseph contends that black children would not receive parity with whites through the ruling. Instead, he convinces his peers to appeal the case to a higher court in order to achieve their original objective of obtaining equal access to services and facilities enjoyed by white students. Despite the clichés and simplistic characterizations, the drama provides a moving historical portrait of valiant individuals bound by a common cause in the civil rights movement.

A more recent work—*Miss Waters, To You*—is based on the life of Ethel Waters. A series of scenes with musical numbers depict Waters's transition from a struggling 17-year-old divorcée to an accomplished actress and singer. The play includes appearances by such noted entertainers as Bessie Smith, Lena Horne, Duke Ellington, and Cab Calloway. These blacks provide each other with moral support and teach Waters how to endure the racial prejudice and indignities of their profession. However, such scenes weaken the credibility of the play as a true portrait of Waters's life. In fact, her animosity toward some black entertainers, such as Miss Horne, is quite well known. The drama also glosses over certain of Waters's ignoble traits which would place her in a less exalted light. As in his other tributes to black entertainers—*Bubbling Brown Sugar* and *Star of the Morning: Scenes in the Life of Bert Williams*—Mitchell chose to portray black role models of high esteem with few, if any, unadmirable attributes.

—Addell Austin Anderson

MOSEL, Tad.

Born in Steubenville, Ohio, 1 May 1922. Educated at Amherst College, Massachusetts, B.A. 1947; Yale University, New Haven, Connecticut, 1947–49; Columbia University, New York, M.A. 1953. Served in the United States Army Air Force, 1943–46: sergeant. Clerk, Northwest Airlines, 1951–53. Visiting critic in television writing, Yale University School of Drama, 1957–58. Member of the Executive Board, *Television Quarterly*, Syracuse, New York; member of the Executive Council, Writers Guild of America. Recipient: Pulitzer prize, 1961; New York Drama Critics Circle award, 1961. D. Litt.: College of Wooster, Ohio, 1963; D.F.A.: College of Steubenville,

1969. Agent: William Morris Agency, 1350 Avenue of the Americas, New York, New York 10019. Address: 400 East 57th Street, New York, New York 10022, U.S.A.

Publications

PLAYS

The Happiest Years (produced 1942).

The Lion Hunter (produced 1952).

Madame Aphrodite (televised 1953; revised version, music by Jerry Herman, produced 1962).

My Lost Saints (televised 1955). In *Best Television Plays*, edited by Gore Vidal, 1956.

Other People's Houses: Six Television Plays (includes *Ernie Barger Is Fifty, The Haven, The Lawn Party, Star in the Summer Night, The Waiting Place*). 1956.

The Out-of-Towners (televised 1956). In *Television Plays for Writers: Eight Television Plays*, edited by A.S. Burack, 1957.

The Five-Dollar Bill (televised 1957). 1958.

Presence of the Enemy (televised 1958). In *Best Short Plays 1957–1958*, edited by Margaret Mayorga, 1958.

All the Way Home, adaptation of the novel *A Death in the Family* by James Agee (produced 1960). 1961.

Impromptu (produced 1961). 1961.

That's Where the Town's Going (televised 1962). 1962.

SCREENPLAYS: *Dear Heart*, 1964; *Up the Down Staircase*, 1967.

TELEVISION PLAYS: *Jinxed*, 1949; *The Figgerin' of Aunt Wilma*, 1953; *This Little Kitty Stayed Cool*, 1953; *The Remarkable Case of Mr. Bruhl*, 1953; *Ernie Barger Is Fifty*, 1953; *Other People's Houses*, 1953; *The Haven*, 1953; *Madame Aphrodite*, 1953; *The Lawn Party*, 1955; *Star in the Summer Night*, 1955; *Guilty Is the Stranger*, 1955; *My Lost Saints*, 1955; *The Waiting Place*, 1955; *The Out-of-Towners*, 1956; *The Five-Dollar Bill*, 1957; *The Morning Place*, 1957; *Presence of the Enemy*, 1958; *The Innocent Sleep*, 1958; *A Corner of the Garden*, 1959; *Sarah's Laughter*, 1959; *The Invincible Teddy*, 1960; *Three Roads to Rome: Venus Ascendant, Roman Fever, The Rest Cure*, from stories by Martha Gellhorn, Edith Wharton, and Aldous Huxley, 1960; *That's Where the Town's Going*, 1962.

OTHER

Leading Lady: The World and Theatre of Katharine Cornell, with Gertrude Macy. 1978.

Tad Mosel gained attention as one of the leading American writers for live television in the 1950s. His scripts were ideally suited for the medium in their restricted scope, focus on intimate details, and Chekhovian naturalism within a thoroughly contemporary American suburban milieu. An earlier one-act play written for the stage, *Impromptu*, has become a minor classic in its treatment of illusion and reality by means of a theatrical metaphor. A group of actors find themselves on a stage to which they have been summoned in order to improvise a play. Their groping efforts point up the recognition that life itself is essentially an improvisation in which roles are assumed and identity is elusive. Mosel handles this potentially trite and sentimental concept with wit and restraint.

Mosel's most successful work, however, was *All the Way Home*, a stage adaptation of James Agee's novel, *A Death in the Family*. Mosel's play captures the essence of the subjective, introspective novel while providing it with an external, theatrical form. In its depiction of several generations of a family and its compassionate rendering of death, birth, and the process of emotional maturing, the work has echoes of Thornton Wilder, an impression that is reinforced by Mosel's fluid handling of time and space. Especially noteworthy is the economy of dialogue, which is related to Mosel's sure sense of the power of the stage to communicate in unverbalized, visual terms.

—Jarka M. Burian

N

NELSON, Richard.

Born in Chicago, Illinois, 17 October 1950. Educated at Hamilton College, Clinton, New York, 1968–72, B.A. 1972. Married Cynthia B. Bacon in 1972; one daughter. Literary manager, BAM Theater Company, Brooklyn, New York, 1979–81; associate director, Goodman Theatre, Chicago, 1980–83; dramaturg, Guthrie Theatre, Minneapolis, 1981–82. Recipient: Watson fellowship, 1972; Rockefeller grant, 1979; Obie award, 1979, 1980; National Endowment for the Arts fellowship, 1980, 1985; Guggenheim fellowship, 1983; ABC award, 1985; Playwrights USA award, 1986; HBO award, 1986; *Time Out* award (London), 1987. Agent: Peter Franklin, William Morris Agency, 1350 Avenue of the Americas, New York, New York 10019. Address: 32 South Street, Rhinebeck, New York 12572, U.S.A.

Publications

PLAYS

The Killing of Yablonski (produced 1975).
Conjuring an Event (produced 1976). In *An American Comedy and Other Plays*, 1984.
Scooping (produced 1977).
Jungle Coup (produced 1978). In *Plays from Playwrights Horizons*, 1987.
The Vienna Notes (produced 1978). In *Wordplays 1*, 1980.
Don Juan, adaptation of a play by Molière (produced 1979).
The Wedding, with Helga Ciulei, adaptation of a play by Brecht (produced 1980).
The Suicide, adaptation of a play by Nikolai Erdman (produced 1980).
Bal (produced 1980). In *American Comedy and Other Plays*, 1984.
Rip Van Winkle; or, "The Works" (produced 1981). 1986.
Il Campiello, adaptation of the play by Goldoni (produced 1981). 1981.
Jungle of Cities, adaptation of a play by Brecht (produced 1981).
The Marriage of Figaro, adaptation of a play by Beaumarchais (produced 1982).
The Return of Pinocchio (produced 1983). In *An American Comedy and Other Plays*, 1984.
An American Comedy (produced 1983). In *An American Comedy and Other Plays*, 1984.
Accidental Death of an Anarchist, adaptation of a play by Dario Fo (produced 1984). 1987.

Three Sisters, adaptation of a play by Chekhov (produced 1984).
Between East and West (also co-director: produced 1984). In *New Plays USA 3*, edited by James Leverett and M. Elizabeth Osborn, 1986.
An American Comedy and Other Plays. 1984.
Principia Scriptoriae (produced 1986). 1986.
Chess (revised version), with Tim Rice, music by Benny Andersson, lyrics by Björn Ulvaeus (produced 1988).
Some Americans Abroad (produced 1989). 1989.
Eating Words (broadcast 1989). In *Best Radio Plays of 1989*, 1990.
Sensibility and Sense (televised 1990). 1989.
Two Shakespearean Actors (produced 1990). 1990.
Columbus and the Discovery of Japan (produced 1992). 1992.
Misha's Party, with Alexander Gelman (produced 1993).
Life Sentences (produced 1993).

RADIO PLAYS: *Languages Spoken Here*, 1987; *Roots in Water*, 1989; *Eating Words*, 1989; *Advice to Eastern Europe*, 1990.

TELEVISION PLAY: *Sensibility and Sense*, 1990.

OTHER
Editor, *Strictly Dishonorable and Other Lost American Plays*. 1986.

THEATRICAL ACTIVITIES
DIRECTOR: **Play**—*Between East and West* (co-director, with Ted D'Arms), 1984.

Richard Nelson is seriously funny: his writing is often comic, but never frivolous, and he uses laughter to deepen an audience's understanding of character and situation. Farcical misunderstanding is one of the ways he achieves that, and it is no surprise to find a Broadway adaptation of Dario Fo's *Accidental Death of an Anarchist* among his scripts (along with versions of Goldoni and Molière), but his plays are perhaps even more notable for a rare thoughtfulness. For a few seasons that thoughtfulness caught audiences in his native United States by surprise, and he was considered suspiciously foreign and probably political.

In a nicely ironic turn of fortune, his reputation in the American theatre grew when he achieved considerable success in a foreign country. His 1986 play *Principia Scriptoriae* was tepidly received in its first production in New York but won prizes and a flurry of admiring reviews when David Jones directed it for the Royal Shakespeare Company. It proved to be only the first of several highly successful plays for the RSC, plays which were subsequently produced to great effect in the United States.

His next play for the RSC, *Some Americans Abroad*, was a comedy about a group of American tourists on a cultural tour of the literary landmarks of England. A knowing and witty piece about American pretension, subterfuge, and enthusiasm, it ingeniously forced spectators into recognition of aspects of themselves. The majority of the audience was naturally British, but they were laughing at the Americans on stage while sharing the theatre with a healthy number of culture-hungry Americans who were finding large parts of their own itinerary recreated in the play.

The later long-running New York production at Lincoln Center demonstrated just how subtly Nelson had pitched his comedy. Where London audiences had been greatly amused by the eagerness of the tourists to experience British culture, New Yorkers accepted such enthusiasm as natural, an understandable white Anglo-Saxon search for European roots. They found their laughter in the acutely observed academic rivalries in the play.

Some Americans Abroad shares with much of Nelson's work a concern with roots and rootlessness, with that endemic 20th-century condition of exile. His play *The Return of Pinocchio* imagines that the wooden puppet who became a boy had left Italy to star in a Walt Disney movie and later became a wealthy entertainer. After World War II he returns to his Italian village where he finds the misery of starvation, prostitution, and theft. But the play is about an American cloak of protective naïvety which permits the American dream of "making it big" to thrive by ignoring the reality of the world.

Between East and West is another story of the uprooted, about Gregor and Erna Hasek, Czech emigrés in their 50's who confront the American experience as Gregor attempts to rebuild his career as a stage and film director in America. The Communist Party, by lying, has made it possible for Gregor to return, but succeeds only in luring the homesick Erna back. Gregor remains alone in a country he still sees as the land of opportunity, directing a play which is finally dismissed as "too European." It contains some of his finest writing, including a scene where Gregor rehearses Erna in Chekhov's *Three Sisters*, trying to correct her English pronunciation while she defiantly reverts to Czech—it is entirely acted in English and uses his own adaptation of Chekhov.

Between East and West also represents another of Nelson's concerns, the function of the intellectual in society. The play which most thoroughly examines that in an American context is *Sensibility and Sense*. It is a fine and delicate drama about the aging of ideals and idealists, focusing particularly on two women as they were in 1937 and as they are in 1986. Their history parallels the history of the intellectual left in those years, and articulates the painful divisions as one woman writes scathingly about the other—who is dying, but certainly not going gently.

The RSC offered the premieres of the next two major plays by Nelson. *Two Shakespearean Actors* was his retelling of the rivalry of two actors, the American Edwin Forrest and the Englishman William Charles Macready. In 1849 they were presenting competing Macbeths in neighbouring theatres in New York's Astor Place and the jingoistic followers of Forrest started a riot which resulted in 34 deaths.

Nelson's play had fun recreating the contrasting styles of the two actors with simultaneous rehearsals of *Macbeth*, and there is loving comic detail in the backstage and bar room banter of the theatrical companies, but the key to the play is an artistic coming-together of Forrest and Macready on the stage of a shuttered theatre as the riot rages in the streets. Despite all the posturing that has gone before, they find their artistic intentions share a belief that could be called sacred. Like *Some Americans Abroad*, it demonstrated Nelson's understanding of audiences on each side of the Atlantic. His British audiences chose the side of Macready, and laughed at the American's perceived crudity. On Broadway, where the play proved itself as a large-scale work, it was injected with American pace yet somehow tilted decisively in Forrest's favour.

Columbus and the Discovery of Japan, his contribution to the 500th anniversary of the discovery of America, suffered a severe critical divide on the RSC's main London stage. Many reviewers felt that the three-hour piece, mistakenly performed in rather small boxes on the vast Barbican stage, was a small-scale play. But the play very effectively dramatizes the contradictions of Columbus himself. His greatness of vision and pettiness of character combine to get him his ships and get him to America and the issues of the play are exceptionally large-scale. To achieve this, Nelson called on the opposing techniques of Brecht and Chekhov to create a "Chekhovian epic," vast and intimate. Passionate admirers of the play recognized that and also recognized the way in which his recurring theme of rootlessness applied to the drifting life of Columbus.

Perhaps his play *Roots in Water* (which has yet to receive a full production on stage), a sequence of 12 short plays spanning the years 1977 to 1988, contains his most specific statement on rootlessness. A husband comforting his ex-wife as her new marriage fails recites something he has been writing: "'Roots in water. We live but there's nowhere to settle.' A poem. That I've been working on for a long time." Coming at the end of the sequence, when year by year he has demonstrated the post-Vietnam, post-Watergate malaise that affected his generation in particular, it none the less seemed to indicate that he himself was continuing to work on that poem, on that clear statement about how Americans had come to that particular disaffected point.

His skill at mastering dramatic forms has also extended to prize-winning radio plays for the BBC, where Americans abroad were directly confronted with cultural conflicts in part prompted by their disaffection with their own country. In *Languages Spoken Here*, a second-generation Polish-American in London finds himself out of his depth when he tries to help an exiled Polish novelist with a translation; in *Eating Words*, a self-exiled American novelist finds a brotherhood through his friendship with an English novelist dying of AIDS; in *Advice to Eastern Europe* a young American would-be filmmaker finds romance and utter political confusion when he gets romantically entangled with a young Czech woman, a filmmaker who idealizes the United States.

—Ned Chaillet

NOONAN, John Ford.

Born in New York City, 7 October 1943. Educated at Fairfield Preparatory School, Connecticut, graduated 1959; Brown University, Providence, Rhode Island, A.B. in philosophy 1964; Carnegie Institute of Technology, Pittsburgh, M.A. in dramatic literature 1966. Married Marcia Lunt in 1962 (divorced 1965); three children. Taught Latin, English, and history at Buckley Country Day School, North Hills, Long Island, New York, 1966–69; stage-hand, Fillmore East Rock Theatre, New York, 1969–71; stock-broker, E.F. Hutton Company, New York, 1971–72; professor of drama, Villanova University, Pennsylvania, 1972–73. Recipient: Rockefeller grant, 1973. Agent: Joan Scott

Inc., 162 West 56th Street, New York, New York 10019. Address: 484 West 43rd Street, New York, New York 10036, U.S.A.

Publications

PLAYS

The Year Boston Won the Pennant (produced 1969). 1970.
Lazarus Was a Lady (produced 1970).
Rainbows for Sale (produced 1971). In *The Off-Off-Broadway Book*, edited by Albert Poland and Bruce Mailman, 1972.
Concerning the Effects of Trimethylchloride (produced 1971).
Monday Night Varieties (produced 1972).
Older People (also director: produced 1972).
Good-By and Keep Cold (produced 1973).
A Noonan Night (produced 1973).
A Sneaky Bit to Raise the Blind, and Pick Pack Pock Puck (produced 1974).
Where Do We Go from Here? (produced 1974).
Getting Through the Night (produced 1976).
A Coupla White Chicks Sitting Around Talking (produced 1979). 1981.
Listen to the Lions (produced 1979).
Some Men Need Help (produced 1982). 1983.
Talking Things Over with Chekhov (produced 1987).
Nothing But Bukowski (includes *The Raunchy Dame in the Chinese Raincoat, The Heterosexual Temperature in West Hollywood*) (produced 1987).
All She Cares About Is the Yankees. 1988.
My Daddy's Serious American Gift (produced 1989).
Stay Away a Little Closer (produced 1990).
Recent Developments in Southern Connecticut (produced 1990).
The Drowning of Manhattan. In *The Best American Short Plays 1992–1993*, edited by Howard Stein and Glenn Young, 1993.
Music From Down the Hill (produced 1994).

SCREENPLAYS: *Septuagenarian Substitute Ball*, 1970; *The Summer the Snows Came*, 1972.

MANUSCRIPT COLLECTION: Lincoln Center Library of the Performing Arts, New York.

CRITICAL STUDIES: "Theatre as Mystery," in *Evergreen Magazine*, December 1969, and reviews in *Village Voice*, May 1971 and May 1972, all by John Lahr; "John Ford Noonan Dons Glad Rags at Stockton" by Noreen Turner, in *The Press*, June 1989.

THEATRICAL ACTIVITIES

DIRECTOR: **Play**—*Older People*, 1972.
ACTOR: Since 1967 in summer stock, regional and off-Broadway theatres, and in television and films.

John Ford Noonan comments:

In *The Year Boston Won the Pennant*, Marcus Sykowski, a once legendary baseball pitcher who has mysteriously lost his glove arm and is now in search of a chrome limb to take its place, discusses pitching as follows:

> I am a pitcher. Pitching is my job. I have lost an arm, but I will earn it back. I have science on my side. I'm no college man. I never got a degree. I am no thinker, no man whose job it is to lead or be understood. I am a pitcher. I stand on the mound. I hold the ball, smile, get the feel I'm ready. I rear, I fire, and that ball goes exactly where I tell it 'cause I tell it to, 'cause it was me who threw it, the great Sykowski. What else must they know. . . . One strike, two strikes, three strikes, four, five, six, seven, eight, nine . . . the whole side, 'cause when you're pouring rhythm sweet, when you got it, really got it, they can't see it, they can't smell it, they can't touch it, they can't believe it. . . . It's yours, all yours . . . it's magic.

I believe Marcus is speaking of more than throwing a baseball.

John Ford Noonan's plays veer in style from conventional realism to fantasy and contain a range of American character types from baseball players and firemen to transvestites, gangsters, old people, and deserted wives. They have earned Noonan critical and popular attention since his first full-length play's production in 1969. Themes interweaving his plays encompass Saroyanesque concern for the vulnerability of the world's little people and the need to help one another. While believing in the communion of saints, Noonan largely avoids sentimentality in his work and sees the dark forces lurking in the sunlight. Characters in early plays tend toward caricatures and are often enmeshed in conflicts with mythic implications.

His more recent work discloses characters of realistic dimension while thematically supporting W.H. Auden's thought that "we must love one another or die." *A Coupla White Chicks Sitting Around Talking*, Noonan's deservedly most popular work, is a two-character comedy effectively emphasizing that good can come from unlikely relationships. In Westchester County suburbia a prim WASP housewife, Maude Mix, angry and lost at the latest desertion by her philandering husband, finds herself called upon by Hannah Mae, a prying Texan wife and new next-door neighbor, who makes uninvited daily visits and offers practical but unwelcome advice after deducing Maude's situation. Maude cannot rid herself of the loud-mouth do-gooder even when she truthfully reports that Hannah's oafish husband has forced her into bed on a surprise visit. Hannah leaves her husband and moves in with Maude; a symbiotic friendship develops. Maude learns to accept her marriage's futility and regains self-esteem and the strength to go it alone, while Hannah returns to her now-penitent husband but promises to maintain daily visits to Maude. The comedy offers a perceptive look at two delightfully defined contemporary women undergoing loss and gain. Although differing in details, a reverse-gender repetition of the above play appears in the more recent but less successful *Some Men Need Help*. A career-disillusioned young WASP advertising executive, Singleton, deserted by his wife, is drowning himself in liquor and self-loathing in his Connecticut home when he is visited by an overbearing lower-class ex-Mafioso neighbor who inexplicably insists on saving him. Singleton cannot eject the unwelcome Good Samaritan, even with racist slurs, yet eventually is persuaded to undergo detoxification and to change his self-destructive attitude. While overly reminiscent of its predecessor, this well-intentioned comedy about two men who grow to like each other relays Noonan's message that help is possible when you love your neighbor.

More characteristic of his individual voice, Noonan's earlier plays are often less realistic in style and context than these later ones. *The Year Boston Won the Pennant* employs fantasy and Brechtian techniques to chronicle the odyssey through a callous society of the maimed baseball pitcher Marcus Sykowski, who wishes to regain his former fame and the ability he enjoyed before mysteriously losing his arm. Throughout 14 mockingly titled scenes, the impractical but courageously aspiring Sykowski visits family and friends seeking solace and money to buy a prosthetic limb, only bewilderingly to encounter attempted exploitation and unprovoked betrayal or violence, while at the same time an anti-war revolution occurs in the streets unnoticed by all. Constantly pursued by a mysteriously menacing gangster, Sykowski is assassinated when pitching a dream-like comeback game. The victimized hero seems to be a metaphor for a baffled, maimed Vietnam-era America self-destructively pursuing an impossible quest for lost prestige and driven by forces of greed and unconscionable irrationality. This dark comedy, sometimes ambiguously uneven in style and characterization, does more than confirm Leo Durocher's observation that "good guys finish last."

The hysteria and inclination toward fantasy of ordinary people are often subjects in Noonan's work of the 1970s. In *Rainbows for Sale*, a youthful firehouse custodian meets his older self to find him a deceased racist fireman who has gone on a maniacal shooting spree in an ethnic neighborhood. The play effectively mixes fantasy with forcibly graphic narrative. The difficulties of ageing are well represented with empathy and irony in *Older People*, a cycle of 15 sketch-like short plays with interludes of song—a Noonan characteristic —dealing with the new fears and waning sexual powers of the elderly. While the sketches range in quality, the work's contrast between its sad and wistful subject matter and its farcical form is engaging.

Concern with fantasy and the bizarre as well as domestic alienation is sustained in several Noonan plays of the 1980's, which tend to be less successful than earlier works. In *Talking Things Over with Chekhov*, a budding playwright has hallucinatory conversations with Chekhov about literary philosophy. The playwright renews a friendship with a former actress lover, desperate for a comeback after suffering a nervous breakdown, by offering her a starring role in his explicit autobiographical play about their past relationship. Her casting has been confirmed by a willing producer. However, when the playwright secures a more advantageous producer who will cast another actress, she is desolate despite the writer's claim that the play is the truly major star. The two-character piece begins awkwardly and totters between comedy and an uneven examination of obsession. *Listen to the Lions* deals with a Boston Irish family, peopled by insufficiently drawn yet colorful characters unable to relate to each other. *My Daddy's Serious American Gift* focuses on a girl who tells of having found her father dead in her home with a killer wanting her to call it suicide. The implausible story is not sufficiently rescued by its bizarre quality.

In a 1989 interview, Noonan claimed that a playwright has to listen to the child in himself and to write about things that pop into his head. That philosophy continues to be borne out, not always with success, in his work. Yet Noonan remains a talented dramatist with a zany, acerbic, and perceptive comic vision of the world. He continues to be an individual voice worthy of attention.

—Christian H. Moe

NORMAN, Marsha (née Williams).

Born in Louisville, Kentucky, 21 September 1947. Educated at Durrett High School, Louisville; Agnes Scott College, Decatur, Georgia, B.A. in philosophy 1969; University of Louisville, 1969–71, M.A. 1971. Married 1) Michael Norman in 1969 (divorced 1974); 2) Dann C. Byck, Jr., in 1978 (divorced 1986); 3) Tim Dykma in 1987. Worked with disturbed children at Kentucky Central State Hospital, 1969–71; teacher, Brown School, Louisville, from 1973; book reviewer and editor of children's supplement (*Jelly Bean Journal*), Louisville *Times*, mid-1970's; playwright-in-residence, Actors Theatre, Louisville, 1977–78, and Mark Taper Forum, Los Angeles, 1979; since 1988 treasurer, the Dramatists Guild. Recipient: American Theater Critics Association prize, 1978; National Endowment for the Arts grant, 1978; Rockefeller grant, 1979; John Gassner award, 1979; Oppenheimer award, 1979; Susan Smith Blackburn prize, 1983; Pulitzer prize, 1983; American Academy award, 1986; Tony award, 1991. Lives in Long Island, New York. Agent: Jack Tantleff, The Tantleff Agency, 375 Greenwich Street, New York, New York 10013, U.S.A.

Publications

PLAYS

Getting Out (produced 1977). 1980.
Third and Oak: The Laundromat (produced 1978). 1980.
Third and Oak: The Pool Hall (produced 1978). 1985.
Circus Valentine (produced 1979).
Merry Christmas, in *Holidays* (produced 1979).
'Night, Mother (produced 1982). 1984.
The Holdup (produced 1983). 1987.
Traveler in the Dark (produced 1984; revised version produced 1985).
Four Plays (includes *Getting Out*, *Third and Oak*, *The Holdup*, *Traveler in the Dark*). 1988.
Sarah and Abraham (produced 1988).
The Secret Garden, music by Lucy Simon, adaptation of the novel by Frances Hodgson Burnett (produced 1990).
D. Boone (produced 1992).
The Red Shoes, from the 1948 movie, music by Jule Styne, lyrics by Marsha Norman and Paul Stryker (produced 1993).

TELEVISION PLAYS: *It's the Willingness* (*Visions* series), 1978; *In Trouble at Fifteen* (*Skag* series), 1980.

NOVEL
The Fortune Teller. 1987.

BIBLIOGRAPHY: *American Playwrights since 1945: A Guide to Scholarship, Criticism, and Performance* by Philip C. Kolin, 1989.

CRITICAL STUDIES: *American Voices: Five Contemporary Playwrights in Essays and Interviews* by Esther Harriott, 1988; "'I thought You Were Mine': Marsha Norman's *'Night, Mother"* by Sally Browder in *Mother Puzzles: Daughters and Mothers in Contemporary American Literature*, edited by Mickey Pearlman, 1989; "Marsha Norman's She-Tragedies" by Jenny S. Spencer in *Making a Spectacle: Feminist Essays on Contemporary Women's Theatre*, edited by Lynda Hart, 1989; *Taking Center Stage: Feminism in Contemporary US Drama*, 1991.

THEATRICAL ACTIVITIES
DIRECTOR: **Play**—*Semi-Precious Things* by Terri Wagener, 1980.

"I know now, all these years and plays later, that I always write about solitary confinement." If this realisation only came to Marsha Norman with the anthologising of *Getting Out* in 1988, it also eluded critics who generalised on her early successes and tended to find a playwright grasping at various fragments of social significance and dissecting them within a broad spectrum of dramaturgic experimentation. Yet the focalising drive towards the character locked within herself certainly is a recurrent motif, and relates suggestively to another of Norman's statements quoted in *The Feminist Companion to Literature in English*: "What you cannot escape seeing is that we are all disturbed kids."

Norman's perception derives from her early experience working with disturbed children, partly at the Kentucky Central State Hospital, and is most obviously illustrated in *Getting Out*. But most of her plays take place at the intersection of the confined and the disturbed. *Third and Oak: The Laundromat* parodies the idea of "standing by your man" in its portrait of two women accidentally meeting in the middle of the night carrying shirts which are the relics of relationships they want to think still survive; but it ends with an assertion of the strength of solitude. If *The Holdup* presents itself as a parody of the frontier myth, it is also a study of a very naïve young man's detachment from a suffocating mother to a point of self-sufficient isolation. *Traveler in the Dark* is more complex in its structuring of relationships, but the same dynamics recur in the central character of Sam, the famous surgeon trying to place himself as father, husband, and son, fleeing back to his (now absent) mother when his professional skills leave him stranded and helpless beside a dying friend. But it is Norman's two full-length plays with female protagonists that most amply illustrate her skills at feminising and contemporising the problem play.

If the material of *Getting Out* sounds in synopsis rather like a case study with obvious elements of social didacticism, its technique is reminiscent of O'Neill's *Strange Interlude* in its schizoid presentation of the main character: the whole action follows the first day of notional freedom for Arlene, just released on parole after serving a murder sentence, but unable to detach from her "criminal" self, Angie, played by another actor. Detachment, however, is just the obverse of the integration she seeks into society, into a straight career, and into her fragmented family, but the quest for some kind of bonding is thwarted by the people she meets: her former pimp and her prison guard, both with an agenda of brutal exploitation, her mother who in effect rejects her, and her new neighbour, another ex-con who still carries the ambience of the prison with her. Instead, integration comes with the self she has tried to exorcise, and the play's ending has Arlie and Arlene laughing playfully together, an interesting anticipation of Caryl Churchill's finale to *Cloud Nine*.

Jessie Cates, whose suicide is the entire action of *'Night, Mother*, is a restatement and development of this integration. As the often-quoted introductory statement emphasises, she has only just got herself together: only in the last year has she "gained control of her own mind and body," and the choice of suicide is the triumphant result of that control. But in the period before that control, there is a quest for identity as daughter, wife, and mother, a search through pockets of silence most graphically illustrated by her epileptic fits. This abnormality, read as a biological deviance parallel to Arlie's anti-social propensities, means that Jessie too has constantly been generating her own state of solitary confinement.

Because they have both in different senses been "inside," Jessie and Arlene are both highly receptive to "reports" of the personal history that they have been out of touch with. The murder for which Angie was locked up is relayed back to her by people who saw it covered on television. Jessie wants to know what she, her other self, looks like during fits, and this is directly related to the search for control that is central to all of Norman's protagonists. Arlene's hunt for normal work will bring her to meet strangers who nevertheless know the television image of Arlie, a gaze as brutal, as impersonal, and as invasive as the thought of the two-way mirrors in the prison washrooms. The reductiveness of this is severe, a total denial of adult dignity, like Jessie regressing to a condition of infantile dependence when she wets herself during fits—and only knowing it has happened because others told her that they cleaned her up.

Such a crisis of identity reflects the blur of societal positioning that both women face. An absent father confronts them with an Oedipal/Electral ambiguity. Society tells both of them that they have failed as mothers of the sons who are having their own problems of integration. And both are threatened by the blackmail of dependence from one of Jane Gallop's "phallic mothers," through whom, in Luce Irigaray's terms, there is the prospect of "femininity" being "effaced to leave room for maternity"—especially as these mothers do not hesitate to hit them with evidence of their own incompetence as mothers. But in their ultimate refusal to disavow themselves in the face of such pressures, or to annihilate the "disturbed kid" in themselves and now in society at large, there is the defiant insistence that the dismantling of structures may not just be anarchic but may bring a more integrated sense of self—if, necessarily, in confinement. Jessie's final wish for her son may serve as Norman's final gloss on the anxieties of modern mothercraft: if he spends his inheritance on dope, she hopes it is at least good dope.

—Howard McNaughton

See the essay on *'Night, Mother*.

O

ODETS, Clifford.

Born in Philadelphia, Pennsylvania, 18 July 1906; grew up in the Bronx, New York. Educated at Morris High School, New York, 1921–23. Married 1) the actor Luise Rainer in 1937 (divorced 1941); 2) Bette Grayson in 1943 (divorced 1951), one son and one daughter. Actor on radio and on Broadway, 1923–28, and with Theatre Guild Productions, New York, 1928–30; wrote for the stage, particularly for the Group Theatre, from 1933; joined Communist Party, 1934 (resigned 1934). Recipient: New Theatre League prize, 1935; Yale Drama prize, 1935; American Academy Award of Merit Medal, 1961. *Died 14 August 1963.*

Publications

PLAYS

Waiting for Lefty (produced 1935). In *Three Plays*, 1935.
Awake and Sing! (produced 1935). In *Three Plays*, 1935.
Till the Day I Die (produced 1935). In *Three Plays*, 1935.
Three Plays (includes *Waiting for Lefty; Awake and Sing!; Till the Day I Die*). 1935.
I Can't Sleep: A Monologue (produced 1935). In *New Theatre 3*, 1936.
Paradise Lost (produced 1935). 1936.
Golden Boy (produced 1937). 1937.
Rocket to the Moon (produced 1938). 1939.
Six Plays (includes *Waiting for Lefty; Awake and Sing; Till the Day I Die; Paradise Lost; Golden Boy; Rocket to the Moon*). 1939.
Night Music (produced 1940). 1940.
Clash by Night (produced 1941). 1942.
The Russian People, from a play by Konstantin Simonov (produced 1942). In *Seven Soviet Plays*, edited by H.W.L. Dana, 1946.
None But the Lonely Heart (screenplay). In *Best Film Plays 1945*, edited by John Gassner and Dudley Nichols, 1946.
The Big Knife (produced 1949). 1949.
The Country Girl (produced 1950). 1951; revised version, as *Winter Journey* (produced 1952), 1955.
The Flowering Peach (produced 1954). 1954.
The Silent Partner (produced 1972).

SCREENPLAYS: *The General Died at Dawn*, 1936; *Black Sea Fighters*, 1943; *None But the Lonely Heart*, 1944 ; *Deadline at Dawn*, 1946; *Humoresque* with Zachary Gold, 1946; *Sweet Smell of Success*, with Ernest Lehman, 1957; *The Story on Page One*, 1960; *Wild in the Country*, 1961.

TELEVISION PLAYS: *Big Mitch*, 1963, and *The Mafia Man*, 1964 (both for *The Richard Boone Show*).

OTHER

Rifle Rule in Cuba, with Carleton Beals. 1935.
The Time is Ripe: The 1940 Journal of Clifford Odets. 1988.

BIBLIOGRAPHY: *Clifford Odets: An Annotated Bibliography 1935–1989* by Robert Cooperman, 1990.

CRITICAL STUDIES: *Clifford Odets: The Thirties and After*, by Edward Murray, 1968; *Clifford Odets: Humane Dramatist* by Michael J. Mendelsohn, 1969; *Clifford Odets: Playwright-Poet* by Harold Cantor, 1978; *Clifford Odets: Playwright*, by Gerald Weales, 1971, revised edition, 1985; *Clifford Odets, American Playwright: The Years from 1906 to 1940* by Margaret Brenman-Gibson, 1981; *Clifford Odets*, by Gabriel Miller, 1989; *Clifford Odets: A Research and Production Sourcebook* by William W. Demastes, 1991; *Critical Essays on Clifford Odets*, edited by Gabriel Miller, 1991.

When Odets told the House Un-American Activities Committee that he had written his first play to be staged, *Waiting for Lefty*, entirely from his imagination, and that he had never been involved in a strike, he was widely thought to be lying in self-defence. Certainly, the play reflected—and in audience terms extended—the violent 40-day strike by 40,000 New York taxi drivers in 1934, and its production by the Group Theatre obviously endorsed the left-wing values of the strikers. But, as John Gassner said of that play, Odets may also be seen to be "playing Pindar to a working class to which he belonged only by bohemian adoption". If that view is accepted, then the elements of Hollywood sentimentality and Broadway realism in his subsequent output may be construed not as a betrayal of his first ideology, but as a regression to his more basic propensity.

The theatrical significance of *Waiting for Lefty* was enormous. Almost immediately it was being produced internationally from gestetnered scripts circulated by the Communist Party before the published text was available. It continued to be central to the canon of "Unity" and "Workers" theatres in the 1950s, and it became a model for much other left-wing agit-prop drama. Predictably, the play was pirated and reshaped into localised versions, and—a dimension often forgotten—Odets' use of the vernacular valorised a relatively new theatre language. But, ideology aside, few playwrights would want to commit their careers to the 40–minute form that was effectively the limit of agit-prop, and Odets had already completed more conventional full-length work when *Waiting for Lefty* was first performed.

Six other plays were done for the Group Theatre, and although none of them is as uncompromisingly propagandist as *Waiting for Lefty*, most do have an embedded argument that addresses issues of social significance, and the one-act *Till the Day I Die* is an overt anti-Nazi polemic. *Awake and Sing!*, the most famous of his full-length plays, presents its characters as products and victims of the Depression, and has dimensions of subtext and social realism that are much subtler than in most of the other Group plays. Much of the play's irony and pessimism is generated by the Jewish characters' search for a promised land in the face of hopeless adversity, and in *Paradise Lost*, the other early full-length play, a middle-class family—also from the Bronx, but this time not explicitly Jewish—goes through an odyssey of disaster in the face of capitalism. This play has more obvious symbolic elements, and most of the male characters are debilitated in some way, ranging from an impotent businessman to a former sports hero who now has a weak heart; the latter is the prototype of several of Odets' later characters, and may also be seen as an ironic glimpse of the American Dream as Albee would develop it in the 1960s.

Odets' move from the Group Theatre to Hollywood was planned as a short-term money-making venture to support stage production, but the models of success he encountered there influenced both his ambitions and his style. *The Silent Partner*, not produced until after his death, is in the vein of *Paradise Lost*, and Harold Clurman's demand for a rewrite because the theme seemed *passé* fundamentally affected Odets' relationship with the Group; shortly before his death, he told a *Theatre Arts* interviewer that it was "the best labor play that was ever written in the United States". He went on to say that "in the development of my work it was very necessary, and I should have insisted that the play be produced. It's the kind of writing that I have not done since, and I don't think I'm capable of now . . . if I had continued writing from there on . . . something extraordinary might have come out".

Odets' first screenplay, *The General Died at Dawn*, deals with a Chinese peasants' revolt, but its obvious socialist elements are crudely sensationalised, and his next major stage-play, *Golden Boy*, was first subtitled "A Modern Allegory", which clearly increased its acceptability to the Group. For all that, the play's commercial success (which Odets was consciously aiming at) was predictable, in that it does not compel audiences to go beneath the strata of sentimentality and melodramatic devices that reviewers widely labelled "cinematic". As a narrative of the spectacular rise and eventual suicide of a sporting hero, it had an unashamedly popular theme which instantly reached the mass imagination, but it also further developed the American Dream motif through the boxer's success story and subjected it to criticism through the many other conflicts in the competitive society that elevates fighting to such status.

Odets' last two Group plays, *Rocket to the Moon* and *Night Music*, are even softer in their audience manipulation, though their treatment of personal relationships introduces factors such as alcoholism and media-constructed identity which would be developed in the post-war plays. *Clash by Night* deals with marital conflict in terms which occasionally evoke the Strindbergian sex war and marked his final dissociation from the (nearly defunct) Group, although its cast, led by Tallulah Bankhead and Lee J. Cobb, was directed by Lee Strasberg.

Apart from *The Flowering Peach*, which remobilises elements of the allegory, poetry, and judaism of the plays of the 1930s, Odets' later plays have been seen as the work of a man fatigued and conditioned by years of screenwriting. Some of his screenplays—notably *None But the Lonely Heart*—had been recognised as distinguished, but his sense of achievement was eroded by recurrent official accusations from 1947 until 1952 of being "active in Communist work in film colony". Most importantly though, the last stageplays were written with an awareness that the audience of the 1930s no longer existed, and that Group members were now dominating the Actors' Studio and achieving major successes with the plays of Miller and Williams. *The Big Knife* and *The Country Girl* are both studies of actors as products of an industry, and alcoholism is presented in an unglamorised—if not exactly sordid—manner. These plays were taken by moralistic critics as pivoting on "weakness of character", augmented by shallowness of characterisation; however, their lasting effectiveness has more to do with their vision of people degenerating as the victims of a falsely-constructed public identity.

—Howard McNaughton

See the essay on *Awake and Sing!*

O'NEILL, Eugene (Gladstone).

Born in New York City, 16 October 1888; son of the actor James O'Neill. Toured with his father as a child, and educated at Catholic boarding schools, and at Betts Academy, Stamford, Connecticut; attended Princeton University, New Jersey, 1906–07, and George Pierce Baker's "47 Workshop" at Harvard University, Cambridge, Massachusetts, 1914–15. Married 1) Kathleen Jenkins in 1909 (divorced 1912), one son; 2) Agnes Boulton in 1918 (divorced 1929), one son and one daughter; 3) the actor Carlotta Monterey in 1929. Worked for New York-Chicago Supply Company mail order firm, New York, 1907–08; gold prospector in Honduras, 1909; seaman on a Norwegian freighter to Buenos Aires, and advance agent and box-office man for his father's company, 1910–11; reporter, New London *Telegraph*, Connecticut, 1912; patient in a tuberculosis sanitarium, 1912–13; full-time writer from 1914; writer and actor with the Provincetown Players, based in Provincetown, Massachusetts, and, from 1916, at the Playwrights' Theatre (also known as the Provincetown Playhouse), New York, 1916–20; co-director, with Kenneth Macgowan and the designer Robert Edmond Jones, of the reconstituted Provincetown Players, now based at the Provincetown and Greenwich Village theatres, New York, 1923–27; founding editor, *American Spectator*, 1934; in ill-health from 1934: in later years suffered from a degenerative brain disease. Recipient: Pulitzer prize, 1920, 1922, 1928, 1957; American Academy of Arts and Letters Gold Medal, 1922; Nobel prize for literature, 1936; New York Drama Critics Circle award, 1957. Litt.D: Yale University, New Haven, Connecticut, 1926. Member, American Academy, 1923, and Irish Academy of Letters. *Died 27 November 1953.*

Publications

PLAYS

Thirst and Other One Act Plays (includes *The Web; Warnings; Fog; Recklessness*). 1914.

Thirst (produced 1916). In *Thirst and Other Plays*, 1914.

Fog (produced 1917). In *Thirst and Other Plays*, 1914.

Bound East for Cardiff (produced 1916). In *The Moon of the Caribbees and Six Other Plays of the Sea*, 1919.

Before Breakfast (produced 1916). 1916.

The Sniper (produced 1917). In *Lost Plays*, 1950.

In the Zone (produced 1917). In *The Moon of the Caribbees and Six Other Plays of the Sea*, 1919.

The Long Voyage Home (produced 1917). In *The Moon of the Caribbees and Six Other Plays of the Sea*, 1919.

Ile (produced 1917). In *The Moon of the Caribbees and Six Other Plays of the Sea*, 1919.

The Rope (produced 1918). In *The Moon of the Caribbees and Six Other Plays of the Sea*, 1919.

Where the Cross is Made (produced 1918). In *The Moon of the Caribbees and Six Other Plays of the Sea*, 1919.

The Moon of the Caribbees (produced 1918). In *The Moon of the Caribbees and Six Other Plays of the Sea*, 1919.

The Moon of the Caribbees and Six Other Plays of the Sea. (includes *In the Zone; The Long Voyage Home; Ile; The Rope; Where the Cross is Made*). 1919.

The Dreamy Kid (produced 1919). In *Complete Works 2*, 1924.

Beyond the Horizon (produced 1920). 1920.

Anna Christie (as *Chris*, produced 1920; revised version, as *Anna Christie*, (produced 1921). With *The Hairy Ape, The First Man*, 1922; original version, as *Chris Christophersen*, 1982.

Exorcism (produced 1920).

The Emperor Jones (produced 1920). With *Diff'rent, The Straw*, 1921.

Diff'rent (produced 1920). With *The Emperor Jones, The Straw*, 1921.

The Straw (produced 1921). With *The Emperor Jones, Diff'rent*, 1921.

Gold (produced 1921). 1921.

The First Man (produced 1922). With *The Hairy Ape, Anna Christie*, 1922.

The Hairy Ape (produced 1922). With *The First Man, Anna Christie*, 1922.

Welded (produced 1924). With *All God's Chillun Got Wings*, 1924.

The Ancient Mariner: A Dramatic Arrangement of Coleridge's Poem (produced 1924).

All God's Chillun Got Wings (produced 1924). With *Welded*, 1924.

Desire under the Elms (produced 1924). In *Complete Works 2*, 1924.

Complete Works (2 vols.). 1924.

The Fountain (produced 1925). With *The Great God Brown, The Moon of the Caribbees*, 1926.

The Great God Brown (produced 1926). With *The Fountain, The Moon of the Caribbees*, 1926.

S.S. Glencairn: Four Plays of the Sea (includes *Bound East for Cardiff; In the Zone; The Long Voyage Home; The Moon of the Caribbees*). 1926.

Marco Millions (produced 1928). 1927.

Lazarus Laughed (produced 1928). 1927.

Strange Interlude (produced 1928). 1928.

Dynamo (produced 1929). 1929.

Mourning Becomes Electra: A Trilogy (produced 1931). 1931.
Ah, Wilderness! (produced 1933). 1933.
Days Without End (produced 1934). 1934.
The Iceman Cometh (produced 1946). 1946.
A Moon for the Misbegotten (produced 1947). 1952.
Lost Plays (includes *Abortion*; *The Movie Man*; *The Sniper*; *Servitude*; *A Wife for a Life*), edited by Lawrence Gellert. 1950.
Servitude (produced 1960). In *Lost Plays*, 1950.
Long Day's Journey into Night (produced 1956). 1956.
A Touch of the Poet (produced 1957). 1957.
Hughie (produced 1958). 1959.
More Stately Mansions (produced 1962). 1964.
Ten "Lost" Plays. 1964.
Children of the Sea and Three Other Unpublished Plays (includes *Bread and Butter*; *Now I Ask You*; *Shell Shock*), edited by Jennifer McCabe Atkinson. 1972.
The Calms of Capricorn scenario by O'Neill, completed by Donald Gallup. 1982.
The Unknown O'Neill (includes *The Personal Equation*; *The Reckoning*; *The Guilty One*), edited by Travis Bogard. 1988.
Complete Plays (3 vols.), edited by Travis Bogard. 1988.

VERSE
Poems 1912–1944, edited by Donald Gallup. 1980.

OTHER
Inscriptions: O'Neill to Carlotta Monterey O'Neill, edited by Donald Gallup. 1960.
O'Neill at Work: Newly Released Ideas for Plays, edited by Virginia Floyd. 1981.
The Theatre We Worked For: The Letters of O'Neill to Kenneth Macgowan, edited by Jackson R. Bryer. 1982.
As Ever, Gene: The Letters of Eugene O'Neill to George Jean Nathan, edited by Nancy L. and Arthur W. Roberts. 1987.
Selected Letters, edited by Travis Bogard and Jackson Bryer. 1988.
The Unfinished Plays (notes and drafts), edited by Virginia Floyd. 1988.

BIBLIOGRAPHIES: *Eugene O'Neill: A Descriptive Bibliography* by Jennifer M. Atkinson, 1974; *Eugene O'Neill and the American Critic: A Bibliographical Checklist* (second edition) by Jordan Y. Miller, 1973; *Eugene O'Neill: An Annotated Bibliography*, by Madeleine Smith and Richard Eaton, 1988.

CRITICAL STUDIES (a selection): *The Haunted Heroes of Eugene O'Neill* by Edwin A. Engel, 1953; *Eugene O'Neill and the Tragic Tension* (second edition) by Doris V. Falk, 1958, revised edition, 1982; *Eugene O'Neill and His Plays: Four Decades of Criticism* edited by Oscar Cargill and others, 1961; *The Tempering of Eugene O'Neill* by Doris Alexander, 1962; *O'Neill* by Arthur and Barbara Gelb, 1962; revised edition, 1974; *Eugene O'Neill* by Frederick I. Carpenter, 1963, revised edition, 1979; *Playwright's Progress:*

O'Neill and the American Critic by Jordan Y. Miller, 1965; *Eugene O'Neill* by
Olivia E. Coolidge, 1966; *O'Neill, Son and Playwright* (biography) by Louis
Shaeffer, 1968, as *O'Neill, Son and Artist*, 1973; *O'Neill's Scenic Images* by
Timo Tiusanen, 1968; *The Late Plays of O'Neill* by Rolf Scheibler, 1970;
Eugene O'Neill by Horst Frenz, 1971; *Contour in Time: The Plays of Eugene
O'Neill* by Travis Bogard, 1972, revised edition, 1988; *Ritual and Pathos: The
Theater of O'Neill* by Leonard Chabrowe, 1976; *Eugene O'Neill, Irish and
American: A Study in Cultural Context* by Harry Cronin, 1976: *Eugene
O'Neill: A Collection of Criticism* edited by Ernest G. Griffin, 1976; *Forging a
Language: A Study of the Plays of Eugene O'Neill* by Jean Chothia, 1979;
Eugene O'Neill: A World View edited by Virginia Floyd, 1979; *Eugene
O'Neill* by Normand Berlin, 1982; *O'Neill on Film* by John Orlandello, 1982;
Eugene O'Neill's Critics: Voices from Abroad edited by Horst Frenz and
Susan Tuck, 1984; *Critical Essays on Eugene O'Neill* edited by James J.
Martine, 1984; *The Eugene O'Neill Companion* by Margaret L. Ranald,
1984; *Final Acts: The Creation of Three Late O'Neill Plays* by Judith E.
Barlow, 1985; *Eugene O'Neill: Life, Work, and Criticism* by Foster Hirsch,
1986; *Eugene O'Neill: Modern Critical Views* edited by Harold Bloom, 1987;
The Plays of Eugene O'Neill: A New Assessment by Virginia Floyd, 1987;
Perspectives on O'Neill: New Essays edited by Shyamal Bagchee, 1988; *The
Banished Prince: Time, Memory, and Ritual in the Late Plays of Eugene
O'Neill* by Laurin R. Porter, 1988; *Eugene O'Neill in Ireland: The Critical
Reception* by Edward L. Shaughnessy, 1988; *Critical Approaches to O'Neill*
edited by John H. Stroupe, 1988; *Staging O'Neill: The Experimental Years
1920–1934* by Ronald H. Wainscott, 1988; *Eugene O'Neill: Three Plays: A
Collection of Critical Essays* edited by Normand Berlin, 1989; *Eugene O'Neill
and the Emergence of American Drama*, edited by Marc Maufort, 1989;
Conversation with O'Neill edited by Mark W. Estrin, 1990; *Eugene O'Neill's
Century: Centennial Views on America's Foremost Tragic Dramatist* edited by
Richard F. Moorton, 1991.

The author of over 60 completed and partly written plays, Eugene O'Neill
brought high seriousness to the American drama. From the beginning of his
career, he reacted against the escapist theatre of his actor-father, epitomized by
James O'Neill Sr.'s financially successful role as Edmond Dantès in *The Count
of Monte Cristo*.

From the earliest plays (produced at the Provincetown Playhouse,
Massachusetts, and its New York City theatre) O'Neill presented the perennial
cosmic theme, humanity's powerlessness before fate. This is shown in enslavement to the sea in the S.S. Glencairn plays, *Ile*, and *Anna Christie*. But equally
as important, O'Neill continually insisted on the need of an artist to honor and
use his gift. Throughout the O'Neill canon, denial of one's talent causes
destruction of the individual, from Robert Mayo in *Beyond the Horizon*,
O'Neill's first Broadway success, to Simon Harford in *A Touch of the Poet*.
This theme is also the basis of other plays in that proposed saga of American
acquisitiveness, "A Tale of Possessors, Self-Dispossessed".

Another important O'Neill theme is that of "belonging", and this shades
into nostalgia for a pre-mechanistic past—the days of sail, for instance. He
excoriates the depersonalization of the individual in modern society, particu-

larly in the expressionistic drama *The Hairy Ape*, in which Yank, the servant and apostle of the machine, is psychologically castrated by a female member of the ruling class in a mere seven words: "Take me away! Oh! The filthy beast!". This play is the only one in which the politics of class struggle are fully relevant, though two other works, *The Personal Equation* and *The Reckoning* (published 1988) are concerned with aspects of trade unionism.

O'Neill was a pioneer in theatrical race relations. His very early one-act play *Thirst* had a West-Indian mulatto sailor, played by O'Neill himself, as one of the three characters on a life raft, while a second one-acter, *The Dreamy Kid*, concerned a small-time black gangster. This was the first occasion on which a white company hired an entire company of black actors to play black roles. *The Emperor Jones* went further by making use of integrated casting. Charles Gilpin, a black actor, created the central role in this Jungian-influenced expressionistic monologue portraying African-American history in reverse. Gilpin's success led to a partial opening of the doors to professional theatre for African-American actors.

Even more controversial was *All God's Chillun Got Wings*, recounting the marriage of the white girl, Ella Downey, to the African-American Jim Harris. Though this play caused a furore of prejudice on its original production, race relations are not its true theme, which, once again, is that of the artist-figure, here the ambitious law student, Jim Harris, who is thwarted and destroyed by his wife's possessiveness and lack of understanding.

Ever the experimenter, O'Neill now turned to masks, and with *The Great God Brown* he offered his first fully masked play. He had already used an African mask in *All God's Chillun* as a means of showing the threat offered to the white, effete Ella Downey by Jim's alien and elemental world. In *The Hairy Ape* he had employed masks in the Fifth Avenue expressionistic scene, at the suggestion of Blanche Hays, the costume designer; but in *The Great God Brown* he wished to develop "a drama of souls" to gain "insight into the inner forces motivating the actions and reactions of men and women". As O'Neill himself put it, "one's outer life passes in a solitude haunted by the masks of others; one's inner life passes in a solitude haunted by the masks of oneself" (in his "Memoranda on Masks").

With *Lazarus Laughed*, a "play for an imaginative theatre", in four acts, eight scenes, and over 420 roles, O'Neill used masks for all characters except Lazarus, who celebrates life, having no fear of death. In this play, which goes beyond the economic limits of the professional theatre, and has, at the time of writing, yet to achieve a fully professional performance, he tried to recreate ritual theatre, analogous to that which grew out of the ancient worship of Dionysus, which could serve again as "practical interpretation and celebration of life". Later, in *Days Without End*, he returned to the use of masks to distinguish the protagonist John from his antagonist *alter ego*, Loving.

O'Neill tested his theories of drama in the further experimental plays *The Fountain* and *Marco Millions*. With the sympathetic co-operation of Kenneth Macgowan as director, and Robert Edmond Jones as scene designer, he aimed at presenting total theatre, or plastic theatre, pressing on the limits of the stage, and applying imaginative techniques to dramatic form, theme, and scenic design. Ambitiously, he now wished to educate his audience in philosophy through a comprehensive theatrical experience. These plays, along with

Lazarus Laughed, are all intellectually and speculatively important, but are only stageable in the theatre of the mind, even though O'Neill showed in them some of his best writing and deepest poetic thought, in attempting a synthesis of history, satire, religion, reconciliation, and love.

His next technical experiment was the nine-act drama *Strange Interlude*, which dealt openly with the taboo subjects of abortion and adultery. Here, O'Neill later wished he had used masks, but instead employed interior monologue to convey the secret thoughts of the protagonists. Thus, the double action portrays outward reality contrasted with inward contemplation and evaluation of that reality. Conflicts, then, are both overt and psychic as O'Neill also played with time, projecting the final act 17 years beyond the date of the play's original production. The true theme is the psychological life of woman in the three manifestations imaged by O'Neill—mother, wife, mistress-whore —within a dramatic structure of gestation and the eternal return.

O'Neill's tragic vision, with its solid grounding in the resonances of myth, naturally led him to attempt the creation of a new, original mythology to reflect the concerns of the 20th century, a task that occupied him for the remainder of his life. Two plays, *Desire Under the Elms* and *Dynamo*, demonstrate O'Neill as an excellent *myth user*, but less successful as *myth maker*. Consequently, it is something of a tragedy for American drama that he spent so much of his productive life endeavoring to produce the ultimate myth of acquisitive American civilization in his proposed 11-play cycle "A Tale of Possessors, Self-Dispossessed".

In *Mourning Becomes Electra*, his next experiment in mythology, O'Neill recreated the classical trilogy format in its three full-length plays, *The Homecoming*, *The Hunted*, and *The Haunted*. Here, as with his larger experiments in total theatre, *The Fountain* and *Lazarus Laughed*, O'Neill appealed to the theatre of the mind, rather than the limitations of the professional stage. In this work, his most creative employment and amalgamation of diverse myths, he used the fate of the House of Atreus as a basis, deliberately adapting the myth to an archetypal American time and place, fashioning "a modern drama in which the Greek fates are replaced by forces which are more comprehensible in an age without religion and without commitment to gods".

O'Neill then turned to myth-making. After the completion of *Marco Millions* he began to think in terms of a trilogy to be called "Myth-Plays for the God-Forsaken". Here he hoped to reforge a modern belief independent of established religions, and suitable for a world that had lost its spiritual way. He set out to reveal the sickness of materialistic American society as he attacked "repressive organized religion with its fear of human sexuality and physicality". In the first of these plays, *Dynamo*, O'Neill seized on the suggestion of Henry Adams in "The Dynamo and the Virgin" that for the 20th century the force and energy of the dynamo are analogous to the medieval cultural and constructive creativity generated by worship of the Virgin. O'Neill portrayed the fate of young Reuben Light who worships the dynamo as his anthropomorphic earth mother/goddess and is destroyed by it, perhaps because he is unworthy. After the unsuccessful *Days Without End*, the second play of this abortive trilogy, O'Neill abandoned the project.

However, *Days Without End* represents a development that led to the last cycle, "A Tale of Possessors, Self-Dispossessed", which "planned to use the saga of one family to illustrate the central theme of the corrupting influence of possessions upon their owners" (see *The Eugene O'Neill Companion*); and more than coincidentally, it emphasizes a series of marriages and family dramas in much the same way as O'Neill finally used his own family to create a new mythology of human relationships.

Familial relationships are, in fact, a central thematic strand of much of O'Neill's work, from *Bread and Butter* and *Servitude*; in the latter a major theme is "Servitude in love! Love in servitude!". This is taken up in *Welded*, *The First Man*, by Elsa Loving in *Days Without End*, and by both Nora and Sara Melody in *A Touch of the Poet*, though later, in *More Stately Mansions*, Sara displays the acquisitive, sensual side of her personality. But O'Neill's family members are almost invariably at each other's throats—except in *Ah, Wilderness!*, a traditionally sentimental, comedic exercise in wish-fulfilled remembrance.

Even *The Iceman Cometh* is a kind of familial drama, because the denizens of the "Last Chance Bar" form a community which is temporarily shattered by the intrusion of Theodore Hickman, who brings death and disruption to those who are bonded by their withdrawal from life. Conversely, *Hughie*, a self-contained monologue, features, in "Erie" Smith, a character who is trying to reach out, "to belong", one who, like the characters of *The Iceman Cometh* and Cornelius Melody in *A Touch of the Poet*, takes refuge in the Ibsenesque "saving lie" to continue living. In effect, all "these last plays continue the theme of the mask which hides the psychic identity of the individual . . . while the action shows characters being stripped of pretense" (see *The Eugene O'Neill Companion*).

With his Pulitzer Prize-winning *Long Day's Journey Into Night* and *A Moon for the Misbegotten*, O'Neill developed his personal, psychological myth-making into high art, paradoxically by returning to realistic techniques. With selective memory, he whitewashed himself by omitting his first marriage, and made peace with his father and brother, paying tribute to their idiosyncrasies, while sympathizing with their weaknesses. However, he never forgave his mother. She remains unhistorically unsalvable, just as the portrait of James O'Neill as irremediable alcoholic and miser is untrue. Indeed, O'Neill seems never to have appreciated the struggle Ella O'Neill underwent in overcoming her addiction to morphine. But then again, his attitude towards women throughout the plays is flawed. For him, woman is virgin/mother/whore, one who must serve man: Josie Hogan in *A Moon for the Misbegotten* is her earth-mother epitome as she cradles Jamie's head in her lap in a Pietà.

Ironically, by the end of his working life, O'Neill had become disenchanted with the theatre—*Hughie* was the only completed play of another projected series, entitled "By Way of Obit". Each of the proposed eight monologue-plays was meant to consist of one scene, with one character and one life-size marionette, the Good Listener. The reactions of this listener, if one can take *Hughie* as representative, are almost entirely non-verbal, and clues to his reactions are in the stage directions, rather than in the dialogue.

"Eclectic to a fault" (as one critic, Christopher Bigsby, has described O'Neill) and permanently experimental, O'Neill's distinguishing character-istics include high seriousness, contrived mass effects, heavy use of irony, melodramatic situations, sardonic humour, imaginative intellectual exploration, and genuine dramatic talent. In his synthesis of myth, past and present, he was pre-eminently successful in giving to the American theatre a unique sense of the tragic human condition.

—Margaret Loftus Ranald

See the essay on *Long Day's Journey Into Night*.

OVERMYER, Eric.

Born in Boulder, Colorado, 25 September 1951. Educated at Reed College, Portland, Oregon, B.A. 1976; Florida State University, Tallahassee, 1977; Brooklyn College, City University of New York, 1979–81. Married 1) Melissa Cooper in 1978; 2) Ellen McElduff in 1991. Literary manager, Playwrights Horizons, New York, 1981–84; associate artist, Center Stage, Baltimore, Maryland, 1984–91; story editor, *St. Elsewhere* television series, 1986–87; visiting associate professor of playwriting, Yale University, and associate artist, Yale Repertory Theater, New Haven, Connecticut, 1991–92. Recipient: Le Comte du Nouy, 1984; McKnight fellowship, 1986; National Endowment for the Arts fellowship, 1987; New York Foundation for the Arts fellowship, 1987; Rockefeller fellowship, 1987. Agent: George Lane, William Morris Agency, 1350 Avenue of the Americas, New York, New York 10019. Address: 366 West 11th Street, New York, New York 10014, U.S.A.

Publications

PLAYS

Native Speech (produced 1983). 1984.
On the Verge, or The Geography of Yearning (produced 1985). 1986.
The Double Bass, with Harry Newman, adaptation of the play by Patrick Süskind (produced 1986).
In a Pig's Valise, music by August Darnell (produced 1986). 1989.
In Perpetuity Throughout the Universe (produced 1988). 1988.
Hawker. In *Plays from New Dramatists*, edited by Christopher Gould, 1989.
Mi Vida Loca (produced 1990). 1991.
Don Quixote de La Jolla (produced 1990).
Kafka's Radio (produced 1990).
The Heliotrope Bouquet by Scott Joplin and Louis Chauvin (produced 1991).
Dark Rapture (produced 1992).

TELEVISION PLAYS: *St. Elsewhere* series, 1985–88; *The Days and Nights of Molly Dodd* series, 1988–90; *Sisters* series, 1990–91.

Eric Overmyer comments:

I am interested in the authentically theatrical. Hermann Broch stated that he wrote novels in order to discover that which can only be discovered by writing a novel. I write plays in order to discover what can only be discovered by writing plays. I am interested in discovering the limits of the theatre, its possibilities and its impossibilities. I am interested in language, first and always: a charged, mythic, poetic, theatrical language. And imagination:

mythic, poetic, epic. I am interested in bravura performance style which is necessary to an authentically theatrical experience. I am not interested in naturalism, in small plays with small ideas which need small performances, in plays which are really faux cinema; in short, in the kind of plays the dramaturg James Magruder refers to as "talking about my problems in your living room." I am interested in plays which are contradictory, complex, many-layered, and many-faceted, which are unencumbered by reductive, mechanistic psychology, motive, and biography. In other words, I am interested in reversal instead of transition, in wrought language rather than humdrum speech, in leaps of the imagination not tedious exposition, in classic plays, and in contemporary plays which embody classical virtues and present classical challenges. I prefer to work with directors who direct classical plays as if they were contemporary, and contemporary plays as if they were classical. I am not an avant-gardist, I am a nouveau-classicist.

As one of only two playwrights currently toiling in the American theater for whom language is both object and muse (the other is Mac Wellman), Eric Overmyer suffers many fools. Directors, actors, and the critical establishment charge him with wilfull obscurity and arrant pedantry, and chide him for a perceived resistance to closure. He runs foul of editors and proofreaders who insisted, for example, upon changing his line "Give it me" in *In Perpetuity Throughout the Universe* to "Give it *to* me" through every stage of publication. The choice of "give it me" over "give it to me" is no trifling matter in an Overmyer play; those deaf to the difference deny the characters their territory. Smoothing over this particular imperative, or paraphrasing Overmyer into standard usage, denies the author his right to remain a non-naturalistic word jockey spinning lines outside the adamantly realist boundaries of the American theater. The standard new American play—standard play in standard prose—can be boiled down to the formula "Talking about *my* problems in *your* apartment." Apartments count for nothing in Overmyer's euphonic universe; his people more often than not turn up in dreams or on the airwaves or on terra incognita. Their language, their logorrheic pulse, is their main chance to talk their way into a known state of being and recognize themselves. How well the audience knows them when they get there is another matter.

Overmyer's second play, *On the Verge, or The Geography of Yearning*, is one of the most important new works to emerge in American drama in the last 30 years. Mary, Alex, and Fanny, three intrepid Victorian lady explorers, set out for adventure with machetes and pith helmets in 1888. As they progress, the terrain becomes increasingly unfamiliar. Unknown objects—eggbeaters, side-view mirrors—turn up; words and phrases they've never heard or used before spring to their lips—I like Ike, Cool Whip, tractor opera. They discover that they are, in fact, bivouacking their way along the continuum of American pop. They pause in 1955; Alex and Fanny, enthralled by post-war consumer culture, remain in this most ideal of climates, leaving Mary to venture ever forward, yearning into the future. *On the Verge* traverses the twin peaks of American literature, the urge to know and the urge to go, charting with unflagging theatricality the giddy debasement of American speech on the open market. "I have seen the future and it is slang."

The theme of what control an artist, particularly the writer, can exert over his work—in a sense, the question of reception theory—recurs throughout Overmyer's work. *In Perpetuity Throughout the Universe* is a dark, vertiginous ride through the conspiracist mentality of racist America in which a doubled cast of good guys and bad guys ghost-write hate primers, creating enemies to keep the populace permanently paranoid and off-kilter. The title is a phrase from an author's contract regarding future rights to sequels and spinoffs. *Don Quixote de La Jolla*, built during five weeks of site-specific collaboration at the La Jolla Playhouse, is an insidiously faithful tweak on the tale of the mad knight and his doughty sidekick. Overmyer offers a baleful rumination on what weight, if any, that mighty and mightily unread 16th-century classic would have on a Southern Californian populace raised on "Lady of Spain" and the terminally trashy *Man of La Mancha*. Not surprisingly, the lambada leaves Cervantes in the dust in another one of Overmyer's hilarious acts of cultural anthropology.

In his 1991 play (the fifth to be presented at Baltimore's Center Stage), *The Heliotrope Bouquet by Scott Joplin and Louis Chauvin*, Overmyer creates a fluid, overlapping dreamscape that encompasses both historical and hallucinatory locations. Joplin, the foremost composer of piano ragtime, and Chauvin, an illiterate contemporary whose musical gifts were said to have surpassed Joplin's, wrote "The Heliotrope Bouquet," a slow-drag two-step, in 1906. This rhapsodic moment occasions the play. Inasmuch as the historical material is scarce and largely conjectural, *Heliotrope* is less an historical restitution of Chauvin's place in American culture and African-American history than it is a dialectical meditation on artistic collaboration. Although grounded in the sporting house context of ragtime America, the conflict between "slow and cautious Joplin," who lives with an eye on the future, and Chauvin, who burns brightly in the moment and believes that it only lasts "as long as a man stays awake," raises larger, unanswered questions "still to be heard in the ether and the House of God." What is posterity to a dead man? What is success—does it come from a rag well performed before friends or in copies of sheet music tucked inside a stranger's piano bench? What is worth recalling—bundles of heliotrope set down on a table or notes bunched on the musical stave? Is art the moment of creativity or the fact of duration?

As with all of Overmyer's work, a main source of *Heliotrope*'s drama is its poetic idiom. As richly syncopated as ragtime, the play can be said to mimic the structure of a piano rag as certain lines are repeated throughout, passed from character to character like a musical phrase set in different keys. *Heliotrope*'s language is sensational; better than merely original, it is particular. Overmyer states his own case best when he writes in his production notes for *On the Verge*: "The language of the play . . . cannot, must not, should not be naturalized or paraphrased. Rhythm and sound are sense."

—James Magruder

OWENS, Rochelle.

Pseudonym for Rochelle Bass. Born in Brooklyn, New York, 2 April 1936. Educated at Lafayette High School, Brooklyn, graduated 1953. Married George Economou in 1962. Worked as a clerk, typist, telephone operator. Founding member, New York Theatre Strategy. Visiting lecturer, University of California, San Diego, 1982; adjunct professor, and host of radio program *The Writer's Mind*, University of Oklahoma, Norman, 1984; distinguished writer-in-residence, Brown University, Providence, Rhode Island. Recipient: Rockefeller grant, 1965, 1975; Ford grant, 1965; Creative Artists Public Service grant, 1966, 1973; Yale University School of Drama fellowship, 1968; Obie award, 1968, 1971, 1982; Guggenheim fellowship, 1971; National Endowment for the Arts grant, 1974; Villager award, 1982; New York Drama Critics Circle award, 1983. Agent: Dramatists Guild, 234 West 44th Street, New York, New York 10036. Address: 1401 Magnolia, Norman, Oklahoma 73072, U.S.A.

Publications

PLAYS

Futz (produced 1965). 1961; revised version in *Futz and What Came After*, 1968, in *New Short Plays 2*, 1969.
The String Game (produced 1965). In *Futz and What Came After*, 1968.
Istanboul (produced 1965). In *Futz and What Came After*, 1968.
Homo (produced 1966). In *Futz and What Came After*, 1968.
Beclch (produced 1968). In *Futz and What Came After*, 1968.
Futz and What Came After. 1968.
The Karl Marx Play, music by Galt MacDermot, lyrics by Owens (produced 1973). In *The Karl Marx Play and Others*, 1974.
The Karl Marx Play and Others (includes *Kontraption, He Wants Shih!, Farmer's Almanac, Coconut Folksinger, O.K. Certaldo*). 1974.
He Wants Shih! (produced 1975). In *The Karl Marx Play and Others*, 1974.
Coconut Folksinger (broadcast 1976). In *The Karl Marx Play and Others*, 1974.
Kontraption (produced 1978). In *The Karl Marx Play and Others*, 1974.
Emma Instigated Me, in *Performing Arts Journal 1*, Spring 1976.
The Widow, and The Colonel, in *The Best Short Plays 1977*, edited by Stanley Richards. 1977.
Mountain Rites, in *The Best Short Plays 1978*, edited by Stanley Richards. 1978.
Chucky's Hunch (produced 1981). In *Wordplays 2*, 1982.
Who Do You Want, Peire Vidal? (produced 1982). With *Futz*, 1986.
Screenplay: *Futz* (additional dialogue), 1969.

RADIO PLAYS: *Coconut Folksinger*, 1976; *Sweet Potatoes*, 1977.

TELEVISION PLAY (video): *Oklahoma Too: Rabbits and Nuggets*, 1987.

SHORT STORIES

The Girl on the Garage Wall. 1962.
The Obscenities of Reva Cigarnik. 1963.

VERSE

Not Be Essence That Cannot Be. 1961.
Four Young Lady Poets, with others, edited by LeRoi Jones. 1962.
Salt and Core. 1968.
I Am the Babe of Joseph Stalin's Daughter. 1972.
Poems from Joe's Garage. 1973.
The Joe 82 Creation Poems. 1974.
The Joe Chronicles 2. 1979.
Shemuel. 1979.
French Light. 1984.
Constructs. 1985.
Anthropologists at a Dinner Party. 1985.
W. C. Fields in French Light. 1986.
How Much Paint Does the Painting Need? 1988.
Paysanne: New and Selected Poems 1961–1988. 1990.

RECORDINGS: *A Reading of Primitive and Archaic Poetry,* with others; *From a Shaman's Notebook,* with others; *The Karl Marx Play,* 1975; *Totally Corrupt,* 1976; *Black Box 17,* 1979.

OTHER

Editor, *Spontaneous Combustion: Eight New American Plays.*   1972.

MANUSCRIPT COLLECTIONS: Mugar Memorial Library, Boston University; University of California, Davis; University of Oklahoma, Norman; Lincoln Center Library of the Performing Arts, New York; Smith College, Northampton, Massachusetts.

CRITICAL STUDIES: *American Playwrights: A Critical Survey* by Bonnie Marranca and Gautam Dasgupta, 1981; *Women in American Theatre* edited by Helen Krich Chinoy and Linda Walsh Jenkins, 1981; *American Women Writers* by Linda Mainiero, 1981; article by Owens in *Contemporary Authors Autobiography Series 2* edited by Adele Sarkissian, 1985.

THEATRICAL ACTIVITIES

DIRECTOR AND ACTOR: **Television**—*Oklahoma Too: Rabbits and Nuggets,* 1987.

Rochelle Owens comments:

I am interested in the flow of imagination between the actors and the director, the boundless possibilities of interpretation of a script. Different theatrical realities are created and/or destroyed depending upon the multitudinous perceptions and points of view of the actors and director who share in the creation of the design of the unique journey of playing the play. There are as many ways to approach my plays as there as combinations of people who might involve themselves.

The inter-media video *Oklahoma Too* uses poetry and images juxtaposed. The structures both linguistic and visual offer exciting projections of my continuous investigation of making art.

Rochelle Owens came to the attention of the theatre public with her first play, *Futz*, whose shocking subject and inventive language launched her theatrical career. Owens's plays are distinguished by intense poetic imagery that springs from primordial human impulses of the subconscious and by the passionate and often violent struggle of her characters to survive within their repressive societies. Although a moralist who satirizes human frailty with parody, dialect, and the comic grotesque, Owens is also a compassionate observer who imbues her characters with tragic dimensions.

Futz is preceded by a quotation from Corinthians: "Now concerning the things whereof ye wrote to me: It is good for a man not to touch a woman." Cyrus Futz loves his pig, Amanda, and is persecuted by the community. Majorie Satz lusts for all men and wheedles an invitation to share Futz's sexual pleasure with his pig. Oscar Loop is driven to madness and murders Ann Fox when they inadvertently witness the Futz-Amanda-Majorie orgy. Majorie kills Amanda for revenge. Oscar is condemned to hang and Futz is sent to prison where he is stabbed by Majorie's brother. Puritanical society punishes innocent sensuality.

The String Game also explores the conflict between puritanism and natural impulse. Greenland Eskimos play the string game to ward off winter boredom. They are admonished for creating erotic images by their Italian priest, Father Bontempo; yet he longs for his own string game: warm spaghetti. Half-breed Cecil tempts Bontempo with a promise of pasta in exchange for the support of Cecil's commercial schemes. While gluttonously feasting, the priest chokes to death. The saddened Eskimos refuse to comply with Cecil's business venture and stoically return to their string games.

Istanboul dramatizes a cultural clash and *Homo* a class struggle. In *Istanboul* Norman men are fascinated by hirsute Byzantine women, and their wives by the smooth-skinned Byzantine men. In a religious frenzy St. Mary of Egypt murders the barbaric Norman, Godfrigh, and sensual Leo makes love to Godfrigh's wife as they wait for the Saracens to attack. *Homo* presents the mutual greed and contempt of Nordic and Asiatic. A surrealistic exploration of racial and class conflict the dramatic energy of the play in which revolution comes and goes, and workers continue their brutality.

Human perversion and bloody primitive rites prevail in Owens's most savage play, *Beclch*. In a fantasy Africa, four white adventurers intrude upon the natural innocence of a village. Queen Beclch, a monster of excess, professes her love for young Jose, then introduces him to the cruelty of cock-fighting. She promises Yago Kingship, if he will contract elephantiasis. When Yago cannot transcend the pain of his deformity, he is forced mercilessly by the villagers to strangle himself. Beclch moves further into excess, and Jose flees in disgust. Since a queen cannot rule without a male consort, Beclch prepares herself for death as voluptuously as she lived.

A promise of social progress resides in Owens's first play with music, *The Karl Marx Play*. As in *Homo*, linear time is ignored and through a montage of scenes, past and present, a human portrait of Marx emerges in this, Owens's most joyful play. Her Marx is drained by illness, poverty, and lust for his aristocratic wife. All those who surround him demand that he complete *Das Kapital*, particularly his friend Engels and a 20th-century American black, Leadbelly. Though Marx denies his Jewish heritage, he invokes Yahweh for consolation, but it is finally Leadbelly who actively ignites the man of destiny to fulfill his mission.

He Wants Shih! is an elegant poetic tragedy. Lan, son of the last Empress of the Manchu dynasty, abdicates the warlike legacy of his mother, ignores the adoring Princess Ling, loves his stepbrother Bok, and is enthralled with his stern mentor Feng. Steeped in Eastern philosophy and the supernatural, this surrealistic archetypal myth of individuation is dramatized with ritual, masks, and pseudo-Chinese dialect. The dismembered head of the Empress continues to speak on stage while Western imperialists decimate the Chinese. Acknowledging his homosexuality in the final scene, Lan-he transforms into Lanshe. Total renunciation of sex and empire ends this fantastic play.

As *He Wants Shih!* explores the quest for selfhood, *Kontraption* examines dehumanization in a technological world. On an empty terrain Abdul and Hortten share their lives and sexual fantasies. Abdul's intolerance of their repulsive laundryman, Strauss, drives him to murder, and he is in turn transformed by a magician into a mechanical contraption. When Abdul attempts to transcend his own grotesque condition he falls to his death, leaving behind a disconsolate Hortten.

Owens returns to historical biography in *Emma Instigated Me*. The life of Emma Goldman, the 19th-century anarchist, is juxtaposed against a contemporary Author, Director, and female revolutionaries. Once again linear time is dissolved. The characters change from one to another, from character into actor into bystander. The theatricality of the play becomes its most important objective.

Owens continues to experiment. *Chucky's Hunch* was acclaimed by New York critics as hilarious and impelling. In contrast to her multi-character dramas, the solitary Chucky, a middle-aged failure, narrates a series of recriminating letters to one of his three ex-wives. Similarly in *Who Do You Want, Peire Vidal?*, two characters assume multiple roles. In this play-within-a-play a Japanese-American professor is among the transformational characters in a series of episodic confrontations. Owens's fantastic imagery, charged language, and daring confrontation with subconscious impulse remains unique in American theatre.

—Elaine Shragge

OyamO.

Born Charles F. Gordon in Elyria, Ohio, 7 September 1943. Educated at Admiral King High School, Lorain, Ohio, graduated 1962; Miami University, Oxford, Ohio, 1963–65; studied journalism, U.S. Naval Reserve, 1966 (honorable discharge); New York University, 1967–68; theater lighting program, Brooklyn College, New York, 1968; Harlem Youth Speaks/First Light Video Institute, New York, 1974; College of New Rochelle, New York, B.A.

1979; Yale University School of Drama, New Haven, Connecticut, M.F.A. 1981. Assistant technical director, New Lafayette Theatre, 1967–69, assistant stage manager, American Place Theatre, 1970, founder, The Black Magicians, theatre company, 1970, and master electrician, Negro Ensemble Company, 1971, all New York; teacher in creative writing, Afro-American Cultural Center, Buffalo, New York, 1972, Street Theatre, Eastern Correctional Institute, Napanoch, New York, 1975–76, Afro-American Cultural Center, New Haven, Connecticut, 1978, and College of New Rochelle, New York, 1979–82; writer-in-residence, Emory University, Atlanta, Georgia, 1982–83, and Playwrights Center, Minneapolis, 1984; visiting lecturer, Playwrights Workshop, Princeton University, New Jersey, 1986–87. Adjunct associate professor in playwriting, 1989–90, and since 1990 associate professor, University of Michigan, Ann Arbor. Recipient: Rockefeller grant, 1972, 1983; New York State Council on the Arts fellowship, 1972, 1975, 1982, 1985; Guggenheim fellowship, 1973; Ohio Arts Council award, 1979; Yale University School of Drama Molly Kazan award, 1980; McKnight fellowship, 1984; National Endowment for the Arts fellowship, 1985, 1992. Address: 814 Stimson, Ann Arbor, Michigan 48103; or, 157 West 120th Street, No. 3, New York, New York 10027, U.S.A.

Publications

PLAYS

Chumpanzees (produced 1970).
The Negroes (produced 1970). In *Black Troupe Magazine*, vol.1, no.2, 1970.
Outta Site (produced 1970). In *Black Theatre Magazine*, vol.1, no.4, 1970.
The Thieves (produced 1970).
Willie Bignigga (produced 1970). In *Dramatika*, vol.3, no.1, 1970.
The Last Party (produced 1970).
The Lovers (also director: produced 1971).
The Advantage of Dope (produced 1971).
His First Step in *The Corner* (produced 1972). In *The New LaFayette Theatre Presents*, edited by Ed Bullins, 1974.
The Breakout (produced 1972). In *Black Drama: An Anthology*, edited by Woodie King and Ron Milner, 1972.
The Juice Problem (produced 1974).
Crazy Niggas (produced 1975).
A Star Is Born Again (for children) (produced 1978).
Mary Goldstein and the Author (produced 1979). 1989.
The Place of the Spirit Dance (produced 1980).
The Resurrection of Lady Lester (produced 1981). In *Plays U.S.A.: 1*, edited by James Leverett, 1981.
Distraughter and the Great Panda Scanda (musical; produced 1983).
Old Black Joe (produced 1984).
Every Moment (produced 1986).
The Temple of Youth (for children) (produced 1987).
Fried Chicken and Invisibility (produced 1988).
Singing Joy (produced 1988).
An Evening of Living Colors, music by Olu Dara (produced 1988).

The Stalwarts (produced 1988).
Return of the Been-To (produced 1988).
Let Me Live (produced 1991).
One Third of a Nation, adaptation of a play by Arthur Arent (produced 1991).
Famous Orpheus (produced 1991).
Angels in the Men's Room (produced 1992).
Sanctuary (sketches) (produced 1992).

OTHER
The Star That Could Not Play (for children). 1974.
Hillbilly Liberation (collection of plays and prose). 1976.

The dramas of OyamO are rarely confined by a realistic style. His works often juxtapose myth and reality and require actors to play multiple roles. His gift for the use of language evokes an intense emotional impact, while creating vivid visual images.

Although inspired by the life of Lester Young, the author does not profess his play, *The Resurrection of Lady Lester*, to be a docudrama of the famed saxophonist. Termed as a "poetic mood song," the lyrical quality of the dialogue provides one with impressions of the man and his music, instead of the cold facts which usually encumber bio-dramas. Although not featured in chronological order, scenes from the musician's life seem to flow seamlessly into one another as though streaming from Young's memory. Perhaps the most poignant of these scenes are those which illustrate his intimate professional and personal relationship with legendary singer Billie Holiday. In the end, the play manages not to be a lament for Young's tragic death, but celebrates the musician who plays his instrument from the depths of his soul.

Set in the early 1970s, *Fried Chicken and Invisibility* examines a former militant who believes he has found a scheme to obtain success in a racist American society. Traveling to a writer's conference by train, William Price and Winston McRutherford share rum and fried chicken, while discussing their experiences as African-Americans. Price, a strong-willed young man in his late 20s, recalls his turbulent youth in an impoverished neighborhood and his revolutionary activities during the 1960s. Reminiscent of the hero in Ralph Ellison's novel *The Invisible Man*, Price argues for invisibility as a strategy for survival. As long as he fits the ineffectual, stereotypical image whites have created for blacks, he believes whites will not see him as a threat and therefore target him for death. Price assumes the posture of a black revolutionary; by play's end, however, his true disposition is revealed. The young man tries to proposition McRutherford's wife who he mistakenly assumes is white, and the opinion of the whites at the writer's conference seems unduly important to him even though McRutherford informs him of its ineffectuality in furthering one's career. Thus, the drama indicts Price as a hypocritical man of few convictions unless in regard to his own self-interest.

Set in Atlanta in 1932, *Let Me Live* gives a moving portrayal of men caught in an unjust and cruel penitentiary system. The drama provides glimpses into the lives of eight African-American prisoners with scenes alternating between their current predicament and episodes revealed by memory. Mirroring prevailing socio-political conditions of the outside world, the penal system encourages the men to turn on each other for their basic needs or perversions. One recently imprisoned man, Angelo Herndon, struggles not to fall prey to the base intentions of his captors. An ardent communist jailed for organizing the disenfranchised, Herndon provides the other prisoners with the hope his socialist allies will provide the legal assistance needed to free them from their hellish existence. Drawing on his strong convictions as a source of inspiration, he refuses to despair when one of his cellmates dies from lack of medical attention or when the attorney sent to advise them proves unsympathetic and ineffectual. Attempting to break his spirit, a masochistic prison informant and enforcer—Shonuff—brutally rapes Herndon after intoxicating him with liquor. However, at play's end, when given the opportunity to deal his abuser a fatal blow, he chooses against the animalistic action. Although another prisoner decides to kill Shonuff, Herndon's personal stance against barbarism represents a tribute to those who refuse to relinquish their humanity under inhumane conditions.

Famous Orpheus is based on the mythological legend of the lovers Orpheus and Eurydice, and inspired by the film adaptation of the story, *Black Orpheus*. The poetic drama uses touches of humor to explore the connection between myth and reality. In Trinidad, an acting troupe of singing and dancing performers portrays the story guided by a "Calypsonian Griot." Orpheus—a famed guitarist—appears eager to marry his fiancée, Mariella, even though she does not share his passion for music. However, when collecting his newly made guitar, Orpheus falls desperately in love with the instrument maker's niece, Eurydice. During the revelry of Carnival, a mysterious figure representing death stalks Eurydice as he has done since she left her home in Tobago. When the figure reveals his presence to Eurydice, she runs for her life with the figure in pursuit. Orpheus gives chase as far as the wharf and tries in vain to fight the figure. Eurydice becomes entangled in an electric cable and falls to her death in the ocean. Obsessed with his love for Eurydice, Orpheus attempts to retrieve her from the Underworld. There he meets such mythological beings as Charon, Pluto, and Persephone. Ironically, these legendary figures speak in the rhythms and style of the Trinidadian people, sprinkling their dialogue with specific references to modern-day popular culture. Receiving his request to retrieve the dead Eurydice, Orpheus is allowed to return with her to the land of the living provided he does not look at her until they have left the Underworld. Unfortunately, Eurydice's feelings of neglect compel her to force Orpheus into looking at her, thus breaking his agreement. A heartbroken Orpheus returns to his own world, only to be killed by his jealously insane ex-fiancée.

—Addell Austin Anderson

P

PARKS, Suzan-Lori.

Educated at Mount Holyoke College, South Hadley, Massachusetts, B.A. in English and German literature (Phi Beta Kappa) 1985; the Drama studio, London, 1986. Guest lecturer, Pratt Institute, New York, 1988, University of Michigan, Ann Arbor, 1990, and Yale University, New Haven, Connecticut, and New York University, both 1990 and 1991; playwriting professor, Eugene Lang College, New York, 1990; writer-in-residence, New School for Social Research, New York, 1991–92. Recipient: Mary E. Woolley fellowship, 1989; Naomi Kitay fellowship, 1989; National Endowment for the Arts grant, 1990, and playwriting fellowship, 1990, 1991; New York Foundation for the Arts grant, 1990; Rockefeller Foundation grant, 1990; Obie award, 1990. Agent: Wiley Hausam, International Creative Management, 40 West 57th Street, New York, New York 10019, U.S.A.

Publications

PLAYS

The Sinner's Place (produced 1984).
Betting on the Dust Commander (produced 1987). 1990.
Imperceptible Mutabilities in the Third Kingdom (produced 1989).
Greeks (produced 1990).
The Death of the Last Black Man in the Whole Entire World (produced 1990). In *Theatre*, Summer/Fall 1990.
The America Play (produced 1991).
Devotees in the Garden of Love (produced 1991).

SCREENPLAY: *Anemone Me*, 1990.

RADIO PLAYS: *Pickling*, 1990; *The Third Kingdom*, 1990; *Locomotive*, 1991.

VIDEO: *Poetry Spots*, 1989; *Alive from Off Center*, 1991.

A playwright with the linguistic sensibilities of a Gertrude Stein or James Joyce, who recognizes that "the world is in the word" and attempts to stage that world following the example of Samuel Beckett; who eschews stage directions, citing the model of Shakespeare: "If you're writing the play—why not put the directions in the writing"; and who draws on her own experiences as an African-American woman living in a white, male culture but who denies

458

that her works are only about being black: "I don't want to be categorized in any way." This is Suzan-Lori Parks.

Parks sees her main task as writer to "Make words from world but set them on the page—setting them loose on the world." Others may employ neologisms, lexical transformations, phonetic shifts, spelling variations, and repetitions to further the plot and point to the theme. In Parks's plays language is the theme, and the omission of even a letter can change the direction of a play or the life of a people. "Before Columbus thuh worl usta be *roun* they put uh /d/ on thuh end of roun makin roun. Thusly they set in motion thuh end. Without that /d/ we coulda gone on spinnin for ever. Thuh /d/ think ended things ended" says Queen-then-Pharaoh Hatshepsut in *The Death of the Last Black Man in the Whole Entire World*. Fixed in place by an imposed language that defines them but is not their own, Parks's people—just as Joyce's and Beckett's—seek to get out from under the weight of words. "Talk right or you're outa here," Molly is told by her boss in *Imperceptible Mutabilities in the Third Kingdom*. A phoneme, the /sk/ in ask, defeats her as she struggles against a language—and a world—in which "Everything in its place."

Parks's first produced play is a tetraptych, whose title she carefully defines: *Imperceptible*: "That which by its nature cannot be perceived or discerned by the mind or the senses"; *Mutabilities*: "things disposed to change"; *in the Third Kingdom*: ". . . that of fungi. Small, overlooked, out of sight, of lesser consequence. All of that. And also: the space between." The four playlets— *Snails*, *Third Kingdom*, *Open House*, *Third Kingdom (reprise)*, and *Greeks* offer a composite picture of African-American experience, starting with contemporary time, moving backward to a mythic retelling of the black forced journey from Africa and concluding with two "family plays" depicting the terrible results of such displacement and estrangement from both language and self.

The absence of traditional narrative is counteracted by formal structures: all have five characters whose names either rhyme or are the same; *Snails*, is divided into six and *Open House*, and *Greeks* seven sections. Each makes use of slides and photographs offering an intertextual archival history. In each the angle of vision is, to invoke Beckett, "trine: centripetal, centrifugal and . . . not": the characters seen by white society, see themselves thus reflected but still struggle to see beyond the stereotype, the "not."

Snails describes three roommates, each wounded by words and each carrying two names: the one she chooses and the one by which she is known in the white community, names that "whuduhnt ours." They are visited by a robber who "didn't have no answer cause he didn't have no speech" and his opposite, a loquacious Naturalist named Lutsky, spouting the latest anthropological terminology, who comes to study the habits of the women, disguised as cockroach, the contemporary version of the fly on the wall, and who also doubles as the "exterminator" called to rid the women of the pest. Of the two it is Lutsky, Parks suggests, who is the true thief: he steals their voice by fixing them with his words the better to classify and study them.

Third Kingdom offers a melodic, mythic retelling of the black voyage from Africa to America, chanted by characters whose names range from Kin-Seer, Us-Seer, Shark-Seer, Soul-seer, to Over-seer. A refrain opens the section and punctuates the piece and the reprise: "Last night I dreamed of where I comed from. But where I comed from diduhnt look like nowhere like I been." The speakers evoke images of a lost home, of a voyage, and of the boat that carried them. While Shark-Seer denies their collective experience, "But we are not in uh boat!" Us-Seer insists, "But we iz."

Open House is a composite black/white family portrait in which Aretha Saxon, a black servant/surrogate mother to a white girl and boy is being "let go because she's gone slack." But before she leaves/expires she is subjected to "an extraction" in which her teeth are tortuously yanked from her mouth by the efficient Miss Faith, who records in the process the parallel extraction/eradication of African-American history from white memory.

Parks's last play, *Greeks*, is her most powerful. The modern retelling of the Odysseus legend, focuses on the Smith family—Sergeant, Mrs. Sergeant, Buffy, Muffy, and Duffy—the mother and children awaiting the return of the father who will bring with him "his Distinction" won by faithfully serving his country in the white man's army. While they make periodic visits to "see their maker" each furlough followed by the birth of a child, and Mrs. Smith takes pride in her own mark of distinction—looking as if "You ain't traveled a mile nor sweated a drop"—Sergeant Smith waits in vain, returning finally in old age, like Odysseus, to a family that barely recognizes him. Legless, broken, he helplessly explains his dream: "Always wanted to do me somethin noble. . . . Like what they did in thuh olden days." The only glory open to him, however, is to break the fall of "that boy fallin out thuh sky. . . . I saved his life. I aint seen him since." This section ends where the first play began: the character recognizing the position of blacks in America: "we'se slugs."

The Death of the Last Black Man in the Whole Entire World is even more experimental and language-centered: a series of poetic phrases or melodious riffs depicting the life and times of Parks's composite African-American couple—Black Man with Watermelon and Black Woman with Fried Drumstick—surrounded by characters with names evoking black soul food—Lots of Grease and Lots of Pork—literary figures—And Bigger and Bigger and Bigger (after Richard Wright), and ancient times—Queen-then-Pharaoh Hatshepsut.

Beginning with the line, "The Black man moves his hands," Parks takes her people on a linguistic voyage back through African-American experience, historic and literary, animating her characters as she plays with a set of phrases and transformations, concluding with "Thuh black man he move. He move. He hans," words carved on a rock to be remembered: "because if you dont write it down we will come along and tell the future that we did not exist." Unlike the earlier play, the characters laugh at the end, having thrown off and stomped on the controlling "/d/."

Again strict form undergirds the work. The title is repeated nine times through the seven sections of the play, the first six times ending in "world," the last three "worl," allowing the Black Man to go from a fixed figure in a borrowed language to a self-animated speaker. The commensurate female experience moves from provider of chicken to supporter and encourager. Her words end the play.

Parks's work is audacious, upending traditional dramaturgy and replacing action with language shifts. Building on the earlier experiments of Ntozake

Shange and Adrienne Kennedy, Parks moves even further, creating a theatre of poetry, in which the very power of language is reaffirmed by showing its potential to stand as subject and theme.

—Linda Ben-Zvi

PATRICK, John.

Born John Patrick Goggan in Louisville, Kentucky, 17 May 1905. Educated at Holy Cross School, New Orleans; St. Edward's School, Austin, Texas; St. Mary's Seminary, LaPorte, Texas. Served in the American Field Service in India and Burma, 1942–44: captain. Radio writer, NBC, San Francisco, 1933–36; freelance writer, Hollywood, 1936–38. Recipient: Pulitzer prize, 1954; New York Drama Critics Circle award, 1954; Tony award, 1954; Donaldson award, 1954; Foreign Correspondents award, 1957; Screen Writers Guild award, 1957; William Inge award for lifetime achievement in theater, 1986. D.F.A.: Baldwin Wallace College, Berea, Ohio, 1972. Address: 22801 Wilderness Way, Boca Raton, Florida 33428, U.S.A.

Publications

PLAYS

Hell Freezes Over (produced 1935).
The Willow and I (produced 1942). 1943.
The Hasty Heart (produced 1945). 1945.
The Story of Mary Surratt (produced 1947). 1947.
The Curious Savage (produced 1950). 1951.
Lo and Behold! (produced 1951). 1952.
The Teahouse of the August Moon, adaptation of a novel by Vern Sneider (produced 1953). 1954; revised version as *Lovely Ladies, Kind Gentlemen,* music and lyrics by Stan Freeman and Franklin Underwood (produced 1970), 1970.
Good as Gold, adaptation of a novel by Alfred Toombs (produced 1957).
Juniper and the Pagans, with James Norman (produced 1959).
Everybody Loves Opal (produced 1961). 1962.
It's Been Wonderful (produced 1966). 1976.
Everybody's Girl (produced 1967). 1968.
Scandal Point (produced 1967). 1969.
Love Is a Time of Day (produced 1969). 1970.
A Barrel Full of Pennies (produced 1970). 1971.
Opal Is a Diamond (produced 1971). 1972.
Macbeth Did It (produced 1972). 1972.
The Dancing Mice (produced 1972). 1972.
The Savage Dilemma (produced 1972). 1972.
Anybody Out There? 1972.
Roman Conquest (produced 1973). 1973.
The Enigma (produced 1973). 1974.
Opal's Baby: A New Sequel (produced 1973). 1974.
Sex on the Sixth Floor: Three One Act Plays (includes *Tenacity, Ambiguity, Frustration*). 1974.

Love Nest for Three. 1974.
A Bad Year for Tomatoes (produced 1974). 1975.
Opal's Husband (produced 1975). 1975.
Noah's Animals: A Musical Allegory (produced 1975). 1976.
Divorce, Anyone? (produced 1975). 1976.
Suicide, Anyone? (produced 1976). 1976.
People! Three One Act Plays: Boredom, Christmas Spirit, Aptitude (produced 1976). 1980.
That's Not My Father! Three One Act Plays: Raconteur, Fettucine, Masquerade (produced 1979). 1980.
That's Not My Mother: Three One Act Plays: Seniority, Redemption, Optimism (produced 1979). 1980.
Opal's Million Dollar Duck (produced 1979). 1980.
The Girls of the Garden Club (produced 1979). 1980.
The Magenta Moth. 1983.
It's a Dog's Life (includes *The Gift, Co-Incidence, The Divorce*). 1984.
Danny and the Deep Blue Sea (produced 1984).
The Reluctant Rogue, or, Mother's Day. 1984.
Cheating Cheaters. 1985.
The Gay Deceiver. 1988.
The Doctor Will See You Now. 1991.

SCREENPLAYS: *Educating Father*, with Katharine Kavanaugh and Edward T. Lowe, 1936; *36 Hours to Live*, with Lou Breslow, 1936; *15 Maiden Lane*, with others, 1936; *High Tension*, with others, 1936; *Midnight Taxi*, with Lou Breslow, 1937; *Dangerously Yours*, with Lou Breslow, 1937; *The Holy Terror*, with Lou Breslow, 1937; *Sing and Be Happy*, with Lou Breslow and Ben Markson, 1937; *Look Out, Mr. Moto*, with others, 1937; *Time Out for Romance*, with others, 1937; *Born Reckless*, with others, 1937; *One Mile from Heaven*, with others, 1937; *Big Town Girl*, with others, 1937; *Battle of Broadway*, with Lou Breslow and Norman Houston, 1938; *Five of a Kind*, with Lou Breslow, 1938; *Up the River*, with Lou Breslow and Maurine Watkins, 1938; *International Settlement*, with others, 1938; *Mr. Moto Takes a Chance*, with others, 1938; *Enchantment*, 1948; *The President's Lady*, 1953; *Three Coins in the Fountain*, 1954; *Love Is a Many-Splendored Thing*, 1955; *High Society*, 1956; *The Teahouse of the August Moon*, 1956; *Les Girls*, with Vera Caspary, 1957; *Some Came Running*, with Arthur Sheekman, 1958; *The World of Susie Wong*, 1960; *The Main Attraction*, 1962; *Gigot*, with Jackie Gleason, 1962; *The Shoes of the Fisherman*, with James Kennaway, 1968.

RADIO PLAYS: *Cecil and Sally* series (1100 scripts), 1929–33.

TELEVISION PLAY: *The Small Miracle*, with Arthur Dales, from the novel by Paul Gallico, 1972.

VERSE
Sense and Nonsense. 1989.

MANUSCRIPT COLLECTION: Boston University.

John Patrick began his career as an NBC script writer who became noted for radio dramatizations of novels. He first reached Broadway in 1935 with *Hell Freezes Over*, an unsuccessful and short-lived melodrama concerning polar explorers whose dirigible crash-lands in Antarctica. Patrick continued writing, primarily Hollywood film scripts. His next play, also unsuccessful, was *The Willow and I*, a forced but sensitively written psychological drama about two sisters competing for the love of the same man and destroying each other in the struggle.

During World War II Patrick served as an ambulance driver with the British Army in North Africa, Syria, India, and Burma. His experience furnished the background for *The Hasty Heart*. Set in a military hospital behind the Assam-Burma front, the action centers on a dour Scottish sergeant sent to the convalescent ward unaware that a fatal illness condemns him to early death. His wardmates, knowing the prognosis, extend their friendship. But the Scot's suspicious nature and uncompromising independence nearly wrecks their good intentions. He gradually warms to his companions until he discovers his fatal condition and concludes that their proffered fellowship is merely pity. Ultimately he comes to accept his wardmates' goodwill, poignantly demonstrating Patrick's premise: "the importance of man's acknowledgement of his interdependency." Although some critics doubted that the stubbornly misanthropic protagonist could be capable of change, the majority found the play's effect credible and warming. It enjoyed a substantial run before being made into a motion picture, and evinced its author's growth as a dramatist in dealing more incisively with plot structure, characterization, and the effect of inner states of mind on conduct and character.

Patrick's next three plays failed to win popular approval. Based on historical events, *The Story of Mary Surratt* depicts the trial and conviction of the Washington landlady sentenced to the gallows by a vindictive military tribunal for complicity in the assassination of Abraham Lincoln. Patrick's view was that Mrs. Surratt, whose misguided son had become involved in Booth's plot, was an innocent victim of 1865 postwar hysteria. Although the drama was a compassionate protest against injustice and the vengeful concept of war guilt, playgoers did not want to be reminded of a probable miscarriage of justice in their own history at a time when war crime trials were a present reality. Critical opinion was divided, and the production failed. The drama, despite some turgidity of dialogue and the minor portrait of its title character, still emerges as a substantial work which deserved a better fate.

Patrick turned to comedy in *The Curious Savage*. The story focuses on a charmingly eccentric wealthy widow, insistent on spending her millions on a foundation financing people's daydreams, whose mendacious stepchildren commit her to a sanatorium where she finds her fellow inmates more attractive than her own sane but greedy family; with the help of the former she outwits the latter. While admitting the play's affectionate humor, critics fairly faulted the author for treating his rational "villains" too stridently and his irrational characters too romantically. Although it had only a brief run on Broadway, *The Curious Savage* has been popular with regional theatres. A sequel, *The Savage Dilemma*, was published in 1972, but not presented in New York.

Other comedies followed. *Lo and Behold!* introduces a rich, solitude-loving writer who dies, having stipulated in his will that his house be kept vacant as a sanctuary for his spirit, and returns in ghostly form to find the premises occupied by three incompatible ghosts whom he untimately persuades to leave after all join forces to resolve a stormy courtship between a lingering house-maid and the estate's executor.

In 1953 Patrick achieved a Broadway triumph with *The Teahouse of the August Moon*, based on a novel by Vern Sneider. The play is a satire on the American Army of Occupation's attempts following World War II to bring democracy to the people of Okinawa. Amidst amusing clashes of mores and traditions, a young colonel with a past record of failure abandons standard Occupation procedure, builds the teahouse the villagers have longed for rather than a school-house, and a distillery producing a local brandy which brings them prosperity. His obtuse commanding officer visits the village and hotly orders an end to such unorthodox practices but is overridden by a Congressional declaration that the colonel's methods are the most progressive in Okinawa. Critic John Mason Brown accurately commented that "no plea for tolerance between peoples, no editorial against superimposing American customs on native tradition has ever been less didactic or more persuasive." The comedy captivated audiences and critics alike to become one of America's most successful plays, winning both the Pulitzer Prize and a New York Critics Circle award. Patrick rewrote it as a screenplay and later as a short-lived musical called *Lovely Ladies, Kind Gentlemen*.

Other comedies by Patrick include *Good as Gold* and *Everybody Loves Opal*. The former, a dramatization of a novel by Alfred Toombs, concentrates on a botanist who discovers a formula for changing gold into soil that will grow enormous vegetables but who cannot persuade Congress to give him the contents of Fort Knox. This farcical satire on politics constructed on one joke failed to find support. The title character of *Everybody Loves Opal* is a kindly recluse, living in a dilapidated mansion, who reforms three intruding petty crooks with her faith in the goodness of man. The comedy's fun was inter-mittent and its run short. Patrick has written several sequels.

Several other Patrick plays, mostly comedies, have been published, but not produced on Broadway. Patrick is a prolific writer of radio, film, and play scripts, but his reputation as a major craftsman in the American theatre rests chiefly on *The Teahouse of the August Moon*, one of the most successful American comedies.

—Christian H. Moe

PATRICK, Robert
(Robert Patrick O'Connor).

Born in Kilgore, Texas, 27 September 1937. Educated at Eastern New Mexico University, Portales, three years. Host, La Mama, 1965, secretary to Ruth Yorck, 1965, and doorman, Caffe Cino, 1966–68, all New York; features editor and contributor, *Astrology Magazine*, New York, 1971–72; columnist, *Other Stages*, New York, 1979–81. Artist-in-residence, Jean Cocteau Repertory Theater, New York, 1984. Recipient: *Show Business* award, 1969; Rockefeller grant, 1973; Creative Artists Public Service grant, 1976;

International Thespians Society award, 1980; Janus award, 1983. Address: 2848 Wathen, Atwater, California 95301, U.S.A.

Publications

PLAYS

The Haunted Host (produced 1964). In *Robert Patrick's Cheep Theatricks!*, 1972; in *Homosexual Acts,* 1976.

Mirage (produced 1965). In *One Man, One Woman,* 1978.

Sketches (produced 1966).

The Sleeping Bag (produced 1966).

Halloween Hermit (produced 1966).

Indecent Exposure (produced 1966).

Cheesecake (produced 1966). In *One Man, One Woman,* 1978.

Lights, Camera, Action (includes *Lights, Camera Obscura, Action*) (produced 1966; in *My Dear It Doesn't Mean a Thing,* produced 1976). In *Robert Patrick's Cheep Theatricks!,* 1972.

Warhol Machine (produced 1967).

Still-Love (produced 1968). In *Robert Patrick's Cheep Theatricks!,* 1972.

Cornered (produced 1968). In *Robert Patrick's Cheep Theatricks!,* 1972.

Un Bel Di (produced 1968). In *Performance,* 1972.

Help, I Am (produced 1968). In *Robert Patrick's Cheep Theatricks!,* 1972.

See Other Side (produced 1968). In *Yale/Theatre,* 1969.

Absolute Power over Movie Stars (produced 1968).

Preggin and Liss (produced 1968). In *Robert Patrick's Cheep Theatricks!,* 1972.

The Overseers (produced 1968).

Angels in Agony (produced 1968).

Salvation Army (produced 1968).

Joyce Dynel: An American Zarzuela (as *Dynel,* produced 1968; revised version, as *Joyce Dynel,* produced 1969). In *Robert Patrick's Cheep Theatricks!,* 1972.

Fog (produced 1969). In *G.P.U. News,* 1980.

The Young of Aquarius (produced 1969).

I Came to New York to Write (produced 1969). In *Robert Patrick's Cheep Theatricks!,* 1972.

Oooooooops! (produced 1969).

Lily of the Valley of the Dolls (produced 1969).

One Person: A Monologue (produced 1969). In *Robert Patrick's Cheep Theatricks!,* 1972.

Silver Skies (produced 1969).

Tarquin Truthbeauty (produced 1969).

Presenting Arnold Bliss (produced 1969; in *The Arnold Bliss Show,* produced 1972).

The Actor and the Invader (in *Kinetic Karma,* produced 1969; in *The Arnold Bliss Show,* 1972).

Hymen and Carbuncle (produced 1970). In *Mercy Drop and Other Plays,* 1979.

A Bad Place to Get Your Head (produced 1970).

Bead-Tangle (includes *La Répétition*) (produced 1970).

Sketches and Songs (produced 1970).

I Am Trying to Tell You Something (produced 1970).

Angel, Honey, Baby, Darling, Dear (produced 1970).

The Golden Animal (produced 1970).

Picture Wire (produced 1970).

The Richest Girl in the World Finds Happiness (produced 1970). In *Robert Patrick's Cheep Theatricks!*, 1972.

A Christmas Carol (produced 1971).

Shelter (produced 1971).

The Golden Circle (produced 1972). 1977(?).

Ludwig and Wagner (produced 1972). In *Mercy Drop and Other Plays*, 1979.

Youth Rebellion (produced 1972).

Songs (produced 1972).

Robert Patrick's Cheep Theatricks!, edited by Michael Feingold. 1972.

The Arnold Bliss Show (includes *Presenting Arnold Bliss, The Actor and the Invader, La Répétition, Arnold's Big Break*) (produced 1972). In *Robert Patrick's Cheep Theatricks!*, 1972.

Play-by-Play (also director: produced 1972; revised version produced 1975). 1975.

Something Else (produced 1973; in *My Dear It Doesn't Mean a Thing*, produced 1976). In *One Man, One Woman*, 1978.

Cleaning House (produced 1973). In *One Man, One Woman*, 1978.

The Track of the Narwhal (produced 1973).

Judas (produced 1973). In *West Coast Plays 5*, Fall 1979.

Mercy Drop; or, Marvin Loves Johnny (produced 1973). In *Mercy Drop and Other Plays*, 1980.

The Twisted Root (produced 1973).

Simultaneous Transmissions (produced 1973). In *The Scene/2 (Plays from Off-Off-Broadway)*, edited by Stanley Nelson, 1974.

Hippy as a Lark (produced 1973).

Imp-Prisonment (produced 1973).

Kennedy's Children (produced 1973). 1975.

Love Lace (produced 1974). In *One Man, One Woman*, 1978.

How I Came to Be Here Tonight (produced 1974).

Orpheus and Amerika, music by Rob Felstein (produced 1974).

Fred and Harold, and One Person (produced 1975). In *Homosexual Acts*, 1976.

My Dear It Doesn't Mean a Thing (includes *Lights, Camera Obscura, Action, Something Else*) (produced 1976).

Report to the Mayor (produced 1977).

Dr. Paroo (produced 1981). In *Dramatics*, 1977.

My Cup Ranneth Over (produced 1978). 1979.

Mutual Benefit Life (produced 1978). 1979.

T-Shirts (produced 1978). In *Gay Plays*, edited by William M. Hoffman, 1979.

One Man, One Woman (produced 1979). 1978.

Bank Street Breakfast (produced 1979). In *One Man, One Woman*, 1978.

Communication Gap (produced 1979; as *All in Your Mind*, produced 1981).

The Family Bar (produced 1979). In *Mercy Drop and Other Plays*, 1979.

Mercy Drop and Other Plays (includes *The Family Bar* and *The Loves of the Artists: Ludwig and Wagner, Diaghilev and Nijinsky*, and *Hymen and Carbuncle*). 1979.

Diaghilev and Nijinsky (produced 1981). In *Mercy Drop and Other Plays*, 1979.

Sane Scientist (produced 1981).

Michelangelo's Models (produced 1981). 1983.

24 Inches, music by David Tice, lyrics by Patrick (produced 1982).

The Spinning Tree (produced 1982).

They Really Love Roba (produced 1982).

Sit-Com (produced 1982). In *Blueboy*, June 1982.

Willpower, in *Curtain*, May 1982.

Blue Is for Boys (produced 1983).

Nice Girl (produced 1983).

Beaux-Arts Ball (produced 1983).

The Comeback (produced 1983).

The Holy Hooker (produced 1983).

50's 60's 70's 80's (produced 1984).

Big Sweet, music by LeRoy Dysart (produced 1984). In *Dramatics*, 1984.

That Lovable Laughable Auntie Matter in "Disgustin' Space Lizards" (produced 1985).

Bread Alone (produced 1985).

No Trojan Women, music by Catherine Stornetta (produced 1985).

Left Out (produced 1985). In *Dramatics*, 1985.

The Hostages (produced 1985).

The Trial of Socrates (produced 1986).

Bill Batchelor Road (produced 1986).

On Stage (produced 1986).

Why Are They Like That? (produced 1986).

Desert Waste (produced 1986).

La Balance (produced 1986).

Pouf Positive (produced 1986). In *Out/Write*, 1988.

Lust (produced 1986).

Drowned Out (produced 1986). In *One-Acts for High Schools*, 1986.

The Last Stroke (produced 1987).

Explanation of a Xmas Wedding (produced 1987).

Let Me Not Mar That Perfect Dream (produced 1988). In *The James White Review*, 1987.

Untold Decades (produced 1988). 1988.

The Trojan Women (produced 1988).

Hello, Bob (produced 1990). In *Stages*, 1991.

Evan on Earth (produced 1991).

United States (produced 1991).

Interruptions (produced 1992).

Screenplays: *The Haunted Host*, 1969; *The Credit Game*, 1972.

Manuscript collection: Lincoln Center Library of the Performing Arts, New York.

THEATRICAL ACTIVITIES

DIRECTOR: Plays—*Wonderful, Wonderful* by Douglas Kahn, and excerpt from *The Approach* by Jean Reavey, 1965; artistic director of *Bb Aa Nn Gg!!!*, 1965; created Comic Book Shows at the Caffe Cino, New York, 1966; assistant director to Tom O'Horgan and Jerome Savary, Brandeis University, Waltham, Massachusetts, 1968; originated *Dracula*, 1968; reopened *Bowery Follies*, 1972; *Silver Queen* by Paul Foster, 1973; directed many of his own plays.

ACTOR: Plays—at Caffe Cino, La Mama, and Old Reliable in his own plays and plays by Powell Shepherd, Soren Agenoux, John Hartnett, Stuart Koch, H.M. Koutoukas, and William M. Hoffman.

Robert Patrick comments:

(1973) My plays are dances with words. The words are music for the actors to dance to. They also serve many other purposes, but primarily they give the actors images and rhythms to create visual expressions of the play's essential relationships. The ideal production of one of my plays would be completely understandable even without sound, like a silent movie. Most of my plays are written to be done with a minimum of scenery, although I have done some fairly lavish productions of them. My plays fall into three general classes: 1) simple histories, like *I Came to New York to Write*; 2) surrealistic metaphors, like *The Arnold Bliss Show, Lights, Camera, Action*, and *Joyce Dynel*, and 3) romances, like *Fog, Female Flower* (unproduced), and both *The Golden Animal* and *The Golden Circle*. Basically, I believe the importance of a play to be this: a play is an experience the audience has together; it is stylized to aid in perception and understanding; and, above all, it is done by live players, and it is traced in its minutest particulars, so that it can serve as a warning (if it is a tragedy or comedy) or as a good example. Nothing must be left out or it becomes merely ritual. The time of the ritual is over. The essential experience must replace it.

Robert Patrick's conception of theatrical form and purpose was molded at the Caffe Cino. He had been working there at odd jobs in the early 1960s and, influenced by Joe Cino's creative energy along with playwrights like Lanford Wilson, Paul Foster, David Starkweather, and the entire Cino gang, he wrote his first play, *The Haunted Host*. In fact, he got his name with that production in a typical Cino haphazard manner. Marshall Mason (later artistic director of Circle Repertory Company and chief interpreter of Lanford Wilson's dramas) was rushing out to get *The Haunted Host* programs printed. Patrick, who was acting in his own show, asked that Mason break up his name and list Robert Patrick and Bob O'Connor, one for playwright and the other for actor, because he didn't want people concentrating on the fact that the playwright and actor were the same person. When Mr. Mason came back with the program, Robert Patrick O'Connor was known as Robert Patrick, playwright.

The Cino was a place in which theatrical rules did not exist. Experimentation with form and content was common, and wits-only, wing-it living was the norm. Although when the Cino closed it was shrouded in tragedy, for most of its years the key word there was fun. Entertainment was the only guideline anyone followed, and this free-wheeling, fun-obsessed lifestyle turned a naive young Texan named Bob O'Connor into the most prolific playwright of his generation. As he says of the off-off-Broadway movement which began, in part, at the Cino, "For the first time a theatre movement began, of any scope or duration, in which theatre was considered the equal of the other arts in creativity and responsibility; never before had theatre existed free of academic, commercial, critical, religious, military, and political restraints. For the first time, a playwright wrote from himself, not attempting to tease money, reputation, or licences from an outside authority."

To analyze the numerous plays Patrick has written and produced since 1964 on a script by script basis would be to miss the profound contribution of the overall body of his work. His genius stems not from some artfully crafted style or from deep, intellectual questioning, but rather from an uncanny ability to record and reflect the world around him. *Kennedy's Children*, his best known play, captures the mood of an entire era, and serves as a mirror of morals for a lost decade.

In *Kennedy's Children* the characters, all of whom we now recognize as 1960s stereotypes, sit separately in a bar. We're presented with their interior monologues. The alienation, the loneliness, and the confusion that were so apparent in America's youth throughout the tumultuous years of Vietnam are so accurately portrayed in *Kennedy's Children* that it is difficult to imagine a more perfect example of the crumbling American dream post-Vietnam.

To read Patrick for clues to a specific style is to get trapped. For most of his career, his style has been unique only in its absence, a fact which often drives his critics to despair. It could only be described, perhaps, as Cinoese, or off-off-Broadway eclectic. As he continues to write, he appears to be coalescing his vast mental resources into a genuine effort to produce works which deal with an unchanging human condition. The classical themes of love, greed, pride, and tormented self-doubt abound in all his plays, but never as obviously mirrored as in his most current works. In fact, he now says he is striving to write "classical Greek drama." If his style is elusive, his subject certainly is not. Patrick is pure romantic and in play after play writes primarily about relationships and heterosexual marriage. In recent years he has become known as a gay playwright and, although he is currently using gay themes again, in fact most of his "gay" plays are early works which have been re-discovered in the current rage for gay theatre. Although *Michelangelo's Models* is about how a man and a boy do get together, theirs is a basically traditional relationship, and this play, too, is about how people do or do not form unions. It is this general appeal to the traditional which gives his plays not only an international popularity, but which also accounts for his enormous effect on high school audiences. Young people are drawn to him as to a pied piper and it is to them that he is most expressive about the great excitement the art of theater can generate. He travels extensively to high schools across the country encouraging students to write for and/or to become involved with theater.

Aside from stating the obvious, that his story is the subject of his play, like apples are the subjects of a Cézanne painting, and that his stories are about couples getting together or not getting together and about how society affects a relationship, there is no generalizing about a Patrick play. From the stark classic tragedy of *Judas* to the innovative oratorio of an age, *Kennedy's Children*, to the retrograde Renaissance fantasia of *Michelangelo's Models*, he has been a man in love with playwriting. He has improvised full-scale musicals in four days (*Joyce Dynel* and *A Christmas Carol*), provided occasional entertainments (*The Richest Girl in the World Finds Happiness*, *Play-by-Play*, *Halloween Hermit*), whipped out formal experiments (*Lights, Camera, Action*; *Love Lace*; *Something Else*), manufactured commercial successes (*My Cup Ranneth Over*, *Mutual Benefit Life*), helped the developing gay theatre (*Mercy Drop*, *T-Shirts*, *The Haunted Host*), and piled up eccentricities (*The Golden Animal*, *Lily of the Valley of the Dolls* and the unproduced *Female Flower*). His first collection, *Robert Patrick's Cheep Theatricks!*, was only an arbitrary gleaning of the 150 works he had accumulated by 1972; his second, *One Man, One Woman*, ranged from 1964 to 1979; his third, *Mercy Drop and Other Plays*, from 1965 through 1980. Many works are still unpublished and unproduced.

Patrick believes that words are music for the actors to dance to, and that rhythms have to help the actors build up emotions. He is very conscious of vocabulary and of how words give the actors images to act out, tell an audience story facts and plot facts or jokes or bits of poetry. In *Michelangelo's Models* Ignudo, the peasant boy who wants to marry Michelangelo, talks in Okie dialect. And Michelangelo's speech varies between the formal patterns of the other characters and the slang that unites him to Ignudo. Patrick's fascination with words sometimes gets him tangled in verbiage, but it creates a type of security blanket for this off-off-Broadway baby. Playwrights who regularly work off-off-Broadway never know if they're going to have sets, lights, music, or anything, so writing for a bare floor and some actors is a form of artistic self-preservation. Then, if you can get lights and background music to set the mood it's all the better. If Patrick is sometimes overly expository it can be traced directly to the Caffe Cino where the lights sometimes went out and action had to be described to an audience in the dark.

—Leah D. Frank

PIELMEIER, John.

Born in Altoona, Pennsylvania, 23 February 1949. Educated at Catholic University, Washington, D.C., 1966–70, B.A. (summa cum laude) in speech and drama 1970 (Phil Beta Kappa); Pennsylvania State University, University Park (Shubert Fellow), 1970–73, M.F.A. in playwriting 1978. Married Irene O'Brien in 1982. Actor, 1973–82: numerous roles in regional theatres, including Actors Theatre of Louisville, Guthrie Theatre, Minneapolis, Alaska Repertory Theatre, Anchorage, Center Stage, Baltimore, and Eugene O'Neill Playwrights Conference, Waterford, Connecticut. Recipient: National Endowment for the Arts grant, 1982; Christopher award, for television play, 1984; Humanitas award, for television play, 1984. D.H.L.: St. Edward's University, Austin, Texas, 1984. Agent: Jeannine Edmunds, Artists Agency, 230 West 55th Street, Suite 17–D, New York, New York 10019. Address: R.R.1, Box 108, Horton Road, Cold Spring, New York 10516, U.S.A.

Publications

PLAYS

Soledad Brother (produced 1971).
A Chosen Room (produced 1976).
Agnes of God (produced 1980). 1985.
Jass (produced 1980).
Chapter Twelve: The Frog (produced 1981).
Courage (produced 1983).
Cheek to Cheek (produced 1983).
A Gothic Tale (also director: produced 1983). In *Haunted Lives*, 1984.
Haunted Lives (includes *A Witch's Brew*, *A Ghost Story*, *A Gothic Tale*) (produced 1986). 1984.
The Boys of Winter (produced 1985).
Evening (produced 1986).
In Mortality (produced 1986).
Sleight of Hand (produced 1987).
The Classics Professor (produced 1988).
Steeple Chase (produced 1989).
Impassioned Embraces (produced 1993). 1989.
Willi, music by Matthew Selman (produced 1991).
Young Rube, music and lyrics by Matthew Selman (produced 1992).

SCREENPLAY: *Agnes of God*, 1985.

TELEVISION PLAY: *Choices of the Heart*, 1983.

THEATRICAL ACTIVITIES

DIRECTOR: **Play**—*A Gothic Tale*, 1983.
ACTOR: **Plays**—Jasmine in *Memphis Is Gone* by Dick Hobson, 1975; Tommy in *Female Transport* by Steve Gooch, Lymon in *Ballad of the Sad Café* by Edward Albee, and Boy in *Welcome to Andromeda* by Ron Whyte, 1975; Junior in *Waterman* by Frank B. Ford, Billy in *The Collected Works of Billy the Kid* by Michael Ondaatje, Burnaby in *The Matchmaker* by Thornton Wilder, and Kid in *Cold* by Michael Casale, 1976; Dorcas in *Gazelle Boy* by Ronald Tavel, and Dennis in *Scooter Thomas Makes It to the Top of the World* by Peter Parnell, 1977; roles in *Holidays*, and Mark in *The Shadow Box* by Michael Cristofer, 1979, Mark Levine in *Today a Little Extra* by Michael Kassin, 1980; role in *The Front Page* by Ben Hecht and Charles MacArthur, 1980; Lysander in *A Midsummer Night's Dream*, 1981; and numerous other roles.

John Pielmeier comments:

I consider myself primarily a writer for actors, and then a theatrical storyteller. I am fascinated with music and the myths of history, though *Agnes of God* is an exception to the latter. Some of my best work (*Jass* and *The Boys of Winter*) illustrates this fascination clearly. I consider writing a collaborative effort with actors and audience, and a play is never finished until it is on its feet for several weeks or for several productions. J.M. Barrie and Thornton Wilder are the playwrights closest to my heart—so in the end I suppose I am something of a theatrical romantic.

The playwright and actor John Pielmeier is indebted to regional theatre, where much of his work has been developed and presented. National attention was achieved with *Agnes of God*, whose successful Broadway engagement was preceded by nine regional productions. The drama's concern with the conflict between the real and the imagined, the rational and the irrational, is one constantly catching Pielmeier's interest.

In the published play's introduction, Pielmeier confesses that *Agnes of God* sprang from his questioning concern as a lapsed Catholic with the possibility of saints and miracles today, augmented by an evocative headline about a nunnery infanticide. The drama's circumstances are that a stigmatic and emotionally disturbed young nun, who as a child was abused by a sadistic mother, gives birth in her convent to a child later found strangled in a wastepaper basket. The saintly nun Agnes (from Latin "lamb"), who hears divine voices, claims to remember nothing about the child's conception, birth, or death. A court psychiatrist, a lapsed Catholic woman harboring a grudge against nuns, is sent to discover whether Agnes is sufficiently sane to stand trial for manslaughter. Proceeding as a narrator and detective-like investigator, the anticlerical doctor becomes absorbed with Agnes, beginning to question her own pragmatic values in the face of the situation's supernatural overtones. The overt conflict arises between the doctor and the convent's Mother Superior, later revealed to be Agnes's aunt, who is protective of Agnes and believes in the possibility of a parthenogenetic miracle. At the investigation's climax, Sister Agnes re-enacts under hypnosis the child's conception, still leaving unanswered the question of divine or human fatherhood. Yet the psychiatrist's anguished self-questioning emerges as the central issue. Unavoidable is a comparison to Peter Shaffer's *Equus*, whose plot is similar and which is more successful in the depth of its protagonist physician and in the examination of the questions raised. Nonetheless, Pielmeier has written a theatrically powerful play whose well-orchestrated female characters and strong dramatic climaxes provide an exciting theatre experience. The question of faith and miracles initially posed, while understandably not answered, tends to become obscured by the psychological issues triggering the second act's revelations erupting after an exposition-laden first act. The play stimulates the emotions but leaves the intellect confused. Pielmeier also wrote the screen version of the play.

The enigmatic dichotomy of the natural and unnatural interconnects three three-character one-acts collectively titled *Haunted Lives*. In the least effective but still eerie *A Witch's Brew*, a brother engages his doubting sister and her boyfriend in a grisly childhood game (pretending objects passed around in darkness are human body parts) in a semi-dark farmhouse basement where he claims his mother murdered and buried his long-absent father. The brother has played the game in earnest. *A Ghost Story*, a more successfully developed piece, presents two hiking strangers seeking shelter from a wintry blizzard in an isolated Maine cabin where they are joined by a mysterious girl who participates in telling frightening stories, one involving the throat-cutting of hikers by an unknown murderer. One hiker, once his companions fall asleep, tells the audience of a recurring dream, realized at the play's conclusion, in which his dead sister appears and cuts the throat of a hiker whom she first seduces. In *A Gothic Tale*, the final and most chilling tale, a young woman obsessed with the need to be loved and her manservant imprison a young rake in an island mansion tower, warning him that he will die unless admitting love for the woman. At the end of six weeks, depicted in sex scenes, the gradually starved prisoner's aversion turns to terror and capitulation as he dies discovering the skeletons of men preceding him. The drama's cumulative effect of impending doom is strong. *Haunted Lives* is a well-crafted minor work again demonstrating Pielmeier's theatrical skill.

In addition to *Courage*, a monodrama about J.M. Barrie, and *Choices of the Heart*, a teleplay about a religious worker murdered in El Salvador, two other works show an extension of Pielmeier's range. The musical *Jass* (dialect for "jazz"), with story-and-mood songs by the playwright, tells an unfocused story of the demise of a New Orleans Storyville red-light district house facing legal closure in 1917. An anti-war drama short-lived on Broadway, *The Boys of Winter*, delineates seven Marines who are wiped out on a Vietnam hilltop in 1968, except for their lieutenant who on his return cold-bloodedly kills seven innocent Vietnamese civilians. The atrocity is rationalized in the men's monologues, offering the controversial premise that we all are guilty of My Lais. Despite flaws, the play's dialogue projects a salty reality, and its bloody incidents gather theatrical force.

Pielmeier is a dramatist of proven theatrical expertise; the nature of his development and the durability of his plays will be discovered by the future.

—Christian H. Moe

PIÑERO, Miguel (Antonio Gomez, Jr.).

Born in Gurabo, Puerto Rico, 19 December 1946; brought to New York City, 1950. Educated at public schools in New York; at Otisville State Training School for Boys, New York, two years; Manhattan State Hospital, high school equivalency diploma. Married Juanita Lovette Rameize in 1977 (divorced 1979); one adopted son. Served sentence for burglary, Riker's Island Prison, New York, 1964, and second term for drug possession; served sentence for burglary, Ossining Correctional Facility (Sing Sing prison), Ossining, New York, 1971–73; joining theatre workshop while in prison; founder, Nuyorican Poets Theatre, New York, 1974. Recipient: Obie award, 1974; New York Drama Critics Circle award, 1974. *Died 17 June 1988.*

Publications

PLAYS

All Junkies (produced 1973).
Short Eyes (produced 1974). 1975.
The Sun Always Shines for the Cool (produced 1975). In *The Sun Always*

Shines for the Cool, A Midnight Moon at the Greasy Spoon, Eulogy for a Small-Time Thief, 1984.

The Guntower (produced 1976).

Eulogy for a Small-Time Thief (produced 1977). In *The Sun Always Shines for the Cool, A Midnight Moon at the Greasy Spoon, Eulogy for a Small-Time Thief*, 1984.

Straight from the Ghetto, with Neil Harris (produced 1977).

Paper Toilet (produced 1979?).

Cold Beer (produced 1979–80).

Nuyorican Nights at the Stanton Street Social Club (produced 1980).

Playland Blues (produced 1980).

A Midnight Moon at the Greasy Spoon (produced 1981). In *The Sun Always Shines for the Cool, A Midnight Moon at the Greasy Spoon, Eulogy for a Small-Time Thief*, 1984.

The Sun Always Shines for the Cool, A Midnight Moon at the Greasy Spoon, Eulogy for a Small-Time Thief, 1984.

Outrageous: One-Act Plays. 1986.

SCREENPLAY: *Short Eyes*, 1977.

TELEVISION PLAYS: scripts for *Baretta* series.

VERSE
La Bodega Sold Dreams. 1979.

OTHER

Editor, with Miguel Algarin, *Nuyorican Poetry: An Anthology of Puerto Rican Words and Feelings*. 1975.

THEATRICAL ACTIVITIES

ACTOR: **Play**—God in *Steambath* by Bruce Jay Friedman, 1975. **Films**—*Short Eyes*, 1977; *The Jericho Mile*, 1979; *Fort Apache the Bronx*, 1981. **Television**—*Baretta* and *Kojak* series; *Miami Vice* series, 1984.

When Miguel Piñero won a New York Drama Critics Circle award for his play *Short Eyes*, he emerged as the leading Puerto Rican American dramatist. The play, richly imbued with the detail and insight gained from his own prison experiences, is the most ruthlessly authentic and exciting drama with a prison setting so far produced by the American theatre. Harrowing, brutal, yet suffused with a transforming, unsettling sensuality, it succeeds in imparting a special kind of understated, deliberately minimal poetic beauty and compassion to the rather terrifying events it dramatizes.

The play, set in the House of Detention, concerns what Piñero calls the "underclass", people who are socially deprived or outside the law, and this group with its own code of justice—for Piñero also to be read "just us"—becomes of course an inverse mirror of that other society without. The highly individualized characters, primarily Puerto Rican and black, with two white prisoners and white prison officers come together during the play in the "Dayroom" where their unique personalities, social roles, and ethnic backgrounds are forged into the play's community. Each of the characters, Paco, Ice, "El Raheem", "Longshoe", Mr. Nett, and the others, creates believability and plays a role in the personal and social processes the play depicts, but three of them are crucial: the catalyst Clark Davis, the "short eyes" or child molester of the title, who is murdered; Juan, the listener, "Poet", and choral commentator; and Julio, nicknamed "Cupcakes", everyone's idealized youth, whose initiation into silent complicity with the others in the murder costs him his innocence and ironically completes the community. As he leaves the prison, Juan pronounces judgement: "Oye, espera, no corra, just one thing brother, your fear of this place stole your spirit . . . And this ain't no pawnshop."

Despite its explosive subject matter, Piñero constructed his play with carefully calculated and controlling structural clarity. It consists of two perfectly balanced acts, each building towards a climax in physical violence, and a concluding "Epilogue". Each act also includes a dramatic monologue concerned with sexuality and fantasy that makes incandescent the play's emotional tensions. The correspondence between "underclass", prison, and society in general assures the play's potentially poetic dimension, but the process of poetic transformation of the play's realistic details is skilfully assisted in other ways as well. The terms that make up the play's special language—"short eyes", "homey", "bandido", "run it", and many more—become constant conversational metaphors; the "Dayroom" is a common ground for coming together and revelation; and the monologues declare the power of the transcending imagination. Clark Davis's brilliant monologue in particular, in which he recounts to Juan, for the first time to anyone, his dream-like encounters with little girls, has that special ambiguity of "facts" upon which poetry in part depends. The subtle border between intent and action, the imagined and real, is emphasized when the inmates discover that he was not in fact guilty of the offence that led to his arrest and death.

Piñero's other plays retain the authenticity and some of the visceral excitement of *Short Eyes*, but they lack its sharp focus and the structural unity and pressure provided in part by its prison setting with its shock-of-recognition framework for less familiar revelations. In these plays the dramatic situation is reversed. The characters are "out" and seek a kind of stabilizing home, "A bar in a large city" "where the time is NOW" in *The Sun Always Shines for the Cool*, Gerry's and Joe's "small luncheonette in the Times Square area" in *A Midnight Moon at the Greasy Spoon*, a small apartment in North Philadelphia in *Eulogy for a Small-Time Thief*. But the literal dead-end of the journeys is always the same: death. *The Sun Always Shines* is the best and most vivid of these continuing chronicles of the "underclass". Here the "hustlers and players" climax in the deadly triangle composed of Viejo, who commits suicide, his innocent daughter, and her lover Cat Eyes in a world where "Every player is a poet". In all three plays the vivid talk is in the foreground, the characters and action somewhat submerged beneath the verbal surface.

—Gaynor F. Bradish

POMERANCE, Bernard.

Born in Brooklyn, New York, in 1940. Educated at the University of Chicago. Co-founder, Foco Novo theatre group, London, 1972. Recipient: New York Drama Critics Circle award, Tony award, Obie award, and Outer Circle award, all 1979. Lives in London. Address: c/o Faber and Faber Ltd., 3 Queen Square, London WC1N 3AU, England.

Publications

PLAYS

High in Vietnam, Hot Damn; Hospital; Thanksgiving Before Detroit (produced 1971). In Gambit 6, 1972.
Foco Novo (produced 1972).
Someone Else Is Still Someone (produced 1974).
A Man's a Man, adaptation of a play by Brecht (produced 1975).
The Elephant Man (produced 1977). 1979.
Quantrill in Lawrence (produced 1980). 1981.
Melons (produced 1985).

NOVEL

We Need to Dream All This Again. 1987.

An American living in England, Bernard Pomerance found productions for his early plays in London's fringe theater of the 1970s. Yet it was his play The Elephant Man, produced on Broadway in 1979 subsequent to an English premiere and an off-off Broadway presentation, that established Pomerance as a playwright. An immense critical and popular success, the play won several awards including an Obie and one from the New York Drama Critics Circle.

The title of the biography-drama was a sideshow term applied to John Merrick (1863–90), a noted teratoid "freak" of Victorian England, so hideously malformed by an incurable and then unknown disease (now diagnosed as neuro-fibromatosis) that he was cruelly exploited as a traveling show oddity. Rescued from such exhibition by the anatomist Dr. Frederick Treves, he was given safe shelter in London Hospital, Whitechapel, which raised public donations for his maintenance and became his home for six years before his death in 1890. Merrick became a curio studied by science and visited by fashionable society who found him a man of surprising intelligence and sensitivity. Treves's published account of Merrick's life sparked Pomerance's interest in the subject.

In 22 often trenchant short scenes identified by title placard, The Elephant Man effectively employs a presentational and Brechtian style to tell its story. In Act 1 Treves encounters Merrick in a sideshow, later offers him shelter after a mob almost kills him, and determines with condescending compassion to create for his patient the illusion of normality. To this purpose, he enlists the actress Mrs. Kendal to befriend Merrick. The second act shifts focus from physician to patient as we watch the progress of Treves's social engineering. The "Elephant Man" fits himself into the role of the correct Victorian gentleman, but not without questioning the rules he is told to obey.

As the metamorphosis continues, fashionable society lionizes him for he lets them see him not as an individual but as a mirror of qualities they like to claim. Noting to Mrs. Kendal that sexual loneliness continues to isolate him from other men and that he has never seen a naked woman, the actress kindly obliges by baring her breasts only to be interrupted by a scandalized Treves who orders her out for her impropriety: she does not return. Interpreting the experience as defining his own limitations, Merrick realizes his normality has been an illusion, and he suicidally lets his huge head drop unsupported, causing strangulation. Simultaneously with his patient's development, Treves comes to question his principles and those of his class and painfully perceives Merrick's subtle exploitation by science and society. Pomerance is concerned with the theme that compassion, society and its conventional morality, and the idea of normality are at bottom destructive illusions.

Pomerance's play is at once theatrically effective, emotionally compelling, and intellectually provoking. Yet the drama has some problems. More ideas are unleashed than are developed, and some of these are overstated in the later scenes. Moreover, the shift in focus from Treves to Merrick and then back to the former near the conclusion unbalances the center of the play: the physician's loss of self-assurance demands more preparation. But such problems are minor when considering the play's overriding strengths.

As John Merrick is an exemplary victim of 19th-century greed, intolerance, and samaritanism, the aging Apache leader Caracol alias John Lame Eagle in *Melons* is a noble-turned-vengeful-savage exploited and oppressed by white civilization. Regarded as a messiah by his southwest Pueblo settlement, Caracol confronts his old U.S. Cavalry adversary now (in 1906) representing an oil company with drilling rights on the Indian's land, recalls past humiliations at white hands, and ultimately reveals his ritual decapitation of two geologists sent by the company to find oil on the reservation. This revelation causes at the climax both his death and that of his white antagonist. Caracol's doomed attempts to hold onto the ancient ways and his white enemy's callous materialism reflect the Indian's inability to accommodate the conquering culture. Pomerance employs as a narrator an Indian activist raised by whites who encompasses the tension between both cultures and is powerless to prevent the conflict's bloody conclusion. The narrator strides back in time to tell us the Caracol story in a fractured narrative burdened with commentary, flashbacks, and a lengthy narrator-Caracol debate which hinders the forward momentum and immediate action of the play. Many critics viewing the 1985 London produc- tion by the Royal Shakespeare Company faulted the play's structural and storytelling flaws, and the consequent shortcomings in overall theatrical effectiveness, while praising its ambitions.

Quantrill in Lawrence, an earlier play, displays similar deficiencies in craft and the playwright's characteristic attraction to historical settings and situation. This play combines a plot derived from Euripides's *Bacchae* with the burning of Lawrence, Kansas, in 1863 by the Confederate outlaw Quantrill. The liberation of women and of suppressed desires are the play's thematic concerns.

Pomerance is a talented playwright committed to tackling large themes. His work is notable for its continuing interest in biographical and historical sources as means by which to examine contemporary problems.

—Christian H. Moe

R

RABE, David (William).

Born in Dubuque, Iowa, 10 March 1940. Educated at Loras College, Dubuque, B.A. in English 1962; Villanova University, Pennsylvania, 1963–64, 1967–68, M.A. 1968. Served in the U.S. Army, 1965–67. Married 1) Elizabeth Pan in 1969, one son; 2) the actress Jill Clayburgh in 1979. Feature writer, New Haven *Register*, Connecticut, 1969–70. Assistant professor, 1970–72, and from 1972, consultant, Villanova University. Recipient: Rockefeller grant, 1967; Associated Press award, for journalism, 1970; Obie award, 1971; Tony award, 1972; Outer Circle award, 1972; New York Drama Critics Circle citation, 1972, and award, 1976; *Variety* award, 1972; Dramatists Guild Hull-Warriner award, 1972; American Academy award, 1974; Guggenheim fellowship, 1976. Agent: Ellen Neuwald Inc., 905 West End Avenue, New York, New York 10025. Address: c/o Grove/Atlantic Monthly Press, 841 Broadway, New York, New York 10003, U.S.A.

Publications

PLAYS

Sticks and Bones (produced 1969). With *The Basic Training of Pavlo Hummel*, 1973.

The Basic Training of Pavlo Hummel (produced 1971). With *Sticks and Bones*, 1973.

The Orphan (produced 1973). 1975.

In the Boom Boom Room (as *Boom Boom Room*, produced 1973; revised version, as *In the Boom Boom Room*, produced 1974). 1975; revised version (produced 1986), 1986.

Burning (produced 1974).

Streamers (produced 1976). 1977.

Goose and Tomtom (produced 1982). 1986.

Hurlyburly (produced 1984; also director: revised version produced 1988). 1985; revised edition, 1990.

Those the River Keeps (produced 1991). 1991.

SCREENPLAYS: *I'm Dancing as Fast as I Can*, 1982; *Streamers*, 1983; *Casualties of War*, 1989.

NOVEL

Recital of the Dog. 1993.

BIBLIOGRAPHY: *David Rabe: A Stage History and a Primary and Secondary Bibliography* by Philip C. Kolin, 1988.

MANUSCRIPT COLLECTION: Mugar Memorial Library, Boston University.

David Rabe's corrosive portrait of American life evolves within a series of metaphoric arenas—living rooms, military barracks, disco bars—where his characters collide violently against each other, but where, primarily, they struggle with their own society-fostered delusions. The revised edition of *In the Boom Boom Room*, published in 1986, is mischievously dedicated to "the wolf at the door" but the creature is already well within Rabe's theatrical house and the psyches of those who dwell inside it.

Two Rabe plays, forming with *Streamers* what has come to be known as his Vietnam trilogy, burst onto the New York stage in 1971 when both were produced by Joseph Papp at the Shakespeare Festival Public Theatre. Rabe denies that they are specifically "anti-war" plays, maintaining that he neither expected nor intended them to wield any political effect, that they merely define a condition as endemic to the "eternal human pageant" as family, marriage, or crime. ("A play in which a family looks bad is not called an 'antifamily' play. A play in which a marriage looks bad is not called an 'antimarriage' play. A play about crime is not called an 'anticrime' play.")

But *The Basic Training of Pavlo Hummel* and *Sticks and Bones* portray the dehumanization and senseless horror of the Vietnam era with the sustained raw power now ordinarily associated only with certain films produced well after American troop withdrawal (*Apocalypse Now*, *The Killing Fields*, *Platoon*, *Full Metal Jacket*). Poor Pavlo Hummel's basic training functions as ritual throughout the play, contributing significantly to Rabe's theatrical stylization of an essentially realistic dramatic structure. Rabe's "realism" is invariably a realism heightened, stretched beyond traditional limits through (as in *Sticks and Bones* and *Hurlyburly*) dazzling language-play or (as in *Pavlo Hummel*) surreal fracturing of time and space and the ominous on-and-off-stage drifting of Ardell, a character seen only by Pavlo. Such blending of the real and surreal characterizes Rabe's style and serves both to rattle a viewer's preconceptions and to reinforce (as in *Sticks and Bones*) a given figure's alienation from those closest to him. It also prevents a play with a simple-minded hero from itself becoming simple-minded by complicating the theatrical conventions that develop Pavlo into an Army-trained killer who is ironically killed himself, not on the battlefield but in a brothel squabble. A sense of verisimilitude nevertheless underpins Rabe's stylistic virtuosity, the details of the Vietnam plays clearly emanating not only from the playwright's imagination but from his own Army experience in a hospital support unit at Long Binh as well.

While *Pavlo Hummel* focuses on pre-combat preparation for war, *Sticks and Bones* concerns its grotesque stateside aftermath. The naïve Pavlo may be blind to the reality of war but David, the embittered veteran of *Sticks and Bones*, has been literally—physically—blinded *by* it. Torn by the atrocities he has witnessed, tormented by his psychological and physical infirmity, David must be expelled from the bosom of the family whose artificial tranquility he is determined to destroy. Pavlo knows too little, David too much, and both must therefore die.

Despite its intensely serious subject, the method of *Sticks and Bones* is often wildly comic, dependent upon the clichéd conventions of situation comedy which Rabe transforms into a vehicle for macabre parody of American delusion. The play resonates, however, with overtones of American domestic tragedy, notably Miller's *Death of a Salesman* and O'Neill's *Long Day's Journey into Night*. Generically complex, articulated in language that alternates between poetic and vernacular extremes, *Sticks and Bones* remains the most important American play to come out of the Vietnam experience.

Streamers, adapted to the screen by Rabe and the director Robert Altman in 1983, expands the thematic scope of the earlier plays but most resembles *Pavlo Hummel* in its barracks setting. The violence inherent in the military system is here expanded, linked by Rabe to institutionalized racism and homophobia camouflaged in the rhetoric of patriotism.

Hurlyburly, a title that reflects the chaos of its characters' lives, veers in a different direction. The word appears in the opening lines of *Macbeth*, which Rabe considered using in their entirety to name each of his three acts, respectively: "When Shall We Three Meet Again?," "In Thunder Lightning or in Rain?," and "When the Hurlyburly's Done, When the Battle's Lost and Won." Though he rejected the idea, he writes in the Afterword to the play that he "felt for a long time that the play was in many ways a trilogy, each act an entity, a self-contained action however enhanced it might be by the contents of the other acts and the reflections that might be sent back and forth between all three." (Rabe is an astute commentator on the art of playwriting—his own and others'. See also his Introduction to *Pavlo Hummel* and the Author's Note to *Sticks and Bones*.)

Like that of *Streamers* and *Pavlo Hummel*, the world of *Hurlyburly* is male-centered, but the barracks of those plays shifts to the living room of a small house in the Hollywood Hills, inhabited by Rabe's least sympathetic outcasts. Cut off from their wives and children by divorce or separation, the men of *Hurlyburly* waver violently between macho boasting and episodes of confessional self-loathing as they seek solace in drugs, alcohol, and uncommitted affairs. Their hostility toward women, whom they regard as "broads" or "bitches," masks their inability to reconcile male behavior codes learned as children with expectations demanded by their liberated partners. These boy-men lack a moral center and represent for Rabe a characteristically American rootlessness.

Their anger is articulated in the stylized excesses and violence of the play's language, in the four-letter words that punctuate the dialogue but, more subtly, in the winding convolutions of speech: parenthetical expressions, self-interruptions, thoughts within thoughts, the repetitions and circularity that contribute to the work's considerable length and O'Neillian power. Eddie, Mickey, and Phil fear silence even more than they fear tuning into their own feelings, and thus keep talking, even if doing so runs the risk of accidental self-revelation. In this regard, an early stage direction notes that "in the characters' speeches phrases such as 'whatchamacallit,' 'thingamajig,' 'blah-blah-blah' and 'rapateta' abound. These are phrases used by the characters to keep themselves talking and should be said unhesitatingly with the authority and conviction with which one would have in fact said the missing word." The play's dialogue is extraordinary in its rich mix of funny, vulgar, savagely articulate language.

Rabe maintains that *Hurlyburly* contains no spokesman, that "no one in it knows what it is about." But the Age of Anxiety, documented by the disasters ticked off nightly on the 11 o'clock news, determines how his characters, and his audience, live. Rabe may claim that no single person in his play knows what it means, but *Hurlyburly*'s thematic core is expressed clearly in the drunken Eddie's furious lament for an absent God:

> The Ancients might have had some consolation from a view of the heavens as inhabited by this thoughtful, you know, meditative, maybe a trifle unpredictable and wrathful, but nevertheless UP THERE—this divine onlooker—we have bureaucrats devoted to the accumulation of incomprehensible data—we have connoisseurs of graft and the filibuster —virtuosos of the three-martini lunch for whom we vote on the basis of their personal appearance. The air's bad, the water's got poison in it, and into whose eyes do we find ourselves staring when we look for providence? We have emptied out the heavens and put oblivion in the hands of a bunch of aging insurance salesmen whose jobs are insecure.

Hurlyburly is Rabe's most intricate, verbally dazzling theatrical statement to date, a view even more strikingly apparent since the publication of the dramatist's definitive edition of the play in 1990. In this version Rabe restores and revises text cut or altered for the 1984 production directed by Mike Nichols in Chicago and on Broadway. This new, even more corrosive version of *Hurlyburly* emerges from a process of revision culminating in a 1988 production of the play, directed by Rabe himself, at the Westwood Playhouse in Los Angeles.

Also prominent in Rabe's most recent work are his screenplay for *Casualties of War*—a film with which Rabe expressed dissatisfaction, but one which searingly reflects Rabe's continuing obsession with the Vietnam conflict; and *Those the River Keeps*, a play which returns to the terrain of *Hurlyburly* from a fresh perspective.

—Mark W. Estrin

See the essay on *The Basic Training of Pavlo Hummel*.

REARDON, Dennis J.

Born in Worcester, Massachusetts, 17 September 1944. Educated at Tulane University, New Orleans, 1962–63; University of Kansas, Lawrence (Hopkins Award, 1965, 1966), 1963–66, B.A. in English (cum laude) 1966; Indiana University, Bloomington, 1966–67. Served in the U.S. Army, 1968–69. Married in 1971 (separated); one daughter. Playwright-in-residence, University of Michigan, Ann Arbor (Shubert Fellow, 1970; Hopwood Award, 1971), 1970–71, and Hartwick College, Oneonta, New York. Since 1985 member of the English Department, State University of New York, Albany. Recipient: Creative Artists Public Service grant, 1984; Weissberger Foundation award, 1985; National Play award, 1986; National Endowment for the Arts fellowship, 1986. Lives in Guilderland Center, New York. Agent: Susan Schulman, 454 West 44th Street, New York, New York 10036, U.S.A.

Publications

PLAYS

The Happiness Cage (produced 1970). 1971.

Siamese Connections (produced 1971).

The Leaf People (produced 1975). In *Plays from the New York Shakespeare Festival*, 1986.

The Incredible Standing Man and His Friends (also co-director: produced 1980).

Steeple Jack (produced 1983).

Subterranean Homesick Blues Again (produced 1983).

Comment, music by Merrill Clark (produced 1985).

New Cures for Sunburn (produced 1986).

MANUSCRIPT COLLECTION: Lincoln Center Library of the Performing Arts, New York.

CRITICAL STUDY: *Uneasy Stages* by John Simon, 1975.

THEATRICAL ACTIVITIES

DIRECTOR: **Play**—*The Incredible Standing Man and His Friends* (co-director), 1980.

Dennis J. Reardon comments:

The central dynamic in my plays exists in the tension between what is "real" and what is "made up." I often mix carefully researched and recognizably topical material with the stuff of dreams, and I am seldom precise about where one mode leaves off and the other begins. My intent is to push beyond the suffocating ephemera of journalistic facts into a more iconic realm where the only reality is a metaphor.

Among the plays of America's contemporary dramatists, Dennis J. Reardon's work is distinguished by an energy that assaults the intellect as well as the emotions. With an audacity arising first from his youthful enthusiasm and then from a greater understanding of his craft, Reardon has experimented with theatrical effect in order to enhance his stories and to communicate his vision of man to audiences from whom he clearly demands intellectual involvement while besieging their senses with a variety of staged actions. Yet he remains basically a storyteller, albeit one with a bit of the Irish dark side showing. His subject is the plight of man immemorial, a condition he explores with all of the anxieties, frustrations, and reactions to the violent freedoms of the 1960s that marked his own maturing years. To date, his career divides into two distinct periods. *The Happiness Cage*, *Siamese Connections*, and *The Leaf People* brought him immediate recognition on Broadway as well as a sense of being both victor and victim in a world he did not fully understand. After a period of "self-willed" oblivion he began writing again in 1980 and has produced a half-dozen plays that reveal the vibrancy of his earlier work accentuated through experience and by the more balanced probing of the demons and saints, facts and fates, that persistently follow the modern Everyman.

The plays of Reardon's early period remain as daringly theatrical as anything he has written. Because he is always idea-oriented, however, his heavy emphasis upon a depressing view of humanity in these plays changes in subsequent work without bringing a complete denial to his philosophical stance. Feeling that he has "the power to bring an untold amount of happiness into this miserable world," Dr. Freytag of *The Happiness Cage* experiments upon his patients to find a cure for schizophrenia. Then one patient questions Freytag's assessment of his condition as "lonely, confused, frightened, and thoroughly unhappy" and asserts that he is simply a man, that he is a unique human being. Moreover, he wants to know what happiness means. Apparently sharing Nathaniel Hawthorne's definition of the "unpardonable sin," Reardon mocks the stupid cruelty of the veteran's hospital where Freytag works and the flagrant hypocrisy of its management toward the lonely, confused, frightened, and thoroughly unhappy doctor. The "brooding, barren immensity" of the Kansas farm in *Siamese Connections* provides a metaphor for the story of two brothers—the favored one who was killed in Vietnam and the one who survived but did not know how to kill the ghosts that made him into a homicidal monster, resentful of his brother, unable to escape, condemned. In *The Leaf People*, a most demanding play for actors and technicians, Reardon underscored one of the ironies of life while dramatizing mankind's murderous pathway to power. The action takes place in the Amazon rain forest where a rock star searches for his father, an Irish apostle named Shaughnessey who has discovered, and wants to save the Leaf People. Internal conflict prevents the Leaf People from protecting themselves from the invisible greed of the outside world, the apostle dies, the son fails as a messenger of their danger, and disaster results. Eventually, new residents in the area say that they "never heard of any tribe called the Leaf People."

In all of Reardon's plays since 1980 there is a persistent probing of man's sensitivities and sensibilities, but his overall perspective is obviously comic as he writes about the human comedy. Laughter, however, is not his objective; understanding is. If people laugh, it is as likely the laughter of pain or startled hilarity, a dark and improbable humor. *The Incredible Standing Man and His Friends*, "a parody of dysfunction on both the societal and individual levels," may produce such confused laughter with its stereotypical characters in an absurd world. Who helps and what happens to the inarticulate man in a situation people do not understand? *Steeple Jack*, Reardon's most balanced view of life, dramatizes the trials of a young girl, tortured by fears and despairs, who is guided to hope by an illiterate busboy and a self-anointed apostle who preaches at perpetual man as he trudges on toward Armageddon. In *Subterranean Homesick Blues Again* the cavern tour guide, Charon, appropriately delivers his querulous tourists with ironic politeness to that place where "the turbulence and confusion of your days beneath the Sun are ended." Both *Security* and *Club Renaissance* in *Unauthorized Entries* (written 1984; unpublished) show the insubstantiality of modern times where a whimsical fate controls. A darker humor prevails in *New Cures for Sunburn* where the disastrous impulses of family cruelty and morbidity climax in a loss of human dignity for all. In opposition to such bleak pictures of grotesque man, *Sanctuary for Two Violins (Under Assault)* (written 1984; unpublished) repeats the hope of *Steeple Jack* as two old violinists heroically resist the assaults of life and survive to create the music described in the final line of the play, "How lovely!"

Having chosen the stage on which to project the conflicts and crises of modern man, Reardon finds that he has a great deal to say—about moral obligations, a mechanical society, illusions of security, destructive cynicism, fraudulence and perversity, the destructive forces of vulgarity. In order to underline his concerns, he is an explorer in contemporary theatre. Music plays an important role in his art—rock music, popular ballads, a sonata for two violins. Like many writers—such as Thornton Wilder whom he appears to admire—Reardon experiments with the concept of time and the complexity of its adequate expression on stage. In *Siamese Connections* the dead and the living exist together; in *The Incredible Standing Man* life hangs waiting for a traffic light to change; dance movements in *Sanctuary for Two Violins* project timeless assaults on life. In these experiments with time, some of Reardon's plays suggest the vertical approach of the Nō drama, unfettered by realistic representation or linear progression of thought. Space—on stage or imagined —also stabs Reardon's consciousness and moves him toward shifting scenes divided by numerous blackouts. His work is also marked by that relentless energy, now carefully orchestrated in such plays as *Steeple Jack*, *Standing Man*, and *Sanctuary for Two Violins*, to produce compelling and thoughtful drama.

—Walter J. Meserve

REDDIN, Keith.

Born in New Jersey, 7 July 1956. Educated at Northwestern University, Evanston, Illinois, B.S. 1978; Yale University School of Drama, New Haven, Connecticut, M.A. 1981. Married Leslie Lyles in 1986. Recipient: McArthur award, 1984; San Diego Critics Circle award, 1989, 1990. Agent: Peter Franklin, William Morris Agency, 1350 Avenue of the Americas, New York, New York 10019, U.S.A.

Publications

PLAYS

Throwing Smoke (produced 1980). With *Desperadoes* and *Keyhole Lover*, 1986.
Life and Limb (produced 1984). 1985.
Desperadoes (produced 1985). With *Throwing Smoke* and *Keyhole Lover*, 1986.
Rum and Coke (produced 1985). 1986.
Keyhole Lover (produced 1987). With *Desperadoes* and *Throwing Smoke*, 1986.
Desperadoes, Throwing Smoke, Keyhole Lover. 1986.
Highest Standard of Living (produced 1986). 1987.
After School Special (produced 1987; as *The Big Squirrel*, produced 1987).
Plain Brown Wrapper (5 sketches) (produced 1987).

Big Time (produced 1987). 1988.
Nebraska (produced 1989). 1990.
Life During Wartime (produced 1990). 1991.
Innocents' Crusade (produced 1991).

TELEVISION PLAYS: *Big Time*, 1988; *The Heart of Justice*, 1990; *Praha*, 1991.

THEATRICAL ACTIVITIES

ACTOR: **Plays**—Third red soldier, art student, fifth comrade, fourth airman, and Dockerill in *No End of Blame* by Howard Barker, 1981; Geoffrey in *A Taste of Honey* by Shelagh Delaney, 1981; Melvin McMullen in *Cliffhanger* by James Yaffe, 1985; Leo Davis in *Room Service* by John Murray and Allen Boretz, 1986; Dr. William Polidori in *Bloody Poetry* by Howard Brenton, 1987; role in *Precious Memories* by Romulus Linney, 1988; role in *Just Say No* by Larry Kramer, 1988; Dennis Post in *The Bug* by Richard Strand, 1989; role in *Buzzsaw Berkeley* by Doug Wright, 1989.

That Keith Reddin is considered one of America's most political playwrights is less an accurate assessment of his dramaturgical preoccupations than it is an indictment of a nation of historical amnesiacs. Indeed, Reddin is part of a disenchanted generation of American writers, baby boomers who were raised on television and the homespun, fictitious ideals of American supremacy, who matured post-Watergate and wish to combat the critical forces of amnesia and nostalgia in the national psyche with their writing, an even more pressing task in the wake of 12 years of Republican rule. With varying degrees of *naïveté*, these writers display a political consciousness rather than set any agendas. While many of Reddin's plays are set around textbook "topics" and incidents like the Korean War (*Life and Limb*), the Cold War (*Highest Standard of Living*), the Bay of Pigs invasion (*Rum and Coke*), or the use of nuclear power (*Nebraska*), what Reddin does, like most filmmakers and playwrights in the American grain, is use political events and cultural patterns as a backdrop for an individual's struggle with fractious personal relationships. The political is traduced by the personal, and the result is a sharply satirical, uneasy sketch about one more episode in the ongoing saga of America's moral complacency.

A Reddin play typically centres around a well-meaning, bright, and unsuspecting gull who joins a powerful organization, only to gradually awaken to its incorporated evil. The hero is given opportunities to stand against the juggernaut (or at least get out), but is shown to be either too powerless or too passive to make a difference. When he does speak out, events have passed him by and/or he sustains a sudden and tragic personal loss. The play at hand then becomes an opportunity for the sadder-but-wiser narrator to detail his loss of innocence for the audience; as Jake, the raw CIA recruit who finds himself unable to stem the tide in Cuba, states at the outset of *Rum and Coke*, "this is how I got messed up in something called the Bay of Pigs."

Jake's admission, offhand yet personal, an invitation that deflects pain through mockery, is an example of Reddin's characteristic tone. Reddin is an actor; and, although he doesn't perform in his own work, he writes, for better and for worse, for the actor. The scenes are taut, brisk, and highly verbal, yet the characters often seem underwritten until actors flesh out the conflicts with their presence. Even the minor characters are provided with monologues or non-naturalistic outbursts to the audience that showcase the actor's talents. A Reddin play, unconcerned with subtextual moorings and structural transitions, is performed at high velocity and high pitch, the comedy arising from abrupt shifts in tone and emphasis and a predilection for the grotesque detail in everyday circumstance.

Reddin makes use of a post-modern sensibility. Having the theologian Calvin make a visit from the 16th century to deliver an ad hoc diatribe against the utter debasement of contemporary language and finish with a reference to Yul Brynner in *The King and I* is a very Reddin moment. Since one of his themes is the anaesthetizing effect of popular culture and the media on the individual, his plays bristle with references to ancient advertising slogans, household products, songs, old movies, political buzzwords, etc. In production, his comedies feature virtual "soundtracks" of popular recordings as commentary to the action. Reddin is also something of a fantasist. In two very different plays, the love interests of the heroes die unexpectedly. In *Life and Limb*, just as things are finally looking better for Franklin and Effie in 1950s suburbia, Effie is killed in a freak movie theatre accident, presumably because she has committed adultery and must pay for it. In *Life During Wartime*, Gail is the victim of a senseless murder in which her young lover Tommy is an unwitting yet circumstantial accessory. Both of these deaths—of highly sympathetic characters—are completely shocking. The playwright himself can't seem to part with them or face up to his dramaturgical choice and so, in each instance, he has the dead woman return from the other world and console her grieving man.

Comic resurrection or patent, infantile wish-fulfilment? Reddin would seem to want it both ways, seeking theatrical resolution while showing such a gesture to be false. His heroes and heroines connect best when they are in different spaces. While they walk the earth, they are pulled irresist- ibly to become like everyone else—amoral, compromised, money-mad, power-driven. Time and again Reddin shows that the blows come when least expected, that people are much more evil than one expects, and that the web of complicity is always more extensive than one assumed; in a society administered by the corrupt and controlled by the media, how can one hope to keep one's hands clean? All that one can do is bear witness. If his earliest plays could be seen as fashionably cynical political cartoons, his later work demonstrates a more profound treatment of individual loss. Small wonder then that his latest play, which opened in 1991, is titled the *Innocents' Crusade*.

—James Magruder

RIBMAN, Ronald (Burt).

Born in New York City, 28 May 1932. Educated at Brooklyn College, New York, 1950–51; University of Pittsburgh, B.B.A. 1954, M.Litt. 1958, Ph.D. 1962. Served in the United States Army, 1954–56. Married Alice Rosen in 1967; one son and one daughter. Assistant professor of English, Otterbein College, Westerville, Ohio, 1962–63. Recipient: Obie award, 1966; Rockefeller grant, 1966, 1968, 1975; Guggenheim fellowship, 1970; Straw Hat award, 1973; National Endowment for the Arts grant, 1974, fellowship, 1986–87; Creative Artists Public Service grant, 1976; Dramatists Guild Hull-   :

Warriner award, 1977; Playwrights U.S.A. award, 1984; Kennedy Center
New American Play grant, 1991. Lives in South Salem, New York. Agent:
Samuel Gelfman, B.D.P. and Associates, 10637 Burbank Boulevard, North
Hollywood, California 91601, U.S.A.

Publications

PLAYS

Harry, Noon and Night (produced 1965). With *The Journey of the Fifth
  Horse,* 1967.
The Journey of the Fifth Horse, based in part on "The Diary of a Superfluous
  Man" by Turgenev (produced 1966). With *Harry, Noon and Night,* 1967;
  published separately, 1974.
The Final War of Olly Winter (televised 1967). In *Great Television Plays,*
  1969.
The Ceremony of Innocence (produced 1967). 1968.
Passing Through from Exotic Places (includes *The Son Who Hunted Tigers in
  Jakarta, Sunstroke, The Burial of Esposito*) (produced 1969). 1970.
The Most Beautiful Fish (televised 1969). In *New York Times,* 23 November
  1969.
The Son Who Hunted Tigers in Jakarta (produced 1989). In *Passing Through
  from Exotic Places,* 1970.
Fingernails Blue as Flowers (produced 1971). In *The American Place Theatre,*
  edited by Richard Schotter, 1973.
A Break in the Skin (produced 1972).
The Poison Tree (produced 1973; revised version produced 1975). 1977.
Cold Storage (produced 1977). 1976.
Five Plays (includes *Cold Storage; The Poison Tree; The Ceremony of
  Innocence; The Journey of the Fifth Horse; Harry, Noon and Night*). 1978.
Buck (produced 1983). 1983.
Sweet Table at the Richelieu (produced 1987). In *American Theatre,*
  July/August 1987.
The Cannibal Masque (produced 1987).
A Serpent's Egg (produced 1987).
The Rug Merchants of Chaos (produced 1991).

SCREENPLAY: *The Angel Levine,* with Bill Gunn, 1970.

TELEVISION PLAYS: *The Final War of Olly Winter,* 1967; *The Most Beautiful
Fish,* 1969; *Seize the Day,* from the novella by Saul Bellow, 1985; *The Sunset
Gang* series (includes *Yiddish, The Detective, Home*), from the short stories by
Warren Adler, 1991.

MANUSCRIPT COLLECTION: New York Public Library.

CRITICAL STUDY: *Harvard Guide to Contemporary American Writing* edited by
Daniel Hoffman, 1979.

Ronald Ribman is a difficult playwright to characterize. The surface dissimilar-
ity among his works gives each of his plays a voice of its own, but all are
variations on the dramatist's own voice—on his preoccupation with recurrent
themes, on his commitment to language that is at once complex and dramatic.

Perhaps because he is also a poet (although not so good a poet as he is a playwright), he is essentially a verbal dramatist, fascinated by the nuances of language—the way a well-chosen adverb can alter the first meaning of a sentence, the way an extended metaphor can come to characterize its speaker through both content and style. Yet he is aware of and, often in key scenes, dependent on visual images that give particular force to the words; consider the scene in *Harry, Noon and Night* in which Immanuel cleans a fish while sparring verbally with Archer, the aggressive chop-chop-chop altering seemingly innocent statements.

The chief thematic concern of the playwright is with man caught between aspiration and possibility. "Well, all my characters are crying out against the universe they can't alter," he once told an interviewer, but the inalterable force varies from play to play. Sometimes it seems to lie primarily within the character (Harry of *Harry, Noon and Night*), sometimes to be dictated by the assumptions of society (the prisoners in *The Poison Tree*). More often it is a combination of these two. Finally, in *Cold Storage*, it lies in the fact of human mortality.

His first two plays—*Harry, Noon and Night* and *The Journey of the Fifth Horse*—deal with "failure clowns," "fifth horses," to borrow the "loser" images of the two plays. Underlying *Harry* is a conventional psychological drama about a young man perpetually in the shadow of his successful older brother. Yet, Harry can be victimizer as well as victim, and so can Immanuel, who routs the brother in Scene 2, but is himself the captive clown of Scene 3. Add the German setting with its references to the Nazis, "the Dachau circus," and the metaphor of the failure clown spreads to suggest the human condition. All this in a very funny comedy. The fifth horses of *Journey*, which grows out of Turgenev's "The Diary of a Superfluous Man," are Turgenev's hero and the publisher's reader who finally rejects the manuscript; the second character is only an ironic note in the original story, but Ribman creates him fully, his real and his fantasy lives, and lets him recognize and cry out against the identification he feels with the man whose diary he is reading.

With his television play, *The Final War of Olly Winter*, and *The Ceremony of Innocence*, Ribman seemed to be moving into overt social drama, into a direct pacifist statement brought on by the general distress with the American presence in Vietnam. Similarly *The Poison Tree* seemed to some an explicit commentary on prison conditions and racial bigotry, a reading that perhaps contributed to its commercial failure as the theater moved away from the social/political concerns of the 1960s. Although the social implications of these dramas are real enough, they are plays that deal with familiar Ribman themes and display the complexities of structure and language already familiar from the early plays. *The Ceremony of Innocence* is an historical drama which uses flashback scenes to explain why Ethelred will not come out of seclusion to defend England against the Danish invasion. He prefers to stand aside from a society which, mouthing the rhetoric of honor, chooses war over peace and special privilege over public welfare; still, the failures of his society—so forcefully expressed in a speech of the disillusioned idealist Kent—are reflections of Ethelred's inability to rule even himself, giving way, as he does at crucial moments, to an anger that belies his faith in the rational mind. In *The Poison Tree*, in which the prison is largely peopled by black convicts and white guards, Ribman develops his titular metaphor to show that all the characters are creatures of the situation. The manipulative guard who is his own victim, too easily a caricature in production, is actually the Kent of this play, finally as helpless as the leading prisoner, the one who prefers feeling to dehumanizing theory, but is incapable of non-violent, regenerative action.

With *Cold Storage* Ribman returned to the exuberance, the inventiveness that characterized *Harry, Noon and Night*. Primarily a two-character play, *Cold Storage* is set in the terminal ward of a New York hospital. Given that setting, it is perhaps surprising to find such vitality, so much luxury of language, such wild humor, but these qualities are as important to the play's content as they are to its texture. Parmigian, a dying fruit merchant with an incredible frame of reference and a compulsive need to talk (silence is death), assaults Landau, gets him to release his secret guilt at having survived the Holocaust. As Landau learns to live, Parmigian comes to accept the fact of death. The play ends with a community of two, a conspiracy of sorts against the human condition, and leaves the audience with a marvelously replenishing sense of life.

The "crying out" is more muted in *Buck* and *Sweet Table at the Richelieu*, but they provide opposition to the inevitable—the one an image, the other a character. The titular protagonist of *Buck*, a director for a sex-and-violence television company, fails to humanize his product, to modify the cruel behavior of his colleagues, to solve his offstage personal problems, but the play ends with the new snow falling, bringing the promise of cleansing even though it will quickly turn to dirt and slush. As the patrons of the Richelieu, a metaphorical luxury spa, exit for the last sleighride, the less self-obsessed of the guests is defined as the Lady of Enduring Hope although she knows that no one can stay long enough to taste all the glories on the sweet table.

There is a quartet of failing clowns in *The Rug Merchants of Chaos*, two couples who have wandered the world, trying to succeed with one impossible business after another. When we meet them, escaping on a rattletrap ship from Cape Town, after a fire they set for the insurance got out of hand, it is only the latest installment of lives which one character describes as "hanging so delicately between farce and destruction." At the end there is exhilaration when they go over the side of the ship, ready to risk themselves and their hopes in an open boat miles from any shore.

—Gerald Weales

RICHARDSON, Jack (Carter).

Born in New York City, 18 February 1935. Educated at Columbia University, New York, 1954–57, B.A. (summa cum laude) in philosophy 1957 (Phi Beta Kappa); University of Munich (Adenauer Fellow), 1958. Served in the U.S. Army, in France and Germany, 1951–54. Married Anne Grail Roth in 1957; one daughter. Recipient: Brandeis University Creative Arts award, 1963. Address: c/o Simon and Schuster, 1230 Avenue of the Americas, New York, New York 10020, U.S.A.

Publications

PLAYS

The Prodigal (produced 1960). 1960.
Gallows Humor (produced 1961). 1961.
Lorenzo (produced 1963).
Xmas in Las Vegas (produced 1965). 1966.
As Happy as Kings (produced 1968).
Juan Feldman, in *Pardon Me, Sir, But Is My Eye Hurting Your Elbow?*, edited
   by Bob Booker and George Foster. 1968.

NOVEL

The Prison Life of Harris Filmore. 1961.

OTHER

Memoir of a Gambler. 1979.

THEATRICAL ACTIVITIES

ACTOR: **Film**—*Beyond the Law*, 1968.

At the outset of the 1960s four young playwrights, Edward Albee, Jack
Richardson, Arthur Kopit, and Jack Gelber, held the attention of the American
theatre as its best prospects for the future since the postwar emergence of
Tennessee Williams and Arthur Miller. The four became acquainted, and in
the season of 1962–63 they were simultaneously active in the Playwrights'
Unit of the Actors Studio in New York. Jack Richardson's particular position
in this rather brilliant quartet was achieved by the success of two splendid
plays produced off-Broadway, *The Prodigal*, his retelling in his own contemporary idiom of the Orestes story, and *Gallows Humor*, two linked tragicomic
plays in a modern setting. In these plays Richardson stands apart from his
three immediate contemporaries for certain defining characteristics unmistakably his own, characteristics that also mark his subsequent and somewhat
parallel pair of Broadway plays, *Lorenzo* and *Xmas in Las Vegas*.
   The plays, all vividly theatrical, are intentionally intellectual in the French
tradition—somewhat unusual in American drama, although less so perhaps for
a graduate in philosophy from Columbia University—and for their almost neo-
classical emphasis upon verbal precision and formal control. At the same time,
the plays share a conscious concern for previous dramatic materials and
conventions, classical, medieval, Renaissance, and are unified by Richardson's
persistent and strongly held view of the human predicament as man's forced
participation in a destructive conflict between fundamental opposites: life,
individuality, imaginative illusion, but chaos on the one hand; or death,
conformity, reality, and order on the other.
   The first pair of plays, *The Prodigal* and *Gallows Humor*, are written with
an exhilarating wit and a Shavian exuberance hard to match in recent drama in
English, and they are contrasting but complementary in method, with the
classically inspired play modern by implication and the modern by medieval
allusion universal or timeless in intent. In the former play Richardson personifies his characteristic and paradoxically grouped opposites in the figures of

Aegisthus and Agamemnon, and in their conflicting views of man as either lesser or greater than he is Richardson also reflects Aristotle's definitions of comedy and tragedy. Orestes, the perfect tragicomic hero, succeeds for a time in avoiding either view and the destructive oppositions Aegisthus and Agamemnon represent. He seeks instead to "walk along the shore" and adopts the detachment of "laughter." But this modern stance, interestingly prophetic of the disillusion of youth in the later 1960s, proves a precarious stasis which cannot hold, and the murder of his father compels Orestes's participation in the battle of extremes he sought to avoid. The seeming inevitability of his decision is doubly reinforced in the play by the revenge theme of the myth itself and by the return motif of the biblical reference to the prodigal son, and at the play's close Orestes identifies his own decision with the general fate of man:

> The sea will always roar with Electra's cry; the waters will always rush toward Agamemnon's vengeance. It will cleanse or wash away the earth entirely, but it will never change . . . I can resist these forces no longer. I will go back, murder, and say it's for a better world.

In *Gallows Humor* the two component plays are linked by their common theme and by the fact that each play exactly reverses the central characters, condemned and executioner, and their points of view, and the effect of reversal is heightened by the appearance of the actors in the first play as their counterpart selves in the second. Walter, the condemned murderer, has a surprising passion for order and conformity, strives to keep his cell immaculate, and to go to his death with his "number patch" in place. But in the last hours, at the imminence of death, he is seduced back toward a celebration of life, illusion, and chaos by the prison prostitute Lucy. In the second play, Phillip the executioner, properly "dressed in the trousers, shirt, and tie of his official uniform," has an irresistible attraction toward revolt and wishes for the coming solemnities "to dress up like a headsman from the Middle Ages" in "a black hood." But his cold and practical wife Martha reasons him back toward conformity and order. The hood, Lucy's face, like a "carnival mask," the essential brutality of the execution itself, and the appearance of Death from the old Morality Plays to deliver the Prologue, give the play its comparative time metaphor. Although modern appearances are confusing, and Death complains that it is now difficult for him to "tell the hangman from the hanged," Richardson's essential oppositions, life or death, order or disorder, conformity or individuality, illusion or reality, and hangman or hanged, are reasserted as Walter and Phillip, modern ambiguities to the contrary, do end up playing their destined roles.

To an extent *Lorenzo* is a Renaissance variation of *The Prodigal*, but with a special emphasis upon illusion and reality, and the gambling metaphor in *Xmas in Las Vegas*, with its insistence upon the either/or of winner and loser, repeats the executioner-condemned contraries of *Gallows Humor* in a zany world and manner reminiscent of Kaufman and Hart and *You Can't Take It with You*. Lorenzo, "director of the theatrical troupe 'Theatre of the First Dove,'" is caught up in the midst of a "small war of the Renaissance" in Italy, and like Orestes he tries vainly not to become involved in the destructive conflict of opposites, polarized here in the impractical Duke, Filippo, and his general, the realist Van Miessen. In *Xmas in Las Vegas* Wellspot is the inveterate gambler condemned to lose, and Olympus, the casino owner, is the financial executioner. Olympus, with his suggestion of the gods, gambling as fate or destiny, and the sacrificial connotations of Christmas all enlarge the dimension of this modern parable.

Although there are important contemporary influences and parallels in his work—Anouilh's wryly detached sense of humor, for example, Genet's concern with illusion, especially Genet's and Beckett's preoccupation with opposites—Richardson's plays (and it is their limiting strength) insist upon his own almost geometrically precise view of the human condition where everything is energized as it is drawn toward its opposite and toward its destruction, and it is this underlying and rather formulaic purity which initiates a sense of tragic inevitability beneath the comic facades of his plays.

More recently in other forms of writing, in periodical essays and in a splendid and revealing book *Memoir of a Gambler*, Richardson has continued to develop with his accustomed precision the preoccupations of his plays. But although this non-dramatic writing has been deservedly successful and represents a high level of accomplishment, one hopes that he will once more be lured back to that special, indeed incurable kind of gambling, theater, in which he has in the past so skillfully played his hand.

—Gaynor F. Bradish

S

SACKLER, Howard.

Born in New York City, 19 December 1929. Educated at Brooklyn College, New York, B.A. 1950. Married Greta Lungren in 1963; two children. Director, Caedmon Records, New York, 1953–68. Recipient: Rockefeller grant, 1953; Littauer Foundation grant, 1954; Maxwell Anderson award, 1954; Sergel award, 1959; Pulitzer prize, 1969; New York Drama Critics Circle award, 1969; Tony award, 1969. Died 1982.

Publications

PLAYS

Uriel Acosta (produced 1954).
Mr. Welk and Jersey Jim (produced 1960). In *A Few Enquiries*, 1970.
The Yellow Loves (produced 1960).
A Few Enquiries (produced 1965). In *A Few Equiries*, 1970.
The Nine O'Clock Mail (televised, 1965; produced 1967). In *A Few Enquiries*, 1970.
The Pastime of Monsieur Robert (produced 1966).
The Great White Hope (produced 1967). 1968.
A Few Enquiries (includes *Search*, *The Nine O'Clock Mail*, *Mr. Welk and Jersey Jim*, *Skippy*). 1970.
Semmelweiss (produced 1977).
Goodbye Fidel (produced 1980).

SCREENPLAYS: *Desert Padre* (documentary), 1950; *Fear and Desire*, 1955; *A Midsummer Night's Dream* (English-language version), 1961. *The Great White Hope*, 1970; *Bugsy*, 1973; *Gray Lady Down*, with James Whittaker and Frank P. Rosenberg, 1978; *Jaws 2*, with Carl Gottlieb and Dorothy Tristan, 1978; *Saint Jack*, with Paul Theroux and Peter Bogdanovich, 1979.

TELEVISION PLAY: *The Nine O'Clock Mail*, 1965.

VERSE
Want My Shepherd. 1954.

MANUSCRIPT COLLECTION: University of Texas, Austin.

CRITICAL STUDY: Introduction by Martin Gottfried to *A Few Enquiries*, 1970.

THEATRICAL ACTIVITIES

DIRECTOR: Plays—*King John*, 1953; *The Family Reunion* by T.S. Eliot, 1954; *Women of Trachis* by Sophocles, 1954; *Purgatory* and *The Words upon the Windowpane* by Yeats, 1955; *Hamlet*, 1957; *Krapp's Last Tape* by Samuel Beckett, 1960; *Chin-Chin* by François Billetdoux, 1960; *Suzanna Andler* by Marguerite Duras, 1971, 1972, 1973; *The Duchess of Malfi* by Webster, 1976. Film—*A Midsummer Night's Dream*, English version, 1961. Television— *Shakespeare: Soul of an Age*, 1964.

Written in a rapid, tumbling free verse, Howard Sackler's *The Great White Hope* is clearly designed as an epic—a big play on a big subject, turbulent race relations in America as reflected in the rise and fall of a black world heavy-weight champion. The play is not equal to its subject; its points are made easily, and all its colour and pageantry cannot disguise the threadbare intellectual conception which is its central impulse. As a metaphor for black-white hostilities, the prize fight ring is sure-fire but facile.

Sackler's Jack Jefferson wants to play the game his own way. He doesn't want to be the symbolic victor for his oppressed people; if he wins, he wins for himself. He doesn't want to live according to the law of either white man or black: he flaunts his white girlfriend; he rejects his too-black former girlfriend; he sets up a speakeasy business; he's loud, violent, in trouble with the law. But for all his stature and his heroic determination, Jefferson is defeated by his opponents—the machinery of the white establishment. After his initial victory, his triumphant defeat of the great white hope, Jefferson is thwarted, hounded, challenged by group power against which his loudly proclaimed and insisted-upon independence proves insufficient. He leaves America only to meet repeated defeats abroad, and he winds up, rock-bottom at a German Café where he enacts a burlesque version of *Uncle Tom's Cabin*. His only escape is to agree to a fixed fight; in return for his agreed-upon defeat, he receives a considerable lightening of his sentence (a trumped-up charge in the first place).

Jefferson is a towering character, and Sackler outfitted him with salty, earthy, "ethnic" dialogue. But the frame in which Sackler placed his character is not nearly so capacious as the character himself. The playwright used his character in the service of a standard liberal tract that bears all the marks of apologetic white liberal guilt. The play offers nothing remotely new about elemental tensions between white and black; it settles instead for clichés of black pride and black sexual superiority to repressed and therefore vindictive whites. Sackler's sources are historical, but none the less he made Jefferson's defeat too neat a thing: his indictment of avaricious whites and his sympathy for oppressed blacks are altogether too schematic. The play has visceral impact (given its subject, it could hardly fail in this) but it is never searching enough to compel our full intellectual commitment.

After the popular success enjoyed by *The Great White Hope*, Sackler published, under the collective title *A Few Enquiries*, four one-act plays which he had written about ten years earlier. The plays suggest no real connection to the flamboyant epic that was to follow except, perhaps, in their theatricality, and in their interest in dialect and period. *Sarah* is set backstage at a Victorian ballet company; *Mr. Welk and Jersey Jim* takes place in a dilapidated turn-of-the-century law office; *Skippy* is set in a liquor store run by a husband and wife who might have stepped out of Bernard Malamud's *The Assistant*; significantly, the one unaccented and contemporary play, *The Nine O'Clock Mail*, is the least flavourful and the least convincing.

The plays share loose thematic connections. The characters are engaged in quests; they want either to discover more about each other or to resolve unsettling puzzles, and their "enquiries" are treated as rituals. In *Sarah* the characters re-enact the mysterious circumstances surrounding a ballerina's death by fire; in *The Nine O'Clock Mail* a compulsive man makes a ritual of waiting for the mail as his neglected wife tries unsuccessfully to reason with him; in *Mr Welk and Jersey Jim* a lawyer rehearses his foolish and guilty client in ways of gaining sympathy in court; and in *Skippy* a wife discovers her husband's long-withheld secret of his responsibility for the death of his kid brother. Sackler's manner in these plays is pleasingly elliptical. His style is realism heightened by theatrical proportions. These four short plays are modest enough, inconsequential enough, but they hint of thematic complexities that make them more tantalizing and more promising than the bloated and oversimplified pageant of *The Great White Hope*.

—Foster Hirsch

SAINER, Arthur.

Born in New York City, 12 September 1924. Educated at Washington Square College, New York University (John Golden award, 1946), 1942–46, B.A. 1946; Columbia University, New York, 1947–48, M.A. in philosophy 1948. Married 1) Stefanie Janis in 1956 (divorced 1962); 2) Maryjane Treloar in 1981, two sons and two daughters. New York editor, *TV Guide*, New York, 1956–61; film critic, *Show Business Illustrated*, Chicago, 1961; founding editor, *Ikon*, New York, 1967. Book critic since 1961, book editor, 1962, and drama critic, 1961–65 and since 1969, *Village Voice*, New York; film and theatre editor, *American Book Review*, New York, 1986–90. Member of the English or Theatre department, C.W. Post College, Brookville, New York, 1963–67, 1974–75, Bennington College, Vermont, 1967–69, Chautauqua Writers' Workshop, New York, 1969, Staten Island Community College, New York, 1974–75, Hunter College, New York, 1974, 1980–81, Adelphi University, Garden City, New York, 1975, Wesleyan University, Middletown, Connecticut, 1977–80, Middlebury College, Vermont, 1981–83, since 1985 New School for Social Research, New York, and since 1990 Sarah Lawrence College, Bronxville, New York. Member of the Academic Council and program adviser, Campus-Free College, Boston, 1971–74. Co-producer, Bridge Theatre, New York, 1965–66. Recipient: Office for Advanced Drama Research grant, 1967; Ford grant, 1979, 1980; Berman award, 1984. Agent: Anne Edelstein, 137 Fifth Avenue, New York, New York 10010. Address: 565 West End Avenue, New York, New York 10024, U.S.A.

Publications

PLAYS

The Bitch of Waverly Place (produced 1964).
The Game of the Eye (produced 1964).

The Day Speaks But Cannot Weep (produced 1965).
The Blind Angel (produced 1965).
Untitled Chase (produced 1965).
God Wants What Men Want (also director: produced 1966).
The Bombflower (also director: produced 1966).
The Children's Army Is Late (produced 1967).
The Thing Itself (produced 1967). In *Playwrights for Tomorrow 6*, edited by
    Arthur H. Ballet, 1969.
Noses (produced 1967).
OM: A Sharing Service (produced 1968).
Boat Sun Cavern, music by George Prideaux and Mark Hardwick (produced
    1969).
Van Gogh (produced 1970).
I Piece Smash (produced 1970). In *The Scene/2 (Plays from Off-Off-
    Broadway)*, edited by Stanley Nelson, 1974.
I Hear It Kissing Me, Ladies (produced 1970).
Images of the Coming Dead (produced 1971).
The Celebration: Jooz/Guns/Movies/The Abyss (produced 1972).
Go Children Slowly (produced 1973).
The Spring Offensive (produced 1974).
Charley Chestnut Rides the I.R.T., music by Sainer (produced 1975).
Day Old Bread: The Worst Good Time I Ever Had (produced 1976).
The Rich Man, Poor Man Play, music by David Tice and Paul Dyer (produced
    1976).
Witnesses (also director: produced 1977).
Carol in Winter Sunlight, music by George Prideaux (produced 1977).
After the Baal-Shem Tov (produced 1979).
Sunday Childhood Journeys to Nobody at Home (produced 1980).

TELEVISION PLAYS: *A New Year for Margaret*, 1951; *The Dark Side of the
Moon*, 1957; *A Man Loses His Dog More or Less*, 1972.

OTHER

The Sleepwalker and the Assassin: A Study of the Contemporary Theatre.
    1964.
The Radical Theatre Notebook. 1975.

CRITICAL STUDIES: "The Greening of American-Jewish Drama" by Ellen Schiff,
in *Handbook of American-Jewish Literature*, 1988.

THEATRICAL ACTIVITIES

DIRECTOR: **Plays**—several of his own plays; *Lord Tom Goldsmith* by Victor
Lipton, 1979; *The Desire for a City* by Norah Holmgren, 1985.
ACTOR: **Plays**—*OM: A Sharing Service*, 1968; *The Children's Army Is Late*,
1974.

Arthur Sainer comments:

(1973) I like to believe I write plays to find out something—about self, about
self in cosmos, about the cosmos, I try to make something in order to

understand something. Sometimes the plays use ideological material but they aren't ideological plays. Ultimately if they work they work as felt experience.

For some time I was fascinated by the juxtaposition of live performers and visual projections, concerned with an enlarged arrested image operating on a level other than that of the "real" performer. That period ran from *The Game of the Eye* (1964) through *Boat Sun Cavern* (written in 1967, produced in 1969). But I've lost interest in projections, I want the magic to be live, immediate, home-made. And I want the mistakes to be live ones.

Language—I've gone from many words, *God Wants What Men Want* (written in 1963), to few words, *The Blind Angel* (1965), *The Bombflower* (1966), to some words, *Images of the Coming Dead* (1971). None of these approaches is superior to the others. It depends on what the play needs and what the playwright needs at that time. Bodies are no more or less useful than the utterances that emerge from them. Only truth is useful.

Words are useful, but so is everything else. I don't hold with Grotowski's belief that every conceivable element other than the performer ought to be stripped away. Everything created by God, everything designed or decimated by the hands of man, is potentially viable and important, all of it is a testament to this life. But I've come lately (in *The Spring Offensive*) to believe in an economy of means—forget the lights, forget the setting—to believe in the magic of what is obviously being put together by hand before our eyes.

Much theatre leaves me cold, and most audiences disturb me. I don't want to make audiences particularly happy or excite them anymore. I don't want them to be sitting there judging the play, to be weighing its excellences and faults. I want the audiences to be seized and ultimately to become the play. We like to say that a really fine play changed its audience, but a really fine play also creates the condition where its audience can change it. The play ultimately is the product of this mutual vulnerability.

Theatre's ability to reproduce the external, everyday details of human life is balanced by its need to incorporate the internal, imaginative reality of its characters. Arthur Sainer's plays combine the two kinds of reality by allowing the characters to retain their unique contributions to life, while linking them into a living whole. Whether describing radical politics of the 1960s, the shifting forces at work in love and marriage, the alienation of the poor and dispossessed, a subway conductor's imminent death, or other contemporary struggles with life, Sainer is sensitive to both the effect of daily routines and rituals, and the pressure of people upon one another. His real subjects are not the events that happen to people in the course of a play, but rather the way people change and are changed by life around them.

This concentration on people produces plays that are plotless in the usual sense, but obey a rigorous internal logic. Louis, the protagonist of *The Thing Itself*, says

In the theatre to which we are offering our blood, there are no characters to be created. There are no consistencies, no patterns. Instead there are irrelevancies, inconsistencies, mistakes, broken thoughts. There is an impulse toward chaos, another toward assimilation. In our theatre there is no stage and no story, there is only human life pushed into a corner, threatened with extinction. And human life threatened with human life. And always mistakes.

The statement is unusually blunt for Sainer, whose dialogue is most often more oblique and questioning, and *The Thing Itself* unusually pessimistic and bitter, but Louis does describe Sainer's primary attitude toward drama's means and goals. Louis and his friends—Harold, who eats obsessively; Althea, a sympathetic prostitute who is brutal toward her brutal customers—are coping with the thing itself, the degradation of life in an impersonal, almost savage, city environment.

As in most of Sainer's plays, *The Thing Itself* is frequently interrupted by mimed scenes, fantasies, monologues, songs, slides, and films. Sainer has used most of the techniques available to contemporary playwrights—from Brechtian alienation to improvisation and audience participation—quite skillfully, but in every case they are expressions of the contradictory, tumultuously human life of the plays. A trilogy—*Images of the Coming Dead*, *The Children's Army Is Late* and *Carol in Winter Sunlight*—follows the growth and evolution of a family: the shifting stresses on David and Carol resulting from David's immersion in filmmaking. Carol's increasing desire to escape the trap of the family, the love both bear for their children, and their concern for their aging parents combine to create a broad and penetrating portrait of the family. In addition, the logic of this portrait calls up a series of mythological and allegorical scenes: a group of figures who begin in naked innocence, gradually become a mindlessly hardworking society, and are beset by aggressive renegades; Hector and Achilles fight their epic combat; and two characters named Allan and Albert re-enact the tragedy of Cain and Abel with a modern twist. The evolution of the human race vibrates against the evolution of the family, and the depiction of the family, sharp and sensitive as it is, is extended and expanded.

Sainer's ability to mesh the intimacy of everyday life and the development of civilization combines with his inquiries into the meaning of Jewish history to focus his plays on death. In *The Children's Army Is Late*, David searches to find and film a dying man. *Charley Chestnut Rides the I.R.T.* is filled with the bewilderment and agony of an ordinary subway conductor who suddenly faces death from a terminal illness. However, the interest in death stems from its use as a reflection of life. *After the Baal-Shem Tov* tells the story of a Jew who survives a German concentration camp to start life anew in the United States. Israel is an innocent, gentle man with an irritating habit of questioning everything. As he makes his way in America, visits a kibbutz in Israel, and becomes the editor of a respected Jewish newspaper, he loses his naivety but not his questions. Recalling his liberation from the concentration camp, he sings

> Here in the new world, the absent
> From the dead take on new life,
> The skeletons take on new flesh.
> What's it like now for the absent from the dead?
> What's it like now? Shoving, running,

Piling up things, looking into faces.
It's stupid life, it's joyous days.

Israel gives up everything and everyone he has gained in order to "redeem the promises," and there is throughout Sainer's plays an intensely human attempt to redeem the gift of life, to understand the death of people, of ideas, and of relationships in order to appreciate them more fully.

—Walter Bode

SÁNCHEZ-SCOTT, Milcha.

Born in Bali in 1955. Lived in Colombia and Mexico until 1969. Educated in London and in California. Has lived in California since 1969. Member of New Dramatists, New York. Recipient: Drama-logue award (seven times); Vesta award, 1984; Rockefeller award, 1987. Agent: George Lane, William Morris Agency, 1350 Avenue of the Americas, New York, New York 10019. Address: 2080 Mount Street, Los Angeles, California 90068, U.S.A.

Publications

PLAYS

Latina (produced 1980). In *Necessary Theater: Six Plays About the Chicano Experience*, edited by Jorge A. Huerta, 1989.
Dog Lady and The Cuban Swimmer (produced 1984). In *Plays in Process*, vol.5, no.12, 1984.
Roosters (produced 1987). In *On New Ground: Contemporary Hispanic-American Plays*, edited by M. Elizabeth Osborn, 1987.
Evening Star (produced 1988). 1989.
Stone Wedding (produced 1989).
El Dorado (produced 1990).

Of pan-American and pan-Pacific ancestry, Milcha Sánchez-Scott has felt the shock of sexist prejudice as a Latina in California. Since 1980 she has dramatised the humor and resolution of the disempowered. These qualities, along with the devotion of displaced communities, hold back for a moment the relentless oppression of economics and negative assumptions. Sánchez-Scott finds holes within harsh realities through which stream magical visions, spells, miraculous cures, transformations, and an old religious faith in past and future. Dual language allows her characters an alternative to the dominant one, whether Spanish or English. Words let them escape from mundanity into unique eloquence. Such language supplies a textual correlative for the immediately visualized and physicalized images.

In *Latina*, her first play, a remarkable playwriting voice made Sánchez-Scott's bilingual and bi-level dramatic visions clear, rich, and effective—even for materialistic, English-speaking audiences. In the prologue to *Latina*, New Girl journeys from a Peruvian mountain village to cross the barbed-wire American border. The originally plaintive Peruvian flute resounds "triumphantly" with American pop music and traffic, as we see a bus stop in front of

FELIX SANCHEZ DOMESTIC AGENCY on Wilshire Boulevard in Los Angeles. Two tanned mannequins stand in the window of the comically sleazy entrepreneur's agency; the maternal dummy in white holds a pink doll, and the naughty maid in black holds a feather duster. Dressed carefully in the American style, Sarita enters briskly to say how embarrassing it is to be thought car-less, a maid-for-hire, Latina, or available at 23 in Los Angeles. Overhearing this but speaking no English, old Eugenia the yu-yu vendor and cleaning lady offers "niña Sarita" a cure for her malady. Sarita, still denying, answers in effortless Spanish, rebukes in English, and translates for the audience. Eugenia ritually sprinkles water to sweep, and Sarita, hearing a rooster, admits she sees her grandmother sweeping a dirt road in 1915 Juarez. Then, joking bawdily about using Lava soap, they reveal Sarita's frustrated television-acting career and the old woman's affectionate pride in it. New Girl, dressed in the Peruvian style, furtively seeking domestic work, panics at the word "immigration" in Sarita's reassurance, and bites the hand that places Latinas in WASP households. As Don Felix approaches to open his shop, Eugenia still prays before they make their daily bet: is he wearing his Mickey Mouse or sailboat pajama top today? What's the point of praying? Sarita blurts in Spanish, and before going in, pauses to assure her audience, "I let her win."

These first few moments of *Latina* typify Sánchez-Scott's career. Seven comically disparate Latin women (eight, including Sarita), awaiting jobs in the agency, gossip about their desperate realities and party. The mannequins appear in Sarita's mind, mock her abject servility to WASP's and failure to defend Alma, and don rebozos to go to the park as sisters. What one lets oneself be called is important. New Girl lets them reduce her five names to "Elsa Moreno," accepts Sarita's exchanging her carefully chosen disguise for her Peruvian clothes, and with the help of Eugenia's charm and prayer and everyone's generosity, gets a placement. Sarita—in learning to accept Eugenia's prayer and bet (that her own audition overcame television's prejudice against "exotics") and divest herself of her disguise in order to help others—gets beyond her "mal educada" status to find her own dignity. "Sarita Gomez" will play her television role, and she attacks the intolerable Mrs. Camden. *Latina* ends with an immigration raid arresting all the "illegal" women as another New Girl creeps toward the barbed wire.

The Cuban Swimmer shows the Suarez family from Long Beach in the Pacific Ocean halfway to Catalina Island. Daughter Margarita is swimming in the invitational race, and her father (coach), mother (a former Miss Cuba), the praying Abuela (grandmother), and the younger brother with binoculars and punk sunglasses follow on their boat. Margarita, losing concentration, is apparently drowned by exhaustion, the oil slick ("rainbows"), and the family's hopes and demands, but mostly by the condescension of being called a simple Cuban amateur and brave little loser by the sexist American television reporter in a helicopter. Sinking to the bottom, she swims to the rhythm of "Hail Mary" into blackout. Abuela, who shouted "Assholes!" after the vanishing helicopter, invokes ancestors and saints as the grieving family reports the swimmer lost: "My little fish is not lost!" The same television reporter, in a nicely ambiguous phrase, describes to the family and the world "a miracle!"— the lost, little Cuban swimmer "is now walking on the waters, through the breakers," first "onto the beach." Abuela recognizes "sangre de mi sangre" — blood of my blood.

In *Dog Lady*, pretty, 18-year-old Rosalinda Luna will successfully and literally "run like a dog" to win the big race, and run on beyond the barrio's Castro-street — with the prayerful support of her decorous mother and the yu-yu spell and incantation of old Luisa Ruiz, the mentally and physically unkempt dog-keeper and "healer" next door. But Jesse, the 15-year-old tomboy, receives the audience's attention, her mother's scolding, her sister's trust, and half the bouquet an infatuated 18-year-old intended for the star. Suddenly transformed into a beautiful señorita, Jesse asks, "You really turn into a dog?" Rosalinda puts the yu-yu around Jesse's neck, explaining, "You have to work very hard." The two actions — winning and reluctantly coming-of-age — frame soaring fantasies, functional but very funny misunderstandings, and sparkling dialogue.

Evening Star offers another two houses on Castro Street and another reluctant coming-of-age; Olivia Peña, aged 14, in parochial school uniform, and Junior Rodriguez, aged 16, search for stars from his roof. A 30-year-old male vendor is the keeper of lore and cures (like Eugenia, Abuela, the dog lady, and *Our Town*'s Stage Manager). Grandmother Tina Peña puzzles with the vendor over the significance of a white rose miraculously appearing in her garden that morning. It should signify birth, they agree — before the old man Peña, throwing rocks, drives the vendor off. Both hardworking households are impoverished and have problems with daughters. Peña drove off their lost Sarita who left behind her child Olivia, and the abandoned Mrs. Rodriguez at first does the same when her lanky 15-year-old admits her own pregnancy. However, as Lilly Rodriguez gives birth upstairs in the Peñas' house, little epiphanies, tendernesses, and strengths bloom like roses. Mama Rodriguez rushes in to help her baby, and old Peña, who can't go in and can't pray, throws a humanistic rock at heaven. The vendor is heard: "The sun is rising. Another day of life. Try not to abuse it." Despite gritty details, poetic monologues, Old Peña's comic grouchiness and his daily ritual with Olivia (painstakingly, penuriously crossing off from his mailing list Hispanic names found in the obituaries), real theatrical magic seems slight, and too much of the affirmation gratuitous.

In *Roosters*, a multi-levelled conflict is set among farm workers who are laboring to achieve some dignity and respite. Sánchez-Scott divides allegorically-named males and females into contrasting types and lets the drama bring them to fertile reconciliation. In a prologue the handsome Gallo, in his forties, explains how, at the cost of a prison term for manslaughter, he "borrowed" a high-flying ("like dark avenging angels") Filipino bolina named MacArthur to breed with his old red Cuban hen ("a queen" to whom you would never give "a second look" yet who killed every "stag") to create the prize-fighting cock Zapata. As he stalks and pricks his crossbred Hispanic-Pacific rooster (a male dancer) with a stiletto, Gallo croons "Show Daddy watcha got" and delights when "son" Zapata attacks and draws blood. Now, all anxiously await the homecoming of husband-lover, brother and father. Willed the bird by his grandfather during his father's absence, Gallo's 20-year-old son Hector plans to first-fight Zapata tonight and sell him to finance a better life for his mother (Juana), tortilla-rolling aunt (Chata), and mystical younger sister (Angelita). The women preparing food anticipate more hardship and loneliness. Angelita with her cardboard wings and tombstones, prayers to saints, disappearances, and imaginary tea-parties can see the shadows stalking her father and brother and must choose sides. The predicted cockfight between Hector and Gallo allows rightful shares of nobility to each generation, character, and way of living. Sánchez-Scott achieves this persuasively.

—John G. Kuhn

SAROYAN, William.

Born in Fresno, California, 31 August 1908. Educated at public schools in Fresno to age 15. Served in the U.S. Army, 1942–45. Married Carol Marcus in 1943 (divorced 1949; remarried 1951; divorced 1952); one son (the writer Aram Saroyan) and one daughter. Worked as grocery clerk, vineyard worker, post office employee, clerk, telegraph operator, then office manager, Postal Telegraph Company, San Francisco, 1926–28; co-founder, Conference Press, Los Angeles, 1936; founder and director, Saroyan Theatre, New York, 1942; writer-in-residence, Purdue University, Lafayette, Indiana, 1961. Recipient: New York Drama Critics Circle award, 1940; Pulitzer prize, 1940 (refused); Oscar, for screenplay, 1944. Member, American Academy, 1943. *Died 18 May 1981.*

Publications

PLAYS

The Man with the Heart in the Highlands. In *Contemporary One-Act Plays,* edited by William Kozlenko, 1938; revised version, as *My Heart's in the Highlands* (produced 1939), 1939.

The Time of Your Life (produced 1939). In *The Time of Your Life* (miscellany), 1939.

The Hungerers (produced 1945). 1939.

Love's Old Sweet Song (produced 1940). In *Three Plays,* 1940.

Radio Play (broadcast 1940). In *Razzle Dazzle,* 1942.

Subway Circus. 1940.

Something About a Soldier (produced 1940).

Hero of the World (produced 1940).

Three Plays: My Heart's in the Highlands; The Time of Your Life; Love's Old Sweet Song. 1940.

A Special Announcement (broadcast 1940). 1940.

The Great American Goof (ballet scenario; produced 1940). In *Razzle Dazzle,* 1942.

The Ping-Pong Game (produced 1945). 1940; as *The Ping-Pong Players,* in *Razzle Dazzle,* 1942.

Sweeney in the Trees (produced 1940). In *Three Plays,* 1941.

The Beautiful People (produced 1941). In *Three Plays,* 1941.

Across the Board on Tomorrow Morning (produced 1941). In *Three Plays,* 1941.

Three Plays: The Beautiful People; Sweeney in the Trees; Across the Board on Tomorrow Morning. 1941.

Hello, Out There, music by Jack Beeson (produced 1941).]In *Razzle Dazzle*, 1942.

There's Something I Got to Tell You (broadcast 1941). In *Razzle Dazzle*, 1942.

The People with Light Coming Out of Them (broadcast 1941). In *The Free Company Presents*, 1941.

Jim Dandy (produced 1941). 1941; as *Jim Dandy: Fat Man in a Famine*, 1947.

Talking to You (produced 1942). In *Razzle Dazzle*, 1942.

Razzle Dazzle; or, The Human Opera, Ballet, and Circus; or, There's Something I Got to Tell You: Being Many Kinds of Short Plays As Well As the Story of the Writing of Them (includes *Hello, Out There*; *Coming Through the Rye*; *Talking to You*; *The Great American Goof*; *The Poetic Situation in America*; *Opera, Opera*; *Bad Men in the West*; *The Agony of Little Nations*; *A Special Announcement*; *Radio Play*; *The People with Light Coming Out of Them*; *There's Something I Got to Tell You*; *The Hungerers*; *Elmer and Lily*; *Subway Circus*; *The Ping Pong Players*). 1942; abridged edition, 1945.

Opera, Opera (produced 1955). In *Razzle Dazzle*, 1942.

Bad Men in the West (produced 1971). In *Razzle Dazzle*, 1942.

Get Away Old Man (produced 1943). 1944.

Sam Ego's House (produced 1947). In *Don't Go Away Mad and Two Other Plays*, 1949.

Don't Go Away Mad (produced 1949). In *Don't Go Away Mad and Two Other Plays*, 1949.

Don't Go Away Mad and Two Other Plays: Sam Ego's House; A Decent Birth, A Happy Funeral. 1949.

The Son (produced 1950).

The Oyster and the Pearl (televised 1953). In *Perspectives USA*, Summer 1953.

A Lost Child's Fireflies (produced 1954).

Once Around the Block (produced 1956). 1959.

The Cave Dwellers (produced 1957). 1958.

Ever Been in Love with a Midget (produced 1957).

The Slaughter of the Innocents (produced 1957). 1958.

Cat, Mouse, Man, Woman. In *Contact 1*, 1958.

The Accident. In *Contact 1*, 1958.

The Dogs; or, The Paris Comedy (as *The Paris Comedy; or The Secret of Lily*, produced 1960; as *Lily Dafon*, produced 1960). In *The Dogs; or, The Paris Comedy and Two Other Plays*, 1969.

Settled Out of Court, with Henry Cecil, from the novel by Cecil (produced 1960). 1962.

Sam, The Highest Jumper of Them All; or, The London Comedy (produced 1960). 1961.

High Time along the Wabash (produced 1961).

Ah Man, music by Peter Fricker (produced 1962).

Four Plays: The Playwright and the Public; The Handshakers; The Doctor and the Patient; This I Believe. In *Atlantic*, April 1963.

The Time of Your Life and Other Plays. 1967.

Dentist and Patient. In *The Best Short Plays 1968*, edited by Stanley Richards, 1968.

Husband and Wife. In *The Best Short Plays 1968*, edited by Stanley Richards, 1968.

The Dogs; or, The Paris Comedy and Two Other Plays: Chris Sick; or, Happy New Year Anyway, Making Money, and Nineteen Other Very Short Plays. 1969.

Making Money, and Nineteen Other Very Short Plays (televised 1970). In *The Dogs; or, The Paris Comedy and Two Other Plays: Chris Sick; or, Happy New Year Anyway, Making Money, and Nineteen Other Very Short Plays.* 1969.

The New Play. In *The Best Short Plays 1970*, edited by Stanley Richards, 1970.

People's Lives (produced 1974).

Armenians (produced 1974).

The Rebirth Celebration of the Human Race at Artie Zabala's Off-Broadway Theatre (produced 1975).

Two Short Paris Summertime Plays of 1974 (includes *Assassinations* and *Jim, Sam, and Anna*). 1979.

SCREENPLAYS: *The Good Job* (documentary), 1942; *The Human Comedy*, with Howard Estabrook, 1943.

RADIO PLAYS: *Radio Play*, 1940 ; *A Special Announcement*, 1940; *There's Something I Got to Tell You*, 1941; *The People with Light Coming Out of Them*, 1941.

TELEVISION PLAYS: *The Oyster and the Pearl*, 1953; *Ah Sweet Mystery of Mrs. Murphy*, 1959; *The Unstoppable Gray Fox*, 1962; *Making Money, and Nineteen Other Very Short Plays*, 1970.

NOVELS

The Human Comedy. 1943.

The Adventures of Wesley Jackson. 1946.

The Twin Adventures: The Adventures of Saroyan: A Diary; The Adventures of Wesley Jackson: A Novel. 1950.

Rock Wagram. 1951.

Tracy's Tiger. 1951.

The Laughing Matter. 1953; as *A Secret Story*, 1954.

Mama I Love You. 1956.

Papa You're Crazy. 1957.

Boys and Girls Together. 1963.

One Day in the Afternoon of the World. 1964.

SHORT STORIES

The Daring Young Man on the Flying Trapeze and Other Stories. 1934.

Inhale and Exhale. 1936.

Three Times Three. 1936.

Little Children. 1937.

The Gay and Melancholy Flux: Short Stories. 1937.

Love, Here is My Hat. 1938.

A Native American. 1938.
The Trouble with Tigers. 1938.
Peace, it's Wonderful. 1939.
3 Fragments and a Story. 1939.
My Name is Aram. 1940.
Saroyan's Fables. 1941.
The Insurance Salesman and Other Stories. 1941.
48 Saroyan Stories. 1942.
Best Stories. 1942.
Thirty-One Selected Stories. 1943.
Some Day I'll Be a Millionaire: 34 More Great Stories. 1943.
Dear Baby. 1944.
The Saroyan Special: Selected Short Stories. 1948.
The Fiscal Hoboes. 1949.
The Assyrian and Other Stories. 1950.
The Whole Voyald and Other Stories. 1956.
Love. 1959.
After Thirty Years: The Daring Young Man on the Flying Trapeze (includes
    essays). 1964.
Best Stories of Saroyan. 1964.
My Kind of Crazy Wonderful People: 17 Stories and a Play. 1966.
An Act or Two of Foolish Kindness: Two Stories. 1977.
Madness in the Family, edited by L. Hamalian. 1988.
The Man with the Heart in the Highlands and Other Early Stories. 1989.

VERSE

A Christmas Psalm. 1935.
Christmas 1939. 1939.

OTHER

Those Who Write Them and Those Who Collect Them. 1936.
The Time of Your Life (miscellany). 1939.
Harlem as Seen by Hirschfeld. 1941.
Hilltop Russians in San Francisco. 1941.
Why Abstract?, with Henry Miller and Hilaire Hiler. 1945.
The Bicycle Rider in Beverly Hills (autobiography). 1952.
The Saroyan Reader. 1958.
A Note on Hilaire Hiler. 1962.
Here Comes, There Goes, You Know Who (autobiography). 1962.
Not Dying (autobiography). 1963.
Me (for children). 1963.
Short Drive, Sweet Chariot (autobiography). 1966.
Look at Us: Let's See: Here We Are: Look Hard: Speak Soft: I See, You See,
    We all See; Stop, Look, Listen; Beholder's Eye; Don't Look Now But Isn't
    That You? (us? U.S.). 1967.
Horsey Gorsey and the Frog (for children). 1968.
I Used to Believe I Had Forever; Now I'm Not So Sure. 1968.
Letters from 74 rue Taitbout. 1969; as *Don't Go But If You Must Say Hello to*
    Everybody, 1970.

Days of Life and Death and Escape to the Moon. 1970.
Places Where I've Done Time. 1972.
The Tooth and My Father (for children). 1974.
Morris Hirshfield. 1976.
Famous Faces and Other Friends: A Personal Memoir. 1976.
Sons Come and Go, Mothers Hang in Forever (memoirs). 1976.
Chance Meetings. 1978.
Obituaries. 1979.
Births. 1983.
My Name is Saroyan (miscellany), edited by James H. Tas. 1983.

Editor, *Hairenik 1934–1939: An Anthology of Short Stories and Poems.* 1939.

BIBLIOGRAPHY: *William Saroyan: A Reference Guide* by Elisabeth C. Foard, 1989.

CRITICAL STUDIES: *William Saroyan* by Howard R. Floan, 1966; *Last Rites: The Death of William Saroyan* by Aram Saroyan, 1982; *William Saroyan* by Aram Saroyan, 1983; *Saroyan: A Biography* by Lawrence Lee and Barry Gifford, 1984; *William Saroyan: The Man and the Writer Remembered*, edited by Leo Hamalian, 1987.

It has become almost mandatory to dismiss William Saroyan as a one-play writer, whose enormous output of drama and fiction has never matched the promise of *The Time of Your Life*, the only one of his works to have had extensive professional revival. Critics have patronised him as sentimental, naive, innocent, optimistic, and childlike, and his plays as formless, loose, and melodramatic. Certainly, in his own writing about his plays there is an intellectual slackness that does not encourage close reading of his work. One critic even observed that "if Saroyan would only keep his big mouth shut about the speed with which he writes, he would be regarded by his critics with considerably more sobriety". George Jean Nathan in 1942 wrote a 13-page essay addressing the question, "Is Saroyan crazy?". Yet the playwright himself also stated that the plays of Ionesco "bewilder, delight, annoy, astonish, amaze and amuse me the most", and that "I cherish every cockeyed moment of *Waiting for Godot*". Nor was his appreciation on a level with Bert Lahr's fondness for such plays, which he took essentially as vaudeville; Saroyan could articulate the value of these writers, and then go on to assess their limits, arguing that "they lack size and rage".

The unpretentiousness of Saroyan does not mean triteness. Post-modernist readings in the 1980s of Sam Shepard's use of the Old West in plays like *Geography of a Horse Dreamer* draw attention to the way that in 1939 Saroyan had done precisely the same thing by bringing Kit Carson into the world of *The Time of Your Life*, and thus based the play's premise not on naturalistic issues in the characters' backgrounds but on the sometimes foolish dreams, goals, and ideals they live by. At the same time, in that play he delineated an alcoholic microcosm that has often been compared with O'Neill's (later) *The Iceman Cometh* and a man-versus-machine drama that recalls Rice's *The Adding Machine*.

Before *The Time of Your Life*, Saroyan had written numerous one-acters characterised by a dreamlike atmosphere and an infantilised perspective in which some critics would find the embryo of what they would term his surrealism. *My Heart's in the Highlands*, the most famous of these, was produced as an "experimental" piece by The Group Theatre, Clurman explaining that he had argued against Kazan that it had "freedom, simplicity, hobo charm, delicate sentiment, and humor". The play gradually transmutes the oppressive atmosphere of 1914 into general optimism about humanity through the agency of a Scottish immigrant to California who bolsters up an assortment of waifs with his bravado, tall stories, songs, and playing the title tune on his bugle.

A similar atmosphere and philosophy pervade *Love's Old Sweet Song* and *The Beautiful People*, although the former has a satirical dimension which would be developed to major proportions in *Get Away Old Man*, taking Hollywood as its target. The play is more clearly plotted than any of his others, but its failure on Broadway after only 13 performances led him back to more than a decade of stylised, sometimes defiantly uncommercial dramatic writing. Symbolism, surrealism, insanity, dada, and self-parodying psychoanalysis merge in many of these plays, and though they tend to end happily there is often a pervasive tone of bitterness. *Sweeney in the Trees* chides at capitalism, *Sam Ego's House* is an asylum inhabited by the Urges, and *Jim Dandy* presents a library in the midst of ruins perceived through an eggshell. The situation anticipates that of *The Cave Dwellers* in its clustering of heterogeneous characters in an unlikely refuge, and in the way that the race is poised between collapse (represented on stage by an apeman hybrid) and redemption (through the curiously opportune arrival of materials for a Eucharist).

The Cave Dwellers was Saroyan's first new play on Broadway in 15 years. Written before the notion of "metatheatre" had been legitimised as critical currency, the play is based on an audacious extension of cultural "ready-mades" into a new microcosmic theatrical context, a technique which had been foreshadowed in *The Time of Your Life*. In the new play, a group of down-and-out former entertainers are revealed living underground beneath a New York theatre, while off-stage explosions indicate chaos outside. A process of regression to a neolithic—if not animal—state is occurring, but the characters have taken the names of their former roles: a stage Queen, a clown King, and a boxer Duke. Their apparent degeneration is arrested by the arrival of various other figures including a terrified girl, a man and a pregnant woman, and a trained bear. The bear and new-born baby give some stimulus to the resurgence of the human spirit, and towards the end of the play the King observes: "What are we doing in a cave? We're angels."

A similar dramaturgy lies beneath another play produced in the same year, *The Slaughter of the Innocents*. It is set in the characteristic Saroyan bar, but the alcoholic subculture transmutes into a courtroom where a perverse justice is being administered. The play may be read as a futuristic dystopia or as an alcoholic reverie which turns into nightmare, but again a buoyant faith reasserts itself when the barman slugs the judge and announces freedom for all and drinks on the house. For all that, the central action has an unnerving depiction of the arbitrariness of totalitarian government, and a passionate commitment to socio-political issues that is surprising in Saroyan.

Was Saroyan crazy? Eric Bentley once provocatively put him beside J.B. Priestley to argue that they "are the two prime instances in the dramatic world of highbrows trying to be lowbrows without losing caste. Hence their exaggerated hominess, their forced simplicity, their patriotism and insistent local color, their chronic fear of the esoteric". To which Saroyan indirectly replied, commenting on one of his plays, "I got the idea from alley cats, whom I had watched carefully".

—Howard McNaughton

SCHENKAR, Joan M.

Born in Seattle, Washington, 15 August 1946. Educated at St. Nicholas School, Bennington College, Bennington, Vermont, and a collection of graduate schools. Advertising copywriter, social worker, and researcher, all New York, 1960's; coffee and doughnut vendor, 1973, and church organist, Congregational Church, 1974, both Vermont; playwright-in-residence, Joseph Chaikin's Winter Project, New York, 1977 and 1978, Polish Laboratory, New York, 1977, Florida Studio Theatre, Sarasota, Florida, 1980, Changing Scene, Denver, Colorado, 1982, Centre d'essai des auteurs dramatiques, Montreal, and Composer-Librettist's Workshop, New York, both 1985, Minnesota Opera New Music Theatre Ensemble, Minneapolis, 1986–88, and Kentucky Foundation for Women, Louisville, Kentucky, 1988. Visiting fellow, Cummington Community Arts, Cummington, Massachusetts, 1978, Ragdale Foundation, Lake Forest, Illinois, 1979, and MacDowell Art Colony, Peterborough, New Hampshire, 1980; teacher, School of Visual Arts, New York, 1978–91; founder and artistic director, Force Majeure Productions, New York, from 1987. Since 1992 director, The Performance Series, North Bennington, Vermont. Recipient: National Endowment for the Arts grant, 1977, 1978, 1980, 1982, fellowship, 1981; Creative Artists Public Service fellowship, 1979–80; Lowe Foundation grant, 1983; Playwrights Forum award, 1984; Arthur Foundation grant, 1984, 1989; New York State Council on the Arts grant, 1986, 1989, 1992; Schubert Travel grant, 1988; Vermont Community grant, 1991. Agent: Casarotto Ramsay Ltd., National House, 60–66 Wardour Street, London W1V 3HP, England. Address: P.O. Box 814, North Bennington, Vermont 05257, U.S.A.

Publications

PLAYS

The Next Thing (produced 1976).
Cabin Fever (produced 1976). 1984.
Last Words (produced 1977).
Signs of Life (produced 1979). In The Women's Project Anthology edited by Julia Miles, 1980.
The Lodger (produced 1979).
Mr. Monster (produced 1980).
The Last of Hitler (also director: produced 1981).
Between the Acts (also director: produced 1984).
Fulfilling Koch's Postulate (also director: produced 1985).

Joan of Arc (produced 1986).
Family Pride in the 50's (produced 1986). In *The Kenyon Review*, Spring 1993.
Fire in the Future (produced 1987; also director: produced 1988).
Hunting Down the Sexes (includes *Bucks and Does, The Lodger*) (produced 1987).
Nothing Is Funnier than Death (produced 1988).
The Universal Wolf (produced 1991). 1992.

CRITICAL STUDIES (selection): "Foodtalk in the Plays of Caryl Churchill and Joan Schenkar" by Vivian M. Patraka, in *The Theatre Annual*, 1985; "Mass Culture and Metaphors of Menace in Joan Schenkar's Plays" by Vivian M. Patraka, in *Making a Spectacle, Feminist Essays on Contemporary Women's Theatre* edited by Lynda Hart, 1989; "History and Hysteria, Writing the Body in *Portrait of Dora* and *Signs of Life*" by Ann Wilson, in *Modern Drama*, March 1989; "Crossing the Corpus Callosum" by Elin Diamond, in *The Drama Review*, Summer 1991.

THEATRICAL ACTIVITIES
DIRECTOR: **Plays**—*The Last of Hitler*, 1981; *Between the Acts*, 1984, 1989; *Fulfilling Koch's Postulate*, 1985; *Fire in the Future*, 1988.

Joan Schenkar comments:

My most serious intention as a writer for the stage is to enter a clear condition of nightmare thru the comedy of precise vernacular . . . Some truths are so terrible they can only be approached by laughter—which is why I write comedies of menace. In the best of all possible productions, I will have made you laugh at something horrible.

Dreams, history, and fantasy serve as raw material for the elliptical, determinedly non-naturalistic plays of Joan Schenkar. Her style is heavily influenced by cartoons, comic strips, feminist theory and literature, radio, television, circus, and sideshow. Schenkar's stated purpose "is to make comedies of tragic subjects," and she wields her macabre, demonic sense of humor like a scalpel, dissecting varied topics—the Victorians' destructive attitude toward women, the insidious spread of anti-Semitism, the power and precariousness of a scientific outlook, and the surreal normality of American suburbia.

Schenkar gives a number of her plays the subtitle "a comedy of menace." Her three primary works in this vein—*Cabin Fever, Fulfilling Koch's Postulate*, and *Family Pride in the 50's*—all share this subversive manic humor. *Cabin Fever*, the funniest and most menacing, reads like a Stephen King story as dramatized by Samuel Beckett. Three characters, called One, Two, and Three, never move from their dilapidated New England front porch as they try to stave off the dreaded disease of the title. Underneath their reserved, almost formal manner, terror lurks: they know "it comes in threes." "What does?" one character asks. "Death," assures another. With each repetition of this litany their anxiety spirals. When talk turns to the cannibalism that's been running rampant in this backwoods community, One twitches in her seat as Two and Three recall the last time they sampled human flesh. Although they jocularly threaten to eat One, she gets the last laugh, and the play ends with her brandishing knife and fork.

Influenced by the Katzenjammer Kids comic strip, Schenkar purposefully confines herself to a 300-word vocabulary for *Fulfilling Koch's Postulate*. Like *Cabin Fever*, Schenkar provides her characters with a one-line litany: "Nothing is funnier than death." Her sets are always exaggerated metaphors that serve as an extra character and this one is no exception, featuring a lip-shaped proscenium and a playing space made into an esophagus. Within this frame the stage is split between the kitchen, from which a household chef, based on the infamous historical figure known as Typhoid Mary, spreads her deadly contagion, and the laboratory in which Dr. Koch tries to track down the disease's root. As the cook cooks and the scientist probes, the culinary activities take on shades of sinister experimentation while Koch's dissections become utterly domestic. *Family Pride in the 50's* is a heavy-handed satire on an easy target: the idyllic post-war decade dominated by frosted flakes, family holiday dinners, and fights over the television set. Everyone resembles everyone else—two brothers married two sisters, each with two children. As the eldest child Joan retches violently, everyone blithely continues their family squabbles. When the children play "doctor," they use real knives and instruments, much like the dramatist did: "When I was a kid I used to collect knives. . . . I had a surgeon's puncture tool. . . . And I'd take people's blood samples." The play ends with the children sitting around the table:

> Maureen: You gonna deal those cards? Or do I have to cut 'em with my knife.
> Joan: Tch tch. Such language sis. Tch tch tch. Such *language* at the *dinner* table.

Schenkar's preoccupation with science—or what she calls "false science"—underlies two other historically based plays, *The Last of Hitler* and *Signs of Life*. The former is a dream play picturing the Führer in what Schenkar envisions as his version of Hell—a "Kozy Kabin" in Florida, a state with a large population of Jews. Once again, Schenkar works with a split stage, but this one is divided by an enormous 1940's radio that spews anti-Semitism, less visible than Typhoid Mary's infection but just as deadly. As Dr. Reich and his office skeleton perform ventriloquist routines reminiscent of Charlie McCarthy's, Hitler and Eva Braun fight off cancer and their own Jewishness. *Signs of Life*, the most successful of Schenkar's imaginative treatments of history, features Henry James and Dr. Sloper, the inventor of the "uterine guillotine," taking tea and toasting "the ladies" who Schenkar believes helped make the men famous—Henry's invalid sister Alice, and Jane Merritt, P.T. Barnum's sideshow star dubbed the "Elephant Woman," on whom Sloper performed experimental surgery. The play clearly demonstrates how both women were transformed into freaks, victims of Victorian patriarchy's male-volence toward women.

Between the Acts, an absurdist surreal fairytale set in the garden of the wealthiest man in the world, gives allegorical voice to Schenkar's feminist and political concerns. At a climactic moment, the rich capitalist Martin Barney and his daughter's lesbian lover the artist Romaine Brooks, circle each other like boxers. Instead of trading physical blows, they shout out famous names. When Barney yells "J.P. Morgan" Romaine is momentarily staggered, but she strikes back with "Emily Brontë, Emily Dickinson, Virginia Woolf!" and crumples the industrialist, who wails, "Genius! Good God! I have nothing to fight genius with." Featuring a gigantic Venus Fly Trap that serves as a trysting spot, a riding crop that spews magic dust, and a dog in a tutu performing bourrées in silhouette, this is one of Schenkar's wildest efforts.

Hunting Down the Sexes, composed of two compact and vicious one-acts, literalizes these gender wars. Part One, *Bucks and Does*, focuses on three men, Rap, Ape, and Ab, at their hunting cabin. The play opens with Rap masturbating in synchronized motion with Ab's ritualistic cleaning of the guns. Schenkar then takes Freud's theories to their harrowing extreme: Rap, who insists on calling does "pretty brown girls," tells his mates, "There's nothing like pulling a trigger and watching 'em drop. I always come when they drop." Of course, the does, portrayed by actresses, get their final revenge when Rap staggers into the cabin with his crotch bloodied by a stray bullet. In Part Two, *The Lodger*, a pair of spinsterish women debate the tortures they'll inflict on their male prisoner, captured in the guerilla war between genders raging around their Victorian New England home.

Schenkar's works all limn the body/brain duality. Images of blood, ritualistic "bloodings," and blood samples appear in virtually every play, while the fragile intellectual systems holding reality together go haywire. Schenkar's stagecraft, using varied performance traditions—from cartoons to shadow-puppets—and structural devices—from entr'actes to epilogues—matches her imagination to provide, in the best of her work, insightful entrées to the dualities duelling for body and soul in Western society.

—John Istel

SCHEVILL, James (Erwin).

Born in Berkeley, California, 10 June 1920. Educated at Harvard University, Cambridge, Massachusetts, B.S. 1942. Served in the United States Army, 1942–46. Married Margot Helmuth Blum in 1966; two daughters by an earlier marriage. Member of the faculty, California College of Arts and Crafts, Oakland, 1950–59; member of the Faculty, 1959–68, and director of the Poetry Center, 1961–68, San Francisco State College. Professor of English 1969–85, professor emeritus since 1985, and director of the creative writing program, 1972–75, Brown University, Providence, Rhode Island. Founding member, Wastepaper Theatre, Providence; since 1983 president, Rhode Island Playwrights Theatre. Recipient: National Theatre Competition prize, 1945; Dramatists Alliance Contest prize, 1948; Fund for the Advancement of Education fellowship, 1953; Phelan prize, for biography, 1954, for play, 1958; Ford grant, 1960; Rockefeller grant, 1964; William Carlos Williams award (*Contact* magazine), 1965; Roadstead Foundation award, 1966; Rhode Island Governor's award, 1975; Guggenheim fellowship, 1981; McKnight fellowship, 1984; American Academy award, 1991, literary award, 1992. M.A. (ad eundem): Brown University, 1969; D.H.L.: Rhode Island College, Providence,

1986. Agent: Helen Merrill Ltd., 435 West 23rd Street, No. 1A, New York, New York 10011. Address: 1309 Oxford Street, Berkeley, California, U.S.A.

Publications

PLAYS

High Sinners, Low Angels, music by Schevill, arranged by Robert Commanday (produced 1953). 1953.

The Bloody Tenet (produced 1956). In *The Black President and Other Plays*, 1965.

The Cid, adaptation of the play by Corneille (broadcast 1963). In *The Classic Theatre 4*, edited by Eric Bentley, 1961.

Voices of Mass and Capital A, music by Andrew Imbrie (produced 1962). 1962.

The Master (produced 1963). In *The Black President and Other Plays*, 1965.

American Power: The Space Fan, and The Master (produced 1964). In *The Black President and Other Plays*, 1965.

The Black President and Other Plays. 1965.

The Death of Anton Webern (produced 1966). In *Violence and Glory: Poems 1962–1968*, 1969.

This Is Not True, music by Paul McIntyre (produced 1967).

The Pilots (produced 1970).

Oppenheimer's Chair (produced 1970).

Lovecraft's Follies (produced 1970). 1971.

The Ushers (produced 1971). In *Five Plays*, 1993.

The American Fantasies (produced 1972).

Emperor Norton Lives! (produced 1972; revised version, as *Emperor Norton*, music by Jerome Rosen, produced 1979).

Fay Wray Meets King Kong (produced 1974). In *Wastepaper Theatre Anthology*, edited by Schevill, 1978.

Sunset and Evening Stance; or, Mr. Krapp's New Tapes (produced 1974). In *Wastepaper Theatre Anthology*, edited by Schevill, 1978.

The Telephone Murderer (produced 1975). In *Wastepaper Theatre Anthology*, edited by Schevill, 1978.

Cathedral of Ice (produced 1975). 1975.

Naked in the Garden (produced 1975).

Year after Year (produced 1976).

Questioning Woman (produced 1980).

Mean Man I (also director: produced 1981).

Mean Man II (also director: produced 1982).

Edison's Dream (produced 1982).

Galileo, with Adrian Hall, adaptation of the play by Brecht (produced 1983).

Cult of Youth (produced 1984).

Mean Man III (also director: produced 1985).

Time of the Hand and Eye (produced 1986).

The Planner (also director: produced 1986).

Collected Short Plays. 1986.

The Storyville Doll Lady (also director: produced 1987).

Perelman Monologue (produced 1987).

Mother O; or, The Last American Mother (produced 1990). In *Five Plays*, 1993.
Sisters in the Limelight (produced 1990).
American Fantasies (produced 1990).
The Garden on F Street, with Mary Gail (produced 1992).
Five Plays (includes *Lovecraft's Follies, The Ushers, The Last Romantics, Mother O; or, The Last American Mother, Shadows of Memory: A Double Bill About Dian Fossey and Djuna Barnes*). 1993.

RADIO PLAYS: *The Sound of a Soldier*, 1945; *The Death of a President*, 1945; *The Cid*, 1963 (Canada); *The Death of Anton Webern*, 1972.

NOVEL

The Arena of Ants. 1977.

VERSE

Tensions. 1947.
The American Fantasies. 1951.
The Right to Greet. 1955.
Selected Poems 1945–1959. 1960.
Private Dooms and Public Destinations: Poems 1945–1962. 1962.
The Stalingrad Elegies. 1964.
Release. 1968.
Violence and Glory: Poems 1962–1968. 1969.
The Buddhist Car and Other Characters. 1973.
Pursuing Elegy: A Poem about Haiti. 1974.
The Mayan Poems. 1978.
Fire of Eyes: A Guatemalan Sequence. 1979.
The American Fantasies: Collected Poems 1: 1945–1981. 1983.
The Invisible Volcano. 1985.
Ghost Names/Ghost Numbers. 1986.
Ambiguous Dancers of Fame: Collected Poems 2: 1945–1985. 1987.
Quixote Visions. 1991.

RECORDING: *Performance Poems*, 1984.

OTHER

Sherwood Anderson: His Life and Work. 1951.
The Roaring Market and the Silent Tomb (biographical study of the scientist and artist Bern Porter). 1956.
Bern Porter: A Personal Biography. 1992.

Editor, *Six Historians*, by Ferdinand Schevill. 1956.
Editor, *Break Out! In Search of New Theatrical Environments.* 1973.
Editor, *Wastepaper Theatre Anthology.* 1978.

MANUSCRIPT COLLECTION: John Hay Library, Brown University, Providence, Rhode Island.

THEATRICAL ACTIVITIES
DIRECTOR: Plays—*Mean Man I–III*, 1981–85; *The Planner*, 1986; *The Storyville Doll Lady*, 1987.

James Schevill comments:

(1973) My early plays were verse plays. Recently, my plays have been written in prose. However, as a poet, I still believe in poetry as the roots of the theatre, and do my best to upend a theatre that is too literal and prosaic. I want an action that is both theatrical and poetic, that can use the disturbing images of our time to create a new vitality on stage. To achieve this vitality, I like to use dramatic, historical contrasts to give a play depth and perspective. Today the great possibilities of playwriting lie in the recognition that a play can range in time and space as widely as a film, that it can be as exciting in movement as a film, and that the great advantage it continues to have over film is the live actor who is capable of instantaneous, extraordinary transformations in character and situation.

A lyric poet, James Schevill has been consistently drawn to the theatre, but his plays are written largely in prose. Composed of history, current events, and fantasy, they theatricalize injustice in contemporary America.

The Bloody Tenet takes its title from the self-defense of Roger Williams when he was persecuted for religious unorthodoxy. Schevill's play sets Williams's story as a play within a play, and the outer frame is a dialogue between a middle-aged Journalist and a voluptuous Evangelist. As the inner play dramatizes Williams's condemnation by orthodox authority, the frame play dramatizes a facile orthodoxy paying lip service to liberty. Schevill's play finally confronts his moderns with Williams himself, who refuses to choose between the Journalist's critique of his inadequacies and the Evangelist's idolization of him. In verse Roger Williams re-emphasizes his belief in individual paths to God.

Moving from religion to politics, Schevill paired his next two plays under the title *American Power*. The first play, *The Space Fan*, is subtitled a play of escape, and the second one, *The Master*, a play of commitment. The titular Space Fan is a zany lady who communicates with beings in outer space, and a suspicious government therefore assigns an Investigator to spy on her activities. Through the course of the play the Space Fan converts the Investigator to her free way of life, and as they join in a dance the Investigator declares: "For the first time in my life, I feel that I've become a real investigator."

In the companion play, *The Master*, investigation is more insidious. An attractive young woman, the Candidate, is guided by the Master in examinations which will culminate in a degree of General Mastery. During the examination the Master imposes upon the Candidate various roles, such as Army Officer, Indian squaw, Minute Man, Southern rebel, and finally corpse. Master and Candidate then oppose each other with their respective autobiographies, which erupt into scenes that glorify American power. The subtitles of both plays emerge as ironic: *The Space Fan* is a play of escape from American power, and *The Master*, a play of commitment, satirizes (and implicitly condemns) commitment to American power.

Schevill's next play, *The Black President*, is rooted in American oppression of blacks, but it reaches out to indict the whole white racist world. Moses Jackburn, a black American, is captain of a facsimile slaveship that is manned by the blacks of many countries. He sails the ship up the Thames to London, demanding to speak with the British Prime Minister. He is met with pious platitudes, then mercantile bargaining, and finally threats of force. Rather than surrender the ship, Jackson orders his crew to blow it up. While awaiting extradition to America, he is visited by Spanish Carla with whom he shares a fantasy life in which she helps him campaign for the presidency, to become the first "Black President." Back in the reality of his prison, Jackburn denounces his dream, but still hopes for "a little light."

In *Lovecraft's Follies* Schevill indicates his concern about man's enslavement by technology. H.P. Lovecraft, a Rhode Island recluse, was one of the first science-fiction writers to stress its gothic horrors. The protagonist of Schevill's play, Stanley Millsage, is a physicist at a space center, who has developed a Lovecraft fixation-fear of the horrors that science can perpetrate, which are theatricalized scenically to serve as a cathartic journey for the protagonist. Thus freed from his Lovecraft fixation, Millsage decares: "Well, that's the end of Lovecraft's follies. . . ." But the figure of Lovecraft, alone on stage, says mockingly to the audience: "Maybe!"

That "Maybe" leads to Schevill's next major play, *Cathedral of Ice*, in which technology again brings horror. On stage is a dream machine: "With our machine's modern computer device/We conjure up a vast Cathedral of Ice./ . . . I become Dream-Fuehrer, power to arrange." The drama fancifully traces the results of Hitler's power mania; in seven scenes he confronts historical and imaginary figures. Inspired by Napoleon and Charlemagne, Hitler summons an architect to "create for eternity our famous German ruins." Converting people's weaknesses into cruel and theatrical strengths, Hitler builds on the legends of Karl May and Richard Wagner. He refuses to tarnish his own legend by marrying Eva Braun. Above all he harnesses science to his monstrous destructive dream. But Night and Fog, actual characters, erode his structures. Even as the gas chambers destroy their multitudes, the Nazis are destroyed by their own manias, so that Hitler finally seeks glory in a *Liebestod* in the Cathedral of Ice.

In fantastic theatrical shapes Schevill's drama explores the realities of power and politics. Using music, dance, ritual, projections, Schevill the poet has reached out to embrace many possibilities of theatre.

—Ruby Cohn

SCHISGAL, Murray (Joseph).

Born in Brooklyn, New York, 25 November 1926. Educated at the Brooklyn Conservatory of Music; Long Island University, New York; Brooklyn Law School, LL.B. 1953; New School for Social Research, New York, B.A. 1959. Served as a radioman in the U.S. Navy, 1944–46. Married Reene Schapiro in 1958; one daughter and one son. Jazz musician in 1940's; lawyer, 1953–55; English teacher, Cooper Junior High School, East Harlem, and other private and public schools in New York, 1955–59. Since 1960 full-time writer. Recipient: Vernon Rice award, 1963; Outer Circle award, 1963; Los Angeles and New York Film Critics award, National Society of Film Critics award, and Writers Guild award, all for screenplay, 1983. Lives in New York City. Agent: Bridget Aschenberg, International Creative Management, 40 West 57th Street, New York, New York 10019, U.S.A.

Publications

PLAYS

The Typists, and The Tiger (as Schrecks: The Typists, The Postman, A Simple Kind of Love, produced 1960; revised versions of The Typists and The Postman produced as The Typists, and The Tiger, 1963). 1963.

Ducks and Lovers (produced 1961). 1972.

Luv (produced 1963). 1965.

Knit One, Purl Two (produced 1963).

Windows (produced 1965). In Fragments, Windows and Other Plays, 1965.

Reverberations (produced 1965; as The Basement, produced 1967). In Fragments, Windows and Other Plays, 1965.

Fragments, Windows and Other Plays (includes Reverberations, Memorial Day, The Old Jew). 1965.

The Old Jew, Fragments, and Reverberations (produced 1966). In Fragments, Windows and Other Plays, 1965.

Fragments (includes The Basement and Fragments) (produced 1967). In Fragments, Windows and Other Plays, 1965.

Memorial Day (produced 1968). In Fragments, Windows and Other Plays, 1965.

Jimmy Shine, music by John Sebastian (produced 1968; revised version, as An Original Jimmy Shine, produced 1981). 1969.

A Way of Life (produced 1969; as Roseland, produced 1975; as The Downstairs Boys, produced 1980).

The Chinese, and Dr. Fish (produced 1970). 1970.

An American Millionaire (produced 1974). 1974.

All Over Town (produced 1974). 1975.

Popkins (produced 1978). 1984.

The Pushcart Peddlers (produced 1979). In The Pushcart Peddlers, The Flatulist, and Other Plays, 1980.

Walter, and The Flatulist (produced 1980). In The Pushcart Peddlers, The Flatulist, and Other Plays, 1980.

The Pushcart Peddlers, The Flatulist, and Other Plays (includes A Simple Kind of Love Story, Little Johnny, Walter). 1980.

Twice Around the Park (includes A Need for Brussels Sprouts and A Need for Less Expertise) (produced 1982). In Luv and Other Plays, 1983.

Luv and Other Plays (includes The Typists, The Tiger, Fragments, The Basement, The Chinese, The Pushcart Peddlers, The Flatulist, Twice Around the Park). 1983.

The New Yorkers (produced 1984).

Jealousy (produced 1984). With There Are No Sacher Tortes in Our Society!, 1985.

Closet Madness and Other Plays (includes *The Rabbi and the Toyota Dealer* and *Summer Romance*). 1984.
The Rabbi and the Toyota Dealer (produced 1985). In *Closet Madness and Other Plays*, 1984.
Old Wine in a New Bottle (produced in Flemish, 1985). 1987.
Schneider (produced 1986).
Road Show (produced 1987). 1987.
Man Dangling. 1988.
Oatmeal and Kisses. 1990.
The Japanese Foreign Trade Minister (prroduced 1992).

SCREENPLAYS: *The Tiger Makes Out*, 1967; *Tootsie*, with others, 1983.

TELEVISION PLAYS: *The Love Song of Barney Kempinski*, 1966; *Natasha Kovolina Pipishinsky*, 1976.

NOVEL
Days and Nights of a French Horn Player. 1980.

In the mid-1960s Murray Schisgal's plays were hailed as a step ahead of the avant-garde and more absurd than the work of the absurdists. He was frequently grouped with the new author-stars of American theater—Edward Albee, John Guare, Arthur Kopit, Jack Gelber—whose work, like Schisgal's, was first seen in the United States off-Broadway. As Schisgal notes with irony in the preface to his plays *The Typists, and The Tiger*, this recognition by American critics came only after he had achieved significant success as a playwright in England. *The Typists* and *The Tiger*, two one-acts, and a full-length play, *Ducks and Lovers*, were in fact all first produced in London, and Schisgal's eventual Broadway hit, *Luv*, was optioned in London as early as 1961. After the popular success of *Luv*, which opened in London in 1963 and New York in 1964, Schisgal's career as a playwright seemed assured. He continued to write new plays at a remarkably steady pace through the 1960s and 1970s; most of his new works were produced and published. Critics, however, quickly lost interest in his work, and he has thus become one of the few American playwrights who has genuinely sustained a career in the theater but has no defined place in American culture or drama history.

   Much of the oddity of Schisgal's reception can be discovered in the comic constancy and contemporaneity of his work. He is a satirist of daily life in America and of the clichés of that life. His plays evoke a zany world that teeters between lunacy and good sense. In each of his plays, there is at least one character whose social role is ostensibly ordinary but whose manner of inhabiting that role is eccentric and perverse. Nowhere is this disclosure of the volatile, chaotic energy of ordinary people better accomplished than in *The Tiger*. The plot is simply and potentially melodramatic: Ben, a postman, kidnaps Gloria, a suburban housewife; he intends to rape her. We encounter the two as Ben enters his dingy, cluttered basement apartment with Gloria slung over his shoulder. Any expectations we might have of soap-opera melodrama are quickly thwarted by the peculiar behavior of both characters. Ben's notion of rape begins with a peck on Gloria's cheek and includes playing her a recording of Tchaikovsky's first piano concerto; Gloria is so impressed by

Ben's quasi-philosophic utterances that she repeatedly forgets that she, not he, is the victim in this situation. Ben's hyperbolic frustration turns out to be the perfect match for Gloria's fertile boredom, and, as we laugh at the two equally naïve lovers groping for each other like adolescents, we are finally able to laugh, too, at the self-indulgence of our own overly promoted ennui.

The Tiger delights both because it enables us to laugh at our inflation of contemporary causes and because almost every line is a surprise. While remaining within a recognizable world, Schisgal captures the inanity of our assertions and our memories. Like The Tiger, Schisgal's full-length work Luv is a comedy of contemporary manners and obsessions. The classic triangle—a man, his wife, and his best friend—erupts and renegotiates its connections in Luv with much the same irreverence for marriage and other institutions that emerged in The Tiger. Milt, Harry, and Ellen of Luv clearly deserve each other; no-one else would take any one of them as seriously as they do each other or themselves. In this play, as in The Tiger, Schisgal's magic is that of the true clown; he makes us laugh at every near-catastrophe including the suicide attempts of each character. In the end, however, Luv does not sustain its wit, and one is left with the uneasy sense that, having displayed love itself as a false totem, the play's most lasting image is of a dog peeing on someone's leg.

Relentless in his deflation of each new passion in American society, Schisgal's plays since the late 1960s have become less funny and more acute in the social issues they address. Of the plays written since Luv, two, Jimmy Shine and All Over Town, are particularly rich in the experience they provide for an audience. All Over Town assaults every facile "solution" that was embraced in the late 1960s and early 1970s: welfare, psychiatry, ecology, liberalism, racial and sexual "liberation" are all reduced to confetti in an upper-class New York apartment that becomes a carnival of errors. Although Schisgal has since written other plays in his distinctive satiric mode, All Over Town so expands the madness and so multiplies the cast of characters that it conveys an aura of finality—in this mode at least. In contrast, Jimmy Shine, while orthodox in dramaturgy, exemplifies a powerful new mode in Schisgal's writing. In Jimmy Shine Schisgal quietly controls the tentative, unsatisfied struggles of his artist-hero to find meaning without ornamentation. Schisgal's persistent presentation of the humorous aspects of sexuality and the painful burdens of human love are presented in Jimmy Shine without the usual parodic refractions. Perhaps it is the integrity so transparent in Jimmy Shine that continues to draw community and academic theater companies to Schisgal's plays.

—Helene Keyssar

SHANGE, Ntozake.

Born Paulette Williams in Trenton, New Jersey, 18 October 1948; took name Ntozake Shange in 1971. Educated at schools in St. Louis and New Jersey; Barnard College, New York, 1966–70, B.A. (cum laude) in American studies 1970; University of Southern California, Los Angeles, 1971–73, M.A. in American studies 1973. Married David Murray in 1977 (2nd marriage; divorced); one daughter. Faculty member, Sonoma State College, Rohnert Park, California, 1973–75, Mills College, Oakland, California, 1975, City College, New York, 1975, and Douglass College, New Brunswick, New

Jersey, 1978. Since 1983 associate professor of drama, University of Houston. Artist-in-residence, Equinox Theatre, Houston, from 1981. Recipient: New York Drama Critics Circle award, 1977; Obie award, 1977, 1980; Columbia University medal of excellence, 1981; Los Angeles *Times* award, 1981; Guggenheim fellowship, 1981; New York State Council of the Arts award, 1981. Address: Department of Drama, University of Houston–University Park, 4800 Calhoun Road, Houston, Texas 77004, U.S.A.

Publications

PLAYS

For Colored Girls Who Have Considered Suicide When the Rainbow Is Enuf (produced 1975). 1976; revised version, 1977.

A Photograph: Lovers-in-Motion (as *A Photograph: A Still Life with Shadows*, *A Photograph: A Study of Cruelty*, produced 1977; revised version, as *A Photograph: Lovers-in-Motion*, also director: produced 1979). 1981.

Where the Mississippi Meets the Amazon, with Thulani Nkabinda and Jessica Hagedorn (produced 1977).

Spell #7 (produced 1979). In *Three Pieces*, 1981; published separately, 1985.

Black and White Two-Dimensional Planes (produced 1979). *Boogie Woogie Landscapes* (produced 1980). In *Three Pieces*, 1981.

Mother Courage and Her Children, adaptation of a play by Brecht (produced 1980).

From Okra to Greens: A Different Kinda Love Story (as *Mouths* produced 1981; as *From Okra to Greens*, in *Three for a Full Moon*, produced 1982). 1983.

Three Pieces: Spell #7, A Photograph: Lovers-in-Motion, Boogie Woogie Landscapes. 1981.

Three for a Full Moon, and Bocas (produced 1982).

Educating Rita, adaptation of the play by Willy Russell (produced 1983).

Betsey Brown, adaptation of her own novel, with Emily Mann, music by Baikida Carroll, lyrics by Shange, Mann, and Carroll (also director: produced 1986).

Three Views of Mt. Fuji (produced 1987).

The Love Space Demands: A Continuing Saga (produced 1992). 1991; in *Plays: One*, 1992.

Plays: One (includes *For Colored Girls Who Have Considered Suicide When the Rainbow Is Enuf, Spell #7, I Heard Eric Dolphy in His Eyes, The Love Space Demands: A Continuing Saga*). 1992.

NOVELS

Sassafrass: A Novella. 1977.

Sassafrass, Cypress and Indigo. 1982.

Betsey Brown. 1985.

VERSE

Melissa and Smith. 1976.

Natural Disasters and Other Festive Occasions. 1977.

Nappy Edges. 1978.

A Daughter's Geography. 1983.

From Okra to Greens: Poems. 1984.
Ridin' the Moon West in Texas: Word Paintings. 1988.

OTHER

See No Evil: Prefaces, Essays, and Accounts 1976–1983. 1984.

THEATRICAL ACTIVITIES

DIRECTOR: **Plays**—*The Mighty Gents* by Richard Wesley, 1979; *The Spirit of Sojourner Truth* by Bernice Reagon and June Jordan, 1979; *A Photograph: Lovers-in-Motion,* 1979; *Betsey Brown,* 1989; *Fire's Daughter* by Ina Césaire, 1993.
ACTOR: **Plays**—The Lady in Orange in *For Colored Girls Who Have Considered Suicide When the Rainbow Is Enuf,* 1976; in *Where the Mississippi Meets the Amazon,* 1977; in *Mouths,* 1981.

The production of *For Colored Girls Who Have Considered Suicide When the Rainbow Is Enuf* established Ntozake Shange as a major force in American theatre. True to the Xhosa name she had received in 1971, she was indeed "one who brings her own things" and "walks with lions." Shange has now moved from the spotlight, but she remains one of the finest English-language verse dramatists, forging a poetry compelling in both its social immediacy and its broad vision.

For Colored Girls is a collage of poems mixed with song and dance celebrating the lives of black girls who previously had not been considered a fit subject for dramatic presentation. Structured around rhythmic pulses, the play charts the passage from the self-conscious bravado of "we waz grown," proclaimed at the moment of high school graduation and loss of virginity, through a variety of alternatively funny and painful experiences with men, to the hard-gained knowledge of one's self-worth found in the closing affirmation, "i found god in myself & i loved her fiercely." Belying the women's anguish and seeming predilection towards the negative is their willingness to dance—dance and music being metaphors for the courage to venture into the world with grace, to seek intimate connections with others, and to celebrate the nearly limitless potentiality of life.

The play unlocked emotional doors rarely touched in American theatre. For many women, experiencing a performance became a quasi-religious moment in which some of their deepest feelings were acknowledged and a healing of wounds achieved. For countless other audiences it energized a highly charged debate about male-female relationships and the image of black men in American literature.

Shange's subsequent plays *A Photograph: Lovers-in-Motion* and *Boogie Woogie Landscapes* continue to use a rites-of-passage theme, but the exploration is carried forth within a more clearly delineated social context and a more conventional dramatic form. Thus, in *A Photograph* the male protagonist's identification with both Alexandre Dumas père and the illegitimate Dumas fils serves as a metaphor for his confusion, and the shedding of this fantasy is an indication of the extent to which he moves towards a healthier creative vision. Similarly, Layla in *Boogie Woogie Landscapes* relives her own emotional geography in order to reconcile the possibility of personal love with social struggle. But given the ways in which society distorts personality, love is tenuous, more often a momentary grasping for, rather than solid achievement of, unity.

With *Spell #7* the playwright moves further into the public arena by tackling the iconography of the "nigger." Manipulating the power of music, minstrel performers banish a huge, all-seeing black-face mask along with their stage personae in order to create a safe space in which secret hopes, fears, and dreams may be articulated. But two confessions centering around the shattering of faith puncture the whimsical or contained quality of most of the fantasies and reveal an almost overwhelming anguish. Although the master of ceremonies intervenes to reassure the audience that it will enjoy his black magic, and although the actors conjure forth the joyous spirit of a black church with the chant, "bein colored and love it," the mask returns. In reading the play we are left to wonder whether the actors and audience have indeed enjoyed the freedom of their own definitions and/or whether Shange has performed a sleight of hand which simply allows the drama to end on a positive note. The answer lies finally in the extent to which the communion between actors and audience creates a countervailing force to the hideous ministrel mask and in the audience members' ability to find within their own lives resolutions to the play's purposeful contradictions.

The most recently published play, *From Okra to Greens: A Different Kinda Love Story*, explores further the intersection of the personal and the political. Present are the now-familiar Shange themes of nearly overwhelming brutalization balanced by the transcendence of dance-music-poetry. But significantly new is the shared articulation of many of these experiences by both a male and female protagonist and the effective merger of the personal and the political into a whole which allows them to move forward. Thus, the play closes with the couple bidding their "children" emerge from the ghettoes, bantustans, barrios, and favelas of the world to fight against the old men who would impose death, to dance in affirmation of their unbreakable bond with nature itself.

Within a black theatre tradition Shange seems to have been influenced most by Amiri Baraka and Adrienne Kennedy. Characteristic of her dramaturgy are an attack upon the English language which she as a black woman finds doubly oppressive; a self-consciousness as a writer linked to a determination to reclaim for oppressed peoples the right of self-definition; and a use of poetry, music, and dance to approximate the power of non-linear, supra-rational modes of experience. A poet, Shange brings to the theatre a commitment to it as a locus of eruptive, often contradictory, and potentially healing forces whose ultimate resolution lie beyond the performance space.

—Sandra L. Richards

SHANLEY, John Patrick.

Born in New York City, 13 October 1950. Educated at New York University, B.S. 1977. Recipient: Oscar, 1987; Writers Guild of America award, 1987; Los Angeles Drama Critics Circle award, 1987. Agent: Esther Sherman, William Morris Agency, 1350 Avenue of the Americas, New York, New York 10019. Address: 630 Ninth Avenue, Suite 800, New York, New York 10036, U.S.A.

Publications

PLAYS

Saturday Night at the War (produced 1978).

George and the Dragon (produced 1979).

Welcome to the Moon and Other Plays (includes *The Red Coat, Down and Out, Let Us Go out into the Starry Night, Out West, A Lonely Impulse of Delight*) (produced 1982). 1985.

Danny and the Deep Blue Sea (produced 1983). 1984.

Savage in Limbo (produced 1985). 1986.

the dreamer examines his pillow (produced 1985). 1987.

Women of Manhattan (produced 1986). 1986.

All for Charity (produced 1987).

Italian American Reconciliation (also director: produced 1988). 1989.

The Big Funk (produced 1990). 1991.

Beggars in the House of Plenty (produced 1991). 1992.

Thirteen by Shanley (includes *Danny and the Deep Blue Sea, The Red Coat, Down and Out, Let Us Go out into the Starry Night, Out West, A Lonely Impulse of Delight, Welcome to the Moon, Savage in Limbo, Women of Manhattan, the dreamer examines his pillow, Italian American Reconciliation, The Big Funk, Beggars in the House of Plenty*). 1992.

What is this Everything? (produced 1992).

The Wild Goose (produced 1992).

Four Dogs and a Bone (produced 1993).

SCREENPLAYS: *Moonstruck*, 1987; *Five Corners*, 1988; *The January Man*, 1989; *Joe Versus the Volcano*, 1990; *Alive*, 1993.

The theatre of John Patrick Shanley is primarily about the loss and pain caused by love. In Shanley's plays love leaves none of its converts with sufficient air; it robs people of options, stultifies, sends reason packing, and embraces suffering. People really suffer in Shanley's plays; they are primed for pain, they can't wait to taste its joys, and such longed-for suffering is fully orchestrated through the arrival of the protagonist, love. Love creates a state where everything diminishes other than the pain it generates. People seem to understand that they have lost something but love holds them in a delicious stupor; they seem not to know what has been lost and spend their days heaving, sighing, and breathing heavily.

Shanley has important strengths—in particular a wonderful ear for the sound of working-class Italian-Americans. He portrays the language as having too many syllables, adopting a flatfooted formality, a kind of hardhat existentialism. Probably nobody speaks like this:

> Aldo: . . . a lot of people have an expression of this problem. They had something horrible for a long time, and then they get away from it, and then they miss it.

or like this:

Huey: I feel this pain that makes me weak. The pain is that place in me
where I'm hurt from the divorce. . . . I tried to go into the future and
be new, but it don't work for me.

—*Italian American Reconciliation*

But, for all their verbal constructions and cadences with an authentic ring, for
all their rhetorical poetry of loss and exhortation of grief and baying to
the heavens, Shanley's characters inhabit a self-perpetuating prison. These
protagonists have not found a way of moving past self-absorption into that
place where the world transacts its mundane but necessary business.

Shanley's early collection *Welcome to the Moon and Other Plays* contains
some seemingly uncertain, sometimes uncontrolled pieces, but they do display
an engaging energy and a foreshadowing of both the strengths and weaknesses
of his later works.

Down and Out is raw Shanley, a work consciously without subtext which
comes at us from that cloudy lyricism fashioned by William Saroyan in his
early plays. The allegorical figures are named Love and Poet. Love is fixing a
dinner of water and beans when Poet arrives home sick and discouraged. He
wanted a library book but the library was not open. A shrouded figure now
comes to the house and demands his library card. Poet wants to write new
poems but "I cannot write them. Because I have no pencil." Another shrouded
figure holds out "Money! Money! Money!"

Love: Look how green it is! How green!
Poet: It's beautiful! Can I have it?
Figure: Give me your soul. Give me your soul.
Love: Never! Get out get out get out!

and later:

Poet: No one wants my poetry. The man in the newspaper said I am an
untalented fool. The man in the newspaper was right. We are alone.
Unknown. We live on beans.

But Love inspires the Poet:

Love: The darkest thing has come and led to a moment of despair. But
look! See here! I am your Love who has never left you! I can turn a tiny
lock and open up your soul again! (She opens the box, which is his
soul. It plays music. The poet is bathed in a powerful light. He rises
up.)

In *Let Us Go out into the Starry Night*, ghosts and monsters are chewing at
the head of a tormented young man and clawing at his stomach. The man
explains to the young woman who seeks him out that one of these monsters is
the ghost of his mother.

Man: She doesn't look too bad today really. Some nights she visits me
looking like a rotting side of beef and carrying a big knife.

They kiss and decide to merge their dreams:

Man: How did we get here?
Woman: We got here by being serious.

In *Welcome to the Moon* Stephen abandons his wife and returns to the Bronx, to a "lowdown Bronx bar." He confides in his old buddy, Vinnie, that he has never got over his girlfriend, Shirley, whom he hasn't seen for 14 years but whose memory has poisoned his marriage. Stephen breaks down and weeps and is shortly joined in his weeping by Ronny, another member of the old Bronx gang who has been trying to kill himself because of his own unrequited love. It is hard to establish where Shanley is positioning himself. His overlay of irony seems to be a defense against the expected charge of sentimentality. One is left suspecting that Shanley's characters are unable to deal with the world, that they need to surrender to that controlling creature Love who will mend all pencils, retrieve library cards, cook beans, and keep one from loneliness and suicide.

By 1988 Shanley had developed an almost seamless aesthetic. Huey, in *Italian American Reconciliation*, desperately wants to return to his former wife, Janice, who not only detested him but shot his dog and threatened him with the same gun. Janice is a nightmare and Huey has everything a man could want in sweet, gentle Teresa, but he is convinced that Janice took "his power to stand up and be a man and take. I want it back. I think Janice has it. I think she took that power from me, or it's sitting with her." Shanley seems to identify with Huey's belief system, his people seeing only themselves. Huey is blinded by his belief in the castrating powers of Janice; in an important sense Huey has created his Janice, a woman he can't possibly see. One has to question what kind of consuming love is taking place, how the world of the Bronx and of broken people is ever going to mend. Perhaps Shanley has to borrow Janice's gun and shoot love right out the door. But then what are we left with?

—Arthur Sainer

SHAWN, Wallace.

Born in New York City, 12 November 1943; son of the editor William Shawn. Educated at the Dalton School, New York, 1948–57; Putney School, Vermont, 1958–61; Harvard University, Cambridge, Massachusetts, 1961–65, B.A. in history 1965; Magdalen College, Oxford, 1966–68, B.A. in philosophy, politics, and economics 1968, M.A.; studied acting with Katharine Sergava, New York, 1971. Lives with Deborah Eisenberg. English teacher, Indore Christian College, Madhya Pradesh, India, 1965–66; teacher of English, Latin, and drama, Church of Heavenly Rest Day School, New York, 1968–70; shipping clerk, Laurie Love Ltd., New York, 1974–75; Xerox machine operator, Hamilton Copy Center, New York, 1975–76. Recipient: Obie award, 1975, 1986, 1991; Guggenheim fellowship, 1978. Agent: Casarotto Ramsay Ltd., National House, 60–66 Wardour Street, London W1V 3HP, England.

Publications

PLAYS

Our Late Night (produced 1975). 1984.

In the Dark, music by Allen Shawn (also director: produced 1976). *A Thought in Three Parts* (as *Three Short Plays: Summer Evening, The Youth Hostel,*

Mr. Frivolous, produced 1976; as *A Thought in Three Parts*, produced 1977). In *Wordplays 2*, 1982.
The Mandrake, adaptation of a play by Machiavelli (produced 1977; as *Mandragola*, music and lyrics by Howard Goodall, produced 1984).
The Family Play (produced 1978).
Marie and Bruce (produced 1979). 1980; with *My Dinner with André* (screenplay), 1983.
My Dinner with André, with André Gregory (produced 1980). *My Dinner with André* (screenplay), with André Gregory. 1981; with *Marie and Bruce*, 1983.
The Hotel Play (produced 1981). 1982.
Aunt Dan and Lemon (produced 1985). 1985.
The Fever (produced 1991). 1991.

SCREENPLAY: *My Dinner with André*, with André Gregory, 1981.

THEATRICAL ACTIVITIES
DIRECTOR: **Play**—*In the Dark*, 1976.
ACTOR: **Plays**—in *Alice in Wonderland*, 1974; Prologue and Siro in *The Mandrake*, 1977; Ilya in *Chinchilla* by Robert David MacDonald, 1979; in *My Dinner with André*, 1980; Father, Jasper, and Freddie in *Aunt Dan and Lemon*, 1985; *The Fever*, 1991. **Films**—*Manhattan*, 1979; *Starting Over*, 1979; *All That Jazz*, 1980; *Atlantic City*, 1980; *Simon*, 1980; *My Dinner with André*, 1981; *Lovesick*, 1983; *Strange Invaders*, 1983; *Deal of the Century*, 1983; *Micki and Maude*, 1984; *Crackers*, 1984; *The Bostonians*, 1984; *The Hotel New Hampshire*, 1984; *Heaven Help Us*, 1985; *Prick Up Your Ears*, 1987; *Radio Days*, 1987; *The Moderns*, 1989; *We're No Angels*, 1990; and other films. **Television**—*Saigon: Year of the Cat*, 1983.

Shock has always been one side-effect of Wallace Shawn's dramatic writing, a rather curious side-effect when one thinks of the man himself in his amiable and benign intelligence. Joint Stock's 1977 production of *A Thought in Three Parts* at London's ICA Theatre started the forces of oppression on a particularly merry chase. Within 24 hours of the play's opening there were calls for prosecution on the grounds of obscenity and there were detectives sitting in the audience. Within a week the Charity Commissioners had initiated an inquiry into the ICA's charitable status. Within two months, the Government had announced that it was setting up a committee to consider the law of obscenity generally, at the same time specifically declining to prosecute *A Thought in Three Parts*.

After the dust settled, the reputation of the three one-act plays that made up the evening was invisible for the outrage that had been engendered. Rarely had London's critics been so disturbed by a theatrical event, and that event showed the danger of taking sex seriously in the theatre. The clownish romping of such shows as *Oh! Calcutta!* had given way to something considerably more threatening.

A dangerous aura of violence hung over the evening despite the jokey comedy and naked sexual frolicking of the actors in the second of the plays, the one which caused the greatest outrage. Something more akin to horror than joy came through, and rather than real copulation there was real fear. The first part, *Summer Evening*, takes place in a hotel room in a foreign city where a man and a woman exchange trivial words about eating, reading, and card-playing. Underneath the conversation is the spectre of brutal sexuality, and phrases break through the trivia to reveal the real state of play: "I just had a picture. I thought of you strangling me."

Rather than viewing sex as communication, the second play analyses the essentially solitary experience of orgasm. The selfishness of much sexual gratification percolates through the distractions presented of oral foreplay, intercourse, and group masturbation in *The Youth Hostel*. Shawn compresses time and emotional responses so that the blinding number of orgasms signal changing relationships between five young people spending the night together. The comedy of the dialogue, in language suitable for *True Teenage Romances*, is a deceiving technique that sharpens the human isolation of his characters when their sexual energies are exhausted.

Mr. Frivolous, the final play, begins and remains with the isolation of an individual, an elegant man breakfasting alone in an elegant room. His monologue skates through idle sexual fantasy, from basic heterosexuality to images of gropes with a priest and the possibilities of bondage. Shawn's very public musings on sexuality are finally too dour to be erotic. He stimulates the mind, not the body.

Shawn first made an impact on the off-off-Broadway scene when André Gregory directed the play *Our Late Night* for the experimental company called the Manhattan Project. An obvious precursor to *A Thought in Three Parts*, the play dramatized the drifting unconscious thoughts of two young people quietly going to bed. Around the two there was a swirl of couples discussing sexuality, food, and other encounters.

Shawn's collaboration with Gregory on that production led to the remarkable play by Shawn and Gregory called *My Dinner with André*, which was made into a film by Louis Malle. Gregory had spent the best part of two decades exploring the expanding boundaries of the theatrical avant-garde, finally chasing the aesthetic experience into a forest in Poland, to the Findhorn community in Scotland, to India, Tibet, and the Sahara Desert. Shawn had spent those years consolidating a reputation as an actor in films with Woody Allen, and with such plays as *Marie and Bruce* which drew attention to him without intensifying the scandal.

The form of *My Dinner with André* is seductive and misleading. It pretends to be an account of an actual dinner that Shawn had with Gregory, "a man I'd been avoiding literally for years," and Shawn himself became the character who introduces and frames the play, indeed playing the part of Wally Shawn opposite Gregory's André in both the stage version and the film. The play's conflict is Shawn's New York rationality confronted with Gregory's telling of the "para-theatrical" activities he had had since quitting the theatre after directing *Our Late Night* in 1975.

No such dinner occurred, but the conversation actually took place, extended well beyond the 100 or so pages of the final script. Shawn and Gregory taped lengthy meetings where Gregory detailed his adventures and conclusions against the curious and sane encouragement of Shawn's scepticism. Gregory talked of the project he undertook in a Polish forest with 40 musicians, creating "experiences" with the encouragement of his friend the Polish director Jerzy Grotowski. He elaborated on his search by telling of a Japanese monk he befriended, and with whom he ate sand in the desert. Shawn responded that he liked electric blankets and that happiness could be a cup of cold coffee in which no cockroach had drowned during the night.

The piece is an aesthetic debate of great interest and value, and while the bulk of the ideological contribution is Gregory's, Gregory credits Shawn with the dramatic sensibility that shaped the debate and made the unfolding of the story so mesmerizing. It is Shawn's own characterization of himself as a cynic that gives a forum to Gregory's ideas, and it makes for a significant contribution to the search for artistic forms and meaning that followed the explosion of experiment in the 1960s. Shawn's own openness to thoughtful and radical inquiry into the nature of art and human experience is hearteningly matched by his disciplined skills of expression.

The amused cynicism evident in his own plays was reflected in Shawn's translation and adaptation of Machiavelli's *Mandragola*, with its jaundiced view of human relationships, but it was his original play *Aunt Dan and Lemon* which again stirred the audience into shock. In some ways a meditation on the Nazi atrocities, it was most disturbing for the cold way in which it portrayed the spiritually damaged woman called Lemon, the narrator of the piece. Beginning by welcoming the audience, including the "little children. How sweet you are, how innocent," she went on to tell the story of a friend of her parents, an American academic teaching at Oxford called Aunt Dan, who had regaled her with strange tales when she was 11. Aunt Dan's stories were sometimes about the heroism of Henry Kissinger when he ordered bombing attacks on Vietnam, or about a woman who had been Aunt Dan's lesbian lover and who had killed a man by strangling him with her stockings. The lesson that Lemon learns is that comfort is bought by assigning the killing to others, and that it is really hypocritical to condemn the Nazis who, after all, had been very successful against the Jews. Profoundly disturbing, the play is a mesmerizing blend of narration and enactment which tries, with mixed success, to comprehend the nature of human cruelty and the negotiated truce with justice that affects all non-political people.

Shawn's 1991 play for one character, *The Fever*, was an even more specific meditation on justice and injustice, virtually a call for revolution. "This piece was written," he writes, "so that it could be performed in anyone's flat or home, for an audience of 10 or 12, as well as in public places, and it was designed to fit a very wide spectrum of performers." Shawn himself has performed it in dining-rooms and at London's Royal National Theatre, and it would be very hard to measure its impact for it is basically a call for people to change, for those theatre-going civilized people who have money to switch sides and join the poor.

The performer describes waking up in a hotel room in a poor country, reviewing his or her own reconsideration of the privilege that has come with money. In a post-Marxist world, it rehearses with passion Marx's analysis of the value of things, of commodities, so that the value of labour is recognized. By graphic reference to torture and oppression which protects privilege, he indicts his audience and the comfortable notion of gradual change—but finally the character speaking cannot relinquish his or her own wealth. The dramatic and political journey is never completed.

—Ned Chaillet

SHEPARD, Sam.

Born Samuel Shepard Rogers in Fort Sheridan, Illinois, 5 November 1943. Educated at Duarte High School, California, graduated 1960; Mount San Antonio Junior College, Walnut, California, 1960–61. Married O-Lan Johnson in 1969 (divorced), one son; one daughter by the actress Jessica Lange. Worked as hot walker at the Santa Anita Race Track, stable hand, Connolly Arabian Horse Ranch, Duarte, herdsman, Huff Sheep Ranch, Chino, orange picker in Duarte, and sheep shearer in Pomona, all in California; actor with Bishop's Company Repertory Players, Burbank, California, and U.S. tour, 1962; car wrecker, Charlemont, Massachusetts; bus boy, Village Gate, 1963–64, waiter, Marie's Crisis Café, 1965, and musician with the Holy Modal Rounders, 1968, all in New York; lived in England, 1971–74, and in California since 1974. Founder, with Murray Mednick, John Steppling, and others, Padua Hills Playwrights Workshop and Festival, Los Angeles, 1978. Recipient: Obie award, 1967, 1970, 1973, 1975, 1977, 1978 (twice), 1980, 1984; Yale University fellowship, 1967; Rockefeller grant, 1967; Guggenheim grant, 1968; American Academy grant, 1974; Brandeis University Creative Arts award, 1976, 1985; Pulitzer prize, 1979; New York Drama Critics Circle award, 1986; Outer Circle award, 1986; Drama Desk award, 1986. Agent: Toby Cole, 234 West 44th Street, New York, New York 10036, U.S.A.

Publications

PLAYS

Cowboys (produced 1964).

The Rock Garden (produced 1964; excerpt produced in *Oh! Calcutta!*, 1969). In *The Unseen Hand and Other Plays*, 1971; in *Angel City and Other Plays*, 1976.

Up to Thursday (produced 1965).

Dog (produced 1965).

Rocking Chair (produced 1965).

Chicago (produced 1965). In *Five Plays*, 1967.

Icarus's Mother (produced 1965). In *Five Plays*, 1967.

4–H Club (produced 1965). In *The Unseen Hand and Other Plays*, 1971.

Fourteen Hundred Thousand (produced 1966). In *Five Plays*, 1967.

Red Cross (produced 1966). In *Five Plays*, 1967.

La Turista (produced 1967). 1968.

Melodrama Play (produced 1967). In *Five Plays*, 1967.

Forensic and the Navigators (produced 1967). In *The Unseen Hand and Other Plays*, 1971.

Five Plays: Chicago, Icarus's Mother, Red Cross, Fourteen Hundred

Thousand, Melodrama Play. 1967: as *Chicago and Other Plays,* 1981.

Cowboys #2 (produced 1967). In *Mad Dog Blues and Other Plays,* 1971; in *Angel City and Other Plays,* 1976.

The Holy Ghostly (produced 1969). In *The Unseen Hand and Other Plays,* 1971.

The Unseen Hand (produced 1969). In *The Unseen Hand and Other Plays,* 1971; with *Action,* 1975.

Operation Sidewinder (produced 1970). 1970; in *Four Two-Act Plays,* 1980.

Shaved Splits (produced 1970). In *The Unseen Hand and Other Plays,* 1971.

Cowboy Mouth, with Patti Smith (produced 1971). In *Mad Dog Blues and Other Plays,* 1971; in *Angel City and Other Plays,* 1976.

Mad Dog Blues (produced 1971). In *Mad Dog Blues and Other Plays,* 1971; in *Angel City and Other Plays,* 1976.

Back Bog Beast Bait (produced 1971). In *The Unseen Hand and Other Plays,* 1971.

The Unseen Hand and Other Plays. 1971.

Mad Dog Blues and Other Plays. 1971.

The Tooth of Crime (produced 1972). With *Geography of a Horse Dreamer,* 1974.

Blue Bitch (televised 1972; produced 1973).

Nightwalk, with Megan Terry and Jean-Claude van Itallie (produced 1973). In *Open Theater,* 1975.

Little Ocean (produced 1974).

Geography of a Horse Dreamer (also director: produced 1974). With *The Tooth of Crime,* 1974.

Action (produced 1974). With *The Unseen Hand,* 1975; in *Angel City and Other Plays,* 1976.

Killer's Head (produced 1975). In *Angel City and Other Plays.* 1976.

Angel City (also director: produced 1976). In *Angel City and Other Plays,* 1976.

Angel City and Other Plays (includes *Curse of the Starving Class, Killer's Head, Action, Mad Dog Blues, Cowboy Mouth, The Rock Garden, Cowboys #2*). 1976.

Suicide in B Flat (produced 1976). In *Buried Child and Other Plays,* 1979.

The Sad Lament of Pecos Bill on the Eve of Killing His Wife (produced 1976). With *Fool for Love,* 1983.

Curse of the Starving Class (produced 1976). In *Angel City and Other Plays,* 1976.

Inacoma (produced 1977).

Buried Child (produced 1978). In *Buried Child and Other Plays,* 1979.

Seduced (produced 1978). In *Buried Child and Other Plays,* 1979.

Tongues, with Joseph Chaikin, music by Shepard, Skip LaPlante, and Harry Mann (produced 1978). In *Seven Plays,* 1981.

Savage/Love, with Joseph Chaikin, music by Shepard, Skip LaPlante, and Harry Mann (produced 1979). In *Seven Plays,* 1981.

Buried Child and Other Plays. 1979; as *Buried Child, and Seduced, and Suicide in B Flat,* 1980.

True West (produced 1980). 1981; in *Seven Plays,* 1981.

Jackson's Dance, with Jacques Levy (produced 1980).

Four Two-Act Plays (includes *La Turista, The Tooth of Crime, Geography of a Horse Dreamer, Operation Sidewinder*). 1980.

Seven Plays (includes *Buried Child, Curse of the Starving Class, The Tooth of Crime, La Turista, True West, Tongues, Savage/Love*). 1980.

Superstitions, music by Shepard and Catherine Stone (produced 1983).

Fool for Love (also director: produced 1983). With *The Sad Lament of Pecos Bill on the Eve of Killing His Wife*, 1983.

Fool for Love and Other Plays (includes *Angel City, Cowboy Mouth, Suicide in B Flat, Seduced, Geography of a Horse Dreamer, Melodrama Play*). 1984.

Paris, Texas (screenplay), with Wim Wenders, edited by Chris Sievernich. 1984.

A Lie of the Mind (also director: produced 1985). 1986.

The War in Heaven (broadcast 1985; produced 1987). 1986.

Hawk Moon (produced 1989).

States of Shock (produced 1991).

SCREENPLAYS: *Me and My Brother*, with Robert Frank, 1969; *Zabriskie Point*, with others, 1970; *Ringaleevio*, 1971; *Paris, Texas*, 1984; *Fool for Love*, 1985; *Far North*, 1988.

RADIO PLAY: *The War in Heaven*, 1985.

TELEVISION PLAY: *Blue Bitch*, 1972.

OTHER

Hawk Moon: A Book of Short Stories, Poems, and Monologues. 1973.

Rolling Thunder Logbook. 1977.

Motel Chronicles (includes *Hawk Moon*). 1982; as *Motel Chronicles and Hawk Moon*, 1985.

Joseph Chaikin and Sam Shepard: Letters and Texts 1972–1984, edited by Barry V. Daniels. 1989.

BIBLIOGRAPHY: *Ten Modern American Playwrights* by Kimball King, 1982.

CRITICAL STUDIES: *American Dreams: The Imagination of Sam Shepard* edited by Bonnie Marranca, 1981; *Sam Shepard, Arthur Kopit, and the Off Broadway Theater* by Doris Auerbach, 1982; *Inner Landscapes: The Theater of Sam Shepard* by Ron Mottram, 1984; *Sam Shepard* by Don Shewey, 1985; *Sam Shepard* by Vivian M. Patraka and Mark Siegel, 1985; *Sam Shepard: The Life and Work of an American Dreamer* by Ellen Oumano, 1986; *Sam Shepard's Metaphorical Stages* by Lynda Hart, 1987; *Sam Shepard: A Casebook* by Kimball King, 1988; *File on Shepard* edited by Simon Trussler, 1989.

THEATRICAL ACTIVITIES

DIRECTOR: **Plays**—many of his own plays. **Film**—*Far North*, 1988.

ACTOR: **Plays**—with Bishop's Company; role in *Cowboy Mouth*, 1971. **Films**—*Brand X*, 1970; *Days of Heaven*, 1978; *Resurrection*, 1981; *Raggedy Man*,

1981; *Frances*, 1982; *The Right Stuff*, 1983; *Country*, 1984; *Fool for Love*, 1985; *Crimes of the Heart*, 1987; *Baby Boom*, 1987; *Steel Magnolias*, 1989; *The Hot Spot*, 1990; *Defenseless*, 1991; *Voyager*, 1991.

Sam Shepard comments:

(1973) I'm interested in exploring the writing of plays through attitudes derived from other forms such as music, painting, sculpture, film, all the time keeping in mind that I'm writing for the theatre. I consider theatre and writing to be a home where I bring the adventures of my life and sort them out, making sense or non-sense out of mysterious impressions. I like to start with as little information about where I'm going as possible. A nearly empty space which is the stage where a picture, a sound, a color sneaks in and tells me a certain kind of story. I feel that language is a veil hiding demons and angels which the characters are always out of touch with. Their quest in the play is the same as ours in life—to find those forces, to meet them face to face and end the mystery. I'm pulled toward images that shine in the middle of junk. Like cracked headlights shining on a deer's eyes. I've been influenced by Jackson Pollock, Little Richard, Cajun fiddles, and the Southwest.

In spite of his prolific output—some 40 plays since the mid 1960s—Sam Shepard's invention never flags, and his achievements sometimes tower high. More than any contemporary American playwright, he has woven into his own dramatic idiom the strands of a youth culture thriving on drugs, rock music, astrology, science fiction, old movies, detective stories, cowboy films, and races of cars, horses, dogs. More recently he strives for mythic dimensions in family plays.

Growing up in Southern California, Shepard fell almost accidentally into playwriting when he went to New York City: "The world I was living in was the most interesting thing to me, and I thought the best thing I could do maybe would be to write about it, so I started writing plays." Since the time was the 1960s and the place was the lower East Side, Shepard's short plays were produced off-off-Broadway. Today he finds it difficult to remember these early efforts, which tend to focus on a single event, the characters often talking past one another or breaking into long monologues. However puzzling the action, these plays already ring out with Shepard's deft rhythms.

Within three years of these first efforts, in 1966, 23-year old Shepard produced his first full-length play, *La Turista*, punning on the Spanish word for tourist and the diarrhea that attacks American tourists in Mexico. Perhaps influenced by Beckett's *Waiting for Godot*, *La Turista* is also composed of two acts in which the second virtually repeats the first. However, questionable identities and mythic roles are at once more blantant and more realistic than in Beckett. In both of Shepard's acts Kent is sick, and his wife Salem (both named for cigarette brands) sends for a doctor, who, more or less aided by his son, essays a cure. But the first act is set in a Mexican hotel room and the illness is *la turista*, whereas the second act is set in an American hotel room and the illness is sleeping sickness. Playing through film stereotypes, Kent breaks out of the theater and perhaps out of illness as well.

Other plays followed swiftly, some published in 1971 in two volumes aptly named for the first and longest play in each book. In the six plays of *The Unseen Hand* almost all the main characters are threatened by unseen hands. Two plays of *Mad Dog Blues* camp the popular arts they embrace affectionately. In the title play two friends, Kosmo, a rock star, and Yahoudi, a drug dealer, separate to seek their respective fortunes. Kosmo takes up with Mae West, and Yohoudi with Marlene Dietrich. Each pair becomes a triangle when Kosmo annexes Waco, Texas, and Yahoudi Captain Kidd, for whose treasure they all hunt. Tumbling from adventure to adventure, Yahoudi shoots Captain Kidd, Marlene goes off with Paul Bunyan, Kosmo and Mae West find the treasure, but Jesse James makes off with treasure and Mae West. Finally Mae suggests that they all go to the Missouri home of Jesse James, and the play ends in festive song and dance.

A longer play from 1970 also ends in comic celebration. The punning title *Operation Sidewinder* refers to an American army computer in the shape of a sidewinder rattlesnake. By the play's end, however, it becomes an actual snake and Hopi Indian religious symbol through whose symbiotic power a disoriented young couple is integrated into an organic society—even as in New Comedy. To attain this, the pair has to avoid a revolutionary conspiracy, military backlash, several corpses, and their own highly verbal confusion.

It is generally agreed that *The Tooth of Crime* is Shepard's most impressive play. He has commented: "It started with language—it started with hearing a certain sound which is coming from the voice of this character, Hoss." And the play's strength remains in language, a synthesis of the slangs of rock, crime, astrology, and sports. Hoss has played by the code and moved by the charts, but he senses that he is doomed. Gradually, the doom takes the shape and name of Crow, a gypsy killer. Alerted through Eyes, warned by the charts of Galactic Jack, doped by his doctor, comforted by his moll, Hoss prepares for his fate, "Stuck in my image." In Act 2, Hoss and Crow, has-been and would-be, duel with words and music—"Choose an argot"—as a Referee keeps score. In the third Round the Ref calls a TKO, and Hoss kills the Referee. Unable to bend to Crow's wild ways, Hoss prefers to die, in the manner of classical heroes but in contemporary idiom: "A true gesture that won't never cheat on itself 'cause it's the last of its kind."

Ironically, this American tragedy was written when Shepard was living in London, where his *Geography of a Horse Dreamer* sprang from English dog-racing. On home ground in California, Shepard wrote *Action* about two passive American couples, *Killer's Head* about a cowboy in the electric chair, *Angel City* about horror and horror movies in Hollywood, *Suicide in B Flat* about pressures leading to artistic suicide. These plays are at once newly inventive and stylistically consistent in their nonrealistic images, unpredictable characters, and rich language grounded in colloquialism and soaring to manic monologue. Shepard's most mercurial achievement in pure monologue is the creation of two pieces for the actor Joseph Chaikin—*Tongues and Savage/Love*.

While becoming more involved in his career as a film actor, Shepard has written what he himself calls a "family trilogy," although there is no carryover of characters in *Curse of the Starving Class*, *Buried Child*, and *True West*. In these plays Shepard follows O'Neill in dramatizing a tragic America, mired in sin. In *Curse* the sin is betrayal of the land to soulless speculators. In *Buried Child* it is incest, cruelty, and murder that stifle freedom and creativity in the young. *True West* is at once funnier on its surface and more focused in its opposition of two brothers with divergent lives and attitudes toward the true West.

The love/hate relation within a pair carries over from *True West* to *Fool for Love*, but the pair is now half-siblings and whole lovers. May and Eddie are alternately ecstatic and sadistic in one another's presence in a tawdry motel room, while their father observes them from an offstage vantage. When, at play's end, the motel room goes up in flames, it is not only the end of their inconclusive incest, but of Shepard's own subjection to conventional play-making, with exposition, plot, and resolution. Shepard punctuates this stage of his career by acting the part of Eddie in the movie version, where flashbacks are unfortunately shown.

A Lie of the Mind divides the stage between a rootless and a rooted family, a violent representative of the old West, and a family where the victimized women exude tenderness, Shepard implies that America must look forward with a gentleness that belies its violent past. More boldly, Shepard denounces the violence of war in *States of Shock*. Into a family restaurant a nameless American colonel wheels a wounded young veteran, Stubbs, who may prove to be his son. As conflict escalates between the bellicose colonel and the injured Stubbs, a white man and woman think only of their own appetites, but the black waitress finally heals Stubbs. Percussion and projections cause the action to resonate far beyond the confines of a family restaurant.

Shepard has absorbed American pop art, media myths, and the Southwestern scene to recycle them in many—perhaps too many—image-focused plays in which the characters speak inventive idioms in vivid rhythms. At his best—*La Turista*, *Mad Dog Blues*, *The Tooth of Crime*, *A Lie of the Mind*—Shepard achieves his own distinctive coherence through beautifully bridled fantasy.

—Ruby Cohn

See the essay on *The Tooth of Crime*.

SHERMAN, Martin.

Born in Philadelphia, Pennsylvania, 22 December 1938. Educated at Boston University, 1956–60, B.F.A. 1960. Playwright-in-residence, Playwrights Horizons, New York, 1976–77. Recipient: Wurlitzer Foundation grant, 1973; National Endowment for the Arts fellowship, 1980; Dramatists Guild Hull-Warriner award, 1980; Rockefeller fellowship, 1985. Agent: Casarotto Ramsay Ltd., National House, 60–66 Wardour Street, London W1V 3HP; and, Johnnie Planko, William Morris Agency, 1350 Avenue of the Americas, New York, New York 10019, U.S.A. Address: 35 Leinster Square, London W.2, England.

Publications

PLAYS

A Solitary Thing, music by Stanley Silverman (produced 1963).
Fat Tuesday (produced 1966).

Next Year in Jerusalem (produced 1968).
The Night Before Paris (produced 1969).
Things Went Badly in Westphalia (produced 1971). In *The Best Short Plays 1970*, edited by Stanley Richards, 1970.
Passing By (produced 1974). In *Gay Plays 1*, edited by Michael Wilcox, 1984.
Soaps (produced 1975).
Cracks (produced 1975). In *Gay Plays 2*, edited by Michael Wilcox, 1986.
Rio Grande (produced 1976).
Blackout (produced 1978).
Bent (produced 1978). 1979.
Messiah (produced 1982). 1982.
When She Danced (produced 1985). 1988.
A Madhouse in Goa (includes *A Table for a King* and *Keeps Rainin' All the Time*) (produced 1989). 1989.

TELEVISION PLAY: *The Clothes in the Wardrobe*, adaptation of Alice Thomas Ellis's *The Summerhouse Trilogy*, 1993.

THEATRICAL ACTIVITIES

DIRECTOR: **Play**—*Point Blank* by Alan Pope and Alex Harding, 1980.

Although Martin Sherman is an American playwright born and bred, his parentage is Russian, and he displays a European consciousness as well as an unusual sensitivity to the music of language. Small wonder he prefers historical periods (including earlier in this century) to the present-day and European settings to American. Although *Bent* and *Passing By* focus on male-identified men, in the leading roles of *Rio Grande*, *Messiah*, *When She Danced*, and *A Madhouse in Goa* Sherman has created remarkably complex and individualized portraits of women. Sherman brings a keen intellect to bear on his materials, yet crafts plays which, far from aridly cerebral, are palpably permeated with the deepest feeling. Generalizations about his work, however, are dangerous, for he does not repeat himself. Equally at home with comedy and drama, Sherman works in styles as diverse as his subjects, and his eccentric characters populate works of often audacious originality.

Sherman's volatile and varied subjects include satire of soap operas (*Soaps*); a dying woman who, when visited by an alien from another planet, is tempted to go off with him in his space ship (*Rio Grande*); a charming, light comedy about two gay men who, shortly after meeting, develop hepatitis and care for each other (*Passing By*); and a hippie whodunnit so crazed the killer's identity is never revealed (*Cracks*). That madcap comedy of death, described by a British critic as "Agatha Christie on acid," is a counterculture *Ten Little Indians*, but also a satire of narcissism which Joe Orton might have written had he spent the 1960s in California.

The characters in these and other Sherman plays are outsiders because they are gay or Jewish or foreign or female or strangers in a strange land. In *Messiah*, seeing the Cossacks torture her husband to death has rendered Rebecca mute, while in *A Madhouse in Goa* aphasiac Daniel's language is as dislocated as this gay genius—an "other"—is from his world. Seven languages are spoken in *When She Danced* because nearly everyone in the play is an expatriate from another country. The men in *Bent* represent exiles within their own country, because of their differences thrown into a concentration camp to die.

Although this literal and metaphorical alienation devastates spectators, Sherman's survival kit contains, above all, humor. In *Messiah* his Rachel—a skeptical yet compassionate figure who seems to embody the author's spirit more than any of Sherman's other creations—endures because she is blessed with an ironic sensibility which perceives God's exquisite humor and turns even her denial of God's existence into a scream directed at the Deity.

This dark, personal, and painful play set in 17th-century Poland and Turkey concerns not the title character, who never appears, but a clever yet homely woman whose life the news of the "false Messiah" Sabbatai Sevi profoundly alters. From a claustrophobic village to a barren foreign shore, Rachel and what family remains after her husband dies in a literal leap of faith journey in search of salvation. In liberation from dogma and sexual repression and in self-reliance, however, fear and doubt accompany the removal of boundaries. Such exiles must do without, equally, both restrictions and security. Rich in eroticism, brooding mysticism, and earthy humor, *Messiah* dramatizes a courageous, autonomous woman, a resilient and female Job, experiencing metaphysical conflicts often reserved for male heroes. In her soul, as well as in the play as a whole, doubt, superstition, and disillusionment war against buoyant spirits, wit, kindness, and faith—in God, in the future, and in self.

Whereas religion opposes sexuality in *Messiah*, in *Bent* the source of oppression is governmental. A play which has changed the popular perception of Holocaust victims as solely Jewish, *Bent* has been staged in 35 countries worldwide. Its initial urbane comedy quickly moves into a nightmare about men whom Nazis required to wear, not yellow stars, but pink triangles. Forced into complicity in his lover's murder, in order to survive Max also denies his homosexuality and proves he's not "bent" by having sex with a 13-year-old girl's corpse. Yet Max moves beyond betrayal and self-contempt. In the dehumanizing circumstances of Dachau, his humanity emerges as he affirms the possibility of love and self-sacrifice, embraces his gay identity, and defies those who imprison his soul. In the play's most amazing scene, Max even makes love to another prisoner without their ever making physical contact.

When She Danced finds affirmation, not through intense suffering, but in comedy of wit. This day in the life of Isadora Duncan takes its tone from Preston Sturges's 1940s films because that writer/director grew up around the Duncan household. A touching and amusing valentine to genius, this comedy finds the 46-year-old, improvident, charismatic dancer living in Paris with her young husband Sergei, with whom she shares no common tongue. Much of the humor derives from the troubles communicating experienced by characters speaking in seven languages and from the arrival of a translator. Isadora's instincts that language is highly overrated—"We never had it in America"—prove prophetic, as communication promotes discord and chaos, as well as hilarious misunderstandings.

A Madhouse in Goa moves, like *Bent*, from wit to poignance. Naturally, neither of its two parts takes place in Goa. The brittle, mannered comedy of *A Table for a King* unfolds at a Corfu resort in the 1960s, while the stormy weather of *Keeps Rainin' All the Time* occurs on Santorini "one year from now," after nuclear accidents have altered world weather patterns so drastically that rain continually drenches the Greek isles. The former's narrator is a gay, Jewish, socially awkward young American whose insecurities are assailed by a garrulous southern matron who mocks and mothers him and whose loneliness is momentarily assuaged by the clever Greek waiter who seduces him.

This fellow's wallowing in melancholy seems only minor self-indulgence when contrasted to the second assortment of self-pitying people all wrapped up in their own needs but none too adept at satisfying them. Only gradually does a spectator appreciate that among this self-absorbed crew is the same American, this time in his forties. Not exactly the same man, though, for it appears Daniel is the *author* of the first part, which dramatizes, not the real events of twenty years ago, but a fictionalization which conveniently omits the painful truths that would have reduced his novel's commercial appeal. That sell-out, however, is minor compared to plans for a musical film version of *A Table for a King* presented by a born-again Hollywood producer, who may be the most mercilessly satirized Sherman creation. The self-preoccupied Daniel's stroke-induced aphasia prevents his communicating to the others surrounding him—his male nurse, his dying friend Heather, her hacker son, the producer's girlfriend. Thus when Heather's fears of religious extremists, carcinogenic food, AIDS, and getting nuked require reassurance, Daniel intones "Apple sauce."

The despair underlying Sherman's humor, as well as the imaginative situation and plotting, recall David Mercer, particularly *Duck Song*. Underneath the jokes lurks anguish for a doomed world, a perception which prompted the comical woman of Part 1 to commit herself to the titular Indian asylum. Sherman smashes his other characters' lives, leaving Daniel no audience for his incomprehensible and bitter wit. Unlike the Sherman plays which have dramatized survival, *A Madhouse in Goa*—like Beckett's *Endgame*—distills dread for the very future of humanity.

—Tish Dace

See the essay on *Bent*.

SHERMAN, Stuart.

Born in the United States, 9 November 1945. Has worked at the Kitchen and the Performing Garage, New York. Recipient: National Endowment for the Arts fellowship; Creative Artists Public Service grant; New York State Council on the Arts grant; Northwest Area Foundation grant; Massachusetts Council for the Arts and Humanities grant; Art Matters grant; MacDowell Colony residency; Asian Cultural Council travel grant; prix de Rome, 1991. Address: 166 West 22nd Street, 6A, New York 10011, U.S.A.

Publications

PLAYS

Spectacles (produced 1975–90).
The Classical Trilogy: Hamlet, Oedipus, Faust.
  Hamlet (produced 1981).
  Faust (produced 1982).
  Oedipus (produced 1984).

The Second Trilogy: Chekhov, Strindberg, Brecht (produced 1986).
  Chekhov (produced 1985).
  Brecht (produced 1985).
  Strindberg (produced 1986).
The Man in Room 2538 (produced 1986).
It is Against the Law to Shout "Fire!" in a Crowded Theater: or, "Fire! Fire!"
  (produced 1986).
This House Is Mine Because I Live in It (produced 1986).
Endless Meadows, and So Forth (produced 1986).
Chattanooga Choo-Choo (Für Elise) (produced 1987).
An Evening of One-Act Plays (produced 1987).
Slant (produced 1987).
Crime and Punishment; or, The Book and the Window (produced 1987).
"A" is for "Actor" (produced 1987).
The Yellow Chair (produced 1987).
One Acts and Two Trilogies. 1987.
But What Is the Word for "Bicycle"? (produced 1988). Published as *Aber wie
  heisst das Wort für "Fahrrad"?*, 1990.
*In a Handbag; or, Oscar's Wilde: or, The Importance of Being More or Less
  Earnest* (produced 1988).
Objects of Desire (produced 1989).
The Play of Tea; or, Pinkies Up! (produced 1989).
Knock, Knock, Knock, Knock (produced 1989).
Taal Eulenspiegel (produced 1990).
Solaris, adaptation of the novel by Stanislaw Lem (produced 1992). 1992.

THEATRICAL ACTIVITIES

DIRECTOR AND ACTOR: **Plays**—acted in and directed all his own plays.

It is difficult to write about Stuart Sherman's theatre, for his work is often
complex; yet at moments the complexity speaks to something quite simple.

Sherman's work is generally described as performance art, under which
rubric works as diverse as Charlotte Moorman's naked cello recitals, the
Spalding Gray meditative monologues about wonders and miseries recalled in
tranquillity, and George Jessel's telephone calls to his mother might be
grouped. One of the elements in Sherman's work that assures the categorizers
that Stuart is performance-arting is its non-linear, non-sequential narrative,
but sometimes his plots are sequential and sometimes his plays are non-
narrative. Another element is Sherman's use of the presentational, the mode
that indicates that the players, even when they do not speak directly to the
audience, are always aware of them. Heightening the presentational mode is an
absence of psychological depth, whereby the player often takes on an allegorical persona (e.g., good dental hygiene), or becomes a metaphor for urban
anxiety. Thus we understand that the player is presenting rather than being,
and even as it distances us from emotional catharsis, it permits us to collaborate in the understanding that presumably we (performer and spectator) are all
thinking together. What we are all thinking about is not always clear.

In the early 1970s, Sherman would set up a small card table on West

Broadway in the heart of Soho in New York City. It was always some daytime
hour, a handful of pedestrians might wander by, a few would stop out of
curiosity, allow themselves to be amused or not, and then move on to other
amusements. No one was threatened by the Stuart Sherman who stood behind
the card table. If the work was not always accessible, it was modest enough not
to challenge whatever agenda you might be developing for yourself. In fact
there was something almost incorrigibly domestic, therefore incorrigibly reassuring about these ostensibly sober and brief cartoon-like romps. The very
card table looked as if it had been lifted out of Sherman's mother's kitchen,
and the objects used by Sherman might have come out of that same kitchen
(for example, a homely set of salt and pepper shakers, some plastic cups and
saucers). The whole arsenal of props suggested banal domesticity—before the
street audience floated unthreatening plastic, dime-store paper, cellophane,
kitchen variety glass, bits of linoleum, and the inevitable formica. The Sherman
work might speak of magical or homely events that could befall any reasonable
middle-class urban type, or there might be an abstract portrait of some local
celebrity out of the downtown art scene. There was something particularly
engaging and refreshing about the modesty of means, about the self-
effaciveness of the performer who plied his art with the homeliest of weapons
in full daylight, open to the scrutiny of whoever might be passing. Granted that
the street chosen was fast becoming a major thoroughfare for downtown
gallery-hoppers, there was still a beguiling innocence about the herky-jerky,
open-faced Sherman performance and its rickety card-table technology.

Sherman had already been performing indoors, but within a year or two he
shifted to more sophisticated sites like the Kitchen and the Performing Garage.
His work began to embrace the more complex technology of lights, projections, and other staples from the arena of mixed media. And now it was
customary to see other performers working in tandem with Sherman. What
these performers very often had in common was a seeming ability to convey
that not only were they not acting but they hadn't the first clue as to how one
might create a character onstage. In a very real sense one was still in Stuart's
mother's kitchen, and the performers had decided to dress up in "acting
clothes" and do something that somebody said was "acting." It is not that one
or more of them might not have had considerable training in performance, but
rather that what seemed to be required for Sherman's material, which still
dealt with abstract portraits and non-linear narratives, was a kind of somnam-
bular persona which acted as cipher rather than character. So the "acting," it
seemed, needed to conform to the comforting artifice of gracelessness, "grace-
less" material which was at the same time particularly heartfelt.

In 1986 Sherman premiered *The Man in Room 2538*, a two-character play
set in a bar-restaurant atop a hotel in Tokyo. The customer, played by
Sherman, is waiting at the bar; he wants to eat his dinner at a window seat but
all such seats are occupied. While he waits he and the bartender carry on a
low-key philosophical discourse. The customer, who dines here every night on
"the usual," steak teriyaki and Kirin beer, recounts how he took the elevator to
the 25th floor and stood outside room 2538:

> I don't see, inside the room, a man sitting by the window, looking out,
> holding a book on his lap. I don't see this. I don't see the color of the

walls, which are slightly blue. I don't feel the fit of the man's shoes. . . . I don't see, feel, or hear any of these things.

Later the customer sees himself "more and more clearly, sitting by a window . . . and I order something to eat and something to drink. . . ." The customer is either recounting last night's "usual" or tonight's "usual" which will materialize when a window seat becomes vacant. What seems to connect what he doesn't see inside room 2538 with what he does see in the bar-restaurant are 2,538 dots of light, precisely 2,538 dots joined to make the seen and the unseen. The bartender, a rationalist, is slowly drawn into the customer's mathematical fixation.

The narrative here is linear, but what gives the play its substance is not simply the apparent "content," the intellectual, discursive byplay, but also the exterior of the byplay, the hallucinatory manner within which the byplay carries on its life. The content and its exterior manner are both shaped in the spirit of the mathematical logic of Kurt Godel and the hallucinatory loop drawings of M.C. Escher in which phenomenon come together in an endless, mirror-like "reality." It seems that Sherman is coming into his own in this work. He has been trying to see into things, and many of his works, which he sometimes calls "Spectacles" or "Portraits," have to do with this attempt at seeing. Perhaps that is why representational acting is not appropriate. If one were to accept the premise that representation is the grossest of lies, then there is a particular value in devising the obvious artifice of "structures" wherein performers perform separate events side by side and over and over, sometimes with variations, sometimes with ritual-like actions, none especially "convincing" except that we are convinced that someone is "performing" them.

Sherman's *The Classical Trilogy*, comprising *Hamlet*, *Faust*, and *Oedipus* and his *Second Trilogy*, comprising *Chekhov*, *Brecht*, and *Strindberg*, combine ritual abstractions with readings of fragments from various plays, and seem to be an attempt to "play" these plays in the manner children might "play" them at home. These trilogies could be regarded as analogs, abstractions of the plays, but the obviousness of the playing suggests that this is Sherman's way of making the plays his own, of finding a new reality, of seeing that he is seeing, as if once again he were making a play in the Sherman kitchen of days gone by.

—Arthur Sainer

SIMON, (Marvin) Neil.

Born in the Bronx, New York, 4 July 1927. Educated at De Witt Clinton High School, New York, graduated 1943; New York University, 1944–45; University of Denver, 1945–46. Served in the U.S. Army Air Force, 1945–46: corporal. Married 1) Joan Baim in 1953 (died 1973), two daughters; 2) the actress Marsha Mason in 1973 (divorced 1983); 3) Diane Lander in 1987. Radio and television writer, 1948–60. Recipient: Emmy award, for television writing, 1957, 1959; Tony award, 1965, 1970, 1985, 1991; London *Evening Standard* award, 1967; Shubert award, 1968; Writers Guild of America West award, for screenplay, 1969, 1971, 1976; PEN Los Angeles Center award, 1982; New York Drama Critics Circle award, 1983; Outer Circle award, 1983, 1985; New York State Governor's award, 1986; Pulitzer prize, 1991.

L.H.D.: Hofstra University, Hempstead, New York, 1981; Williams College, Williamstown, Massachusetts, 1984. Address: c/o G. DaSilva, 10100 Santa Monica Boulevard, No. 400, Los Angeles, California 90067, U.S.A.

Publications

PLAYS

Sketches (produced 1952).

Sketches, with Danny Simon, in *Catch a Star!* (produced 1955).

Sketches, with Danny Simon, in *New Faces of 1956* (produced 1956).
   Adventures of Marco Polo: A Musical Fantasy, with William Friedberg, music by Clay Warnick and Mel Pahl. 1959.

Heidi, with William Friedberg, music by Clay Warnick, adaptation of the novel by Johanna Spyri. 1959.

Come Blow Your Horn (produced 1960). 1961.

Little Me, music by Cy Coleman, lyrics by Carolyn Leigh, adaptation of the novel by Patrick Dennis (produced 1962; revised version produced 1982). In *Collected Plays 2*, 1979.

Barefoot in the Park (as *Nobody Loves Me*, produced 1962; as *Barefoot in the Park*, produced 1963). 1964.

The Odd Couple (produced 1965; revised [female] version produced 1985). 1966.

Sweet Charity, music by Cy Coleman, lyrics by Dorothy Fields, based on the screenplay *Nights of Cabiria* by Federico Fellini and others (produced 1966). 1966.

The Star-Spangled Girl (produced 1966). 1967.

Plaza Suite (includes *Visitor from Mamaroneck*, *Visitor from Hollywood*, *Visitor from Forest Hills*) (produced 1968). 1969.

Promises, Promises, music and lyrics by Burt Bacharach and Hal David, based on the screenplay *The Apartment* by Billy Wilder and I.A.L. Diamond (produced 1968). 1969.

Last of the Red Hot Lovers (produced 1969). 1970.

The Gingerbread Lady (produced 1970). 1971.

The Prisoner of Second Avenue (produced 1971). 1972.

The Sunshine Boys (produced 1972). 1973.

The Comedy of Neil Simon (includes *Come Blow Your Horn*; *Barefoot in the Park*; *The Odd Couple*; *The Star-Spangled Girl*; *Plaza Suite*; *Promises, Promises*; *Last of the Red Hot Lovers*). 1972.

The Good Doctor, music by Peter Link, lyrics by Simon, adaptation of stories by Chekhov (produced 1973). 1974.

God's Favorite (produced 1974). 1975.

California Suite (includes *Visitor from New York*, *Visitor from Philadelphia*, *Visitor from London*, *Visitor from Chicago*) (produced 1976). 1977.

The Goodbye Girl (screenplay 1977) stage version, music by Marvin Hamlisch, lyrics by David Zippel (produced 1992).

Chapter Two (produced 1977). 1979.

They're Playing Our Song, music by Marvin Hamlisch, lyrics by Carol Bayer Sager (produced 1978). 1980.

Collected Plays 2 (includes *The Sunshine Boys*, *Little Me*, *The Gingerbread*

Lady, *The Prisoner of Second Avenue*, *The Good Doctor*, *God's Favorite*, *California Suite*, *Chapter Two*). 1979.
I Ought to Be in Pictures (produced 1980). 1981.
Fools (produced 1981). 1982.
Brighton Beach Memoirs (produced 1982). 1984.
Actors and Actresses (produced 1983).
Biloxi Blues (produced 1984). 1986.
Broadway Bound (produced 1986). 1987.
Rumors (produced 1988; revised version produced 1990). 1990.
Jake's Women (produced 1990; revised version produced 1992).
Lost in Yonkers (produced 1991). 1991.
Collected Plays 3 (includes *Sweet Charity*, *They're Playing Our Song*, *I Ought to Be in Pictures*, *Fools*, *The Odd Couple* [female version], *Brighton Beach Memoirs*, *Biloxi Blues*, *Broadway Bound*). 1992.
Laughter on the 23rd Floor (produced 1993).

SCREENPLAYS: *After the Fox*, with Cesare Zavattini, 1966; *Barefoot in the Park*, 1967; *The Odd Couple*, 1968; *The Out-of-Towners*, 1970; *Plaza Suite*, 1971; *The Heartbreak Kid*, 1972; *The Last of the Red Hot Lovers*, 1972; *The Prisoner of Second Avenue*, 1975; *The Sunshine Boys*, 1975; *Murder by Death*, 1976; *The Goodbye Girl*, 1977; *The Cheap Detective*, 1978; *California Suite*, 1978; *Chapter Two*, 1979; *Seems Like Old Times*, 1980; *Only When I Laugh*, 1982; *I Ought to Be in Pictures*, 1982; *Max Dugan Returns*, 1983; *The Lonely Guy*, with Ed Weinberger and Stan Daniels, 1984; *The Slugger's Wife*, 1985; *Brighton Beach Memoirs*, 1987; *Biloxi Blues*, 1988; *The Marrying Man*, 1991.

RADIO: scripts for *Robert Q. Lewis Show*.

TELEVISION: *Phil Silvers Show*, 1948; *Tallulah Bankhead Show*, 1951; *Your Show of Shows*, 1956; *Sid Caesar Show*, 1956–57; *Jerry Lewis Show*; *Jacky Gleason Show*; *Red Buttons Show*; *Sergeant Bilko* series, 1958–59; *Garry Moore Show*, 1959–60; *The Trouble with People*, 1972; *Happy Endings*, with others, 1975; *Broadway Bound*, 1992.

BIBLIOGRAPHY: *Ten Modern American Playwrights* by Kimball King, 1982.

MANUSCRIPT COLLECTION: Harvard University, Cambridge, Massachusetts.

CRITICAL STUDIES: *Neil Simon* by Edythe M. McGovern, 1979; *Neil Simon* by Robert K. Johnson, 1983.

In a time of turmoil and despair in the commercial theatre both in Britain and in America, it is encouraging to note that neither Neil Simon nor Alan Ayckbourn has been seriously deterred by dismissive or hostile criticism. Some fifty years ago on both sides of the Atlantic, there were a number of playwrights who regularly produced new works, confidently expecting professional productions. Today, writers' grants and play-workshops proliferate, as producers, directors, actors, critics, and even audiences wonder where the interesting new plays are to be found. At least in the commercial sector, some already renowned playwrights find it difficult to get a production. In the United States, Simon is almost alone as a successful dramatist who is expected to continue concocting comedies and musicals which please audiences.

Unlike Ayckbourn, who is able to develop and test his new works at Scarborough's Stephen Joseph Theatre before they are shown in the West End, Simon's scripts are customarily commercially mounted and "tried out" in Los Angeles and elsewhere in regional America before coming to Broadway. It has been suggested that Simon may well be the most successful playwright—in terms of royalties and other income from his varied ventures on stage, in films, and on television—who has ever lived. At various times, he has had three and four productions running simultaneously on Broadway, not to mention touring ensembles, stock and amateur productions, and foreign stagings.

His fortunes with many critics, however, have been rather different. Initially, with early domestic comedies such as *Come Blow Your Horn* and *Barefoot in the Park*, he was welcomed as a fresh new voice, with a particular comic talent for pointing up the pangs and problems of urban family life. He was also fortunate in receiving slickly professional productions with impressive performers to bring his visions of contemporary middle-class angst to life. The fact that most new Simon scripts rapidly became long-running hits, significant commercial money-spinners, helped attract even wider audiences. It's an axiom that people would rather see hits than flops. Once in the theatre, however, spectators were obviously amused by Simon's comic techniques, but they also clearly responded to characters and situations they could recognize.

It has been repeatedly pointed out, by regional and foreign critics and producers, that the farther removed from New York a Simon production is, the less easily do audiences respond and empathize. Some explain this by suggesting that Simon's concerns are largely with urban and suburban New Yorkers, which may well be of interest to audiences elsewhere, without striking any personal sparks of instant recognition. A few of Simon's detractors, however, insist that his comedy is not only one of New York insularity, but more specifically of materialistic, middle-class New York Jews, thus making it less immediately accessible to non-Jews beyond the Hudson. Whatever the merits of this argument, in the mid-1980s such nation-wide American Simon successes as his autobiographical *Brighton Beach Memoirs* and *Biloxi Blues* were produced by Britain's subsidized National Theatre rather than by a West End commercial management.

While some object to what they perceive as a regional, cultural, economic, or even ethnic bias in Simon's choice of subject matter, others—notably critics, rather than audiences—complain about what is often seen as the playwright's major fault: his obvious addiction to the "one-liner" comic comment, which seems to elicit boisterous laughter, regardless of the dramatic context in which it occurs. A cursory reading of Simon's comedies and musical comedy books will readily reveal this penchant for the quick, often sarcastic quip, which in fact is more often to be heard in New York conversations than elsewhere in America. This is a distinctive element in Simon's comic writing, and its genesis can be traced to his early collaboration with his brother, Danny Simon, when they were gag-writers for such television series as the *Phil Silvers Show* and the *Sid Caesar Show*, where the smart retort and the devastating comic put-down were major provokers of laughter. The gift of making people laugh in the theatre is to be prized, but this talent in Simon has been viewed, by critics who would like to admire him more, as rather a curse than a dramatic inspiration.

Despite his commercial success and even such official recognitions as the Tony, Shubert, and *Evening Standard* awards, Simon has been sensitive to critical objections. In conversation, he is an informed, concerned, compassionate, serious human being; a Simon interview is not a barrage of hilarious one-liners. He has repeatedly pointed out—to answer critical charges that his comedies are all artificial constructs, manipulations of stereotypes in stock situations—that the most succesful of his works, from the first, have been firmly rooted in his personal experience, or that of close friends and family. That's true of *Come Blow Your Horn* and *The Odd Couple*, in terms of the brothers Simon. As television collaborators, Simon has noted, brother Danny was rumpled and disorganized, while brother Neil was always neat and tidy: out of this experience came the comic conflicts of sloppy Oscar and fussy Felix. *Barefoot in the Park* reprised the New York apartment experiences of the newlywed Neil Simons.

Last of the Red Hot Lovers, a series of amorous miscarriages on the part of a frustrated fish merchant with variously fixated women, was inspired by the so-called Sexual Revolution of the 1960s, when many middle-aged men and women feared the new freedoms were passing them by. (Women in the Broadway audience would shout advice to James Coco, playing the forlorn would-be seducer: "Jimmy! *She's* not right for you!") Whatever demanding critics may say, popular audiences readily respond to Simon's view of man and life.

The Star-Spangled Girl is a construct, as Simon has admitted, acknowledging that it didn't work as he hoped it would. *Plaza Suite*, in which the same suite in the famed New York hotel is the scene of three quite different but amusing encounters, may be viewed as a comic tour de force, but the situations are all based on realities. (In fact, Simon's film *The Out-of-Towners* is a dramatised expansion of an opening *Plaza Suite* monologue, omitted on Broadway.)

When Simon tried to show his critics—and his public—that he was capable of dealing thoughtfully and dramatically with a serious subject, *The Gingerbread Lady* was dismissed or disparaged as having been damaged by his recourse to the familiar device of the comic quip. This play was clearly inspired by the self-destructiveness of Judy Garland. Simon explored the possible reasons for her loss of confidence and bad habits; he also was intrigued by the idea of an often hurt but still loving daughter effectually becoming a mother to her own mother, to protect her from herself. Another show-business situation was probed in *The Sunshine Boys*, exploring the behind-the-scenes hostilities —continuing into old age—of vaudeville teams such as Smith and Dale. *The Prisoner of Second Avenue* continues to excite interest, however, with its mordant humor all the more valid as seemingly successful, highly paid executives are suddenly fired, with no prospects of re-employment. As if to answer those who complain that Simon only writes about New Yorkers, *California Suite* did for Los Angeles what *Plaza Suite* did for Manhattan.

Chapter Two—in which Simon came to terms with the sorrow and rage at the loss of his first wife through cancer and began a new relationship—at last was a serious subject which critics and public could accept as an honest, deeply felt vision of suffering and redemption, leavened with sharp personal satire and comic quips. Curiously, the most recent Simon comedies, the saga of a young playwright's growing up, have been critically praised as a kind of breakthrough in comic technique. Actually, however, the semi-autobiographical *Brighton Beach Memoirs* (childhood in Brooklyn), *Biloxi Blues* (1940s army experience), and *Broadway Bound* (young man with a typewriter) exemplify one of the oldest known dramatic structures. Simon's alter-ego, Eugene Morris Jerome (*pace* Eugene O'Neill), functions as a genial narrator, who interrupts his first-person story to step into dramatised episodes. It's efficient as a technique, but it's hardly an innovation.

Rumors was a disappointment after the trilogy, for the basic situation and characters were stereotypical constructs of no particular interest, animated merely by the confusions and misunderstandings rumors make possible. Simon himself described it as a farce, but it lacked the essential elements of farce, except for a setting with a number of doors. Unlike Feydeau, however, Simon did not know how to use the doors for suspense or comic effect. A colorful, manic Broadway production glossed over the weakness of the script.

After that slump, *Lost in Yonkers* was doubly welcomed by critics and public. It was hailed as even more honest and autobiographical than the trilogy. It focused again on two boys—Simon brothers surrogates—growing up with a tyrannical, embittered, and crippled grandmother in a shabby Yonkers flat, while their loving but feckless father tries to survive the Depression on the road. A gangster uncle and a childlike aunt provide love and occasional adventure for the boys. At last Simon was awarded a Pulitzer prize as well as the 1991 Tony for best play, his work being deemed sufficiently serious. The characters, it is true, were much more distinctive and less generic, but as in previous Simon plays, every one of them had a string of smart "one-liner" retorts which were vintage Simon, and yet not out of character.

Jake's Women, which tried out in San Diego in 1990, only to be halted on its way to Broadway by Simon himself, was rethought and rewritten to achieve a popular—if not critical—success in New York. The dramaturgy was intricate and engaging, as Jake, a Simon-like playwright, summons up his own imaginings of the women in his fantasy and real lives. His long-dead first wife turns up at will, but, like his newer estranged wife, a possible future wife, and his daughter by the first wife, seen at two different ages, she can only express the thoughts, emotions, and words which the playwright assigns her in his fantasies. This play is "*Chapter Two*," also autobiographical as *Chapter Two* was, in that the spectre of a beloved but deceased first wife is ruining the playwright's emotional relationships with subsequent lovers. Even the writer's female therapist is made to see things his way. It's a clever conceit in performance, but it plumbs no new depths in the Simon or human psyche which weren't already explored in *Chapter Two*.

Over the years, Simon has also shown himself a skilled adaptor of other materials, as in the musicals *Little Me* (Patrick Dennis's novel), *Sweet Charity* (Federico Fellini's film), and *Promises, Promises* (Billy Wilder's film), and in the plays *The Good Doctor* (Chekhov's short stories), *God's Favorite* (*The Book of Job* on Long Island's North Shore: Simon's answer to MacLeish's *J.B.*), and *Fools* (suggested by Sholem Alecheim's stories of Chelm). For the cinema, he has drafted effective screenplays of some of his own plays, as well as some originals, such as *The Goodbye Girl* and *Murder by Death*, the first a popular romantic comedy, the second, a puzzling disaster.

Despite periodic renunciations of Broadway, carping critics, the pace of New York life, or East Coast values, Simon does seem to draw his primary inspiration and stimulation from this scene. And, ...'.ough some denigrators would insist that with Simon, "Nothing succeeds like *excess*," his large, impressive, continuing body of comedies, endorsed to a greater or lesser degree by audiences at home and abroad, is an undeniable achievement by a distinctive talent with a penetrating intelligence. It is a record all the more impressive in a time when so few playwrights are regularly creating effective comedies.

—Glenn Loney

See the essay on *Brighton Beach Memoirs*.

SMITH, Michael T(ownsend).

Born in Kansas City, Missouri, 5 October 1935. Educated at the Hotchkiss School, Lakeville, Connecticut, 1951–53; Yale University, New Haven, Connecticut, 1953–55. Married Michele Marie Hawley in 1974 (divorced 1989); two sons. Theatre critic, 1959–74, and associate editor, 1962–65, *Village Voice*, New York (Obie award judge, 1962–68 and 1972–74); teacher, New School for Social Research, New York, 1964–65, Project Radius, Dalton, Georgia, 1972, and Hunter College, New York, 1972; instrument maker, Zuckermann Harpsichords, Stonington, Connecticut, 1974–77 and 1979–85; arts editor, Taos *News*, New Mexico, 1977–78; music, art, and theatre critic, New London *Day*, Connecticut, 1982–86; assistant press secretary to Edward I. Koch, Mayor of New York City, 1986–89; since 1992 music critic, Santa Barbara *News-Press*. Also director, lighting designer, and musician: manager, Sundance Festival Theatre, Upper Black Eddy, Pennsylvania, 1966–68; producer, Caffe Cino, New York, 1968; director, Theatre Genesis, New York, 1971–75, and Boston Early Music Festival and Exhibition, 1983–85; manager, 14th Street Lighting, New York, 1989–90; since 1990 lighting director, The Living Theater, New York. Recipient: Brandeis University Creative Arts award, 1965; Obie award, for directing, 1972; Rockefeller grant; 1975; MacDowell Colony fellowship, 1991. Address: 1801 Olive Avenue, Santa Barbara, California 93101, U.S.A.

Publications

PLAYS

I Like It (also director: produced 1963). In *Kulchur*, 1963.

The Next Thing (produced 1966). In *The Best of Off-Off-Broadway*, edited by Smith, 1969.

More! More! I Want More!, with John P. Dodd and Remy Charlip (produced 1966).

Vorspiel nach Marienstein, with John P. Dodd and Ondine (also director: produced 1967).

Captain Jack's Revenge (also director: produced 1970). In *New American Plays 4*, edited by William M. Hoffman, 1971.

A Dog's Love, music by John Herbert McDowell (produced 1971).

Tony (produced 1971).

Peas (also director: produced 1971).

Country Music (also director: produced 1971). In *The Off-Off-Broadway Book*, edited by Albert Poland and Bruce Mailman, 1972.

Double Solitaire (also director: produced 1973).

Prussian Suite (also director: produced 1974).

A Wedding Party (also director: produced 1974).

Cowgirl Ecstasy (also director: produced 1976).

Life Is Dream, adaptation of a play by Calderón (also director: produced 1979).

Heavy Pockets (also director: produced 1981).

Sameness, with Alfred Brooks (produced 1990).

VERSE

American Baby. 1983.
A Sojourn in Paris. 1985.

OTHER

Theatre Journal, Winter 1967. 1968.
Theatre Trip (critical journal). 1969.

Editor, with Nick Orzel, *Eight Plays from Off-Off-Broadway*. 1966. Editor, *The Best of Off-Off-Broadway*. 1969.

Editor, *More Plays from Off-Off-Broadway*. 1972.

THEATRICAL ACTIVITIES

DIRECTOR: **Plays**—many of his own plays, and *Three Sisters Who Are Not Sisters* by Gertrude Stein, 1964; *Icarus's Mother* by Sam Shepard, 1965; *Chas. Dickens' Christmas Carol* by Soren Agenoux, 1966; *Donovan's Johnson* by Soren Agenoux, 1967; *With Creatures Make My Way* by H.M. Koutoukas, 1967; *The Life of Juanita Castro* by Ronald Tavel, 1968; *Dr. Kheal* by Mariá Irene Fornés, 1968; *Hurricane of the Eye* by Emmanuel Peluso, 1969; *Eat Cake* by Jean-Claude van Itallie, 1971; *XXX* by William M. Hoffman, 1971; *Bigfoot* by Ronald Tavel, 1972; *Tango Palace* by Mariá Irene Fornés, 1973; *Krapp's Last Tape* by Beckett, *The Zoo Story* by Albee, and *West Side Story* by Arthur Laurents, 1977–78; *A Shot in the Dark* by Harry Kurnitz, 1985; *Curse of the Starving Class* by Sam Shepard, 1985.

Michael T. Smith comments:

Circumstances too narrowly personal to be called historical have more to do with the extent and character of my plays than any political or career agenda I may have chosen and willed. It has seemed to me that the real (as opposed to manifest) content of anything I write produces itself from affinities and perceptions that I haven't much control over. In fact they control me, define me. The challenge is to find a form that transmits them, that enables me to share these infinitely intimate flashes of truth and beauty.

> It all seems to refer to something else, but it is difficult to figure out what that something else is.
> — *Country Music*

I offer the following tale as a model for the unconscious process that seems to underlie the plays of Michael T. Smith:

He has gone to a lot of trouble to arrange his materials. The plantain was picked while Venus was ascendant, the hair was surreptitiously cut from the sleeping girl, the circle was drawn in clean sand by the flowing stream, and now the words so carefully memorized are pronounced correctly. All these elements must be in order to produce the *event*.

Dutifully he summons demons to aid him. From the inner recesses of his consciousness and the stream, from his spinal column and the beech tree, from his shoulder and his dog, demons fly to him. He is protected from danger by the limits of his circle.

He perceives the demons as scraps of old arguments, flashes of relieved emotions, a slight feeling of unease. Is he coming down with a cold? Why did he think of his mother? Will he stay with his lover?

His experience tells him to say "Get ye hence" to the demon-thoughts. He must go further. He's tired of emotion, bored with dialectic. "There must be something else," he thinks.

What does he want tonight? To be loved? To hate? Make fertile? Kill? None of these. Tonight he wants to be *wise*. He does not want information; he has plenty of facts. He knows that hens lay eggs, soldiers kill, lovers love. No, he wishes to know how and where to stand in relation to all his knowledge.

He throws a little something on the fire. It flares briefly, and suddenly a similar flare lights his mind. He thinks of nothing at all for some moments of eternity. The muscles of his neck relax.

After which he addresses the world as the wind makes his hair fly: "Who are you, Moon? Who are you, Stream? Who are you, Dog? Who are you, Man?"

I certainly do not wish to say that Smith is a practitioner of black or white arts. What I do mean to suggest is that Smith, like many other artists of this time, wants to explore lines of inquiry that in earlier times might have been called religious.

As the magician or priest juxtaposes disparate and often illogical elements toward a magical goal, Smith arranges his material without the superficially logical glue that audiences since Ibsen have come to expect.

Smith's stories often seem discontinuous in characterization and time. The actress playing the daughter in *Peas* is also asked to play her own mother, grandmother, and lover's other girlfriend. In *Country Music* costumes and make-up are changed drastically and abruptly. In *The Next Thing* the sequence of events is arranged aesthetically; reaction does not necessarily follow action, although within any small section time is "normal." In *Point Blank* (as yet unproduced) the opening stage direction reads, "This is a loop play. Begin anywhere, repeat several times, stop anywhere."

Thus in spite of fairly naturalistic dialogue the audience is somewhat disoriented by a Smith play. In fact because the dialogue is so "normal" Smith creates enormous tension by letting his characters play freely with role and time.

Smith's homely subject matter, which is most often the family, also is at variance with his treatment. Unlike most playwrights who write about the family, Smith is uninterested in commenting either unfavorably or favorably about his subject.

As the priest or witch places such ordinary elements as bread, wine, and plants in the context of the cosmos, so Smith exposes his characters to time, nature, and politics.

In *Country Music* two couples are exposed to the vagaries of time and weather. Their loves seem more affected by these elements than by psychology. Change seems to occur the same way buds grow. In *Captain Jack's Revenge* the characters are subject to art and politics. In the first act the people consciously try to order their awareness by means of television, radio, stereo, slide and movie projectors, telephone, and the doorbell. In the second act we see how the minds of these same people have been shaped by the actions of remote figures in American history.

Yet Smith does not tell us that we are doomed by weather, time, politics, psychology, or the media. He is pointing two ways at once, both at the solidity of certain facts, the bread and the wine, and at the cosmic context of these facts.

Yes, the couple in *Country Music* are subject to powerful forces outside their control, but look at the stars, look at the different kinds of light we can see—candlelight, sunshine, moonlight, twilight, dawn. The actors prepare food on stage and then eat it. All these experiences are called for by the author as his characters love, grow apart, leave.

Yes, the white people in *Captain Jack's Revenge* are doomed to the Indians' revenge for the crimes of their ancestors, but notice the beauty of the revenge, the glorious but mind-numbing media, the alluring but confusing drugs.

From Smith's magical (I might say "objective") point of view comes the curiously unemotional language. Rarely do his people lose their cool. They love passionately, they hate, they murder, but their language does not often reflect this. Does the playwright feel that emotion is such a heavy element on stage that the total stage picture would be unduly dominated by it? As the son says in *Peas*. "I want other people to be there without making a point of it."

Smith's plays are not designed to weigh ten tons of emotions. The audience must not be distracted from being aware they are seeing a model, not a slice, of life. The altar or voodoo dolls are not naturalistic representations either. Perhaps the logic of a Smith play is: If you can portray a situation objectively, with the freedom to be playful, if you can see the total picture, if you can arrange the elements of existence, you can induce a state of mind that allows us to see the magic of everyday life.

—William M. Hoffman

STARKWEATHER, David.

Born in Madison, Wisconsin, 11 September 1935. Educated at the University of Wisconsin, Madison, 1953–57, B.A. in speech 1957. Editor of a visitors newspaper in New York. Recipient: Creative Artists Public Service grant, 1975; Rockefeller grant, 1978. Address: 340 West 11th Street, New York, New York 10014, U.S.A.

Publications

PLAYS

Maggie of the Bargain Basement, music by Starkweather (ballad opera; produced 1956).
Excuse Me, Pardon Me (produced 1957).
You May Go Home Again (produced 1963). In *The Off-Off-Broadway Book*, edited by Albert Poland and Bruce Mailman, 1972.
So Who's Afraid of Edward Albee? (produced 1963).
The Love Pickle (produced 1963).
The Family Joke (produced 1965).
The Assent (produced 1967).
Chamber Comedy (produced 1969).
A Practical Ritual to Exorcise Frustration after Five Days of Rain, music by Allan Landon (also co-director: produced 1970).
The Poet's Papers: Notes for an Event (produced 1971). In *New American Plays 3*, edited by William M. Hoffman, 1970.
The Straights of Messina (produced 1973).
Language (also director: produced 1974).
The Bones of Bacon (produced 1977).

MANUSCRIPT COLLECTION: Lincoln Center Library of the Performing Arts, New York.

THEATRICAL ACTIVITIES
DIRECTOR: several of his own plays.

David Starkweather comments:

(1973) Two mirrors facing what do they reflect?

Slice the mind in fives, Consciousness stage center. One way wings of Memory, staging areas of attention seeking self-ordering re-experience, detouring terror into ritual belief: Subconscious. Opposite wings of Appetite, senses drawn to sources of actuation, pulled always into foreign homes: Superconscious. Deeper still surrounding wings as well as centers, forms in the mind's structure beneath conception, containing all potential concepts like the possibilities of a medium; Unconscious. Facing Other Consciousness awareness of other centers of awareness, the possibilities of union/conflict with/within all potential spectators. The boundaries between these modes of mind-works the symbol, always blocking one way, all ways disappearing another.

My current vision of theatre is a head, the bodies of the audience resonating chambers like the jugs beneath the stage in the classic Nō, feeling their behavioral imaginations. Sound surrounds but the eyes are in front perceiving SENSES in terms of each other. Vision is figure to sound's ground and vice versa because each word has an aural and visual component. A noun is a picture (visual/spatial) and a verb is a melody (aural/temporal) relation. The split between being and doing dissolves when nouns are just states verbs are in at a given moment. The central human art form is the spoken word.

We laugh at people who are out of control. We laugh with people who are shoulder to shoulder. And we call it tragedy when a hero who is behind us loses.

If you write a play and do it badly that play is about incompetence. My plays in their forms hope to suggest what competence is. Moving toward an ideal. And I deal this round. Place your bets. It's a show of competence. All plays are about knowing. Being is where they're at. What I seek in a word is Order. In a feeling a release of energy.

For themes I have recognized a clear line of development in my last three plays: 1) there is nothing you can know without limiting your ability to know something equally true; 2) the only thing we need to believe is that there is nothing we need to believe; and 3) the only taboo is on taboos.

I write consistently about changing minds.

A number of works, my most ambitious, are as yet unproduced: *Owey Wishey Are You There?*, 1965, *The Wish-House*, 1967.

Ham—And where are you?
Noah—I am here and it is now. And all around is mystery.
        —*A Practical Ritual to Exorcise Frustration*
                              after Five Days of Rain.

It's not that he hates his family, his religion, or the rest of the society; it's just that he can't stand their noise. Most people he knows participate in the trivia of family life and the charades of state. They believe that somewhere there is *one* person who will solve the riddle of their emotional needs, that the state must be protected, especially from within, that there is a god who sits on a throne, somewhere.

So the young man leaves his home, not to be mean or ornery, but because he'll go crazy if he stays. He goes Downtown, where there are so many people that no one will notice him, or Downtown to the wilderness, where there are no people. And now he is in the Downtown part of his mind, where memories of his former life rise and beckon him to return and resume the old ties. He replies to their telephone calls and to his dreams that their lives are meaningless and their ways are mindless and hold no allure.

But the old ways are alluring to him in his solitude, and part of him wants to go home. However, gradually, painfully, he withdraws into the land of light, and now he's totally alone with his mind. Soon he *is* his mind and alone he's together. At this still point fears arise in their pure form and threaten his sanity. Fears: of pain, of people, of death, of body functions.

He discovers that these fears cannot be conquered in their essence but must be met in their actuality, and so, here he goes, folks, back to the "real world" to conquer his fears. But this time he's armed; around his waist he carries self-containment; his vest is armored with enlightenment; his helmet is pure reason.

There are no trumpets on his return. People have scarcely noticed he's been gone, so busy have they been with their own wars and marriages. When he approaches the natives he finds that things are as they've always been between him and them: they don't see what he sees. So he withdraws again, and returns again armed with new weapons. The cycle is endless, the man is lonely, but filled with love. His attitude is increasingly ironic.

This portrait of the saintly exile is a composite of the heroes and mock heroes that form the core of David Starkweather's work, the recalcitrant lover Colin of So Who's Afraid of Edward Albee?, the errant son David of You May Go Home Again, the would-be suicide Alan of The Assent, the wandering Poet of The Poet's Papers, and both Sonny and Pittsburgh, who together form the hero of Language. They are all versions of the Odysseus/Christ/dropout anti-heroes of our time.

Colin, one of Starkweather's earliest creations, is merely disgusted by the System and puzzled by his disgust. David, created later, overwhelmed by his ambiguous feelings toward his family, goes into exile. Alan, guilty in exile, longs for death. The Poet, more comfortable in his separation from society, wanders the earth watching it destroy itself. And Sonny and Pittsburgh, who have in different ways plumbed the mysteries of isolation, now seek a way back into a society they have left.

In all of his plays, but especially in The Family Joke and The Wish-House (unproduced), Starkweather provides ample reason for self-exile, and incidentally offers savage but concerned criticism of Western society. In The Family Joke the nuclear family is seen as the System's breeding factory. Children must be raised, no matter what the cost to the parents. The Wish-House presents an almost paranoid view of the methods of mind control that the System is willing to employ. For the enemy, here represented by a Dr. Brill, is in possession of the same knowledge that Starkweather's exile-heroes have struggled so hard to obtain: "All that you consider yourself to be is merely the stopper to contain what you really are. All that you do most easily, by habit and without thought, is only to avoid your most beautiful and dangerous nature."

In counterpoint to some of the most glorious abstractions in contemporary theatre, architectural visions that spring from contemplation of the basic dualities of thought, Starkweather weaves the anxieties that often accompany advanced thought: fears of death, impotence, blood, piss, and shit.

In The Poet's Papers the war between the two divisions of mankind, the Orals and the Anals, is conducted in lyrical language. In The Assent the System prefers control of urination to control of theft: "Petty theft raises the living standard of the worker . . . and stimulates cash flow. Whereas urine . . . involves the production of a non-salable commodity and is therefore a general drain on the corporate effort." In Language Sonny, a virgin, admits: "I think that potency has something to do with murder."

In the plays of Starkweather we have a most complete view of what in olden times would have been called a saint: the man who leaves his society, goes into physical and psychical exile, searches for his god, and brings back the golden fleece to an indifferent world. In play after play, in growing clarity, Starkweather shows us the dangerous yet exciting journey, the abandoned society, and the funny, heartbreaking return. He even allows us glimpses of the fleece:

> He goes away within
> miles from the common road
> to bring back for this world
> something lovely something pure
> Thank you, man.

—William M. Hoffman

STAVIS, Barrie.

Born in New York City, 16 June 1906. Educated at New Utrecht High School, Brooklyn, New York, graduated 1924; Columbia University, New York, 1924–27. Served in the Army Signal Corps, Plans and Training section, 1942–45: technical-sergeant. Married 1) Leona Heyert in 1925 (divorced 1939); 2) Bernice Coe in 1950, one son and one daughter. Foreign correspondent in Europe, 1937–38; freelance journalist after World War II. Co-founder, and member of the board of directors, New Stages theatre group, 1947, and United States Institute for Theatre Technology, 1961–64 and 1969–72; visiting fellow, Institute for the Arts and Humanistic Studies, Pennylvania State University, University Park, 1971. Recipient: Yaddo fellowship, 1939; National Theatre Conference award, 1948, 1949. Fellow, American Theatre Association, 1982. Lives in New York City. Address: c/o Benjamin Zinkin, 635 Madison Avenue, New York, New York 10022, U.S.A.

Publications

PLAYS

In These Times (produced 1932).

The Sun and I (produced 1933; revised version produced 1937).

Refuge: A One-Act Play of the Spanish War (produced 1938). 1939.

Lamp at Midnight: A Play about Galileo (produced 1947). 1948; revised version, 1966; revised version, 1974; one-hour school and church version (produced 1972), 1974.

The Man Who Never Died: A Play about Joe Hill (produced 1955). 1954; revised version, 1972.

Banners of Steel: A Play about John Brown (produced 1962). 1967; revised version, as *Harpers Ferry: A Play about John Brown* (produced 1967).

Coat of Many Colors: A Play about Joseph in Egypt (produced 1966). 1968.

Joe Hill (opera libretto), music by Alan Bush, adaptation of the play *The Man Who Never Died* by Stavis (produced 1970).

Galileo Galilei (oratorio) music by Lee Hoiby, adaptation of the play *Lamp at Midnight* by Stavis (produced 1975).

The Raw Edge of Victory (as *Washington*, produced 1976). In *Dramatics*, April and May 1986.

NOVELS
The Chain of Command (novella). 1945.
Home, Sweet Home! 1949.

OTHER
John Brown: The Sword and the Word. 1970.
Editor, with W. Frank Harmon, *The Songs of Joe Hill.* 1955.

MANUSCRIPT COLLECTIONS: Lincoln Center Library of the Performing Arts, New York; Pennsylvania State University, University Park.

CRITICAL STUDIES: "Barrie Stavis: The Humanist Alternative" by Herbert Shore, in *Educational Theatre Journal*, December 1973; interview in *Astonish Us in the Morning: Tyrone Guthrie Remembered* by Alfred Rossi, 1977; "Humanism Is the Vital Subject" (interview), in *Dramatics*, March-April 1978; "A History, A Portrait, A Memory" by Stavis, in *Time Remembered: Alan Bush: An Eightieth Birthday Symposium* edited by Ronald Stevenson, 1981; "How Broad Should the Theatre's Concerns Be?" by Daniel Larner, in *Dramatics*, May 1981; "Barrie Stavis Issue" of *Religion and Theatre*, August 1981; *American Theater of the 1960's* by Zoltán Szilassy, 1986; "Barrie Stavis: Sixty Years of Craft and Commitment" by Ezra Goldstein, in *Dramatics*, April 1986.

Barrie Stavis comments:

(1973) I wrote my first full-length play when I was 19 years old. I had my first production when I was 26. Fortunately there are no scripts in existence. About a dozen plays followed—all since destroyed.

The material and form of these early plays were derivative, echoing closely the dominant writing and production modes of the American stage. I refer to the Theatre of Illusion where the play is naturalistic in concept and style, generally romantic in approach. The physical envelope of such plays consists of a box set, usually a four-walled room with the fourth wall removed so that the audience can "peek in" and see what happens to those "real" people on the stage.

I was gradually becoming dissatisfied with this kind of stage and its "imitation of life." It could not contain the statements I was trying to make in the theatre. But at that time I did not know how to break away from the narrow restrictions of the romantic-naturalism and the pseudo-realism of the Theatre of Illusion. I knew (though certainly not as clearly as I know it now) that I was concerned with writing plays where the driving force of the characters was the clash of their *ideas*, not their subjective emotions.

Form is dictated by content and should grow out of function. Thus, I was also searching for a form which would be consonant with my material. I was seeking a freedom and a plastic use of the stage which the box set could not give me. I began studying Shakespeare intensively. Shakespeare was, and remains even to this day, my major theatre influence, followed by the Bible for its style, and its ruthlessly candid and objective way of telling a story. My study of the Elizabethan theatre, along with Greek theatre and the Roman amphitheatre, gradually led me to devise what I designated (1933–34) as "Time-Space Stage"—a stage where both time and space could be used with fluidity.

In 1939 I began to work on *Lamp at Midnight*. It took three years to complete. It was in this play that I first achieved a successful synthesis of content and form. The characters in the play are embattled over basic philosophic concepts; and the plastic use of time and space on the stage proved to be the perfect medium for expressing the conflict of ideas.

It was then that I realized I wanted to write further plays exploring this use of the stage. Although all the plays in the series would have the same major theme, each play would be independent unto itself with the common theme developed from a different axis of observation.

The series proved to be a tetralogy exploring the problems of men who have ushered in new and frequent drastic changes in the existing social order—men who are of their time and yet in advance of their time. And I have been concerned with examining the thrust they exercise on their society, and the counter-thrust society exerts on them.

It is the essence of nature and of man to undergo continual change. New forms evolve from old, mature, and, as the inevitable concomitant of their maturation, induce still newer forms which replace them. This is the historical process.

This process of change is gradual. It is not always perceived nor clearly apparent. Yet it is constant and inexorable. At a given moment when historical conditions are ripe, a catalyst enters and fragments the existing culture, setting into motion a new alignment of forces, a new series of relationships, which gradually become stabilized, codified.

It is this process of change that I endeavor to capture in my plays: the precise moment in history when society, ripe for change, gives birth to the catalyst who sets the dynamics of change into accelerated motion.

The four plays in their order are: *Lamp at Midnight* (Galileo Galilei), *The Man Who Never Died* (Joe Hill), *Harpers Ferry* (John Brown), *Coat of Many Colors* (Joseph in Egypt). In the first of these plays, *Lamp at Midnight*, I dramatize the story of Galileo Galilei, the first human being to turn his new, powerful telescope to the night skies, there to discover the true motion of our solar system, a discovery unleashing a host of scientific and social consequence which heralded the coming Industrial Age. In *The Man Who Never Died* I dramatize the story of Joe Hill, troubador, folk poet, and trade union organizer, who was framed on a murder charge and who, during the 22 months of his prison stay, grew to heroic proportions. In *Harpers Ferry* I dramatize the story of John Brown's raid on Harpers Ferry, a raid which was the precursor to the Civil War. In *Coat of Many Colors* I dramatize the story of Joseph in Egypt, the world's first great agronomist and social planner, and I explore the theme of power and its uses. These four plays have been so designed that they can be performed by a single basic acting company. Further, all four plays can be produced on the same basic unit set.

Galileo Galilei, Joe Hill, John Brown, Joseph—these men have certain things in common. They were put on trial for their thoughts and deeds, found guilty, and punished. Yet their very ideas and acts achieved their vindication by later generations. Thus does the heresy of one age become the accepted truth of the next.

I have chosen to write plays about men who have an awareness of social and moral responsibility, plays that have faith in man's capacity to resolve his problems despite the monumental difficulties facing him. Why? Because I believe in ethical commitment. I believe that man is capable of ultimately solving the problems of the Nuclear Age.

Today, much theatre writing is obsessed with frustration and defeat. One trend of such playwriting deals with personality maladjustments and sexual aberration. This theatre is preoccupied with such matters as who goes to bed with whom, the gap in communication between parent and adolescent, the need to show that sex is either rape or submission. There is intense concern with subjective, neurotic problems, very little concern with the objective and social conditions of the world in which the characters live and the impact of the world upon them. It is as though the characters were living in a vacuum tube. Outside is the pulsating, throbbing world, but within the tube they function only insofar as their psyches collide with one another. Of the outside world, there is barely a reflection. A second contemporary trend is the writing of plays which explore the thesis that the human condition is hopeless because man is utterly dislocated in his society, that rational thought is a snare, that human life is purposeless, that action is without point for it will accomplish no result. There is in such plays no release for the affirmative emotion of an audience.

However, I believe with Chekhov that "Every playwright is responsible not only for what man is, but for what man can be." With Aristophanes, I seek to banish the "little man and woman affair" from the stage and to replace it with plays which explore ideas with such force and clarity as to raise them to the level of passion. Today especially, it should be the responsibility of the playwright to search out those situations which, by the inherent nature of the material, will capture the emotions and the intellect of an audience and focus it on men and women striving creatively for a positive goal.

(1988) I am now engaged in another tetralogy. The overall thematic examination of these four plays is *War, Revolution, and Peace.* In them, I explore George Washington, Abraham Lincoln, Miguel Hidalgo, and Simon Bolivar. Thus, I deal with the four liberators of the Western Hemisphere. In these plays I am concerned with the movement of colony to nation, of subject to citizen.

The material I handle is historical, but like the four plays of my first tetralogy, they are highly contemporary. We have been living in a century of war. There was the Japanese-Russian war in the first years of the century. Then came the famous/infamous assassination in Sarajevo which ushered in World War I. From then on until today, the world has been embroiled in wars, large and small. At this moment, there are over 50 different wars raging throughout the world. Thus, focusing on the theme of *War, Revolution, and Peace* is very much of our time.

I have completed the first play of the tetralogy: *The Raw Edge of Victory,* which deals with George Washington and the Revolutionary War. I'm half way through the second play, which focuses on Abraham Lincoln and the Civil War. Since I spend approximately five years on each play, it is obvious that I have accounted for the next ten years of my writing life!

A mere glance at the men Barrie Stavis has chosen to write about is indicative of his own passions, goals, intentions: John Brown, Joe Hill, Galileo, the biblical Joseph, and now in various stages of completion, works about George Washington, Hidalgo, Bolivar, and Lincoln.

There is about Stavis an almost Talmudic fury when he discusses his work and when he writes. This is in strange contrast to the man himself: warm, friendly, hopeful, and eager. Stavis is intellectually always aware ("conscious" might be an even better word) of what he is doing, dramaturgically and theatrically. His experience in theatre goes back further than most, and he has worked with almost every kind of theatre—getting his plays on to stages, everywhere.

Beyond grassroots experiences, there is a playwright, Stavis, who is very like the protagonists in his own plays: a man with a vision. It is a driving, almost monomaniacal vision which he, the artist, holds in careful check.

Just as his first tetralogy dealt with, in his words, "four aspects of mankind," all of his plays are precisely predicated. *Lamp at Midnight* (seen by twenty million in one night on a Hallmark Hall of Fame telecast) is "about Truth" (no small feat to undertake in a single play); *The Man Who Never Died* is "about Human Dignity"; *Harpers Ferry* is "about Freedom"; and *Coat of Many Colors* is "about Power." Stavis writes that kind of play deliberately, and there are abundant audiences and theatres in the United States and abroad eagerly seeking these plays: they have something to say, say it clearly, and are "about" something. As with good textbooks (*good* textbooks, mind), his work is pedantic, fascinating, and satisfying.

Stavis celebrated his 80th birthday shortly after the first play in his projected second tetralogy was published in *Dramatics*. This drama is about George Washington's heroic efforts to hold together the colonial army in the face of foreign intrigues, English military superiority, congressional neglect, domestic opportunism, and defeatism, despair, and dissatisfaction in the ranks. Stavis calls this epic drama *The Raw Edge of Victory*, and it is a potent brew of all the conflicts which raged as the Revolutionary War dragged on and on. The real role of black slaves and women in the war is forcefully demonstrated, as are the grim realities of keeping the troops in line, which Washington does with unflinching severity—even though he understands the reasons for rebellion in the ranks. Unlike the earlier plays, there are touches of humor here—even gallows-humor, as well as contrasts between the roughness of camp life and the sophisticated Court of King Louis XVI. Stavis's extensive research fortunately doesn't parade itself; it is abundantly evident in the dramatic revelation of how Washington and his army won the war and at what cost.

As with any conscientious teacher, Stavis is a superb researcher, who reads and studies about and around the men he will put on stage. Eventually, out of that research comes the spine of the play, the direction dictated by the material. His own humanistic background, of course, controls the aesthetics and even the politics of the play, and his experience controls the shape of the work, but the man and the artist avoid the merely pedantic, the narrowly polemic, the purely didactic. The five years he works on any single play make it fairly inevitable as a work: big, intellectual, more than a little "preachy" but almost always theatrical.

Stavis is a grassroots playwright. Middle America listens to the voice of history, and it is history that Stavis purveys most astutely and clearly. Grandeur and pageantry are second nature to the themes and the shapes of his work. His best work, I think, is *The Man Who Never Died*. It is no small accident that the play deals with an early "liberal," an American labor leader martyred and misplaced in time and place. That this play comes most successfully to the stage finally in the form of a German opera is really no surprise to those most familiar with Stavis's work.

He denies a tendency to romanticism and insists on the classicistic nature of his work. As did Brecht, Stavis claims to be more concerned with the *how* of an action than with the *why*. And in fact, his plays (the Joseph play possibly excepted) tend to Seriousness, with a capital S. There is generally little to amuse one in a Stavis play; the solemnity of the central figure is reflected in the almost complete lack of humor in the play itself. Even love is dealt with clinically and analytically. He leaves it to the total action to *move* his audiences: the themes that last, the appeal to noble if belated stances, the hero out of time.

Stavis, quite seriously and realistically, sees his own work as primarily influenced by both Shakespeare and the Holy Bible. If there are more rabbinic research and prophetic polemicism than there are lyricism and joy, Stavis cannot be faulted: he is after all very much a writer of his time and place, with a keen eye on the lessons of the past.

It might seem overly ambitious or optimistic for a playwright at age 80 to be looking forward to completing three more epics, all linked by the theme *War, Revolution, and Peace*. But Stavis has already been doing his years of research on Bolivar, Miguel Hidalgo, and Lincoln. Indeed, the life of Bolivar —whose own officers betrayed the vision of South American democracy for which he fought the war of liberation from Spain—has obsessed him for some time. The new tetralogy, he says, will explore in depth the "processes of throwing off oppression to gain freedom." He's focusing on "the movement of colony to nation, of subject to citizen," but the processes, as in *The Raw Edge of Victory*, are to be illuminated by the central characters of the liberators. In 1986, he was already halfway through his drama about Lincoln, with 2 epics to go. Knowing Stavis at all is to know that his plays will indeed deliver.

He is a "pro." Methodical, organized, enthusiastic, and almost pristinely professional as he is, there is a double irony in the fact that he has never really had a hit on Broadway. Yet he represents professional theatre to literally dozens of colleges and repertory companies not only in the United States but around the world. To non-Americans, particularly, as Tyrone Guthrie indicated, Stavis represents the clearest and "most American" voice of the time. As perhaps is still true with O'Neill, Stavis seems most American to those who are least American, and he seems most "universal" to his American audiences.

There is, in any event, no mistaking Stavis's intent and purpose. If heroic drama has gone out of fashion in an era of the anti-hero, Stavis persistently views history and man's passage through that history as essentially Heroic with a capital H.

Finally, Stavis is quite the opposite in one crucial aspect from the heroes of his plays. While each of them is a man *out* of joint with his own time, Stavis is *of* his time and writes for that broadest, most fundamental of audiences: people, not critics.

—Arthur H. Ballet

STEPPLING, John.

Born in California, 18 June 1951. Founder, with Sam Shepard and others, Padua Hills Playwrights Workshop and Festival, Los Angeles, 1978; founder and co-artistic director, Heliogabalus Company, 1986–89. Recipient: Rockefeller fellowship, 1984; National Endowment for the Arts grant; PEN West award, 1989. Agent: Michael Peretzian, William Morris Agency, 151 El Camino Drive, Beverly Hills, California 90212. Address: 844 Brooks Avenue, Venice, California 90291, U.S.A.

Publications

PLAYS

The Shaper (produced 1985).
The Dream Coast (produced 1986). 1987.
Pledging My Love (produced 1986).
Standard of the Breed (produced 1988).
Teenage Wedding (produced 1990).
Deep Tropical Tan (produced 1990).
The Thrill (produced 1991).
Storyland and Theory of Miracles. In *Best of the West*, edited by Murray Mednick, 1991.
Sea of Cortez (produced 1992).

SCREENPLAY: *52 Pick-up*, with Elmore Leonard, 1986.

In John Steppling's enigmatic evocations of life on the edge of the emotional abyss, the American Dream has been neither deferred nor exploded. Instead, his characters' aspirations have leaked from their souls like corrosive toxic sludge. His four major full-length plays—*The Shaper*, *The Dream Coast*, *Standard of the Breed*, and *The Thrill*—are all set on a West Coast whose spiritual, if not physical, focus is the scuzzy underside of Los Angeles and Hollywood.

All the plays are written in short, enigmatic blackout scenes that resolutely avoid a traditional dramatic trajectory composed of rising and falling action, therefore structurally mimicking the emptiness of the characters' emotional lives, which seem measured out in small epiphanies that come across as continuous dénouements. His spare use of language and heavy emphasis on silence and pauses are reminiscent of the German playwright Franz Xaver Kroetz. The sometimes glacial pace of his action coupled with his low-life subjects help inject all his plays with a dark, unseen, but pervasive sense of danger and potential menace.

Wilson, the ageing owner of a rundown Los Angeles motel in *The Dream Coast*, perhaps best describes the world view of Steppling's characters when he remembers being with his son: "I took him out—and everything seemed fine. He'd be having fun—he was only a little boy, three, four years old, so it was a kind of fun that little kids have, like it's an easy thing—but it was drab; underneath it not very deep, right under the surface was this drabness—sordid, sad—yeah, very sad, an awful sickness, an illness of sadness. . . ." The play, a *Grapes of Wrath* for the 1980s, finds two transplanted Okies—Marliss, a pliable 23-year-old and Weldon, approaching 40—in residence at Wilson's motel. Marliss doesn't "have any dreams about California"; instead, she's content to hang out by the pool and pop whites, smoke joints, score some coke. She ends up naked and semi-conscious on a transvestite's motel room floor as Bill, a grease-stained auto mechanic, drops his pants and lowers himself onto her. Wilson, haunted throughout the play by his ex-wife's harpings injected onstage via audiotape, finally allows his financially strapped motel to be torched for the insurance money.

The Shaper also explores failed dreams through the increasing insolvency of a small business. Set in Bud and Del's rundown surfboard shop, the title literally refers to Bud's occupation as a surfboard sculptor; metaphorically it suggests the influence of Del, in jail for cocaine possession at the play's outset, who lures Bud not only into acts of infidelity and petty larceny, but also into the whole soulless environment in which their dissipation has occurred. Reesa, Del's half-sister, has recently arrived in California from Ohio and she ogles the other characters' tans and tells them how she always imagined Bud as a "shiny golden beach boy." The great distance between her ideal and the sordid reality forms the vacuous grand canyon at the heart of Steppling's plays.

The Thrill, like The Dream Coast, is an ironic title. Linda, another of Steppling's young impressionable women unable to generate any self-motivation, hangs out at a Southern California shopping mall. There she encounters two small-time con-artists, working their way west from Providence, Rhode Island. Walter found Nat when he was 19 and reminds his partner that he was "the most beautiful thing I'd ever seen." But their partnership, like Bud and Del's, is doomed since Nat has managed to forcefully seduce the docile Linda (one scene consists solely of Nat forcing himself sexually on her in a telephone booth in the mall while her friend Beverly watches). However, the "thrill" of her relationship is all Linda has to fill her life; her passivity is such that when her father sends her a large check for her 21st birthday, she willingly hands it over to Nat, who then disappears with the money. The play ends with Linda sharing lunch with her aunt who runs a small fabric store in the mall—a perfect image of bland domesticity—in which she's recently started working now that the source of her "thrills" has vanished.

Standard of the Breed departs slightly from these other plays in that it takes place not in the Los Angeles area but in Jack's Nevada desert home outside Las Vegas (although the dreams crash just as resoundingly there) where he raises mastiffs, "the largest dogs in the world." A more significant difference is that the characters haven't yet completely surrendered their hopes and dreams to despair. The play unfolds at a dreamlike pace over the course of one night, beginning when twentysomething Cassie, a mixed-up young L.A. girl, arrives at Jack's doorstep after having left her unwitting boyfriend asleep in their room at a Vegas hotel. She's come to buy a mastiff puppy and escape her relationship. Jack explains that the standard for breeding dogs is "perfection," a metaphor for these humans as well (although such a project is ultimately destined for failure). The play is also about leaving, and like all Steppling's work, the characters are in transit to or from some half-idealized existence. Reese, Jack's boss at the casino, deserts his girlfriend Teela, who hoped to go to L.A. to try to make it as a singer. Jack decides to head to Sacramento and get drunk for a while, and encourages Cassie to dump her life and head out into the desert with her puppy by her side: "Leave it—That's a fine thing to do. All you need to take is the yearning." The play ends with Jack letting his prized mastiffs loose into the desert morning where they'll surely die slow painful deaths.

Some critics take exception to Steppling's plays, not only for the manner in which they continually portray young females as hapless victims of older, predatory males, but for their perceived soullessness. In an interview Steppling maintains his prerogative: "we live in patriarchy, it's very sexist. I'm writing what I see. . . . And everyone's a victim, really. Men and women are just subjugated in different kinds of ways." To Steppling's admirers, such arguments are beside the point; for, they feel, few U.S. dramatists so effectively describe the underbelly of human aspiration and futility.

—John Istel

SUNDE, Karen.

Actor, Colorado Shakespeare Festival, Boulder, Colorado, 1967, The New Shakespeare Company, San Francisco, 1967–68, Arrow Rock Lyceum, Arrow Rock, Missouri, 1969–70, and CSC Repertory, New York, 1971–85; associate director, CSC Repertory, New York, 1975–85. Recipient: Bob Hope award, 1963; American Scandinavian Foundation travel grant, 1981; Finnish Literature Center Production grant, 1982; Villager award (three times), 1983; McKnight fellowship, 1986; Aide de la Création grant, 1987. Address: 23 Leroy Street, Number 8, New York, New York 10014, U.S.A.

Publications

PLAYS

The Running of the Deer (produced 1978).

Balloon (produced 1983). 1983.

Philoctetes, adaptation of the play by Sophocles (also director: produced 1983).

Dark Lady (produced 1986). 1985.

Kabuki Othello (produced 1986).

To Moscow (produced 1986).

Quasimodo (musical), adaptation of Victor Hugo's *The Hunchback of Notre Dame*, with Christopher Martin (produced 1987).

Anton, Himself (produced 1988). In *Moscow Art Theatre*, edited by Michael Bigelow Dixon, 1989.

Kabuki Macbeth (produced 1989).

Haiti: A Dream (produced 1990).
Masha, Too (produced 1991).
Achilles (produced 1991).
In a Kingdom by the Sea (produced 1992).

RADIO PLAYS: *The Sound of Sand*, 1963; *Balloon*, 1987; *Haiti: A Dream*, 1991.

MANUSCRIPT COLLECTION: Lincoln Center Library for the Performing Arts, New York.

THEATRICAL ACTIVITIES
DIRECTOR: Plays—*Exit the King* by Ionesco, 1978; *Philoctetes* by Sophocles, 1983.
ACTOR: Plays—some 60 roles performed Off Broadway including: Ruth in *The Homecoming* by Pinter, 1972–76; Celimene in *The Misanthrope* by Molière, and Viola in *Twelfth Night*, 1973–74; Hedda in *Hedda Gabler* by Ibsen, 1974–77; Antigone in *Antigone* by Anouilh, 1975–77; Isabella in *Measure for Measure*, 1975; Hesione in *Heartbreak House* by Shaw, 1976–77; Rebekka West in *Rosmersholm* by Ibsen, 1977–78; Countess Aurelie in *The Madwoman of Chaillot* by Giraudoux, 1978; Portia in *The Merchant of Venice*, 1980; Jocasta and Antigone in *Oedipus Rex, Antigone*, and *Oedipus at Colonus* by Sophocles, 1980–81; Aase in *Peer Gynt* by Ibsen, 1981–82; Lotte in *Big and Little* by Botho Strauss, 1983–84; Alice in *Dance of Death* by Strindberg, 1984; Clytemnestra in *The Orestia* by Aeschylus, 1984–85. Television—Mary Brewster in *The Mayflower*, 1980.

Karen Sunde comments:

I follow my nose—and here's all I know: that rhythm is important to me. And economy. And passion. That the live current between audience and stage is everything.

With a voice both poetic and theatrical, Karen Sunde's plays dramatize historical epochs in epic scope, making hers a distinctive, even unique, contemporary American drama, more akin to European than to other American plays. She tackles topics of war and politics to produce usually presentational, often explosive theatre which many would swear could not have been created by a woman. Yet she imbues her mythic vision of the bellicose and patriarchal nature and direction of the United States and the world with a sense of what women can or do contribute to modifying these.

Sunde's twenty works for stage and screen fall into three related groups: the historical plays, the treatments of classics, and the glimpses of a painful present shaping a deplorable, but possibly salvageable future.

The first of her three consecutive plays set during or immediately after the American Revolution, *The Running of the Deer*, with its huge canvas and varied vistas, dramatizes the ravages of cold, starvation, and battle on George Washington's troops in order to probe the character of American male heroes, while the second, *Balloon*, achieves the same goal by setting in a theatrical framework worthy of Jean Genet another American founding father, Ben Franklin, so he can spar with his Tory son and woo his French mistress, Helvetius, who fears losing her autonomy in marriage to a man as passionately committed to his vocations as to his lovers. An appropriate protagonist for a play about hope and progress, Franklin strives and achieves, yet his painful interpersonal relations have diluted his triumphs.

Deborah: The Adventures of a Soldier (an unproduced television play), like several of Sunde's subsequent plays, investigates female heroism, or, in this case, the male model of heroism achieved by an astonishing woman warrior, Deborah Sampson, who enlists in the Continental Army as "Robert Shurtliffe," and rises to leadership among men while battling with the British. As Sunde remarks of her version of this actual historical woman's triumphs, "When war is real, issues confused, deaths bitter, a woman has to finally decide who she is." This one can outshoot, outthink, and outrun the men, but should she continue to do so? Sunde humorously recounts Deborah's adventures both as a soldier and as a woman trying to pass for a man (with women coming on to "him") and falling in love with a sergeant who thinks she's male. Sunde's background as an actor in Shakespeare's plays certainly sensitized her to the comedic possibilities of employing a woman playing a man. But the dramatist also conveys the war's pathos, its pain, and its cost in lives lost.

Sunde continues to explore female heroism in *The Flower's Lost Child* (an unproduced play), which portrays what the playwright describes as "America's romance with violence." Instead of colonists resisting taxation without representation and throwing off an oppressor's rule, Sunde chooses hippie revolutionaries in 1970 New York. The shift in period changes our perspective, forcing us to distance ourselves from terrorists, to question the appropriateness of bombs in the pursuit of peace. Yet she dramatizes these idealists sympathetically. A resourceful and brave leader, Anne had worked with Martin Luther King and embraced non-violence. Now, disillusioned by his assassination, she has abandoned marches and rallies in favor of dynamite. This tragedy creates a powerful sense of fate because Sunde frames the entire play as flashback by beginning with firemen sifting through rubble and dismembered bodies, and then enhances the suspense by surrounding her characters with explosives.

In her as yet unproduced and untitled gothic thriller about British serial killer John George Haigh, set in 1948, Sunde builds tension by hinting at a murder and the threat to the lives of two courageous women, a spirited teenager and another more mature woman, who struggle to foil their amoral terrorizer.

Sunde again depicts a female hero in *Dark Lady*, which, set against the plague's slaughter, dramatizes the relationship between Shakespeare and Renaissance England's best-known woman poet, Emilia Bassano. Sunde creates in her a passionate woman whose humanity, courage, spirit, and generosity equal—and ultimately exceed—the Bard's.

In three further plays, Sunde dramatizes actual characters in events which plausibly might have occurred. *To Moscow* concerns Chekhov, his actress wife Olga Knipper, Konstantin Stanislavsky, and the beginnings of the Moscow Art Theatre. The title evokes Chekhov's three sisters' unrealized intention to return from their provincial backwater to Moscow. Sunde chooses as four of the six central characters women whom Chekhov exploits. But in one, Olga, he finds (like Shakespeare in Emilia) his equal. Sunde completes her Russian trilogy with two matching one-act portraits, one of the narcissist Chekhov titled *Anton, Himself*, the other, *Masha, Too*, of his sister, as she struggles to summon the courage to tell him she plans to marry. We conclude from *Anton* that her brother will not let her leave him. While viewers need know nothing about Chekhov to enjoy these three, Sunde interlards the action with jokes about the plays and stories, especially intriguing to knowledgeable viewers.

While penning her history plays Sunde undertook a related approach to indicting human folly, by means of our literary myths, one from Victor Hugo, three from Shakespeare's plays, and one from Homer's *Iliad*. Sunde's musical version of *The Hunchback of Notre Dame*, which she wrote with director Christopher Martin, fashions the novel into a fluid work which contrasts with the long, carefully demarcated scenes in that other Hugo musical, *Les Misérables*. More opera than musical and boasting a score ranging from ecclesiastic to gypsy, the galvanic *Quasimodo* dramatizes the theme that people should experience, not repress, their passions: "Man is man, not stone."

Providing further evidence of her versatility, Sunde created four Kabuki plays for Japanese director Shozo Sato, who has staged them in Kabuki style but with American performers. Although *Kabuki Othello* preserves the Shakespearean outlines, Sunde makes Iago's motivation clearer and eliminates the Bard's racism and sexism. Asian ritual reinforces the tragedy's inevitability. Far from inviting any unfavorable comparisons to the original, Sunde creates her own distinc- tive imagery—delicate, tender, and eventually heroic for Desdemona, demonic for the Ainu Othello—and, in Emilia's lines, a healthy sarcasm about machismo and female subservience. In her *Kabuki Macbeth* and, the as yet unproduced, *Kabuki Richard* the dramatist also evokes a theatrical mixture of the original plots and their archetypes with Eastern culture—samurai, shoguns, karma, and Shiva intertwined with ghosts, witches, and severed heads.

In *Achilles* Sunde converts material from *The Iliad* into a mythic anti-war tragedy. She emphasizes the macho lust for glory which leads to the razing of Troy and massive, senseless slaughter, reminding us of the continuing cost of personal and international bravado. Sunde's searing script dramatizes pride, arrogance, and savagery—and their aftermath of grief, when Achilles joins Priam in mourning Hector's death after the bereaved father kisses the "victor's" hand. Focusing her work for us through the eyes of the enslaved Briseis, "only a woman," a prize of battle, who has learned "the purpose of life is war," Sunde employs an archetypal example to promote peace and recognition of our common humanity.

Sunde likewise dramatizes conflicts from a humanist perspective in a series of prescient plays looking towards the global future. *House of Eeyore* (an unproduced play), which takes its title from A. A. Milne's *Winnie the Pooh* stories, employs dream research, a gubernatorial campaign, and an ageless native American psychic (named after the female spirit Gaia) to awaken a prominent American family to its spiritual and social responsibilities.

Whereas the visionary middle-class women in *House of Eeyore* works as a research physician, Gaye in *Countdown: Earth* (an unproduced screenplay),

saves the western half of the planet because of her skill as a geophysicist—not
to mention her bravery in carrying out a daredevil rescue while dangling above
a volcano starting to erupt. Still a third woman scientist, this one discovering a
cure for cancer, plays a prominent role in *Over the Rainbow* (another unproduced screenplay), but here Sunde chooses as her protagonist another healer,
the scientist's little girl. Both *Countdown: Earth* and *Over the Rainbow*
employ science fiction to arouse concern about our planet's survival.

In three further plays Sunde hopes for a better tomorrow even as she
explores the roots of misery today. The prophetic *Haiti: A Dream* dramatizes
the flight to Florida of Haitian boat people by focusing on a man and his wife
and the Old Woman empowered by voodoo who tries unsuccessfully to inspire
them both to recognize their own strength to lead their people. In a similar
spirit of fantasizing about a better way, *How His Bride Came to Abraham* (an
unproduced play), creates an extraordinary modern pacifist myth in which a
wounded male Israeli soldier and a female Palestinian terrorist experience each
other's passionate hunger for their homes and rights. Sunde describes this
tragedy as "today's violent news stories in fairy-tale form," but it indelibly
etches itself upon viewers' souls because of the human encounter, as wary
people drop their guard with an enemy.

The multi-media *In a Kingdom by the Sea*, based upon the abduction of
Marine Lt. Col. William Higgins, presents simultaneously the efforts of the UN
peacekeepers to free one of their own—here named Hogan—and Hogan
himself, who appears in both past and present, in both monologue and
dialogue, to share with us the "key to America," and to his character: football
and women—in Hogan's case the woman whom, since high school, he has
tried to impress with a uniform. In contrast to *How His Bride Came to
Abraham*'s wartime dream of peace and love, *In a Kingdom by the Sea*
dramatizes the subversion of the UN peacekeeping forces' efforts in Lebanon
by those on both sides for whom macho bravado means more than would an
end to hostility.

A balloon will rise, but what, Sunde inquires in *Balloon*, of humanity? Her
plays consider whether we have reason to hope.

—Tish Dace

T

TALLY, Ted.

Born in Winston-Salem, North Carolina, 9 April 1952. Educated at Yale University, New Haven, Connecticut (John Golden fellowship 1976–77; Kazan award, 1977; Field prize, 1977), B.A. 1974, M.F.A. 1977. Married; one son. Taught at Yale University; artist-in-residence, Atlantic Center for the Arts, 1983. Member of the Dramatists Guild, Writers Guild, Academy of Motion Picture Arts and Sciences, and the Artistic Board, Playwrights Horizons, New York. Recipient: CBS-Yale fellowship, 1977; Creative Artists Public Service grant, 1979; John Gassner award, 1981; National Endowment for the Arts fellowship, 1983; Obie award, 1984; Guggenheim fellowship, 1985; Christopher award, 1988; Oscar, 1992; Writers Guild award, 1992; Chicago Film Critics award, 1992; Saturn award, 1992. Lives in Pennsylvania. Agent: (theatre) Helen Merrill Ltd., 361 West 17th Street, New York, New York 10011; (film) Arlene Donovan, International Creative Management, 40 West 57th Street, New York, New York 10019, U.S.A.

Publications

PLAYS

Terra Nova (produced 1977). 1981.
Night Mail and Other Sketches (produced 1977).
Word of Mouth (revue), with others (produced 1978).
Hooters (produced 1978). 1978.
Coming Attractions, music by Jack Feldman, lyrics by Feldman and Bruce Sussman (produced 1980). 1982.
Silver Linings: Revue Sketches. 1983.
Little Footsteps (produced 1986). 1986.
Taxi from Hell in *Urban Blight* (musical revue), based on an idea by John Tillinger, music by David Shire, lyrics by Richard Maltby, Jr. (produced 1988).
The Gettysburg Sound Bite (produced 1989).

SCREENPLAYS: *White Palace*, with Alvin Sargent, 1990; *The Silence of the Lambs*, 1991.

TELEVISION: *The Comedy Zone* series, 1984; *Holy Angels*, with others, 1986; *The Father Clements Story*, with Arthur Heineman, 1987.

Ted Tally comments:

I have sometimes been asked whether my plays share any particular theme. Though they have been diverse both stylistically and in terms of subject matter, I think there are at least two common threads: a fascination with rites of passage, and a concern for the prices one must pay in pursuit of a dream.

Ted Tally writes in versatile voices. Since 1977 productions of his plays at showcase American theaters (including the Yale Repertory Theater, the O'Neill Theater Center in Waterford, Connecticut, the Mark Taper Forum in Los Angeles, and the audaciously innovative Playwrights Horizons in New York City), in Stockholm, and at the Chichester Festival Theatre have earned him recognition as an important dramatic talent.

Tally's prodigious promise is revealed stunningly in *Terra Nova*, his most widely produced and justifiably praised work to date. His subject is specific and based in reality: Englishman Robert Scott's doomed 1911–12 race to the Antarctic against the Norwegian Roald Amundsen. But the play's method and implications are mythic and poetic; they free Tally from the confines of a history play and enable him to universalize his literal subject through stylized language, setting, and dramatic structure. Set in the mind of the dying Scott as he records final entries in his diary, *Terra Nova* portrays its hero's hallucinatory evaluation of the sources that have driven him and his unlucky band of men to the Antarctic. The procession of stage images shifts seamlessly, cinematically, within the frozen present, the past, the future—all reflected through the anguished mind of Scott, whose story co-exists as exciting theatrical adventure and as the wellspring for a series of complex moral debates.

Tally dissects the core of heroism even as he concedes the needs of nations to create heroes and the symbiotic needs of special men, sometimes tragic men like Scott, to enact the roles their societies write for them. Related to the play's central, ambivalent issue are the vanishing points between national pride and jingoism, patriotic sacrifice and familial irresponsibility, a shrinking British Empire and a future (toward which the play points) bereft of Old Style Heroes. "The world is changing," Amundsen says in Scott's imagined future. "England, Norway, Europe—The Great War changed everything, you wouldn't know it today [1932]. It's a smaller place, but not a more neighbourly one. A frightened place, a world of shopkeepers and thieves. Where is the heroic gesture in such a world? The man who can keep his bread on the table is a hero. Where on such an earth are men who walk like gods? Dead and gone, with Columbus and Magellan." In his haunted fear of failure and conflicting drive to defy man's ordinary boundaries, Scott resembles Ibsen's Master Builder Solness. Possibly, as Amundsen calls him, "the most dangerous kind of decent man," possibly a true representative of the last breed of genuine hero, possibly a complete sham. Scott is one of the few realized tragic heroes in the recent American drama.

In *Coming Attractions* the subject is still celebrity but the mode is wild satire. Amundsen's prediction in *Terra Nova* has come true: no heroes are left. But television and the tabloids, memoir publishers and movie writers, hungry for heroes to feed an insatiable American public, fabricate them out of killers, madmen, and Real People. *Coming Attractions* takes deadly aim at many targets: Miss America contests, television news, talk and variety shows, inept law enforcement, an even more inept judicial system, old time religion, advertising, and—especially—an American society that encourages fleeting fame or infamy to masquerade as authentic accomplishment. To appear on television, even for a moment, is the Promised End. Tally's shift from the poetic voices of *Terra Nova* to the parodies in *Coming Attractions* of show biz vernacular, press agentry, and media hype is dazzling. Outrageous puns (Criminal to Judge: "I demand that you give me the chair!" Judge: "Then where would I sit?"), burlesque routines, movie clichés, and mordantly hilarious situations (the play concludes with the televised musical electrocution of its killer-hero: "Live from Death Row—it's—The Execution of Lonnie Wayne Burke!") combine in a lunatic blend of the Marx Brothers, Artaudian theatre of cruelty, Paddy Chayefsky's *Network*, and Sinclair Lewis's *Elmer Gantry*.

Tally's other work reflects his discomfort with stylistic uniformity. *Hooters* is a rites-of-passage sex comedy. Three early unproduced film scripts belong to three separate genres: situation comedy (*Couples Only*); epic (*Empire*, on which Tally worked for a year with director Lindsay Anderson); New York police thriller (*Hush-a-Bye*). In the underrated play *Little Footsteps* ("an exceptionally literate sitcom," *New York Times* critic Frank Rich called it), the teenage courtship dance of *Hooters* evolves into marriage and in law rituals as a young couple await the arrival of their firstborn. "We've got nothing against your religion, Ben; it's you we hate," his mother-in-law casually informs the beleaguered hero in the play's pungent dialogue.

Like most serious American playwrights of the past decade, Tally deplores the exorbitant costs of Broadway theatre which result in productions appealing to "the widest possible audience" and having "more and more to do with sensation and effect, less to do with any food for thought." His plays are primarily associated with strong regional theatre companies and with Playwrights Horizons in New York City, the highly regarded company with which he has been identified periodically since the beginning of his career.

Tally's disenchantment with the theatre appears for now to have driven him entirely to screenwriting, a shift that, with his adaptation of *The Silence of the Lambs*, has brought him financial reward and critical acclaim (including an Oscar) rarely earned for his stage work. He embraces film writing for its opportunities to reach "a wider audience and to be less subject to the whims of critics." He rejects the notion that Hollywood "sucks up writers and destroys them," maintaining that his work with director Jonathan Demme on *The Silence of the Lambs* was a thoroughly enjoyable collaborative effort; he anticipates the prospect of a sequel with relish.

In recognition of what he calls the inevitable "streamlining" that must occur in screen adaptation, Tally's screenplay for the film eliminates the multiple points of view which occur in Thomas Harris's novel. "The book goes inside the minds not just of Clarice Starling, but of Lecter, of Gumb, the killer she is pursuing, and of Jack Crawford, her mentor at the F.B.I.," Tally told a New York Times interviewer. "I thought really that the entire story had to concentrate on Clarice, that every scene had to concentrate as much as possible on what she is seeing and what she is feeling and what she is thinking. The heart of the story was between Clarice and Lecter, that strange sexual power struggle, that chess game between this young woman and this man—this monster." That "this monster," performed memorably by Anthony Hopkins, becomes the film's unforgettable character, a Norman Bates for the 1990's, is a particular consequence of Tally's dialogue, which manages to externalize Lecter's dangerous complexity and dark humour without turning him into a caricature.

"Success is a bitch. Grab her, and have her—but don't stand under her window with a mandolin," says Amundsen, the cynical, pragmatic leveler of Scott's romantic imagination in *Terra Nova*. "Ain't life a bitch?" muses theatrical agent Manny Alter to the man condemned to electrocution in *Coming Attractions*. In *Terra Nova* heroism comes to an end but genuine myths are born. In *Coming Attractions* travesty is the only legitimate vehicle for a society in which violence and bad taste alone capture the public imagination. Hannibal (the Cannibal) Lecter sprang to mythical status as an icon of popular cinema culture following the release of *The Silence of the Lambs*. It is no small irony that Ted Tally's most explicit flirtation with violence and bad taste captured the public imagination as none of his plays has yet been able to do.

—Mark W. Estrin

TAVEL, Ronald.

Born in Brooklyn, New York, 17 May 1941. Educated at Brooklyn College; University of Wyoming, Laramie, B.A., M.A. 1961. Screenwriter, Andy Warhol Films Inc., 1964–66; playwright-in-residence, Play-House of the Ridiculous, New York, 1965–67, Theatre of the Lost Continent, New York, 1971–73, Actors Studio, New York, 1972, Yale University Divinity School, New Haven, Connecticut, 1975, 1977, Williamstown Theatre Festival, Massachusetts, Summer 1977, New Playwrights Theatre, Washington, D.C., 1978–79, Cornell University, Ithaca, New York, 1980–81, Centrum Foundation, Fort Worden State Park, Washington, 1981, and Millay Colony for the Arts, New York, 1986; lecturer in foreign languages, Mahidol University, Thailand, 1981–82; visiting professor of creative writing, University of Colorado, Boulder, 1986. Since 1984 member of the Education Division, Theater for the New City, New York. Literary adviser, *Scripts* magazine, New York, 1971–72; drama critic, *Stages* magazine, Norwood, New Jersey, 1984; theatre editor, *Brooklyn Literary Review*, 1984–85. Recipient: Obie award, 1969, 1973; American Place Theatre grant, 1970; Creative Artists Public Service grant, 1971, 1973; Rockefeller grant, 1972, 1978; Guggenheim fellowship, 1973; National Endowment for the Arts grant, 1974; New York State Council on the Arts grant, 1975; ZBS Foundation grant, 1976; New York Foundation for the Arts fellowship, 1985; Yaddo fellowship, 1986. Agent: Helen Merrill Ltd., 361 West 17th Street, New York, New York 10011. Address: 780 Carroll Street, Brooklyn, New York 11215; or, 438 West Broadway, Apartment 1, New York, New York 10012, U.S.A.

Publications

PLAYS

Christina's World, published in *Chicago Review*, Winter-Spring 1963.
The Life of Juanita Castro (produced 1965). In *Bigfoot and Other Plays*, 1973.
Shower (produced 1965). In *Bigfoot and Other Plays*, 1973.
Tarzan of the Flicks (produced 1965). In *Blacklist 6*, 1965.
Harlot (scenario), published in *Film Culture*, Spring 1966.
The Life of Lady Godiva (produced 1966). In *The New Underground Theatre*, edited by Robert Schroeder, 1968.
Indira Gandhi's Daring Device (produced 1966). In *Bigfoot and Other Plays*, 1973.
Screen Test (produced 1966).
Vinyl (produced 1967). In *Clyde*, vol. 2, no. 2, 1966.
Kitchenette (also director: produced 1967). In *Bigfoot and Other Plays*, 1973.
Gorilla Queen (produced 1967). In *The Best of Off-Off-Broadway*, edited by Michael T. Smith, 1969.
Canticle of the Nightingale (produced 1968).
Cleobis and Bito (oratorio; produced 1968).
Arenas of Lutetia (also director: produced 1968). In *Experiments in Prose*, edited by Eugene Wildman, 1969.
Boy on the Straight-Back Chair, music by Orville Stoeber (produced 1969). In *Bigfoot and Other Plays*, 1973.
Vinyl Visits an FM Station (produced 1970). In *Drama Review*, September 1970.
Bigfoot, music by Jeff Labes (produced 1970). In *Bigfoot and Other Plays*, 1973.
Words for Bryan to Sing and Dance (produced 1971).
Arse Long—Life Short (produced 1972).
Secrets of the Citizens Correction Committee (produced 1973). In *Scripts 3*, January 1972.
Bigfoot and Other Plays. 1973.
Queen of Greece (produced 1973).
The Last Days of British Honduras (produced 1974).
Playbirth (produced 1976).
The Clown's Tail (produced 1977).
Gazelle Boy (produced 1977).
The Ovens of Anita Orangejuice: A History of Modern Florida (produced 1977).
The Ark of God (produced 1978).
The Nutcracker in the Land of Nuts, music by Simeon Westbrooke (produced 1979).
My Foetus Lived on Amboy Street (broadcast 1979; also director: produced 1985).
The Understudy (produced 1981).
Success and Succession (produced 1983).
Notorious Harik Will Kill the Pope (also director: produced 1986).
Thick Dick (also director: produced 1988).

SCREENPLAYS: *Harlot*, 1964; *Phillip's Screen Test*, 1965; *Screen Test*, 1965: *Suicide*, 1965; *The Life of Juanita Castro*, 1965; *Horse*, 1965; *Vinyl*, 1965; *Kitchen*, 1965; *Space*, 1965; *Hedy; or, The 14–Year-Old Girl*, 1966; *Withering Sights*, 1966; *The Chelsea Girls*, 1966; *More Milk Evette*, 1966.

RADIO PLAY: *My Foetus Lived on Amboy Street*, 1979.

NOVEL
Street of Stairs. 1968.

MANUSCRIPT COLLECTIONS: Mugar Memorial Library, Boston University: Lincoln Center Library of the Performing Arts, New York; University of Wisconsin Center for Theatre Research, Madison.

CRITICAL STUDIES: "The Pop Scene," in *Tri-Quarterly* 6, 1966, and "Pop Goes America," in *New Republic*, 9 September 1967, both by Peter Michelson; "Ronald Tavel: Ridiculous Playwright" by Dan Isaac, in *Drama Review*, Spring 1968; "Toward Eroticizing All Thought," in *New York Times*, 5 January 1969, and "Ronald Tavel: Celebration of a Panic Vision," in *Village Voice*, 6 March 1969, both by Gino Rizzo; "A Kid Named Toby" by Jack Kroll, in *Newsweek*, 24 March 1969; *American Playwrights: A Critical Survey* by Bonnie Marranca and Gautam Dasgupta, 1981.

THEATRICAL ACTIVITIES
DIRECTOR: **Plays**—*The Life of Juanita Castro*, 1967; *Kitchenette*, 1967; *Arenas of Lutetia*, 1968; *Infinity*, 1972; *A Streetcar Named Desire* (in Thai, as *Ourrat*) by Tennessee Williams, 1981; *The Zoo Story* (in Thai) by Edward Albee, 1982; *Clash of the Bra Maidens*, 1984; *My Foetus Lived on Amboy Street*, 1985; *The Tell-Tale Heart*, 1985; *Talent*, 1985; *Notorious Harik Will Kill the Pope*, 1986; *Thick Dick*, 1988. **Films**—*Harlot*, 1964; *Phillip's Screen Test*, 1965; *Screen Test*, 1965; *The Life of Juanita Castro*, 1965; *Horse*, 1965; *Vinyl*, 1965; *Space*, 1965; *It Happened in Connecticut*, 1965; *Hedy; or, The 14–Year-Old Girl*, 1966; *Withering Sights*, 1966; *The Chelsea Girls* (*Toby Short* and *Hanoi Hanna* episodes), 1966.
ACTOR: **Plays**—roles in *In Search of the Cobra Jewels* by Harvey Fierstein, 1972, and in all his directed plays. **Films**—in all his directed films, and in *Fifty Fantasticks*, 1964; *Bitch*, 1965; *Jail*, 1967; *Suicide Notations: Fire Escape*, 1972; *Infinity*, 1974.

Ronald Tavel comments:

(1973) My earliest tales were delivered Homerically. At the age of six or seven I took the first step toward giving them permanent form: comic books. While these comics were shameless imitations of the pictorial styles featured in the funnies we read at that time, there was, I fancy, something more urgent in my stories and characterizations. I wrote my first (verse) play (or fragment of one) in my sophomore year in high school and ten verse plays (or fragments of ones) followed that effort. The last of these have reached print but only one (*Cleobis and Bito*) was ever produced. In 1965, after two years of writing, directing, and acting in films, I turned again to playwriting. These were the one-acters that inaugurated The Theatre of the Ridiculous movement—a term I invented to catch the attention of critics and lower them into a category in order to facilitate their work. The term "Ridiculous" should not be taken too seriously (!) unless you want to re-define that word as Professor Peter Michelson did in his essay on the new American absurdity (*New Republic*, 9 September 1967). I sought in these abstract satires to find a distinctly American language for the stage and that is a continuing preoccupation in my later and mercilessly longer "tragedies." In the early plays I also attempted to destroy plot and character, motivation, cause, event, and logic along with their supposed consequences. The word was All: what was spoken did not express the moment's preoccupation; rather, the preoccupation followed the word. In *The Life of Lady Godiva* I reached, cynically, for the Aristotelian principles of playmaking. While cynicism is the major thrust of *Godiva*, a near decade of concern with *The Poetics* was worming its way, re-evaluated, to the core of my chores. *Gorilla Queen* progresses by building and abolishing, rebuilding and reabolishing, etc., the Aristotelian constructs. The full-length plays after *Gorilla Queen* obey, I believe, without too much objection, the Greek's difficult insights. While I have no single favorite, I am particularly fond of *Shower* because it continues to mystify me, am protective of *Arenas of Lutetia* because no one else will be, and consider *Bigfoot* (if you will allow me to play critic) my most ambitious and best play to date.

(1988) Although my recent fellowships and judging and teaching appointments are apparently for my abstract work in theatre, I have continued to create as many formal pieces: partly because I feel that formal values, following the disappearance of American education, are threatened in serious contemporary theatre; and partly because I believe that our present situation is not more keenly scrutinized by the abstract than the formal. (My previous solution, in larger works, was always to combine the two.)

Because of the growing idiosyncratic nature of serious plays, it has become common in the last decade for American dramatists to direct their own work. Reluctantly, I have joined their ranks. Since directing forces a stronger confrontation with space, time, flesh, clothes, and light than words alone do, and requires no rewards or rejuvenations outside itself, it helps the playwright to that closer understanding of the unity of theatre which he irresponsibly surrendered in the past century and a half.

Ronald Tavel is one of the originators of the mode Susan Sontag identified as "camp." From the start he writes with an unmistakable voice, relentlessly punning, answering back to his own word-plays, philosophizing, art-conscious, joking, ridiculous as the Marx Brothers, and turning his formidable energy to the service of a passion for justice, with a Cassandra's terror of self-righteousness, a not-to-be-thwarted demand for meaning, self- and god-knowledge.

This thrust is evident even in a pop joke like *The Life of Juanita Castro* which takes its authenticity from *Life* magazine. *Indira Gandhi's Daring Device* drew a swift protest from the government of India, and *How Jacqueline Kennedy Became Queen of Greece* was muted (but in title only) to *Queen of*

Greece. These plays are travesty, but Tavel is out for serious game, and has loaded them with real facts and arguments.

Gorilla Queen, his first play on a large scale, is a spoof on jungle movies, unique in its crazy playfulness, rococo, smartaleck language, outlandishly scrambled sexuality, and self-consciousness about art. From the epilogue (delivered by a gibbon holding a purple rose): ". . . art ain't never 'bout life, but life *is* only 'bout art. Dis rose?—oh, it ain't no symbol like ya mighta thought, an dat's cause it ain't got nothing' to do wit life either. Dis here rose is all 'bout art. Here, take it—(He throws the rose into the audience.)"

In *Bigfoot* the work began to reveal, not just refer to, its depth and power. Here Tavel's subject is brothers, in the image of Jacob and Esau. On a profound level of derangement the one, an intellectual monastic and school-teacher, suspects the other, a forest ranger, of being not human, confusing him with the Bigfoot, the legendary man-ape of the Pacific Northwest. Set in the majestic forest and the monastery schoolroom, *Bigfoot* is a play of immense complexity. The surface is no longer pop or campy but the post-realist strategies are in flood: a fictional lighting girl gets caught up in the *more real* fiction of the play's far-fetched story; the Playwright's Brother is a character *ex machina*, played in the production Tavel supervised by his own brother—what a thing to do in a play about mythic fratricide!

The Ovens of Anita Orangejuice is a boisterous, savage satire about Anita Bryant's 1977 campaign against gay rights. Subtitled "A History of Modern Florida," it is a wisecrack that turns into a nightmare. For all its frenzied hilarity, it makes a thought-provoking, emotionally compelling case. In *Gazelle Boy* a middle-aged missionary in the north woods loses her head over a wild boy, which leads to tragedy of profoundly unsettling dimensions. It is a beautiful play, dense with religion. Here sex is a reaching for the divine. *The Understudy* is about sex murder: the play's playwright may have done the killings he has written about, which the audience is ultimately shown in literal gore; a demented understudy tries to save him, and steal the writer's being, by recommitting them himself.

My Foetus Lived on Amboy Street takes a far more tender tone. The play appears to be, of all things, a prenatal autobiography. The writer experiments here with an expressionistically abstracted, outwardly geometrical stagecraft. The persona of the play's ego images himself as a spider, while the company of players patch in the various roles as freely as the author counterposes multiple vernaculars of lyricism and melodrama. *Notorious Harik Will Kill the Pope*, which Tavel himself staged at the Theatre for the New City in New York in 1986, crammed the stage with movie types (Turhan Bey and Lana Turner are among the characters) in a flashy complexity of scenes. The frivolity of its trashy satirical style—Tavel never resists a pun—masks a sustained demolition of the religious establishment which, like all his themes, the writer gives every sign of meaning.

—Michael T. Smith

TERRY, Megan.

Born Marguerite Duffy in Seattle, Washington, 22 July 1932. Educated at
Banff School of Fine Arts, Alberta, summers 1950–53, 1956; University of
Washington, Seattle, 1950, 1953–56, B.Ed. 1956; University of Alberta,
Edmonton, 1951–53. Drama teacher and director of the Cornish Players,
Cornish School of Allied Arts, Seattle, 1954–56; founding member, 1963, and
director of the playwrights workshop, 1963–68, Open Theatre, New York;
writer-in-residence, Yale University School of Drama, New Haven,
Connecticut, 1966–67; founding member, Women's Theatre Council, 1971;
founding member and treasurer, New York Theatre Strategy, 1971; Bingham
professor of humanities, University of Louisville, 1981; Hill professor of fine
arts, University of Minnesota, Duluth, 1983; visiting artist University of Iowa,
Iowa City, 1992. Since 1971 resident playwright and literary manager, Omaha
Magic Theatre. Recipient: Stanley award, 1965; Office of Advanced Drama
Research award, 1965; ABC-Yale University fellowship, 1966; Rockefeller
grant, 1968, 1987; Obie award, 1970; National Endowment for the Arts
grant, 1972, fellowship, 1989; Earplay award, 1972; Creative Artists Public
Service grant, 1973; Guggenheim fellowship, 1978; Dramatists Guild award,
1983; Nebraska Artist of the Year Governors award, 1992. Agent: Elisabeth
Marton, 96 Fifth Avenue, New York, New York 10011. Address: 2309
Hanscom Boulevard, Omaha, Nebraska 61805; or, c/o Omaha Magic
Theatre, 1417 Farnam Street, Omaha, Nebraska 68102, U.S.A.

Publications

PLAYS

Beach Grass (also director: produced 1955).
Seascape (also director: produced 1955).
Go Out and Move the Car (also director: produced 1955).
New York Comedy: Two (produced 1961).
Ex-Miss Copper Queen on a Set of Pills (produced 1963). With *The People vs.
   Ranchman*, 1968.
When My Girlhood Was Still All Flowers (produced 1963).
Eat at Joe's (produced 1964).
Calm Down Mother (produced 1965). 1966.
Keep Tightly Closed in a Cool Dry Place (produced 1965). In *Four Plays*,
   1967.
The Magic Realists (produced 1966). In *Three One-Act Plays*, 1972.
Comings and Goings (produced 1966). In *Four Plays*, 1967.
The Gloaming, Oh My Darling (produced 1966). In *Four Plays*, 1967.
Viet Rock: A Folk War Movie (also director: produced 1966). In *Four Plays*,
   1967.
Four Plays. 1967.
The Key Is on the Bottom (produced 1967).
The People vs. Ranchman (produced 1967). With *Ex-Miss Copper Queen on a
   Set of Pills*, 1968.
Home; or, Future Soap (televised 1968; revised version, as *Future Soap*,
   produced 1987). 1972.
Jack-Jack (produced 1968).

Massachusetts Trust (produced 1968). In *The Off-Off-Broadway Book*, edited by Albert Poland and Bruce Mailman, 1972.

Changes, with Tom O'Horgan (produced 1968).

Sanibel and Captiva (broadcast 1968). In *Three One-Act Plays*, 1972.

One More Little Drinkie (televised 1969). In *Three One-Act Plays*, 1972.

Approaching Simone (produced 1970). 1973.

The Tommy Allen Show (also director: produced 1970). In *Scripts* 2, December 1971.

Grooving (produced 1972).

Choose a Spot on the Floor, with Jo Ann Schmidman (produced 1972).

Three One-Act Plays. 1972.

Couplings and Groupings (monologues and sketches). 1973.

Susan Peretz at the Manhattan Theatre Club (produced 1973).

Thoughts (lyrics only), book by Lamar Alford (produced 1973).

Nightwalk, with Sam Shepard and Jean-Claude van Itallie (produced 1973). In *Open Theater*, 1975.

St. Hydro Clemency; or, A Funhouse of the Lord: An Energizing Event (produced 1973).

The Pioneer, and Pro-Game (produced 1973). 1975.

Hothouse (produced 1974). 1975.

Babes in the Bighouse (produced 1974). 1979.

All Them Women, with others (produced 1974).

We Can Feed Everybody Here (produced 1974).

Hospital Play. 1974.

Henna for Endurance. 1974.

The Narco Linguini Bust (produced 1974).

100,001 Horror Stories of the Plains, with others (produced 1976). 1979.

Sleazing Towards Athens. 1977; revised version (produced 1986), 1986.

Willie-Willa-Bill's Dope Garden. 1977.

Brazil Fado (produced 1977). 1977; revised version (produced 1978), 1979.

Lady Rose's Brazil Hide Out (produced 1977).

American King's English for Queens (produced 1978). 1978.

Goona Goona (produced 1979). 1985.

Attempted Rescue on Avenue B: A Beat Fifties Comic Opera (produced 1979). 1979.

Fireworks, in Holidays (produced 1979). 1992.

Running Gag (lyrics only), book by Jo Ann Schmidman (produced 1979). 1981.

Objective Love I (produced 1980). 1985.

Scenes from Maps (produced 1980). 1980.

Advances (produced 1980). 1980.

Flat in Afghanistan (produced 1981). 1981.

Objective Love II (produced 1981). 1985.

The Trees Blew Down (produced 1981). 1981.

Winners (produced 1981).

Kegger (produced 1982).

Fifteen Million Fifteen-Year-Olds (produced 1983). 1983.

Mollie Bailey's Traveling Family Circus, Featuring Scenes from the Life of Mother Jones, music by Jo Anne Metcalf. 1983.

X-rayed-iate (produced 1984).
Katmandu, in *Open Spaces,* 1985.
Family Talk (produced 1986).
Sea of Forms (collaborative work), text and lyrics with Jo Ann Schmidman (produced 1986). 1987.
Walking Through Walls (collaborative work), text and lyrics with Jo Ann Schmidman (produced 1987). 1987.
Dinner's in the Blender (produced 1987). 1987.
Retro (produced 1988).
Amtrak (produced 1988). 1990.
Headlights (produced 1988).
Do You See What I'm Saying? (produced 1990). 1991.
Body Leaks, with Sora Kimberlain and Jo Ann Schmidman (produced 1990).
Breakfast Serial (produced 1991).
Sound Fields: Are We Hear (produced 1992).

RADIO PLAYS: *Sanibel and Captiva,* 1968; *American Wedding Ritual Monitored/Transmitted by the Planet Jupiter,* 1972.

TELEVISION PLAYS: *The Dirt Boat,* 1955; *Home; or, Future Soap,* 1968; *One More Little Drinkie,* 1969.

OTHER

Editor, with Jo Ann Schmidman and Sora Kimberlain, *Right Brain Vacation Photos: New Plays and Production Photographs 1972–1992,* 1992.

MANUSCRIPT COLLECTIONS: Kent State University, Kent, Ohio; Hope College, Holland, Michigan; Lincoln Center Library of the Performing Arts, New York; Omaha Public Library.

CRITICAL STUDIES: "Who Says Only Words Make Great Drama?" by Terry, in *New York Times,* 10 November 1968; "Megan Terry: Mother of American Feminist Theatre," in *Feminist Theatre* by Helene Keyssar, 1984; "(Theoretically) Approaching Megan Terry" by Elin Diamond, in *Art and Cinema 3,* 1987; "Making Magic Public: Megan Terry's Traveling Family Circus" in *Making a Spectacle,* edited by Lynda Hart, 1989.

THEATRICAL ACTIVITIES

DIRECTOR: **Plays**—with the Cornish Players, Seattle: *Beach Grass, Seascape,* and *Go Out and Move the Car,* 1955; with the Open Theatre's Playwrights Workshop, New York, 1962–68; *Viet Rock,* 1966; *The Tommy Allen Show,* 1970; and other plays. **Television**—*The Dirt Book,* 1955.
ACTOR (as Maggie Duffy): **Plays**—Hermia in *A Midsummer's Night Dream,* title role in *Peter Pan* by J.M. Barrie, Kate in *Taming of the Shrew,* and other roles, Banff School of Fine Arts, Alberta, 1950–53; (as Megan Terry): roles in *Body Leaks,* 1991, and *Sound Fields,* 1992.

Megan Terry comments:

I design my plays to provoke laughter—thought may follow.

A prolific author with over 60 plays to her credit, Megan Terry has consistently experimented with different styles, allowing the content of each project to dictate the form of the piece. She has written in a traditional, realistic format, most notably in *Hothouse*, a play about three generations of women in a single family during the 1950s, and in *Home; or, Future Soap*, which carefully creates a futuristic world based on the assumption of over-population. More frequently, however, Terry's plays are episodic and presentational, emphasizing the importance of the performance event rather than the complete representation of a fictional world. She is probably best known for her innovative use of "transformation" in which character, time, and place shift rapidly in full view of the audience. *Comings and Goings*, subtitled "a theatre game", is a series of seemingly unrelated scenes designed to engage performers and audience in a spirited imaginative exercise. In *Calm Down Mother*, three actresses explore various aspects of women's roles through a series of different characters. *Keep Tightly Closed in a Cool Dry Place* is set initially in a prison, but the three male performers, in addition to assuming traditional character identities as inmates, play out scenes derived from history, the movies, and their own real or imagined pasts.

These transformation-plays from the 1960s were developed while Terry was associated with the Open Theatre (1963–68) in New York and reflect that company's experimentation with techniques to circumvent typecasting and psychological realism. *Viet Rock*, perhaps Terry's most famous play, and one of the first rock musicals, was developed in workshop with Open Theatre actors, and combined the use of changing realities with political comment as it explored the effects of the war in Vietnam. Terry has continued to incorporate music in plays that address serious issues and has remained committed to developing scripts in collaboration with other theatre artists. Since she joined the Omaha Magic Theatre as playwright-in-residence, Terry has worked closely with visual artists to create vibrant, often humorous, performances. Trained as a designer, Terry typically relies heavily on visual images to convey emotional and intellectual content, a characteristic accentuated in her collaborative work. Some of these Magic Theatre productions, such as *Sea of Forms* and *Walking Through Walls*, have completely converted the performance space into a new, abstract environment for audience and performers.

Terry's willingness to experiment with theatrical form has allowed her to tackle a wide variety of subject matter. In 1983 she was recognized by the Dramatists Guild as a "writer of conscience and controversy", emphasizing the fact that she has dealt with large social, political, and ethical issues perhaps more than any other contemporary playwright in the U.S.A. Along with the U.S. involvement in Vietnam, her early work addressed such topics as the single-minded pursuit of monetary gain (*The Magic Realists*), political assassination (*Massachusetts Trust*), and the sensationalism of a rape trial (*The People vs. Ranchman*). At the Magic Theatre she and her colleagues have continued this commitment to socially aware theatre, often working closely with their audiences and using the tools of research and interview to develop meaningful scripts of particular topical concern. *Kegger*, for example, deals with teenage use and abuse of alcohol; *Goona Goona* is concerned with domestic violence, *Dinner's in the Blender* with family communication, and *Headlights* with the national problem of illiteracy.

Terry is recognized by critics as a pioneer in feminist theatre, frequently putting women and gender-related problems at the center of her plays. *Approaching Simone*, which won the Obie award for best play in 1970, explores the life of philosopher Simone Weil through a series of scenes demonstrating her strength of spirit and determination to learn and serve, in spite of the limitations placed upon her by society. *Mollie Bailey's Traveling Family Circus, Featuring Scenes from the Life of Mother Jones* juxtaposes the lives of the 19th-century mother-and-show-business-entrepreneur with that of the more well-known labor activist to create a portrait of two strong, maternal, but otherwise very different historical figures. In examining the stark reality of the lives of women in prison, *Babes in the Bighouse* utilized the same actors to play both guards and inmates and both men and women to play female characters in order to emphasize the adopted characteristics of social roles.

Recurring themes in Terry's work include the relationship of the individual to larger social units (family, peer groups, government) and to the natural environment, power relationships (domination and submission), and the interplay of reason and intellectual control with the more primitive, biological self. She often addresses the world of people who are outside the power structures of the capitalist society—battered women, teenagers, children, prisoners, the illiterate, the elderly—and the content of her plays is intimately connected with the professional choices she has made. Terry has consistently worked outside of the established system of commercial theatre in the USA. The Magic Theatre tours frequently to prisons, schools, and other communities in an attempt to reach the widest audience possible. When her work suggests a course of action, it tends to be an awakening of conscience and consciousness, or a rejection of victimization and discovery of individual strength. *Body Leaks*, Terry's recent collaboration with Schmidman and Sora Kim which deals with insecurity and self-censorship, encapsulates this strain of Terry's work with its refrain of "Take a risk, darling!".

Because of the commitment to a type of theatre in which the text is only one element in the total production experience, Terry's printed plays may be difficult to read and visualize. They range from complex works, in which the layering of image and dialogue repay careful and intense study, to the straightforward presentation of message. In much of her work, Terry challenges the notion that "serious" drama must, of necessity, end pessimistically; in doing so she serves as a voice of hope in the American theatre.

—Kathy Fletcher

See the essay on *Approaching Simone*.

TESICH, Steve.

Born Stoyan Tesich in Titovo Uzice, Yugoslavia, 29 September 1943; emigrated to the United States, 1957; became citizen, 1961. Educated at Indiana University, Bloomington, B.A. 1965 (Phi Beta Kappa); Columbia University, New York, M.A. in Russian 1967, and further graduate study. Married Rebecca Fletcher in 1971. Caseworker, Brooklyn Department of Welfare, late 1960's. Recipient: Rockefeller grant, 1972; New York Film Critics award, Writers Guild award, and Oscar, all for screenplay, 1979. Agent: International

Creative Management, 40 West 57th Street, New York, New York 10019,
U.S.A.

Publications

PLAYS

The Carpenters (produced 1970). 1971.
Lake of the Woods (produced 1971). In *Division Street and Other Plays*,
   1981.
Baba Goya (produced 1973). In *Division Street and Other Plays*, 1981; as
   Nourish the Beast (produced 1973), 1974.
Gorky, music by Mel Marvin (produced 1975). 1976.
Passing Game (produced 1977). 1978.
Touching Bottom (*The Road, A Life, Baptismal*) (produced 1978). 1980.
Breaking Away (screenplay). 1979.
Division Street (produced 1980; revised version produced 1987). In *Division
   Street and Other Plays*, 1981.
Division Street and Other Plays (includes *Baba Goya, Lake of the Woods,
   Passing Game*). 1981.
The Speed of Darkness (produced 1989). 1991.
Square One (produced 1990). 1990.
On the Open Road (produced 1992). 1992.

SCREENPLAYS: *Breaking Away*, 1979; *Eyewitness* (*The Janitor*), 1981; *Four
Friends* (*Georgia's Friends*), 1981; *The World According to Garp*, 1982;
American Flyers, 1985; *Eleni*, 1986.

NOVEL
Summer Crossing. 1982.

Though still best known as the Oscar-winning writer of the film *Breaking
Away*, Yugoslavian-born Steve Tesich launched his writing career in the
theatre and continues to work primarily in that medium. Like David Mamet,
Tesich loves "the rhythm of alternating between the mediums, the fact that
whatever is confining in one form isn't in the other." His plays are generally
quirkier and more personal than his screenplays, and have received sympathetic but mixed critical comments.

   The typical Tesich play centers around family relationships. His characters
are often archetypal and eccentric, his themes moral and societal. He writes in
a variety of genres, from comedy and tragicomedy to musicals, farces, and even
Beckett-like absurdism.

   Tesich's early plays, written in the 1970s for the American Place and other
Off-Broadway theatres, were mostly upbeat paeans to the progressive,
economically-secure America that had welcomed the young Tesich and his
family. In his more recent plays, however, Tesich's outlook has grown decidedly darker.

   His first produced play, *The Carpenters*, has been called *The Master Builder*
in reverse. Whereas Ibsen's Solness builds a beautiful house for a family he has
helped ruin, the inept father in *The Carpenters* struggles to keep his home from

collapsing around his wife and children, all of whom search desperately for happier, purer, more natural lives. The play was well received by the critics: John Simon called it "a play of witty insight and fierce foresight," and Clive Barnes sensed "an air of Greek tragedy about it."

Nourish the Beast, originally entitled *Baba Goya*, garnered Tesich his best notices. In this serious comedy, a matriarch struggles to hold together a diverse extended family, which includes her dying fifth husband, an unhappy daughter, a son in the police force, and other engaging characters. To *Newsweek*'s Jack Kroll, this play proved Tesich "one of the most promising young American playwrights," whose work echoed Archie Bunker, Ionesco, and Sam Shepard, though it lacked "the shock that comes with the real moral force of [David Rabe's] *Sticks and Bones*." Richard Watts likened it to Saroyan's work in its "warm friendliness," and other critics compared it to George Kaufman and Moss Hart's Pulitzer prize-winning *You Can't Take It with You*. Despite these strong notices, the play has not aged well: after a 1989 revival, even Tesich acknowledged that it seemed dated.

Tesich wrote several more notable off-Broadway plays, including *Passing Game* and *Touching Bottom*, before *Division Street* opened on Broadway. In this knockabout farce, a 1960s student leader seeks obscurity in 1980 Chicago as an insurance adjuster, but is immediately surrounded by the same type of people he is trying to avoid, including some old comrades. Some critics praised its colorful cast of characters, but others considered it either an anachronistic radical call to arms, or (missing Tesich's purpose entirely) a piece of shallow American chauvinism. Even after a 1987 rewrite, which changed the original rousing ending to a more somber meditation, *Newsweek*'s Mark Chalon Smith still dismissed the play as "a flag-waver" with "a cloyingly goofy side." Though the critics were cool, audience enthusiasm has since made it Tesich's most-produced play.

Tesich wrote no new plays for almost a decade, devoting himself almost exclusively to film writing until *The Speed of Darkness*. In this stark drama, a pillar of society is visited by his now-homeless old Vietnam buddy, who forces him and his family to confront the moral and physical pollution of America. The play was compared by critics to Ibsen's *An Enemy of the People* and Miller's *All My Sons*, but as Edwin Wilson noted in the *Wall Street Journal*, it has "too many issues crammed into an obvious dramatic structure." Frank Rich wrote that although it is "at times its author's most pretentious play, it is also his most ambitious and, potentially, a major breakthrough." Unhappily, the play's Broadway production coincided exactly with the Gulf War, and it closed after only 36 performances.

Square One is a love story set in a tidy, structured brave new world where all art is purified for public consumption by a huge governmental bureaucracy. Reviewers responded warmly to the work's relevance to the controversy over government sponsorship of the arts. *Time* called it a "witty and touching work . . . likely to be topical again all too soon," and Liz Nicholls of the *Edmonton Journal* was impressed by "its radical argument that artists themselves are corrupt . . . in that their ends are always suspect."

In Tesich's latest play, *On the Open Road*, two tramps meet during an unspecified "time of civil war," decide to travel to "The Land of the Free," and are crucified alongside a mute Christ. Commenting on this work, Tesich has said that he has no doubt man will survive, "but I'm not so sure he'll survive as a human being." To *Time*'s Georgia Harbison, the play blends "metaphysical ambition and gothic excess," and is filled with "echoes of Kerouac, Beckett and Reaganomics interwoven with Tesich's moral fervor." The play's "philosophical and theological vaudeville" reminds Hedy Weiss of the *Chicago Sun-Times* of Beckett, Dostoevsky, Brecht, Hannah Arendt, and "doomsday landscapes of Mad Max"; its characters, though, "too often sound like mouthpieces rather than human beings."

A talented and committed writer, Tesich's work continues to evolve, and he continues to give much of his most personal and heartfelt work to the stage rather than to the screen. "Now the only thing I will write for the theater," he said recently, "is something that involves a moral issue. Nothing else interests me."

—Paul Nadler

U

UHRY, Alfred.

Born in Atlanta, Georgia, 3 December 1936. Educated at Brown University, Providence, Rhode Island, 1958. Married Joanna Kellogg in 1959; four daughters. Member, 1987, and since 1990 president, Young Playwrights Foundation, New York; since 1988 council member, Dramatists Guild, New York; since 1991 member of the faculty, New York University School of the Arts. Recipient: Pulitzer prize, 1988; Marton award, 1988; Outer Critics Circle award, 1988; Los Angeles Drama Critics Circle award, 1989; Oscar, 1990. Lives in New York. Agent: Flora Roberts, 157 West 57th Street, New York, New York 10019, U.S.A.

Publications

PLAYS

Here's Where I Belong, adaptation of East of Eden by John Steinbeck, book by
  Alex Gordon, music by Robert Waldman (produced 1968).
The Robber Bridegroom, adaptation of the novella by Eudora Welty, music by
  Robert Waldman (produced 1974). 1978.
Swing, book by Conn Fleming, music by Robert Waldman (produced 1980).
Little Johnny Jones, adaptation of a musical by George M. Cohan (produced
  1982).
America's Sweetheart, adaptation of a novel by John Kobler, with John
  Weidman, music by Robert Waldman (produced 1985).
Driving Miss Daisy (produced 1987). 1987.

SCREENPLAYS: Mystic Pizza, 1988; Driving Miss Daisy, 1989; Rich in Love,
1992.

Alfred Uhry was awarded the Pulitzer prize in 1988 for his first and only full-length play, Driving Miss Daisy, and an Oscar for the best screenplay adaptation of the play. Uhry's earlier work was primarily as a lyricist and librettist. His long-time collaboration with composer Robert Waldman resulted in Tony and Drama Desk award nominations in 1976 as lyricist and librettist for The Robber Bridegroom. Waldman composed the incidental music for the Playwrights Horizons première of Driving Miss Daisy. Uhry's work prior to the success of Driving Miss Daisy was primarily on lesser-known musicals including, Here's Where I Belong, based on Steinbeck's East of Eden; Swing; Little Johnny Jones, which starred Donny Osmond; and America's Sweetheart, about Al Capone. None of these musicals received critical acclaim. Even *The Robber Bridegroom*, a musical based on the novella by Eudora Welty, met with mixed reviews, with one reviewer noting that the score was "self-consciously rural" with "few bright moments." However, Uhry's work on such musicals along with his long stint as a teacher of play- and lyric-writing proved to be beneficial once the playwright decided to write about his childhood in Atlanta and of his grandmother, an elderly Southern woman who had a black chauffeur who drove her for nearly 25 years.

Driving Miss Daisy is really a long one-act, that takes place in various locations in Atlanta from 1948 to 1973. There are 24 "shifts" in scene, though the play is not formally divided into scenes. The action centers around Daisy Werthan, a widow who progresses in age from 72 to 97 during the course of the play. Her son Boolie Werthan, who ages from 40 to 65, hires a black chauffeur, Hoke Coleburn. Hoke is 60 when the play begins.

The play is deceptively simple in presentation. There is no traditional plot or conflict. The structure is episodic, moving chronologically forward, but the large span of time does not resonate with meaning; nor does it punctuate any vast issues or polemics. The dramatic action is sustained through the growing relationship between Daisy and Hoke. Boolie serves more as a transitional device than as a pivotal character, though the playwright does use Boolie to demonstrate the up-and-coming Southern Jewish businessman.

What distinguishes *Driving Miss Daisy* from other plays written during the 1980s is the subtlety with which the playwright empowers his dramaturgy, enabling him to address issues of race and ethnicity and to explore conflicts of old versus young, rich versus poor, Jew versus gentile, while maintaining the emphasis on the very human relationship that develops between Daisy and Hoke. Uhry's dramaturgy is economical in every way. Exposition is provided via dialogue concerning cars and insurance and the church that people attend, so that necessary information regarding geography, economy, and time is provided by scant verbal signposts.

When the subject of hiring a driver for the ageing Miss Daisy is broached by Boolie, Daisy responds innocently with "I still have rights. And one of my rights is the right to invite who I want—not who you want—into my house. . . . What I do not want—and absolutely will not have is some—some chauffeur sitting in my kitchen. . . ." This technique of introducing ideas and issues—in this case, that of human rights—is a technique that Urhy employs subtly, but also deftly. The notion of prejudice is handled in the same way—both issues are strong undercurrents in the play; and issues that Daisy comes to understand better through her friendship with Hoke, though she never articulates anything beyond saying to Hoke "You're my best friend."

Uhry is a master of understatement. What is not said in *Driving Miss Daisy* is significant. Equally compelling is Uhry's use of metaphor which serves both to punctuate the humor and to reveal the differences in characters' lifestyles and points of view. Hoke's response to Boolie's inquiry regarding Hoke's ability to handle Miss Daisy is a good example. Hoke replies with "I use to wrastle hogs to the ground at killin' time, and ain' no hog get away from me yet."

Driving Miss Daisy is a play about dignity in which all the characters strive to hold onto their personal integrity against an environment of prejudice, change, and economic instability. The Southern dialect in counterpoint with the colloquial expressions create a lyrical rhythm that greatly contributes to the overall effect of the play. The simple images called for by Uhry throughout the play are meant to capture glimpses of these characters' lives, so that in effect these people become representative of types as well as individuals. The play, then, becomes representative of a time in history and tells about that time via this one story.

Perhaps the only drawback of Uhry's play is that with the simplicity of the dramaturgy the play requires a strong cast to sustain the subtextual notions of the play as well as to sustain the constant leaps in time and place. In addition the juxtaposition of one "scene" to the next has no symbolic meaning so that the shifts become predictable and tension is difficult to sustain. Still, *Driving Miss Daisy* reflects Uhry's expertise in cinematic dramaturgy, and it is a play that continues to be produced successfully in regional theatres.

—Judy Lee Oliva

V

VALDEZ, Luis (Miguel).

Born 26 June 1940. Educated at San Jose State University, California. Married Guadalupe Valdez in 1969; three children. Union organizer, United Farmworkers, Delano, California, to 1967. Since 1965 founding director, El Teatro Campesino, Delano, 1965–69, Fresno, 1969–71, and since 1971 San Juan Bautista, California. Recipient: Obie award, 1968; Emmy award, for directing, 1973; Rockefeller grant, 1978. Address: 705 Fourth Street, San Juan Bautista, California 95045, U.S.A.

Publications

PLAYS

Las dos caras del patroncito (produced 1965). In *Actos*, 1971.
La quinta temporada (produced 1966). In *Actos*, 1971.
Los vendidos (produced 1967). In *Actos*, 1971.
The Shrunken Head of Pancho Villa (produced 1968).
La conquista de Mexico (puppet play; produced 1968). In *Actos*, 1971.
No saco nada de la escuela (produced 1969). In *Actos*, 1971.
The Militants (produced 1969). In *Actos*, 1971.
Vietnam campesino (produced 1970). In *Actos*, 1971.
Soldado razo (produced 1970). In *Actos*, 1971.
Huelguistas (produced 1970). In *Actos*, 1971.
Bernabé (produced 1970). In *Contemporary Chicano Theatre*, edited by Roberto Garza, 1976.
Actos. 1971.
El Virgen del Tepeyac (produced 1971).
Dark Root of a Scream (produced 1971). In *From the Barrio: A Chicano Anthology*, edited by Lillian Faderman and Luis Omar, 1973.
Los olivos pits (produced 1972).
Mundo (produced 1973).
La gran carpa de los rasquachis (produced 1973).
El baille de los gigantes (produced 1973).
El fin del mundo (produced 1975).
Zoot Suit (produced 1978). In *Zoot Suit and Other Plays*, 1992.
I Don't Have to Show You No Stinking Badgers (produced 1986).
Zoot Suit and Other Plays. 1992.

SCREENPLAYS: *Zoot Suit*, 1982; *La Bamba*, 1987.

OTHER

Pensamiento Serpentino: A Chicano Approach to the Theatre of Reality. 1973.
Editor, with Stan Steiner, *Aztlan: An Anthology of Mexican American
Literature.* 1972.

THEATRICAL ACTIVITIES

DIRECTOR: **Plays**—most of his own plays. **Films**—*Zoot Suit*, 1982; *La Bamba*,
1987.
ACTOR: **Film**—*Which Way Is Up?*, 1977. **Television**—*Visions* series, 1976.

Best known as the founder of the Teatro Campesino (Farmworkers Theatre) in
1965, Luis Valdez is a man of many talents: actor, playwright, screenwriter,
essayist, stage and film director, and he is the leading practitioner of Chicano
theater in the United States. From the earliest agit-prop pieces he directed and
wrote, termed *actos*, to his professionally produced *Zoot Suit*, first a play and
then a film, Valdez has attempted to portray the Chicano's reality.
   The very term "Chicano" connotes a political attitude, cognizant of a
distinctive place in the so-called "American melting-pot," and Valdez became
a major proponent of this self-imposed designation when his teatro toured the
country asserting a cultural and political distinction. Valdez has termed *Zoot
Suit* an "American play," this in deference to his belief that Chicanos are a part
of the American society and should not be excluded from what this society has
to offer its citizens. Valdez's dramatic themes always reflect Chicanos in crisis,
never pretending that Chicanos have been fully accepted into the American
mainstream. His characters are always in conflict with some aspect of the
system, and more often than not, that manifestation of the power structure is
presented by non-Chicanos, or "Anglos." Although the characters in power
find it easy to manipulate the subordinate Chicanos, Valdez's audiences discover that whether the heroes win or lose it is they who can win through
collective action.
   Las dos caras del patroncito (The Two Faces of the Boss) and *La quinta
temporada* (The Fifth Season) are *actos* that reveal the plight of striking
farmworkers, solved through unionization. When Valdez decided to leave the
union in 1967 he sought an independent theater company, not focused solely
on labor movement and farmworker themes. The next *acto*, *Los vendidos* (The
Sellouts), explored various stereotypes of Chicanos and satirized the "sellout"
who attempted to assimilate into a white, racist society. *No saco nada de la
escuela* (I Don't Get Anything Out of School) exposed some inequities in the
educational process and *La conquista de Mexico* (The Conquest of Mexico)
paralleled the fall of the Aztecs with the disunity of Chicano activists of the
day. The use of masks, farcical exaggeration, stereotyped characters, improvisation, and social commentary in the *actos* reflects Valdez's work with the San
Francisco Mime Troupe prior to his founding the teatro. While the *actos* are
brief agit-prop statements, Valdez's plays explore other theatrical forms.
   Beginning with his first play, *The Shrunken Head of Pancho Villa*, originally
written and produced while he was a student, Valdez has written non-realistic
statements, mingling fantasy and farce, comedy and pathos. All of Valdez's
plays issue forth from a family structure. *The Shrunken Head of Pancho Villa*

pits the assimilationist against the *pachuco* social bandit: two brothers whose
life-styles reflect the extremes within the barrio. *Bernabé* revolves around a
village idiot who gains a spiritual release when he symbolically marries *La
Tierra* (The Earth) who appears to him as a symbol of the Mexican Revolution
of 1910.

There is much of the Spanish religious folk theatre in Valdez's plays,
combined with a new message of social justice. The playwright uses allegorical
and mythological figures to present his messages, combatting the evils of the
war in Vietnam in the *actos Vietnam campesino* and *Soldado razo* (Private
Soldier) or the expressionist play *Dark Root of a Scream*. He exposes the need
for a balance with Mother Nature in the ritualistic *El fin del mundo* (The End
of the World), *La gran carpa de los rasquachis* (The Great Tent of the
Underdogs), and *Mundo* (a title based on the name of the protagonist,
Reimundo, or "king of the world"). Beginning with *Bernabé*, each of the
plays combines indigenous mythology with contemporary problems. *La gran
carpa de los rasquachis* most notably unites the Virgin of Guadalupe with
Quetzalcoatl, the meso-American Christ-figure, calling for unity among all
people.

In *Zoot Suit* Valdez unites all the elements of his theater to create a
statement that cannot be classified without listing its parts: the *acto*, Living
Newspaper, the *corrido* (dramatized Mexican ballads), selective realism, and
fantasy. The play is narrated by an archetypal "pachuco," a barrio character
type that has always fascinated the playwright. This enigmatic figure glides in
and out of the action, a fantastical symbol of the Chicano's defiance and ability
to survive between two cultures: the Mexican and the Anglo. *Zoot Suit* was the
first Chicano play to reach Broadway, and though the New York critics
generally disliked the play, it broke box-office records in Los Angeles. The play
reminded its audiences that current Chicano struggles have their precedents in
such events as the Sleepy Lagoon Murder Trial, which exposed a biased system
of justice in the 1940s. Valdez's hit film *La Bamba*, the story of Chicano pop
singer Ritchie Valens, reached the Anglo audience in a big way in 1987.

From *actos* to *Zoot Suit*, Valdez remains a singular example of a Chicano
who has consistently recreated the struggles and successes of the Chicanos with
a clarity of vision and style, however controversial the themes, that makes him
a true man of the theater.

—Jorge A. Huerta

van ITALLIE, Jean-Claude.

Born in Brussels, Belgium, 25 May 1936; moved to the United States, 1940;
became citizen, 1952. Educated at Great Neck High School, New York;
Deerfield Academy, Massachusetts; Harvard University, Cambridge, Massachusetts, A.B. 1958; New York University, 1959; studied acting at the Neighborhood Playhouse, New York. Editor, *Transatlantic Review*, New York,
1960–63; playwright-in-residence, Open Theatre, New York, 1963–68;
freelance writer on public affairs for NBC and CBS television, New York,
1963–67; taught playwriting at the New School for Social Research,
New York, 1967–68, 1972, Yale University School of Drama, New Haven,

Connecticut, 1969, 1978, 1984–85, and Naropa Institute, Boulder, Colorado, 1976–83; lecturer, Princeton University, New Jersey, 1973–86, New York University, 1982–86, 1992, University of Colorado, Boulder, Fall 1985, 1987–91, and Columbia University, New York, Spring 1986; visiting Mellon professor, Amherst College, Massachusetts, Fall 1976, and Middlebury College, Vermont, 1990. Recipient: Rockefeller grant, 1962; Vernon Rice award, 1967; Outer Circle award, 1967; Obie award, 1968; Guggenheim fellowship, 1973, 1980; Creative Artists Public Service grant, 1973; National Endowment for the Arts fellowship, 1986. Ph.D.: Kent State University, Kent, Ohio, 1977. Address: Box 729, Charlemont, Massachusetts 01339, U.S.A.

Publications

PLAYS

War (produced 1963). In *War and Four Other Plays*, 1967; in *America Hurrah: Five Short Plays*, 1967.

Almost Like Being (produced 1964). In *War and Four Other Plays*, 1967; in *America Hurrah: Five Short Plays*, 1967.

I'm Really Here (produced 1964). In *War and Four Other Plays*, 1967.

The Hunter and the Bird (produced 1964). In *War and Four Other Plays*, 1967.

Interview (as *Pavane*, produced 1965; revised version, as *Interview*, produced 1966). In *America Hurrah: Five Short Plays*, 1967.

Where Is de Queen? (as *Dream*, produced 1965; revised version, as *Where Is de Queen?*, produced 1965). In *War and Four Other Plays*, 1967.

Motel (as *America Hurrah*, produced 1965; revised version, as *Motel*, produced 1966). In *America Hurrah: Five Short Plays*, 1967.

America Hurrah (includes *Interview*, *TV*, *Motel*) (produced 1966). 1967; with *War* and *Almost Like Being*, as *America Hurrah: Five Short Plays*, 1967.

The Girl and the Soldier (produced 1967). In *Seven Short and Very Short Plays*, 1975.

War and Four Other Plays. 1967.

Thoughts on the Instant of Greeting a Friend on the Street, with Sharon Thie (produced 1967; in *Collision Course*, produced 1968). In *Seven Short and Very Short Plays*, 1975.

The Serpent: A Ceremony, with the Open Theatre (produced 1968). 1969.

Take a Deep Breath (televised 1969). In *Seven Short and Very Short Plays*, 1975.

Photographs: Mary and Howard (produced 1969). In *Seven Short and Very Short Plays*, 1975.

Eat Cake (produced 1971). In *Seven Short and Very Short Plays*, 1975.

Mystery Play (produced 1973). 1973; revised version, as *The King of the United States*, music by Richard Peaslee (also director: produced 1973), 1975.

Nightwalk, with Megan Terry and Sam Shepard (produced 1973). In *Open Theater*, 1975.

The Sea Gull, adaptation of a play by Chekhov (produced 1973). 1977.

A Fable, music by Richard Peaslee (produced 1975). 1976.

Seven Short and Very Short Plays (includes *Photographs*, *Eat Cake*, *The Girl and the Soldier, Take a Deep Breath, Rosary, Harold, Thoughts on the Instant of Greeting a Friend on the Street).* 1975.

The Cherry Orchard, adaptation of a play by Chekhov (produced 1977). 1977.

America Hurrah and Other Plays (includes *The Serpent, A Fable, The Hunter and the Bird, Almost Like Being).* 1978.

Medea, adaptation of the play by Euripides (produced 1979).

Three Sisters (produced 1979). 1979.

Bag Lady (produced 1979). 1980.

Uncle Vanya, adaptation of a play by Chekhov (produced 1983). 1980.

Naropa, music by Steve Gorn (produced 1982). In *Wordplays 1,* 1980.

Early Warnings (includes *Bag Lady, Sunset Freeway, Final Orders)* (produced 1983). 1983.

The Tibetan Book of the Dead; or, How Not to Do It Again, music by Steve Gorn (produced 1983). 1983.

Pride, in *Faustus in Hell* (produced 1985).

The Balcony, adaptation of a play by Jean Genet (produced 1986).

The Traveler (produced 1987).

Struck Dumb (produced 1989). In *Best One-Act Plays: 1990–1991,* 1991.

Ancient Boys (produced 1990).

SCREENPLAYS: *The Box Is Empty,* 1965; *Three Lives for Mississippi,* 1971.

TELEVISION WRITING: scripts for *Look Up and Live* series, 1963–65; *Hobbies; or, Things Are All Right with the Forbushers,* 1967; *Take a Deep Breath,* 1969; *Picasso: A Painter's Diary,* 1980.

OTHER
Calcutta (journal). 1987.

MANUSCRIPT COLLECTIONS: Kent State University, Ohio; Harvard University Library, Cambridge, Massachusetts.

CRITICAL STUDIES: "Three Views of America," in *The Third Theatre* by Robert Brustein, 1969, 1970; *Up Against the Fourth Wall* by John Lahr, 1970; "Jean-Claude van Itallie Issue" of *Serif,* Winter 1972.

THEATRICAL ACTIVITIES
DIRECTOR: **Plays**—*The King of the United States,* 1973; *The Tempest* by Shakespeare, 1984; *The Balcony,* 1989.

Jean-Claude van Itallie comments:

I seem to have been most intent on playing with new forms that might express a clear theatre optic. I have worked as a playwright in solitude. I have adapted and translated into English from a foreign language. I have worked as a poet in collaboration with a theatre director and actors, and with actors alone. I have written for puppets. I have written screenplays and specifically for television. I question theatre but I remain married to it, more or less. I agree that language itself helps to keep us isolated but I continue to write. I want to write with greater clarity, but from the heart. I like to work with other artists in the theatre, and to imagine the audience as a community of friends.

The 1960s were an exciting time of revolt and reformation. In the vanguard, theater destroyed preconceptions and invented new disciplines to express re-found truths underlying the mendacity of the commercial and political world. The 1970s were a time of retrenchment; I worked on new versions of classics making contact with my heritage as a playwright, my lineage. What now? In form, working to synthesize the discoveries of the 1960s, and the rediscoveries of the 1970s. Political lies and corruption of power have become mundane; we are concerned now with our self-caused possible destruction of the world. What is the relationship between runaway technology and short-sighted pollu-tion of air, food, and water, on the one hand, and spiritual poverty on the other? This is a time to clarify and acknowledge the split between body and mind in the individual and the world, and in that acknowledgement to effect a healing.

The early plays of Jean-Claude van Itallie, in terms of their brevity, wit, and social commentary, may be taken to resemble the early one-acts of Ionesco or, better, Chekhov—and later in his career van Itallie composed luminous American versions of the major Chekhov plays. The decisive difference be-tween van Itallie's drama and that of the classic moderns lies in the realm of form. He is preoccupied with multiple levels of experience, with the mask behind the mask, and with states of awareness outside the province of the everyday. His crystalline perceptions give rise to complex modes of character-ization, a concern with indeterminate time, and a montage approach to dramatic activity and language.

Van Itallie's essential stage vocabulary is there at the start, in his off-off-Broadway debut with *War*. He describes the play as a "formal war game, a duel" between two male actors of different generations who metamorphose into father and son. They are visited by the shimmering vision of a nameless great actress of the Edwardian era who addresses them as her children and transforms their gritty New York loft which is crammed with theatrical paraphernalia, into a sunny, cheerful park. At the end the men form an emblem of a two-headed eagle of war, each male identity locked into that of the other.

The rich theatrical implications of this meditation on appearances, on essential conflict, and on the role-nature of personality quickly matured when in the same year van Itallie began writing for the newly organized Open Theatre under the direction of Joseph Chaikin. In its shattering of received theatrical forms, its canonization of the workshop process, and its philosophi-cal daring, the Open Theatre provided van Itallie with a subtle instrument for testing the limits of theatrical representation. For the Open Theatre he con-tributed numerous sketches, improvisations, and short plays, including *The Hunter and the Bird*; among his most successful are the pop-art Hollywood comedies informally known as "the Doris Day plays": *Almost Like Being* and *I'm Really Here*, with a wacky Doris D. in love with Just Rock and then the deadly Rossano.

Van Itallie's chief works for the Open Theatre came in his last years with the company. A triptych of one-acts under the title *America Hurrah* begins with *Interview*, a rhythmic weaving of ritualized daily behavior and speech that starts and concludes in the anonymous offices of an employment agency where all the applicants are named Smith. *TV* dramatizes the menace and trivializing power of the mass media, with a trio watching television in the viewing room of a television-ratings company: the television images break free of the set and engulf the viewers. *Motel: A Masque for Three Dolls* unfolds within a tacky midwestern motel room where a huge Doll Motel-Keeper spews forth an unctuous monologue about the room and its furnishings which represent the mail-order-catalogue surface of a violent America. Man Doll and Woman Doll enter the room and proceed to tear the place apart, have sex, and destroy the Motel-Keeper.

The theme of violence done to persons through the exigencies of the social contract is taken up again in *The Serpent*. Here, in an even more sophisticated interplay of layered actions, contemporary violence is linked back to its ancient sources and seen as a central aspect of the human condition. As it simultaneously presents and confronts the values in its story, this "ceremony" for actors explores the themes and the events of Genesis, and the Tree of Life is a tangle of men who embody the serpent. God's fixing of limits upon Adam and Eve is viewed as humanity's projection of its own need for limits, and the self-consciousness that results from the Fall leads to Cain and Abel and the unending human battle, in which each is "caught between the beginning and the end" and unable to remake the past.

After leaving the Open Theatre, van Itallie wrote and staged *The King of the United States*, a stark political fable about the need for an office of rule supported by agents of the status quo to give order to life. *Mystery Play* recycles the characters and themes of *The King* and inverts its tone and style in an elegantly paced farce-parody of the whodunnit, presided over by a Mystery Writer who likes to play detective.

In 1975 van Itallie collaborated again with Chaikin on *A Fable*, a folktale for adults. In picaresque episodes a Journeyor leaves her impoverished village in search of help, and in her wanderings over a wide and storied landscape she comes to celebrate the need to transcend the beast within.

With *Early Warnings* van Itallie returned to smaller forms and a second triptych, on the theme of accommodation. The warnings are directed at the audience, for the characters already have made their choices. *Bag Lady* presents a day in the street life of the witty Clara who is organizing her bags and keeping only the essential shards of her identity. The perky actress Judy Jensen in *Sunset Freeway* breezes along in her car at dusk on the L.A. freeway, immersed in her identity of commercial actress. She speaks to her toy giraffe, imagines a nuclear holocaust, spots Warren Beatty, and, looking out upon the glories of consumer culture, she's in heaven. In *Final Orders* space program agents Angus and Mike listen to instructions from a computer and hold on to one another, poised for the holocaust that now is at hand.

Among van Itallie's most ambitious projects is a theatrical version of *The Tibetan Book of the Dead; or, How Not To Do It Again*, a ritual for the dead in which the characters are emanations of the Dead One, speaking, chanting, and dancing within a huge skull and upon a floor mandala. In its style and complexity, and in its debt to an ancient text, it resembles *The Serpent*, but its landscape lies beyond history and legend in an essentialized world of the spirit.

The whole of van Itallie's dramatic universe is dedicated to a process of vital experimentation through the counterpoint of language, mask, and gesture. His is a philosophy of theatrical play underscored with social critique. Central to his vision are the inadequacies of being and a knowledge of exile. And above all, a knowledge too of the brutalities that are visited upon the self as it seeks to make its way in a world almost willfully estranged from organic life.

—Bill Coco

VIDAL, Gore
(Eugene Luther Gore Vidal, Jr.).

Born in West Point, New York, 3 October 1925. Educated at Los Alamos School, New Mexico, 1939–40; Phillips Exeter Academy, New Hampshire, 1940–43. Served in the United States Army, 1943–46: warrant officer. Editor, E.P. Dutton, publishers, New York, 1946. Lived in Antigua, Guatemala, 1947–49, and Italy, 1967–76. Member of the advisory board, *Partisan Review*, New Brunswick, New Jersey, 1960–71; Democratic-Liberal candidate for Congress, New York, 1960; member of the President's Advisory Committee on the Arts, 1961–63; co-chair, New Party, 1968–71. Recipient: Mystery Writers of America award, for television play, 1954; Cannes Film Critics award, for screenplay, 1964; National Book Critics Circle award, for criticism, 1983. Address: La Rondinaia, Ravello, Salerno, Italy; or c/o Random House Inc., 201 East 50th Street, New York, New York 10022, U.S.A.

Publications

PLAYS

Visit to a Small Planet (televised 1955). In *Visit to a Small Planet and Other Television Plays*, 1956; revised version (produced 1957), 1957; in *Three Plays*, 1962.

Honor (televised 1956). In *Television Plays for Writers: Eight Television Plays*, edited by A.S. Burack, 1957; revised version as *On the March to the Sea: A Southron Comedy* (produced 1961), in *Three Plays*, 1962.

Visit to a Small Planet and Other Television Plays (includes *Barn Burning, Dark Possession, The Death of Billy the Kid, A Sense of Justice, Smoke, Summer Pavilion, The Turn of the Screw*). 1956.

The Best Man: A Play about Politics (produced 1960). 1960; in *Three Plays*, 1962.

Three Plays (includes *Visit to a Small Planet, The Best Man, On the March to the Sea*). 1962.

Romulus: A New Comedy, adaptation of a play by Friedrich Dürrenmatt (produced 1962). 1962.

Weekend (produced 1968). 1968.

An Evening with Richard Nixon and . . . (produced 1972). 1972.

SCREENPLAYS: *The Catered Affair*, 1956; *I Accuse*, 1958; *The Scapegoat*, with Robert Hamer, 1959; *Suddenly, Last Summer*, with Tennessee Williams, 1959; *The Best Man*, 1964; *Is Paris Burning?*, with Francis Ford Coppola, 1966; *Last of the Mobile Hot-Shots*, 1970; *The Sicilian*, 1970; *Gore Vidal's Billy the Kid*, 1989.

TELEVISION PLAYS: *Barn Burning*, from the story by Faulkner, 1954; *Dark Possession*, 1954; *Smoke*, from the story by Faulkner, 1954; *Visit to a Small Planet*, 1955; *The Death of Billy the Kid*, 1955; *A Sense of Justice*, 1955; *Summer Pavilion*, 1955; *The Turn of the Screw*, from the story by Henry James, 1955; *Honor*, 1956; *The Indestructible Mr. Gore*, 1960; *Vidal in Venice* (documentary), 1985; *Dress Gray*, from the novel by Lucian K. Truscott IV, 1986.

NOVELS
Williwaw. 1946.
In a Yellow Wood. 1947.
The City and the Pillar. 1948; revised edition, 1965.
The Season of Comfort. 1949.
Dark Green, Bright Red. 1950.
A Search for the King: A Twelfth Century Legend. 1950.
The Judgment of Paris. 1952; revised edition, 1965.
Messiah. 1954; revised edition, 1965.
Three: Williwaw, A Thirsty Evil, Julian the Apostate. 1962.
Julian. 1964.
Washington, D.C. 1967.
Myra Breckinridge. 1968.
Two Sisters: A Memoir in the Form of a Novel. 1970.
Burr. 1973.
Myron. 1974.
1876. 1976.
Kalki. 1978.
Creation. 1981.
Duluth. 1983.
Lincoln. 1984.
Empire. 1987.
Hollywood. 1990.

Novels as Edgar Box
Death in the Fifth Position. 1952.
Death Before Bedtime. 1953.
Death Likes It Hot. 1954.

SHORT STORIES
A Thirsty Evil: Seven Short Stories. 1956.

OTHER
Rocking the Boat (essays). 1962.
Sex, Death, and Money (essays). 1968.
Reflections upon a Sinking Ship (essays). 1969.

Homage to Daniel Shays: Collected Essays 1952–1972. 1972; as *Collected Essays 1952–1972*, 1974.
Matters of Fact and of Fiction: Essays 1973–1976. 1977.
Sex Is Politics and Vice Versa (essay). 1979.
Views from a Window: Conversations with Gore Vidal, with Robert J. Stanton. 1980.
The Second American Revolution and Other Essays 1976–1982. 1982; as *Pink Triangle and Yellow Star and Other Essays*, 1982.
Vidal in Venice, edited by George Armstrong, photographs by Tore Gill. 1985.
Armegeddon? Essays 1983–1987. 1987; as *At Home*, 1988.
A View From the Diner's Club: Essays 1987–1991. 1991.
The Decline and Fall of the American Empire (essays). 1992.
Screening History. 1992.

Editor, *Best Television Plays*. 1956.

BIBLIOGRAPHY: *Gore Vidal: A Primary and Secondary Bibliography* by Robert J. Stanton, 1978.

MANUSCRIPT COLLECTION: University of Wisconsin, Madison.

CRITICAL STUDIES: *Gore Vidal* by Ray Lewis White, 1968; *The Apostate Angel: A Critical Study of Gore Vidal* by Bernard F. Dick, 1974; *Gore Vidal* by Robert F. Kiernan, 1982.

THEATRICAL ACTIVITIES
ACTOR: **Film**—*Roma* (*Fellini Roma*), 1972.

Eschewing all consideration of Gore Vidal as a novelist and short story writer the critic must associate his theatrical production with its kinship to cinema and television, i.e., Vidal's plays are quite stageable yet are intrinsically cinematographic or televisionistic. They have a modernity about them that facilitates their being restructured for each medium—because they are thematically and linguistically hinged loosely but integrally, and the characters drawn in such a manner that in displacing a character, in changing a tempo, or shifting psychology for a particular medium, Vidal does not violate the play's integrity. Critics have envied Vidal's facile success on television and stage; but his success would not be forthcoming were he not an extremely proficient stylist. True, Vidal has a grudge against a complacent "bourgeois" society and likes to jab at sensitive and vulnerable spots, and he succeeded cinematographically in *Suddenly Last Summer*. The film *Lefthanded Gun* (based on his television play on the Billy the Kid legend) succeeded; but *Myra Breckinridge* failed because the producers were not faithful to Vidal.

His themes—extreme and tabooistic in his novels—are more traditional in his plays, mainly war and politics. But the persistent leitmotiv in all his works is man bereft in the modern world. Should man relinquish certain values? Find new ones? Vidal assigns satire for the first alternative, irony for the second. Vidal the person seems to opt for relative values, and creates types (as do all playwrights) to epitomize these values; yet Vidal the writer, in creating the antagonistic types to exemplify certain absolutes, finds himself with characters possessing more dramatic qualities and effectiveness—which indicates that Vidal the writer is instinctively more sage than Vidal the person. Since the antagonist stands well in his own defence he wins dramatic or tragic sympathy; hence, the thesis comes to no social conclusion and the spectator is left with the unresolved futility of modern life. This is good dramaturgy.

Weekend is the least effective of Vidal's plays. It is an attempt to profit from the topical concern about miscegenation which the author encrusts on a political campaign (not unlike *The Best Man*); but the situation and the characters are not real enough for good satire, nor exaggerated enough to make good farce. Vidal's merit as a playwright, however, is best demonstrated in his trilogy: *Visit to a Small Planet, On the March to the Sea, The Best Man*.

Visit to a Small Planet is the story of a one-man invasion from outer space—an extraterrestrial being who is intent on creating a state of war between his world and ours. This "man" is called Kreton (may all warmongers bear this epithet!) and almost succeeds in creating a war hysteria on earth through certain well-conceived comic situations. It was because of these situations that the play became a very successful television series. However, its anti-war theme is ineffective because we cannot associate the Kreton's world with our own cretin world. After all, it was they who wanted war, not us humans. The audience can't help but feel self-righteous at the end when Kreton is led off to his celestial kindergarten. In attempting a satire on war Vidal created an excellent science-fiction farce with characterizations that are memorable—the pixie Kreton, the prototype of the war-loving general, Tom Powers, and Roger Felding, an equally ambitious television commentator.

Although the theme of *On the March to the Sea* is shopworn—the disasters wrought on Southern families, particularly that of John Hinks, by the ravages of the Civil War—this play is poignant and highly dramatic. The characters are all believable, with the possible exception of Captain Taylor of the Union Army—flamboyant, too philosophic (war participants, i.e., soldiers, are never introspective not contemplative, at least about ethical or social problems, during bellicose engagements). Vidal thought a lot of this character and gave him the final words of the play; but the character really caught in the maelstrom of life and war, John Hinks, was the authentic tragic figure of the play. The play is in a war setting and the war pervades all. Yet as the title aptly indicates, the main theme is not Sherman's march to the sea, but a series of incidents that take place *on* the march to the sea. The question of what is human dignity (the answer to one's own conscience) and honor (the answer to social conscience) is put literally through a trial by fire. The characters, even though typified (intentionally so) are all quite well drawn, except for Colonel Thayer, who is the "heavy."

But Colonel Thayer is too celluloidish a character to be really cruel. The cruelty prize goes to Clayton, son of John Hinks, too young and self-centered to understand his father's anguish. Though *Visit to a Small Planet* was intended as a satire on war, *On the March to the Sea* is infinitely more effective as an anti-war drama.

The Best Man shows the struggle between two presidential aspirants, jockeying, scratching, and grubbing for the nomination of their party. The play is a well-wrought urn, perfectly structured, containing political characters that emulate Hollywoodian stereotypes (Vidal had every intention of doing this), effective dialogue, with each character keeping to his program. The suspenseful outcome of the nomination is solved by an honorable, classical, and justified theatrical technique: President ex-machina. The solution is not only theatrically perfect, but thematically perfect, in that the person eventually to be nominated is of little importance.

The main theme—does one have to be a demogogue to be successful in political life? Vidal gives us such a selection of presidential aspirants that they seem *inverosimil* and incredible. But as the old Italian quip says, "If it's not a wolf, it's a dog." This is ingeniously planted in the mind of the spectator and this is why *The Best Man* is extremely good satire.

—John V. Falconieri

VOGEL, Paula (Anne).

Born in Washington, D.C., 16 November 1951. Educated at Bryn Mawr College, Pennsylvania, 1969–70, 1971–72; Catholic University, Washington, D.C., 1972–74, B.A.; Cornell University, Ithaca, New York, 1974–77, A.B.D. Various jobs including secretary, moving van company packer, factory packer, computor processor, electronics factory worker, 1969–71; lecturer in women's studies and theatre, Cornell University, Ithaca, New York, 1977–82; artistic director, Theater with Teeth, New York, 1982–85; production supervisor, theatre on film and tape, Lincoln Center, New York, 1983–85; associate professor and director of graduate playwriting program, Brown University, Providence, Rhode Island, from 1985. Since 1990 artistic director, Theatre Eleanor Roosevelt, Providence, Rhode Island; since 1992 board member, Circle Repertory Company, New York. Recipient: Heerbes-McCalmon award, 1975, 1976; American College Theatre Festival award, 1976; Samuel French award, 1976; American National Theatre and Academy-West award, 1977; National Endowment for the Arts fellowship, 1980, 1991; MacDowell Colony fellowship, 1981, 1989; Bunting fellowship, 1990; Yaddo fellowship, 1992; McKnight fellowship, 1992; Bellagio fellowship, 1992; AT&T award, 1992; Obie award, 1992. Agent: Peter Franklin, William Morris Agency, 1350 Avenue of the Americas, New York, New York 10019. Address: c/o Box 1852, Brown University, Department of Creative Writing, Providence, Rhode Island 02912, U.S.A.

Publications

PLAYS

Swan Song of Sir Henry (produced 1974).
Meg (produced 1977). 1977.
Apple-Brown Betty (produced 1979).
The Last Pat Epstein Show Before the Reruns (produced 1979).
Desdemona: A Play About a Handkerchief (produced 1979).
Bertha in Blue (produced 1981).
The Oldest Profession (produced 1981).
And Baby Makes Seven (produced 1986).

The Baltimore Waltz (produced 1992). 1992.
Hot 'n' Throbbing (produced 1992).

THEATRICAL ACTIVITIES
DIRECTOR: **Plays**—*The Lower Rooms* by Eliza Anderson.
ACTOR: **Plays**—Sister George in *The Killing of Sister George* by Frank Marcus,
1972.

Paula Vogel's plays, while imaginatively dramatizing the conflict between the
life force and death, prompt us to re-examine such topics as the feminization of
poverty, the non-traditional family, the AIDS epidemic, and domestic violence
(both in late 20th-century America and in the context of a revisit to
Shakespeare's *Othello*). Despite the topicality of her comedies sporting a sting,
these plays tend to salute the salutary nature of fantasy. Although clearly
writing from a feminist perspective, Vogel does not portray her women
uncritically or her men unsympathetically.

Nevertheless Vogel laments the unnecessarily Darwinian nature of people's
odds of survival—a sort of law of the jungle by which the more muscular,
wealthy, or powerful white, Protestant men enjoy the advantage. Prodigy
Cecil, one of three fantasy children in *And Baby Makes Seven*, quotes Darwin
to this effect: "Never forget that every single organic being around us strives to
increase in numbers; that each lives by a struggle at some period in its life; that
heavy destruction inevitably falls either on the young or the old. . . . Thus,
from war or nature, from famine and death, all organic beings advance by one
general law—namely, Multiply, Vary, Let the Strongest Live, and the Weakest
Die. . . ."

The Oldest Profession depicts the effects wrought by the feminization of
poverty among the elderly during the Reagan years. In a tiny New York City
park at 72nd and Broadway, four still-working prostitutes in their 70's and
their madame, aged 83, quietly chat about their fees, their clients and their
simple meals—which provide a precarious pleasure and sustenance, given their
low incomes. These hookers preserve their self-respect and their dignity except
for the occasional necessity of beating off the incursions of a rival's encroach-
ment on their territory. Although Vogel's premise that ladies of the night keep
plying their trade till they drop might seem far-fetched, *The Oldest Profession*
reflects the reality that senior citizens do service their own generation in this
manner—what else are they trained to do and how else, deprived of health
insurance and Social Security payments, can they eke out an existence? Vogel's
shrewd social criticism even locates them in the building occupied by Zabar's
Delicatessen, which really did evict the elderly tenants living upstairs when it
expanded into selling housewares.

Vogel evinces a keen ear for her characters' colloquial speech, an intuitive
understanding of their honor, pride, and enjoyment in their work, and subtlety
in dramatizing their deprivations, ambitions, conflicts, and mutual nurturing.
She gives us 10 minutes or so to warm to these women before we learn that
they are anything more than just widows enjoying the sun. By this time we're
perfectly prepared to recognize their importance to their clients and their value
as people—for this represents the most respectful play ever written on this
topic. As we laugh at such quips as "Vera's not just a woman with a Past; she's

a woman with an Epic," we respond to Vogel's views of their struggle to survive on income insufficient to meet expenses, their efforts to exercise some control over their destinies, their compassion, their sisterhood, their respect for others and themselves, and their loneliness as, one by one, they die.

Although a comedy (especially in its, as yet unreleased, cinematic version, which takes the women away from their park bench and includes their satisfied customers), *The Oldest Profession*, like Vogel's other plays, stresses the women's mortality. *And Baby Makes Seven* initially seems a more carefree comedy about a contented though non-traditional family composed of Ruth, her pregnant partner Anna, Peter (the gay man who has fathered Anna's child), and three imaginary children made quite real to the adults (and to us) by Ruth and Anna. The situation quickly grows sinister, however, after Peter insists the kids must go before baby arrives. Once more Vogel hooks us with her characters' charm before telling us the truth about them. When we hear the boys talking in the dark about how babies are made, we can't resist lovable Henri from Albert Lamorisse's 1955 film *The Red Balloon*, prodigy Cecil, and Orphan—a wild boy brought up by a pack of dogs, who wants to name the baby Lassie. Soon infanticide occupies the grown ups. Combining whimsy and menace, the fantasy threatens to career off into violence while still encompassing the playful interaction of the lesbian lovers and their friend. After eight-year-old Henri tries to blackmail Anna into buying him a pony by claiming to be the father of her child, all three kids are killed off. (Orphan, most amusingly, dies of rabies, while quoting dog references from Shakespeare, such as "Out, damned spot.") Yet the parents come to appreciate their need for both illusions and playfulness and, in Vogel's happiest ending, quickly recapture both.

Vogel repeats this mingling of fantasy and death in *The Baltimore Waltz*, this time replacing the earlier plays' realism with a fluid presentational approach which combines narrative, lectures, language lessons, a slide show, and quick two- and three-person scenes set in the United States and Europe. Vogel creates simultaneously a compassionate comedy about death, a bedroom farce, and a satire on American AIDS policy, which fails urgently to pursue a cure because so many of the victims have been those "different" (from our rulers) and powerless. "If just one grandchild of George Bush caught this thing during toilet training, that would be the last we'd hear about the space program," laments a character.

But Vogel conjures a disease which targets single elementary school teachers, because they haven't a mother's immunity to their pupils' viruses. Although set in a ward at Baltimore's Johns Hopkins Hospital, this fantasy waltzes protagonist Anna around Europe in a two-fold quest: to find a cure for Acquired Toilet Disease and to enjoy sex, so that she can, before her untimely demise, make up for all those years of celibacy while forcing herself to remain a good little girl. Vogel forces spectators not in a high-risk group to consider for the first time the possibility of their own impending deaths, struck down by a mysterious illness the government doesn't care to fight fiercely. An AIDS play for those unaware souls who ignore the epidemic's ravages, *The Baltimore Waltz* proves another Vogel comedy which wins our sympathies before showing its hand: only after we can't help caring about Anna does the play, by substituting slides of Baltimore for views of Europe, let us know she's merely a surrogate for her dying sibling, AIDS-victim Carl (Vogel's brother, to whose memory she dedicates the play "because I cannot sew"). This ferocious comedy, playful and poignant, written in lieu of a panel for the AIDS memorial quilt, veers quickly then from nightmarish satire of medical quackery, to bereavement, to a magical waltz.

The plays which tackle violence, however, cannot offer such an upbeat conclusion. *Hot 'n' Throbbing* tells the truth: domestic violence escalates to murder. And *Desdemona* creates no happy ending to avoid its protagonist's death. We're stuck with how Shakespeare ends his play—though Vogel stops her comedy's action prior to that tragedy's crisis. Yet the intersection of their plots at *Desdemona*'s conclusion in the hair-brushing scene renders chilling the loss of life awaiting the high-spirited woman we've been delighting in earlier.

Vogel's imaginative recreation of Desdemona provides us with everything which Shakespeare denies us: full portraits of the three women (the only characters here), high spirits which do not willingly suffer their men's foolishness, no easy acquiescence to being victimized, even a lusty, frank sexuality. This provocative, startling comedy takes from Shakespeare its setting in Cyprus, Amelia's theft of the handkerchief, and the women's names. But where Shakespeare's Desdemona today must appear foolish to endure Othello's violent and unwarranted jealousy, Vogel's gives him cause to be jealous by exulting in an earthy, exuberant sexuality as she beds every man on the island save Cassio. Weaving such irony through her short, pithy episodes Vogel depicts women as often coarse, mainly honest, and so sensual they seem on the verge of seducing each other. The women's relations are marred, however, by petty jealousies, betrayals, and rivalries.

Vogel shows us we must blame the social system, implicitly responsible for denying the women sisterhood in a common cause, forcing them instead to depend on destructive men who exercise over them the power of life and death. Denied meaningful, remunerative employment, a woman can slave in a kitchen while promoting the advancement of a husband she despises (Amelia's choice), run a bawdy house (Bianca's choice), or prostitute herself (Desdemona's choice). Separated by class, financial status, and education (like the women in Wendy Kesselman's *My Sister in This House*), the women trust each other too little, too late—and therefore Desdemona will die, ironically having just made plans to leave her husband the next morning.

Ostensibly more in control, *Hot 'n' Throbbing*'s Charlene, an empowered, professional woman and feminist, has obtained a restraining order against the husband who has beaten her for years. At her computer, she supports herself and her kids by writing women's erotica for a feminist film company; like Desdemona's hooking, this has earned her independence. Yet gender power imbalances leave her vulnerable to violence. The husband breaks down the door, manipulates both her compassion for him and their teenagers' responses, and finally kills her.

Charlene has created powerful images of a dominant woman and submissive partner, but later, just before she is murdered, a male crew reverse the roles and turn the script into a snuff film. Even the daughter has fantasized about bondage and pain. If Vogel permits us any hope for women at this funny but dark and frightening play's conclusion, it emerges when the daughter dons knee-socks, flannel shirt, overalls, and heavy boots, thereby ensuring she's no sex object, before taking her own place at the computer. There she begins to write the play we've just seen, the sort of play Paula Vogel dramatizes, with the power to transform people and thus alter the world.

—Tish Dace

WALKER, Joseph A.

Born in Washington, D.C., 23 February 1935. Educated at Howard University, Washington, D.C., B.A. in philosophy 1956; Catholic University, Washington, D.C., M.F.A. 1970. Served in the United States Air Force: 2nd lieutenant. Married 1) Barbara Brown (divorced 1965); 2) Dorothy A. Dinroe in 1970. Worked as taxi driver, salesman, and postal clerk; English teacher in Washington, D.C., and New York; actor with the Negro Ensemble Company, New York, from 1969; playwright-in-residence, Yale University, New Haven, Connecticut, 1970; taught at City College, New York, 1970's; currently member of the drama department, Howard University. Address: Department of Drama, Howard University, 2400 6th Street, N.W., Washington, D.C. 20059, U.S.A.

Publications

PLAYS

The Believers, with Josephine Jackson, music and lyrics by Benjamin Carter and others (produced 1968).
The Harangues (produced 1969). Shortened version, as *Tribal Harangue Two*, in *The Best Short Plays 1971*, edited by Stanley Richards, 1971.
Ododo (also director: produced 1970). In *Black Drama Anthology*, edited by Ron Milner and Woodie King, 1971.
The River Niger (produced 1972). 1973.
Yin Yang, music by Dorothy A. Dinroe-Walker (also director: produced 1973).
Antigone Africanus (produced 1975).
The Lion Is a Soul Brother (also director: produced 1976).
District Line (produced 1984).
Screenplay: *The River Niger*, 1976.

THEATRICAL ACTIVITIES

DIRECTOR: several of his own plays.
ACTOR: **Plays**—*The Believers*, 1968; *Cities in Bezique* by Adrienne Kennedy, 1969. **Films**—*April Fools*, 1969; *Bananas*, 1971. **Television**—*NYPD* series; *In Black America* (narrator).

The dramas of Joseph A. Walker explore various aspects of black life such as male-female relationships, interracial strife, and family and community bonds.

However, the focus of most of his works is on the psyche of black American males. Cut off from their ancestral home and exploited by whites, these disoriented men are portrayed as lacking a sense of identity, purpose, and self-worth. Efforts by some of these men to obtain power and wealth are most often thwarted by white America's black sycophants. Whether or not one agrees with this simplistic ideology, frequently exhorted in the 1960s and 1970s, Walker's plays are still relevant because of their compelling depictions of those black males stagnated by feelings of impotence, frustration, and hopelessness.

While the black male characters are deftly drawn and complex, Walker's portraits of black women and whites rarely escape the limitations of stereotypes. Black women seldom have any personal goals, but instead function as either supporters or "castrators" of their men. White women serve as sexual playmates and status symbols for their black lovers. White men exploit blacks and destroy those who pose a threat to their way of life. Lacking depth and plausible motivations for their actions, these characters weaken the credibility of Walker's plays.

As its title suggests, *The Harangues* is used as a vehicle for the playwright to vent his opinions. Composed of two episodes and two one-act plays, the work portrays a despairing view of black life. In the first episode, a 15th-century West African man chooses to kill his son rather than subject him to life as a slave in the New World. The second episode mirrors the first by showing a contemporary black American revolutionary who kills his child rather than allow him to grow up in a despondent society. Black women plead for their children's lives in the episodes, but are conspicuously absent in the one-acts. The first one-act, set in Washington, D.C., concerns a black male and his pregnant white fiancée. Incredibly, with little hesitation, the white woman agrees to assist her lover in the murder of her father who will disinherit her if she marries. However, the plan backfires and results in the death of the scheming black man due to the actions of a traitorous black "friend." In the second one-act, unless they can convince him of their worthiness to live, a deranged black man threatens to kill his three captives: a white liberal and an assimilationist black man and his white lover. After exposing their perverted lives, only the white woman who endures several sexual indignities is deemed to be virtuous. However, as the death penalty is being carried out, the woman takes a bullet meant for her contemptible black lover. In an ensuing struggle, the assimilationist gains control of his captor's gun and kills him. As in the first one-act, a desperate black man dies at the hands of a black minion of the white race.

In sharp contrast to the pessimistic outlook which envelopes *The Harangues, The River Niger* celebrates the enduring qualities of the black man and offers a hopeful vision of the future. Johnny Williams, a middle-aged house painter and poet living in Harlem, uses liquor to escape the bleak reality of a life stagnated by unrealized dreams. Johnny places his hopes for the future in his son Jeff's career in the air force. But his son's homecoming brings another disappointment to Johnny's life. Jeff admits that he was dismissed from the military which he abhorred. He contends his ouster was due to his refusal to be a "supernigger"—a black man who tries to prove he has capabilities comparable to whites. He further announces he will no longer be bound by familial and societal expectations but will instead seek only to fulfill his own needs and desires. Despite his intentions, Jeff soon finds himself involved in the self-destructive affairs of his former gang. When prison terms appear imminent for Jeff and the gang after they are betrayed by one of their members, Johnny has a shoot-out with the traitor which results in both of their deaths. But before Johnny dies, he demands to take the rap for the shooting and the gang's alleged offense. Johnny's wife Mattie admonishes her family and the gang not to fail to cooperate and carry out her husband's wishes. Johnny's heroic gesture provides Jeff and other gang members with a new lease on life and a powerful example of the unconditional selfless love that a father can have for his son.

The portraits of the men are well crafted and realistic. The characters function as representatives of differing moral values, abilities, aspirations, and perspectives within the black community. Johnny emerges as the most eloquent and convincing spokesman who, through his poem "The River Niger," speaks of the need to be cognizant of one's unbreakable link to all people of African descent.

Although the play's black women represent various age groups and cultures, they share similar attitudes toward their men. The women serve their men's needs with little concern for their own desires or ambitions. Mattie even accepts the fact that her husband chooses to confide in his West Indian friend instead of her. Incredibly, during a conversation between Mattie and Jeff's South African lover, Johnny's wife agrees with the younger woman that women are incapable of having a similar type of relationship because "women don't trust one another." Despite this and several other questionable remarks made by the women, their behavior as selfless and loyal supporters of their men foreshadows the concluding message of the play. As Johnny's final actions and his demand for cooperation demonstrate, survival of the race requires a communal effort with little thought of self-interest.

A Washington, D.C. taxi-stand serves as the setting for *District Line*. The play depicts a day in the lives of six cab drivers: two white and three black males and one black female. The drivers reveal their past experiences, present concerns, and aspirations as they interact with each other and their passengers. Black males continue to be Walker's most poignant characterizations. Of greatest interest are the scenes concerning two drivers—Doc, a moonlighting Howard University professor and Zilikazi, an exiled South African revolutionary. Women characters, whether black or white, appear to be gratuitous in the drama and remain stereotypes. However, the playwright does portray white men in roles other than the liberal or oppressor of blacks. Still, the work suffers in comparison to Walker's other plays because of a few fundamental flaws. Dramatic action is not adequately developed and sustained throughout the play and the work lacks a central theme to tie all the scenes together. Consequently, the drama fails to create the intense emotional impact characteristic of Walker's other plays.

—Addell Austin Anderson

WARD, Douglas Turner.

Born in Burnside, Louisiana, 5 May 1930. Educated at Xavier University Preparatory School, New Orleans, 1941–46; Wilberforce University, Ohio, 1946–47; University of Michigan, Ann Arbor, 1947–48; Paul Mann's Actors Workshop, New York, 1955–58. Married Diana Hoyt Powell in 1966; one son and one daughter. Co-founder, 1967, and artistic director, Negro Ensemble Company, New York. Recipient: Vernon Rice award, 1966; Obie award 1966, 1970, for acting, 1973; Drama Desk award, for acting, 1970; Boston Theatre Critics Circle award, for directing, 1986. Agent: William Morris Agency, 1350 Avenue of the Americas, New York, New York 10019. Address: Negro Ensemble Company, 165 West 46th Street, Suite 800, New York, New York 10036, U.S.A.

Publications

PLAYS

Happy Ending, and Day of Absence (produced 1965). 1966; as Two Plays, 1971.
The Reckoning (produced 1969). 1970.
Brotherhood (also director: produced 1970). 1970.
Redeemer, in Holidays (produced 1979; in About Heaven and Earth, also director: produced 1983).

CRITICAL STUDY: introduction by Sheila Rush to Two Plays by Ward, 1971.

THEATRICAL ACTIVITIES

DIRECTOR: Plays—Daddy Goodness by Richard Wright and Louis Sapin, 1968; Man Better Man by Errol Hill, 1969; Contribution by Ted Shine, 1969; Brotherhood and Day of Absence, 1970; Ride a Black Horse by John Scott, 1971; Perry's Mission by Clarence Young III, 1971; The River Niger by Joseph A. Walker, 1972; A Ballet Behind the Bridge by Lennox Brown, 1972; The Great MacDaddy by Paul Carter Harrison, 1974, 1977; The First Breeze of Summer by Leslie Lee, 1975; Waiting for Mongo by Silas Jones, 1975; Livin' Fat by Judi Ann Mason, 1976; The Offering by Gus Edwards, 1977; The Twilight Dinner by Lennox Brown, 1978; The Raft by John Pepper Clark, 1978; Black Body Blues by Gus Edwards, 1978; Zooman and the Sign by Charles Fuller, 1980; Home by Samm-Art Williams, 1980; Weep Not for Me by Gus Edwards, 1981; A Soldier's Play by Charles Fuller, 1981; The Isle Is Full of Noises by Derek Walcott, 1982; About Heaven and Earth by Ward, Julie Jensen, and Ali Wadad, 1983; Manhattan Made Me by Gus Edwards, 1983; District Line by Joseph A. Walker, 1984; Ceremonies in Dark Old Men by Lonne Elder III, 1985; The War Party by Leslie Lee, 1986; Jonah and the Wonder Dog by Judi Ann Mason, 1986; Louie and Ophelia by Gus Edwards, 1986; We (includes Sally and Prince) by Charles Fuller, 1988; Jonquil by Charles Fuller, 1990; Lifetimes on the Streets by Gus Edwards, 1990.
ACTOR as Douglas Turner and Douglas Turner Ward: Plays—Joe Mott in The Iceman Cometh by O'Neill, 1957; Matthew Kumalo in Lost in the Stars by Maxwell Anderson; Moving Man, then Walter Younger, in A Raisin in the Sun by Lorraine Hansberry, 1959; Archibald in The Blacks by Jean Genet,

1961; Porter in *Pullman Car Hiawatha* by Thornton Wilder, 1962; understudied Fredericks in *One Flew over the Cuckoo's Nest* by Dale Wasserman, 1963; Zachariah Pieterson in *The Blood Knot* by Athol Fugard, 1964; Fitzroy in *Rich Little Rich Girl* by Hugh Wheeler, 1964; Roman Citizen in *Coriolanus*, 1965; Arthur in *Happy Ending*, 1965; Mayor and Clan in *Day of Absence*, 1965; Oba Danlola in *Kongi's Harvest* by Wole Soyinka, 1968, in *Summer of the Seventeenth Doll* by Ray Lawler, 1968, Thomas in *Daddy Goodness* by Richard Wright and Louis Sapin, 1968, Russell B. Parker in *Ceremonies in Dark Old Men* by Lonne Elder III, 1969, 1985, Scar in *The Reckoning*, 1969, Black Man and Asura in *The Harangues* by Joseph A. Walker, 1969, in *Frederick Douglass Through His Own Words*, 1972, Johnny Williams in *The River Niger* by Joseph A. Walker, 1972, Harper Edwards in *The First Breeze of Summer* by Leslie Lee, 1975, Mingo Saunders in *The Brownsville Raid* by Charles Fuller, 1976, Bob Tyrone in *The Offering* by Gus Edwards, 1977, Fletcher in *Black Body Blues* by Gus Edwards, 1978, Flick in *The Michigan* by Dan Owens, 1979, Technical Sergeant Vernon C. Waters in *A Soldier's Play* by Charles Fuller, Edinburgh, 1984, Jonah Howard in *Jonah and the Wonder Dog* by Judi Ann Mason, 1986, and Louie in *Louie and Ophelia* by Gus Edwards, 1986; Papa in *This Isle Is Full of Noises* by Derek Walcott, 1982; New Ice Age and New Ice Age II in *Lifetimes on the Streets* by Gus Edwards, 1990.

Douglas Turner Ward comments:

I am a black playwright, of black sensibilities, primarily utilizing the devices of satire, exaggeration, and mordant humor to explore and express themes of contemporary life, particularly as they relate to black survival.

Douglas Turner Ward, a black American, is one of those rare individuals who have successfully combined careers as actor, writer, and director. He has twice won Obie awards for plays which he wrote and in which he performed: in 1966 for *Happy Ending* and *Day of Absence*, and in 1970 for *The Reckoning*. Since 1967 he has been artistic director of the Negro Ensemble Company, an important repertory company which he and actor-director Robert Hooks founded.

Despite his success as an actor, Ward is better known as a dramatist, particularly for his first two plays, *Happy Ending* and *Day of Absence*, which treat satirically the relationships between blacks and whites. The history of these award-winning one-acts is almost as ironic as their subject matter. Although both plays were completed by 1960, Ward could not find a producer until, five years later, Robert Hooks, operating on limited financing, arranged to have them produced at St. Mark's Theatre.

As *Happy Ending* opens, two black female domestics are lamenting their employer's decision to divorce his promiscuous wife. Their sorrow is interrupted by their dapper nephew, who rebukes them for pitying people who have overworked and underpaid them. This, he informs them, is their chance to escape from domestic labor. Then, they educate him to the ironies of life: as middle-aged black women, with limited formal education (four strikes against them), they can expect only low-paying jobs which will barely provide subsistence. In contrast, as domestic laborers, though they have received little money, they have provided their nephew with fashionable clothes not missed from the employer's wardrobe and with food smuggled from the employer's larder. As the nephew joins in their sorrows, they receive the happy news that the employers have become reconciled.

Day of Absence is a one-act satirical fantasy about the turmoil in a southern city on a day when all blacks disappear. White couples begin to argue as they discover that they have no experience tending the house or caring for their children. The Ku Klux Klan is bitter because, with black people gone, it no longer has a pretext for existence and victims for sadistic practices. Elected repeatedly on a campaign of keeping blacks in their places, the mayor proves incompetent to manage the affairs of the town. In the midst of the despair, the reappearance of one black reassures the whites that others will return. The play ends, however, with the question of whether the whites have fully learned how much they depend upon blacks.

Ward's first full-length play, *The Reckoning*, produced by the Negro Ensemble Company in 1969, focuses on a confrontation between a black pimp and a southern governor. Ward continued his satire in the one-act *Brotherhood*, in which a white husband and wife try to mask their anti-black sentiments from a middle-class black couple whom they have invited to their house. The blacks are not deceived. In 1966, in an article published in the Sunday *New York Times*, Ward adumbrated the need for a predominantly black audience "to readily understand, debate, confirm, or reject the truth or falsity" of the creations of the black playwright. Ward insisted that whenever a black playwright writes for a predominantly white audience— "least equipped to understand his intentions, woefully apathetic or anesthetized to his experience, often prone to distort his purpose"—that writer must restrict himself to the rudimentary re-education of that audience. Consequently, he has no opportunity to develop artistically. Although he admitted that a black playwright could gain the necessary "theatre of Negro identity" in a black community, Ward saw no possibility for such a theatre prior to massive reconstruction of the urban ghettos.

His hope of such a black-oriented theatre inspired the founding of the Negro Ensemble Company, whose notable successes include Lonne Elder III's *Ceremonies in Dark Old Men* and Charles Fuller's *A Soldier's Play*.

—Darwin T. Turner

WASSERSTEIN, Wendy.

Born in Brooklyn, New York, 18 October 1950. Educated at Calhoun School, Manhattan; Mount Holyoke College, South Hadley, Massachusetts, B.A. 1971; City College, City University of New York, M.A. 1973; Yale University School of Drama, New Haven, Connecticut, M.F.A. 1976. Recipient: Pulitzer prize, 1989; New York Drama Critics Circle award, 1989; Susan Smith Blackburn award, 1989; Tony award, 1989; National Endowment for the Arts grant; Guggenheim grant. Lives in New York. Agent: International Creative Management, 40 West 57th Street, New York, New York 10019, U.S.A.

Publications

PLAYS

Any Woman Can't (produced 1973).

Happy Birthday, Montpelier Pizz-zazz (produced 1974).

When Dinah Shore Ruled the Earth, with Christopher Durang (produced 1975).

Uncommon Women and Others (produced 1975). 1979.

Isn't It Romantic (produced 1981; revised version produced 1983). 1985.

Tender Offer (produced 1983).

The Man in a Case, adaptation of a story by Chekhov, in *Orchards* (produced 1985). 1986.

Miami, music and lyrics by Bruce Sussman and Jack Feldman (produced 1986).

Smart Women/Brilliant Choices in *Urban Blight* (musical revue), based on an idea by John Tillinger, music by David Shire, lyrics by Richard Maltby, Jr. (produced 1988).

The Heidi Chronicles (produced 1988). 1990.

The Heidi Chronicles and Other Plays (includes *Uncommon Women and Others, Isn't It Romantic*). 1990.

The Sisters Rosensweig (produced 1992). 1993.

TELEVISION PLAY: *The Sorrows of Gin*, from the story by John Cheever, 1979.

OTHER

Bachelor Girls (essays). 1990.

THEATRICAL ACTIVITIES

ACTOR: **Play**—in *The Hotel Play* by Wallace Shawn, 1981.

Identity is the theme in all of Wendy Wasserstein's plays, but is most fully integrated in her major works—*Uncommon Women and Others, Isn't It Romantic*, and *The Heidi Chronicles*. Wasserstein's commercial success with *The Heidi Chronicles*, which received both the Pulitzer prize and the Tony award for best play in 1989, has placed her in the slippery position of championing women's causes and feminist concerns. However, the playwright is more concerned with genetics than gender; and more likely to employ humor than humanism in creating her female characters. Her early works, which are not published, are precursory exercises exploring themes of sexuality, marriage, and relationships using episodic structure, music, and comic caricatures. Male characters are primarily used as foils and are rarely fully developed. Most of Wasserstein's female characters are not traditionally developed either, and are often representative of types. What unifies and sustains her dramaturgy is Wasserstein's coy sense of humor supported by keen observations of everyday life.

Wasserstein uses traditional American rituals as a means to exploit traditional roles. In two early plays, *When Dinah Shore Ruled the Earth* and *Any Woman Can't*, she uses a beauty pageant in the former and a dance audition in the latter to both exhort and extol the eclectic roles of ambitious females in a male-dominated society. In *Happy Birthday, Montpelier Pizz-zazz*, the college party scene is the backdrop for the exploitation of both stereotypical roles and stereotypical expectations of college students. The primary issues center around women's options but the play depends too much on caricature to be taken seriously. *Uncommon Women and Others*, Wasserstein's first major work, makes better use of college rituals as a means to explore both character and issue.

Uncommon Women and Others is not unique but it is risky in terms of subject matter. The reunion format of five women who meet in 1978 and then travel back six years to their final year at Mount Holyoke College provides the structure of the all-female play. What makes the play compelling are the concerns that each of the five women have regarding their role in society, in relation to each other, and to themselves. There is no real plot that unifies the play, and no real ending. A disembodied male voice is heard between each scene reciting extracts from a traditional graduation address. The technique serves to unify the play not only structurally but also thematically, since each excerpt raises issues that the women are trying to work through and choices that they are facing in the future.

Isn't It Romantic is similar to *Uncommon Women and Others* in terms of episodic structure, the use of music to create mood and exploit ritual, and in terms of the disembodied voice, which takes the form of telephone messages from various characters in the play and characters who are not physically present. *Isn't It Romantic* offers a better developed plot, characters with more dimension, and thematically the strongest philosophical bent of any Wasserstein work. The play, benefiting from some major rewrites after its initial New York première, contains the best linguistic foreplay of wit and wisdom stemming from Wasserstein's keen sense of irony and honest portrayal of the two major characters.

The central character, Janie Blumberg, is "a little kooky, a little sweet, a little unconfident." By contrast, her best friend Harriet Cornwall could be "the cover girl on the best working women's magazine." With Janie, her friends, and her parents along with Harriet and her mother, Wasserstein creates a Chekhovian *Cherry Orchard* where the plot is simple and the characters, each of whom is a bit eccentric and lives in his or her own world, discover that each must fulfill his or her own desires; that each must have his or her own dream. Janie grows by recognizing the discrepancies in everyone else's desires. The final tableau shows Janie as she begins to dance to "Isn't It Romantic" while the audience hears the voice of a friend leaving a desperate message on the telephone machine. Janie's dancing becomes more confident until she is "dancing beautifully," symbolizing her growth and celebrating an optimistic future.

The final tableau in Wasserstein's most celebrated work, that of Heidi sitting in a rocker singing softly to her adopted child, is in stark contrast to that of Janie's ebullient face and dancing silhouette. Unfortunately, *The Heidi Chronicles* overshadows the merits of *Isn't It Romantic*. The plays are similar, both dealing with a single woman looking for her place in society and in life. However, Heidi more closely resembles Harriet or Kate from *Uncommon Women and Others*. All are successful in their careers, but all have paid a price for success.

Wasserstein's most prize-winning play is not without merit, but it does not live up to its potential as a well-documented play that promises a comparison of "lost women painters" from the 16th century to the "lost feminists" of the 20th century.

Heidi, an art historian, opens the play in mid-lecture in front of a slide screen of a Sofonisba Anguissola painting. The painting and the lecture serve as both a literal and symbolic framing device. Scenes move back in time from 1965 to 1977, and from 1980 to 1989. The play explores Heidi's disillusionment with the women's movement, dramatizing its history at the same time. It raises serious and important issues only to undercut them with a loosely constructed plot and a contrived ending. Homosexuality, single parenting, politics, and art are all subjects that remain unexplored. As the heroine of the play, Heidi has an unusual role in that much of the time she is a spectator. And most of the action is that of encountering and re-encountering the various people in her life who have influenced her. The humor is closer to that of television sit-com and lacks the risqué verbiage of *Uncommon Women and Others* or the strong philosophical wit of *Isn't It Romantic*. Wasserstein's strengths lie in her ability to create characters who laugh at themselves while questioning others. She serves as a role model for women who wish to be successful in the New York theatre venue. All her plays are quirky and interesting and offer strong roles for women.

—Judy Lee Oliva

See the essay on *The Heidi Chronicles*.

WEIDMAN, Jerome.

Born in New York City, 4 April 1913. Educated at City College, New York, 1931–33; Washington Square College, New York, 1933–34; New York University Law School, 1934–37. Served in the United States Office of War Information, 1942–45. Married Elizabeth Ann Payne in 1943; two sons. President, Authors League of America, 1969–74; Recipient: Pulitzer prize, 1960; New York Drama Critics Circle award, 1960; Tony award, 1960. Agent: Brandt and Brandt, 1501 Broadway, New York, New York 10036. Address: 1966 Pacific Avenue, San Francisco, California 94109, U.S.A.

Publications

PLAYS

Fiorello!, with George Abbott, music and lyrics by Sheldon Harnick and Jerry Bock (produced 1959). 1960.

Tenderloin, with George Abbott, music and lyrics by Sheldon Harnick and Jerry Bock, adaptation of the work by Samuel Hopkins Adams (produced 1960). 1961.

I Can Get It for You Wholesale, music by Harold Rome, adaptation of the novel by Weidman (produced 1962). 1962.

Cool Off!, music by Howard Blackman (produced 1964).

Pousse-Café, music by Duke Ellington, lyrics by Marshall Barer and Frank Tobias (produced 1966).
Ivory Tower, with James Yaffe (produced 1968). 1969.
The Mother Lover (produced 1969). 1969.
Asterisk! A Comedy of Terrors (produced 1969). 1969.

SCREENPLAYS: *The Damned Don't Cry*, with Harold Medford, 1950; *The Eddie Cantor Story*, with Ted Sherdeman and Sidney Skolsky, 1953; *Slander*, 1957.

TELEVISION PLAYS: *The Reporter* series, 1964.

NOVELS
I Can Get It for You Wholesale. 1937.
What's in It for Me? 1938.
I'll Never Go There Any More. 1941.
The Lights Around the Shore. 1943.
Too Early to Tell. 1946.
The Price is Right. 1949.
The Hand of the Hunter. 1951.
Give Me Your Love. 1952.
The Third Angel. 1953.
Your Daughter Iris. 1955.
The Enemy Camp. 1958.
Before You Go. 1960.
The Sound of Bow Bells. 1962.
Word of Mouth. 1964.
Other People's Money. 1967.
The Center of the Action. 1969.
Fourth Street East. 1970.
Last Respects. 1972.
Tiffany Street. 1974.
The Temple. 1975.
A Family Fortune. 1978.
Counselors-at-Law. 1980.

SHORT STORIES
The Horse That Could Whistle 'Dixie' and Other Stories. 1939.
The Captain's Tiger. 1947.
A Dime a Throw. 1957.
Nine Stories. 1960.
My Father Sits in the Dark and Other Selected Stories. 1961.
Where the Sun Never Sets and Other Stories. 1964.
The Death of Dickie Draper and Nine Other Stories. 1965.
I, and I Alone. 1972.

OTHER
Letter of Credit (travel). 1940.
Back Talk (essays). 1963.

Praying for Rain: An Autobiography. 1986.

Editor: *The W. Somerset Maugham Sampler.* 1943; as *The Somerset Maugham Pocket Book*, 1944.
Editor, *Traveler's Cheque.* 1954.
Editor, with others, *The First College Bowl Question Book.* 1961.

MANUSCRIPT COLLECTION: Humanities Research Center, University of Texas, Austin.

The best of Jerome Weidman's musical comedies are concerned with some aspect of New York life: *Fiorello!*, which traces the rise of the city's illustrious mayor, deals with problems of politics; *Tenderloin* with vice and corruption in a particular area of New York; and *I Can Get It for You Wholesale* with the trials, tribulations and ethos of the garment district. Yet, the plays are far from parochial, because character and theme transcend the narrow confines of their specific period and geographic location. Nor is there any question that such themes are appropriate for the musical stage. They are, after all, part of a tradition which dates back at least as far as Gay's *Beggar's Opera* via Gilbert and Sullivan's 'intellectual comedies'.

The protagonists of these three plays are men of considerable ambition. But there is a difference between the aspirations of La Guardia, the moral fervour of Reverend Brock, and Harry Bogan's crooked deals which Weidman, in his equally sympathetic treatment of all three, tends to obscure and thereby undermines the moral dimension on which he insists. Both La Guardia and Brock are lively and sympathetic, but Harry Bogan's shady operations — breaking a strike, unloading a trusting partner, blowing the firm's money on a 'fashion consultant', and throwing the blame for a bankruptcy on another partner — are neither exhilarating matter for the musical theatre, nor treated with the cynicism of Brecht.

With *Ivory Tower*, Weidman moves from musical comedy to drama. Although Weidman and his collaborator, James Yaffe, explicitly disclaim any specific identification with historical personages, the fate of the protagonist strongly resembles that of Ezra Pound. Simon Otway is a famous expatriate poet who broadcast propaganda for the German army during World War II: the intended subject is the relationship between the artist and society and the action involves his trial for sedition after the armistice. All this should make for an interesting play but, unfortunately, the authors' use of the material does not measure up to its potential.

The dramatis personae include an array of stereotypes, such as Harold Gutman, the Jewish prosecutor, Wendel Drew, an English professor in charge of the 'Save Otway Committee', and Vincent Rimini, the young defence attorney who stakes his career on this case. There is the pseudo-Freudian exploration of Otway's childhood and early marriage to a waitress. But the main problem with the play is that we are meant to see Simon Otway as a major artist, even if politically irresponsible. We are told, for example, that his work embodies 'the greatest experiment with language this century has seen', and even one of his critics calls him, 'the finest master of the short story in this century'. Otway, however, spouts little more than literary and philosophical clichés. In the end he breaks under the pressure of Gutman's questions and, his megalomania and paranoia no longer disguised, suffers a psychotic episode.

Weidman is generally most successful in musical comedy where his talent to dramatize the big city atmosphere can be augmented by music and lyrics.

—Erica Aronson

WEINSTEIN, Arnold.

Born in New York City, 10 June 1927. Educated at Hunter College, New York, B.A. in classics 1951 (Phi Beta Kappa); University of London, 1949–50; Harvard University, Cambridge, Massachusetts, A.M. in comparative literature 1952; University of Florence (Fulbright Fellow), 1958–60. Served in the United States Navy, 1944–46. Married Suzanne Burgess in 1969. Visiting lecturer, New York University, 1955–56, and University of Southern California, Los Angeles; United States Information Service Lecturer, Italy, 1958–60; director of Drama Workshop, Wagner College, Staten Island, New York, summers 1964, 1965; visiting professor, Hollins College, Virginia, 1964–65; professor of dramatic literature, New School for Social Research, New York, 1965–66; chair of the department of playwriting, Yale University, New Haven, Connecticut, 1966–69; visiting professor, University of Colorado, Boulder, Summer 1969; chair of the department of drama, Columbia College, Chicago, 1969–70; visiting professor, Southampton College, Southampton, New York, 1978–79, and Columbia University, New York, from 1979. Co-director, with Paul Sills, Second City, and other improvisational groups; director, Free Theatre, Chicago, Actors Studio, New York and Los Angeles, and Rock Theatre and Guerilla Theatre, Los Angeles. Recipient: Guggenheim fellowship, 1965. Agent: Sam Cohn, International Creative Management, 40 West 57th Street, New York, New York 10019. Address: Department of English and Comparative Literature, Columbia University, New York, New York 10027, U.S.A.

Publications

PLAYS

Red Eye of Love (produced 1958). 1962.

White Cap (produced 1960).

Fortuna, music by Francis Thorne, adaptation of a play by Eduardo De Filippo and Armando Curcio (produced 1962).

The Twenty Five Cent White Hat (in 3 x 3, produced 1962).

Food for Thought: A Play about Food, with Jay and Fran Landesman (produced 1962).

Dynamite Tonite, music by William Bolcom (produced 1963; revised version produced 1964). 1964.

Party (produced 1964; revised version, music by Laurence Rosenthal, produced 1976).

They (produced 1965).

Reg. U.S. Pat. Off., in Pardon Me, Sir, But Is My Eye Hurting Your Elbow, edited by Bob Booker and George Foster. 1968.

Story Theatre (produced 1968).

Greatshot, music by William Bolcom (produced 1969).

Ovid, music by The True Brethren, adaptation of *Metamorphoses* by Ovid (produced 1969).

Mahagonny, adaptation of the libretto by Brecht, music by Kurt Weill (produced 1970). Excerpts in *Yale/Theatre*, 1969.

The American Revolution, with Paul Sills, music by Tony Greco, lyrics by Weinstein (produced 1973).

More Metamorphoses, adaptation of the work by Ovid (produced 1973).

Gypsy New York (produced 1974).

Lady Liberty's Ice Cream Cone (produced 1974).

Captain Jinks, adaptation of the play by Clyde Fitch, music arranged by William Bolcom (produced 1976).

America More or Less, music by Tony Greco (produced 1976).

Monkey, with Paul Sills (produced 1978).

Stories for Theatre (produced 1979).

Casino Paradise, with Thomas Babe, music by William Bolcom (produced 1990).

McTeague, with Robert Altman, music by William Bolcom (produced 1992).

IMPROVISATIONAL MATERIAL; *Second City*, 1963–64.

TELEVISION PLAYS: *Improvisation*; *The Last Ingredient*, music by David Amram.

VERSE

Different Poems by the Same Author. 1960.

Recording: lyrics for *Black Max: Cabaret Songs*, music by William Bolcom, 1985.

OTHER

What Did I Do?, with Larry Rivers, 1992.

MANUSCRIPT COLLECTION: Yale University, New Haven, Connecticut.

CRITICAL STUDIES: *American Drama since World War II*, 1962, and *The Jumping-Off Place*, 1969, both by Gerald Weales; *A Theatre Divided*, 1967, and *Opening Nights*, 1969, both by Martin Gottfried; *Common and Uncommon Masks* by Richard Gilman, 1971.

THEATRICAL ACTIVITIES

DIRECTOR: **Plays**—*Second City* (co-director, with Paul Sills), and other improvisational groups; his own and other plays at the Free Theatre, Chicago, Actors Studio, New York and Los Angeles, and the Rock Theatre and the Guerilla Theatre, Los Angeles; *A Memory of Two Mondays* by Arthur Miller, 1979; *The White House Murder Case* by Jules Feiffer, 1980.

Arnold Weinstein comments:

I try to write the history and mythology of today. The schoolroom, the churchroom, the theatre are one, or all are lost. Drama and karma are one. Look them up. Look them up and down. The audience is half the action, the actors the other half; the author starts the fight. Power. The passing of power. It really is life there in the dark, here. The lightning of television terrifies most. Right in the word the intrusion of fear—fear of loss of control, loss of sale, loss of sorcery. Loss of power. Our fear sends us through the channels, puts us on our tracks. If the trinity does not control the power, what's left? Only everything. Everything running around in formless rampant ranks waiting for daring brutes to pick up the wire reins.

The generation of American playwrights that followed Arthur Miller and Tennessee Williams was a troubled one, reflecting a country that was emerging from a history of brute domination into a future of questions and complexities. These playwrights were similarly trapped between the theater styles and values of an outgoing past and the uncertainty of a fast-approaching future. Such writers as Jack Gelber and Jack Richardson have never fulfilled their early promise, but Arnold Weinstein's inability to find himself as a playwright is perhaps the most painful, for he is the most artistic, talented, and original of the lot. But he has been hurt by a combination of critical rejection and changing taste, and though the author of charming plays and libretti, his career seems frustrated.

His New York professional debut was a production by the Living Theatre of *Red Eye of Love*, which remains his best known full-length play. The Living Theatre at the time was in its Brecht stage and so was Weinstein, who was to prove too affected by changing fashion and too insecure in his own style. The play is a romantic fable about American capitalism. Its hero is a toy inventor in love with a girl who feels it her "duty to marry money." She turns to the owner of a 13-storey meat market, which grows beyond 40 stories as the play progresses. This girl vacillates between the inventor (artist) and the butcher (capitalist) while the play does vaudeville turns to Joycean word games with a whimsicality that would prove a Weinstein signature. The author's stage energy, his antic humor, his feel for America, and his deep love of cheap sentiment are established as they would persist through his subsequent work, but the play is too often precious and almost blatantly Brechtian.

In 1962 he wrote the libretto for an off-Broadway musical of inspired zaniness—*Fortuna* (Weinstein was to become involved with many musical projects, one of America's rare artistic playwrights to appreciate their value, but though several were planned, none reached Broadway). *Fortuna*, adapted from an Italian comedy, told of the impoverished and luckless title character who inherits a fortune on the condition that he have no sons. After a series of farcical complications, Fortuna gets his fortune. Once again, Weinstein was dealing with a Schweikian hero-victim (expressionist and absurdist influences would for too long influence his work and keep him from self-discovery).

His one-act absurdist play, *The Twenty Five Cent White Hat*, opened and closed off-Broadway, unappreciated by New York's critics. Though the play was a trite plea for the importance of individuality, it was filled with Weinstein's lively and poetic comedy writing.

The turning point in the playwright's career came with *Dynamite Tonite*, his "comic opera for actors" written with composer William Bolcom. Though not without relation to Brecht, the work had a brisk originality of its own. For though it was a legitimate opera, it was indeed written for actors—that is, non-singers. Weinstein's libretto was intensely pacifist, yet romantic and comic, tender and suffused with affection for a vulnerable mankind. Its operetta-style hero and heroine sang hilarious Wagnerian parodies in counterpoint to flat-footed soldiers doing soft shoe dances, and set as the work was on the battleground of a neverneverland it had an odd mixture of expressionism and Americana that somehow worked.

Dynamite Tonite is a superb theater work, but it was so brutally criticized that it closed on its first night. Several attempts were made to revive it, first by the Repertory Theatre at Yale Drama School and once more off-Broadway, but it seemed doomed to rejection despite (or perhaps because of) its artistic superiority.

Greatshot, another musical work with Bolcom—also produced at Yale—was in the style of the then-popular self-creative companies (such as his friends at the Living Theatre had developed), but there was no soul to the work, nor clarity of intention. The structured, verbal theater to which the playwright naturally inclined did not mesh with physical, improvisational, anti-verbal theater he was emulating.

Meanwhile, Weinstein had been long preparing a new translation of the great Brecht-Weill opera, *Mahoganny*, and when it was finally produced after many years of effort, his work proved mediocre, though hardly showcased by the disastrous production.

Weinstein's history, then, is one of victimization by the American theater's commercialism, which leaves little room for so creative, artistic, and poetic a playwright; it is a victimization by British-American theater generally, with its overwhelming sense of trend (absurdism, once hailed as *the* style for moderns, was obsolete after no more than five years of fashion); and it is a victimization by rejection. His past shows some fulfillment and great promise; his present is in limbo; his future depends on his own resolve and his treatment at the hands of both the theater and circumstance.

—Martin Gottfried

WELLER, Michael.

Born in New York City, 26 September 1942. Educated at Stockbridge School; Windham College; Brandeis University, Waltham, Massachusetts, B.A. in music 1965; Manchester University, Lancashire. Recipient: Creative Artists Public Service grant, 1976. Agent: Michael Imison Playwrights, 28 Almeida Street, London N1 1TD, England. Address: 215 East 5th Street, New York, New York 10003, U.S.A.

Publications

PLAYS

Cello Days at Dixon's Palace (produced 1965).
Fred, music by Weller, adaptation of the novel *Malcolm* by James Purdy (produced 1965).

How Ho-Ho Rose and Fell in Seven Short Scenes, music by Weller (produced 1966).

The Making of Theodore Thomas, Citizen, adaptation of the play *Johnny Johnson* by Paul Green (produced 1968).

Happy Valley (produced 1969).

The Bodybuilders, and Now There's Just the Three of Us (produced 1969). With *Tira Tells Everything There Is to Know about Herself*, 1972; in *Off-Broadway Plays 2*, 1972.

Poison Come Poison (produced 1970).

Cancer (produced 1970). 1971; as *Moonchildren* (produced 1971), 1971.

Grant's Movie (produced 1971). With *Tira*, 1972.

Tira Tells Everything There Is to Know about Herself (produced 1971). With *The Bodybuilders*, 1972; as *Tira* (produced 1975), with *Grant's Movie*, 1972.

The Bodybuilders, and Tira Tells Everything There Is to Know about Herself. 1972.

More Than You Deserve, music by Jim Steinman, lyrics by Weller and Steinman (produced 1973).

Twenty-Three Years Later (produced 1973).

Fishing (produced 1975). 1975.

Alice, in *After Calcutta* (produced 1976).

Split (one-act version; produced 1977). 1979; as *Abroad* in *Split* (full-length version), 1981.

Loose Ends (produced 1979). 1980.

Barbarians, with Kitty Hunter Blair and Jeremy Brooks, adaptation of a play by Gorky (produced 1980). 1982.

Dwarfman, Master of a Million Shapes (produced 1981).

At Home (produced 1981). In *Split* (full-length version), 1981.

Split (full-length version; includes *At Home* [*Split*, part 1] and *Abroad* [*Split*, part 2]. 1981.

Five Plays (includes *Moonchildren, Fishing, At Home, Abroad, Loose Ends*). 1982.

The Ballad of Soapy Smith (produced 1983). 1985.

Ghost on Fire (produced 1985). 1987.

A Dopey Fairy Tale, adaptation of a story by Chekhov, in *Orchards* (produced 1985). 1986.

Spoils of War (produced 1988). 1989.

Lake No Bottom (produced 1990). 1991.

SCREENPLAYS: *Hair*, 1979; *Ragtime*, 1982; *Lost Angels*, 1989; *God Bless You Mr. Rosewater*, 1991.

THEATRICAL ACTIVITIES

ACTOR: **Play**—Star-Man in *The Tooth of Crime* by Sam Shepard, 1972.

Chronicling his own generation, Michael Weller has sent interim reports from the front lines of bourgeois American youth as students moved from universities into communes, from the city to the country, and from idealism to

Madison Avenue competitiveness. Whatever the surrounding environment, his basic concern has been with personal relationships and their vulnerability.

Many of his early plays were introduced to London by the American expatriate Charles Marowitz of the Open Space Theatre, and Weller had an English reputation before he had an American one, despite earning his first production while he was still a student at Brandeis University. His plays generally appeared in a kind of hyper-ventilating realism which matched the extremes of emotion that afflict his characters without detailing too completely their day-to-day existence.

His first play to have a genuine transatlantic impact was the very specifically American drama which was called *Cancer* when it had its premiere at London's Royal Court Theatre. Cancer is, of course, an astrological sign as well as a disease, and the play was retitled *Moonchildren* for its first American performance at the Arena Stage in Washington D.C. Although written and first produced in 1970, there was something nostalgic and historical in its portrait of a group of college students sharing an apartment during the heady days of resistance to President Nixon and the war in Vietnam.

Perhaps Weller drew the battle lines too clearly, placing his young people in a sort of drug-armed camp opposing the adult society which was represented by police, landlords, and relatives. The sharp details of the young people's conversational exchanges spoke well for his dramatist's ear, however, and there was an optimism in his writing which suggested that goodwill, high spirits, and visionary certitude would break down the barriers between police and students, an idea which grew sour in the later plays where the broken barriers more often represented a capitulation of idealism. What balanced the comical anarchy in *Cancer* was finally the familial call across generations, the news given to one boy that his mother was dying of cancer—actually, painfully, and beyond the relief of metaphor.

Grant's Movie followed *Cancer* almost immediately, and drew harsher lines between the generations. Police and anti-war demonstrators have come to serious violence, and a policeman is kidnapped by three peace-seeking hippies who believe the man might have murdered the brother of a friend during a demonstration. The friend is Grant and the planned torment of the policeman is according to his script: everybody is in Grant's movie.

Weller's next leap was a review of the hippie alternative as it appeared in 1975: *Fishing*, a play that came to be seen as the second part of an extended trilogy that began with *Cancer*. Three drop-outs are discovered in a backwater of the Pacific Northwest, short on cannabis, short on cash, and exploring a new fantasy of beginning a commercial fishery—if they can raise $1,500 to buy a boat. In the course of the play, real death again enters the fable when the man who was selling the boat dies, and again when the chicken who was becoming a pet is killed, plucked for eating, and pulled apart in rage. Another death is flirted with, when one of the three plans suicide on his motorcycle before changing his mind in favour of the fishing: "Oh you're right, it's a dumb idea, no doubt about it. You and me. Two of the finest minds of our generation. But it's something to do. And, you know, if we approach it just the right way, after a while, if we manage to stick to it, and we don't get seasick and we do catch fish we might find there's a good reason for doing it."

Weller's ear for dialogue had become more acute by then, and the acid wit was refined, but the play that best represented his developing perspective was *Loose Ends*, his 1979 report on the progress of the alternative society of the 1960s. It was panoramic in intention, first evoking an accidental meeting on the hippie road to paradise when a young couple come together on a beach in Bali, he returning to America from a depressing tour in the Peace Corps, and she on her way to enlightenment in India. Weller's comedy and optimism survive his story of that relationship, which stretches forward from 1970 across the decade of Vietnam, Watergate, and disillusion.

With the panoramic structure of *Loose Ends*, Weller constructed a play consisting entirely of dramatic touchpoints: the form remained realistic but every meeting was a contrast to what had gone before and what would have been a gradual evolution of a drop-out into a hip property speculator becomes a comical commentary as the woodsman becomes a long-haired man in a business suit. Gurus and passing fashions are recorded for their worth, then brushed aside while the original couple fall into competition with each other, rejecting then courting financial success. Their path was to divorce instead of enlightenment and although their careers remain on the edge of art, in photography and filmmaking, the world is busy overcoming their ideals.

With *Cancer* and *Fishing* it forms a rounded trilogy of reportage, and the plays make a dramatic document of value. Weller remains a writer for the theatre, contributing new, short pieces such as *Split* and important longer works such as *Ghost on Fire* and *Spoils of War*. With such adaptations for the cinema as his screenplay for E.L. Doctorow's *Ragtime*, his reputation has also been growing elsewhere.

—Ned Chaillet

WELLMAN, Mac (John McDowell).

Born in Cleveland, Ohio, 7 March 1945. Educated at University School, Shaker Heights, Ohio, graduated 1963; School of International Service, American University, Washington D.C., B.A. in international relations and organization 1967; University of Wisconsin, Madison, M.A. in English literature 1968. Associate professor of English, Montgomery College, Rockville, Maryland, 1969–72; playwright-in-residence, New York University, 1981–82, Yale University School of Drama, New Haven, Connecticut, 1992, and Princeton University, New Jersey, 1992–93; teacher of playwriting, Mentor Playwrights' Project at the Mark Taper Forum, Los Angeles, University of New Mexico, Albuquerque, New York University, Iowa Playwright's Lab, Iowa City, Brown University, Providence, Rhode Island, and New Dramatists, New Voices, Boston, Massachusetts, 1984–92; resident, Bellagio Study and Conference Centre, the Rockefeller Foundation, Bellagio, Italy, 1991; PNM distinguished chair in playwriting, University of New Mexico, Albuquerque, 1991; master artist, Atlantic Center for the Arts, New Smyrna, Florida, 1991. Recipient: New York Foundation for the Arts fellowship, 1986, 1990; McKnight fellowship, 1989; Rockefeller fellowship, 1989; Guggenheim fellowship, 1990; National Endowment for the Arts fellowship, 1990; Obie award, 1990 (three times), 1991; Outer Circle Critics award,

1990; Bessie award, 1992; American Theater Critics Association award, 1992. Lives in New York. Agent: Wiley Hausam, International Creative Management, 40 West 57th Street, New York, New York 10019, U.S.A.

Publications

PLAYS

Fama Combinatoria (broadcast 1973; produced 1975).

The Memory Theatre of Giordano Bruno (broadcast 1976; produced 1976).

Opera Brevis. 1977.

Starluster (produced 1979). In *Wordplays 1*, edited by Bonnie Marranca, 1980.

Dog in the Manger, adaptation of a play by Lope de Vega (produced 1982).

The Self-Begotten (produced 1982).

Phantomnation, with Constance Congdon and Bennett Cohen, music by James Ragland (produced 1983).

The Professional Frenchman (produced 1984). In *Theatre of Wonders*, edited by Wellman, 1985.

Harm's Way, music by Bob Jewett and Jack Maeby (broadcast 1984; produced 1985). 1984.

Energumen (produced 1985). In *Women with Guns*, edited by Christopher Gould, 1986.

The Bad Infinity (produced 1985). In *7 Different Plays*, edited by Wellman, 1988.

1951, with Anne Bogart and Michael Roth (produced 1986).

The Nain Rouge, music by Michael Roth (produced 1986).

The Distance to the Moon, music by Melissa Shiftlett (produced 1986).

Cleveland (produced 1986).

Dracula, adaptation of the novel by Bram Stoker (produced 1987).

Bodacious Flapdoodle. 1987.

Albanian Softshoe (produced 1988).

Peach Bottom Nuclear Reactor Full of Sleepers (produced 1988).

Cellophane (produced 1988). 1988.

Without Colors, adaptation of *Cosmicomics* by Italo Calvino, music by Melissa Shiftlett (produced 1989).

Whirligig (produced 1989). In *Plays in Process*, vol.10, no.7, 1989.

Bad Penny (produced 1989). 1990.

The Ninth World (produced 1989).

Terminal Hip (also director: produced 1989). In *Performing Arts Journal*, no.40, 1992.

Crowbar (produced 1990).

Sincerity Forever (produced 1990).

7 Blowjobs (produced 1991). In *TheaterForum*, no.1, 1992.

A Murder of Crows (produced 1991). In *Plays in Process*, 1992.

Tallahassee, adaptation of Ovid's *Metamorphoses*, with Len Jenkin, (produced 1991).

Coat Hanger (produced 1992).

Strange Feet (produced 1993).

The Land of Fog and Whistles (produced 1993).

RADIO PLAYS: *Nobody*, 1972; *Fama Combinatoria*, 1973; *Mantices*, 1973; *Two Natural Drummers*, 1973; *The Memory Theatre of Giordano Bruno*, 1976; *Harm's Way*, 1984.

NOVEL

The Fortuneteller. 1991.

VERSE

In Praise of Secrecy. 1977.
Satires. 1985.
A Shelf in Woop's Clothing. 1990.

OTHER

Editor, *Breathing Space: An Anthology of Sound-Text Art*. 1977.
Editor, *Theatre of Wonders*. 1985.
Editor, *7 Different Plays*. 1988.
Editor, *Slant Six*. 1990.

THEATRICAL ACTIVITIES

DIRECTOR: **Play**—*Terminal Hip*, 1990.

Mac Wellman is one of the most original, daring, and important playwrights in America. His work is spiky, challenging, fiercely funny, radical in its formal strategies and in its politics, and in every line a rebuke to the timid, dull, stultifying, and sentimental naturalism that still dominates the American theatre. Consequently, his work has rarely been produced outside New York City, other than in small fringe theatres around the country, and rarely, if ever, performed on the strait-laced stages of the mainstream regional theatres. Artistic directors may admire Wellman's work, but few have the courage or recklessness to produce his plays and risk awakening and alienating their slumbering subscription audiences.

Wellman is also a poet and novelist, and is one of a handful of American playwrights who care about writing, who are investigating the possibilities of the American language, whose language is carefully wrought and poetically charged, and whose plays are always, in some part, whatever their other concerns, about the American language (and hence, about American culture and American politics). In his disdain for naturalism, his rejection of linear narrative, psychological subtext, and traditional notions of character, his deliberate subversion and mockery of mainstream theatrical convention, and his love of (in his words) "Gritty, dirty, slimy American language when spoken in the theatre," Wellman is colleague and kindred spirit to a group of playwrights who include Len Jenkin, Eric Overmyer, and Jeffrey Jones, writers who are, in Jones's words, "the Huck Finns" of the American theatre.

Wellman is also a critic, editor, and teacher, and has tried, along with the playwrights mentioned above, to generate a new movement in American playwriting, a movement based in American language, and in rebellion against mainstream American playwriting, against the kind of play characterized by the dramaturge James Magruder as "the talking about my problems in your living room kind of play." To this end, he has edited two influential anthologies, *Theatre of Wonders* and *7 Different Plays*, and published numerous articles.

Wellman was born and raised in Cleveland, Ohio, and his writing evinces the dry humor and flat twang of his Midwestern roots:

Lights up on a pair of boots protruding from a washtub.

Nella: That's not Andy. That's dad, and he's dead.

Nella: When the kids were young the sea was normal. Of the logic of the sea my younger one, Susannah, said: It's lucky the shallow end is near the beach.

—*A Murder of Crows*

His Cleveland background shows in recurring images of toxicity and pollution; the plays are full of poisoned landscapes and poisoned families. It is not surprising that a playwright from Cleveland should be concerned with blight, death, and decay. After all, the river which flows through the middle of the city is so polluted it once caught fire, a landmark event in the history of the American ecology movement. That image, a burning river of sludge, seems to inform Wellman's work in a pervasive, subterranean way, its smudgy fumes percolating up from the depths of his writing.

Nella: Not to mention the county dump, where that hellacious grease pit is. The rivers in this part of the state all look like bubble baths, and the air's all mustardy. Even the local ocean's a little oily and waxy. Like a big bowl of custard, wiggly custard.

Howard: Nella's alright. Only she's never been the same since the avalanche by the . . . grease pit. Landfill or whatever it was. Godawful sludge heap. That ghastly, wolfish slime.

—*A Murder of Crows*

Wellman's concern with blight extends, of course, to the American language, "as she is spoke" in the theatre. He is attempting to dig himself out from under the avalanche of advertising hype, sentimental cliché, received ideas and politically correct jargon, and sheer mendacity which poison public discourse, tyrannize and terrorize the artist in America, and reduce most American theatre to ersatz television. Two of his newest plays, *7 Blowjobs* and *Sincerity Forever*, are direct responses to the right-wing attack on art and artists in America, and to the assault on the National Endowment for the Arts led by the conservative senator from North Carolina, Jesse Helms. *Sincerity Forever* is about, among other things, the Ku Klux Klan, and with typical puckish humor, Wellman dedicated the play to Senator Helms and sent him a copy. *7 Blowjobs* was inspired by the furore over Robert Mapplethorpe's homoerotic photographs. Both pieces generated considerable public controversy. Ironically, the terrified bureaucrats at the NEA tried to disassociate themselves from *Sincerity Forever*, not wanting the unreliable Wellman as an ally.

Wellman has said he is interested in "bad language," a term which means non-standard American language, and which originates with H.L. Mencken. In an interview, Wellman said, "I think there are deep truths about the American psyche that you can understand better by a little of the downside, the dark side of American language. There is a powerful yearning that is present there, a powerful urge for transcendence. A very deep and spiritual side to all Americans that's most evident when we're not being correct grammatically or stylistically, in our use of language." (interview with Allan Havis in *Theatre Forum* [San Diego], Spring 1992)

A typical example of Wellman "bad language," in which he mines American folk talk and twists and forges it into his own idiom, occurs in *A Murder of Crows:*

> Raymond: . . . Crows jerk and juke about and the winds wind up a medley of talkative hacksaws. We edge near the pit, back off and think by baking apple pie we've got the key to the whole shitwagon and maybe we do. Maybe we don't. I'd love to know what the inside of a storm feels like to be one. I really do. But if it were up to me I'd skin the cat with a touch more care, seeing as how the consequences of what passes for luck at gin rummy, poker and horses has a strange way of barking up the wrong tree.

Another of Wellman's principal linguistic strategies is the use of free verse. His lines are broken in such a way, and with such care, that they acquire a terrific sprung rhythm, a tin-can tied to a tail-pipe sort of clatter, great energy, and unexpected humor. The use of verse also acts as a series of linguistic speed bumps, slowing the headlong hurtle of the actor and the audience as one speaks and the other listens, revitalizing the language, and subverting expectations and assumptions. Much of Wellman's recent work, like *Cellophane*, a long dramatic poem for an ensemble of actors, and *Terminal Hip*, a demented tour-de-force monologue, is pure language, without conventional narrative or action or character: tirades from the edge of darkness which harangue an American culture twisted and scarred and maimed by advertising and television and politics.

Mac Wellman's other major works include *The Bad Infinity*, *Harm's Way*, *Crowbar*, and *Bad Penny*. *Harm's Way*, a Western (or rather, a Midwestern), is a meditation upon violence, upon the language of violence, and upon the American culture of violence. Violence is America's original sin, the dark stain on the American psyche; it is a subject too little explored in serious non-exploitative endeavors in any medium, and almost never in the theatre. *Harm's Way* is a dark, brooding meditation on the conquest of the frontier and, by extension, on subsequent American foreign policy, an x-ray of American myth, and American history, both official and counter-cultural. Its hero is a gun-fighter named Santouche, a glorified psychopath and serial killer, and the play probes the American penchant for making heroes of such monsters. (See the recent popularity of Dr. Hannibal Lecter in *The Silence of the Lambs*.) The play ends with Santouche murdering his woman, a whore named Isle of Mercy, while a crowd of children taunt the gunslinger: "You gonna kill everyone, Mister? You gonna kill everyone, Mister? You gonna kill everyone, Mister?", a haunting refrain which evokes the scorched-earth tragedy of Vietnam, as well as countless Hollywood movies, both Western and contemporary. *Harm's Way* is an American *Woyzcek*.

> You know the story of Rip
> Van Winkle? Well the true

story of Rip Van Winkle
runs as follows: there's
this old fart who went
to sleep for twenty years
and woke up to find
everything. THE SAME.
(pause)
Except him. He was twenty
years older.
Was he ever surprised.
And horrified.
EXACTLY THE SAME.
          —*The Bad Infinity*

A "Bad Infinity" is a flawed system which replicates itself forever—like most human systems. More correctly, the term is from Hegel, and means any series of logical operations which never reaches a final result or accelerates to another level, a dialectic which never achieves synthesis or transcends itself. In *The Bad Infinity* Wellman explores a number of such systems: geopolitics, fashion, economics, professional sports, crime, international banking, art, criticism, media, and the theatre itself. Or, rather, the shopworn conventions of the conventional theatre. The American theatre: a bad infinity if ever there was one.

Bad Penny and *Crowbar* are site-specific pieces, written for En Garde Arts, a New York-based producing organization run by Anne Hamburger which produces on-site theatrical events. *Crowbar* was written for and produced in the Victory Theatre, an old, *grande dame* of a Broadway house which was reclaimed and refurbished for the event. (It had fallen on hard times; long ago abandoned as a legit theatre, it had become, in recent years, a porno house, showing terrifying triple-bills at bargain basement prices.) *Crowbar* used the history of the Victory Theatre as inspiration for an evocative, ghostly, ultimately tender and sad piece about the decay of Broadway, the theatre, and the city itself, and its present crime-ridden, derelict, end-of-days condition as a great, hulking, once-magnificent, now dangerous, ruin.

Bad Penny is one of Wellman's best plays, playful, funny, and exhilarating. Produced at, and written for, Bow Bridge in Central Park, *Bad Penny* is a comic sonata of urban life, alienation, and insanity. A hapless motorist from Big Ugly, Montana, breaks down in the big city, and finds himself stranded in the middle of Central Park, surrounded by inspired New York lunacy. *Bad Penny* is spare and taut, and contains some of Wellman's most inspired writing. The following passage is the monologue which ends the play:

First Woman: For all things beneath the sky are
lovely, except those which
are ugly; and these are odious
and reprehensible and must be
destroyed, must be torn limb from limb howling,
to prepare the ritual banquet, the
ritual of the Slaughter of Innocents.
For the Way is ever difficult to discover

in the wilderness of thorns and mirrors
and the ways of the righteous are full
strange and possess strange hats and
feet. For the Way leads over from the
Fountains of Bethesda, where the Lord
performed certain acts, acts unknown to
us, across the Bow Bridge of our human
unknowability, pigheadedness, and the
wisenheimer attitude problem of our
undeserving, slimeball cheesiness; and
scuttles into the Ramble, there, of
utterly craven, totally lost, desperate
and driven incomprehensibility—friend
neither to fin, to feather, nor tusk
of bat, bird, weasel, porcupine, nor gnat.
And we who are not who we are must forever
bury the toxic waste of our hidden hates
in the dark, plutonic abysm of our human
hearts, and be always blessed in the empty promise
of the sky that looks down upon us with
a smile, a divine smile, even as she
crushes us all beneath her silver foot.

Mac Wellman's plays are political in every line. They are not direct. They are oblique, ironic, and have multiple, even contradictory meanings. They are many-faceted. They are dense and extraordinary. In a word, they are poetic, theatrical. They are, to use an image from *The Bad Infinity*, like horizontal avalanches. An avalanche of images, language, and ideas, moving the viewer from his or her received ideas and assumptions as relentlessly and irresistibly as a wall of mud or a glacier grinding down a canyon. I understand Wellman's plays as I understand poetry, on a deep, cellular level that almost resists reason and explanation. There is much in life that is mysterious, that resists reduction and categorization and simple-minded explanation. Such are Wellman's plays. They are beautiful, subversive works, important works, and deserve to be more frequently produced and better known.

—Eric Overmyer

WESLEY, Richard (Errol).

Born in Newark, New Jersey, 11 July 1945. Educated at Howard University, Washington, D.C., 1963–67, B.F.A. 1967. Married Valerie Deane Wilson in 1972; three children. Passenger service agent, United Airlines, Newark, 1967–69; member of the New Lafayette Theatre Company and managing editor of *Black Theatre* magazine, New York, 1969–73; founding member, 1973, and member of the Board of Directors, 1976–80, Frank Silvera Writers Workshop, New York; teacher of black theatre history, Manhattanville College, Purchase, New York, Wesleyan University, Middletown, Connecticut, 1973–74, and Manhattan Community College, New York, 1980–83; member of the board of directors, Theatre of Universal Images,

Newark, 1979–82; teacher, Rutgers University, New Brunswick, New Jersey, 1984. Recipient: Drama Desk award, 1972; Rockefeller grant, 1973; Audelco award, 1974, 1977; NAACP Image award, 1974, 1975. Agent: Jay C. Kramer, 135 East 55th Street, New York, New York 10022. Address: P.O. Box 43091, Upper Montclair, New Jersey 07043, U.S.A.

Publications

PLAYS

Put My Dignity on 307 (produced 1967).
The Street Corner (produced 1970).
Headline News (produced 1970).
Knock Knock, Who Dat (produced 1970).
The Black Terror (produced 1970). In *The New Lafayette Theatre Presents*, edited by Ed Bullins, 1974.
Gettin' It Together (produced 1971). With *The Past Is the Past*, 1979.
Strike Heaven on the Face! (produced 1973).
Alicia (produced 1973; as *Goin' Thru Changes*, produced 1974).
Eight Ball (produced 1973).
The Sirens (produced 1974). 1975.
The Mighty Gents (produced 1974; as *The Last Street Play*, produced 1978; as *The Mighty Gents*, produced 1978). 1979.
The Past Is the Past (produced 1974). With *Gettin' It Together*, 1979.
On the Road to Babylon, music and lyrics by Peter Link, based on a concept by Brent Nicholson (produced 1980).
Butterfly (produced 1985).
The Talented Tenth (produced 1989).

SCREENPLAYS: *Uptown Saturday Night*, 1974; *Let's Do It Again*, 1975; *Fast Forward*, 1985; *Native Son*, 1986.

TELEVISION PLAY: *The House of Dies Drear*, from the novel by Virginia Hamilton, 1974.

MANUSCRIPT COLLECTION: Dramatists Play Service, New York.

Richard Wesley writes about the black community of America's urban ghettos. He charts the stoops, poolrooms, and tenements of the inner city and the ways of the people who live there: pimps, prostitutes, derelicts, street gangs. While his sensibility is lyrical, his intentions are political. Wesley questions the values that entrap his characters in aimless days and barren futures. He examines the rules by which they try to survive and the human and social costs when these rules prove inadequate.

While black playwrights such as Ed Bullins and Ron Milner really came from the ghettos they dramatize, Wesley grew up in a middle-class family in Newark, New Jersey. He was, he says, nearly a teenager before he discovered that college wasn't compulsory. At Howard University he not only came under the influence of the fabled Owen Dobson, mentor of many black theatre artists, but also embraced the black nationalist movement which took root on campuses in the 1960s. Upon graduation in 1967, he joined Bullins at the Black Playwrights Workshop of Harlem's New Lafayette Theatre, known for its activist posture and the cross-pollination it encouraged between the stage and the surrounding street culture.

His early play *The Black Terror* is a satire on the contradictions Wesley now detected in cultural nationalism. The playwright introduces us to members of a radical cadre pledged to revolutionary suicide in the service of urban guerrilla warfare. Through the character of Keusi, a pragmatic Vietnam veteran, Wesley debates the movement's tactics and its leaders' image of themselves as a kamikaze vanguard. "To die for the revolution is the greatest thing in life," says one of the militants. "But revolution is about life, I thought," Keusi answers. "Our first duty as revolutionaries is to live. . . . Why we gotta fight a revolution with a value system directed toward death?"

Although its ideological emphasis is unique among his plays, *The Black Terror* incorporates many stylistic traits, blended impressionistically, that Wesley would refine in his increasingly humanistic later works. Raised more on television than live entertainment, he favors the stage equivalents of filmic crossfades, superimpositions, and jump cuts to shift locations rapidly, juxtapose moods, and suggest simultaneous action—an approach which subsequently brought him several Hollywood contracts. From the classics he borrows choral and ritualistic elements which he mingles with characters and scenes more typical of contemporary naturalistic drama. His dialogue, a pungent street argot, is expanded by poetic rhythms and refrains, while his monologues approach direct address soliloquies.

For the series of short plays he produced between 1972 and 1974, Wesley muted the stylistic exuberance of *The Black Terror* in favor of compassionate yet unsentimental character studies. In *Gettin' It Together* and *Goin' Thru Changes* polarized young couples struggle both against each other and against cheapening odds to piece together a future. *Strike Heaven on the Face!* brings a war hero home to peacetime defeat. *The Past Is the Past* is set in a poolhall, where a son in search of his heritage confronts the father who long ago abandoned him. Inspired in part by Fellini's *Nights of Cabiria*, a second reunion play, *The Sirens*, probes the life of a prostitute, eventually faced with a choice between her hard won but precarious independence and reconciliation with the husband who vanished a decade before to chase a dream now belatedly come true.

Individually, the plots of these five miniatures are casual, mere hooks on which Wesley's hangs family portraits. Taken as montage, however, they together gain a thematic solidarity which presents the scenography of a condition. A number of issues that played supporting roles in *The Black Terror* here become Wesley's preoccupations: the breakdown of family structures, leading to alienation among men and women, parents and children; connections between past and present, through which a legacy of defeat passes from generation to generation; thwarted efforts to wrench self-worth from deluded hopes and to stake out a little turf from which pride can be harvested. How, Wesley asks, can the quest for manhood succeed opposite frustrations that lead to inertia on one hand and savagery on the other?

His cinematic style refined, his ability to draw tenderly detailed characters matured, Wesley assembled his thematic concerns in a full-length drama about the important present and harsh destiny in store for the remnants of an expired Newark street gang. *The Last Street Play* opened to enthusiastic reviews, some of which compared Wesley's inner city tragedy to Kurosawa's *The Seven Samurai* and Fellini's *I vitelloni*, film classics concerning disoriented young toughs, now past their prime, who confront tomorrow with a gallows bravado as deluded as it is fatal. Under the title *The Mighty Gents*, the play transferred to Broadway, a commercial tribute that remains rare for legitimate dramas by black authors, and which italicizes the universality of Wesley's subject: the American dream, examined from a black perspective. Frankie Sojourner, onetime Gents leader, owes a debt to Studs Lonigan, the Irish Catholic title character of James T. Farrell's Depression novel of another squandered youth, another wasted generation. Among fellow playwrights who came of age in the 1970s, Wesley has most in common with David Mamet, whose *American Buffalo* in many ways resembles *The Mighty Gents*. In both plays, might-have-been men cling to a past in which, briefly, they were somebody. In both, desperation ignites violent schemes to regain self-esteem in the eyes of a world where, as Frankie puts it, "The census don't count us and welfare don't even know we alive." More largely, each evaluates American society in our times and the standards we use to govern it.

—C. Lee Jenner

WHITE, Edgar Nkosi.

Born in Montserrat, West Indies, 4 April 1947. Brought to the United States in 1952. Educated at the City College, City University of New York, 1964–65; New York University, 1966–69, B.A.; Yale University School of Drama, New Haven, Connecticut, 1971–73; since 1992, the New York Theological Seminary. Playwright-in-residence, Yale University School of Drama, New Haven, Connecticut, New York Shakespeare Festival Joseph Papp Public Theater, 1971–72, and Cafe La Mama, New York, 1992; artistic director, Yardbird Players Company, New York, 1974–77. Recipient: New York State Council on the Arts grant, 1975; O'Neill award, 1977; Rockefeller grant, 1989. Agent: Helen Merrill, 361 West 17th Street, New York, New York 10011, U.S.A; and, Marion Boyars, 24 Lacy Road, London SW15 1NL, England.

Publications

PLAYS

The Mummer's Play (produced 1965). In *Underground*, 1970.
The Wonderful Yeare (produced 1969). In *Underground*, 1970.
The Figures at Chartres (produced 1969).
The Life and Times of J. Walter Smintheus (produced 1971). With *The Crucificado*, 1973.
The Burghers of Calais (produced 1971). In *Underground*, 1970.
Fun in Lethe; or, The Feast of Misrule (produced 1974). In *Underground*, 1970.
Underground: Four Plays. 1970.
Seigismundo's Tricycle: A Dialogue of Self and Soul (produced 1971).

Lament for Rastafari (produced 1971). In *Lament for Rastafari and Other Plays*, 1983.

Transformations: A Church Ritual (produced 1972).

The Crucificado (produced 1972). With *The Life and Times of J. Walter Smintheus*, 1973.

La Gente (produced 1973).

Ode to Charlie Parker (produced 1973).

Offering for Nightworld (produced 1973).

Les Femmes Noires (produced 1974). In *Redemption Song and Other Plays*, 1985.

The Pygmies and the Pyramid (produced 1976).

The Defense (produced 1976).

Trinity: The Long and Cheerful Road to Slavery (includes *Man and Soul, The Case of Dr. Kola, That Generation*) (produced 1982). In *Lament for Rastafari and Other Plays*, 1983.

Lament for Rastafari and Other Plays. 1983.

Like Them That Dream (produced 1988). In *Lament for Rastafari and Other Plays*, 1983.

The Nine Night (produced 1983). With *Ritual by Water*, 1984.

Ritual by Water (produced 1983). With *The Nine Night*, 1984.

Redemption Song (produced 1984). In *Redemption Song and Other Plays*, 1985.

The Boot Dance (produced 1984). In *Redemption Song and Other Plays*, 1985.

Ritual (produced 1985).

Redemption Song and Other Plays. 1985.

Moon Dance Night (produced 1987).

I Marcus Garvey (also director: produced 1992).

Live from Galilee (produced 1992).

OTHER

Sati, the Rastafarian (for children). 1973.

Omar at Christmas (for children). 1973.

The Yardbird Reader. 1973.

Children of Night (for children). 1974.

The Rising. 1988.

CRITICAL STUDIES: *The Drama of Nommo* by Paul Carter Harrison, 1972; *Drumbeats, Masks, and Metaphors: Contemporary Afro-American Theatre* by Genevieve Fabre, 1983.

Edgar Nkosi White comments:

My work mainly has to do with ritual. The central theme of my work is the business between man and God. My interest in theatre began with the church (African, Caribbean, American). I am at present studying for my Masters in Divinity at the New York Theological Seminary.

I am a very slow writer. I have no control over what direction my work, my interest, my craft will lead me. I also find myself falling in love with film. I am still a black writer. After 20 years of writing I am beginning to learn the craft. My perspective is global.

Edgar Nkosi White's drama is concerned with the black predicament within a predominantly white universe. And for him a black is a black whether he comes from Africa or the Caribbean, and he is even more so to the white man. His plays highlight the deprivation and hardship of the developing nations and the usual dreams of a better life in the developed nations. It is hardly surprising that migration, exile, and alienation are the central focus as he follows black exiles through their humiliations and disappointments in the cities of Europe and North America.

White's first collection of plays, *Underground*, contains *The Burghers of Calais*, *Fun in Lethe*, *The Mummer's Play* and *The Wonderful Yeare*. *The Burghers of Calais* deals with the wrongful conviction of the Scottsboro boys for rape. The play centres around Bagatelle and his mates in prison as their fate is thrown from one court to another without much hope for a reprieve. White here shows his concern with the manifest injustice which black people face. Of the four plays in the collection, this is the one with the largest focal range and is the one in which White is closest to his fellow victims of racism. The play's structure is very complex, displaying the playwright's bold experiments with dramatic form. Of especial interest is his application of a highly developed cinematic sensibility to create plays that very often challenge the audience's ability to integrate diverse material. His scenes are as varied as the huge canvas on which his characters conduct their complex relationships.

Fun in Lethe explores the theme of migration, exile, and alienation by dramatizing the journey of a West Indian poet through Great Britain. Harmatia represents the numerous "citizens of Empire" who return to claim their own piece of the "motherland" and his experience typifies the problems and disillusionment of the black son who stakes his claim on mother England. It is even worse for the pretentious ones like Harmatia and like Legion in *Redemption Song* who are writers trying to eke out a living through their craft in a very hostile environment. This play is typically a mishmash of characters, events, and ideas that though amusing aren't always effective structurally.

The Mummer's Play returns to an America described as "one large unflushed toilet." A note of impatient anger creeps into White's writing, a note which he retains, up to *Redemption Song*. The black victims, because they merely laze around and do nothing to help themselves, get sympathy neither from White nor from the audience. Here, as in other plays, White explores the various myths about West Indians and in the end he tries to explode some of them. When he looks at alienation in *Redemption Song*, *The Mummer's Play*, *The Wonderful Yeare*, and *The Boot Dance*, he does not simply blame America or Europe but also the victims who through an enervating anguish allow themselves to become alienated. And when he deals with migration and exile as he does in most of his plays, he seeks to expose the deeper structures of social inequality in Caribbean society which is responsible for the famed migratory consciousness of West Indians. And he does this well in *Redemption Song* as he follows Legion, the failed and alienated migrant who returns to his island only to face further alienation and subsequent death from the oppressors of Redemption City.

The Wonderful Yeare is set in a New York slum and deals with social deprivation among and petty racial jealousies between America's oppressed ethnic minorities. This deeply ironic play in which White shows his understanding of the lazzis and improvisation of the commedia dell' arte is about the "gift of life in the midst of death." Even as the plague rages, life goes on, and on a positive note, unlike White's other artists, Misserimus does something in the end—he marries Maria and goes to work.

White's second collection contains Lament for Rastafari, Like Them That Dream, and Trinity. Lament for Rastafari is structurally episodic and narrative continuity is maintained safely through characters. It is about the spiritual as well as physical journey of a West Indian family first to England and then to America. Lindsay, Barret, and Laputa, like White's other migrants and exiles, are driven by want and racial oppression to leave home and scour the cities of Europe and North America. In this play White begins his experiments with the West Indian dialect which we see in full flow in Redemption Song. Like Them That Dream is about Sparrow, a South African painter, who flees apartheid only to encounter it in other forms in America. In the end he has to make a choice, either to keep running or stand and confront apartheid head on. And it is only when he does the latter that he is able to appreciate the love and stability which Sharon offers him. The play is in many respects like The Boot Dance, which concerns Lazarus, another exile who in fleeing oppressive apartheid finds himself oppressed and powerless in an English mental asylum where only blacks are the inmates and the doctor is white. All in all, what emerges from this and other plays is White's extreme despairing vision of the black condition.

Trinity is a group of three plays—Man and Soul, which deals with the misunderstanding and antagonism between blacks from Africa and those from the West Indies, and also the racist law which lumps them together as criminals; The Case of Dr. Kola, which shows the idiocies of African governments and corrupt politicians, as well as the equally hopeless military men who replace them through coups; and finally, That Generation, which follows Wallace and Phyllis on the journey from a very comfortable life in the West Indies to one of penury and denigration in England. Again, a sense of despair pervades these plays since they are coloured by White's essential pessimism.

Les Femmes Noires displays all the characteristics of White's dramaturgy and, as he himself points out, it is "polyscenic" and was conceived as representing the "viewpoint of a blind man perceiving sound." The action progresses as if seen through the roving lens of a movie camera or the playing-out of sounds and motion in a dream as it follows the dreary lives, individual anguish, and fading hopes of a group of black women in New York City. However, the play is rescued from White's usual pessimism by the sisterly striving and support which these women offer to each other, and it is their basic humanity which survives.

White's plays suggest that each is a personal journey, and the central characters—often black artists struggling to survive in the unfriendly cities of Europe and North America—are projections of his own psyche which he probes in order to come to terms with his exile and alienation. His central characters are thus one person seen in different situations, sometimes speaking the same lines as in *Fun in Lethe* and *Lament for Rastafari* but always the exile. The plays capture White's lonely and restless search for meaning through their cinematic structure. It is this dialectic between content and form which makes White an interesting dramatist.

—Osita Okagbue

WHITE, John (Sylvester).

Born in Philadelphia, Pennsylvania, 31 October 1919. Educated at Gonzaga High School, Washington, D.C., 1933–37; University of Notre Dame, Indiana, 1937–41, A.B. in English 1941. Married Vasiliki Sarant in 1966. Actor for 25 years: charter member, Actors Studio, New York. Lives in Hawaii. Address: c/o Greenevine Agency, 9021 Melrose Avenue, Suite 304, Los Angeles, California 90069, U.S.A.

Publications

PLAYS

Twist (produced 1963).
Bugs (produced 1964). With *Veronica*, 1966.
Sand (produced 1964).
Veronica (produced 1965). With *Bugs*, 1966.
Bananas (produced 1968).
The Dog School (produced 1969).
Lady Laura Pritchett, American (produced 1969).
Mirage (produced 1969).
The Passing of Milldown Muldern (produced 1974).
Ombres (produced 1975).
Les Punaises (produced 1975).

SCREENPLAY: *Skyscraper*, 1959.

OTHER

Editor (American version), *Report from Palermo*, by Danilo Dolci. 1958.

MANUSCRIPT COLLECTION: Lincoln Center Library of the Performing Arts, New York.

THEATRICAL ACTIVITIES

ACTOR: **Plays**—as John Sylvester: roles in *Richard III*, 1943; *Sundown Beach* by Bessie Brewer, 1948; *Danny Larkin* by James V. McGee, 1948; *All You Need Is One Good Break* by Arnold Manoff, 1950. **Television**—Mr. Woodman in *Welcome Back, Kotter* series, 1975–79; roles in other television and radio plays.

John White comments:

(1973) Unless writing for hire, I write privately, from within, using for material the backwash of fifty years of existence, sometimes even living. I cannot work from the daily paper or the latest vogue. Indeed, I am turned off by the world. When I think about it, I can't write. I have been accused of being formless and have been applauded, on the other hand, for good form. I detest critics (in the main; there are a few splendid exceptions) and professional "knowers-how." Lonely is the word.

Though represented by professional productions of just one full-length and a few one-act plays, John White in the 1960s established himself as one of the freshest and most talented playwrights in America. Writing in a strikingly idiosyncratic style—the hallmark of any artist—he applied modern surrealism (less than absurdist, more than naturalist) to find a mythology in American roots. His small body of work is uneven—*Bugs* a good one-act play, *Veronica* a superlative one, and *Bananas* a prematurely produced full-length play that, with polishing, would have been a major work. But like too many playwrights producing in New York during this period, White was hurt by a powerful and ignorant fraternity of critics (it was an era when *Waiting for Godot*, *Entertaining Mr. Sloane*, and *The Homecoming* by Beckett, Orton, and Pinter were rejected). The playwright fled to Hollywood to seek a living wage at least. Ironically, the style that he plumbed has since become familiar (and therefore palatable) through the work of playwrights from Pinter to Sam Shepard.

Bugs (American vernacular for mad) is about a disturbed young man who has escaped from a hospital and returned to a home where things aren't much saner. His mother and girlfriend are respectively and insanely cheerful and stupid. His father, when not hidden behind a newspaper, is a ranting menace. Though the play might have been more, it gave clear promise of the author's specialness.

Veronica fulfilled the promise. Its central characters are a popular American songwriting team of the 1930s. They are holed up in a hotel room, trying desperately to repeat the huge success they had with a song called "Veronica." They are interrupted by a most peculiar burglar whose very philosophy of life, as it turns out, was inspired by the lyrics of that song.

These lyrics, in accurate satire of the period's popular music, spell out the passé, nostalgic, American dream as once advertised—a dream of beautiful blonds and money and trips to tropical islands. But has this sweet, silly dream now grown obsolete, only to be superseded by mundane social responsibility? One of the songwriters is too absorbed by war and disease to write again about June and moon. His partner is furious—"People haven't changed—a kiss is still a kiss, a sigh is still a sigh."

This yearning for a country once foolish and lovable—this choice of inno-cence over sophistication—was more deeply explored in the ambitious *Bananas*. The play is set in a period burlesque house during a rehearsal by three comics and an actress. A critic arrives. A series of sketches begins in which the author relates the techniques for burlesque to those of absurdism, suggesting that in a nostalgic, truthful-sardonic way, everything is bananas (another American slangword for madness, obviously White's view of exist-ence). As the play continues, the metaphor of a show as life changes from the burlesque theater to a modern television studio, but everyday conversation remains as a replica of dialogue we have heard on some stage, somewhere.

The idea is excellent and much of the technique is virtuosic, but the play was produced prematurely, and is ultimately confusing, though its argument seems clear enough—a preference for the innocence of actors, entertaining, over the hopeless attempts by intellectuals to make sense of life. Without being repetitious, White—like most fine playwrights—had from the start a consistency to his style and content.

But sadly, a start seems to be all that his playwriting career will have. Like too many in the brutal, competitive, business controlled, and mindlessly commercial and anti-artistic American theater, his sensitivity as a playwright seems to have been beaten down by senseless rejection and unappreciation.

—Martin Gottfried

WILDER, Thornton (Niven).

Born in Madison, Wisconsin, 17 April 1897. Educated at Thacher School, Ojai, California, 1912–13; Berkeley High School, California, graduated 1915; Oberlin College, Ohio, 1915–17; Yale University, New Haven, Connecticut, 1917, 1919–20, A.B. 1920; American Academy in Rome, 1920–21; Princeton University, New Jersey, 1925–26, A.M. 1926. Served in the US Coast Artillery Corps, 1918; served in the US Army Air Intelligence, rising to the rank of Lieutenant-Colonel, 1942–45: honorary M.B.E. (Member, Order of the British Empire), 1945. French teacher, 1921–25, and house master, 1927–28, Lawrenceville School, New Jersey; part-time lecturer in comparative literature, University of Chicago, 1930–36; visiting professor, University of Hawaii, Honolulu, 1935; Charles Eliot Norton professor of poetry, Harvard University, Cambridge, Massachusetts, 1950–51. U.S. Delegate: Institut de Coopération Intellectuelle, Paris, 1937, International PEN Club Congress, England, 1941, Unesco Conference of the Arts, Venice, 1952. Recipient: Pulitzer prize, for fiction, 1928, for drama, 1938, 1943; American Academy gold medal, 1952; Freedom Prize (Frankfurt), 1957; MacDowell medal, 1960; presidential medal of freedom, 1963; national medal for literature, 1965; national book award, for fiction, 1968. D. Litt.: New York University, 1930; Yale University, 1947; Kenyon College, Gambier, Ohio, 1948; College of Wooster, Ohio, 1950; Northeastern University, Boston, 1951; Oberlin College, 1952; University of New Hampshire, Durham, 1953; Goethe University, Frankfurt, 1957; University of Zurich, 1961; LL.D: Harvard University, 1951. Chevalier, Légion d'Honneur (France), 1951; member, Order of Merit (Peru); Order of Merit (Germany), 1957; honorary member, Bavarian Academy of Fine Arts; Mainz Academy of Science and Literature; member, American Academy. *Died 7 December 1975.*

Publications

PLAYS

St. Francis Lake. In *Oberlin Literary Magazine*, December 1915.
Flamingo Red. In *Oberlin Literary Magazine*, January 1916.

Brother Fire. In *Oberlin Literary Magazine*, May 1916.

A Christmas Interlude. In *Oberlin Literary Magazine*, December 1916.

The Walled City. In *Yale Literary Magazine.* April 1918.

In Praise of Guynemer. In *Yale Literary Magazine*, December 1918.

The Trumpet Shall Sound (produced 1926). In *Yale Literary Magazine*, October-December 1919, January 1920.

The Angel That Troubled the Waters and Other Plays (includes *Nascuntur Poetae; Proserpina and the Devil; Fanny Otcott; Brother Fire; The Penny That Beauty Spent; The Angel on the Ship; The Message and Jehanne; Childe Roland to the Dark Tower Came; Centaurs; Leviathan; And the Sea Shall Give Up Its Dead; Now the Servant's Name Was Malchus; Mozart and the Gray Steward; Hast Thou Considered My Servant Job?; The Flight into Egypt*). 1928.

The Long Christmas Dinner (produced 1931). In *The Long Christmas Dinner and Other Plays*, 1931; libretto for opera version, as *Das Lange Weihnachtsmahl*, music by Paul Hindemith (produced 1961), libretto published, 1961.

The Long Christmas Dinner and Other Plays in One Act (includes *Queens of France; Pullman Car Hiawatha; Love and How to Cure It; Such Things Only Happen in Books; The Happy Journey to Trenton and Camden*). 1931.

The Happy Journey to Trenton and Camden (produced 1931). In *The Long Christmas Dinner and Other Plays*, 1931; revised version, as *The Happy Journey*, 1934.

Such Things Only Happen in Books (produced 1931). In *The Long Christmas Dinner and Other Plays*, 1931.

Love and How to Cure It (produced 1931). In *The Long Christmas Dinner and Other Plays*, 1931.

Queens of France (produced 1932). In *The Long Christmas Dinner and Other Plays*, 1931.

Pullman Car Hiawatha (produced 1962). In *The Long Christmas Dinner and Other Plays*, 1931.

Lucrèce, from a play by André Obey (produced 1932). 1933.

A Doll's House, from a play by Ibsen (produced 1937).

Our Town (produced 1938). 1938.

The Merchant of Yonkers, from a play by Johann Nestroy, based on *A Well-Spent Day* by John Oxenford (produced 1938). 1939; revised version, as *The Matchmaker* (produced 1954), in *Three Plays*, 1957.

The Skin of Our Teeth (produced 1942). 1942.

Our Century (produced by 1947). 1947.

The Victors, from a play by Sartre (produced 1949).

Die Alkestiade (as *A Life in the Sun*, produced 1955; as *Die Alkestiade*, music by Louise Talma, produced 1962). 1960; as *The Alcestiad; or, A Life in the Sun*, with *The Drunken Sisters: A Satyr Play*, 1977.

Three Plays (includes *Our Town; The Skin of Our Teeth; The Matchmaker*). 1957.

Bernice (produced 1957).

The Wreck of the 5:25 (produced 1957).

The Drunken Sisters (produced 1970). 1957.

Infancy in *Plays for Bleecker Street* (produced 1962). 1960.
Childhood in *Plays for Bleecker Street* (produced 1962). 1961.
Someone from Assissi in *Plays for Bleecker Street* (produced 1962). 1961.
The Emperor (unfinished). In *The Journals 1939–1961*, 1985.

SCREENPLAYS: *We Live Again*, with others, 1934; *Our Town*, with Frank
Craven and Harry Chandlee, 1940; *Shadow of a Doubt*, with others, 1943.

NOVELS

The Cabala. 1926.
The Bridge of San Luis Rey. 1927.
The Woman of Andros. 1930.
Heaven's My Destination. 1934.
The Ides of March. 1948.
The Eighth Day. 1967.
Theophilus North. 1973.

OTHER

The Intent of the Artist, with others. 1941.
James Joyce 1882–1941. 1944.
Kultur in einer Demokratie. 1957.
Goethe und die Weltliteratur. 1958.
American Characteristics and Other Essays, edited by Donald Gallup. 1979.
The Journals 1939–1961 (includes unfinished play *The Emporium*), edited by
   Donald Gallup. 1985.

BIBLIOGRAPHY: *Wilder: A Bibliographical Checklist of Works by and About
Wilder* by Richard Goldstone and Gary Anderson, 1982.

CRITICAL STUDIES (a selection): *The Enthusiast: A Life of Thornton Wilder* by
Gilbert A. Harrison, 1983; *Thornton Wilder* by David Castronovo, 1986.

In a decade dominated by realistic domestic melodrama, Thornton Wilder was
one of the very few significant playwrights to resist the pull of verisimilitude,
the pretense of portraying real life on stage, in favor of the exploration of the
theatre's potential for universality and magic. From the openly experimental
one-act plays of the 1931 volume *The Long Christmas Dinner* through his
masterpieces *Our Town* and *The Skin of Our Teeth*, he exploited the drama's
plasticity of time and space, making full use of the ability of a stage scene to
represent any place, and for time to pass with the speed of an onstage
announcement or a programme note. And in a decade during which both
writers and audiences could be excused for lapsing into pessimism and doubt,
he affirmed, in commercially successful and entertaining plays, a faith in the
goodness of life and the value of humanity.

The one-act plays function almost as sketches for the longer works. In *The
Long Christmas Dinner*, Wilder manipulates time by condensing 90 years into
the table talk of a single meal, showing that an audience can be guided to

believe what it is told more than what it sees. *The Happy Journey to Trenton and Camden* and *Pullman Car Hiawatha* prove that a bare stage can appear filled with scenery if the audience is led by the dialogue to provide through imagination what is missing, and that the most ordinary events can be made to seem dramatically interesting if they are presented as such.

In *Our Town*, Wilder celebrates the intrinsic holiness of ordinary life by presenting a simple story of love, marriage, and death in totally unadorned fashion. As is well known (the play, a staple of the amateur and student repertories, is perhaps the most widely known of great American plays), it is played on an almost bare stage, with minimal furniture and the actors' mime replacing realistic sets. The fictional small town of Grover's Corners, New Hampshire, is described by a narrating Stage Manager who leads us through the growing up, falling in love, and marriage of the very ordinary George Gibbs and Emily Webb. The Stage Manager plays secondary parts, fills in narrative gaps, and controls the sequence of events to limit our focus to the bare essentials of the story and characters. All three devices—the absence of scenery, the deliberately uneventful plot, and the narrative manipulation— make what is shown seem important simply because it is all that *is* shown. Combined with Wilder's open and unembarrassed appeals to the emotions, most powerfully in the scenes after Emily's death, when she is allowed to revisit earth and realize the beauty she had overlooked while alive, these technical devices guide the audience to accept the play's assertion that the most mundane elements of everyday life are almost too precious and significant to be appreciated.

If *Our Town* disarms through the illusion of simplicity, *The Skin of Our Teeth* is meant to dazzle through the illusion of extraordinary complexity; but in fact the plays are technically similar in manipulating time and space to focus the audience's attention on universals. Mr. and Mrs. Antrobus are simul- taneously an ordinary suburban couple and also Adam and Eve, Noah and his wife, and the spirits of man- and womankind personified. By happily juggling these several levels (having Mr. Antrobus come home from a hard day at the office where he's been inventing the alphabet, for example, or setting Noah's Flood during a Lodge convention in Atlantic City), and while carefully keeping the thread of the narrative clear, Wilder dramatizes the continuity of the human experience, reminding us that the greatest accomplishments of myth and history were the products of people not unlike ourselves. And thus he can reassure us that, like our ancestors, we have the innate human capacity to survive any challenge, if only (as the title suggests) just barely.

Even the lesser comedy *The Merchant of Yonkers* (later revised as *The Matchmaker*, and even later the basis for the musical *Hello, Dolly!*) toys with stage realism through the pointed use of 19th-century conventions such as direct audience address and plot complications based on accident and coinci- dence. Its conclusion, that every life should contain a little adventure, but ultimately homely pleasures are best, reaffirms Wilder's celebration of the ordinary.

There is no "school of Wilder" among later American dramatists; the American stage was dominated by domestic realism for another 20 years or more before some playwrights of the 1960s rediscovered the pleasures of violating the conventions of realism through self-conscious theatricality, and

their inspiration was more likely Brecht and Beckett than Wilder. His importance lies in the plays themselves, affirmations of both theatrical imagination
and faith in humanity in accessible and effective popular art.

—Gerald Berkowitz

See the essay on *Our Town*.

WILLIAMS, Tennessee.

Born Thomas Lanier Williams in Columbus, Mississippi, 26 March 1911.
Educated at the University of Missouri, Columbia, 1929–31; Washington
University, St. Louis, 1936; University of Iowa, Iowa City, 1938, A.B. 1938.
Clerical worker and manual labourer, International Shoe Company, St. Louis,
Missouri, 1934–35; held various jobs, including waiter and elevator operator,
New Orleans, 1939; teletype operator, Jacksonville, Florida, 1940; worked at
odd jobs, New York, 1942, and as screenwriter for MGM, Hollywood, 1943;
full-time writer from 1944; distinguished writer-in-residence, University of
British Columbia, Vancouver, 1980. Recipient: American Academy gold
medal, 1969; New York Drama Critics Circle award, 1945, 1948, 1955,
1962; Sidney Howard award, 1945; Donaldson award, 1945, 1948; Pulitzer
prize, 1948, 1955; medal of freedom, 1980. L.H.D.: Harvard University,
Cambridge, Massachusetts, 1982. Member, American Academy, 1976. *Died
25 February 1983.*

Publications

PLAYS

Beauty is the Word (produced 1930). In *Missouri Review*, 7, 1984.
Cairo, Shanghai, Bombay!, with Doris Shapiro (produced 1935).
The Magic Tower (produced 1936).
Headlines (produced 1936).
Candles to the Sun (produced 1937).
Fugitive Kind (produced 1937).
Spring Song (produced 1938).
The Long Goodbye (produced 1940). In *27 Wagons Full of Cotton*, 1946.
Battle of Angels (produced 1940). 1945; revised version, as *Orpheus
    Descending* (produced 1957), with *Battle of Angels*, 1958; further revised
    version, 1976.
At Liberty (produced 1978). In *American Scenes*, edited by William Kozlenko,
    1941.
This Property is Condemned (produced 1942). In *27 Wagons Full of Cotton*,
    1946.
You Touched Me!, with Donald Windham, from the story by D.H. Lawrence
    (produced 1943). 1947.
The Glass Menagerie (produced 1944). 1945; revised version, 1970.
The Unsatisfactory Supper (produced 1986). In *Best One Act Plays of 1945*,
    1945.
27 Wagons Full of Cotton and Other One-Act Plays (includes *The*

Purification; *The Lady of Larkspur Lotion*; *The Last of My Solid Gold Watches*; *Portrait of a Madonna*; *Auto-da-Fé*; *Lord Byron's Love Letter*; *The Strangest Kind of Romance*; *The Long Goodbye*; *Hello from Bertha*; *This Property is Condemned*). 1946; augmented edition (also includes *Talk to Me Like the Rain and Let Me Listen*; *Something Unspoken*), 1953.

Portrait of a Madonna (produced 1946). In *27 Wagons Full of Cotton*, 1946.

The Last of My Solid Gold Watches (produced 1947). In *27 Wagons Full of Cotton*, 1946.

Lord Byron's Love Letter (produced 1947). In *27 Wagons Full of Cotton*, 1946; revised version, music by Raffaello de Banfield (produced 1955), 1955.

Auto-da-Fé (produced 1986). In *27 Wagons Full of Cotton*, 1946.

The Lady of Larkspur Lotion (produced 1947). In *27 Wagons Full of Cotton*, 1946.

The Purification (produced 1954). In *27 Wagons Full of Cotton*, 1946.

27 Wagons Full of Cotton (produced 1955). In *27 Wagons Full of Cotton*, 1946.

Hello from Bertha (produced 1961). In *27 Wagons Full of Cotton*, 1946.

The Strangest Kind of Romance (produced 1969). In *27 Wagons Full of Cotton*, 1946.

Moony's Kid Don't Cry (produced 1946). In *American Blues*, 1948.

Stairs to the Roof (produced 1947).

A Streetcar Named Desire (produced 1947). 1947.

Summer and Smoke (produced 1947). 1948; revised version, as *The Eccentricities of a Nightingale* (produced 1964), with *Summer and Smoke*, 1965; further revised version (produced 1976).

American Blues: Five Short Plays (includes *Moony's Kid Don't Cry*; *The Dark Room*; *The Case of the Crushed Petunias*; *The Long Stay Cut Short, or, The Unsatisfactory Supper*; *Ten Blocks on the Camino Real*). 1948.

Ten Blocks on the Camino Real. In *American Blues*, 1948; revised version, as *Camino Real* (produced 1953), 1953.

The Case of the Crushed Petunias (produced 1973). In *American Blues*, 1948.

The Dark Room (produced 1966). In *American Blues*, 1948.

The Rose Tattoo (produced 1951). 1951.

I Rise in Flame, Cried the Phoenix: A Play About D.H. Lawrence (produced 1959). 1951.

Something Unspoken (produced 1955). In *27 Wagons Full of Cotton*, 1953.

Talk to Me Like the Rain and Let Me Listen (produced 1958). In *27 Wagons Full of Cotton*, 1953.

Cat on a Hot Tin Roof (produced 1955). 1955; revised version (produced 1973), 1975.

Three Players of a Summer Game (produced 1955).

Baby Doll (screenplay). 1956.

Sweet Bird of Youth (produced 1956). 1959.

Period of Adjustment: High Point over a Cavern: A Serious Comedy (produced 1958). 1960.

The Fugitive Kind (screenplay), with Meade Roberts. 1958.

A Perfect Analysis Given by a Parrot (produced 1976). 1958.

The Enemy: Time. In *Theatre*, March 1959.

The Night of the Iguana (produced 1959; revised version, produced 1961). 1962.

To Heaven in a Golden Coach (produced 1961).

The Milk Train Doesn't Stop Here Anymore (produced 1962; revised versions, produced 1963, 1964, 1968). 1964.

The Mutilated (produced 1966). In *Esquire*, August 1965.

The Gnädiges Fräulein (produced 1966). In *Esquire*, August 1965; revised version, as *The Latter Days of a Celebrated Soubrette* (produced 1974).

Kingdom of Earth. In *Esquire*, February 1967; revised version, as *The Seven Descents of Myrtle* (produced 1968), published as *Kingdom of Earth (The Seven Descents of Myrtle)*, 1968; further revised version, in *Theatre 5*, 1976.

The Two-Character Play (produced 1967; revised version, produced 1969). 1969; revised version, as *Out Cry* (produced 1971), 1973; further revised version (produced 1974).

In the Bar of a Tokyo Hotel (produced 1969). 1969.

I Can't Imagine Tomorrow (televised 1970; produced 1976). In *Dragon Country*, 1970.

Confessional (produced 1970). In *Dragon Country*, 1970; revised version, as *Small Craft Warnings* (produced 1972), 1972.

The Frosted Glass Coffin (produced 1970). In *Dragon Country*, 1970.

Dragon Country: A Book of Plays (includes *In the Bar of a Tokyo Hotel*; *I Rise in Flame, Cried the Phoenix*; *The Mutilated*; *I Can't Imagine Tomorrow*; *Confessional*; *The Frosted Glass Coffin*; *The Gnädiges Fräulein*; *A Perfect Analysis Given by a Parrot*). 1970.

Tennessee Laughs: Three One-Act Plays (*Some Problems for the Moose Lodge*; *A Perfect Analysis Given by a Parrot*; *The Frosted Glass Coffin*) (produced 1980; revised version of *Some Problems for the Moose Lodge*, as *A House Not Meant to Stand*, produced 1981, revised version, 1982). *The Frosted Glass Coffin* and *A Perfect Analysis Given by a Parrot* in *Dragon Country*, 1970.

Senso, with Paul Bowles, in *Two Screenplays*, by Luigi Visconti, 1970.

A Streetcar Named Desire (screenplay), in *Film Scripts 1*, edited by George Garrett, O.B. Hardison, Jr., and Jane Gelfman, 1971.

The Theatre of Tennessee Williams:

1. *Battle of Angels; A Streetcar Named Desire; The Glass Menagerie.* 1972.
2. *The Eccentricities of a Nightingale; Summer and Smoke; The Rose Tattoo; Camino Real.* 1972.
3. *Cat on a Hot Tin Roof; Orpheus Descending; Suddenly Last Summer.* 1972.
4. *Sweet Bird of Youth; Period of Adjustment; Night of the Iguana.* 1972.
5. *The Milk Train Doesn't Stop Here Anymore; Kingdom of Earth*; revised version; *Small Craft Warnings; The Two-Character Play*, revised version. 1976.
6. *27 Wagons Full of Cotton and Other One Act Plays* (includes *The Unsatisfactory Supper; Steps Must Be Gentle; The Demolition Downtown: Count Ten in Arabic*). 1981.
7. *Dragon Country; Lifeboat Drill; Now the Cats with Jewelled Claws; Now the Peaceable Kingdom.* 1981.

The Red Devil Battery Sign (produced 1975; revised version, produced 1976). 1988.

Demolition Downtown: Count Ten in Arabic—Then Run (produced 1976). In *Theatre*, 6, 1981.

This is an Entertainment (produced 1976).

Vieux Carré (produced 1977). 1979.

Tiger Tail (produced 1978). With *Baby Doll* (screenplay), 1991.

A Lovely Sunday for Creve Coeur (as *Creve Coeur*, produced 1978; as *A Lovely Sunday for Creve Coeur*, produced 1979). 1980.

Lifeboat Drill (produced 1979). In *Theatre*, 7, 1981.

Some Problems for the Moose Lodge (produced 1980; revised versions, as *A House Not Meant to Stand*, produced 1981).

Steps Must Be Gentle: A Dramatic Reading (produced 1983). 1980.

Kirche, Küchen, und Kinder (produced 1980). 1981.

Clothes for a Summer Hotel (produced 1980). 1983.

Will Mr. Merriwether Return from Memphis? (produced 1980).

Something Cloudy, Something Clear (produced 1981).

The Notebook of Trigorin, from a play by Chekhov (produced 1981).

The Remarkable Rooming-House of Mme. Le Monde. 1984.

Stopped Rocking and Other Screenplays (includes *All Gaul is Divided; The Loss of a Teardrop Diamond; One Arm*). 1984.

SCREENPLAYS: *Senso* (*The Wanton Countess*; English dialogue, with Paul Bowles), 1949; *The Glass Menagerie*, with Peter Berneis, 1950; *A Streetcar Named Desire*, with Oscar Saul, 1951; *The Rose Tattoo*, with Hal Kanter, 1955; *Baby Doll*, 1956; *Suddenly Last Summer*, with Gore Vidal, 1959; *The Fugitive Kind*, with Meade Roberts, 1960; *Boom*, 1968; *All Gaul is Divided*, *The Loss of a Teardrop Diamond*, *One Arm*.

TELEVISION PLAYS: *Lord Byron's Love Letter*, 1953; *I Can't Imagine Tomorrow*, 1970; *Stopped Rocking*, 1975.

NOVELS

The Roman Spring of Mrs. Stone. 1950.

Moise and the World of Reason. 1975.

SHORT STORIES

One Arm and Other Stories. 1948.

Hard Candy: A Book of Stories. 1954.

Three Players of a Summer Game and Other Stories. 1960.

Grand. 1964.

The Knightly Quest: A Novella and Four Short Stories. 1967; augmented edition, as *The Knightly Quest: A Novella and Twelve Short Stories*, 1968.

Eight Mortal Ladies Possessed: A Book of Stories. 1974.

It Happened the Day the Sun Rose and Other Stories. 1982.

Collected Stories. 1985.

VERSE

Five Young American Poets, with others. 1944.
In the Winter of Cities. 1956.
Androgyne, Mon Amour. 1977.

OTHER

Memoirs. 1975.
Letters to Donald Windham 1940–1965, edited by Donald Windham. 1976.
Where I Live: Selected Essays, edited by Christine R. Day and Bob Woods.
   1978.
Conversations with Williams (interviews), edited by Albert J. Devlin. 1986.
Five O'Clock Angel: Letters to Maria St. Just, edited by Maria St. Just and Kit
   Harvey. 1990.

BIBLIOGRAPHIES: *The Critical Reputation of Tennessee Williams: A Reference
Guide* by John S. McCann, 1983; *Tennessee Williams: A Bibliography* (second
edition) by Drewey Wayne Gunn, 1991.

CRITICAL STUDIES (a selection): *Tennessee Williams* (second edition) by Signi
Falk, 1961; revised edition, 1978; *Tennessee Williams: The Man and His
Work* by Benjamin Nelson, 1961; *The Dramatic World of Tennessee Williams*
by Francis Donahue, 1964; *The Broken Worlds of Tennessee Williams* by
Esther Jackson, 1965; *Tennessee Williams and Friends* by Gilbert Maxwell,
1965; *Tennessee Williams* by Gerald Weales, 1965; *The Influence of D.H.
Lawrence on Tennessee Williams* by Norman J. Fedder, 1966; *Tennessee
Williams* by Christian M. Jauslin, 1969; *A Look at Tennessee Williams* by
Mike Steen, 1969; *Tennessee Williams* by Nancy M. Tischler, 1969; *Tennessee
Williams* by Carol Petersen, 1975; *Tennessee Williams: A Moralist's Answers
to the Perils of Life* by Ingrid Rogers, 1976; *Tennessee Williams and Film* by
Maurice Yacowar, 1977; *Tennessee Williams: A Collection of Critical Essays*
edited by Stephen S. Stanton, 1977; *Tennessee Williams: A Tribute* edited by
Jac Tharpe, 1977; *Tennessee Williams: The Tragic Tension* by Emmanuel B.
Asibong, 1978; *Tennessee Williams in Tangier* by Mohamed Choukri, 1979;
A Portrait of the Artist: The Plays of Tennessee Williams by Foster Hirsch,
1979; *Tennessee Williams* by Felicia H. Londré, 1979; *The Films of Tennessee
Williams* by Gene D. Phillips, 1980; *Tennessee Williams: An Intimate
Biography* by Dakin Williams and Shepherd Mead, 1983; *Tennessee Williams:
An Illustrated Chronicle*, edited by Margaret A.Van Antwerp and Sally Johns,
1984; *Tennessee Williams on File*, edited by Catherine Arnott, 1985;
Tennessee, Cry of the Heart by Dotson Rader, 1985; *The Kindness of
Strangers: The Life of Tennessee Williams* by Donald Spoto, 1985;
Conversations with Tennessee Williams by Albert J. Devlin, 1986; *Tennessee
Williams: An Intimate Memoir* by Dotson Rader, 1986; *Tennessee Williams:
A Portrait in Laughter and Lamentation* by Harry Rasky, 1986; *Tennessee
Williams: Modern Critical Views*, edited by Harold Bloom, 1987; *Tennessee
Williams* by Roger Boxill, 1987; *Tennessee Williams on the Soviet Stage* by
Irene Shaland, 1987; *Lost Friendships: A Memoir of Truman Capote,
Tennessee Williams, and Others* by Donald Windham, 1987; *Tennessee*

Williams' Plays: Memory, Myth and Symbol by Judith Thompson, 1987; *Evolving Texts: The Writing of Tennessee Williams* by Timothy D. Murray, 1988; *Tennessee Williams: Life, Work, Criticism* by Felicia Londré, 1989; *Costly Performances: Tennessee Williams: The Last Stage* by Bruce Smith, 1990.

The revitalisation of American drama begun by Eugene O'Neill was ably, if unevenly, continued by Tennessee Williams. The territory changed from O'Neill's New England and New York to the Deep South, but the theme of people tearing themselves and each other apart by the intensity of their passions survived.

Williams's work is best approached through his three most successful plays, *The Glass Menagerie*, *A Streetcar Named Desire* and *Cat on a Hot Tin Roof*. The first has a lyrical, sad gentleness that separates it from the savage cruelty of much of his later work. Its focus on the withdrawn, immature Laura, crippled emotionally as much as physically, shows the playwright's sympathetic insight into female psychology which, despite occasional sentimentalisation, is distinctive of Williams's dramas. Similarly, the use of the eponymous collection of fragile animal-models in the play establishes the delight in symbolism that in later plays is often overworked. The play is non-realistic in its sectionalised house-and-exterior set, in its use of lighting and music, and in the choric use of one character to stress that it is a "memory play".

A Streetcar Named Desire, grimmer altogether, resumes the theme of a woman's self-destructive urge for sexual fulfilment (again in a squalid urban environment suggested by a sectionalised house-and-street set), but this time the heroine is more ambivalently presented as partly the architect of her own destruction. Like Laura, Blanche DuBois has her fantasy world, which is symbolically suggested by her references to Belle Reve (beautiful dream), the old family plantation home. Unlike Laura, she has a sexual appetite which can be predatory and cruel—yet her vulnerable sensitivity is indisputable, and she too is the victim of others. Living dangerously near to the edge of sanity and dependent on "the kindness of strangers", Blanche is the first of a line of characters to protect themselves by "mendacity", a key word in *Cat on a Hot Tin Roof*.

Before this play, however, came three less successful works. In *Summer and Smoke*, Williams's debt to D.H. Lawrence is plain. Less frequently remarked upon is the similarity between many of Williams's characters and the "grotesques" who populate Sherwood Anderson's *Winesburg, Ohio* of 1919. *Summer and Smoke*, like Anderson's short stories, has problems in engaging our complete sympathy for, and comprehension of, these small-town misfits. *The Rose Tattoo*, a turbulently melodramatic celebration of the sexual vigour of Sicilian immigrants, has at least the dramatic robustness to give it a theatrical vitality which, like other Williams plays, transferred effectively to the cinema screen. *Camino Real* sustained his reputation for imaginatively exploring the possibilities of different dramatic idioms, but its expressionism, its laboured symbolism, its lack of realism, and its romanticisation of loneliness ended up bewildering or alienating its audiences.

Cat on a Hot Tin Roof is dedicated to Elia Kazan, who admired its "freedom and flexibility of form" but whose much-discussed influence on it (he directed it) was crucial. As Williams's most vivid excursion into the tensions of family life, it is tightly and more conventionally constructed, displaying a lively, if bitter, sense of humour and a powerful vitality. It balances skilfully the self-destructive stubborn inertia of Brick, the loner, against the sexual energy of his wife Maggie, the cat who stays on the hot tin roof by virtue of her indestructible tenacity. Her will to survive is as dynamic as that of her father-in-law, Big Daddy, who is fighting against terminal cancer and the internecine warfare and malice of his divided, larger-than-life family. Brick is Williams's first full-scale exploration of the homosexuality that was to figure increasingly in the later plays and in his own life. His readiness to rework his plays is exemplified by the alternative versions of the last act—his own and the Kazan-inspired one—however each is evaluated.

After *Cat on a Hot Tin Roof*, Williams concentrated more on the loners than on the family, and the Gothic element of Southern decadence that earned *Streetcar* its initial notoriety became more sensationally sinister. Sexual and other forms of perversity, including cannibalism in *Suddenly Last Summer* and castration in *Sweet Bird of Youth*, figured prominently, and what he once identified as "the passion for declivity" in human nature became paramount. Yet the obsession with cruelty, loneliness, depravity, desperation, and death in these plays is often Jacobean in intensity, feeling, and dramatic energy.

A compulsive writer, Williams also published poetry, short stories, and two novels (*The Roman Spring of Mrs. Stone* and *Moise and the World of Reason*), as well as a volume of *Memoirs* from which his personality emerges as more ebullient than the blackness of his plays might lead one to expect. Some of the fiction he subsequently dramatised, and a study of the non-dramatic work, can often illuminate the dramatist's personality, aims, and achievements. So, too, can the forewords and afterwords which abound. (*Camino Real* has one of each, which reward detailed comparison.) He also had an interesting habit of digressing, in his stage directions, into asides on his intentions.

Comparisons and contrasts with the work of Arthur Miller, whose career coincides with and in many ways complements Williams's, are inevitable. Setting *The Glass Menagerie* so squarely in the Depression of the 1930s seemed to prefigure the emphasis on social context more characteristic of Miller, but this area was not developed further. The afterword to *Camino Real* tries to explain the play's failure by a resentful distinction between "thinking playwrights" and "us who are only permitted to feel": the self-deprecatory emphasis on feeling did the play no good and also did the playwright a disservice, yet his work would have benefitted in many places from a tighter rein on emotionalism and a more rigorous self-discipline. The Williams canon, though larger than Miller's, lacks Miller's abiding urge to explore new subjects and new dramatic forms, showing instead a preference for re-examining a limited range of themes and styles. At his best, however, Williams achieved unforgettably powerful, resonant, and moving theatre.

—Dennis Welland

See the essay on *A Streetcar Named Desire.*

WILSON, August.

Born in Pittsburgh, Pennsylvania, 27 April 1945. Educated at Gladstone High School, Pittsburgh, 1960–61. Married Judy Oliver in 1981; one daughter. Founder, Black Horizons Theatre Company, Pittsburgh, 1968. Member, New Dramatists, New York. Recipient: Jerome fellowship, 1980; Bush fellowship, 1982; Rockefeller fellowship, 1984; McKnight fellowship, 1985; New York Drama Critics Circle award, 1985, 1987, 1988, 1992; Guggenheim fellowship, 1986; Whiting Foundation award, 1986; American Theatre Critics award, 1986, 1989, 1991; Outer Circle award, 1987; Drama Desk award, 1987; John Gassner award, 1987; Tony award, 1987; Pulitzer prize, 1987, 1990; Helen Hayes award, 1988; Los Angeles Drama Critics Circle award, 1988. Member, American Academy of Arts and Sciences. Agent (attorney): John Breglio, Paul Weiss Rifkind Wharton and Garrison, 1285 Avenue of the Americas, New York, New York 10019. Address: c/o Emily Kretschmer, Assistant, 1290 Grand Avenue, Suite 105, St. Paul, Minnesota 55101, U.S.A.

Publications

PLAYS

Black Bart and the Sacred Hills (produced 1981).
Jitney (produced 1982).
The Mill Hand's Lunch Bucket (produced 1983).
Ma Rainey's Black Bottom (produced 1984). 1985; with *Fences*, 1988.
Fences (produced 1985). 1986; with *Ma Rainey's Black Bottom*, 1988.
Joe Turner's Come and Gone (produced 1986). 1988.
The Piano Lesson (produced 1987; revised version produced 1990). 1990.
Two Trains Running (produced 1990).
Three Plays (includes *Ma Rainey's Black Bottom*, *Fences*, *Joe Turner's Come and Gone*). 1991.

August Wilson comments:

I write about the black experience in America and try to explore in terms of the life I know best those things which are common to all cultures. I see myself as answering James Baldwin's call for a profound articulation of the black experience, which he defined as "that field of manners and ritual of intercourse that can sustain a man once he has left his father's house." I try to concretize the values of the black American and place them on stage in loud action to demonstrate the existence of the above "field of manners" and point to some avenues of sustenance.

August Wilson is one of America's most significant playwrights. His acclaimed major works comprise his proposed cycle of dramas depicting African-American life in each decade of the 20th century. Cut off from their African roots due to the legacy of slavery, Wilson's black characters are often victims of racism and economic oppression. Feeling powerless to change their bleak condition, some even vent their frustrations on each other. Those able to reclaim their history and spirituality not only find a way to survive, but are inspired to challenge the injustices which plague their lives.

Set in a Pittsburgh boarding house in 1911, *Joe Turner's Come and Gone* portrays a man, Herald Loomis, in search of "his song"—that elusive element which would make his life meaningful. Seven years prior to his journey to Pittsburgh, Loomis lived in Tennessee with his wife and young daughter. Falsely jailed on a trumped-up charge, he was forced to work in one of the chain gangs run by the governor's brother. The years of hard labor broke Loomis's spirit. When released from jail, he finds his wife has left his daughter in the care of her mother. Loomis and his daughter travel to Pittsburgh ostensibly in search of his wife. However, a "conjure" man named Bynum shows him it is not the loss of his wife, but a lack of direction in his life which has been plaguing him. Despite the painful hardships he has endured, Loomis learns to look within himself to find the unique and life-affirming quality which will serve as the source of inspiration and guidance throughout the remainder of his years.

One of Wilson's few plays set outside of Pittsburgh, *Ma Rainey's Black Bottom* examines the consequence of black rage which can find no other outlet for expression except through violence. Set in Chicago in 1927, the play has less to do with the famed blues singer Gertrude "Ma" Rainey, than her studio band. Most of the musicians trade retorts and stories about life, while accepting the exploitation of their talents by whites as an inherent part of the entertainment business. A cocky but gifted young trumpeter, Levee, mistakenly believes he can break through the racial barriers which have prohibited his peers from reaping their rightful rewards. However, when rebuffed by the establishment he sought to join, he does not lash out at his oppressors. Instead, his wrath results in the death of one of his black musician colleagues. Thus, the playwright suggests black-on-black crime to be a direct result of the prevailing inequitable socio-economic system.

Set in 1936 in Pittsburgh, *The Piano Lesson* concerns the trials and tribulations a family endures over the legacy of a piano. As slaves in the mid-19th century, two members of the Charles family were exchanged by their owners, the Sutter family, for a piano. When the Sutters order one of the remaining members of the Charles family to carve decorations into the piano, the sculptor instead creates a memorial not only to those recently sold, but to his ancestors who survived from the middle passage to the present time. Stolen for the Sutter family by the grandsons of the sculptor, 80 years later the piano is now in the possession of Berniece, whose father was killed in retaliation for the theft. Two of the Charles descendants, Berniece and her brother Boy Willie, fight over the piano, not fully understanding its symbolic and emotional worth. Obsessed with the anguish suffered by her mother over the piano, Berniece fails to recognize the more important connection it has with her family's legacy. Boy Willie sees more value in the piano as a commodity to sell in order to purchase land. At play's end, the family is reconciled as each member comes to realize that the piano must remain as a living symbol of the family's painful, yet proud heritage.

Set in Pittsburgh in 1957, *Fences* tells the story of a garbage man named Troy Maxson and his family. A former player in the Negro baseball leagues, Troy had developed into a fine batter. However, he became embittered when the major leagues finally opened its door to black athletes and Troy, being past his prime, could not compete with younger players. In Pittsburgh, he married a woman named Rose who bore him a son, Cory. Troy found himself in a seemingly endless routine revolving around his work and familial responsibilities. He also recognized bitterly that he could not have purchased his house or adequately supported his family if it were not for the income supplements from his brother's disability checks. Thus, Troy understands that poverty and racism have kept him from achieving the American dream. His dissatisfaction with his life consequently leads Troy to betray his family through infidelity and a misguided sense of what is best for them. His ill-fated actions threaten to tear the family apart, while leaving deep emotional scars on those he loved the most. Through the play, Wilson teaches that blacks cannot survive on bitterness or thoughts of what should have been. Instead, blacks must learn that adaptation is the key to their survival. Indeed, it is this ability to adjust to new situations which has allowed African-Americans to endure horrific experiences.

Though set in the volatile 1960s, the great political and social upheaval of the times seem to have little effect on the characters of Wilson's more recent play, *Two Trains Running*. Set in Pittsburgh, the characters who pass through a diner owned by Memphis Lee enjoy spinning tales and appear to have a passive view of life. A frustrated and embittered man, Memphis struggles with his own feelings of self-worth as exemplified by the conflict he has with white city officials over the price offered for his home for an urban development project. Ironically, it is a mentally impaired handyman who first illustrates that one does not have to accept the role of being a victim in a racist society. For nine years, each day he demands the agreed payment of a ham for the painting of a butcher's fence. His refusal to acquiesce to the butcher's offering of a chicken as compensation inspires others finally to take a stand for their rights. With the added encouragement and wisdom of an ancient sage, Memphis is motivated to demand and acquire his just rewards from those formerly thought to be immovable, omnipotent opponents.

—Addell Austin Anderson

See the essay on *Fences*.

WILSON, Doric.

Born in Los Angeles, California, 24 February 1939. Studied with Lorraine Larson, Tri-Cities, Washington, 1955–58; apprenticed to Richland Players, Washington, 1952–58; attended University of Washington, Seattle, 1958–59. Founding member and playwright-in-residence, Barr/Wilder/Albee Playwrights Unit, New York, 1963–65; artistic director, Ensemble Project, New York, 1965–68; founding member and playwright-in-residence, Circle Repertory Company, New York, 1969–71; founding, artistic director, TOSOS Theatre Company, New York, 1973–77; playwright-in-residence, The Glines, New York, 1978–82, and Jerry West's Funtastic Shows, Portland, Oregon, 1983–84; director, New City Theatre Playwright's Workshop, Seattle, 1985. Since 1986 director and playwright-in-residence, Pioneer Square Theater, Seattle. Recipient: San Francisco Cable Car award, 1981; Chambers-Blackwell award, 1982; Villager award, 1983; Newsmaker award, 1984. Address: 506 9th Avenue, Apartment 3FN, New York, New York 10018, U.S.A.

Publications

PLAYS

And He Made a Her (produced 1961).
Babel, Babel, Little Tower (produced 1961).
Now She Dances! (produced 1961; revised version produced 1975).
Pretty People (produced 1961).
In Absence (produced 1968).
It Was a Very Good Year (produced 1970).
Body Count (produced 1971).
The West Street Gang (also director: produced 1977). In *Two Plays*, 1979.
Ad Hoc Committee (produced 1978).
Surprise (produced 1978).
Turnabout (as Howard Aldon) (produced 1979).
A Perfect Relationship (produced 1979). In *Two Plays*, 1979.
Forever After: A Vivisection of Gaymale Love, Without Intermission (also director: produced 1980). 1980.
Street Theater: The Twenty-Seventh of June, 1969 (produced 1981). 1983.

MANUSCRIPT COLLECTION: Lincoln Center Library of the Performing Arts, New York.

CRITICAL STUDIES: introduction by William M. Hoffman to *Gay Plays*, 1979; *Lavender Culture* by Karla Jay and Allen Young, 1979: "Caffe Cino" by Wilson, in *Other Stages*, 8 March 1979; interview with Robert Chesley, in *Advocate*, 5 April 1979; "Gay Plays, Gay Theatre, Gay Performance" by Terry Helbing, in *Drama Review*, March 1981.

THEATRICAL ACTIVITIES

DIRECTOR: Plays—many productions in New York, including *The Madness of Lady Bright* by Lanford Wilson, 1974; *The Hostage* by Brendan Behan, 1975; *What the Butler Saw* by Joe Orton, 1975; *Now She Dances!*, 1976; *The West Street Gang*, 1977; *Forever After*, 1980.

Doric Wilson is a quintessentially urban dramatist who grew up in rural Washington State but lived in New York City for more than two decades. He specializes in stylish farce, ironic comedy of wit, and urbane satire. His combination of fantasy and whimsy and his intellectual dialectic may suggest the touch of a Giraudoux or a Shaw, a Wilder or a Wycherley. Yet underlying his often caustic comedy is a surprisingly romantic sensibility which finds him subtly rooting for happy ever afters.

And He Made a Her (1961) may have been the first play written specifically for Caffe Cino—and therefore for off-off-Broadway. Like many of the Cino writers, Wilson is gay, and, after stints as an original member of both the

Barr/Wilder/Albee Playwrights Unit and the Circle Repertory Company, in 1973 he formed the first professional gay company, TOSOS (The Other Side of Silence), which he founded with his income as a bartender.

Wilson excels at accurate observation of life, particularly gay life, which he satirizes but with which he also sympathizes. He was the first to write openly about gay characters who are neither sick nor miserable. Although he dislikes the word "gay," this is a linguistic rather than a political stance. A pioneer in his efforts to write about gay subjects and produce for gay audiences, Wilson has been a leader among up-front homosexuals combating gay self-hatred, and his sharpest satire is reserved for homophobes, whether straight or gay. Wilson's plays speak particularly to gay spectators, but they promote tolerance, affection, honesty, and understanding among people of any sexuality.

Wilson's work is characterized by its playfulness, its fantasy, and its feminism. *And He Made a Her*, for example, dramatizes the displeasure among Adam and the angels caused by Eve's creation. The angelic host—including one described as "of liberal size and liberal party but not left winged enough to fly—or fall—with Lucifer"—worry about Eve, who's disturbing the natural animosity of the animals, domesticating the plants, and intent upon reproduction. Clearly superior to Adam, she provokes amazement "that woman is able to look up at someone shorter than she is." More surprising, perhaps, as early as 1961 is Wilson's substitution—for the response "Amen"—of "A Women." Other early Wilson one-acts which exemplify these characteristics are his satire of narcissism *Pretty People*, set in a museum displaying live people, and the political satire *Babel, Babel, Little Tower*, in which the narcissists are warmongers and religious freaks from several historical periods.

Although these early Wilson plays are not specifically gay in subject, another piece from that period which is concerned with homosexuality has been expanded into a full-length play. *Now She Dances!* comments upon both Oscar Wilde's imprisonment and contemporary America by dramatizing the Salome story according to the dramatic conventions of *The Importance of Being Earnest*. As Lane the butler ("with excellent references from another play") puts it, *Now She Dances!* gives us "farce fencing force over tea." In both versions, Lady Herodias's daughter, Miss Salome, demands and finally receives a man's head on a tray covered with a tea cozy; in the full-length version the word "head" is subject to double entendre which may go over the heads of some. In the original, Wilde is the prisoner, and he won't come out of the closet; in the rewrite, the prisoner is an unashamed and clever contemporary American homosexual whom Salome tries to seduce. The words she speaks as she unbuttons her bodice typify Wilson's simultaneous accomplishment of more than one objective: "In years to come, when you talk of this, and you will, be kind."

Those famous lines directed, in Robert Anderson's *Tea and Sympathy*, toward a boy who is sympathetic because he is *not* gay, serve as implicit critique of years of theatrical treatment of the homosexual, who, until recently, is usually ignored or despised or pitied. Wilson hardly misses an opportunity to mix in comments on the theatre with his wider political satire. Among jabs at animal symbols of women (seagull, wild duck), Actors Studio nonsense about an actress who plays a maid "identifying" with the soup she's serving, and tedious first scenes ("a lovely bouquet of blue expositions"), Wilson spoofs gay dramatists such as Genet and Wilde who do not give us a reasonable facsimile of the life thousands of homosexuals actually live.

In *Street Theater*, his play about the hours preceding the Stonewall riots (which gave birth to the gay rights movement), Wilson mocks the self-contemptuous pair from *The Boys in the Band* and a closet queen as well as the heterosexual mobster bar owner who exploits his "queer" customers and a couple of Vice Squad cops, one of whom arrests the other. Set on the street near the Stonewall gay bar, this comedy offers politically provocative wit plus an array of New York homosexuals deftly characterized and suggests what sort of homophobic treatment prompted them to turn on their tormentors in revolt.

Another treatment of the street-bar scene by one of its own aficionados is *The West Street Gang*, which likewise dramatizes the victimization of gays by homophobes, opportunists, and each other. Set in a downtown west-side leather bar, it was also performed in one (the Spike). It shows the bar's patrons threatened by a gang of teenage fag bashers of the type who regularly try to murder gays with baseball bats and tire chains. Their efforts at self-protection are led by a transvestite and are hampered by a so-called gay rights leader, by Arthur Klang (a thinly disguised Arthur Bell of the *Village Voice*), and Bonita Aryant (a still more thinly disguised Anita Bryant, then waging a nationwide anti-homosexuality crusade). *The West Street Gang* offers more than just appropriate politics. It's a hilarious treatment of some familiar New Yorkers, who turn out to be more than mere stereotypes. There's the hustler who gets rolled, the pacifist who urges violence, and, best of all, the drag queen who leads the fight against the marauding street gang. "She" initially follows the butch dress code on her entrance, then heads for the head and simpers back on in a dress. Whether hero or heroine, she stands up very well not only to the homophobic cops and bar owner and to Bonita (who mistakes the bar's patrons for longshoremen) but to her less than broadminded gay fellow bar patrons. Indeed, the varied characters lead us to conclude that tolerance, cooperation, and mutual respect are the qualities Wilson most admires.

Among his domestic love stories, *Turnabout* is one of several Wilson satires of straight relationships; *A Perfect Relationship* depicts the friendship of two men who don't recognize that they ought to be lovers; and *Forever After* is both a romantic comedy and a parody of same.

Written under the pseudonym "Howard Aldon" *Turnabout* is a suburban sit com in which a wife teaches her adulterous husband a lesson without actually sleeping with other men. A play in which non-stop one-liners compete with very funny situations as sources of humor, *Turnabout* devastates the complacent husband's double standard. It demonstrates Wilson's capacity for exactly the sort of heterosexual commercial comedy with which he could regale Broadway if he weren't more interested in a different kind of dramaturgy. He has, however, written several other satires of heterosexual relations, including *In Absence, It Was a Very Good Year, Body Count*, and *Surprise*.

In *A Perfect Relationship* the protagonists, Ward and Greg, are roommates whose lifestyle is built upon a commitment to non-commitment. Both thrive on cruising, which Greg practices at discos and Ward at backroom bars. Although they aren't lovers, they bicker as though they were—over who does the laundry, or cooks dinner, or takes the first shower. They even keep score, as though it were an organized sport, while denigrating each other's masculinity. They have a "perfect" relationship until both sleep with the same trick, a young opportunist who uses this one-night stand to acquire Ward and Greg's desirable Christopher Street apartment. Along the way to discovering that they ought to be lovers, Ward and Greg deal with the kooky heterosexual woman from whom they are subletting. She and her boyfriends behave as though they're at a zoo and the young men are the animals, yet her preconceptions about gays aren't much sillier than their own. Although she outdoes them in promiscuous non-involvement, she helps the roommates to recognize that they share a lot more than the rent.

The kind of love story which Wilson writes in *A Perfect Relationship* he sets out to parody in *Forever After*, yet he maintains an effective tension in the latter between amusement at romanticism and acceptance of long-term commitment between men. Tom and David's amorous remarks are jeered by two mocking muses in drag seated in proscenium boxes. Actually it's Melpomene, the tragic muse, who sets out to destroy the affair. It is her descent into the fray to coach the lovers in suspicion and disharmony which prompts the comic muse Thalia to follow and defend the playwright's prerogative to give the young men a happy-ever-after conclusion. Something of a descendant of Sheridan's *The Critic* or the Duke of Buckingham's *The Rehearsal*, *Forever After* mixes presentational and representational styles while lampooning such theatrical targets as Sam Shepard's *Buried Child*, Martin Sherman's *Bent*, Edward Albee's *The Lady from Dubuque*, Robert Patrick's *T-Shirts*, general negativity in drama, and the claims made by performers in gay plays that they're straight. The particular object of Wilson's wrath—and wisecracks— however, is melodramas in which the homosexual is a tormented degenerate.

Wilson's ear for the varieties of gay attitudes, jargon, and quips is as good as ever in *Forever After*, and his penchant for punning is true to his best form. The dialogue is among his most raunchy and real. As to his appraisal of the dispute between the muses, Wilson shares Thalia's views; he sees the funny and playful side of everything, including love, but on the subjects of human relations and aesthetics he's no cynic. Although *Forever After* demonstrates it's easier to fight than to sustain a relationship, Wilson sets us to cheering those who succeed at commitment.

—Tish Dace

WILSON, Lanford (Eugene).

Born in Lebanon, Missouri, 13 April 1937. Educated at Ozark High School, Missouri; Southwest Missouri State College, Springfield, 1955–56; San Diego State College, California, 1956–57; University of Chicago, 1957–58. Worked at various jobs, and in advertising, Chicago, 1957–62; director, actor, and designer for Caffe Cino and Cafe La Mama theatres, New York, and other theatres. Since 1969 co-founder and resident playwright, Circle Repertory Company, New York. Recipient: Rockefeller grant, 1967, 1974; Vernon Rice award, 1968; ABC-Yale University fellowship, 1969; New York Drama Critics Circle award, 1973, 1980; Obie award, 1973, 1975, 1983; Outer Circle award, 1973; American Academy award, 1974; Drama-Logue award,

1978, 1979; Pulitzer Prize 1980; Brandeis University Creative Arts award
1981. Agent: Bridget Aschenberg, International Creative Management, 40
West 57th Street, New York, New York 10019. Address: c/o Hill and Wang,
19 Union Square West, New York, New York 10003, U.S.A.

Publications

PLAYS

So Long at the Fair (produced 1963).

No Trespassing (produced 1964).

Home Free! (also director: produced 1964). In *Balm in Gilead and Other Plays*, 1965; with *The Madness of Lady Bright*, 1968.

Balm in Gilead (produced 1964). In *Balm in Gilead and Other Plays*, 1965.

The Madness of Lady Bright (also director: produced 1964). In *The Rimers of Eldritch and Other Plays*, 1967; with *Home Free!*, 1968.

Ludlow Fair (produced 1965). In *Balm in Gilead and Other Plays*, 1965.

Balm in Gilead and Other Plays. 1965.

Sex Is Between Two People (produced 1965).

The Rimers of Eldritch (also director: produced 1965). In *The Rimers of Eldritch and Other Plays*, 1967.

This is the Rill Speaking (also director: produced 1965). In *The Rimers of Eldritch and Other Plays*, 1967.

Days Ahead (produced 1965). In *The Rimers of Eldritch and Other Plays*, 1967.

The Sand Castle (produced 1965). In *The Sand Castle and Three Other Plays*, 1970.

Wandering: A Turn (produced 1966). In *The Rimers of Eldritch and Other Plays*, 1967.

The Rimers of Eldritch and Other Plays. 1967.

Miss Williams: A Turn (produced 1967).

Untitled Play, music by Al Carmines (produced 1967).

The Gingham Dog (produced 1968). 1969.

The Great Nebula in Orion (produced 1970). In *The Great Nebula in Orion and Three Other Plays*, 1973.

Lemon Sky (produced 1970). 1970.

Serenading Louie (produced 1970). 1976; revised version (produced 1984), 1984.

The Sand Castle and Three Other Plays (includes *Wandering, Stoop: A Turn, Sextet (Yes): A Play for Voices*). 1970.

Sextet (Yes): A Play for Voices (produced 1971). In *The Sand Castle and Three Other Plays*, 1970.

Summer and Smoke, music by Lee Hoiby, adaptation of the play by Tennessee Williams (produced 1971). 1972.

Ikke, Ikke, Nye, Nye, Nye (produced 1971). In *The Great Nebula in Orion and Three Other Plays*, 1973.

The Family Continues (produced 1972). In *The Great Nebula in Orion and Three Other Plays*, 1973.

The Great Nebula in Orion and Three Other Plays (includes *Ikke, Ikke, Nye, Nye, Nye; The Family Continues; Victory on Mrs. Dandywine's Island*). 1973.

The Hot l Baltimore (produced 1973). 1973.
The Mound Builders (produced 1975). 1976.
Brontosaurus (produced 1977). 1978.
5th of July (produced 1978). 1979.
Talley's Folly (produced 1979). 1980.
Bar Play, in *Holidays* (produced 1979).
Talley and Son (as *A Tale Told*, produced 1981; revised version, as *Talley and Son*, produced 1985). 1986.
Angels Fall (produced 1982). 1983.
Thymus Vulgaris (produced 1982). 1982.
Three Sisters, adaptation of a play by Chekhov (produced 1985; revised version produced 1992).
Say deKooning (produced 1985). In *Hall of North American Forests*, 1988.
Sa-Hurt? (produced 1986).
A Betrothal (produced 1986). In *Hall of North American Forests*, 1988.
Burn This (produced 1987). 1988.
Dying Breed (produced 1987).
A Poster of the Cosmos (produced 1987).
Hall of North American Forests (includes *The Bottle Harp*, *Say deKooning*, *A Betrothal*) (produced 1987). 1988.
The Moonshot Tape (produced 1990).
Redwood Curtain (produced 1992).
Eukiah (produced 1992).

SCREENPLAYS: *One Arm*, 1970; *Burn This*, 1992; *Talley's Folly*, 1992.

TELEVISION PLAYS: *The Migrants*, from a story by Tennessee Williams, 1974; *Taxi!*, 1979.

BIBLIOGRAPHY: *Ten Modern American Playwrights* by Kimball King, 1982.

THEATRICAL ACTIVITIES

DIRECTOR: **Plays**—many of his own plays, including *Home Free!*, 1964; *The Madness of Lady Bright*, 1964; *The Rimers of Eldritch*, 1965; *This Is the Rill Speaking*, 1965; *Indecent Exposure* by Robert Patrick, 1968; *Not to Worry* by A.E. Santaniello, 1975; *In Vienna* by Roy London, 1980. Actor: **Plays**—in *The Clown*, 1968; *Wandering*, 1968; *Him* by E.E. Cummings, 1974.

Lanford Wilson's plays are deeply concerned with the conflict between the traditional values of the past and the insidious pressures of modern life. While he has been only intermittently successful at resolving this conflict, it has provided him with dramatic material of great variety and interest. The eccentric characters of *Balm in Gilead* and *The Madness of Lady Bright* fight or flee convention, and their desperation is sharply and sympathetically drawn. *The Rimers of Eldritch* or *This Is the Rill Speaking* ridicule the hypocrisy, bigotry, and convention of a small town while they rejoice in the confused innocence and energy of its adolescents. These "collage" plays, in which different strands of dialogue interweave, scenes overlap, and actors double their roles, allowed Wilson deftly to juxtapose the rooted strengths and values of the old with the energy and explorations of the young.

Wilson's experiments with the collage style resolved themselves in *The Hot l Baltimore*, set in a deteriorating flophouse (whose sign has lost its "e") peopled by whores, retirees, outcasts, and deadbeats. At the Hotel Baltimore, however, it is the old who have rejected convention, and the young Girl who fights to recover the past. This callgirl is as dismayed that no one will fight to save the hotel—"That's why nothing gets done anymore. Nobody's got the conviction of their passions"—as she is furious that a young stranger gives up the search for his grandfather too easily. More naturalistic than earlier plays, *The Hot l Baltimore* uses a clear and simple prose and the physical symbol of the hotel to focus on Wilson's basic concerns.

Wilson's trilogy about the Talley family again used buildings as the symbol of an emotional and social conflict between past and present. *5th of July*, set in the present, reunites the scattered Talleys: Aunt Sally Talley, her nephew Ken and his homosexual lover, and Sally's niece June and her illegitimate daughter. Since Ken (whose legs were paralyzed in Vietnam) and June are offering the house to two old friends who were fellow radicals in the 1960s, the play was frequently described as an evaluation of the decade's politics. However, the politics are not deeply felt, and quickly become secondary to the sale of the house, which comes to represent the rejection of the family's roots in favor of a future they don't want or like. *Talley and Son* (set in World War II but the last play to be written) hinges on the struggle between Sally Talley's father and grandfather over control of the family business. While this play was excessively (and clumsily) complex, *Talley's Folly* (whose action is concurrent with that of *Talley and Son*) concerns the elegantly compact and dramatically clear court-ship of Sally Talley by a New York lawyer, Matt Friedmann. Described as "a valentine" by Matt (who frequently and non-naturalistically addresses the audience), the play unites tradition and progress through Matt's warm, obsti-nately honest, and ultimately successful wooing of Sally.

While *Talley's Folly* avoided topical issues to its benefit, *Angels Fall* used an accident at a nearby nuclear plant to trap characters in a small Catholic church (compare *Bus Stop*). Parallelling a young, intelligent Navaho's rejection of his responsibility to his community with an art historian's sudden and violent rejection of his life's work, the play's pretext seems gratuitous and its resol-ution of the characters' spiritual crises mechanical.

A talented craftsman of dialogue, Wilson often fails to weld his situations seamlessly to his deepest concerns. However, when his primary values—honesty and the love of friends, family, and home—are tied closely to his dramatic situations his plays enact crucial questions about how the fabric of society is woven and cared for over generations.

—Walter Bode

WILSON, Robert M.

Born in Waco, Texas, 4 October 1941. Educated at the University of Texas, Austin, 1959–62; Pratt Institute, Brooklyn, New York, 1962–65, B.F.A. 1965; studied painting with George McNeil, Paris, 1962; apprentice in architecture to Paolo Soleri, Acrosanti community, Phoenix, Arizona, 1966. Since 1970 artistic director, Byrd Hoffman Foundation, New York; frequent lecturer at seminars and workshops from 1970. Artist: individual shows since 1971.

Recipient: Best Foreign Play award (France), 1970; Guggenheim fellowship, 1971, 1980; Drama Desk award, for directing, 1971; Obie award, for directing, 1974, 1986; Rockefeller fellowship, 1975, and award, 1981; Maharam award, for design, 1975; BITEF, Belgrade Grand prize, 1977; Lumen award, for design, 1977; French Critics award, for musical theatre, 1977, for best foreign play, 1987; German Critics award, 1979; Der Rosenstrauss, Munich, 1982; Harvard University citation, 1982; San Sebastian Film Festival award, 1984; Berlin Theatre Festival award, 1984, 1987; Malaga Theatre Festival Picasso award, 1986; Boston Theatre Critics Circle award, 1986; Skowhegan medal, for drawing, 1986; Bessie award, 1987; American Theatre Wing Design award, for noteworthy unusual effects, 1987; Mondello award, Palermo, 1988; The American Institute of Architects honor, 1988; New York Public Library Lion of the Performing Arts, 1989; São Paulo great prize, for best event, 1989; Italian Theatre Critics award, 1989; Barcelona Festival of Cinema Art grand prize, for video, 1989; Paris Film Festival special mention, for video, 1989; German Theatre Critics award, 1990. Address: Byrd Hoffman Foundation, 131 Varick Street, Number 908, New York, New York 10013, U.S.A.

Publications

PLAYS

Dance Event (produced 1965).
Solo Performance (produced 1966).
Theater Activity (produced 1967).
ByrdwoMAN (produced 1968).
Alley Cats (produced 1968).
Watermill (produced 1969).
The King of Spain (produced 1969). In *New American Plays 3*, edited by William M. Hoffman, 1970.
The Life and Times of Sigmund Freud (produced 1969).
Deafman Glance (produced 1970).
Program Prologue Now, Overture for a Deafman (produced 1971).
Overture (produced 1972).
Ka Mountain and GUARDenia Terrace: A Story about a Family and some People Changing (produced 1972).
King Lyre and Lady in the Wasteland (produced 1973).
The Life and Times of Joseph Stalin (produced 1973).
Dia Log/A Mad Man a Mad Giant a Mad Dog a Mad Urge a Mad Face (produced 1974).
The Life and Times of Dave Clark (produced 1974).
"Prologue" to A Letter for Queen Victoria (produced 1974).
A Letter for Queen Victoria (produced 1974). 1974.
To Street (produced 1975).
The $ Value of Man (produced 1975).
Dia Log, with Christopher Knowles (produced 1975).
Spaceman, with Ralph Hilton (produced 1976).
Einstein on the Beach, music and lyrics by Philip Glass (produced 1976). 1976.
I Was Sitting on My Patio This Guy Appeared I Thought I Was Hallucinating (produced 1977). 1978.

Dia Log/Network, with Christopher Knowles (produced 1978).
Overture to the Fourth Act of Deafman Glance (produced 1978).
Death, Destruction, and Detroit (produced 1979). 1978.
Dia Log/Curious George, with Christopher Knowles (produced 1979).
Edison (produced 1979).
The Man in the Raincoat (produced 1981).
Medea, with Gavin Bryars (produced 1981).
Great Day in the Morning, with Jessye Norman (produced 1982).
The Golden Windows (produced 1982). 1982.
the CIVIL warS: *a tree is best measured when it is down* (sections produced
    1983; with Heiner Müller, 1984; with Maita di Niscemi, 1984; with *The
    Knee Plays*, music and lyrics by David Byrne, 1984). Sections published
    1983, 1984; with *The Knee Plays*, with David Byrne, 1984; with Heiner
    Müller, 1985.
King Lear (produced 1985).
Readings (produced 1985).
Alcestis, adaptation of the play by Euripides, with Heiner Müller (produced
    1986). 1987.
Death, Destruction, and Detroit II (produced 1987).
Parzival, with Tankred Dorst (produced 1988). 1987.
Cosmopolitan Greetings (book only), music by Rolf Liebermann and George
    Gruntz, text by Allen Ginsberg (produced 1988).
The Forest (book only), music by David Byrne, text by Heiner Müller and
    Darryl Pinckney (produced 1988). 1988.
De Materie, music by Louis Andriessen (produced 1989).
Orlando, adaptation of the novel by Virginia Woolf, text by Darryl Pinckney
    (produced 1989).
The Black Rider: The Casting of Magic Bullets, music and lyrics by Tom
    Waits, text by William S. Burroughs (produced 1990).

SCREENPLAY: *Overture for a Deafman*, 1971.

VIDEO: *Spaceman*, with Ralf Hilton, 1976; *Video 50*, 1978; *Deafman Glance*,
1981; *Stations*, 1982; *La Femme à la Cafetière*, 1989; *The Death of King Lear*,
1989.

RECORDINGS: *The Life and Times of Joseph Stalin*, 1973; *Einstein on the
Beach*, music and lyrics by Philip Glass, 1979; *the CIVIL warS: Knee Plays*,
music and lyrics by David Byrne, 1985.

MANUSCRIPT COLLECTION: Rare Book and Manuscript Library, Columbia
University, New York.

CRITICAL STUDIES (selection): *The Theatre of Visions: Robert Wilson* by Stefan
Brecht, 1979; *Robert Wilson: The Theater of Images* edited by Craig Nelson,
1980, revised edition, 1984; *Robert Wilson and His Collaborators* by
Laurence Shyer, 1990.

THEATRICAL ACTIVITIES

DIRECTOR AND DESIGNER: **Plays**—all his own plays; *American Hurrah* by Jean-
Claude van Itallie, 1966 (design only); *A Letter to Queen Victoria*, 1974;

Hamletmachine by Heiner Müller, 1986; *Quartet* by Heiner Müller, 1987 ; *Swan Song* by Chekhov, 1989; *King Lear* by Shakespeare, 1990; *When We Dead Awaken*, adaptation of the play by Ibsen, 1991. Opera—*Medée* by Marc-Antoine Charpentier, 1984; *Alceste* by C.W. Gluck, 1986; *Salome* by Richard Strauss, 1987; *Le Martyre de Saint Sebastian* by Claude Debussy (choreographed with Suzushi Hanayagi), 1988; *Doktor Faustus*, adaptation of the novel by Thomas Mann, music by Giacomo Manzoni, 1989; *La Nuit d'avant le jour*, 1989; *Parsifal* by Richard Wagner, 1991. Films—*The House*, 1963; *Slant*, 1963; *Overture for a Deafman*, 1971.

Robert M. Wilson is an atypical dramatist in that he composes with pictures rather than words, and creates through directing his works (few of which have been published) on the stage. Early productions with his Byrd Hoffman School of Byrds (named after Wilson's dance therapist) had affinities with the 1930s surrealists. Drama therapy work with a deaf mute, and a man with severe brain damage, showed that one picked up sounds in the form of vibrations or "interior impressions," while the other created a "graphic" logic from the aural shape of words independent of conventional sense.

Wilson's "performance pieces" express this "autistic" perception of the world, from his first, relatively simple piece—*Deafman Glance* which formed part of the epic *Ka Mountain and GUARDenia Terrace*—through to recent collaborations with Heiner Müller. Their structure is an architectural arrange-ment of sounds, words, and movement, in which images are restated or varied to form thematic motifs. The presentation is designed to sensitize the spectator to the same subliminal range of nuances as a brain-damaged deaf mute. Seeing autism as an increasingly common psychological response to the pressures of contemporary life, Wilson's aim is therapeutic: to open the audience to "inter-ior impressions." The result is an audio-visual collage of dream-like and seemingly disconnected images, deliberately presented with obsessive repetiti-veness and painful slowness. This kind of temporal fourth dimension reached its fullest extension with *Ka Mountain* at the Shiraz festival, which spread over seven days, and moved from a picture-frame stage to cover a whole mountain-side.

At one point the only movement was that of a live turtle crossing the empty stage, which took almost an hour, while the mountain behind was dotted with unrelated two-dimensional cardboard cut-outs: Noah's ark, a dinosaur, flamingoes, the Acropolis surrounded by a ring of ICBM rockets, Jonah's whale, a graveyard, and the Manhattan skyline on the summit. This last cut-out was burnt to the ground on the final day of the performance, and replaced by a Chinese pagoda with the Lamb of God inside. (The original plan, vetoed by the Iranian festival authorities, had been to blow up the mountain top or paint it entirely white.) There was no intellectual sense to be made out of this apocalyptic collage. The dialogue resembled automatic writing, or dadaist free association. Yet there were obvious mythical con-notations: the creation of the world corresponding to the seven-day perform-ance of the play, "ka" representing the soul, and a seasonal birth/death/resurrection pattern.

Wilson's "chamber" pieces tend to draw their dream-imagery from social rather than religious archetypes, as in *A Letter for Queen Victoria*. Queen

Victoria listens while a long and totally meaningless letter is read out. Couples in white sit at café tables gesticulating frenetically and speaking the same lines—"chitter-chatter, chitter-chatter"—simultaneously. However, the effect is disorienting rather than satiric, with two ballet dancers slowly spinning either side of the stage throughout the performance, and somnambulistic characters talking in endless *non sequiturs*. Again, there are apocalyptic overtones: a sniper shoots the couples who collapse one by one across their tables; and the performance ends with a long-drawn-out scream. But the focus is on perception itself, instead of on what is perceived. Four aviators/Lindberghs stand with their backs to the audience, looking at a changing land/cloudscape through a huge window; a Chinese man stands behind another enormous window-frame staring out at the audience through a continually opening and closing Venetian blind.

Coexisting independently in their collaborative work, Müller's verbal poetry and Wilson's visual imagery—like the separated halves of metaphor—form overlapping layers of sign versus signifier, where the multiple possible meanings are more than the sum of the statements, making rational comprehension almost impossible. This surrealistic unrelatedness and conflict of opposites, the hallmark of Wilson's later drama, is represented by *the CIVIL warS: a tree is best measured when it is down.*

Originally intended for performance at the 1984 Olympics, this multi-lingual, multimedia epic has reached the stage only in fragmented segments. Texts by both Wilson and Müller—plus excerpts from letters by Frederick the Great and Kafka, and fragmented passages from Empedocles, Goethe, Hölderlin, Shakespeare, and Racine—accompanied a sequence of pictures drawn by Wilson (the initial step in any of his productions from which movements and tableaux are developed). The flow of images turned history into a multinational stream-of-consciousness; and a major theme was the way events get recorded in art. The starting point of Act III scene E—produced with Act IV, scene A, and the Epilogue, in Cologne and at the ART—was Mathew Brady's American Civil War photographs, with the anachronistic presence of Frederick the Great leading into other types of conflict: Frederick's invasion of neighbouring territories to unify Germany (which spread to North America, becoming a prototype for modern world wars); Frederick's battles with his father representing familial conflict; Frederick's schizoid combination of Enlightenment liberalism and militaristic brutality as the emblem of a single person at war with himself. The apocalyptic final section presented documentary film of New York high-rise buildings being demolished.

Although the material can be described in such linear terms, the effect was hallucinatory. Fantastical figures—elongated black scribes bearing huge black quills like swords; a white scribe, dressed in ornate folds of paper and transfixed by a massive pencil; a half-human dog; waltzing polar bears—share the stage with historical characters. Frederick the Great was played by several different actors, both male and female. In the epilogue, Abraham Lincoln (a stick-like 20-foot top-hatted puppet, which topples like a felled tree) is juxtaposed with mythical Hopi Indian beings—Snow Owl, and Earth Mother—and with King Lear mourning the dead Cordelia (actually a pile of crumpled newspaper).

History as hallucination, time scales that distort conventional modes of perception, deconstructed reality as myth—these are the defining features of Wilson's drama.

—Christopher Innes

WOLFE, George C.

Born in Frankfort, Kentucky in 1954. Educated at Pomona College, Claremont, California, B.A.; New York University, M.F.A. in dramatic writing and musical theatre. From 1993, artistic director, New York Shakespeare Festival. Recipient: Hull-Warriner award, 1986; Playwrights U.S.A. award, 1988; Obie award, for direction, 1990 Tony award, 1992. Address: c/o Grove/Atlantic Monthly Press, 841 Broadway, New York, New York 10003, U.S.A.

Publications

PLAYS

Paradise!, music by Robert Forest (produced 1985).

The Colored Museum (produced 1986). 1987.

Queenie Pie, music by Duke Ellington (produced 1987).

Over There in *Urban Blight* (musical revue), based on an idea by John Tillinger, music by David Shire, lyrics by Richard Maltby, Jr. (produced 1988).

Spunk, adaptation of stories by Zora Neale Hurston, music by Chic Street Man (includes *Sweat, Story in Harlem Slang, The Gilded Six-Bits*) (also director: produced 1989). 1991.

Jelly's Last Jam (also director: produced 1992).

Besides August Wilson, George C. Wolfe is probably the most prominent African-American dramatist writing at the present time. Wolfe's most popular play, *The Colored Museum*, presents 11 satirical skits, called "exhibits," which deftly portray modern-day African-American life. The first exhibit, "Git on Board," depicts a gleeful stewardess on a "celebrity slaveship" who takes her passengers on a trip at warp speed through African-American history. In "Cookin' with Aunt Ethel," an earthy, black woman recalling an "Aunt Jemima" stereotype sings a biting blues song about the ingredients needed to make up a "batch of Negroes." "The Photo Session" lampoons blacks who are stylish in dress, but lack any substantive thoughts or feelings. "Soldier with a Secret" portrays a facet of black life characterized by a sense of hopelessness which drives people to seek desperate measures to eliminate the pain of their existence. In the skit, the ghost of a Vietnam soldier kills members of his platoon to spare them from enduring lives of anguish they are sure to experience once they return home. "The Gospel According to Miss Roj" depicts a "snap queen" who initially compels one to laugh at his outrageous attire, speech, and behavior. However, just as one becomes comfortable being amused by this self-styled "extraterrestrial" being, he forces us to examine our own smugness and disinterest in the wellbeing of others. "The Hairpiece" is a hilarious look at the preoccupation blacks have in reconciling their dual identities as Africans and Americans. "The Last Mama-on-the-Couch Play" parodies such dramas as Lorraine Hansberry's *A Raisin in the Sun* and Ntozake Shange's *For Colored Girls Who Have Considered Suicide*, while also satirizing classical training for blacks and the unrealistic portrayal of blacks in musicals. In "Symbiosis," a middle-class black man finds he cannot discard his ethnic past in order to better assimilate into the dominant white society of which he wants so desperately to be a part. "Lala's Opening" reveals an entertainer of international prominence who, like the man in the previous skit, tries unsuccessfully to ignore all traces of her African-American heritage. In "Permutations," a once-neglected and denigrated young woman creates a new image of self-worth through the experience of giving birth and nurturing her newborn. In the final exhibit, "The Party," a number of famous African-Americans gather to celebrate their cultural heritage. Through the character of Topsy Washington the play's theme is revealed. The survival of blacks as a people comes from an appreciation of one's past and a "madness" which allows one to adapt to and endure the absurdities and needless pain of African-American life.

Wolfe's next major work, *Spunk*, is based on three short stories concerning male-female relationships by the famed writer, folklorist, and anthropologist Zora Neale Hurston. Throughout the show, the songs of the Guitar Man and Blues Speak Woman complement the scenes. The first tale, *Sweat*, depicts a destructive relationship in rural Florida. The sole support of the household, Delia, leads an unpleasant life with her abusive and adulterous husband, Sykes. Although Delia has purchased and cared for their home, Sykes decides to drive her out of it so he can share the house with his lover, Bertha. Knowing his wife is greatly afraid of reptiles, Sykes attempts to terrorize her by bringing a rattlesnake into the home. Though frightened, Delia refuses to succumb to his act of intimidation. Growing impatient, Sykes decides to attack Delia in bed, but ironically meets his own doom when the snake gives him a fatal bite. In stark contrast to the preceding scene, *Story in Harlem Slang*, is a comical look at male-female relations told in the vernacular of the people of Harlem. Two gigolos, Jelly and Sweet Back, boast of their seductive talents and decide to test their appeal on a young woman. However, after sizing them up, the woman quickly deflates their egos as she belittles them both for believing her to be so naïve as to yield to their dubious charms. Perhaps the most poignant of the three tales is *The Gilded Six-Bits*. The wife in a once-happy marriage is seduced by the allure of gold possessed by a businessman. Catching his wife in an adulterous act, the husband proves her lover to be nothing more than a con artist deceiving people with his gilded coins. Although the couple remain married, their relationship changes drastically as the husband takes on an aloof posture toward his wife. However, after she gives birth to a son, the husband finds he can forgive her and begins to nurture their relationship once again. Thus, the power of love overcomes the deceptions of the past.

Wolfe wrote the book for a more recent work, the musical *Jelly's Last Jam*, based on the life of the first great jazz composer, Jelly Roll Morton. The play is unlike those musicals which are little more than an excuse for blacks to sing and dance or those historical dramas which only provide praise of its subject. Instead, the musical takes a critical look at Morton's accomplishments, as well as his ignoble traits. Set on the eve of his death, the play dramatizes events of his life and dares to question whether the Creole musician neglected to credit his African-American heritage for the uniqueness and appeal of the musical style he helped to make popular.

—Addell Austin Anderson

See the essay on *The Colored Museum.*

WYMARK, Olwen (Margaret, née Buck).

Born in Oakland, California, 14 February 1932. Educated at Pomona College, Claremont, California, 1949–51; University College, London, 1951–52. Married the actor Patrick Wymark in 1950 (died 1970); two daughters and two sons. Writer-in-residence, Unicorn Theatre for Young People, London, 1974–75, and Kingston Polytechnic, Surrey, 1977; script consultant, Tricycle Theatre, London; lecturer in playwriting, New York University; part-time tutor in playwriting, University of Birmingham, 1989–91. Member, Arts Council of Great Britain Drama Panel, 1980–84. Recipient: Zagreb Drama Festival prize, 1967; Actors Theatre of Louisville Best New Play award, 1978. Lives in London. Agent: Lemons Unna, and Durbridge, 24 Pottery Lane, Holland Park, London W11 4LZ, England.

Publications

PLAYS

Lunchtime Concert (produced 1966). In *Three Plays*, 1967; in *The Best Short Plays 1975*, edited by Stanley Richards, 1975.

Three Plays (as *Triple Image: Coda, Lunchtime Concert, The Inhabitants,* produced 1967; *The Inhabitants*, produced 1974). 1967.

The Gymnasium (produced 1967). In *The Gymnasium and Other Plays*, 1971.

The Technicians (produced 1969). In *The Gymnasium and Other Plays*, 1971.

Stay Where You Are (produced 1969). In *The Gymnasium and Other Plays*, 1971; in *The Best Short Plays 1972*, edited by Stanley Richards, 1972.

No Talking (for children; produced 1970).

Neither Here nor There (produced 1971). In *The Gymnasium and Other Plays*, 1971.

Speak Now (produced 1971; revised version produced 1975).

The Committee (produced 1971). In *Best Friends, The Committee, The Twenty-Second Day*, 1984.

The Gymnasium and Other Plays. 1971.

Jack the Giant Killer (produced 1972). In *The Gymnasium and Other Plays*, 1971.

Tales from Whitechapel (produced 1972).

Daniel's Epic (for children), with Daniel Henry (produced 1972).

Chinigchinich (for children; produced 1973).

Watch the Woman, with Brian Phelan (produced 1973).

The Bolting Sisters (for children; produced 1974).

Southwark Originals (collaborative work for children; produced 1975).

The Twenty-Second Day (broadcast 1975; produced 1975). In *Best Friends, The Committee, The Twenty-Second Day*, 1984.

Starters (collaborative work for children; includes *The Giant and the Dancing*

Fairies, The Time Loop, The Spellbound Jellybaby, The Robbing of Elvis Parsley, I Spy) (produced 1975).

Three For All (collaborative work for children; includes *Box Play, Family Business, Extended Play*) (produced 1976).

We Three, and After Nature, Art (produced 1977). In *Play Ten*, edited by Robin Rook, 1977.

Find Me (produced 1977). 1980.

The Winners, and Missing Persons (for children; produced 1978).

Loved (produced 1978). 1980.

The Child (broadcast 1979). 1979.

Please Shine Down on Me (produced 1980).

Female Parts: One Woman Plays (includes *Waking Up, A Woman Alone, The Same Old Story, Medea*), adaptations of plays by Dario Fo and Franca Rame, translated by Margaret Kunzle and Stuart Hood (produced 1981). 1981.

Best Friends (produced 1981). In *Best Friends, The Committee, The Twenty-Second Day*, 1984.

Buried Treasure (produced 1983).

Best Friends, The Committee, The Twenty-Second Day. 1984.

Lessons and Lovers (produced 1985). 1986.

Nana, adaptation of the novel by Zola (produced 1987). 1990.

Strike Up the Banns (produced 1988). 1988.

Brezhnev's Children (produced 1991). 1992.

Mirror Mirror (opera; produced 1992).

RADIO PLAYS: *The Ransom*, 1957; *The Unexpected Country*, 1957; *California Here We Come*, 1958; *The Twenty-Second Day*, 1975; *You Come Too*, 1977; *The Child*, 1979; *Vivien the Blockbuster*, 1980; *Mothering Sunday*, 1980; *Sea Changes*, 1984; *A Wreath of Roses*, from the novel by Elizabeth Taylor, 1985; *Mothers and Shadows*, from a novel by Marta Traba, 1987; *Christopher Columbus*, from the novel by Elizabeth von Arnim, with Barbara Clegg, 1989; *Oroonoko*, from the novel by Aphra Behn, 1990.

TELEVISION PLAYS: *Mrs. Moresby's Scrapbook*, 1973, *Vermin*, 1974, *Marathon*, 1975, *Mother Love*, 1975, *Dead Drunk*, 1975, and *Her Father's Daughter*, 1984 (all in *Crown Court* series); *Oceans Apart*, 1984; *Not That Kind of People*, 1984.

Olwen Wymark comments:

I didn't start writing plays until my mid-thirties and for the first few years wrote only one-act, rather experimental plays; Harold Hobson called them "atonal." I also wrote about eight plays for children. Since 1977 I've written full-length plays in a more naturalistic form as well as some adaptations. I've recently written an opera which was performed in 1992 and hope I will write more. I'm currently concentrating on writing for television.

Olwen Wymark has written some three dozen plays for radio, television, and stage. These range from one-act plays through full-length ones, and her children's plays typify the playful side of her personality. Indeed smallness figures again and again in her work—though, like so much else, one has to unmask it from her work even as she herself relies on a series of unmasking for dramatic effect. *Find Me*, for example, is a documentary play about a mentally disturbed girl who had, in real life, died in a special hospital. Those expecting the play to concentrate sympathy on the little girl must have been disappointed: it is far easier to sympathize with the restaurant owners, friends, and family who have their peace and property destroyed by the girl's predilection for starting fires. Indeed, though she died in the hospital, viewers find themselves sympathizing with the desperate hospital authorities rather than with Verity. She is so small as to disappear in the maelstroms she creates. It is difficult to find her, let alone love her. For the play was sparked off by letters which the girl had written, and which her family had allowed Wymark to read; one began, "Dear Whoeveryouare. Please find me and have me as your beloved." Here, in Wymark's view, is everyman's dilemma: you feel unsure of yourself, and yet it is precisely that self-doubt which fuels creativity. At least it is so in her own case.

Her early plays are exteriorizations of internal anguish, games devised by the characters to reflect and exercise their griefs and dissatisfactions. In *The Gymnasium*, two friends begin a friendly boxing match, with the elderly and gentlemanly one requesting his pretty cockney partner not to talk. They have hardly commenced sparring when the boy turns on a stream of vitriolic abuse. There is plenty of time to attempt puzzling this through, before one realizes that this is a regular marriage therapy session, in which the cockney plays the gentleman's wife and incites his partner to beat him up instead of the wife who is protected by the fine walls of custom and civility.

Most of Wymark's plays are about boringly familiar situations, rooted as they are in the emotional hothouse of upper-middle-class life. What makes the plays dramatic is a lively sense of timing; she offers to her audience the pleasure of solving marvellously constructed puzzles. It is not always possible to sort out the stories, however; and, as in *Neither Here nor There*, "a series of false certainties recede in infinite perspective. Her characters fall through one trapdoor to the solid ground beneath, only to find that collapsing beneath them as well" (Irving Wardle's review in the *Times*). Is the play a comment on the nightmarish quality of experience? Hardly, because the schoolgirls are inventing the whole game themselves.

Situation and theme; anxieties, tensions, and emotional states; guilt, futility, and desperation—these come across in her bizarre and intense plays much more strongly than characters and situations, though these are presented starkly enough. Whenever it is possible to piece her stories together, one begins to care for her characters. Otherwise her plays remain merely ingenious. Witty, arresting at their best, their lack of shape reflects a deeper problem. *Stay Where You Are* shows us a girl at the mercy of two people who appear to be lunatics. Their lunacy turns out, however, to be designed to wake her from her complacency. Quasi-existentialism no longer brings the excitement it did in the 1960s, and this is Wymark's biggest problem: she needs to find something new or fresh or more substantial that she can say through the pressure and sparkle of her work.

What saves her work is that she is aware of this, and that she laughs at herself: *The Technicians* is a marvellous attack on technical cunning which operates in a moral vacuum. Modern experimental theatre is here hoist with its own petard, and what makes the attack poignant is that Wymark loves modern theatre; in it she lives and moves and has her being.

—Prabhu S. Guptara

Y

YANKOWITZ, Susan.

Born in Newark, New Jersey, 20 February 1941. Educated at Sarah Lawrence College, Bronxville, New York, B.A. 1963; Yale University School of Drama, New Haven, Connecticut, M.F.A. 1968. Married Herbert Leibowitz in 1978; one son. Recipient: Vernon Rice award, 1970; MacDowell Colony fellowship, 1971, 1973; National Endowment for the Arts fellowship, 1972, 1979; Rockefeller grant, 1973; Guggenheim fellowship, 1974; Creative Artists Public Service grant, 1974; New York State Council on the Arts grant, 1984; Japan/US Friendship Commission grant, 1985. Agent: Flora Roberts, 157 West 57th Street, New York, New York 10019. Address: 205 West 89th Street, New York, New York 10024, U.S.A.

Publications

PLAYS

The Cage (produced 1965).

Nightmare (produced 1967).

Terminal (produced 1969). In *Three Works by the Open Theatre*, edited by Karen Malpede, 1974.

The Ha-Ha Play (produced 1970). In *Scripts 10*, October 1972.

The Lamb (produced 1970).

Slaughterhouse Play (produced 1971). In *New American Plays 4*, edited by William M. Hoffman, 1971.

Transplant (produced 1971).

Basics, in *Tabula Rasa* (produced 1972).

Positions, in *Up* (produced 1972).

Boxes (produced 1972). In *Playwrights for Tomorrow 11*, edited by Arthur H. Ballet, 1973.

Acts of Love (produced 1973).

Monologues for *Wicked Women Revue* (produced 1973).

Wooden Nickels (produced 1973).

America Piece, with the Provisional Theatre (produced 1974).

Still Life (produced 1977).

True Romances, music by Elmer Bernstein (produced 1977).

Qui Est Anna Marks? (Who Done It?) (produced 1978).

A Knife in the Heart (produced 1983).

Baby (original story), book by Sybille Pearson, music by David Shire, lyrics by Richard Maltby, Jr. (produced 1983).

Alarms (produced 1987).
Night Sky (produced 1991). 1992.

SCREENPLAYS: *Danny AWOL*, 1968; *The Land of Milk and Funny*, 1968; *Silent Witness*, 1979.

RADIO PLAYS: *Rats' Alley*, 1969; *Kali*, 1969.

TELEVISION WRITING: *The Prison Game* (*Visions* series), 1976;
The Forerunner: Charlotte Perkins Gilman, 1979; *Arrow to the Sun: The Poetry of Sylvia Plath*, 1987.

NOVEL
Silent Witness. 1976.

MANUSCRIPT COLLECTION: Kent State University, Kent, Ohio.

CRITICAL STUDIES: *Interviews with Contemporary Women Playwrights* edited by Kathleen Betsko and Rachel Koenig, 1987.

Susan Yankowitz comments (1973):

Most of my work for the theatre has been an attempt to explore what is intrinsically unique in the theatrical situation. That is, I've been interested in sound, gesture, and movement as a corollary to language; in the interaction between the visual and verbal elements of stage life; in the fact of live performers engaged with live audience members in an exchange; and in the development of a theatrical vocabulary. My work has been generally informed by the social and political realities which impinge on all our lives; these, to a large extent, influence and shape my plays. In addition, I have been interested in a collective or collaborative approach to evolving works for the theatre and in working improvisationally with actors and directors to "find" a play which is a creative expression of our shared concerns.

At present, I am growing more concerned with the question of language—its limits and possibilities—and am moving into the realm of fiction which I feel is a more appropriate medium for that adventure.

Susan Yankowitz enlivens non-realistic, highly theatrical images of sociological problems with music, dance, pantomime, patterned speech, bold sets and costumes. These devices reinforce her verbal attacks on such contemporary social sins as conformity, alienation, racism, and sexism. These devices also enable her to avoid didacticism. Yankowitz's emphasis on *theatre* was undoubtedly encouraged by the Open Theatre, whose ensemble work contributed to the several versions of the published text of *Terminal*. *Terminal* cannot be understood apart from the Open Theatre production; the text merely suggests the performance and may be altered by other groups.

Terminal achieves unity through ritual rather than through coherent plot. It argues that people must face their deaths, and satirizes people who do not. The dying in *Terminal* turn to "Team Members" who offer them a mass-produced panacea for death. The living conduct this impersonal ritual; they also embalm and touch up the dead to hide the fact of death. The dead pierce the subterfuge practiced by and upon the dying; they "come through" the dying to judge the living and themselves. The enactment of necrophilia or the graphic description of embalming involves the audience in this common human fate.

As ritual is the binding thread in *Terminal*, so the structure of a parable unifies *The Ha-Ha Play*. Like *Terminal*, this play exposes a general human failing, but emphasizes rectification rather than exposure. Children, abducted to a woods (in which the audience sits) by hyenas wearing masks, learn to communicate through laughter. Communication is thus not only possible between groups, but it also dissolves enmity between them.

In contrast to *Terminal* and *The Ha-Ha Play*, *Slaughterhouse Play* traces the growth of consciousness of a unifying character, the black slaughterhouse worker, Junius. *Slaughterhouse Play* attacks racism: its central symbol is the slaughterhouse, which whites run and in which blacks work, slaughtering black troublemakers and selling their "meat" to whites. As in *Terminal*, action and dialogue involve the audience. The most prized black meat is that of the male genitals, which a white butcher displays in his shop, and which Junius and other rebellious blacks steal to wear around their necks as symbols of their rebellion. *Slaughterhouse Play* ends with a sequence in which blacks stab whites and whites shoot blacks repeatedly.

Not only is *Boxes* in a much lighter vein than *Slaughterhouse Play*, but literal boxes function theatrically as a fictional slaughterhouse cannot. Characters carve windows in boxes, and from within those boxes define themselves according to type and speak in clichés. Yankowitz underlines this conformity by having the characters wear hats with boxes that match their box dwellings. People in their separate boxes perform their daily chores at the same time that others experience great pain or joy. Such caricature unifies *Boxes*. Ultimately the boxes become coffins.

Yankowitz dramatizes individual or social problems and involves her audience either by shock or mimicry. Once engaged, the audience is forced to admit its responsibility for such failures as avoiding death, alienation, conformity, and racism. And this is Yankowitz's aim.

—Frances Rademacher Anderson

Z

ZINDEL, Paul.

Born in Staten Island, New York, 15 May 1936. Educated at Port Richmond High School, Staten Island; Wagner College, New York, B.S. in chemistry 1958, M.Sc. 1959. Married Bonnie Hildebrand in 1973; one son and one daughter. Technical writer for chemical company, New York, 1959; chemistry teacher, Tottenville High School, New York, 1960–69; playwright-in-residence, Alley Theatre, Houston, 1967. Recipient: Ford grant, 1967; Obie award, 1970; Vernon Rice award, 1970; New York Drama Critics Circle award, 1970; Pulitzer prize, 1971. D.H.L.: Wagner College, 1971. Lives in New York City. Agent: Curtis Brown, 10 Astor Place, New York, New York 10003. Address: c/o Harper and Row, 10 East 53rd Street, New York, New York 10022, U.S.A.

Publications

PLAYS

Dimensions of Peacocks (produced 1959).
Euthanasia and the Endless Hearts (produced 1960).
A Dream of Swallows (produced 1964).
The Effect of Gamma Rays on Man-in-the-Moon Marigolds (produced 1965). 1971; in *Plays and Players*, December 1972.
And Miss Reardon Drinks a Little (produced 1967). 1972.
Let Me Hear You Whisper (televised 1969). 1974.
The Secret Affairs of Mildred Wild (produced 1972). 1973.
The Ladies Should Be in Bed (produced 1978). With *Let Me Hear You Whisper*, 1973.
Ladies at the Alamo (also director: produced 1975).
A Destiny with Half Moon Street (produced 1983), revised version as *Amulets Against the Dragon Forces* (produced 1989). 1989.

SCREENPLAYS: *Up the Sandbox*, 1973; *Mame*, 1974; *Maria's Lovers*, with others, 1984; *Runaway Train*, with Djordje Milicevic and Edward Bunker, 1985.

TELEVISION PLAY: *Let Me Hear You Whisper*, 1969.

NOVEL

When a Darkness Falls. 1984.

FICTION (for children)
The Pigman. 1968.
My Darling, My Hamburger. 1969.
I Never Loved Your Mind. 1970.
I Love My Mother, illustrated by John Melo. 1975.
Pardon Me, You're Stepping on My Eyeball! 1976.
Confessions of a Teenage Baboon. 1977.
The Undertaker's Gone Bananas. 1978.
The Pigman's Legacy. 1980.
A Star for the Latecomer, with Bonnie Zindel. 1980.
The Girl Who Wanted a Boy. 1981.
To Take a Dare, with Crescent Dragonwagon. 1982.
Harry and Hortense at Hormone High. 1984.
The Amazing and Death-Defying Diary of Eugene Dingman. 1987.
A Begonia for Miss Applebaum. 1989.
The Pigman and Me. 1991.

MANUSCRIPT COLLECTION: Boston University.

CRITICAL STUDY: *Presenting Paul Zindel* by Jack Jacob Forman, 1988.

THEATRICAL ACTIVITIES
DIRECTOR: **Play**—*Ladies at the Alamo*, 1975.

Most parts in most plays are male. In realist and humorist Paul Zindel's work, however, almost all the roles are for women. They aren't very nice women because they tend, like so many of Tennessee Williams's women, to be neurotic freaks. The tormented women who people his plays are dumpy and defensive, lonely and lacerating, bitter and—psychologically, at least—brutal. Yet Zindel stirs our compassion by imparting to them a vulnerability which guarantees that they must endure at least as much pain as they inflict.

Not all of Zindel's characters are adults. Perhaps because he was initially a high school chemistry teacher on his native Staten Island, he has taken an interest in the distress of young people, not only in his best known play, *The Effect of Gamma Rays on Man-in-the-Moon Marigolds*, but also in such teen novels as *My Darling, My Hamburger*, *The Pigman*, and *The Pigman's Legacy*. He likewise introduces animals in his scripts with considerable frequency.

Regardless of who their victims may be, Zindel's characters damage those for whom they have reason to feel affection and to whom they are bound, either by blood or in other ways. Where the relationship is familial or a surrogate for the sibling, parental, or conjugal bond, the suffocating intimacies create a dramatic tension familiar from the work of such other American writers of domestic drama as Inge, Williams, O'Neill, and Miller. Most of Zindel's characters are sexually unfulfilled. Despite their tenacity in surviving, his creations are clinging to unlived lives or, in the nuclear terminology of *Marigolds*, half lives, which in some of the plays are shadowed by the dead and the doomed. Yet the terrible plight in which Zindel's characters find themselves is relieved by considerable humor.

The melodrama *Marigolds* has enjoyed far more success than any other of Zindel's plays. Its original New York production ran for over two years and won its author several prizes. This play takes its remarkable title from the project on this subject which withdrawn Tillie, a girl in her early teens, has prepared for her school science fair. Tillie finds solace in the perspective of her place in the whole history of evolution beginning with the creation of the universe. Understanding the continuity of life, of energy and matter, encourages her to look beyond her own squalid surroundings. Her attitude contrasts sharply to the narcissism shared by her crude older sister Ruth and cynical mother Beatrice.

Beatrice is at once eccentric, selfish, and pathetic. She forces Tillie to miss school and then lies about it to the teacher. When she's angry at the other kids' derision of Tillie, her resentment stems not from sympathy with her daughter but from a suspicion they're really ridiculing her. She flirts with the teacher on the phone but insults him behind his back, talks constantly of hairbrained get-rich-quick schemes, taunts and torments her helpless senile boarder and her emotionally crippled daughters. And she kills the girls' pet rabbit.

Yet we grow fond of Beatrice, and of Ruth too, in spite of her resemblance to her mother, with whom she shares lipstick, cigarettes, hostilities, and neuroses. We observe Ruth's dread of thunder and death and her mother's fear of failure and life, we watch them wound and comfort each other, and we find Zindel's craft compelling us to care for women who might well have seemed monsters. When Ruth destroys her mother's confidence and makes her miss the science fair in which Tillie's project wins first prize, we even appreciate the agony out of which she chloroforms Ruth's rabbit.

Marigolds dramatizes a recurrent Zindel subject, disturbed women, and a recurrent Zindel theme, the suffering friends and relatives inflict on their "loved ones." All three women are "crazies" whose behavior reflects that of more controlled but no less destructive "normal" people. Just as the marigolds have been exposed to gamma rays, these women have been subjected to high concentrations of anguish; Ruth and Beatrice correspond to the dwarfed plants and Tillie to the rare mutants made beautiful by more moderate radiation.

In *And Miss Reardon Drinks a Little*, another play which depicts women who both cause pain and suffer from it, Zindel sides with the vulnerable but abnormal against the ruthless or insensitive but normal. Each Miss Reardon—one alcoholic, the other depressive—is harmless compared to their executive sister and her unsupportive husband. In one respect, that couple resemble Mildred and her spouse in *The Secret Affairs of Mildred Wild*. The sexual repression which is mostly implicit in the earlier play, however, becomes an explicit issue in the latter. Mildred absorbs herself in movie magazines and cinematic fantasies instead of her marriage, and her husband in his turn fails to consummate an extra-marital affair because he's distracted by his sweet tooth. While Mildred watches movies day and night, her diabetic candy-store owner of a husband is swallowing all his merchandise. Naturally both the business and the relationship are bankrupt. Yet somehow the pair survive their eccentricities and—more importantly—their disillusionment with each other to subscribe to the further fantasy of reconciliation.

The farce of *Mildred Wild*—complete with a modernization of the screen scene from *The School for Scandal*—is less successful than the acerbic wit—replete with profanity and obscenity—of *Ladies at the Alamo*. More of a cat fight than a literal shoot-out, this play does take place in Texas, where control of a regional theatre constitutes the battle's stakes. Even though the Alamo is only a theatre, a massacre of sorts does occur, with devastating destruction wrought to each of the five women's egos. Funny, foul-mouthed insults fly amid women feuding over whether the Artistic Director, Dede, will continue to run the theatre she's built from a little box into an empire. The loyalties are complex, the betrayals still more so. Dede is far from admirable and probably wins because she's the biggest bully, but when the dust settles we're somehow glad she's survived. *Alamo* is another Zindel triumph in manipulation of audience sympathies.

The drunken neurotics of that play resemble the bridge players of a short work, *The Ladies Should Be in Bed*. The principal action in this play forms a minor incident as well in *Alamo*, when one of the women maliciously phones parents of teenagers and reports sexual activity with a "pervert." But it's the ladies themselves who are sex obsessed and therefore "should be in bed." Sexuality is likewise a subject of *Amulets Against the Dragon Forces* in which a boy unsure of his sexual preference is thrust temporarily, by his mother's employment as a nurse, into a gay male household. But, with alcoholic longshoreman Floyd and teenage Chris, Zindel especially depicts the products of dysfunctional families. This play rivals *Marigolds* in its dramatization of a youngster's effort at self-protection when threatened by tormented and tormenting adults. Unusual in Zindel's menagerie of female misfits, *Amulets*'s neurotics (or dragons) include both men and women.

—Tish Dace

WORKS

AMERICAN BUFFALO
by David Mamet.

First Publication: 1977.
First Production: 1975.

American Buffalo is set in a junk shop run by Don Dubrow, a man in his late 40s. In the first act, Don and his young friend, Bobby, prepare to steal a coin collection from a man who, a week earlier, bought a buffalo-head nickel from Don. Angered by the man's condescension and a suspicion that the coin was worth much more than he was paid, Don has arranged a heist with Bobby as the one to do the actual robbery. Teach, a "friend and associate", convinces Don to take him on as a partner instead and to cut Bobby out of the deal. In Act II, tension runs high as Don and Teach wait for Fletcher, another friend Don has insisted on taking into the partnership. When Bobby appears with a buffalo nickel to sell and the story that Fletch is in the hospital, Teach becomes suspicious and convinces Don that they have been betrayed, and Bobby and Fletch have stolen the coin collection themselves. When Bobby cannot answer their questions satisfactorily, Teach viciously bashes him on the side of the head with a heavy object. A phone call corroborates Bobby's story; a fight erupts between Don and Teach, and Teach goes berserk, trashing the junk shop. After the emotional storm has passed, the three men awkwardly make peace with one another and leave to take Bobby to the hospital.

As is typical of Mamet's work, *American Buffalo* depicts a very specific segment of society, but raises issues of more general concern about the American way of life. Don, Teach, and Bobby inhabit an urban world of resident hotels, cheap diners, and pawn shops. They are petty crooks without the intelligence or forethought necessary actually to carry out the robbery they plan, but the projected heist serves to illuminate the values of the characters and to focus attention on their relationships. Don serves as a father or mentor figure to the inept Bobby, and early in the play, he tries to explain the difference between "business", which he sees as "People taking care of themselves", and friendship: "When you walk around you *hear* a lot of things, and what you got to do is keep clear who your friends are, and who treated you like what. Or else the rest is garbage, Bob, because I want to tell you something . . . Things are not always what they seem to be". The garrulous Teach, who fancies himself a profound thinker, is obsessed by the need for loyalty among friends, yet he has little trouble convincing Don to dump Bobby from their financial deal or to believe that the boy's inarticulateness and Fletcher's absence are proof of a double-cross. Teach rewrites his code of ethics and behavior at a moment's notice in order to follow the most crucial of his objectives, which is to look out for his own economic interests, even at the cost of someone else. Having internalized a warped notion of the traditional American value of independence, Teach defines "free enterprise" as "The freedom . . . Of the *Individual* . . . To Embark on Any Fucking Course that he sees fit . . . In order to secure his honest chance to make a profit".

The junk shop full of discarded merchandise becomes a metaphor for this morally bankrupt world as the characters continually contradict their own empty profession of ethics in the absence of any objective standard. The buffalo-head nickel, the central image of the play, is, significantly, a coin whose sliding value depends upon circumstances and the knowledge of its beholder. Characteristic of Mamet in its poetic manipulation of rhythm, the language of the play reflects the inner emptiness of the characters. Their limited vocabulary, omission of words, tortured grammar, and reliance on profanity reflect a lack of command over their lives and emotions. In a world devoid of guiding principles, the men are always perilously close to chaos, as shown by the eruption of violence at the play's end, yet in the midst of their moral confusion, they long for the humane interaction which their own actions constantly subvert. Bobby reveals that he lied about a crucial detail of the robbery and purchased the second buffalo nickel in an effort to please Don and gain his approval. As Teach ransacks his friend's shop with an instrument formerly used to drain the blood from a slaughtered pig, he voices his own perception of reality: "The Whole Entire World./There Is No Law./There Is No Right And Wrong./The World Is Lies./There Is No Friendship./Every Fucking Thing . . . Every God-forsaken Thing . . . We all live like the cavemen". The final, ineffectual groping of the men toward a reconciliation is a sad illustration of their need and their essential isolation.

Mamet's characters are both funny and pathetic in their evasions, manipulations, and excesses. The halting rhythms of the dialogue are designed to provoke both laughter and thought. In performance, the violence of the play's conclusion is disturbing, but it is a fitting image for the author's depiction of a society in which the pursuit of personal monetary gain has supplanted or perverted all other patterns of behavior.

—Kathy Fletcher

ANGELS IN AMERICA:
A Gay Fantasia on National Themes
by Tony Kushner.

First Publication: *Part One: Millenium Approaches*, 1992; *Part Two: Perestroika*, 1994.
First Production: *Part One: Millenium Approaches*, 1991; *Part Two: Perestroika*, 1992.

An extended fantasy set in New York in the mid-1980s, *Angels in America* follows the lives of two couples and their friends, relatives, and visionary visitors as they struggle to come to terms with the realities of the late 20th-century. Prior Walter has AIDS; unable to cope, his lover, Louis, leaves him and begins an affair with Joe, a Mormon lawyer who is on the point of leaving his wife. Abandoned and dying, Prior begins to have visions of an angel; at the same time Joe is drawn into the orbit of Roy M. Cohn, a corrupt lawyer and political operator who is himself dying of AIDS. As Prior's condition worsens his visions intensify—by the beginning of *Part Two: Perestroika*, he accepts (albeit reluctantly) that he is a prophet with a message for mankind.

Visiting the local Mormon temple he meets Harper, Joe's wife, and learns that it is her husband who is Louis' new lover. Louis is surprised to learn that Joe is a Mormon; he is horrified when he discovers, not much later, that Joe is a protégé of Roy Cohn, whom he sees as the very embodiment of evil. The pair fight, and Joe leaves to attempt a reconciliation with Harper. But Harper (who has been having her own visions) refuses to take him back; she forgives him but explains that her life has changed and she now has another course to follow. While all this has been happening Roy Cohn has died, and Prior has visited heaven: he has a message of his own to give his angelic visitor. The fantasy ends with the main characters, battered but surviving, grouped round a symbolic fountain in Central Park.

With *Angels in America* Tony Kushner has become a celebrity. Critics on both sides of the Atlantic have waxed lyrical over his talent, one declaring him to be the most important American playwright since David Mamet. Time, ultimately, will tell whether such praise is warranted; meanwhile it is certain that in scale and ambition *Angels in America* stands alone on the contemporary stage.

The first point to make about Kushner's piece is that it is not a play in the ordinary sense of the word. It is in fact subtitled *A Gay Fantasia on National Themes*, and this is an accurate description, for in its imaginative flights and deliberate staginess it resembles less a typical modern drama than opera or masque. There is, altogether, a theatrical quality about it: characters see angels crash through their ceilings, or suffer visits from the dead, or climb to heaven on magic ladders to hand back sacred books. Not since Jacobean times have special effects been used for such serious purposes, and Kushner's language, too, veering as it does between earthy witticism and lush poetry, has something of the Jacobean about it. If, on occasion, it all seems a little over the top—and Kushner's characters themselves often feel it is—then such a style is perhaps only apt for our fevered, millennial age.

That we are nearing the "End Time" is the central message of *Millennium Approaches*. As Harper puts it at the beginning of the play, "Everywhere things are collapsing, lies surfacing, systems of defence giving way." It is not just society that is disintegrating: at the biological level bodies are falling apart, attacked by strange new diseases, while globally the ozone layer is being depleted by deadly fluorocarbons. Each character, gay or heterosexual, black or white, Christian or Jew, is haunted by foreboding: *Millennium Approaches* is largely about their attempts to continue living their old lives in the face of this knowledge.

For Prior, dying of AIDS, the problem is especially acute; possibly for this reason he becomes the moral centre of the play, a blind prophet who receives angelic visitors. That he is, initially, extremely reluctant to take on his new role does not mark him out—all the characters in *Millennium Approaches* are, in their own way, unwilling to face reality. In particular they are unwilling to accept who they are (Joe, for example, must recognize his homosexuality) and what they have done (Louis, for instance, must recognize his moral failure in abandoning Prior). But accept it they must; the alternative is to perish amid old, worn-out illusions.

If a sense of foreboding permeates *Millenium Approaches*, the necessity for change dominates Kushner's second play, *Perestroika*. "Can we change?" thunders Aleksii Antedilluvianovich Prelapsarianov, the world's oldest living

Bolshevik, and over and over again, in their different ways, the various characters repeat this basic question. Change, certainly, there must be—humanity, plainly, is in a mess and dragging the rest of creation down with it. According to Prior's angelic visitor the fault lies with man's erring restlessness: his promiscuous mobility has driven God away from the world and as a result the planet is falling apart. Man, the angel asserts, must stop moving—only then will God return and matters mend. But Prior rejects this message—as he says, "The world spins only forward." Man must change, he knows, but into something new and unknown. This, at heart, is the work each of Kushner's characters undertakes in *Perestroika*. It is not easy—as the Mormon mother explains to Harper, changing is like having your guts torn out—but each does nevertheless begin the task. And as the characters change, so they are forgiven: Joe by Harper, Roy by Louis, Louis by Prior. With forgiveness, the conditions for new life are created, and even the damage done to the world can be repaired—Harper's final vision, as she flies off into an unknown future, is of the souls of the sick and dying rising to remake the torn ozone layer. At the end of the play we see the main characters grouped round the Bethesda fountain in Central Park—legend has it that at the end of time the original fountain in Jerusalem will flow again and heal the afflicted. It is an image of hope: we can face the apocalypse, *Angels in America* tells us, and survive.

—John O'Leary

APPROACHING SIMONE
by Megan Terry.

First Publication: 1973.
First Production: 1970.

Set in France, America, and England during the first half of the century, *Approaching Simone* depicts the life and death of Simone Weil, the French thinker and worker who committed suicide by starvation during World War II. Starting at the beginning Megan Terry shows us Simone as a demanding and intelligent child who rejects the comforts of her home in order to share, precociously, in the burdens of humanity. As she grows Simone's originality and curiousity only deepen; this leads to trouble at the schools where she teaches, and she is repeatedly fired. Unable and unwilling to continue her career, Simone works in factories and joins the Left; a little later she goes to Spain to fight. In Spain she witnesses atrocities that cause her to question whether politics can help man achieve freedom and justice; it is these doubts, in fact, that pave the way for the mystical experience she undergoes while trying to flee Nazi-occupied France. Her conviction that love for one's fellow man is the necessary transforming agent in human life grows during her exile in America and England—so great is her desire to share in the sufferings of her French compatriots that she attempts to return to Europe despite the great danger to herself. But authority rebuffs her. In the end, out of solidarity with her starving countrymen, she starves herself to death.

Approaching Simone is one of Terry's best known plays, and this is understandable, for in it her style and technique, developed over many years, are used in an approachable manner to portray the life of one of the century's more attractive thinkers. Elements of the surreal persist, it is true—at one point a group of schoolgirls become machine parts, at another a rain of sweets descends on the audience—but on the whole such moments are rare, and serve less to distract or puzzle than to heighten dramatic impact. *Approaching Simone*, in short, might be said to represent a balance between the strangeness of Terry's earlier works and the naturalism of some of her later pieces—a balance which, if not absolutely steady, is nonetheless successfully maintained.

An important point to make about *Approaching Simone* is that it is not, and does not try to be, an exhaustive and detailed account of Simone Weil's life. As the title indicates, it is rather an approach, an attempt to discover something of the essence of this complex and difficult woman. That said, Terry's method is fairly conventional in terms of staging and chronology—we begin at the beginning, so to speak, with the infant Simone and her family, and progress, more or less steadily, through her youth and adulthood. We see Simone's friends, we see her work; we witness, in the end, her suicide. The result is a play that is undeniably solid, but not earthbound—a drama through which we glimpse, if not plumb, Simone's depths.

"Simone" says one of Terry's actors, "taught herself the art of perpetual attention", and it is this rigorous examination of society and self that is key to Simone's character as Terry conceives it. Thus Simone is shown as a child rejecting the bourgeois comfort of her home—she mails her sugar to the soldiers at the front—while craving simultaneously to share in the burdens of humanity, here symbolized by the family luggage she tries to carry. The puzzlement and concern of Simone's parents is well conveyed by Terry—even better portrayed is the outraged reaction of authority when, now a young schoolteacher, Simone takes her pupils on a hike through frozen countryside. Three girls, the board of governors complain, have contracted pneumonia; Simone they explain, is near to being charged with kidnapping. Simone is unrepentant—she wished, she says, to educate her pupils in what they might do. It is, altogether, a typical situation: throughout her life Simone makes demands on herself, and others, that bring her into conflict with received wisdom and established authority. Nor is it only bourgeois society Simone confronts—Terry is careful to show us that any rigid system is liable to face Simone's scrutiny, as when she argues with Stalinist co-workers at a political meeting. The Simone Terry shows us is, in a word, heroic—but also, perhaps naive (she is almost killed at the meeting, and is saved only because her friends rescue her).

Open-minded as she is, there is one experience which Simone will not admit, and that is love. Love, she tells her pupils, is a serious thing—she for her part has decided not to experience it till she knows more about herself. But love finds Simone willy nilly, not in the form of the rose-coloured romance her girls dream of, but in the shape of a mystical visitation in which Christ comes down and possesses her. The change—or rather, perhaps, deepening—of Simone's life wrought by the advent of love is the subject, more or less, of the second act of *Approaching Simone*. Terry's portrayal of this is moving and credible: changed as she is, Simone remains very much herself (she says her prayers, for example, in the original Greek). In a sense she becomes *more* herself—it is in the end only logical, given her desire to share in the sufferings of humanity, that she rejects the safety of exile in America and England and tries to return to occupied France. Her attempt is brusquely rejected by authority ('there's a war on'); as a result, in an act of solidarity with her compatriots across the Channel, Simone refuses to eat and starves herself to death. "Strange suicide" murmur Terry's chorus of women, as they contemplate Simone's tiny coffin; again we are asked to judge whether Simone's action is saintly or naive.

Maybe, Terry is saying, it is both, which is why we in our complicated, compromised world find it so difficult to understand. It is a tribute to Terry, ultimately, that we comprehend it through her play—that, however fleetingly or partially, we have approached Simone.

—John O'Leary

AWAKE AND SING!
by Clifford Odets.

First Publication: in *Three Plays*, 1935.
First Production: 1935.

Five flights up is the Bronx apartment of Bessie Berger. She dominates the family and determines what goes: light shall be shut out, the shades pulled down ("I like my house to look respectable"), telephone calls from her son's girl shall be censored, father shall be ordered out into the snow to walk the dog, and phonograph records promising a new Eden for America shall be smashed.

No one can raise his voice in this house because "they'll hear you down the dumbwaiter". Bessie ironically offers to serve "a special blue plate supper in the garden", but there is no garden; there's no patch of green to escape to. The roof offers two options; you can go there to walk the dog, or you can go there to jump off. Threats of self-elimination abound. The proud beauty of a daughter, Hennie, is burdened with a pregnancy by a stranger she can't trace; the father is someone "from out of town", the true New Yorker's phrase for the rest of the world beyond one's neighborhood. She says she'll "jump out the window" if they don't lay off the pressure for her to find a marital stand-in to mask her disgrace. It's the heart of the Depression, and many choose the same escape route: "Still jumping off the high buildings like flies—the big shots who lost all their cocoanuts". In Bessie's waking nightmare, she too ends up on the streets, but not from self-propelled velocity: "They threw out a family on Dawson Street today. All the furniture on the sidewalk. A fine old woman with gray hair". She's determined nobody will do that to her. She grabs onto her options to feed her family and keep them together. Like Brecht's Mother Courage, she earns our grudging admiration for her wit and her competency.

Competing visions of paradise are presented. For Moe, street-wise but not lucky enough to emerge from the Great War with both legs, "Par-a-dise" is Hennie. His campaign is for her to escape: "Sure, kids you'll have, gold teeth, get fat, big in the tangerines . . . Cut your throat, sweetheart. Save time". He offers, instead, a moonlit cruise to Yama Yama land.

Jacob, the patriarch of the Berger family, clings to a vision of paradise he's sure the workers of the world can attain. It's part Edenic myth fed by the voice of Caruso ("From *L'Africana* . . . a big explorer comes on a new land . . . 'Oh paradise on earth! Oh blue sky, oh fragrant air—'") and part Old Testament prophesy ("Awake and sing, ye that dwell in dust"). Though Jacob can spout Isaiah and quote from *Exodus* in Hebrew, he has, in fact, rejected God and taken Marxism as his new religion. His hopes are pinned on a future for his grandson Ralph.

In the play's climax, key deceptions the family lives with are revealed. At this juncture, Odets audaciously yokes together Bessie scolding her father to walk the dog with her father's evocation of Judaism's central patriarchal tenet, faith in one master of the universe:

> Bessie: Don't stand around Poppa! Take Tootsie on the roof. And don't
>   let her go under the water tank.
> Jacob: Schmah Yisroeal. Behold!

With stunning understatement, Jacob exits into the snow with, "Tootsie is my favorite lady in the house". He's never heard from again. We're given this report from the immigrant janitor: "He shlipped maybe in the snow . . . Your fadder fell off de roof".

What is Jacob's legacy, besides the $3,000 insurance policy he leaves to Ralph? Jacob was an out-of-work barber who claimed, "I'm studying from books a whole lifetime"; but when Ralph inherits his leftist library, he discovers that "the pages ain't cut in half of them". As in Ibsen's *Wild Duck*, as in Miller's *Death of a Salesman*, we're left to assess the value of the big talk, the shock of the human sacrifice. Will Jacob's vision lead to revolution or must we agree with his more modest self-portrait—"Look on this failure and see for seventy years he talked . . . A man who had golden opportunities but drank instead a glass tea".

Odets' original title was not the affirmation of Isaiah about dwellers in the dust arising to a new world. The original title was from a line of Hennie's, *I Got the Blues*. In that version, Moe is picked up for bookmaking; therefore, Hennie does not get to desert her child and her deceived husband to join Moe (if ever so temporarily) in Yama Yama land. Odets had both Bessie and Ralph withhold much needed money from the family. Harold Clurman insisted that Odets' original conclusion was "almost masochistically pessimistic", and the leverage of the stage director altered the shape the playwright had crafted.

And so we're presented with Ralph abruptly abandoning his pursuit of his girl. His grandfather died to provide him with a means of escape from this family, but suddenly Ralph feels no need for the inheritance, no need for his much awaited declaration of independence. Instead, he's content to move into Jacob's old room, cut the pages of those books, and become a labor organizer.

Odets is an important link between the European pioneers of realism and America's own theatrical flourishing after World War II. He has an unerring ear for self-depracating humor, the Yiddish inflection of urban American speech. One factor that might be holding back a full appreciation of this, his best-realized play, is the patched together jolt of the optimistic ending Clurman helped to impose.

—Roger Sorkin

THE BASIC TRAINING OF PAVLO HUMMEL
by David Rabe.

First Publication: 1972.
First Production: 1971.

In a Vietnamese brothel, Pavlo Hummel is blown apart by a grenade thrown in the window. Then the black soldier Ardell, an alter ego, appears and prompts a replay for the dying Pavlo of his army life, and this forms the fractured action of the play. In the Georgia boot-camp, Pavlo emerges as a friendless young man desperate to "belong". His quirky need to be "individual", including his way of telling tall stories to "show-boat", gets him into trouble with the other recruits. But with his inner voice of Ardell, he survives the motory brutality of basic training, and masters its physical skills. After training, he briefly re-visits his dysfunctional "family" of mother and half-brother. When he is posted to Vietnam as a medic, he experiences his first sex with a prostitute and his first real intimations of mortality when tending a human "stump". When he urgently opts for combat duty, he is wounded three times; on Ardell's prompting, he applies for a transfer back home, but instead is given the award of the Purple Heart. Then the action comes full circle—and we learn that the fatal grenade was lobbed by a fellow soldier, an older man he squabbled with over the prostitute's favors. At the end, he is goaded by Ardell to say what he now thinks of "the cause"; he repeatedly screams that it is "Shit" before Ardell slams his coffin shut.

David Rabe's *The Basic Training of Pavlo Hummel* was the first American play of stature to deal with the Vietnam war experience, by a playwright who had served there. Its first major professional production by Joseph Papp was well received and Rabe followed it with another play, *Sticks and Bones*, dealing with the return of a blind Vietnam veteran to his uncomprehending and stereotypical middle-class family. But *The Basic Training of Pavlo Hummel*, partly because it is less contrived in its technique, and partly because it presents the war directly, is the more powerful play of the two.

Rabe himself emphasises that *Pavlo Hummel* is not an "anti-war" play in the political sense, and his attitude to some of the values and skills the army inculcates seems ambivalent. Martin Gottfried (in the *New York Post*) perceptively commented in his review of the 1977 production that "Rabe has treated military basic training as an American rite . . . [He] captures the rite uncannily and elevates it to mythic stature. And he takes the metaphor of basic training one stop further, making it a ritual that must conclude with death, whether in the army or out of it".

But the U.S. Army and its treatment of Pavlo is also a metaphor for Rabe's deeper thematic concern: the coercive power of an institution on the individual. For Pavlo finds that his "rite of passage" is a journey to nowhere, and that the army has not fostered either his individuality or his manhood. Neither does it act as a surrogate "family". At the end of Act I, it re-fashions him into a killing mask in dress-uniform and dark glasses, and the kind of resilience it gives him accrues almost totally from his military function. In Act II, he finally begins to realise both what he has missed and what his possibilities are. But by then the institutional trap has closed and he is swallowed whole, denied even an "heroic" end in the field. Several critics felt that Pavlo remains an uncomprehending cipher, and that this weakens the play. It is true that he never achieves self-realisation and that his talent is for "leaping into the fire"; but if played resourcefully, as he was by William Atherton in the first New York production and later by Pacino on Broadway, Pavlo can be touching in his eagerness for individuality and for street-wisdom. He is an archetype for all those who lack the means within themselves to develop an identity and a sense of belonging, who look to an external "system" to provide those needs, and who are betrayed.

Two dramaturgical devices serve to "characterize" Pavlo in this way and to stress the pathos of his "incompleteness", as well as depict a potential in him that is never realised. The first is the language that Rabe uses, for it clearly establishes differences between the institutionalized, "societal" idioms of the military, and the more fractured, inchoate, and personalized talk of Pavlo himself. His co-option by military values is signalled partly by his taking over more of this imposed idiom in the later scenes of the play. The other device is more problematic: Ardell, the "invisible" black alter ego, draws Pavlo out, establishes his confusions, and forms a conduit for Pavlo's "inner self" to be manifested. But Ardell's functions are too varied, and the values of his different personae too inconsistent—conscience, devil's advocate, mentor, teacher, surrogate sergeant, "angel of death"—for the device to come into focus for the audience and register as a strong, discrete theatrical element in its own right. But this flaw does not fatally compromise the play, and the shifting functions for Ardell have their own fascination.

The scenography forms an ideal trampoline for characterisation and structure—and the structure is a perfect embodiment of the violence of the training ritual as well as that of the field, and an apt analogue for Pavlo's "progress". The training tower in the back suggests the impersonal power of the system that dominates Pavlo; and the indeterminate and fluid locations of the downstage areas, together with the area lighting, emphasise the evanescence and instability of memory and the fact that Pavlo has no clearly defined "private space" to grow in.

The Basic Training of Pavlo Hummel will surely remain one of the classic dramatic treatments of the Vietnam war, but also an enduring treatment of the theme of the individual vainly searching for sustenance and development within an indifferent institutional structure.

—Dennis Carroll

BENT

by Martin Sherman.

First Publication: 1979.
First Production: 1978.

Set in Germany just before World War II, *Bent* depicts the suffering of a group of gay men at the hands of the Nazis. Central to the play is Max, a rather seedy wheeler-dealer, who at the start of the action is living with Rudy, a dancer. Max is in the habit of picking up "rough trade"; unwisely, he brings home one night the boyfriend of a local SA leader. This folly gains him the attention of the Nazis, who have begun their campaign against homosexuals. As a result he and Rudy are obliged to flee Berlin. While making for the Dutch border they are caught and shipped off to Dachau. It is on this journey that Max, shocked and terrified, is forced to participate in killing Rudy; but it is on this journey, also, that he meets Horst, a decent "pink triangle" who assists him and with whom, gradually, he falls in love. Despite the degradation of camp life Max grows in humanity through this relationship: in the end, when Horst is exterminated, he puts on his lover's coat with its pink triangle in a gesture of solidarity and love, so sealing his own death warrant.

Bent occupies a central place in Martin Sherman's work, for in it the themes of alienation, identity and love, present in his other plays, are most perfectly presented and explored. So finely crafted is *Bent*, in fact—so effortlessly "right"—that there is a danger of taking its art for granted, of our not noticing, in the sweep of action and emotion, how beautifully Sherman has constructed his play. Only on reading, and reading again, does one begin to appreciate the piece's almost classical perfection.

More than anything else, *Bent* is about acceptance. Not merely acceptance of minorities (gays, Jews) by the majority, but acceptance of the self, with all its terrible faults, by the self. This is Max's central problem: "Oh God!" he exclaims, at the beginning of the play, on seeing himself in a mirror, and his words aptly convey his self-loathing. *Bent*, in fact, is largely about Max's journey toward self-acceptance: the journey he must make if he is to be able to love; the journey, in the end, we must all make if we are to become fully human.

That said, Max is not, initially, a promising candidate. A petty criminal, drunk and drug-abuser, he treats his lover, Rudy, with indifference, if not contempt. When they are forced to quit Berlin he looks after Rudy, one has the impression, only out of habit—and when, shocked and dazed, he participates in Rudy's killing, one is horrified but not wholly surprised. Max, then, is definitely not a hero—he does not even have the glamour of an anti-hero, but is, in effect, very much an average human being, slightly more cunning, perhaps, than his fellow men but otherwise much like all of us. There are, in fact, no heroes in *Bent*: not only are the Nazis shown to be as brutal and hypocritical as they undoubtedly were, but even the more sympathetic characters (Greta, the transvestite nightclub owner and Uncle Freddie, Max's gay relation) are portrayed as fearful and treacherous, concerned entirely with their own survival. Only Horst, the camp inmate who befriends Max after

Rudy's death, has glimmerings of greater humanity: and it is this humanity that proves to be Max's salvation.

Sherman, however, does not sentimentalize their relationship. Beyond offering basic kindness Horst, at least at first, is wary of Max, as Max is of Horst; in particular he finds it difficult to accept Max's denial of his own homosexuality, symbolized by Max's adoption of a yellow star instead of a pink triangle (hell, it seems, has its gradations, and Max, cunning as ever, has worked out that his chances of survival are better if he pretends to be Jewish). Even when the two men become, in effect, lovers (they are forbidden actually to touch) there are still squabbles and fights. Little by little, however, as they carry out their pointless, degrading tasks, they are drawn together, Horst learning to love Max and Max, in turn, learning to love Horst. But as their feelings for each other grow, so, ominously, does the probability of death, for Horst is sick and in Dachau the sick do not last long. In the end, despite Max's efforts, Horst is killed by guards who think it a joke to force prisoners to escape over an electrified fence. For a moment it appears as if Max, bereft, will be left to survive alone, till in a moment of grace and love he puts on Horst's coat with its pink triangle and throws himself on to the fence. He dies in a blaze of light that illuminates, not merely the theatre stage, but our whole world—in a blaze of love and truth.

—John O'Leary

BRIGHTON BEACH MEMOIRS
by Neil Simon.

First Publication: 1984.
First Production: 1982.

Brighton Beach Memoirs is an autobiographical play depicting a series of family crises in the Jerome family of the Brighton Beach section of Brooklyn in September 1937. The play is set against the Depression and the approaching war in Europe. By the play's end all the family problems—career decisions, illnesses, finances, sibling rivalry, family relationships—are resolved, and the Jeromes look forward with dignity and unity to the future and to the arrival of refugee relatives from Hitler's Europe.

The first in a trilogy (the other two are *Biloxi Blues* and *Broadway Bound*), *Brighton Beach Memoirs* is Neil Simon's *Remembrance of Things Past*, a look back at his adolescence. Like Tennessee Williams' *The Glass Menagerie*, *Brighton Beach Memoirs* is a memory play; it reaches back into the family past with more affection than Williams' play, but with less lyricism. Like Williams' play, it employs the perspective of a single character to provide exposition, move the action ahead, and comment on characters and situations. In *Brighton Beach Memoirs*, this character is 15-year-old Eugene Morris Jerome. Composition book in hand, Eugene is an ideal narrator for he hopes to be a writer some day. The family crises he records will become the matter for his writing as did Simon's family and situations become the matter of his own plays.

Certainly there is enough material in the Jerome family saga for several plays. As Jack, the father, points out, "If you didn't have a problem, you wouldn't live in this house". Eugene's immediate ambition is to tryout for the Yankees, but he would be willing to give up both baseball and writing "if I could see a naked girl while I was eating ice cream". His older brother Stanley — "either I worshiped the ground he walked on or I hated him so much I wanted to kill him" — is in danger of losing his job; later, he gambles away the family's food money. Jack — "a real hard worker. He was born at the age of 42" — holds down two jobs to make ends meet and in Act II is felled by a heart attack. Big-hearted though she is, Kate, the mother, lays guilt upon her family, and over the years has built up resentment against her widowed sister, Blanche, who lives with the Jeromes: "I was the workhorse and you were the pretty one". Blanche has two daughters: Laurie suffers from asthma, and Nora wants to quit school for a career on stage. Then there are concerns over the fate of numerous relatives in Europe.

Eugene, the audience's guide to the world of the Jeromes, is a much put-upon youngster, forever setting the table or running for groceries — "Next year I'm entering the Grocery Store Olympics" — forever being blamed for minor household mishaps. For all problems, big or small, Eugene has a wisecrack; he is able to look with humor at what life deals out. He also has most of the play's funniest lines; as filtered through Eugene's perceptive and gently ironic consciousness, the soap opera situations seem less calamitous and clichéd. But as guide, commentator, and Greek chorus, Eugene is less a character in a play than an observer. His is the central consciousness, yet he is on the periphery of the action rather than at its center. Although he comments, "How am I going to become a writer if I don't know how to suffer", he suffers little: liver and cabbage for dinner ("a Jewish medieval torture" is his description of it) and the frustrations of puberty.

One can fault the play for its too many plot lines. Some dovetail, commenting on each other; others, like that dealing with Blanche's aborted date with an eligible Irish bachelor, could easily have been dropped. There is also an excess of similar scenes. Act II has a shrill quarrel and reconciliation between Blanche and Nora, and an even shriller quarrel and reconciliation between Blanche and Kate. Moreover, problems are too neatly wrapped up, the rough edges of family relationships too easily sanded.

Still, the play's strengths more than compensate for its weaknesses. Simon skillfully combines the comic and the serious without taking away from either. The one-liners, the hallmark of Simon's earlier plays, give way here to humor that comes naturally from character and situation, not from some joke book. The quiet conversations between Jack and Stanley are genuinely effective in their understatement. The scene in which Nora tells Laurie how she realized their father really was dead — when she put her hand in his overcoat pocket "and everything was emptied and dry-cleaned and it felt cold" — is movingly poignant. The exchange between Eugene and Stanley about masturbation is both hilariously funny and in good taste. These scenes and others have an honest ring to them. Although *Brighton Beach Memoirs* at times settles too easily for happy endings and the easy laugh, it is a play that looks back with honest affection and humor at all our family pasts, and reminds us of our common humanity.

—Richard B. Gidez

CHILDREN OF A LESSER GOD
by Mark Medoff.

First Publication: 1980.
First Production: 1979.

The action of *Children of a Lesser God* "takes place in the mind of James Leeds". Time is fluid in the play, as characters "step from his memory for anything from a full scene to several lines", and place changes rapidly on the stage which holds "only a few benches and a blackboard". James is a speech teacher, aged "thirtyish", at a State School for the Deaf. Upon his arrival at the school, he encounters Sarah Norman, a former student, now in her mid-20s, who has been deaf from birth. Sarah lives and works at the school as a maid, and has steadfastly refused to try to speak, or read lips. James is immediately attracted to this bright, abrasive young woman, and is determined to break through her wall of resistance and lead her into interaction with the larger world. The action of the play follows their problematic courtship, marriage, and finally separation, as Sarah comes to the realization of her own need for independence.

While the love affair of Sarah and James gives the play a particular human interest, the importance of the work lies in its depiction of two separate cultures—hearing and deaf—and the difficulties encountered by those who try to bridge the two. Mr. Franklin, the supervising teacher at the school, prohibits the love affair and then questions the marriage, warning James that "Whether you intend it or not, you're about to uproot Sarah from the only home she's ever known . . . You're asking Sarah to step away from the community of the deaf". The second act begins with Sarah's first card party—a test of how completely she has been integrated into the middle-class hearing world. While she turns in a splendid performance designed to impress both Franklin and her newly reconciled mother, Sarah later confesses to James, "I feel split down the middle, caught between two worlds". James soon becomes exhausted serving as translator for Sarah. He finds it impossible to enjoy music, one of his great loves, because his wife cannot share it, and he is constantly frustrated in his attempts to comprehend fully the experience of a world without sound.

The deaf and hearing cultures of the play are characterized by separate languages. Sarah, who is profoundly deaf, communicates totally in sign language, but variations in communication methods within the deaf community are represented by Orin and Lydia, both students at the school, who have some residual hearing, read lips, and speak as well as use sign language. Sarah, however, refuses to do anything she cannot do well, and late in the play argues for the acceptance of her own language: "my hands are my voice; and my language, my speech, my ability to communicate is as great as yours. Greater, maybe, because I can communicate to you in one image an idea more complex than you can speak to each other in fifty words". Medoff solves the problem of a hearing audience's unfamiliarity with sign language by having James translate Sarah's side of their conversations as if for his own benefit, and much of the play's visual interest in performance comes from the beauty of this physical language.

The personal difficulties of Sarah and James become more obviously connected to political issues when Orin enlists Sarah's help in a campaign to charge the school with discrimination for not hiring enough deaf teachers. Many of the misconceptions and mistakes made by well-meaning people from the hearing community are illustrated by Edna Klein, a lawyer brought in to help in the challenge. Sarah comes to realize that, as Miss Klein wishes to speak for all deaf people, James wants to speak for her, and in the process of trying to articulate her feelings in a speech to be given before a committee, Sarah explains that she has always been devalued as somehow defective because "everyone was supposed to hear but I couldn't and that was bad". Everyone has assumed that she could not understand and could not speak for herself. The very integrity of her own identity as a separate person has been ignored: "Until you let me be an individual, an *I*, just as you are, you will never truly be able to come inside my silence and know me. And until you do that, I will never let myself know you. Until that time, we cannot be joined. We cannot share a relationship".

After a climactic argument in which James forces Sarah to try to speak, she leaves him, and, despite his remorse and awakening understanding of her position, she refuses to return: "I'm afraid I would just go on trying to change you. We would have to meet in another place; not in silence or in sound but somewhere else. I don't know where that is now. I have to go it alone". While the play does not minimize their difficulties, it ends with the hope of reconciliation as James dreams of her returning so they can be joined once again.

Written especially for the actress Phyllis Frelich, *Children of a Lesser God* is important historically as a play for the hearing theatre which includes a part for a deaf performer. The simplicity and directness of its style emphasize the beauty of its two languages, and the presentation of prejudice and misunderstanding give the play a valuable social function. Its emotional appeal, however, comes from the sensitive handling of the story of two people who struggle to understand, and to love, amidst enormous difficulties.

—Kathy Fletcher

THE CHILDREN'S HOUR
by Lillian Hellman.

First Publication: 1934.
First Production: 1934.

Karen Wright and Martha Dobie run a girls' school in a small New England town. Their relationship, Wright's imminent marriage, and the future of the school are threatened when a neurotically vindictive pupil publicly accuses the headmistresses of lesbianism. The child's grandmother forces the parents to withdraw their children, Wright and Dobie sue for damages, and a scandal erupts. The incriminating testimony is subsequently exposed as bogus and the lawsuit is paid in full, but not before Dobie commits suicide and Wright breaks off her engagement. The play ends with a stinging indictment of the criminally indulgent grandmother.

Hellman marked her playwriting debut in 1934 with this searing examination of good and evil, taken from an actual case in 19th-century Scotland, which was suggested to her by her close companion, the crime novelist Dashiell Hammett. The play's boldness was distinguished by more than the intrigue of sexual deviation. There is genuine malevolence in the portrayal of Mary Tilford, the disturbed, adolescent informer, which transcends most of the American plays of the period, and which prefigures much of Hellman's writing for the next three decades. Time and again her characters threaten with the chilling aplomb of this precocious prototype. Mary bullies the timid and flatters the vain with the perverse vehemence of a changeling.

The central target, however, is a petty, narrow community eager to act on circumstantial evidence resulting in the eventual destruction of the accusers and the innocent alike. The title, as such, is acutely ironic. For Hellman, above all, is an adult dramatist, revealing precisely how far people will manipulate others to advantage. In this respect, a film version, written by Hellman and released in 1936, lost little in transforming the intrigue into adulterous betrayal. The blackmail is worked just as convincingly as in the original, the indictment as strong. The theme of scare-mongering gives the play a political dimension which made its revival in 1952 particularly apposite (Hellman was called to testify before a House Un-American Activities Committee, and was later prevented from working in Hollywood; Hammett was actually imprisoned).

Hellman was often accused of admitting a melodramatic strain into her writing. There is evidence of it here in the final confrontation between Wright and Mrs. Tilford. The author recognized that she may have been, as she said, a bit too much "on the nose" in her meting out of justice. The focus is perhaps too slight to bear such tragically formal retribution. "It's over for me", Wright says, "but it will never be over for you", in the closing moments. It is probably sufficient for the audience to see for themselves the damaging effects of the gossip. In a national drama corn-fed on palliatives, however, Hellman's bald assertion against the status quo is, to some extent, justified. It will be remembered that *The Children's Hour* opened on Broadway in the same season as Odets's *Awake and Sing!* and Sherwood's *The Petrified Forest*—three harbingers of cultural revolution. Hellman's attack was the more invidious. With 691 performances, too, it proved to be her greatest commercial success. And although she consistently dealt with themes of abiding social moment, never again did she confront so directly the theme of the public lie. Brought into new focus by her victimisation at the hands of McCarthy witch-hunters, this play established her as a controversial, American spokesperson for the next half century.

—James MacDonald

THE COLORED MUSEUM
by George C. Wolfe.

First Publication: 1988.
First Production: 1986.

George C. Wolfe represents one of the African-American dramatists of the 1980s writing to address the conflicts within the Black community without feeling the need to explain these tensions to a white audience. The playwright's work exposes these discords with no apologies for the nerves which may be frayed in the process. *The Coloured Museum* portrays eleven vignettes of contemporary African-American life. The play begins with a satirical journey through key historical events in Black American history, then lampoons cultural icons and the pretensions of the middle class. Not all of the "exhibits" are humorous as a few evoke debilitating tensions and despair within the Black community. At the end, the drama suggests that the key to survival for African Americans is the ability to reconcile the contradictions of the past while adapting to the needs of the present and future within an African-American cultural context. The play also evokes a spirit of celebration of a complex and dynamic Black heritage.

The play conforms to several important characteristics of the Black Theatre. The drama adheres to the Aristotelian concept of dramatic structure in which spectacle is the least important element. The production of the work has minimal scenic requirements. Like most Black Theatre productions, the satire invites the audience to actively participate with the play in an antiphonal, improvised manner (known as "call and response") similar to the style seen in African-American Baptist, Pentecostal, and charismatic church services. Examples of such responses include comments, verbal interjections, applause, and signifying through hand gestures. During the performance, these audience responses provide the actors with immediate criticism of their work.

Wolfe's "museum" seeks not to preserve these portraits of Black life, but to transform them. The play challenges Blacks to hold up a mirror of introspection to assess their own complicity in maintaining the beliefs which cause Blacks to question the value of their heritage. The satire also exposes stereotypes imposed on Blacks; however, rather than attempting to expunge them from the African-American psyche, they are recognized as part of the legacy of Black people which influences, but does not necessarily dictate one's sense of self.

One of the most dominant themes of the work concerns the conflict of African Americans trying to come to terms with a history of oppression, while attempting to become a part of the culture which had denied Blacks access to the basic rights and privileges of that society. This conflict is best exemplified in the scene, "Symbiosis". In this exhibit, a professional Black man seeks to disown his heritage in order to better fit the American corporate image. Into a trash bin, he throws away his first *dashiki*, first box of curl relaxer, autographed photographs of Stokley Carmichael, Jomo Kenyata and Donna Summer, and records by Jimi Hendrix, Sly Stone, the Jackson Five, and the Temptations. The man is confronted by his alter ego, the Kid, who represents his racial past. The Kid contends the man cannot deny him; however, the desperate executive strangles the boy. He disposes of the Kid's lifeless body in the trash bin. A Temptations album catches his attention and inspires him to hum one of the tunes. Just as he opens the bin to throw away the record, the Kid emerges and grasps the man's arm in a "death grip". This conflict illustrates that survival is dependent of the recognition that one's history and culture define one's identity and cannot be trashed without destroying oneself.

Several African-American elements are prominent in this work—language and music. Wolfe deftly utilizes various styles of the Black vernacular—rural, urban, lower class, and sophisticated modes of speech. Most of the monologues have a lyrical quality reflecting the importance of rhythm in African-American language. The use of African-American music and references to its great artists within the script recognizes the significance of the art to the Black cultural heritage. Music provides an apt vehicle for the "Mammy" inspired character in the skit, "Cookin' with Aunt Ethel", to call forth the history, attitudes, and talents which interacted to produce a rich Black cultural legacy. The play also begins and ends with drumming to mark the inextricable relationship between Black Americans and their African ancestors. In the first scene, "Git on Board", Blacks are forbidden to play their drums for fear of instigating a revolt. However, in the Black culture, drums represent more than a musical instrument or tool of insurrection. In the final exhibit, "The Party", one of the characters—Topsy Washington—reminds the audience that the "drums" are reflected within her mind, body, and soul. In this way, drums are symbolic of the spiritual bond between African-Americans and their homeland, as well as the tie that binds and strengthens the Black community.

—Addell Austin Anderson

THE CONDUCT OF LIFE
by María Irene Fornés.

First Publication: 1985.
First Production: 1985.

In a brief opening soliloquy Orlando tells us of his ambitions for promotion; of his willingness to cultivate people in power; to "marry a woman in high circles", discarding his current wife Leticia; and of his fear that his sexual drive stands in his way. No sooner are these blunt declarations uttered than we see him in the uniform of a higher rank. In a scene of plain exposition he and his wife tell his colleague and friend Alejo of how each sees the other. Leticia tells Alejo her husband is "an animal. Nothing touches him except sensuality. . . . He is romantic but he is not aware of what you are feeling". In an almost wordless scene we see Orlando raping a twelve-year-old girl (represented in a stylized way). She is a homeless girl he has enticed into his van and now keeps locked first in his warehouse and, later in the play, in his cellar. The fourth scene introduces us to the final character, Olimpia, a servant who treats Leticia and us to a long account of her stifling routines, whose daily ordinariness cannot help but contrast with the rape we have just witnessed. Leticia is eager to educate herself and change, but seems as locked into her life as Olimpia.

Olimpia has no time to help her; and in his one line, at the end of the exposition scene, Alejo says "Do you think you can change anything? Do you think anyone can change anything?".

The play proceeds in a series of generally brief scenes. Orlando's promotion has come when he joined a unit torturing people. He brings home with him both the tensions and the attitudes of the job. We see him with the homeless girl, Nena, explaining "What I do to you is out of love. Out of want. It's not what you think. I wish you didn't have to be hurt. I don't do it out of hatred". Late in the play we get Nena's point of view: "He puts his fingers in my parts and he keeps reciting [poetry]. Then he turns me on my stomach and puts himself inside me. And he says I belong to him. (*There is a pause.*) I want to conduct each day of my life in the best possible way. . . . And I should value the kindness that others bestow upon me. And if someone should treat me unkindly, I should not blind myself with rage, but I should see them and receive them, since they are maybe in worse pain than me." By the last scene of the play he has not only taken to beating Nena, but we see him physically interrogating his wife about a lover she has taken. She shoots him dead and puts the pistol into Nena's hand, who, the final stage direction tells us, "*is in a state of terror and numb acceptance*".

The title, the setting of the play (*A Latin American country. The present*), and the stage setting all suggest that we are to see the play as a paradigm of relationships. The setting presents five locales—living room, dining room, hallway, basement, and warehouse—one behind the other, each the width of the stage. Are we looking through the public facade represented by the rooms where formal entertainment takes place to the hidden places where the real values of the society are revealed? To what extent are the roles of husband and wife, employer and servant, torturer and victim to be seen as analogues of one another? And do such relationships represent the way life is conducted? If so, do we read ironically Nena's line about how she wishes to conduct her life, in that it is true of no one else in the play and only marks her as a victim? Or, since she is most sympathetically presented, are we also intended to admire her all-accepting humility? If so, is it only an outside, someone not indoctrinated in the values of the society, who can conduct her life in such a way? Fornés seems to invite us to have such thoughts.

Unlike many of her plays, *The Conduct of Life* has a male protagonist, an Orlando who is *furioso* but no warrior-hero. The effect of the man's actions on the women in the play, therefore, we see directly. Another of her plays from the same time, the early 1980s, *Mud*, has such striking similarities that it seems to be designed as both the converse of, and parallel in situation to, *The Conduct of Life*. The differences are that it has a female protagonist and that the characters are rural and semi-literate and lack the fluence of speech and self-exposition of those in *The Conduct of Life*. But Mae, "a spirited young woman", is like Leticia in wishing to educate herself; brings a second lover into her home as Orlando brings Nena into his, and like Orlando is shot dead at the end. It is as though Fornés was illustrating the damage that the will to dominate does to sexual relationships between men and women in contexts as widely different as she could make them. Together, they are the closest Fornés has come to writing didactic plays.

—Anthony Graham-White

DEATH OF A SALESMAN:
Certain Private Conversations in Two Acts and a Requiem
by Arthur Miller.

First Publication: 1949.
First Production: 1949.

Willy Loman, the hero—or anti-hero—of *Death of a Salesman* is said by his elder son, Biff, to have had "all the wrong dreams. All, all wrong. He never knew who he was". The play tells through flashbacks intercut into present-day action, of the false aims, degradation, and final decline of a salesman who believes he is "vital in New England" but who, in reality, is a failure—as salesman, as father, and, in Biff's eyes, as husband. The two-act play has a sub-title, "Certain Private Conversations in Two Acts and a Requiem". At first this seems a trifle portentous, but it accurately describes the behind-the-scenes life of the public salesman. One thread of the story shows an aging Willy Loman (he has a Jonsonian-style symbolic name), disappointed in his children (Biff and Happy), with failing car and worn-out fridge, less and less able to cope with his daily round, despite the support of his faithful wife, Linda. He is failing to sell, and when he calls on his boss, Howard Wagner, to request to be transferred to New York, he discovers he is not wanted, and is fired. Even his little patch of garden grows nothing. The second act ends with the sound of Willy driving off at high speed to commit suicide. His funeral takes place on the very day the house is paid off. "We're free and clear . . . We're free . . .", says Linda, as the curtain falls, "And there'll be nobody home".

The play's original title was "The Inside of His Head" and that aptly described both the delusions Willy has about himself and his sons and the world of memories which are enacted within the main action. Biff, a fine athlete, fails to win a college place and calls at Willy's hotel in Boston unexpectedly to persuade Willy to see his teacher, "Because if he saw the kind of man you are, and you just talked to him in your [salesman] way . . . I'm sure he'd come through for you". Then a woman appears through the bathroom door, dressed only in a black slip, and there is a brilliant moment of humiliation for all three expressed in the most economical dramatic terms. This exposure of Willy's infidelity to his son comes almost at the end of the play but, chronologically, years earlier. We have had a subtle hint that Willy took women companions on his sales-trips early in the play when the voices of Linda and an unnamed woman overlap, but Willy's deception of his wife and its revelation to Biff are deliberately placed much later. Miller has adapted Ibsen's technique of retrospective exposition—the technique whereby the events that led to the present are only fully revealed at the climax of the present. Shortly after the scene in the Boston hotel room, Biff confronts Willy with a length of hose that he suspects Willy intended to use to commit suicide with, by gassing himself. He reveals that his father was no more than an assistant to an assistant salesman, and that he, Biff, is a wastrel who has spent three months in gaol for stealing a suit in Kansas City. He has now just stolen a valuable pen from the desk of the man from whom he hoped to get a good job. He realises, as he tells his father, "I'm a dime a dozen, and so are you!". Almost comically, yet pathetically, Willy, "in an uncontrolled outburst", breaks out, "I am not a dime a dozen! I am Willy Loman, and you are Biff Loman!". Biff has to be restrained from attacking his father and sums up their common failures:

> I am not a leader of men, Willy, and neither are you. You were never anything but a hard-working drummer who landed in the ash can like all the rest of them! I'm one dollar an hour, Willy! I tried seven states and couldn't raise it. A buck an hour! Do you gather my meaning?

It would be wrong to dismiss Willy as a mean, rather pathetic, hypocrite. It is easy, and not wholly incorrect, to see him as epitomising a society in which money and sales-talk count for more than human values. Willy's values, like those of his society, are false, but the tragedy for Willy is that they are rooted in a genuine love for his wife, even though loneliness and failure draw him to seek consolation in passing women. He has a real desire to build something worthwhile for his family and to provide his children with a good start in life. His dream world is, perhaps not wholly convincingly, further dramatised by his conversations with Ben who beckons to a world out there where fortunes are to be made—to the riches of Africa or the timberlands of Alaska—but the deception he has worked on Linda makes her dissuade him: "Why must everybody conquer the world? You're well liked, and the boys love you, and someday . . . [you'll] be a member of the firm . . .".

Death of a Salesman could easily be a depressing story of failure, but it has much humour. Often scenes begin with lightness, even joy and hope, and the comic and melodramatic are juxtaposed so that the overall effect can reasonably claim to be a tragedy of the common man (upon which subject Miller has written perceptively). It is a cliché to say that *Death of a Salesman* dramatises the failure of the American Dream; but it is also true that not many salesman are driven to Willy's end. The tragedy is Willy's tragedy, our tragedy, not specifically America's.

—Peter Davison

DUTCHMAN
by Amiri Baraka [LeRoi Jones].

First Publication: In *Dutchman and The Slave*, 1964.
First Production: 1964.

On a hot summer's day in New York City, Clay, a young black man, rides the subway to a friend's party. A white woman, Lula, boards the train, having previously observed Clay; she engages him in conversation, at first desultory and flirtatious, then increasingly abusive and threatening. Provoked, Clay finally explodes in anger, assaulting both Lula and a drunk, watched silently throughout by other white travellers. In an abrupt reversal, Lula stabs Clay, killing him; then she orders the other passengers to throw his body from the car, covering the murder. As the play ends, another young black man boards the train, attracting Lula's attention; her approach is delayed by the arrival of an old black conductor, but as he leaves the now almost empty car, Lula turns her gaze back to her likely next victim.

Dutchman played first at the Cherry Lane Theatre in Greenwich Village, New York, in 1964, winning an Obie award; it later transfered to the Black Arts Repertory Theatre in Harlem, a theatre founded by Imamu Amiri Baraka himself, with an exclusively black audience. Essentially a two-hander, this one-act piece is extraordinarily compressed and controlled: full of powerful anger, resonant far beyond the confines of its apparently simple situation. It should properly be viewed in the context of 1960s America, for it was first produced in the year following the assassination of John F. Kennedy, and the first American troop involvement in Vietnam; and against the backdrop of the rise of the Civil Rights movement and the Black Power initiative, following in the wake of the school bombing in Birmingham, Alabama, and the burning of Watts, a black section of Los Angeles. Baraka saw his plays as interventions in the political struggle, addressing a particular issue: black pride and self-image.

The play is therefore primarily addressed to a black audience, though it did not truly find its audience until Baraka moved it to the Harlem theatre. Its success off-Broadway—during the explosion of fringe theatre in New York in the 1960s—derives not only from its vibrant language and tight structure but also from its central issue, which offered some resonances also to white audiences. American writing at this time was preoccupied with questions of personal identity and the problematic relationship between the individual and society, in particular, with the compromises and questionable choices with which the individual is confronted. For the American black population at this time, such questions were formulated in terms of assimilation and colonisation, and were of immediate political and social import, but for many in the white audiences, the questions were also urgent and immediate.

Dutchman's ability to address both constituencies resides in Baraka's use of a mythic structure, both ancient and modern. The title recalls the myth of the "Flying Dutchman", condemned forever to sail with his undead crew as punishment for an offence against the natural order. The "loop" structure of the play, which suggests an ongoing cycle of black/white, male/female, violent aggression echoes the Dutchman's eternal voyage. But more contemporary myths are also addressed, the myths of black existence in late 20th-century America: myths which underpin and propel the black struggle. Baraka offers an uncompromising confrontation with these and with black history.

Clay, Baraka's 20-year-old male protagonist, is offered as an articulate and pleasant character at the outset. Provoked by the louche and sexually predatory Lula, he is, by turns, amused and exasperated by her insistence; he tries to placate her with civility, imitating her tone and manner, seemingly both attracted and also unnerved by her. But the more he maintains this approach, refusing to be baited by her racial gibes and slurs, the more aggressive Lula becomes, dominating him in an inexorable fashion. Clay prides himself upon his articulacy, using language to defend himself, to deflect the offensiveness of her underlying attitude. When he is ultimately pushed beyond the limits of tolerance—and of his linguistic evasions—Jones gives him both a physical action, the attack upon the drunk, and also a verbal assault upon all the white passengers including Lula. It is a stream of pungently expressed invective, chilling in its statement of the impossibility of reconciliation and cohabitation between black and white. It is a speech of great impact, stripping away the codes of black culture which Clay—and Baraka—claims whites utterly mis-read, and attempt to appropriate.

Lula's identification of Clay's attempted assimilation into the dominant white culture—traceable in the very articulacy and civility upon which he prides himself—is the source of her contempt and ultimate violence. Lula offers an emblematic representation of the white position, from the black viewpoint and from a male viewpoint; the ritual action of *Dutchman*, as well as being viewed within the context of the Black movement, can also be read against another 1960s socio-political phenomenon, the Women's Liberation initiative. As the repository of the negative aspects of the play, Lula is also very much a female stereotype; she is irrational, emotionally unstable, sexually confrontational, and homicidally violent. Her verbal attacks upon Clay can also be read as a form of castration, continually denigrating his masculinity. Yet there are possibilities of exploring the boundaries of the stereotype, too; for she is as trapped and oppressed by the ritual action as is Clay. Both are betrayed, and betraying. It is this openness of the text that renders it accessible to the white audience also; *Dutchman*, set in the subway "*heaped in modern myth*" as Baraka's stage direction claims, is a human, rather than simply a black, play.

—Val Taylor

FENCES
by August Wilson.

First Publication: 1986.
First Production: 1985.

As he runs from his home in the American South, Troy Maxson, the son of a black sharecropper, is borne north by the great migration of his people searching for the promised land. Unskilled and unwanted, he searches the streets of distant cities until the day he kills a man to stay alive. He learns how to play baseball in jail, rises to prominence in the Negro leagues, but is barred from playing in the major leagues because of the color of his skin. He was great before the game was fair, and the game will "never, never, never, never, never" come again. "There ought not never have been no time called too early" is how he puts it, as he tries to understand why his father beat him as a child.

Fences is a play about a national, American pastime. The greatest white baseball player, Babe Ruth, died at 53 years of age; Troy is 53 as the play begins, and a comparison of Troy and Babe Ruth is both compelling and to the point. Babe Ruth was everything Troy is: large-spirited, a drinker, and womanizer, physically imposing, and a slugger. It suits August Wilson's pur-pose, perhaps, to imply their divergent destinies. If Yankee Stadium is, by repute, linked with Ruth, then Troy gives rise to a quite different set of associations: a back-alley of Pittsburgh, the life his family leads on his garbage collector's pay, the rag ball he hits with a dusty bat.

The era which Wilson describes—the late 1950s and the dawn of the civil rights movement—enables a bitter experience of the past to clash with the awakening hope of the future. Troy, distrustful of his own experience, consequently fails to understand his son's aspirations. Troy, a responsible man belittled by an irresponsible society and its racism, needs the strength beyond endurance to accommodate his wasted potential. Under the pressure, he becomes irresponsible, hurting family and friends. His personality conspires with his victimization in an horrific image of the self-inflicted wound of racism. Many questions are raised. With more greatness in him, Troy has more to lose; he is more bitter as a consequence. But with greatness in him, he also has it in him to change. And yet he is beaten down; he even beats himself—"Hallelujah! I can't taste nothing no more!".

With the negative response to oppression so much in evidence, it is nevertheless important to note that Wilson is not fashioning a martyr. If Troy is a victim of racism, not all victims of racism become like Troy. How deeply Wilson explores the race issue is a question. He kills Troy before the end, with the final word being spoken over his grave. He thereby avoids an issue and misses an opportunity. What happened to Troy in the missing intervening years between the final scenes? Did he come to understand why his father beat him as a child? Did he come to understand his son? These questions are left open.

—Michael Bertin

THE HEIDI CHRONICLES
by Wendy Wasserstein.

First Publication: 1990.
First Production: 1988.

The Heidi Chronicles offers a truthful and slightly wistful comic look at the life and times of the fictional heroine, Heidi Holland, and of the "baby boom" generation. Heidi, like the play's author Wendy Wasserstein, is a young Jewish woman living in America in the 1980s. While it focuses on Heidi as the central character, and while women's relationships are treated sympathetically and humourously, the play is designed to appeal to both women and men.

The play opens with a Prologue, set in 1989. The eponymous Heidi delivers a lecture at Columbia University, New York. Slides of women painters and their work are projected behind her as she speaks; the audience is positioned as part of her class. She begins by discussing the marginalization of women in art history books, pointing out that: ". . . Although Sofonisba was praised in the seventeenth century as being a portraitist equal to Titian, and at least thirty of her paintings remain known to us, there is no trace of her or any other woman artist prior to the twentieth century in your current Art History Survey textbook. Of course, in my day, this same standard text mentioned no women, 'from the Dawn of History to the Present.' Are you with me? Okay."

Here, the lecturer Heidi, and through her the dramatist Wendy Wasserstein, engages in the feminist project of "writing women into history". She does so with humour and verve; with a mixture of academic argument and colloquial, conversational language. This opening speech is winning, amusing, convincing. So is the play as a whole.

The play's central theme is communication: between friends, between lovers, between a woman and her memory and understanding of her past. All the main characters demonstrate sharp wits and tongues. Heidi's responses are usually understated, and Wasserstein has created some wonderfully authentic scenes in which Heidi is repeatedly interrupted by men—even those who most love and respect her—contrasted quite effectively with the scenes in which she holds her own, in the authority position of lecturer. The characters are clearly and sympathetically drawn: Heidi, the strong independent woman; Peter, Heidi's closest friend, whose life experiences parallel Heidi's and with whom she might have formed a relationship if he were not gay; Scoop, the wise-guy journalist with whom Heidi first falls in love, and who remains a friend throughout; and a number of close women friends whose lives develop quite differently to Heidi's, showing the range and diversity of women's experiences, and of men's. For instance, Peter explains himself in this way in Act 1, scene 4, set in 1974 at the Chicago Art Institute: ". . . According to my mental health friends, we are moving into a decade of self-obsession. I am simply at the forefront of the movement." But Peter turns out to be less self-obsessed than other characters, each of whom is faced with decisions and changes indicative of the "me-first" baby boom generation in America. Indeed, Scoop's magazine is called "Boomer": it is a chronicle of the times, which develops alongside the lives of the characters in the play.

The Heidi Chronicles is episodic in form. The rest of Act One flashes back to significant moments in Heidi's past, all staged in public spaces in academic contexts. These scenes take us through Heidi's formative years: her college days; the forging of a significant friendship with Peter; her first romance with Scoop; her girlhood insecurities and young woman's friendships and alliances with a range of women, all of whom get involved in feminist consciousness-raising groups as well as each other's personal lives. Act Two takes us back to New York, but the time frame is Heidi's present (the 1980s) and the scenes contrast public and private spaces, moving from public lecture halls to TV studios, a restaurant, and a hospital ward (where privacy is both most necessary and hardest to come by), and finally to Heidi's apartment.

The device of using contemporary music helps to set the scene and mood of each episode, weaving together events and moods as they reflect on the central characters. Major events are mentioned, setting Heidi's life in context and allowing her personal chronicle to become something more universal.

At play's end: Scoop sells his magazine and sets out to do something else, perhaps politics (he ends up more self-obsessed than ever); Peter works as a successful pediatrician—"the most eligible Dr. under forty"—finds a partner and lives in the country, though this seemingly idyllic life is counterpoised by his job on a medical wing for immune-deficient children, and the revelation that his former partner "is not well" (he probably has AIDS); while Heidi adopts a daughter. We last see her rocking the child to sleep, singing the same song she sang as a younger woman:

Darling, You send me.
You send me.
Honest you do, honest you do, honest you do.
Lights fade as Heidi rocks.

In ending the play with this image and song, Wasserstein takes up the major theme of earlier women's drama such as Caryl Churchill's *Top Girls*, wherein the central character gave up her daughter in order to invest her time and energy in her career. Heidi adopts a daughter and has a career, but lacks a relationship, and is described as content rather than happy. Each generation gains and loses something. *This* generation gains something important in *The Heidi Chronicles*, which makes a major contribution to the field of drama.

—Lizbeth Goodman

THE HOUSE OF BLUE LEAVES
by John Guare.

First Publication: 1972.
First Production: 1971.

John Guare's *The House of Blue Leaves* opens with Artie Shaughnessy performing at the El Dorado Bar Amateur Night. He fails to get the attention of either audience—not those attending the El Dorado nor those attending Guare's play, because his tacky songs are performed to Guare's spectators, as the stage directions indicate, *"while the house lights are still on, and the audience is still being seated"*. He wants recognition and "a blue spotlight"; he gets neither. He needs to believe that his musical potential is his way out of a life tending animals all day at the zoo, then returning at night to tend his deranged wife, Bananas. Depressive but acute, a potent threat to his pipe dream, she can hear the blatant plagiarism of his music and is willing to say so.

On the other hand, Artie's lover, Bunny Flingus, is enthusiastically support-ive of him. She knows her man is going to make it big and drag her along with him. She has claims to all sorts of special knowledge from her myriad jobs. Being a movie usher at women's weepies let her "know these sick wives" and the way to deal with them—electric shock therapy (by virtue of her experience at Con Edison). A theatrical furniture store taught her "the score" about "casting couches"! Her conclusion is to leap onto them. She dispenses sexual pleasure with largesse but withholds her secret weapon of culinary joy in order to achieve marriage and celebrity. When Artie's old friend Billy, the Hollywood success story, breezes through, she immediately abandons Artie's cause and uses her cooking to earn a place with the famous man.

The working-class neighborhood of New York which is the setting for *The House of Blue Leaves* is called Sunnyside, yet *"the only illumination in the room is the light from the television"*. Though the Pope is making his first visit ever to America, the closest Artie Shaughnessy can get his demented wife to the curative powers of the chief prelate is to have her kneel before his passing parade on the television. She obeys her husband's order to "kiss him . . . He'll cure you! Kiss him". Even the nuns who descend from the roof down to the modest apartment kneel before this icon which glows in the dark. Of the three habited sisters, only the Little Nun escapes with her life; her last words in the play as she kisses the television are "A shrine . . . I wanted to be a Bride of Christ but I guess now I'm a gay divorcée". The Pope's broadcast is reassuring:

> We feel, too, that the entire American people is here present with its noblest and most characteristic traits: a people basing its conception of life on spiritual values, on a religious sense, on freedom, on loyalty, on work, on the respect of duty, on family affection, on generosity and courage—

Guare's dark comedy is a brilliant and hilarious debunking of the current status of those values in a land where the book that teaches men how to live is the *Reader's Digest* and the pulpit that dispenses the word is the Johnny Carson Show. In this world the only religion that everyone bows to is fame.

Guare's commonplace people do not consider themselves fully human: "The famous ones—they're the real people". Only clerical and cinematic superstars are considered real. Artie is a zoo-keeper who turns his back on his wife and on the wonder of all the animals giving birth at once: "I've become this Dreaming Boy. I make all these Fatimas out of the future. Lourdes and Fatimas. All these shrines of the future and I keep crawling to them". Approaching the pinnacle of fame too closely cost Corrinna Stroller, Billy's girlfriend, first her hearing and then her life. Ronnie Shaughnessy, Artie's army son about to be shipped to Vietnam, will do anything to appear on the evening news, even assassinate the Pope (Guare invented this extremity; the plot on the Pope's life had not yet occurred when the play had its premiere in 1971). The Pope survives Ronnie's first attempt, but Ronnie's mother, Bananas, does have the life choked out of her before the audience's disbelieving eyes. The woman who praised his music (Bunny) gone, Artie is left with Bananas, the one who sees through it. It is necessary for Artie to shut her up; she can hear that he has no musical talent. He realizes that he will never escape Sunnyside; he will never get Hollywood recognition. He confronts his dime-a-dozen reality by choking the life out of his wife. Only now does the "blue spotlight appear". And who knows, even if Artie the songwriter never made it to the Academy Awards ceremony, maybe Artie the wife-killer will appear on the evening news after all. Guare's disturbing ending affirms that addiction to fame is fatal.

—Roger Sorkin

INDIANS
by Arthur Kopit.

First Publication: 1969.
First Production: 1968.

Arthur Kopit's *Indians* is composed of 13 scenes which alternate between Buffalo Bill's Wild West Show and an 1886 Indian Commission hearing. In these scenes a combination of historical and non-historical figures participate in acts in the show or are involved in treaty discussions between United States government officials and Indians. Besides being hailed as one of the "best plays of 1969–70" in America, it met with critical acclaim in France, Germany, Japan, and the Scandinavian countries, and was the basis for an unsuccessful film version by Robert Altman in 1976 under the title *Buffalo Bill and the Indians: Or Sitting Bull's History Lesson*.

Kopit's underlying concept for the play dates from March 1966 when he read a statement made by General William Westmoreland, the Commander-in-Chief of American forces in Vietnam. Speaking about reports that American soldiers had killed Vietnamese civilians, Westmoreland said, "Of course innocent people have been killed. In war they always are. And of course our hearts go out to the innocent victims of this". The dramatist realized that Westmoreland's sentiment runs throughout American history, and he recalls listening to Charles Ives' *Fourth Symphony* in which two orchestras in counterpoint play opposing pieces of music based on American folk songs ("Shenandoah" and "Columbia, the Gem of the Ocean"): "you have this serene, seraphic music based on these folk songs, and then the violent opposition of a marching band drowning it out". In Kopit's mind this music was juxtaposed with Westmoreland's quote. Thus, the dramatist uses those exact words as part of Colonel Forsythe's dialogue in his comments on the massacre of a group of Indians.

Although capturing the essence of American history, Kopit has admitted that "most of the scenes in the play are based on real incidents that were distorted". The tension in the play derives from his pairing of the scenes. He uses the extravagant Wild West Show segments to illustrate American prejudices, to reveal Buffalo Bill's character, and to examine a theme that has run through some of his earlier plays—the concept of mythic heroism. Opposed to the Wild West Show segments are scenes from the Indian Commission hearing that demonstrate how alien the White and Indian societies appear to each other. On the one hand the Whites do not understand why Indians do not abide by the signed treaties and do not recognize that they are innately inferior to the White race. On the other hand the Indians do not understand the concept of treaties based on land ownership, a notion which does not make sense to them because they do not believe that the land can be owned. They also question why the Whites do not abide by the agreed-upon terms of the treaties if they are valid. Obviously neither side understands nor respects the other and therefore is unable to recognize the dignity of its opponent.

To emphasize the contrast between the basic cultural instincts of the two sides, Kopit twice incorporates into the play words that Chief Joseph uttered in 1877:

> I am tired of fighting. Our chiefs have been killed . . . the old men are all dead. It is cold and we have no blankets. The children are freezing. My people, some of them, have fled to the hills and have no food . . . no one knows where they are—perhaps frozen. I want to have time to look for my children and see how many of them I can find. Maybe I shall find them among the dead. Hear me, my chiefs. I am tired. My heart is sick and sad! From where the sun now stands, I will fight no more, forever.

This quotation stands in stark contrast to Westmoreland's words (cited above) and thereby epitomizes the conflict that Kopit is representing.

As demonstrated by the "Chronology for a Dreamer" that is included in the printed version of the play, it is clear that Kopit does not intend *Indians* to be taken on a literal, realistic level. This dramatic structure—an emotional Gestalt in the impressionistic, surrealistic representation of his themes through a deliberately confusing, Brechtian style—leads the audience to an awareness of the man-made nature of the historical process. For example, through the delineation of Buffalo Bill's character, combined with historical events and America's need to create heroes—which make him instrumental in destroying a people and a way of life that he admires—the dramatist shows that history is composed of human, not natural, forces, and are thus alterable.

—Steven H. Gale

LONG DAY'S JOURNEY INTO NIGHT
by Eugene O'Neill.

First Publication: 1956; corrected edition, 1989.
First Production: 1956.

Long Day's Journey Into Night begins at 8.30 a.m. in the Tyrone summer home in Connecticut and ends around midnight of the same, hot August day. The year is 1912. As bright daylight fades into fog-shrouded night, Mary Tyrone resumes taking morphine, dashing her family's hopes that she has been cured of her addiction. James Tyrone is an aging actor who, in the course of the play, confronts not only his family's accusations of cheapness but his own regret over wasting his talents in a popular melodrama. Their elder son, Jamie, devastated by his mother's return to drugs and by his brother Edmund's illness, tries to ease his sorrow with copious amounts of liquor and a visit to the local brothel. The youngest member of the family is Edmund, who learns that he has consumption and must enter a sanitarium. A tapestry of recriminations, regrets, apologies, and confessions, the play ends with the men sunk in a haze of alcohol and the heavily drugged Mary reliving, in her mind, the happier times of her youth.

After O'Neill completed this autobiographical work, one of his last plays, he placed it in a vault with the stipulation that it not be opened until 25 years after his death. Shortly after he died, his widow and heir, Carlotta Monterey

O'Neill, removed the play and authorized its publication and production. Following the Swedish premiere it was performed in New York and earned O'Neill a posthumous fourth Pulitzer prize. The production of *Journey* was instrumental in the resurrection of the playwright's reputation that began in the 1950s; frequent stage revivals as well as films have helped place the drama among O'Neill's most famous works.

The majority of critics consider *Journey* to be O'Neill's best play, and it is arguably one of the finest dramas created by an American. Using a form favored by American writers, the realistic family play, O'Neill painted a searing portrait of four people caught in a web of resentment and need, anger and love. And while the Tyrone family is in many ways unique, based on O'Neill's own immediate kin, it is also a kind of "Everyfamily" writ large. Monumental as their battles may be, the Tyrones harbor grievances that are instantly recognizable: the failure of spouses and children to live up to expectations, the inevitable jealousy between siblings, the regrets and recriminations over dreams that have been shattered by time.

Except for Mary's return to drugs and the doctor's confirmation of Edmund's consumption, nothing actually happens in *Journey*; adhering to the Aristotelian Unities, O'Neill creates a drama that emphasizes character rather than plot (a fact that explains the play's appeal to a legion of fine actors). Confrontations between characters—involving accusations that are often hastily withdrawn or modified—form the building blocks of the first three acts. As the day progresses in linear fashion from early morning to night, the characters move in a circular pattern of memory through the past events that have brought them to their present plight. The emotional center of the work is Mary Tyrone, the most fully-realized female character in the O'Neill canon. Mary is the play's apostle of determinism, claiming that "none of us can help the things life has done to us", yet her constant complaints against her husband and sons reveal her belief in individual responsibility. The convent-educated Mary is trapped in a world for which she was never prepared; she retreats into reveries induced by drugs and spends the last moments of the play looking for her faith and the childhood innocence she has lost. A woman who chafes at the overwhelming familial demands placed upon her, and who imagines—albeit in a drug fantasy—a world in which she would have a story separate from that written by her male kin, Mary is one of O'Neill's most complex and theatrically compelling female creations.

The world of O'Neill's late plays is a painful one; men and women wander bewildered in a spiritual and emotional fog; indeed they deliberately attempt to drown themselves in drugs or drink. But few of his characters wholly succeed in escaping their anguish, and the final act of *Journey* is composed of a series of confessions by the distraught Tyrone men. A self-educated immigrant whose fear of poverty conflicts with his concern for his family, Tyrone comes to understand how he has betrayed his own potential by wasting his talents in "the big money-maker" he starred in too long. Like many another O'Neill character, Jamie is a lost soul traveling on a path to self-destruction (a path O'Neill would trace more fully in his last play, *A Moon for the Misbegotten*, which focuses on Jamie). But even Jamie gains tragic stature as he confesses his attachment to his doomed mother and his jealousy of Edmund.

In a play that revolves around betrayal and blame, it is not wholly surprising to find a character accused of the crime of being born. Edmund's difficult birth was the immediate cause of his mother's addiction; he came into the world guilty of virtual matricide. In his guilt and guiltlessness, Edmund embodies O'Neill's interpretation of the concept of original sin, as well as his modern translation of the Greek sense of fate. Edmund, a young writer based on the playwright himself, is also the moral touchstone of the play. The only member of the family with the possibility for a future, he learns compassion for his less fortunate kin.

Journey is a beautifully structured play, moving inexorably through recriminations, confrontations, and confessions to a stunning theatrical climax. The tragic counterpart to *Ah, Wilderness!*, O'Neill's sunny comedy of family life, *Journey* is an excoriating trip through a world where past mistakes circumscribe the present and destroy the future. But it is also, as O'Neill insisted in his dedication of *Long Day's Journey Into Night* to his third wife, Carlotta, a work written "with deep pity and understanding and forgiveness for *all* the four haunted Tyrones".

—Judith E. Barlow

M. BUTTERFLY
by David Henry Hwang.

First Publication: 1989.
First Production: 1989.

The action of *M.Butterfly* takes place in Beijing and Paris between 1960 and 1986. The plot is based on a cause célèbre of the latter year—the trial in Paris of a French diplomat and his Chinese lover on a charge of spying for China. What made the trial especially newsworthy was that during its course the Chinese spy, with whom the diplomat had conducted a twenty-year liaison, revealed that "she" was a man. More extraordinary still, the diplomat resolutely insisted that he had always been ignorant of this fact.

On these historical facts, bizarre in themselves, Hwang has framed his play. In an "Afterword" attached to the text he fully explains the nature of his interest in the story. His thesis (the "arc" of the play) is that what we have here is the plot of Puccini's *Madame Butterfly* in ironic reversal—"the Frenchman fantasises that he is Pinkerton and his lover is Butterfly. By the end of the piece he realises that it is he who has been Butterfly, in that the Frenchman has been duped by love; the Chinese spy, who exploited that love, is the real Pinkerton."

This reversal of a theme familiar in Western literature since at least the middle of the last century—that of a predatory white male exploiting the love of a submissive Asian female—enables Hwang to explore the half-truths and exaggerations which underpin the myth (and which in some quarters still conspire to keep it alive) and the unhappy personal consequences of those enmeshed in it.

However those consequences are not, as Hwang claims in his "Afterword" and contrives to bring out in the action of his play, limited to the "merely" personal sphere of sexual and racial relations. There is also, he suggests, a political dimension to the Butterfly myth: "It is reasonable to assume that influences and attitudes so pervasively displayed in popular culture might also influence policy-makers as they consider the world." Hwang's contention is that [Western] politicians become, consciously or unconsciously, Pinkertons when dealing with Asian cultures in that they perceive the latter to be passive, submissive, and "feminine" in nature. Thus in his play Hwang adds a political dimension—the spying—lacking in the original opera plot which widens the scope of the Butterfly myth beyond the personal motivations of the two principal characters. However, consonant with Hwang's reversal of the myth it is the Westerner who this time suffers the machinations of a ruthless Asian power.

Hwang's extension of the significance of the Butterfly myth into politics is certainly novel but it is contentious—as one British critic has pointed out, Asian societies have in this century produced leaders (Mao, Pol Pot, Ho Che Min to name but a few) who have been anything but submissive in their relations with the West and whom most Western governments have speedily recognised as vigorous, competent men. It would, however, be a mistake to regard this play as a serious critique of Western attitudes, both private and public, towards Asia and then attack it for the tendentious assertions and dubious generalisations it undoubtedly contains. It is meant first and foremost to be a theatrical event, as the playwright's careful stage directions—especially as to positioning of the actors, lighting, and sound effects—amply demonstrate and ultimately this is both its real strength and true weakness. Hwang's characters are made to articulate his beliefs so precisely and so obviously that it is difficult to see them as "real" people. They seem to have more in common with the "types" in a medieval drama, limited by the humours they must illustrate. There are, literally and figuratively, very few grey areas on Hwang's stage, always brightly lit or plunged into darkness, to render his characters more human. For the same reason, if properly directed with careful reference to the playwright's directions, this play undoubtedly makes for provocative (in every sense), eye-catching drama. No character speaks more than a dozen lines at a time, the dialogue is punchily aggressive with a good deal of amusing slang and Hwang makes imaginative use of stage, light, and sound effects to under-line the action and dialogue on stage. This, as much as the intriguing story on which it is based, makes the play good theatre and accounts for its box-office popularity.

—D.H. O'Leary

A MOVIE STAR HAS TO STAR IN BLACK AND WHITE

by Adrienne Kennedy.

First Publication: 1984.
First Production: 1976.

Clara waits in a hospital room at the bedside of her brother, who is in a coma after an auto accident. She is joined there by her parents, who are separated because her father left "to marry a girl who talked to willow trees", and her husband, from whom she is separated. As she keeps vigil memories—mostly traumatic—run through her mind: of segregation in the small Georgia town where she grew up, of her marriage and move to Cleveland, of a miscarriage she suffered ('All that bleeding. I'll never forgive him') while her husband was in the army in Korea, her father's attempted suicide. At the end of the play the doctor tells her "that my brother will live; he will be brain damaged and paralyzed".

To summarize the play in this way is to misrepresent it. *A Movie Star Has to Star in Black and White* is short but complex in form. Clara tells us that her husband says of her that she "can't accept the passage of time, and that my diaries consume me and that my diaries make me a spectator watching my life like watching a black and white movie. He thinks sometimes . . . to me my life is one of my black and white movies that I love so . . . with me playing a bit part". But this explanation comes near the end of the play; meanwhile, we have already experienced the rather mysterious mingling of life and movies.

The play opens with the appearance of the Columbia Pictures Lady, the draped woman holding a torch who appears at the beginning of Columbia Pictures' movies, who tells us we will see scenes from *Now Voyager*, *Viva Zapata* and *A Place in the Sun*, and names the stars who appear in them. "Supporting roles are played by the mother, the father, the husband. A bit role is played by Clara". Nevertheless, with the line "Lately I often think of killing myself" she begins speaking Clara's thoughts. The lights fade down on her and up on Clara, who speaks three sentences before the lighting takes us to the deck of the ocean liner in *Now Voyager* and Bette Davis speaks Clara's thoughts for her. So the play continues, passing from one movie to the next, with Clara and the members of the family sometimes in the movie settings and sometimes in the hospital. In each movie scene the female star speaks for Clara and the male star is silent. In the scene from *Viva Zapata* Jean Peters kisses Marlon Brando—it is their wedding night—but "*She is bleeding. She falls back on her bed. Brando pulls a sheet out from under her. The sheets are black*". This action is later repeated and then done over and over again until the end of the play. The scene from *A Place in the Sun* ends, just before Kennedy's play ends, with Shelley Winters falling from a boat into the water. Montgomery Clift watches her continue to call silently for help through the last few lines of the play.

To complicate the play further, Clara refers on several occasions to her writings, of diaries, poems and a play, which is "going to be called a Lesson in Dead Language. The main image is a girl in a white organdy dress covered with menstrual blood". *Lesson in Dead Language* is an earlier play of Adrienne Kennedy. Furthermore, the character of Clara appeared in *The Owl Answers*, and when Clara says "I call God and the Owl answers" she clearly refers us to that earlier play, from which most of the lines that she speaks in her own persona are taken.

That Clara is writing a play as we witness Kennedy's play suggests an ordering of the otherwise cruelly meaningless experience of her brother's accident or self-destruction. It is the one positive note to set against the grimness of what we see and hear. The function of the movie scenes is more problematic. They seem to suggest that Clara is not in control of her life—just as she cannot influence what happens to her brother—and so looks for its reflection elsewhere, as though reaching for models or images against which she can measure her own life—as though a movie star has to star *for* black and white alike. But those images may also suggest the alienation of the African-American woman from the popular images of the dominant culture. Kennedy was named for a movie actress and tells us in her memoir *People who Led to My Plays* that as a child she identified with Bette Davis in *Now Voyager*. Yet she also writes there that "my father often called me good-looking when in the mirror I saw a strange-looking face". The dissonance is conveyed in the play, not only by the members of Clara's black family wandering onto the deck of the ocean liner of *Now Voyage,* and from the distortion of the chaste wedding night of *Viva Zapata* into the image of the ever-bleeding bridal figure, but also by the irony that Adrienne Kennedy uses the images of once-popular movies to write a play that is unconventional in form, and one in which the audience is allowed only slowly to grasp the significance of what they see.

—Anthony Graham-White

'NIGHT, MOTHER
by Marsha Norman.

First Publication: 1983.
First Production: 1982.

Her daughter informs Thelma Cates five minutes into *'Night, Mother* that Jessie plans to kill herself. Although Mama tries to josh her out of it, tries to phone Jessie's brother Dawson, tries to argue her to reason, and begs her to change her mind, nothing works. Right to the end, Jessie maintains her determination to kill herself, and Mama keeps attempting passionately, but ineffectually, to stop her. Along the way, Jessie prepares Mama for life alone, shows her where kitchen supplies and detergent are stored, explains how to have her favorite candies delivered, and advises her how, after Jessie's death, to manage the police, the wake, and the food the neighbors will bring. She has thought of everything, has dry-cleaned the dress her mother should wear to the funeral, and now even rehearses Thelma in washing a pan until somebody arrives. Jessie also elicits from Mama the answers to her unanswered questions: Did Mama love Jessie's father? What does Jessie look like during her epileptic seizures—which Mama still refers to as "fits"? Mama, in turn, supplies unexpected news: Jessie's ex-husband cheated on her, and Jessie's epilepsy began years earlier than she has always thought.

After begging "Don't leave me, Jessie", Thelma's goal moves from saving Jessie to protecting herself—from guilt, from abandonment, from others' curiosity, from a lonely old age, from the disruption of a life she's ordered just the way she likes it. Thelma's survival after Jessie's death concerns them both in the daughter's final minutes. Jessie instructs Mama in how to deal with questions about motives; Thelma must ascribe the suicide to "something personal". By this time, Mama has run out of roadblocks to erect in front of a daughter rapidly approaching the moment when she will whisper "'night, Mother" and lock herself in her room. We know, of course, that a gunshot will quickly follow, and we dread that moment, even as we anticipate it. For, make no mistake, the play's tragic conclusion must arrive.

'Night, Mother could not be labeled melodrama. Norman provides no ranting and raving, no soap-opera accidents, no possibility of reprieve from the inexorable sweep towards Jessie's inevitable death. The 90-minutes run without intermission, which prevents anything from interfering with the cumulative tensions, from diluting the potent pity and fear which Jessie's final minutes alive generate in those of us who remain behind after she has pulled the trigger. We experience mounting suspense and dread and then, with Mama, heartbreak.

Norman's exceptionally linear plot construction contains two simultaneous actions: Jessie tries to prepare her mother for the daughter's suicide, and Mama tries to dissuade her or prevent it. This amounts to the irresistible force meeting the immovable object. Yet Mama's efforts also lead to both achieving some measure of understanding how Jessie arrived at the point where she would rather get off the bus than continue on the aimless ride which in the end would only drop her at the same destination—death.

Marsha Norman wrote 'Night, Mother to try to understand how someone could decide to take her own life. She selected as her protagonist a woman who chooses suicide as the logical step. "You're not even upset!" exclaims Mama, for Jessie does not feign ending her life as a disguised cry for help. Nor does she suddenly despair and impulsively grab a gun, aim it at her head, and pull the trigger. In her past, she has not even manifested self-destructive tendencies. Far from indicating she's out of touch with reality or has had a bad day, Jessie makes an existential choice—the exercise of her free will—from which she never waivers. She has examined her options, made a considered choice of what appeals to her most, and engaged in careful preparations, which conclude with her attempt to explain her decision to her horrified mother—and to us, the spectators.

By dramatizing an hour and a half of intense crisis and conflict, leavened by bursts of wry humor, Norman thrusts us inside the souls of both Jessie and Thelma. We care for them, and we also come to align ourselves with both women, simultaneously. We accept that ending her life will please Jessie most and eventually we regard her position as not unreasonable. Yet even as we comprehend her motives we join traumatized Mama in aching to stop her daughter. Mama experiences the greater ordeal because nothing has prepared her for this, for the struggle to prevent her daughter's death, and also for its aftermath. By comparison, Jessie benefits from her conviction, her certainty that she has selected the proper course and soon will achieve peace. But 'Night, Mother dramatizes, not only Jessie's will to die, but the efforts she makes to tutor her mother in survival.

Norman has not created eccentric oddballs such as Beth Henley might have imagined. Norman's Jessie and Thelma represent the ordinary "simple people" whose lives generally go unchronicled. Norman speaks for them. As she does so, she demonstrates an extraordinary ear for language, not highfalutin dialogue, but precisely the right words to convey what the characters would say—their mood, class, circumstances, gender, relationship—everything, in short, which makes them themselves. The spare, uncluttered and natural conversations move us readily to tears and laughter.

We respond to the women's experience so intensely in part because Norman has chosen a dramatic style so representational as to be termed naturalistic. The two women inhabit a fully realized living room and kitchen, with the menacing door to the room where Jessie plans to die clearly visible. We observe a slice of life—on a day which concludes that life—and it appears unusually real, as though we really were voyeurs at the actual event, peering through the fourth wall removed.

As we watch, we come to appreciate how the past has led these women to this moment. We can appreciate that Jessie doesn't enjoy life and has relinquished hope it will improve. Why should she stick around? Her mother can only try to tantalize her with suggestions they rearrange the furniture or go buy groceries at the A&P. When Jessie argues that the "self" she has hoped to become will never "show up, so there's no reason to stay," we can't refute her any more persuasively than Mama can.

Of course Mama must try, not just because any mother would, but because she has spent all Jessie's life controlling her daughter and expects she can do so now. One of the reasons Jessie has never before taken control of her life surely involves the fact Mama has never let her, but instead has always determined who Jessie has been, was, and would be—non-epileptic, even though Mama knew better, a wife to the man Mama chose for her, and eventually a comfort to Mama in her old age. Norman's astute psychological perceptions of this mother/daughter relationship lead the playwright to ascribe to Thelma the thought that Jessie belongs to her, "I thought you were mine", shorthand for the belief she has the right to meddle, manipulate, possess, and control her. When Mama insists she "won't let" Jessie take her life, however, Jessie reminds her "It's not up to you." She firmly insists her life belongs to her, not to Thelma. For 'Night, Mother dramatizes Jessie taking control of her life by ending it. She has decided to escape prosaic circumstances she can't abide. Having "waited until I felt good enough," she now has marshalled the strength to declare about her life, "it's all I really have that's mine, and I'm going to say what happens to it." With exceptional emotional honesty and power, this modern masterpiece permits Jessie to do just that, and thus to achieve "everybody and everything I ever knew, gone."

—Tish Dace

OUR TOWN
by Thornton Wilder.

First Publication: 1938.
First Production: 1938.

One of the most successful American plays of the 20th century, Thornton Wilder's *Our Town* owes its fame chiefly to the skill with which its author dramatizes the age-old theme of the importance of ordinary day-to-day human existence: namely, by means of a daring rearrangement of conventional stage-craft. To depict the supreme worth of savoring life fully while we possess it, Wilder drew upon such classic models as Homer's *Odyssey* and Dante's *Purgatorio*, both of which offer poignant contrasts between the fleeting beauty of the living and the dreary permanence of the dead, as in Achilles's dour comment in Hades that he would rather be a living slave than a dead king. In *Our Town*, Wilder converted the universal message implicit in this scene into an allegory involving birth, marriage, and death in the United States of the 1930s. By his bold methods of staging his drama, his artful manipulation of time and place, he related the here and now of an insignificant New England village to the timeless concerns of human nature everywhere. His aim, he wrote, was "an attempt to find a value above all price for the smallest events in our daily life. I have made the claim as preposterous as possible, for I have set the village against the largest dimensions of time and place".

Wilder's two major innovations enabling him to fulfill his aim were the use of a bare stage and a centralizing character, the Stage Manager, a throwback to both the Chorus in classical Greek drama and the Property Man in Chinese theatre. As a stand-in for author and director, he not only arranges stage props, but also initiates, controls, and interprets setting and action, explaining directly to the audience from the outset that they are going to witness a play about life in an ordinary little town in New Hampshire, Grover's Corners, beginning just before dawn on 7 May 1901. After pointing to some of its notable imaginary features, including the cemetery, he gives a brief history of the town, identifies some of its leading citizens, focusing on several members of the two neighboring families, the Webbs and the Gibbses, whose interrelation-ships will dominate the action from there on. As the Stage Manager develops their typical encounters with one another that day throughout Act I, he also offers further commentary, from time to time, which illustrates the common-placeness of routine in the Webb and Gibbs households, but also suggests its broader, metaphysical significance. The blessed tie that binds Grover's Corners to the Universe and the mind of God is then circuitously expressed in the colloquy between young George Gibbs and his sister Rebecca at the end of the first act.

Similar techniques are employed in the second and third acts to strengthen and clarify the union of theme and action. In Act II, which deals with the courtship and marriage of George Gibbs and Emily Webb three years later, the Stage Manager serves as both the minister who weds them and the commentator who disparages the glamour of the ceremony, which, he says, is interesting only "once in a thousand times". Nevertheless, as he muses on the fact that millions of folk since the dawn of time have celebrated such marriage rites as these, it becomes clear that the wedding of this particular young couple, however commonplace it appears, symbolizes a universal "fusion of nature's physical and spiritual purposes".

Again, in Act III, Wilder boldly extends his basic analogy by literally juxtaposing life and death on the stage. Nine more years have elapsed, and some of the town's recent dead who were alive in Act II are now seated on chairs representing their graves in the cemetery, where they are witnessing the burial of Emily, who has just died in childbirth. As she joins them in the vacant chair next to her mother-in-law, she becomes the catalyst for the swift evocation of Wilder's deepest meaning. The granting of her desire to relive just a single day of her former life, her 12th birthday, leads to her discovery that the living can neither appreciate nor understand the beauty of life till they have lost it. Crying "Oh, earth you're too wonderful for anybody to realize you", she is ready to return to the passionless Dead, whom the Stage Manager had described at the opening of the act as "waitin' for something they feel is comin'. Something important and great". The action has built up steadily throughout the play toward the dramatic revelation that human life, however painful, dreary, or inconsequential its quotidian events, is both a precious gift in itself as well as part of a mysterious plan that rests in the "Mind of God".

—Eugene Current-Garcia

PICNIC
by William Inge.

First Publication: 1953.
First Production: 1953.

"Women are gettin desperate," says the hunky, unintelligent and unsophisticated Hal Carter to his old college friend, Seymour, and that statement sums up the situation in *Picnic*. William Inge set his Pulitzer prize-winning drama in a small, Kansas town, the sort of place in which he had himself grown up, with the typical sun-baked landscape of the Midwest with its grain elevator, a great silo, and a railway that seems to be the only link between the endless prairie and the world outside. As in classical drama that respects the unity of place, there is a single setting, a realistic one showing "the porches and the yards of two small houses", and this helps to create a sense of a closed community which receives a stranger into its midst and from which some will want to escape while others realize they cannot. There is also something not unlike the unity of time, the action beginning early one day and finishing a few hours later the following morning, and, still in classical style, the scantiness of action, the most spectacular portions of which occur off-stage, is more than made up for by the great force of psychological tensions as past, present, and future come into sharp focus in the lives of two sets of essentially similar but also sharply differentiated characters. The play takes place on Labor Day, the first Monday in September, which marks the end of the summer and the start of the difficulties of autumn and winter. The irony of it is that this holiday will, as often happens when there is a break from work, be a fraught time of self-questioning and even downright unhappiness; as for the traditional picnic, not only does it, of course, mean extra work for the women, but it is also an occasion when human values will be questioned. This is indeed a Labor Day to remember, but not for the customary reasons.

The two modest houses shown on stage are inhabited by women. The first of them that we see is Mrs Helen Potts, described in the first stage-direction as a "merry, dumpy little woman close to sixty", but we realize before long we should not let ourselves be deceived by appearances. Her life is still largely controlled by her imperious, bed-ridden mother who, years back, had intervened to have her daughter's marriage annulled, and we ask ourselves if it is simply kind-heartedness that impels Helen not to turn away "bums" like Hal when they turn up on her doorstep offering to do odd jobs in return for a bite to eat. Her neighbour, Flo Owens, also has no husband any longer. He had been affectionate enough at the time of the birth of Madge, their first daughter, but was already seeking his pleasure elsewhere when Millie was born a couple of years later, and soon after he went his way. 18-year-old Madge is "unusually beautiful", and though, according to Inge's stage direction she "seems to take her beauty very much for granted", she puts some effort into making herself attractive, shampooing her hair, painting her nails and so on. Her mother is not slow to point out the need to capitalize on good looks to ensure a comfortable future with a grateful husband. Millie, on the other hand, is more intellectual, a girl who won a scholarship to the local school and likes reading; it is she who says most clearly that she wants a more exciting future than a small town in Kansas can promise. "Anyone mind if an old-maid schoolteacher joins their company?", is the entry line of Rosemary Sydney, who is rooming in Flo's house. She is a miniature masterpiece of characterization, its seemingly resigned self-depreciation paradoxically high-lighting what is really a cry of enraged frustration. The irony becomes perhaps a little too blatant when she is joined by two other spinster representatives of the teaching profession, one of whom specializes in the subject of Feminine Hygiene.

The four male characters are all, in a sense, intruders into this world of women. Bomber, the newspaper boy, makes only brief appearances, but Millie's readiness to quarrel with him is significant of her desire for more than he can ever provide. As for Alan Seymour, he is Madge's beau, a nice enough college lad with some prospects in business in the small town, but he is shy and uncharismatic. His deficiencies of physique and personality are shown up in a most unflattering light by Hal. Anything but economically prosperous, Hal arrives in T-shirt, dungarees, and cowboy boots, ready to undertake menial tasks to assuage his hunger and thirst, but there is no denying the physical attractions of this young man who was able, for a time, to hold down a football scholarship at the college Seymour attended. It is true he has not got a lot of brains, and whenever he dreams of the future he talks of a most banal existence. This lack of imagination, like his social gaucheness, does not seem to matter when he appears stripped to the waist, the image of healthy, West Coast manhood. His relationship with Millie is essentially sexual; it is brief too. By the end of the play we realize, however, that though he has played a vital role in her emancipation, he cannot provide her with all that she will need if she is to develop fully. The link between Rosemary and Howard, a middle-aged man in business as a haberdasher, offers a somewhat less serious parallel to the main action of the play as the man who hitherto had been quite content simply to be a steady, if somewhat uninspiring admirer is cajoled into taking the step of at last agreeing to marry her.

Picnic is a powerful play, its homely realism as a portrayal of the life of ordinary people in the Midwest being given a cutting edge as Inge develops his theme with great, psychological insight. Occasionally the contrivance may appear a little too obvious, as is the symbolism too, but in the detail, as in the style of the dialogue, there is much that has the ring of authenticity. All the craftsmanship and observation that make up this very American play are put to the service of a vision of life whose disabused bleakness is redeemed by a breath of a vital optimism that, in the last analysis, refuses to be gainsaid.

In 1955 a filmed version of *Picnic* was released, directed by Joshua Logan. It appears, however, that in the long run, the very success of the film has led to an unjustifiable neglect of *Picnic* as a piece of writing for the stage that is as skilful as it is powerful.

—Christopher Smith

A RAISIN IN THE SUN
by Lorraine Hansberry.

First Publication: 1959.
First Production: 1959.

Lorraine Hansberry was 28 when *A Raisin in the Sun* opened at the Ethel Barrymore Theatre in 1959. She was the first black woman to have her work produced on Broadway, and Lloyd Richards, the director, was the first black man to direct a play for the Broadway stage. The play won the New York Critics' Circle award, and Hansberry also became the first black writer and the first woman to receive that prize.

The title of the play, a line from Langston Hughes's poem "Dream Deferred", refers to both the subject and plot of the drama: the Younger family, trapped in poverty and overcrowded housing conditions, await the arrival of an insurance policy cheque for $10,000, following the death of the father. Act I deals with the family's situation and attitudes towards their condition and in a series of confrontations, members of the family reveal their different dreams in relation to the insurance cheque. The central tensions between Mama's dream and that of her son Walter, provide the axis and ultimately the action of the play. Walter proposes investing the money in a liquor-store business, which he believes to be the only way to break the cycle of servitude and poverty in which the family is trapped. His dream offers the potential to regain his pride and dignity, which has been eroded by his work as a chauffeur for a white man: "I open and close car doors all day long. I drive a man around in his limousine and I say, 'Yes, sir; no, sir; very good, sir; shall I take the Drive, sir?' Mama, that ain't no kind of job . . . that ain't nothing at all".

Mama begins to fulfil her dream in Act II when she announces that she has put a payment down on a house for the family, a place where she hopes the three generations of Youngers can thrive. The house is located in a white suburb, and this adds fuel to Walter's bitterness as his hope of opening a store fades. He articulates his anger in terms of his dream: "So you butchered up a dream of mine—you—who always talking 'bout your children's dreams". Fearful that his bitterness will destroy him, Mama entrusts the remainder of the $10,000 to Walter. Walter is duped by a friend who, instead of using the money to open the liquor store, steals it and disappears.

In Act III Walter, diminished and beaten as much by his failure of judgement as by the loss of the money, proposes to accept a lucrative bribe offered by a white man in an effort to keep the Youngers out of the white suburb where Mama has chosen their house. Walter plays out for the horrified family the full portrait of his humiliation, which is couched in terms of the social degradation to which black Americans are subjected and the roles which Whites expect them to play. Finally, Walter finds the strength and pride to reject the bribe, and the play ends with the Youngers moving out of their cramped apartment, on their way to their new home in the suburbs. An earlier draft of the play ended with the Youngers in their new home, preparing to face racial attack and, for some, the absence of a clear recognition of this future confrontation within the final draft of the play undermines the note of hope on which *A Raisin in the Sun* ends.

Interest in the play, at the time of its first performance, was undoubtedly fuelled by the unusual experience, for a Broadway audience, of watching a play in which all but one character was black. Furthermore, the tone of the play was not didactic. Its values were familiar, even if its characters and setting were not, and to some extent audiences and critics, both predominantly white, must have felt some relief that the protest implicit in the play was not belligerent. One of the dilemmas confronting black playwrights attempting to gain access to Broadway in 1959, was that their audiences were both the consumers and the object of the black writer's protest, and there is certainly, within the play, an acceptance of some of the myths inherent in the American dream and a lack of critical scrutiny of the values embedded in those aspirations. This led later critics to regard the play as middle-class and assimilationist. Opinions continue to differ as to whether it is a play of social protest or a soap opera. But, in 1959, the central tenet of the Civil Rights policy was to demand access to such aspirations, rather than to challenge them and, in this sense, *A Raisin in the Sun* is true to its cultural and political environment.

In form, the play is conventionally naturalistic, a three-act play within a single set. Dialogue and action are gently, even humorously, home-spun. The characters, whilst being affectionately drawn, are familiar types, only occasionally rising above the stock. There are, however, some fine moments of realisation and self-confrontation in the play, particularly when the aspirations of individuals encounter the constraints of social reality. The focus of the play centres on the characters' struggle to make choices of value, despite social constraints, and out of those choices to retain integrity. This may place *A Raisin in the Sun* within the tradition of Miller's *Death of a Salesman*, to which

Hansberry acknowledged her debt, but the Younger family's search for dignity has a specific and inevitable resonance in relation to the political struggle current in black America in 1959.

—Glendyr Sacks

A STREETCAR NAMED DESIRE
by Tennessee Williams.

First Publication: 1947.
First Production: 1947.

The plot of *A Streetcar Named Desire* is deceptively simple. Stanley and Stella Kowalski live in a poor section of New Orleans. Stanley, a northerner of Polish descent, has recently returned from fighting in World War II. He is between 28 and 30 years old. Stella is a "gentle young woman" of about 25. She was raised in genteel surroundings on Belle Reeve, a former plantation in Mississippi. Blanche, Stella's older sister, comes to visit. During her visit, it becomes apparent that Blanche's refined bearing is objectionable to Stanley, and his animalistic crudity is offensive to her. It is soon revealed that Stella is pregnant, but she has not told Stanley because she is not sure how he will react. In the meantime, Mitch, a friend of Stanley's, becomes romantically interested in Blanche. It is also revealed that Blanche has been married and feels guilty for the suicide of her young husband who took his own life when she confronted him with her knowledge of his homosexuality. Stanley learns of this incident along with the fact that Blanche has been fired in her home town as a schoolteacher because of her sexual escapades with young men. As a result of this knowledge, Stanley declares that he does not want Blanche to have any more contact with Mitch.

Soon afterwards Stella goes to the hospital to have the baby. While his wife is giving birth, Stanley rapes Blanche. In the play's final scene, which takes place some weeks later, it is apparent that Blanche has suffered a nervous breakdown because of the incident. As Stanley and his friends are engaged in a poker game, he, Stella, and Eunice watch a doctor and a nurse arrive to take Blanche to a mental institution. As the curtain falls, the card game continues and Stanley caresses Stella.

At least part of the reason for the immense success of the play must lie in the casting for the premiere production, directed by Elia Kazan, which featured Marlon Brando in the role of Stanley (and established his star status), along with Kim Hunter as Stella, Karl Malden as Mitch, and Jessica Tandy as Blanche. Four years later, in 1951, a multi-Oscar-winning film version of *Streetcar* was released. Directed by Kazan, the cinematic adaptation starred Brando, Hunter, and Malden, with Vivien Leigh replacing Tandy.

The initial appearance of Stanley (indeed the first words in the play) set the tone for what is to follow. Dressed as a blue-collar laborer and carrying a blood-stained package from the butcher's, Stanley bellows, "Hey, there! Stella, Baby!". The image produced is that of the male warrior returning home from the hunt with meat for his mate. Throughout the drama Stanley's animalistic nature is emphasized: he is uncouth, rough, and blunt. Physical comfort seems to be one of his prime considerations; he is uninhibited and does not give a second thought to appearing in public wearing a T-shirt.

Given Stanley's crude nature, it is difficult for some to understand how the refined, cultured, sophisticated Stella could find him attractive—let alone marry him and bear his child. As the play develops, however, it is apparent that these characteristics are part of his appeal for Stella. George Bernard Shaw posited the existence of a "life force": the most vital men and women were attracted to one another and the result was that they would ultimately produce a race of supermen which combined the best aspects of the mother and father. Shaw also indicated that he did not think that social class was a determining factor, (and frequently his heroes and heroines were from disparate classes). Stella's actions make sense if they are seen as analogous to this concept. It is clear that Stella represents the best of her society, the ante bellum South; even though that civilization no longer exists and what is left has degenerated considerably. Stanley, on the other hand, is alive in the fullest sense of that word. The strength and power that he exudes, therefore, is a magnet that draws Stella to him. When Stanley mistreats Stella it is not because he does not love her. And, Stella, who loves Stanley, recognizes this. Their love is based on the mutual attraction of the two strongest characters in the play.

Blanche is a representative of the same civilization that produced Stella, but her character has become perverted by the destruction of that civilization. The homosexuality of her dead young husband, and the music of the "rapid, feverish polka tune", the "Varsouviana", exemplify the old South that she grew up in and is unable to escape. Her pursuit of young men was, ironically, an attempt to recapture the innocence of her youth and the past. When that old South is finally, absolutely, lost to her—when Belle Reeve has been sold and all of the family connections have been severed—she has no one to turn to but her younger sister. Stanley immediately understands the threat that Blanche represents to his relationship with Stella. For her own survival Blanche must supplant Stanley in Stella's affections. The resultant conflict can only bring the destruction of one or the other of these two characters.

The garish, ruthless, sensual world of *Streetcar* is captured in one of the primary scenes of the play, the poker night. Interestingly, Williams had originally titled this drama *The Poker Night* (and the importance of this scene is underscored by Thomas Hart Benton's painting of the poker game to represent the play). Besides demonstrating the essence of the lower-class New Orleans culture in which *Streetcar* takes place, the poker game also functions metaphorically, for it represents the concept of game playing that runs throughout the play (particularly in Blanche's actions); the melting-pot concept of America; the male bonding and camaraderie that epitomize Stanley's nature; and the exclusion of the outsider. Blanche had had the strength to keep Belle Reeve together for a long time, but when it was lost the source of her strength was also removed; yet Stanley senses her underlying strength of character and the family ties that bind her and Stella together. To defeat his adversary he must employ his attributes represented metaphorically by the poker night.

Stanley knows therefore that he must expel Blanche, the intruder, in order to save his marriage. Whether from animal cunning or intelligence or a combination of both, he also knows that he must do this in such a way that Stella participates in the expulsion. His rape of Blanche is brutal, ruthless, callous, and premeditated. He knows that Blanche will tell Stella about the attack; he knows that Stella *cannot* believe Blanche or she will have to give him up. And he is right. Stella *chooses* to believe that Blanche has tried to seduce Stanley. Since Stella participates in rejecting her sister, she will not be able to bring her back. Blanche is not capable of handling this rejection. Ironically, Blanche, for whom family was the most important thing, is reduced to uttering the most poignant statement in the entire drama with her last words: "I have always depended on the kindness of strangers".

Blanche's concluding statement makes this play terribly bleak and depressing. There is hope, however, at the end. Stanley and Stella are together, and they end where they began, with their relationship reconfirmed. While there is a lack of concern for what has had to be rejected in order to insure the survival of their relationship, the baby remains as the ultimate symbol of hope. Stanley and Stella's child can be interpreted as a combination of the best of both cultures.

Some interpretations of *Streetcar* add a further symbolic dimension. If Stanley is seen as a representative of the North in American society and Stella is seen as representing the South, the play is a metaphor for a specific period in American history. The harsh, raw, realistic, insensitive, masculine, new, industrial part of the nation is brought into contact with the old, feminine, romantic, agrarian, cultured part of the nation, and the blending of the two produces a vital, new, nation.

Williams's craftsmanship allowed him to create realistic characters, place them in a significant situation, and bring together layers of emotional, intellectual, and historical meaning in ways that make this play his masterpiece. Whatever interpretation or combination of interpretations is accepted, *A Streetcar Named Desire* remains a landmark in the American theatre.

—Steven H. Gale

THE TOOTH OF CRIME
by Sam Shepard.

First Publication: In *The Tooth of Crime*; *Geography of a Horse*, 1974.
First Production: 1972.

Sam Shepard, probably the most highly regarded American playwright of the 1970s, brings to *The Tooth of Crime* his background as a drummer for the "rockabilly" band Holy Moly Rounders. The play, actually "a sort of talking opera" about the violent paranoia experienced by rock stars at the top, is the work of a musician whose playwrighting has endured far beyond his music-making. Using an inventive hip lingo of the future (in the manner of the Anthony Burgess novel *Clockwork Orange*), Shepard places at the heart of *Tooth of Crime* the ritualized musical battle between an older style of performance, one with its roots deeply embedded in the African-American blues, and a newer threat to that style, one that is brittle, androgynous, heartless. As the reigning star, Hoss, is challenged by the rising star, Crow, the threatening language often involves the hardware of combat; but the central showdown is a musical *agon*; but the battle to the death is performed with microphones, not knives. The contest is over the heart of the culture: will it be represented by music with a soul or will it be taken over by a harsher brand of punk, where the essence is in the body moves and not in the sound, where the content is "nothin' but flash"?

The people of the not-so-distant future who inhabit Shepard's dramatic space are *aficionados*, not only of the nuances between blues and rock entertainers of different decades and different styles—Ma Rainey vs. Mongo Santamaria, Keith Richards vs. Keith Moon, Bob Dylan vs. The Velvet Underground—but also they are *aficionados* of a range of hard drugs, gleaming weaponry ("really beautiful and clean"), and Italian racing cars. An entourage satisfies the immediate craving for exhilaration, whether that excitement is provided by speed shot intravenously or experienced on the interstate highways; astrological and sexual comforts are available at the snap of a finger. In a Sam Shepard play, there are inevitable evocations of the old West, of gangster shoot-outs, of teenage class combat in southern California. A young woman presents the struggle of a date rape where she plays both the abuser and the abused; she must both protect herself from exposure and also rip off her own psychic and material layers of protection.

Act I is devoted to Hoss fixated on impending doom. Uneasy lies the head that wears this bopper's crown. He knows that the sharp edge of his art is losing its visionary gleam: "We ain't flyin' in the eye of contempt. We've become respectable and safe. Soft, mushy, chewable . . . What's happened to our killer heart? . . . We were warriors once". What popular art aims for is to "knock 'em dead", to "make a killing". Shepard picks up on this aggressive showbiz terminology, takes it a step further, turns his musicians into "warriors". Hoss surely is named to invoke the cowboy West; Crow to suggest the eaters of carrion, the cleansers who dispose of road kill. From the grandeur of his perch at the top of the charts, "lonely as an ocean", Hoss hunches over, brooding about who will come to challenge his authority. He recognizes his former self in the potential challenger: "I can smell blood. It's right. The time is right! I'm fallin' behind". Act I ends with the announcement that the *Doppelgänger* has arrived: "He's my brother and I gotta kill him. He's gotta kill me".

Act II is the musical *agon*. Inevitably the reigning monarch loses. Though Euripides and Shakespeare did not have basketball referees overseeing the combat and cheerleaders mooning the audience, *Tooth of Crime* is open to comparisons with dramas of the past: Dionysus will outsmart his cousin Pentheus; Bolingbroke will outmaneuver his cousin Richard; Crow will overwhelm his blues brother Hoss.

At the height of his power, this youthful playwright was already obsessed with being corrupted by success, with selling out to a dehumanized system. Just off stage are "the keepers", who exact obedience and threaten liquidation if the artist does not strictly follow their system of "points" and "penalties"; does not strictly adhere to their "code" of rules. The play explicitly celebrates the martyrs of recent popular and high culture, Jimmy Dean, Jackson Pollock,

Duane Allman. There is a strong sense of the ephemeral nature of an artistic career: "Sure you'll have a few moments of global glow, maybe even an interplanetary flash. But it won't last, Hoss, it won't last".

—Roger Sorkin

TORCH SONG TRILOGY
by Harvey Fierstein.

First Publication: 1981.
First Production: 1981.

Torch Song Trilogy comprises three plays so different in style that at first sight they seem totally self-contained; only the central character, a professional drag queen named Arnold, provides a nominal link. However, the stylistic differences are important to the whole concept in that they comment on and enrich one another in complex ways.

The first play, *The International Stud*, opens with Arnold in full warpaint in the eponymous gay bar and charts the ups and downs of his relationship with his lover, Ed, a man uncertain about his sexuality, his willingness to come out of the closet, and his commitment to Arnold. The second play, *Fugue in a Nursery*, takes place one year later. Ed is now married and Arnold has a new lover. The two couples meet at Ed's upstate farmhouse and discover crosscurrents of desire, jealousy, and insecurity running between them. Ed sleeps with Alan, finds that he is still drawn to Arnold, and finally marries Laurel, while Alan and Arnold arrange a wedding of their own. The final play, *Widows and Children First!* takes place five years later. Alan has been brutally murdered. Arnold is fostering a gay teenage boy, David, a project he originally undertook with Alan, and it is clear that the centre of his life is now the father-son relationship he soon hopes to make official. He is visited by Ed, estranged from Laurel, and his own mother. In the course of the play he tries to make his mother come to terms not just with his sexuality but his feelings as Alan's "widow" and David's father. Meanwhile David does some strenuous matchmaking between Arnold and Ed.

The movement of the whole trilogy is towards the values of commitment and a reinterpreted ideal of the family, symbolised by the changing on-stage patterns created by the characters. *The International Stud* consists almost entirely of soliloquies. Arnold addresses us, Ed addresses an unseen Arnold, Arnold makes love to an anonymous figure in the backroom of the bar, again unseen. Arnold and Ed speak on the phone, both visible to us but not to each other. It is in fact only in the last scene that they are both present in each other's space on stage, in what starts out as Ed's farewell visit to Arnold's dressing room and becomes some kind of reconciliation. The play explores the tension between Arnold's two kinds of desire for love: one the urge for a relationship stronger and more meaningful than the joyless one-night stands of the back room; the other springing from an insatiable desire for security. This tension removes the play from the territory of easy answers, because one desire is never entirely untouched by the other. Fierstein, writing before the AIDS crisis changed American gay life beyond recognition, allows the limited free-dom of the bar its place in the scheme of things, and in his dedication wishes its *habitués* "the courage to leave it when they can, and the good sense to come back to it when they must". Arnold clear-sightedly recognises that his search for secure love is both his curse and part of his vulnerable charm; he say of Ed, "Maybe I use him to give me that tragic torch-singer status I admire so in others".

Fugue in a Nursery follows logically by exploring love in a wider commu-nity. Its setting has a surreal edge: the action takes place in a bed which represents all the rooms in Ed's house. The effect is multi-layered. First, the bed stresses the erotic groundbase of all the relationships in the play. All the characters are to some extent romantics, in that they have not fully relin-quished the ideal of a single, lasting, sexual love. Secondly, it creates an atmosphere of intimacy that makes credible the four-cornered rapport, the confidences flying thick and fast. Thirdly, it adds an element of stylisation which emphasises that this play is ultimately a comedy of manners. As Arnold points out, however, in the world of the new sexual mores, manners have to be improvised as you go along. "You were wrong to do what you did! . . . Though I know why you did . . . And Laurel was wrong to use what you two did! . . . Though I know why she did. And I was wrong to do everything I did! But I did. I don't know, maybe it all evens out . . .".

Widows and Children First! takes Arnold away from the circle of lovers into a wider world: of families, of the law of the land. Reminders of how the latter has failed the gay community are ever present in the frequent allusions to Alan's fate; the family we have to judge for ourselves—but here Fierstein shows his optimism by his chosen style, that of sitcom, the form created specifically to exalt family values. Arnold's wisecracking mother, the farcical misunderstandings when she assumes David is Arnold's lover, her ridiculous rabbit slippers and her home cooking—all belong to sitcom; but while the play never questions the status of the family as the vital unit in society, it suggests that one can construct a "family" to suit one's individual needs and desires. The success of *Torch Song Trilogy* is perhaps owed to the fact that it does not simply celebrate gay life but the right of the individual, straight or gay, to create the family unit in which that individuality can be expressed.

—Frances Gray

THE WASH
by Philip Kan Gotanda.

First Publication: 1990.
First Production: 1985.

The Wash takes its title from the one point of contact between an elderly Japanese American, Nobu, and his wife Masi, who have, at her insistence, separated a year earlier. Each week she delivers his cleaned clothes to his apartment and picks up the dirty ones. In the last, silent scene of the play she decides not to take the bag of dirty clothes, thus ending their tenuous relation-ship. Each becomes involved in a new relationship, he very tentatively with the proprietor of a restaurant where he eats lunch every day, she in an affair with a widower, Sadao. When she tells Nobu that she wants a divorce in order to remarry, he feels so humiliated by her rejection, and by the suspicion that she and their two daughters have conspired to hide her new relationship from him, that he hides in his apartment, refusing to answer the phone or the door. The telephone rings once more—doubtless it is the best friend of the restaurant proprietor calling—as the play ends.

He, it seems, lives in the past and cannot change. In one of his rare conversations with Masi he argues about how a store he worked at should be run but, as she points out, the store closed down nine years earlier. He also cannot express his emotions, either to Masi or to the restaurant proprietor. In one scene he does ask Masi to stay the night, but he can do so only indirectly, by asking her to make him breakfast—and since it is evening when he asks her his intention is clear. But in one significant way, he does change. He has been alienated from one of his daughters because she married an African American. He has refused to meet him, but in the course of the play he holds their baby and even gives him the elaborate kite he has been constructing to console himself. Perhaps, then, at some point he will answer the phone.

Philip Kan Gotanda has written the play in twenty-six short scenes whose brevity is perfect for recording the micro-events in which the developing relationships are measured. The play is unusual in that it is about both aging and about an awkward and tentative reaching for romance. This gives *The Wash* great poignancy. It is also unusual in that the central focus is not on the person who changes and "finds" herself, but on the person who will not change. That focus is reflected in the author's imagined setting: Nobu's apartment is center stage with the restaurant and Masi's apartment on either side.

The Wash has particular meaning in the Japanese-American context. As Michael Toshiyuki Uno, the director of the 1988 film of the play said, "if you're talking about Asian-American images in the past, there is no sexuality". But Gotanda's play deals openly with the characters' sexual needs. Those sexual and psychological needs run up against traditional Asian-American values. Devotion to family is probably the reason Masi stayed in a marriage with a man she now says she never particularly liked. And the central problem in her relationship with Nobu has been his internalized prohibition on the expression of emotion, which now prevents him from either saying to her, as one of his daughters points out, "Three lousy words, 'please come back'", or from accepting the affection offered by the widow who runs the restaurant. That prohibition is perhaps particularly strong among second-generation Japanese Americans because of their internment during the Second World War, to which Nobu's mind keeps returning, and the difficulties in their lives that that experience created.

But if there are aspects of the play which have particular significance for Japanese Americans, anyone can empathize with the play's characters and their situations. *The Wash* is quiet, realistic, and very moving.

—Anthony Graham-White

WEDDING BAND:
A Love/Hate Story in Black and White
by Alice Childress.

First Publication: 1974.
First Production: 1966.

Subtitled *A Love/Hate Story in Black and White*, *Wedding Band* is set in South Carolina during the summer of 1918. At the centre of the play is the love affair between a black woman, Julia Augustine, and a white man, Herman. State laws prohibit inter-racial marriages and social codes virtually prohibit any inter-racial relationships; yet the couple have survived ten years together. They imagine the freedom they might achieve by moving to New York City (where such laws do not prevail), but are prevented from leaving first by Herman's sense of familial responsibility to his mother and sister, and then, at the end of the play, by his death from influenza.

Wedding Band is not a typical Childress play, nor has it always been well received. Her choice of an inter-racial relationship makes it unlike her other works, which have only black protagonists, and the relationship itself has provoked censure from both black and white critics. The premiere performance of *Wedding Band* on the New York stage, as well as its later transmission on ABC television, broke a taboo in both media about representing inter-racial relationships, and this gave Childress's text an immediate notoriety. Black critics felt that *Wedding Band* should have concentrated on a black couple or that, at least, Julia should have rejected Herman. As *Wedding Band* demonstrates, however, Childress is more interested in staging the world which so many people experience than in offering an idealized portrayal of positive role models and their successes. White critics of the play felt that Herman should have left South Carolina, that he should have been strong enough to reject the claims of his mother and sister. Both types of criticism neglect Childress's ability to look with compassion at both black and white poor in the context of Julia and Herman's culturally unacceptable love. The play suggests the possibility, despite immense economic hardship, not only of survival, but of survival in loving relationships. With the death of Herman, however, it is evident that while the characters are, for the most part, survivors, they are always and especially vulnerable.

The play's opening set indicates the naturalism of Childress's dramatic method. The scene is three houses in a backyard, and Julia is the new tenant in the middle house. In this setting, we see the problems which dominate the everyday actions of working-class Blacks and the pressures these place on familial and community relations. As well as being physically situated in the middle, Julia is also in the middle culturally. While she cannot even be acknowledged by her lover's racial group, she is also distanced from fellow Blacks by that alliance. Her history is, as she says, one of constant moving in an attempt to avoid the apparently inevitable disapproval.

Through the presentation of the landlady and other tenants, as well as through Julia, Childress demonstrates the economic conditions and cultural values which inform and shape the experience of working-class Blacks.

Another tenant, Mattie, has an absent husband and her attempts to survive as a single parent are juxtaposed with Julia's economically easier, but socially impossible, situation with Herman. While both Julia and Mattie react to their circumstances with a persistent and determined dignity, events show that to be black and to be a woman is to be doubly disadvantaged. Yet Herman, white and male, is not portrayed as the play's villain.

Herman is trapped by his bakery store which he feels obliged to maintain in order to repay an earlier loan from his mother. While Herman's procrastinations might seem to be the direct cause of Julia's troubles, Childress points out that Herman's endeavours to fulfill class, race, and gender norms leave him as much a victim as Julia. At the end of Act I, Herman falls sick at Julia's home and the tension that having a white man stay in the black neighbourhood provokes is signalled by the act's stark closing line: the landlady makes the social unacceptability and, indeed, the risk of such an action all too apparent in her simple command to Julia: "Get him out of my yard".

In the second act, Herman's mother and sister arrive to take him back and much of the action centres on schemes to move him discreetly out of Julia's home. As the neighbours function as representatives of black social values, so Herman's mother and sister provide stereotypic white responses. In many ways the intolerance shown to Julia and Herman's relationship by both communities stems from those people's sense of the difficulty in simply surviving, let alone with the extra burden of dealing with the claustrophobia of a society so rigidly divided on grounds of class, race, and gender.

The wedding band of the title that Herman gives to Julia (significantly to wear on a chain around her neck rather than on her finger) in celebration of their ten years "together" signifies survival despite racial prejudice. But what *all* the characters fight against is economic oppression. The black couple (Mattie and her absent husband), evidently as much "in love" as Julia and Herman, struggle endlessly and painfully like the latter to avoid destruction at the hands of class-determined economics. Moreover, Herman's mother describes her own life as putting up with a man who breathed stale whiskey in her face every night and enduring the birth of seven babies, five stillborn. For Annabelle, Herman's sister, the chance to marry for love depends on Herman's agreement to marry Celestine, his mother's choice.

Although based on a true story and on common circumstance, Julia and Herman's relationship is perhaps less than convincing. Nonetheless for the audience/reader who responds not only to the central couple but to all the characters Childress draws, *Wedding Band* underscores the dependence of everyone's individual happiness on prevailing social and political conditions.

—Susan Bennett

WHO'S AFRAID OF VIRGINIA WOOLF?
by Edward Albee.

First Publication: 1962.
First Production: 1962.

The action of the play takes place late one evening in the New England campus home of a childless, middle-aged couple. George has an impressive record of academic mediocrity teaching in the history department of the college where, in spite of having married the principal's daughter early in his career, he has failed to fulfil the overpowering expectations of his wife and her father. George's personal failings and lack of professional ambition have provided abundant ammunition for the vitriolic war of attrition waged by Martha against him. However, the years of abuse have enabled George to develop his own verbal arsenal and sharpen an acerbic wit, equally skilled in offensive as well as defensive capability. The domestic battleground has become entrenched with its own strategies and rules of engagement, complicated by the invention of a non-existent son, who inhabits the most private quarter of their game-playing province. The chief rule is that under no circumstances should the boy be mentioned to anyone.

Into this arena, Martha invites a new appointee to the college, the handsome young biologist Nick, and his wife Honey, to continue an inaugural party hosted on campus earlier in the evening. The liberal quantities of liquor and the arrival of the younger couple, who in many ways mirror the sterility of George and Martha's own marriage, provoke an explosive confrontation with the realities of past and present. Nick confesses his material motives for marrying the once hysterically pregnant Honey. She, in turn, reveals her fear of bearing a child. The exorcism of the illusory aspects of all their lives is symbolically achieved when George, prompted by Martha's forbidden disclosure of the "fact" of their son's forthcoming 21st birthday and then sickened by her attempted sexual liaison with an incapable Nick, announces the death of the boy in an automobile accident.

The appearance of *Who's Afraid of Virginia Woolf?* on Broadway in 1962 briefly established Edward Albee's reputation as the inheritor of a predominantly naturalistic postwar American playwriting tradition. Yet Albee's subsequent plays were to baffle critical and popular audiences alike, with their marked and uncompromising departure from a familiar realism. It is possible to see that while *Who's Afraid of Virginia Woolf?* may appear to be essentially naturalistic, several features serve to undermine the conventional domestic situation of the "battle-of-the-sexes" kind that Strindberg and Ibsen were dramatising decades earlier. Albee creates a confining theatrical space within which the role-play of private disputation assumes a larger, public significance. In spite of the success of the film version of the play with Richard Burton and Elizabeth Taylor, its adaptation for the screen sacrificed the self-consciousness, the illusory and ephemeral nature of the medium of the theatre for which it was written and for which it is so appropriate.

The historical resonance with the Washingtons is clearly not meant to go unnoticed, as George and Martha's relationship to Western cultural values and the edifice of dreams and self-deceptions that New World mythology has long cherished become apparent. The character of Nick might be seen as one of these dreams made flesh, the blond-haired, blue-eyed quarterback with a promise of a genetically engineered future who proves to be such an attractive sexual lure for Martha. (Such a figure appears as the Young Man in another of Albee's plays from the same period, *The American Dream* of 1962). Yet Nick's impotence in this adulterous encounter suggests a deeper relevance: the hollow ring of an empty vessel. These symbolic undercurrents run beneath a dramatic setting which enables Albee to juxtapose representatives from the intellectual worlds of scientific objectivity and historical inevitability through the campus meeting of the younger and older man.

George's history is ambiguous. Is he, in part at least, the subject of his own story of the boy who accidentally shot his mother and a year later saw his father killed in a car crash? Was it an autobiographical narrative in the book ridiculed by Martha and her father? Such an explanation might account for motivations in a naturalistic sense, but we need not have the facts of this history verified in order to experience an intensification of the characters' sense of loss through this metaphorical tale. Edward Albee's preoccupation with the gaping wound of missing parents and lost children must be rooted in his own experience of having been abandoned by his mother and father in the late 1920s and subsequently adopted. Central to the play is the notion of absence: the child whose painful absence has been filled with an imagined presence; the absence of love in a marriage which has had its unconfronted truths veneered.

Who's Afraid of Virginia Woolf? is a raw, moving, emotionally exhausting play to witness in performance. Albee has constructed, through the characters of George and Martha, two of the most demanding roles in modern dramatic writing. The deadly struggle between them unleashes a chain of events which pursues its inevitable course of destruction. Yet there is renewal in this tragedy of loss, epitomized by the rising light in the darkened sky at the play's conclusion, when night begins to turn to dawn. Here there is at last affirmation of the strength gained from mutual support, the promise of courage through reconciliation, and the final abandonment of an unsustainable lie.

—Chris Banfield

TITLE INDEX

The following list includes the titles of all stage, screen, radio, and television plays cited in the entries. The name in parenthesis directs the reader to the appropriate entry where fuller information is given. Titles appearing in **bold** are subjects of individual essays in the Works section. The date is that of first production or publication. These abbreviations are used:

s   screenplay
r   radio play
t   television play

A (Fratti), 1965
"A" is for "Actor" (S. Sherman), 1987
A Whale of a Killing (t S. Miller)
Aber wie heisst das Wort für "Fahrrad"? (S. Sherman), 1990
Abingdon Square (Fornés), 1984
Abortion (O'Neill), 1950
About Time (Hailey), 1982
Abraham (Goodman), 1953
Abroad (Weller), 1981
Absolute Power over Movie Stars (R. Patrick), 1968
Absolute Strangers (r Anderson), 1991
Abundance (Henley), 1989
Academic Murders (Koch), 1966
Academy (Fratti), 1963
Academy Award Show (t Gelbart), 1985
Accademia (Fratti), 1964
Accident (Saroyan), 1958
Accidental Death of an Anarchist (Nelson), 1984
Achilles (Sunde), 1991
Acrobats (Horovitz), 1968
Across a Crowded Room (Machado), 1991
Across the Board on Tomorrow Morning (Saroyan), 1941
Across the River and into the Jungle (Kopit), 1958
Act (Furth), 1977
Action (R. Patrick), 1966
Action (Shepard), 1974
Action at a Distance (Foreman), 1977
Action in the North Atlantic (s Lawson), 1943
Actor (t Lawrence, Lee), 1978
Actor and the Invader (R. Patrick), 1969
Actors and Actresses (Simon), 1983
Actors' Delicatessen (Mednick), 1984
Actor's Nightmare (Durang), 1981
Actos (Valdez), 1971
Acts of Love (Yankowitz), 1973
Ad Hoc Committee (D. Wilson), 1978
Adam (Carter), 1966
Adams County, Illinois (Mac Low), 1963
Adam's Rib (s Kanin), 1949
Adaptation (May), 1969
Admiral (MacLeish), 1944
Adoring the Madonna (Havis), 1992
Adrian (Birimisa), 1974
Advances (Terry), 1980

Advantage of Dope (OyamO), 1971
Adventures of Karagöz (Ludlam), 1976
Adventures of Marco Polo (Simon), 1959
Advice to Eastern Europe (r Nelson), 1990
Africanis Instructus (Foreman), 1986
After Calcutta (Weller), 1976
After Nature, Art (Wymark), 1977
After School Special (Reddin), 1987
After the Baal-Shem Tov (Sainer), 1979
After the Fall (A. Miller), 1964
After the Fox (s Simon), 1966
After You (Dietz), 1990
After You've Gone (Busch), 1982
Agamemnon (Alfred), 1953
Age d'Or (McNally), 1993
Agnes of God (Pielmeier), 1980
Agony of Little Nations (Saroyan), 1942
Ah Man (Saroyan), 1962
Ah Sweet Mystery of Mrs. Murphy (t Saroyan), 1959
Ah, Wilderness! (O'Neill), 1933
Ah! Wine! (Melfi), 1974
A.I.D.S. (Fratti), 1987
Air Raid (MacLeish), 1938
Akhmatova (Linney), 1989
Alarms (Yankowitz), 1987
Albanian Softshoe (Wellman), 1988
Alcestiad (Wilder), 1977
Alcestis (R. Wilson), 1986
Alfred Dies (Horovitz), 1976
Alfred the Great (Horovitz), 1972
Alfredo (s Horovitz), 1970
Algiers (s Lawson), 1938
Alice (Weller), 1976
Alice in Wonder (Davis), 1952
Alicia (Wesley), 1973
Alive (s Shanley), 1993
All Day for a Dollar (Koutoukas), 1966
All Fall Down (s Inge), 1962
All for Charity (Shanley), 1987
All Gaul is Divided (Williams), 1984
All God's Chillun Got Wings (O'Neill), 1924
All in the Family (t Kalcheim), 1971
All in Your Mind (R. Patrick), 1981
All Junkies (Piñero), 1973
All Men Are Whores (Mamet), 1977
All My Sons (A. Miller), 1947
All Over (Albee), 1971

Doctor and the Patient (Saroyan), 1963
Dr. Bull (s Green), 1933
Dr. Christian (r Laurents), 1939
Doctor Detroit (s Friedman), 1983
Dr. Fish (Schisgal), 1970
Dr. Hero (Horovitz), 1972
Dr. Kheal (Fornés), 1968
Dr. Paroo (R. Patrick), 1981
Dr. Selavy's Magic Theatre (Foreman), 1972
Doctor Will See You Now (J. Patrick), 1991
Dog (Mamet), 1983
Dog (Shepard), 1965
Dog in the Manger (Wellman), 1982
Dog Lady and The Cuban Swimmer (Sánchez-Scott), 1984
Dog School (J. White), 1969
Dog Show (Bogosian), 1992
Dog Sitters (Chase), 1963
Dogs (Saroyan), 1960
Dog's Love (Smith), 1971
Doing a Good One for the Red Man (Medoff), 1969
Doing the Beast (Greenspan), 1988
$ Value of Man (R. Wilson), 1975
Doll's House (Wilder), 1937
Dolls No More (Fratti), 1975
Domanda (Fratti), 1961
Domino Courts (Hauptman), 1975
Don Juan (Nelson), 1979
Don Juan in New York City (Machado), 1988
Don Juan in Texas (Kopit), 1957
Don Quixote de La Jolla (Overmyer), 1990
Don't Fall for the Lights (Gurney, McNally), 1988
Don't Get God Started (Milner), 1987
Don't Go Away Mad (Saroyan), 1949
Don't Go Gentle, (Inge), 1968
Doorbell (Fratti), 1970
Dopey Fairy Tale (Weller), 1985
Dorothy (Furth), 1971
Double Bass (Overmyer), 1986
Double Life (s Kanin), 1947
Double Solitaire (Smith), 1973
Doubletalk (Carlino), 1964
Dove (Barnes), 1926
Down and Out (Shanley), 1982
Down by the River Where Waterlilies Are Disfigured Every Day (Bovasso), 1972
Down in the Dumps (Babe), 1989
Down the Road (Blessing), 1989
Downstairs Boys (Schisgal), 1980
Dowsing (Mamet), 1984
Dracula (Wellman), 1987
Dragon Country (Williams), 1970
Dragon Lady's Revenge (Holden), 1971
Dramatic License (Ludwig), 1985
Drapes Come (t Dizenzo), 1965
Dream (van Itallie), 1965
Dream Coast (Steppling), 1986
Dream of Kitamura (Gotanda), 1985
Dream of Love (s Lawson), 1928
Dream of Swallows (Zindel), 1964

Dream Tantras for Western Massachusetts (Foreman), 1971
dreamer examines his pillow (Shanley), 1985
Dreams of Glory (Gilroy), 1979
Dreamy Kid (O'Neill), 1919
Dress Gray (t Vidal), 1986
Dress Made of Diamonds (Birimisa), 1976
Dreyfus in Rehearsal (Kanin), 1974
Drinking Gourd (Hansberry), 1972
Drinking in America (Bogosian), 1986
Driving Miss Daisy (Uhry), 1987
Drowned Out (R. Patrick), 1986
Drowning (Fornés), 1985
Drowning of Manhattan (Noonan), 1993
Drugstore (t Foote), 1956
Drumbeats in Georgia (Green), 1973
Drunken Sisters (Wilder), 1957
Duck Variations (Mamet), 1972
Ducks and Lovers (Schisgal), 1961
Dudes (Duberman), 1972
Duet for Three (Havis), 1986
Duffy's Tavern (r Gelbart), 1945
Dulcy (Connelly), 1921
Dunnigan's Daughter (Behrman), 1945
Duplex (Bullins), 1970
Durango Flash (Hauptman), 1977
Dusk (Goodman), 1941
Dutch Landscape (Baitz), 1989
Dutchman (Baraka), 1964
Dwarfman, Master of a Million Shapes (Weller), 1981
Dying Breed (L. Wilson), 1987
Dynamite (s Lawson), 1929
Dynamite Tonite (Weinstein), 1963
Dynamo (O'Neill), 1929
Dynel (R. Patrick), 1968

Early Frost (t Cowen), 1985
Early Warnings (van Itallie), 1983
Earth Worms (Innaurato), 1974
Earthbound (s Lawson), 1940
East Side, West Side (t Davis)
Easter (Koch), 1966
Eastern Standard (Greenberg), 1988
Eat at Joe's (Terry), 1964
Eat Cake (van Itallie), 1971
Eating Words (r Nelson), 1989
Eccentricities of a Nightingale (Williams), 1964
Ecole Normale (Koch), 1973
Ed Sierer's New Zealand (t Chin), 1967
Eddie and Susanna in Love (Melfi), 1976
Eddie Cantor Show (r Gelbart), 1947
Eddie Cantor Story (s Weidman), 1953
Eddie Goes to Poetry City (Foreman), 1991
Eden Rose (Anderson), 1949
Edison (R. Wilson), 1979
Edison's Dream (Schevill), 1982
Edmond (Mamet), 1982
Educating Father (s J. Patrick), 1936
Educating Rita (Shange), 1983

Little Book of Professor Enigma (Kondoleon), 1992
Little David (Connelly), 1937
Little Duchess (s Connelly), 1934
Little Footsteps (Tally), 1986
Little Foxes (Hellman), 1939
Little Gloria . . . Happy at Last (t Hanley), 1982
Little Hero (Goodman), 1957
Little Hero, After Moliére (Goodman), 1970
Little Johnny (Schisgal), 1980
Little Johnny Jones (Uhry), 1982
Little Journey (Crothers), 1918
Little Light (Koch), 1972
Little Me (Simon), 1962
Little More Light Around the Place (Gordone), 1964
Little Murders (Feiffer), 1966
Little Ocean (Shepard), 1974
Little Odes, Poems, and a Play (McClure), 1969
Little Salt (Kesselman), 1975
Little Venice Makes a Good Drink (Melfi), 1985
Live from Galilee (E. White), 1992
Live Spelled Backwards (Lawrence), 1966
Live Wire (Kanin), 1950
Livre de Splendeurs (Foreman), 1976
Lo and Behold! (J. Patrick), 1951
Lobby (Drexler), 1984
Locks (r Mac Low), 1984
Locomotive (r Parks), 1991
Lodger (Schenkar), 1987
Lolita (Albee), 1981
Lolita (Chase), 1954
Lolita in the Garden (Fornés), 1977
London Comedy (Saroyan), 1960
Lone Canoe (Mamet), 1979
Lone Star (Green), 1977
Lone Star (McLure), 1979
Lonely (Foote), 1943
Lonely Guy (s Simon), 1984
Lonely Impulse of Delight (Shanley), 1982
Lonely Planet (Dietz), 1992
Lonesome Road (Green), 1926
Long Christmas Dinner (Wilder), 1931
Long Day's Journey into Night (O'Neill), 1956
Long Goodbye (Williams), 1940
Long Night (Green), 1920
Long Stay Cut Short (Williams), 1948
Long Voyage Home (O'Neill), 1917
Longtime Companion (s Lucas), 1990
Look, Ma, I'm Dancin' (Lawrence, Lee), 1948
Look Out, Mr. Moto (s J. Patrick), 1937
Look Up and Live (t van Itallie), 1963
Loon's Rage (Holden), 1977
Loose Ends (Weller), 1979
Lord Alfred's Lover (Bentley), 1979
Lord Byron's Love Letter (Williams), 1946
Lord Love a Duck (s Axelrod), 1966
Lord Pengo (Behrman), 1962

Lord's Will (Green), 1922
Lorenzo (Richardson), 1963
Los olivos pits (Valdez), 1972
Los Siete (Holden), 1980
Los vendidos (Valdez), 1967
Loss of a Teardrop Diamond (Williams), 1984
Loss of Memory (Laurents), 1981
Loss of Roses (Inge), 1959
Loss of Teardrop Diamond (s Williams)
Lost Angels (s Weller), 1989
Lost Child's Fireflies (Saroyan), 1954
Lost Colony (Green), 1937
Lost Feed (Koch), 1966
Lost in Yonkers (Simon), 1991
Lost Ones (Breuer), 1977
Lost Plays (O'Neill), 1950
Lou Gehrig Did Not Die of Cancer, (J. Miller), 1970
Loudest Whisper (s Hellman), 1961
Loudspeaker (Lawson), 1927
Louisiana Cavalier (Green), 1976
Louisiana Territory (Kopit), 1975
Lounge Player (Horovitz), 1977
Love and How to Cure It (Wilder), 1931
Love and Science (Foreman), 1987
Love and the Invention of Punctuation (Krauss), 1973
Love and/or Death (Gardner), 1979
Love Course (Gurney), 1970
Love Death (Inge), 1975
Love Death Plays (Inge), 1969
Love Diatribe (Kondoleon), 1990
Love 'em and Leave 'em (Abbott), 1926
Love in Buffalo (Gurney), 1958
Love Is a Many-Splendored Thing (s J. Patrick), 1955
Love Is a Time of Day (J. Patrick), 1969
Love Is Like That (Behrman), 1927
Love Lace (R. Patrick), 1974
Love Letters (Gurney), 1988
Love Me Or Leave Me (Cristofer), 1989
Love Nest for Three (J. Patrick), 1974
Love Pickle (Starkweather), 1963
Love Reconciled to War (Hivnor), 1968
Love Revisited (Anderson), 1951
Love Song of Barney Kempinski (t Schisgal), 1966
Love Space Demands (Shange), 1992
Love Story (Behrman), 1933
Love Suicide at Schofield Barracks (Linney), 1972
Love Suicides at Kaluka (Koch), 1965
Love! Valour! Compassion (McNally), 1993
Lovecraft's Follies (Schevill), 1970
Loved (Wymark), 1978
Loveliest Afternoon of the Year (Guare), 1972
Lovely Ladies, Kind Gentlemen (J. Patrick), 1970
Lovely Sunday for Creve Coeur (Williams), 1979
Lovers (Bernard), 1969
Lovers (Fratti), 1992

Miracle Worker (Gibson), 1957
Mirage (R. Patrick), 1965
Mirage (J. White), 1969
Mirror (McClure), 1979
Mirror Mirror (Wymark), 1992
Misadventures of Candide (Guare), 1973
Miser (Congdon), 1990
Misfits (s A. Miller), 1961
Misha's Party (Nelson), 1993
Miss Firecracker (s Henley), 1990
Miss Firecracker Contest (Henley), 1980
Miss Lou (Foote), 1943
Miss Universal Happiness (Foreman), 1985
Miss Waters, To You (Mitchell), 1983
Miss Williams (L. Wilson), 1967
Missing Persons (Lucas), 1985
Missing Persons (Wymark), 1978
Mission (Jenkin), 1975
Mission XQ3 (Fornés), 1968
Mister Jello (Birimisa), 1968
Mitchell (t Fuller), 1968
Mizlansky/Zilinsky (Baitz), 1985
Moby Dick (Koch), 1973
Modern Ladies of Guanabacoa (Machado), 1983
Mojo (Childress), 1970
Mojo Candy (Babe), 1975
Moke-Eater (Bernard), 1968
Mole on Lincoln's Cheek (r Connelly), 1941
Mollie Bailey's Traveling Family Circus (Terry), 1983
Molly's Dream (Fornés), 1968
Moms (Childress), 1987
Monday after the Miracle (Gibson), 1982
Monday Night Varieties (Noonan), 1972
Monday on the Way to Mercury Island (Bovasso), 1971
Money (Baraka), 1982
Monkey (Weinstein), 1978
Monkeys of the Organ Grinder (Bernard), 1970
Monster (Milner), 1969
Monster in a Box (Gray), 1990
Monstrous Martyrdoms (Bentley), 1985
Montserrat (Hellman), 1949
Moon Balloon (Koch), 1969
Moon Dance Night (E. White), 1987
Moon Dreamers (Bovasso), 1967
Moon for the Misbegotten (O'Neill), 1947
Moon in Capricorn (Herlihy), 1953
Moon of the Caribbees (O'Neill), 1919
Moon over Miami (Guare), 1989
Moon Watcher (s Henley), 1983
Moonchildren (Weller), 1971
Moonshot Tape (L. Wilson), 1990
Moonstruck (s Shanley), 1987
Moony's Kid Don't Cry (Williams), 1946
More Fun Than Bowling (Dietz), 1986
More Metamorphoses (Weinstein), 1973
More Milk Evette (s Tavel), 1966
More! More! I Want More! (Smith), 1966
More Stately Mansions (O'Neill), 1962

More Than You Deserve (Weller), 1973
More the Merrier (s Kanin), 1943
More Things in Heaven and Earth (t Jenkin), 1976
More War in Store (Carter), 1970
Morning (Horovitz), 1968
Morning, Noon and Night (Horovitz, McNally, Melfi), 1968
Morning Place (t Mosel), 1957
Morocco (Havis), 1984
Morris and Joe (Mamet), 1985
Mortadella (s Melfi), 1971
Most Beautiful Fish (Ribman), 1969
Motel (van Itallie), 1966
Mother (t Chayefsky), 1954
Mother Carey's Chickens (Crothers), 1917
Mother Courage and Her Children (Shange), 1980
Mother Earth (s Duberman), 1971
Mother Goose (Congdon), 1990
Mother Love (t Wymark), 1975
Mother Lover (Weidman), 1969
Mother O (Schevill), 1990
Mothering Sunday (r Wymark), 1980
Motherlode (Ferlinghetti), 1963
Mothers (Fornés), 1986
Mothers and Shadows (r Wymark), 1987
Mothers and Sons (Carter), 1987
Mother's Aria (Havis), 1986
Mother's Day (J. Patrick), 1984
Mother's Kisses (Friedman), 1968
Motion of History (Baraka), 1977
Mound Builders (L. Wilson), 1975
Mountain Rites (Owens), 1978
Mountains and Electricity (Koch), 1973
Mourning Becomes Electra (O'Neill), 1931
Mouths (Shange), 1981
Movie Man (O'Neill), 1950
Movie Movie (s Gelbart), 1978
Movie Star Has to Star in Black and White (Kennedy), 1976
Moving (Kalcheim), 1991
Moviola (t Hanley), 1980
Mozamgola Caper (Holden), 1986
Mozart and the Gray Steward (Wilder), 1928
Mrs. Dally Has a Lover (Hanley), 1963
Mrs. John Hobbs (Crothers), 1899
Mrs McThing (Chase), 1952
Mrs. Moresby's Scrapbook (t Wymark), 1973
Mr. Broadway (t Kanin), 1963
Mr. Flannery's Ocean (Carlino), 1961
Mr. Frivolous (Shawn), 1976
Mr Gogol and Mr Preen (May), 1991
Mr. Happiness (Mamet), 1978
Mr. Krapp's New Tapes (Schevill), 1974
Mr. Monster (Schenkar), 1980
Mr. Moto Takes a Chance (s J. Patrick), 1938
Mr. Tucker's Taxi (Melfi), 1980
Mr. Welk and Jersey Jim (Sackler), 1960
Mud (Fornés), 1983
Mud Angel (Cloud), 1990
Mummer's Play (E. White), 1965

Pitch (Mednick), 1985
Place of the Spirit Dance (OyamO), 1980
Place + Target (Foreman), 1979
Plain Brown Wrapper (Reddin), 1987
Planet Fires (Babe), 1985
Planner (Schevill), 1986
Play for Germs (Horovitz), 1972
Play for Trees (t Horovitz), 1969
Play of Herod (MacLeish), 1968
Play of Tea (S. Sherman), 1989
Play of the Play (Bullins), 1973
Play with an Ending (Bernard), 1984
Play Yourself (Kondoleon), 1988
Playbirth (Tavel), 1976
Play-by-Play (R. Patrick), 1972
Playhouse 90 (t Gilroy)
Playing for Time (A. Miller), 1980
Playland Blues (Piñero), 1980
Plays and Manifestos (Foreman), 1976
Plays for Bleecker Street (Wilder), 1961
Playwright and the Public (Saroyan), 1963
Plaza Suite (Simon), 1968
Please Shine Down on Me (Wymark), 1980
Pledging My Love (Steppling), 1986
Plot Counter Plot (Cristofer), 1971
Plumb Loco (Carter), 1970
Poet and the Rent (Mamet), 1974
Poetic Situation in America (Saroyan), 1942
Poet's Corner (Kondoleon), 1988
Poet's Papers (Starkweather), 1971
Pogey Bait! (Birimisa), 1976
Point Judith (Gray), 1979
Point of View (Crothers), 1904
Poison Come Poison (Weller), 1970
Poison Tree (Ribman), 1973
Police (Baraka), 1968
Polymorphous Pirates (McClure), 1972
Pomegranada (Koutoukas), 1966
Pool Hall (Norman), 1978
Poor Folks Pleasure (Jenkin), 1987
Popeye (s Feiffer), 1980
Popeye among the Polar Bears (Koch), 1986
Popkins (Schisgal), 1978
Pops (Linney), 1986
Porcelain Time (Cowen), 1972
Porno Stars at Home (Melfi), 1976
Portable Yenberry (Connelly), 1962
Port-au-Prince (Mac Low), 1963
Portrait of a Madonna (Williams), 1946
Portrait of the Artist (Greenspan), 1988
Positions (Yankowitz), 1972
Poster of the Cosmos (L. Wilson), 1987
Postlude (Carlino), 1962
Postman (Schisgal), 1960
Postman Always Rings Twice (s Mamet), 1981
Postmortem (Ludwig), 1984
Potter's Field (Green), 1934
Pouf Positive (R. Patrick), 1986
Pousse-Café (Weidman), 1966
Power and the Prize (s Ardrey), 1956
Power Failure (Gelbart), 1991

Power Outrage (Mamet), 1985
Power Play (Holden), 1975
Practical Ritual to Exorcise Frustration after Five Days of Rain (Starkweather), 1970
Prague Spring (Kalcheim), 1975
Praha (t Reddin), 1991
Prairie du Chien (Mamet), 1978
Prayer for My Daughter (Babe), 1977
Prayer Meeting (Green), 1926
Precious Memories (Linney), 1988
Precious Sons (Furth), 1986
Preggin and Liss (R. Patrick), 1968
Prelude and Liebstod (McNally), 1989
Prelude to a Kiss (Lucas), 1988
Prelude to Death in Venice (Breuer), 1980
Presence of the Enemy (Mosel), 1958
Present Tense (Gilroy), 1972
Presenting Arnold Bliss (R. Patrick), 1969
President's Lady (s J. Patrick), 1953
Pretty People (D. Wilson), 1961
Price (A. Miller), 1968
Pride (van Itallie), 1985
Primary English Class (Horovitz), 1975
Primitive World (Baraka), 1984
Prince (Fuller), 1988
Prince of Peasantmania (Inny) (Gagliano), 1968
Principia (Greenspan), 1987
Principia Scriptoriae (Nelson), 1986
Printer's Measure, (t Chayefsky), 1953
Prison Game (t Yankowitz), 1976
Prisoner of Second Avenue (Simon), 1971
Private Eye of Hiram Bodoni (Gagliano), 1978
Prize Play (Chase), 1961
Problem (Gurney), 1968
Processional (Lawson), 1925
Prodigal (Richardson), 1960
Production of Mysteries (Ludlam), 1980
Professional Frenchman (Wellman), 1984
Professor Bedlam's Educational Punch and Judy Show (Ludlam), 1975
Pro-Game (Terry), 1973
Program Prologue Now, Overture for a Deafman (R. Wilson), 1971
"Prologue" to A Letter for Queen Victoria (R. Wilson), 1974
Promenade (Fornés), 1965
Prometheus Bound (Lowell), 1967
Promises, Promises (Simon), 1968
Promontory Point Revisited (t Kopit), 1969
Proserpina and the Devil (Wilder), 1928
Prussian Suite (Smith), 1974
Psychic Pretenders (Bullins), 1972
Psycho Beach Party (Busch), 1987
Public Affairs (Gurney), 1992
Puck! Puck! Puck! (t Melfi), 1968
Pugnale Marocchino (Fratti), 1982
Pullman Car Hiawatha (Wilder), 1931
Pure in Heart (Lawson), 1934
Purification (Williams), 1946
Purlie (Davis), 1970